Writer's Guide to Book Editors, Publishers, and Literary Agents

2002–2003

Writer's Guide to Book Editors, Publishers, and Literary Agents

2002–2003

Who They Are! What They Want!

And How to Win Them Over!

JEFF HERMAN

PRIMA PUBLISHING

3000 Lava Ridge Court • Roseville, California 95661
(800) 632-8676 • www.primalifestyles.com

ISBN: 0-7615-3023-1
ISBN: 0-7615-3024-X (CD-ROM Deluxe Edition)
ISSN: 1089-3369

01 02 03 04 BB 10 9 8 7 6 5 4 3 2 1
Printed in the United States of America

How to Order

Single copies may be ordered from Prima Publishing, 3000 Lava Ridge Court, Roseville, CA 95661; telephone (800) 632-8676. Quantity discounts are also available. On your letterhead, include information concerning the intended use of the books and the number of books you wish to purchase.

Visit us online at www.primalifestyles.com

This work is dedicated to the people who live to create words that give the world progress and pleasure.

The power to publish is the power to create or destroy. It is not for the publishers to issue the call; that is determined by a source beyond them. By merits granted or earned, some will be chosen. The gates should therefore never be sealed, and those with the power to publish always revealed.

—*An Anonymous Literary Agent*

About the Author

Jeff Herman is the founder of The Jeff Herman Literary Agency, LLC, in New York City and Columbus, Ohio. One of the most innovative agents in the book business, he represents more than 100 writers and has sold more than 450 titles in the United States and internationally. Herman has been extensively written and talked about in numerous print publications and broadcast programs, and he speaks at writer's conferences around the country. He is the coauthor with Deborah Levine Herman of *Write The Perfect Book Proposal*. Be sure to visit his high-content Web site at: www.jeffherman.com.

Contributors

Deborah Levine Herman is vice president of The Jeff Herman Literary Agency and coauthor of *Write The Perfect Book Proposal: 10 Proposals That Sold and Why* (John Wiley & Sons).

Gene Busnar is an author, collaborator, ghostwriter, and publishing consultant with dozens of books to his credit.

William Hamilton is the publisher at University of Hawaii Press.

Greg Ioannou is director of the Editorial Centre in Toronto, Ontario, Canada.

Jamie M. Forbes is a publishing and media consultant based in New York.

Morris Rosenthal is an author and translator. His computer books have been published in Chinese and Spanish editions, and you can visit his internationally recognized Web site at: www.daileyint.com.

Katherine Ramsland has published 17 nonfiction books, including biographies of Anne Rice and Dean Koontz, and nonfiction narratives about the vampire subculture, ghost hunting, and death investigations. Currently, she is writing about forensic science for Court TV and working on a novel. Her latest books are *Cemetery Stories* and *The Forensic Science of CSI.*

Contents

Acknowledgments

Every edition of this work creates a new trial of endurance for myself and my dedicated associates who help me with this annual endeavor.

They include:

Deborah Herman, still my honey.

Amanda White, still my right hand.

Johanna Haney, who's always good for last minute assignments.

Susan Silva, Shawn Vreeland, and David Richardson—my Prima editors, who are among the best in the business.

Introduction

Dear Reader,

I am happy to say that several hundred thousand copies of the *Writer's Guide* are in print. What I also find to be personally gratifying is that everyone from novices to seasoned veterans claim this work to be one of the most valuable tools available for and about the book publishing business.

More than ten years ago, when I was a twenty-something and still new to this business of agenting, I did not like the obstacles, fixed attitudes, or sense of exclusionary elitism I experienced along the way. In many ways, the murky world of agents and editors struck me as being some kind of secret society. I felt like this was wrong on many levels. All people deserved a fair shot at being a part of our nation's publishing infrastructure, and the distribution of ideas and words needed to flow like flood waters without arbitrary dams. I was an idealist. Plus, I wanted a way to attract more clients.

Back then, and today, the mission of the *Writer's Guide* hasn't changed: To expose as many of the key publishing decision-makers as possible, provide clear information and directions for ways to challenge the abstract obstacles, and penetrate the entire process to the point of success. Because of this book, countless editors and agents have more work to do than they otherwise would have. But that has always been the point, and the results are good for all who participate.

This book is an opportunity for you to learn and grow as it relates to the special endeavors of writing and publishing. I will appreciate hearing about your experiences, comments, and (okay) submissions. Thank you.

Best wishes,

Jeffrey H. Herman

Jeffrey H. Herman

The Jeff Herman Literary Agency
332 Bleecker Street, Suite G-31, New York, NY 10014
212-941-0540   fax: 212-941-0614
www.jeffherman.com   (e-mail) jeff@jeffherman.com

Directory of Book Publishers and Editors

A

United States Publishers

2.13.61 PUBLICATIONS, INC.

P.O. Box 1910, Los Angeles, CA 90078
213-969-8043 (information hotline)
www.two1361.com

2.13.61 Publications offers new fiction and creative narratives, creative prose nonfiction, poetry, cultural events and critical works, photographic books, and audiovisual products. The house was founded in 1988.

Titles from 2.13.61 include: *Smile, You're Traveling; The Portable Henry Rollins; Solipsist; Do I Come Here Often?; Black Coffee Blues; The First Five; See a Grown Man Cry; Get in the Van; Every Scream,* all by Henry Rollins; *Letters to Rollins* by Rob Overton; *The Cowardice of Amnesia* by Ellyn Maybe; *Go Tell the Mountain* by Jeffrey Lee Pierce; *Boy in the Air* by Don Bajema; *Attack God Inside* by Tricia Warden; *The Consumer* by Michael Gira; *Fish in a Barrel* by Peter Milne; *Dream Baby Dream* by Stephanie Chernikowski; *Planet Joe* by Joe Cole; *Metallica,* photographs by Ross Halfin; *Rock & Pop Narcotic* by Joe Carducci; and *Human Shrapnel* by Bill Shields.

Oh, incidentally: It's no big secret, but this operation is under the watchful eye of none other than poet-rocker Henry Rollins himself. Want to start a contest? Guess what 2.13.61 means; a fancy facsimile of Henry Rollins's birth certificate goes to the winner.

2.13.61 Publications, Inc., distributes to the trade through Publishers Group West. Query letters and SASEs should be directed to:

Carol Bua, Director

ABBEVILLE PUBLISHING GROUP

Abbeville Kids

Artabras

Canopy Books

Cross River

A

22 Cortlandt Street, New York, NY 10007
212-577-5555   fax: 212-577-5579
www.abbeville.com

Abbeville is renowned for finely produced, award-winning volumes in the areas of fine arts, art history, architecture, graphic arts, design, lifestyle, cuisine, handicrafts, nature, collectibles, popular culture, sports, and illustrated historical works. Abbeville also produces postcard books, stationery items, pop-up children's books, artists' portfolios, and titles in biography, letters, literature, and humor. Abbeville issues hardcover and trade paperback editions—all published with attention to quality in design, illustration, and production standards. Abbeville Publishing Group includes: Abbeville Press, Abbeville Kids, Artabras, Edition Stemmle, Touring Club of Italy, Skira, Van der Meer, and Flammarion. Abbeville Kids is the house's children's imprint (see subentry further on). Tiny Folios is a line of small, handsome, reasonably priced gift volumes. Editions Abbeville is the house's enterprising French imprint. Artabras is a house imprimatur for specially priced promotional/premium volumes. Abbeville is the exclusive distributor for English-language publications, based in Zurich, and for the Touring Club of Italy, Skira, and Van der Meer. They are publishers of fine art and photographic books.

Abbeville Publishing Group is an international firm with offices in New York and Paris. Abbeville upholds a tradition of bookmaking established by the publisher Harry N. Abrams, who with his son Robert E. Abrams started Abbeville Press (in 1977) subsequent to the purchase of the eponymous publishing house Harry N. Abrams, Inc. by the Times Mirror Company (see entry for Abrams in this directory).

Representing the Abbeville list: *The Civil Rights Movement: A Photographic History, 1954–68* by Stephen Kasher; *Covering the New Yorker: Cutting Edge Covers from a Literary Institution* by Francoise Mouly; *The Great Book of French Impressionism* by Diane Kjelder; *A History of Women Photographers* by Nancy Rosenblum; *The House of Philip Johnson* by David Mohney; *The Magic Flute* by Davide Pizzigoni; *Manhattan Lightscape* by Nathaniel Lieberman; *Parisians* by Peter Turnley; *Robert Doisneau: A Photographer's Life* by Peter Hamilton; *Smoke Gets in Your Eyes: Branding and Design in Cigarette Packaging* by Michael Thibodeau and Jana Martin; *The White House: Its Historic Furnishings and First Families* by Betty Monkman.

Tiny Folios accents miniature books—for those who love gifts that come in small packages. Series titles: *Hugs & Kisses* by Mimi Coucher; *Dogs Up Close* by Vicki Croke; *100 Classic Cocktails* by Barry Shelby; *Frank Lloyd Wright: American Master Architect* by Kathryn Smith; *Treasures of the Museum of Fine Arts, Boston* (chapter introductions by Gillian Wohlauer); *Edgar Degas* by George T. M. Shackelford; *Treasures of the Hermitage* (introduction by Vitaly A. Suslov); *Provence* by Sonja Bullaty and Angelo Domeo. Artabras (quality books at bargain prices) titles: *Norman Rockwell: 332 Magazine Covers* by Christopher Finch; *Ethnic Style: From Mexico to the Mediterranean* by Miranda Innes; *Cats Up Close* by Vicki Croke; *Piaget: Watches and Wonders Since 1874* by Franco Cologni and Giampiero Negretti; *Venetian Taste* by Adam Tihany.

Abbeville's colleagues at Paris-based Flammarion publish a vigorous list with international appeal. The Flammarion program includes: *Dressed to Kill: James Bond, the Suited Hero* by Jay McInerney, Nicholas Foulkes, Neil Norman, and Nick Sullivan; *The Violin*

A

by Yehudi Menuhin; *City of Ambition: Artists and New York, 1900–1960* by Elizabeth Sussman and John G. Hanhardt; *Messengers of Modernism: American Studio Jewelry* by Toni Greenbaum; *Impressions of Arabia: Architecture and Frescoes of the Asir Region* by Thierry Mauger.

Abbeville Press distributes its own books throughout the United States and also distributes for Flammarion; international distribution is handled by regional representatives, including John Murray Ltd. for the United Kingdom.

Unsolicited manuscripts are rarely accepted, but query letters and SASEs can be directed to:

Susan Costello, Editorial Director—Gardening, nature, folk art, general.

Christopher Lyon, Executive Editor—Fine arts, general.

Kerrie Baldwin, Assistant Editor—Children's, general.

Abbeville Kids

Abbeville Kids produces a lineup designed to introduce younger folk to the world of art and design—as well as to hone the tastes of younger artists and connoisseurs. Abbeville Kids offers breakthrough series of interactive, inquiry-based books designed to teach children about art by looking at the world and about the world by looking at art. Abbeville Kids also offers books with a broader scope that cover the finer pleasures of living and life.

Titles from Abbeville Kids: Abbeville Animals series; *Father and Daughter Tales* by Josephine Evetts-Secker (illustrated by Helen Cann); *Felix Activity Book* by Marc Tyler Nobleman and Leslie Mosely; *In the Paint* by Patrick Ewing and Linda L. Louis; *The Story of Chess* by Horacio Cardo; *Women of Camelot: Queens and Enchantresses at the Court of King Arthur* by Mary Hoffman. How Artists See . . . is a series from Abbeville Kids with such titles as *How Artists See Feelings, How Artists See the Elements, How Artists See People, How Artists See Families, How Artists See Work,* and *How Artists See Animals* (all by Colleen Carroll).

Abrams

100 Fifth Avenue, New York, NY 10011
212-206-7715   fax: 212-645-8437
www.abramsbooks.com

Abrams publishes in the fields of fine art, architecture, design; anthropology, archaeology, ethnology, and culture; gardening and the home; literary and art criticism; world history; travel and the natural sciences; creative use of technology and new media.

The Abrams list accents fine illustrated volumes, mainly in hardcover, with some trade paperback editions and series, as well as a selection of works in electronic format. Many Abrams books are published in cooperation with institutions such as museums, foundations, or art galleries; these works bring together top-quality illustrative materials and expert text. Abrams publishes a strong seasonal list of new titles and maintains an extensive backlist.

A

Abrams was founded in 1949 as an independent house (then known as Harry N. Abrams, Inc.) and has been a subsidiary of the Times Mirror Company from 1977 to 1997. In that year, Abrams was acquired by Groupe Latingy (now La Martiniere Groupe). From its inception, the firm has been among the leaders in the field of fine bookmaking in the areas of art, design, and illustrated works.

From Abrams: *African Ceremonies* by Carol Beckwith and Angela Fisher; *African Rock Art* by Alec Campbell; *Art Nouveau 1890–1914* (edited by Paul Greenhalgh); *Chicken Run: Hatching the Movie* by Brian Shelby; *Colonial Wiliamsburg* by Philip Kopper; *Design and Detail in the Home* by David Linley; *Diego Rivera* by Pete Hamill; *Earth from Above,* with photographs by Yann Arthur-Bertrand; *Flowers A to Z: Buying, Growing, Cutting, Arranging* by Cecilia Heffernan; *Giorgio Armani* by Germano Celant and Harold Koda; *Hearst Castle: The Biography of a Country House* by Victoria Kastner; *History of Art* by Anthony F. Janson; *Hollywood Candid,* with photographs by Murray Garrett; *Hollywood Moms,* with photographs by Joyce Ostin; *Home: A Collection of Poetry and Art* by Stan Tymorek; *How to Look at Everything* by David Finn; *Laurie Anderson* by Roselee Goldberg; *Leonardo da Vinci: The Complete Paintings* by Pietro Marani; *Loving Picasso: The Private Journal of Fernande Oliver; The Magic of M.C. Escher,* created by Joost Elffers and Andreas Landshoff; *Mark Pickford Rediscovered* by Kevin Brownlow; *Matisse: Father and Son* by John Russell; *Norman Rockwell: Pictures for the American People* (edited by Maureen Hart Hennessey and Anne Knutson); *Physics in the 20th Century* by Curt Suplee; *The Red Rose Girls* by Alice Carter; *Tiffany Jewels* by John Loring; *Valley of the Golden Mummies* by Zahi Hawass; *YES: Yoko Ono* by Alexandra Monroe with John Hendricks.

Abrams children's books include *Babar and the Succotash Bird* by Laurent de Brunhoff; *Hello Kitty Hello World; Sally Goes to the Beach* by Stephen Huneck; *The Worst Band in the Universe* by Graeme Base.

Abrams trade paperback lines include Discoveries (books covering history, archaeology, natural history, culture, and the arts, over the full range of house subject areas of interest).

Titles here: *Alexander the Great* by Pierre Briant; *The Aztecs* by Serge Gnuzinski; *The Birth of Greece* by Pierre Leveque; and *Einstein* by Francoise Balibar.

It should be noted that Abrams is a specialist house and acquires projects on a highly selective basis that gives particular weight to such factors as the national or international renown and credentials of participant artists, photographers, and writers.

Abrams distributes its own books in the United States and Canada.

Query letters and SASEs should be directed to:

Eric Himmel, Editor in Chief

Mark Magowan, Publisher

ACADEMY CHICAGO PUBLISHERS

363 West Erie Street, Chicago, IL 60610
312-751-7300, 800-248-7323   fax: 312-751-7306
www.academychicago.com   e-mail: academy363@aol.com

Academy Chicago publishes general nonfiction, art, history, and gender and cultural studies, as well as fiction (including mysteries). The house also offers a line of classic reprints. Academy Chicago Publishers (established in 1975), a small press with an inspired list, is a major player in American letters.

A

Nonfiction from Academy Chicago includes popular works with an emphasis on contemporary culture, current events, and historical interpretation. Titles here: *Kings and Queens of Early Britain* by Geoffrey Ashe; *The Provincial Lady in Russia* by E. M. Delafield; *Before and After Zachariah: A True Story About a Family and a Different Kind of Courage* by Fern Kupfer; *Titanic: A Survivor's Story & the Sinking of the S.S. Titanic* by Colonel Archibald Gracie/John B. Thayer; *The Five Weeks of Giuseppe Zangara: The Man Who Would Assassinate FDR* by Blaise Picchi; *The Celtic and Scandinavian Religions* by J. A. MacCulloch; *Ireland: A Concise History from the Twelfth Century to the Present Day* by Paul Johnson; *Night Witches: The Amazing Story of Russia's Women Pilots in World War II* by Bruce Myles.

The Academy Chicago program in fiction and letters encompasses English-language originals, often with a historical or cultural hook; a solid number of these titles feature the mystery and suspense modes. Academy Chicago also publishes a variety of contemporary and vintage novels in translation, many of which bear the Plover Press imprint.

Frontlist fiction includes: *Cutter's Island* by Vincent Panella; *The Marquise & Pauline: Two Novellas* by George Sand (translated by Sylvie Charron and Sue Huseman); *Murder at Heartbreak Hospital* by Henry Slesar; *A Writer of Books* by George Paston (Emily Morse Symonds); *The Man Who Once Played Catch with Nellie Fox* by John Manderino; *Freedom in the Dismal* by Monifa A. Love; *Death and Blintzes* by Dorothy and Sidney Rosen; *Leone Leoni* by George Sand; *Homer's Daughter* by Robert Graves; *The Monkey's Paw: And Other Tales of Mystery and the Macabre* by W. W. Jacobs (compiled and with an introduction by Gary Hoppenstand); *In a Dark Wood Wandering: A Novel of the Middle Ages* by Hella S. Haasse (translated by Anita Miller); *Thirteen Uncollected Stories* by John Cheever (edited by Franklin H. Dennis); *Indiana* by George Sand (translated by George Burnham Ives); *The White Guard* by Mikhail Bulgakov (translated by Michael Glenny).

Representing the range of Academy Chicago fiction and literary works: *The Fat Woman's Joke* by Fay Weldon; *The Life and Times of Deacon A. L. Wiley* by Gregory Alan-Williams (drama/African-American studies); *The Perfect Murder* by H. R. F. Keating. Academy Chicago is the American publisher of the successful British series of humorous and profound Miss Read novels, including *Fresh from the Country*.

Fiction from Plover Press: *Gambusino* by Carlos Montemayor (translated by John Copeland); *On the Seventh Day: Portrait of the Artist as a Creative Writer* by John Mitchell.

Academy Chicago handles its own distribution.

Query letters and SASEs should be directed to:

Anita Miller, Senior Editor

Jordan Miller, Vice President and Editor

ADAMS MEDIA CORPORATION

57 Littlefield Street, 2nd Floor, Avon, MA 02322
781-767-8100   fax: 781-767-0994
www.adamsmedia.com

A

Adams Media Corporation has experienced dramatic growth over the past few years and, looking to the future, is poised for even greater title acquisition, higher store presence, and increased marketing sales, and media clout. One of the fast-growing publishers in the country, the now mid-sized trade house boats a list of well over 500 titles and currently publishes approximately 100–120 books per year during its two seasonal lists. Adams has created a truly unique and distinct publishing universe, with magnificent cover designs, eye-catching trademark brands, high-quality content, and competitive retail packaging.

The Adams Editorial Group is now structured to accommodate both bestselling Single Titles and powerhouse Series Publishing programs for trade, mass-market, special sales, gift markets, library sales, and other burgeoning outlets and channels.

In the Single Title area, the publisher has had tremendous success in the areas of self-help/self-improvement, women's issues, relationships, spirituality, popular psychology, digital business, personal finance, business management, and pets. Adams also considers proposals with broad popular appeal and unique marketing hooks in the areas of parenting, cooking, careers, fitness/leisure how-to, and sales/marketing how-to.

The highly commercial Spring 2001 list features such lead titles as *The Book of Rudy* by Rudy Boesch; *How Can You Tell If You're Really In Love?* by Sol Gordon, Ph.D.; *God Is My CEO* by Larry Julian; *Heaven & Beyond: Conversations with Souls in Transition* by Barbara Mark and Trudy Griswold; *Outwitting Fish* by Bill Adler, Jr.; *Thank Heaven for Little Girls* by Sister Carol Ann Nawracaj and Monica Rich Kosann; *Wisdom of the Animals* by Raphaela Pope and Elizabeth Morrison; and *A Woman's Way to Incredible Success in Business* by Mary-Ellen Drummond.

Among the company's Single Title backlist hot sellers are *The Angelspeake Storybook* by Barbara Mark and Trudy Griswold; *In Search of Our Ancestors* by Megan Smolenyak; *First Time Resume* by William McNeill; *22 Keys to Creating a Meaningful Workplace* by Tom Perez; and *A String of Pearls* by Bettie B. Youngs.

The Adams Series Publishing Program continues to yield unparalleled results and now has an in-house acquisitions and development team to keep up with the insatiable market demand. The staff is actively seeking professional writers to build upon the phenomenal success of the flagship Everything series, which now boats over 80 titles in more than a dozen publishing categories, including parenting, cooking, hobbies, spirituality, New Age, personal finance, pets, weddings, relationships, careers, gardening, and more. Among the series' top sellers are *The Everything Pregnancy Book, The Everything Baby Names Book, The Everything Bartenders Book, The Everything Dreams Book, The Everything Money Book, The Everything Wedding Book, The Everything Etiquette Book, The Everything Cat Book, The Everything Astrology Book,* and *The Everything Barbecue Book.*

The series has also spawned two hugely successful spinoff series, Everything Kids' and Everything Mini. The Kids' books include *The Everything Kids' Baseball Book, The Everything Kids' Witches and Wizards Book, The Everything Kids' Online Book, The Everything Kids' Puzzle Book,* and *The Everything Kids' Nature Book.* Among the Minis are *The Everything Dreams Mini Book, The Everything Baby Names Mini Book, The Everything Bedtime Story Mini Book, The Everything Pregnancy Mini Book,* and *The Everything Get Ready for Baby Mini Book.*

While shorter in terms of title count than the Everything series, with four books, the Small Miracles franchise has sold 1.5 million copies and continues to enlighten readers around the world. Authors Yitta Halberstam and Judith Leventhal have assembled an astonishing collection of remarkable coincidences in *Small Miracles, Small Miracles II, Small Miracles for Women,* and *Small Miracles of Love and Friendship.*

Among Adams's many other series are: Streetwise, which now features two dozen business books, ranging from *Streetwise Managing People* to *Streetwise Internet Business Plan; Heartwarmers* by Azriela Jaffe, now firmly established with a second title, *Heartwarmers of Love:* fastread, a series for people with limited reading time; Knock Em' Dead, a series of career books by Martin Yate, as well as Job Banks, Adams Almanacs, The 100 Best (Stocks, Mutual Funds), Mr. Cheap's, and 365 Ways to . . .

Adams orchestrates its own worldwide distribution network. In the United States, Adams distributes directly to bookstore chains and independents, and also operates through wholesales and jobbers; in the United Kingdom and elsewhere in the world, the publisher distributes via overseas distributors.

Query letters with SASEs should be directed to:

Gary M. Krebs, Director of Series and Single Title Publishing. Handles a variety of trade properties, both in series and single title. Will often pass to appropriate editors.

Single Title Publishing:

Dawn Thompson, Assistant Editor

Elizabeth Gilbert, Editorial Assistant

Series Publishing:

Cheryl Kimball, Acquisitions Editor, Series Publishing. Acquisitions champion for the Everything Kids' series.

Leah Bloom, Editorial Assistant

Clair Gerus, Editor

ADDISON WESLEY LONGMAN PUBLISHING COMPANY
Addison Wesley is now strictly a textbook publisher.

ALGONQUIN BOOKS OF CHAPEL HILL
(A DIVISION OF WORKMAN PUBLISHING COMPANY)
P.O. Box 2225, Chapel Hill, NC 27515
919-767-0108
www.algonquin.com

This division of Workman Publishing Company has a primarily literary orientation in commercial nonfiction and fiction. The house list represents the American tradition, ranging from the homespun to the avant-garde. Algonquin Books of Chapel Hill presents its titles in hardcover and trade paper editions with a look and feel befitting the publisher's

A

emphasis on both the classical and contemporary—books designed to be comfortably handled when read. The Algonquin editorial organization operates from both the Chapel Hill and New York Workman offices.

Algonquin nonfiction includes: *Return of the Osprey* by David Gessnee; *Godforsaken Sea* by Derek Lundy; *Educating Esme* by Esme Raji Codell; *Sugar Pie & Jelly Roll* by Robbin Gourleg; and *Somehow for a Family,* essays by Tony Earleg.

Algonquin fiction and literary works: *Gap Creek* by Robert Morgan; *Tea* by Stacey D'Erasino; *Fay* by Larry Brown; *In the Name of Salome* by Julia Aluarez; and *A Perfect Arrangement* by Suzanne Berne.

Algonquin Books of Chapel Hill is distributed by the parent Workman Publishing Company. Query letters and SASEs should be directed to:

Duncan Murrell, Editor, Algonqin Books

Elisabeth Scharlatt, Publisher, Algonquin Books

Shannon Ravenel, Editorial Director, Shannon Ravenel Books

Kathy Pories, Editor, Algonquin Books

Antonia Fusco, Editor, Algonquin Books

Amy Gash, Editor, Algonquin Books

AMACOM (AMERICAN MANAGEMENT ASSOCIATION)

1601 Broadway, New York, NY 10019-7420
212-586-8100
www.amnet.org

AMACOM publishes business and management books, primarily for a professional readership. AMACOM trade nonfiction lines include works that cover the fields of accounting and finance, career, customer service, management issues, general business and management, human resources, management skills, international business, manufacturing, quality, reference books, personal finance, project management, marketing, advertising and public relations, personal development, small business, supervision, sales and sales management, and training.

Managers in large and small companies are encouraged to use AMACOM books as an inexpensive and effective way to energize their staff, explain new concepts, teach specific skills, and inspire employees at all levels. AMACOM challenges companies to empower employees at all levels to teach themselves!

Titles from AMACOM: *The Complete Guide to Training Development* by Stephen B. King, Marsha King, and William J. Rothwell; *Mentoring: Helping Employees Reach Their Full Potential* by Gordon F. Shea; *The Presentation Skills Workshop* by Sherron Bienveau, Ph.D.; *The Team Building Workshop* by Melinda Nykamp; *Business Writing Skills* by Joseph Dobrian; *Empower Yourself!* by Dr. Marlene Caroselli; *The Board Book* by Susan F. Schultz; *The Business Analyzer and Planner* by Michael Zambruski; *Customer Centered Products* by Ivy F. Hooks and Kristin A. Farry; *How to Resolve Conflicts at Work* by Florence M. Stone; *Powerful Products* by Roger Baen and Russell Radford; *The Supply Chain Network @ Internet Speed* by Fred A. Kuglin and Barbara A. Rosen-

A

baum; *The E-Commerce Question and Answer Book* by Anita Rosen; *E-Factor* by Martin T. Focazio; *The Brave New Service Strategy* by Barbara A. Gutek and Theresa Welsh; *E-Service* by Ron Zemke and Tom Connellan; and *Cash Is Still King* by Keith Checkley.

Prospective writers might keep in mind the AMACOM readership profile (not to typecast, but rather to offer guidelines): AMACOM readers are definitely not mass-market consumers; they want specialized materials and information on business issues that concern them most. AMACOM book buyers want more than a quick fix. They crave in-depth ideas and practical approaches they can try out on the job. They like to be on the leading edge and get a jump on the competition. They do not want secondhand information. They want to go straight to the source.

AMACOM distributes its own products through multiple marketing channels, including retail trade, direct marketing, special sales, and international sales (through McGraw-Hill). Query letters and SASEs should be directed to:

Adrienne Hickey, Executive Editor—General and human resource management, organization development, leadership, strategy.

Ellen Kadin, Senior Acquisitions Editor—Career skills, sales and marketing, customer service, self-development.

Jacquie Flynn, Acquisitions Editor—Information technology applications, e-commerce, training.

Neil Levine, Senior Acquisitions Editor—Manufacturing, supply chain management, operations management, facilities management.

Ray O'Connell, Senior Acquisitions Editor—Corporate finance and accounting, personal finance, project management.

Born: September 23, 1951.

Education: B.A. in Political Science and a M.A. in History.

Employment history/editor career path: Started as a salesman in college publishing, which led to becoming a trade professional editor.

Personal interests: Elected official, issues concerning planning and zoning.

What would you be doing if you were not an editor? Teaching history.

What has been your most successful book that you have acquired to date? *Business Ethics* by Manuel Valascast (1982), in its 8th edition.

What books that you have acquired reflect the types of books you like to represent? *Scientific Dimensional Management;* an interior design book that was a bestseller; philosophy books.

Do you represent fiction? No.

Do you represent nonfiction? Yes.

Do you require book proposals? If so, what do you look for in evaluating a book proposal? Yes. Draft preface, an annotated table of contents, and a market statement; who the reader is.

Are certain aspects of a book proposal given more weight than others? Preface and table of contents.

What process do you use for making a decision? What is the process for acquisition, is there a committee? If the proposal is good, we send it to a committee and then may have an outside reader read it and give a report.

What kinds of nonfiction books do you want to see less of? Less "Me-too" books.

Do you think that agents are important? Why? Yes. They are good at getting the proposals to us.

Do you like new writers? What should new writers do to break into the business? Yes. Put together a good proposal.

How should writers approach you? Call me or write me an e-mail letting me know that you are sending me a proposal.

What are some common mistakes writers make? What really gets on your nerves? Telling me that "I have the next bestseller"; just tell me what the market is.

What can writers do to get your attention and to avoid the slush pile? Just write a good proposal.

What have been some of your craziest experiences with submissions? I haven't had too many crazy submissions.

What, if anything, makes you different from other editors? I will probably read just about anything.

Any advice for writers? Keep swinging.

AMERICAN BAR ASSOCIATION BOOK PUBLISHING

750 North Lake Shore Drive, Chicago, IL 60611
312-988-5000   fax: 312-988-5528
www.abanet.org e-mail: abasvcctr@abanet.org

The American Bar Association publishes a variety of resources for wide categories of specialty legal fields. The publishing division offers books, periodicals, pamphlets, CD-ROMs, and videotapes. The American Bar Association is the national organization of the legal profession. The Association is committed to keeping its members and the general public informed of the latest developments in law and law-related fields. To accomplish this goal, it publishes numerous books and pamphlets and, on a regular basis, a variety of magazines, journals, and newsletters. The prospective writer should note that the American Bar Association publishes for the professional market, and each ABA division publishes its own line of books. Please inquire as to which divisional line your project fits before querying.

For general-interest professional-legal projects, query letters and SASEs may be directed to:

Robert Roen, Director of Publications (books)

Kerry Klumpy, Managing Editor—*ABA Journal.*

Susan Yessne, Executive Editor—ABA periodicals.

AMERICAN PSYCHIATRIC PUBLISHING, INC.
(FORMERLY AMERICAN PSYCHIATRIC PRESS, INC.)

1400 K Street, NW, Washington, DC 20005
202-682-6268, 800-368-5777   fax: 202-789-2648
www.appi.org

In March 2001, American Psychiatric Press, Inc. (APPI), will celebrate its 20th anniversary. By then, the Press will have published more than 800 titles, launched five journals, and merged all publishing operations of the American Psychiatric Association into a single corporation entity known as American Psychiatric Publishing, Inc.

American Psychiatric Press Publishing, Inc., publishes professional, reference, and trade books, as well as college textbooks. The press's spheres of interest include the behavioral and social sciences, psychiatry, and medicine. The house publishes a mid-sized booklist in hardcover and trade paper and also produces a number of professional journals; selected reference works are issued in electronic formats (including diskettes and CD-ROMs).

Although by far the major portion of the American Psychiatric list is geared toward the professional and academic markets, the house catalogs a number of books in the areas of patient information and books for the general public, among which are selected titles marketed through trade channels.

Representative of the American Psychiatric popular-interest list: *Trauma, Memory, and Disassociation* (edited by J. Douglas Bremner, M.D., and Charles R. Marmar, M.D.); *The Selfish Brain: Learning from Addiction* by Robert L. DuPont, M.D.; *Women's Health Research: A Medical and Policy Primer,* from the Society for the Advancement of Women's Health Research; *Posttraumatic Stress Disorder: Acute and Long-Term Responses to Trauma and Disaster* (edited by Carol S. Fullerton, Ph.D., and Robert J. Ursano, M.D.); *The Broken Connection: On Death and the Continuity of Life* by Robert Jay Lifton; *Wrestle with Demons: A Psychiatrist Struggles to Understand His Patients and Himself* by Keith Russell Ablow; *Lies! Lies! Lies! The Psychology of Deceit* by Charles V. Ford; *Bad Men Do What Good Men Dream* by Robert I. Simon; *Talking About Sex* by Derek C. Polonsky; *How to Help Your Child Overcome Your Divorce* by Elissa P. Benedek and Catherine F. Brown; *Surviving Childhood Cancer: A Guide for Families* by Margot Joan Fromer; and *The Preteen's First Book About Love, Sex, and AIDS* by Michelle Harrison (illustrated by Lynn Beckstrom).

Professional titles from American Psychiatric: *The American Psychiatric Press Textbook of Psychiatry,* 3rd edition (edited by Robert E. Hales, M.D., and Stuart C. Yudofaley, M.D.); *DSM-IV Casebook* by Spitzer et al.; and *Psychodynamic Psychiatry in Clinical Practice,* 3rd edition by Glen O. Gabbard, M.D.

Practice Guidelines (guidelines were formulated to improve patient care and to assist with clinical decision making) titles: *American Psychiatric Association Practice Guideline for the Treatment of Patients with Schizophrenia; American Psychiatric Association Practice Guideline for the Treatment of Patients with Nicotine Dependence; American Psychiatric Association Practice Guideline for the Treatment of Patients with Alzheimer's Disease and Other Dementias of Late Life;* and the *American Psychiatric Association Practice Guideline for the Treatment of Patients with Substance Use Disorders: Alcohol, Cocaine, Opioids; American Psychiatric Association Practice Guideline for Eating Disorders.*

American Psychiatric Publishing is the publisher of the psychiatric profession's accredited clinical guidebook, *Diagnostic and Statistical Manual of Mental Disorders* (4th edition text revision), also known as *DSM-IV.*

American Psychiatric Publishing distributes through several regional distribution services. Query letters and SASEs should be directed to:

Carol C. Nadelson, M.D., Editor in Chief

Claire Reinburg, Editorial Director

A

AMERICAN PSYCHOLOGICAL ASSOCIATION, INC.

750 First Street, NE, Washington, DC 20002-4242
202-336-5793   fax: 202-336-5502
www.apa.org e-mail: order@apa.org

Areas of American Psychological Association publishing interest include virtually all aspects of the field of psychology: methodology, history, student aids, teaching, health, business strategies, violence, personality, and clinical issues. APA publications include books, journals, publishing resources, continuing-education/home-study programs, audiocassettes, videotapes, and databases.

The information resources produced by APA are grounded in a long publishing tradition of scholarly and professional works that encompass diverse topics and applications in the arena of human behavior, from basic research to practical therapies, including the teaching curriculum of psychology as well as the contributions of psychology to progressive education, from personality disorders to implications for psychology of public policies. The American Psychological Association (founded in 1892) is the major psychological organization in the United States.

On the APA list: *Uniting Psychology and Biology: Integrative Perspectives on Human Development* (edited by Nancy L. Segal, Glenn E. Weisfeld, and Carol C. Weisfeld); *A Spiritual Strategy for Counseling and Psychotherapy* by P. Scott Richards and Allen E. Bergin; *After the Crash: Assessment and Treatment of Motor Vehicle Accident Survivors* by Edward B. Blanchard and Edward J. Hickling; *The Science of Prevention: Methodological Advances from Alcohol and Substance Abuse Research* (edited by Kendall J. Bryant, Michael Windle, and Stephen G. West); *In Defense of Human Consciousness* by Joseph F. Rychlak; *The Psychological Meaning of Chaos: Translating Theory into Practice* (edited by Frank Masterpasqua and Phyllis A. Perna); *Health Care for Women: Psychological, Social, and Behavioral Influences* (edited by Sheryle J. Gallant, Gwendolyn Puryear Keita, and Reneé Royāk-Schaler); *Shaping the Future of Feminist Psychology: Education, Research, and Practice* (edited by Judith Worell and Norine G. Johnson); *Treating Patients with Memories of Abuse: Legal Risk Management* by Samuel J. Knapp and Leon VandeCreek; *Understanding Sleep: The Evaluation and Treatment of Sleep Disorders* (edited by Mark R. Pressman and William C. Orr); *William James: The Center of His Vision* by Daniel W. Bjork; *Measuring Patient Changes in Mood, Anxiety, and Personality Disorders: Toward a Core Battery* (edited by Hans H. Strupp, Leonard M. Horowitz, and Michael J. Lambert).

A publication of the American Psychological Association that has wide influence in all areas of scholarly publishing, especially the social and behavioral sciences, is the *Publication Manual of the American Psychological Association* (now in its 4th edition), a resource that guides writers and editors through manuscript preparation and production. Query letters and SASEs should be directed to:

Julia Frank-McNeil, Director, APA Books

AMERICAN SOCIETY FOR TRAINING AND DEVELOPMENT (ASTD) BOOKS

A

1640 King Street, P.O. Box 1443, Alexandria, VA 22313-2043
703-683-8100   fax: 703-683-1523
www.astd.org e-mail: CustomerCare@astd.org

American Society for Training and Development (ASTD) Books is a business-information specialist. Among ASTD's major categories are workplace learning and performance, human resource development, training, management development, career development, workforce issues, consulting, teamwork, technology, games, and problem solving and creativity. In addition to books, ASTD offers training kits, diagnostic tools, presentation materials, games and simulations, videos, audiocassettes, and computer software.

ASTD Books (founded in 1944) is the book-publishing wing of American Society for Training and Development, a nonprofit membership organization. The house's professional books cover such areas as employee education, training, and development; human resource development; organization management; career development; and performance improvement. Within this business arena, ASTD strives to put forth a list that represents the most current topics, the most innovative techniques, and the most gifted authors in the field. ASTD publishes selected titles in conjunction with other business-oriented houses, such as Berrett-Koehler, Jossey-Bass, and McGraw-Hill.

Books listed in the ASTD catalog are reviewed and selected by a distinguished and professional peer group.

Titles from ASTD: *The Targeted Evaluation Process A Performance Consultant's Guide* by Wendy L. Combs and Salvatore V. Falletta; *ISD from the Ground Up: A No-Nonsense Approach to Instructional Design* by Chuck Hodell; *Project Management for Trainers: Stop "Winging It" and Get Control of Your Training Projects* by Lou Russell; *Managing Web Based Training: How to Keep Your Program on Track and Make It Successful* by Alan L. Ellis, Ellen D. Wagner, and Warren R. Longmire; *In Action: Leading Knowledge Management and Learning* by Dede Booner; *Interactive Distance Learning Exercises That Really Work!* by Karen Mantyla; *Distance Learning: A Step-by-Step Guide for Trainers* by Karen and Gividen Mantyla; *The ASTD Media Selection Tool for Workplace Learning* by Raymond J. Marx; *Promoting Emotional Intelligence in Organizations* by Cary Cherniss and Mitchel Adler; *Consulting on the Inside* by Scott Beverly.

ASTD's new learning technology series includes *A Trainer's Guide to Web-Based Instruction, Managing Web-Based Training, How to Develop Web-Based Training, Developing a Web-Based Training Strategy,* and others.

Writers: If you are working on a book targeted to trainers that you think ASTD might like to publish, please contact Nancy Olson, Vice President for Publications (703-683-8131), or e-mail at nolson@astd.org. Guidelines for submitting a book proposal are available upon request.

ASTD Books distributes its own list via an in-house easy-ordering program; selected ASTD books are available through other publishing houses, for which ASTD returns the favor by cataloging business titles from a variety of other publishers—not limited to business specialists: John Wiley; Random House; Scott, Foresman; and Van Nostrand Reinhold.

Query letters and SASEs should be directed to:

A

Mark Morrow, Senior Acquisitions Editor

Nancy Olson, Vice President for Publications

Ruth Stadius, Publications Manager

ANDREWS MCMEEL PUBLISHING
4520 Main Street, Kansas City, MO 64111-7701
816-932-6700   fax: 816-932-6749

Andrews McMeel Publishing (founded in 1970) is an Andrews McMeel Universal company that publishes a wide assortment of general trade nonfiction books and gift books, humor (including cartoon books), and calendars. Areas of interest include popular culture and lifestyles, psychology and self-help, health and medicine, New Age and inspiration, women's issues. Andrews McMeel publishes over 100 calendars each year in day-to-day, wall, and desk-diary format.

Titles from Andrews McMeel: *The Millionaire Mind* by Thomas J. Stanley; *The Blue Day Book* by Bradley Trevor Greive; *Simplify Your Life with Kids* and *365 Simple Reminders* by Elaine St. James; *We Really Love Dogs* by Kim Levin; *What's the Number for 911?: America's Wackiest 911 Calls* by Leland Gregory III; *I Believe* by Allan Stark; *The Pyne Stewart Story* by Larry Guest; *Raising a Nonviolent Child* by John Rosemond; *The Joyful Soul: Messages from a Saint for Our Times* by Pope John XXIII; *The Ten Commandments of Relationships* by Catherine Cardinal, Ph.D.; *Abounding Grace: An Anthology of Wisdom* (edited by M. Scott Peck, M.D.); *The Babe Book: Baseball's Greatest Legend Remembered* by Ernestine Miller; *Why We Love Cats* by Bob Walker and Frances Mooney; *Ornaments: Creating Handmade Tree Decorations* by Carol Endler Sterbenz; *The Story of the Other Wise Man* by Henry Van Dyke, retold by Michael Lynberg; *Life Messages: Inspiration for the Woman's Spirit* by Josephine Carlton; *The Book of Birthday Letters* by Bobbi Conner; *Golfers* by Dick Durrance II (A Lionheart Book); *Couples: A Celebration of Commitment* by Catherine Whitney; *The Best Advice Ever for Golfers* by Robert McCord; *The Best Advice Ever for Teachers* by Charles McGuire and Dianna Abitz; *Fame at Last: Who Was Who According to the New York Times Obituaries* by John Ball and Jill Jonnes; *Dear Isaac: A Father's Legacy to His Son* by Joel Friedman, M.D.; *The Two of Us* by Ellen Small and James Dale; *The Too Bad It's Your Birthday Book: Tender Thoughts to Put a Smile on Your Wrinkly Little Face* by James Dale; *Why Dogs Are Better Than Kids* by Jennifer Berman; *1,003 Great Things About Teachers* by Lisa Birnbach, Patricia Marx, and Ann Hodgman; *It's a Girl Thing: The Hilarious Truth About Women* by Jan King; *The Fudge Factor: The Easy Way to Burn Up to 1,000 Extra Calories Every Day* by Frank and Victor Katch with Gene Brown; *Villains: The Bad Boys (and Girls) of Sports* by Barry Wilner and Ken Rappaport (A Lionheart Book); *The Joy of Christmas* by Hane Hughes Paulson; *The New Millionaires Handbook: A Guide to Contemporary Social Climbing* by Chris Fountain; *The Joy of Being a Woman* by Amy Hall; *Mort Walker's Private Scrapbook: A Celebration of 50 Years of Comic Excellence* by Mort Walker.

From Andrews Gift Books: *Thanks Mom!* by Claire Murray; *Warm and Fuzzy: A Ferret Guide to Friendship; Dogs Are Funny* by Kim Levin; *Jane Austen Speaks to Women* by

A

Edith Lank; *Happy Birthday* by Joan Walsh Anglund; *Bee Happy: It's Your Birthday* by Sue Dreamer; *Thanks! You're the Best* by Sue Dreamer; *Isn't She Beautiful? And Isn't He Beautiful?* by Lynn Johnston; *The Happy Book for Friends: 501 Happy Thoughts; What Love Is* by Laura Straus; and *Kristi Yamaguchi: Triumph on Ice.*

Tiny Tomes are tiny, of course—as well as topical, traditional, tactile, tempting, and targeted. These teeny books from Andrews and McMeel are less than half the size of their little gift books—the tactile allure of these palm-size volumes is said to be irresistible. Titles include: *Mom: You're the Greatest; A Tiny Treasury of African Proverbs; Sex: A Book of Quotations;* and *The Little Book of Coffee.*

Each volume in the Cader Unstamped Books line presents 16 sheets of exquisitely designed and printed stamps. Use them to personalize and decorate correspondence, collect them, or frame them. Titles here include: *Nature Unstamped; Holidays Unstamped;* and *Angels Unstamped.*

Representative of Andrews McMeel Children's Books are the following titles: *Rosie Plants a Radish* and *Sam Plants a Sunflower* (both Lift-the-Flap Books with Real Seeds) by Kate Petty and Axel Scheffler; *Hummingbirds: A Book and Build-Your-Own-Feeder Kit* by Luann Colombo; *Where Does Rain Come From?* and *Where Does the Sun Go at Night?* (both from the Junior Scientist Series) by C. E. Thompson; *Hit the Trail! The Camping Kit for Kids* by Cecilia Dinio-Durkin and Peter Durkin (illustrated by Rick Brown). We do not publish new children's titles anymore. Agents, please query. No unsolicited manuscripts are accepted. Query letters should be directed to:

Christine Schillig, Vice President and Editorial Director—General nonfiction, all categories.

Dorothy O'Brien, Assistant Vice President and Managing Director—Humor and general nonfiction.

Patty Rice, Senior Editor and Editorial Director—Gift Books and general nonfiction.

Jean Lucas, Editor—General nonfiction, gift books, humor.

Jennifer Fox, Editor—General nonfiction, gift books, humor.
   Born: December 10, 1973.
   Education: B.A. in Journalism from University of Missouri-Columbia.
   Employment history/editor career path: Began as an Editorial Assistant at Andrews McMeel in 1996.
   Personal interests: Wildlife conservation, environmental issues, cats/dogs, poetry, tennis, travel, music, movies.
   What would you be doing if you were not an editor? If I were not able to work in publishing of any kind, I would probably be working in the zoology field.
   What has been your most successful book that you have acquired to date? *You're Already a Success: Thoughts on Beginning Your New Career* by Peggy Ballard.
   What books have you acquired that make you the most proud? What books that you have acquired reflect the types of books you like to represent? *You're Already a Success: Thoughts on Beginning Your New Career* by Peggy Ballard; *2001 Ways to Pamper Yourself* by Lorraine Bodger; *Maggie's Way: Observations from Below Your Knees* by Bill Stanton; *Little Books,* written and illustrated by Joan Walsh Anglund.
   Do you represent fiction? No.

A

Do you represent nonfiction? Yes.

Do you require book proposals? If so, what do you look for in evaluating a book proposal? Yes. Solid summary, outline of book, competition, author bio, and sample text.

Are certain aspects of a book proposal given more weight than others? Summary, sample chapters, author bio.

What process do you use for making a decision? What is the process for acquisition, is there a committee? I usually get a couple of reads from other editors before taking it to an acquisitions meeting with the committee.

What kinds of nonfiction books do you want to see less of? Parenting, business, serious self-help.

Are you interested in work geared for the masses (readers of *People, The Star,* etc.)? Yes, very much so.

Are agents important? Why? Yes, they're great for screening the material and sending it to the right publishing houses. They are also helpful in dealing with difficult authors.

Do you like new writers? What should new writers do to break into the business? I mostly edit gift books where the author's name is usually not as important as the subject matter.

How should writers approach you? They should approach me with a hook—what makes their idea different and salable.

What are some common mistakes writers make? What really gets on your nerves? Writers who expect a great deal of attention and publicity for a small book. Writers who don't trust the publisher to make the right decisions. Writers who are too hands-on.

What can writers do to get your attention and to avoid the slush pile? Call me directly or address the proposal to my attention. But the best way is to have an agent.

What have been some of your craziest experiences with submissions? Receiving sloppy proposals, where it is obvious the writer spent about 30 seconds pulling it together.

What have been some of your best experiences with writers or in your job? Working with talented, hard-working, and professional writers whose books actually succeed. Then, signing up more books with those authors.

Is there anything you would like to see changed in the industry? Better pay!!

Any advice for writers? Any way to improve the system for you? Any additional thoughts? I'm always looking for gift books, light self-help, pop culture, and humor books. Remember to get an agent.

THE ANONYMOUS PRESS, INC.

332 Bleecker Street , New York, NY 10014

The Anonymous Press specializes in high-velocity projects that tap the current cultural pulse. The house is on the lookout for commercial, inherently marketable nonfiction in such areas as investigative and journalistic accounts; issue-oriented human-interest stories; celebrity biographies and memoirs; ultimate conspiracies, exposés, and scandalous affairs; and popular reference works (including high-interest single-volume encyclopedias, personal and professional how-to, and awareness).

The Anonymous Press, Inc. (founded in 1996), is an independent publisher dedicated to open expression and individual liberty. This is viewed as an activist mission, not a statement of guaranteed privilege. People must take it upon themselves to carry the ongoing fight for their personal right to pursue the life that's best for them. The press publishes in recognition of the primary designs of the book-buying public: looking good, feeling good, making money.

The Anonymous Press featured as its initial release *Sleeping with the President: My Intimate Years with Bill Clinton* by Gennifer Flowers—a powerful personal memoir written as a riveting political love story. Another Anonymous hit, *The Elvis Cover-Up* by Gail Brewer-Giorgio, explores the secret life of Elvis Presley, his connection to United States government law-enforcement agencies, and his involvement with a deep-cover sting operation; Elvis may have hoaxed his own death to lead a new life underground. This brandnew investigatory biography follows the author's *Is Elvis Alive?* (multimillion-copy *New York Times* bestseller); several highly rated, syndicated television specials and video documentaries; and *Orion* (bestselling pop-cultural fiction; dramatic story of a mercurial musical performer).

Anonymous wishes to break through old barriers to create new publishing frontiers; the house is open to a wide variety of creative projects that will inspire the publisher's marketing vision. It is essential that submitted materials be imaginatively conceived and in professional book-proposal format. Authors must demonstrate expertise in the chosen topic area and must offer thorough and credible documentation.

Do not send materials via registered mail, overnight express delivery, or any other means requiring a recipient's signature. Please query first.

Query letters and SASEs should be directed to:

(Mr.) Gilchrist (Chris) Bonner, Acquisitions

THE APEX PRESS

The Bootstrap Press

Council on International and Public Affairs
777 United Nations Plaza, Suite 3C, New York, NY 10017
914-271-6500
e-mail: cipany@igc.apc.org

Branch office:
Box 337, Croton-on-Hudson, NY 10520

Apex accents nonfiction titles in such fields as corporate accountability, grassroots and worker participation, and intercultural understanding. One special publishing focus is on economic and social justice, human rights, and the impact of technology on contemporary society.

The Apex Press (introduced in 1990) is an imprint of the nonprofit research, education, and publishing group Council on International and Public Affairs (CIPA). Apex publishes hardcover and paperback books that provide critical analyses of and new approaches to

A

significant economic, social, and political issues in the United States, other industrialized nations, and the Third World.

The Apex publishing program has a special focus on economic and social justice, human rights, and the impact of technology on contemporary society. The Council on International and Public Affairs was founded in 1954 and is a nonprofit research, education, and publishing group. The Council seeks to further the study and public understanding of problems and affairs of the peoples of the United States and other nations of the world through conferences, research, seminars and workshops, publications, and other means.

From Apex Press: *Inhuman Rights: The Western System and Global Human Rights Abuses* by Winin Pereira; *Washington's New Poor Law: Welfare "Reform" and the Roads Not Taken, 1935–1996* by Sheila D. Collins and Gertrude Schaffner Goldberg; *Corporate Power and the American Dream: Toward an Economic Agenda for Working People* (9th edition) by the Labor Institute; *Don't Lose Your Unemployment Benefits: A Handbook for Workers and the Unemployed* by Jose I. Portela; *The Good Neighbor Handbook: A Community-Based Strategy for Sustainable Industry* by Sanford J. Lewis; *Greenwash: The Reality Behind Corporate Environmentalism* by Jed Greer and Kenny Bruno; *Taking Care of Business: The Underbelly of the U.S. Economy: Joblessness and Pauperization of Work* by David Dembo and Ward Morehouse; *Human Rights: The Universal Declaration of Human Rights* by Winin Pereira; *Nuclear Weapons Are Illegal: The Opinions and Story Behind the Historic Decision of the World Court* (edited by Ann Fagan Giner); *Nurtured by Knowledge: Learning by Doing Participatory Action-Research* (edited by Susan E. Smith and Dennis G. Willms with Nancy A. Johnson); and *When Workers Decide: Workplace Democracy Takes Root in North America* (edited by Len Krimerman and Frank Lindenfeld).

The Apex Press handles its own distribution; the house catalog includes books and additional resources (including videos) from a number of publishers worldwide.

The Bootstrap Press

Intermediate Technology Development Group of North America

Bootstrap's publishing interest focuses on social economics and community economic change; the house covers small-scale and intermediate-scale or appropriate technology in both industrialized and emerging countries, with an aim to promote more just and sustainable societies. Its books explore business and industry theory and how-to, gardening and agriculture, building and construction, and communications.

The Bootstrap Press (inaugurated in 1988) is an imprint of Intermediate Technology Development Group of North America (ITDG/North America) in cooperation with the Council on International and Public Affairs.

Titles from Bootstrap: *Greening Cities: Building Just and Sustainable Communities* by Joan Reolofs; *Building Sustainable Communities: Tools and Concepts for Self-Reliant Economic Change* by C. George Benello, Robert Swann, and Shann Turnbull; *Chicken Little, Tomato Sauce and Agriculture: Who Will Produce Tomorrow's Food?* by Joan Dye Gussow.

Titles of Intermediate Technology Publications (London), previously distributed by the Bootstrap Press, are now available through Stylus Publishing.

A

Bootstrap publications are distributed with those of sibling operation the Apex Press. Query letters and SASEs should be directed to:

Judi Rizzi, Publications Manager

Ward Morehouse, President

APPLAUSE THEATRE BOOK PUBLISHERS

151 West 46th Street, 8th Floor, New York, NY 10036
212-575-9265   fax: 646-562-5852

Applause Theatre Book Publishers (established in 1983) produces a list geared to fields of stage, cinema, and the entertainment arts. Applause produces collections, compendiums, biographies, histories, resource books, reference works, and guides keyed to the needs of the house's wide readership of seasoned pros, rookies, and aficionados.

The Applause program covers hardback and paperback editions, among them a number of generously illustrated and well-produced works. Applause issues stage plays and screenplays (many in translation and many in professional working-script format) that run the gamut from the classical repertory to contemporary works in drama, comedy, and musicals. Applause also offers audio works and a video library. The publisher's backlist is comprehensive (it has never declared a single title out of print and goes back to press for as few as 500 copies of a backlist standby).

Special-production volumes encompass works that detail the background and history behind the creation of works for stage and screen, in addition to containing complete scripts.

Titles from Applause: *The Real Life of Laurence Olivier* by Roger Lewis; *An Actor and His Time* by John Gielgud; *Ralph Richardson: An Actor's Life* by Garry O'Connor; *Seats: The Insider's Guide to the Performing Arts and Sports in New York* by Sandy Millman; *The Other Way: An Alternative Approach to Acting and Directing* by Charles Morowitz; *Fundamental Acting: A Practical Guide* by Paul Kuritz; *Theatre on the Edge: New Visions, New Voices* by Mel Gussow; *The Smart Set: George Jean Nathan and H. L. Mencken* by Thomas Quinn Curtiss; *London Theatre Walks* by Jim DeYoung.

For theatrical professionals and students as well, Applause offers: *Acting in Film* (from the Applause Acting Series) by Michael Caine; *Telling Moments: 15 Gay Monologues* by Robert C. Reinhart; *The Actor and the Text* by Cicely Berry; and *The Secret of Theatrical Space* by Josef Svoboda.

Applause Theatre Books are distributed by R. R. Donnelley & Sons. Query letters and SASEs should be directed to:

Glenn Young, Publisher

ARCADE PUBLISHING

141 Fifth Avenue, New York, NY 10010
212-475-2633

A

Arcade Publishing (founded in 1988 by Jeannette and Richard Seaver) produces commercial and literary nonfiction and fiction, as well as selected poetry. Nonfiction standouts include issue-oriented titles, contemporary human-interest stories, and cultural historical works. Arcade's fiction list includes entrants in such categories as mystery, suspense, and thrillers. Arcade's program leans toward learned and enlightened reading.

From Arcade nonfiction: *The Queen and Di: The Untold Story* by Ingrid Seward; *The Hinge Factor: How Chance and Stupidity Have Changed History* and *The Weather Factor: How Nature Has Changed History* by Erik Durschmied; *Belief or Nonbelief?* by Umberto Eco and Cardinal Carlo Maria Martini; *Dealing with the Dragon* by Jonathan Fenby; *Ann the Word: The True Story of Ann Lee* by Richard Francis; *Hitler's Gift* by Jean Medawar and David Pyke; *Sorcerer's Apprentice* by Tahir Shah; *Roanoke: Solving the Mystery of England's Lost Colony* by Lee Miller; *The Emperor's Codes: The Breaking of Japan's Secret Ciphers* by Michael Smith; *Red Sorrow: A Memoir* by Nanchu; *Masquerade* by Tivadar Soros; *Sex in the Future* by Robin Baker.

Arcade fiction and literature: *Gardener to the King* by Frederic Richaud; *Destiny* by Tim Parks; *The Anyan Tree* by Christopher Nolan; *The Mystified Magistrate and Other Tales,* translated by Richard Seaver; *The Salt of Broken Tears* by Michael Meehan; *The Brush-Off* by Shane Maloney; *The Big Ask* by Sane Maloney; *Virgin* by Robin Maxwell; *The Chalon Heads* by Barry Maitland; *The Republic of Wine* by Mo Yan; *Shifu, You'll Do Anything for a Laugh* by Mo Yan, translated by Howard Goldblatt; *Requiem for a Lost Empire* by Andrei Makine, translated by Geoffrey Strachan.

Arcade Publishing is distributed by Little, Brown.

Prospective authors please note that Arcade does not accept unsolicited submissions. Query letters and SASEs should be directed to:

Calvert Barksdale, Senior Editor—All areas of house interest.

Jeannette Seaver, Executive Editor—Fiction: literary. Nonfiction: history, politics, literary criticism, cookbooks, illustrated books.

Richard Seaver, President—Fiction: literary. Nonfiction: history, politics, literary criticism, illustrated books.

JASON ARONSON INC., PUBLISHERS

230 Livingston Street, Northvale, NJ 07647
201-767-4093
www.aronson.com

Jason Aronson Inc., Publishers, marks two main sectors of publishing concentration: One Aronson line comprises psychotherapy, offering professional books (as well as some trade-oriented titles) in psychiatry, psychoanalysis, counseling (including pastoral care), and the behavioral sciences. The other Aronson publishing arena is Judaica, covering contemporary thought as well as traditional works. (Please see Aronson listing in Directory of Religious, Spiritual, and Inspirational Publishers.) Aronson's strong backlist encompasses a wide range of publications well regarded in the fields of psychotherapy and Judaica.

A

Among Aronson highlights in psychotherapy: *Creating the Capacity for Attachment: Treating Addictions and the Alienated Self* by Karen B. Walant; *Winning Cooperation from Your Child! A Comprehensive Method to Stop Defiant and Aggressive Behavior in Children* by Kenneth Winning; *Dancing with Fear: Overcoming Anxiety in a World of Stress and Uncertainty* by Paul Foxman; *Cognitive Therapy: Basic Principles and Applications* by Robert Leahy; *Sons, Lovers, and Fathers: Understanding Male Sexuality* by Didier Dumas; *Psychic Deadness* by Michael Eigen; *The Adolescent Journey: Development, Identity Formation, and Psychotherapy* by Marsha Levy-Warren; *Using DSM-IV: A Clinician's Guide to Psychiatric Diagnosis* by Anthony L. LaBruzza and José Méndez-Villarrubia; *A Curious Calling: Unconscious Motivations for Practicing Psychotherapy* by Michael R. Sussman.

Among Aronson highlights in *Judaica: The Thirteen Petalled Rose* by Adin Steinsaltz; *The Jewish Time Line Encyclopedia* by Mattis Kantor; *Night, Dawn, Day* by Elie Wiesel; *Reincarnation and Judaism* by Dov Ber Pinson; *The Synagogue Survival Kit* by Jordan Lee Wagner.

Jason Aronson Inc., Publishers (started in 1965), oversees a distribution network that utilizes its own in-house services as well as independent trade-fulfillment services. Aronson also features a direct-mail catalog that includes special-interest titles from other presses.

Query letters and SASEs should be directed to:

Arthur Kurzweil, Editor in Chief, Publisher (Judaica)

ARTE PÚBLICO PRESS

Piñata Books

University of Houston, 4800 Calhoun, Houston, TX 77204-2090
713-743-2841
http://bentley.uh.edu/arte_publico

Arte Público Press (founded in 1979) publishes books of fiction, poetry, drama, literary criticism, and art by the leading figures in Mexican-American, Puerto Rican, Cuban, and U.S. Hispanic literature. In addition, the press has a particular focus on Hispanic women's literature. Arte Público is the oldest and largest publisher of Spanish-American writing of the United States. The house publishes works in both the English and Spanish languages, as well as in bilingual editions. Arte Público's Piñata Books imprint is devoted to books for children and young adults that address the United States Hispanic experience. Arte Público issues a full roster of new titles each season and maintains a steadfast backlist.

The U.S. Hispanic Literary Heritage Series project locates, recovers from perishing, and publishes single titles and collections of primary literary sources written by Hispanics in the geographic area that is now the United States from the Colonial Period to 1960. The project will issue important titles to be considered for inclusion in the study of American literature. This project intends to fill the large gap that exists in American literature: the Hispanic contribution. The broad scope of the project includes recovery of all of the conventional literary genres, as well as such forms as letters, diaries, oral lore, and popular

A

culture by Cuban, Mexican, Puerto Rican, Spanish, and other Hispanic residents of what has become the United States.

Arte Público was the original publisher of *The House on Mango Street* by Sandra Cisneros (in 1985), and has published *The Last of the Menu Girls* by Denise Chavez, as well as the works of Victor Villaseñor, Rolando Hinojosa, and Luis Valdez. On the Arte Público list: *Giuseppe Rocco* by Ronald L. Ruiz; *Ask a Policeman: A Rafe Buenrostro Mystery* by Rolando Hinojosa; *Brand New Memory* by Elias Miguel Munoz; *South Wind Come* by Tina Juarez; *Havana Split* by Teresa Bevin; *Delia's Way* by Olga Berrocal Essex; *The Shadow* by Americo Paredes; *The Real Billy the Kid* by Miguel Antonio Otero, Jr. (introduction by John-Michael Rivera); *Tropical Town and Other Poems* (edited by Salomon de la Selva, with an introduction by Silvio Sirias); *Salsa* by Lilian Colon-Vila; *The Year of Our Revolution* by Judith Ortiz Cofer; *Rina's Family Secret: A Roosevelt High School Series Book* by Gloria Velasquez; *The Tall Mexican: The Life of Hank Aguirre, All-Star Pitcher, Businessman, Humanitarian* by Bob Copley; *A Wake in Ybor City* by Jose Yglesias; *The Cutter* by Virgil Suarez; *A People Forgotten, a Dream Pursued: The American GI Forum, 1948–1983* by Henry Ramos; *Women Don't Need to Write,* by Raquel Puig Zaldivar; *The Big Banana,* by Roberto Quesada (translated by Walter Krochmal).

Arte Público handles its own distribution and distributes Hispanic literature for smaller presses, in addition to publishing *The Americas Review* literary journal. Query letters and SASEs should be directed to:

Clifford Crouch, Executive Editor

Nicolás Kanellos, Publisher

Piñata Books

Piñata Books (launched in 1994) is the first imprint devoted to providing literary materials for children and young adults that authentically and realistically portray themes, characters, and customs unique to Hispanic culture in the United States. Selections include picture books, novels, and short story collections.

Titles from Piñata: *Hispanic, Female and Young: An Anthology* (edited by Phyllis Tashlik); *Jumping Off to Freedom* (novel) by Anilú Bernardo; *The Gift of the Poinsettia* (children's picture book) by Pat Mora and Charles Ramírez Berg (illustrated by Daniel Lechón); *Walking Stars* (memoir) by Victor Villeseñor; *Mexican Ghost Tales of the Southwest* (folktales) by Alfred Avila (edited by Kat Avila); and *Aplanso! Hispanic Children's Theater* (edited by Joe Rosenberg).

ATHENEUM PUBLISHERS

See Scribner Rawson Associates.

AUTONOMEDIA/SEMIOTEXT(E)

55 South Eleventh Street, P.O. Box 568, Williamsburgh Station, Brooklyn, NY 11211-0568
phone/fax: 718-963-2603
www.autonomedia.org

Autonomedia/Semiotext(e) accents radical culture, media and politics; gender and ethnicity; fiction and belles lettres; and contemporary, futurist, and historical criticism. The two divisional imprints overlap in their respective areas of interest; however, Autonomedia and Semiotext(e) remain distinctive entities with regard to editorial approach and featured series lines.

Although Autonomedia/Semiotext(e) publications are not intended for specialist market sectors, individual titles are of particular appeal to media buffs, political watchers, pop-culture hounds, and aficionados of the arts, as well as artistic practitioners; the publishing scope also includes works that speak distinctly to an academic audience.

Autonomedia/Semiotext(e) is a publisher with a vision and a mission. Begun in 1983, this double-barreled house produces a powerful list of what is portrayed as movement literature. Whatever the designation—traditional book-publishing labels simply do not stick—Autonomedia/Semiotext(e) describes its role as that of an antiauthoritarian publisher; it shows a bent for literature that examines culture from a perspective that is against work and all forms of exploitation, and promotes actively the abolition thereof.

The house oversees its own distribution.

Autonomedia

Autonomedia emphasizes cultural theory and criticism. The house features original artistic and literary expression on topics that radiate from perspectives of ethnicity and race (black radicalism), notions of gender and sexuality (gay, lesbian, feminist), and spirited renditions of personalized philosophical viewpoints. Autonomedia produces a gamut of creative thought that, although perhaps implicitly active in political arenas, is essentially unfettered by conventional notions of partisanship.

Indicative of the Autonomedia list: *The Ibogaine Story: Report on the Staten Island Project* by Paul Di Rienzo and Dana Beal; *On Anarchy & Schizoanalysis* by Rolando Perez; *God & Plastic Surgery: Marx, Nietzsche, Freud & the Obvious* by Jeremy Barris; *Model Children: Inside the Republic of Red Scarves* by Paul Thorez; *About Face: Race in Postmodern America* by Maliqalim Simone; *The Rotting Goddess: Classical Origins of the Witch Cult* by Jacob Rabinowitz; *Gone to Croatan: Origins of American Dropout Culture* (edited by Saklolsky and Koehnline); *File Under Popular: Theoretical and Critical Writings on Music* by Chris Cutler; *Cassette Mythos: The New Music Underground* (edited by Robin James); *Rethinking Marxism* (edited by Resnick and Wolff); *By Any Means Necessary: Outlaw Manifestos, 1965–1970* (edited by Stansill and Mairowitz); and *The Daughter* by Roberta Allen.

New Autonomy is a series of anarchist and antihierarchical works in the areas of literature, politics, and culture. Bob Black (author of the successful title *Friendly Fire*) and Tad Kepley are coeditors of *Zero Work: The Anti-Work Anthology*—a collection of writings that in large measure epitomizes the publisher's primary stance.

Query letters and SASEs should be directed to:

Kevin Coogan, Submissions Editor

Semiotext(e)

www.semiotexte.org

The Semiotext(e) lineup features series keyed to such fields as radical European continental philosophy (including works by Jean Baudrillard, Pierre Clastres, and Michel

A

Foucault); social and cultural theory; gender expression and sexuality (including fiction, essay, and memoir); artistic and political affairs; and native Asian feminist and gay literature (including fiction and poetry).

Representative titles from Semiotext(e): *Walking Through Clear Water in a Pool Painted Black* by Cookie Mueller; *Hannibal Lecter, My Father* by Kathy Acker; *How I Became One of the Invisible* by David Rattray; *Reading Brooke Shields: The Garden of Failure* by Eldon Garnet; *If You're a Girl* by Ann Rower; *Polysexuality* (edited by François Peraldi); *Semiotext(e): Architecture* (edited by Hraztan Zeitlian); *Semiotext(e) USA* (edited by Jim Fleming and Peter Lamborn Wilson); *In the Shadow of the Silent Majorities* by Jean Baudrillard; and *Speed and Politics* by Paul Virilio.

Query letters and SASEs should be directed to:

Jim Fleming, Editor

Sylvere Lotringer, Editor

AVALON BOOKS

160 Madison Avenue, New York, NY 10016
212-598-0222   fax: 212-979-1862
www.avalonbooks.com   e-mail: avalon-books@att.net

Avalon Books produces fiction lines primarily for distribution to library and institutional markets on a subscriber basis. Avalon editions are wholesome family stories in the following categories: traditional mysteries; mainstream romance; career romance; traditional genre Westerns. Avalon produces a line of literary classics in reprint (on the Airmont Classics imprint).

Avalon Books (a subsidiary of Thomas Bouregy & Company, founded in 1950) publishes a primarily hardcover fiction list. The house emphasis on new original novels caters to the tastes and preferences of the all-important library readership; stories should consist of those likely to be of high interest to the patrons of this core market.

From the Avalon list: *Cyber Bride* by Annette Couch Jared; *In a Wink* by Lacey Green; *Only You* by Joye Ames; *Sweet Surrender* by Janet Cookson; *Endangered* by Eric C. Evans; *Face Down* by Jack Lewis; *Last Dance* by Joyce and Jim Lavene; *Ten and Me* by Johnny D. Boggs; and *The Gold of Black Mountain* by Kent Conwell.

Distribution is primarily through library sales. Query letters and SASEs should be directed to:

Veronica Mixon, Editor

Erin Cartwright, Senior Editor
Avalon Books, 401 Lafayette Street, New York, NY 10003
fax: 212-979-1862
www.avalonbooks.com
   Born: January 20.
   Education: B.A., in English and History from University of Delaware.
   Employment history/editor career path: I grew up in the Bahamas, and I always knew I wanted to be a novelist and live in New York City. I discovered that I liked to edit

A

much more than I liked the actual writing, so I became an Editor. I started out at a small magazine company called *Details Magazine*. I moved from there to Simon & Schuster for five years and then to Harper Collins for two years. I have been a Senior Editor at Avalon Books for one year.

Personal interests: Biking, running, snow boarding, travel, writing.

What would you be doing if you were not an editor? Teaching.

What has been your most successful book that you have acquired to date? *The Vitamin E Factor* and *Worst Fears Realized*, both on the *New York Times* Bestseller Lists.

What books have you acquired that make you the most proud? What books that you have acquired reflect the types of books you like to represent? *Love is Friendship Caught on Fire* by Guy Zona.

Do you represent fiction? If so, what do you look for? Yes. Romance, mysteries, Westerns. I look for good writing, good stories, believable characters, and something that has a different edge to it.

Do you represent nonfiction? No.

Do you require book proposals? If so, what do you look for in evaluating a book proposal? No book proposal, but I do ask for a brief synopsis and the first three chapters with an SASE. If I like what I see, I will then request the entire manuscript.

What process do you use for making a decision? What is the process for acquisition, is there a committee? There is not a committee, but I will give the manuscript to about two or three people to also read. If they agree that it is a good buy, we will then discuss it in more detail.

Are agents important? Why? Yes, they are important for people who have published multiple books. I think first-time authors don't necessarily need an agent, it's when you decided to move on with more books, to the bigger houses, with a complicated contract, that you need an agent.

Do you like new writers? What should new writers do to break into the business? Yes. Most of my authors are first or second time authors. I think it's always good to have a fresh voice. To break into the business, you should take writing classes, always write, never give up even when the rejections are pouring in, and have others read and critique your work.

How should writers approach you? Go to the LMP or similar resources and find out what my submission guidelines are. Always give away the ending to your story in your cover letter to me; you don't have to "hook" an editor.

What are some common mistakes writers make? What really gets on your nerves? I tend to see the same kind of romances over and over again. There are too many cowboy romance stories. I don't like when the characters get killed in the stories in car accidents. It bothers me when people don't do their homework and submit something outside of my guidelines.

What can writers do to get your attention and to avoid the slush pile? Follow my submission guidelines.

What have been some of your craziest experiences with submissions? I've gotten some pretty weird stuff from people in prison. Manuscripts sent in from teenagers.

What have been some of your best experiences with writers or in your job? I have recently bought an author's first book—she's 80 years old! She just started writing about

A

10 years ago and was thrilled! This is the most wonderful feeling, to get to be the one to make someone's day.

What, if anything, makes you different from other editors? I am willing and happy to give anyone a chance. I will work with you even if everything is not perfect the first time around. If you have talent, and I don't feel I can buy your manuscript, I will take the time to suggest other editors who may like to take a look.

Is there anything you would like to see changed in the industry? I would like to see authors make more money.

Any advice for writers? Keep writing, do your homework, find out everyone's submission guidelines, and *never quit!* Keep writing and submitting until someone says "yes," because eventually someone will.

AVALON PUBLISHING GROUP
See also: Carroll & Graf and Avalon Travel Publishing.

Thunder's Mouth Press, Marlowe & Company, and Blue Moon Books
841 Broadway, Fourth Floor, New York, NY 10003
fax: 212-614-7887

Carroll & Graf
19 West 21st Street, Suite 601, New York, NY 10010

Avalon Travel Publishing
5855 Beaudry Street, Emeryville, CA 94608
e-mail: avalonpub@aol.com

The Avalon Publishing Group combines five unique firms, each component maintaining its own distinct publishing persons, and is distributed by Publishers Group West.

In mid-2001 Thunder's Mouth Press, Marlowe & Company, Blue Moon Books, and Carroll & Graf will relocate to 161 William Street, New York, NY 10038.

Thunder's Mouth Press publishes adult trade books in a variety of subject areas, concentrating most heavily on popular culture, film, music, current events, contemporary culture, biography/personality, fantasy, role-playing games, the arts, and popular reference. Thunder's Mouth Press copublishes, with Balliett and Fitzgerald, Adrenaline Books, which features a series of anthologies written about extreme adventure sports and stories, and Adrenaline Classics, reprints of adventure classics. Thunder's Mouth also collaborates with the National Institute on an imprint called Nation Books, which features selections from this premier independent magazine of politics and culture.

Marlowe & Company focuses on personal growth, spirituality, psychology, self-help, health, and healthful cooking. Marlowe & Company is involved in a copublishing venture with Balliett & Fitzgerald called Illumina Books, which draws therapy and self-help from the world's finest literature.

Blue Moon Books, founded by longtime Grove Press publisher Barney Rosset, publishes mass-market erotic fiction, with an emphasis on Victorian erotica and discipline.

Carroll & Graf publishes a combination of original and reprinted fiction and nonfiction. It has become known for its history and current affairs titles, as well as high-quality fiction and mysteries.

A

Avalon Travel Publishing guides features a combination of practicality and spirit, offering a unique traveler-to-traveler perspective perfect for an afternoon hike, around-the-world journey, or anything in between. Avalon Publishing Group publishes many guides by Rick Steves.

Representative of Thunder's Mouth Press: *The Book of Rick* by Philip Dodd; *Requiem for a Dream* by Hubert Selby, Jr.; *Gangs of New York* by Herbert Asbury; *Dreams: The Art of Boris Vallejo* by Boris Vallejo; *The Outlaw Bible of American Poetry* (edited by Alan Daufman); *Miles Davis* by Ian Carr; *Rebel for the Hell of It* by Armond White; *Soft as Steel* by Julie Bell; *Black Beauty* by Ben Arogundade; *Lobotomy: Surviving the Ramones* by Dee Dee Ramone.

Representative of Adrenaline Books: Storm: *Stories of Survival from Land, Sea and Sky* (edited by Clint Willis); *Adrenaline: The Year's Best Stories of Adventure and Survival 2000* (edited by Clint Willis); *Explore: Stories of Survival from Off the Map* (edited by Jennifer Sehwamm); *Climb: Stories of Survival from Rock, Snow and Ice* (edited by Clint Willis).

Representative of Adrenaline Classics: *Shackleton's Forgotten Men* by Lennard Binckel; *Annapurna South Face* by Sir Chris Bonington; *A Slender Thread* by Stephen Venables.

Representative of Nation Books: *The Best of the Nation* (edited by Victor Navasky and Katrina Vanden Hueval); *Cinema Nation: The Best Writing on Film from* The Nation *1913–2000* (edited by Carl Bromley); *Burning All Illusions: Writing from* The Nation *on Race* (edited by Paula Giddings).

Representative of Marlowe & Company: *The Glucose Revolution* by Jennie Brand-Miller, Kaye Foster-Powell, Thomas M. S. Wolever, and Stephen Colagiuri; *The Parent's Tao Te Ching* by William Martin; *Beach: Stories by the Sand and Sea* (edited by Lena Lencek and Gideon Bosker); *Eating for IBS* by Heather Van Vorous; *Soul Mapping* by Nina Frost, Kenneth Ruge, and Richard Shoup; *Vastu Living* by Kathleen Cox; *When the Little Things Count and They Always Count* by Barbara Pachier with Susan Magee; *Tofu Mania* by Brita Housez; *Best Food Writing 2000* (edited by Holly Hughes).

Representative of Illumina Books: *Heart: Stories of Learning to Love Again* by series Editor Thomas Dyja; *Cure: Stories of Healing the Mind and Body* by series Editor Thomas Dyja; *Why Meditate? The Essential Book About How Meditation Can Enrich Your Life* (edited by Clint Willis).

Representative of Blue Moon Books: *The Blue Moon Erotic Reader* (edited by Barney Rosser); *Shoe Leather* by Stan Kent; *Gynecocracy* by Viscount Ladywood; *CyberWebs* by Niranda Reigns; *Shadow Land II: Return to Random Point* by Eve Howard; *Suburban Souls* by Anonymous.

Representative of Carroll & Graf: *Master Georgie* by Beryl Bainbridge; *Close to the Wind* by Pete Goss; *Stanley Kubrick: A Biography* by John Baxter; *Faust's Metropolis* by Alexandra Richie; *One of Us* by David Freeman; *The Well* by Katie Hafner; *The Mammoth Book of Unsolved Crime* (edited by Roger Wilkes); *Military Blunders* by Saul David.

Representative of Avalon Travel Publishing: *Rick Steves' Europe Through the Back Door* by Rick Steves; *Road Trip USA: Cross-Country Adventures on America's Two-Lane Highways* by Jamie Jensen; *Travelers' Tales Greece* (edited by Larry Habegger and Sean O'Reilly); *Hidden Baja* by Richard Harris; *Moon Handbooks: Yellowstone/Grand Tetons* by Don Pitcher; *Foghorn Outdoors: Colorado Camping* by Tom Stienstra; *Great American Motorcycle Tours* by Gary McKechnie.

Avalon Publishing Group is unable to accept unsolicited manuscripts or queries at this time. Query letters and SASEs should be directed to:

Neil Ortenberg: Thunder's Mouth Press

Matthew Lore: Marlowe & Company

Claiborne Hancock: Carroll & Graf

Heather Tidrick: Avalon Travel Publishing

Philip Turner, Carroll & Graf

AVERY PUBLISHING GROUP

375 Hudson Street, New York, NY 10014
212-366-2000

Avery was recently purchased by the Putnam Berkley Group. It will remain an active imprint.

Health and nutrition titles: *Smart Medicine for Healthier Living: A Practical A-to-Z Reference to Natural and Conventional Treatments for Adults* by Janet Zand, Allan Spreen, and James B. LaValle; *Smart Medicine for Your Eyes: A Guide to Safe and Effective Relief of Common Eye Disorders* by Jeffrey Anshel; *Prescription for Herbal Healing: A Practical A-Z Reference to Drug-Free Remedies Using Herbs and Herbal Preparations* by Robert Rister; *Japanese Herbal Medicine: The Healing Art of Kampo,* also by Robert Rister; *Secrets of Cooking for Long Life: Over 175 Fat-Free and Low-Fat Dishes from Exquisite Appetizers to Decadent Desserts* by Sandra Woodruff; *Barefoot Shiatsu: The Japanese Art of Healing the Body Through Massage* by Shizuko Yamamoto and Patrick McCarty; *Pregnancy to Parenthood: Your Personal Step-by-Step Journey Through the Childbirth Experience* by Linda Goldberg, Ginny Brinkley, and Janice Kukar; *The No-Time-to-Cook Cookbook: Fabulous Dishes for Today's Fast-Paced Lifestyle* by Marie Caratozzolo and Joanne Abrams; *The Real Vitamin & Mineral Book*—2nd edition by Shari Lieberman and Nancy Bruning; *Probiotics: Nature's Internal Healers* by Natasha Trenev; *Coping with Breast Cancer: A Practical Guide to Understanding, Treating, and Living with Breast Cancer* by Robert Phillips and Paula Goldstein; *The Skin Cancer Answer: The Natural Treatment for Basal and Squamous Cell Carcinomas and Keratoses* by I. William Lane and Linda Comac; and *St. John's Wort* by Hyla Cass.

John Duff, Editorial Director

Laura Shepherd, Executive Editor

AVON BOOKS (A DIVISION OF THE HEARST BOOK GROUP)

www.AvonBooks.com

The entire Hearst Book Group (Avon, Wm. Morrow) was acquired by News Corporation in late 1999. The acquisition brings Morrow/Avon together with News Corporation's HarperCollins Publishers, joining two companies with complementary strengths to create a full-service publishing leader.

All operations have been moved to the Harper address, and the Avon imprint is being re-reorganized within the Harper program.

BAEN PUBLISHING ENTERPRISES (BAEN BOOKS)

P.O. Box 1403, Riverdale, NY 10471
718-548-3100
www.baen.com

Baen publishes science fiction and fantasy writing. The house's new releases are generally published in mass-market paperback format, with targeted lead titles produced in trade paper and hardcover editions. Baen is a prominent publisher of series in science fiction and fantasy, and also publishes a notable lineup of collections and anthologies geared to various subgenre traditions and the works of individual writers.

Baen Publishing Enterprises (founded in 1984) concentrates its concise list on its proven categories of publishing strength. Baen's roster of writers includes James P. Hogan, John Ringo, David Weber, Marion Zimmer Bradley, Lois McMaster Bujold, John Dalmas, Robert A. Heinlein, Mercedes Lackey, Anne McCaffrey, Eric Flint, Spider and Jeanne Robinson.

From Baen: *Lt. Leary, Commanding* by David Drake; *Beyond World's End* by Mercedes Lackey and Rosemary Edgill; *Changer of Worlds* (edited by David Weber); *March Upcountry* by David Weber and John Ringo; *The Philosophical Strangler* by Eric Flint; *Thrice Bound* by Roberta Gellis; *The Spheres of Heaven* by Charles Sheffield; *Time Traders* by Andrea Norton; *The Legend That Was Earth* by James P. Hogan.

Baen Books is distributed by Simon & Schuster. Query letters and SASEs should be directed to:

James Baen, Editor in Chief

Toni Weisscoft, Executive Editor

THE BALLANTINE PUBLISHING GROUP (A DIVISION OF RANDOM HOUSE)

Ballantine

Del Rey

Fawcett

Ivy Books

One World

299 Park Avenue, New York, NY 10171
212-751-2600

The Ballantine Publishing Group is a Random House division that produces trade paperbacks and hardcovers, in addition to its traditionally commanding presence in mass-market paperbacks. The house is active in a full range of commercial fiction and nonfiction areas—originals as well as reprints. Hardcover originals bear the Ballantine or Fawcett logo; general trade paperbacks are likewise released under these two stamps. The other imprints in this division are typified by their respective specialist lines (see elsewhere in this guide). Ballantine is also home to a number of imprints geared to young-reader interest.

Ballantine and Fawcett fiction accents novels with a popular orientation, including mainstream, literary, and category works, with particular emphasis in mysteries, suspense, and thrillers. Representative titles: *The Kindness of Strangers* by Julie Smith; *The Lethal Partner* by Jake Page; *Imagine Love* by Katherine Stone; *A Shred of Evidence* by Jill McGown; *That Day the Rabbi Left Town* by Harry Kemelman; *Pentecost Alley* by Anne Perry; *My Lover Is a Woman: Contemporary Lesbian Love Poems* (edited by Lesléa Newman); and *Buck Naked* by Joyce Burditt.

Ballantine and Fawcett nonfiction plays to the high-interest commercial arena. Titles include *Spontaneous Healing* by Andrew Weil, M.D.; *Creating from the Spirit: Living Each Day as a Creative Act* by Dan Wakefield; *Without Child: Challenging the Stigma of Childlessness* by Laurie Lisle; *The 5-Day Miracle Diet* by Adele Puhn; and *Sun Pin: The Art of Warfare* (translated by D. C. Lau and Roger T. Ames).

Del Rey publishes science fiction and fantasy titles (originals and reprints) in hardcover, trade paper, and mass-market paperback formats, including major series offerings. Titles here are *The Crystal Singer Trilogy* by Anne McCaffrey; *The Ringworld Throne* by Larry Niven; *First King of Shannara* by Terry Brooks; *The Warrior Returns* (an epic fantasy of the Anteros) by Allan Cole; and *Slow River* by Nicola Griffith.

Ivy Books is a mass-market paperback imprint that covers a wide range of fiction and nonfiction.

One World is a distinguished imprint that presents commercial and literary writing from authors representing a variety of world cultures. One World books include *Getting Good Loving: How Black Men and Women Can Make Love Work* by Audrey B. Chapman; *Low-Fat Soul* by Jonell Nash; *Messengers of the Wind: Native American Women Tell Their Life Stories* (edited by Jane Katz); *Crossing over Jordan* by Linda Beatrice Brown; *Brotherman: The Odyssey of Black Men in America—An Anthology* (edited by Herb Boyd and Robert L. Allen); and *Native Wisdom for White Minds: Daily Reflections Inspired by the Native Peoples of the World* by Anne Wilson Schaef.

Query letters and SASEs should be directed to:

Cathy Repetti, Associate Publisher—Mass market nonfiction: health, biographies, diet, popular culture.

Anita Diggs, Senior Editor—One World Books (multicultural imprint).

Dan Smetanka, Senior Editor—Literary fiction and nonfiction.

Elisa Wares, Senior Editor—Fiction: commercial women's, Regency romances, some historicals.

Joanne Wyckoff, Senior Editor—Nonfiction: history, women's issues, biography, current events. Some literary fiction.

Joe Blades, Executive Editor and Associate Publisher—Fiction: hardcover and mass-market originals; mysteries, suspense, espionage.

Judith Curr, Publisher and Editor in Chief—Oversees entire hardcover and mass-market programs. Wide range of how-to/self-help nonfiction titles. Frontlist fiction.

Leona Nevler, Editorial Director—Commercial fiction.

Maureen O'Neal, Editorial Director, Trade Paperbacks—Upscale, commercial nonfiction. Literary and commercial fiction. In charge of trade paperback program.

Shana Summers, Senior Editor—Women's fiction and romance.

Shelly Shapiro, Editorial Director—Science fiction and fantasy.

Nancy Miller, Editor—General nonfiction and fiction.

Linda Marrow, Editor—General nonfiction and fiction.

BANTAM BOOKS

1540 Broadway, New York, NY 10036
212-354-6500

Bantam is active in virtually every nonfiction area and fiction genre, including frontlist commercial categories and literary works. The fighting-cock logo of Bantam Books (founded in 1945) was for decades synonymous with paperbacks in mass-market editions. Bantam currently publishes hardcover and paperback originals, while carrying on its stalwart mass-market tradition (in both originals and reprints). Special Bantam frontlist titles enjoy simultaneous release on BDD Audio.

Bantam nonfiction: *Bones of the Master: A Buddhist's Monk Search for the Lost Heart of China* by George Crane; *Super Casino: Inside the "New" Las Vegas* by Pete Earley; *Flags of Our Fathers* by James Bradley with Ron Powers; *Pain Free: A Revolutionary Method for Stopping Chronic Pain* by Pete Egoscue with Roger Gittines; *After the Ecstasy, the Laundry: How the Heart Grows Wise on the Spiritual Path* by Jack Kornfield; *Strong Women Stay Slim* and *Strong Women Stay Young* by Miriam E. Nelson, Ph.D., with Sarah Wernick, Ph.D.; *Brave Journeys: Profiles in Gay and Lesbian Courage* by David Mixner and Dennis Bradley; *Dogs Behaving Badly* by Dr. Nicholas Dodman; *The Soup Has Many Eyes: From Shtetl to Chicago—A Memoir of One Family's Journey Through History* by Joann Rose Leonard; *Circling the Sacred Mountain: A Spiritual Adventure through the Himalayas* by Robert Thurman and Tad Wise; *Baby Minds: Brain Building Games Your Baby Will Love* by Linda Acredolo, Ph.D., and Susan Goodwyn, Ph.D.; *Calling the Circle: The First and Future Culture* by Christina Baldwin; *Yoga: Discipline of Freedom: The Yoga Sutra Attributed to Patanjali* (translated by Barbara Stoler Miller); *High-Tech Conception: A Comprehensive Book for Consumers* by Brian Kearney, Ph.D.); *The Manipulative Child: How to Regain Control and Raise Resilient, Resourceful, and Independent Kids* by E. W. Swihart, Jr., M.D., and Patrick Cotter, Ph.D.

Bantam fiction encompasses commercial novels; mysteries, suspense, and thrillers; science fiction and fantasy; romance and women's fiction; and select literary works. Crime Line is a Bantam imprint that accents topnotch suspense and detective fiction.

Titles here: *False Memory* by Dean Koontz; *The Least Likely Bride* by Jane Feather; *Fierce Invalids Home from Hot Climates* by Tom Robbins; *Jane and the Stillroom Maid:*

Being the Fifth Jane Austen Mystery by Stephanie Barron; *Grant: A Novel* by Max Byrd; *Follow the Stars Home* by Luanne Rice; *Chill Factor* by Chris Rogers; *Sold Down the River* by Barbara Hambly; *Deep Sound Channel* by Joe Buff; *Ship of Destiny* by Robin Hobb; *Star Wars: I, Jedi* by Michael Stackpole; *Wicked Widow* by Amanda Quick; *Pawing Through the Past* by Rita May Brown and Sneaky Pie Brown; *Places in the Dark* by Thomas H. Cook; *The Patient* by Michael Palmer; *Tough Cookie* by Diane Mott Davidson.

Query letters and SASEs should be directed to:

Ann Harris, Senior Editor—Nonfiction interests consistent with the house list.

Anne Lesley Groell, Editor—Fiction: Bantam Spectra science fiction/fantasy imprint.

Beverly Lewis, Senior Editor—Broad interests consistent with the house list.

Nita Taublib, Deputy Publisher—Projects consistent with the Bantam list.

Toni Burbank, Vice President and Executive Editor—Spirituality, addiction/recovery, health.

Wendy McCurdy, Senior Editor—Women's fiction, romance. Commercial nonfiction, popular culture.

Robin Michaelson, Editor—Nonfiction.

BANTAM DOUBLEDAY DELL PUBLISHING GROUP, INC.

Bantam Classics

Bantam Doubleday Dell Books for Young Readers

Bantam Hardcover

Bantam Trade Paperback

Bantam Mass Market

Crimeline

Domain

Fanfare

Spectra

Delacorte Press

The Dial Press

Delta

DTP

Dell

Island

1540 Broadway, New York, NY 10036
212-354-6500

Bantam Dell Publishing Group addresses the entire mainstream book-publishing spectrum, from frontlist commercial products to specialty nonfiction titles and genre fiction;

the house issues titles published in hardcover, trade paperback, and mass-market paperback rack editions. Bantam Dell publishes for adult and children's markets and catalogs an audio-publishing specialty list (BDD Audio). Bantam Dell Books for Young Readers hosts the house's children's program. (Please see subentries.)

Bantam Dell is a colossal enterprise that comprises under one canopy several formerly independent major houses (primarily Bantam and Dell/Delacorte) plus new lines (such as Broadway Books). Bantam Dell is itself owned by the German-based communications conglomerate Bertelsmann Publishing Group International.

Broadway Books is a dynamic trade division that accents highly marketable nonfiction projects, as well as selected titles in fiction. (Please see separate entry for Broadway Books.)

WaterBrook Press is a new venture in Christian publishing, an autonomous subsidiary of BDD located in Oregon (see WaterBrook Press in Directory of Religious, Spiritual, and Inspirational Publishers).

Bantam Dell Publishing Group handles its own distribution.

BARRICADE BOOKS INC.

185 Bridge Plaza North, Suite 308-A, Fort Lee, NJ 07024
201-944-7600
www.barricadebooks.com

Barricade's publishing interests include arts and entertainment; how-to/self-help; biography, history, politics, and current events; humor; natural sciences; New Age, occult, and religion; psychology, health, and sexuality; recreation; and true crime.

Barricade Books was founded in 1991 by the veteran publisher Lyle Stuart who had previously founded Lyle Stuart Books (Lyle Stuart Books eventually became the Carol Publishing Group before Carol closed its doors in late 1999). Barricade Books was launched in order to continue the tradition begun in 1956 when Lyle Stuart became a publisher—to specialize in books other publishers might hesitate to publish because they were too controversial.

Barricade sought bankruptcy protection in 1999, due to an expensive libel suit against them by Las Vegas gambling tycoon Steve Wynn, but the firm continues to operate.

Barricade publisher Carole Stuart is the author of a number of successful books, including *I'll Never Be Fat Again* and *Why Was I Adopted?* She has worked in book publishing her entire adult life. Lyle Stuart is a former newspaper reporter who launched his career as a book publisher with $8,000 that he won in a libel action against Walter Winchell. Stuart sold that company three decades later for $12 million. The Barricade catalog expands this tradition with a roster of freethinking writers that is perhaps unrivaled in the international commercial-publishing arena. Barricade's list is exemplary of publishing courage in action.

From Barricade: *The African American Woman's Health Book* by Dr. Valiere Alcena; *Wicked Women* by Betty Alt and Sandra Wells; *50 Years at the Craps Table* by "Malcolm Jay"; *Physician: The Life of Paul Beeson* by Richard Rappoport, M.D.; *Gas Station Thoughts and the Daily Journal of Wheeler Antabanez* by Matt Kent; *Don't Play the Slot Machines (Until You've Read This Book)* by Michael Gellar; *How to Survive the IRS* by

B

Michael Minns, Esq.; *Diamonds: Famous and Fatal* by Leo P. Kendall; *The Dead Pool* by Mike "Stretch" Gelfand and Mike Wilkinson; *The Charney Report* by Leon Charney; *The Complete Book of Werewolves* by Leonard R. N. Ashley; *The Encyclopedia of World War II Spies* by Peter Kross; *When Capone's Mob Murdered Roger Touhy* by John Touhy; *The Lazy Person's Guide to Fitness* by Charles Swencionis, Ph.D., and E. Davis Ryan; *Getting a Jump Start on Fitness* by Barbara Marrott; *Dirty Jokes for Women* by Liz Hughes; *Smiles for Seniors* by "J" (illustrated by Arthur Robins); *The Great Jewish Cartoon Book* by Neil Kerber; *Promises to Keep* by Ernest W. Michel; *Mark It with Stone* by Joseph Horn; and *The Nouvelle Yenta Cookbook* by Jeannie Sakol.

Popular fiction titles from Barricade: *Best Japanese Science Fiction Stories* by John L. Apostolou and Martin H. Green; *Boys and Girls Together* by William Saroyan; *I Love You! I Hate You, Drop Dead!* by Artie Shaw; *A Man of Respect* by Darryl London; *Measuring Lives* by Tom Foley; *Norman Corwini's Letters* (edited by A. J. Langguth); *Not Dying: A Memoir* by William Saroyan; *Orion: The Story of a Rape* by Ralph Graves; *Sister Cat* by Felix Gould; *Where The Money Is: A Novel of Las Vegas* by Ivan G. Goldman; *The William Saroyan Reader* (edited by Aram Saroyan).

Query letters and SASEs should be directed to:

Carole Stuart, Publisher

BARRON'S/BARRON'S EDUCATIONAL SERIES, INC.

250 Wireless Boulevard, Hauppauge, NY 11788
631-434-3311   fax: 631-434-3723
www.barronseduc.com

Barron's hosts a broad publishing operation that encompasses books in business and finance; gift books; titles in cooking, family and health, gardening, nature, pets, and retirement lifestyle; as well as selected titles in arts, crafts, and hobbying. Barron's produces computer books and software. The house highlights a children's line.

Barron's (founded in 1945) was originally known for its comprehensive line of study notes and test-preparation guides in business, literature, and languages, and standardized tests in individual subject and professional fields. The house offers a number of practical business series, retirement and parenting keys, programs on skills development in foreign languages (as well as in English), and specialty reference titles in allied areas of interest.

Barron's cookbooks address international cuisines as well as healthful cookery. Dictionaries of health-related terms and many other specialized topics are offered. Under the rubric of special-interest titles, Barron's produces series on arts and crafts techniques, biographies of well-known artists, and home and garden. Books on pets and pet care include numerous titles keyed to particular breeds and species of birds, fish, dogs, and cats.

Children's and young-adult books and books of family interest include series on pets, nature and the environment, dinosaurs, sports, fantasy, adventure, and humor. Many of these are picture storybooks, illustrated works, and popular reference titles of general interest.

Barron's Children's and young adult titles include: *What's That?* by Isobel Gamble (illustrations by Tim Warnes); *Hide and Seek Birthday Treat* by Linda Jennings (illustrations by Joanne Partis); *Touch, Taste and Other Feelings* by Ingrid Gordon; *Flop Ear* by

Guido Van Genechten; *Bunnies: Animal Babies Series; One, Two, Guess Who?* by Colin and Jacqui Hawkins; *Yucky Stuff* by Moira Butterfield, illustrations by Chris Fisher; and *The U.S. Constitution and You* by Syl A. Sobel, J.D.

Barron's offers an extensive general-interest series lineup of interest to students and educators: Masters of Music series, Megascope series, Bravo series, the History series, the Natural World series, and Literature Made Easy series.

Barron's Study Guides subjects include: book notes, college review, easy-way series, English language arts, EZ-101 Study Keys, foreign language, law, literature, mathematics, philosophy/religion, science, social studies, study tips/reference, and test preparation.

From Barron's: *The Perfect Life of Lovers* by Monique Pivot; *The Perfect Life of Fishermen* by Pierre Affre; *Love Potions & Charms: 50 Ways to Seduce, Bewitch, and Cherish Your Lover* by Francis Melville; *The New Food Lover's Companion,* 3rd edition by Sharon Tyler Herbst; Stained Glass by Pere Balldeperez; *Running* by Thomas Wessinghage, M.D.; *Junior Gold* by Nick Wright; *The Family Dog* by David Taylor; *Real Estate Handbook,* 5th edition by Jack P. Friedman, Ph.D., C.P.A., and Jack C. Harris, Ph.D.; *100+ Tactics for Office Politics* by Casey Hawley; *100 Careers in the Music Business* by Tanja Crouch; *Guide to Law Enforcement Careers,* 2nd edition by Donald B. Hutton and Anna Mydlarz; *Barron's Science Study Dictionary* by Chris Prescott; and *Let's Prepare for the Grade 8 Intermediate Social Studies Test* by Curt Lader.

Barron's handles its own distribution.

Send query letters with SASEs to:

Mark Miele, Managing Editor

Max Reed, Senior Editor

Linda Turner, Senior Editor

BASIC BOOKS

Perseus Publishing

10 East 53rd Street, 23rd Floor, New York, NY 10022-5299
212-207-7600   fax: 212-207-7703

Basic Books focuses on nonfiction in the areas of psychology and self-help, history and cultural studies, business and economics, women's studies, science, contemporary affairs, and politics.

Basic Books (founded in 1952), a former division of HarperCollins, became a subsidiary of the Perseus Books Group in 1997. Basic had published many distinguished academic, scientific, and philosophical titles, including works by Thomas Sowell, Charles Murray, and Amitai Etzioni. This backlist should form a solid foundation to Basic as it moves into the Perseus Books Group.

Basic has a rich heritage and a strong future as a bridge between trade books and the academy. Recent trends within the publishing business reinforce the conviction that the kind of targeted, serious, niche publishing that Basic does is culturally necessary and economically viable. Basic Books' sense of the word *basic* is not elementary but fundamental. Its goal is to publish books of reliable excellence: provocative books rooted in disciplinary thought but intended for a wider audience, books argued with intellectual vigor and told with narrative drive and literary voice.

Basic has always traded on its ability to commercially publish serious works and respond quickly to a variety of marketplaces. In a sense, Basic is a start-up business as well as a grand tradition.

Basic Book nonfiction titles: *Myths of Rich and Poor: The Long Triumph of the American Economy* by Michael W. Cox and Richard Alm; *George III* by Christopher Hibbert; *The Custody Wars: Why Children Are Losing the Legal Battle and What We Can Do About It* by Mary Ann Mason; *The Pity of War* by Niall Ferguson; *Living to 100 (The Art and Science of Living Longer and Better)* by Thomas T. Perls and Margery Hutter-Silver with John F. Lauerman; *Dangerous Waters: A Biography of the Boy Who Became Mark Twain* by Ron Powers; *Floods, Famines, and Emperors: El Nino and Fate of Civilizations* by Brian Fagan; *Tales of the Lavender Menace: A Memoir of Liberation* by Karla Jay; *The Verona Secrets: The Soviet Union's World War II Espionage Campaign Against the United States—And How America Fought Back* by Eric Breindel and Herbert Romerstein; *The Computers of Star Trek* by Lois Gresh and Robert Weinberg.

Perseus Publishing

Perseus Publishing publishes in the fields of business, science, health, parenting, psychology, and general nonfiction. Founded more than 20 years ago as the General Publishing Group of Addison Wesley, Perseus Publishing continues to bring readers some of the most stimulating and important books being published today. Some of the distinguished authors the house has published are Richard P. Feynman, Sir Martin Rees, Warren Bennis, Donald Vickery, M.D., James F. Fries, M.D., and William Bridges. Within Perseus Publishing are two special imprints: Helix Books, publishing trade and academic science books; and Merloyd Lawrence Books, publishing critically acclaimed books by many notable authors, especially in the areas of child development and health (T. Berry Brazelton, M.D.; Stanley Greenspan, M.D.; and Dr. Susan Love).

Basic will continue to distribute its books through HarperCollins. Query letters and SASEs should be directed to:

Brian Desmond, Managing Editor

Caroline Sparrow, Editorial Assistant

Don Fehr, Executive Editor—History and religion, biography, autobiography and memoir, narrative nonfiction, politics, and current affairs.

Glenda Johnson, Assistant to Publisher

Jessica Erace, Editorial Assistant

Jo Ann Miller, Executive Editor and Director of Behavioral Science Program—Psychology and contemporary social issues, including narrative nonfiction, memoirs, and books in education, women's issues, psychotherapy, health, and cognitive science.

John Donatich, Publisher and Vice President

Libby Garland, Editorial Assistant

Marian Brown, Director of Publicity

Matty Goldberg, Marketing Director

Sabrina Bracco, Sales and Marketing Coordinator

Timothy Bartlett, Senior Editor—Politics and current affairs.

Liz Maguire, Associate Publisher, Editorial Director

William Frucht, Senior Editor—Science. Frucht is the coauthor, with Dr. Larry Siever, of *The New View of Self: How Genes and Neurotransmitters Shape Your Mind, Your Personality, and Your Mental Health.*

Jacquelyn Murphy, Editor—Business subjects.

BEACON PRESS

25 Beacon Street, Boston, MA 02108
617-742-2110   fax: 617-742-2290
www.beacon.org

Beacon is primarily a publisher of nonfiction works (along with the annual winner of the Barnard New Women Poets Prize and some fiction reprints). Beacon's areas of publishing interest include contemporary affairs; gender, ethnic, and cultural studies; the life of the mind and spirit; history; science; and the spectrum of global and environmental concerns. The publisher also hosts a short, strong list of titles in literary essays and poetry. The house no longer publishes children's titles. Beacon Press tenders an extensive backlist.

Beacon Press has been a light of independent American publishing since 1854, when the house was established by the Unitarian Universalist Church. The Beacon Press list is presented as a complement to corporate publishing's rapt attention to commercially correct topics and as a publishing platform for those whose search for meaning draws them to fresh points of view. Indeed, the house's estimable reputation thrives on the diversity and divergence of the ideas and stances advanced by Beacon authors.

Beacon titles: *Notes of a Native Son* by James Baldwin; *The Winged Serpent: American Indian Prose* (edited by Margo Astov); *Sacrificed for Honor: Italian Infant Abandonment and the Politics of Reproductive Control* by David I. Kertzer; *An Autobiography: The Story of My Experiments with Truth* by Mohandas K. Gandhi, foreword by Sissela Bok; *Fist Stick Knife Gun: A Personal History of Violence in America* by Geoffrey Canada; *Talking About Death: A Dialogue Between Parent and Child* by Earl A. Grollman; *Tales of the Ashanti Father* by Peggy Appiah; *Thousand Pieces of Gold* by Ruthanne Lum Mc-Cunn; *Kindred* by Octavia E. Butler; *Transgender Warriors: Making History from Joan of Arc to Dennis Rodman* by Leslie Feinberg; *You Can't Be Neutral on a Moving Train: A Personal History of Our Times* by Howard Zinn; *Nice Jewish Girls: A Lesbian Anthology* (edited by Evelyn Torton Beck); *The Tribe of Dina: A Jewish Woman's Anthology* (edited by Melanie Kaye/Kantrowitz and Irena Klepfisz); *Heretic's Heart* by Margot Adler; *Nature and Walking* by Ralph Waldo Emerson and Henry David Thoreau (introduction by John Elder); *The Poetics of Space* by Gaston Bachelard; *House of Light* by Mary Oliver; *The Wrong Way Home: Uncovering the Patterns of Cult Behavior in American Society* by Arthur J. Deikman, M.D.; *A Buddhist Bible* (edited by Dwight Goddard); *Beyond God the Father: Toward a Philosophy of Women's Liberation* by Mary Daly.

B

Scholarly highlight: Beacon's edition of the seventeenth-century classic *Lieutenant Nun: Memoir of a Transvestite in the New World* by Catalina de Erauso (translated by Michele Stepto and Gabriele Stepto; foreword by Marjorie Garber).

Writers, please note these Beacon titles that address themes in the writing life: *Ruined by Reading: A Life in Books* by Lynne Sharon Schwartz; *Facing the Lion: Writers on Life and Craft* (edited by Kurt Brown); *Talking to Angels: A Life Spent at High Latitudes* by Robert Perkins.

Beacon Press is distributed to the trade by Ballantine Books, a division of Random House. In order to stem the tide of unsolicited manuscripts and unwanted queries, the house's stance is to accept agented manuscripts only (this means no unagented submissions). Agented query letters and SASEs should be directed to:

Camille Andrews, Editorial Assistant (direct all agented query letters to her attention).

Deanne Urmy, Executive Editor—Environmental and nature studies, family issues.

Deborah Chasman, Editorial Director—Gay/lesbian studies; African American, Jewish, Latino, and Native American studies.

PETER BEDRICK BOOKS

156 Fifth Avenue, New York, NY 10010
212-206-3738   fax: 212-206-3741
e-mail: bedrick@panix.com

Bedrick's list focuses on popular reference works in history, folklore and mythology, and women's studies; the Bedrick children's list accents highly illustrated nonfiction, including several ongoing series in world history and cultures, and numerous educational titles.

Peter Bedrick Books was established in 1983, following the founder's long and successful association with Schocken Books. Today a mid-sized publishing house with a fetching swan logo, Bedrick still has a personal touch—evident from the first Bedrick list, which featured adult and children's books and introduced the initial three titles in the Library of the World's Myths and Legends.

Special from Bedrick: *The World of the Pirate* by Valerie Garwood (illustrated by Richard Berridge); *The World of Native Americans* by Marion Wood (illustrated by Antonella Pastorelli and Federico Michelli); *The Atlas of the Classical World* by Piero Bardi (illustrated by Paola Ravaglia and Matteo Chesi); *The Atlas of World Cultures* by Brunetto Chiarelli and Anna Lisa Bebi (illustrated by Paola Ravaglia); *Slavery: From Africa to the Americans* by Christine Hatt.

The Inside Story series offers titles filled with full-color cutaway illustrations and informative text. Notable entrants here: *The Roman Colosseum* by Fiona Macdonald (illustrated by Mark Bergin); *A Renaissance Town* by Jacqueline Morley (illustrated by Mark Peppe).

First Facts Series titles: *First Facts About the American Frontier* and *First Facts About the Ancient Romans* by Fiona Macdonald; *First Facts About the Ancient Egyptians* and *First Facts About the Vikings* by Jacqueline Morley.

Peter Bedrick Books has been acquired by NTC/Contemporary Publishing. They do not accept any unsolicited manuscripts. Query letters and SASEs should be directed to:

Peter Bedrick, President and Publisher

B

MATTHEW BENDER & COMPANY, INC.
1275 Broadway, Albany, NY 12204
518-487-3000   fax: 518-487-3027
www.bender.com

Bender produces works in the fields of law, accounting, banking, insurance, and related professions. Areas of Bender concentration include general accounting, administrative law, admiralty, bankruptcy, civil rights law, computer law, elder law, employment/labor, environmental, estate and financial planning, federal practice and procedure, government, health care, immigration, insurance, intellectual property, law-office management, personal injury/medico-legal, products liability, real estate, securities, taxation, and worker's compensation.

Matthew Bender (founded in 1887), a member of the Reed Elsevier plc group, is a specialist publisher of professional information in print and electronic format. Bender publishes general references as well as state-specific works. Bender produces treatises, textbooks, manuals, and form books, as well as newsletters and periodicals. Many Matthew Bender publications are available in the CD-ROM format (Authority CD-ROM libraries make available the most comprehensive and accurate information for the practice of law) on the Internet and on Lexis-Nexis.

Matthew Bender has served professionals for more than 108 years and has achieved its unique status as a specialty publisher in diverse areas of the law. Matthew Bender combines in-house editorial talent and publishing ties with the foremost experts in the legal profession to produce a product that will fit its customers' needs. Practicing attorneys often serve as contributing legal writers in their areas of expertise. Matthew Bender is one of the world's leading publishers of legal analysis and case law and pours this experience and expertise into more than 500 publications in print and electronic formats and serves professionals in more than 160 countries.

Matthew Bender considers itself an essential partner with law professionals, providing integrated information, resources, and tools, and delivering that information in formats useful to its customers, to help them reach solutions with confidence.

Representative titles from Matthew Bender: *Computer Contracts* by Esther C. Roditt; *Cable Television Law: A Video Communications Practice Guide* by Charles D. Ferris, Frank W. Lloyd, and Thomas J. Casey; *Franchising* by Gladys Glickman; *The Law of Advertising* by George Eric Rosden and Peter Eric Rosden; *Business Organizations with Tax Planning* by Zolman Cavitch; *Employment Discrimination* by Lex K. Larson; *Moore's Federal Practice* by James William Moore and the Moore's Editorial Board; *Immigration Law and Procedure* by Charles Gordon, Stanley Mailman, and Stephen Yale-Loehr; *Responsibilities of Insurance Agents and Brokers* by Bertram Harnett; *World Patent Law and Practice: Patent Statutes, Regulations and Treaties* by John P. Sinnott and William

Joseph Cotreau; *Environmental Law Practice Guide* by Michael B. Berrard (General Editor); *Environmental Law in Real Estate and Business Transactions* by David R. Berz and Stanley M. Spracker.

Matthew Bender handles its own distribution. Query letters and SASEs should be directed to:

George Bearese, Vice President and Editor in Chief

B

BERRETT-KOEHLER PUBLISHERS

450 Sansome Street, Suite 1200, San Francisco, CA 94111-3320
415-288-0260
www.bkconnection.com   e-mail: bkpub@aol.com

Berrett-Koehler's nonfiction program accents the areas of work and the workplace, business, management, leadership, career development, entrepreneurship, human resources, and global sustainability. Berrett-Koehler Publishers (instituted in 1992) is an independent press that produces books, periodicals, journals, newsletters, and audiocassettes.

The Berrett-Koehler booklist is produced in well-crafted, ecologically aware hardcover and paperback editions.

Berrett-Koehler stands for a commitment to produce publications that support the movement toward a more enlightened world of work and more free, open, humane, effective, and globally sustainable organizations. They are committed to do publications that challenge conventional views of work and management, that create new lenses for understanding organizations, that pioneer new purposes and values in business, and that open up new sources of guidance for today's complex work world.

Their focus is seeking to make each book they publish successful, which seems natural, yet goes against the prevailing "numbers game" model in conglomerate publishing: put out large numbers of titles and see which ones succeed with little support from the publisher. Unfortunately, most conglomerates' titles do not succeed and have only a short shelf life before they go out of print. Berrett-Koehler is committed to keeping books in print far longer than the big publishers' norm, and, in fact, none of our first five years' titles has yet gone out of print. A key to making each book successful and keeping books in print is Berrett-Koehler's marketing through multiple channels in addition to bookstores (such as direct mail, corporate sales, and association sales) to not only support bookstore sales but to also provide an ongoing life for books when their bookstore shelf life is past.

Titles: *301 More Ways to Have Fun at Work* by Dave Hemsath; *Downshifting* by John D. Drake; *E-Supply Chain* by Charles C. Poirier and Michael J. Bauer; *Helping Your New Employee Succeed* by Elwood F. Holton, III, and Sharon S. Naquin; *How to Succeed in Your First Job* by Elwood F. Holton, III and Sharon S. Naquin; *Leadership and the New Science* by Margaret J. Wheatley; *Love 'Em or Lose 'Em* by Beverly Kaye and Sharon Jordan-Evans; *The 21 Success Secrets of Self-Made Millionaires* by Brian Tracy; *The Influence Edge* by Alan A. Vengel; *The New Super Leadership* by Charles C. Manz, Ph.D., and Henry P. Sims, Jr.; and *Whistle While You Work* by Richard J. Leider and David A. Shapiro.

Bestselling titles from Berrett-Koehler include: *Emotional Value* by Janelle Barlow and Dianna Maul; *Taking Back Our Lives in the Age of Corporate Dominance* by Ellen Schwartz and Suzanne Stoddard; *Managing Your Own Learning* by James R. Davis and Adelaide B. Davis; *Future Search* by Marvin R. Weisbord and Sandra Janoff; *Identity Is Destiny* by Laurence D. Ackerman; and *Results* by Richard A. Swanson and Elwood F. Holton, III.

Koehler tends its own multichanneled distribution, through bookstores, direct-mail brochures, catalogs, a toll-free telephone-order number, book clubs, association book services, and special sales to business, government, and nonprofit organizations; the house is distributed to the trade via Publishers Group West. Query letters and SASEs should be directed to:

Steven Piersanti, President and Publisher

Jeevan Sivasubramaniam, Managing Editor

B

BLOOMBERG PRESS

100 Business Park Drive, P.O. Box 888, Princeton, NJ 08542-0888
609-279-7049, 800-388-2749   fax: 917-369-8288
www.bloomberg.com/books   e-mail: press@bloomberg.com

Bloomberg publishes books in finance, personal finance, business, economics, management, investments, financial planning, and works within related categories. House imprints and specialty lines include: Bloomberg Professional Library (primarily for financial professionals), Bloomberg Personal Bookshelf (consumer-oriented personal finance and investing titles), and Bloomberg Entrepreneur (small businesses and entrepreneurship).

Bloomberg Press (founded in 1996) is part of Bloomberg L.P., a global, multimedia-based information service that combines news, data, and analysis for financial markets and businesses. The company runs a real-time financial-information network, as well as a number of news-service operations (supplying news and stories to, among other clients, reporters, editors, and news bureaus), and radio, Web, and television enterprises (Bloomberg Radio, Bloomberg.com, Bloomberg Television).

The goal at Bloomberg Press has been to cut through the technical static of the markets and provide a clear picture. Bloomberg Press books pack a lot of information into a small package. They are designed to be functional as well as factual, and are organized and designed to take the reader's busy schedule into account. Authors are prominent authorities and writers.

Bloomberg publishes books for brokers, traders, portfolio managers, analysts, money managers, CEOs, CFOs, bankers, and other financial professionals, as well as for small-business people, consultants, and sophisticated investors worldwide. Subject areas include: investment intelligence, portfolio management, markets, financial analytics, economic analysis of use to traders and other financial professionals.

Representative titles: *Best Practices for Financial Advisors* by Mary Rowland; *Thriving as a Broker in the 21st Century* by Thomas J. Dorsey; *New Thinking in Technical Analysis* (edited by Rick Bensignor); *Small Cap Dynamics* by Satya Pradhumah.

Categories for consumers, business people, and professionals include: investing; managing personal wealth; choosing products and services, including insurance, health care,

B

banking services, and real estate; personal-finance reference, education, use of personal computers for investment decisions, and online information; and other topics, from a personal-finance angle, such as credit, taxes, and estate planning.

Titles include: *Investing in Small-Cap Stocks* by Christopher Graja and Elizabeth Ungar, Ph.D.; *Investing 101* by Kathy Kristof; *In Defense of Free Capital Markets* by David F. DeRosa; *The Pied Pipers of Wall Street* by Benjamin Cole.

Bloomberg markets its products and services internationally, through a creative variety of outlets, including traditional print venues as well as electronic distribution. Bloomberg Press is distributed by W. W. Norton & Company.

Query letters and SASEs should be directed to:

Tracy Tait, Assistant Editor

Blue Moon Books
(A Subsidiary of the Avalon Publishing Group)

841 Broadway, New York, NY 10003
212-505-6880
www.bluemoonbooks.com

Blue Moon's Web site contains a complete listing of available books, cover art, the Blue Notes newsletter, ordering information, writer's guidelines, and snippets of erotica. Blue Moon's erotica includes some of the finest novels and stories in the field. Blue Moon Books also publishes selected trade fiction and nonfiction. Blue Moon Books was established in 1987 by Barney Rosset, the trailblazing publisher who earlier founded Grove Press and developed that enterprise into a house of international literary, cultural, and commercial renown.

Blue Moon erotica: *The Encounter* by Maria Madison; *Romance of Lust* by Anonymous; *Mariska* by Olga Tergora; *Shogun's Agent* by Akahige Namban; *Sundancer* by Briony Shilton; *Ironwood Revisited* by Don Winslow; *Shadow Lane III: The Romance of Discipline* by Eve Howard; *Souvenirs from a Boarding School* by Anonymous; *The Pearl* by Anonymous; *Julia* by Elaine Rice; *Carousel* by Daniel Vian; *Our Scene* by Wilma Kauffen; *The Captive III* by Anonymous; *My Secret Life* by Anonymous; *Laura* by Patrick Hendren; *The Reckoning* by Anonymous; and *Ellen's Story* by Anonymous.

In addition to fervid classical romances, Blue Moon offers erotic works with such contemporary themes as psychosexual suspense thrillers; the house offers a significant listing of erotic fiction by women.

Blue Moon Books oversees its own distribution. The house no longer accepts unsolicited submissions. All work must be submitted by literary agents.

Bonus Books, Inc.

160 East Illinois Street, Chicago, IL, 60611-3880
312-467-0580   fax: 312-467-9271
www.bonus-books.com   e-mail: bb@bonus-books.com

Bonus publishes general nonfiction, accenting titles in automotive, broadcasting, business and careers, collectibles, consumer, legal, self-help, health and fitness, cooking, autobiography and biography, books of regional interest (including the Chicago area), sports, gambling, and current affairs. Titles from the Precept Press imprint are written by and for fundraising professionals, physicians, and the broadcasting industry.

Bonus Books, Inc. (founded in 1985) had an original focus on sports titles and grew quickly into a trade book publisher with nationwide prominence. Strong Bonus growth categories have been sports books and gambling books. As Bonus publisher Aaron Cohodes remarked in a letter to booksellers, "I don't know what this says about our society, but perhaps that's just as well."

Bonus highlights include: *Score!* by Gene Hart with Buzz Ringe; *The Best of the Ring* by Stanley Weston; *Insider's Guide to Stock Car Racing* by Richard Huff; *Ditka: An Autobiography* by Mike Ditka with Don Pierson; *The Game I'll Never Forget* by George Vass; *Be My Love: A Celebration of Mario Lanza* by Bob Dolfi, Damon Lanza, and Mark Muller; *What Will My Mother Say?* by Dympna Ugwu-Oju; *Reading Between the Lips* by Lew Golan; *Buttermilk: The Rest of the Carton* by Susan Costello and Anna Heller; *Opaa! Greek Cooking New York Style* by George J. Gekas; *Prairie Recipes and Kitchen Antiques: Bella and Me* by Herbert Block; *Stuck in the Seventies,* 2nd edition by Scott Matthews; *Forever Craps* by Frank Scoblete; *Thrifty Gambling* by John Brokopp; *The Coin Collector's Survival Manual,* 4th edition by Scott A. Travers; *Chicago's Best Restaurants,* 9th edition by Sherman Kaplan; and *The Complete Win at Spades* by Joseph Andrews.

Bonus's watershed title, *Ditka: An Autobiography* by Mike Ditka with Don Pierson, remains in print on a sturdy backlist. Other Bonus backlist favorites are their bestselling gambling titles: *Best Blackjack* and *Break the One-Armed Bandits* by Frank Scoblete; *Getting Lucky* by Ben Johnson. More strong backlist titles include: *101 Ways to Make Money in the Trading-Card Market Right Now!* by Paul Green and Kit Kiefer; *Overlay: How to Bet Horses Like a Pro* by Bill Heller; *Quarterblack: Shattering the NFL Myth* by Doug Williams with Bruce Hunter; *Settle It Yourself: When You Need a Lawyer—And When You Don't* by Fred Benjamin and Dorothea Kaplan.

Bonus Books distributes its own list and utilizes a number of national sales representatives. Query letters and SASEs should be directed to:

Devon Freeny, Managing Editor

Karen Housler, Promotion Manager

MARION BOYARS PUBLISHING

U.K. Office:
Marion Boyars Publishing, 24 Lacy Road, London SW15 INL, England, U.K.
Note: Marion Boyars' New York office has closed.

The Marion Boyars publishing program gives preeminence to fine writing and is open to considering the highest level of expression in virtually any category. Areas of particular Marion Boyars accomplishment are in the fields of fiction, poetry, belles lettres, memoirs, literary criticism, biography, music, theater, sociology, and travel. Marion Boyars Publishing (founded in 1978) has achieved international renown and commercial presence in

B

letters with an individualist precision and personalized disposition. Marion Boyars releases a moderate-sized seasonal list; the house tends a strong backlist. Though not technically a United States publishing house (projects emanate editorially from the London base), Boyars presents writers whose works may have more of an international appeal than a strictly commercial-American flavor. The publisher acquires on the basis of enthusiasm for a given work—and this is not necessarily based on projections of huge initial sales. Indeed, Marion Boyars herself has remarked that overlooked books and translations are often the house's jewels.

A representative coup is the English-language publication of *Nip the Buds, Shoot the Kids* by Nobel Laureate Kenzaburo Oe. On the Marion Boyars list: *Gents* by Warwick Collins; *Asher* by Mark Fyfe; *The Ministry of Hope* by Roy Heath; *Four Black Revolutionary Plays* by Amiri Baraka; *Creativity and Disease* by Dr. Philip Sandblom.

Marion Boyars Publishing is distributed by Rizzoli International; books are also available to the trade through the LPC Group. Query letters and SASEs should be directed to:

Cathy Kilgarriff, President, Editor in Chief

BOYDS MILLS PRESS
(A SUBSIDIARY OF HIGHLIGHTS FOR CHILDREN)
815 Church Street, Honesdale, PA 18431
570-253-1164, 800-490-5111   fax: 717-253-0179

Boyds Mills produces books for children, picture books, novels, nonfiction, and poetry—nonsensical verse, as well as more serious fare. The press promotes a solid seasonal list of new titles and hosts a hefty backlist. Boyds Mills Press (founded in 1990) is a subsidiary of Highlights for Children.

Boyds Mills wants books that challenge, inspire, and entertain young people the world over. Boyds Mills has published such international bestsellers as Dougal Dixon's *Dinosaurs* (over a dozen editions in 10 languages, plus multivolume spinoffs).

Boyds Mills releases: *The Farmer in the Dell* (illustrated by John O'Brien); *The World of Animals by Day and Night* by Ron Hirschi (photographs by Thomas D. Mangelsen); *See the Stars: Your First Guide to the Night Sky* by Ken Croswell; *How God Fix Jonah* by Lorenz Graham (illustrated by Ashley Bryan); *Rio Grande: From the Rocky Mountains to the Gulf of Mexico* by Peter Lourie; *Mississippi River: A Journey Down the Father of Waters* by Peter Lourie; *Happy Hanukkah* (edited by Jeff O'Hare, illustrated by Arthur Friedman and Mary Rhinelander); *Two Bad Babies* by Jeffie Ross Gordon (illustrated by Chris L. Edemarest); *Just Like My Dad* by Tricia Gardella (illustrated by Margot Apple); *Saint Nicholas* by Ann Tompert (illustrated by Michael Garland); *The Golden City* by Neil Waldman; *The Wisdom Bird* by Sheldon Oberman (illustrated by Neil Waldman); *What's Opposite?* by Stephen R. Swinburne; *Cat on Wheels* by Larry Dane Brimner (illustrated by Mary Peterson); *Look What You Can Make* (edited by Betsy Ochester); *Farmers Garden: Rhymes for Two Voices* by David L. Harrison (illustrated by Arden Johnson-Petro); *Santa and the Three Bears* by Dominic Catalano; *Uncommon Champions* by Marty Kaminsky; *Mr. Beans* by Dayton O. Hyde; *An Aligator Ate My Brother* by Mary

Olson (illustrated by Tammie Lyon); *New Moon* by Pegi Deitz Shea (illustrated by Cathryn Falwell); *Wanda's Roses* by Pat Brisson (illustrated by Maryann Cocca-Leffler).

Among featured Boyds Mills authors is Jane Yolen, award-winning author of more than 170 books. A sampling of her titles include: *All in the Woodland Early: An ABC Book; Before the Storm; How Beastly! A Menagerie of Nonsense Poems; An Invitation to the Butterfly Ball: A Counting Rhyme; Jane Yolen's Mother Goose Songbook; Weather Report: A Book of Poems; Street Rhymes Around the World; Once Upon Ice; Water Music;* and *Color Me a Rhyme.*

Boyds Mills Press handles its own distribution. Query letters and SASEs should be directed to:

Beth Troop, Manuscript Coordinator

B

BRASSEY'S INC.

22841 Quicksilver Drive, Dulles, VA 20166
703-661-1548   fax: 703-661-1547
www.brassey'sinc.com

Brassey's is a leading publisher in military history, biography, defense, national and international affairs, foreign policy, military reference, and intelligence. The Brassey's Sports imprint publishes trade titles related to various sports topics.

Forthcoming Brassey's titles include: *Aces in Command: Fighter Pilots as Combat Leaders* by Walter Boyne; *Legacy of Discord: Voices of the Vietnam War Era* by Gil Dorland; *The Fate of America: An Inquiry into National Character* by Michael Gellert; *Stealing Secrets, Telling Lies: How Spies and Codebreakers Helped Shape the Twentieth Century* by James Gannon; *Record Breakers of the North Atlantic: Blue Riband Liners 1838–1952* by Arnold Kludas; *The Final Crucible: U.S. Marines in Korea, Vol. II: 1953* by Lee Ballenger; *Hitler's Personal Pilot: The Life and Times of Hans Baur* by C. G. Sweeting; *Brassey's International Intelligence Yearbook: 2001 Edition* by Robert D. A. Henderson; *Baseball Prospectus: 2001 Edition* by Joseph Sheehan by Chris Kahrl et al.; *Rebel with a Cause: A Season with NASCAR Star Tony Stewart* by Monte Dutton; *Football's Most Wanted: The Top Ten Book of the Game's Outrageous Characters, Fortunate Fumbles, and Other Oddities* by Floyd Conner.

Query letter with SASE should be directed to:

Donald Jacobs, Senior Assistant Editor

Don McKeon, Publisher
   Born: April 15, 1952.
   Education: B.A., English, College of Holy Cross.
   Employment history/editor career path: My editorial career path had several detours, but the route was basically as follows: bookstore Clerk, Proofreader and Copy Editor, Managing Editor of a monthly defense and foreign affairs magazine, and then Publishing Manager of what was then Pergamon-Brassey's International Defense Publishers, Inc. I have been with Brassey's for 14 years.
   Personal interests: Reading (of course), volleyball, and motorcycling.

What would you be doing if you were not an editor? I'd possibly be working in international development. I served in the Peace Corps in West Africa after college.

What has been your most successful book that you have acquired to date? *Baseball Prospectus* by Chris Kahrl et al., a highly praised and entertaining annual analysis of baseball statistics, from the major league level down to the lowest minor leagues. Sales have improved each year, and now we're developing a *Football Prospectus* and a *Hockey Prospectus.*

What books have you acquired that make you the most proud? What books that you have acquired reflect the types of books you like to represent? I'm most proud of our books that make a real contribution to the literature, such as *Dien Bien Phu: The Epic Battle America Forgot* by Howard R. Simpson and *One War at a Time: The International Dimensions of the American Civil Wa*r by Dean B. Mahin. Other books that reflect the types of books I like to represent include *Baseball Prospectus* by Chris Kahrl et al.; *Military Geography* by John M. Collins; *A Mind in Prison : The Memoir of a Son and Soldier of the Third Reich* by Bruno Manz; *A Chain of Events: The Government Cover-Up of the Black Hawk Incident and the Friendly-Fire Death of Lt. Laura Piper* by Joan L. Piper; and *The Outpost War: The U.S. Marine Corps in Korea, 1952* by Lee Ballenger. I should add that I am now seeking more titles that can be used in courses at the military academies, in ROTC units, and at the military postgraduate schools.

Do you represent fiction? Brassey's no longer publishes fiction.

What do you want to see less of? Since we no longer publish fiction, I'd naturally like to see no more proposals for novels. Also, with all due respect to veterans, I'd like to see fewer proposals for unremarkable wartime memoirs. They must be unique and well written.

Do you represent nonfiction? Brassey's publishes nonfiction in the following areas: history (especially military history), world and national affairs, foreign policy, defense, intelligence, and biography. In addition, Brassey's is now developing books about transportation (especially automobiles) and about the personalities and events of national and international athletic competition.

Do you require book proposals? If so, what do you look for in evaluating a book proposal? We do require book proposals. We ask for a one-page synopsis, a table of contents or outline, one or two sample chapters, the author's thoughts on the book's market and competition, his or her qualifications, and photocopies of any sample photos. In evaluating proposals, besides deciding whether the topic itself interests us, we look for clarity and organization and for relevance in the author's credentials.

Are certain aspects of a book proposal given more weight than others? A proposal by an author with a strong publishing record will certainly get our attention.

What process do you use for making a decision? What is the process for acquisition, is there a committee? The first hurdle, I reject perhaps 95 percent of submissions out of hand. The rest are discussed at an editorial meeting, where the decision is made whether to have the proposal or manuscript read by outside experts. We regularly consult an informal network of authorities in our publishing areas.

Are you interested in work geared for the masses (readers of *People, The Star,* etc.)? We are interested to some degree in work geared to the masses, but only if it's somehow related to our core list. For example, this year we're publishing an account by a mother whose daughter, an Air Force officer, was killed in a friendly-fire incident and who fought government bureaucracies for years for accountability. Stories such as this have broad general appeal.

Are agents important? Why? Agents are important to publishers because they presumably don't waste their time on projects of little value, and the better agents know what kind of projects will be of interest to specific publishers.

Do you like new writers? What should new writers do to break into the business? We've had a lot of success with first-time authors, although it's usually easier to work with an author who already knows the game. I'm not sure what to suggest to new authors who want to break into the business except that perhaps they should find a new angle on a topic of broad interest and be able to summarize their project in 25 words or less.

How should writers approach you? By mail or e-mail, although we do not open unsolicited attached files. Please note that our new address is 22841 Quicksilver Drive, Dulles, VA 20166. I can be reached by e-mail at Don@BooksIntl.com.

What are some common mistakes writers make? What really gets on your nerves? Perhaps the biggest mistake I see is some authors' compulsion to use all the information dredged up during the book's research. They just cannot bring themselves to throw anything away. Authors should continually ask themselves how important each fact is to their thesis. What does it add? As to what really gets on my nerves, I'd have to say authors who don't make deadlines, who are disorganized, and who don't fact-check their own work.

What can writers do to get your attention and to avoid the slush pile? Potential authors could provide me with their proposal in a brief, clear, concise cover letter that tells me what the book is about, why it would be important, why it would sell, and why he or she is the proper person to write it.

What have been some of your craziest experiences with submissions? I can't think offhand of any particular example of a crazy submission experience, but we do occasionally receive those kinds of proposals on which every marginless page is completely filled with tiny handwriting and contains references to an extremely personal relationship with God.

What have been some of your best experiences with writers or in your job? My best publishing experiences have been with authors of memoirs—people who have led exemplary, sometimes courageous lives—some of whom I now consider friends.

What, if anything, makes you different from other editors? Although I've never been an author, I believe I have the ability to look at the publishing process from the author's perspective and can empathize with him or her. I wouldn't be doing my job if I always agreed with the authors, of course, but I'm patient, and many authors have said they enjoy working with me. Brassey's prides itself on its repeat authors.

Is there anything you would like to see changed in the industry? I wouldn't mind if the industry were more lucrative at the lower editorial and production levels so that it attracted and retained more bright young people.

Any advice for writers? Any way to change the system for you? Any additional thought? I would advise authors to remember who their main audience is and to write for that group, but also to try to get feedback from people who would not normally read their kind of book. Different perspectives can be valuable.

B

GEORGE BRAZILLER, INC.

171 Madison Avenue, New York, NY 10016
212-889-0909

George Braziller accents fine editions in art and design, architecture, and art movements and history. The house also publishes selected literary titles, as well as philosophy, science, history, criticism, and biographical works. The house hosts a solid backlist.

George Braziller, Inc. (founded in 1955), is perhaps most widely known for original fine books in the fields of art and architecture. Much of Braziller's fiction and poetry is foreign literature in translation, although the publisher does publish original literary novels (such as works by Janet Frame) and works in the English language that have received initial publication elsewhere.

Braziller also has a strong interest in literary criticism and writing relating to the arts, in addition to a small selection of contemporary and modern poetry. Essential Readings in Black Literature is a Braziller series that features world-class writers from around the globe. Other Braziller series include Library of Far Eastern Art and New Directions in Architecture.

From Braziller: *Impressionism: Reflections and Perceptions* by Meyer Schapiro; *Painted Prayers: The Book of Hours in Medieval and Renaissance Art* by Roger S. Wieck; *Picturing Hong Kong: Photography 1855–1910* by Roberta Wue, Edwin K. Lai, and Joanna Waley-Cohen; *The Gallery of Maps in the Vatican* by Lucio Gambi (translated by Francoise Pouncey Chiarini); *Georgia O'Keeffe: A Celebration of Music and Dance* by Katherine Hoffman; *Dreamings: The Art of Aboriginal Australia* (edited by Peter Sutton).

Great Frescoes of the Italian Renaissance series (10 volumes of the world's major fresco cycles from the early 14th–17th centuries): *Giotto: The Schrovegnia Chapel, Padua* by Bruce Cole; *The Brancacci Chapel, Florence* by Andrew Ladis; *Raphael: The Stanza Della Segnatura, Rome* by James Beck; *Ambrogio Lorenzetti: The Palazzo Pubblico, Siena* by Randolph Starn; *Andrea Mantegna: Padua and Mantua* by Keith Christiansen; *Piero Della Francesca: San Francesco, Arezzo* by Marilyn Aronberg Lavin; *Annibale Carracci: The Farnese Gallery, Rome* by Charles Dempsey; *Fra Angelico: San Marco, Florence* by William Hood; *Luca Signorelli: The San Brizio Chapel, Orvieto* by Jonathan B. Riess; *Michelangelo: The Sistine Chapel Ceiling, Rome* by Loren Partridge.

Braziller titles are distributed by W.W. Norton & Co. Query letters and SASEs should be directed to:

George Braziller, Publisher—All areas consistent with publisher description.

BROADWAY BOOKS (A DIVISION OF RANDOM HOUSE INC.)

1540 Broadway, New York, NY 10036
212-782-6500

Broadway generates commercial nonfiction in celebrity autobiography and biography; historical, political, and cultural biography and memoirs; politics and current affairs; multicultural topics; popular culture; cookbooks, diet, and nutrition; consumer reference, business, and personal finance; popular psychology, spirituality, and women's issues. The house also provides selective commercial/literary frontlist fiction, primarily by established and/or highly promotable authors.

Broadway's emporium strategy involves publishing unique, marketable books of the highest editorial quality by authors who are authorities in their field and who use their credibility and expertise to promote their work.

Broadway Books began operation in mid-1995, with a mission to publish high-quality nonfiction hardcovers and trade paperbacks. In 1999 it was merged with Doubleday to form the Doubleday Broadway Publishing Group, with Stephen Rubin as the group's publisher.

The publishing house's namesake street and logo (a diagonally bisected letter B) are emblematic of the publisher's mandate. Broadway is New York's oldest thoroughfare and runs obliquely through the diversity of Manhattan's multicultural neighborhoods, from the original harbor and the financial district, along the city's centers of government, literature, music, theater, communications, retail shops, and educational and medical institutions.

Broadway frontlist nonfiction includes: *The O'Reilly Factor* by Bill O'Reilly; *Bella Tuscany in Tuscany* by Frances Mayes; *Fair Ball* by Bob Costas; *The Corner: A Year in the Life of an Inner-City Neighborhood* by David Simon and Edward Burns; *Life Makeovers* by Cheryl Richardson; *Smart Women Finish Rich* by David Bach; *Vegetarian Cooking for Everyone* by Deborah Madison; *Webonomics: Nine Essential Principles for Growing Your Business on the World Wide Web* by Evan I. Schwartz.

Broadway's general nonfiction program includes kitchen-arts and lifestyle; relationships, parenting, and the family; popular business; popular issues; humor; and popular psychology, inspirational, and self-help/self-awareness works. Sample projects here: *Eat Your Way Across the USA* by Jane and Michael Stern; *A Fresh Taste of Italy* by Michele Scicolone; *Polenta* by Michele Anna Jordan; *Becoming the Parent You Want to Be* by Laura Davis and Janis Keyser; *A Family Like Any Other* (a work on stepfamilies in America) by James Bray; *Big Bertha and Me* by Ely Callaway (founder of Callaway Golf); *It's Here Now (Are You?)* by Bhagavan Das; *With God on Our Side: The Rise of the Religious Right in America* by William Martin; *Let's Pave the Stupid Rainforests & Give School Teachers Stun Guns and Other Ways to Save America* by Ed Anger; *The Wise Woman's Guide to Erotic Videos* by Angela Cohen and Sarah Gardner Fox.

On Broadway's preferred fiction list: *Freedomland* by Richard Price; *Tomcat in Love* by Tim O'Brien; *The Emperor's General* by James Webb; *The Prodigal Spy* by Joseph Kanon; and *Equal Music* by Vikram Seth.

Please query the house's acquisition stance prior to submitting projects—Broadway wishes to receive no unsolicited manuscripts; only agented works will be considered. Query letters and SASEs should be directed to:

Jennifer Josephy, Executive Editor—Cookbooks.

Ann Campbell, Editor—Narrative nonfiction, women's history, health and fitness, spirituality.

Charles Conrad, Vice President and Executive Editor—New nonfiction projects: popular culture, social history, literary nonfiction. Contemporary literary and quality fiction. In charge of trade-paperback reprints.

Lauren Marino, Executive Editor—Nonfiction, especially popular culture, entertainment, humor, spirituality.

Luke Dempsey, Senior Editor—Fiction and general interest nonfiction.

Suzanne Oaks, Editor—Commercial nonfiction, investigative and other business stories.

Gerald Howard, Editorial Director—Narrative nonfiction and literary fiction.

B

BURNHAM PUBLISHERS

111 North Canal Street, Suite 955, Chicago, IL 60606
312-930-9446

Burnham (formerly Nelson-Hall) publishes college textbooks in political science, sociology, and mass communications.

Samples of recent Burnham titles include: *Living Off Crime* by Ken Tunnell; *Three Black Generations at the Crossroads* by Lois Benjamin; *Cities in the Third Wave* by Leonard Ruchelman; and *History of Nazi Germany* by Joseph Bendersky. Virtually all of our authors are college professors at various institutions around the nation.

Burnham handles its own distribution and welcomes manuscript submissions (please write directly to Burnham for proposal guidelines). Query letters and SASEs should be directed to:

Richard Meade, General Manager

BUSINESS ONE IRWIN

See Irwin Professional Publishing.

CAPRA PRESS

P.O. Box 2068, Santa Barbara, CA 93120
805-966-4590   fax: 805-965-8020

Capra presents cultivated nonfiction and contemporary literary fiction in trade formats. Capra's specialties include books in the categories of Santa Barbara regional, natural history, wine, and health.

Capra Press (founded in 1970) is a small house with a highly select catalog geared to the general trade. Capra's respected goat colophon mascot was initially associated with fine books on the American West. The Capra interest has since expanded, and the current backlist features a solid assortment of the house's own originals as well as literary works in reprint.

The publisher expresses this view of publishing in the 1990s: "Independent publishers and booksellers, besieged as they are by the roughshod centralization of the superstores and superpublishers, are nevertheless bringing out a greater diversity of books than ever before in direct response to America's insatiable need to hear voices in the crowd. The strength of our culture comes not from our unity, but from our very salmagundi. We thrive in tolerance, not single-mindedness, and that's where the midlist books live. The publishers with Consortium represent a microcosm of what books in America are all about."

Capra Press titles are distributed to the book trade by Consortium Book Sales and Distribution. Titles are also available to individuals via mail order. Query letters and SASEs should be directed to:

Noel Young, President

CAREER PRESS

3 Tice Road, P.O. Box 687, Franklin Lakes, NJ 07417
201-848-0310

Career Press is established as a hard-driving, entrepreneurial publisher of essential career, business, reference, and personal finance titles. The still-independent company celebrated its 15th anniversary in March 2000. The year 2000 also saw a new Career Press imprint called New Page Books, which features general nonfiction books centered in these categories: weddings, Judaica, New Age, self-help, and health.

Between the two imprints, Career Press has published 65 titles in 2000. There is an active backlist of more than 200 strong-selling and well-promoted titles. The publisher promotes aggressively and resourcefully and stocks booksellers with titles geared to receive major nationwide publicity.

Highlights from the Spring 2001 list: *100 Ways to Motivate Yourself* by Steve Chandler; *High Selling Performance* by Jerry Beck; *101 Best Home Businesses* by Dan Ramsey; *50 Companies That Changed the World* by Howard Rothman; *Building Your Career Portfolio* by Carol A. Poore; *The Innovative Woman: Creative Ways to Reach Your Potential in Business and Beyond* by Norma Carr-Ruffino; *The Editors Speak* by Jeff Herman; *Good Service Is Good Business: 7 Simple Strategies for Success* by Catherine DeVrye; *Repair Your Own Credit* (3rd edition) by Bob Hammond; *Capturing Customers.com* by George Columbo; *How to Study* (5th edition); by Ron Fry; *Winning Teams: Making Your Team Productive and Successful; 50 Ways to Create Great Relationships* by Steve Chandler; *Look Within or Do Without: 13 Qualities Winners All Share* by Tom Bay; *21 Day Countdown to Success: Take Charge of Your Life in Less Than a Month* by Chris Witting, Jr.; *365 Ways to Connect with Your Kids* by Charlene Baumbich; *How to Be an Instant Expert* by Stephen Spignesi; *101 Best Weekend Businesses* by Dan Ramsey; *101 Home Office Success Secrets* by Lisa Kanarek; *Toasts for All Occasions* by Jeff and Deborah Herman; *Double Your Income in Real Estate Sales* by Danielle Kennedy; *Business Letters for Busy People* by Jim Dugger; *Management Mess-Ups: 57 Pitfalls You Can Avoid (and Stories of Those Who Didn't)* by Mark Eppler; *The Very Very Rich, How They Got That Way, and How You Can Too!* by Steve Mariotti and Mike Caslin with Debra DeSalvo.

Go to careerpress.com for complete information. Career Press distributes its own list. Query letters and SASEs should be directed to:

Ronald Fry, President

CAROL PUBLISHING GROUP

This large and respected independent house went bankrupt and permanently shut its doors in late 1999. It is missed.

CARROLL & GRAF PUBLISHERS, INC.

19 West 21st Street, Suite 601, New York, NY 10010-6805
212-627-8590   fax: 212-627-8490
www.pgw.com

Carroll & Graf publishes commercial trade nonfiction and literary and commercial fiction (including a strong list in mystery and suspense). Carroll & Graf (founded in 1983) is a compact house with a catalog as select and well targeted as it is diverse. In addition to its original titles, Carroll & Graf reprints American classics and genre works, along with foreign literature in translation. The house issues a full raft of genre-specific anthologies. Carroll & Graf produces hardcover, trade paper, and mass-market paperback editions.

Carroll & Graf nonfiction emphasizes contemporary culture, current events, and issue-oriented perspectives (including investigative accounts, political and historical works, and top-end true crime); business, finance, and economics; self-improvement; humor and games; and high-interest topical reference.

In fiction and the literary arts, Carroll & Graf produces mainstream novels; tales of the supernatural, fantasy, science fiction; and is particularly adventuresome in suspense categories, publishing an array of titles that runs from traditional mysteries to future-horror crime thrillers with a literary bent.

Titles from Carroll & Graf: *According to Queeny; Angelica's Grotto; April Rising; Baby Boomer's Guide to Getting It Right the Second Time Around; The Barrens; Bloody Mary's Martyrs; The Book of Cain; Clint; Cozy; Creative Loveplay; Dead Secret; Death by Horoscope; Death of Kings; The Devil's Oasis; Dr. Mortimer and the Barking Man Mystery; The Dragon Syndicates; Fairness; A Few Minutes Past Midnight; The Flight of the Maidens; A Good Man in Evil Times; The House of Death; In the Heat of the Night; Kids' Letters to Harry Potter; The Last Battle; The Mammoth Book of UFOs; The Mammoth Book of Astounding Puzzles; The Mammoth Book of Legal Thrillers; Mouthing the Words; The Oppermanns; The Orange Curtain; A Prize for Princess; Pulp Masters; A Pure Clear Light; A Purple Thread for Sky; Russia's Heroes; The Sea Warriors; Soldier Sahibs; Star-Spangled Eden; Time; The Transfer Agreement; The Well; Within the Dark Man Calls;* and *With a Gem-Like Flame.*

Mammoth Books is a line from Carroll & Graf that accents quantity as well as quality: the Mammoth list includes literary anthologies, works of topical appeal, and specialist interests. Titles here: *The Mammoth Book of New Sherlock Holmes Adventures* (edited by Mike Ashley); *The Mammoth Book of the Third Reich at War* (edited by Michael Veranov); *The Mammoth Book of Chess* by Graham Burgess; *The Mammoth Book of Carnival Puzzles* by David J. Bodycombe; *The Mammoth Book of Fortune Telling* by Celestine.

Carroll & Graf books is now completely owned by its distributor, Publishers Group West. Kent Carroll will be leaving the firm in early 2001, though his good name will continue to grace the firm he co-founded with Herman Graf.

Carroll & Graf Publishers no longer accepts unsolicited submissions. The house only accepts agented submissions. Query letters and SASEs should be directed to:

Philip Turner, Editor

Kent Carroll, former Publisher and Editor in Chief

Born: Early June.

Education: Princeton University.

Employment history/editor career path: I came to New York to work in the publishing or movie business. My thoughts were that if I was going to have to work, I better do something I enjoy doing. I started out in publishing at Walt Disney Co. and within six months we all were fired. I then went to work at *Variety,* reviewing films. Shortly after this I was at Grove Press in the film division. I stayed with Grove for 10 years. I then moved on to start my own company with Herman Graf in 1983.

Personal interests: I have a house on Long Island where I love to go on the weekends and work in the yard. I also love dinners in the evenings.

What would you be doing if you were not an editor? I don't know. I might be working in the movie business.

What has been your most successful book that you have acquired to date? It was a reprint titled *Endurance* by Elfred Lansing. It was originally published in 1955 and we reprinted it in 1986. The sales increased steadily over the years, and finally last year it became a bestseller.

What books have you acquired that make you the most proud? What books that you have acquired reflect the types of books you like to represent? *The Twilight Years* by William Weiser; *The Birthday Boys* and *Every Man For Himself* by Barrel Bambridge; *Time* by Alexander Walsh.

Do you represent fiction? If so, what do you look for? Yes. Mysteries, thrillers, commercial, historical, and literary fiction.

What do you want to see less of? We only read things that are submitted through an agent, so most manuscripts are right on target for what we like to see.

Do you represent nonfiction? Yes. Biographies, current affairs, history.

Do you require book proposals? If so, what do you look for in evaluating a book proposal? I would prefer to see a complete manuscript for nonfiction, but if it's a good book proposal I will buy it. With fiction, it's more of looking at the actual writing.

What process do you use for making a decision? What is the process for acquisition, is there a committee? Not necessarily a committee, but we do sit down and discuss the project in detail.

What kinds of nonfiction books do you want to see less of? Diet books, New Age, spirituality, self-help in general.

Are you interested in work geared for the masses (readers of *People, The Star,* etc.)? On occasion. We did a biography on Woody Allen that did very well.

Are agents important? Why? Yes, agents play an important role for writers, but more so today than 15 or 20 years ago. From the publishing aspect it's easier to deal with an agent rather than with a writer simply because the agent is very knowledgeable about the publishing business.

Do you like new writers? What should new writers do to break into the business? Yes, new writers usually have new, fresh, and imaginative ideas. To break into the business, I would say, get an agent. Good writing is something that is difficult and rare, but write something really good and you will for sure get in.

How should writers approach you? Through an agent.

What are some common mistakes writers make? What really gets on your nerves? When people imitate others' work. It's okay to research and find out what sells, but don't copy the work, write something that is different and new.

What can writers do to get your attention and to avoid the slush pile? Not much; when we have a slush pile, it gets sent back.

What have been some of your craziest experiences with submissions? We once published the wrong book by mistake. We were trying to reprint a thriller called *The Man from Lisbon* and somewhere along the line we ended up publishing a title called *The Man Who Stole Portugal*.

What have been some of your best experiences with writers or in your job? All of the authors I work with are wonderful, talented authors who make the whole experience enjoyable. I genuinely like the people I work with and am always learning from them.

What, if anything, makes you different from other editors? We are a relatively small house, which brings everything down to a much more personal level. I can keep my promises, and we stay with our authors; we won't turn them loose after their first book is published.

Is there anything you would like to see changed in the industry? There are too many conflicting processes. There is an enormous amount of competition, and more books are being published than need to be. Because of the large advances that are going out today, it seems those are the only books getting any real attention, which is sad that we are ignoring very good books that start off slow.

Any advice for writers? Read more books and learn about publishing by paying attention to what's going on.

CATBIRD PRESS/GARRIGUE BOOKS

16 Windsor Road, North Haven, CT 06473
203-230-2391
e-mail: catbird@pipeline.com

Catbird Press (founded in 1987), along with its Garrigue Books imprint, is a small publisher with concentration in the areas of American fiction, general humor, legal humor, and Central European literature.

Fiction, humor, and titles with a literary appeal: *Performing Without a Stage: The Art of Literary Translation* by Robert Wechsler; *The Poetry of Jaroslav Seifert* (edited by George Gibian, translated from the Czech by Ewald Osers; largest English-language collection of poetry by the Nobel Prize–winning poet); *The Breath of an Unfee'd Lawyer: Shakespeare on Lawyers and the Law* (edited by Edward J. Bander; illustrated by Jerry

Warshaw); *Daylight in Nightclub Inferno: Czech Fiction from the Post-Kundera Generation* (edited by Elena Lappin); *Lifetime Employment* (fiction) by Floyd Kemske; *It Came with the House* (short stories) by Jeffrey Shaffer.

Catbird epitomizes small-press savvy in its continuing success in garnering industry publicity and promotion: Catbird was among the first presses to post selected works-in-progress via the electronic Online Bookstore.

Catbird Press and Garrigue Books are distributed to the trade by Independent Publishers Group. Proposals and SASEs should be directed to:

Robert Wechsler, Publisher

C

CCC PUBLICATIONS

9725 Lurline Avenue, Chatsworth, CA 91311
818-718-0507   fax: 818-718-0655

CCC Publications accents nonfiction trade books in crisply targeted categories: relationships, self-help/how-to, humor, inspiration, humorous inspirational titles, age-related and over-the-hill titles, games and puzzles, party books, cartoon books, gift books and merchandise, gag and blank books—and a group of titles mischievously cataloged as On the Edge. CCC publishes a number of books by bestselling author Jan King.

CCC produces primarily trade paperbacks, smaller gift-size editions, accessories (such as bags and bookmarks), and a line of audio works (including collections of answering-machine messages and sound effects).

In addition to books, CCC Publications also has a sidelines division: CCC Novel Tease Apparel Co. is one of the largest producers of embroidered occasion merchandise. Our themes include Bridal, New Parent, Baby, Age-Related, Anniversary, Over-the-Hill, Maternity, Graduation & Prom, and novelty items. Our fiberoptic design division is producing light-up caps and jackets for numerous major accounts.

On the CCC list: *Golfaholics* by Bob Zahn; *So, You're Getting Married* by Fred Sahner (illustrated by Lennie Peterson); *The Last Diet Book: You'll Ever Need!* by Dr. David Fisch; *Why God Makes Bald Guys* by Paul Della Valle (illustrated by Lennie Peterson); *Are We Dysfunctional Yet?* by Randy Glasbergen; *You Know He's a Two-Timing, Egomaniacal, Womanizing, Slimeball When . . .* by Jon Michaels; *Technology Bytes!* by Randy Glasbergen; *Cat Love: 150 Wonderful Things You Can Do for Your Cat* by Jill Kramer; *How to Survive a Jewish Mother: A Guilt-Ridden Guide* by Steven Arnold; *Red-Hot Monogamy in Just 60 Seconds a Day* by Patrick T. Hunt, M.D.; *50 Ways to Hustle Your Friends* by Jim Karol.

From On the Edge: *Men Are Pigs, Women Are Bitches* by Jerry King; *The Definitive Fart Book* by Desmond Mullan; *The Very Very Sexy Adult Dot-to-Dot Book* by Tony Goffe; *The Complete Wimp's Guide to Sex* by Jed Pascoe.

Jan King books: *Over the Hill . . . Deal with It!; Ladies, Start Your Engines: The Secrets for Restoring Romance, Passion and Great Sex in Your Relationship; Why Men Don't Have a Clue; Hormones from Hell; Killer Bras (and Other Hazards of the 50s).*

CCC (founded in 1983) orchestrates its own distribution. Query letters and SASEs should be directed to:

Cliff Carle, Editorial Director
Mark Chutnick, Publisher

CHAPMAN AND HALL

Wolters-Kluwer Academic Publishers has purchased Chapman and Hall. The Chapman and Hall office has been closed.

C

CHAPTERS PUBLISHING

222 Berkeley Street, Boston, MA 02116
617-351-3855

Chapters specializes in books on cooking and nutrition, health and fitness, gardening, nature, country living, and home and family (including a series of weekend-projects books). The house offers a line of calendars with themes linked to its overall publishing interests. Chapters productions are recognized for their excellent book design and feature top-quality paper and binding.

Chapters Publishing (founded in 1991) publishes a select number of new titles each season and tends toward larger print runs; many Chapters titles enjoy sales through established book clubs. Chapters' evolution as a small commercial press has been markedly winning; and writers might note that the publisher's advances are generally comparable with those expected of large houses.

On the Chapters list: *The Joy of Coffee: The Essential Guide to Buying, Brewing and Enjoying* by Corby Kummer; *The New Games Treasury: More Than 500 Indoor and Outdoor Favorites with Strategies, Rules and Traditions* by Merilyn Dimonds Mohr; *The Complete Italian Vegetarian Cookbook: 350 Essential Recipes for Inspired, Everyday Eating* by Jack Bishop; *Mission Furniture You Can Build: Authentic Techniques and Designs for the Home Woodworker* by John Wagner; *Passing Strange: True Tales of New England Hauntings and Horrors* by Joseph A. Citro; *Eating Thin for Life: Food Secrets and Recipes from People Who Have Lost Weight and Kept It Off* by Anne M. Fletcher, M.S., R.D.; *Just the Weigh You Are: How to Be Fit and Healthy, Whatever Your Size* by Steven Jonas, M.D., and Linda Konner; *Tender Roses for Tough Climates* by Douglas Green; *Hummingbird Gardens: Attracting Nature's Jewels to Your Backyard* by Nancy L. Newfield and Barbara Nielsen; *Orchid Simplified: An Indoor Gardening Guide* by Henry Jaworski.

Among Chapters series: Simply Healthful Cookbooks (recipes for tasty, healthful dishes without a lot of fuss and bother); How to Spot . . . (books written by professional naturalists that give a thorough description of a specific animal's habitat, range, diet, and breeding habits to increase amateur naturalists' enjoyment of animal watching).

The Curious Naturalist Series promotes works (in handsome trade paperback editions) from some of North America's finest naturalist writers, such as Peter Mathiessen, R. D. Lawrence, Adrian Forsyth, and Sy Montgomery. Titles here include: *A Natural History of Sex: The Ecology and Evolution of Mating Behavior* by Adrian Forsyth; *Birds of Tropical*

America by Steven J. Hilty; *Nature's Everyday Mysteries: A Field Guide to the World in Your Backyard* by Sy Montgomery; *Shark! Nature's Masterpiece* by R. D. Lawrence; *The Wind Birds: Shorebirds of North America* by Peter Mathiessen.

Chapters is distributed in the United States by W. W. Norton; Canadian distribution is handled by Key Porter Books. Chapters Publishing is now part of Houghton Mifflin Company. Query letters and SASEs should be directed to:

Lori Galvin-Frost, Assistant Managing Editor—Cookbooks.

Chelsea Green Publishing Company

205 Gates-Briggs Building, P.O. Box 428, White River Junction, VT 05001
802-295-6300   fax: 802-295-6444
www.chelseagreen.com

Chelsea Green publishes trade nonfiction in natural gardening and food, energy and shelter, nature and the environment, and regional books (including travel, social issues, history, and culture). Chelsea Green projects include a publishing co-venture with Real Goods Trading Company, designated by the imprimatur *Real Goods Independent Living Book.*

Chelsea Green Publishing Company (founded in 1984) is a compact, independent firm of individualistic spirit; the house continues to hone its publishing program through a small number of new seasonal releases (in hardcover and trade paper formats) and a hardy backlist. Chelsea Green's goal is to improve the visibility of sustainability by showing that even a small, home-based business can be instrumental in bringing about social change on a global scale.

On the Chelsea Green list: *The Neighborhood Forager: A Guide for the Wild Food* by Robert Kottenderson; *The Natural House: Energy Efficient Environment Homes* by Daniel Chiras; *From the Redwood Forest: A Headwaters Epiphany* by Joan Dunning; *The Good Woodcutter's Guide: Chainsaws, Portable Sawmills, and Woodlots* by Dave Johnson; *The NEW Independent Home: People and Houses That Harvest the Sun* by Michael Potts; *The Straw Bale House* by Athena Swentzell Steen, Bill Steen, and David Bainbridge with David Eisenberon; *The Apple Grower: A Guide for the Organic Orchardist* by Michael Phillips; *The Blooming Lawn: Creating a Flower Meadow* by Yvette Verner; *The Earth-Sheltered House: An Architect's Sketchbook* by Malcolm Wells; *Bamboo Rediscovered* by Victor Cusack; *Gaviotas: A Village to Reinvent the World* by Alan Weisman; *Hammer. Nail. Wood.: The Compulsion to Build* by Thomas P. Glynn; *The Bread Builders: Hearth Loaves and Masonry Ovens* by Daniel Wing and Alan Scott; *Global Spin: The Corporate Assault on Environmentalism* by Sharon Beder.

Chelsea Green handles its own distribution and distributes for a number of other small, innovative independent presses such as Green Books, Ltd., Orwell Cove, OttoGraphics, Ecological Design Press, Harmonious Press, and Seed Savers Exchange. Query letters and SASEs should be directed to:

Hannah Silverstein, Production Editor

Stephen Morris, President and Publisher

Alan Berolzheimer, Acquisitions Editor

Jim Schley, Editor in Chief (Editor off the Grid)

Born: November 13, 1956.

Education: I went to Dartmouth College and have a B.A. in Literature and Creative Writing, a minor in Native American studies, and a M.A. in Poetry from Warren Wilson College.

Employment history/editor career path: I have always loved books so I knew early on that I wanted to teach or be involved in publishing. I started as an intern at *New England Review* magazine and climbed very quickly up the ladder to become an Editor.

Personal interests: Reading, books, being outside, hiking, camping, activist politics; I built my house from scratch.

What would you be doing if you were not an editor? It's impossible for me to imagine, but I would probably be teaching or doing some kind of freelance work.

What has been your most successful book that you have acquired to date? *The Straw Bail House* by Athena Stein et al.

What books have you acquired that make you the most proud? What books that you have acquired reflect the types of books you like to represent? *Gaviotias* by Alan Weisman.

Do you represent fiction? If so, what do you look for? Yes. *Hammer. Nail. Wood* by Thomas Glynn; *Toyle,* which is a diary of someone working construction.

Do you represent nonfiction? Yes, unusual how-to books, gardening, building.

Do you require book proposals? If so, what do you look for in evaluating a book proposal? Yes, I need something written. In some cases I can help the author to do this, but in most I would expect to see an outline, writing samples, and so on.

What process do you use for making a decision? What is the process for acquisition, is there a committee? Yes, there is a committee made up of the publisher, editor in chief, acquiring editor, and the production and marketing team.

What kinds of nonfiction books do you want to see less of? I would like to see fewer submissions of material that we do not handle. We publish books that are related to ecology in some way. It needs to have something to do with environmentalism for us to take a look at it.

Are you interested in work geared for the masses (readers of *People, The Star,* etc.)? No.

Are agents important? Why? Yes, I think they are important. I've learned a lot about agents over the last couple of years; due to higher advances, they seem to be around more and more. Agents are very editor-savvy, they can think editorially and have good marketing skills. In most cases they are more sophisticated about the publishing business than the author, which helps to make the process go as smoothly as possible.

Do you like new writers? What should new writers do to break into the business? Yes, we publish many first-time authors. To break into the business an author should learn how to write. Start out by getting something published in magazines, newspapers, and so on.

How should writers approach you? Look at our Web site, chealseagreen.com, for our guidelines. To approach me, send me a letter or an e-mail. I would rather have something in writing than a phone call.

What are some common mistakes writers make? What really gets on your nerves? Writers concentrate so much sometimes on their subject, they forget about all the other aspects of writing. To be a writer, you need to have more than a good idea and it takes more than saying, "Everyone I know loves this idea!"

What can writers do to get your attention and to avoid the slush pile? Our slush pile is quite thin. But to avoid it, be clear and articulate and have a unique idea. We're a writer-friendly house and try to keep the slush to a minimum.

What have been some of your craziest experiences with submissions? Someone once brought me an idea for a book that was all about using human feces as fertilizer.

What have been some of your best experiences with writers or in your job? I love being an editor and working with my colleagues. I love the working relationship between the author and the editor. The editor gets to learn all aspects of a writer, his or her strengths, weaknesses, and so on. Some authors turn into your best friends.

What, if anything, makes you different from other editors? I'm a very literary person, I read on my own time, I bring the skills of being a literary editor to a practical level.

Is there anything you would like to see changed in the industry? I can't answer what I would change, but I can tell you what *not* to change. What I would not like to see is the intimacy that reading represents for some people being lost.

Any advice for writers? Be clear, be inventive, and take pleasure in the task.

CHELSEA HOUSE PUBLISHERS
(A SUBSIDIARY OF HAIGHTS CROSS COMMUNICATIONS)

1974 Sproul Road, Suite 400, Broomall, PA 19008-0914
610-353-5166   fax: 610-359-1439
www.chelseahouse.com   e-mail: Sales@Chelseahouse.com

The entire Chelsea House catalog is available on the Internet's World Wide Web.

Chelsea House produces books for older children and young adults. The Chelsea House program accents the educational and institutional market in history, young-adult nonfiction, reference works, and literary criticism, as well as some works of broader appeal. Books on the Chelsea House list are most often produced in library-bound hardcover volumes, with some titles offered in trade paperback editions.

The editorial focus is on biography, culture, and history (American and worldwide). Broad interest areas include multicultural studies, social studies, literary criticism/English, general biography, mythology, sports, science, health/drug education, art, Spanish-language books, economics/business and personal finance, and law.

This approach is underscored by developmental marketing of such series as the Asian-American Experience, Folk Tales and Fables, the Immigrant Experience, Lives of the Physically Challenged, Milestones in Black American History, Mysterious Places, Pop Culture Legends, Science Discoveries, Sports Legends.

Chelsea House Publishers was originally instituted (founded in 1967) as a small press (then located in New York City) devoted to trade and reference titles on American history and popular culture. The company was bought in 1983 by Main Line Book Company, a library distributor based in suburban Philadelphia—whereupon the house's emphasis turned toward nonfiction for a young-adult readership.

Chelsea House series and highlights:

Famous Figures of the Civil War Era: *Jefferson Davis; Frederick Douglas; Ulysses S. Grant; Robert E. Lee; Abraham Lincoln; Children of the World; Civil War Leaders; Egyptian Kings and Queens; Classical Deities; Good Luck Symbols and Talismans;* and *Greetings of the World.*

Cats and Dogs: A Basic Training, Caring, and Understanding Library: *Kittens & Cats; Skin Care for Cats; The Myth & Magic of Cats; The Well Trained Dog; Adopting a Dog; The Perfect Retriever; Traveling with Dogs; Puppy Training.*

Funtastic Science Activities for Kids: *Sound Fundamentals; Electricity & Magnetism Fundamentals; Heat Fundamentals.*

Major World Nations: *Albania, Argentina, Australia, Vietnam, West Bank, West Indies, Zimbabwe.*

Overcoming Adversity: *Tim Allen; Jim Carrey; James Earl Jones; Abraham Lincoln; William Penn.*

Superstars of Film: *Robert DeNiro; Johnny Depp; Brad Pitt; Keanu Reeves; John Travolta.*

They Died Too Young: *Kurt Cobain; Jimi Hendrix; Bruce Lee; John Lennon; Elvis Presley.*

Great Disasters: *Reforms and Ramifications; The Bombing of Hiroshima; The Exxon Valdez; Pearl Harbor; Three Mile Island; The Titanic.*

Male/Female Sports Stars: *Baseball Legends: Roger Clemens, Randy Johnson, Chipper Jones, Mark McGwire, Larry Walker; Superstars of Men's Figure Skating; Superstars of Men's Track and Field; Superstars of Women's Golf; Superstars of Women's Tennis; Superstars of Women's Gymnastics.*

The Illustrated Living History Series: *Tall Ships of the World; Woodland Indians; Revolutionary Medicine; Homebuilding and Woodworking in Colonial America.*

Women of Achievement: *Madeleine Albright; Hillary Rodham Clinton; Diana, Princess of Wales; Rosie O'Donnell; Elizabeth Taylor; Barbara Walters.*

Women Writers of English and Their Words: *Native American Women Writers; Jewish Women Fiction Writers; Asian-American Women Writers; British Women Fiction Writers of the 19th Century.*

Explorers of New Worlds: *Daniel Boone, Vasco de Gama; Lewis and Clark; Juan Ponce de Leon; The Viking Explorers.*

Crime, Justice, and Punishment: *Detectives, Private Investigators, and Bounty Hunters; Hate Crimes; The Jury System.*

Administrative, editorial, and warehousing facilities are currently located in the Philadelphia area. Query letters and SASEs should be directed to:

Sally Cheney, Editor in Chief

Kim Shinners, Associate Editor in Chief

Pamela Loos, Production Manager

Sara Davis, Art Director

Judy L. Hasday, Director of Photography

James D. Gallagher, Managing Editor

J. Christopher Higgins, Senior Production Editor

CHRONICLE BOOKS

Chronicle Children's Books

85 Second Street, Sixth Floor, San Francisco, CA 94105

415-537-3730, 415-537-4441   fax: 415-537-4470

www.chroniclebooks.com   e-mail: customerfrontdesk@chroniclebooks.com

It was announced in late 1999 that this respected, independent firm was acquired from its corporate parent by the Associate Publisher, Nion McEvoy. McEvoy is the great-grandson of Michel de Young, who co-founded the *San Francisco Chronicle* with his brother Charles in 1865.

Founded in 1968, Chronicle Books publishes 300 new titles each year across its three divisions—Adult Trade, Children's, and Gift—in the subject areas of food, photography, art, architecture, interior design, gardening, pop culture, and fiction. It also distributes the publishing programs of the Princeton Architectural Press, North South Books, and innovative KIDS.

Chronicle's areas of interest include architecture and fine arts, design, photography, history and popular culture, the outdoors lifestyle (cuisine, pets, travel, home, and family), business and finance, and sports; the house issues a separate catalog for its children's books and for the gift list.

Chronicle Books was initially best known for its glossy paperback series of illustrated theme cookbooks. Since that era, Chronicle has gradually ventured further afield and currently publishes general nonfiction in both hardback and paperback. Chronicle Books also publishes selected fiction and literary works.

The Chronicle program features many selections of California regional interest (food, architecture, outdoors), with a focus on San Francisco and the Bay Area in particular (on both frontlist and backlist). The publisher has expanded its regional scope: Chronicle is open to an increasing variety of titles keyed to areas and travel destinations worldwide. Chronicle scored major bestseller hits with Nick Bantock's Griffin & Sabine fiction trilogy: *Griffin & Sabine, Sabine's Notebook,* and *The Golden Mean.*

Representative Chronicle titles: *The Worst Case Scenario Survival Handbook* by Joshua Piven and David Borgenicht; *Illuminations: Living by Candlelight* by Wally Arnold; *Weber's Big Book of Grilling* by Jamie Purviance and Sandra McRae; *Fern House* by Deborah Schenck; *The Voice of the Butterfly* by John Nichols; *Dog Bless America: Tails from the Road* by Jeff Selis; *The Home Renovation Workbook* by Jain Lemos; *Poker: Bets, Bluffs, and Bad Beats* by A. Alvarey; *Discover Zen: A Practical Guide to Personal Serenity* by David Fontana, Ph.D.; *Quick Pickles: Easy Recipes with Big Flavor,* by Chris Schlesinger, John Willoughby, and Dan George; *The Wishing Box* by Dashka Slater; *Things Unspoken* by Anitra Sheen; *The Perfect Day: 40 Years of* Surfer *Magazine,* edited by Sam George; *Great Eats and Great Sleeps Paris* by Sandra Gustafson; *The Gift to Be Simple: Life in Amish Country* by Bill Coleman.

Chronicle Children's Books

Chronicle's children's lineup has a reputation for high quality and innovation in traditional and not-so-traditional formats. From the Chronicle children's list: *Hush Little Baby* by Sylvia Long; *If I Had a Horse* by Jonathan London (illustrated by Brooke Scudder); *Desert Dwellers: Native People of the American Southwest* by Scott Warren; *The Clubhouse Crew's Joker's Bag of Tricks* by Anne Civardi and Ruth Thomson (illustrated by Mark Oliver); *The Merchant of Marvels and the Peddler of Dreams* by Frederick Clement; *Beneath the Sea in 3-D* by Mark Blum; *Star Wars, The Empire Strikes Back,* and *Return of the Jedi* by John Whitman (illustrated by Brandon McKinney); *A Rainbow at Night: The World in Words and Pictures by Navajo Children* by Bruce Hucko.

Query letters and SASEs should be directed to:

Victoria Rock, Director and Associate Publisher—Children's books.

Alan Rapp, Associate Editor—Design books, travel.

Bill LeBlond, Senior Editor—Cookbooks.

Christine Carswell, Associate Publisher—All publisher's described areas.

Jay Schaefer, Senior Editor—Fiction: send complete manuscript, synopsis, and SASE. No queries, please.

Leslie Jonath, Editor—Gardening, crafts, lifestyle.

Sarah Malarky, Editor—Popular culture: all areas.

Mikyla Brunder, Editor—Craft/lifestyle.

CITY LIGHTS PUBLISHERS

261 Columbus Avenue, San Francisco, CA 94133
415-362-1901   fax: 415-362-4921
www.citylights.com   e-mail: staff@citylights.com

City Lights publishes literary essays and criticism, biography, philosophy, literary fiction (including first novels), and poetry, books on political and social issues, as well as artistically ecumenical volumes featuring both words and visual images.

City Lights Booksellers and Publishers (founded in 1953 by the poet-publisher Lawrence Ferlinghetti) is a San Francisco treasure, its bookstore a North Beach landmark and, above all else, a resolute cultural institution and self-embodied tradition. City Lights initially featured the Pocket Poets series, which introduced such writers as Gregory Corso, Allen Ginsberg, Jack Kerouac, and other Beats to a wider audience. Since then, as successive literary generations have commenced and terminated, City Lights remains most assuredly commercially viable.

Highlights from City Lights: *Reclaiming San Francisco: History, Politics, Culture* (edited by James Brook, Chris Carlson, and Nancy J. Peters); *Sarajevo Blues* by Semezdin Mehmedinovic (translated from the Bosnian by Ammiel Alcalay); *The Dogs: A Modern Bestiary* by Rebecca Brown; *Hectic Ethics* by Francisco Hinojosta (translated from the Spanish by Kurt Hollander); *Ploughing the Clouds: The Search for Irish Soma* by Peter Lamborn Wilson; *Revolutionary Romanticism* (edited by Max Bleehman); *City Lights Blank Journal; The Monstrous and the Marvelous* by Rikki Ducornet; *Postcards from the Underground: Portraits of the Beat Era* by Larry Keenana; *Distance No Object Stories* by Gloria Frym; *History as Mystery* by Michael Parenti; *Memories of Our Future* by Ammiel Alcalay; *The Back Room* by Carmen Martin Gaite (translated from the Spanish by Helen Lane); and *Whose Song? And Other Stories* by Thomas Glave.

The City Lights backlist embraces many of this publishing house's classic publications, such as *Howl and Other Poems* by Allen Ginsberg (available in the original Pocket Poets format as well as lavish trade-paper reprint); *Gasoline* (poetry) by Gregory Corso; *Scripture of the Golden Eternity* (literary writings) by Jack Kerouac; *William S. Burroughs's Yage Letters* (creative essays and imaginative correspondence with Allen Ginsberg); and *Shock Treatment* (monologues from performance artist Karen Finley). Each fall, the publisher issues *City Lights Review: Annual Journal of Literature and Politics,* which brims with original poetry, essays, and fiction.

City Lights is distributed by Consortium Book Sales and Distribution and has its own in-house mail-order fulfillment department. Query letters and SASEs should be directed to:

Elaine Katzenberger, Acquisitions Editor—Latin American literature, women's studies, fiction.

James Brook, Acquisitions Editor—Nonfiction.

Nancy J. Peters, Publisher and Executive Editor

Robert Sharrard, Acquisitions Editor—Poetry and literature.

CLEIS PRESS

P.O. Box 14684, San Francisco, CA 94114
415-575-4700

Cleis Press publishes books on sexual politics and self-help, lesbian and gay studies and culture, feminism, fiction, erotica, humor, and translations of world-class women's literature. Cleis titles cross-market from niches of gender and sexuality to reach the widest possible audiences.

Projects from Cleis Press (founded in 1980) garner numerous awards and reviews—and include many bestselling books. The house is committed to publishing the most original, creative, and provocative works by women (and a few men) in the United States and Canada.

From the Cleis list: *Sexually Speaking* by Gore Vidal; *The New Good Vibrations Guide to Sex: Tips and Techniques from America's Favorite Sex Toy Store* by Cathy Winds and Anne Semans; *The Woman Who Knew Too Much* by B. Reece Johnson.

Cleis fiction includes: *Memory Mambo* by Achy Obejas; *A Ghost in the Closet* (mystery featuring Nancy Clue and the Hardly Boys) by Mabel Maney; *Best Gay Erotica* (published annually; series Editor Richard Labonté); *Best Lesbian Erotica* (published annually; series Editor Tristan Taormino).

Cleis Books is represented to the book trade by Publishers Group West. Query letters and SASEs should be directed to:

Felice Newman, Publisher and Acquisitions Editor
Frédérique Delacoste, Publisher and Acquisitions Editor

COBBLEHILL BOOKS
See Penguin USA.

C

COFFEE HOUSE PRESS
27 North Fourth Street, Suite 400, Minneapolis, MN 55401
612-338-0125   fax: 612-338-4004
www.coffeehousepress.org

Coffee House produces contemporary poetry, short fiction, and novels. The press is a source of contemporary writing that is challenging and thought-provoking, funny and furious, wildly diverse, even downright wacky, vibrant, and lyrical.

Coffee House Press is a nonprofit publisher dedicated to presenting visionary books of contemporary literature by diverse authors. The mission of Coffee House Press is to promote exciting, vital, and enduring authors of our time; to delight and inspire readers; to increase awareness of and appreciation for the traditional book arts; to enrich our literary heritage; and to contribute to the cultural life of our community. Coffee House Press publishes books that advance the craft of writing; books that present the dreams and ambitions of people who have been underrepresented in published literature; books that help build a sense of community; and books that help to shape our national consciousness.

Coffee House descends from what was originally (in the 1970s) a letterpress specialty firm, with a small list and an intimate circle of readers. The publisher then introduced titles geared toward an expanded readership; happily, conviviality and craft remain in strong evidence. Coffee House Press (established in 1984) is a publisher of trade titles and fine editions in a program that features a creative approach to the publishing arts. The house colophon is a steaming book, which is chosen to let the reader know (as the Coffee House motto runs) "where good books are brewing."

Titles from Coffee House: *Girl Reel; Captain Blackman; Our Sometime Sister; Garden Primitives; Summit Avenue; The Annotated Here; Breakers; Glory Goes and Gets Some; Write Letter to Billy; Hand of Buddha;* and *Shiny Pencils at the Edge of Things.*

Coffee House books are printed on acid-free paper stock and have sewn bindings for long life and comfortable reading—as well they might, for the house features a comprehensive and enduring backlist.

Coffee House Press oversees its own marketing and sales network with the assistance of regional representatives; trade distribution is handled by Consortium. Query letters and SASEs should be directed to:

Allan Kornblum, Editor and Publisher
Christopher Fischbach, Managing Editor

COLLECTOR BOOKS
(A DIVISION OF THE SCHROEDER PUBLISHING COMPANY)

5801 Kentucky Dam Road, Paducah, KY 42001
270-898-6211   fax: 270-898-8890
www.collectorbooks.com   e-mail: editor@collectorbooks.com
Mailing address:
P.O. Box 3009, Paducah, KY 42002-3009

Collector Books produces books for collectors in such fields as Depression glass, glassware, pottery and porcelain, china and dinnerware, cookie jars and salt shakers, stoneware, paper collectibles, Barbie dolls, dolls, toys, quilts, tools and weapons, jewelry and accessories, furniture, advertising memorabilia, bottles, Christmas collectibles, cigarette lighters, decoys, doorstops, and gas station memorabilia.

Collector Books (founded in 1969) is a division of Schroeder Publishing Company. Collector Books is dedicated to bringing the most up-to-date information and values to collectors in an attractive, high-quality format. Books are designed to be practical, easy-to-use tools that assist dealers and collectors in their pursuit of antiques and collectibles. Collector's publications are liberally illustrated editions, generally filled with histories, production facts and lore, research sources, and identification information. Collector Books also produces inventory ledgers for professional dealers and avid collectors.

The house produces a mid-sized list of new offerings each year and maintains a sizable backlist. Springing from its original principles of offering quality products, customer satisfaction, giving customers the most for their dollar, and one-day sudden service, Collector Books has grown from one title on fruit jars to over 500 titles, and from a firm of two employees to over 70. Fueled by strong customer support, the publisher's list of new releases continues its recent growth.

Every August, Collector publishes *Schroeder's Antiques Price Guide,* which features more than 50,000 listings and hundreds of photographs for identification and current values as well as background and historical information.

Sample titles: *Huxford's Collectible Advertising,* 4th edition by Bob and Sharon Huxford; *Collector's Guide to Ideal Dolls, Identification & Values,* 2nd edition by Judith Izen; *Collector's Guide to Children's Books, 1850–1950,* volume 2 by Diane McClure Jones and Rosemary Jones; *Cartoon Toys & Collectibles, Identification & Value Guide* by David Longest; *Dugan & Diamond Carnival Glass, 1909–1931* by Carl O. Burns; *B. J. Summers' Guide to Coca-Cola* by B. J. Summers; *World of Beer Memorabilia* by Herb and Helen Haydock; *A Decade of Barbie Dolls and Collectibles, 1981–1991* by Beth Summers; *Pocket Guide to Depression Glass and More (1920s–1960s)* (10th edition); *Very Rare Glassware of the Depression Years* (5th edition); *Stemware Identification Featuring Cordials with Values, 1920s–1960s* by Gene Florence; *McCoy Pottery: Collector's Reference and Value Guide* by Bob Hanson, Craig Nissen, and Margaret Hanson; *Figural Nodders: Identification and Value Guide—Includes Bobbin' Heads and Swayers* by Hilma R. Irtz; *Antique and Collectible Buttons: Identification and Values* by Debra J. Wisniewski; *Antique and Vintage Clothing: A Guide to Dating and Valuation of Women's Clothing, 1850–1940* by Diane Snyder-Haug; *The Standard Knife Collector's Guide* (3rd edition) by Roy Ritchie and Ron Stewart; *Garage Sale and Flea Market Annual,* 9th edition by Bob and Sharon Huxford; *Schroeder's Collectible Toys* by Bob and Sharon Huxford; *Collector's Guide to Lunch Boxes* by Carole Bess White and L. M. White.

Collector Books looks for its authors to be knowledgeable people considered experts within their fields. Writers who feel there is a real need for a book on their collectible subject and have available a large comprehensive collection are invited to contact the publisher at the house's mailing address.

Collector Books distributes its own list, targeting particularly bookstore buyers and antiques-trade professionals. Collector Books operates an especially strong mail-order program and purveys selected works from other publishers, including out-of-print titles in the collectibles and antiques field. Query letters and SASEs should be directed to:

Billy Schroeder, Publisher

Lisa Stroup, Editor

COMPUTE BOOKS

Compute Books (a computer-book specialist founded in 1979) is no longer doing business.

CONARI PRESS

2550 Ninth Street, Suite 101, Berkeley, CA 94710
510-649-7185
www.conari.com

Conari Press (founded in 1987) accents works in relationships, self-awareness, spirituality, and the family. In addition to books, Conari produces a select line of audiocassettes, project packets, buttons, and posters. The house began as a small press and has grown step by step, expanding cogently on its strong backlist base. Conari is one of the most successful regional independent publishers.

Conari titles: *Living Legacies* by Coleen Le Drew and Duane Elgin; *In Her Footsteps* by Annette Madden; *Food Men Love* by Margie Lapanja; *The Book of Love* by Daphne Kingma; *Doing It* by Isadora Alman; *Uppity Women of the New World* by Vicki Leon; *Out of the Mouths of Babes* by Autumn Stephens; *The Ladies' Room Reader* by Alicia Alvrez; *Embracing Persephone* by Virginia Beane Rutter; *Aromatherapy Through the Seasons* by Paula M. Bousquet and Judith Fitzsimmons.

Conari Press seeks to be a catalyst for profound change by providing enlightening books on topics that range from spirituality and women's issues to sexuality, relationships, and personal growth. Conari values integrity, process, compassion, and receptivity, in publishing projects as well as the house's internal workings.

Conari is distributed to the trade by Publishers Group West; gift store distribution is handled through Sourcebooks, Inc.

Query letters and SASEs should be directed to:

Heather McArthur, Managing Editor

Leslie Berriman, Executive Editor

CONSUMER REPORTS BOOKS

101 Truman Avenue, Yonkers, NY 10703
914-378-2000

Consumer Reports Books is active in a number of consumer-information spheres. Among them: product-buying guides and consumer reference; automotive; children and teenagers; consumer issues; food, cooking, and nutrition (including cookbooks); general interest; health and fitness; home and environment; law for consumers; personal finance; and travel.

Consumer Reports Books is the book-publishing wing of the Consumers Union (founded in 1936), which publishes *Consumer Reports* magazine. Consumer Reports Books specializes in nonfiction works (most of them in trade paperback format, along with a few hardcovers) designed as guides for consumers as they make purchasing decisions or participate in the demands of certain sectors of contemporary corporate and commercial society—especially health care, personal finance, and the law. Some Consumer Reports titles hone a controversial edge. The publisher typically offers a small number of new books each season (plus periodically revised editions of some of the house's more popular and important works). Consumer Reports maintains a steadfast backlist.

Many Consumer Reports titles originate in house and are researched and written by *Consumer Reports* editors; however, the house acquires and produces a limited number of works from independent authors.

Representative guides (often in updated editions): *Guide to Baby Products; Best Travel Deals 2001; Complete Drug Reference 2001; Guide to Health Care for Seniors; Home Computer Buying Guide 2001; How to Plan for a Secure Retirement; Consumer Reports Money Book; Used Car Buying Guide 2001; New Car Preview 2001; Used Car Yearbook; Sport Utility Special 2001; House and Home Buying Guide 2001; Best Buys for Your Home 2001;* and *Guide to Online Shopping.*

Featured Consumer Reports trade titles: *How to Clean Practically Anything; How to Buy a House, Condo, or Co-op; How to Avoid Auto Repair Rip-Offs; Easy Lawn and Garden Care; Complete Book of Bathroom Design; Mind/Body Medicine; Health Schemes, Scams and Frauds; 101 Health Questions; AIDS: Trading Fears for Facts; Women's Sexual Health; Sumptuous Desserts; Consumer Reports Money Book: How to Get It, Save It, and Spend It Wisely; Below the Line: Living Poor in America.*

Consumer Reports Books distributes to the trade through St. Martin's Press.

Query letters and SASEs should be directed to:

Andrea Scott, Director of Special Publications

CONTINUUM PUBLISHING GROUP

370 Lexington Avenue, New York, NY 10017-6550
212-953-5858   fax: 212-953-5944
www.continuum-books.com   e-mail: contin@tiac.net

Continuum's Web site contains details on forthcoming, current, and previously published titles, as well as links to Chiron Publications, Daimon Publications, Spring Publications, Templeton Foundation, and Paragon House.

Continuum publishes general trade books, texts, scholarly monographs, and reference works in the areas of literature and the arts, psychology, history and social thought, women's studies, and religion. Continuum offers more than 100 new publications a year, as well as 700 established backlist titles.

Continuum's broad focus integrates the fields of literature and criticism, psychology and counseling, women's studies, and social issues of contemporary public interest. The house is known for its select line of books in popular and scholarly approaches to religion and philosophy. The Frederick Ungar imprint specializes in literature, film, and the performing arts.

Continuum and Crossroad Publishing Company were editorially independent components of the Crossroad/Continuum Publishing Group from 1980 into the early 1990s, since which time Continuum has pursued its own independent publishing trajectory. (For Crossroad Publishing, see entry in the Directory of Religious, Spiritual, and Inspirational Publishers.)

From the Continuum trade list: *The Religious Art of Andy Warhol* by Jane Daggett Dillenberger; *Breaking the Fine Rain of Death: African American Health Issues and the Womanist Ethic of Care* by Emilie M. Townes; *The Family and HIV Today: Recent Research and Practice* (edited by Robert Bor and Jonathan Elford); *Legal Queeries* (edited by Leslie Moran, Sarah Beresford, and Daniel Monk); *The Lesbian and Gay Christian Movement: Campaigning for Justice, Truth and Love* (edited by Sean Gill); *Love Does No Harm: Sexual Ethics for the Rest of Us* by Marie M. Fortune; *Text and Psyche: Experiencing the Scripture Today* by Schuyler Brown; *The Way of Compassion: Survival Strategies for a World in Crisis* (edited by Martin Rowe); *Genetic Knowledge, Human Values, and Responsibility: An Essential Guidebook to the Moral and Scientific Issues in Gene Therapy* (edited by Jacquelyn Kegley); *Beyond the Human Species: The Life and Work of Sri Aurobindo and the Mother* by Georges Van Vrekham. Continuum's Hollywood-related titles: *Robert Altman: Hollywood Survivor* by Daniel O'Brien; *The Cinema of Oliver Stone* by Norman Kagan; *The Cinema of Stanley Kubrick* by Norman Kagan; *Steven Spielberg: The Man, His Movies, and Their Meaning* by Philip M. Taylor.

Continuum is distributed through Books International. Continuum also distributes the distinguished publishing programs of Chiron Publications, Daimon Publications, Spring Publications, and Paragon House. Query letters and SASEs should be directed to:

Evander Lomke, Managing Editor—Psychological counseling, history and the arts, literary criticism, current affairs, women's studies.

Frank Oveis, Publishing Director—Academic religious and biblical studies, world religions, spirituality.

DAVID C. COOK PUBLISHING COMPANY
See listing for Chariot/Victor in Directory of Religious, Spiritual, and Inspirational Publishers.

COPPER CANYON PRESS

P.O. Box 271, Port Townsend, WA 98368
360-385-4925   fax: 360-385-4985
coppercanyonpress.org

The Copper Canyon mission is to publish poetry distinguished in both content and design, within the context of belief that the publisher's art—like the poet's—is sacramental. Copper Canyon Press (founded in 1972) publishes in hardcover and paperback.

Within this ambitious vision, there are limitations; Copper Canyon generally does not sign many new writers. The house assigns its resources to furthering its established roster. The publisher's success in its aim is proven through abundant and continuing recognition of its authors via honors, awards, grants, and fellowships.

Copper Canyon Press publishes a list with such titles as these: *Always Beginning* by Maxine Kumin; *Armored Hearts* by David Bottoms; *August Zero* by Jane Miller; *Below Cold Mountain* by Joseph Stroud; *Black Iris* by Denise Levertov; *The Book of Questions* by Pablo Neruda; *Carrying Over,* by Carolyn Kizer; *Communion* by Primaus St. John; *Cool, Calm, & Collected* by Carolyn Kizer; *Daughter's Latitude* by Karen Swenson; *Death Son* by Thomas McGrath; *East Window* by W. S. Merwin; *Exiled in the Word* by Jerome Rothenberg and Harris Lenowitz; *Heart of Bamboo* by Sam Hamill; *Iris of Creation* by Marvin Bell; *Like Underground Water* by Edward Lueders; *The Leaf Path* by Emily Warn; *Moment to Moment* by David Budbill; *Nightworks* by Marvin Bell; *On Poetry and Craft* by Theodor Roethke; *Rivers of Sale* by Shirley Kaufman; *The Sea and the Bells* by Pablo Neruda; *Selected Essays and Reviews* by Hayden Carruth; *The Steel Cricket* by Stephen Berg; *The Mercy Seat* by Norman Dubie; *The Wandering Border* by Jann Kaplinski; and *Words for My Daughter* by John Balaban.

Copper Canyon distributes to the trade via Consortium.

Manuscripts for first, second, or third books are considered only in conjunction with the Hayden Carruth Award. Contact the press with an SASE for the entry form in September; submissions are accepted during the month of November, and the winner will be announced in February. The winner of the first Hayden Carruth Award is Sascha Feinstein, for his poems *Blues Departures*. Visit our Web site at www.ccpress.org for details.

All queries must include SASE. We do not accept manuscript queries by e-mail. Copper Canyon generally does not sign many new writers. Query letters and SASEs should be directed to:

Sam Hamill, Editor

CRAIN BOOKS

See NTC Business Books/VGM Career Horizons.

CRISP PUBLICATIONS

1200 Hamilton Court, Menlo Park, CA 94025
650-323-6100

Crisp Publications produces nonfiction business books and media packages; topic areas include: management, personal improvement, human resources and wellness, communications and creativity, customer service, sales, small businesses, financial planning, adult literacy and learning, careers, and retirement and life planning. The house is known for a number of successful lines: 50-Minute Book, series in small-business ventures, and business titles keyed to use of new media.

Crisp Publications (founded in 1985) is a specialist in target business publishing and is equally expert at marketing the resultant product. Crisp offers an extensive selection of training programs (including self-study formats) that incorporate books, manuals, and audiovisual materials. The house's aim is to provide high-quality cost-effective books and videos that can help business organizations succeed in competitive times.

The 50-Minute Book is Crisp's signature designation for books produced with the concept of being concise, easily read, and readily understood through personal involvement with exercises, activities, and assessments. Other Crisp lines are the Quick Read Series, the Small Business and Entrepreneurship Series, and the Crisp Management Library.

Highlights from Crisp: *Organizing Your Workspace* by Odette Pollar; *Measure and Manage Stress* by Herbert Kindler and Marilyn Ginsburg; *Motivating at Work: Empowering Employees to Give Their Best* by Twyla Dell; *Preventing Job Burnout* by Beverly A. Potter; *Preventing Workplace Violence* by Marianne Minor; *The Art of Communicating* by Bert Decker; *The New Supervisor* by Elwood N. Chapman; *Training Managers to Train* by Brother Herman Zaccarelli; *A Legal Guide for Small Business* by Charles Lickson.

Crisp Publications distributes through a commission sales force. Query letters and SASEs should be directed to:

George Young, Editor

CROWN PUBLISHING GROUP (PART OF RANDOM HOUSE)

Crown Books

Crown Business

Three Rivers Press

Clarkson Potter/Publishers

Harmony Books

Prima Publishing: Lifestyles and Health

299 Park Avenue, New York, NY 10171

Crown publishes a variety of trade-oriented fiction and nonfiction titles in hardcover and paperback. Crown (acquired by Random House in 1988) incorporates a number of Random House imprints and acquisitions that together make up the Crown Publishing Group.

Crown imprints include Harmony Books, the Crown imprint, Crown Business, Clarkson Potter, Shaye Areheart Books, Three Rivers Press, Prima Publishing, and Bell Tower.

Three Rivers Press is a new designation for what was formerly Crown Trade Paperbacks. Titles include: *Britney Spears' Heart to Heart* by Britney and Lynne Spears; *Our Dumb Century* from The Onion Web site; *Business Plan for the Body* by Jim Karas; *Nine Steps to Financial Freedom* by Suze Orman; *Kovel's Antiques and Collectibles Pricelist;* and *The New York Times Parent's Guide to the Best Books for Children* by Eden Ross Lipson.

The House of Collectibles line of books is the definitive leader in price guides for a broad spectrum of collectibles from coins to teacups to bottles, and includes the *Official Beckett Price Guides* to sports cards.

Crown's fiction includes commercial novels across the trade spectrum, including mystery and suspense; Harmony Books embraces a typically more vanguard literary tone.

Crown's fiction list and works of cultural and literary interest are exemplified by *Another City, Not My Own: A Novel in the Form of a Memoir* by Dominick Dunne; *Road Rage: A Novel* by Ruth Rendell; *Summer Island* by Kristen Hannah; as well as *Starting Out in the Evening* by Brian Morton.

Crown nonfiction encompasses popular titles in biography, history, art, antiques and collectibles, contemporary culture, crime, sports, travel, languages, cookbooks, and self-help/how-to, as well as popular-reference works.

Cuisine and lifestyle are areas of Clarkson Potter emphasis. Releases here include Martha Stewart's coffee-table editions and *The Barefoot Contessa* books by Ina Garten, the contemporary and innovative hostess guru of the Hamptons. They've also recently published Melinda and Robert Blanchard's *A Trip to the Beach.*

From Crown nonfiction: *Isaac's Storm* by Eric Larson; *Tupac Shakur* by the Editors of *VIBE Magazine,* foreword by Quincy Jones, introduction by Danyl Smith; *Dogs Never Lie About Love: Reflections on the Emotional World of Dogs* by Jeffrey Moussaieff Masson; *The Intelligence Edge: How to Profit in the Information Age* by George Friedman, Meredith Friedman, John S. Baker, Jr., and Colin Chapman; *Cactus Tracks and Cowboy Philosophy* by Baxter Black; *Dave Barry Is from Mars and Venus* by Dave Barry; *Lest We Forget: The Passage from Africa to Slavery and Emancipation* by Graham Hancock and Robert Bauval; *How We Remember and Why We Forget: The Art and Science of Memory* by Rebecca Rupp; *Stealing Jesus: How Fundamentalism Betrays Christianity* by Bruce Bawer.

From Harmony and Shaye Areheart Books, quality fiction such as Chris Bohjalian's *Midwives* and Jeanne Ray's *Julie and Romeo.* A solid non-fiction list includes Deepak Chopra's *How to Know God;* Tara Bennett-Goleman's *Emotional Alchemy;* Stephen Mitchell's translation of *Bhagavad Gita;* Suzanne Finstad's biography of Natalie Wood, *Natasha;* and Stephen Jay Gould's *The Lying Stones of Marakesh.*

Query letters and SASEs should be directed to:

Bob Mecoy, Vice President and Executive Editor—Adult trade fiction and nonfiction. Does not accept unsolicited manuscripts.

Doug Pepper, Vice President and Senior Editor—Literary fiction and issue-oriented nonfiction.

Kristin Kiser, Senior Editor—Thrillers and literary fiction; special interests, popular culture, music, sports, popular science, and narrative nonfiction.

C

Pete Fornatale, Associate Editor—Adult trade fiction and nonfiction. Does not accept unsolicited manuscripts.

Rachel Kahan, Associate Editor—Historical fiction, narrative nonfiction, contemporary fiction.

Steve Ross, Senior Vice President and Editorial Director—Adult trade fiction and nonfiction. Also oversees Times Books and Times Business Imprints. Does not accept unsolicited manuscripts.

John Mahaney, Executive Editor Crown Business

Elizabeth Rapoport, Executive Editor—Health, parenting, psychology.

Emily Loose, Executive Editor—Politics, history, current events.

Chris Jackson, Senior Editor

Ruth Mills, Editor—Business.

Caroline Sincerbeaux, Assistant Editor

Toisan Craigg, Assistant Editor

Stephanie Higgs, Editorial Assistant

Jonathan Sloim, Editorial Assistant

Kate Donovan, Editorial Assistant

Dorianne Steele, Editorial Assistant

Claudia Gable, Editorial Assistant

Clarkson Potter/Publishers

Annetta Hanna, Senior Editor—Design, gardening, biography, popular culture, how-to style and decorating books.

Lauren Shakely, Senior Vice President and Editorial Director—How-to style and decorating books, art books, gardening, biography.

Margot Schupf, Associate Editor

Pam Krauss, Vice President and Executive Editor—Cooking and food, how-to style and decorating books, gardening, narrative nonfiction.

Roy Finamore, Editor and Special Projects—Cooking and food, design and architecture, special projects, style and decorating, biography, popular culture.

Katie Workman, Senior Editor—Cooking and food, popular culture, how-to style and decorating books.

Clarkson Potter
299 Park Avenue, New York, NY 10171

   Born: March 11, 1968.
   Education: Major in British American Literature; Minor in Psychology and Minor in Philosophy from George Washington University.
   Employment history/editor career path: I am a rare case; I started working at Clarkson Potter right out of college and have been here ever since—10 years.

Personal interests: Cooking, food related things, volunteer work, working out, and I have a new baby.

What would you be doing if you were not an editor? Something in the food world or doing volunteer work. Maybe working on the Internet.

What has been your most successful book that you have acquired to date? The *Pillsbury* series; we just published the ninth one. Probably the most successful was *The Pillsbury Best to the Bake-Off*. This sold over one million copies.

What books have you acquired that make you the most proud? What books that you have acquired reflect the types of books you like to represent? *Almost Vegetarian* by Diana Shaw (sold 200,000) copies; *The Blue Ribbon Country Cookbook* by Diane Roupe (it has over 1,000 recipes from over 10 years of award-winning blue ribbon food in Iowa).

Do you represent fiction? No.

Do you represent nonfiction? Yes, mostly branded books (company-connected books) such as Pillsbury, Omaha Steaks, and so on.

Do you require book proposals? If so, what do you look for in evaluating a book proposal? Yes. The right balance of editorial integrity, must have a strong emphasis on the market for the book, who the audience is, and what is your competition.

What process do you use for making a decision? What is the process for acquisition, is there a committee? We have an editorial meeting once a week with all the editors, sales, and marketing people at Clarkson.

Are you interested in work geared for the masses (readers of *People, The Star,* etc.)? Yes.

Are agents important? Why? Yes, they are part of the screening process.

Do you like new writers? What should new writers do to break into the business? It's tough to break into this business. I think getting an agent helps. Go to the bookstore and read books like the one you are proposing to write, read the acknowledgments section of the book to find the agents acknowledged. This is a good way to find an agent who obviously represents work in your field. Put together a good proposal and use all of your contacts that you know.

How should writers approach you? I look at everything that comes to me; do your homework and know what I like to see and then mail me something (snail mail).

What are some common mistakes writers make? What really gets on your nerves? Lateness. Authors who cannot meet deadlines. When querying me, don't tell me that no one has written a book like yours; chances are if you do your research, someone has.

What can writers do to get your attention and to avoid the slush pile? Write a good concise cover letter telling me why you should be the person to write this book. Do your homework!!

What have been some of your best experiences with writers or in your job? Some of my authors have become really good friends of mine. The Pillsbury relationship has been wonderful. I love when something unique happens with a book.

What, if anything, makes you different from other editors? I do think of things from a sales and marketing perspective. I like to be involved with all aspects of the book, not just editing.

Is there anything you would like to see changed in the industry? We should all remember that the focus of book publishing is on the authors and books themselves. I would like to see everyone in the industry having more fun and enjoying the publishing process.

Any advice for writers? Hand in the best manuscript that you can; it will result in the best product in the end.

Harmony Books

Linda Lowenthal, Vice President, Executive Editorial Director, Harmony Books and Three Rivers Press—Narrative non-fiction, spirituality, psychology.

Becky Cabaza, Executive Editor, Three Rivers Press—Health, fitness, parenting, humor, business, pop science, narrative non-fiction.

Rebecca Strong, Senior Editor, Harmony—Literary non-fiction, science, literary fiction.

Carrie Thornton, Editor, Three Rivers Press—Pop culture, music, humor, gay and lesbian, dating and relationships, film.

Sarah Silbert, Editor, Three Rivers Press—Pop-culture, beauty, light Judaica, narrative non-fiction, health, pets, and parenting.

Shaye Areheart, Vice President, Editorial Director, Shaye Areheart Books/Harmony Books—Literary fiction, biographies, humor. Wide general nonfiction interests.

Toinette Lippe, Editorial Director, Bell Tower—Spirituality and inspiration (not reincarnation, astrology, crystals, and the like).

Prima Publishing: Lifestyles and Health

3000 Lava Ridge Court, Roseville, CA 95661
916-787-7000   fax: 916-787-7001
www.primapublishing.com

In late March of 2001, the Crown Publishing Group under Random House acquired Prima Publishing (founded in 1984). With a fluid and innovative list, Prima Publishing's Lifestyles and Health groups publish books in a wide variety of categories, including business, parenting and education, network marketing, pets, crafts, natural medicine, reference, and travel. Prima is also the publisher of the book you are now reading, *Writer's Guide to Book Editors, Publishers, and Literary Agents, 2002–2003: Who They Are! What They Want! And How to Win Them Over!* by Jeff Herman.

Prima Lifestyles publishes general trade books. Representative titles include: *Walt Disney World with Kids* by Kim Wright Wiley; *Wave 3* and *Wave 4* by Richard Poe; *Glenn Dickey's 49ers* by Glenn Dickey; THE RELOCATING series; *Homeschooling Almanac* by Michael and Mary Leppert; *The New Color of Success* by Niki Butler Mitchell; *Setting Limits with Your Strong-Willed Child* by J. Robert MacKenzie; *Parent's Complete Guide to Soccer* by Joe Provey; *The Servant* by James Hunter; *Sacred Dying* by Megory Anderson; the POSITIVE DISCIPLINE series by Jane Nelsen, Ed.D.; *Your Over-35 Pregnancy Week-by-Week Pregnancy Guide* by M. Kelly Shanahan, M.D.; YOUR PET'S LIFE series edited by Joanne Howl, D.V.M.; the BETTER IN 5 MINUTES series; and A GIRL'S WORLD series by A Girl's World Productions Inc.

Forum, Prima's serious nonfiction imprint, covers topics such as current affairs, public policy, libertarian/conservative thought, high-level management, individual empowerment, and historical biography. Recent titles include: *Let Us Talk of Many Things* by William F. Buckley Jr.; *The Seven Myths of Gun Control* by Richard Poe; *Cisco: Unauthorized* by Jeffrey S. Young; and the latest in the ON LEADERSHIP series, *Theodore Roosevelt on Leadership* by James Strock.

Prima Girls provides positive, realistic, and current books for preteen and early teen girls on relevant topics related to growing up. All of the books are based on input from girls, are interactive in format, and address the issues, concerns, hopes, and dreams for the growing young adult market. Key titles include: A GIRL'S WORLD series for girls by girls and *Girls: What's So Bad About Being Good?* by Harriet S. Mosatche, Ph.D.

Prima Home publishes a variety of titles in the areas of crafts and hobbies, weddings, and the home. Representative titles include: *How to Have an Elegant Wedding for $5,000 or Less* by Jan Wilson and Beth Wilson Hickman; *The Ultimate Wedding Idea Book* by Cynthia Muchnick; *Housekeeping Secrets My Mother Never Taught Me* by Joni Hilton; *How to Decorate & Furnish Your Apartment on a Budget* by Lourdes Dumke; the FOR FUN & PROFIT series; and the GOOD GIFTS FROM THE HOME series.

Prima Money provides current, reliable, and sophisticated finance books for professionals on trading and investing. Representative titles include: *The Wealthy Barber* by David Chilton; *Electronic Day Trading Made Easy* by Misha T. Sarkovich, Ph.D.; *The Complete Guide to Offshore Money Havens, Revised 4th Edition,* by Jerome Schneider; and *Successful Biotech Investing* by Joe Duarte, M.D.

Prima Pets is dedicated to building a trusted library of books to provide owners with the vital information they need to keep their animal friends happy and healthy. Prima Pets also offers warm and inviting books that touch the hearts of animal lovers everywhere. Titles include: The YOUR PET'S LIFE series, which encompasses breed-specific titles for dogs, as well as titles devoted to cats, reptiles, and birds; THE NATURAL VEt series by Dr. Shawn Messonnier; *Emergency Animal Rescue Stories* by Terri Crisp, founder and director of EARS; *You Can Save the Animals* by Ingrid Newkirk and published in conjunction with PETA; *What Animals Teach Us* by Mary Hessler-Key, Ph.D., and *The Compassion of Animals* by Kristin von Kreisler.

Prima SOHO provides small office/home office entrepreneurs with information on establishing and growing their businesses. These entry-level books cover a wide range of topics—from making the decision to go into business to marketing and promotion strategies. Titles include: *101 Best Home-Based Businesses for Women, Revised 2nd Edition* by Priscilla Y. Huff; *The Stay-at-Home Mom's Guide to Making Money, Revised 2nd Edition* by Liz Folger; and *101 Great Mail-Order Businesses, Revised 2nd Edition* by Tyler G. Hicks. In addition, Prima is the leading publisher of network marketing titles, including: *Wave 4* by Richard Poe; *Your First Year in Network Marketing* by Mark Yarnell and Rene Reid Yarnell; and *Pre-Paid Legal Handbook* by Harland C. Stonecipher and James Robinson.

Prima Venture gives entrepreneurs and executives the tools to thrive in the New Economy with professional books on growing and innovating businesses. Venture titles include: *Deep Branding on the Internet* by Marc Braunstein and Edward H. Levine; *The*

Complete Guide to Valuing and Selling Your Business by Frederick D. Lipman; and *Lessons from the E-Front* by Matthew W. Ragas.

Prima Health publishes books on natural medicine and its integration into the medical mainstream. Latest titles include: *The Natural Pharmacist: Natural Health Bible* (edited by Steven Bratman, M.D., and David Kroll, Ph.D.); THE NATURAL PHARMACIST series; *SAMe* by Sol Grazi, M.D., and Marie Costa; *Encyclopedia of Natural Medicine* by Michael T. Murray, N.D.; *The Omega* Solution by Jonathan Goodman, N.D.; and *New Hope for People with Bipolar Disorder* by Jan Fawcett, M.D., Bernard Golden, Ph.D., and Nancy Rosenfeld.

Query letters and SASEs for Prima Lifestyles and Health should be directed to:

Alice Feinstein, Editorial and Publishing Director

David Richardson, Acquisitions Editor—Prima Money and Prima Venture: business, management, marketing, finance, and investing.

Denise Sternad, Acquisitions Editor—Prima Home, Prima Girls, Prima Pets, and Prima SOHO.

Jamie Miller, Acquisitions Editor—Parenting and education, Prima Health.

DALKEY ARCHIVE PRESS

Illinois State University, Campus Box 4241, Normal, IL 61790-4241
309-438-7555   fax: 309-438-7422
www.dalkeyarchive.com   e-mail: cwpost@dalkeyarchive.com

Dalkey Archive (founded in 1984) is dedicated to breakthrough artistic expression in fiction. Dalkey's writers are among the most influential stylists on the printed page. Dalkey Archive Press is a division of the Review of Contemporary Fiction.

From the Dalkey Archive list: *The Age of Wire and String* by Ben Marcus; *Take Five* by D. Keith Mano; *Cigarettes: A Novel* by Harry Mathews; *Tlooth: A Novel,* also by Harry Mathews; *Excitability* by Diane Williams; *A Short Rhetoric for Leaving the Family* by Peter Dimock; *The Polish Complex* by Tadeusz Konwicki (introduction by the translator Richard Lourie); *The Dick Gibson Show* by Stanley Elkin; *Pushkin House* by Andrei Bitov; *Chromos* by Felipe Alfau; *Odile* by Raymond Queneau; *The Engineer of Human Souls* by Josef Skvorecky (translated by Paul Wilson).

Dalkey Archive distributes through Chicago Distribution Center. Query letters and SASEs should be directed to:

Chad Post, Editor

DAW BOOKS, INC.

375 Hudson Street, New York, NY 10014
212-366-2096

DAW Books publishes science fiction, fantasy, science fantasy, future fiction and future fantasy, dark suspense, and horror. DAW publishes mass-market paperbound originals and reprints, as well as hardcovers and trade paperbacks.

The DAW line includes masterful genre-keyed anthologies that showcase some of the most respected writers in their respective literary provinces. DAW typically produces a medium-sized seasonal list of new titles. The DAW backlist is replete with successful individual titles, along with a host of perennially selling series.

DAW Books (founded in 1971) is at the forefront of the literary categories and genres in which it specializes. The house is affiliated with Penguin USA.

From DAW Books: *Death Watch* by Elizabeth Forrest; *Fire in the Sky* by Jo Clayton; *Murder at the Galactic Writers' Society* by Janet Asimov; *Northlight* by Deborah Wheeler; *The Winds of Darkover* by Marion Zimmer Bradley; *Vampire Detectives* (edited by Martin H. Greenberg).

DAW distribution is through an affiliation with Penguin USA. Query letters and SASEs should be directed to:

Peter Stampfel, Submissions Editor

D

DCI PUBLISHING
See Chronimed Publishing.

DEACONESS PRESS
See Fairview Press.

DEARBORN TRADE
A Kaplan Professional Company
155 North Wacker Drive, Chicago, IL 60606-1719
312-836-4400   fax: 312-836-1021
www.dearborn.com

Dearborn Trade is the nation's premier provider of personal finance, investment, real estate, and business information resources for consumers and professionals. In 1998, Dearborn Publishing Group, Inc., was acquired by Kaplan Educational Centers, opening significant opportunities for growth in both the professional and consumer areas. Kaplan is a wholly owned subsidiary of the Washington Post Company. All imprints of Dearborn (Dearborn Trade, Dearborn Financial Publishing, Inc., and Upstart Publishing Company) have been folded into one imprint—Dearborn—representing an integrated approach to its future. Dearborn Trade has moved into publishing information geared to the general business and management arenas.

Dearborn has been constantly redefining and refining its direction ever since the trade division started actively publishing practical how-to books for consumers and investors in

1986. Prior to that, the company (founded in 1967) focused on training for financial professionals in real estate, insurance, and securities. Dearborn remains the premier provider—worldwide—of prelicensing, continuing professional education and training in the financial services and real estate industries. Dearborn Trade publishes titles intended for individual book buyers, whether they are general consumers or CEOs of corporations. Topics including personal finance, securities, trading, tax issues, estate planning, consumer real estate, general management, corporate biographies, business leader biographies, and entrepreneurship.

From Dearborn: *The Power of Six Sigma* by Subir Chowdhury; *If You're Clueless About Accounting and Want to Know More* by Seth Godin; *The New "Retirementality"* by Mitch Anthony; *Real Estate a la Carte* by Julie Gordon Good; *Everyone's Money Book* by Jordan Goodman; *Collaborative Communities* by Jeffrey Sherman, Janiu M. Twombly, and David I Rottenbers.

Query letters and SASEs should be directed to

Don Hull, Editorial Director— Finance and investing.

Evan Cooper, Publisher—Professional real estate.

Mary B. Good, Acquisitions Editor—Consumer real estate and entrepreneurship.

Jean Iversen, Senior Acquisitions Editor—Management and general business.

Born: September 21.

Education: B.A. in Journalism from Columbia College, Chicago, Illinois.

Employment history/editor career path: I was a magazine Editor and writer before coming to the book publishing industry. I was an Acquisitions Editor at Publications International, a consumer book Publisher in the suburbs of Chicago, for three years before coming to Dearborn, where I have been for almost two years now. I love being back in the city!

Personal interests: Reading, of course. I also do some freelance writing for local newspapers and music publications on rock and entertainment in general. My original major was piano performance, and I sung/played in rock bands for over 10 years. About 5 years ago I discovered scuba diving and have since been to Mexico, the Bahamas, and Bonaire. It's one of those incredible experiences in life.

What would you be doing if you were not an editor? On the other side of the fence—writing. Or an underwater photographer.

What has been your most successful book that you have acquired to date? A couple of titles: *Web Rules* by Tom Murphy, which chronicles the return of power to the consumer via the Internet; and *Handy Ma'am*, a how-to home repair and decorating guide by PBS's femme fatale Beverly DeJulio.

What books have you acquired that make you the most proud? What books that you have acquired reflect the types of books you like to represent? *Lightning in a Bottle* by author David Baum, a collection of over 60 stories and anecdotes on the subject of corporate change. It's David's first book and we received so much positive feedback when it came out. It was humorous and enlightening, captivating and compelling—all the things we were trying to be. And because we succeeded, it's been a very positive and fulfilling book to be a part of. I've actually attracted very credible authors who saw and read the book and wanted to be a part of the Dearborn fold.

Do you represent fiction? No.

What do you want to see less of? Too many proposals are on dated topics or written from an unoriginal perspective.

Do you represent nonfiction? Yes. Management/general business.

Do you require book proposals? If so what do you look for in evaluating a book proposal? Generally, I prefer a completed proposal and either one sample chapter or relevant writing samples. However, a query letter with a detailed description and compelling book synopsis can also be effective. In evaluating proposals, I look for timely topics or topics with a fresh spin or perspective on them. The author *must* be shedding new light on the subject. I also look for authors who are aggressive promoters and who bear impressive credentials.

Are certain aspects of a book proposal given more weight than others? Obviously, the ability of the author (or ghostwriter) to write, but also their credentials and name recognition.

What process do you use for making a decision? What is the process for acquisition, it there a committee? We are a small house, so the process is probably quicker than most; though because we are small, each project is scrutinized very carefully. I generally present each project to our editorial committee, which consists of key sales, marketing, and editorial staff. Based on the feedback at this meeting, I will make an offer to the author. Our current president lets us acquire projects on our own, thereby giving us the autonomy we need to function as a growing, innovative publishing house.

What kinds of nonfiction books do you want to see less of? Ones that tell the same old story that we heard last year, the year before, and so on. Tell us something new!

Are you interested in work geared for the masses (readers of *People, The Star,* etc.)? No. We're a business publisher. Though one of our books, *Rags to Riches*, did get excerpted in the *National Enquirer!*

Are agents important? Why? Yes, especially for first-time authors. I see many proposals that are good, but way too rough, and suggest that the writer contract an agent or editorial adviser to help out in the proposal process. A good agent can also help an author through the contract negotiation process, as some authors need an objective party to explain the terms. I wouldn't say that every author needs an agent, but it is crucial in many cases.

Do you like new writers? What should new writers do to break into the business? I sign new writers and repeat writers. I've been very successful with many new writers. Because they are new to the process, it can be a lot of fun to work with them and be creative and guide them through the process. It's nice to hear, at the end of the development process, that they'd like to do another book with you and that they enjoyed the process. Writing a book can certainly be a very grueling process.

How should writers approach you? Either a query letter or a completed proposal with a sample chapter or relevant writing samples. I've gotten phone calls from referrals, and that can be okay, too, because I've already heard about their idea and they've been referred to me, but those are exceptions. Maybe it's just me, but I don't like it when authors or agents e-mail unsolicited proposals to me.

What are some common mistakes writers make? What really gets on your nerves? If you misspell my name or anything in your query letter, then you're representing yourself

D

as unprofessional and I can't take you very seriously. Also, proposals on topics that we would obviously never publish. Please read our catalogs, visit our Web site, or do some research at the bookstore or library. Get to know us before you send us a proposal.

What can writers do to get your attention and to avoid the slush pile? Again, propose timely topics with a fresh spin that are consistent with our publishing program. Present yourself as a credible, promotable author. If your writing is weak, get help—from the proposal stage on up. Convince us that we can't afford to not publish your title, and be realistic. Editors see through hyperbole more than anyone else.

What have been some of your craziest experiences with submissions? I received a submission for a book on *How to Start Your Own Organic Farm.*

What have been some of your best experiences with writers or in your job? Some of my best experiences have been with writers who were very willing collaborators and found creative ways to either write/organize or promote their books and saw their book as one piece of their professional portfolio.

What, if anything, makes you different from other editors? This can only be told by those who have worked with me! I have been told, however, that I involve myself quite a bit more than other editors and truly assist in the development of the manuscript, rather than putting the rubber stamp of approval on their first draft and pushing it on the copyeditor. I take a personal interest in every detail of each author's book and do my best to help each author realize his or her fullest potential.

Is there anything you would like to see changed in the industry? It is, of course, extremely tough to be in an industry where almost all of your product is sold on a consignment basis. That said, I think the evolution of electronic publishing is crucial to being competitive in this marketplace and should be developed in a way that is fruitful to both authors and publishers.

Any advice for writers? Do your homework. Research publishers. Know your topic inside and out—you want to be perceived as the "expert" on your topic. And seek editorial assistance—whether you're a published author or not—because too many authors work in a vacuum and become myopic in the development of their work.

DELACORTE PRESS
See Dell Publishing.

DELL PUBLISHING
(A DIVISION OF BANTAM DOUBLEDAY DELL PUBLISHING)
Delacorte Press

The Dial Press

DTP Trade Paperbacks

Laurel

See also: Bantam Doubleday Dell Publishing Group

1540 Broadway, New York, NY 10036
212-354-6500

The Dell/Delacorte wing spans commercial nonfiction and popular fiction, including mainstream titles as well as mystery, suspense, and thrillers. Dell/Delacorte has a strong presence in hardcover, trade paperback, and mass-market areas.

Dell Publishing produces trade and mass-market paperbacks in virtually all fiction and nonfiction categories, along with selected hardcover originals. Dell (founded in 1921) upholds a traditional position as one of the major players in paperback publishing. The DTP imprint covers practical and inspirational nonfiction in trade paperback. Delta Trade Paperbacks include serious (and fun) contemporary fiction, narrative nonfiction, popular culture, popular science, and issue-oriented psychology. The Laurel imprint includes literary and reference titles in trade paper and mass-market paperback. Dell mass-market paperbacks feature reprints of Delacorte hardcovers, mass-market editions of hardcover originals from other BDD divisions, and a raft of paperback originals.

Delacorte Press concentrates on hardcover frontlist releases. Among Delacorte's nonfiction areas of interest are popular psychology, self-help, child care, humor, politics, true crime, and current issues and events. Delacorte trade fiction includes commercial novels, mystery, romance, historical sagas, and futurist works. A good number of Delacorte's frontlist titles are presented with simultaneous release on BDD Audio Cassette.

Delacorte Press nonfiction and popular works: *Last Call: 10 Common-Sense Solutions to America's Biggest Problems* by Rob Nelson; *Lost in the Funhouse* by Bill Zehme; *For the Bride* and *For the Groom* by Colin Cowie; *If Only* by Geri Halliwell; *How I Accidentally Joined the Vast Right-Wing Conspiracy (and Found Inner Peace)* by Harry Stein; *Civil Warriors: The Legal Siege on the Tobacco Industry* by Dan Zegart.

Delacorte commercial fiction and literary works: *Losing Julia* by Jonathan Hull; *Handyman* by Linda Nichols; *The House on Hope Street* and *The Wedding* by Danielle Steel; *The Runner* by Christopher Reich; *After the Fire* by Belva Plain; *Lost Girls* by Andrew Pyper; *The Tidal Poole* (an Elizabeth I mystery) by Karen Harper; *Cuba Libre* by Elmore Leonard; *The Horse Whisperer* by Nicholas Evans; *The Marriage Prize* by Virginia Henley; *Move to Strike* by Peri O'Shaughnessy.

The Dial Press is a revived presence in the Dell Publishing division of Bantam Doubleday Dell Publishing Group. Dial offers a short, selective commercial-literary list (fiction and serious nonfiction) published primarily in hardcover editions under its own lion-and-cupid logo.

The Dial Press literary purview in fiction: *Deep in the Heart* by Sharon Oard Warner; *Dating Big Bird* by Laura Zigman; *A Trip to the Stars* by Nicholas Christopher. Creative nonfiction from Dial: *Driving Mr. Albert* by Michael Paterniti.

DTP Trade Paperbacks presents up-to-the-minute trends in a principally mainline nonfiction list that also hits specialty sectors such as humor and puzzles. The DTP nonfiction program covers: *How to Think Like Leonardo Da Vinci* by Michael J. Gelb; *What Einstein Told His Barber* by Robert L. Wolke; *Lea's Book of Rules for the World* by Lea DeLaria with Maggie Cassella; *Champions Are Raised, Not Born* by Summer Sanders with Melinda Marshall; *Contemplative Living* by Joan Duncan Oliver.

D

Delta trade paperbacks embrace both originals and reprints in mainstream nonfiction and in popular and cutting-edge fiction. Representing the Delta line: *Rocket Boys: A Memoir* by Homer H. Hickam, Jr.; *After Long Silence: A Memoir* by Helen Fremont; *Writer's Harvest 3: A Collection of New Fiction* (edited and with an introduction by Tobias Wolf); *Black and Blue* by Anna Quindlen; *Mother of My Mother* by Hope Edelman; *Cuba Libre* by Elmore Leonard; *Last Things* (novel) by Jenny Offill.

Laurel publishes the writing and editing reference *The 21st Century Manual of Style* (edited by the Princeton Language Institute) on a primarily reprint trade-paper and mass-market list.

Query letters and SASEs should be directed to:

Jackie Cantor, Executive Editor, Delacorte Press—Fiction: women's fiction, mysteries, historical romance, and quality/literary fiction.

Kathleen Jayes, Editor, Dell— Quality fiction, popular culture, humor, lifestyle, women's issues.

Mary Ellen O'Neill, Senior Editor, Dell—Projects consistent with house interest.

Michael Shohl, Editor—Commercial nonfiction, literary and commercial fiction.

Susan Kamil, Vice President and Executive Editor, Delacorte; Editorial Director, Dial Press—Quality nonfiction; literary fiction.

THE DERRYDALE PRESS

4720 Boston Way, Lanham, MD 20706
fax: 301-429-5748
www.derrydalepress.com

The Derrydale Press was founded in 1927 by Eugene V. Connett III and then quickly became America's preeminent publisher of books on outdoor sports. An avid sportsman himself, Connett sought out manuscripts by the leading sportsmen and sportswomen of his generation, for whom he published books of the highest quality materials.

The Derrydale Press currently has over 150 titles in print and continues to publish in the areas of fishing, hunting, equestrian sports, sporting art, the outdoors, and other aspects of nature. The Derrydale Press is an imprint of the Rowman & Littlefield Publishing Group, whose sister company, National Book Network (NBN), is responsible for the distribution of Derrydale books.

Please direct query letters with SASEs to:

Stephen Driver, Associate Editor

DIOGENES PUBLISHING

965 Alamo Drive, Unit 336, Vacaville, CA 95687
707-447-6482   fax: 707-447-6482
www.diogenespublishing.com   e-mail: sales@diogenespublishing.com

Diogenes is a small-sized house with a strong emphasis on nonfiction titles, specializing in satire, social issues, philosophy, psychology, contemporary interests, and humor. Diogenes is committed to publishing culturally significant material that challenges mainstream beliefs, promotes independent thought, and takes an honest and critical look at society and social institutions.

Most recent publication: *Happiness and Other Lies* by Mary Massaro. Diogenes distributes to the trade through Ingram, Baker & Taylor, Hushion Unlimited, Book People, and Quality Books. Web site links to Amazon and Barnes & Noble.

Query letters should be directed to:

Chris Primi, Marketing Director

Mary Gillissie, Editor in Chief

THE DOUBLEDAY BROADWAY PUBLISHING GROUP

Nan A. Talese Books

Broadway Books

Currency

Doubleday

Doubleday Religious Publishing

Doubleday/Image

Main Street Press

1540 Broadway, New York, NY 10036
212-354-6500

Doubleday (founded in 1897) is one of America's cherished publishing names; the house's emblematic colophon (a dolphin entwined round a ship's anchor) is equally beloved among book buyers, booksellers, and critics. Doubleday & Company is known for its potent commercial list in fiction and nonfiction, with major concentration in mainstream popular nonfiction and genre fiction (Double D Westerns, Perfect Crime, Loveswept), as well as works of literary note.

Doubleday publishes hardcover and paperback editions. The Anchor imprint features original nonfiction and fiction in hardcover and trade paper, as well as paperback reprints. Doubleday/Currency produces a list of high-interest books in business, finance, management, and human relations. Doubleday Equestrian Library publishes top-of-the-line titles in the art and sport of horsemanship. Doubleday is also the home of Nan A. Talese's personalized trade imprint (see separate subentry further on).

Doubleday spins off many of its lead titles on BDD Audio.

Indicative of Doubleday fiction and popular literature: *Meg* (a Jurassic shark thriller) by Steve Alten; *Some Love, Some Pain, Sometime* (stories) by J. California Cooper; *Parsley, Sage, Rosemary, and Crime: A Pennsylvania Dutch Mystery with Recipes* by Tamar Myers; *The War Trail North: A New Novel of the Cherokee People* by Robert J. Conley;

D

Wilderness of Mirrors by Linda Davies; *Pandora's Clock* by John J. Nance; *St. Famous* by Jonathan Dee.

Doubleday is the publisher of *The Partner* by John Grisham, as well as his earlier works in the legal-thriller field (*The Firm; The Pelican Brief; The Client; The Chamber; The Rainmaker; The Runaway Jury*). Doubleday hosts a notable lineup by the 1988 winner of the Nobel Prize for literature, Naguib Mahfouz, which includes *The Cairo Trilogy:* (I) *Palace Walk;* (II) *Palace of Desire;* and (III) *Sugar Street.*

Representing Doubleday nonfiction: *Animalogies* (humor) by Michael Macrone; *Racial Healing: Confronting the Fear Between Blacks and Whites* by Harlon L. Dalton; *The "21" Cookbook: Recipes and Lore from New York's Fabled Restaurant* by Michael Lomonaco with Donna Forsman; *The Last Word on Power: Reinvention for Executives Who Want to Change Their World* by Tracy Goss (edited by Betty Sue Flowers); *The Sixth Extinction: Patterns of Life and the Future of Humankind* by Richard Leakey and Roger Lewin; *The Way of Woman: Awakening the Perennial Feminine* by Helen Luke.

On the Anchor Books list: *The Book of Ruth,* by Jane Hamilton; *Into the Wild,* by Jon Krakauer; *Virtual Equality: The Mainstreaming of Gay and Lesbian Liberation* by Urvashi Vaid; *Dark Carnival: The Secret World of Tod Browning—Hollywood's Master of the Macabre* by David J. Skal and Elias Savada; *Sister to Sister: Women Write About the Unbreakable Bond* (edited by Patricia Foster); *Nine Poets of Desire: The Hidden World of Islamic Women* by Geraldine Brooks.

Query letters and SASEs should be directed to:

Bill Thomas, Senior Editor—General nonfiction, politics, current affairs.

Eric Major, Director, Religious Publishing—Scholarly and popular works on religion and spirituality; titles likely to provoke religious controversy; books covering a wide range of religious thought, including Hinduism and Buddhism; Judaica.

Jackie Gill, Editor, Doubleday Books for Young Readers—Fiction and nonfiction for children to age 10; seeking primarily illustrated volumes.

Janet Hill, Senior Editor, Doubleday—African-American studies, commercial fiction, and nonfiction.

Judith Kern, Senior Editor—Fiction: quality commercial, historical romance. Nonfiction: cookbooks, diet books, self-help, and how-to, illustrated.

Marjorie Braman, Senior Editor—Fiction and nonfiction.

Mark Fletz, Senior Editor, Religious Publishing—Scholarly and popular works on religion and spirituality.

Pat Mulcahy, Vice President and Editor in Chief, Doubleday—Commercial and literary fiction. Does a lot of suspense, thriller, and mystery fiction. General nonfiction; special interests include music and other popular culture.

Roger Scholl, Senior Editor, Doubleday, Executive Editor, Anchor Books—Currency Books, Doubleday's business imprint; also acquires for Doubleday and Anchor in serious nonfiction, history, literary fiction, popular science, sociology, innovative business books.

Trace Murphy, Editor, Religious Publishing—Scholarly and popular works on religion and spirituality.

Shawn Coyne, Senior Editor, Doubleday—Commercial fiction and nonfiction. Some specialties: mysteries, psychological suspense, sports, crime and investigative stories, popular culture.

Sign: Leo.

Education: B.A., in Microbiology from Harvard.

Employment history/editor career path: I originally was going to go to medical school when I graduated high school and I then changed my mind to come to New York to start acting. This is how I met my wife; she's an actor as well. We decided that one of us was going to have to get a real job sooner or later and since she was the better actor, it was going to have to be me. This is when I got into publishing. I started at Dell in 1992 and worked my way up to an Editor. I then went to St. Martin's for a short time and have been with Doubleday & Co. for four and a half years.

Personal interests: Golf, reading, acting.

What would you be doing if you were not an editor? I would find another job in publishing. I love this job because it's a job where you actually have something to show for your work. If I couldn't be in publishing at all, I would be in some kind of creative field in Hollywood.

What has been your most successful book that you have acquired to date? *Gates of Fire* by Gloria Paton; *Cinderella Story* by Bill Murray; *The Putting Bible* by Dave Pelz; *Loose Balls* by Jason Williams.

Do you represent fiction? If so, what do you look for? Yes, crime fiction, thrillers, military thrillers, historical fiction, commercial fiction.

What do you want to see less of? Writers overflooding the market with whatever works (i.e., historical novels).

Do you represent nonfiction? Yes.

Do you require book proposals? If so, what do you look for in evaluating a book proposal? Yes, I require a book proposal for nonfiction work. I look for passion, really tight and strong writing, and some sample material.

What process do you use for making a decision? What is the process for acquisition, is there a committee? I am the only editor at Doubleday for fiction, so there is no committee to really talk it over with, but for nonfiction, yes, we do have an acquisitions board. With any submission we will talk it over with the Editor in Chief.

What kinds of nonfiction books do you want to see less of? I would like to see books being published based on passion rather than being based on a business decision.

Are you interested in work geared for the masses (readers of *People, The Star,* etc.)? When you start to publish for a large audience, you get in trouble, you then have to ask questions like, "Who will like this book?" and "Why will they buy this book"?

Are agents important? Why? Yes, they are really important. It is extremely important for a writer to have an advocate in his or her corner and an agent can be this firsthand. All of the agents whom I know personally are as dedicated to publishing as myself and other hard-working editors.

Do you like new writers? What should new writers do to break into the business? Yes, we are always looking for new writers. I would say you can break into the business by writing the material over and over and over again. You have to make a conscience decision that you are going to be a writer; not just say that you are one.

How should writers approach you? Through an agent.

What are some common mistakes writers make? What really gets on your nerves? Every writer should find a way to remove every cliché from his or her work. Proofread all of your work.

What can writers do to get your attention and to avoid the slush pile? Get representation from an agent.

What have been some of your craziest experiences with submissions? When I was working as an assistant, I would go through the slush pile and read the material. Somehow I had read a manuscript from a woman who had managed to find out my name. She would continually send me Tootsie Rolls every day. I enjoyed the candy.

What, if anything, makes you different from other editors? I will fight until the end of the day to make sure that everything is being done correctly. I edit as hard as I can.

Any advice for writers? Broaden your circle of friends by going to writing groups, classes, and so on. Get out of your house or your studio to work on your book.

D

Nan A. Talese Books

The personalized imprint of Nan A. Talese promotes topical issues of widespread interest addressed through commercial nonfiction and selected fiction. The Talese roster is particularly strong in works that tie in with contemporary cultural themes.

Representative of the Talese list: *Alias Grace* (novel) by Margaret Atwood; *What Falls Away* (memoir) by Mia Farrow; *The Voyage* (novel) by Robert MacNeil; *Beach Music* (novel) by Pat Conroy; *Choices* (novel) by Mary Lee Settle; *Milton in America* (speculative fiction) by Peter Ackroyd; *How the Irish Saved Civilization: The Untold Story of Ireland's Historic Role from the Fall of Rome to the Rise of Medieval Europe* by Thomas Cahill; *"Feminism Is Not the Story of My Life": How Today's Feminist Elite Has Lost Touch with the Real Concerns of Women* by Elizabeth Fox-Genovese; *Skin Deep: Black Women and White Women Write About Race* (edited by Marita Golden and Susan Richards Shreve).

Talese does not wish to receive unagented/unsolicited submissions. Query letters and SASEs should be directed to:

Jesse Cohen, Editor—Fiction: literary (particularly women authors on a variety of female issues); occasional commercial works. Nonfiction: biographies of fine and performing artists, essays, subjects of popular or contemporary cultural interest.

Nan A. Talese, Publisher

Dove Books/NewStar Media, Inc.

8955 Beverly Boulevard, West Hollywood, CA 90048
310-786-1600

Dove Books is a major player in publication of innovative and quality nonfiction, concentrating on areas of self-help, business, entertainment, California interest, and exposes.

Dove titles: *When Money Is King: How Revlon's Ron Perelman Mastered the World of Finance to Create One of America's Greatest Business Empires, and Found Glamour,*

Beauty, and the High Life in the Bargain by Richard Hack; *Getting to Howard: The Two Year Odyssey of an Obsessed Howard Stern Fan* by Dan Wagner; *Mercury Rising* by Rich Lynch; *The Naked Truth: A Woman Inside the Corporate Ranks of Playboy* by Stephanie Wells-Walper, with Judith Estrine; *Close but No Cigar: A Look Back at 30 Wonderful Years with George Burns—An Unusual Love Story* by Melissa Miller.

Backlist favorites: *You'll Never Make Love in This Town Again* by Robin, Liza, Linda, and Tiffany (as told to Joanne Parrent); *Nicole Brown Simpson: The Private Diary of a Life Interrupted* by Faye D. Resnick; *Fatal Subtraction: The Inside Story of Buchwald vs. Paramount* by Pierce O'Donnell and Dennis McDougal (introduction by Art Buchwald).

Dove's founder and president, Michael Riner, has recently left the company and the book division has been reorganized.

Dove Books handles its own distribution.

Dove does not accept unsolicited manuscripts directly from authors.

ECCO (AN IMPRINT OF HARPER COLLINS PUBLISHERS)

10 East 53rd Street, New York, NY 10022
212-207-7000

Ecco Press was acquired by HarperCollins in 2000. The Ecco list presents literary fiction, general nonfiction, poetry, and essays, as well as selected imaginative and practical works on travel, food, culture, and sports. Ecco (founded in 1970) is a small, distinguished publisher of trade books (many in special fine editions).

Stalwarts on Ecco's roster of poets include Louise Glück, Robert Hass, Zbigniew Herbert, Carolyn Kizer, Czeslaw Milosz, Robert Pinsky, and Charles Simic. The house also offers classic reprints in the Essential Poets series. In addition, Ecco publishes the literary journal *Antæus.*

Ecco's original mandate remains in effect—to publish significant books of enduring quality.

Popular features from Ecco: *The Gardener's Son,* a never-before-published screenplay from Cormac McCarthy; *Sun Under Wood,* the long-awaited new book of poems from U.S. Poet Laureate Robert Hass; two first novels: *Hallucinating Foucault* by Patricia Duncker, and *Blue Italian* by Rita Ciresi; the newest volume in the Essential Poets Series, *The Essential Dickinson* (edited by Joyce Carol Oates); *Kiki's Memoirs* (a bold and sassy autobiography of the model who became the reigning queen of 1920s Montparnasse, banned by U.S. Customs in 1929 and only now published in America for the first time) (edited and annotated by Billy Klüver and Julie Martin; with an introduction by Ernest Hemingway).

Representative titles: *Memoir of the Hawk* by James Tate; *Cuisines of India: The Art of Regional Indian Cooking* by Smita and Sanjeev Chandra; *The Red of His Shadow* by Mayra Montero; *Blonde* by Joyce Carol Oates (National Book Award Finalist); *Kitchen Confidential* by Anthony Bourdain; *Trattorias of Rome, Florence, and Venice* by Maureen B. Fant; *Swarm* by Jorie Graham; *The Last Night I Spent with You* by Mayra Montero;

E

Skating to Antarctica: A Journey to the End of the World by Jenny Diski; *Road Atlas: Prose and Other Poems* by Campbell McGrath.

Query letters and SASEs should be directed to:

Daniel Halpern, Vice President and Editorial Director

ENTREPRENEUR PRESS

2445 McCabe Way, 4th Floor, Irvine, CA 92614
949-261-2325   fax: 949-261-7729
www.smallbizbooks.com   e-mail: jcalmes@entrepreneur.com

Entrepreneur Press, a division of Entrepreneur Media, Inc., publishes trade books offering practical advice and inspirational success stories for business owners and aspiring entrepreneurs. Our areas of expertise include instructional business books, motivational, management, marketing, new economy, e-commerce, and personal finance titles that appeal to a broad spectrum of the business book–buying audience. Steady sellers include: *Start Your Own Business,* and *Entrepreneur* magazine's Start-Up Series.

They are distributed to the trade by NBN. Query letters and SASEs should be directed to:

Jere Calmes, Editorial Director

M. EVANS & COMPANY, INC.

216 East 49th Street, New York, NY 10017
212-688-2810   fax: 212-486-4544
e-mail: editorial@mevans.com

The M. Evans frontlist features high-profile offerings in topical issues; investigative stories in politics, business, and entertainment; and popular biography. The core Evans program accents popular nonfiction books in the areas of health and fitness, human relationships, business and finance, and lifestyle and cuisine. Evans also issues a small list in popular fiction. The house tends a strong and varied backlist.

M. Evans and Company (founded in 1963) thrives as a selective trade publisher (in hardcover and trade paperback) with a clear, constantly honed commercial focus in its favored market niches.

Evans fiction is exemplified by: *The Kill Box* by Chris Stewart; *Shattered Bone* by Chris Stewart; *Down the Common* by Ann Baer; *First Victim* by Douglas MacKinnon; *A Fine Italian Hand* (a Shifty Lou Anderson mystery) by William Murray.

M. Evans books are distributed to the trade via National Book Network. Query letters and SASEs should be directed to:

George C. de Kay, President and Publisher—Popular psychology, health, cookbooks, commercial fiction.

PJ Dempsey, Senior Editor

FACTS ON FILE

11 Penn Plaza, 15th Floor, New York, NY 10001-2006
212-967-8800   fax: 212-967-9196
www.factsonfile.com   e-mail: Custserv@factsonfile.com

Facts On File specializes in reference and information titles in a broad popular range, including science, nature, technology, world history, American history, business, popular culture, fashion, design, sports, health, current affairs and politics, and the environment—in addition to general reference works. Facts On File offers a broad selection of historical and cultural atlases, dictionaries, and encyclopedias geared toward professional as well as popular interests and is one of the pioneers of the electronic multimedia-publishing frontier.

Facts On File (founded in 1940) is a dynamic popular-reference publisher. The house has a full skein of award-winning titles to its credit, and many Facts On File publications feature an innovative production approach. The publisher is extremely well tuned to specific category markets, which it targets with marked commercial consistency.

Facts On File has made a renewed commitment to its goal of becoming the premier print and electronic reference publisher in the industry. It is striving to be a beacon and a guide for librarians, teachers, students, parents, and researchers to look to for award-winning materials, cutting-edge trends, and innovative products. This is the publisher you seek when the requirements are nebulous and the transitions are turbulent.

The year 1998 brought the launch of the trade imprint Checkmark Books. It was created to provide booksellers and consumers with quality resources focused on topics such as: business, careers, fitness, health and nutrition, history, nature, parenting, pop culture, and self-help.

Facts On File titles include: *The History of Archaeology; Vice Presidents; Working in America; Encyclopedia of African History and Culture; Capital Punishment; Chronology of American Indian History; Encyclopedia of Cold War Politics; The Facts on File Handbook of Earth Science; Plate Tectonics; Animal Habitats; Elephants; Alien Encounters; The Facts on File Dictionary of Astronomy; The Encyclopedia of Child Abuse; New Complete Book of Herbs, Spices & Condiments; The Encyclopedia of Schizophrenia and Other Psychotic Disorders; British English from A to Zed; Edgar Allan Poe A to Z; The Literary 100; Words to Rhyme With; Career Opportunities for Writers; The Executors' Handbook; Best Baby Names in World; Black Belt Tae Kwon Do; Forbidden Films; Athletic Scholarships;* and *Career Ideas for Kids Who Like Money.*

On File is an award-winning collection of reference materials. Spanning virtually every subject in the middle- and high-school curricula, each On File contains hundreds of images that visually depict complex subjects in a way that will both engage and inform young people. Even students at the elementary and college levels will find the material useful. Filled with hundreds of exciting hands-on activities, projects, exercises, and experiments, On File volumes encourage critical thinking and allow students to actively participate in their educational process.

Facts On File utilizes individualized marketing and distribution programs that are particularly strong in the areas of corporate, institutional, and library sales. Query letters and SASEs should be directed to:

Anne Savarese, Editor—Reference books: language and literature.

Laurie Likoff, Editorial Director—Family, parenting, trade books, science, music, history.

Nicole Bowen, Executive Editor—Reference books: American history and culture, multicultural; and nonfiction young-adult reference books about military history, sports, American culture and history, music.

Jim Chambers, Editor—Trade books, entertainment subjects, TV, and reference books on entertainment subjects, TV, movies, Broadway, sports.

Frank Darmstadt, Senior Editor—Reference books, science, technology, nature.

Claudia Schrab, Editor—Reference books, world history, geography, religion.

FAIRVIEW PRESS

2450 Riverside Avenue South, Minneapolis, MN 55454
612-672-4228   fax: 612-672-4980
www.Press.Fairview.org e-mail: press@webex.fairview.org

Fairview Press publishes books on issues that affect adults, families, children, and the communities in which they live. These issues include relationships, parenting, domestic violence, divorce, family activities, aging, health, self-esteem, social issues, and addictions.

Fairview's commitment to its customers is that the materials Fairview publishes will offer the advice and support that individuals and families need to face stressful situations, difficult choices, and the trials and changes of everyday life. In addition, Fairview Press books are tools to help families enjoy and appreciate each other and strengthen family bonds. Fairview usually offers several special series especially for kids.

Fairview Press (formerly Deaconess Press; founded in 1988) is a service of Fairview Health System and a division of Fairview Riverside Medical Center.

On the Fairview list: *Cry Until You Laugh: Comforting Guidance for Coping with Grief* by Richard J. Obershaw, M.S.W., L.I.C.S.W.; *A Women's Guide to Personal Safety* by Janee Harteau and Holly Keegel; *Sports Medicine for Young Athletes: A Guide for Parents, Teachers, and Coaches* by the Institute for Athletic Medicine (edited by Scott Kulstad, Med., A.T.C./R.); *Any Girl Can Rule the World* by Susan Brooks; *Daily Imperfections: 364 Surprising and Delightful Ways to Celebrate the Imperfect You* by Enid Howarth and Jan Tras; *Naomi Wants to Know: Letters from a Little Girl to the Big Big World* by Naomi Shavin; *Sex Smart: A Sexuality Resource for Teenagers* by Susan Browning Pogany; *Coaching Coaches: A Guide for Coaches from Youth Leagues to College* by John Anderson and Rick Aberman, Ph.D.; *When Men Grieve: Why Men Grieve Differently and How You Can Help* by Elizabeth LeVang, Ph.D.; *How We Made the World a Better Place: Kids and Teens Write on How They Changed Their Corner of the World,* compiled by Editors of Fairview Press.

Slim Goodbody, award-winning star of children's public TV, celebrates "Wonderful You" in a unique series—*The Body, The Mind, The Spirit,* and *The Cycle of Life* by Slim

Goodbody (illustrated by Terry Boles). Slim Goodbody, developed over 20 years ago, is the creation of performer John Burnstein.

Woodland Press Children Can Cope Series (illustrated by children) is a line of workbooks developed to help children work through feelings about traumatic events and changes. Titles include: *When Someone Very Special Dies; When Mom and Dad Separate; When Someone Has a Very Serious Illness.*

Fairview Press, a specialist publisher and distributor, operates through a variety of sales venues; the press is distributed to the trade through the National Book Network. Query letters and SASEs should be directed to:

Lane Stiles, Publisher

Stephanie Billecke, Editor

FANTAGRAPHICS BOOKS

7563 Lake City Way NE, Seattle, WA 98115
206-524-1967

Fantagraphics produces comics and comic art. The house accents a list of mainstream, classic, and borderline offerings in this specialty arena and also purveys a strong line of erotic comics and books. Fantagraphics Books (inaugurated in 1976) produces trade paperbacks, hardbound editions, and quality fine-art album editions of graphic productions, in addition to comic books, comics-related magazines, and a line of gift items dedicated to this most accessible literary form.

The Fantagraphics catalog lists, in addition to its own lines, products from additional publishers of comics and books, as well as audio, video, and multimedia works.

The Fantagraphics roster features some of the finest cartoonists of America and around the world—underground masters, political satirists, artists in the realms of science fiction and fantasy, and reprints of classic newspaper comic-strip series—as well as works from the emerging young Turks in the field.

Comics creators cataloged by Fantagraphics include Peter Bagge, Vaughn Bode, Daniel Clowes, Guido Crepax, Robert Crumb, Dame Darcy, Kim Deitch, Julie Doucet, Jules Feiffer, Frank Frazetta, Drew Friedman, Rick Geary, Los Bros. Hernandez, Peter Kuper, Terry LeBan, Douglas Michael, Joe Sacco, Gilbert Shelton, Art Spiegelman, Ralph Steadman, Basil Wolverton, and Wallace Wood.

Fantagraphics projects: *Whoa, Nellie! Graphic Novel* by Jaime Hernandez; *Tales of Terror—The Complete EC Compendium* by Grant Geissman and Fred von Bernewitz; *Complete Crumb Comics Volume 14; The Early 80's and WEIRDO Magazine* by Robert Crumb; *Maakies* by Tony Millionaire; *Mirror, Window: An Artbabe Collection* by Jessica Abel; *Drawing Sexy Women* by Frank Thorne; *Jimmy Corrigan* by Chris Ware; *Cumple* by Dave Cooper; *The Strange Cases of Edward Gorey* by Alexander Theroux; *Dirty Stories Volume 2* (edited by Eric Reynolds); and *Black Hole #8* by Charles Burns.

Fantagraphics also offers Burne Hogarth's set of art-instruction books.

Fantagraphics distributes its own list and catalogs selections from a number of other comics- and graphics-oriented publishers, in addition to audio CDs, computer CD-ROMs,

F

videotapes, and books, posters, and calendars. Query letters should be accompanied by short, carefully selected samples.

Michael Dowers, Submissions Editor

FARRAR STRAUS & GIROUX

Farrar Straus & Giroux Books for Young Readers

Hill and Wang

Noonday Press

North Point Press

19 Union Square West, New York, NY 10003
212-741-6900

Farrar Straus & Giroux is a trade house that produces a wide range of general-interest and specialist nonfiction as well as top-of-the-line fiction and literature. FS&G is known for its commercial list of finely designed hardcover and trade paperback editions.

Among FS&G divisions and imprints are Hill and Wang and North Point Press (see separate subentries further on); the primarily trade-paperback imprints are Noonday Press for adult titles and Sunburst Books for young readers. FS&G tends a solid backlist and issues a line of classic works in reprint.

Long a mainstay among independently owned American publishing houses, Farrar Straus & Giroux (founded in 1946) was bought by Verlagsgruppe Georg von Holtzbrinck. In this multinational corporate phase, FS&G retains an affluent spirit that seeks to represent writing at its commercial-literary best, presented under the esteemed and widely recognized FS&G logo of three abstract fish.

In an era when there is great market leverage obtained from a publisher's offer of full-spectrum publishing packages for high-interest projects, FS&G's absence in the mass-market and trade paperback arena proved a hitch in acquiring certain prime properties. Farrar Straus therefore employs combination hardcover/paperback acquisition deals, with paperback-reprint rights slotted to the mass-market paperback programs of other United States–based Holtzbrinck properties, such as Henry Holt and Company and St. Martin's Press, and Picador USA

FS&G nonfiction offerings cover topical issues and current events; popular and fine arts; contemporary culture; popular history, biography, and memoir; popular science; family, relationships, and awareness; lifestyle, travel, and cuisine.

Representative nonfiction: *Frozen Desire: The Psychology of Money* by James Buchan; *The Spirit Catches You and You Fall Down: A Hmong Child, Her Doctors, and an American Tragedy* by Anne Fadiman; *Bloodlines: From Ethnic Pride to Ethnic Terrorism* by Vamik Volkan; *Painting by Numbers: Komar and Melamid's Scientific Guide to Art* by Vitaly Komar and Alexander Melamid (edited by JoAnn Wypijewski); *Trickster Makes This World: Mischief, Myth, and Art* by Lewis Hyde; *The Idea of India* by Sunil Khilnani.

FS&G's interest in literature and the arts encompasses novels, short stories, drama (and other theatrical works), history, essays and criticism, biography, memoirs, and poetry. In this area, the house's offerings often feature an adventuresome approach to both form and content. FS&G has published such diverse writers as Joseph Brodsky, Carlos Fuentes, John McPhee, Philip Roth, Aleksandr Solzhenitsyn, Calvin Trillin, Scott Turow, Mario Vargas Llosa, Tom Wolfe, and Susan Sontag. In addition to the FS&G roster of established and marketable literary talent, the house is alert to hitherto lesser-appreciated literary voices primed for the commercial spotlight.

Farrar Straus & Giroux fiction, literature, and criticism: *Four Letters of Love* by Niall Williams; *Required Reading: Why Our American Classics Matter Now* by Andrew Delbanco; *All Around Atlantis* by Deborah Eisenberg; *Jane Austen: A Life* by David Nokes; *The Zigzag Kid* by David Grossman (translated from the Hebrew by Betsy Rosenberg); *The Crystal Frontier: A Novel in Nine Stories* by Carlos Fuentes (translated from the Spanish by Alfred Mac Adam); *Heroes Like Us* by Thomas Brussig (translated from the German by John Brownjohn); *My Brother* by Jamaica Kincaid; *Hogarth: A Life and a World* by Jenny Uglow; *Charming Billy* by Alice McDermott; *Shadows on the Hudson: A Novel* by Isaac Bashevis Singer (translated from the Yiddish by Joseph Sherman); *Granite and Rainbow: The Life of Virginia Woolf* by Mitchell Leaska; *Just as I Thought* by Grace Paley; *The House Gun* by Nadine Gordimer; *Tales of the Night* by Peter Høeg (translated from the Danish by Barbara Haveland); *Notes from Hampstead: The Writer's Notes 1954–1971* by Elias Canetti (translated from the German by John Hargraves); *The Picasso Papers* by Rosiland E. Krauss; *Eccentric Neighbors: A Novel* by Rosario Ferré; *The Life of Insects: A Novel* by Victor Pelevin (translated from the Russian by Andrew Bromfield).

Poetry from FS&G: *History of My Heart* by Robert Pinsky; *The Inferno of Dante* (Deluxe Bilingual Edition) by Robert Pinsky (illustrated by Michael Mazur); *The Odes of Horace* by David Ferry; *Desire* by Frank Bidart; *Tales from Ovid: 24 Passages from the Metamorphoses* (A New Verse Translation) by Ted Hughes; *Keats* by Andrew Motion; *Collected Poems 1916–1956* (Bilingual Edition) by Eugenio Montale (translated from the Italian and annotated by Jonathon Galassi); *Mysticism for Beginners* by Adam Zagajewski (translated from the Polish by Clare Cavanagh).

FS&G's sales catalog and promotional endeavors include services for a number of smaller houses with literary orientations, such as Soho, Aperture, Fromm International, and Harvill Press.

Query letters and SASEs should be directed to:

Elisabeth Dyssegaard, Senior Editor—Fiction: literary, German and Scandinavian translations. Nonfiction: child care, education, popular reference.

Elisabeth Sifton, Vice President and Senior Editor—History, politics, current events and issues, biography, and literary fiction. Oversees the Hill and Wang program (see subentry).

John Glusman, Executive Vice President—Literary fiction, history, biography, science, politics, current events.

Jonathan Galassi, Editor in Chief, Publisher— Fiction, nonfiction, art history, belles lettres, business, poetry.

Paul Elie, Editor—Literary nonfiction, music, religion, translation.

Rebecca Saletan, Senior Editor—Fiction, nonfiction, personal memoir.

Elisabeth Sifton, Senior Editor—Fiction, nonfiction, biography, history, politics, translation.

Farrar Straus & Giroux Books for Young Readers

Farrar Straus & Giroux Books for Young Readers publishes for a wide-ranging audience, from picture-book age to young adult. Imprints include Sunburst and Aerial books, which are paperback reprints (FS&G does not publish paperback originals or series books). Among FS&G's authors are William Steig, Madeline L'Engle, Suzanne Fisher Staples, and Jack Gantos.

Recent titles: *Snow* by Uri Shulevitz; *The Gardener* by Sarah Stewart (illustrated by David Small); *Madlenka* by Peter Sis; *Me and My Cat?* by Satoshi Kitamura; *Not My Dog* by Colby Rodowsky; *Holes* by Louis Sachar; *The Trolls* by Polly Horvath; *Speak* by Laurie Halse Anderson; *Joey Piqza Swallowed the Key* by Jack Gantos; *Leon's Story* by Leon Walter Tillage.

Query letters and SASEs should be directed to:

Frances Foster, Publisher, Frances Foster Books

Margaret Ferguson, Vice President, Associate Publisher, and Editorial Director

Wes Adams, Senior Editor

Melanie Kroupa, Publisher—Melanie Kroupa Books

Hill and Wang

Hill and Wang highlights trade nonfiction, as well as selected titles in drama as literature. Otherwise (and traditionally) viewed as a leader in the academic and trade books in the humanities and social sciences, the Hill and Wang program is also active commercially, with titles keyed to popular interests and cultural themes as well as current issues.

From Hill and Wang: *Understanding China: A Guide to China's Economy, History, and Political Structure* by John Bryan Starr; *First Generations: Women in Colonial America* by Carol Berkin; *A Very Different Age: Americans of the Progressive Era* by Steven J. Diner; *American Frontiers: Cultural Encounters and Continental Conquest* by Gregory H. Nobles; *Tangled Web: The Making of Nixon's Foreign Policy, 1968–1974* by William P. Bundy.

Query letters and SASEs should be directed to:

Elisabeth Sifton, Publisher, Hill and Wang—American History, politics, public-policy issues.

Lauren Osborne, Editor

North Point Press

North Point Press features a list that accents trade and literary nonfiction. Strong North Point categories include: nature writing and natural history; literary, food, travel, and sports writing; Asian literature; books about spirituality and religion (but no New Age); biographies, memoirs, and essays.

Founded in Berkeley, California, in 1980, North Point Press is now a division of Farrar Straus & Giroux.

On the North Point list are titles such as: *Where the Roots Reach for Water: A Personal and Natural History of Melancholia* by Jeffrey Smith; *Living on the Wind: Across the*

Hemisphere with Migratory Birds by Scott Wiedensaul; *My Kitchen Wars* by Betty Fussell; *Tigers in the Snow* by Peter Matthiessen; *Cleaving: The Story of a Marriage* by Dennis and Vicki Covington; *Gothic: Four Hundred Years of Excess, Horror, Evil and Ruin* by Richard Davenport-Hines; *Out of Sheer Rage: Wrestling with D. H. Lawrence* by Geoff Dyer; *Butter Beans to Blackberries: Recipes from the Southern Garden* by Ronni Lundi; *The Potato: How the Humble Spud Rescued the Western World* by Larry Zuckerman.

More North Point titles and projects are: *Son of the Morning Star: Custer and Little Big Horn* by Evan S. Connell; *Come Hell or High Water* by Gregory Jaynes; *The New Testament* (translated by Richmond Lattimore); *Indian Tales* by Jaime de Angulo (illustrated by the author, with a new foreword by Howard Norman); *Inside Bluegel: The Play of Images in Children's Games* by Edward Snow; *Paradise by Design: Native Plants and the New American Landscape* by Kathryn Phillips; *The Couch and the Tree: Dialogues Between Psychoanalysts and Buddhism* (edited by Anthony Molino); *Through Another Lens: My Years with Edward Weston* by Charis Wilson and Wendy Madar.

Query letters and SASEs should be directed to:

Rebecca Saletan, Editorial Director

Ethan Nosowsky, Editor
  Born: 1967.
  Education: B.A., Columbia; M.A., University of California at Berkeley.
  Employment history/editor career path: After a brief stint at Oxford University Press, I attended graduate school. I returned to publishing as an Assistant at FSG, where I've worked for seven years. About half of the books I work on are published under FSG's North Point Press imprint.
  What has been your most successful book that you have acquired to date? Success for a book can be defined in different ways, but I'm very proud of two works of nonfiction that we published under FSG's North Point imprint: Geoff Dyer's *Out of Sheer Rage: Wrestling with D. H. Lawrence,* which was a finalist for a National Book Critics Circle Award; and Scott Weidensaul's *Living on the Wind: Across the Hemisphere with Migratory Birds,* which was a finalist for the Pulitzer Prize. Jenny Offill's debut novel, *Last Things,* which FSG published in 1998, appeared on the regional bestseller lists and was a finalist for a *Los Angeles Times* Book Prize.
  What books have you acquired that make you the most proud? What books that you have acquired reflect the types of books you like to represent? See previous entry for most successful book. Also, a biography: *A Dream of Life* by Leslie Staint.
  Do you represent fiction? If so what do you look for? Yes, about half of my list is fiction. I look for voice, primarily, and authors willing to take risks. I like books that teach you how to read them.
  What do you want to see less of? Bad novels.
  Do you represent nonfiction? Yes.
  Do you require book proposals? If so, what do you look for in evaluating a book proposal? If something is unagented, a query letter is the best way to start. I look for untraditional takes on traditional subjects or books about things that have previously been overlooked.
  Are certain aspects of a book proposal given more weight than others? Well, for FSG and North Point the writing is of primary importance, so sample chapters are crucial.

F

What process do you use for making a decision? What is the process for acquisition, is there a committee? There is no editorial board, but the Editor in Chief and the President of the company must approve everything I acquire.

What kinds of nonfiction books do you want to see less of? Copy-cat books. Too many people are writing to the market rather than pursuing a subject that is of deep and obsessive interest to them.

Are you interested in work geared for the masses (readers of *People, The Star,* etc.)? Well, I hope my books will be widely popular, but I think the answer to the question as phrased is no.

Do you think that agents are important? Why? Agents are an excellent filter and help draw editors' attention to where it's merited. More than that, though, in taking care of the negotiating process, which can be tense, they help the author/editor relationship stay focused on the book itself. I do work with unagented authors, but most of them had been previously published.

Do you like new writers? What should new writers do to break into the business? Sure—there's little that's as exciting for a publisher as discovering a new voice. New writers can help themselves by first publishing in literary journals and magazines.

How should writers approach you? By query letter. Follow-ups don't particularly help; if we haven't responded to you in a couple of months, it's fair to call, but eventually we respond to everyone.

What are some common mistakes writers make? What really gets on your nerves? Insufficient research. I get an enormous number of submissions that are inappropriate for our firm—it's a waste of my time and theirs.

What can writers do to get your attention and to avoid the slush pile? Make sure to address your submission to a particular editor. Avoid the harsh sell.

What have been some of your best experiences with writers or in your job? Working with the authors. Getting my hands dirty with the author working on the manuscript.

What, if anything, makes you different from other editors? I think every editor hopes his taste is singular.

Any advice for writers? Writers have to be really good self-critics—before getting wrapped up trying to sell a book, make sure you've really finished writing it, make sure you've done all that the book wants you to do.

FOUR WALLS EIGHT WINDOWS

39 West 14th Street, Suite 503, New York, NY 10011
212-206-8965   fax: 212-206-8799
www.fourwallseightwindows.com   e-mail: edit@fourwallseightwindows.com

Four Walls Eight Windows offers a select seasonal list in creative nonfiction and literary fiction oriented toward topical issues and current culture. The house is known for journalistic forays into progressive politics; experimental fiction that features a stylistic and intellectual edge (including illustrated narrative); American and world culture expressed and portrayed through the essay; penetrating literary and critical studies; and individualistic poetry.

This is a publisher with a list far from the norm: Four Walls Eight Windows catalogs cultural artifacts in book form. The house hosts a healthy backlist laden with critically acclaimed, accomplished sellers, as well as an array of literary reprints.

Four Walls Eight Windows (established in 1987) was founded by John Oakes and Daniel Simon. Repeat: Contrary to speculation, when Dan Simon split to found the independent press Seven Stories (in early 1995; see separate entry for Seven Stories in this directory), John Oakes did not even contemplate a name change to Two Walls Four Windows.

Representative titles from Four Walls include: *How Wall Street Created a Nation* by Ovidio Diaz Espino; *Desert Survivor: An Adventurer's Guide to Exploring the Great American Desert* by John Annerino; *The Thank You Book* by Carole Stuart (illustrated by Arthur Robins); *The Choices We Made: Twenty-Five Women and Men Speak Out About Abortion* by Angela Bonavoglai; *Jane Sexes It Up: True Confessions of Feminist Desire* by Merri Lisa Johnson; *The Jaguar Hunter* by Lucas Shepard; *The Cornelius Quartet* by Michael Moorcock; *Headbanger* by Hugo Hamilton; *The Angel Quickest for Flight* by Steven Kotler; *Here Comes the Bride* by Jaclyn Geller; *The Autobiography of Abbie Hoffman* by Abbie Hoffman; *Before the Big Bang: The Origins of the Universe and the Nature of Matter* by Ernest J. Sternglass; *The Keys to Conflict Resolution: Proven Methods of Resolving Disputes Voluntarily* by Theodore W. Kheel, Esq.; *Running Scared: The Life and Treacherous Times of Las Vegas Casino King Steve Wynn* by John L. Smith; *Lebanese Cuisine: More than 200 Simple, Delicious, Authentic Recipes* by Madelain Farah; *City Come a-Walkin* by John Shirley; *White Light* by Rudy Rucker; *Sleeping with Jane Austen* by David Aitken; and *Scorpion Rising* by Anthony Frewin.

Four Walls Eight Windows books are distributed to the trade by Publishers Group West; foreign rights are administered by Writers House. Query letters and SASEs should be directed to:

Jofie Ferrari-Adler, Associate Editor

FOXROCK, INC.

61 Fourth Avenue, #4, New York, NY 10003
e-mail: evergreen@nyc.rr.com

Foxrock, Inc., features fine writing in both hardcover and paperback. Foxrock hosts literary anthologies, poetic works, shorter and longer fiction, as well as general trade titles.

On the Foxrock list: *Stirrings Still* by Samuel Beckett; *The Man Sitting in the Corridor* (fiction) by Marguerite Duras; *The Correct Sadist* (novel) by Terence Sellers; *Lament: A Novel About How the West Was Blown* by David (Sunset) Carson; *The Ghost Ship* (poetry) by Henry Hart; *Triangulation from a Known Point* (poetry) by Ruth Danon; *New and Selected Poems 1930–1990* by Richard Eberhart; *The Colors of Infinity* (poetry) by Donald E. Axinn; and *Two Dogs and Freedom: The Open School in Soweto* (schoolchildren from South Africa's Open School speak out).

The Foxrock Line has republished a number of classic literary compilations: *The Olympia Reader* and *The New Olympia Reader* (edited by Maurice Girodias) are filled

F

with ribald and erotic writings first published in Paris by the germinal publisher of Olympia Press, Maurice Girodias; these volumes feature the work of such authors as Jean Genet, Henry Miller, Chester Himes, Lawrence Durrell, William S. Burroughs, Gregory Corso, George Bataille, John Cleland, Pauline Réage, Samuel Beckett, and the Marquis de Sade. Blue Moon Publisher Barney Rosset, along with associates, has edited *Evergreen Review Reader 1957–1966,* featuring selections from *Evergreen,* America's fabled journal of literary provocateurism.

Query letters and SASEs should be directed to:

Barney Rosset, President

Astrid Myers, Publisher's Assistant

F

THE FREE PRESS (A UNIT OF PEARSON U.K.)

1230 Avenue of the Americas, New York, NY 10020
212-698-7000

The Free Press produces trade nonfiction titles with emphasis on business, biography, psychology, history, and current affairs; the division also presents general-interest works that address popular contemporary themes. In addition, the Free Press publishes professional and academic books in the fields of psychology and business.

Popular titles from the Free Press list: *Abuse of Power: The New Nixon Tapes* by Stanley I. Kutler; *At the Water's Edge* by Carl Zimmer; *Being Single in a Couple's World* by Xavier Amador and Judith Kiersky; *The Blood and the Shroud* by Ian Wilson; *Competitive Strategy* by Michael E. Porter; *Drawing Life: Surviving the Unabomber* by David Gelernter; *Ernie Pyle's War* by James Tobin; *The Intelligence of Dogs* by Stanley Coren; *Ronald Reagan* by Dinesh D'Souza; *Spin Cycle: Inside the Clinton Propaganda Machine* by Howard Kurtz; *The World According to Peter Drucker* by Jack Beatty.

Query letters and SASEs should be directed to:

Martha Levin

Fred Hills, Editor, general business motivation, spirituality, current issues, history.

Dominick Anfuso, Editor, general nonfiction.

Rachel Klayman, Editor, current events.

Bruce Nichols, Vice President/Senior Editor—serious nonfiction.

The Free Press (an imprint of Simon & Schuster)
1230 Avenue of the Americas, New York, NY 10020
212-698-7000

Born: March 23, 1964.
Education: B.A., Yale, 1986.
Employment history/editor career path: Sales Representative, Little Brown, Brown College Publishing, 1986–1988; Editor, Little Brown College Publishing, 1988–1989; Editor/Senior Editor, Macmillan College Publishing 1989–1992; Senior Editor, The Free Press, 1992–present.

Personal interests: Music, backpacking.

What would you be doing if you were not an editor? I dunno. Maybe writing a best-seller, playing a trombone, or hiking around Scotland.

What has been your most successful book that you have acquired to date? *Darwin's Black Box* by Michael Behe.

What books have you acquired that make you the most proud? What books that you have acquired reflect the types of books you like to represent? *Darwin's Black Box*, Behe; *Ernie Pyle's War*, Tobin; *The Great Poems of the Bible*, Kugel.

Do you represent fiction? If so, what do you look for? I do not represent fiction.

What do you want to see less of? I want to see less books on public policy.

Do you represent nonfiction? Yes, exclusively.

Do you require book proposals? If so, what do you look for in evaluating a book proposal? I look for the author's credentials, strength of argument, and ability to draw in readers.

Are certain aspects of a book proposal given more weight than others? The aspects of a book proposal that matter most include author's credentials, demonstration of writing style, and power of the thesis. Aspects that matter least include assessment of the market (it shouldn't need defense).

What process do you use for making a decision? What is the process for acquisition, is there a committee? We have an Editorial Board that meets weekly to consider proposals.

Are you interested in work geared for the masses (readers of *People, The Star,* etc.)? We do not publish mass market nonfiction.

Are agents important? Why? Agents are very important in most cases. They help educate authors, and they help in the publishing process.

Do you like new writers? What should new writers do to break into the business? In serious nonfiction, it is rare for new writers to have major success. Many of our authors are experts (academics, e.g.) who have already published books for specialized markets and are finally ready to write for a broad audience.

How should writers approach you? Through agents.

What are some common mistakes writers make? What really gets on your nerves? Writing in a vacuum, without seeking feedback at an early stage. Writing only for his or her peers, ignoring the needs and interests of a broader audience.

What can writers do to get your attention and to avoid the slush pile? Writers need an agent.

What have been some of your craziest experiences with submissions? I won't offer "crazy" experiences, to protect the innocent and not-so-innocent.

What have been some of your best experiences with writers or in your job? Helping writers with important research but no previous writing experience to reach a large audience (the previously mentioned Michael Behe; also Robert Stinnett, author of *Day of Deceit: The Truth About FDR and Pearl Harbor*, e.g.) Also, helping a first-time writer shape a book that went on to win prizes (James Tobins's *Ernie Pyle's War*) and allowed him to devote himself full time to writing.

What, if anything, makes you different from other editors? I publish serious nonfiction exclusively, for a large commercial publisher. Unlike university presses, I look for books that can sell to a broad public; unlike (some) other commercial publishers, I also look for authors with original research or unique expertise.

F

Is there anything you would like to see changed in the industry? There are lots of things I would like to see changed in the industry, but nothing that would be of use to your readers. It is what it is, after all.

FREE SPIRIT PUBLISHING

217 Fifth Avenue North, Suite 200, Minneapolis, MN 55401-1299
612-338-2068   fax: 612-337-5050
www.freespirit.com   e-mail: help4kids@freespirit.com

Free Spirit Publishing produces trade nonfiction arenas keyed to parenting, human development, the family, education, and relationships. Areas of special concentration: self-help for kids; self-help for teens; gifted and talented education, learning differences (LD), creative learning, parenting and teaching, social action, service learning, school success. Free Spirit Publishing offers creative learning materials that enrich the lives of children and teens.

Free Spirit publications include education guides for students, educators, parents, and mental health professionals, as well as self-help for parents, educators, children, and teens. The publisher (founded in 1983) has been particularly successful with its Self-Help for Kids line of books and educational materials. Free Spirit also catalogs posters and other creative learning wares.

Free Spirit highlights: *The Gifted Kid's Survival Guide for Ages 10 & Under* by Judy Galbraith, M.A.; *Jump Starters: Quick Classroom Activities That Develop Self-Esteem, Creativity and Cooperation* by Linda Nason McElhern, M.A.; *Cliques, Phonies, and Other Baloney* by Trevor Romain; *I'm Like You, You're Like Me: A Child's Book About Understanding and Celebrating Each Other,* written and illustrated by Cindy Gainer; *The Bully Free Classroom: Over 100 Tips and Strategies for Teachers K–12* by Allan Beane, Ph.D.; *How to Handle a Hard-to-Handle Kid: A Parent's Guide to Understanding and Changing Problem Behaviors* by C. Drew Edwards, Ph.D.; *Wonderful Way Books* by Judy Ford, M.S.W.; *The Reading Tutor's Handbook: A Commonsense Guide to Helping Students Read and Write* by Jeanne Shay Schumm, Ph.D., and Gerald E. Schumm, Jr., D.Min.; *What Kids Need to Succeed* by Peter Benson, Ph.D., Judy Galbraith, M.A., and Pamela Espeland; *Teaching Gifted Kids in the Regular Classroom* by Susan Winebrenner; *How Rude!* by Alex Packer; *Gutsy Girls* by Tina Schwager, P.T.A., A.T.C., and Michele Schuerger.

Free Spirit's distribution is through the trade market as well as direct to schools and other youth-serving venues. Query letters and SASEs should be directed to:

Katrina Wentzel, Acquisitions Editor

W. H. FREEMAN AND COMPANY PUBLISHERS

Computer Science Press

Scientific American Books

41 Madison Avenue, New York, NY 10010
212-576-9400   fax: 212-561-8273
www.whfreeman.com

W. H. Freeman accents mathematics and the sciences; the house roster features trade titles of general interest, textbooks, and professional books. Areas of trade interest include anthropology, astronomy, current issues, nature and the environment, health and medicine, life sciences, parenting, and psychology.

W. H. Freeman represents a tradition of outstanding and innovative publishing in the sciences. Freeman books—especially the popular works—often display superb graphics and fine design. W. H. Freeman and Company (established in 1946) is a subsidiary of Scientific American, Inc. The house logs a trusty backlist.

From Freeman: *Star Trek on the Brain: Alien Minds, Human Minds* by Robert Sekuler and Randolph Blake; *Night Comes to the Cretaceous: Dinosaur Extinction and the Transformation of Modern Geology* by James Lawrence Powell; *Why Geese Don't Get Obese (and We Do): How Evolution's Strategies for Survival Affect Our Everyday Lives* by Eric P. Widmaier; *The Nine Myths of Aging: Maximizing the Quality of Later Life* by Douglas H. Powell; *The Earth in Turmoil: Earthquakes, Volcanoes, and Their Impact on Humankind* by Kerry Sieh and Simon LeVay; *The Eleventh Plague: The Politics of Biological and Chemical Warfare* by Leonard A. Cole; *The Secret of Life: Redesigning the Living World* by Joseph Levine and Davis Suzuki; *Children of the Ice Age: How a Global Catastrophe Allowed Humans to Evolve* by Steven M. Stanley; *Why Zebras Don't Get Ulcers: An Updated Guide to Stress, Stress-Related Diseases, and Coping* by Robert M. Sapolsky.

From Scientific American Library, a line of trade-oriented books authored by celebrated scientists, come titles geared to particular fields, in addition to works of general-readership appeal. Sample titles: *Visual Computing* by Richard Mark Friedhoff and Mark S. Peercy; *Gravity's Fatal Attraction: Black Holes in the Universe* by Mitchell Begelman and Martin Rees; *Investigating Disease Patterns: The Science of Epidemiology* by Paul S. Stolley and Tamar Lasky; *The Origin of Modern Humans* by Roger Lewin.

A special coproduction of Infon, Inc., Scientific American, and W. H. Freeman is *Molecular Cell Biology* (CD-ROM).

W. H. Freeman oversees its own distribution. Query letters and SASEs should be directed to:

Michelle Julet, Acquisitions Editor—Chemistry.

Nicole Folchetti, Sponsoring Editor for Life Science.

Richard Bonacci, Acquisitions Editor—Mathematics.

Sara Tenney, Senior Editor—Life Science.

Erika Goldman, Senior Editor—Narrative nonfiction.

John Michael, Executive Editor—Trade areas of house interest.
   Education: B.A., Physics.
   Employment history/editor career path: After college I worked for about a year and a half in a marketing position and then decided I wanted to get into publishing. I started working at HarperCollins and I have been with W. H. Freeman for 3 years. I have 17 years of experience in the publishing industry.
   Personal interests: I have a son who's eight and a half years old.
   What would you be doing if you were not an editor? I would be teaching English (poetry) to jocks or to people who didn't want to learn it.
   Do you represent fiction? No.

Do you represent nonfiction? Yes, exclusively science.

Do you require book proposals? If so, what do you look for in evaluating a book proposal? Yes. I look for an extraordinary topic and a good writer.

Are certain aspects of a book proposal given more weight than others? The way it's written.

What process do you use for making a decision? What is the process for acquisition, is there a committee? Yes, we have a small and informal "committee." We will come together and discuss manuscripts, but we don't really have an official meeting.

What kinds of nonfiction books do you want to see less of? Repeat books. Books that are already out there.

Are agents important? Why? I do believe they are important, but they are not necessary for everyone. They are familiar with the business and know how to help authors get more money and get the best deal with the best house for their book. They will fight for the authors' rights.

Do you like new writers? What should new writers do to break into the business? Breaking into the business is like trying to find an apartment in Manhattan. You need to pull out all of the stops, talk to everyone you know, and find and make connections.

How should writers approach you? With a 30-page proposal that states up front what the book is about and can get my attention within a couple of pages.

What are some common mistakes writers make? What really gets on your nerves? It gets on my nerves when authors will tell me how to do my job; how to do the marketing, how to publish the book, and so on.

What can writers do to get your attention and to avoid the slush pile? Get referred from someone and you will avoid the slush pile. To get my attention, have a good title and opening page.

What have been some of your craziest experiences with submissions? I once had a guy (when I worked at Harper) who would submit his book *Charlotte's Web* and said that E. B. White had stolen his book and that he wanted all rights and royalties to be reverted to him at once and he also wanted to be booked on the Carson show right away. I also had a guy once come to the office and tell me that he had a book that was going to save the world; the entire book was on 5 × 7 index cards.

What have been some of your best experiences with writers or in your job? I had an author that I worked with follow me to three different houses; just so I could be the editor for his material. We worked together for 10 years and finally finished the project, which won the John Burroughs award.

What, if anything, makes you different from other editors? I have a willingness and a desire to work closely with the author. I do all forms of editing, starting with the down and dirty line editing.

Is there anything you would like to see changed in the industry? I would like to see all of the conglomerates broken up into tiny houses. "When will they realize this is a cottage business?" (Francis Lindley).

Any advice for writers? Write for yourself, don't write for fame (you will be disappointed). Don't fall into the John Kennedy Toole trap.

Susan Brennan, Executive Editor/Publisher
  Born: September 1961.

Education: B.A., in Medieval History from Cornell University.

Employment history/editor career path: After college I went into retail, working as an Assistant Buyer for A&S department stores; went to Prentice Hall as a sales rep. And shortly afterward was promoted to an Editor.

Personal interests: Theater, I have two children, aged nine months and three years, and my husband. Restaurants, jogging, hiking.

What would you be doing if you were not an editor? I never really thought about it. I feel lucky that I happened to end up in this position.

What has been your most successful book that you have acquired to date? *Abnormal Psychology* book by Rathus and Nevid, 1st edition around 1990.

What books have you acquired that make you the most proud? What books that you have acquired reflect the types of books you like to represent? Innovative books. In college publishing you are always publishing for a particular market; college professors don't change quickly. Freeman is an innovative publisher.

Do you represent fiction? If so, what do you look for? No.

Do you represent nonfiction? Yes.

Do you require book proposals? If so, what do you look for in evaluating a book proposal? Yes. Most textbooks that we sign, it's something that we have been pursuing. It's not like trade publishing where you get hundreds of submissions per day. Proposals are usually joint adventures between the publisher and the author for textbooks.

Are certain aspects of a book proposal given more weight than others? Yes, do you have an idea that will set your book apart from other books? The quality of the author. How well do you understand your market and competition?

What process do you use for making a decision? What is the process for acquisition, is there a committee? No committees. I read the material and I then send the material out to the people who teach that specific course to review. We get the responses from the reviews and send them to the author and try to revise the book from there.

What kinds of nonfiction books do you want to see less of? Vanilla-flavored textbooks—you can't tell why it is different from the books that are already there.

Are agents important? Why? No. Once in a blue moon. I don't like working with an agent, I like to work directly with the author.

How should writers approach you? Contact me directly by e-mail or mail. Don't call.

What are some common mistakes writers make? What really gets on your nerves? Everyone's book is too long, constantly trying to rein it in. Having to spend a lot of time cutting material out.

What have been some of your craziest experiences with submissions? Schizos from prison who will send you handwritten material that is really crazy. Crazy times for us are when we are involved in a competitive signing and end up doing things that we never thought we would do to obtain the deal.

What have been some of your craziest experiences with writers or in your job? When you are working with an author and something "clicks." You know when you are right on target. It's very rewarding when you sell a lot of books.

What, if anything, makes you different from other editors? Authors love to work with me, I'm straight with my authors, I tell them exactly what I think the issues are, how they should be addressed, and so on. I am in contact with them a lot, and I think a lot of other authors have problems with this, they feel neglected.

Is there anything you would like to see changed in the industry? I don't like the high cost of the textbooks for the students.

Computer Science Press

Computer Science Press publishes in computer science and information technology, with an eye on emerging areas within these quick-moving fields. The house offers introductory- to advanced-level college texts in computer sciences, telecommunications, and computer mathematics, as well as related areas. Computer Science Press, founded in 1974, became an imprint of W. H. Freeman in 1988. Query letters and SASEs should be directed to:

Richard Bonacci, Publisher

FROMM INTERNATIONAL PUBLISHING CORPORATION

979 East Third Avenue, New York, NY 10022
212-308-4010

Fromm International, a German-based company with a New York presence since 1980, ceased all United States operations on May 31, 2001. Fromm International is a small-sized house with a strong literary nonfiction list. Originally known for modern and contemporary fiction from around the globe (originals and reprints), Fromm now publishes primarily a line of diverse and high-quality writings in such nonfiction categories as history, biography, memoirs, belles lettres, essays, cultural and performing arts, analytical psychology, and issues of contemporary interest. The house produces hardcovers, trade paperbacks, and special fine editions.

Fromm International (founded in 1982) has branch offices in Germany and Switzerland.

From Fromm: *The Hermitage: The Biography of a Great Museum* by Geraldine Norman; *Harvey Keitel: The Art of Darkness, the Unauthorized Biography* by Marshall Fine; *Simon & Garfunkel: The Biography* by Victoria Kingston; *Fairweather Eden: Life Half a Million Years Ago as Revealed by the Excavations at Boxgrove* by Michael Pitts and Mark Roberts; *In My Life: Encounters with the Beatles* (edited by Robert Cording, Shelli Jankowski-Smith, and E. J. Miller Laino); *The Art of the Impossible: Politics as Morality in Practice, Speeches and Writings, 1990–1996* by Václav Havel (translated from the Czech by Paul Wilson and others); *Allen Ginsberg in America* by Jane Kramer; *The Life of Sinatra: All or Nothing at All* by Donald Clarke.

Fromm orchestrates its own distributional schemes.

FULCRUM PUBLISHING

16100 Table Mountain Parkway, Suite 300, Golden, CO 80403-5093
303-277-1623, 800-992-2908
www.fulcrum-books.com

Fulcrum publishes general trade nonfiction books, with emphasis in gardening, nature and the outdoors; food; travel guides; business and the environment; Colorado and the Rockies; parenting; health; humor; and American history, world history, and cultural history.

Fulcrum imprints and lines include the Library of Congress series of Americana, educational books (for children and adults), and the Starwood line of books and calendars; the house also issues selected audiocassettes on the Fulcrum Audio Book imprint. Native American writers and subjects are a vital part of the Fulcrum program.

Fulcrum Publishing (founded in 1984) is a growing firm with an ambitious list. It is the Fulcrum vision to produce works that provide a link to the experiences and wisdom of the past. This image fits in neatly with the publisher's characterization of the editorial relationship:

In his autobiography, Anthony Trollope wrote, "Of all the needs that a book has, the chief need is that it be readable." When that happens, it is due to excellent writers and professional and understanding editors. It is difficult and sometimes lonely being a writer, but a good editor is a supporter, a confidant, a representative of the reader, and often can assist the writer in producing a book far better than the writer is capable of creating alone. Sometimes the changes are obvious, sometimes subtle, but they are always aimed at making the book readable. Bob Baron, Publisher, would like to praise and thank Fulcrum's dedicated editors who have made all of their 250 books possible and who have tried to achieve the standards of Trollope.

This is good news for Fulcrum readers, and good news for writers, too. Fulcrum supports a hefty backlist.

Special Fulcrum projects: *The Book in America* by Richard Clement, which used the vast resources in the Library of Congress to trace the history of the American book. *All the World's a Stage,* a volume that combines writing from William Shakespeare with the calligraphy and full-color illustrations of Dorothy Boux. Fulcrum is working with colleagues in England to celebrate the building of the new Globe Theatre in London. *Faces of a Nation: The Rise and Fall of the Soviet Union, 1917–1991,* is a photo essay featuring Dmitri Daltermants, Russia's most famous photographer, with text by noted historian Theodore H. Von Laue.

On the Fulcrum list: *The Colorado Guide,* 5th edition by Bruce Caughey and Dean Winstanley; *Canine Colorado: Where to Go and What to Do with Your Dog* by Cindy Hirschfeld; *Colorado's Thirteeners: From Hikes to Climbs* by Gerry Roach and Jennifer Roach; *Colorado's Lost Creek Wilderness: Classic Summit Hikes* by Gerry Roach and Jennifer Roach; *Biblioholism: A Literary Addiction* by Tom Raabe; *Eating Up the Santa Fe Trail* by Samuel P. Arnold (illustrated by Carrie Arnold); *The Hollywood West: Lives of Film Legends Who Shaped It* (edited by Richard W. Etulain and Glenda Riley); *Going Over East: Reflections of a Woman Rancher; In Search of Kinship: Modern Pioneering on the Western Landscape* by Page Lambert; *Children of the Storm: The True Story of the Pleasant Hill School Bus Tragedy* by Ariana Harner and Clark Secrest; and *Amidst the Gold Dust: Women Who Forged the West* by Julie Danneberg.

Children's titles: *Keepers of the Earth: Native American Stories and Environmental Activities for Children; Keepers of the Animals: Native American Stories and Wildlife Activities for Children; Keepers of Life: Discovering Plants Through Native American Stories and Earth Activities for Children* by Michael J. Caduto and Joseph Bruchac; *From*

Butterflies to Thunderbolts: Discovering Science with Books Kids Love by Anthony D. Fredericks (illustrated by Rebecca Fredericks); *Do Bees Sneeze? And Other Questions Kids Ask About Insects* by James K. Wangberg (illustrated by Ellen Parker).

Fulcrum Publishing handles its own distribution. Query letters and SASEs should be directed to:

Susan Zernial, Editor—Education.

T. J. Baker, Acquisitions Editor—Projects consistent with the house list.

Naomi Horii, Acquisitions Editor
Fulcrum Resources, 350 Indiana Street, Suite 350, Golden, CO 80401-5093
800-992-2908
> **Sign:** Capricorn
> **Education:** B.S. in Journalism; M.A. in Literature.
> **Employment history or editor career path:** Editor at Scientific Publishing House; Editor at *Many Mountains Moving,* a literary journal; Editor at Fulcrum.
> **Personal interests:** Literature, writing, nature.
> **What would you be doing if you were not an editor?** I'd be a teacher.
> **What has been your most successful book that you have acquired to date?** I've acquired poetry, fiction, essays, and art for *Many Mountains Moving,* an internationally distributed literary journal that has had work reprinted in *Best American* and the *Pushcart Prize* anthology. I've worked with some of the world's best writers—Sherman Alexie, Allen Ginsberg, Naomi Shihab Nye, and many more.
> **What books that you have acquired reflect the types of books you like to represent?** I acquired a book on teaching poetry, which I love.
> **Do you represent fiction? If so, what do you look for?** We are considering fiction geared to grades 3 to 8. I look for an engaging voice and a story that stays with me long after I've finished the last page.
> **What do you want to see less of?** I would like to see less work that talks down to young readers.
> **Do you represent nonfiction?** Yes.
> **Do you require book proposals? If so, what do you look for in evaluating a book proposal?** We do require book proposals. In evaluating them, I want to know that the author has carefully thought out the concept and audience of his or her book. I also like to see sample chapters.
> **Are certain areas of a book proposal given more weight than others?** The main thing I evaluate in a book proposal is whether the topic seems like something that people would be interested in.
> **What process do you use for making a decision? What is the process for acquisition, is there a committee?** I immediately reject about 90% of the proposals that come in. The other 10% I will re-read and perhaps pass on to other members of our publishing team for a second opinion.
> **What kinds of nonfiction books do you want to see less of?** Less therapy books.
> **Are you interested in work geared for the masses (readers of *People, The Star,* etc.)?** Yes, as long as it is intelligently written and not dumbed down for the lowest common denominator.

Are agents important? Why? I try to read all manuscripts with an open mind, whether or not the author has an agent. But good agents can be invaluable to an author to help find appropriate forums for the manuscript and to help make things go smoothly for the author.

Do you like new writers? What should new writers do to break into the business? I always keep an eye out for new writers and encourage them to submit work. The most important advice I would give new writers is to know the market. Before even thinking about sending a piece to a certain publishing house, the writer should be familiar with the kinds of books that house has published. To send submissions blindly is a waste of everyone's time.

How should writers approach you? I prefer that writers simply send in a book proposal and a sample chapter with a brief cover letter.

What are some common mistakes writers make? What really gets on your nerves? I dislike manuscripts that write down to readers, whether they be children or adults. I loathe overly cutesy manuscripts.

What can writers do to get your attention and to avoid the slush pile? I try to read every manuscript that comes through the door with equal attention. A good manuscript will always get my attention.

What have been some of your craziest experiences with submissions? I have read for a number of publishers and have read the same manuscript for three different publishing houses. I've also had authors become irate when we've turned down their work.

What have been some of your best experiences with writers or in your job? I delight in discovering new writers but love to work with any author who cares passionately about his or her work.

Is there anything you would like to see changed in the industry? In general, I think that sometimes the market, or the perceived market, dictates what is published. The book industry, as well as Hollywood, has been ruled too long by what some executives think will sell. I think it's important that publishers publish what is good and then decide how they will market or sell that material, rather than trying to figure out whether or not it will sell. There's always room for good material.

Any advice for new writers? My advice to writers is to know your market and to not be discouraged. Some of the books that have become classics were initially rejected by numerous publishers.

GARRETT PUBLISHING

384 South Military Trail, Deerfield Beach, FL 33442
954-480-8543   fax: 954-698-0057
www.garrettpub.com

Garrett's focus is on books in business, finance, law, and personal finance. Garrett books are practical, often featuring a self-help/how-to approach that highlights sample forms, ready-to-use templates, checklists, instructions, resources, and informative examples. A major Garrett imprint is E-Z Legal Books.

Garrett Publishing (founded in 1990) is on the lookout for authors with marketable projects: authors who are expert in their fields and know how to get their point across clearly and enthusiastically. Garrett's marketing department is staffed with professionals skilled in publicity, promotions, advertising, and editorial services. Garrett promotes its authors' books through print advertising, television appearances, and radio spots. The house offers competitive advances and royalties.

With sales representatives located strategically across the United States, Garrett's books are available in the giant trade bookseller chains and are obtainable from major wholesalers and distributors. Over the past several seasons, the publisher has expanded its retail distribution.

Representative of the Garrett program: *Asset Protection Secrets; How to Settle with the IRS—For Pennies on the Dollar; Building Your Financial Fortress: How to Protect Your Assets from the 10 Deadly Threats to Your Wealth!; The Limited Partnership Book.*

Garrett Publishing distributes through its own house operation, as well as via such outlets as Quality Book Distributors, Ingram, and Baker and Taylor. Query letters and SASEs should be directed to:

Arnold Goldstein, Editor/Owner

GENERAL PUBLISHING GROUP

This young West Coast start-up fell victim to the harsh realities of independent publishing and closed shop.

G

THE GLOBE PEQUOT PRESS

Morris Communications Corporation
246 Goose Lane #200, P.O. Box 480, Guilford, CT 06437-0833
860-395-0440   fax: 860-395-0312
www.globe-pequot.com   e-mail: info@globe-pequot.com

Globe Pequot is a specialist in travel and outdoor recreation, with additional interest in cooking, personal finance, and home-based business. The publisher accents titles marketed to both trade and specialty market slots.

Within this program, Globe Pequot looks for works in a number of important categories: travel books—regional and special-interest travel guides; family adventure guides; travel annuals, accommodations guides, itinerary-format guides, and travel how-to's; outdoor recreation—any outdoor sport; how-to and where-to guides; and home-based business. Authors should have firsthand experience running the featured home-based business.

In the travel arena, Globe Pequot is well regarded for several bestselling series and also distributes for a number of travel-specialist houses. Among Globe Pequot lines: Quick Escapes (weekend and day trips keyed to metropolitan areas or regions); Romantic Days and Nights; Recommended Bed & Breakfasts; Fun with the Family Guides; Cadogan Guides to destinations worldwide for the discriminating traveler; and the popular Off-the-Beaten-Path series. Globe Pequot also updates a variety of annuals, among them Europe by Eurorail. Globe Pequot's regionally keyed books also cover such interest areas as biking, hiking, mountaineering, skiing, and family activities in wilderness and on the beach.

Globe Pequot representative titles: *The Essential Little Cruise Book: Secrets from a Cruise Director for a Perfect Cruise Vacation* by Jim West; *Take Your Kids to Europe: How to Travel Safely (and Sanely) in Europe with Your Children* by Cynthia W. Harriman; *Hostels USA: The Comprehensive, Unofficial, Opinionated Guide to Hostels in the United States* by Paul Karr and Evan Halper.

The Globe Pequot Press (originated in 1947) operates from publishing headquarters in Old Saybrook and warehouse facilities in the Nashville area. The press distributes its own list through its home-office facilities, as well as through a network of regional sales representatives. The house handles distribution for such houses as Appalachian Mountain Club Books, Berlitz Publishing, Bradt Publications, Cadogan Guides, Interstate America, New Holland, Ltd., Ulysses, Woodall Publications, and Moorland Publishing.

Globe Pequot was purchased in early 1997 by Morris Communications Corporation, a privately held company (founded in 1795) with nationwide, diversified holdings in newspaper and magazine publishing, radio, outdoor advertising, and computer services. Query letters and SASEs should be directed to:

Lafe Low, Acquisitions Editor—Outdoor submissions.

Shelley Wolf, Submissions Editor—General submissions.

Laura Strom, Executive Editor—Travel submissions.
Globe Pequot Press, 246 Goose Lane #200, P.O. Box 480, Guilford, CT 06437-0833

Born: April 24.

Education: B.A., English Literature.

Employment history/editor career path: I started out in an unrelated industry out of college, but shortly after that I worked in an entry-level position at a vanity press and then shortly after that I moved to Connecticut and got an editorial/proofreading position. Four years later Globe Pequot was hiring, and I have been with the company for 11 years.

Personal interests: Traveling, swing dancing, gardening, being outdoors.

What would you be doing if you were not an editor? I would be a farmer.

What has been your most successful book that you have acquired to date? A companion book to a PBS genre on legendary lighthouses (fall 1998), it's been back to press four times.

What books have you acquired that make you the most proud? What books that you have acquired reflect the types of books you like to represent? The companion book is one of them, also a book titled *New York Neighborhoods,* which is a food lovers' guide to the ethnic community by Elenor Berman (1999). I also developed a romantic travel book called *Romantic Days and Nights.*

Do you represent fiction? If so, what do you look for? No.

Do you represent nonfiction? Yes. In our specific areas (travel).

Do you require book proposals? If so, what do you look for in evaluating a book proposal? Yes. First I look to see if it's something we actually publish; well-credentialed authors; new ideas that can be sold into nontrade; any previous writing experience.

Are certain aspects of a book proposal given more weight than others? We look for excellent writing, the marketability and promotability of the author.

G

What process do you use for making a decision? What is the process for acquisition, is there a committee? We do have a committee that meets every couple of weeks and the Acquisitions Editors usually present the new ideas to the committee. The committee is made up of sales representatives, as well as our administration and editorial staff. We discuss new ideas that we have and if everyone agrees, we do a thorough competition search, and so on.

What kinds of nonfiction books do you want to see less of? Motor home travel books.

Do you think that agents are important? Why? Yes, agents are really important. They tend to represent some of the better authors. We also work with unagented authors or previous authors of ours.

Do you like new writers? What should new writers do to break into the business? Yes, especially for our regional guidebooks. New writers are often very enthusiastic.

How should writers approach you? With a query letter via snail mail.

What are some common mistakes writers make? What really gets on your nerves? Query letters that sound like they are a sales pitch or gimmick.

What can writers do to get your attention and to avoid the slush pile? Be polite, nondemanding, do periodic follow-ups by e-mail or through the mail. No phone calls.

What have been some of your best experiences with writers or in your job? Working with authors who really know how to write.

What, if anything, makes you different from other editors? I really care about my authors.

G

David R. Godine, Publisher, Inc.

9 Hamilton Place, Boston, MA 02108
617-451-9600   fax: 617-350-0250

Godine publishes trade nonfiction in such areas as history and criticism, typography and graphic arts, art and architecture, horticulture, cooking, Americana, and regional-interest books. The house also publishes fiction (including mysteries), literature and essays, and poetry, as well as children's books. Godine offers a line of classic works in reprint, as well as works in translation.

The Godine program is committed to quality. Godine specializes in attentively produced hardcover and trade paperback editions. The house issues a small catalog of new titles each year while maintaining an active backlist. Godine's imprints include Country Classics, Double Detectives, and Nonpareil Books.

David R. Godine, Publisher (founded in 1969), was started in an abandoned cow barn, where David R. Godine both worked and lived; the expanding operation later moved to Boston.

Godine has intentionally kept itself small, the list eclectic, and the quality consistently high, with a stronger concentration on titles with backlist potential (particularly nonfiction). The house maintains its fortunate position of being able to ask: What do we really believe is superior? rather than, What are we confident will sell? The editors at Godine have learned to trust their instincts. By staying small, this house is lucky enough to have kept most of its goals attainable. They do not need to sell 10,000 copies of a book to make money. They do not need to put authors on tour or to indulge in massive hype. Good books, like water, find their own levels. It sometimes takes years, but it is inevitable.

In short, David R. Godine, Publisher, remains what it was 30 years ago: a true cottage industry, surviving on a very small budget, and doing what it does and what it knows best: publishing books that matter for people who care.

General trade nonfiction from Godine: *Tyranny of the Normal: Essays on Bioethics, Theology, and Myth* by Leslie Fiedler; *Great Camps of the Adirondacks* by Harvey H. Kaiser (now back in print); *The Grand Resort Hotels of the White Mountains: A Vanishing Architectural Legacy* by Bryant F. Tolles, Jr.; *Schola Illustris: The Roxbury Latin School, 1645–1995* by F. Washington Jarvis; *Crowning Glory: Silver Torah Ornaments of the Jewish Museum, New York* by Rafi Grafman (edited by Vivian B. Mann); *Bright Stars, Dark Trees, Clear Water: Natural Writing from North of the Border* (edited by Wayne Grady).

Representative of Godine special-interest nonfiction: *The Art of the Printed Book, 1455–1955* by Joseph Blumenthal; *Into Print: Selected Writings on Printing History, Typography, and Book Production,* by John Dreyfus; *Calligraphic Flourishing: A New Approach to an Ancient Art* by Bill Hildebrandt; *Giving Up the Gun: Japan's Reversion to the Sword, 1545–1879* by Noel Perrin.

On the Godine fiction list: *The Disobedience of Water* (stories) by Sena Jeter Naslund; *Last Trolley from Beethovenstraat,* by Grete Weil (translated from the German by John Barrett); *Life: A User's Manual* by Georges Perec (translated from the French by David Ellos); and works by Andre Dubus, William H. Gass, William Maxwell, and Walter Abish and others.

Mystery and suspense titles include: *The Man Who Liked Slow Tomatoes* by K. C. Constantine; *Adventures of Richard Hannay* by John Buchan.

Godine's children's books backlist includes: *We Didn't Mean to Go to the Sea* by Arthur Ransome; and *Crime and Puzzlement: 24 Solve-Them-Yourself Picture Mysteries* by Lawrence Treat (illustrated by Leslie Cabarga).

Query letters and SASEs should be directed to:

Carl W. Scarbrough, Publicity Director

G

GRAYWOLF PRESS

2402 University Avenue, Suite 203, Saint Paul, MN 55114
651-641-0077   fax: 651-641-0036
www.graywolfpress.org

Graywolf publishes poetry, fiction, and nonfiction and essays. Graywolf produces works by writers past and present, with particular emphasis on the scene of contemporary international letters, as well as a line of literary anthologies and reissues. Graywolf hosts a solid backlist of featured titles.

About the Graywolf Press trade motto: Creative writing for creative reading. This distinctive approach to publishing signifies Graywolf Press as an independent, not-for-profit publisher dedicated to the creation and promotion of thoughtful and imaginative contemporary literature essential to a vital and diverse culture.

Graywolf backs up its authors and its literary claims with publishing prowess: the Graywolves have been successful in finding an audience for their works, and the Graywolf Press list has been augmented, confirming the achievement of a program that runs contrary to the stream of contemporary commercial publishing.

Begun in 1974, Graywolf Press exemplifies the small-scale independent American literary house. The publisher's wolf pack logo marks a list rippling with award-winners and critical endorsement.

The Graywolf Forum series was launched with the publication of Graywolf Forum One: *Tolstoy's Dictaphone: Technology and the Muse,* a collection of new essays edited by Sven Birkerts (author of the hotly debated *Gutenberg Elegies*).

General-interest trade books include: *If You Want to Write: A Book About Art, Independence and Spirit* by Brenca Ueland; *Burning Down the House: Essays on Fiction* by Charles Baxter; *The Outermost Dream: Literary Sketches* by William Maxwell; *Diary of a Left-Handed Birdwatcher* by Leonard Nathan.

Graywolf fiction and literary works: *War Memorials* by Clint McCown; *Otherwise: New & Selected Poems* by Jane Kenyon; *A Four-Sided Bed* by Elizabeth Searle; *Pastoral* by Carl Phillips; *Domestic Work* by Natasha Trethewey; *Some Ether* by Nick Flynn; *The Way It Is: New and Selected Poems* by William Statford; *Ana Imagined* by Perrin Ireland.

Graywolf Press utilizes a network of regional sales representatives; books are proffered to the trade through Consortium Book Sales and Distribution. Query letters and SASEs should be directed to:

Katie Dublinski, Editor—Fiction.

Anne Czarniecki, Executive Editor—Fiction and Nonfiction.

Daniel Kos, Publishing Assistant

Fiona McCrae, Publisher

G

GREENWOOD PUBLISHING GROUP

Auburn House

Bergin & Garvey

Greenwood Press

Praeger Publishers

Quorum Books

88 Post Road West, P.O. Box 5007, Westport, CT 06881-5007
203-226-3571   fax: 203-222-1502
www.greenwood.com

The Greenwood publishing program encompasses general trade nonfiction, along with a traditional emphasis on professional, academic, and reference books in economics, business, social sciences and humanities, law enforcement, business, law, and current affairs, as well as special series of reference works. In addition, Greenwood produces reprints of scholarly monographs and journals. The house issues editions in hardcover and trade paperback.

Greenwood Publishing Group (instituted in 1967) comprises a number of imprints and divisions that include Auburn House, Bergin & Garvey, Greenwood Press, Quorum Books, and Praeger Publishers. (See separate subentries elsewhere in this guide.) Greenwood imprints generally maintain extensive backlists.

Greenwood Publishing Group orchestrates its own distribution. A major portion of Greenwood's sales are aimed at the library, institutional, and corporate markets. Query letters and SASEs should be directed to:

Cynthia Harris, History (reference), economics.

George Butler, Senior Acquisitions Editor—Literature and drama.

Jane Garry, Acquisitions Editor—Anthropology and education.

Michael Herman, Acquisitions Editor—Political science.

Nita Romer, Acquisitions Editor—Literature and drama.

Greenwood Academic and Trade Publishing

Auburn House

Bergin & Garvey

Praeger Publishers

Greenwood Publishing Group's general nonfiction trade books and academic works are published under the imprints Auburn House, Bergin & Garvey, and Praeger Publishers. Each imprint has its own individual publishing orbit and distinct editorial approach.

Auburn House emphasizes professional and academic works in economics, business, health care, labor relations, and public policy.

Bergin & Garvey concentrates on scholarly monographs in the social sciences and humanities, as well as general nonfiction works in a similar subject range geared toward a popular audience.

Praeger Publishers promotes a vigorous approach to trade nonfiction and areas of scholarly specialist attention. Categories of publishing interest include history (including cultural history), military studies (including history, espionage, and military operations), political science and international relations, women's studies, business and economics, psychology, and urban affairs.

Sample works in the social and behavioral sciences (political science, history, economics, sociology, anthropology, education, psychology, health and medicine, and science and computers): *The Future of Ethnicity, Race, and Nationality* by Walter L. Wallace; *An Introduction to the Psychology of Dreaming* by Kelly Bukleley; *Setting Psychological Boundaries: A Handbook for Women* by Anne Cope Wallace; *Women and Soap Opera: A Cultural Feminist Perspective* by Dannielle Blumenthal; *Abused Men: The Hidden Side of Domestic Violence* by Philip W. Cook; *Hardball Without an Umpire: The Sociology of Morality* by Melvyn L. Fein; *Maximizing Your Health Insurance Benefits: A Consumer's Guide to New and Traditional Plans* by Richard Epstein; *Lesbian Family Relationships in American Society: The Making of an Ethnographic Film* by Maureen A. Asten; *A Lost Cause: Bill Clinton's Campaign for National Health Insurance* by Nicholas Laham; *Jimmy Carter as Peacemaker: A Post-Presidential Biography* by Rod Troester.

Representing the humanities (literature, music, theater and drama, religion, philosophy, popular culture, communication and mass media, library and information science, and art and architecture): *The Meanings of Love: An Introduction to the Philosophy of Love* by Robert E. Wagoner; *Moral Reasoning for Journalists: Cases and Commentary* by Steven R. Knowlton; *Teaching Shakespeare with Film and Television: A Guide* by H. R. Coursen; *The Short Fiction of Kurt Vonnegut* by Peter J. Reed; *Sam Shepard and the American Theatre* by Leslie A. Wade; *Fred Astaire: A Bio-Bibliography* by Larry Billman; *Harold Pinter and the New British Theatre* by D. Keith Peacock; *Enchanted Places: The Use of Setting in F. Scott Fitzgerald's Fiction* by Aiping Zhang.

Query letters and SASEs should be directed to:

Heather Staines, Acquisitions Editor—History, monographs, legal studies.

Lynne Taylor, Assistant Vice President for Editorial Reference.

Pamala St. Clair, Associate Acquisitions Editor—Music and dance.

Peter Krack, Executive Editor for Academic Programs

Greenwood Reference Publishing

The Greenwood Reference Publishing imprint offers popular, educational, scholarly, and professional reference works. The house counts among its specialty areas library and information sciences; social sciences, humanities, the arts, and works covering contemporary trends in cultural studies and criticism.

Greenwood reference series are diverse and comprehensive, and are authored and edited primarily by academics working in their respective fields of concentration. Series include: Critical Companions to Popular Contemporary Writers, Student Companions to Classic Writers, Histories of the Modern Nations, Daily Life Through History, Professional Guides in School Librarianship. (Some individual series titles are cited in the previous listing for Greenwood Academic and Trade division.) Greenwood publishes popular, educational, scholarly, and professional reference works, including library and information sciences; social sciences, humanities, the arts, and works covering contemporary trends in cultural studies and criticism.

Query letters and SASEs should be directed to:

Barbara Rader, Executive Editor—School and public library reference.

Quorum Books

At Quorum Books, the business books imprint of Greenwood Publishing Group, Inc., the accent is on titles keyed to areas of topical interest, including timely issues in business, finance, and law. Sectors of this division's scope are management trends; business ethics; international business and economics; business, law, and public policy; environment and energy; information and corporate communications; human resource management; organizational behavior and development; finance, investment, and banking; accounting and taxation; marketing, advertising, and sales; and public and not-for-profit management.

Quorum Books is a dedicated imprint for professional and scholarly books in business, business-related law, and applied economics. Quorum scholarly studies recount findings and hypotheses derived from significant academic research and offer well-reasoned analysis, interpretations, and opinions.

Quorum professional books are more applied in scope and presentation. These works are intended for people who are skilled in their work, who are rising in their organizations, and who have urgent need for highly technical, timely, and specialized knowledge. These books thus provide readers with a blend of theory and practice not easily found or produced; it is significant that among Quorum readers are also many Quorum authors.

Titles here include: *The Muted Conscience: Moral Silence and the Practice of Ethics in Business* by Frederick Bruce Bird; *Leadership and the Job of the Executive* by Jeffrey A. Barach and D. Reed Eckhardt; *Scaling the Ivory Tower: Stories from Women in Business School Faculties* (edited by Dianne Cyr and Blaize Horner Reich); *Toxic Leaders: When Organizations Go Bad* by Marcia Lynn Whicker; *Virtual Reality Systems for Business* by Robert J. Thierauf; *Cross-Cultural Business Negotiations* by Donald W. Hendon, Rebecca Angeles Hendon, and Paul Herbig; *Measuring the Employment Effects of Regulations: Where Did the Jobs Go?* by Neal S. Zank; *The Future of the Space Industry: Private Enterprise and Public Policy* by Roger Handberg; *Reflexive Communication in the Culturally Diverse Workplace* by John E. Kikoski and Catherine Kano Kikoski; *Business Decisions, Human Choices: Restoring the Partnership Between People and Their Organizations* by Lloyd C. Williams; *Selling Sin: The Marketing of Socially Unacceptable Products* by D. Kirk Davidson.

Query letters and SASEs should be directed to:

Eric Valentine, Publisher, Quorum Books

GROLIER CHILDREN'S PUBLISHING/GROLIER INCORPORATED

Children's Press

Orchard Books

www.publishing.grolier.com

Grolier Children's Publishing is the umbrella under which the separate book-publishing houses Children's Press, Franklin Watts, and Orchard Books operate their independent, distinctive lists geared to children's and young-adult markets. (See separate subentries further on.)

Children's Press

Representative titles for the Children's Press are as follows:

Cornerstones of Freedom series titles: *African-Americans in the Thirteen Colonies* and *The Disability Rights Movement* by Deborah Kent; *The Transcontinental Railroad* by Peter Anderson; *The Liberty Bell* by Gail Sakurai; and *Building the Capital City* by Marlene Targ Brill.

Little Brown Bear series titles: *Little Brown Bear Dresses Himself; Little Brown Bear Helps His Mama; Little Brown Bear Is Going on a Trip;* and *Little Brown Bear Takes a Bath.*

New True Books is a series that seeks to provide answers to many basic questions children may have about animals, the environment, the human body, space, sports, and the like.

Grolier All-Pro Biographies represents a new series targeted at ages 9 to 12. Perseverance, courage, and the personal will to succeed are the qualities that bind the athletes profiled in this new series of sports biographies. Selected titles include *Cedrick Ceballos; John Elway; Dan Marino; Orlando Merced; Hakeem Olajuwon; Lyn St. James;* and *Steve Young.*

Orchard Books

95 Madison Avenue, New York, NY 10016
212-951-2649

Orchard Books produces mainstream trade children's fiction books, many of them illustrated works—and here again, award-winning titles and authors abound. Storybooks, boardbooks, novelty books, picture books, and middle grade and young adult novels are among areas of particular house emphasis.

Orchard emphasizes individual trade titles. Representative titles: *One Seal* by John Stadler; *A Is for the Americas* by Cynthia Chin-Lee (illustrated by Sanchez); *Zagazoo* by Quentin Blake; *Simply Delicious* by Margaret Mahey (illustrated by Jonathon Allen); *Montezuma's Revenge* by Cari Best (illustrated by Diane Palmisciano); *The Other Side* by Angela Johnson; and *Rode a Horse of Milk White Jade* by Diane Lee Wilson.

Query letters and SASEs should be directed to:

Ana Cerro, Editor

Judy V. Wilson, President and Publisher

Lisa Hammond, Assistant Editor

Rebecca Davis, Senior Editor

Sarah Caguiat, Editor

Tamson Weston, Assistant Editor

G

GROVE/ATLANTIC, INC.

Atlantic Monthly Press

Grove Press

841 Broadway, New York, NY 10003
212-614-7850

Grove/Atlantic publishes trade nonfiction and fiction; these works often display a contemporary cultural bent or an issue-oriented edge. Grove Press and Atlantic Monthly Press, two previously independent houses, are united under the Grove/Atlantic, Inc., corporate crest. Grove/Atlantic operates from the former Grove headquarters on Broadway (with Atlantic having relocated from its previous digs at nearby Union Square West). Grove/Atlantic operates essentially as one house, while maintaining the distinction of two major imprints. (See separate subentries further on for both Atlantic Monthly Press and Grove Press.)

Grove/Atlantic holds a tradition of publishing arresting literature—from the writing of Samuel Beckett and William S. Burroughs to Jean Genet and Marguerite Duras, from John Kennedy Toole and J. P. Donleavy to Henry Miller and Jeanette Winterson. The house initiated an aggressive program to repackage these modern classics, as well as to return to print the work of such celebrated writers as Terry Southern, Robert Coover, Jerzy Kosinski, Frederick Barthelme, Patricia Highsmith, Aharon Appelfeld, Barry Hannah, and Kenzaburo Oe. In a marketplace it sees as increasingly dominated by ephemera, Grove/Atlantic is committed to publishing serious books that last and to introducing classic books to a new generation of readers.

Subsequent to the previously noted Grove/Atlantic merger—with Atlantic most decidedly the major partner—speculation was that Atlantic had bought Grove essentially for Grove's extensive, internationally renowned backlist; Atlantic would presumably vampirize Grove's backlist, then cast aside the dry husk of Grove Press to any interested bidders. Happily, such tiresome prognostications have not come to pass; the publishing image of Grove/Atlantic is, if anything, more finely honed under the auspices of the umbrella house.

Grove/Atlantic books are distributed by Publishers Group West.

Grove/Atlantic does not accept unsolicited manuscripts. Query letters and SASEs should be directed to:

Amy Hundley, Associate Editor

Andrew Miller, Editor

Brendan Cahill, Assistant Editor

G

Atlantic Monthly Press

Atlantic Monthly Press paces the spectrum of commercial categories, publishing hardcover and trade paperback editions in memoirs, belles lettres, history, social sciences, current affairs, natural history, ethnology, lifestyle, fashion, and cuisine, in addition to literary and popular fiction. AMP authors have over the years garnered an enormous wealth of recognition for their work, including Pulitzers, Nobels, and National Book Awards. The AMP Traveler series encompasses nonfiction works that offer unstinting looks at nations, cultures, and peoples of the world.

Atlantic Monthly Press has long been representative of the highest aims of American publishing—with a list that features quality writing, fine production, and strong commercial presence. Atlantic Monthly Press was inaugurated originally (in 1917) to be primarily a book-publishing vehicle for writers associated with *Atlantic Monthly* magazine. From 1925 through 1984 the press was an imprint of Boston's Little, Brown. Atlantic Monthly Press was bought by Carl Navarre in 1985, and under current owner-publisher Morgan Entrekin (who bought out Navarre in 1991), AMP (now in consort with Grove) continues as a leading force in American letters.

AMP is publisher of the *New York Times* bestseller *Cold Mountain,* the astonishing debut Civil War novel by Charles Frazier.

Representing Atlantic nonfiction: *Black Hawk Down: A Story of Modern War* by Mark Bowden; *Throwim Way Leg: Tree Kangaroos, Possums and Penis Gourds—On the Trail of Unknown Mammals in Wildest New Guinea* by Tim Flannery; *Eat the Rich* by P. J. O'Rourke; *The Earth Shall Weep: A History of Native America* by James Wilson.

Fiction and literature from AMP: *The Road Home* by Jim Harrison; *Mr. Darwin's Shooter* by Roger McDonald; *The Pleasing Hour* by Lily King; *Having Everything* by John L'Heureux; *By the Shore* by Galaxy Craze. Prospective authors please note that Grove/Atlantic no longer accepts unsolicited material.

Grove Press

Grove Press accents trade nonfiction and fiction with a sharp cultural consciousness and literary flair. The house continues to expand on its powerful backlist base by engaging at the forefront of publishing trends: Grove publishes a line of feature-film screenplays and has instituted a new poetry series.

Grove Press was founded in 1951 by literary trailblazer Barney Rosset, who established a tradition of enterprising lists that featured some of the finest and most fearless writing from around the globe. This literary institution was purchased by Ann Getty in 1985; in league with the British-based house of Weidenfeld & Nicholson, the publisher (briefly) operated under the sobriquet Grove Weidenfeld. With the early retreat of the Weidenfeld interests, the fate of Grove was a popular topic of publishing tattle—rumored by some to be perpetually on the block, both prior and subsequent to the house's merger with Atlantic Monthly Press.

Throughout these corporate shifts, Grove nevertheless extended its distinguished reputation, with a masterly mix of backlist offerings as well as commercially successful and stimulating new titles—as befits the Grove tradition.

The Grove nonfiction list covers biography and memoirs, popular culture worldwide, literary criticism, history and politics.

Grove nonfiction titles include: *The Century of Sex: Playboy's History of the Sexual Revolution 1900–1999* by James R. Peterson (edited and with a foreword by Hugh M. Hefner); *My War Gone By, I Miss It So* by Anthony Loyd; *Daughter of the River: An Autobiography* by Hong Ying; *Charles Bukowski: Locked in the Arms of a Crazy Life* by Howard Sounes.

In fiction, Grove owes a historic commitment to literature that explodes boundaries, having published such authors as Kathy Acker, William S. Burroughs, Robert Coover, Thulani Davis, Jack Kerouac, Milan Kundera, Henry Miller, Bharati Mukherjee, Hubert Selby, Jr., and Diane Williams. Grove publishes a wide variety of world literature in translation, has a strong drama list, and produces a significant poetry list.

Indicative of Grove fiction and literary works: *Word Virus: The Selected Writings of William S. Burroughs* (edited by James Grauerholz and Ira Silverberg); *Mr. Spaceman* by Robert Olen Butler; *The Sweet Smell of Psychosis* by Will Self; *Lovers for a Day* by Ivan Klima; *What It Takes to Get to Vegas* by Yxta Maya Murray; *Lord of the Barnyard* by Tristan Egolf; *The Blue Room* by David Hare; *The Place You Return Is Home* by Kirsty Gunn.

Backlist literary classics include the freshly designed reissue of major works (including collections) authored by the Marquis de Sade: *The 120 Days of Sodom and Other Writings; Juliette; Justine; Philosophy in the Bedroom and Other Writings.*

G

Grove/Atlantic Monthly editors acquire in all areas consistent with house description. Prospective authors please note that Grove/Atlantic no longer accepts unsolicited material. However, you may still send a query or (occasionally) talk directly with an editor before sending a manuscript. Query letters and SASEs should be directed to:

Joan Bingham, Executive Editor

Morgan Entrekin, Publisher

GULF PUBLISHING COMPANY

All operations ceased in 2000.

HARCOURT INC.

Harcourt Trade Children's Books

Harvest Books

San Diego office:
525 B Street, Suite 1900, San Diego, CA 92101-4495
619-231-6616

New York office:
15 East 26th Street, New York, NY 10010

The Harcourt trade division publishes the gamut of nonfiction categories, as well as some serious and commercial fiction, in hardcover and paperback editions. Special lines include Harcourt's Judaica backlist, literary works in translation, the Harvest imprint (which accents American and international literature and culture in trade paper originals and reprints), Gulliver Books (popular works in hardcover and trade paper for readers of all ages.

Harcourt (founded in 1919) has through the decades evolved into a publishing house of prodigious reach. Harcourt's multidimensional sprawl encompasses offices in such diverse locations as Chicago, Orlando, San Diego, Toronto, and New York. Although the trade-publishing program was trimmed markedly through the late 1980s into the early 1990s, Harcourt (formerly Harcourt Brace Jovanovich) remains particularly potent in the arena of educational materials and texts, as well as professional reference.

Among Harcourt subsidiaries are Academic Press, Harcourt Legal and Professional Publications, Johnson Reprint (scholarly and special-interest titles), W. B. Saunders (professional and academic medical publications), and Holt, Rinehart, & Winston (focusing on the educational market from elementary through university levels).

On the Harcourt list: *Riddle of the Compass* by Amir D. Aczel; *Double Down* by Frederick and Steven Barthelme; *A Hole in the Earth* by Robert Bausch; *Advent of the Algorithm* by David Berlinski; *Presidential Inaugurations* by Paul. F. Boller, Jr.; *Devil's Valley* and *Rights of Desire* by Andre Brink; *Spytime and Elvis in the Morning* by William F.

H

Buckley Jr.; *An Honorable Defeat* by William C. Davis; *Allegiance* by David Detzer; *Slammerkin* by Emma Donoghue; *Peppered Moth* by Margaret Drabble; *Under the Skin* by Michael Faber; *Troy* by Adele Geras; *Talking in the Dark* by Laura Glen Louis; *Other Statue* by Edward Gorey; *At End of the Day* by George V. Higgins; *Soulcatcher* by Charles Johnson; *Unwinding the Clock* by Jonsson Bodil; *Painter of Birds* by Lidia Jorge; *Head Game* by Roger Kahn; *Blue Bedspread* by Raj Damal Jha; *A Case of Curiosities* by Allen Kurzweil; *America's Undeclared War* by Daniel Lazare; *Tales from Earthsea* by Ursula K. Le Guin; *Six Figures* by Fred G. Leebron; *Stolen Words* by Thomas Mallon; *Hunters* by Claire Messud; *Knick Knack Paddy Whack* by Ardal O'Hanlon; *Home Run* by George Plimpton; *Mermaids Explained* by Christopher Reid; *Lost Legends of New Jersey* by Rederick Reiken; *Rails Under My Back* by Jeffery Renard Allen; *Scandalmonger* by William Safire; *Journey to Portugal* by Jose Saramago; *Nebula Awards Showcase 2001* by Robert Silverberg; *Jumping Fire* by Murray A. Taylor; *Confessions of Mycroft Holmes* by Marcel Theroux; *Half Empty, Half Full* by Susan C. Vaughan; *Why We Hurt* by Frank T. Vertosick, Jr.; *Word Count* by Barbara Wallraff; *Secret Lives of Word* by Paul West; and *One Man's Justice* by Akira Yoshimura.

Harcourt handles its own distribution. Send query letters with SASEs to:

Walter Bode, Senior Editor—Literary fiction and nonfiction.

Ann Patty, Executive Editor—Literary fiction, women's fiction.

Andrew Bernard, Editor in Chief—Harvest Books; literary fiction, poetry.

Harcourt Trade Children's Books

Gulliver Books
Gulliver Green
Red Wagon Books

Harcourt children's categories include picture books, easy readers, nonfiction, fiction, poetry, big books, older readers, and reference books.

Harcourt produces a full offering of children's books in hardcover and paperback. Many Harcourt titles are presented as books for all ages—intended to embrace a wide readership range.

The house features several distinct imprints for young readers. Among them: Gulliver Books, Gulliver Green, Gulliver Books in Paperback, Red Wagon Books, Magic Carpet Books, Harcourt Big Books, Harcourt Creative Curriculum Connections, and the paperback lines Odyssey and Voyager Books—along with a lineup of author videos. Libros Viajeros is the Voyager line of Spanish-language books.

On the Harcourt children's list: *Lou Gehrig* by David A. Adler; *Baby Duck's New Friend* by Frank and David Asch; *Stella's Dancing Days* by Sandy Asher; *Little Green* by Keith Baker; *Twinnies* by Eve Bunting; *Marco's Run* by Wesley Cartier; *Miles Away from Home* by Joan Vcottle; *Splash!* by Driane and Aruego Jose Dewey; *Deep Wizardry* by Diane Duane; *Lizards, Frogs and Polliwogs,* and *Kipper and the Egg* by Mick Inkpen.

Unsolicited manuscripts are no longer accepted. Editors now work exclusively through literary agents.

Harvest Books
Kurt and Helen Wolff Books

Harvest Books, the trade paperback imprint of Harcourt Inc., offers the best from the house's illustrious 77-year publishing history, as well as from its distinguished present. The Harvest in Translation Series publishes some of the world's finest literature, many from the distinguished Helen and Kurt Wolff imprint.

Harvest Books publishes fiction, nonfiction, and poetry by some of the most exciting writers and celebrities. Many Harcourt Brace hardcovers are published simultaneously in paperback by Harvest Books. Representative titles include: *Mister Sandman: A Novel* by Barbara Gowdy; *A Goat's Song* by Dermot Healy; *Every Parent's Guide to the Law* by Deborah L. Forman; *The House of Moses All-Stars* by Charley Rosen; *Buckley: The Right Word* (edited by Samuel S. Vaughan); *Inventions of the March Hare: Poems 1909–1917* by T. S. Eliot (edited by Christopher Ricks); *A Book of Luminous Things: An International Anthology of Poetry* (edited and with an introduction by Czeslaw Milosz); *Nebula Awards 32: SFWA's Choices for the Best Science Fiction and Fantasy of the Year* (edited by Jack Dann, winner of the Nebula Award for Best Novella); and *The Highwaymen* (business/ current affairs) by Ken Auletta.

The Wilderness Experience series (Harvest originals) volumes are written by top nature writers, who act as guides, selecting pieces on a chosen theme from the best writers, environmentalists, and naturalists.

New Wilderness titles: *Echoes from the Summit* (edited by Paul Schullery); *Call of the River* (edited by Page Stegner); and *Lure of the Sea* (edited by Joseph E. Brown).

Although Harcourt has greatly reduced its acquisitions of commercially oriented titles, the house is still active in the trade arena. Query letters and SASEs should be directed to:

Daniel H. Farley, Vice President and Publisher (New York and San Diego)—Adult trade books.

Diane Sterling, Senior Editor (San Diego)—Translations. Test-preparation books.

Drenka Willen, Editor (New York)—Literary fiction, translations; some poetry.

Jane Isay, Executive Editor (New York)—Nonfiction books; hardcover originals; also works intended for the Harvest trade paper line.

Vicki Austin-Smith, Senior Editor (San Diego)—Serious and general fiction and nonfiction in hardcover and paperback, with emphasis on backlist titles. Some humor.

Walter Bode, Editor (New York)

Yoji Yamaguchi, Associate Editor (New York)

H

HARLEQUIN BOOKS/SILHOUETTE BOOKS

300 East 42nd Street, 6th Floor, New York, NY 10017
212-682-6080

Harlequin and Silhouette publish romance novels, love stories, and women's fiction. With commanding emphasis on these interrelated categories, the publisher is always experimenting with inventive, distinctive lines that explore new approaches to the age-old tradition of tales of amour.

The Harlequin Books New York office issues several Harlequin series; the rest of the list is published from the Harlequin Enterprises base in Ontario, Canada (please see directory of Canadian publishers and editors), and the house's United Kingdom branch (contact information for which is listed under the Harlequin listing in the Canadian section). Silhouette Books (a division of Harlequin with editorial offices in New York) is profiled here in a separate subentry further on.

Both Harlequin and Silhouette provide editorial guidelines for writers who wish to submit manuscripts for publishing consideration. Included in these materials are series requirements—including tips for authors regarding plot and character (some of which are applicable to other fiction-genre areas), as well as nuts-and-bolts advice pertaining to the preferred physical properties of manuscripts they review.

Harlequin Books

Harlequin Books is an innovator—not only in the romance category field, but in defining and refining the market for women's fiction in general. The Harlequin enterprise continues to access that important market sector through venues that range from direct marketing to discount-department-store wire racks to the woodgrained shelves of major book-chain superstores.

A précis of the Harlequin Books American lines follows.

Harlequin American Romance is an exciting series of passionate and emotional love stories—contemporary, engrossing, and uniquely American. These are longer, satisfying novels of conflict and challenge, stories of modern men and women dealing with life and love in today's changing world. Harlequin American Romance offers a lineup of contemporary, upbeat, action-packed novels, set in a world where everything is possible—not problem-based or introspective. These stories feature a characteristically self-assured, perceptive American woman as heroine. The hero is a dynamic American man who is irresistible, whether he's rough around the edges, earthy, slick, or sophisticated. Sizzling repartee and one-upmanship are hallmarks of the characters' attraction.

Because romance is all about mystery . . . Harlequin Intrigue offers something unique in the world of romance fiction: a compelling blend of romance, action, and suspense. These complex contemporary stories are chock-full of dynamic drama in the finest Harlequin tradition. Harlequin Intrigue is an exciting presentation of romance within such genre formats as a hidden identity, a woman-in-jeopardy, who did its, and thrillers. The love story is central to the mystery at the level of the novel's premise. The heroine and her hero must be indispensable in solving the mystery or completing whatever adventure they undertake. Their lives are on the line, as are their hearts.

Harlequin Historicals are tales of yesterday written for today's women. This distinctly different line delivers a compelling and quickly paced love story with all the scope of a traditional historical novel. Passionate romance and historical richness combine to give Harlequin Historicals a unique flavor. Harlequin Historicals are conceived as sweeping period romances and range from Medieval sagas to lighthearted Westerns and everything in between. These romance titles should be authentically detailed and realistic (to provide atmosphere, rather than a history lesson). Heroes and heroines are equally strong-willed, with their relationship the focus of the story. The writing should be rich and evocative, with the characters bringing the material alive so that the reader may connect with and appreciate the attributes of the historical setting. The story focus is on the heroine and how one man changes her life forever; the stories must have depth and complexity: subplots and important secondary characters are necessary items here.

Length of manuscript and level of sensuality vary from series to series; contact Harlequin for detailed editorial guidelines. When corresponding with Harlequin, please specify the series for which your manuscript is intended. Query letters and SASEs should be directed to:

Angela Catalano, Associate Editor

Denise O'Sullivan, Associate Senior Editor

Margaret O'Neill Marbury, Editor

Melissa Endlich, Associate Editor

Melissa Jeglinski, Associate Senior Editor—Harlequin American Romance.

Patience Smith, Assistant Editor

Tara Garin, Editorial Director

Tracy Farrell, Senior Editor/Editorial Coordinator—Harlequin Historicals and Steeple Hill Love Inspired.

Silhouette Books

Silhouette Books publishes adult category romances set in a contemporary milieu. Authors must indicate with their submissions for which series their work is intended. Silhouette Books was previously a major competitor of Harlequin Enterprises, its current parent company. A summary of the Silhouette romance lines follows.

Silhouette Romance is the house's original line of romance fiction. Silhouette Romance novels are contemporary, tender, emotional stories for today's reader, featuring the challenges and changes that occur as a couple falls in love. The wonder of a reassuring romance is that it can touch every woman's heart, no matter her age or experience. Although the hero and the heroine do not make love unless married, continuing sexual tension and a strong romantic and emotional awareness keep the reader engaged. Silhouette encourages writers to come up with fresh twists to classic themes, as well as innovative, original stories. New writers are always welcome.

Silhouette Desire is a passionate, powerful, and provocative series with a strong emotional impact. Built on believable situations about how two people grow and develop, the plots capture the intensity of falling in love and explore the emotional and physical aspects of a meaningful relationship. Silhouette Desire accents the sensuous side of romance. These books are written for today's woman, whether innocent or experienced. The conflict should be emotional, springing naturally from within the characters. The characters do not have to be married to make love, but lovemaking is not taken lightly. New slants on classic formulas are welcome. Secondary characters and subplots must blend with the core story.

Silhouette Special Edition novels are substantial, contemporary romances that explore issues that heighten the drama of living and loving through true-to-life characters and compelling, romantic plots. Sophisticated and packed with emotion, these novels are for every woman who dreams of building a home with a very special man. With grace, courage, and determination, each of these vivacious heroines is empowered to be all that she can—lover, wife, mother—as she makes her dreams come true. Sensuality may be sizzling or subtle. The plot can run the gamut from the wildly innovative to the comfortably traditional. The novel's depth and emotional richness should contribute to the overall effect of a very special romance between unforgettable, fully developed characters.

Silhouette Intimate Moments features characters swept into a passionate world that is larger than life. These novels explore new directions by setting the core romance within the framework of today's mainstream novels: glamour, melodrama, suspense, and adventure, even occasionally paranormal. Let your imagination be your guide. Excitement is the key to a successful intimate moment novel. Your reader should be swept along with your characters as emotions run high against the backdrop of a compelling, complex, and always dramatic plot. Manuscript length and other series requirements vary; detailed editorial guidelines are available from the publisher. When querying, please specify the series for which your work is intended. Query letters and SASEs should be directed to:

Ann Leslie Tuttle, Associate Editor

Debra Robertson, Associate Editor

Gail Chasan, Editor

Jennifer Walsh, Associate Editor

Joan Marlow Golan, Senior Editor—Silhouette Desire.

Karen Kosztolnyik, Editor

Karen Taylor Richman, Senior Editor—Silhouette Special Edition.

Kim Nadelson, Assistant Editor

Leslie Wainger, Executive Senior Editor

Lynda Curnyn, Editor

Mary Theresa Hussey, Editor—Silhouette Romance.

Rachel Sharpin, Assistant Editor

Tara Gavin, Editorial Director

Tina Colombo, Assistant Editor

The Editorial Staff, Harlequin/Silhouette/Mills & Boon/Steeple Hill

Born/Sign: Editorial age range is from early 20s to over 50, and we include every sign of the zodiac.

Employment history/editor career path: It varies with the editor. Some of the senior editorial staff have been with the company over 20 years; some of the junior and senior staff have worked at other publishing houses, both in romance publishing and other genres.

Personal interests: Responses include: Reading (of course!); walking; aerobics; fishing; salsa dancing; squash; art and sculpture; theater; architecture; interior design; dining out; psychology; travel; photography; watching television and movies; kids; playing the stock market.

What would you be doing if you were not an editor? Responses include: Unhappy accountant who reads romance at every opportunity; personal trainer and fitness instructor; veterinarian; archaeologist; film camera person; architect; classical actress or drama coach; librarian; teacher; bookstore employee; researcher or producer for a Web site.

What has been your most successful book that you have acquired to date? We are proud of the success of a wide variety of authors who write or have written category romances for one or more of our various series and imprints and of the dedication to their readership that has led to many of our original authors, including some who've gone on to major mainstream success, to continue to contribute to our category lines. The honors garnered by our authors include positions on the *New York Times*, *USA Today,* and *Publishers Weekly* bestseller lists, as well as numerous awards such as the coveted RITA awards bestowed by the Romance Writers of America.

What books have you acquired that make you the most proud? What books that you have acquired reflect the types of books you like to represent? We're proud of all our books, and we're especially proud that in order to satisfy the demands of our readership—to be something beloved and familiar they can rely on, as well as something fresh and unique that will capture their imagination—we've more than doubled our output of incremental offerings during the past 10 years and increased the number of series as well. These devoted readers can count on our books to both celebrate their values and provide a respite from the daily stress and demands of their lives, reinvigorating their spirit. Harlequin celebrated its 50th anniversary in 1999; Silhouette is celebrating its 20th anniversary in 2000, and Mills & Boon has been publishing romance novels for more than 7 decades. Our category publishing activity has steadily increased and continues to be vibrant in 24 languages in more than 100 international markets.

Do you represent fiction? If so, what do you look for? Yes. We are always looking for writers with a distinctive, appealing, and upbeat voice who can create vivid sympathetic characters and offer fresh approaches to the classic romance themes, along with compelling storytelling.

What do you want to see less of? It's not what you do but how you do it—but keep in mind that we are a romance publisher. A happy ending is a must. Also, while there may be other elements in our romance novels, like a mystery or secondary plot, the focus must be on the love story between the hero and heroine. Please note that we do not accept e-mailed submissions or multiple submissions.

Do you represent nonfiction? No. We publish category romance, including inspirational romance, all of which is fiction.

Do you require book proposals? If so, what do you look for in evaluating a book proposal? Yes. We ask for a query letter that includes a word count and pertinent facts about the author as a writer, including familiarity with the romance genre and publishing history, and what series the project is appropriate for, as well as a brief synopsis (no more than two single-spaced pages). When we request a submission, we want to see a complete manuscript from unpublished authors and a proposal consisting of the first three chapters and an outline from published authors. We look for a clear idea of both plot and characters and an exciting new author voice.

Are certain aspects of a book proposal given more weight than others? A distinctive, appealing voice and compelling characterization are distinguishing factors that often get an editor's attention.

H

What process do you use for making a decision? What is the process for acquisition, is there a committee? If the proposal works for us, we ask to see the complete manuscript from unpublished authors and an outline and three sample chapters from previously published authors. The submission may be sent to an outside reader for evaluation before being considered in house. Both an acquiring editor and the senior editor of the series for which the work is targeted have to read and approve the submission in order for it to be bought.

Are you interested in work geared for the masses (readers of *People, The Star,* etc.)? With romance novels comprising close to half of all mass-market books sold, the romance genre continues its decades-long domination of the marketplace. As the world's largest publisher of category romance novels, Harlequin, with its imprints Harlequin, Silhouette, Steeple Hill, Mills & Boon, and its foreign language imprints, constantly strives to meet the needs of our growing marketplace.

Are agents important? Why? Harlequin/Silhouette/Mills & Boon are looking for romance authors with fresh, compelling voices. An agent is not necessary—we consider each and every submission, whether it comes in over the transom or from an agent—but we urge interested authors to research the genre fully and write in for our current guidelines before sending us any material. For over 15 years, most of our lines have requested unagented authors to send query letters with SASEs, while agented authors skip the query letter stage in favor of complete manuscripts (new authors) and proposals (published authors). Both methods have resulted in publication and long-term careers with us for large numbers of authors.

Do you like new writers? What should new writers do to break into the business? Yes! We publish new authors all the time within all of our series. A talented writer will bring her own special magic to whatever type of romance she writes, and a talented editor will discern it.

How should writers approach you? After reviewing our submission requirements on our Web site, eHarlequin.com, or sending in an SASE and request for our guidelines, please send a query letter and 2-page synopsis to the romance series you're targeting. Information can also be obtained from libraries, which often carry writers' guides, and some authors join writers' organizations—one specifically focused on romance writers and writing is Romance Writers of America (RWA).

What are some common mistakes writers make? What really gets on your nerves? Some new writers take too long to get into their story, whereas ideally the reader should be hooked from page one. If the most compelling material is "saved" for chapter 3 or 4, it's too late. Within the shorter category romances, new writers sometimes neglect to focus on the hero and heroine and allot too many pages to minor characters. Too often writers are not aware of our guidelines or lack an understanding of category romance and submit manuscripts that are inappropriate for our series. Swooning, passing out heroines are a thing of the past and are not welcome. We do publish "bodice rippers." New writers will sometimes stagnate because they can't put aside a rejected manuscript and start writing a new one. Be aware that many category writers experience a few rejections before they make their first sale. Our biggest headaches are the result of contracted manuscripts not being delivered in a timely fashion, especially when we aren't given adequate notice of delays.

H

What can writers do to get your attention and to avoid the slush pile? Read widely in the series you've targeted. Research our books before submitting your manuscript. All of our guidelines are available at our Web site, eHarlequin.com. Keep in mind, too, that ultimately it is the emotional appeal of a given story, not its trendiness or lack thereof, that makes it a reader's favorite.

What have been some of your best experiences with writers or in your job? We are proud that authors who were among the original authors for each of our imprints are still writing for us, and that close to 100 of our current authors have published 20 or more books with Harlequin/Silhouette and/or Mills & Boon. We value as well the many letters we get from readers telling us how much our books mean to them and the ways in which our authors' stories have touched and even changed their lives.

What, if anything, makes you different from other editors? The strength of our brand allows us to acquire never-before-published authors and publish them effectively. And while our titles must, of course, always meet our readers' expectations, because we are a unique publisher, we can let authors experiment with stories that never would have been published at a midlist house. We also publish many authors and many books from each author and, therefore, work with her editorially to develop her voice and a successful career. Within category romance, we offer our authors a variety of options to accommodate their particular talents and styles—their books may be contemporary or historical; tender or sexy; short enough to be read in one sitting or longer and more complex; pure romance or romance with elements of mystery, suspense, or paranormal; stand-alone books or miniseries; and in addition to category romance, we also offer authors the opportunity to contribute to short story anthologies and to write single titles that often evolve from a popular miniseries.

Is there anything you would like to see changed in the industry? We'd like to see a heightened perception of the romance genre and an elimination of negative bias against romance. In terms of author relations, we would like to see a timely delivery of manuscripts, as well as a willingness to work with the publisher to find effective solutions to problems.

Any advice for writers? Any way to improve the system for you? Any additional thought? Please keep in mind that inadequately thought-through or unsalable submissions take up significant editorial time and lengthen response time. Authors who are responsive to reader tastes and present polished, professionally presented material avoid this.

H

HARPERCOLLINS PUBLISHERS

Avon

Basic Books

HarperBusiness

HarperCollins Children's Books

HarperCollins San Francisco

HarperCollins Trade Division

HarperEntertainment

HarperPerennial

HarperPrism

Harper Reference

Rayo

ReganBooks

Westview Press

William Morrow

New York offices:
10 East 53rd Street, New York, NY 10022-5299
212-207-7000
www.harpercollins.com

HarperCollins Publishers offers a program that spans a full spectrum of commercial, trade, professional, and academic interests within a number of interlocked divisions (located on both the East and West Coasts, as well as in the Rockies). HarperCollins projects are released in hardcover and paperback, as well as multimedia editions.

Among the HarperCollins East Coast American components are HarperPerennial (trade paper originals and reprints) and HarperPaperback (mass-market). A special high-concept HarperCollins program is the ReganBooks imprint.

HarperLibros publishes a wide range of works in the Spanish language. HarperCollins is home to a number of children's-book and reference divisions. (See separate subentries further on.)

The HarperCollins San Francisco wing features the HarperSanFrancisco division, with its special emphasis on trade titles in spirituality, awareness, and healing (please see HarperSanFrancisco entry in the directory of Religious, Spiritual, and Inspirational publishers).

Westview Press accents scholarly and academic works, with some trade crossover. HarperCollins also owns Hazelden Publishing Group and Zondervan (see entries for Hazelden and Zondervan in the directory of Religious, Spiritual, and Inspirational publishers).

HarperCollins Publishers is the current corporate embodiment of the venerable firm (founded in 1817) previously known as Harper & Row. HarperCollins is part of Rupert Murdoch's transnational communications empire, which includes the *New York Post* newspaper and Twentieth Century Fox. For all its international divisions, imprints, and subsidiaries, HarperCollins is a publishing colossus with a well-defined image: The house's flaming-torch logo signifies a reputation for superior editorial quality and mighty commercial carriage.

In 1996, George Craig, President and Chief Executive Officer, HarperCollins Publishers, issued a corporate mandate: HarperCollins intends to meet the unprecedented challenges that face the publishing industry and is committed to being an organization that leads in those behaviors and practices critical to shared success. In order to achieve this goal, HarperCollins has embarked on an initiative called Vision & Values. At the core of this initiative is our Vision Statement:

Our goal is to be the world's best publisher, a growth company with excellence in products, customer service, and financial performance. We will treat each other, our authors, customers, and business partners with care, integrity, and respect. We will attract and retain the best people by creating an environment where managers act as leaders and coaches and all employees are encouraged to develop and excel. We will face reality and embrace change in all aspects of our business life.

Within months of these 1996 declarations George Craig was replaced. To engage corporate challenges head on, Anthea Disney, President and Chief Executive Officer Harper-Collins, announced realignment of the trade-publishing wing as well as elimination of former HarperCollins divisions HarperReference and BasicBooks (including the firing of all HarperReference and BasicBooks editors). HarperCollins then announced cancellation of a major portion of its list, in order to concentrate on the books most worthy of editorial and marketing resources.

The trade group was synthesized into three primary divisions, each with its own entrepreneurial mission: HarperCollins Trade (commercial nonfiction and fiction); Harper-Business (top-of-the-list nonfiction in business and finance); HarperPrism (thrillers, suspense fiction). BasicBooks was sold to Perseus Books Group in 1997.

HarperCollins handles its own distribution. Query letters and SASEs should be directed to:

Carolyn Marino, Vice President, Editorial Director, HarperCollins—Commercial fiction, including mysteries, suspense, and women's fiction.

Laura Cifelli, Editor, HarperPaperbacks—Mass-market fiction: women's stories, romances.

Leslie Stern, Associate Editor, HarperPaperbacks—Women's fiction, romances, nonfiction.

Adrian Zackheim, Associate Publisher/HarperCollins; Editor in Chief/Senior Vice President/Harper Information

Born: 9/19/51.

Education: B.A., Grinnell College, M.A., University of Toronto.

Employment history/editor career path: 1975–1977, Assistant at Putnam; 1977–1979, Associate Editor at St. Martin's Press; 1979–1985, Editor/Senior Editor at Doubleday; 1986–1994, Senior Editor/Editorial Director at William Morrow & Co.; 1994–present, President at HarperCollins.

Personal interests: Family, exercise, travel, computers.

What would you be doing if you were not an editor? Writing, teaching.

What has been your most successful book that you have acquired to date? *Mayo Clinic Family Health Book.*

What books have you acquired that make you the most proud? What books that you have acquired reflect the types of books you like to represent? *Love & Profit* by Jim Astry; *Head to Head* by Lester Thurow; *Critical Cave* by Rick Dooling; *In Her Defense* by Stephen Horn; *Consulting Demons* by Lewis Pincultt; *If the Gods Had Meant for Us to Vote They'd Have Seven Us Candidates* by Jim Hightower; *The Year of Living Dangerously* by Christopher Koch.

Do you represent fiction? If so, what do you look for? Yes. Voice, character, idea.

Do you represent nonfiction? Yes.

Do you require book proposals? If so, what do you look for in evaluating a book proposal? Love the idea, capacity to write, plot form.

Are certain aspects of a book proposal given more weight than others? It depends.

Are you interested in work geared for the masses (readers of *People, The Star,* etc.)? Yes.

Are agents important? Why? Yes. They help the author focus on the work. A good agent improves communication and helps resolve conflict.

Do you like new writers? What should new writers do to break into the business? Yes. Keep at it!

How should writers approach you? Query or e-mail.

What are some common mistakes writers make? What really gets on your nerves? Follow-up calls in less than a week.

What can writers do to get your attention and to avoid the slush pile? Address query letter to an editor by name.

HarperBusiness

HarperBusiness heralds the latest trends of thought in such fields as management, finance, and international business. Business books from HarperCollins are most often (but not always) presented under the HarperBusiness banner. The HarperCollins business list is distinguished by gifted, individualistic author voices geared to attract a wide popular readership in addition to interested business professionals. HarperCollins also releases comprehensive and specifically targeted professional reference works and career how-to's.

On the HarperCollins business list: *Winning Everyday* by Lou Holtz; *Behind Enemy Lines: A Mossad Combatant's Guide to Business Conduct* by Gerald Westerby; *The Interpretation of Financial Statements: The Classic 1937 Edition* by Benjamin Graham and Spencer B. Meredith (introduction by Michael F. Price); *On the Firing Line: My 500 Days at Apple Computer* by Gil Amelio and William Simon; *Thoughts of Chairman Buffett: Thirty Years of Unconventional Wisdom from the Sage of Omaha* (compiled by Simon Reynolds); *The E-Myth Manager: Why Management Doesn't Work—And What to Do About It* by Michael E. Gerber; *Getting It Done: Even When You're Not in Charge* by Roger Fisher and Alan Sharp; *How Hits Happen: Forecasting Predictability in a Chaotic Marketplace* by Winslow Farrell.

Query letters and SASEs should be directed to:

Adrian Zackheim, Senior Vice President and Publisher—Business books; general nonfiction.

David Conti, Executive Editor—Investment subjects, nonfiction business stories.

Joe Veltre, Editor—General business.

HarperCollins Children's Books

HarperCollins Children's Books produces hardcovers, paperbacks, and novelty titles in fiction and nonfiction for all readership levels, from preschool through young adult.

HarperCollins Children's Books does not currently accept unsolicited picture book manuscripts.

HarperCollins children's titles include: *Today I Feel Silly* by Jamie Lee Curtis; *Ella Enchanted* by Gail Carson Levine; *Zoom City* by Thacher Hue; and *If You Give a Pig a Pancake* by Laura Numeroff.

Favorites from the backlist: *Charlotte's Web* by E. B. White; *Goodnight Moon* by Margaret Wise Brown; and *Where the Wild Things Are* by Maurice Sendak.

Query letters, manuscripts, and SASEs regarding novels should be directed to:

Alix Reid, Executive Editor

Joanna Cotler, Senior Vice President and Publisher—Joanna Cotler Books.

Kate Morgan Jackson, Senior Vice President, Associate Publisher, and Editor in Chief

Laura Geringer, Senior Vice President and Publisher—Laura Geringer Books.

Emily Brenner, Editorial Director—HarperFestival.

Phoebe Yeh, Editorial Director

Robert Warren, Editorial Director

Elise Howard, Vice President and Director of Paperback Publishing

Susan Hirschman, Greenwillow Books—Senior Vice President and Publisher

Barbara Lalicki, Senior Vice President and Editorial Director

HarperCollins San Francisco

353 Sacramento Street, Suite 500, San Francisco, CA 94111
415-477-4400

HarperCollins San Francisco incorporates several California-based divisions. HarperCollins San Francisco International Editions publishes imported original titles and reprints originating from HarperCollins divisions outside the U.S. sphere (Australia, New Zealand, South Africa, Canada, and the United Kingdom).

The former imprint Collins Publishers San Francisco moved in the fall of 1996 to New York and combined with HarperStyle to form the illustrated division of HarperCollins Trade.

HarperSanFrancisco (please see the Directory of Religious, Spiritual, and Inspirational Publishers) is a general publishing house with a list that accents books that inspire the mind, body, and spirit, as well as trends in world culture.

Renee Sedliar, Assistant Editor, HarperSanFrancisco

Born: October 28, 1970.

Education: B.A., English and Liberal Arts; M.A., Fine Arts and Creative Writing from the University of Michigan.

Employment history/editor career path: I came to HarperSanFrancisco through a temp. agency and have now been working here for three and a half years.

Personal interests: Reading, writing, poetry, working out, sports.

What would you be doing if you were not an editor? I would teach creative writing on a high school or undergraduate level.

What has been your most successful book that you have acquired to date? I'm new in the Editor position, but I have worked with other editors to acquire successful books.

What books have you acquired that make you the most proud? What books that you have acquired reflect the types of books you like to represent? I'm currently working on *Meditation Secrets for Women, The Healing Companion,* and *Fruit Fresh,* a book of meditations and exercises for women writers.

Do you represent fiction? If so, what are you looking for? We do very little fiction; it must have a spiritual angle.

Do you represent nonfiction? Yes, women's issues, spirituality, religion, inspirational memoirs.

Do you require book proposals? If so, what do you look for in evaluating a book proposal? Yes, I do require book proposals. I look for clarity, directness of purpose, creativity, how well authors know what they want to do (where they are going), good outline, author credentials, and sample material.

Are certain aspects of a book proposal given more weight than others? It's on a per-project basis—author credentials, sample chapters.

What process do you use for making a decision? What is the process for acquisition, is there a committee? Yes, we have weekly meetings with a committee composed of the editorial staff, publicity people, marketing people, and the publisher. Before presenting it to the committee, I will usually have a couple of other editors read it to get their feedback also.

Are you interested in work geared for the masses (readers of *People, The Star,* etc.)? Yes and no. Yes, we look for projects that will appeal to a large audience, but I would say no if it would compress the quality of the material.

Are agents important? Why? Yes, they make the whole publishing process go much smoother. They know which editors to send what projects to, and they help authors to understand the publishing business.

Do you like new writers? What should new writers do to break into the business? Yes, I champion the underdog. I would say to break into the business, you need to get a good agent and pay attention to the market.

How should writers approach you? A query letter with SASE. Or—flowers, chocolate, and so on, can always do the trick as well.

What are some common mistakes writers make? What really gets on your nerves? It gets on my nerves when authors act like their book is the only one in the world. As editors we have other books and authors to work with and deadlines to meet as well.

What can writers do to get your attention and to avoid the slush pile? Have a topic that catches my attention or write about something that appeals to me. If it doesn't appeal to me but I know of a colleague that it does, I will pass it on to him or her. I do try to read everything that comes across my desk.

What have been some of your craziest experiences with submissions? I've received some proposals with strangely creative content. Mostly in the New Age category—making outrageous claims along the lines of things you would find in the tabloids/*Weekly World News.*

What have been some of your best experiences with writers or in your job? When things go smoothly and work out and when the authors are wonderful to work with. Working with authors I like personally and professionally.

Any advice for writers? Be conscientious, be neat and careful, pay attention to the market and whom you are sending material to, don't waste valuable time, and realize that there is a lot of work involved in writing a book.

Gideon Weil, Associate Editor, HarperSanFrancisco
  Born: August 16, 1971.
  Education: Vassar College—English Major.
  Employment history/editor career path: I started out working at New York Press. I then worked at Witherspoon Associates as a literary agent for four years, and I have now been at HarperSanFrancisco for seven months.
  Personal interests: Being outside, watching sports, and reading.
  What would you be doing if you were not an editor? Running a small restaurant.
  What has been your most successful book that you have acquired to date? None have been published yet.
  What books have you acquired that make you the most proud? What books that you have acquired reflect the types of books you like to represent? *Seeking Peace* by Scott Hunt; *Forgive for Good* by Dr. Frederick Luskin.
  Do you represent fiction? We do acquire some fiction, but not very much.
  Do you represent nonfiction? Yes, inspiration, self-help, narrative nonfiction.
  Do you require book proposals? If so, what do you look for in evaluating a book proposal? Yes, I like to see the structure of the book, sample chapters, outline, and tell me where it fits in the marketplace.
  Are certain aspects of a book proposal given more weight than others? Sample chapters.
  What process do you use for making a decision? What is the process for acquisition, is there a committee? Yes, it consists of the publisher, editorial staff, and marketing and sales people.
  What kinds of nonfiction books do you want to see less of? Random memoirs with no direction.
  Are you interested in work geared for the masses (readers of *People, The Star,* etc.)? Yes, in *People* in particular, there are inspirational stories.
  Are agents important? Why? Yes. Good agents make everything run smoothly.
  Do you like new writers? What should new writers do to break into the business? Yes. Be confident writing for an audience and know who your audience is. Read books. Know how to effectively get your point across to the reader. Take your time. Know why you are writing. Sell yourself in two paragraphs.
  How should writers approach you? Send a query letter with SASE. I would rather have proposals sent to me through agents.
  What are some common mistakes writers make? What really gets on your nerves? Laziness, putting little thought into something.
  What can writers do to get your attention and to avoid the slush pile? Write good, clear, concise cover letters. Put your best foot forward.
  What have been some of your craziest experiences with submissions? After I have rejected a project, having family members call and convince me of why I am making a mistake.

H

What have been some of your best experiences with writers or in your job? Creating the author and editor relationship is the most fulfilling part of my job.

What, if anything, makes you different from other editors? I make myself available to the author, I'm conscientious, I come from the agent side so I know what is important to authors. I can negotiate and know what the common problems are that writers have and know how to effectively solve them.

Is there anything you would like to see changed in the industry? I would like to see publishers work together more and for books to have a longer shelf-life.

Any advice for writers? Be aggressive, sell yourself, get an agent. Nothing will happen if you are passive in this business; be aggressive but don't nag.

HarperCollins Trade Division

HarperCollins produces adult hardcover books, trade paperbacks, and mass-market paperback editions that cover the breadth of trade publishing categories, including feature biographies (celebrity, sports, and historical), business books, mysteries and thrillers, popular culture, humor, inspiration, and how-to (including cookbooks and health), in addition to works across most popular reference categories. HarperStyle specializes in illustrated works keyed to contemporary lifestyle, design, and culture. Many HarperCollins frontlist titles are also available on HarperAudio.

Representing HarperCollins' general nonfiction and popular titles: *Ghosts of Manila: The Fateful Blood Feud Between Muhammad Ali and Joe Frazier* by Mark Kram; *Country Matters: The Pleasures and Tribulations of Moving from a Big City to an Old Country Farmhouse* by Michael Korda; *Racing the Antelope: What Animals Can Teach Us About Running and Life* by Bernd Heinrich; *Just for Fun: The Story of an Accidental Revolutionary* by Linus Torvalds with David Diamond; *Vegetarian Classics* by Jeanne Lemlin; *The Grrl Genius Guide to Life: A Twelve Step Program on How to Become a Grrl Genius According to Me* by Cathryn Michon; *The Real Age Diet: Make Yourself Younger with What You Eat* by Michael F. Roizen, M.D., and John La Puma, M.D.; *American Terrorist: Timothy McVeigh and the Oklahoma City Bombings* by Lou Michael and Dan Herbeck; *Jackie Style* by Pamela Clarke Keogh; *Chi Fitness: A Workout for Mind, Body and Spirit* by Sue Benton and Drew Denbaum; *Rulers of Evil: Useful Knowledge About Governing Bodies* by F. Tupper Saussy; *No Apparent Danger: The True Story of a Volcano's Deadly Power* by Victoria Bruce; *The Twelve Gifts of Birth* by Charlene Costanzo; *Sherman: A Soldier's Life* by Lee Kennett; *A Voyage for Madmen* by Peter Nichols; and *Beyond the Grave: the Right and Wrong Way of Leaving Money to Your Children (and Others)* by Gerald M. Condon, Esq., and Jeffrey L. Condon, Esq.

HarperCollins offers fiction and literary works on a diversified program that includes commercial novels and standout category titles, in addition to select literary works. Harper Collins has published such authors as Anne Rivers Siddons, Ursula K. Le Guin, Sue Miller, Len Deighton, Allen Ginsberg, Barbara Taylor Bradford, Oscar Hijuelos, Tony Hillerman, Leon Uris, and William Lashner. HarperPrism is the imprint designation for selected high-concept titles in science fiction, fantasy, horror, and thrillers.

Fiction from HarperCollins: *Soul Mountain* by Gao Xingjian (translated from the Chinese by Dr. Mable Lee); *The Shark Mutiny* by Patrick Robinson; *Thief of Time* by Terry Pratchett; *A King's Ransom* by James Grippando; *Who's Afraid of Virginia Ham?* by Phyllis Richman; *Bel Canto* by Ann Patchett; *Sharpe's Trafalgar* by Bernard Cornwell; *Down by the Water* by Caroline Upcher; *A Mulligan for Bobby Joe* by Bob Cullen; *A Theory of Relativity* by Jacquelyn Mitchard; *The Catsitters* by James Wolcott; *Where We Lived* by Christina Fitzpatrick.

The HarperPaperbacks program includes a strong lineup in mystery, suspense, and thrillers (primarily reprints, along with a few originals). HarperPaperbacks also publishes a select number of mass-market true crime titles, as well as a few hardcover originals in commercial fiction genres. HarperMonogram is a mass-market imprint that specializes in women's fiction, including historical romances, time-travel, and commercial contemporaries.

Query letters and SASEs should be directed to:

Carrie Feron, Editor—Commercial fiction and nonfiction.

David Hirshey, Executive Editor—Popular culture, celebrity books, politics, current affairs.

Gladys Justin Carr, Associate Publisher—Fiction: literary and commercial. Nonfiction: biographies and memoirs, military and general history, nutrition, medicine, celebrity stories, popular culture, true crime, sports, current events, business.

Harriet Bell, Editor—Cookbooks.

Hugh Van Dusen, Executive Editor, HarperPerennial—History, biography, spirituality, self-help. Fiction and nonfiction reprints and originals in quality paperback.

Lawrence Ashmead, Executive Editor—Fiction: mysteries, thrillers. Nonfiction: biographies and autobiographies, gardening, general self-help.

Mauro DiPreta, Executive Editor, HarperEntertainment—Nonfiction: pop-culture, humor, commercial nonfiction.

Megan Newman, Editor—General nonfiction, how-to, self-help trade paperback originals.

Robert Jones, Executive Editor, HarperPerennial—Quality literary fiction. Nonfiction: social issues, current affairs, psychology.

Susan Friedland, Executive Editor—Food, cookbooks, literary history.

Terry Karten, Executive Editor—Quality literary and commercial women's fiction. Nonfiction: biographies and autobiographies, history, current issues, women's issues.

Edwin Tan, Associate Editor—Business and other nonfiction narratives, business and general humor, motivation/self-help/advice, the arts, sex and sexuality, social studies, and general fiction.

Susan Weinberg, Editor—General fiction and nonfiction.

Tim Duggan, Senior Editor—Serious nonfiction, literary fiction.

H

Tom Dupre, Senior Editor—Rock biographies, comic novels.

Dan Conaway, Executive Editor

HarperPrism

HarperPrism concentrates on commercial, high-concept thrillers and hones the leading edge in frontlist suspense fiction. HarperPrism has produced a limited selection of popular nonfiction with a contemporary-to-futurist bent. HarperPrism fiction and literary works cover a select group of suspense and thriller categories and modes: fantasy and science fiction, technical thrillers, medical thrillers, action tales and adventure novels, military fiction, mystery and suspense fiction, occasional outstanding horror. Nonfiction areas of interest include: popular science, history and future of science and technology, topical commentary, and unexplained phenomena (including UFOs and the like). Query letters and SASEs should be directed to:

Caitlin Blasdell, Editor—HarperPrism. Science fiction, fantasy, media tie-ins, techno-thrillers.

Lois Brown, Senior Editor—HarperHorizon. Brand-related publishing; for example, sport franchises, consumer goods companies.

Mike Campbell, Director of Product Development—HarperPrism/HarperHorizon. Media-related merchandise, including calendars, maps, games.

Pat Teberg, Director of Brand Publishing—HarperHorizon. Brand-related publishing; for example, sport franchises, consumer goods companies.

ReganBooks

ReganBooks, the imprint of publishing virtuoso Judith Regan, hosts a selective list of general nonfiction and fiction. The house scouts properties with bestseller and high commercial promise, as well as serious literary merit. Nonfiction categories include personality, politics medical, self-help, style, science humor, biography, how-to, adventure, spirituality, history, cooking, and memoir. In fiction, the house ranges from extremely commercial high-concept novels to serious fiction —with a special emphasis on projects with television or film potential.

Recent nonfiction includes: *The Soy Zone: 101 Delicious and Easy-to-Prepare Recipes* by Barry Sears, Ph.D.; *The 7 O'Clock Bedtime: Early to Bed, Early to Rise, Makes a Child Playful, Healthy and Wise* by Inda Schaenen; *What Is a Man?* by Waller R. Newell; *How to Manage Your Mother: Understanding the Most Difficult, Complicated, and Fascinating Relationship in Your Life* by Alyce Faye Cleese and Brian Bates; *Hawk* by Tony Hawk with Sean Mortimer; *The 30 Day Total Health Makeover* by Marilu Henner; *The Dirt: Confessions of the World's Most Notorious Rock Band* by Motley Crue; *Digital Hustlers: Living Large and Falling Hard in Silicon Valley* by Casey Kait and Stephen Weiss; *Dark City Dames* by Eddie Muller; *Trust No One* by Dave Navarro with Neil Strauss; *What Color Is Your Diet?* by David Heber, M.D., Ph.D., with Susan Bowerman;

Every Mistake in the Book: A Business How-NOT-to by F. J. Lennon; *Cooking Thin with Chef Kathleen* by Kathleen Daelemans.

Regan fiction: *I Know This Much Is True* by Wally Lamb; *Wicked: The Life and Times of the Wicked Witch of the West* and *Confessions of an Ugly Stepsister* by Gregory Maguire; *Getting Over It* by Anna Maxted; *Microserfs* and *Girlfriend in a Coma* by Douglas Coupland; and *These Is My Words* by Nancy Turner.

Query letters and SASEs should be directed to:

Judith Regan, President and Publisher

Calvert Morgan, Editorial Director

Doug Corcoran, Editor—Health subjects.

Westview Press

5500 Central Avenue, Boulder, CO 80301-2877
303-444-3541   fax: 303-449-3356
www.westviewpress.com   e-mail: westview@harpercollins.com

Westview's publishing interests include works of nonfiction for the general trade readership, in addition to the hefty Westview list in college texts, reference materials, and professional academic publications. Westview is known for its scholarly lines in social sciences, international relations, area studies, domestic and international development, military affairs, political science, history, anthropology, sociology, government, economics, philosophy, religion, communication, criminology, law, environment, and energy.

Titles representative of Westview: *Extinct Humans* by Ian Tattersall and Jeffrey Schwartz; *Comeback Cities: A Blueprint for Urban Neighborhood Revival* by Paul Grogan and Tony Proscio; *Madeleine Albright and the New American Diplomacy* by Thomas Lippman; *The Perpetual Prisoner Machine: How America Profits from Crime* by Joel Dyer; *Fire in the Sky: The Air War in the South Pacific* by Eric Bergerud; *Through the Eyes of Innocents: Children Witness World War II* by Emmy E. Werner; *Inside Sudan: Political Islam, Conflict, and Catastrophe* by Donald Petterson.

Westview Press is a member of the Perseus Books Group, accenting scholarly and academic works for professionals and works in related topics geared for a popular readership. Westview catalogs numerous mainstream-interest titles in current affairs and popular culture. In addition to its Colorado operation, the Westview enterprise (founded in 1975) includes a vast United Kingdom division and additional offices in San Francisco and New York. Query letters and SASEs should be directed to:

Jill Rothenberg, Editor

Carol Jones, Associate Editor—History, Europe/Russia, Jewish studies, Asia.

David Perrin, Editor

Cass Canfield, ICON imprint—Art, architecture, and art history.

Karl Yambert, Senior Editor

Sarah Warner, Editor—Film studies, religion, philosophy.

H

THE HARVARD COMMON PRESS

535 Albany Street, Boston, MA 02118
617-423-5803   fax: 617-695-9794

Harvard Common Press accents trade nonfiction in the areas of food, home and the family, small-business guides, travel, and lifestyle, and in addition offers a select list of children's books.

The Harvard Common Press (founded in 1976) is a smaller house devoted to the publication of general nonfiction books in hardcover and trade paperback; the press maintains a solid backlist. The company colophon features a representation of a classical javelin thrower on the run—emblematic of the house's athletic publishing vigor.

Harvard Common issues the Best Places to Stay series as part of its travel line; the Gambit Books imprint covers how-to business titles geared to starting up and operating enterprises such as small restaurants, small newspapers, and small theaters, as well as alternative careers for teachers. Parenting and the family are sectors where Harvard Common shows particular traditional success.

Titles: *The Italian American Cookbook: A Feast of Food from a Great American Cooking Tradition* by John Mariani and Galina Mariani; *Starting a Small Restaurant: Revised Edition* by Daniel Miller; *Buller's Professional Course in Bartending for Home Study* by John Buller; *The Blue Strawberry Cookbook: Cooking (Brilliantly) Without Recipes* and *Another Blue Strawberry: More Brilliant Cooking Without Recipes* by James Haller; *Norman Van Aken's Feast of Sunlight: 200 Inspired Recipes from the Master of New World Cuisine* by Norman Van Aken; *The Best Quick Breads* by Beth Hansperger; *The Bread Lover's Bread Machine Cookbook* by Beth Hansperger; *The Butterfly Garden: Turning Your Garden, Window Box, or Backyard into a Beautiful Home for Butterflies* by Matthew Tekulsky; *The Dictionary of American Bird Names* by Dr. Ernest A. Choate; *The Hummingbird Garden* by Matthew Tekulsky; *You and Your Newborn Baby: A Guide to the First Months After Birth* by Linda Todd, M.P.H.; *The VBAC Companion: The Expectant Mother's Guide to Vaginal Birth After Cesarean* by Diana Korte; *Essential Exercises for Breast Cancer Survivors* by Amy Halverstadt and Andrea Leonard.

The Harvard Common Press is represented to the trade by National Book Network. Query letters and SASEs should be directed to:

Bruce Shaw, President

Pam Hoenig, Executive Editor

H

HEALTH COMMUNICATIONS, INC.

3201 Southwest 15th Street, Deerfield Beach, FL 33442
954-360-0909   fax: 954-360-0034
www.hci-online.com

Health Communications features nonfiction trade titles in relationships, finance, spirituality, health, empowerment, esteem, and social issues. The publisher has achieved notable success with topical approaches to personal growth, women's issues, addiction and other compulsive behaviors, abuse and trauma, family relationships, and healing.

Health Communications (founded in 1976) publishes with the intent to provide direction for the journey of living. The publisher's issue-orientation is apparent in a list that addresses a family spectrum of interest, encompassing books geared to be read by early readers through adults, as well as targeted market interest segments. Health Communications publishes books in affordable hardcover and trade paperback editions and also produces a line of audiobooks.

Health Communications operates in tandem with sister companies US Journal, US Journal Training, A & D Publications, and Children Are People Too! The program brings together professional caregivers and the broader community in a publishing forum that embraces books, journals, pamphlets, and conferences.

Exemplifying the Health Communications list: *Addictive Relationships: Reclaiming Your Boundaries* by Joy Miller; *An Adult Child's Guide to What's Normal* by John Friel, Ph.D., and Linda Friel, M.A.; *Before It's Too Late: Helping Women in Controlling an Abusive Relationship* by Robert J. Ackerman, Ph.D., and Susan E. Pickering; *Healing the Human Condition* by Charles L. Whitfield; *Healing the Child Within: Discovering and Recovery for Adult Children of Dysfunctional Families* by Charles L. Whitfield; *Gentle Reminders for Co-Dependents* by Mitzi Chandler; *From the First Bite: A Complete Guide to Recovery from Food Addiction* by Kay Sheppard; *Learning to Love Yourself* by Sharon Wegscheider-Cruise; *Lifeskills for Adult Children* by Janet Woilitz, Ed.D., and Alan Gurner, M.A.; *Perfect Daughters: Adult Daughters of Alcoholics* by Robert J. Ackerman; *Time for Joy* by Ruth Fishel; *Eternal Blessings* by Brahma Kurmaris; *Pearls of Wisdom* by Dadi Janki; *The Soulful Money Manual: 9 Keys to Being Effective, Happy and at Peace with Money* by Richard Mitz; *Becoming a Father* by John L. Hart, Ph.D.; *Fun Facts About Cats* and *Fun Facts About Dogs* by Richard Torregrossa; *How to Change Your Life* by Ernest Holmes and Michael Beckwith; *Lives Charmed: Intimate Conversations with Extraordinary People* by Linda Sivertsen; *Taste Berries for Teens* by Bettie B. Youngs, Ph.D., and Jennifer Leigh Youngs; *Struggle for Intimacy* by Janet C. Woitiz; *The Lost Boy* by Dave Pelzer; *Healing Shame That Binds You* by John Bradshaw; *The Flying Boy: Healing the Wounded Man* by John Lee; *Choicemaking: For Spirituality Seekers, Co-Dependents and Adult Children* by Sharon Wegscheider-Cruse; *A Child Called It: An Abused Child's Journey from Victim to Victor* by Dave Pelzer; *The 7 Worst Things Parents Can Do* by John C. Friel, Ph.D., and Linda D. Friel, M.A.; and *Bradshaw On: The Family, Revised Edition* by John Bradshaw.

Health Communications published *Chicken Soup for the Soul: 101 Stories to Open the Heart and Rekindle the Spirit* (written and compiled by Jack Canfield and Mark Victor Hansen), an entertaining, uplifting work that features selections from a wide variety of writers. As this book goes to press, the original *Chicken Soup* has been an international bestseller for several years. This book has spawned a number of successful *Chicken Soup* collections. Indeed, if imitation is the sincerest form of flattery, the number of works with allied themes that currently appear under other publishers' imprints is a genuine tribute from the industry to this popular genre originated by the authors and Health Communications. More titles in this series: *Chicken Soup for the Christian Soul: 101 Stories to Open the Heart and Rekindle the Spirit* by Jack Canfield, Mark Victor Hansen, Patty Aubery,

H

and Nancy Mitchell; *Chicken Soup for the Woman's Soul: 101 Stories to Open the Hearts and Rekindle the Spirits of Women* by Jack Canfield, Mark Victor Hansen, Jennifer Read Hawthorne, and Marci Shimoff; *Condensed Chicken Soup for the Soul* by Jack Canfield, Mark Victor Hansen, and Patty Hansen; *Chicken Soup for the Soul at Work: 101 Stories of Courage, Compassion & Creativity in the Workplace* by Jack Canfield, Mark Victor Hansen, Martin Rutte, Maida Rogerson, and Tim Clauss.

In the tradition of *Chicken Soup for the Soul,* Health Communications also publishes *Chicken Soup for Little Souls.* Each captivating book introduces a wondrous story revealing sincere messages of kindness and generosity for ages 4–8. Titles include: *Chicken Soup for Little Souls: The Never-Forgotten Doll* by Jack Canfield and Mark Victor Hansen (illustrated by Mary O'Keefe Young); *Chicken Soup for Little Souls: The Goodness Gorillas* by Jack Canfield and Mark Victor Hansen (illustrated by Pat Porter); *Chicken Soup for Little Souls: The Best Night Out with Dad* by Jack Canfield and Mark Victor Hansen (illustrated by Bert Dodson).

Health Communications distributes its own list, as well as those of its sister companies US Journal, Children Are People Too!, US Journal Training, and A & D Publications. Query letters and SASEs should be directed to:

Allison Janse, Senior Editor

Lisa Drucker, Senior Editor

Susan Tobias, Editor

Christine Belleris, Editorial Director
   Sign: Leo.
   Education: B.A., Journalism, from the University of Colorado.
   Employment history/editor career path: I have always been interested in reading and writing. After I graduated from college, I was a Legislative Assistant for a U.S. congressman in Washington, D.C., for about four years. I decided I didn't want to stay in politics, so I started doing freelance work for *The Colorado Statesman.* I then moved to Boca Raton, Florida, and started working at Sirs, publishing research material. I then came to Health Communications and have been here for about six and a half years.
   Personal interests: Reading, writing, bicycling; I have a two-year-old and a new baby on the way.
   What would you be doing if you were not an editor? I would be a travel writer.
   What has been your most successful book that you have acquired to date? *The Schwarz Bein Principal.*
   What book have you acquired that makes you the most proud? What books that you have acquired reflect the types of books you like to represent? *The Tom Trap* and *Aristotle Would Have Liked Oprah.*
   Do you represent fiction? If so, what do you look for? Yes, we do occasionally, but not much. Visionary fiction, New Age.
   Do you represent nonfiction? Yes, self-help, books for teenagers, books on healthy aging, and anything that is new and different.
   Do you require book proposals? If so, what do you look for in evaluating a book proposal? Yes, I look for two sample chapters, a table of contents, a detailed pro-

H

file of the author, and marketing ideas. It has to be well written, neat, and follow our guidelines.

Are certain aspects of a book proposal given more weight than others? It helps if the author is an expert in his/her field, but we use a strategy known as HART. H stands for healing. A is affirming or positive. R stands for whether the material is readable. T is timely. We need the proposal to meet all of these categories.

What process do you use for making a decision? What is the process for acquisition, is there a committee? We use the HART system and, yes, we have a committee. The committee meets once a month and consists of staff from sales, marketing, and the editorial department.

What kinds of nonfiction books do you want to see less of? Personal memoirs that can't help a general audience.

Are you interested in work geared for the masses (readers of *People, The Star,* etc.)? Yes.

Are agents important? Why? Yes, they are very important. They bring a higher caliber of authors and manuscripts to us. They can "weed-out" all the material that is not what we're looking for.

Do you like new writers? What should new writers do to break into the business? Yes, we're always looking for new writers. I would say to join a writers group and try to publish some work in periodicals.

How should writers approach you? First send me a query letter in the mail. If I like the material, I will call you to request the manuscript.

What are some common mistakes that writers make? What really gets on your nerves? When people call after you've asked them not to call. Most authors don't realize just how busy editors are. When authors don't do their homework and send me material that we don't even publish (i.e., poetry). When authors send unsolicited material without an SASE and expect that we will return it. We read unsolicited material as a courtesy, not as an obligation.

What can writers do to get your attention and to avoid the slush pile? The way to get my attention is to send a professional-looking package with a well-written proposal inside.

What have been some of your craziest experiences with submissions? Getting gifts with the submissions. I've gotten everything from cookies, to stuffed animals, gum, rocks, you name it. A colleague of mine once received a dozen red roses.

What have been some of your best experiences with writers or in your job? Getting to know people. I always have good professional advice in this profession (diet, therapy). I'm always learning new things and I love to develop a wonderful relationship with the authors.

What, if anything, makes you different from other editors? I'm a good listener and am good at compromise. It's important in this job and business that you are willing to "bend" a little.

Is there anything that you would like to see changed in the industry? I would like to see less consolidating of bookstores, I like the independent bookstores.

Any advice for writers? Be persistent. Don't get discouraged because one person turned you down, and get many different viewpoints.

H

THE HEARST BOOK GROUP

The entire Hearst Book Group was acquired by HarperCollins in late 1999.

HILL STREET PRESS, LLC

191 East Broad Street, Suite 209, Athens, GA 30601-2848
fax: 706-613-7204
www.hillstreetpress.com

Hill Street Press was founded in May 1998 and currently has 35 titles in print. Hill Street Press is a publisher of regional focus and international interest. We plan to increase our number of literary and popular fiction titles, ranging from the hard-edged to the homespun, as our backlist grows. HSP is particularly interested in nonfiction titles of various kinds, particularly contemporary issues. We do not publish children's or juvenile literature, science fiction, or romance. We are nationally and internationally distributed through LCP/InBook and Source Books and sell to all major chains and independents, as well as through the major e-commerce outlets.

Representative titles include: *Before Scarlet: Girlhood Writings of Margaret Mitchell* by Margaret Mitchell; *Bevelyn Blair's Everyday Cakes* by Bevelyn Blair; *Special Kay: The Wisdom of Terry Kay* by Terry Kay; *Celestine Sibley: A Granddaughter's Reminiscence* by Celestine Sibley Fleming; *Southern Belly: The Ultimate Food Lover's Companion to the South* by John T. Edge; *The Total View of Taftly* by Scott Morris; *Literary Washington DC* by Patrick Allen; *Flannery O'Connor: A Celebration of Genius* by Sarah Gordon; and *Fatal Flowers* by Rosemary Daniell.

Please direct query letters with SASEs to:

Patrick Allen, Senior Editor

HIPPOCRENE BOOKS

171 Madison Avenue, New York, NY 10016
212-685-4371   fax: 212-779-9338
www.hippocrenebooks.com   e-mail: hippocre@ix.netcom.com

Hippocrene accents history, military science, international literature, music, travel, cuisine, and scholarly Judaica and Polonica. The house offers selected works in the areas of current affairs and popular culture, in addition to comprehensive lines of foreign-language dictionaries, maps, and atlases—the house publishes dictionaries and instruction books in over 100 languages. Hippocrene Books (founded in 1971) publishes hardcovers and trade paperbacks. The house also produces a line of audiobooks.

Hippocrene has undertaken publication of the works of Polish writer Henryk Sienkiewicz (1905 Nobel Laureate in literature) in English translation.

Hippocrene titles for the general trade: *You Can't Do Business (or Most Anything Else) Without Yiddish* by Leon H. Gildin; *Wedded Strangers: The Challenges of Russian-*

American Marriages, Expanded Edition by Lynn Vision; *Jews in Old China, Expanded Edition* by Sidney Shapiro; *Greece: An Illustrated History* by Tom Sloane; *China: An Illustrated History* by Yong Ho.

Hippocrene Books prides itself on being the foremost United States publisher of international cookbooks and foreign language dictionaries.

International cookbook titles: *Taste of Latvia* by Siri Lise Doub; *The Indian Spice Kitchen* by Monisha Bharadwaj; *Afghan Food & Cookery* by Helen Saberi; *The Best of Croatian Cooking* by Liliana Pavicic and Gordana Pirker-Mosher; *Hungarian Cookbook: Old World Recipes for New World Cooks* by Yolanda Nagy Fintor; *Imperial Mongolian Cooking: Recipes from the Kingdoms of Genghis Khan* by Marc Cramer.

Hippocrene's Bilingual series titles include: *Swahili Practical Dictionary* by Nicholas Awde; *Japanese Dictionary & Phrasebook* by Evgeny Steiner; *Croatian Dictionary & Phrasebook* by Ante Susnjar; *Beginner's Italian* by Joseph Privitera; *Beginner's Slovac* by Elena Letnanova.

Hippocrene offers practical and concise dictionaries as well as unabridged and comprehensive dictionaries, specialty dictionaries, proverbs dictionaries, and standard dictionaries in over 100 languages.

Mastering Advanced . . . guides make up a line that offers the student reasonably priced, contemporary foreign-language instruction. The Hippocrene Beginner's series is designed for students with little or no background in a foreign language. The goal of each volume is to provide readers with a basic knowledge to travel independently, speak and understand, and read and write essential words.

Hippocrene distributes its own list. Query letters and SASEs should be directed to:

Carol Chitnis Gress, Managing Editor—Oversees international cooking, travel, library of world folklore and general history titles.

George Blagowidow, President and Editorial Director

Paul Simpson, Associate Editor—Oversees illustrated histories, series, international proverbs.

Caroline Gates, Associate Editor—Oversees all foreign language dictionaries and learning guides.

H

HOLIDAY HOUSE

425 Madison Avenue, New York, NY 10017
212-688-0085

Holiday House specializes in children's and young-adult books in a program that encompasses quality trade hardcover picture books, short-chapter books, and middle-grade readers, as well as selected novels for young adults. Holiday House publishes general nonfiction works for all age levels, ethnic stories and nonfiction, fast-paced adventure stories, historical fiction, boys' books, humorous stories, folktales, fairy tales, poetry, and fantasy.

Holiday House (established in 1935) is a small independent publisher with a large and varied backlist of fiction and nonfiction children's books. The publisher is open to well-written, new ideas.

Sample picture-book titles: *A Child's Calendar* by John Updike (illustrated by Trina Schart Hyman) and *Under New York* by Linda Oatman Hyh (illustrated by Robert Royersby).

Further representative of the Holiday House list: *Gods and Goddesses of the Ancient Maya* by Leonard Everett Fisher (illustrated by the author); *A Right Fine Life: Kit Carson on the Santa Fe Trail* by Andrew Glass (illustrated by the author); *The Ghost in Room II* by Betty Ren Wright (drawings by Jacqueline Rogers); *Hiding from the Nazis* by David A. Adler (illustrated by Karen Ritz); *Celebrity Passover* by Diane Hoyt-Goldsmith (photographs by Lawrence Migdale); *The Uncivil War* by Sheila Solomon Klass; *School Spirits* by Michael O. Tunnell; *Under Our Skin: Kids Talk About Race* by Debbie Holsclaw Birdseye and Tom Birdseye (photographs by Robert Crum); *The Year My Parents Ruined My Life* by Martha Freeman.

From the Holiday House Readers (large type, simple vocabulary, and short manageable chapters, specially written for children who have just learned to read on their own): *Christmas in the Forest* by Marion Dane Bauer (illustrated by Diane Dawson); *Cats Are Like That* by Martha Weston (illustrated by the author).

From the Picture Book Biographies line: *A Picture Book of George Washington Carver* by David A. Adler (illustrated by Dan Brown). Mr. Adler has written 27 other Picture Book Biographies, including: *A Picture Book of Louis Braille; A Picture Book of John F. Kennedy; A Picture Book of Martin Luther King, Jr.; A Picture Book of Eleanor Roosevelt; A Picture Book of Paul Revere; A Picture Book of Florence Nightingale.*

Holiday House's authors' guidelines contain concise advice that all authors of children's books would do well to follow; contact the publisher for detailed information regarding manuscript submissions.

Holiday House handles its own distribution. Query letters and SASEs should be directed to:

Suzanne Reinoehl, Assistant Editor

H

HOLLOWAY HOUSE PUBLISHING GROUP

8060 Melrose Avenue, Los Angeles, CA 90046-7082
323-653-8060   fax: 323-655-9452

Holloway House publishes nonfiction and fiction within its areas of publishing interest, including African American, American Indian, and Hispanic literature, as well as selected titles in games and gambling. Holloway House (founded in 1960) is the world's largest publisher of paperbacks representing the American Black experience.

The publisher is noted for hard-hitting novels, historical anthologies and biographical series (including the Educator's Library and the Black American Series, which is a widely acclaimed continuing series of profusely illustrated biographies, meticulously researched, featuring famous African Americans), and selected public-interest nonfiction. The house is also known for reprint editions of classic works by such authors as Donald Goines and Iceberg Slim. Among Holloway House imprints are Avanti, Heartline Romances, Mankind, Premiere, and Melrose Square. Holloway also produces calendars, postcard books, and posters. The publisher typically publishes a mid-sized list of new titles each year and maintains a strong backlist.

On the Holloway House fiction list: *The Listening Sky* by Bernice Anderson Poole; *The Revenge of June Daley* by Rina Keaton; *Buffalo Soldier* by C. R. Goodman; *Shack Town* by Glen T. Brock; *Black Bait* by Leo Guild; *Daddy Must Die* by William O. Brown; *Coming of Age* by Lorri Hewett; *Black Cheyenne* by Charles R. Goodman.

Nonfiction includes: *Arthur Ashe* by Ed Weissberg; *B. B. King* by J. Nazel; *Bill Cosby* by M. Ruuth; *Billie Holiday* by Bud Kliment; *James Baldwin* by Lisa Rosset; *Jackie Robinson* by Richard Scott; *Jesse Owens* by Tony Gentry; *Muhammad Ali* by C. Riccella; *Oprah Winfrey* by M. Ruuth; *Women in History* by D. L. Shepherd; *To Kill a Black Man* (dual biography of Martin Luther King and Malcolm X) by Louis E. Lomax; *Dizzy Gillespie* by Tony Gentry; *Kathleen Dunham* by Darlene Donloe; *Book of the Navajo* by Raymond Locke.

The Holloway House list is handled by All America Distributors Corporation.

Query letters and SASEs should be directed to:

Ray Locke, Senior Editor

HENRY HOLT AND COMPANY (PART OF THE VERLAGSGRUPPE GEORG VON HOLTZBRINCK)

Henry Holt and Company Books for Young Readers

Henry Holt Reference

John Macrae Books

Metropolitan Books

Owl Books

Times Books

21st Century Books

115 West 18th Street, New York, NY 10011
212-886-9200

Henry Holt and Company publishes a full range of trade nonfiction, as well as a strong complement of fiction and literary works. In addition, Holt maintains a number of individualized imprints and divisions. Holt emphasizes hardcover and trade paperback editions.

Metropolitan Books is an imprint that features an international lineup of topical-interest nonfiction and literary fiction; Metropolitan is open to different genres, unconventional points of view, controversial opinions, and perhaps a few new voices in fiction. Other Holt trade hardcover imprints include John Macrae Books and Times Books. Owl Books is host to the house line of trade paperbacks. (See subentry further on.)

The house presents several fine children's and young-adult lines under the aegis of Henry Holt's Books for Young Readers (please see subentry further on).

Henry Holt and Company nurtures a healthy backlist.

Henry Holt and Company (founded in 1866) is part of the German-based international Verlagsgruppe Georg von Holtzbrinck. Holt was previously a thriving independent publisher, subsequent to the sale of former umbrella operation Holt Rinehart & Winston's textbook division to Harcourt Brace in 1987.

The Henry Holt nonfiction scope spans the trade spectrum. Areas of interest include politics and current events; contemporary issues; business and economics; history, military history; nature and ecology; literary commentary; popular and scholarly biography and memoir; business, personal finance, and career; psychology and medicine; health, exercise, and nutrition; spirituality and awareness; and reference works keyed to popular, academic, and professional topics.

From the Holt nonfiction list: *For Women Only: A Revolutionary Guide to Overcoming Sexual Dysfunction and Reclaiming Your Sex Life* by Jennifer Berman, M.D., and Laura Berman, M.D.; *Below Another Sky* by Rick Ridgway; *The Origin Diet* by Elizabeth Somer, MA., R.D.; *The Queen's Conjurer* by Benjamin Woolley; *Love the Work You're With: A Practical Guide to Finding New Joy and Productivity in Your Job* by Richard Whiteley; *Painbuster: A Breakthrough 4 Step Program for Ending Pain* by John Stamatos, M.D., with Jane O'Boyle; *Beer and Circus: How Big Time College Sports Is Crippling Undergraduate Education* by Murray Sperber; *After the Darkest Hour* by Kathleen Brehony, Ph.D.; *The Complete Letters of Oscar Wilde* (edited by Merlin Holland and Rupert Hart-Davis); *Alexander Hamilton: "A Life"* by Willard Sterne Randall; *In Harm's Way* by Doug Santon; *Richard Wright: The Life and Times* by Hazel Rowley; *A Perfect Fit: Clothes, Character, and the Promise of America* by Jenna Weissman Joselit.

Henry Holt fiction includes frontlist commercial novels and literary works, as well as topflight mystery and suspense fiction. Representative titles here: *Iced* by Jenny Silver; *Greetings from the Golden State* by Leslie; *Singing Boy* by Dennis McFarland; *Field Guide* by Gwendolen Gross; *A Good House* by Bonnie Burnard; *Author Unknown* by Don Foster; *Sylvia and Ted* by Emma Tennant; *The Artist's Wife* by Max Philips; *The Looking Glass* by Michele Roberts; *On the Night Plain* by J. Robert Lennon.

Backlist features (including Owl trade-paper reprints of recent Holt hardcover originals): *Edisto Revisited* by Padgett Powell; *The Debt to Pleasure* by John Lanchester; *Amnesiascope* by Steve Erickson; *The Death of Frank Sinatra* by Michael Ventura; *Sandra Nichols Found Dead* (a Jerry Kennedy novel) by George V. Higgins; *Angel Maker: The Collected Short Stories of Sara Maitland* by Sara Maitland; *Go the Way Your Blood Beats: An Anthology of Gay and Lesbian Literary Writings* by African Americans (edited by Shawn Stewart Ruff). Holt also features John Harvey's Charlie Resnick mysteries, John Lutz's Fred Carver mysteries, Collin Wilcox's San Francisco police procedurals, and Sue Grafton's alphabetically titled Kinsey Millhone detective series. Henry Holt and Company handles its own distribution.

Query letters and SASEs should be directed to:

David Sobel, Editorial Director, Times Books—Science travel adventure, business, personal finance, parenting.

Elizabeth Stein, Editor—History, biography, current events, military history.

Jack Macrae, Editorial Director, John Macrae Books—American history and biography, scientific inquiry, travel, and nature.

H

Jennifer Barth, Editor in Chief, Holt—Commercial and literary fiction, biography, memoir, narrative nonfiction.

Sara Bershtel, Associate Publisher, Metropolitan Books—Individualistic nonfiction and literary fiction.

Tom Bissell, Associate Editor, Holt—Literary fiction and nonfiction.

Robin Dennis, Associate Editor, Times Books—Business.

Riva Hocherman, Editor, Metropolitan

Henry Holt and Company Books for Young Readers

Henry Holt and Company Books for Young Readers publishes in categories that range from the youngest readers through young-adult. The list includes illustrated storybooks, fiction, and nonfiction volumes of popular educational appeal.

Imprints, series, and specialty lines include books by Michael Hague; books by Bill Martin, Jr.; Reference; Edge Books; Redfeather Books; and Owlet Paperbacks. The hardcover young-adult Edge imprint features themes keyed to contemporary culture and multicultural titles from around the world. Among Holt productions in the children's arena are those issued in finely crafted, elegantly understated editions.

Representative of the Holt Books for Young Readers list: *When Zachary Beaver Came to Town* by Kimberly Willis Holt; *Mama Cat Has Three Kittens* by Denise Fleming; *Mole Music* by David McPhail; *Little Bunny on the Move* by Peter McCarty; *Scrambled States of America* by Laurie Keller; *What Happened on Planet Kid* by Jane Leslie Conly.

From the Edge Books imprint: *Remix: Conversations with Immigrant Teenagers* by Marina Budhos; *Forbidden Love: The Secret History of Mixed Race America* by Gary Nash.

Query letters and SASEs should be directed to:

Laura Godwin, Associate Publisher

Owl Books

Owl Books publishes a wide range of nonfiction (commercial, popular, and literary) and no new fiction, only backlist. Owl is a Holt division recognized for its trade-paperback program in both originals and reprints.

Owl is expanding its nonfiction program with more books in more areas of interest to trade-paperback readers. Owl areas of interest include: topical issues and popular culture; literary essay; biography and memoir; business, personal finance, and career; popular psychology, health and nutrition, and awareness; popular and scholarly reference.

Owl has also opened a distinctive fiction line that features reprints of novels and stories from some of the most celebrated contemporary writers: Irene Dische, John Lanchester, Paul Beatty, Salman Rushdie, Tom De Haven, Padgett Powell, Alison Lurie, Robert Olmstead, Steve Erickson, Tibor Fischer, Alexander Theroux, George V. Higgins, and Hilary Mantel.

Though an established imprint at Holt, the premiere Owl Books catalog was issued for the spring and summer of 1997—the Year of the Owl.

Owl nonfiction originals: *Yukon Alone: The World's Toughest Adventure Race* by John Balzer; *Retire Early and Live the Life You Want Now* by John Wasik; *The Kitchen Table Investor* by John Wasik; *Till Death Do Us Part (Unless I Kill You First): A Step by Step Guide for Resolving Marital Conflict* by Jamie Turndorf, Ph.D.; *You've Got Ketchup on Your Muumuu: An A-Z Guide to English Words Around the World* by Eugene Ehrlich; *Patrick O'Brian: A Life* by Dean King; *The Time Bind: When Work Becomes Home and Home Becomes Work* by Arlie Russell Horchschild; *Teller of Tales: The Life of Arthur Conan Doyle* by Danill Stashower; *Bury My Heart at Wounded Knee* by Dee Brown; *Mao: A Life* by Philip Short; *Abe: A Novel of the Young Lincoln* by Richard Slotkin; *Wild Minds: What Animals Really Think* by Marc D. Hauser; *Time Management from the Inside Out* by Julie Morgenstern; *Day of Infamy* by Walter Lord.

Owl fiction and popular literature: *Mason and Dixon* by Thomas Pynchon; *The Black Flower: A Novel of the Civil War* by Howard Bahr; *Two by Carrère: Class Trip/The Mustache* by Emmanuel Carrère (translated by Lanie Goodman and Linda Coverdale); *First, Body* by Melanie Rae Thon; *Imagine Being More Afraid of Freedom Than Slavery: Poems* by Pamela Sneed; *The Story of the Night: A Novel* by Colm Tóibín; *Out of the Sun: A Novel* by Robert Goddard; *The Church of Dead Girls: A Novel* by Stephen Dobyns; *A Crime in the Neighborhood: A Novel* by Suzanne Berne; *The Last Station: A Novel* by Jay Parini; *The Fool's Progress: An Honest Novel* by Edward Abbey; *A Trail of Heart's Blood Wherever We Go: A Novel* by Robert Olmstead; *Despair* by Andre Alixix; *The Friends of Eddie Coyle* and *Boomers Law* by George Aiggino; *G Is for Grafton* by Natalie Hevener.

All editors are now Henry Holt and Company editors. There is no separate Owl editorial body.

Times Books

Times Books publishes general trade nonfiction across the gamut of commercial areas, including business and career, finance, current affairs, social issues, science, how-to, cooking, education, travel, humor, reference, and puzzles and games. Times is particularly strong in the crossword-puzzle publishing arena.

Times Books (founded in 1959 by the *New York Times* newspaper) is among the houses acquired by Henry Holt in 2000–2001.

On the Times book list: *How Race Is Lived in America* by Joseph Lelyveld; *Alternative Consumers Health Guide To* by Jane E. Brody, Denise Grady, and Reporters for the *New York Times; Writers on Writing: Collected Essays from the* New York Times by John Parnton; *Leadership Ensemble* by Harvey Seifter and Peter Economy; New York Times *Management Reader* by Brent Bowers and Deidre Leipzinger.

All editors are now Henry Holt and Company editors. There is no separate Times editorial body.

Houghton Mifflin Company
CAT
Clarion Books

College Division

Great Source

Houghton Mifflin Books for Children

International Division

McDougal Littell

Riverside Publishing Company

School Division

Sunburst Technology

Trade and Reference Division

Boston office:
222 Berkeley Street, Boston, MA 02116-3764
617-351-5000
www.houghtonmifflinbooks.com

New York office:
215 Park Avenue South, New York, NY 10003
212-420-5800

Houghton Mifflin produces general trade nonfiction and fiction in hardcover and paperback, as well as a strong general-reference list. Mariner is a trade-paperback imprint covering house interests in fiction and nonfiction. Children's divisions include Houghton Mifflin Books for Children, and the editorially independent juveniles' imprint Clarion Books (see subentries further on). The backlist of formerly independent Ticknor & Fields has been incorporated into the core Houghton Mifflin catalog.

Houghton Mifflin (founded in 1832) is one of the grand names of American publishing tradition. The house's renowned leaping-dolphin emblem embellishes a distinguished list.

Houghton Mifflin nonfiction encompasses mainstream titles in such areas as current events, international affairs, business, journalism, lifestyle and travel, and natural history.

Reference works from Houghton Mifflin include: *American Heritage Dictionary of the English Language* (an excellent resource for American writers); *The Columbia Encyclopedia* (copublished with Columbia University); and *Cannon's Concise Guide to Rules of Order.*

Also on the Houghton Mifflin list are travel and nature series that include the Peterson Field Guides, and Best Places to Stay Guides. Houghton Mifflin is also known for publishing the ever popular *American Heritage Dictionary.*

Popular Houghton Mifflin nonfiction: *Building Big* by David Macaulay; *Carson Mc-Cullers: A Life* by Josyane Savigneau; *A Life in the Twentieth Century: Innocent Beginnings* by James Carroll; *Fast Food Nation: The Dark Side of the All American Meal* by Eric Schlosser; *Surviving Galeras* by Stanley Williams and Fen Montaigne; *The Perfect Recipe* by Pam Anderson; *Birds of North America* by Kenn Kaufman; *Sober for Good* by Anne M. Fletcher; *The Ultimate Workout Log* by Suzanne Schlosberg; *The Algeria Hotel* by Adam Nossister; *Beyond Innocence* by Jane Goodall; and *The Ultimate Baseball Book: The Classic Illustrated History of the World's Greatest Game* (edited by Daniel Okrent and Harris Lewine).

H

Fiction and works with literary and cultural scope: *Gathering Blue* by Lois Lowry; *The Best American Mystery Stories of the Century* by Tony Hillerman; *Taps* by Willie Morris; *Sheba* by Nicholas Clapp; *The Far Field* by Edie Meidav; *The Silmarillion* by J. R. R. Tolkien; *The Lord of the Ring* by J. R. R. Tolkien; *All We Know of Heaven* by Remy Rougeau; *Hotel Honolulu* by Paul Theroux; *Dupont Circle* by Paul Kafka-Gibbons; *The Dying Animal* by Philip Roth; *Doghouse Roses* by Steve Earle; and *Interpreter of Maladies* by Jhumpa Lahiri.

The publisher also issues selected works of poetry, including: *Time & Money: New Poems* by William Matthews; and *Nature: Poems Old and New* by May Swenson.

Houghton Mifflin distributes its own list. Query letters and SASEs should be directed to:

Eamon Dolan, Executive Editor (New York)—Business, technology, nonfiction; travel guides.

Elaine Pfefferblit, Editor at Large (New York)—Philosophy, history, biography, general nonfiction; literary fiction; nonfiction consistent with the house list.

Eric Chinski, Senior Editor (New York)—Philosophy, history, Jewish studies, biography, general.

Harry L. Foster, Jr., Senior Editor (Boston)—Nature and history.

Janet Silver, Vice President and Editor in Chief (Boston)—Literary nonfiction and fiction. Nonfiction: biographies, arts and culture, women's issues. Focus on developing writers.

Laura van Dam, Science Editor (Boston)—Hard science, medicine, technology; practical nonfiction.

Pat Strachan, Executive Editor (New York)—Poetry, literary fiction and nonfiction, gardening, general reference works.

Rex Martin, Senior Editor (Boston)—Cooking, health, self-help, poetry, biography, literary nonfiction.

Wendy Strothman, Executive Vice President (Boston)

Anton Mueller, Senior Editor (Boston)

Susan Canavan, Associate Editor (Boston)

Heidi Pitlor, Editor (Boston)

Lori Galvin-Frost, Assistant Managing Editor,(Boston)—Cookbooks.

Lisa White, Associate Director (Boston)—Field Guides.

Deanne Urmy, Senior Editor—Science, nature, serious nonfiction

Frances Tenenbaum, Imprint Editor/Senior Editor Houghton Mifflin (Boston)—Gardening books. Oversees Taylor gardening guides and Tasha Tudor books.

Education: University of Michigan and Columbia School of Journalism.

Employment history/editor career path: I have worked here for over 25 years. I started as a journalist and then moved on to work for a small publisher. I then worked for a small book club and was writing a book on gardening and wildflowers. Soon after, I moved out of Long Island and came to work for Houghton Mifflin.

Personal interests: Gardening, nonfiction editing, I love editing—don't like writing.

What would you be doing if you were not an editor? I don't know—I don't even want to think about it.

What has been your most successful book that you have acquired to date? *Tasha Tudor's Garden* by Tovah Martin and Richard Brown. It's a large, beautiful book that is full of color. It was published in 1994 and is in its ninth printing. I am also the editor of a whole series of gardening books called *The Tailor's Guide to Gardening.*

What books have you acquired that make you the most proud? What books that you have acquired reflect the types of books you like to represent? I am the Editor for three of Henry Mitchell's books, who is a late columnist of the *Washington Post.* He is one of the most opinionated writers in gardening.

Do you represent nonfiction? Yes.

Do you require book proposals? If so, what do you look for in evaluating a book proposal? Yes, from people I don't know. Subject is the first thing, writing is the second. What is the salability of the project? It must have a unique voice.

What process do you use for making a decision? What is the process for acquisition, is there a committee? Because I'm the "expert" on gardening at Houghton Mifflin, I'm the one who usually reads the gardening books. I might go to other people who may be interested, such as the sales/marketing division. We do have an acquisitions committee.

Are agents important? Why? Yes and no. I work with some agents and I also work with people who do not have agents.

How should writers approach you? Not by phone.

What are some common mistakes writers make? What really gets on your nerves? When someone tells me that his or her project is unique, when I know that it's not. I don't like books that are rehashes, the same thing over and over again. I also don't like books that are manufactured in the author's head. As far as gardening books, it gets on my nerves when people have just taken it up, and they want to tell everyone else about it.

What can writers do to get your attention and to avoid the slush pile? If you write it directly to me, it doesn't go to the slush pile.

What have been some of your craziest experiences with submissions? My assistant usually goes through everything first, so she sees most of the "crazy" submissions.

What have been some of your best experiences with writers or in your job? I have some wonderful writers who turn out to be my best friends. I have recently found out that an organization that is giving a book party for one of my authors is actually giving the party for both of us. That's never happened to me before.

Is there anything that you would like to see changed in the industry? Yes, the whole industry.

Clarion Books

215 Park Avenue South, 10th floor, New York, NY 10003
212-420-5800

Clarion publishes books geared for the youngest readers up through the early teen years. Clarion Books is an award-winning children's book division that is editorially independent of Houghton Mifflin's other lines.

On Clarion's list in fiction and picture books: *The Three Pigs* by David Wiesner; *Riding the Tiger* by Eve Bunting (illustrated by David Frampton); *A Pocketful of Poems* by Nikki Grimes (illustrated by Javaka Steptoe); *The Secrets of Ms. Snickle's Class* by Laurie Miller Hornik (illustrated by Debbie Tilley); *A Single Shard* by Linda Sue Park; *Sigmund Freud: Pioneer of the Mind* by Catherine Reef; *Heroine of the Titanic: The Real Unsinkable Molly Brown* by Elaine Landau.

Query letters and SASEs should be directed to:

Dinah Stevenson, Vice President and Editorial Director

Jennifer Greene, Associate Editor

Julie Strauss-Gabel, Associate Editor

Michele Coppola, Editor

Houghton Mifflin Books for Children

The Houghton Mifflin children's-book division stands out with a broad list that addresses topics of wide import; at all reading levels, the Houghton program accents works of thematic complexity and emotional depth. Imprints and lines include Walter Lorraine Books (illustrated and novelty titles) and Sandpiper Paperbacks.

Houghton Mifflin Books for Children publishes hardcover and paperback titles from picture books for the youngest readers to fiction for young adults, audio products, foldout books, board books, lift-the-flap books—and the house showcases a brace of successful authors as well. Caldecott and Newbery medallions abound in the tradition of Houghton Mifflin Books for Children.

Representing the Houghton Mifflin approach: *Baby Buggy, Buggy Baby* by Harriet Ziefert (illustrated by Richard Brown); *Curious George: A Pop-Up Book* by H. A. Ray (illustrated by the author); *Under the Cherry Blossom Tree: An Old Japanese Tale* (retold and illustrated by Allen Say); *Secrets of Animal Flight* by Nic Bishop (illustrated by the author); *Mist over the Mountains: Appalachia and Its People* by Raymond Bial (illustrated by the author); *Shoes: Their History in Words and Pictures* by Charlotte and David Yue (illustrated by the authors; bibliography and index included).

Sandpiper Paperbacks include: *Table, Chair, Bear: A Book in Many Languages* by Jane Feder (illustrated by the author); *Turtle Time* by Sandol Stoddard (illustrated by Lynn Munsinger); *Nights of the Pufflings* by Bruce McMillan (illustrated by the author); *The Haunting of Cassie Palmer* by Vivien Alcock.

Query letters and SASEs should be directed to:

Margaret Raymo, Acquisitions Editor (Boston)

HUMANICS PUBLISHING GROUP
Humanics Learning
P.O. Box 7400, Atlanta, GA 30357
404-874-2176   fax: 404-874-1976
e-mail: humanics@mindspring.com

The Humanics publishing program covers the categories of self-help, how-to, psychology, human relations, health and nutrition, creative expression (in art, crafts, literature), education, humor, and spirituality. Special emphasis is on subjects such as personal growth, love and relationships, environment, peace, and Taoism. Market areas of concentration include elementary child and child development, teachers' resource books, child care, and the family.

Humanics produces children's books under the Humanics Children's House imprint. The Humanics line of teachers' resource books and materials in child development is directed in part to colleges and institutional markets; popular works in this arena are published under the Humanics Learning imprint.

Humanics Publishing Group (founded in 1976) publishes a small- to medium-sized list of paperback trade books, a line of special fine editions, and audiocassettes.

Humanics titles: *The Millennium Myth: The Ever-Ending Story* by Sean O'Shea and Meryl Walker; *Garden of the Sufi: Insights into the Nature of Man* by Jim Aghevli; *While You Are Expecting: Your Own Prenatal Classroom* by F. Rene Van DeCarr and Marc Lehrer, M.D.; *The Adlerian Primer: How to Manage Children at Home and in the Classroom* by Alex Chew, Ed.D.; *The Way of Virtue: The Ancient Wisdom of Confucius Adapted for a New Age* by James Vollbracht; *Many Paths, One Truth: The Common Thread* by Carole Addlestone; *The Magic of Zen* by Inez D. Stein; *The I Ching of Management* by William E. Sadler; *Inner Bridges: A Guide to Energy Movement and Body Structure* by Fritz Frederick Smith, M.D; *All Presidents' Sexual Styles* by John Berice.

The Humanics Tao series offers a variety of titles: *The Tao of Recovery: A Quiet Path to Wellness* by Jim McGregor; *The Creative Tao: Lao Tzu's Tao Te Ching Adopted for a New Age* by Pamela Metz; *The Tao of Design: Taoist Elements for Designers* by Carl Garant; *The Tao of Leadership* by John Heider, Ph.D.; *The Tao of Women* by Pamela Meets and Jacqueline Tobin; *The Tao Te Ching: A New Approach—Backward Down the Path* by Jerry Dalton; *The Tao of Sailing* by Ray Grigg.

Humanics oversees its own distribution. Query letters and SASEs should be directed to:

Arthur Bligh, Acquisitions Editor—Adult trade books.

Humanics Learning

The accent at Humanics Learning is on original stories and tales targeted for younger readers, in a program geared primarily toward illustrated works. The Fun E. Friends series is one of the house's successful lines. Humanics produces guides for caregivers and educators under the Humanics Learning logo.

On the Humanics Learning list: *Bottle Cap Activities: Recycled Crafts for All Ages* by Kathy Cisneros; *Homespun Curriculum: A Developmentally Appropriate Activities Guide* by Denise Theobold; *Cambio Chameleon* by Mauro Magellan; *The Planet of the Dinosaurs* by Barbara Carr (illustrated by Alice Bear); *The Adventure of Paz in the Land of Numbers* by Miriam Bowden; *Giggle E. Goose, Fibber E. Frog, Fraid E. Cat,* and *Greb E. Dog* by Al Newman (illustrated by Jim Doody).

Titles for teachers and caregivers under the Humanics Learning imprint: *Science, Math and Nutrition for Toddlers: Setting the Stage for Lifelong Skills* by Rita Schrank; *The Planet of the Parental Classroom: A Parent's Guide for Teaching Your Baby in the Womb* by Rene Van De Carr and Marc Lehrer; *Teaching Terrific Twos* by Terry Graham and Linda Camp; *The Infant and Toddler Handbook* by Kathryn Castle; *Toddlers Learn by Doing* by Rita Schrank.

Query letters and SASEs should be directed to:

Arthur Bligh, Humanics Learning

HUMAN KINETICS

1607 North Market Street, P.O. Box 5076, Champaign, IL 61825-5076
217-351-5076   fax: 217-351-1549
www.humankinetics.com

Human Kinetics produces works in recreational and competitive sports, physical education, sports medicine, and fitness. Human Kinetics (founded in 1974) offers a list of trade and academic works (including college textbooks) that cover a wide range of athletic pursuits, with books geared for professional-level coaches, trainers, and participants, in addition to serious leisure-time athletes. Human Kinetics has established the Human Kinetics Foundation to issue grants promoting youth sports and school physical education.

A notable HK imprint is YMCA of America Books. Human Kinetics books are issued primarily in trade paperback editions, with special editions in hardcover. The press also publishes a number of periodicals in its areas of interest. Human Kinetics bills itself as the premier publisher for sports and fitness.

Frontlist titles: *Creative Coaching* by Jerry Lynch; *Sports Talent* by Jim Brown; *WBCA's Defensive Basketball Drills* by the Women's Basketball Coaches Association; *Youth Basketball Drills* by Burrall Paye and Patrick Paye; *Mind & Muscle* by Blair Whitmarsh, Ph.D.; *Bollettieri's Tennis Handbook* by Nick Bollettieri; *Advanced Marathoning* by Pete Pfitzinger and Scott Douglas; *Swim, Bike, Run* by Wes Hobson, Clark Campbell, and Mike Vickers; *Lactate Threshold Training* by Peter Janssen; *The Swim Coaching Bible* by Dick Hannula and Nort Thorton, Editors; *Active Living Every Day* by Steven N. Blair, Andrea L. Dunn, Bess H. Marcus, Ruth Ann Carpenter, and Peter Jaret; *Coaching Golf Successfully* by Bill Madonna; *Complete Conditioning for Martial Arts* by Sean Cochran; *Judo Techniques & Tactics* by Jimmy Pedro; *The Young Athlete's Handbook* by Youth Sport Trust; *Juggling* by Dave, Dorothy, and Ben Finnigan.

The Fitness Spectrum series offers books that take the guesswork out of working out. Each book is packed with easy-to-use, color-coded workouts that add variety and produce results. Titles here: *Fitness Cross-Country Skiing* by Steven E. Gaskill; *Fitness Aquatics* by LeAnne Case; *Fitness Stepping* by Debi Pillarella and Scott O. Roberts.

Outdoor Pursuits is a series that emphasizes safety, environmental responsibility, and outdoor activity. Some titles: *Orienteering* by Tom Renfrew; *Rock Climbing* by Phil Watts; *Snowshoeing* by Sally Edwards and Melissa McKenzie.

Steps to Success Activity books represent a line designed to serve as primary resources for beginners in a variety of sports and activities. Readers learn to perform basic skills quickly and easily. Representative titles: *Archery* by Kathleen M. Haywood and Catherine F. Lewis; *Team Handball* by Reita E. Clanton and Mary Phyl Dwight; *Social Dance* by Judy Patterson Wright, Ph.D.

Backlist favorites: *Sculpting Her Body Perfect* by Brad Schoenfeld; *LPGA's Guide to Every Shot* by the Ladies Professional Golf Association; *The Baseball Coaching Bible* by Jerry Kindall and John Winkin, Editors; *In Pursuit of Excellence* by Terry Orlick, Ph.D.; *Precision Pool* by Gerry Kanov and Shari Stauch; *Muscle Mechanics* by Everett Aaberg; *Total Training for Young Champions* by Tudor O. Bompa, Ph.D.; *Stronger Abs and Back* by Dean and Greg Brittenham; *Complete Conditioning for Baseball* by Pat Murphy and Jeff Forney.

Human Kinetics oversees its own distribution. Query letters and SASEs should be directed to:

Rainer Martens, Publisher and President

HUNGRY MINDS (FORMERLY IDG)

909 Third Avenue, New York, NY 10022
Chicago address: 645 N. Michigan Avenue, Chicago IL, 60611
212-884-5000

Hungry Minds is a leading publishing content company with a diverse offering of technology, consumer, reference and general how-to book brands, computer-based learning tools, Web sites, and Internet e-services. HMI's bestselling brands include . . . *For Dummies, 3-D Visual, Bible, Unofficial Guides, Cliff Notes, Frommer's, Betty Crocker's, Weight Watchers,* and *Webster's New World.*

HMI has well over 600 selections in the popular . . . *For Dummies* series, including titles in computer-related, business, and general interest areas. 3-D Visuals accents such areas as Windows, DOS, and network security; Macworld Books concentrates on the universe of Apple users; PC World handbooks are hands-on tutorial reference works. Many HMI books come packaged with bonus software. Technical books are often packaged with useful shareware, freeware, and macros. Some HMI business books are packaged with templates for up-to-date business documents.

Hungry Minds, formerly IDG Books Worldwide (founded in 1990), is a publicly traded company (HMIN). Expanding beyond its original sphere of computer titles, HMI is interested in authors and/or potential projects that are appropriate for single titles and series in all areas of business and general reference. Hungry Minds takes pride in issuing books chock full of information and valuable advice the reader is not likely to get anywhere else—brought together with attention to quality, selection, value, and convenience.

Representative computing titles from Hungry Minds Books Worldwide: *Researching Online for Dummies, 2nd Edition* by Reva Basch and Mary Ellen Bates; *Linux Programming for Dummies* by Francis Litterio; *Windows 2000 Professional Simplified* by Ruth Maran; *Teach Yourself Visual Basic 6* by Patricia Hartman; *Standard C++ Bible* by Al Stevens and Clayton Walnum.

Consumer, business, and how-to hit titles: *Investing for Dummies, 2nd Edition* by Eric Tyson; *Champagne for Dummies* by Ed McCarthy; *The Unofficial Guide to Picking Stocks* by Paul Mladjenovic; *Betty Crocker's Cooking for Two: How to Cook Everything* by Mark Bittman; *Spanish for Dummies* by Susana Wald and the Language Experts at Berlitz; *Astronomy for Dummies* by Stephen P. Maran, Ph.D.; *Golf for Dummies* by Gary McCord; *Ken Schultz's Fishing Encyclopedia: Worldwide Angling Guide* by Ken Schultz.

H

Hungry Minds directs its own distribution services.

For technical (computer-related) titles, queries, proposals, and SASEs should be directed to: Queries & Proposals—Technical Publishing, Hungry Minds, 919 E. Hillsdale Boulevard, Suite 400, Foster City, CA 94404.

Nontechnical queries and proposals are only accepted for review if they are submitted through a literary agent.

For all business titles, queries, proposals, and SASEs should be directed to: Queries & Proposals—Business Publishing, Hungry Minds, 645 N. Michigan Avenue, Suite 800, Chicago, IL 60611.

Kathleen Welton, Vice President and Publisher, IL

Mark Butler, Executive Editor—Personal finance; taxes; small business; e-commerce, IL.

Holly McGuire, Executive Editor—Management and skills training, business self-help; technical/how-to, NY.

Karen Hansen, Acquisitions Editor—Careers, IL.

For education and reference titles, queries, proposals, and SASEs should be directed to: Queries & Proposals—Education and Reference, Hungry Minds, 10475 Crosspoint Boulevard, Indianapolis, IN 46256.

Diane Steele, VP/Publisher—General education titles; science; foreign language.

Greg Tubach, Publishing Director—Cliffs Notes; literature; test prep.

Mike Agnes, Editor in Chief—Webster's New World.

For lifestyle titles, queries, proposals, and SASEs should be directed to: Queries & Proposals—Lifestyles Publishing, Hungry Minds, 909 Third Avenue, New York, NY 10022.

Kathy Nebenhaus, VP/Publisher—General lifestyles.

Mike Spring, VP/Publisher—Travel.

Jennifer Feldman, Asst. VP/Publisher—Cooking, gardening.

Dominique DeVito, Asst. VP/Publisher—Pets.

H

HYPERION

Disney Press

Hyperion Books for Children

Miramax Books

77 W. 66th Street, New York, NY 10023-6298
212-456-0100

Hyperion Books for Children offices:
114 Fifth Avenue, New York, NY 10011-5690
212-633-4400

Hyperion (founded in 1991) publishes commercial fiction and literary works, and frontlist nonfiction in the areas of popular culture, health and wellness, business, current topical interest, popular psychology and self-help, and humor. The house publishes books in hardcover, trade paperback, and mass-market paperback formats. Hyperion operates a strong children's program that encompasses Hyperion Books for Children and Disney Press. (See separate subentry further on.) Miramax Books (see separate subentry further on) concentrates on projects that tie in with the world of film.

Hyperion is part of Disney—the transnational corporate entity noted for its bountiful theme parks, hotels, and resorts, as well as its considerable ledger of film and television enterprises (including ABC, ESPN, Touchstone, Miramax, and Disney studios). Disney launched Hyperion as a full-fledged, well-funded book-publishing division, and the house's top-of-the-line reputation commenced with its initial well-chosen list.

Exemplifying the arrangements available for coveted properties via major media enterprises, Hyperion acquired publishing rights to *Takedown: The Pursuit and Capture of America's Most Wanted Computer Criminal* by cybersleuth Tsutomu Shinomura and journalist John Markoff (of the *New York Times*); Miramax Films simultaneously consummated a contract for dramatic (stage and screen) rights, as well as CD-ROM/interactive (computer game) rights to the project.

Representing Hyperion: *ABC Sports College Football All Time All Americans* by Keith Jackson; *Buried Evidence* by Nancy Taylor Rosenberg; *Chosen by God* by Joshua Hammer; *Don't Sweat the Small Stuff for Teens* by Richard Carlson, Ph.D.; *The Fourth Mega-Market* by Ralph Acampora; *Joe Torre's Ground Rules for Winners* by Joe Torre; *Line of Sight* by Jack Kelly; *The Naked Chef* by Jamie Oliver; *The Red Rose Crew* by Daniel J. Boyne; *Almost History* by Roger Bruns; *The Book of My Pet* by David Marshall and Kate Marshall; *Don't Sweat the Small Stuff in Love* by Richard Carlson, Ph.D., and Kristine Carlson; *The Ice Master* by Jennifer Niven; *Latina Beauty* by the Editors of *Latina* magazine and Belen Aranda-Alvarado; *Teen Talks Parents Must Have with Their Children About Sex and Character* by Pepper Schwartz, Ph.D., and Dominic Cappello; *2001 ESPN Information Please Sports Almanac* by Gerry Brown, Michael Morrison, and the Editors of Information Please; *Christmas: Lost & Found* by John A. Jenson; *Money Talk* by Lorraine Spurge; *Relationship Rescue* by Philip C. McGraw, Ph.D.; *Simplify Your Work Life* by Elaine St. James; *Angel Whiskers* (edited by Laurel E. Hunt); *The Hearse You Came in On* by Tim Cockey; *Irish Wedding Traditions* by Shannon McMahon-Lichte; *Breaking Apart* by Wendy Swallow; *Don't Sweat the Small Stuff for Women* by Kristine Carlson; *The Lost Daughter of Happiness* by Geiling Yan; *No Parachute* by Jeff Gunhus; *Don't Send a Resume* by Jeffrey J. Fox; *The Devil's Cure* by Kenneth Oppel; *Why Is Everyone So Cranky?* by C. Leslie Charles; *Becoming American* by Merl Nana-Ama Danquah; *Sex Tips for the Living* by Dan Saferstein, Ph.D.; *Betrayal of Trust* by Laurie Garrett; *What Women Want Men to Know* by Barbara D Angelis, Ph.D; and *The Workshop* by Tom Grimes.

Emblematic of Hyperion fiction and literary works (including mystery, suspense, and thrillers): *The Men of Brewster Place: A Novel* by Gloria Naylor; *An Ocean in Iowa* by Peter Hedges; *The Job* by Douglas Kennedy; *The Pied Piper* by Ridley Pearson; *Stigmata: A Novel* by Phyllis Alesia Perry;

Other notable projects have included *Secrets of the Cube: The Ancient Visualization Game That Reveals Your True Self* by Annie Gottlieb and Slobodan D. Pesic; *Myst: The Book of Atrus* (based on the bestselling CD-ROM game) by Robyn and Rand Miller; *Act of Betrayal* by Edna Buchanan; *Tropical Depression* by Laurence Shames.

H

Hyperion hardcover and trade paperback books are distributed to the trade by Little, Brown; Warner Books handles special sales as well as the mass-market paperback list.

Hyperion is not currently accepting unsolicited manuscripts. Any materials received will be returned without review.

Alison Lowenstein, Assistant Editor

Gretchen Young, Editor

Jennifer Long, Associate Editor

Katherine Brown Tegen, Editor in Chief—Hyperion Books for Children.

Leigh Haber, Executive Editor

(Ms.) Leslie Wells, Senior Editor

Maureen O'Brien, Senior Editor—Major nonfiction: popular culture, current affairs, the media.

Michael DiCapua, Publisher—Michael DiCapua Books. A new imprint within Hyperion's Children's Program. Formerly an imprint at HarperCollins.

Peternelle Van Arsdale, Executive Editor

Wendy Lefkon, Executive Editor—Disney-related projects.—Has own Disney imprint.

Will Schwalbe, Executive Editor

Mary Ellen O'Neill, Senior Editor

Hyperion Books for Children
Hyperion Paperbacks for Children
Disney Press

The children's book division of Hyperion publishes titles for younger readers through young adult via a number of series, imprints, and lines. On the Hyperion children's division list are volumes that are finely designed and luxuriously produced in hardcover and paperback.

Hyperion Books for Children produces illustrated fairy tales, picture storybooks, poetry, illustrated fiction, calendars, and activity books—many of which are lavish, inventively presented works. Disney Press concentrates on illustrated works that tie in with Disney children's cinema classics, old and new—including series novelizations and books with cinematically conceived formats.

From Hyperion Books for Children: *McDuff and the Baby* by Rosemary Wells (illustrated by Susan Jeffers); *Dinorella: A Prehistoric Fairytale* by Pamela Duncan Edwards (illustrated by Henry Cole); *Pat the Beastie Hand Puppet* by Henrik Drescher; *Breakfast at the Liberty Diner* by Daniel Kirk; *The Secret of the Lost Kingdom* by Michael Bolton (illustrated by David Jermann); *William Wegman Puppies* by William Wegman; *The Peacock's Pride* by Melissa Kajpust (illustrated by Jo Anne Kelly); *The Bone Man: A Native American Modoc Tale* by Laura Simms (illustrated by Michael McCurdy); *Phoebe and the Spelling Bee* by Barney Saltzberg; *The Little Mermaid* by Hans Christian Anderson (illustrated with Disney Archival Art); *Teddy's Christmas: A Pop-up Book with Mini Christmas Cards* by Margie Palatini (illustrated by Mike Reed); *El Arbol de Navidad/The Christmas Tree* by Alma Flor Ada (illustrated by Terry Ybañez); *The Farolitos of Christmas* by Rudolfo Anaya (illustrated by Edward Gonzalez); *Armadillos Sleep in Dugouts: And Other Places Animals Live* by Pam Muñoz Ryan (illustrated by Diane deGroat); *The Buried City of Pompeii: What It Was Like When Vesuvius Exploded* by Shelley Tanaka (illustrated by Greg Ruhl); *The Wonder Worm Wars* by Margie Palatini; *Sons of Liberty* by Adele Griffin; *Wolf Shadows* by Mary Casanova.

Other noteworthy titles: *Tim Burton's Vincent* by Tim Burton; illustrated by the author (his first picture book, which he wrote and illustrated, was *The Nightmare Before Christmas*); *Anastasia's Album* by Shelley Tanaka (edited by Hugh Brewster; the true story of the youngest daughter of Czar Nicholas II of Russia and her incredible life, told through her own snapshots, diaries, and letters); *On Board the Titanic: An I Was There Book* by Shelly Tanaka (illustrated by Ken Marschall; true-story account of the famous ocean liner's fate told through the eyes of two young survivors).

Fiendly Corners by E. W. Leroe is a new Hyperion series that features paperback originals with eye-popping die-cut covers: *Fiendly Corners No. 1: Monster Vision; Fiendly Corners No. 2: Pizza Zombies; Fiendly Corners No. 3: Revenge of the Hairy Horror; Fiendly Corners No. 4: Nasty the Snowman.*

Hyperion is proud to announce an ongoing series of FamilyPC books designed to grow as families grow. The FamilyPC book series is intended as the absolute best option for parents who want to get the most productivity and fun out of their home computers—in tandem with the Editors of award-winning *FamilyPC* magazine. Titles: *The FamilyPC Guide to Homework* by Gregg Keizer and the Editors of *FamilyPC; The FamilyPC Software Buyer's Guide* by Kurt Carlson, Valle Dwight, and the Editors of *FamilyPC; The FamilyPC Guide to Cool PC Projects* by Sam Mea and the Editors of *FamilyPC.*

Disney Press produces a lineup that includes picture books, board books, pop-up books, novels, and activity books. Many of these works are derived from such successful Disney cinematic productions as *101 Dalmatians, The Hunchback of Notre Dame, The Lion King, Beauty and the Beast, James and the Giant Peach, Aladdin, Pocahontas, Lady and the Tramp, Bambi, The Mighty Ducks,* and *The Little Mermaid.*

Special Hyperion project: *Since the World Began: Walt Disney World's First 25 Years* by Jeff Kurtti. This work celebrates the 25th anniversary of the Disney World theme park. The book is a lavish, entertaining, and absolutely unique history of Walt's city of dreams—and the world's most popular tourist destination.

Hyperion Books for Children and products from Disney Press are distributed to the trade by Little, Brown.

Hyperion Books for Children is not currently accepting unsolicited manuscripts. Any materials received will be returned without review.

Andrea Cascardi, Associate Publisher

Gretchen Young, Editor—Also works with core Hyperion adult-trade list.

Ken Geist, Associate Publisher

Lisa Holton, Vice President and Publisher

H

Miramax Books

Miramax Books accents titles keyed to cinema—as a profession, industry, lifestyle, or avocation. The Miramax imprint develops a wide range of markets within this interest area. The Miramax list includes select original fiction (usually with a high-concept media link, or at least a halfway-celebrity author), reprints of novels that serve as the basis for films, and other movie tie-in projects.

From Miramax Books: *From Dusk Till Dawn* (a script by Quentin Tarantino); *The Last of the High Kings* (novel keyed to a film project) by Ferdia MacAnna; a currently untitled dark-comic novel by David Lipsky (author of *The Pallbearer*); *The Piano* (a script by Jane Campion); *The Postman* (a script by Antonio Skarmeta); *Jane Eyre* by Charlotte Brontë (classic fiction produced in a film tie-in reprint edition); *Pulp Fiction* (a script by Quentin Tarantino and Roger Avary).

Miramax Books is not currently accepting unsolicited manuscripts. Any materials received will be returned without review.

Susan Costello, Vice President of Publishing—Film-related projects.

IDG BOOKS WORLDWIDE
See Hungry Minds.

INDUSTRIAL PRESS

200 Madison Avenue, New York, NY 10016
212-889-6330 888-528-7852   fax: 212-545-8327
www.industrialpress.com   e-mail: induspress@aol.com

Industrial Press produces scientific works, technical handbooks, professional guides, and reference books in the areas of engineering and the law, manufacturing processes and materials, design engineering, and quality control. The house offers a line of works designed for plant and industrial engineering interface with management and logistics. In addition to advanced professional books, Industrial Press produces basic references in its fields of interest.

Industrial Press (founded in 1883) is a leading specialist house in the professional, scientific, and scholarly publishing arenas. The publisher typically offers several handpicked new titles a year in addition to its ongoing backlist of established sellers.

Industrial Press continues to offer its classic *Machinery's Handbook* by Erik Oberg, Franklin D. Jones, Holbrook L. Horton, and Henry H. Ryffel (elaborated from the Green-McCauley original in both print and CD-ROM), along with a companion guidebook (in fully revised formats).

Representative of the Industrial Press list: *Interpretation of Geometric Dimensioning and Tolerancing* by Daniel E. Puncochar; *Engineering Formulas, Conversions, Definitions, and Tables* by Frank Sims; *CNC Machining Handbook* by James Madison; *Setup Reduction Through Effective Workholding* by Edward G. Hoffman; *Blueprint Reading Basics,* 2nd edition by Warren Hammer; *Plastic Component Design* by Paul Campbell;

Why Systems Fail: And How to Make Sure Yours Doesn't by David A. Turbide; *Purchasing for Manufacturing* by Harry E. Hough; *Lubrication for Industry* by Kenneth E. Bannister; *The Handbook of Maintenance Management* by Joel Levitt; *Microbiologically Influenced Corrosion Handbook* by Susan Watkins Borenstein; *Fundamentals of Product Liability Law for Engineers* by Linda K. Enghagen; and *Pipefitter's Handbook* by Forrest R. Lindsey.

Industrial Press handles its own distribution.

Industrial Press is expanding its list of professional and educational titles and also starting a new program in electronic publishing. For guidelines and suggestions regarding submitting proposals, check out the Web site or contact John Carleo.

John F. Carleo, Editorial Director

IRWIN PROFESSIONAL PUBLISHING (A DIVISION OF MCGRAW-HILL)

1333 Burr Ridge Parkway, Burr Ridge, IL 60521
630-789-4000

Irwin Professional Publishing (a division of McGraw-Hill) produces a comprehensive lineup of business and professional publications. Areas within the Irwin scope include accounting, banking, corporate finance, employee benefits, financial advising, futures and options, general business, health-care management, individual investing, institutional investing, management, manufacturing, marketing, quality, and sales.

Irwin slots such topical niches as business economics, international trade, real estate, small business, personal finance, fixed income, lending and retail banking, global investing, mutual funds, stocks, portfolio management, business strategy, communication, customer satisfaction, diversity, global management, executive management, sales management, operations, auditing, compliance, human resources, fraud prevention/security, insurance, leadership, teams, and training.

Irwin Professional Publishing (part of McGraw-Hill) is the single largest publisher devoted to business publishing in the United States. Irwin strives constantly to create unique, innovative products tailored to meet the information demands of today's busiest people. The publisher produces an array of books, video seminars, and other media products of interest to seasoned corporate veterans as well as to rookie recruits—keyed to professional business markets worldwide.

Irwin Professional Publishing has a strong sales focus on the corporate and institutional market (featuring quantity discounts); of particular interest is the house's customer advisory service, which involves working with individual companies to develop specially tailored in-house training programs that feature Irwin Professional Publishing products. In addition, Irwin Professional Publishing has a section that specializes in custom-published and copublished corporate projects.

ASQC Quality Press and Irwin Professional Publishing have a conjoint arrangement; the fruits of this endeavor include the Malcolm Baldridge National Quality Award Series, as well as a line that focuses on issues of quality.

Irwin Professional (founded in 1965) went by the name of Dow Jones-Irwin until Dow Jones sold its interest in 1990; for several years subsequently, the house published under the Business One Irwin imprint. Irwin merged with formerly independent Probus Publishing Company in late 1994.

Prior to its acquisition by Irwin Professional, Probus Publishing Company (founded in 1984) was a privately held house specializing in trade and professional books for investors, business professionals, and entrepreneurs. Combining the complementary strengths of Irwin and Probus creates a market leader with increased publishing savvy and financial strength—of potential benefit to authors and booksellers alike. The plan goes forward with a large and varied publishing program dedicated to the development and marketing of business and financial books—as well as other information of significance to professionals around the world.

Irwin Professional Publishing is part of the McGraw-Hill group of specialty publishers.

Titles: *Fraud: Bringing Light to the Dark Side of Business* by W. Steve Albrecht, Gerald Wernz, and Timothy L. Williams; *Getting the Money You Need: Solutions for Financing Your Small Business* by Gibson Heath; *Healthcare Marketing in Transition: Practical Answers to Pressing Questions* by Terrence J. Rynne; *Soros: The Life, Times, and Trading Secrets of the World's Greatest Investor* by Robert Slater; *Stocks for the Long Run: A Guide to Selecting Markets for Long-Term Growth* by Jeremy J. Siegel; *Bogle on Mutual Funds: New Perspectives for the Intelligent Investor* by John C. Bogle; *The WOW Factor: Creating a Customer Focus Revolution in Your Business* by Paul Levesque; *Riding the Waves of Culture: Understanding Diversity in Global Business* by Fons Trompenaars; *The Ultimate Guide to Sport Event Management and Marketing* by Stedman Graham, Joe Jeff Goldblatt, and Lisa Delpy; *ISO 14000: A Guide to the New Environmental Management Standards* by Tom Tibor with Ira Feldman; *The Paradox Principles: How High-Performance Companies Manage Chaos, Complexity, and Contradiction to Achieve Superior Results* by Price Waterhouse Change Integration Team.

Irwin Professional Publishing handles its own distribution. Query letters and SASEs should be directed to:

Jeffrey A. Krames, Associate Publisher and Editor in Chief—Individual investing, personal finance, management, sales and marketing management, employee benefits.

Stephen Isaacs, Editor—Finance and investment.

Kelli Christiansen, Editor—Finance, and investment.

Catherine Dassopoulus, Editor—Supply chain, risk, telecommunications, project management, finance.

Ela Aktay, Editor—Finance, accounting, marketing, management.

ISLAND PRESS

Editorial office:
1718 Connecticut Avenue, NW, Suite 300, Washington, DC 20009
202-232-7933   fax: 202-234-1328
www.islandpress.org

West Coast operations:
P.O. Box 7, Covelo, CA 95428

Island Press issues books for resource conservation professionals and activists. The Island Press list is keyed to topics and issues in ecology, conservation, nature, regional studies, science (including biology and natural sciences), landscape architecture, land use, education, policy and planning, economics, and reference. Island publishes hardcover and trade paperback editions. The Shearwater Books imprint accents books of mainstream trade appeal and topical interest in hardbound and trade paper.

Island Press (founded in 1979; a subsidiary of Center for Resource Economics) pronounces itself: "the environmental publisher." Many Island Press books are authored in association with research groups, funds, and institutes with environmental focus.

From Island Press: *Strangers in Paradise: Impact and Management of Nonindigenous Species in Florida* (edited by Daniel Simberloff, Don C. Schmitz, and Tom C. Brown); *The Florida Panther: Life and Death of a Vanishing Carnivore* by David S. Maehr; *Nature's Services: Societal Dependence on Natural Ecosystems* (edited by Gretchen C. Daily; forewords by John Peterson Myers and Joshua S. Reichert); *The Work of Nature: How the Diversity of Life Sustains Us* by Yvonne Baskin; *Coastal Waters of the World: Trends, Threats, and Strategies* by Don Hinrichsen; *Placing Nature: Culture and Landscape Ecology* (edited by Joan Iverson Nassauer); *Discovering the Unknown Landscape: A History of America's Wetlands* by Ann Vileisis; *The Next West: Public Lands, Community, and Economy in the American West* (edited by John A. Baden and Donald Snow); *In the Dust of Kilimanjaro* by David Western.

Titles from Shearwater: *Fishcamp: Life on an Alaskan Shore* by Nancy Lord (illustrated by Laura Simonds Southworth); *Kinship to Mastery: Biophilia in Human Evolution and Development* by Stephen R. Kellert; *The Value of Life: Biological Diversity and Human Society* by Stephen R. Kellert; *The Others: How Animals Made Us Human* by Paul Shepard.

Island Press handles its own distribution.

Acquisitions are made primarily through the Washington office. Initial contact names and locations should be confirmed prior to any query. Query letters and SASEs should be directed to:

Barbara Dean, Executive Editor

Dan Sayre, Editor in Chief

Jonathon Cobb, Executive Editor—Shearwater Books

JOSSEY-BASS, INC., PUBLISHERS (A WILEY COMPANY)
Pfeiffer & Company

350 Sansome Street, Fifth Floor, San Francisco, CA 94104-1342
415-433-1740   fax: 415-433-0499
www.pfeiffer.com

Jossey-Bass, Inc., Publishers (established in 1967), produces nonfiction in professional and advanced trade categories covering business, management, and administration in public and nonprofit sectors, as well as issues in psychology, social and health sciences, religion, and education. Major Jossey-Bass divisions include Pfeiffer & Company. The house sustains an extensive backlist and publishes specialist journals in fields allied to editors.

The firm was acquired by John Wiley & Sons in 1999.

Pfeiffer & Company is a formerly independent business-and-workplace specialist press acquired by Jossey-Bass in 1996 (see separate entry further on).

Jossey-Bass has an editorial commitment to provide useful, leading-edge resources grounded in research and proven in practice. These works present substantive ideas that will help individuals and organizations to learn, develop, and improve their effectiveness.

The Jossey-Bass publishing niche accents theory-to-practice books for thinking professionals, often in larger corporations, who are progressive and curious, and who are in a position to influence their organizations. Most J-B books are grounded in primary research by the authors and are aimed at the twin concerns of development of the organization as a whole, as well as the individuals within the organization.

Jossey-Bass sells via a half-dozen channels; about 20 to 25 percent of J-B business and management titles get general-market trade-bookstore distribution, while the balance is sold through direct mail, direct to corporations, via catalog companies, through agency bookstore accounts (mostly large, independent professional booksellers), and for use in college-level courses.

Titles: *A New Beginning for Pastors and Congregations: Building an Excellent Match Upon Your Shared Strengths* by Kennor L. Callahan; *On Becoming a Servant Leader: The Private Writings of Robert K. Greenleaf* by Don M. Frick and Larry C. Spears; *Our Lives as Torah: Finding God in Our Own Stories* by Carol Ochs; *Living with Paradox: Religious Leadership and the Genius of Double Vision* by Newton Malony; *Jewish Spiritual Guidance: Finding Our Way to God* by Carol Ochs and Kerry Olitzky; *Reaching for Higher Ground in Conflict Resolution* by E. Ranklin Dukes, Marina A. Piscolish, and John B. Stephens; *Resolving Personal and Organizational Conflict* by Kenneth Cloke and John Goldsmith; *Narrative Mediation: A New Approach to Conflict Resolution* by John Winslade and Gerald Monk; *Peace Skills* by Alice Frazer Evans, Robert A. Evans, and Ronald S. Kraybill; *Collaborating: Finding Common Ground for Multiparty Problems* by Barbara Gray; *Work and Motivation* by Victor H. Vroom; *Working Scared: Achieving Success in Trying Times* by Kenneth N. Wexley and Stanley B. Silverman; *Working with Family Businesses: A Guide for Professionals* by David Bork, Dennis T. Jaffe, Sam H. Lane, and Leslie Dashew; *Visionary Leadership: Creating a Compelling Sense of Direction for Your Organization* by Burt Nanus; *Telecommuting: A Manager's Guide to Flexible Work Arrangements* by Joel Kugelmass; *Thought Leaders: Insights on the Future of Business* by Joel Kurtzman; *Strategic Pay: Aligning Organizational Strategies and Pay Systems* by Edward E. Lawler; *Smart Alliances: A Practical Guide to Repeatable Success* by John R. Harbison and Peter Pekar; and *Spirit at Work: Discovering the Spirituality in Leadership* by Jay A. Conger.

A representative Drucker Foundation Future series book: *The Leader of the Future: New Visions, Strategies, and Practices for the Next Era* (edited by Frances Hesselbein, Marshall Goldsmith, and Richard Beckhard; foreword by Peter F. Drucker). This Drucker Foundation Future Series book asks the leaders of today to imagine the leadership of tomorrow.

Books from Warren Bennis Executive Briefing series: *The 21st Century Organization: Reinventing Through Reengineering* by Warren Bennis and Michael Mische; *Why Lead-*

J

ers Can't Lead: The Unconscious Conspiracy Continues by Warren Bennis; *Fabled Service: Ordinary Acts, Extraordinary Outcomes* by Betsy Sanders; *The Absolutes of Leadership* by Philip B. Crosby.

Query letters and SASEs should be directed to:

Alan Rinzler, Executive Editor—Professional books in adult, child, and adolescent clinical psychology; trade/consumer titles in marriage, family, parenting, children and youth development, professional and trade books in conflict resolution, mediation, and international negotiation.

Andy Pasternack, Senior Editor—Health policy, administration, governance, and leadership; health-care systems and organizational development; public health; HIV and AIDS; physician issues.

Byron Schneider, Development Editor—Industrial and organizational psychology; organizational behavior, theory, development, and change; business communication; personal and professional career development; creativity, ethics, spirituality.

Cedric Crocker, Executive Editor—Global business; strategy; and e-business models.

Gale Erlandson, Senior Editor—Higher education administration, governance, leadership, and policy; student services and student development (in college); adult and continuing education; teaching and learning in colleges and universities; curriculum and faculty development.

Juliana Gustafson—Human resources management; industrial/organizational psychology.

Kathe Sweeney—Creativity/innovation; entrepreneurship (especially women); growing companies, post start-up; high-tech management; women in business; communications; transitions, third age; leadership development (CCL); and work/life balance.

Lesley Iura, Senior Editor—School administration, leadership, and policy; teaching and teacher education; student assessment; child development and welfare; multicultural issues.

Sarah Polster, Editor—Leadership and management of congregations and religious non-profits, and other faith-based organizations; congregational and organizational studies; practical theology; education, growth, and development of both lay and ordained religious leaders.

Susan Williams, Editor—Leadership; organizing development/change; emerging managers/leaders; career/personal development; women in business; teams; project management; hiring/retaining talent; decision-making; negotiation; facilitation; diversity; coaching/mentoring.

Pfeiffer & Company

Pfeiffer's trade business list targets such areas as career/personal development and general business/management. Pfeiffer also produces a dynamic array of training games, simulation/experiential-learning leader's manuals, computer software/CD-ROM, and audio- and videocassettes.

Pfeiffer & Company (formerly an independent business-and-workplace specialist press acquired by Jossey-Bass in 1996) is an international house that specializes in business topics directed particularly toward trainers, consultants, and managers; with offices in

Amsterdam, Johannesburg, London, Sydney, and Toronto, in addition to its former United States home in San Diego, the Pfeiffer & Company scope is adamantly global. As an imprint of Jossey-Bass Inc., Publishers, Pfeiffer & Company offers innovative products for Human Resource Development.

From Pfeiffer & Company: *Getting Together: Icebreakers and Group Energizers* by Lorraine L. Ukens; *Feeding the Zircon Gorilla and Other Team Building Activities* by Sam Sikes; *Team Players and Teamwork: The New Competitive Business Strategy* by Glenn M. Parker; *The Skilled Facilitator: Practical Wisdom for Developing Effective Groups* by Roger M. Schwarz; *Leading with Soul: An Uncommon Journey of Spirit* by Lee G. Bolman and Terrence E. Deal; *Empowerment Takes More Than a Minute* by Ken Blanchard, John P. Carlos, and Alan Randolph.

Query letters and SASEs should be directed to:

Matt Holt, Editor—Practical materials in human resource development and management; organization development.

Susan Rachmeier, Associate Editor—Management, careers, training.

KENSINGTON PUBLISHING CORPORATION
Pinnacle Books

Zebra Books

Dafina Books

Citadel Books

Citadel Press

850 Third Avenue, 16th Floor, New York, NY 10022-6222
212-407-1500
www.kensingtonbooks.com

The Kensington, Zebra, and Pinnacle programs cover all major categories of commercial and popular trade nonfiction and fiction. Kensington nonfiction is strong in issue-oriented investigatory works of topical interest, humor, health, self-help and awareness, true crime, and popular biography. Areas of fiction concentration include romance fiction (historical and contemporary), horror, mystery and suspense, thrillers, and women's fiction.

Kensington is one of the largest independently owned book publishers. Kensington Publishing Corporation is home to such divisional imprints as Kensington Books (primarily hardcover and trade paperback originals), along with Zebra and Pinnacle (mainly mass-market paperback editions, as well as selected hardcovers). Long a leader in the paperback category arena, the house has expanded its publishing emphasis along the commercial spectrum; under the Kensington and Zebra/Pinnacle banners, the house is a vital hardcover presence. Kensington recently bought the Carol Publishing Group's backlist.

The Kensington mass-market imprint publishes quality and commercial fiction and nonfiction, both original titles and reprints.

Zebra Books (founded in 1975) and its sibling house Pinnacle Books (acquired in 1987) publish a colossal list of mass-market paperback originals that span the spectrum of mainstream and genre categories. Zebra and Pinnacle also produce mass-market reprints of hardcover originals, as well as fiction and nonfiction in trade paper, and designated high-profile titles in original hardcover editions.

The paperback-originals division of the house maintains a firm backlist of books—however, in keeping with mass-market rack tradition, titles that don't move are soon gone.

Kensington continues its romance program under such imprints, series, and lines as Bouquet Romance, Regency Romance, Historical Romance, and Arabesque (a line of multicultural romances).

Sample Kensington titles: *Landing It: My Life On and Off the Ice* by Scott Hamilton; *The Complete Encyclopedia of Natural Healing: A Comprehensive A–Z Listing of Common and Chronic Illnesses and Their Proven Natural Treatments* by Gary Null, Ph.D.; *Cradle and All* by Zachary Alan Fox; *Hanging Curve* by Troy Soos; *Power Juices, Super Drinks* by Steve Seyerownitz.

Representative Zebra titles: *Sara's Song* by Fern Michaels; *Tempting Fate* by Meryl Sawyer; *Once in a Lifetime* by Constance O'Day Flannery; *Patchwork Angel* by Laurel Collins; *Irish Magic II: Four Unforgettable Novellas of Love and Enchantment* by Morgan Llewelyn, Barbara Samuel, Susan Wiggs, and Roberta Gellis.

From Pinnacle: *The Mentor* by R. A. Forster (legal thriller); *Wingman: Return of Sky Ghost* (men's adventure) by Mack Maloney; *Dawn of the Vampire* (horror) by William Hall; *Mom's New Little Instruction Book: More Wit and Wisdom for Mothers* by Annie Pigeon; *Arabesque: Love Everlasting* by Anna Larence.

Also on the house roster within the various fiction genres and categories are these backlist successes: *Vegas Heat* by Fern Michaels; *Murder Among Friends* (a Kate Austen mystery) by Jonnie Jacobs (from Partners in Crime); *Back\Slash: A Cyber Thriller* by William H. Lovejoy; *Pig Town* by William Caunitz.

Kensington oversees its own distributional operations.

All listed Kensington editors have a wide range of interests in fiction and nonfiction; some of their personal specialties are noted as follows. Query letters and SASEs should be directed to:

Ann LaFarge, Executive Editor, Zebra—Women's fiction.

Hilary Sares, Consulting Editor—Precious Gems Romances.

John Scognamiglio, Editorial Director, Fiction—Horror, psychological suspense, mysteries, romance.

Karen Haas, Consulting Editor—True crime and Westerns.

Karen Thomas, Executive Editor—American fiction.

Kate Duffy, Editorial Director, Romance—Commercial fiction; women's stories, romance—especially Regencies, mysteries; nonfiction.

Lee Heiman, Consulting Editor—Alternative, health.

Paul Dinas, Editor in Chief—Supervises all hardcover trade and mass-market titles, as well as the Zebra and Pinnacle imprints. Specialties: true crime, nonfiction.

Richard Ember, Associate Editor—Citadel Books, all commercial nonfiction.

K

Bruce Bender, Director of Publishing—Citadel Books

Margaret Wolf, Editor—Citadel Books

Bob Shuman, Editor—General nonfiction, popular reference.

Amy Garvey, Consulting Editor. Editor—Romance.
  Sign: Aries.
  Education: College—English degree.
  Employment history/editor career path: Luck. I started at a small newspaper part time after my son was born. I had a friend who worked at Walker & Co. and said she could get me a job. I now have been at Kensington for six and a half years.
  Personal interests: Reading, movies, I have two sons ages eight and a half and three.
  What would you be doing if you were not an editor? Writing or working at a bookstore.
  What has been your most successful book that you have acquired to date? A nonfiction book titled *Do Your Kids Know You Love Them* by Barbara Pierce and Martine Bern. I also work on a popular fiction series that is sold exclusively through WalMart called *Precious Gems.*
  Do you represent fiction? If so, what do you look for? Yes, I do acquire mostly fiction. Romance, mainstream, commercial, and women's fiction.
  What do you want to see less of? Science fiction. Authors who are trying to follow a formula, especially in women's fiction.
  Do you represent nonfiction? Yes, parenting, relationship books.
  Do you require book proposals? If so, what do you look for in evaluating a book proposal? Yes. A really developed outline, why are you the person most qualified to write this book? What are your background, credentials, and so on?
  Are certain aspects of a book proposal given more weight than others? No, I look at the whole package.
  What process do you use for making a decision? What is the process for acquisition, is there a committee? We have an equal opportunity editorial department; everyone is free to propose a project. The fist step is to take it to an editorial meeting and have others read it. Then it will go to further discussion.
  What kinds of nonfiction books do you want to see less of? Diet books, they really aren't effective; relationship books.
  Are you interested in work geared for the masses (readers of *People, The Star,* etc.)? Yes.
  Are agents important? Why? Yes, they can be. But it depends on the project.
  Do you like new writers? What should new writers do to break into the business? It depends on what they're writing. An agent would be helpful to persuade me to read a new writer's material.
  How should writers approach you? Snail mail. I need to see the actual writing, and give me a decent amount of time to respond.
  What are some common mistakes writers make? What really gets on your nerves? People who have not done their homework. Example: Kensington does not handle science fiction, poetry, and so on, yet people will still send them. Also, do not send money rather than an SASE. Just send a simple envelope with enough postage for your manuscript to be returned if necessary.

K

What can writers do to get your attention and to avoid the slush pile? I read agented material first. Don't address your material to me with Dear Romance Editor, and don't send material to people who don't work here any longer.

What have been some of your craziest experiences with submissions? We once received a manuscript from someone in prison who had the entire manuscript handwritten on tiny pieces of paper, in a sandwich baggie.

What have been some of your best experiences with writers or in your job? Working with authors who are getting published for the first time. It's wonderful to be the person to make the phone call to tell them they are getting published and then listen to their reaction.

What, if anything, makes you different from other editors? I'm a writer as well as an editor. I can relate to both positions. I am willing to write a personal rejection letter offering advice on how to improve your manuscript.

Is there anything you would like to see changed in the industry? I would like to see more success stories such as Charles Frazier.

Any advice for writers? Be patient, it's not going to happen overnight. Be willing to change, do your homework about the industry itself. Ask lots of questions, talk to people at bookstores.

MICHAEL KESEND PUBLISHING, LTD.

1025 Fifth Avenue, New York, NY 10028
212-249-5150   fax: 212-249-2129

Kesend's publishing scope is focused on travel, leisure, animals, pets, nature, the outdoors, hiking, health, and sports. The house also produces a line of belles lettres and biographies (often with themes related to the core house interest areas). Kesend in addition publishes occasional serious new fiction as well as classic literary reprints, along with some general trade nonfiction (especially in health-care issues).

Michael Kesend Publishing (begun in 1979) is an intimate house that offers personalized attention to the authors and books on its choice list. Kesend intends to pursue its program of publishing books with lasting quality that appeal to a broad readership.

Michael Kesend Publishing, Ltd., is now in its third decade. The publishing successes of recent years—primarily national and regional travel guidebooks—have resulted in numerous updated editions. The house typically releases a small number of new hardcover and trade paperback titles each year and maintains a backlist featuring the publisher's many perennial sellers.

Representing the Kesend list in travel, leisure, and the outdoors: *Terra Cotta, Don't Take It for Granite: Three Walks in New York City Neighborhoods* by Susan Tunick; *George and Edward Blum Texture & Design in New York City Apartment House Architecture* by Andrew S. Dolkart and Susan Tunick; *Gardenwalks: 101 of the Best Gardens from Maine to Virginia* and *Recommended Gardens Throughout the Country* by Marina Harrison and Lucy D. Rosenfeld; *Guide to the Sculpture Parks and Gardens of America* by Jane McCarthy and Laurily K. Epstein; *The Essential Guide to Wilderness Camping and Backpacking in the United States* by Charles Cook; *Mountainsigns/Mountain Life* (in

K

the illustrated Pocket Nature Guidebook series) by Gerald Cox; *Care of the Wild, Feathered and Furred: Treating and Feeding Injured Birds and Animals* by Mae Hickman and Maxine Guy (with foreword by Cleveland Amory).

A novel with a travel theme is *Season of the Migration to the North* by Tayeb Salih (translated from the Arabic by Denys Johnson-Davies). Literary travel writing includes a reprint of the classic *A Poet's Bazaar: A Journey to Greece, Turkey, and Up the Danube* by Hans Christian Andersen.

Kesend books in sports and athletics: *Basketball's Best 50 Players in the Last 50 Years* by Ken Shouler; *The Historical Dictionary of Golfing Terms: From 1500 to the Present* by Peter Davies; *Swee'pea and Other Playground Legends: Tales of Drugs, Violence and Basketball* by John Valenti with Ron Naclerio; *Butch Beard's Basic Baseball: The Complete Player* by Butch Beard with Glenn Popowitz and David Samson (with foreword by Julius Erving).

Health and popular medicine from Kesend: *Hysterectomy: Learning the Facts, Coping with the Feelings, Facing the Future* by Wanda Wigfall-Williams; *Understanding Pacemakers* by David Sonnenburg, Michael Birnbaum, and Emil A. Naclerio; and *Southern Gardenwalks* and *West Coast Gardenwalks.*

Michael Kesend Publishing handles its own distribution. Query letters and SASEs should be directed to:

Judy Wilder, Senior Editor

Michael Kesend, Publisher

KIVAKÍ PRESS

P.O. Box 1053, Skyland, NC 28776
704-684-1988   fax: 704-684-7372
www.kivaki.com

Kivakí Press is a small house with a focus on three editorial areas: environmental restoration; community renewal and education; and personal and holistic healing. Kivakí exists to provide people with practical strategies for restoring their ecosystems, for reconnecting with their places and local cultures, and for renewing their bodies holistically. Kivakí addresses academic, holistic health, and environmental book markets. Located in the mountains of North Carolina, the press produces a small number of new titles on a seasonal basis to add to a strong backlist.

Indicative of Kivakí interest: *A Wilder Life: Essays from Home* by Ken Wright; *The Company of Others: Essays in Celebration of Paul Shepard* (edited by Max Oelschlaeger); *Look to the Mountain: An Ecology of Indigenous Education* by Gregory Cajete; *Seasons of Change: Growing Through Pregnancy and Birth* by Suzanne Arms; *Restoration Forestry: An International Guide to Sustainable Forestry Practices* (edited by Michael Pilarski); *Flora of the San Juans: A Field Guide to the Mountain Plants of Southwestern Colorado* by Sue Komarek; *Sacred Land Sacred Sex: Rapture of the Deep—Concerning Deep Ecology and Celebrating Life* by Dolores Lachapelle; *Deep Powder Snow* by Dolores Lachapelle; *Igniting the Sparkle: An Indigenous Science Education Model* by Gregory Cajete; *David Johns: On the Trail of Beauty* by Lois and Jerry Jack.

K

Kivakí oversees its own distribution, including direct mail-order, and a trade distribution network that utilizes the facilities of several national fulfillment and distribution firms. Query letters and SASEs should be directed to:

Fred Gray, Publisher

KNOPF PUBLISHING GROUP (A SUBSIDIARY OF RANDOM HOUSE)

Alfred A. Knopf Books for Young Readers

Everyman's Library

Pantheon Books

Schocken Books

Vintage Anchor Publishing

299 Park Avenue, New York, NY 10171
212-751-2600

The publishing firm of Alfred A. Knopf was long associated with fine bookmaking and the literary tradition. The regime of publisher Sonny Mehta (begun in 1990) has seen a bestselling radiance to the house, now astutely positioned in the arena of commercial contemporary letters in its corporate incarnation as Knopf Publishing Group, which, in addition to the Alfred A. Knopf imprint, covers Vintage, Pantheon, and Schocken (see separate subentries). Knopf Books for Young Readers stakes a solid claim in the kids' books domain. Random House corporate marketing and promotion support combines with Knopf editorial and publishing tradition to make for a truly formidable house.

The Knopf roster of eminent authors includes major voices worldwide in virtually every field of fiction and nonfiction. Regardless of the category or genre affiliation or lack thereof, these books are Knopf: The volumes are consummately designed products, and Knopf's running-dog colophon—the illustrious Borzoi—can in and of itself signal a potential reviewer's priorities.

Knopf fiction and literary works express established traditions as well as new domains in popular contemporary writing, including provocatively styled mysteries and suspense fiction, inventive approaches in nonfiction, and literary writing in travel, food, and lifestyle. Knopf has published such writers as Ann Beattie, John le Carré, Sandra Cisneros, Michael Crichton, Brett Easton Ellis, James Ellroy, Carl Hiaasen, P. D. James, Dean R. Koontz, Peter Maass, Cormac McCarthy, Susanna Moore, Toni Morrison, Anne Rice, Donna Tartt, John Updike, and Andrew Vachss.

Titles here include: *Toward the End of Time: A Novel* by John Updike; *The Wind-Up Bird Chronicle: A Novel* by Haruki Murakami; *Memoirs of a Geisha: A Novel* by Arthur Golden; *Lucky You: A Novel* by Carl Hiaasen; *Plays Well with Others: A Novel* by Allan Gurganus; *The Wonder Worker: A Novel* by Susan Howatch; *A Certain Justice: An Adam Dalgliesh Mystery* by P. D. James; *Doctor Faustus: The Life of the German Composer Adrian Leverkühn as Told by a Friend: A Novel* by Thomas Mann; *Barney's Version: A Novel* by Mordecai Richler; *Preston Falls: A Novel* by David Gates; *Cities of the Plain* by Cormac McCarthy.

K

Knopf lists a notable array of poetry, including *I Can't Remember* by Cynthia Macdonald; *Odes, Elegies, and Epigrams* (edited by Peter Washington); *Ghost Ship* by Mary Kinzie; *Flight Among the Tombs* by Anthony Hecht; *The Fire Fetched Down* by George Bradley; *The Willow Grove* by Laurie Sheck.

Knopf nonfiction accents contemporary culture, issues of public interest, art and architecture, biography and memoir, and titles in health, fitness, and lifestyle; otherwise, Knopf titles roam virtually anywhere across the reaches of the mainstream publishing emporium, including popular reference and humor.

The Knopf list in nonfiction and popular works is represented by *The Ultimate Guitar Book* by Tony Bacon; *Jane Austen: A Biography* by Claire Tomalin; *Compañero: The Life and Death of Che Guevara* by Jorge G. Castañeda; *Eyes of the Nation: A Visual History of the United States* by Vincent Virga and Curators of the Library of Congress, with Alan Brinkley; *The Man Who Ate Everything: And Other Gastronomic Feats, Disputes, and Pleasurable Pursuits* by Jeffrey Steingarten; *Heart and Blood: Living with Deer in America* by Richard Nelson; *Albert Camus: A Life* by Oliver Todd; *Cagney* by James McCabe; *Degas in New Orleans: Encounters in the Creole World of Kate Chopin and George Washington Cable* by Christopher Benfey; *Conquering Schizophrenia: A Father, His Son, and a Medical Breakthrough* by Peter Wyden; *Remaking the World: Adventures in Engineering* by Henry Petroski.

Knopf is home to the National Audubon Society Pocket Guides (field guides) series; the Knopf Guides series includes regionally keyed handbooks to such areas of travel interest as Ireland and the route of the Mayas; Chic Simple books highlight ingenious approaches to the good life.

Prospective authors please note that Knopf's address is currently in flux; please call to verify it before submitting materials. Query letters and SASEs should be directed to:

Ann Close, Editor—Literary fiction, literary fiction.

Gary Fisketjon, Editor—Literary fiction; varied serious nonfiction interests.

Jane Garrett, Editor—United States history, some European and Middle Eastern history, craft and hobby books.

Jonathan Segal, Senior Editor—Twentieth-century history, contemporary events and issues.

Judith Jones, Senior Editor and Vice President—Literary fiction, cookbooks, cultural history, the arts.

Ken Schneider, Assistant Editor—Contemporary fiction. Nonfiction: cultural history, the arts (drama, music, ballet). Works with Judith Jones.

Robin Desser, Senior Editor—Contemporary fiction; works with international/multicultural outlook; narrative nonfiction, including literary travel.

Susan Ralston, Editorial Director of Schocken, Senior Editor of Knopf

Victoria Wilson, Senior Editor—Nonfiction: biography and memoir; cultural and social history; performing and creative arts, including film. Literary fiction.

Deb Garrision, Poetry Editor at Knopf, Senior Editor of Pantheon

K

Alfred A. Knopf Books for Young Readers
Crown Books for Young Readers

The Knopf and Crown programs for young readers provide works geared to all age ranges in hardcover and paperback formats. This division produces trade reference and entertainment titles, as well as works for the educational market. Knopf and Crown cover a broad range that includes picture books, reference books, readers, fiction and nonfiction, novelty and gift productions, and series.

Crown's children's list is distinguished by illustrated works in hardcover and paperback, mainly for kids between the ages of 3 and 12; the program offers a few nonfiction titles for older grade-school readers. Crown has a special emphasis on picture books for preschoolers and quality nonfiction.

The Knopf children's book program produces a hardy list of picture books, books for middle readers, and young adult fiction and nonfiction.

Knopf Paperbacks Young Adult fiction and middle grade fiction includes Dragonfly Books, which are picture books (for the very young).

This division prefers submissions that go through agents. Unsolicited manuscripts are no longer accepted or considered. Query letters and SASEs from authors should be directed to the Editorial Department; agented submissions may be sent to:

Joan Slattery, Executive Editor—Paperbacks.

Nancy Siscoe, Editor

Simon Boughton, Publishing Director

Tracy Gates, Senior Editor

Pantheon Books

Pantheon accents nonfiction books in current events, international affairs, contemporary culture, literary criticism and the arts, popular business, psychology, travel, nature, science, and history. The house also has a strong list in contemporary fiction, poetry, and drama. Pantheon also offers the Fairytale and Folktale Library.

Pantheon Books was founded in 1942 by German Jewish émigrés and, from its United States base, forged an international reputation as a publisher of exemplary titles in fiction and nonfiction while remaining a viable business entity. Pantheon was bought by Random House in 1990, subsequent to which occurred the famous and abrupt departure of director André Schiffrin, followed by the resignation of members of the editorial staff and the shift of major authors to other houses. Although awestruck literary commentators were quick to offer epitaphs, Pantheon regrouped along a profile similar to that previously pursued; the house continues its product success with seasonally vigorous lists and a refined editorial eye.

Pantheon books include: *The Feast of Love* by Charles Baxter; *The Diagnosis* by Alan Lightman; *Master of the Crossroads* by Madison Smartt Bell; *Waiting* by Ha Jin; *The Consolations of Philosophy* by Alain de Botton; *House of Leaves* by Mark Danielevski; *Passage to Juneau* by Jonathan Raban; *Jimmy Corrigan: The Smartest Kids on Earth* by Chris Ware; *Four Wings and a Prayer: Caught in the Mystery of the Monarch Butterfly* by

K

Sue Halpern; *An American Story* by Debra Dickerson; *Compass Points: How I Lived* by Edward Hoagland.

Query letters and SASEs should be directed to:

Daniel Frank, Vice President and Editorial Director—Pantheon Books. Nonfiction: serious subjects, history, science, and current issues. Literary fiction.

Erroll McDonald, Executive Editor—Pantheon Books. Literary fiction. Nonfiction: politics, current issues, and contemporary culture.

Shelley Wanger, Senior Editor—Literary fiction, memoir, nonfiction, culture, science, film.

Deborah Garrison, Senior Editor

Schocken Books

With strong footholds in both academic and commercial publishing, Schocken produces titles in cultural, religious, and women's studies; Judaica; literature; science and health; and the social sciences.

Schocken Books was founded in Germany in 1931 by Salman Schocken, a noted bibliophile, Zionist, and department-store kingpin. The house's German division was shut down after Kristallnacht (the formal institution of the full brunt of the Nazi pogram on November 9, 1938), but much of Schocken's holdings had been moved to Jerusalem and Tel Aviv by that time. In 1945 Schocken opened New York offices and flourished as an independent until acquired by Random House in 1987. Schocken controls the world rights to the works of Franz Kafka and otherwise includes works by Jean-Paul Sartre, Claude Lévi-Strauss, Susannah Heschel, Gershom Scholem, Elie Wiesel, Primo Levi, and Harold Kushner.

Schocken (under Editorial Director Susan Ralston, who is also a Senior Editor at Knopf) is now part of the Knopf publishing group at Random House, Inc. It has adopted a robust approach across the contemporary cultural horizon and does much of Random House's religion publishing.

Schocken's list sports a logo based on the Bauhaus-style S that was emblematic of Salman Schocken's business enterprises in Germany earlier in the century.

On the Schocken list: *Montessori in the Classroom: A Teacher's Account of How Children Really Learn* by Paula Polk Lillard; *The Five Books of Moses,* a riveting translation by Everett Fox, is the first volume of a four-volume Bible-translation project in progress: the *Schocken Bible; The Sunflower: On the Possibilities of Forgiveness* by Simon Wiesenthal; *The Monk and the Philosopher* by Jean-Francois Revel and Matthiew Ricard; *A Good Enough Daughter* by Alix Kates Shulman; and *Saying Kaddish: How to Comfort the Dying, Bury the Dead, and Mourn as a Jew* by Anita Diamant.

Literary writing from Schocken includes new translations of Kafka's *The Castle* and *The Trial; The Iron Tracks* and *The Conversion* by Aharon Appelfeld; *The Schocken Book of Contemporary Jewish Fiction* (edited by Ted Solortaroff and Nessa Rapoport); *Yiddish Folktales* (edited by Beatrice Silverman Weinreich, translated by Leonard Wolf); *All the Rivers Run to the Sea* (autobiography) by Elie Wiesel; *A Book That Was Lost and Other Stories* by S. Y. Agnon.

Proposals and SASEs should be directed to:

K

Altie Karper, Editor

Cecelia Cancellaro, Editor

Susan Ralston, Editorial Director

Vintage Books

Vintage trade paperbacks are renowned for high style in design and production standards as well as their substantial content. Vintage accents new titles in the fields of contemporary global and American literature and current-interest nonfiction, along with its preponderance of reprints in trade fiction and nonfiction. Among Vintage series are Vintage International, Vintage Contemporaries, Vintage Departures, Vintage Books/The Library of America, Vintage Classics, Vintage Spiritual Classics, Vintage Español, and Vintage/ Black Lizard Crime.

Indicative of the Vintage list: *Memoirs of a Geisha* by Arthur Golden; *Meditations from a Movable Chair* by Andre Dubus; *Ecology of Fear* by Mike Davis; *King of the World* by David Remnick; *Two in the Wild* by Susan Fox Rodgers; *Cold Mountain* by Charles Frazier; *Slapboxing with Jesus* by Victor La Valle; *Titan: The Life of John D. Rockefeller, Sr.* by Ron Chernow; *Midwives* by Chris Bohjalian; *Crime Wave* by James Ellroy; *Everybody Pays* by Andrew Vachss; *Civil Action* by Jonathan Harr; *The Reader* by Bernhard Schlink.

Query letters and SASEs should be directed to:

Martin Asher, Editor in Chief

KODANSHA AMERICA/KODANSHA INTERNATIONAL

Kodansha's last U.S. list was fall 1999. The firm's New York offices have been closed and all publications are now being done from their parent company in Tokyo. Kodansha's interests are autobiography and biography, business and psychology, garden and design, health and lifestyle, parenting, self-help, history and sociology, natural history, world culture, religion and spirituality, and women's studies.

KRAUSE PUBLICATIONS

700 East State Street, Iola, WI 54990-0001
888-457-2873
www.krause.com

Krause is a large publisher of trade nonfiction, with a concentration in antiques, collectibles, sewing, ceramics, and crafts and hobbies, as well as technical and professional topics (in such areas as engineering). Series include Contemporary Quilting, Creative Machine Arts, and a full lineup of consumer/trade titles that lists current market values for a wide range of antiques and collectibles (usually in periodically updated editions).

Representative of the list: *Radio & TV Premiums: Value and History from Tom Mix to Space Patrol* by Jim Harmon; *Decorating with Collectibles* by Annette Lough; *Silver Christmas Ornaments: A Collector's Identification and Price Guide* by Clara Johnson

K

Scroggins; *Antique Golf Collectibles: A Price and Reference Guide* by Chuck Furjanic; *Old Car Wrecks* by Ron Kowalke; *Chevrolet Police Cars, 1956–1996* by Edwin J. Sanow; *Ancient Coin Collecting II: Numismatic Art of the Greek World* by Wayne G. Sayles; *Japanese Folded Patchwork* by Mare Clare Clark; *Painted Wooden Furniture* by Cate Withacy; *Modern Custom Guns: Walnut, Steel, and Uncommon Artistry* by Tom Turpin; *Warman's Coins & Currency* (in updated editions) by Allen G. Berman and Alex G. Malloy; *Collectors' Information Bureau's Collectibles Market Guide & Price Index* (in updated editions); *Coykendall's Complete Guide to Sporting Collectibles* by Ralph Coykendall, Jr.; *The Doulton Figure Collectors Handbook* (in updated editions).

Query letters and SASEs should be directed to:

Deb Faupel, Editor—Book Division.

Don Johnson, Vice President of Publishing—Magazines and periodicals.

LATIN AMERICAN LITERARY REVIEW PRESS

121 Edgewood Avenue, Pittsburgh, PA 15218
fax: 412-371-9025
www.lalrp.org e-mail: latin@angstrom.net

Latin American Literary Review Press produces reference books, trade books, and specialty publications in Latin American interest and studies. The press produces books in art, architecture, literature, and poetry; history, biography, and natural science; country studies (Spain, Europe, United States, Latin America); and children's books.

Latin American Literary Review Press (founded in 1980) is an independent house that is particularly vigorous in such fields as Latin American literature in English translation, Spanish-language art books, and literary criticism in Spanish. The press also publishes the journal *Latin American Literary Review,* the only journal in the United States devoted solely to the study of Latin American literature.

Representative titles in fiction and literature: *Clara* by Luisa Valenzuela (translated by Andrea G. Labinger); *Ceremonial Songs* by Chilean Nobel Laureate Pablo Neruda (translated by Maria Jacketti); *The Island of Cundeamor* by Rene Vazquez Diaz (translated by David E. Davis); *The Medicine Man* by Francisco Rojas Gonzalez (translated by Robert Rudder and Gloria Arjona); *Scent of Love* by Edla Van Steen (translated by David S. George); *Strange Forces* by Leopoldo Lugones (translated by Gilbert Alter-Gilbert); *People on the Prowl* by Jaime Collyer (translated by Lillian Lorca de Tagle); *Melodious Women* by Jarjorie Agosin (edited by Croi L. Gabbard, translated by Monica Bruno Galmozzi); *Bebbeh* by Sabina Berman (translated by Andrea G. Labinger); *Yo-Yo Boing!* by Giannina Braschi; *Beer Cans in the Rio de la Plata* by Jorge Stamadianos (translated by Leland Chambers); *Maria de Estrada, Gypsy Conquistadora* by Gloria Duran; *The Cuban Mile* by Alejandro Hernandez Diaz (translated by Dick Cluster); and *Sultry Moon* by Mempo Giardinelli.

Nonfiction and critical works: *XVIII Century Spanish Music Villancicos of Juan Francés de Iribarren* by Marta Sánchez; *Mexican American Theater: Legacy and Reality* by Nicolás Kanellos; *The Art of Mariano Azuela* by Eliud Martínez.

K

Latin American Literary Review Press has its own in-house distribution operation; in addition, the house markets through direct-mail catalog dissemination and utilizes a variety of national and regional distribution houses. Major markets include public libraries, trade booksellers, and university and college libraries. Latin American Literary Review Press handles distribution for a number of domestic and international presses. Query letters and SASEs should be directed to:

Yvette E. Miller, President and Editor in Chief

Maria G. Trujillo, Assistant Editor

LEARNING EXPRESS

900 Broadway, Suite 604, New York, NY 10003
212-995-2566   fax: 212-995-5512
www.learnx.com

Learning Express's mission is to help prepare people for a brighter future by offering "unique, customized test preparation, career information, and skill-enhancing books." Books are distributed by Random House, Inc. Learning Express is interested in test preparation, basic skills, and career guidance books. Query letters and SASEs should be directed to:

Jan Gallagher, Senior Editor

LEISURE BOOKS

276 Fifth Avenue, Suite 1008, New York, NY 10001
212-725-8811

Leisure's publishing program centers on mass-market paperback originals in fiction, with a short list of hardcover reprints. Leisure's category fiction embraces historical romance, horror, technothrillers, thrillers, and Westerns.

Leisure hosts a fine list from established genre writers and also offers works from newer authors; the house publishes several brand-name category series and issues a notable number of deluxe double editions. The innovative Love Spell line has defined new market territory with experimental marketing slates in paranormal, futuristic, time travel, legendary lovers, perfect heroes, and faerie tale romance. Love Spell is developing a new line of humorous contemporary romance, and also launched a new line of gothic romances. Leisure Books (founded in 1970) and Love Spell are divisions of Dorchester Publishing Company.

Indicative of Leisure Books interest: *Spirit's Song* by Madeline Baker; *The Cowboys: Sean* by Leigh Greenwood; *Savage Joy* by Cassie Edwards; *Pirate* by Connie Mason; *Lark* by Norah Hess; *The Bewitched Viking* by Sandra Hill; *Mine to Take* by Dara Joy; *Two Sixes* by Max Brand; *Danger Ridge* by Tim McGuire; *The Halloween Man* by Douglas Clegg; *Drawn to the Grave* by Mary Ann Mitchell.

L

Leisure is distributed by Hearst Distribution Group. Query letters and SASEs should be directed to:

Alicia Condon, Editorial Director

Christopher Keeslar, Editor

Don D'Auria, Senior Editor

Leah Hultenschmidt, Editorial Assistant

Joanna Rulf, Editorial Assistant

Kate Seaver, Associate Editor

LifeLine Press (An Imprint of Regnery Publishing)

See also: Regnery Publishing

One Massachusetts Avenue NW, Washington, DC 20001
202-216-0600   fax: 202-216-0612

LifeLine Press is a new imprint of Regnery Publishing, which is dedicated to health, wellness, and child care. The press is committed to publishing the latest ground-breaking medical research in the fields of alternative health, nutrition, wellness, and child development. LifeLine's mission is "to provide timely and accurate information for consumers concerned about their health." LifeLine Press is committed to building a successful partnership with authors that could lead to the publication of not only the authors' first books, but their second and third books as well. Query letters and SASEs should be directed to:

Marji Ross, Vice President and Group Publisher

Little, Brown and Company (Part of Time Warner)

Bulfinch Press

Little, Brown and Company Books for Children and Young Adults

New York office:
Time & Life Building, 1271 Avenue of the Americas, New York, NY 10020
212-522-8700   fax: 212-522-2062

Boston office:
3 Center Plaza, Boston, MA 02108

Little, Brown publishes commercial trade nonfiction and fiction. Nonfiction interests encompass popular and literary biography, history, travel, art, medicine and allied health education, law, science, cuisine and lifestyle, reference, inspiration, and keepsake volumes/gift books. Little, Brown also produces commercial and literary fiction, essays, and memoirs; cultural, literary, and art criticism; and selected poetry. Little, Brown publishes in hardcover, trade paper, and mass-market paperback editions, and produces selected deluxe editions of bestselling works, coffee-table volumes, and a line of calendars.

L

Little, Brown and Company (founded in 1837) originated as an independent house with a Boston home base. Little, Brown earned renown as a publisher with a dynamic, commercially successful line as well as an outstanding literary list. Little, Brown, now a subsidiary of Time Warner, functions autonomously, primarily from within the Time & Life building (where its main trade offices reside), and releases titles under its stately colophon image of an eagle-topped column. Bulfinch Press (a division still based in Boston; see subentry further on) is one of the leading houses to specialize in fine-arts publishing and illustrated volumes.

Back Bay Books is a Little, Brown trade paperback imprint that accents contemporary fiction; Back Bay titles are generally cataloged with the core Little, Brown list. Little, Brown and Company Books for Young Adults is among the strongest and most respected imprints in its field. (Please see separate subentry.)

Little, Brown nonfiction and popular works: *Shooting the Moon* by David Harris; *The Oldest Rookie: Big League Dreams from a Small Town Guy* by Jim Morris and Joel Engel; *Atom: An Odyssey from the Big Bang to Life on Earth* by Lawrence M. Krauss; *Believing It All* by Marc Parent; *A Baby's Garden* by Elizabeth St. Cloud Muse; *Pasquale's Nose* by Michael Rips; *One Band Could Be Your Life* by Michael Azemad; *Where Dead Voices Gather* by Nick Tosches*; My Really Cool Baby Book* by Todd Parr; *The Road to Success Is Paved with Failure* by Joey Green; *The Prostate Cancer Protection Plan* by Bob Arnot; *Where There's Smoke, There's Flavor* by Richard Langer; *The Attachment Parenting Book* by William Sears, M.D., and Martha Sears, R.N.

Little, Brown fiction and belles lettres encompass topnotch commercial novels and popular literature, as well as a high-profile selection of thrillers, suspense stories, and mysteries. Featured titles: *1st to Die* by James Patterson; *The Last Time They Met* by Anita Shrove; *The Gospel of Judas* by Simon Mawer; *I Don't Want to Go to Jail* by Jimmy Breslin; *Fearless Jones* by Walter Mosley; *All the Fine Girls* by Alexander Styron; *Suzanne's Diary for Nicholas* by James Patterson; *Do What You Are* by Paul Tieger and Barbara Barron-Tieger.

The Ansel Adams Publishing Program: Little, Brown is the sole authorized publisher of the Ansel Adams line of books, calendars, and posters, authorized by the Publishing Rights Trust established by Ansel Adams. Top-quality design and papers and meticulous attention to detail ensure the enduring legacy of America's great landscape photographer.

Little, Brown maintains an extensive backlist, which is especially strong in literary fiction and nonfiction. Little, Brown distributes its own titles as well as those of a changing list of other publishing houses both large and small, including Arcade Publishing, Bilingual Books, Food and Wine, Hyperion Books, and Miramax.

Please note: There are currently no Little, Brown adult-trade editors in Boston full-time. Query letters and SASEs should be directed to these New York editors:

J. Scott Oberacker, Editorial Assistant (Boston)

Judy Clain, Senior Editor—Literary and commercial fiction; serious nonfiction.

Kim McArthur, President

Michael Pietsch, Vice President and Editor in Chief—Literary fiction and thrillers; general nonfiction, music biography and autobiography. Authors published or under contract include Peter Blanner, Michael Connelly, John Feinstein, Peter Guralnick, Joe McGinnis, Rick Moody, Walter Mostley, and the Neville Brothers.

L

Sarah Burnes, Editor—General nonfiction. Literary and serious commercial fiction.

Terry Adams, Director—Trade Paperbacks.

William D. Phillips, Editor in Chief—General nonfiction; some literary fiction; fiction, essays, and memoirs; cultural, literary, and art criticism; and selected poetry.

Geoff Shandler, Executive Editor

Deborah Baker, Senior Editor

Bulfinch Press

Bulfinch Press is a Little, Brown and Company division (based in Boston) that specializes in fine arts, architecture, photography, and design, as well as finely produced collections of literary classics and illustrated volumes with a historical, cultural, or geographical accent. The house produces lush hardcover and paperback volumes, as well as merchandise lines, including posters and calendars.

Representative of the Bulfinch list: *Faces of Time: 75 Years of Time Cover Portraits* (essay by Frederick C. Voss); *David Hockney's Dog Days* by David Hockney; A *Murmur on the Trees* by Emily Dickinson (selected and illustrated by Ferris Cook); *The Bulfinch Illustrated Encyclopedia of Antiques* by Paul Atterbury and Lars Tharp; *Stuart Davis* (edited by Philip Rylands); *The Illustrated Book of Women Gardeners* by Deborah Kellaway; *De Chirico* by Paolo Baldacci; *If Only You Knew How Much I Smell You: True Portraits of Dogs* by Roy Blount, Jr. (photographs by Valerie Shaff); *Á Propos de Paris* by Henri Cartier-Bresson; *Masterpieces of the Metropolitan Museum of Art* by the Metropolitan Museum of Art (introduction by Phillippe de Montebello); *Women in Love: Portraits and Stories of Lesbian Mothers and Their Families* (photographs and interviews by Barbara Seyda and Diana Herrera); *Crabtree and Evelyn Fragrant Herbal: Enhancing Your Life with Aromatic Herbs and Essential Oils* by Lesley Bremness (recipes by Marie-Pierre Moine, photographs by Clay Perry and Jean Cazal); *LIFE Legends: The Century's Most Unforgettable Faces* by the Editors of *LIFE*; *Patrick Demarchelier: Photographs* by Patrick Demarchelier; *Fun Along the Road: American Tourist Attractions* by John Margolies; *Branded Youth and Other Stories* by Bruce Weber.

A special Bulfinch project: *All Quiet on the Western Front: The Illustrated Edition* by Erich Maria Remarque. This classic war novel was first published by Little, Brown and Company in 1929 and is here illustrated for the first time with fascinating and moving historical photographs from World War I.

Query letters and SASEs should be directed to:

Carol Judy Leslie, Vice President and Publisher

Janet Swan Bush, Executive Editor

Terry Hackford, Senior Editor

Dorothy Williams, Senior Editor

Karen Dane, Editor

Michael Sand, Managing Editor

Stephanie Lucianovic, Assistant Editor

Helen Watt, Assistant Editor

L

Little, Brown and Company Books for Children and Young Adults

Three Center Plaza, Boston, MA 02108
617-227-0730

Little, Brown's children's books division (headquartered in Boston) produces picture books, board books, pop-up and lift-the-flap editions, chapter books, and general fiction and nonfiction titles for middle and young adult readers.

This division also issues resource guides and reference titles in careers, social issues, and intellectual topics for higher grade levels and the college-bound. Marc Brown's Arthur books and Matt's Christopher sports series are especially successful. The house offers volumes in Spanish language and in dual Spanish/English editions and is on the lookout for multicultural titles.

Sample titles: Caldecott winner *Saint George and the Dragon* (illustrated by Trina Schart Hyman); Newbery winner *Maniac Magee* by Jerry Spinelli; *Toot & Puddle* by Holly Hobbie; *Daisy and the Egg* by Jane Simmons; *Kevin and His Dad* by Irene Smalls; *Go Away, Big Green Monster!* by Ed Emberley; *Animal Crackers* by Jane Dyer; and *The Jolly Pocket Postman* by Janet and Allen Ahlberg.

Little Brown & Company recently added the imprint Megan Tingley Books to its children's division. (See Megan Tingley Books.) The house distributes the publications of Disney Press and Hyperion Books for Children.

Prospective authors please note: Little Brown's children's division does not accept unsolicited manuscripts directly from authors. Manuscripts must go through an agent to: Children's Editorial Dept.

LODESTAR BOOKS (AN IMPRINT OF DUTTON)

See Penguin USA.

LONELY PLANET PUBLICATIONS

150 Linden Street, Oakland, CA 94607
510-893-8555   fax: 510-893-8563
www.lonelyplanet.com   e-mail: info@lonelyplanet.com

Lonely Planet's Web site includes up-to-date, down-to-earth travel information.

Lonely Planet specializes in travel guides and phrasebooks for the practical traveler, city guides, walking guides, and guides for those on a shoestring budget. Lonely Planet's list offers travel survival kits that provide in-depth coverage of a single country or group of countries, with travel options for a range of budgets and styles. Lonely Planet also offers a line of literary travel narratives.

Lonely Planet Travel Atlas series comprise detailed full-color maps in a sturdy atlas format with comprehensive road and rail details and countrywide introductory sections. City Guides offer the best of the world's great cities in a pocket-sized format. Walking Guides offer informative and reliable route descriptions, easy-to-follow maps and advice on preparation, equipment, and supplies for some of the world's most exciting trekking

L

routes. Phrasebooks are handy, pocket-sized books covering essential words and phrases for almost every travel situation.

Lonely Planet Journeys is a series that delves into the world's hidden places, capturing the spirit of a place and the nature of travel. These are books to read while you are planning a trip, while you are on the road, or while you are at home in your favorite armchair.

Lonely Planet Publications also offers audio packs that include unique language recordings to help travelers learn essential words and phrases and their correct pronunciation by participating in realistic travel situations. Lonely Planet videos offer original footage of today's most interesting destinations. These videos (as seen on the cable television Travel Channel) offer the same approach to travel as Lonely Planet guidebooks—get off the beaten track, be informed about where you are going, get to know the locals, and have fun!

Recent titles: *Antarctica: Travel Survival Kit* by Jeff Rubin; *Full Circle: A South American Journey* by Luis Sepulveda; *Trekking in the Karakoram & Hindukush* by John Mock and Kimberley O'Neil.

The people at Lonely Planet (founded in 1975) strongly believe that travelers can make a positive contribution to the countries they visit, both through their appreciation of the countries' culture, wildlife, and natural features, and through the money they spend. In addition, Lonely Planet makes a direct contribution to the countries and regions it covers. Since 1986 a percentage of the income from each book has been donated to ventures such as famine relief in Africa, aid projects in India, agricultural projects in Central America, Greenpeace's efforts to halt French nuclear testing in the Pacific, and Amnesty International.

As the publisher's message suggests: "I hope we send the people out with the right attitude about travel. You realize when you travel that there are many different perspectives about the world, so we hope these books will make people more interested in what they see. These are guidebooks, but you can't really guide people. All you can do is point them in the right direction."

Lonely Planet produces an anecdotal and informative travel newsletter and distributes its own list in America through its United States office. The Lonely Planet Publications editorial division is located in Australia—though manuscripts and proposals are given preliminary consideration at the stateside contact address. Query letters and SASEs should be directed to:

Eric Kettunen, U.S. Manager (at United States office)

LONGMEADOW PRESS USA

Longmeadow Press, begun in 1984, is no longer operating as a publisher. The house was a proprietary publishing division of the powerful retail-bookstore chain WaldenBooks.

LONGSTREET PRESS

2140 Newmarket Parkway, Suite 122, Marietta, GA 30067
770-980-1488, 800-927-1488   fax: 770-859-9894
www.lspress.com

L

Longstreet publishes general nonfiction and fiction (often with a Southern regional accent), self-help, gardening, sports, health, photography and art, gift books, and calendars. Longstreet distributes a series of books published by the Arthritis Foundation.

Longstreet nonfiction: *No Such Thing as a Bad Day* by Hamilton Jordan; *The Millionaire Next Door* by Thomas Stanley and William Danko; *Get Clark Smart: The Ultimate Guide for the Savvy Consumer* by Clark Howard and Mark Meltzer; *Strong at the Broken Places* by U.S. Senator Max Cleland; *Month-by-Month Gardening in the South* by Don Hastings; *Guided by Angels: Divinely Inspired Paintings* by Amanda Dunbar.

Fiction and literary works: *Princess Naughty and the Voodoo Cadillac* by Fred Willard; *Home Across the Road* by Nancy Peacock; *True Women* by Janice Woods Windle.

With the Arthritis Foundation: *250 Tips for Making Life with Arthritis Easier; Your Personal Guide to Living Well with Fibromyalgia; Arthritis 101: Answers to Your Questions About Arthritis* (all volumes by the Arthritis Foundation).

Longstreet oversees its own distribution. Query letters and SASEs should be directed to:

John Yow, Senior Editor

Scott Bard, Publisher and President

Tysie Whitman, Senior Editor

Loompanics Unlimited

Box 1197, Port Townsend, WA 98368
360-385-2230   fax: 360-385-7785
www.loompanics.com   e-mail: editorial@loompanics.com

Loompanics Unlimited produces books of nonfiction trade interest in addition to professional and special-interest nonfiction. The Loompanics list accents practical self-help and how-to, contemporary and historical culture, and sociopolitical and issue-oriented works. The house offers a selective fiction list (primarily reprints of hitherto overlooked masterworks).

Loompanics offers books in such categories as underground economy, tax "avoision," money-making opportunities, individual privacy, fake identification, Big Brother is watching you, conducting investigations, crime and police science, locks and locksmithing, self-defense, revenge, guns, weapons, bombs and explosives, guerrilla warfare, murder and torture, survival, self-sufficiency, head for the hills, gimme shelter, health and life extension, paralegal skills, sex, drugs, rock and roll, intelligence increase, science and technology, heresy/weird ideas, anarchism and egoism, work, mass media, censorship, reality creation, self-publishing—and an enigmatic category of works classified solely as miscellaneous.

Since its foundation in 1973, Loompanics titles have been among the most controversial and unusual publications available, and the publishing program has produced recognized classics in a number of fields.

Many Loompanics publications test the edge of the free-speech envelope—and often do so with humorous subversiveness and literary zest; some of the more treacherous materials are clearly intended exclusively for amusement, informational, or scholarly reference purposes.

L

Loompanics features: *Secrets of Methamphetamine Manufacture* by Uncle Fester; *The Outlaw's Bible* by E. X. Boozhie; *Natural Law: Or Don't Put a Rubber on Your Willy* by Robert Anton Wilson; *Take No Prisoners: Destroying Enemies with Dirty and Malicious Tricks* by Mack Nasty; *Gaslighting: How to Drive Your Enemies Crazy* by Victor Santoro; *Poison Pen Letters* by Keith Wade; *Getting Started in the Underground Economy* by Adam Cask; *Anarchic Harmony: The Spirituality of Social Disobedience* by William J. Murray; *Principia Discordia: Or How I Found the Goddess and What I Did to Her When I Found Her* by Malaclypse the Younger; *How to Sneak into the Movies* by Dan Zamudio; *Practical LSD Manufacture* by Uncle Fester; *Secondhand Success: How to Turn Discards into Dollars* by Jordan L. Cooper; *The Hitchhiker's Handbook* by James MacLaren; *The Politics of Consciousness: A Practical Guide to Personal Freedom* by Steve Kubby; *Stoned Free: How to Get High Without Drugs* by Patrick Wells with Douglas Rushkoff; *You Are Going to Prison* (a survival guide) by Jim Hogshire.

From the arena of literary fiction: *The Gas* (another classic literary work in reissue) by Charles Platt.

Some backlist Loompanics hits: *Bad Girls Do It! An Encyclopedia of Female Murderers* by Michael Newton (author of *Serial Slaughter: What's Behind America's Murder Epidemic?*); *Hunting Humans: An Encyclopedia of Modern Serial Killers; Psychedelic Shamanism* by Jim DeKorne; *Secrets of a Superhacker* by an incognito information superhighwayman known as the Knightmare; *Shadow Merchants: Successful Retailing Without a Storefront* by Jordan L. Cooper; *The Art & Science of Dumpster Diving* by John Hoffman (with original comix by Ace Backwords); *Community Technology* by Karl Hess; *Free Space: Real Alternatives for Reaching Outer Space* by B. Alexander Howerton; *How to Obtain a Second Passport and Citizenship and Why You Want To* by Adam Starchild; *The Rape of the American Constitution* by Chuck Shiver; *The Wild and Free Cookbook* by Tom Squire; *Travel-Trailer Homesteading Under $5,000* by Brian D. Kelly; *Screw the Bitch: Divorce Tactics for Men* by Dick Hart.

Special Loompanics compilations: *Loompanics' Greatest Hits: Articles and Features from the Best Book Catalog in the World* (edited by Michael Hoy); *Loompanics Unlimited Live! in Las Vegas* (edited by Michael Hoy).

Loompanics Unlimited is editorially a reclusive house. Writers who wish to work with Loompanics should note that their business is the printed word, and potential authors should approach Loompanics through the printed word (via mail—do not telephone or e-mail proposals or submissions). The publisher also notes that the press tends toward small advances and works through literary agents only on occasion.

The Loompanics Unlimited direct-order catalog (emblazoned with the publisher's free-booter-spaceship colophon) depicts a wealth of titles from its own list, as well as select offerings from other houses in a luscious newsprint format that includes graphics, essays, and short fiction, along with blurbs from reviewers and satisfied customers testifying to the potency of the house's list and the efficacy of the Loompanics distribution and fulfillment services.

Query letters and SASEs should be directed to:

Michael Hoy, President

Gia Cosindas, Editor

LOTHROP, LEE & SHEPARD BOOKS
See William Morrow & Company, Inc.

LOWELL HOUSE
Lowell House was acquired as part of McGraw Hills acquisition of parent company, Contemporary Books. The Lowell House backlist will be maintained, but there will be no new title acquisitions and the office has been closed.

THE LYONS PRESS
123 West 18th Street, New York, NY 10010
212-620-9580   fax: 212-929-1836

The Lyons Press produces trade nonfiction, especially books on country living, horses, fly fishing, adventure, travel, military history, natural history, and outdoor recreation and sports; the house also produces works aimed at regional interests worldwide, selected literary fiction and essays, and reference.

From Lyons Press: *Hemingway on Fishing* (edited by Nick Lyons); *Bacchus & Me* by Jay McInerney; *Some Horses* by Thomas McGuane; *The Faraway Horse* by Buck Brannaman; *Toro* by Mark Sundeen; *Last Flight Out* by Randy Wayne White; *Twelve Days of Terror* by Richard G. Fernicola; *A Life Worth Living* by Jack Hemingway; *The Greatest Dog Stories Ever Told* (edited by Patricia M. Sherwood); *The Last Posse* by Gale Christianson; *My Faraway Home* by Mary Maynard; *Cougar Attacks!* by Kathy Etling; *Advanced Fly Tying* by A. K. Best; *The Hunter, The Hammer, and Heaven* by Robert Young Pelton; *Ill Nature* by Joy Williams; *The Greatest Baseball Stories Ever Told* (edited by Jeff Silverman); *L. L. Bean Fly Fishing Handbook* by Dave Whitlock; *Pocket Waters* by William Tappley; *Outwitting Deer* by Bill Adler, Jr.; *The Long Walk* by Slavomir Rawicz; *We Die Alone* by David Howarth. The Lyons Press has ongoing series with the Nature Conservancy, L. L, Bean, *Field & Stream,* The Orvis Company, *Outdoor Life,* Outward Bound, and *The New York Times*.

Fiction and literature: *Guiding Elliott* (novel) by Robert Lee; *Dry Rain* (stories) by Pete Fromm; *Travers Corners* (stories about the Lake Wobegon of fly fishing) by Scott Waldie.

The company logo shows a leaping trout poised gracefully midair over the publisher's ingenious LP colophon. Lyons Press produces a midsize roster of new titles and keeps a substantial backlist.

The Lyons Press is now an imprint of the Globe Pequot. Query letters and SASEs should be directed to:

Becky Koh, Senior Editor—Sports and fitness, adventure and exploration, country living.

Lilly Golden, Editor-at-large—Literary fiction, essays.

L

M

M & T Books

M & T has been acquired by IDG, which has been renamed Hungry Minds.

Macmillan Books

CGE Books Canada, Inc.

Macmillan Heinemann ELT

Palgrave

Sams Publishing

Macmillan Reference

Grove's Dictionaries

1185 Avenue of the Americas, New York, NY 10036
212-782-3406   fax: 212-654-8929

The entire Macmillan Program was spun-off in various directions as part of Viacom's liquidation of its book publishing assets. As of this writing, the Lasser Program was acquired by John Wiley & Sons. The *Unofficial Guides,* travel, cooking, gardening, and computer divisions have been acquired by IDG, renamed Hungry Minds. The Alpha Books program, primarily known for its *Complete Idiots Guide* series, has remained intact as part of Macmillan Books, which is now owned by Pearson Education, the British-based firm whose assets include Prentice Hall.

Marlowe & Thunder's Mouth
(Part of the Avalon Publishing Group)

Marlowe & Company

Thunder's Mouth Press

841 Broadway, Fourth Floor, New York, NY 10003
212-614-7880   fax: 212-614-7887

Marlowe & Thunder's Mouth emphasizes trade nonfiction in current events, contemporary culture, biography/personality, the arts, and popular reference. Marlowe & Thunder's Mouth combines two previously independent firms, Thunder's Mouth Press and Marlowe & Company, each with overlapping fields of concentration and its own distinct publishing persona.

Thunder's Mouth Press (founded in 1980) upholds a tradition of producing high-interest nonfiction (as well as selected fiction with media/cultural cross-publicity potential). Thunder's Mouth is known for works of quirky ambiance and decidedly popular appeal. An overview of the Thunder's Mouth nonfiction program provides a list particularly strong in the areas of topical issues, popular culture, and specialty reference. In fiction, Thunder's Mouth spouts modern and contemporary literary writing, in addition to classic

M

genre fiction, poetry, and works for stage and screen, with additional focus on the African-American tradition, works from the Beat generation, and hitherto underappreciated women authors (many of these works published in reprint editions).

During early 1995, Thunder's Mouth initiated a radical restructuring. Thunder's Mouth publisher Neil Ortenberg announced that substantially all assets of the house had been acquired by Avalon Publishing Group, an affiliate of Publishers Group West (the distribution house with an East Coast office located conveniently adjacent to the Thunder's Mouth digs). The Thunder's Mouth program was downsized dramatically—everyone was fired, leaving Ortenberg the sole crew. The house was poised for consolidation and regrowth, with a projected scenario reminiscent of that at Grove/Atlantic.

Thunder's Mouth merged with Marlowe & Company, a new, independent house headed by John Webber. Marlowe was previously part of Universal Sales and Marketing, a promotional and remaindering operation; the new Marlowe operation purchased the Paragon Publishing backlist. In tandem with the Thunder's Mouth literary resources, this evolving publishing entity (known corporately as Marlowe & Thunder's Mouth) features two main imprints (Marlowe and Thunder's Mouth) and covers the publishing spectrum from commercial to controversial.

Please note: The overall house focus and imprint identities are currently believed to be in transition.

Representative general nonfiction: *Fidel's Cuba: A Revolution in Pictures* photographs by Osvaldo Salas and Roberto Salas (introduction by Gregory Tozian); *Francis Ford Coppola: Close Up: The Making of His Movies* by Ronald Bergan; *The World of Warhammer: The Official Encyclopedia of the Best-Selling Fighting Fantasy Game* by Richard Wolfrik Galland; *Erotique: Masterpieces of Erotic Photography* by Rod Ashford; *Albert Camus Notebooks 1935–1951* by Albert Camus; *Trainsong* by Jan Kerouac (with an introduction by Gerald Nicosia); *Firebrands: The Heroines of Science Fiction and Fantasy* by Pamela Sargent (illustrated by Ron Miller); *Pueblo Children of the Earth Mother* by Thomas Mails; *Who Killed Martin Luther King Jr.?* by James Earl Ray; *A Black Man's Hell: From Slavery to the CIA-Crack Connection* by Philip Nobile, Joe Madison, and John Newman; *Easy Prey: The Fleecing of America's Senior Citizens—And How to Stop It* by Senator William S. Cohen; *Not in Your Lifetime: The Definitive Book on the JFK Assassination* by Anthony Summers; *Beyond Roswell: The Alien Autopsy Film, Area 51, and the U.S. Government Cover-Up of UFOs* by Michael Hesemann and Philip Mantle.

Works with a cultural/personality tilt: *Led Zeppelin Dazed and Confused: The Stories Behind Every Song* by Chris Welch; *Robin Williams: A Biography* by Andy Dougan; *Better to Burn Out: The Cult of Death in Rock 'n' Roll* by David Thompson; *Rebel for the Hell of It: The Life of Tupac Shakur* by Armond White; *Live Fast—Die Young: Remembering the Short Life of James Dean* by John Gilmore; *Captain Trips: A Biography of Jerry Garcia* by Sandy Troy; *John Lennon: In My Life* by Pete Shotton with Nicholas Shaffner; *The Velvet Years, 1965–1967: Warhol's Factory* (photographs, graphics, and essay by Stephen Shore and Lynne Tillman).

Sample fiction and literary works: *Amistad* by David Pesci; *High Latitudes: A Romance* by James Buchan; *The Polish Lover* by Anthony Weller; *Dr. Rat* by William Kotzwinkle; *A Treasury of African Folklore* (edited, retold, and with commentary by Harold Courlander); *Life Is Hot in Cracktown* by Buddy Giovinazzo; *Goodbye, Sweetwa-*

M

ter: New and Selected Stories by Henry Dumas; *City of Light* by Cyrus Colter; *Panther* by Melvin Van Peebles (who authored the screenplay for the film of the same name, directed by his son Mario Van Peebles—whose first movie appearance was as a kid in Melvin's own classic *Sweet Sweetback's Baadasssss Song*).

Another event of media interest was the publication of *Marita* (memoir) by Marita Lorenz, Fidel Castro's former mistress. In a related development, Thunder's Mouth publisher Ortenberg was wed to Lorenz's daughter, the internationally known cultural luminary Monica Mercedes.

Meanwhile: What has the name Thunder's Mouth got to do with all this? William Shakespeare's King John provides the source: "O that my tongue were in the thunder's mouth! Then with a passion would I shake the world."

Marlowe & Thunder's Mouth Press is distributed by Publishers Group West. The house no longer accepts unsolicited submissions. All work must be submitted by literary agents. Query letters and SASEs should be directed to:

John Webber, Publisher, Marlowe

Neil Ortenberg, Senior Editor and Publisher, Thunder's Mouth

Matthew Lore, Editorial Director, Marlow & Company

Education: B.A. in Art & Literature from Swarthmore College, Pennsylvania.

Employment history/editor career path: I have been in the publishing industry for about 12 years. I started at HarperSanFrancisco in the religious/psychology section. I was there for five and a half years and had worked my way up to a marketing manager. I took a couple of years off from publishing and did a variety of things, and then returned to it and started working at Fodors Travel Guide. I did mostly line editing for them for about two years. I then came to Marlow & Co. and have been here for about two years.

What would you be doing if you were not an editor? I would be an adventurer of some kind. I would be an advocate of alternative transportation, bicycling in particular.

What has been your most successful book that you have acquired to date? I was the marketing manager for *The Alchemist* by Paulo Coelho, which was a very big international bestseller. I have acquired as an editor: *The Glucose Revolution: The Authoritative Guide to the Glycemic Index* by Jennie Brand-Miller, Thomas Wolever, and others.

What books have you acquired that make you the most proud? What books that you have acquired reflect the types of books you like to represent? *The Parents Tao Teaching Agent* by William Martin; *Vast Living: Creating a Home for the Soul* by Kathleen Cox; *Going on Faith,* edited by William Zinsser.

Do you represent fiction? If so, what do you look for? I do fiction anthologies only; no original fiction.

Do you represent nonfiction? Yes, mind, body, spirit, health, healthful cooking.

Do you require book proposals? If so, what do you look for in evaluating a book proposal? Yes. I look for originality of an idea, clarity of the presentation, great writing, author credentials, author analysis of the competition and market, and marketing potential.

Are certain aspects of a book proposal given more weight than others? It depends on the project.

What process do you use for making a decision? What is the process for acquisition, is there a committee? Yes, there is a small acquisitions committee.

What kinds of nonfiction books do you want to see less of? Personal stories dealing with personal misfortune.

Are you interested in work geared for the masses (readers of *People, The Star,* etc.)? No.

Are agents important? Why? Yes. They help to pre-screen the material and help authors to shape their projects.

Do you like new writers? What should new writers do to break into the business? Yes, although with many of the books I acquire, many of them already write. To break into the business I would say have an important message, have original work, and send something that interests me strongly.

How should writers approach you? With a query letter or through an agent.

What are some common mistakes writers make? What really gets on your nerves? When they don't present a clear, concise query letter.

What can writers do to get your attention and to avoid the slush pile? Propose a fresh, interesting idea.

What have been some of your craziest experiences with submissions? N/A.

What have been some of your best experiences with writers or in your job? Every day there is a new wonderful experience. The process of working with the writers to shape their manuscripts into the best possible books that they can be is an ongoing pleasure.

What, if anything, makes you different from other editors? I have had over seven years of marketing experience; the number of books I have published; the fact that I myself do everything from the marketing, to the editing to designing the art jackets.

Is there anything that you would like to see changed in the industry? I would like to see faster turn-around time for reprints and faster publishing.

Any advice for writers? Any way to improve the system for you? Any additional thoughts? Be bold and know how to write.

MASQUERADE BOOKS

Has discontinued its publishing operations.

McFARLAND & COMPANY, INC., PUBLISHERS

Box 611960, Highway 88 West, Jefferson, NC 28640-0611
336-246-4460   fax: 336-246-5018
www.mcfarlandpub.com   e-mail: info@mcfarlandpub.com

McFarland & Company, Inc., Publishers, is an independent nontrade publisher specializing in general reference, performing arts (especially film, radio, television and theater), baseball, popular culture, automotive history, chess, Appalachian studies, history (U.S., Civil War, world), international studies, criminal justice, women's studies, and African-American studies. Publishes nonfiction only; around 190 titles a year.

Query letters and SASEs should be directed to:

M

Robert Franklin, President and Editor in Chief

Virginia Tobiassen, Editor

Steve Wilson, Senior Editor
Born: November 27, 1968.
Education: B.A., summa cum laude, in English, UNC-Chapel Hill, 1991.
Employment history/editor career path: Started at McFarland as Assistant Editor shortly after graduating from college; no prior publishing experience.
Personal interests: Automotive technology, Southern literature, woodworking, scale automotive modeling.
What would you be doing if you were not an editor? I suppose I'd be writing, perhaps for a newspaper or magazine.
What books have you acquired that make you the most proud? What books that you have acquired reflect the types of books you like to represent? Two works, both coincidentally on North Carolina history, come to mind: Fred Mallison's *The Civil War on the Outer Banks* and R. G (Hank) Utley and Scott Verner's *The Independent Carolina Baseball League, 1936–1938; Baseball Outlaws.* They're both labors of love, the kind of lifelong research efforts that can only be accomplished by someone deeply involved with the subject material. Moreover, they're both charming and fascinating. Both books also represented unknown marketing quantities that performed well.
Do you represent fiction? No.
Do you represent nonfiction? Yes, exclusively.
Do you require book proposals? If so, what do you look for in evaluating a book proposal? If the manuscript is complete when the author first contacts us, we generally go directly to the manuscript if it sounds plausible. At the opposite extreme, we're willing to launch a discussion based on nothing more than an idea, particularly if we have worked with the author before. At some point prior to a contract offer we do need a proposal, though—preferably an outline, length estimate, draft of introduction or preface, two sample chapters, and description of special elements such as illustrations or appendices. We look for authoritative and complete coverage of a subject that is not already exhausted; competent research and organization; and reliability (we don't want to be forced to verify absolutely every fact and spelling).
Are certain aspects of a book proposal given more weight than others? Yes, but varying according to the type of book. In a work of film reference, for example, we look hard at the depth of filmographic data; in a biography the freshness of the material tends to be a key factor; in a book of library cartoons, the question is whether they're funny. Authors tend to waste time with us in developing elaborate marketing plans in their proposals, thus revealing that they haven't researched us very well (we're a nontrade publisher, handling mainly scholarly and reference material; our marketing is pretty well set) and often showing that they have impossible expectations.
What process do you use for making a decision? What is the process for acquisition, is there a committee? All members of our editorial staff are involved in acquisitions. Proposals are distributed as they arrive, and the editors meet once a week to discuss the new proposals they've received. A decision is made in the meeting and usually the editor who examined the proposal retains it to begin the correspondence if we are interested.

M

What kinds of nonfiction books do you want to see less of? We do not publish devotional works, stories of personal triumph over adversity, theories about the functioning of the cosmos (a very frequent offering), or children's books, all of which are proposed to us regularly.

Are you interested in work geared for the masses (readers of *People, The Star,* etc.)? Generally, no. Our market consists of (1) libraries and (2) individuals with a strongly focused interest in any of several specialty subjects (film, old-time radio, baseball, chess, automotive history, and others).

Are agents important? Why? From our perspective, no. The agents we have dealt with have tended to lack an understanding of nontrade publishing in general or of us in particular. Agents very often send manuscripts that are categorically inappropriate for us, indicating they haven't done their homework. We use a standard contract that does not vary from book to book, so an agent has no real negotiating role in signing a contract with us. Communication with an author is smoother, too, when it is direct.

Do you like new writers? What should writers do to break into the business? We do like new writers. Perhaps as many as half our authors had not published a book before coming to McFarland, and many have gone on to publish several successful books with us. (We enjoy a very high rate of repeat authors.) For breaking in with a publisher like us, the best advice to a new author is to concentrate on the uniqueness of the manuscript and produce a fairly substantial sample before contacting us. Our Web site lists some useful guidelines.

How should writers approach you? The traditional query letter, followed up by a formal proposal if we express interest, is hard to beat. We accept queries by telephone or even by e-mail (no attachments please), but a letter tends to make the best impression.

What are some common mistakes writers make? What really gets on your nerves? Writers are better off not phoning every few days to see if we've looked at a proposal yet. We're really quite prompt—we respond inside of two weeks in most cases, and it almost never takes us more than a month—but some authors can't stand even that wait. The innocent "Have you gotten to my proposal yet" question is almost impossible to answer by phone. We receive too many proposals to remember them all instantly (especially before actually looking through them), and a given proposal may be with any of four or five of us. An author who phones two or three times in the short period before we can reply signals a possible "personality problem."

What can writers do to get your attention and to avoid the slush pile? As noted earlier, we're actually very good about keeping up with incoming proposals. We have no "slush pile" in the usual sense.

What have been some of your craziest experiences with submissions? Authors reproposing previously rejected manuscripts three or four times or writing us under a different name after a rejection. One or two have refused to reveal the subject of the manuscript without a commitment of interest and a written confidentiality agreement.

What have been some of your best experiences with writers or in your job? Well, there's really nothing more satisfying than a happy author. Editors sometimes forget the sheer work that goes into a manuscript. When an author's long labor has produced something really good, we've done our job right and turned out a beautiful book, and the author senses that we've made the manuscript better, I feel good. That sense of productive partnership doesn't happen every time, but it's enormously rewarding.

M

McGRAW-HILL PUBLISHING GROUP

Business McGraw-Hill

Computing McGraw-Hill

Osborne/McGraw-Hill

2 Penn Plaza, New York, NY 10121
212-512-2000

McGraw-Hill operates specialty programs in a variety of professional, business, and educational fields, such as law, health care, high-tech industries, and college textbooks. The house produces books for professional, institutional, and trade markets; journals keyed to core areas of interest; seminar and group workshop materials; and issues a selection of electronic products (including CD-ROMs).

McGraw-Hill officially disbanded its adult general trade book-publishing operation in 1989; since then, the house's lineup of professional and reference book divisions has continued to thrive. Still geared primarily toward business and professional titles, McGraw-Hill is again venturing into the broader range of commercial trade arenas. In the United States, this international house publishes titles in business, trades and technical fields, computing, architecture, engineering/electronics, science, and leisure. (See subentries further on.)

An area of particular McGraw-Hill presence encompasses the interface of business, personal computing, and computer science; many of these titles are published from within the McGraw-Hill list and that of the Osborne/McGraw-Hill subsidiary. (See separate subentries further on.)

McGraw-Hill distributes for all its divisions. Query letters and SASEs should be directed to:

Amy Murphy, Editor—Business and General Reference division.

Business McGraw-Hill

Business McGraw-Hill produces trade and professional titles in business, finance, entrepreneurship, marketing, training, human resources, investing, management, advertising, sales, self-help, and communication.

Indicative of the Business McGraw-Hill list: *Storage and Stability* by Benjamin Graham; *Economic Smarts: Using Economic Indicators in "Investor's Business Daily" to Pick Winning Stocks* by Dhun H. Sethna; *Heart at Work: Stories and Strategies for Building Self-Esteem and Reawakening the Soul at Work* by Jack Canfield and Jacqueline Miller; *Financial Planning for the Utterly Confused* (5th edition) by Joel Lerner; *Job Hunting for the Utterly Confused* by Jason R. Rich; *Winning the Loser's Game: Timeless Strategies for Successful Investing* (3rd edition) by Charles D. Ellis; *Robert Erwin's Pocket Guide for Home Buyers: 101 Questions and Answers for Every Home Buyer* by Robert Irwin; *The Business Traveler's World Guide: Key Information on 150 Cities Around the World* by Philip Seldon; *When Smart People Work for Dumb Bosses: How to Survive in a Crazy and Dysfunctional Workplace* by William Lundin, Ph.D., and Kathleen

M

Lundin; *Tips and Traps for Entrepreneurs: Real-Life Ideas and Solutions for the Toughest Problems Facing Entrepreneurs* by Courtney Price and Kathleen Allen; *The Economics of Life: From Baseball to Affirmative Action to Immigration, How Real-World Issues Affect Our Everyday Life* by Gary Becker and Guity Nashat Necker; *Send 'Em One White Sock: 66 Outrageously Simple Ideas from Around the World for Building Your Business or Brand* by Stan Rapp and Thomas L. Collins.

McGraw-Hill Business is proud to announce a new imprint, BusinessWeek Books. In the award-winning tradition of *BusinessWeek* magazine, BusinessWeek Books will offer cutting-edge information from the international business community's movers, shakers, and experts. Representative titles include: *Mastering the Art of Creative Collaboration* by Robert Hargrove; *Conquering Uncertainty: Understanding Corporate Cycles and Positioning Your Company to Survive the Changing Environment*, by Theodore Modis; *Beyond Competition: From Competition and Collaboration to Transcompetition*, by Harvey Robbins and Michael Finley.

Query letters and SASEs should be directed to:

Mary E. Glenn, Editor—Management and management theory, self-help with a business focus, some marketing and sales; topical books with global appeal that can cross over into serious nonfiction.

Philip Ruppel, Publisher—All areas indicated in house description, including marketing, management, quality, human resources, training, operations management.

Richard Narramore, Senior Editor—Training and development, organizational development, management.

Computing McGraw-Hill

Computing McGraw-Hill is the trade designation (used widely in advertising and promotional venues) for titles in computing that emerge from the various McGraw-Hill divisions, including a number of projects acquired through the trade/business wing, as well as some from the Osborne/McGraw-Hill subsidiary (please see subentry further on).

Computing titles from McGraw-Hill: *Hands-on ATM* by David McDysan and Darren Spohn; *The Complete Guide to Java Database Programming* by Ken North; *Public Key Infrastructure* by the CommerceNet PKI Task Force; *Webmaster Engineer Certification Handbook* by Net Guru Technologies, Inc.; *Web Objects* by Ron Ben-Natan; *Internet Explorer 4.0: Browsing and Beyond* by Dave Johnson.

Osborne/McGraw-Hill

2600 Tenth Street, Berkeley, CA 94710
510-549-6600

Osborne/McGraw-Hill targets the hands-on user approach to computer software, hardware, and systems, with many titles geared toward specific types of projects or proprietary systems and programs. Many titles on the Osborne/McGraw-Hill list are book/software packages.

M

Primary areas of Osborne/McGraw-Hill interest include spreadsheets, accounting, integrated software, graphics, word processing, desktop publishing, computer-aided design, telecommunications, networking, operating systems, hardware, programming languages, databanks, and business applications, as well as games and entertainment. The house also frontlists select titles with broader appeal for a wide range of computer-friendly readers.

Sample titles: *The Internet Kids and Family Yellow Pages* by Jean Armour Polly; *Great American Websites: An Almanac of All Things American* by Edward J. Renehan, Jr.; *The Webmaster's Toolkit* by Michael Erwin; *The McGraw-Hill Encyclopedia of Networking* by Tom Sheldon.

Osborne/McGraw-Hill distributes its titles via the order-services center shared with and operated through TAB/McGraw-Hill.

MEADOWBROOK PRESS

5451 Smetana Drive, Minnetonka, MN 55343
952-930-1100   fax: 952-930-1940

Meadowbrook publishes books with a family outlook, encompassing the areas of pregnancy and child care, parenting, health, the environment, business, travel, cooking, reference, party-planning, and children's-activity books. Meadowbrook Press (established in 1975) is a small trade-oriented house that has particular success pinpointing such specialty markets as baby names, family humor, and the facts of life.

Frontlist releases: *The Joy of Sisters* by Karen Brown; *Free Stuff for Kids* (in periodically updated editions) by the Free Stuff Editors; *Eating Expectantly* by Bridget Swinney; *The Toddler's Busy Book* by Trish Kuffner; *Storybook Parties* by Penny Warner; *The Best Bachelorette Party Book* by Becky Long; *Pregnancy, Childbirth and the Newborn* by Penny Simkin and Janet Whalley; *52 Romantic Evenings* by Liya Lee Oertel.

From the Meadowbrook backlist: *The Very Best Baby Name Book in the Whole Wide World* by Bruce Lansky; *Feed Me! I'm Yours* by Vicki Lansky; *First-Year Baby Care* (edited by Paula Kelly); *The Joy of Grandparenting* by Audrey Sherins and Joan Holleman; *Baby and Child Emergency First Aid Handbook* by Mitchell J. Enzig; *The Working Woman's Guide to Breastfeeding* by Nancy Dana and Anne Price; *The Joy of Marriage* by Monica and Bill Dodds; *Birth Partner's Handbook* by Carl Jones; *The Baby Journal* by Matthew Bennett (illustrated by Breck Wilson).

Meadowbrook Press is distributed by Simon & Schuster. Query letters and SASEs should be directed to:

Bruce Lansky, Publisher

MECKLERMEDIA CORPORATION

Mecklermedia (founded in 1971; earlier known as Meckler Publishing) is no longer publishing. The house was a specialist publisher with emphasis on informational books, directories, and databases keyed to a wide range of subjects and applications.

MEGAN TINGLEY BOOKS (AN IMPRINT OF LITTLE, BROWN AND CO)

Three Center Plaza, Boston, MA 02108

Megan Tingley Books, an imprint of Little, Brown and Company, publishes mainly picture books, with some fiction and nonfiction for middle-grade and young adult readers. This imprint does not consider "genre" novels for publication (including mystery, romance, and science fiction).

Titles from Megan Tingley include: *Look Alikes* by Joan Steiner; *Just Like a Baby* by Rebecca Bond; *The Girls' Guide to Life* by Catherine Dee; *The Okay Book* by Todd Parr; *Define Normal* by Anne Peters; *This Land Is Your Land* by Woody Guthrie and Kathy Jakobsen; and *One of Each* by Mary Ann Hoberman and Marjorie Priceman.

While the submission guidelines for Megan Tingley Books remain the same as Little Brown's, unpublished authors may submit one-page query letters for fiction and nonfiction. Please mark the envelope "Query" and address to:

Alvina Ling, Editorial Assistant, Megan Tingley Books, Little Brown & Company, Three Center Plaza, Boston, MA 02108. Include an SASE for response.

MERCURY HOUSE, INC.

3004 Sixteenth Street, Suite 101, San Francisco, CA 94103
415-626-7874   fax: 415-626-7875

Mercury House produces a list strong in contemporary fiction, world literature in translation, literary classics, Asian literature and philosophy, cultural studies, film and performing arts, current affairs, nature and environment, and general nonfiction. The press issues hardcovers and trade paperbacks.

Mercury House (a nonprofit corporation founded in 1984) is a publisher guided by literary values; categories of house interest encompass quality fiction; biographies and autobiographies; history and narrative nonfiction; multiethnic and cross-cultural literary expression (including essays and true-life narratives, as well as fiction); arts and entertainment; literary travel. The Mercury House logo is a graphic representation of a winged manuscript scroll in flight.

From Mercury House: *Pharmako/Dynamics: Plant Teachers and the Poison Path* by Dale Pendell; *Narrow Road to the Deep North: A Journey into the Interior of Alaska* by Katherine McNamara; *House with the Blue Bed* by Alfred Arteaga; *The House by the Sea: A Portrait of the Holocaust in Greece* by Rebecca Fromer; *In the Ring of Fire: A Pacific Basin Journey* by James D. Houston; *A Girl with a Monkey: New and Selected Stories* by Leonard Michaels.

Mercury House issues the journal *Artes: An International Reader of Literature, Art and Music* (new editions released periodically; edited by Bengst Jangfeldt and Gunnar Harding).

Mercury House distributes through Consortium. Query letters and SASEs should be directed to:

K. Janene-Nelson, Executive Editor

Justin Edgar, Assistant Editor

M

MICROSOFT PRESS

One Microsoft Way, Redmond, WA 98052-6399
206-882-8080, 800-677-7377
http://mspress.microsoft.com

Microsoft Press specializes in solution-oriented computer books—especially those relating to the corpus of Microsoft products, the Microsoft operating system, and selected titles pertaining to the Apple Macintosh world. Microsoft Press lists titles in general personal-computer applications, programming, and general-interest computing areas. The house brochure features books, book-and-software packages (including diskettes and CD-ROMs), and training videos. Microsoft Press (founded in 1983) is a product unit within the Microsoft Corporation and a leading source of comprehensive self-paced learning, training, evaluation, and support resources designed to help everyone from developers and IT professionals to end users get the most from Microsoft technology. Users can choose from more than 250 current titles in print, multimedia, and network-ready formats—learning solutions made by Microsoft. More information is available at http://mspress.microsoft.com.

Microsoft Press titles are constantly updated and released in newly revised versions in order to anticipate advances in hardware and software systems, as well as the underlying technology to which they pertain. The house aims to produce information that is reliable, timely, and easy to use so that readers can get their work done faster and without frustration.

Series from Microsoft Press include At a Glance Series (get answers in a picture, not a thousand words); Step by Step (self-paced training); Running (in-depth reference and inside tips from the software experts); Field Guide (quick, easy answers); WYSIWYG (What You See Is What You Get—books for beginners); Best Practices (candid accounts of the new movement in software development—highly readable accounts of what works in the real world); Microsoft Professional Editions (technical information straight from the source); Microsoft Programming (the foundations of software development); Solution Developer (expert development strategies for creating custom business solutions).

The Mastering series is a line of CD-ROM–based interactive training titles created to help intermediate and advanced developers' master tasks and concepts for writing sophisticated solutions with Microsoft tools.

A representative general reference work is Microsoft Press Computer Dictionary.

Microsoft Press distributes its own books; the list is also available through electronic mail via CompuServe. Query letters and SASEs should be directed to:

Alex Blanton, Acquisitions Editor

Bookidea@microsoft.com

MILKWEED EDITIONS

1011 Washington Avenue South, Suite 300, Minneapolis, MN 55415
612-332-3192   fax: 612-215-2550
www.milkweed.org and www.worldashome.org

Milkweed publishes fiction, essays and literature, poetry anthologies, poetry, as well as literary nonfiction about the natural world in its the World as Home publishing program. Milkweeds for Young Readers is the house's children's line. Milkweed Editions (instituted in 1984) presents a personalized small-house approach that accents high standards of content and production.

Milkweed was founded (in 1979) as a nonprofit literary press, publishing with the intention of making a humane impact on society, in the belief that literature is a transformative art uniquely able to convey the essential experiences of the human heart and spirit. The house presents distinctive voices of literary merit in handsomely designed, visually dynamic books, exploring the ethical, cultural, and aesthetic issues that free societies must continually address.

Under Emilie Buchwald (Publisher/CEO), the house maintains its position to make a humane impact on society. Milkweed Editions offers an award-winning list of distinctive literary voices, with a line of handsomely designed, visually dynamic volumes that address ethical, cultural, and aesthetic issues.

Milkweed publishes diverse, nonhomogenous literary books that take artistic and financial risks and that give readers access to the richness, aliveness, and possibilities afforded by the written word. Milkweed exists to publish, promote, and keep alive this important literature for readers today and in the future.

The company's continued marketing success augments the publisher's stance in support of exceptional books with appeal to discerning readers. Milkweed Editions hosts a substantial backlist of hardcovers, paperbacks, and chapbooks.

Poetry: *Turning Over the Earth* by Ralph Black; *Son of the World Becoming: Poems New & Collected 1981–2000* by Pattiann Rogers.

Nonfiction about the natural world: *Ecology of a Cracker Childhood* by Janisse Ray; *Swimming with Giants* by Anne Collet; *Brown Dog of the Yaak* by Rick Bass; *Boundary Waters: The Grace of the Wild* by Paul Gruchow.

Milkweed Fiction Titles: *Thrist* and *Pu-239 and Other Russian Fantasies* by Ken Kalfus; *Falling Dark* by Tim Tharp.

Milkweed is the publisher of Susan Straight's acclaimed *Aquaboogie: A Novel in Stories* (among a number of novels-in-stories projects); *The Historian: Six Fantasies of the American Experience* by Eugene K. Garber (with paintings by Kathryn Nobbe); and *Minnesota Gothic* (in the Seeing Double series of collaborative books; poetry by Mark Vinz; photographs by Wayne Gudmundson).

Contact the editorial department for information pertaining to the Milkweed Prize for Children's Literature and the Milkweed National Fiction Prize.

Books from Milkweed Editions are available via direct order from the publisher; the house's titles are distributed to the trade through Publishers Group West.

Milkweeds for Young Readers

Milkweeds for Young Readers produces children's books of literary merit that embody humane values. Books that ask the most of young readers, the publisher maintains, have the staying power to influence them for a lifetime. Milkweed also produces a series of teaching guides.

Titles from Milkweed's children's program: *The $66 Summer* by John Armistead; *The Ocean Within* by V. M. Caldwell; *The Secret of the Ruby Ring* by Yvonne MacGrory; *Behind the Bedroom Wall* by Laura E. Williams.

Query letters and SASEs should be directed to:

Elisabeth Fitz, First Reader

Emilie Buchwald, Publisher

WILLIAM MORROW & COMPANY

The following was taken verbatim from the publisher's catalogue:

William Morrow was sold to HarperCollins in late 1999. William Morrow first opened its doors in January 1926. It was the Jazz Age. The age of Jack Dempsey and Babe Ruth. The year Fidel Castro, Allen Ginsberg, and Marilyn Monroe were born and Rudolph Valentino died. Calvin Coolidge as president, and the canine star Rin Tin Tin became Hollywood's biggest box-office draw. It was also a time of exciting events in the world of publishing. Sinclair Lewis was at the top of the bestseller lists. The year before had seen the publications of *The Great Gatsby* and the birth of the *New Yorker.* The following year would see the founding of The Literary Guild and Random House. It was into this best of times that Morrow introduced its first list, headed by *On to Oregon,* a historical novel by Honore Willsie Morrow, a noted author and the wife of our founder. After 75 years it is still in print.

Over the ensuing three-quarters of a century Morrow has published a broad spectrum of titles in the early days, books as diverse as *Coming of Age in Samoa* by Margaret Mead and *Perry Mason Solves the Case of the Fiery Fingers* by Erle Stanley Gardner, *National Velvet* by Enid Bangnold and *Lost Horizon* by James Hilton, and later *Black Feeling, Black Talk* by Nikki Giovanni and *The Summer of '49* by David Halberstam, *Zen and the Art of Motorcycle Maintenance* by Robert M. Pirsig, and *The One Minute Manager* by Ken Blanchard and Spencer Johnson; biographies as different as *Mommie Dearest* by Christina Crawford and *Bearing the Cross* by David J.Garrow. Fiction as wide-ranging as Jacqueline Susanne's *Once Is Not Enough* and *The Jewel in the Crown* by Paul Scott, *The Merlin Trilogy* by Mary Stewart, *The Other Side of Midnight* by Sidney Sheldon, and John Irving's *The Cider House Rules.*

The Morrow list has always reflected a wide variety of tastes, interests, and opinions, works of poetry and belles lettres alongside blockbuster bestsellers. We promise that it will remain an eclectic selection of books, a mixture of culture and commerce to read for knowledge and enjoyment. Our winter list continues in this tradition, offering works that will make an impact now and some we believe will still be selling when we celebrate our 100th birthday in 2026.

Direct query letters with SASEs to:

Meaghan Dowling, Senior Editor—women's fiction, commercial fiction.

Kelli Martin, Assistant Editor—Literary and commercial fiction, current events.

Ben Schafer, Associate Editor

William Morrow, an Imprint of HarperCollins

1350 Avenue of the Americas, New York, NY 10019

212-261-6500

M

Born: March 20, 1972.

Education: B.A., English, Earlharm College, Richmond, Indiana.

Employment history/editor career path: Allen Ginsberg & Associates (management office), New York City. Hanuman Books, New York City, Four Walls, Eight Windows, New York City.

Personal interests: Music, counterculture history.

What would you be doing if you were not an editor? Wearing a bolo tie and playing bass in a Texan house honky-tonk band.

What has been your most successful book that you have acquired to date: *Hell's Angel* by Ralph "Sonny" Barger (acquired with Paul Bresnick).

What books have you acquired that make you the most proud? What books that you have acquired reflect the types of books you like to represent? The *Hubert Huncke Reader* by Hubert Huncke; *Jackin' for Beats* by Jesse Washington; *Bob Dylan: Behind the Shades* by Clinton Heylin; *Paradise Outlaws* by John Tytell; *Boy Island* by Camdin Joy.

Do you represent fiction? If so, what do you look for? Yes. Originality, above all.

What do you want to see less of? Stories of near-alcoholic police officers with father issues.

Do you represent nonfiction? Yes.

Do you require book proposals? If so, what do you look for in evaluating a book proposal? Author credentials, a large outlook, a stellar sample chapter(s). Nonfiction only—never for novels.

Are certain aspects of a book proposal given more weight than others? Sample chapter(s) and author credentials are very important.

What process do you use for making a decision? What is the process of acquisition, is there a committee? Gather second opinions in house. Find key marketing and sales people to support it. Yes, there is an editorial committee.

What kinds of nonfiction books do you want to see less of? Books on bands or artists best suited for "Behind the Music."

Are you interested in work geared for the masses (readers of *People, The Star,* etc.)? Yes.

Are agents important? Why? Good screening process.

Do you like new writers? What should new writers do to break into the business? Depends on the writer. A new writer should find an agent and get some stories published in literary journals.

How should writers approach you? Through an agent.

What are some common mistakes writers make? What really gets on your nerves? Calling and badgering an editor after he or she has turned a book down.

What can writers do to get your attention and to avoid the slush pile? Get an agent, in New York City.

What have been some of your craziest experiences with submissions? Daily faxes from the self-proclaimed Messiah, demanding that I publish his book or the world would end: "God is my Agent"!

What have been some of your best experiences with writers or in your job? Lasting friendships, good mixed tapes, a beautiful book we're both proud to be associated with.

What, if anything, makes you different from other editors? I'm from the Midwest.

M

Is there anything you would like to see changed in the industry? Would like to see it become less a part of the entertainment—industrial complex.

Any advice for writers? Believe in your own creations—don't seek or crave validation from corporate publishers. Don't pride yourself on being outside of the mainstream and then get bitter when the mainstream fails to recognize you. Fame is the biggest golden calf of all.

THE MOUNTAINEERS BOOKS

1001 Southwest Klickitat Way, Suite 201, Seattle, WA 98134
206-223-6303, 800-553-4453   fax: 206-223-6306
www.mountaineerbooks.org e-mail: mbooks@mountaineers.org

The Mountaineers produces adventure narratives; mountaineering histories and guides; books on bicycling, kayaking/canoeing, hiking, and rock climbing; instructional guides to the outdoors and winter trekking; maps; historical works related to the house themes; natural history guides, and works on environmental conservation.

The Mountaineers (founded in 1906) is a conservation and outdoor-activity group with a mission to explore, study, preserve, and enjoy the natural beauty of the outdoors.

The Mountaineers Books was founded in 1961 as a nonprofit publishing program of the club. The Mountaineers sponsors the Barbara Savage/Miles from Nowhere Memorial Award competition for outstanding unpublished nonfiction adventure-narrative manuscripts. The initial title offered by Mountaineers Books, *Mountaineering: The Freedom of the Hills,* is still in print in a fully revised edition.

Series from Mountaineers: 100 Hikes, 100 Classic Hikes, Hiking Geology, Best Short Hikes, State Parks, Afoot and Afloat, Exploring Wild Areas by Bike, and Mountain Bike Adventures.

Mountaineers titles: *Kiss or Kill, Confessions of a Serial Climber* by Mark Twight; *Where the Pavement Ends, One Woman's Bicycle Trip through Mongolia, China & Vietnam* by Erika Warmbruss; *Rock and Ice Goldline: Stories of Climbing Adventure and Tradition* by Gregory Crouch; *Extreme Rock and Ice, 25 of the World's Great Climbs* by Garth Hattingh; *Everest, Eighty Years of Triumph and Tragedy* (2nd edition) by Peter and Leni Gillman; *River Running* (2nd edition) by Verne Huser; *Hiking the Triple Crown* by Karen Berger; *Fearless on Everest: The Quest for Sandy Irvine* by Julie Summers; and *Conquistadors of the Useless: From the Alps to Annapurna* by Lionel Terray.

Winners of the Barbara Savage "Miles from Nowhere" competition (biennial award for a previously unpublished adventure narrative manuscript): *Himalayan Passage: Seven Months in the High Country of Tibet, Nepal, China, India, and Pakistan* by Jeremy Schmidt (photographs by Patrick Morrow); *American Discoveries: Scouting the First Coast-to-Coast Recreational Trail* by Dudley and Seaborg.

The Mountaineers Books distributes its list via direct orders and also utilizes the services of regional and national wholesalers and trade representatives. The American Alpine Club Press is now distributed by the Mountaineers Books.

Query letters and SASEs should be directed to:

M

Margaret Sullivan, Acquisitions Assistant

David Emblidge, Editor in Chief

Cassandra Conyers, Acquisitions Editor

MOYER BELL LIMITED

54 Phillips Street, Wickford, RI 02852
401-789-0074   fax: 401-789-3793
e-mail: sales@moyerbell.com

Moyer Bell Limited specializes in literary works, reference works, and books in art and design. Many general-interest nonfiction works from this smaller house evidence a high-interest cultural or public-issues slant. Within this specialty arena, Moyer Bell produces original titles, reprints, and translations. The house also maintains a strong commitment to poetry. The Asphodel Press imprint was founded as a nonprofit organization in 1990 and concentrates on fine literary titles.

Moyer Bell Limited was established in 1984 by Jennifer Moyer and Britt Bell; this notably independent house (with a U.K. base in London, in addition to its U.S. operations) has received worldwide accolades for its roster of fine writers and stylish product.

Moyer Bell nonfiction: *World Enough and Time: A Political Chronicle* by Jonathan Schell; *The Art of Lucien Pissarro* by Lora Urbanelli; *Don't Look Back: A Memoir* by Patrick O'Connor; *Walking to LaMilpa: Living in Guatemala with Armies, Demons, Abrazos, and Death* by Marcos McPeek Villatoro; *The New Genetics: Challenges for Science, Faith, and Politics* by Roger L. Shinn; *In the Wake of Death: Surviving the Loss of a Child* by Mark Cosman; *Rebirth of Thought: Light from the East* by Ruth Nanda Anshen; *The Elixirs of Nostradamus: Nostradamus' Original Recipes for Elixirs, Scented Water, Beauty Potions and Sweetmeats* by Knut Boeser (illustrated by Leonhard Fuchs); *A Trifle, a Coddle, a Fry: An Irish Literary Cookbook* by Veronica Jane O'Mara and Fionnuala O'Reilly.

Fiction and literary titles: *The Only Piece of Furniture in the House* by Diana Glancy; *The Orchard on Fire* by Shene Mackay; *The Raven: With the Philosophy of Composition* by Edgar Allan Poe (poetry and essay; illustrated by Alan James Robinson); *Peace Breaks Out, Private Enterprise,* and *The Demon in the House* by Angela Thirkell (granddaughter of Edward Burne-Jones and a cousin of Rudyard Kipling); *Peony* by Pearl S. Buck.

On Moyer Bell's reference-book list are the periodically revised *Grant Seekers Guide* by James McGrath Morris and Laura Adler, and *Directory of American Poetry Books* from Poets House.

From Asphodel Press: *Directory of Literary Magazines* (updated annually) by the Council of Literary Magazines and Presses.

Moyer Bell Limited books are distributed to the trade by Publishers Group West. Query letters and SASEs should be directed to:

Britt Bell, Editor and Publisher

Jennifer Moyer, Editor and Publisher

M

MUSEUM OF NEW MEXICO PRESS

Deliveries and physical address: 228 East Palace Avenue, Santa Fe, NM 87501
505-827-6454   fax: 505-827-5741

Mailing address: P.O. Box 2087, Santa Fe, NM 87504-2087
e-mail: mwachs@oca.state.nm.vs

Museum of New Mexico Press is a nationally distributed publisher affiliated with the Museum of New Mexico. Museum of New Mexico Press publishes high-quality illustrated books on the arts and culture of the Southwest, such as Native America, the Hispanic Southwest, 20th-century fine art, folk art from around the world, Latin American arts, nature and gardening, architecture and style, folklore.

Query letters and SASEs should be directed to:

Mary Wachs, Editorial Director

MUSTANG PUBLISHING COMPANY

P.O. Box 770426, Memphis, TN 38177
901-684-1200   fax: 901-684-1256
e-mail: MustangPub@aol.com

Mustang produces trade nonfiction books in hardcover and paperback. Mustang is especially successful with its lines of specialty how-to's and titles in the fields of humor, games, outdoor recreation, sports, travel, and careers. Mustang Publishing Company (founded in 1983) is a modest-sized house with a concise publishing vision and compactly tailored list.

Representative frontlist titles: *101 Classic Jewish Jokes: Jewish Humor from Groucho Marx to Jerry Seinfeld* by Robert Menchin (illustrated by Joel Kohl); *Dear Elvis: Graffiti from Graceland* by Daniel Wright; *Lucky Pants and Other Golf Myths* by Joe Kohl; *The Complete Book of Golf Games* by Scott Johnston; *How to Be a Way Cool Grandfather* by Verne Steen.

Mustang's specialty books include those geared to expansive lifestyles. Titles here: *Paintball! Strategies and Tactics* by Bill Barnes with Peter Wrenn; *Bet on It! The Ultimate Guide to Nevada* by Mary Jane and Greg Edwards; and *The Hangover Handbook: 101 Cures for Humanity's Oldest Malady* by Nic van Oudtshoorn. There's also the immensely popular *The Complete Book of Beer Drinking Games* by Andy Griscom, Ben Rand, and Scott Johnson—as well as *Beer Games II: The Exploitative Sequel.*

The "For Free" series is a godsend for people scared by the high cost of travel and for everyone who loves a bargain. Each book describes hundreds of terrific things to do and see, and nothing costs one single penny, lire, franc, or pfennig. Titles: *Europe for Free, London for Free,* and *DC for Free* by Brian Butler; *The Southwest for Free* by Mary Jane and Greg Edwards; *Hawaii for Free,* by Frances Carter; *Paris for Free (or Extremely Cheap)* by Mark Beffart.

The touring and travel list also includes: *Festival Europe! Fairs and Celebrations Throughout Europe* by Margaret M. Johnson; *The Nepal Trekker's Handbook* by Amy R.

M

Kaplan, with Michael Keller; *Europe on 10 Salads a Day* by Mary Jane and Greg Edwards; plus, the hilariously revised and expanded edition of *Let's Blow Thru Europe: How to Have a Blast on Your Whirlwind Trip Through Europe* by Thomas Neenan and Greg Hancock.

A solid group of Mustang books targets a higher education–bound audience, including series for students and graduate-school applicants, often geared toward particular professional curricula: *The One Hour College Applicant* by Lois Rochester and Judy Mandell; *Medical School Admissions: The Insider's Guide* by John A. Zebala and Daniel B. Jones.

The Essays That Worked series inspires thousands of students to write the best essays they can. There's also lots of practical advice on the application process. Titles: *Essays That Worked for College Applicants* and *Essays That Worked for Business Schools* (edited by Boykin Curry and Brian Kasbar); *Essays That Worked for Law Schools* (edited by Boykin Curry).

Representative career title: *Working in T.V. News: The Insider's Guide* by Carl Filoreto with Lynn Setzer; *Medical School Admissions: The Insider's Guide* (4th edition) by John Zebala, Daniel Jones, and Stephanie Jones.

Mustang also offers Alan and Theresa von Altendorf's general reference *ISMs: A Compendium of Concepts and Beliefs from Abolitionism to Zygodactylism.*

Writers should note that Mustang welcomes book proposals on almost any nonfiction topic. The publisher prefers to see an outline and two to three sample chapters—and urges authors to be sure to enclose a self-addressed stamped envelope (the ubiquitous SASE) with each submission. No phone calls, please.

Mustang's books are distributed through National Book Network. Query letters and SASEs should be directed to:

Rollin A. Riggs, President and Publisher

THE MYSTERIOUS PRESS (AN IMPRINT OF WARNER BOOKS)

Time & Life Building, 1271 Avenue of the Americas, New York, NY 10020
212-522-7200

The Mysterious Press features novels of crime and suspense, detective fiction, and thrillers, as well as anthologies within these fields. The house also produces literary criticism, some true crime, and reference works for writers and aficionados of mystery and detection. Mysterious Press issues titles in hardcover, trade paperback, and mass-market paper formats, and also releases opulent series of slipcased editions signed by the authors. The Mysterious Press was founded as an independent house in 1976.

Mysterious Press publishes works by such writers as Robert Campbell, Jerome Charyn, George C. Chesbro, Mary Higgins Clark, Janet Dailey, Aaron Elkins, Nicolas Freeling, Elmore Leonard, Charlotte MacLeod, Margaret Maron, Marcia Muller, Elizabeth Peters, Ellis Peters, Ruth Rendell, Julie Smith, David Stout, Donald E. Westlake, Teri White, and Margaret Yorke.

Indicative of Mysterious Press fiction: *A Dying Light in Coruba* by Lindsey Davis; *Suspense (A Stanley Hastings Mystery Novel)* by Parnell Hall; *The Devil's Backbone* by

Robert Greer; *The Rape of Ganymede* by John Peyton Cooke; *Brushback (A Mario Balzic Novel)* by K. C. Constantine; *One More River* by Nicholas Freeling.

Time Warner Electronic Publishing and Simultronics Corporation launched *Modus Operandi,* an online, multi-player computer mystery game series, with interactive plots based on scenarios created by authors and editors of Mysterious Press.

The Mysterious Press list is distributed by Warner Books. Query letters and SASEs should be directed to:

Sara Ann Freed, Executive Editor

William Malloy, Editor in Chief

THE NAIAD PRESS

P.O. Box 10543, Tallahassee, FL 32302
850-539-5965   fax: 850-539-9731
www.naiadpress.com

Naiad publishes lesbian and feminist fiction, essays, poetry, short stories, humor, translations, and bibliographies. The Naiad emphasis in category fiction includes stylish and traditional mysteries, espionage thrillers, adventure yarns, science fiction, fantasy, romances, historical fiction, erotica, and Westerns. Naiad Press (established in 1973) remains joyously the oldest and largest lesbian publishing company in the world, going from one title to being the publisher of over 400 books.

Naiad has been particularly innovative among book-publishing operations in the development of specialized target-marketing techniques. The house has expanded its media presence to become active in the wider arena of audio books, videos, and theatrical film. The romantic fiction *Claire of the Moon* by Nicole Conn (writer and director of the feature film of the same name), represents a groundbreaking Naiad project that embraces documentary, music, and storytelling in cinema, video, audiocassette, CD, and print. Naiad Books maintains a comprehensive backlist.

Nonfiction from Naiad: *Sapphistory* by Pat Califia; *For Love and for Life* and *Intimate Portraits of Lesbian Couples* by Susan Johnson; *Sex Variant Women in Literature* by Jeanette H. Foster; *There's Something I've Been Meaning to Tell You* by Loralee MacPike; *The Loving Lesbian* by Claire McNabl; *Parents Matter* by Ann Muller; *Before Stonewall* by Weiss and Schiller.

Sample Naiad fiction and belles lettres: *Both Sides* by Saxon Bennett; *Claire of the Moon* by Nicole Conn; *Curious Wine* by Katherine V. Forrest; *Greener than Grass* by Jennifer Fulton; *City Lights Country Candles* by Penny Hayes; *Car Pool* by Karin Kallmaker; *Cherished Love* by Evelyn Kennedy; *Dawn of the Dance* by Marianne Martin; *Window Garden* by Janet McClellan; *Yes I Said Yes I Will* by Judith McDaniel; *The Finer Grain* by Denise Ohio; *The Other Woman* by Ann O'Leary; *Endless Love* by Lisa Shapiro; *The Drive* by Trisha Todd; and *Piece of My Heart* by Julia Watts.

The women of Naiad Press continue in pursuit of their essential goal—which is to make sure that someday, any woman, anyplace, can recognize her lesbianism and be able to walk into a bookstore and pick up a book that says to her: "Yes, you are a lesbian and you are wonderful." With that aim in mind, Naiad has adopted the following slogan for use in its potent mailing-list campaigns: Lesbians always know; if it's a book by Naiad Press, it's a book you want to own.

Naiad Press books are available directly from the publisher via a toll-free telephone-order number and from the following distributors as well: Bookpeople, LPC Group, Borders, Ingram. Query letters and SASEs should be directed to:

Barbara Grier, Chief Executive Officer

NATIONAL GEOGRAPHIC SOCIETY BOOKS

1145 17th Street Northwest, Washington, DC 20036
202-857-7000   fax: 202-429-5727

National Geographic Society Books' motto is "to diffuse geographic knowledge." Books are distributed by Random House, Inc. National Geographic Society Books is interested in any type of book written from a geographic perspective. Query letters and SASEs should be directed to:

William Gray, Vice President and Director of Book Division

NEW AMERICAN LIBRARY/NAL

See Penguin USA.

NEW AMSTERDAM BOOKS

101 Main Street, P.O. Box C, Franklin, NY 13775
212-685-6005

New Amsterdam's publishing scope encompasses art and art history, literature and fiction, biography and letters, food and drink, drama and performing arts, travel, photography, architecture, design, archaeology, Islamic studies, publishing, and design.

New Amsterdam Books (begun in 1987) is a small house that publishes a preferred list of trade titles in targeted fiction and nonfiction topic areas. Featured on the New Amsterdam list are books of an eclectic European cultural viewpoint, as well as American editions of European books. New Amsterdam editions are produced in paperback and clothbound formats. The press typically issues a few new original works seasonally, acquires selected reprint rights from overseas publishers, and maintains a comprehensive backlist.

Characteristic of New Amsterdam general trade titles: *Anarchism and Anarchists* by George Woodcock; *Life and Food in the Caribbean* by Cristine Mackie; *Alastair Sawday's Guide to French Bed & Breakfast* (updated edition by arrangement with Alastair Sawday Publishing); *The Whiskies of Scotland* by R. J. S. McDowell; *The Great Fire at Hampton Court* by Michael Fishlock (with foreword by HRH, the Prince of Wales).

Literary and critical works, the fine and popular arts, and culturally themed projects: *Killing the Mandaris* (popular multicultural fiction) by Juan Alonso; *The Three-Arched Bridge* (literary novel) by Albanian writer Ismail Kildare; *Tennyson: An Illustrated Life* by Norman Page; *Walt Whitman's New York: From Manhattan to Montauk* (edited by Henry M. Christman); *Victorian Theatre: The Theatre of Its Time* (edited by Russell Jackson); *British Landscape Watercolors, 1750–1850* by Jane Munro; *The Story of Western Furniture* by Phyllis Bennett Oates (illustrated by Mary Seymour); *Typefaces for Books* by James Sutton and Alan Bartram; *Mrs. Delany, Her Life and Her Flowers* by Ruth Hayden.

New Amsterdam issues the illustrated historical series Manuscripts in the British Library.

New Amsterdam Books handles its own distribution. Query letters and SASEs should be directed to:

Emile Capouya, Managing Director

NEW CENTURY BOOKS

P.O. Box 7113, The Woodlands, TX 77387-7113
936-295-5357

New Century publishes several lines of nonfiction books in association with XLibris, the electronic print-on-demand publisher in Philadelphia. (New Century was established in 2000.)

Its first list includes the Exceptional Lives series. Titles include: *A Desert Daughter's Odyssey: For All Those Whose Lives Have Been Touched* by *Cancer—Personally, Professionally or Through a Loved One* by Sharon Wanslee; *The Man Who Was Dr. Seuss: The Life and Work of Theodor Seuss Geisel; The Man Who Was Walter Mitty: The Life and Work of James Thurber,* and others forthcoming.

In its Communication, Culture and Literature Series: New Century has *Writing Solutions: Beginnings, Middles & Endings* and others.

New Century is also developing a series of "Top Secret" books.

New Century is interested in: autobiographies and biographies, business and personal success, communication/journalism, current affairs, parenting, popular culture, history, multicultural (Hispanic), how-to, Southwestern and mountain states subjects, sports, trends, women's issues/women's health, and perhaps a selected few children's books and mysteries.

Not interested in: Computer books, gothic romances, horror, poetry, sci-fi, screenplays, Westerns, or anything of a non-book-length nature. Note: The house's list will likely continue to be 99 percent nonfiction.

Pays royalties. Rate: varies. Pays quarterly. Plans 5–15 books per year.

New Century Books are available from XLibris in hardcover, mass-market paperback, in downloadable form via the Internet to any computer, and in a "palm reader" version.

Queries and SASEs should be directed to:

Thomas Fensch, Publisher

NEW HORIZON PRESS

Small Horizons

34 Church Street, Liberty Corner, NJ 07938
908-604-6311   fax: 908-604-6330

Mailing address:
P.O. Box 669, Far Hills, NJ 07931

New Horizon Press: Real people . . . incredible stories. That's right. The New Horizon list accents true-life events with narrative nonfiction accounts told by actual participants. In its broader program, the house addresses topics of social concern, including corporate and professional responsibility, behavioral diversity, and politics, as well as personal self-help, how-to, and mainstream business books.

New Horizon Press (established in 1983) was originally an imprint of Horizon Press; now a separate publishing entity, New Horizon Press is remarkable for its pinpoint commercial vision in the arena of nonfiction stories of courageous individuals. These incredible tales of real people display an intense human-interest appeal and often embody an investigative journalistic stance that probes related public issues. The house maintains a solid backlist that is particularly strong in self-help titles.

New Horizon is configured as a small press: Projects are often initiated with restrained author advances; more money accrues to the writer through subsequent sales. The publisher has had conspicuous success in expanding the scope of its projects via targeted promotion, advertising, touring, and subsidiary rights, both in print via book-club selections and in the electronic arena in the form of related television docudramas, talk show appearances by authors, and feature items on television journals.

From the New Horizon list: *Tainted Roses: A True Story of Murder, Mystery and a Dangerous Love* (movie rights sold to CBS) by Margie Danielson; *The Other Side: The True Story of the Boy Who Sees Ghosts* by Denice Jones; *Secret Weapons: Two Sisters' Terrifying True Story of Sex, Spies and Sabotage* by Cheryl and Lynn Hersha with Dale Griffs and Ted Schwarz; *Canine Capers: Real Life Tales of a Female Pet Vigilante* by Rose Black and Delilah Abrendt.

Reality-based self-help: *Older Women, Younger Men: New Options for Love and Romance* by Felicia Brings and Susan Winter; *Second Wives: The Pitfalls and Rewards* by Susan Shapiro Barahs; *Empowering Underachievers: How to Guide Failing Kids (8–18) to Personal Excellence* by Dr. Peter A. Spevak and Maryann Karinch; *Small Criminals Among Us: How to Recognize and Change Children's Antisocial Behavior—Before They Explode* by Gad Czuder, Ph.D.

New Horizon Press is distributed by National Book Network, Inc.

Query letters and SASEs should be directed to:

Joan S. Dunphy, Editor in Chief
   Sign: Leo/Virgo.
   Education: Ph.D., from Miami University; English, Psychology, and Philosophy.
   Employment history/editor career path: Assistant Professor at Rutgers University.
   Personal interests: Reading, rock specimens.

N

What would you be doing if you were not an editor? Teaching English at a college level and writing.

What has been your most successful book that you have acquired to date? *Black Widow/False Arrest.*

What books have you acquired that make you the most proud? What books that you have acquired reflect the types of books you like to represent? *In Africa with Schweitzer; My Life on the Streets.*

Do you represent fiction? No.

What do you want to see less of? Nonfiction generalized manuscripts on the educational system, life, and so forth and so on.

Do you represent nonfiction? Yes.

Do you require book proposals? If so, what do you look for in evaluating a book proposal? A subject matter that matters.

Are certain aspects of a book proposal given more weight than others? The plot and whether the author is the prime mover of the action.

What process do you use for making a decision? What is the process for acquisition, is there a committee? No committee, but we meet to discuss the merits, or lack of, on manuscripts we feel deserve attention.

Are you interested in work geared for the masses (readers of *People, The Star,* etc.)? Yes. I believe as Virgil said: Often times the common people see "rightly."

Are agents important? Why? At times, very. Often an agent can recognize and send us the real essence of a true story whereas the author who has lived it may not recognize its significance.

Do you like new writers? What should new writers do to break into the business? Since we are geared toward finding modern heroes who've made a difference, changing the status quo and present problems, we like new writers and subjects.

How should writers approach you? In writing, send: query, chapter synopsis, and at least two chapters. Please don't call.

What are some common mistakes writers make? What really gets on your nerves? Trying to get the editor's attention by diffuse methods (i.e., My story is the most dramatic, heartrending tale ever written and then not saying what it is).

What can writers do to get your attention and to avoid the slush pile? Tell the story. In a synopsis tell us why it's important and make sure it is.

What have been some of your craziest experiences with submissions? The niece of Mary Phagan, a young girl murdered in the South, whose death brought back the KKK, sent a one-pager with red ink stains in the shape of tears. However, her story became the basis for a strong book and Emmy Award–winning mini-series.

What have been some of your best experiences with writers or in your job? Meeting brave and significant people who have fought for what they believe in.

What, if anything, makes you different from other editors? I look for true stories with a social issues and we are willing, if we find them, to do heavy rewriting in house.

Is there anything you would like to see changed in the industry? First and foremost: more diversity. I would like to see more interdisciplinary accords between film, Internet, and print so that the publishing industry does not vanish.

N

Any advice for writers? Any way to improve the system for you? For writers: Do not embellish, simplify. For the critics, Remember the books that have transcended their times were often ridiculed or overlooked in them. And for our industry: "Change is here: it's not going away, it's gonna keep on happening; so, let's find a way to adapt to it."

Small Horizons

Small Horizons is an imprint offering self-help books for children written by teachers and mental-health professionals. Small Horizons Self-Help Books for Children: *The Stick Family: Helping Children Cope with Divorce* by Natalie Reilly; *I Am So Angry, I Could Scream: Helping Children Deal with Anger* by Laura Fox; *The Boy Who Sat by the Window: Helping Children Cope with Violence* by Chris Loftis; *There's a Skunk in My Bunk: Teaching Children Tolerance for Others* by Dr. Joseph McCann.

NEWMARKET PRESS

18 East 48th Street, New York, NY 10017
212-832-3575

Newmarket concentrates on general nonfiction, accenting such categories as contemporary issues, history and biography, psychology, parenting, health, nutrition, cooking, personal finance, and business. A major Newmarket program salutes classic literary figures, other media, and performing arts, featuring titles in film (including shooting scripts) and music. Newmarket also issues a small number of children's titles (Newmarket Medallion imprint), as well as occasional works of high-interest fiction (the house was the original publisher of the hardcover edition of Michael Blake's novel *Dances with Wolves*).

Newmarket Press (founded in 1981) is a division of Newmarket Publishing and Communications Company. The house produces books in hardcover, trade paper, and mass-market paperback editions.

General trade titles: *Success@Life: How To Catch and Live Your Dream* by Ron Rubin and Stuart Avery Gold; *Tracing the Past* (edited by Tom Twomey); *Bankroll Your Future: Retirement with Help from Uncle Sam* by Ellen Hoffman; *When Someone You Love Needs Nursing Care* by Robert Bernstein, Ph.D., and Mary Languiroud, Ph.D.; *Mommy, My Head Hurts* by Sarah Cheyette, M.D.; *How to Help Your Child Overcome Your Divorce* by Elissa Benedek, M.D., and Catherine Brown; *Beyond the Big Talk* by Debra Haffner, M.P.H.; *My Feelings Myself: A Growing Up Journal for Girls* by Lynda Madaras and Area Madaras.

Special Newmarket editions: *The Words of Gandhi* (selected and introduced by Sir Richard Attenborough); *The Words of Albert Schweitzer* (selected and introduced by Norman Cousins); *The Words of Martin Luther King, Jr.* (selected and introduced by Coretta Scott King).

Film-related books: *Cast Away,* screenplay and introduction by William Broyles, Jr.; *Traffic,* screenplay by Stephen Gaghan; *Erin Brockovich,* screenplay and introduction by Susannah Grant; *Snatch,* screenplay and introduction by Guy Ritchie; *The Jaws Log* by Carl Gottlieb (introduction by Peter Benchley); and *Crouching Tiger, Hidden Dragon.*

Newmarket distributes its list through Random House and maintains a network that utilizes a number of regional sales representatives. No children's titles. Query letters and SASEs should be directed to:

Keith Hollaman, Managing Editor

Esther Margolis, President and Publisher

Michelle Howry, Editor

N

THE NOBLE PRESS

The Noble Press is no longer doing business.

NOLO.COM

950 Parker Street, Berkeley, CA 94710
510-549-1976
www.nolo.com

Nolo.com, formerly Nolo Press, presents a glittering array of self-help titles in law and business. The house promotes a related list in lifestyle, recreation, travel, and retirement. Nolo also produces law-form kits, legal software, electronic books, and videotapes.

Nolo's consumerist perspective encompasses homeowners, landlords, and tenants; going to court; money matters; estate planning and probate; business; legal reform; patents, copyrights, and trademarks; employee rights and the workplace; family matters; immigration; research and reference; older Americans; and humor titles.

Nolo.com is the pioneer publisher of self-help legal books and software. The house (started in 1971) was founded by two Legal Aid lawyers who were fed up with the public's lack of access to affordable legal information and advice. Convinced that with good, reliable information Americans could handle routine legal problems without hiring an attorney, they began writing plain-English law books for the general readership.

Nolo led off its first list with *How to Do Your Own Divorce in California* and has been going strong since, with a steady stream of titles addressing consumer needs in a wide range of general and specialist areas. Whereas lawyers have historically sold information only to the few who can afford their services, Nolo aims to provide comprehensive low-cost information to the public at large.

The Nolo Web site (www.nolo.com) is an award-winning destination for consumers, businesspersons, and not a few lawyers. The *Nolo Encyclopedia,* available free on the site, gives plain English answers to commonly asked questions. All of Nolo's books and software can be downloaded from the site or ordered in hard copy. Nolo also offers "e-Guides," "e-Form Kits," and "Web Forms," which are electronic products that allow users to buy legal information and tools "by the drink."

All Nolo publications are regularly revised and are issued in updated editions, and the publisher maintains a hardy backlist. Most Nolo titles are written by practicing attorneys who are specialists in their fields of authorship. A major portion of the Nolo list exhibits a national orientation, while some titles are specifically geared to regional markets.

Representative titles: *License Your Invention: Take Your Great Idea to Market with a Solid Legal Agreement* by Attorney Richard Stim; *Every Landlord's Legal Guide* by Marcia Stewart and attorneys Ralph Warner and Janet Portman; and *WillMaker,* 50-state estate-planning software; *Patent It Yourself* (revised edition) by Attorney David Pressman.

Social, community, career, lifestyle, and issue-oriented titles: *Get a Life: You Don't Need a Million to Retire Well* by Ralph Warner; *The Copyright Handbook: How to Protect and Use Written Works* by Stephen Fishman; *How to Buy a House in California* by Attorney Ralph Warner, Ira Serkes, and George Devine; *Stand Up to the IRS* by Frederick W. Daily; *Dog Law* by Mary Randolph; *Neighbor Law: Fences, Trees, Boundaries & Noise* by Cora Jordan; *A Legal Guide for Lesbian and Gay Couples* by Hayden Curry, Denis Clifford, and Robin Leonard; *The Independent Paralegal's Handbook* (revised edition) by Attorney Ralph Warner; *How to Mediate Your Dispute: Find a Solution You Can Live with Quickly and Cheaply Outside the Courtroom* by Peter Lovenheim.

Some humor!: *29 Reasons Not to Go to Law School* by Ralph Warner, Toni Ihara, and Barbara Kate Repa; *Poetic Justice: The Funniest, Meanest Things Ever Said About Lawyers* (edited by Jonathan and Andrew Roth); *The Devil's Advocates: The Unnatural History of Lawyers* by Andrew and Jonathan Roth.

Nolo.com distributes its own books to the trade (along with selected titles from other publishers) and also utilizes several distribution services; in addition, Nolo sells to consumers via direct mail and from its Web site and operates its own bookstore in Berkeley. Query letters and SASEs should be directed to:

Janet Portman, Publisher—Books and software.

W. W. NORTON AND COMPANY, INC.

Countryman Press/Backcountry Publications

Foul Play Books

500 Fifth Avenue, New York, NY 10110
212-354-5500   fax: 212-869-0856
www.wwnorton.com

Norton publishes trade nonfiction and belles lettres, and works for professional and academic markets. W. W. Norton (founded in 1923) offers prime-caliber publications in all areas of its trade program; the house is equally esteemed for its line of college texts and professional reference titles.

W. W. Norton produces hardcover and trade paperback editions under its celebrated gliding-seagull colophon, as well as through a variety of imprints, including Liveright and Countryman. Norton nourishes a comprehensive backlist of books in all areas of its publishing interest.

Norton nonfiction accents trade titles in topics of current interest, with a range of works featuring the popular as well as scholarly approach to fields, including cultural criticism, biography, psychology, history, economics, politics, natural history, the sciences, fine arts and design, photography, and lifestyle. Norton also offers a line of books for enthusiasts of sailing and publishes Blue Guide travel books.

Nonfiction from Norton: *America's Black Architects and Builders* by Stephen A. Kliment; *The Country Houses of David Adler* by Steven M. Salny; *New York for New Yorkers,* 2nd edition by Liza M. Greene; *Between Lives: An Artist and Her World* by Dorothea Tanning; *Basil Street Blues: A Memoir* by Michael Holroyd; *The Life of Jung* by Ronald Hayman; *Next: The Invisible Revolution* by Michael Lewis; *Latinos: A Biography of the People* by Earl Shorris; *The Bush Dyslexicon* by Mark Crispin Miller; *Something Under the Sun: An Environmental History of the Twentieth Century World* by J. R. McNeill; *Vital Signs 2001: The Environmental Trends That Are Shaping Our Future* by Worldwatch Institute; *Stone in the Garden: Inspiring Designs and Practical Projects* by Gordon Hayward; *The Body Silence: The Different World from the Disabled* by Robert F. Murphy; *Around America: A Tour of Our Magnificent Coastline* by Walter Cronkite; *Children of the West: Family Life on the Frontier* by Cathy Luchetti; *Ariel's Gift: Ted Hughes, Sylvia Plath, and the Story of Birthday Letters* by Erica Wagner; *The Pushcart Prize XXV: Best of the Small Presses,* 2001 edition by Bill Henderson, Editor, with the Pushcart Prize Editors; and *How Can We Keep from Singing: Music and the Passionate Life* by Joan Oliver Goldsmith.

In fiction and literary writing Norton publishes novels, poetry (including the Norton Anthologies series), and short story collections—from established, distinguished scribes and from a select few marketable new voices. In addition, the house publishes critical essays, biographies, and literary histories. The Norton fiction list covers classical, modern, contemporary, and experimental styles, as well as novels showing a mainstream commercial profile; the Norton program also encompasses mystery and suspense fiction.

Examples from the Norton fiction list: *Babe in Paradise* by Marisa Silver; *The Edge of Marriage Stories* by Hester Kaplan; *Glue* by Irvine Welsh; *Hussein: An Entertainment* by Patrick O'Brian; *The Partnership* by Barry Unsworth; *Strange Fire* by Melvin Jules Bukiet; *Strangers on a Train* by Patricia Highsmith; *A Suspension of Mercy* by Patricia Highsmith; and *The Miracle Life of Edgar Mint* by Brady Udall.

Norton poetry includes: *Blackbird Singing: Lyrics and Poems, 1963–1999* by Paul McCartney; *Collected Poems 1951–1971* by A. A. Ammons; *Landscape with Chainsaw: Poems* by James Lasdum; *Last Blue: Poems* by Gerald Stern; *The Making of a Poem: A Norton Anthology of Poetic Forms* (edited by Mark Strand and Eavan Boland); *A Mayan Astronomer in Hell's Kitchen: Poems* by Martin Espada; and *Worldly Hopes: Poems* by A. R. Ammons.

Works of speculative literary configuration: *The Coral Sea* (poetry, fiction, and essay) by Patti Smith; *In Short: A Collection of Brief Creative Nonfiction* (edited by Judith Kitchen and Mary Paumier Jones); *Sudden Fiction (Continued): 60 New Short-Short Stories* (edited by Robert Shepard and James Thomas); *When the Air Hits Your Brain: Tales of Neurosurgery* by Frank Vertosick; *Wise Women: Over 2,000 Years of Spiritual Writing by Women* (edited by Susan Cahill); *Holy Land: A Suburban Memoir* by D. J. Waldie.

W. W. Norton distributes its own list and handles distribution for its subsidiaries and imprints, as well as for a number of other publishers. Norton's distribution network includes: Chapters Publishing, Countryman Press, Ecco Press, Liveright Publishing Corporation, New Directions Books, The New Press, Pushcart Press, The Taunton Press, Thames and Hudson, and Verso.

Query letters and SASEs should be directed to:

Alane Mason, Editor—Serious nonfiction for a general audience, particularly cultural and intellectual history, some illustrated books. Literary fiction and memoir.

Amy Cherry, Senior Editor—History, biography, women's issues, African American, health, fiction.

Angela von der Lippe, Senior Editor—Trade nonfiction. Serious works in behavioral sciences, earth sciences, astronomy, neuroscience, education.

Carol Houck Smith, Editor at Large—Literary fiction, travel memoirs, behavioral sciences, nature.

Edwin Barber, Senior Editor—Acquires for the full range of house interests.

Jill Bialosky, Senior Editor—Literary fiction. Biographies, memoirs. poetry.

Jim Mairs, Senior Editor—History, illustrated books, photography.

Robert Weil, Executive Editor—Literature in translation, intellectual history, social science, German and Jewish interests.

Starling Lawrence, Editor in Chief—Acquires for the full range of house interests.

W. Drake McFeely, President—Nonfiction of all kinds, particularly science and social science.

Maria Guarnaschelli, Senior Editor—Cookbooks, serious nonfiction.

Countryman Press/Backcountry Publications

New England office:
P.O. Box 748, Woodstock, VT 05091
802-457-4826   fax: 802-457-1678

Countryman specializes in regional history, recreation, travel, gardening, nature, environment, how-to, regional hiking, walking, bicycling, fishing, cross-country skiing, and canoeing guides. Imprints include Countryman Press and Backcountry Publications. Previously developers and proprietors of the Foul Play line, the house has a successful heritage in mystery and suspense fiction.

Countryman (founded in 1973) has been on the cusp of the small, regional press initiative that has enriched the North American publishing scope through editorial acumen and niche-marketing panache. Now affiliated with W. W. Norton, Countryman remains editorially independent.

Representative Countryman titles: *Alaska on Foot: Wilderness Techniques for the Far North* by Erik Molvar; *The Lake Champlain Corridor: Touring Historic Battle Sites from Saratoga to Quebec* by Howard Coffin and Will and Jane Curtis; *Covered Bridges of Vermont* by Ed Barna; *The Architecture of the Shakers* by Julie Nicoletta (photographs by Bret Morgan).

Backcountry Publications: *Walks and Rambles in Ohio's Western Reserve: Discovering Nature and History in the Northeastern Corner* by Jay Abercrombie; *25 Mountain Bike Tours in the Hudson Valley* by Peter Kick; *50 Hikes in Connecticut: From the Berkshires to the Coast* by David, Sue, and Gerry Hardy.

Sales and distribution for Countryman are handled by the parent corporation, W. W. Norton. Query letters and SASEs should be directed to:

Kermit Hummel, Editorial Director

Foul Play Press

Foul Play is heavy on traditional mystery and suspense fiction, including classic reprints, United States editions of British originals, and a short list of homegrown originals. Foul Play Press was until 1996 part of Countryman Press, which developed the Foul Play imprint with careful small-press attention and independent-press savvy.

From Foul Play: *Slaughter Music* by Russell James; *Penance* (a Holland Taylor mystery) by David Housewright; *Astride a Grave* by Bill James; *Fête Fatale* by Robert Barnard; *Family Business* by Michael Z. Lewin.

Query letters and SASEs should be directed to:

Candace Watt, Editor (New York)

OAK TREE PRESS

915 W. Foothill Blvd., Suite 411, Claremont, CA 91711-3356
fax: 909-624-3930
OakTreeBooks.com

Oak Tree Press is an independent publisher of a wide variety of fiction and nonfiction, with a concentration on the mystery genre. Founded in 1998 to offer a counterpoint to shrinking publishing opportunities, Oak Tree maintains its welcoming attitude toward new authors. Since 1999, the publisher has sponsored the Dark Oak Mystery Contest and published the winning entry.

Oak Tree policies include dynamic cover design, aggressive outreach, strong backlist promotion, and an open editorial policy. We will consider almost any subject—so long as there is no gratuitous violence against women.

Trade fiction titles include: *Tulsa Time* by Letha Albright; *The Damned Never Die* by J. McKay; *Callie and the Dealer* and *A Dog Named Jake* by Wendy Howell Mills; and *An Affinity for Murder* by Anne White. In addition, Oak Tree is re-releasing a number of classic out-of-print titles from Odie Hawkins, beginning with *Ghetto Sketches* in spring 2001.

Nonfiction titles include: *Of Weeds and Views* by Frances U. Crain; *Mid-life Mojo: A Guide for the Newly Single Male* by Robert M. Davis, Ph.D., and *Business Buyer's Handbook* by Jim Calkins.

In Spring of 2001, Oak Tree made an entry into the audio and music realm through its sister company, WEGOTSKILLZ music, which will distribute and produce the work of independent artists.

Oak Tree Press handles its own marketing, sales and distribution. Query letters with SASEs should be directed to:

Billie Johnson, Publisher
Anthony Cruz, Operations Manager
Sarah Wasson, Editorial Assistant

ORYX PRESS

4041 North Central Avenue, Suite 700, Phoenix, AZ 85012-3397
602-265-2651
www.oryxpress.com   e-mail: info@oryxpress.com

The Oryx Web site includes sample chapters from selected books, online versions of Oryx Press catalogs, book reviews, and author biographies.

Oryx covers reference and informational publications in such fields as business and careers, medicine and consumer health, popular culture, popular science (including nature and environment), technical science, sports, elderly population and services, social services, education, human growth and development, gender studies, multicultural studies, international government and politics, and regional or period American history.

Oryx Press (founded in 1975) targets the informational marketplace, specializing in directories, databases, CD-ROMs, periodicals, looseleaf services, library and information science readers, and educational texts, as well as general reference works. Many Oryx releases are geared toward the library, corporate, institutional, educational, academic, and technical research arenas. The press issues special catalogs for the school market and also publishes books in cooperation with the University Continuing Education Association (UCEA) as part of the ACE/Oryx Continuing Higher Education Series.

Other Oryx Press series include: Oryx American Family Tree—this series is the first to explain the how-to's of genealogical research in simple, jargon-free language. The series explores how to research family history for 12 different ethnic groups: African American, British American, Japanese American, Polish American, German American, Scandinavian American, Italian American, Native American, Chinese American, Jewish American, and Mexican American. Exploring the Constitution Series—helps students develop critical-thinking skills as they investigate four key civil liberties areas of the U.S. Constitution. Exploring the United States Through Literature Series—each volume covers a difference geographic area and describes the best fiction and nonfiction books, computer programs, periodicals, videos, audiocassettes, maps, and atlases. The Oryx Reading Motivation Series—five different approaches merge the best in young adult literature with student interests to improve and enhance reading skills.

From the Oryx list: *Talking About People: A Guide to Fair and Accurate Language* by Rosalie Maggio; *Childhood and Children: A Compendium of Customs, Superstitions, Theories, Profiles, and Facts* by Joan Bel Geddes; *Storytelling Encyclopedia: Historical, Cultural, and Multiethnic Approaches to Oral Traditions Around the World* (Project Editor Marion Sader); *The Reference Guide to the World's Famous Landmarks: Bridges, Tunnels, Dams, Roads, and Other Structures* by Lawrence H. Berlow; *Encyclopedia of Women and Sport in America* (edited by Carole A. Oglesby); *Ethnic Groups Worldwide: A Ready Reference Handbook* by David Levinson; *Multicultural Folktales for the Feltboard and Readers' Theater* by Judy Sierra; *Children's Reference and Information Services* by Greg Byerly and Carolyn S. Brodie.

The Oryx Press handles its own distribution.

Editors listed below acquire in all areas consistent with publisher description. Query letters and SASEs should be directed to:

Martha Wilke, Acquisitions Editor

Mary Jo Godwin, Director of Marketing—Sales and promotional services.

Phyllis Steckler, President and CEO

THE OVERLOOK PRESS

368 West Broadway, New York, NY 10012
212-477-7162
www.overlookpress.com

Overlook focuses on general nonfiction and offers a respected line in fiction, belles lettres, and poetry. The nonfiction purview encompasses biography, crafts, how-to, fine arts, architecture and design, Hudson Valley regionals, cookbooks, and natural history. The house releases a limited number of titles directed toward the young reader.

The Overlook Press was founded in 1971 by Peter Mayer (until recently also Chief Executive of the Worldwide Penguin Group) and his father. Overlook is a smaller publisher with a diverse and select list. Under its enigmatic logo (a mythical beast in cartouche that calls to mind a winged elephantine species), Overlook produces books in special fine editions, hardcover, and trade paperback. The house nurtures a thriving backlist that features such titles as the business-martial arts classic *Book of Five Rings* by Miyamoto Musashi (translated by Victor Harris); *The Gormenghast Trilogy* by Mervyn Peake; and *Tiny Houses* by Lester Walker.

Overlook was founded with the intent to publish against the grain. Here was a new publishing company that did not exactly imitate the policies of large companies. The editors did not pursue bestsellers; they wanted good-sellers. And they believed in the backlist. They did not want to be a niche publisher, just a small general publisher. They wanted to publish books that very likely had been "overlooked" by larger houses—although the Overlook name actually came from a mountain in Woodstock, New York.

Overlook made a name by publishing useful books in areas where none existed. It published the first book on wood stoves in the early 1970s, anticipating a major trend; when the house produced the first book on Kendo published in the United States (*A Book of Five Rings*)—who knew it would become famous as a metaphor for business strategy?

In 1977 Overlook launched the Ivory Press to publish unusual books in the visual arts, joining Tusk paperbacks in the Overlook family of imprints.

Overlook's authors roster is one of the finest in the land. Fiction: Paul West, Geoff Nicholson, Steve Weiner, Richard Foreman, Robert Schneider, David Shapiro, and Paul Auster. Film books: Howard Koch, Peter Bogdanovich, Ian McKellen, Derek Jarman, Ang Lee, Guin Turner, Rose Troche, Michael Ritchie, Cyril Collard, and Bruce Robinson. Nonfiction: Buckminster Fuller, Erving Goffman, Martin Esslin, Armond White, and

Howard Jacobson. Design: Milton Glaser, Raymond Loewy, Terence Conran, Osborne and Little, Judith Miller, and Caroline Wrey.

Overlook nonfiction titles: *Dramatic Effects with Architectural Plants* by Noël Kingsbury; *The Complete Home Lighting Book: Contemporary Interior and Exterior Lighting for the Home* by James Davidson; *The Nashville Music Machine: The Unwritten Rules of the Country Music Business* by Dan Daley; *Pottery Decoration* by John Gibson; *The Hale Clinic Guide to Good Health: How to Choose the Right Complementary Therapy* by Teresa Hale.

Indicative of the Overlook backlist: *Chanel: The Couturière at Work* by Amy De La Haye and Shelley Tobin; *100 Great Albums of the Sixties* by John Tobler; *Diagnosis for Disaster: The Devastating Truth About False Memory Syndrome and Its Impact on Accusers and Families* by Claudette Wassil-Grimm; *The Zen of Cooking: Creative Cooking With and Without Recipes* by Claire Hyman and Lucille Naimer.

Overlook's literary emphasis is on vanguard fiction, poetry, biography, memoirs, travel, and criticism. Fiction from Overlook: *Parties: A Literary Companion* (edited by Susanna Johnston); *Kicking the Pricks* by Derek Jarman; *Dead Glamorous: The Autobiography of Seduction and Self-Destruction* by Carole Morin; *Kafka, Love and Courage: The Life of Milena Jesenská,* by Mary Hockaday; *The Music Teacher* by Robert Starer; *Promised Lands* by Jane Rogers; *Children of Albion Rovers: An Anthology of New Scottish Writing* (edited by Kevin Williamson); *Forbidden Journey: The Life of Alexandra David-Neel* by Barbara and Michael Foster.

Backlist entrants here include *X-Ray: The Unauthorized Autobiography* by Ray Davies; *The Ukimwi Road: From Kenya to Zimbabwe* by Dervla Murphy; *In Catskill Country: Collected Essays on Mountain History, Life and Lore* by Alf Evers; *Chroma* by Derek Jarman; *Nico: The End* by James Young.

Overlook Press is distributed by Penguin USA. Query letters and SASEs should be directed to:

Peter Mayer, Publisher

Tracy Karns, Editor

PALADIN PRESS

Paladin Enterprises, P.O. Box 1307, Boulder, CO 80306
303-443-7250   fax: 303-442-8741
www.paladin-press.com

Paladin issues new titles and reprints in such categories as new identity and personal freedom, espionage and investigation, weapons, military science, revenge and humor, special forces, survival, martial arts, action careers, sniping, knives and knife fighting, locksmithing, self-defense, police science, silencers, and history and culture relating to the previous fields, as well as selected general-interest books. Paladin also purveys a video library. Paladin Press (established in 1970) is a division of Paladin Enterprises.

Certain Paladin titles exhibit a markedly subversive approach and are intended as high-edge, satiric amusement. It should be further noted that particular works on the Paladin list contain material that may be restricted in some jurisdictions and are sold for academic, research, or informational reference purposes only.

Frontlist catalog entrants: *Cowboy Action Pistol Shooting: Secrets of Fast and Accurate Gunplay* by Charles K. Stephens; *The Jeet Kune Do Experience: Understanding Bruce Lee's Ultimate Martial Art* by Jerry Beasley, Ed.D.; *The Logic of Steel: A Fighter's View of Blade and Shank Encounters* by James LaFond; *No Waiting: How to Get What You Want, When You Want It* by Andy Kane; *Stopping Power: A Practical Analysis of the Latest Handgun Ammunition* by Evan P. Marshall and Edwin J. Sanow; *Surviving Street Patrol: The Officer's Guide to Safe and Effective Policing* by Steve Albrecht; *The Passport Report: Over 100 Ways and Many Good Reasons to Obtain a Second Foreign Passport* by Dr. W. G. Hill; *The Perpetual Traveler 2: A Coherent Plan for a Stress-Free, Healthy and Prosperous Life Without Government Interference, Taxes or Coercion* by Dr. W. G. Hill; and *The Moment of Truth: How to Physically, Mentally, and Legally Survive a Street Fight* by Lucianao Silveria.

Highlights from the backlist (including all-time Paladin hits): *Hard-Won Wisdom from the School of Hard Knocks: How to Avoid a Fight and Things to Do When You Can't or Don't Want to* by Alain Burrese; *Protect Your Assets: How to Avoid Falling Victim to the Government's Forfeiture Laws* by Adam Starchild; *Running a Ring of Spies: Spycraft and Black Operations in the Real World of Espionage* by Jefferson Mack; *SWAT Battle Tactics: How to Organize, Train, and Equip a SWAT Team for Law Enforcement or Self-Defense* by Pat Cascio and John McSweeney; *Mega-Marketing for the Private Investigator: How to Drastically Increase Your Agency Business with Effective Mega-Marketing Techniques* by Ralph D. Thomas; *Body for Sale: An Inside Look at Medical Research, Drug Testing, and Organ Transplants and How You Can Profit from Them* by Ed Brassard; *How to Investigate* by *Computer* by Ralph D. Thomas.

Paladin Press looks for original manuscripts on combat shooting, firearms and exotic weapons, personal and financial freedom, military science, and other action topics. For more information, call or write the publisher for a copy of the Author Style Guide and Insider Newsletter.

Paladin Press distributes its own list and in addition services individual orders via toll-free ordering numbers. Query letters and SASEs should be directed to:

Jon Ford, Editorial Director

PATHFINDER PRESS

410 West Street, New York, NY 10014
212-741-0690   fax: 212-727-0150
e-mail: pathfinderpress@compuserve.com

The Pathfinder program catalogs such fields as black and African studies; women's rights; the Cuban revolution in world politics; revolutionaries and working-class fighters; fascism, big business, and the labor movement; Russia, Eastern Europe, and the Balkans; scientific views of politics and economics; trade unions: past, present, and future; United

States history and political issues; Latin America and the Caribbean; the Middle East and China; and art, culture, and politics. Pathfinder titles often suggest such streams of thought as populism, internationalism, utopianism, socialism, and communism.

Pathfinder Press (established in 1940) issues books, booklets, pamphlets, posters, and postcards keyed to issues affecting working people worldwide. Pathfinder produces titles in English, Spanish, French, Swedish, Farsi, Greek, Icelandic, and Russian. Pathfinder distributes the journal *New International.*

The Pathfinder Mural that once adorned the company's editorial and manufacturing digs in Manhattan's Far West Village featured a depiction of a gargantuan printing press in action, as well as portraits of revolutionary leaders whose writings and speeches are published by Pathfinder; this community cultural icon represented the work of more than 80 artists from 20 countries.

Representative Pathfinder books: *Episodes of the Cuban Revolutionary War, 1956–58* by Ernesto Che Guevara (firsthand account of the military campaigns and political events that culminated in the January 1959 popular insurrection that overthrew the U.S.-backed dictatorship in Cuba); *Lenin's Final Fight: Speeches and Writings, 1922–23* by V. I. Lenin; *In Defense of Marxism: The Social and Political Contradictions of the Soviet Union* by Leon Trotsky; and *The Second Declaration of Havana* by Fidel Castro.

On Pathfinder's staunch backlist: *Bolivian Diary* by Ernesto (Che) Guevara); *Peru's Shining Path: Anatomy of a Reactionary Sect* by Martín Koppel; *Lenny Bruce: The Comedian as Social Critic and Secular Moralist* by Frank Kofsky; *The Revolution Betrayed: What Is the Soviet Union and Where Is It Going?* by Leon Trotsky; *The Politics of Chicano Liberation* (edited by Olga Rodriguez); *Polemics in Marxist Philosophy* by George Novack; *The Communist Manifesto* by Karl Marx and Frederick Engels; *Cuba's Internationalist Foreign Policy, 1975–80* by Fidel Castro; *To Speak the Truth: Why Washington's "Cold War" Against Cuba Doesn't End* by Fidel Castro and Che Guevara; *How Far We Slaves Have Come! South Africa and Cuba in Today's World* by Nelson Mandela, Fidel Castro; *Che Guevara: Economics and Politics in the Transition to Socialism* by Carlos Tablada.

Pathfinder's *New International* is a magazine of Marxist politics and theory. Many of the articles that appear in *New International* are available in Spanish, French, and Swedish. The magazine is a numbered series in trade paperback format.

Special Pathfinder series include *Malcolm X: Speeches and Writings,* as well as written works and spoken words from James P. Cannon, Eugene V. Debs, Farrell Dobbs, Carlos Fonseca, Mother Jones, Rosa Luxemburg, Nelson Mandela, Fidel Castro, and Ernesto (Che) Guevara; the house also publishes the works of Karl Marx, Frederick Engels, V. I. Lenin, and Leon Trotsky.

A number of bookstores around the world distribute Pathfinder's titles and offers membership in a readers' club for an annual fee (entitling members to enjoy special Pathfinder discounts); individual orders are payable via Visa and MasterCard. Pathfinder Press distributes its own publications in the United States and worldwide primarily through its own fulfillment centers.

Query letters and SASEs should be directed to:

Michael Taber, Editorial Director—Projects consistent with the Pathfinder list.

Peachpit Press (A Division of Pearson Education)

1249 Eighth Street, Berkeley, CA 94710
510-524-2178   fax: 510-524-2221
www.peachpit.com

Peachpit is a specialist computer-publishing house with a list in personal computing and desktop publishing for business and recreational users. Peachpit publishes books and book/software packages (including CD-ROM products) that tackle basic practical tasks and troubleshooting, as well as advanced applications.

Peachpit covers a number of categories: general introductory works on computing, general works about the Macintosh computer system, Macintosh Bible series, Visual Quick Start series, On the Web series, the Real World series, The Non-Designer's series, desktop publishing, graphics, Windows and Windows applications, word processing, and related topics. Many Peachpit releases are keyed to particular proprietary products.

Visual Quick Start Guides provide exactly what the title implies: a fast, simple way to get up and running with a new program—which is perhaps the secret to the popularity of this successful line.

Peachpit's editorial approach is to make the computing world relevant, make it dramatic, and make it fun. Peachpit authors are at the forefront of ongoing technological developments and trends in computer hardware and software development, and masterful at teasing out the nuances of end-user potential in print.

Publisher's statement: Peachpit is not only in the book business and not only a player on the computer-business stage; Peachpit is also in the teaching business. In addition to trade bookstores and computer venues, Peachpit hits a variety of market sectors such as schools and educational enterprises (including evening classes and adult education); library, institutional, and corporate consumers; and end-user and professional groups.

Peachpit Press (founded in 1986) was acquired by Addison-Wesley in late 1994, and the house is now a division of Pearson Education. Within this corporate structure, Peachpit maintains its independent editorial stance and gains financial and distributional leverage from the new ownership to the benefit of Peachpit's worthy list.

Titles from Peachpit: *HTML 4 for the World Wide Web* (4th edition), *Visual Quick Start Guide* by Elizabeth Castro; *Robin Williams Design Workshop* by Robin Williams; *Real World Bryce 4* by Susan Kitchens and Victor Gavenda; *The Illustrator 9 Wow! Book* by Sharon Steuer; *Dreamweaver 3 Hands-On Training* by Lynda Weinman; *Flash 5! Creative Web Animation* by Derek Franklin and Brooks Patton; *Community Building on the Web* by Amy Jo Kim; *The Little iMac Book* by Robin Williams; *Sad Macs, Bombs, and Other Disasters,* 4th edition by Ted Landau.

Peachpit Press is distributed through the parent company Pearson Education.

To suggest a book idea or submit a book proposal, contact Marjorie Baer (510-524-2178) or e-mail (marjorie@peachpit.com). Query letters and SASEs should be directed to:

Nancy Ruenzel, Publisher

Peachtree Publishers, Ltd

Peachtree Children's Books

1700 Chattahoochee Avenue, Atlanta, GA 30318-2112
404-876-8761   fax: 404-875-2578

Peachtree publishes children's books and general trade, and offers a substantial and growing children's list. Peachtree has a concentration in markedly innovative books in self-help, self-awareness, health, and parenting. A special area of Peachtree publishing interest encompasses regional topics, including the American South in general and the state of Georgia in particular. Peachtree is also known for its storytelling series.

Peachtree Publishers (established in 1978) is a midsize house that produces books in hardcover and trade paperback editions. Peachtree hosts a hardy backlist.

From Peachtree: *Cheap Psychological Tricks: What to Do When Hard Work, Honesty, and Perseverance Fail!* by Perry Buffington (illustrated by Mitzi Cartee); *Archival Atlanta: Electric Street Dummies, The Great Stonehenge Explosion, Nerve Tonics and Bovine Laws* by Perry Buffington and Kim Underwood; *The Hiking Trails of North Georgia* by Tim Homan with the Georgia Conservancy; *Margaret Mitchell & John Marsh: The Love Story Behind Gone With the Wind* by Marianne Walker; *The Single Mother's Book: A Practical Guide to Managing Your Children, Career, Home, Finances, and Everything Else* by Joan Anderson.

Standout Peachtree projects: *The Celestine Sibley Sampler: Writings and Photographs with Tributes to the Beloved Author and Journalist* by Celestine Sibley (edited by Sibley Fleming); *Over What Hill? Notes from the Pasture* by Effie Leland Wilder (illustrated by Laurie Klein); *Growing Up Cuban in Decatur, Georgia* by Carmen Agra Deedy; *The New Austerities* by Tito Perdue.

Peachtree distributes its own list to the trade with the assistance of regional sales representatives. Query letters and SASEs should be directed to:

Sarah Helyar Smith, Acquisitions and Development Editor

Peachtree Children's Books

Children's editions from Peachtree encompass award-winning frontlist illustrated storybooks for younger readers, as well as a select group of works directed toward parents. Peachtree Jr. is a line of chapter books targeted for ages 8 years and up. The AllStar SportStory series combines contemporary tales with sports history and statistics. Freestone is a line of novels for today's teenagers, ages 12 to 16.

Titles here: *The Secret of Old Zeb* by Carmen Agra Deedy (illustrated by Michael P. White); *Oh No, Anna!* by Vivian French (illustrated by Alex Ayliffe); *Gilbert de la Frogponde: A Swamp Story* by Jennifer Rae (illustrated by Rose Cowles); *Lillian's Fish* by James Menk (illustrated by Louisa Bauer); *Charlie's Story* by Maeve Friel; *Hero* by S. I. Rottman.

Query letters and SASEs should be directed to:

Sarah Helyar Smith, Acquisitions and Development Editor

PELICAN PUBLISHING COMPANY

P.O. Box 3110, Gretna, LA 70054-3110
504-368-1175 800-843-1724 (orders)   fax: 504-368-1195
www.pelicanpub.com   e-mail: editorial@pelicanpub.com

Pelican Publishing Company (founded in 1926) produces a general trade list with special interests in travel and lifestyle guides, Americana, cookbooks, art and architecture, photography, humor, sports, motivational, and inspirational titles. Many Pelican titles offer a regional or cultural perspective in such areas as the American South, Civil War history, Louisiana and the New Orleans environs, and Scottish American heritage. Pelican produces a short menu of children's books and offers a select group of fiction works, many of which have a regional or historical twist.

Pelican's travel series include the Maverick Guides (for the independent traveler—these guides include history, customs, language, and attractions, as well as current prices and recommendations for accommodations, dining spots, etc.); the Marmac Guides (up-to-date information on population, services, recreation, accommodations, restaurants in various American cities); At Cost Travel Guide series (for the value-conscious traveler); the Pelican Guide series (designed to give the discriminating traveler insight into some of the most interesting locations within the United States).

Other Pelican series include the Majesty Architecture series, the New Orleans Architecture series, the Best Editorial Cartoons of the Year series, the Editorial Cartoonists series, the Cruising Guides series, and the Clovis Crawfish Series for kids.

From Pelican: *Creating Ever-Cool: A Marketer's Guide to a Kid's Heart* by Gene Del Vecchio; *A Redneck Night Before Christmas* by David Davis (illustrated by James Rice); *The Gardens of Florida* by Steven Brooke and Laura Cerwinske.

Pelican's Top-30 list includes: *See You at the Top* by Zig Ziglar; *The Justin Wilson Cook Book, The Justin Wilson Gourmet and Gourmand Cookbook,* and *Justin Wilson's Outdoor Cooking with Inside Help* by Justin Wilson

Representing the Pelican's children's list favorites: *Pennsylvania Dutch Night Before Christmas* by Cet Williamson (illustrated by James Rice); *Why Cowgirls Are Such Sweet Talkers* by Laurie Lazzoro Knowlton (illustrated by James Rice); *Lucky O'Leprechaun Comes to America,* written and illustrated by Jane Dillon.

Pelican Publishing Company handles its own distribution. Query letters and SASEs should be directed to:

Nina Kooij, Editor in Chief

PENGUIN USA

Dutton

Penguin

Penguin USA Children's Divisions

Viking

Puffin

Ladybird

Frederick Warne

G. P. Putnam's Sons

Berkley Books

Riverhead Books

Plume

Signet

375 Hudson Street, New York, NY 10014
212-366-2000

Penguin USA is a major component of Penguin Putnam, Inc. Beneath the spread of its two primary branches—Viking Penguin and Dutton Signet—Penguin USA offers a wealth of distinctive and distinguished lines and imprints. The house produces books in hardcover, trade paper, and mass-market paperback editions.

In early 1997 Penguin USA and the Putnam Berkley Group—two huge book-publishing enterprises—merged to form Penguin Putnam, Inc. Within this expansive domain, Penguin USA remains an imposing publishing group, one of North America's leading houses.

Penguin earns an admirable industry presence through a diverse program that includes a solid seasonal list of new commercial titles, as well as a select group of imprints featuring some of publishing's classic lines in poetry, belles lettres, and literary fiction (established backlist sellers, newer reprints, and originals). The Viking Penguin division incorporates such imprints as Viking, Penguin, and Penguin Studio. The Dutton Signet division includes Dutton, Mentor, New American Library, Obelisk, Onyx, Plume, Roc, Signet, and Topaz.

In the Penguin USA lineup are a number of children's-book divisions, among them Cobblehill, Dial Books for Young Readers, Dutton Children's Books, Lodestar, Puffin, and Viking Children's Books (please see subentry further on for Penguin USA Children's Divisions).

Penguin USA is also home to the Frederick Warne imprint, Arkana, Virago Modern Classics, and the autonomous imprint Truman M. Talley Books, as well as the subsidiary Stephen Greene Press.

Dutton/Plume, a division of Penguin USA, includes Truman M. Talley Books and the William Abrahams line. Plume publishes primarily trade paperback nonfiction and fiction, original titles as well as reprints. Plume accents commercial nonfiction and selected high-interest contemporary fiction, as well as classics and literary works. Plume also produces a variety of television and film tie-ins and a strong line of popular nutrition, health, and self-improvement titles.

NAL, the mass-market side of Penguin USA, includes such imprints as Mentor, Onyx, Roc, Signet, Topaz, and the affiliated DAW Books (see DAW main entry). These imprints address popular nonfiction (how-to, self-improvement, topical stories) and produce category fiction lineups in mystery and suspense, thrillers, romance, science fiction and fantasy, horror, and Westerns).

New American Library is a designation given to a portion of the Signet/NAL mass-market rack-size paperback list, covering broad categories in nonfiction and fiction.

Penguin Putnam distributes for all its divisions and imprints; Penguin also handles distribution for books published by a variety of houses, including Sports Illustrated, DAW, Dove Books, Overlook Press, Hamish Hamilton, and Michael Joseph.

The Viking Penguin program informs us that it does not accept unsolicited manuscripts or queries. Any materials sent to the house with an SASE are returned unread. Anything without an SASE is recycled. The house accepts only agented or otherwise solicited work. The acquisitions contacts listed below are for information and reference purposes.

Dutton

Dutton spans the spectrum of trade categories in fiction and nonfiction. Dutton is a major player in popular nonfiction areas, covering personality and celebrity books, topical interest, current events, biography and memoirs, business and careers, parenting and the family, psychology and inspiration, cultural studies, history, science, and reference. The house produces a substantial list in contemporary fiction, with an emphasis in top-rank suspense and mystery novels, science fiction and fantasy, Westerns, and popular literary works.

The Dutton division of Penguin Putnam, Inc., is a corporate incarnation of the former E. P. Dutton. Under the Dutton umbrella are a number of imprints, including Signet, Onyx, Topaz, and the William Abrahams line.

Indicative of the Dutton program in fiction, literary works, and letters: *The World on Blood* by Jonathan Nasaw; *Millionaires Row* by Norman Katkov; *Gossip* by Christopher Bram; *Touched* by Carolyn Haines; *Streets of Fire* by Soledad Santiago; *Fearful Symmetry* by Greg Bills; *Infamous* by Joan Collins; *No Use Dying over Spilled Milk: A Pennsylvania Dutch Mystery with Recipes* by Tamar Myers; *Bad Angel* by Helen Benedict; and *First Cases: First Appearances of Classic Private Eyes* (edited by Robert J. Randisi).

Dutton has published such authors as Nancy Taylor Rosenberg, Helena Maria Viramontes, Lisa Appignanesi, Lisa Alther, Dorothy Allison, Joyce Carol Oates, Julia Alvarez, Max Allan Collins, Joan Hess, Lawrence Block, and Christopher Bram.

Representative Dutton nonfiction: *What Women Want* by Patricia Ireland; *Harriet Roth's Deliciously Healthy Jewish Cooking: 350 New Low-Fat, Low-Cholesterol, Low-Sodium Recipes for Holidays and Every Day* by Harriet Roth; *Facing the Wolf: Inside the Process of Deep Feeling Therapy* by Theresa Sheppard Alexander; *The Directory of Saints: A Concise Guide to Patron Saints* by Annette Sandoval; *Howard Hughes: The Untold Story* by Peter Harry Brown and Pat H. Broeske; *Behind Blue Eyes: The Life of Pete Townsend* by Geoffrey Giuliano; *Split Image: The Life of Anthony Perkins* by Charles Winecoff; *Growing Myself: A Spiritual Journey Through Gardening* by Judith Handelsman; *Faith of Our Fathers: African-American Men Reflect on Fatherhood* (edited by Andre Willis); *Mama's Boy: The True Story of a Serial Killer and His Mother* by Richard T. Pienciak; *Orion's Legacy: A Cultural History of Man as Hunter* by Charles Bergman.

Acquisition contacts (agented only):

Audrey LaFehr, Executive Editor, Dutton Signet; Editorial Director, Topaz—Commercial fiction, romance, suspense.

Carole DeSanti, Vice President, Editor at Large—Women's issues, literary fiction, cookbooks, health.

Hamilton Cain, Senior Editor—Narrative nonfiction, business, politics/current affairs, literary fiction.

Hillary Ross, Associate Executive Editor—Women's fiction, romance, suspense, thrillers, commercial fiction, general nonfiction.

Hugh Rawson, Editorial Director, Penguin Reference—Reference, general nonfiction.

Joanna Cagan, Senior Editor—Romance, women's fiction, other commercial fiction and nonfiction.

Laurie Chittenden, Senior Editor—Popular and commercial works in nonfiction. Occasional fiction.

Julia Serebinsky, Associate Editor—Journalism, psychology, film, novelty books, cookbooks, literary fiction.

Kari Paschall, Associate Manuscript Editor

Laura Ann Gilman, Executive Editor—Acquires for Roc science fiction and fantasy line; mysteries.

Lisa Hibler, Associate Manuscript Editor

Lori Lipsky, Vice President, Associate Publisher, Editor in Chief, Adult Trade—Commercial fiction, thrillers, suspense; general nonfiction, cookbooks, novelty books. Presides over Dutton hardcover and Plume.

Mitch Hoffman, Editor—Mysteries, thrillers, narrative nonfiction, and humor.

Donald I. Fine Books

Donald I. Fine Books imprint has been dissolved as Mr. Fine has passed away.

Penguin

Penguin (founded in 1935) is an imprint of the Viking Penguin division of Penguin Putnam. Penguin's original publishing vision was to make great books available—and affordable—to a broad audience. Publishing under the widely recognized imprint of its emblematic penguin cartouche, the house retains a paperback orientation and operates a program that encompasses both originals and reprints. Many Viking hardcover books are reprinted in Penguin paperback editions.

In addition to the celebrated Penguin Classics line, the imprint features the Viking Portable series, the Viking Critical Library, the Penguin Nature Classics, and Penguin Twentieth-Century Classics. Penguin offers an acclaimed assortment of poetry that accents contemporary voices (including titles in the Penguin Poets line). The Arkana imprint is devoted to spirituality and philosophy. Penguin is always on the lookout for strong original trade-paperback titles.

In 1996, Penguin launched Penguin Ediciones, a paperback line of books written in Spanish; authors include Carlos Fuentes, Gabriel Garcia Marques, and Manuel Puig.

Representative Viking Penguin nonfiction: *Places Left Unfinished at the Time of Creation* by John Phillip Santos; *A People's History of the Supreme Court* by Peter Irons; *Breakout* by Martin Russ; *Black Hawk Down* by Mark Bowden; *Difficult Conversations* by Douglas Stone, Bruce Patton, and Sheila Heen; *Eleanor Roosevelt,* volumes 1 and 2 by Blanche Wiesen Cook. Viking Penguin fiction and literary highlights: *Borges Collected Fiction; Death in Summer* by William Trevor; *The Girls' Guide to Hunting and Fishing* by Melissa Bank; *Bridget Jones's Diary* by Helen Fielding; *Stories* by T. C. Boyle; *Farming of Bones* by Edwindge Danicat. The house has success with a roster of bestselling novels from popular authors: *Felicia's Journey* by William Trevor; *The Cunning Man* by Robertson Davies; *Redeye* by Clyde Edgerton; *Songs in Ordinary Time* by Mary McGarry Morris; *Rose Madder* by Stephen King; *Speaking in Tongues* by Jeffrey Deaver; and *At Home in Mitford* by Jan Karon.

Acquisition contacts (agented only):

Caroline White, Editor—Literary fiction, women's issues, memoirs, sociology, religion, film and television, popular culture, Penguin Classics.

Jane von Mehren, Associate Publisher—Health and social issues, self-help, child care and parenting, nature, memoir, history, popular culture, and personal stories, as well as contemporary and historical literary fiction.

Kathryn Court, Publisher—Literary and commercial fiction, including Third World and European fiction. Nonfiction interests include humor, travel writing, biography, current affairs, business, nature, women's issues, and true crime.

Laurie Walsh, Assistant Editor—Literary and commercial fiction.

Michael Millman, Senior Editor—Oversees the Penguin Classics and Twentieth-Century Classics, the Viking Portable Library, and the Penguin Nature Classics series.

Sarah Baker, Senior Editor—Nonfiction paperback originals with backlist potential in several areas: popular culture, music, humor, current events, environment. Also hardcover and/or paperback originals for the Arkana imprint, which publishes spiritual literature.

Penguin USA Children's Divisions

The Penguin children's book-publishing operations offer a panoply of distinctive divisions, imprints, and affiliates of Penguin's component houses, including Cobblehill Books, Dial Books for Young Readers, Dutton Children's Books, Lodestar Books, Puffin Books, and Viking Children's Books. Each imprint publishes a wide range of titles in a variety of formats, and each children's house is a recognized name in the industry; taken together, this Penguin lineup represents a powerhouse in the young-reader arena.

The Cobblehill Books affiliate accents picture books with stories to tell, as well as nonfiction for the range of youthful readership. Among Cobblehill titles: *When the Wolves Return* (photoessay) by Ron Hirschi (photographs by Thomas D. Mangelsen); *Kids In and Out of Trouble* by Margaret O. Hyde; *The Chicks' Trick* by Jeni Bassett (illustrated by the author); *Emeka's Gift: An African Counting Story* by Ifeoma Onyefulu (photographs by the author); *The Haunting of Holroyd Hill* by Brenda Seabrooke.

Dial Books for Young Readers is a division that publishes the spectrum from preschoolers through older readers. On the Dial list: *Boundless Grace* by Mary Hoffman; *It's a Spoon, Not a Shovel* by Caralyn Buehner (illustrated by Mark Buehner); *Titanic Crossing* by Barbara Williams; *The Secret Code Book* (with press-out code-busters) by Helen Huckle; *Do the Whales Still Sing?* by Dianne Hofmeyr (illustrated by Jude Daly).

The Dutton Children's Books program includes humorous and serious titles for the youngest readers through young adult. Indicative of the Dutton list are *Jeremy Kooloo* by Tim Mahurin; *Dinner at Magritte's* by Michael Garland (illustrated by the author); *Jimmy, the Pickpocket of the Palace* by Donna Jo Napoli (illustrated by Judith Byron Schachner); and *It's for You: An Amazing Picture-Puzzle Book* by John Talbot.

Lodestar Books offers a vigorous approach to fiction and nonfiction for all age groups, as well as an innovative line of activity books and specialty items. Lodestar fiction and nonfiction titles often have a social-issue edge and deal with such phenomena as ethnic experience, gender relations, art and culture, and sexual preference.

Representative Lodestar titles are *For Home and Country: A Civil War Scrapbook* by Norma Bolotin and Angela Herb; *Toads and Diamonds* (retold and illustrated by Robert Bender); *Paco and the Witch: A Puerto Rican Folktale,* retold by Felix Pitre (illustrated by Christy Hale; also available in Spanish as *Paco y la Bruja* (translated by Osvaldo Blanco); *Earth, Sky, and Beyond: A Journey Through Space* by Jean-Pierre Verdet (illustrated by Pierre Bon).

Puffin Books is a division that produces the gamut of mainstream children's categories, with emphasis on popular-priced paperback picture-book editions for the youngest readers and novels and nonfiction for the older group. Sample Puffin entrants: *Glasses—Who Needs 'Em?* by Lane Smith; *The Day the Goose Got Loose* by Reeve Lindbergh (illustrated by Steven Kellogg); *Springtime* by Ann Schweninger; *The Sea Lion* by Ken Kesey (illustrated by Neil Waldman). Puffin Classics issues a line of traditional children's works in new editions. The house also produces Spanish-language books.

F. Warne & Company concentrates on reissues of works by such historic masters as Beatrix Potter and Cicely Mary Barker.

Viking Children's Books publishes a well-rounded list that includes picture books for the youngest readers as well as works aimed toward middle and older readership in fiction and nonfiction (some keyed to high-interest contemporary topics); the house also produces a respected reference line. Titles here are *Taking Flight: My Story* by Vicki Van Meter with Dan Gutman; *Two's Company* by Amanda Benjamin; *Dinosaurs: The Fastest, the Fiercest, the Most Amazing* by Elizabeth McLeod (illustrated by Gordon Sauvé); *The Encyclopedia of Native America* (edited by Trudy Griffin-Pierce); and *Undone! More Mad Endings* by Paul Jennings.

Query letters and SASEs should be directed to:

Deborah Brodie, Executive Editor, Viking Children's Books

Jane O'Connor, President and Publisher, Grosset & Dunlap

Joe Ann Daly, Editorial Director, Cobblehill Books

Lauri Hornik, Editorial Director

Nancy Paulsen, President and Publisher, G. P. Putnam's Sons

Patricia Gauch, Vice President and Editorial Director, Philomel Books

Regina Hayes, Publisher, Viking Children's Books

Toby Sherry, Senior Editor, Dial Books for Young Readers

Tracy Tang, Publisher, Puffin Books and Alloy Books

Joy Peskin, Editor, Puffin Books (imprint of Penguin/Putnam)
   Born: February 8, 1974.
   Education: Vassar College, Sociology major, and I have completed the Radcliffe Publishing Course.
   Employment history/editor career path: I started at Course Crafters, Inc., a small education packager in Newburyport, Massachusetts. I have been with Puffin Books since February 1997.
   Personal interests: I have been a volunteer tutor for three years and I love it. I have also taken several writing classes and am currently trying to start my own writer's group.
   What would you be doing if you were not an editor? I would be a social worker.
   What has been your most successful book that you have acquired to date? I was just promoted to Editor in May so books I have acquired have not yet been published. I have worked with other editors on successful books.
   What books have you acquired that make you the most proud? What books that you have acquired reflect the types of books you like to represent? I have acquired several Lift-the-Flap and Easy-to-Read books, which I enjoy working on because I love the challenge of telling an engaging story in only a few words and with art.
   Do you represent fiction? If so, what do you look for? Not at this point, but I am interested in working with young adult fiction in the future.
   Do you represent nonfiction? Yes, Lift-the-Flap books (2–6-year-old range, which are fiction and nonfiction).
   Do you require book proposals? If so, what do you look for in evaluating a book proposal? Yes, most of the material that I acquire is short, so I don't mind seeing the whole text. In a query letter I look for the author to sum up the proposed material in a few good sentences.
   Are certain aspects of a book proposal given more weight than others? Author credentials help to get my attention, but I can usually tell right away if I like the material by the style of the author's writing.
   What process do you use for making a decision? What is the process for acquisition, is there a committee? At Puffin we publish mostly paperback reprints. So, we don't have editorial meetings. The acquisition process happens informally. I read the author's work and if I like it, I begin a correspondence with the author. Once the manuscript is in good shape, I take it directly to the publisher for her review. If she likes it, I make the author an offer.
   What kinds of nonfiction books do you want to see less of? Alphabet books—fruit alphabet books, and other uninspired ideas.

Are you interested in work geared for the masses (readers of *People, The Star,* etc.)? Yes, sometimes. Celebrity bios are popular with teenagers, and I'm always looking for ways to reach the teen market.

Are agents important? Why? Yes, I think they are, although I haven't worked with many agents yet. I have done most of my work directly with the author, but I've seen others work very successfully with agents.

Do you like new writers? What should new writers do to break into the business? Yes, I like new writers. Breaking into the business can be frustrating! I would advise aspiring writers to be persistent with a gentle touch. I've had writers just "show-up" at the office unannounced and put me on the spot—this is *not* a good idea. Just put something in the mail and follow up with a friendly reminder note.

How should writers approach you? Send me your material through the mail. Be sure to address it directly to me with my correct title. If material comes addressed to me as an Editorial Assistant, I know the sender is looking at an old publication of something.

What are some common mistakes writers make? It's annoying when writers haven't done their homework, when they don't know what each publishing house publishes. I'd advise writers to know what each house is known for. This will save writers time and postage money in the end. Another annoying thing some writers do is to follow up too frequently. I had one writer sending demanding e-mails weekly. That's a big mistake. It makes me think—if this person is acting like this at this stage, what will she be like to work with if I acquire her book?

What can writers do to get your attention and to avoid the slush pile? Address material directly to me with the correct title and refer to one of our programs (Lift-the-Flap, Easy-to-Read) here at Puffin in your cover letter, if it applies.

What have been some of your craziest experiences with submissions? When people send items to enhance their project idea (whistles, T-shirts, champagne, etc.).

What have been some of your best experiences with writers or in your job? I love getting the finished art in for a book. I love working with artists and authors who are really inspiring. It's also wonderful to develop a relationship with an author and to see his/her work evolve.

What, if anything, makes you different from other editors? Each editor has different interests and passions. I try to acquire books that I am interested in and passionate about.

Is there anything you would like to see changed in the industry? In child readers, we tend to lose boys around the ages of 11 or 12. We don't have many male children's book editors, and I would like to see more men involved in editing books for boys. It may sound sexist, but I think men have a better sense of what boys like to read. "Boy humor" can be a bit vulgar—some female children's book editors don't get it. I certainly don't fully appreciate it. I think men are more in touch with that. They can remember being an 11-year-old boy; they can remember what they liked to read about at that age. Humor is a great way to keep boys reading.

Any advice for writers? Do research into the different houses so you can place your story in the best possible hands. Research the market—if you see 10 books on a certain subject, don't write a book on that topic. Find a different angle. Most important: Don't give up. Hang in there. All it takes is one editor to pick up your work and love it.

Viking

Viking covers the trade spectrum in nonfiction and fiction. Nonfiction areas include current events, popular and academic history, personal finance, business, lifestyle and design, travel, health, music, popular philosophy, self-help, religion and spirituality, women's studies, history, general reference, essays, biography and autobiography, and literary criticism. Viking fiction hits all the popular categories, including popular literature, international fiction, literary fiction, thrillers, mystery, and suspense. Viking's output includes books for young readers (see information under Penguin USA Children's Divisions).

Viking produces primarily hardcover trade editions under its captivating, illustrious logo of a seafaring dragon ship. Viking's publishing program spins off many of its originals into paper editions via the Penguin and Dutton reprint lists.

Acquisition contacts (agented only):

Rick Kot, Senior Editor—Commercial works in nonfiction; some fiction.

Doug Grad, Senior Editor—Narrative nonfiction, thrillers, historical.

Paul Slovak, Vice President Viking Publishing, Senior Editor, Assistant Publisher—Poetry, literary fiction, beat work (Kerouac and the like) intellectual nonfiction.

Carolyn Carlson, Senior Editor—Narrative nonfiction, cultural history, biography, women's issues, commercial nonfiction, commercial and literary fiction, mysteries.

Clare Feraro, President—Commercial fiction and nonfiction.

Janet Goldstein, Executive Editor—Spirituality, health, psychology, narrative nonfiction.

Pamela Dorman, Executive Editor—Commercial fiction, especially women's fiction and suspense. Nonfiction interests include self-help and psychology, investigative stories and narrative nonfiction, popular inspiration, popular reference, and women's issues.

Susan Hans O'Connor, Associate Editor—Commercial and literary fiction, mysteries, dance/theater/arts.

Wendy Wolf, Senior Editor—Nonfiction, especially music, culture, humor.

Viking Studio (formerly Penguin Studio)

Viking Studio publishes illustrated books of mainstream interest for adults in all subject categories and in all price ranges. Studio titles tend toward high-interest frontlist offerings in art and culture, fashion and design, lifestyle, and sports, with interests that cross over into such arenas as health and nutrition, popular psychology and inspiration, humor, works with social and historical themes, and literary writing.

Representing the Studio lineup: *Strange Sisters* by Jaye Zimet; *Pug Shots* by Jim Dratfield; *Rolling Stones: A Life on the Road* by the Rolling Stones; *David Bailey: Birth of the Cool* by Martin Harrison; *Siblings* by Nick Kelsh and Anna Quindlen; *The Secret Language of Relationships* by Gary Goldschneider and Joost Elffers; *The Secret Language of Destiny* by Gary Goldschneider and Joost Elffers; *The Holy Bible* (illustrated by Barry Moser); *The Tibetans* by Art Perry; *Outside the Bungalow* by Paul Duchscherer and Douglas Keister; *Confessions of a Window Dresser* by Simon Doonan; *Novena: The Power of Prayer* by Barbara Calimari and Sandra DiPasqua; *Laetitia Casta* by Laetitia Casta;

World Ceramics by Hugo and Margorie Munsterberg; *House Styles in America* by James Massey and Shirley Maxwell; *The English Rose* by David Austin; *The Chateaux of the Loire* by Pierre Miquel and Jean-Baptiste Leroux.

  Acquisition contacts (agented only):

Christopher Sweet, Executive Editor—Popular culture, art, photography, music, history, fashion, style.

Cyril Nelson, Senior Editor—Folk art and crafts, gardening, quilting, collecting, antiques, and architecture.

Marie Timell, Senior Editor—Occult, astrology, New Age, reference, recovery, psychology, medicine.

Rachel Tsutsumi, Associate Editor—Fashion, design, photography, architecture, and art.

P

THE PERMANENT PRESS/SECOND CHANCE PRESS

4170 Noyac Road, Sag Harbor, NY 11963
fax: 631-725-1101

Founded in 1978 by copublishers Judith and Martin Shepard, the Permanent Press produces expressive, vital, and exciting nongenre fiction. The sine qua non here for titles is that they be artfully written. The Permanent Press publishes 12 books a year in cloth editions only. Selected out-of-print books are released in reprint under the Second Chance Press imprint.

  Judith and Martin Shepard have endeavored to bring out quality writing, primarily fiction, without regard to authors' reputations or track records. The publisher presents a handpicked list in which it firmly believes. Such dedication is not without payoff: Permanent Press titles generate considerable and favorable word of mouth among readers and booksellers, and reap the kinds of reviews that pique wide interest (particularly in the realm of subsidiary rights).

  While publishing only 12 books a year, Permanent Press has, since 1986, gained 49 literary awards for its titles (including an American Book Award and a National Book Award finalist). The press has launched the careers of such novelists as Bill Albert, Larry Duberstein, David Galef, Andrew Klavan, Howard Owen, Sandra Scofield, and William Browning Spencer. Permanent has published a Nobel Prize–winner (Halldor Laxness) and a Nobel Prize–nominee (Berry Fleming). This is the house that gave a fresh start to Clifford Irving after his misadventures involving the Howard Hughes "autobiography," by publishing Irving's account of that episode (*The Hoax*).

  To celebrate Permanent's 20th year, the list presents 20 titles (8 more than it has ever done before) selected from the over 8,000 submissions received: 16 novels, 3 works of nonfiction, and a short-story collection.

  Fiction on the Permanent Press list: *Marginalia* by Doran Larsen; *Natural Bridges* by Debbie Lynn McCampbell; *The Trap* by Rink van der Velde (originally published in the Netherlands in 1966); *Geometry of Love* by Joan Fay Cuccio; *Up, Down, & Sideways* and *Life Between Wars* by Robert H. Patton; *The Deer Mouse* by Ken Grant; *The Speed of*

Light by Susan Pashman; *Bending Time* by Stephen Minot (short stories); *Queen of the Silver Dollar* by Edward Hower; *Apology for Big Rod* by Charles Holdefer; *They Don't Play Stickball in Milwaukee* by Reed Farrel Coleman; *Going to Chicago* by Rob Levandoski.

Nonfiction titles: *So's Your Old Man: A Curmudgeon's Words to His Son* by Peter Cross; *Fishing in the Stars: The Education of Namory Keita* by Donald Lawder; *Home to India* by Jacqueline Singh (originally published in New Delhi by Penguin, India).

News from the sub-rights front: *Résumé with Monsters* (science fiction) by William Browning Spencer, has garnered foreign rights in at least two countries—Germany and Italy. The film option for *An Occasional Hell* (mystery) by Randall Silvis, became an official purchase when the cameras started to roll.

The house has also brought back all the original works (and some new ones) by Marco Vassi—works that gained Vassi a reputation as the best erotic writer of his generation. The Vassi Collection is a 10-volume offering of erotic fiction that has hitherto been long out of print and generally unavailable. Titles in the Vassi Collection: T*he Stoned Apocalypse; Mind Blower; The Gentle Degenerate; The Saline Solution; Contours of Darkness; The Devil's Sperm Is Cold; The Sensual Mirror; Slave Lover.* More from Vassi: *A Driving Passion; The Erotic Comedies; The Other Hand Clapping.*

Permanent Press handles its own distribution. Query letters and SASEs should be directed to:

Judith Shepard, Editor and Copublisher

PERSEA BOOKS, INC.
171 Madison Avenue, New York, NY 10016
212-779-7668

Persea produces a discriminating list in trade and reference nonfiction, fiction and belles lettres, and poetry. Persea's categories include essays, memoirs, literary criticism, novels and stories, fine arts and art history, scholarly works, social sciences, and gender and cultural studies.

Persea Books (founded by Michael Braziller in 1975) is an independently owned press. The house's titles in the arts are brought out in handsomely designed and produced editions. Persea's contemporary literature has an international cast of eminent writers.

Entrants from the Persea program: *Beyond Telling: Stories* by Jewel Mogan; *Paper Dance: 55 Latino Poets* (edited by Victor Hernández Cruz, Leroy V. Quintana, and Virgil Suarez); *Rhapsodies of a Repeat Offender: Poems* by Wayne Koestenbaum; *Show Me a Hero: Great Contemporary Stories About Sports* (edited by Jeanne Schinto); *The Heart Knows Something Different: Teenage Voices from the Foster Care System* by Youth Communication (edited by Al Desetta); *Things Shaped in Passing: More "Poets of Life" Writing from the AIDS Pandemic* (edited by Michael Klein and Richard McCann).

From Ontario Review Press: *Women, Animals, and Vegetables: Essays and Stories* by Maxine Kumin; and *Doris Lessing: Conversations* (edited by Earl G. Ingersoll).

Persea shares office space with and is distributed by W. W. Norton & Company. Query letters and SASEs should be directed to:

Karen Braziller, Editorial Director
Gabriel Fried, Associate Editor

PETERSON'S

202 Carnegie Center, P.O. Box 2123, Princeton, NJ 08540
609-243-9111   fax: 609-243-9150
www.petersons.com

Peterson's is the country's largest educational information/communications company, providing the academic, consumer, and professional communities with books, software, and online services in support of lifelong education access and career choice. Peterson's, founded in 1966, publishes such well-known references as its annual guides to graduate and professional job hunting programs, colleges and universities, financial aid, private schools, standardized test-prep, summer programs, international study, executive education, job hunting, and career opportunities, as well as a full line of software offering career guidance and information for adult learners. Many of Peterson's reference works are updated annually. Peterson's is a Thomson company.

Peterson's markets strongly to libraries and institutions, as well as to the corporate sector.

Newly authored frontlist titles include: *The Ultimate College Survival Guide* by Janet Farrar Worthington and Ronald Farrar; *The Ultimate Job Search Guide* by Paul L. Dyer; *The Ultimate New Employee Survival Guide* by Ed Holton; and *The Ultimate Home Office Survival Guide* by Sunny Baker and Kim Baker. Authored backlist titles include: *The Colorblind Career* by Ollie Stevenson; *Portfolio Power* by Martin Kimeldorf; *How to Write a Winning Personal Statement for Graduate and Professional School* by Richard J. Seltzer; *Paralegal* by Barbara Bernardo; *Virtual College* by Pam Dixon; *Financing Graduate School* by Patricia McWade; and *Smart Parents' Guide to College* by Dr. Ernest Boyer and Paul Boyer.

Query letters and SASEs should be directed to:

Eileen Fiore, Executive Assistant, Research and Editorial Development—Interests consistent with house list.

Ian Gallagher, Senior Editor—Test preparation.

PFEIFER-HAMILTON PUBLISHERS & WHOLE PERSON ASSOCIATES

210 West Michigan Street, Duluth, MN 55802-1908
218-727-0500   fax: 218-727-0505
www.wholeperson.com   e-mail: books@wholeperson.com

Pfeiffer-Hamilton produces publications in self-awareness, motivation, and improvement; inspirational works; books on peace and healing; and select children's titles. Additional Pfeiffer focus is on gift books and books that celebrate the special beauty and unique lifestyle of the North Country.

This house offers books that awaken your senses, excite your imagination, make you laugh, make you cry, touch your heart, and give you hope; books that inspire creativity, critical thinking, inner change, and personal growth.

Whole Person Associates, which was founded in 1977, develops a noteworthy lineup of stress-management and wellness training materials, including books, audiotapes, and videotapes. The house has achieved increasing market penetration. P-H's marketing strategy is to concentrate promotional efforts regionally prior to inaugurating national campaigns.

Titles by Sam Cook, Pfeifer-Hamilton's first author: *If This Is Mid-Life, Where's the Crisis?; Up North; Quiet Magic; CampSights* (illustrated by Bob Cary).

On the Pfeiffer-Hamilton list: *Connections & Reflections: Mothers & Daughters in Their Own Light, in Their Own Words* by Catherine Koemptgen; *Christmas Song of the North* by Marsha Bonicatto (watercolors by Karlyn Holman); *Time at the Lake: A Minnesota Album* by William Albert Allard; *Not Now—I'm Having a No-Hair Day: Humor and Healing for People with Cancer* by Christine Clifford (illustrated by Jack Lindstrom); *Journey of the Heart: Spiritual Insights on the Road to a Transplant* by Beth Bartlett; *Kicking Your Holiday Stress Habits* by Donald A. Tubesing and Nancy Loving Tubesing (W.P.A.); *Our Family Has Cancer, Too!* by Christine Clifford (illustrated by Jack Lindstrom).

Whole Person Associates develops and publishes stress-management and wellness-promotion training and self-care resources for health professionals, counselors, trainers, therapists, consultants, educators, and group leaders. Titles here: *Instant Icebreakers: 50 Powerful Catalysts for Group Interaction and High-Impact Learning* by Sandy Stewart Christian and Nancy Loving Tubesing; *Sleep Secrets for Shift Workers & People with Off-Beat Schedules* by David Morgan; *Don't Get Mad, Get Funny!: A Light-Hearted Approach to Stress Management* by Leigh Anne Jasheway (illustrated by Geoffrey M. Welles); *Working with Groups to Overcome Panic, Anxiety, & Phobias: Structured Exercises in Healing* by Shirley Babior and Carol Goldman.

Whole Person Associates also offers a wide variety of relaxation and healing audiotapes, as well as videotapes on achieving healthful lifestyles and managing job stress. On the video list: *Team Esteem Overview; Building Communication in the Workplace; Empowerment and Wellness in the Workplace; Developing Mission and Purpose; Putting Team Esteem to Work.*

Pfeifer-Hamilton Publishers oversees its own distribution. Query letters and SASEs should be directed to:

Carlene Sippola, Publisher, Whole Person Associates

PLENUM PUBLISHING GROUP

The entire Plenum program was acquired in 1999 by the independent Perseus Group. Its frontlist acquisition program is being reorganized. The Spring Street offices have been closed.

POCKET BOOKS (PART OF SIMON & SCHUSTER)

Pocket Books

Pocket Books for Young Adults

Star Trek Books

Washington Square Press

Simon & Schuster, 1230 Avenue of the Americas, New York, NY 10020
212-698-7000

The Pocket Books division of Simon & Schuster produces commercial fiction and nonfiction in hardcover and trade paperback editions while maintaining its tradition of mammoth mass-market paperback presence. Pocket Books is currently structured into three separate units: adult fiction and nonfiction; Star Trek Books; and Pocket Books for Young Adults.

Nonfiction from Pocket hits all sectors of the popular spectrum, including current issues, contemporary culture, health and fitness, relationships, self-awareness, personal finance, celebrity-based stories, humor, games and puzzles, and popular reference.

Pocket Books maintains a powerful category-fiction list that includes originals and reprints in such genres as thrillers and suspense, romance, science fiction (including the Star Trek series), fantasy, action adventure, and horror; in addition, the house produces original commercial and literary fiction (with many of the literary works issued under the Washington Square Press imprint).

Pocket Books offers a line of books for young adults, including a number of solid fiction and nonfiction series.

Nonfiction and popular works from the Pocket Books list: *Renovating Woman: A Guide to Home Repair, Maintenance, and Real Men* by Allegra Bennett; *Pimps, Whores, and Welfare Brats: The Reformation of a Welfare Queen* by Star Parker; *Children of the Troubles: Our Lives in the Crossfire of Northern Ireland* by Laurel Holliday; *Wings of Fury: From Vietnam to the Gulf War—The Astonishing, True Stories of America's Elite Fighter Pilots* by Robert Wilcox; *The Day After Roswell* by Colonel Philip J. Corso with William J. Birnes; *Heart and Soul: A Psychological and Spiritual Guide to Preventing and Healing Heart Disease* by Bruno Cortis, M.D.; *The Gods of Golf* by David L. Smith and John P. Holms; *Leadership Secrets of the Rogue Warrior* (and others in the series) by Richard Marchinko; *A Dog in Heat Is a Hot Dog and Other Rules to Live By* by E. Jean Carroll.

Pocket Books fiction, literary writing, and cultural chronicles: *She's Come Undone* by Wally Lamb; *Dark Homecoming* by Eric Lustbader; *Audrey Hepburn's Neck* by Alan Brown; *Avenger* by William Shatner (part of the Star Trek line); *I Still Miss My Man, But My Aim Is Getting Better* by Sarah Shankman; *Jackson Street and Other Soldier Stories* by John A. Miller; *Hidden Latitudes* by Alison Anderson; *Hoopi Shoopi Donna* by Suzanne Strempek Shea; *Hiding My Candy* by the Lady Chablis with Theodore Bouloukos II; *Lord of the Dead* by Tom Holland; *Tarnished Gold* by V. C. Andrews; *Knights* by Linda Lael Miller; *Defiance County* by Jay Brandon; *The Journal of Callie Wade* by Dawn Miller.

From Paradox Graphic Mysteries: *A History of Violence* by John Wagner (illustrated by Vince Locke); *Green Candles* by Tom DeHaven (illustrated by Robin Smith).

Pocket Books (founded in 1937) was America's first publisher to specialize in customized drugstore/newsstand rack-size paperback editions. Today, the house excels in both original titles and reprint lines brought out under its well-known reading-kangaroo logo (what better animal to convey the notion of a pouch-size edition?). Query letters and SASEs should be directed to:

Amanda Ayer, Assistant Editor

Amy Pierpont, Assistant Editor

Caroline Tolley, Senior Editor—Historical romances.

Emily Bestler, Vice President and Editorial Director—Varied nonfiction, including health, family, parenting, inspirational, popular science, lifestyle. Commercial fiction: thrillers, mysteries.

George Lucas, Senior Editor

Greer Kessel-Hendricks, Senior Editor, Pocket Books—Popular nonfiction. Health, sports, popular culture, some humor. Literary fiction from established as well as emerging voices.

Brenda Copeland, Editor

Jason Kaufiran, Senior Editor

Kate Collins, Editor

Kim Kanner, Associate Editor

Kip Hakala, Associate Editor

Marco Palmieri, Editor

Mitchell Ivers, Senior Editor—Commercial fiction and celebrity nonfiction.

Maggie Crawford, Vice President and Editorial Director—Women's fiction.

Rosemary Ahern, Executive Editor, Washington Square Press

Tracy Bernstein, Editor—Health, pop psychology, general nonfiction.

Tracy Sherrod, Editor—Serious nonfiction and literary fiction written by and/or for African Americans and lesbians and gays; women's issues.
 Born: June 27, 1965.
 Education: B.A.—Political Philosophy; minor English and Economics, James Madison College at Michigan State University. Cambridge University, England—Literature.
 Employment history/editor career path: The Feminist Press, *Essence* Magazine, Marie Brown Literary Services, Henry Holt, Pocket Books.
 Personal interests: Tennis, health issues, decorating, vegan cooking.
 What would you be doing if you were not an editor? Designing clothes for large women.

What has been your most successful book that you have acquired to date? *The Rose That Grew from Concrete* by Tupac Shakur.

What books have you acquired that make you the most proud? What books that you have acquired reflect the types of books that you like to represent? *Dead Above Ground* by Jervey Tervalon; *The White Boy Shuffle* by Paul Beatty; *First Body* by Melanie Rae Thorn; *Healing Fibroids* by Allan Warshowsky; *Douglass's Women* by Jewell Parker Rhodes; *Still Life in Harlem* by Eddy L. Harris; *The Rose That Grew from Concrete* by Tupac Shakur; *Wounds of Passion* by bell hooks.

Do you represent fiction? If so, what do you look for? Yes, a strong voice.

What do you want to see less of? Memoirs about how "I was down and out and got up and over." "Sistergirl" fiction.

Do you represent nonfiction? Yes.

Do you require book proposals? If so, what do you look for in evaluating a book proposal? Marketable idea; strong, complimentary, professional credentials. A strong, informative sample chapter.

Are certain aspects of a book proposal given more weight than others? Sample chapter. Too many authors take the easy way out and write the simple, easy sample chapter, rather than provide a chapter that gets to the heart and originality of their idea.

What process do you use for making a decision? What is the process for acquisition? Is there a committee? I only acquire/pursue books that stir a passion within me. I prefer to make a trend, rather than follow one. Yes, there is a committee.

What kinds of nonfiction books do you want to see less of? Humor; general natural healing. I find that natural healing books for a specific ailment are best. Nature books. What I learned on the road books.

Are you interested in work geared for the masses (readers of *People, The Star,* etc.)? Some.

Are agents important? Why? They do the footwork that editors don't have time to do, such as pursue nonfiction writers.

Do you like new writers? What should new writers do to break into the business? Concentrate on the craft of writing and not just on getting published.

How should writers approach you? By writing a letter.

What are some common mistakes writers make? What really gets on your nerves? Calling, e-mailing, single spacing a manuscript, sending me a manuscript with a handwritten note, a note with the manuscript that says it's unedited, providing an unattractive, self-designed cover with a manuscript.

What can writers do to get your attention and to avoid the slush pile? Avoid making common mistakes and getting on my nerves (see previous answer).

What have been some of your craziest experiences with submissions? Writers slipping them into my bag when I'm not looking.

What have been some of your best experiences with writers or in your job? Being mentored by Marian Wood, and even being rescued by her on several occasions! I love that there are so many truly intelligent and devoted people in publishing.

What, if anything, makes you different from other editors? I don't know how different this is, but once a month I go to bookstores and chat with customers to find out why they buy the books that they do.

Is there anything you would like to see changed in the industry? More editors of diverse races, as well as publicists and designers.

Any advice for writers? Listen to your editors—they have published more books than you as a writer ever will.

Pocket Books for Young Adults

Query letters and SASEs should be directed to:

Anne Greenberg, Executive Editor

Ingrid vander Leeden, Senior Editor

Lisa Clancy, Executive Editor

Nancy Pines, Vice President and Associate Publisher

Patricia MacDonald, Vice President and Editorial Director

Star Trek Books

Query letters and SASEs should be directed to:

John Ordover, Senior Editor

Margaret Clark, Senior Editor

Scott Shannon, Director

POMEGRANATE COMMUNICATIONS, INC.

Box 6099, Rohnert Park, CA 94927
707-586-5500   fax: 707-586-5518

Pomegranate publishes an attractive array of graphically lavish books and specialty items geared to interests such as fine art, contemporary art, architecture, travel, ethnic culture, and crafts. Pomegranate is among the premier publishers of calendars of all types and stripes, posters and poster art, note cards, games and puzzles, specialty sets, and popular topical card decks.

Sample titles include: *Sunday Afternoon, Looking for the Car: The Aberrant Art of Barry Kite* by Alan Bisbort; *Cultivating Sacred Space: Gardening for the Soul* by Elizabeth Murray; *CatDreams* by B. Kliban; *Maxfield Parrish: A Retrospective* by Laurence S. Cutler and Judy Goffman Cutler; *Edward Hopper's New England* by Carl Little; *The Collectible Art of Susan Seddon Boulet.* The Little Wright Books Series showcases the work of Frank Lloyd Wright, with each volume focusing on a particular topic. Titles by Carla Lind: *Frank Lloyd Wright's California Houses; Frank Lloyd Wright's First Houses; Frank Lloyd Wright's Public Buildings; Frank Lloyd Wright's Prairie Houses; Frank Lloyd Wright's Lost Buildings; Frank Lloyd Wright's Fireplaces; Frank Lloyd Wright's Dining Rooms.*

Pomegranate is an independent house and operates its own distributional network, including foreign representation worldwide. Query letters and SASEs should be directed to:

Submissions Department

Praeger Publishers

See Greenwood Publishing Group.

Prentice Hall Direct (part of Pearson Education Group)

Prentice Hall Press

240 Frisch Court, Paramus, NJ 07652
201-909-6200

Prentice Hall produces an extensive trade list in hardcover and trade paperback that accents books keyed to diverse career and business orientations, as well as noteworthy lines in such areas as health, fitness, and lifestyle

In addition to a strong and growing trade presence, Prentice Hall is a respected publisher in the educational arena; the educational and textbook divisions of Prentice Hall produce series in all subject and curricula areas for the youngest students through postgraduates, along with professional reference works in such fields as law and engineering.

This house specializes in direct marketing and sales to the individual, corporate, and institutional markets. The business and professional division is widely known for the targeted mailing lists it compiles; some of these lists contain more than a million names and addresses. Trade distribution is handled by Penguin Putnam, Inc.

Sample titles: *Elizabeth I CEO* and *Patton on Leadership* by Alan Axelrod; *Top Grading* by Brad Smart; *Wizards of Wall Street* by Kirk Kazanjian; *How to Say It* by Rosalie Tlaggio; *Technical Analysis of the Financial Market* by John Murphy; *Heineman's Encyclopedia of Healing Juices* by John Heineman; *12 Simple Secrets of Happiness* by Glenn van Erkeren.

Query letters and SASEs should be directed to:

Edward Claflin, Executive Editor, Health—Health and fitness books, with emphasis on natural healing.

Ellen Schneid Coleman, Associate Publisher—Professional and personal finance and investing, business, management, self-improvement.

Eugene F. Brissie, Vice President and Publisher—Business, management, finance and investing, health, and self-improvement.

Luis Gonzales, Senior Editor, Marketing and Sales—Accounting, corporate finance, human resources, training.

Tom Power, Senior Editor—General how-to business titles, management, career, spoken and written communications.

    Born: September 16, 1946.

    Education: B.A., English, at Manhattan College.

    Employment history/editor career path: I have been in publishing for many years. I started in sales of college textbooks and then came to the editorial side. I have been at Prentice Hall for 21 years.

    Personal interests: Running, swimming, tennis.

What has been your most successful book that you have acquired to date? *How to Say It* by Rosalie Maggio.

What books have you acquired that make you the most proud? What books have you acquired that reflect the types of books you like to represent? *How to Say It* by Rosalie Maggio*; Patton on Leadership*; *Cigars, Whiskey & Winning.*

Do you represent fiction? If so, what do you look for? No.

Do you represent nonfiction? Yes, small business, management, practical nonfiction, leadership, communications, careers.

Do you require book proposals? If so, what do you look for in evaluating a book proposal? Yes. I look for the material to be presented intelligently, be well organized, have good writing, have a clear understanding of the market and competition, describe author credentials, and convince me how promotable the book and the author are.

Are certain aspects of a book proposal given more weight than others? Yes, who is the audience and what is the market need for this book?

What process do you use for making a decision? What is the process for acquisition, is there a committee? Yes, there is a committee. It consists of the editorial department, marketing, and financial people.

Are you interested in work geared for the masses (readers of *People, The Star,* etc.)? No.

Are agents important? Why? Yes. I enjoy working with them. Agents can usually send editors proposals that we want because they know what we're looking for. They also help the author to learn about the publishing industry and to shape their proposals and manuscripts.

Do you like new writers? What should new writers do to break into the business? Yes; however, new writers are at a disadvantage today, due to the tremendous amount of competition in the market. New authors can bring a fresh voice and new view to the market. I think, to break into the business, they need to establish their credentials, learn about the market they're writing for, familiarize themselves with bookstores, and make themselves visible.

How should writers approach you? Mail a query or a proposal with an SASE.

What are some common mistakes writers make? What really gets on your nerves? Pestering in all forms. Authors who don't understand the business and who have unrealistic expectations and time frames. Authors who don't take editors' advice.

What can writers do to get your attention and to avoid the slush pile? Write a great proposal, one that is attention-grabbing and well thought out, as well as well written.

What have been some of your best experiences with writers or in your job? Authors who become your friends. Authors whose books will surprise you, they exceed your expectations.

Is there anything you would like to see changed in the industry? I think that there has been an "over-publishing" syndrome for quite a while now, and I would like to see there be more selectivity. I would also like to see editors have higher salaries.

Any advice for writers? Be optimistic, learn all that you can. Buy Jeff Herman's books. Learn how to put together proposals.

Gloria Fuzia, Editor
Born: October 24, 1964.
Education: B.A. in English.

Employment history/editor career path: I had a friend call and tell me that there was an opening at John Wiley & Sons; that's where I got my start. I have been with Prentice Hall for one and a half years.

Personal interests: I don't have many. I have two children, ages 6 and 10.

What would you be doing if you were not an editor? I would be a full-time parent, freelance writer, or teach. Would get a linguistics degree.

What books have you acquired that make you the most proud? What books that you have acquired reflect the types of books you like to represent? I like books that are useful to readers and that will really make a difference in people's lives.

Do you represent fiction? If so, what do you look for? No.

Do you represent nonfiction? Yes, parenting, spirituality, self-help.

Do you require book proposals? If so, what do you look for in evaluating a book proposal? Yes. I look for a good idea with a unique angle. Is the proposal put together well and how can it be developed?

Are certain aspects of a book proposal given more weight than others? Not really. If you are a first-time author, the proposal needs to be put together better than someone's who has already had multiple books.

What process do you use for making a decision? What is the process for acquisition, is there a committee? The first step is to go through me and, yes, the next step is to our editorial committee.

Are you interested in work geared for the masses (readers of *People, The Star,* etc.)? No.

Are agents important? Why? Yes. A lot of good projects come from agents and they are very helpful to the authors. They help authors put their books together.

Do you like new writers? What should new writers do to break into the business? Yes. You need to have an important message or point to sell. Make yourself different from everyone else by taking a unique angle.

How should writers approach you? Mail a proposal and SASE.

What are some common mistakes writers make? What really gets on your nerves? Sloppy writing, not seeing the project through, relying on the editor too much.

What have been some of your craziest experiences with submissions? Single line concepts in the form of a query.

What, if anything, makes you different from other editors? I read everything thoroughly.

Susan McDermott, Acquisitions Editor

Born: September 10.

Education: M.A. in Marketing and English undergrad.

Employment history/editor career path: I started out of college at a commerce clearing house. I then moved to Hourback and finally come to Prentice Hall. I have always done technical publishing.

Personal interests: Reading, movies, going to the beach.

What would you be doing if you were not an editor? I would work in advertising or public relations.

What has been your most successful book that you have acquired to date? Several *Is Management* books and *Everyday Miracles.*

What books have you acquired that make you the most proud? What books that you have acquired reflect the types of books you like to represent? Successful *Is Management* books and *Everyday Miracles.* Also *The Best of Everything for Your Baby.*

Do you represent fiction? No.

What do you want to see less of? I am actually only looking for *Is* authors. I don't receive many things that are unsolicited.

Do you represent nonfiction? Yes.

Do you require book proposals? If so, what do you look for in evaluating a book proposal? Yes, thoroughness of coverage, analysis of competition, and table of contents.

Are certain aspects of a book proposal given more weight than others? Table of contents.

What process do you use for making a decision? What is the process for acquisition, is there a committee? Yes, there is a committee that consists of editors and people with *Is* backgrounds for technical writing.

What kinds of nonfiction books do you want to see less of? Nothing, really. I think that there is a good mix of books on the market.

Are you interested in work geared for the masses (readers of *People, The Star,* etc.)? We do self-help material, but not much is actually pop-culture.

Are agents important? Why? Yes, they are important because material coming from an agent is usually high-quality material.

Do you like new writers? What should new writers do to break into the business? Yes, we always need new writers. To break into the business, I would say to get an agent.

How should writers approach you? Through an agent.

What are some common mistakes writers make? What really gets on your nerves? Not doing enough research and giving me material that is a less than thorough synopsis.

What can writers do to get your attention and to avoid the slush pile? Have a package that you have put a lot of thought into and have it look very professional.

What have been some of your best experiences with writers or in your job? Meeting new writers and helping them through the writing process. I love working with authors and watching their success with them.

What, if anything, makes you different from other editors? I'm not sure that this is different from other editors, but I am committed to helping authors in any way that I can.

Any advice for writers? Know what your goal is and see it through to the finished product.

PRESIDIO PRESS
P.O. Box 1764, Novato, CA 94948-1764
415-898-1081   fax: 415-898-0383

Presidio is known for works in such areas as general military history, American history, aviation, biography and memoirs, World Wars, Korean War, Vietnam, African-American studies, military theory, and professional studies. Presidio also issues a small number of superior fiction titles that favor a military-historical milieu.

Presidio Press (founded in 1974) is America's foremost publisher of military history. The house emphasizes both popular and scholarly works, especially those with potential for backlist endurance. Presidio publishes in hardcover and quality paperback editions.

Nonfiction from Presidio: *Mr. Michel's War, from Manila to Mukden: An American Naval Officer's War with the Japanese, 1941–1945* by John J. A. Michel; *Patton's Ghost Corps: Cracking the Seigfried Line* by Nathan Prefer; *What They Didn't Teach You About the Civil War* by Mike Wright; *My Just War: The Memoir of a Jewish Red Army Soldier in World War II* by Gabriel Temkin; *Easy Target: The Long, Strange Trip of a Scout Pilot in Vietnam* (memoir by Tom Smith); *When the Odds Were Even: The Vosges Mountains Campaign, October 1944–January 1945* by Keith E. Bonn; *The Biographical Dictionary of World War II* by Mark M. Boatner III; *Destroyer Skipper: A Memoir of Command at Sea* by Don Sheppard; *Phantom over Vietnam: Fighter Pilot, USMC* by John Trotti; *Operation Dragoon: The Allied Invasion of the South of France* by William B. Breuer; *Spec Ops: Case Studies in Special Operations Warfare—Theory and Practice* by William H. McRaven; *They Had a Dream: The Story of African-American Astronauts* by J. Alfred Phelps; *Elvis in the Army: The King of Rock 'n' Roll as Seen by an Officer Who Served with Him* by William J. Taylor, Jr.

Presidio's Gulf War memoir, *She Went to War: The Rhonda Cornum Story* by flight surgeon Rhonda Cornum, as told to Peter Copeland, garnered considerable subsidiary-rights interest—including a high-profile television-movie.

Presidio Press titles, as well as those associated imprints (such as British military publisher Greenhill Books), are distributed to the book trade in the United States and Canada through National Book Network. Query letters and SASEs should be directed to:

E. J. McCarthy, Executive Editor

PROBUS PUBLISHING COMPANY
See Irwin Professional Publishing.

PROFESSIONAL PUBLICATIONS, INC.
1250 Fifth Avenue, Belmont, CA 94002-3863
650-593-9119
www.ppi2pass.com

Professional Publications publishes titles in engineering, architecture, and interior design, as well as works aimed toward the broader business and professional trade arena. The house produces books and educational aids (such as audiocassettes, videos, software, and study guides) for the professional market.

Professional Publications (established in 1981) earned initial success with examination-preparation packages (reference manuals, ancillary workbooks, sample exams, and solved problem books) for the professional engineering license examination given to applicants in the major engineering disciplines. Once this niche market was secured, the house branched into wider publishing territory.

On the Professional Publications list: *FE Review Manual, Civil Engineering Reference Manual,* and *Mechanical Engineering Reference Manual,* all by Michael R. Lindeburg; *Interior Construction and Detailing for Designers and Architects* and *Interior Design Reference Manual,* both by David K. Ballast.

Professional Publications oversees its own distribution. Query letters and SASEs should be directed to:

Aline S. Magee, Acquisitions Editor

PROMETHEUS BOOKS

59 John Glenn Drive, Amherst, NY 14228-2197
716-691-0133   fax: 716-564-2711
www.prometheusbooks.com   e-mail: Pbooks6205@aol.com

Prometheus catalogs works with challenging stances on contemporary issues. The house is particularly strong in popular science, science and the paranormal, biblical criticism, religion and politics, politics and current events, consumer health and fitness, philosophy, humanism, free thought, sports, human sexuality and sexual autobiography, literature and literary history, popular culture, creation versus evolution, religion, and education, as well as reference works in allied fields, and occasional works of fiction. Prometheus also publishes books for young readers, produces a line of titles on human aging, and serves the educational market with several series of modestly priced classics in reprint (including Great Books in Philosophy, Literary Classics, and Great Minds). The house offers select works in electronic format.

Prometheus Books (established in 1969) produces an ambitious frontlist that embraces a wide range of perennially popular nonfiction topics; more enduring titles are backlisted indefinitely.

Prometheus also publishes the following periodicals: *Scientific Review of Alternative Medicine* (a peer-reviewed medical journal providing objective, scientific assessments of the treatments, methods, and hypotheses of unconventional medicine—the realm of acupuncture, homeopathy, herbal therapies, therapeutic touch, "miraculous" cancer treatments, and more); *Nutrition Forum* (bimonthly newsletter on the frontline of the anti–health fraud movement); *The Journal for the Critical Study of Religion, Ethics, and Society* (articles in the area of religious studies and scholarly assessments of society, ethics, and culture that have a bearing on the understanding of religion; the journal seeks to promote a broadly humanistic understanding of culture).

On the Prometheus list: *The Psychic Mafia* by M. Lamar Keene (as told to Allen Spraggett); *The Roswell UFO Crash: What They Don't Want You to Know* by Karl K. Korff; *The Christ Myth* by Arthur Drews; *Women and the Koran: The Status of Women in Islam* by Anwar Hekmat; *Child Sexual Abuse and False Memory Syndrome* (edited by Robert A. Baker, Ph.D.); *Slaughterhouse: The Shocking Story of Greed, Neglect, and Inhumane Treatment Inside the U.S. Meat Industry* by Gail A. Eisnitz; *All About Adam & Eve: How We Came to Believe in Gods, Demons, Miracles & Magical Rites* by Robert J. Gillooly; *Generations Apart: Xers vs. Boomers vs. the Elderly* (edited by Richard D. Than and Jay S. Heflin); *Affirmative Action: Social Justice or Reverse Discrimination?*

(edited by Francis J. Beckwith and Todd E. Jones); *Suicide: Right or Wrong?* (edited by John Donnelly); *Dirty Talk: Diary of a Phone Sex "Mistress"* by Gary Anthony with Rocky Bennett; *Cigarettes: What the Warning Label Doesn't Tell You* by the American Council on Science and Health; *Vampires: Emotional Predators Who Want to Suck the Life Out of You* by Daniel Rhodes and Kathleen Rhodes; *The Truth About Everything: An Irreverent History of Philosophy, with Illustrations* by Matthew Stewart, D.Phil.

Prometheus Books introduces the Literary Classics line. This is a series of attractive, moderately priced paperback editions of classic authors (in both poetry and prose) whose works embody free inquiry and free thought. Titles here: *The Turn of the Screw: The Lesson of the Master* by Henry James; *The Awakening* by Kate Chopin; *Main Street* by Sinclair Lewis; *The Confidence Man* by Herman Melville.

Please note: Though known primarily as a house that operates on an advance/royalty arrangement, Prometheus has on occasion offered agreements to authors through which the author invests cooperatively in the costs and thus subsidizes publication.

Prometheus distributes its own list. Query letters and SASEs should be directed to:

Steven L. Mitchell, Editorial Director

Mark Hall, Ph.D., Managing Editor/Creative Marketing Coordinator
Born/ Sign: May 29, 1952/Gemini.
Education: Ph.D. from the University of Pennsylvania in Ancient Near Eastern Studies; B.A. in Classics from the University of New York in Buffalo.
Employment history/editor career path: I originally went to grad school for ancient history with the intent of teaching on a university level. I found out while in school that there were few positions available in the area that I was specializing; nonetheless, I finished the degree. In 1990 I applied to Prometheus Books and got the job. I started as the Production Manager and then went to edit trade books. The production demand to edit trade books was much too high for me, so I eventually left and went to marketing. I also do freelance medical editing for John Wiley & Sons in the department of Psychology.
Personal interests: Ancient Near Eastern History, archaeology, history of the Bible, following modern fiction, I used to write poetry, so I try to keep up with that.
What would you be doing if you were not an editor? If there had been good opportunities in academics, I would love to be in that field.
What has been your most successful book that you have acquired to date? Prometheus is known for its midlist books.
What books have you acquired that make you the most proud? What books that you have acquired reflect the types of books you like to represent? *End of Days* by Erna Paris, which is a story of expulsion of the Jews in Spain at the time of Ferdinand and Isabella. She is a wonderful presenter and can do so in a way that is in great detail and has very interesting twists.
Do you represent fiction? If so, what do you look for? Prometheus doesn't publish much fiction.
What do you want to see less of ? Works that tend to be narcissistic, self-indulgent, or that talk about boredom of the wealthy.
Do you represent nonfiction? Yes.
Do you require book proposals? If so, what do you look for in evaluating a book proposal? Yes. I look for a good, brief synopsis of what the book is about, a table of

contents, a sample chapter, who is the competition. I don't usually like to see the entire manuscript.

What process do you use for making a decision? What is the process for acquisition, is there a committee? The editor in chief looks at almost every serious submission. We have recently hired two acquisitions editors to present material to the committee.

What kinds of nonfiction books do you want to see less of? Self-help, psychology, diet books, New Age, committed scientific evaluations.

Are agents important? Why? Agents are a fact of life in this business. They bring important authors to my attention.

Do you like new writers? Sometimes.

How should writers approach you? With a simple query letter. I would advise authors that sending a proposal on the first attempt is totally inappropriate.

What can writers do to get your attention and to avoid the slush pile? Do your homework.

What have been some of your craziest experiences with submissions? I once received a submission from a man who was recounting his experience 25 years ago in the Himalayas. He was searching for the meaning of life and went up the mountain and almost died. He was then rescued by a hermit and the hermit revealed to him the secrets of the universe.

What have been some of your best experiences with writers or in your job? Steve Allen, who wrote *Dumbth,* has been wonderful to work with. Peter Ustinov has also been a great joy to work with.

What, if anything, makes you different from other editors? My background in ancient eastern history.

Is there anything you would like to see changed in the industry? I would like to see less of a tendency to go with the conglomerates. The rise of Barnes & Noble and Borders, limiting the bookselling markets.

PUBLICAFFAIRS

250 West 57th Street, Suite 1825, New York, NY 10107
212-397-6666   fax: 212-397-4277
e-mail: pubaff@interport.net

PublicAffairs (founded in 1997) is a nonfiction book publisher specializing in works of journalism, history, biography, memoirs, and social criticism by today's most influential writers and public figures. The company was founded by publisher and chief executive Peter Osnos (former publisher of the Times Books imprint of Random House and of books by Bill Clinton, Robert McNamara, Jim Lehrer, and Natan Sharansky, among others).

PublicAffairs is among the group of publishing companies founded or financed by the Perseus Capital investment firm, headed by Frank H. Pearl. Sister companies include: Basic Books, Counterpoint, and Civitas. Though associated with Perseus, PublicAffairs remains an independent and editorially autonomous company. Other investors in the company include Peter Jennings of *ABC News;* Martin V. Koldyke, chairman of WTTW, the PBS station in Chicago; Peter Malkin, a real estate lawyer and founder of the Grand Central Partnership; Dr. Robert Osnos, a psychiatrist in New York City; Robert Rosencrans, the former chairman of C-SPAN; Eli Segal, the founder and CEO of Americorps and now chairman of the Welfare to Work Foundation; and Peter Osnos.

Osnos has dedicated PublicAffairs to publishing intelligent nonfiction for general readers creatively and enthusiastically, at a time when larger publishers are finding it economically unattractive to do so. The company plans to publish 25 to 30 titles per year, including both originals and reprints in hardcover and trade paperback formats.

PublicAffairs, in Osnos's words, "is intended as a tribute to the standards, values and flair of three persons who have served as mentors to countless reporters, writers, editors and book people of all kinds, including me": the late independent journalist and First Amendment advocate I. F. Stone; Benjamin C. Bradlee of the *Washington Post;* and Robert L. Bernstein, founder of Human Rights Watch and the longtime chief executive of Random House. A note about them, and an honorary colophon, will appear in every PublicAffairs book.

PublicAffairs intends to interpret the meaning of "public affairs" broadly and to publish engaging books that tell good stories and that reflect a diversity of experiences and opinions on subjects of social, historical, cultural, and political significance. From penetrating scholarship to political exposé to personal narrative, a PublicAffairs book will be one that broadens your understanding of the world.

Each season, PublicAffairs will publish a short, exclusive list of books and conduct a well-focused promotion and publicity campaign for each book. Unlike larger publishers who devote the lion's share of their marketing energies to a few leading titles, PublicAffairs intends to publish only the books—and the number of books—it feels it is able to promote with enthusiasm.

Sample titles/subjects include: *When the War Was Over: Cambodia's Revolution and the Voice of Its People* by Elizabeth Becker; *Last Wish* by Betty Rollin; *Fear No Evil* by Natan Sharansky (includes a new chapter in which Sharansky discusses his return visit to Russia in 1996 and his experiences in Israel).

PublicAffairs will publish a paperback series focusing on classic works of reportage and analysis (many of which will be substantially updated and revised to reflect current understandings and the progress of history). The publisher has formed publishing partnerships with PBS's Frontline series and with the Twentieth Century Fund/the Century Foundation, and will continue to seek other innovative ways to support writers, develop projects, and market and publicize its books through targeted mailings, newsletters, special events, and online promotions.

Distribution to the trade will be handled by HarperCollins. Query letters and SASEs should be directed to:

Erica Brown, Assistant to the Publisher

Kate Darnton, Editor—Current events, biographies, memoirs, women authors.

Mary-Claire Flynn, Assistant to the Editors

PUSHCART PRESS

Box 380, Wainscott, NY 11975
631-324-9300

Pushcart Press (established in 1972) is a small, personalized house that is emblematic of the mission to provide useful as well as entertaining trade books and reference volumes directed primarily toward writers, editors, small publishers, and literary aficionados; Pushcart Press is also a dedicated forum for fiction and nonfiction works of literary merit, and the house list includes many award-winning volumes.

Pushcart is known as the house that issues the established annual literary anthology *The Pushcart Prize: Best of the Small Presses,* in addition to the classic *The Publish-It-Yourself Handbook: Literary Tradition and How-to Without Commercial or Vanity Publishers* (both works edited by Pushcart Publisher Bill Henderson). *The Pushcart Book of Essays* (edited by Anthony Brandt) expands the house's line of exemplary writing collections.

Ongoing Pushcart Press publishing projects include the Literary Companion series and the Editors' Book Award series.

Titles from Pushcart: *To a Violent Grave: An Oral Biography of Jackson Pollock* by Jeffrey Potter; *Yeshua: The Gospel of St. Thomas* by Alan Decker McNary; *Garden State: A Novel* by Rick Moody; *Imagine a Great White Light* by Sheila Schwartz; *Writing for Your Life* by Sybil Steinberg; the anonymous *Autobiography of an Elderly Woman* (with an afterword by Doris Grumbach); and *The Tale of the Ring: A Kaddish* by Frank Stiffel.

Pushcart Press is distributed by W. W. Norton. Query letters and SASEs should be directed to:

Bill Henderson, President

THE PUTNAM BERKLEY GROUP

The Berkley Publishing Group

Perigee Books

Price Stern Sloan

The Putnam Publishing Group

The Putnam & Grosset Book Group

Riverhead Books

Tarcher

375 Hudson Street, New York, NY 10014
212-366-2000
www.penguinputnam.com

The Putnam Berkley Group is part of Penguin Putnam, Inc. Founded in 1838 and subsequently known as G. P. Putnam's Sons, this house achieved renown as one of America's principal publishers. Over the past several decades the company has expanded dramatically. In 1965 Putnam acquired Berkley Books, and in 1975 the augmented enterprise was acquired by the communications conglomerate MCA, itself now part of the Seagram's Corporation wing that also incorporates Universal Studios. All of Penguin Putnam is now part and parcel of Pearson (U.K.).

The group's primary trade paper imprint, Perigee Books, was established in 1979, and since then additional divisions have been instituted, including the children's houses Philomel Books and Grosset & Dunlap (see under Putnam & Grosset subentry). During the early 1990s, two formerly independent entities, Jeremy P. Tarcher and Price Stern Sloan (please see subentries), have been brought under the corporate shield. Riverhead Books, created in the mid-1990s, features fiction and nonfiction with a contemporary cultural slant.

In early 1997 Seagram's/MCA divested itself of the entire Putnam Berkley Group. Putnam Berkley merged with Penguin USA (home of the Viking, Penguin, and Dutton programs) to form Penguin Putnam, Inc. This mammoth book-publishing eminence combines what had been two of North America's grandest trade-publishing establishments into a single powerful marketing force.

The Putnam Publishing Group assumes a profile at once streamlined and eclectic—this division's mission is to launch top-of-the-charts titles across the board. Thus, the relentlessly commercial Putnam frontlist, during a given season, can accent any and all popular fiction and nonfiction areas. The Berkley Publishing Group—which comprises such lines as Berkley, Jove, Ace, and Boulevard—publishes trade and mass-market paperback reprints and originals in nonfiction and fiction, as well as selected hardcover originals.

The nomenclature and categorization of Putnam Berkley lists is flexible; designated projects can assume many different formats and experimental imprints—as in, for instance, hardcover genre-fiction releases bearing the Ace/Putnam stamp, Riverhead titles catalogued under both Putnam (for hardcovers) and Berkley (trade paper originals and reprints), and trade titles in business, finance, and topical spirituality interest released as Tarcher/Putnam books. Putnam also recently acquired the large independent health field publisher, Avery.

Putnam New Media was initiated to ride the multimedia tide; for a rash of corporate reasons, during 1995, this division's assets were shifted under the umbrella of another of MCA's media enterprises.

Penguin Putnam distributes its own list, as well as providing services for a number of other houses, including Farrar Straus & Giroux

The Berkley Publishing Group

Boulevard

Jove

Ace

Prime Crime

The Berkley Publishing Group produces a solid commercial list of fiction and nonfiction, including frontlist titles in trade paper and hardcover editions; the house also accents a mass-market paperback list. Berkley fiction encompasses such categories as romance and women's fiction, action adventure, Westerns, mysteries, science fiction, and fantasy. Nonfiction interests run the gamut of commercial categories. Berkley publishes reprints (many of them originally on the Putnam list) as well as original fiction and nonfiction under the Berkley, Jove, and Ace imprints.

Berkley's nonfiction range includes self-help and awareness, business, true crime, popular culture, and parenting. Boulevard is a media-oriented imprint with an accent on popular culture. Perigee Books concentrates on commercial nonfiction in trade paperback.

Nonfiction titles from Berkley include *It's Not About the Bike* by Lance Armstrong with Sally Jenkins; *Failure Is Not an Option* by Gene Kranz; *Teaching Right from Wrong: 40 Things You Can Do to Raise a Moral Child* by Arthur Dobrin; *Heart to Heart* by Patricia Gottlieb Shapiro; *This Is No Drill!: Living Memories of the Attack on Pearl Harbor* by Henry Berry; *Taking Center Stage: Masterful Public Speaking Using Acting Skills You Never Knew You Had* by Deb Grottesman and Buzz Mauro; *Navy Seals: A History of the Early Years* by Kevin Dockery; *The Boxer Rebellion* by Diana Preston; *Quitting the Nairobi Trio* by Jim Knipfel; *Food Fights and Bed Time Battles* by Tim Jordan, M.D.; *The Complete Herb Book* by Maggie Stuckey; *Math Coach: A Parent's Guide to Helping Children Succeed in Math* by Wayne Wickelgren, Ph.D., and Ingrid Wickelgren; *The Navy Times Book of Submarines* by Brayton Harris and Walter Boyne.

Berkley Group fiction authors include Tom Clancy, John Sandford, and LaVyrle Spencer; a significant portion of the list crosses over from Putnam hardcover originals into Berkley paperback reprint editions. Prime Crime is an imprint that emphasizes original frontlist mysteries and suspense fiction. The Berkley romance line includes such bestselling writers as Nora Roberts, Kathleen Sutcliff, Laura Kinsale, and Mary Balogh.

Features from Berkley Prime Crime include *The Tainted Snuff Box* by Rosemary Stevens; *Death Dines at 8:30* (edited by Claudia Bishop and Nick DiChirio); *The Big Nap* by Ayelet Waldman; *The Crossword Connection* by Nero Blanc; *A Dying Art* by Nageeba Davis; and *Death on the Downs* by Simon Brett.

The Ace Books list denotes the forefront of science fiction and fantasy, including original titles as well as reprints. On the Ace list: *The Tower at Stony Wood* by Patricia A McKillie; *Chronospace* by Allen Steele; *Revelation Space* by Alastair Reynolds; *Son of the Sword* by J. Ardian Lee; *First Landing* by Robert Zubrin; *The House in the High Woods* by Jeffrey Barlough; *Empty Cities of the Full Moon* by Howard Hendrix.

Jove produces a primarily mass-market fiction list, including originals and reprints in romance, historical romance, suspense, action adventure, mysteries, and Westerns.

Query letters and SASEs should be directed to:

Sara Carder, Editor

Denise Silvestro, Senior Editor—Women's fiction and nonfiction, health, self-help, popular culture, inspirational, and New Age books.

Gail Fortune, Editor—Women's fiction, romance, mystery.

Christine Zika, Senior Editor—Commercial nonfiction; business subjects.

Judith Palais, Senior Editor—Women's fiction, general fiction, commercial/literary works, romance.

Leslie Gelbman, Publisher, President, and Editor in Chief for Berkley—Wide range of projects in commercial fiction and nonfiction. Works with such authors as Nora Roberts, Laura Kinsale, and Erich Segal.

Natalie Rosenstein, Vice President, Senior Executive Editor—General fiction, mystery.

Susan Allison, Vice President, Editor in Chief, Ace Books—Science fiction, fantasy, horror.

Tom Colgan, Senior Editor—Wide range of commercial nonfiction and fiction. Nonfiction: history, business, inspiration, biography. Fiction: suspense, mysteries, thrillers, adventure, police, espionage.

Allison McCabe, Senior Editor—General fiction and nonfiction, commercial/literary works.

The Putnam Publishing Group
Penguin Putnam, Inc.

The Putnam Publishing Group produces fiction and nonfiction hardcover trade books. Putnam fiction highlights commercially bankable novels, popular literary fare, and top-of-the-list entrants in category fiction, including mystery, science fiction, suspense, and historical novels. Putnam nonfiction covers the range of topical, popular, and commercial interests.

Putnam trade books are published primarily under the G. P. Putnam's Sons imprint. Putnam from time to time combines with other Putnam Berkley imprints for special projects issued under such banners as Ace/Putnam (frontlist category novels), and Tarcher/Putnam (business and professional; awareness; current issues and trends).

Putnam fiction offers a star-studded lineup of authors, including such works as *Here on Earth* by Alice Hoffman; *No Hiding Place* by Valerie Wilson Wesley; *Night Passage* by Robert B. Parker; *News of the Spirit: Stories* by Lee Smith; *Only Love* by Erich Segal (author of *Love Story*); *The Burning Plain* by Michael Nava; *Torchlight* by Robert Louis Stevenson III; *State of Emergency* by Steve Pieczenik; *The Investigators: A Badge of Honor Novel* by W. E. B. Griffin; *Singing in the Back of the Comeback Choir* by Bebe Moore Campbell; *The Cat Who Sang for the Birds* by Lillian Jackson Braun; *When Last Seen Alive* by Gar Anthony Haywood.

Putnam produces spectacular omnibus fiction anthologies, featuring such powerhouse authors as Tom Clancy, W. E. B. Griffin, Lillian Jackson Braun, Dean Koontz, and LaVyrle Spencer.

The Putnam nonfiction list includes *Initiation: A Woman's Spiritual Adventure in the Heart of the Andes* by Elizabeth B. Jenkins; *God Is a Verb: Kabbalah and the Practice of Mystical Judaism* by Rabbi David Cooper; *Straight, No Chaser: How I Became a Grown-Up Black Woman* by Jill Nelson; *12 Secrets, 12 Strategies, and 8 Compromises* by Tova Borgnine; *Angels Along the Way: My Life with Help from Above* by Della Reese; *The New Men: Inside the Vatican's Elite School for Priests* by Brian Murphy; *The Seamstress: A Memoir of Survival* by Sara Tuvel Bernstein; *The Message and the Kingdom: How Jesus and Paul Ignited a Revolution and Transformed the Ancient World* by Richard A. Horsley and Neil Asher Silberman.

Putnam distributes its own list to the trade. Query letters and SASEs should be directed to:

Christine Pepe, Senior Editor—Fiction: mysteries, thrillers, horror. Nonfiction: business, health, celebrity stories.

David Highfill, Senior Editor—Fiction: mysteries and mainstream novels, commercial nonfiction.

John Duff, Vice President and Senior Editor—Nonfiction, self-help, popular reference. (See also listing for John Duff under Perigee Books.)

Laura Mathews, Senior Editor—Serious, women-oriented fiction and nonfiction.

Neil Nyren, Publisher, G. P. Putnam's Sons—Serious and commercial fiction and nonfiction.

Stacy Creamer, Vice President and Senior Editor—Fiction: thrillers, crime and detective novels, horror, medical themes. Nonfiction: true crime.

Hillery Borton, Editor—Literary fiction and serious biography.

Jeremy Katz, Senior Editor—Prescriptive nonfiction, including health, relationships, finance, and self-help. Narrative nonfiction and nonfiction novels.

  Sign: Virgo

  Education: English major.

  Employment history/editor career path: I started as a Literary Agent and then shifted to a publishing house and moved up in ranks.

  Personal interests: Family, reading books whenever possible, I like to read anything.

  What would you be doing if you were not an editor? I don't know, I don't plan life that way.

  What books have you acquired that make you the most proud? What books that you have acquired reflect the types of books you like to represent? *The Arthritis Cure; Hostile Waters.*

  Do you represent fiction? No.

  Do you represent nonfiction? Yes.

  Do you require book proposals? If so, what do you look for in evaluating a book proposal? Yes. Cogent writing, a unique idea, something that fulfills a need, a clear market, author credentials, something that is translatable into book format.

  What process do you use for making a decision? What is the process for acquisition, is there a committee? I do the first screen, and then it is taken to a committee.

  Are agents important? Why? Yes, they make editors' lives easier. They are familiar with the publishing business.

Perigee Books

Perigee Books is Penguin Putnam Inc.'s mainline trade paperback nonfiction imprint. Perigee acquires originals and reprints, with emphasis on prescriptive nonfiction.

Titles from Perigee include: *What's Next?* by Rena Penderson; *From Chaos to Calm* by Janet Heininger, Ph.D., and Sharon Weiss; *The Amazing Dad: More Than 400 Ways to*

Wow Your Kids by Giovanni Livera and Ken Preuss; *Home Made* by Alexa Lett; *In Our Humble Opinion:* Car Talk's *Click and Clack Rant and Rave* by Tom and Ray Magliozzi; *What He Can't Tell You . . . and Needs to Say* by Brenda Shoshanna, Ph.D.; *Spiritual Maturity* by Joseph Sharp; *Dilemmas: What Would You Do?* by James Saywell and Anne Marie Roffi; *Strong Women, Strong Bones* by Miriam Nelson, Ph.D., and Sarah Wernick, Ph.D.; *What Your Unborn Baby Wants You to Know* by Boris Petrikovsky, Ph.D., Jessica Jacob, M.D., and Lisa Aiken, Ph.D.; *Blackjack: A Winner's Hand* by Jerry Patterson; *Bright Minds, Poor Grades* by Michael D. Whitley, Ph.D.; *7 Steps to Successful Selling* by Traci Bild.

Please direct query letters with SASEs to:

Jennifer Repo, Editor—Spirituality, women's issues, health, relationships, pop culture.

John Duff, Publisher—Wide range of commercial nonfiction, cookbooks, self-help/how-to, popular psychology, and the newly acquired Avery Health Line.

Sheila Curry Oakes, Executive Editor—Spirituality, general nonfiction, health, and fitness. Perigee

375 Hudson Sreet, New York City, NY 10014

Born: December 6, 1960.

Education: Major in English and History.

Employment history/editor career path: 16 years ago I started as a receptionist at a publishing company and from there I worked my way into an editorial position.

Personal interests: Squash, cycling, movies, art, travel.

What has been your most successful book that you have acquired to date? *The Out of Sync Child*, March 1998.

What books have you acquired that make you the most proud? What books that you have acquired reflect the types of books you like to represent? *The Out of Sync Child; Writing the Wave; Parenting Survival Kit; Talking with Children About Loss.*

Do you represent fiction? No.

Do you represent nonfiction? Yes.

Do you require book proposals? If so, what do you look for in evaluating a book proposal? Yes. What the book is, who is it for, who's writing it, why are you the one most qualified to write this book? Include a sample chapter.

Are certain aspects of a book proposal given more weight than others? I look more for a balanced proposal. Every aspect is important.

What kinds of nonfiction books do you want to see less of? Diet/health books and books on how to get a man.

Are you interested in work geared for the masses (readers of *People, The Star,* etc.)? Our books appeal to all kinds of people and readers.

Are agents important? Why? Yes, they are a valuable tool for the author in the sense that they know the editors very well and they can help with the big picture of publishing.

Do you like new writers? What do you think new writers should do to break into the business? A lot of my writers are first-time authors who have spent their lifetimes developing their ideas.

How should writers approach you? I prefer to see things on paper.

What are some common mistakes writers make? What really gets on your nerves? Having my name spelled wrong. Cover letters that don't get to the point immediately.

What can writers do to get your attention and to avoid the slush pile? If a manuscript comes directly addressed to me, it won't end up in a slush pile. Writers can avoid others' slush piles by having it addressed correctly and to the correct person; editors change jobs frequently.

What have been some of your craziest experiences with submissions? I have received a few submissions in crayon.

What have been some of your best experiences with writers or in your job? I like to edit. It's a different experience every time because of the writers. Most are interesting people to talk to.

Price Stern Sloan

212-414-3610

Price Stern Sloan's main business involves producing books for children and young adults, featuring activity books, craft kits, pop-ups, audiocassettes, and other specialty publications. (See description of overall Putnam children's program under the Putnam & Grosset Book Group subentry.) The house also produces occasional humor titles for the adult market.

Price Stern Sloan was founded as an independent in 1964; since 1993 PSS has been a part of the Putnam Publishing Group. The house was moved from its previous Los Angeles offices to New York in mid-1997. Currently, Price Stern Sloan is focusing on its children's line (mainly novelty). The house also requests that people do not send unsolicited manuscript submissions at this time. Query letters and SASEs should be directed to:

Jon Anderson, Publisher

The Putnam & Grosset Book Group

The Putnam & Grosset Book Group produces children's books under such imprints as G. P. Putnam's Sons, Philomel Books, Sandcastle Books, Grosset & Dunlap, and Platt & Munk. Children's books from the Price Stern Sloan division are coordinated with the Putnam & Grosset program. The list ranges from picture books for toddlers to novels for young adults, covering the full spectrum of nonfiction and fiction areas, board books, first reading books, novelty books, miniature editions, foreign-language books, and holiday books.

Titles include *Flora and Tiger: 19 Very Short Stories from My Life* by Eric Carle (illustrated by the author); *The Seven Songs of Merlin* by T. A. Barron; *Santa's Time Off* by Bill Maynard (illustrated by Tom Browning); *Posters à la Miss Piggy: With Fabulous Jewel Stickers!* from Muppet Books.

Query letters and SASEs should be directed to:

Jane O'Connor, President, Grosset & Dunlap

Lara Bergen, Editorial Director, Price Stern Sloan

Nancy Paulsen, Publisher, G. P. Putnam's Sons

Patricia Lee Gauch, Publisher, Philomel Books

Riverhead Books

Riverhead publishes fiction and nonfiction hardcover and trade paperback originals and reprints. Riverhead fiction and literary works cover an array of serious, lively, and imaginative arenas; explore the frontiers of expression; and resound with the variety and depth of cultural experience. Nonfiction at Riverhead embraces psychology, narrative nonfiction, and popular culture; the house is also on the lookout for strong, creative works in religious and spiritual thought.

The Riverhead name was chosen because of its variety of metaphorical themes. "River" expresses the power of moving water to nurture, terrorize, creep, or inundate; "head" resounds with images of authority and unity.

On Riverhead's nonfiction list: *Ethics for the New Millennium* by His Holiness the Dalai Lama; *Still Here: Embracing Aging, Changing, and Dying* by Ram Dass; *A Place in the Country* by Laura Shaine Cunningham; *Verses from the Center* by Stephen Batchelor; *Woe Is I* by Patricia T. O'Connor; *Our Last Best Shot* by Laura Sessions Stepp; *Changing Places* by Judy Kramer

Fiction and literary works from Riverhead: *Gesture Life* by Chang-rae Lee; *The Man in the Box* by Thomas Moran; *The Beach* by Alex Garland; *Catch the Fire!!! A Cross-Generational Anthology of Contemporary African-American Poetry* (edited by Derrick I. M. Gilbert); *Lovesick* by Ángeles Mastretta; *The Holy Man* by Susan Trott; *Soul Kiss* by Shay Youngblood; *Caucasia* by Danzy Senna; *High Fidelity* by Nick Hornby; *Laura Blundy* by Julie Myerson; and *Light House* by William Monahan.

Query letters and SASEs should be directed to:

Amy Hertz, Executive Editor

Celina (Cindy) Spiegel, Co-Editorial Director

Chris Knutsen, Editor

Julie Grau, Co-Editorial Director

Susan J. Petersen, Publisher

Wendy Carlton-Kennedy, Senior Editor

Tarcher/Putnam

212-951-8800

The Tarcher/Putnam imprint is the corporate banner of the formerly independent Jeremy P. Tarcher, Inc. (founded in 1964), which grew from a small West Coast house to a midsize publisher of hardcover and trade paperback titles in adult trade nonfiction. Subsequent to Tarcher's acquisition by the Putnam Publishing Group (in 1994), the operation was relocated from its Los Angeles base to Putnam Berkley's New York offices. Tarcher's overall editorial goal is to focus on frontlist, cutting-edge, quality nonfiction on a variety of topics: science, memoir and narrative nonfiction, health, anthropology, philosophy, psychology, and spirituality.

On the Tarcher list: *Hope Is the Thing with Feathers: A Personal Chronicle of Vanished Birds* by Christopher Cokinos; *The Lost Daughters of China: Abandoned Girls, the Journey to America, and the Search for a Missing Past* by Karin Evans; *The New Drawing on the Right Side of the Brain: A Course in Enhancing Creativity and Artistic Confidence* by Betty Edwards; *In Search of Captain Zero: A Surfer's Road Trip Beyond the End of the Road* by Allan C. Weisbecker; *Slackjaw* by Jim Knipfel; *Age of Access: The New Culture of Hypercapitalism Where All of Life Is a Paid-for Experience* by Jeremy Rifkin; *Trust Us, We're Experts: How Industry Manipulates Science and Gambles with Your Future* by Sheldon Rampton and John Stauber; and the works of Julia Cameron, including *The Artist's Way: A Spiritual Path to Higher Creativity; Vein of Gold: A Journey to Your Creative Heart;* and *The Right to Write: An Invitation and Initiation into the Writing Life.*

Query letters and SASEs should be directed to:

Sara Carder, Editor

Mitch Horowitz, Senior Editor—Focuses on new trends in spirituality, science, social thought, and personal growth.

Wendy Hubbert, Senior Editor—Focuses on science, psychology, narrative nonfiction, and memoir.

P

QUE CORPORATION

See Macmillan Computer Publishing USA.

RANDOM HOUSE

Fickling Books

Random House Audio Publishing and Large Print Books

Random House Books for Young Readers

Random House Reference and Information Publishing

Random House Trade Group

Random House Value Publishing

Times Books

Villard Books

See also: Ballantine Publishing Group; Crown Publishing Group; Knopf Publishing Group (including: Alfred A. Knopf Books for Young Readers; Crown Books for Young Readers; Clarkson Potter Juvenile Books; Pantheon Books; Schocken Books; Vintage Books)

299 Park Avenue, New York, NY 10171
212-751-2600
www.randomhouse.com

Random House (founded in 1925) is among the celebrated names of the American book trade. As a major domain of the Newhouse publishing empire, Random House has evolved into an intricate commonwealth of publishing groups, divisions, and imprints with a far-flung web of interests and diverse specialties in virtually all categories of commercial fiction and nonfiction. Random House publishes books in hardcover, trade paperback, and mass-market rack editions.

The house's breadth is indicated by the central trade group that encompasses the mainstream sweep of Random House adult trade books; the resolute commercial orientation of the Villard hardcover imprint; the discriminating trade-paper scheme of Vintage Books; and the Modern Library Classics series. Random House publishing entities include Ballantine Publishing Group, Crown Publishing Group, Knopf Publishing Group/Alfred A. Knopf, Pantheon, Schocken, and Times Books. Random House publishing groups also produce an equally fine medley of lines for young readers. (Please see separate subentries elsewhere in this guide.)

Random House distributes for itself and its subsidiaries, as well as for a raft of other publishers, including National Geographic Books, Shambhala Publications, and Sierra Club Books.

Random House Audio Publishing Group
Bantam Doubleday Dell Audio Publishing
Random House Audiobooks
Listening Library
Random House Audible

Assuming a mainstream commercial profile, Random House presents popular books as AudioBooks and as large-print editions. Areas of interest are trade fiction and nonfiction, including current events; history, biography, memoirs; investigative stories, narrative nonfiction; lifestyles and the arts; popular science, frontlist novels; outstanding mysteries, suspense tales, thrillers; and commercial literary works.

Random House Books for Young Readers

Random House Books for Young Readers publishes books for preschoolers through young adults, with a preponderance of its highly commercial list slated for the younger audience.

Established Random House lines include *Babar the Elephant* productions, Dr. Seuss titles, *The Magic Treehouse, Junie B. Jones* and other chapter books, plus *Sesame Street* books. Step-into-Reading books are the preeminent, stepped paperback reader series.

The house engages in a variety of preschool formats, including lift-the-flap books, chunky-shaped books, cuddle-cloth books, scratch 'n' sniff books, books with phosphorescent ink, and vinyl bath books.

This division no longer accepts unsolicited manuscripts directly from authors; all projects go through agents. Query letters and SASEs should be directed to:

Kate Klimo, Publisher

By publisher request, we have printed the following statement from the publisher verbatim:

Random House Children's Books

Random House Children's Books, a division of Random House, Inc., which includes the Alfred A. Knopf, Bantam, Crown, Delacorte, Dell, Disney, Doubleday, Laurel-Leaf, Random House, and Yearling imprints, regretfully informs you that because of the volume of the materials we receive, we now accept unsolicited manuscripts only if they are submitted to one of our two contests: the Marguerite de Angeli Contest for a first middle-grade novel, written for children 7 to 10 years old, and the Delacorte Press Contest for a first young adult novel, written for readers 12 to 18 years old.

If your work meets the criteria for one of the contests, please submit your manuscript. You can find rules and guidelines at our Web site, www.randomhouse.com/kids. You can also make a written request for rules and guidelines; please include a self-addressed stamped envelope.

Information for new writers is also available from the Children's Book Council (www.chcbooks.org) and from the Society for Children's Book Writers and Illustrators (www.scbwi.org).

Beverly Horowitz, Vice President and Publisher

Random House Reference and Information Publishing

Prima Games

Prima Tech

Random House Reference and Information Publishing offers a tight, well-developed list that focuses on a strong dictionary program, with some consumer reference titles.

Random House consumer reference titles include: *The Order of Things* by Barbara Ann Kipfer; *Random House Book of Jokes and Anecdotes* by Joe Claro; *Spy Book* by Norman Polmar and Thomas B. Allen. In the perennially strong standard-reference arena, with a new twist or two, are *Random House Unabridged Dictionary* (book and CD-ROM) and a revised version of the hardy Webster's desktop stand-by, *Random House Webster's College Reference* works.

Query letters and SASEs should be directed to:

Wendalyn Nichols, Editorial Director—Reference Titles.

Chad Bunning, Associate Publisher—Reference Titles.

Prima Games

The world's leader in electronic entertainment publishing, Prima Games publishes strategy guides for PC and console games. For a full list of titles, visit the Prima Games Web site at www.primagames.com. If you're an experienced strategy guide author or an expert gamer who loves to write, please send a resume and writing sample to freelance@primagames.com.

Prima Tech

36 South Pennsylvania Avenue, Suite 610, Indianapolis, IN 46204
317-488-4300
www.prima-tech.com

Prima Tech publishes basic tutorials for the layperson on popular software applications, as well as advanced tutorials and comprehensive reference books for programmers and other computer professionals. Prima Tech delivers up-to-date coverage on operating environments, word processing, data management, graphic design, desktop and Web publishing, multimedia, programming languages, networking, and the Internet. Prima Tech places special emphasis on Game Development, Linux, and SAP communities with titles such as Isometric Game Programming, The Art and Design of Creating Games, and PHP Essentials. Prima's FAST & EASY series consists of highly graphical, step-by-step guides for novices, including such titles as *Office XP, Photoshop for Windows, iMac and Family Tree Maker 8*. Prima's IN A WEEKEND series presents a series of sessions that can be completed in a single weekend to accomplish a project with technology, such as *Create Your First Web Page in a Weekend* and *Learn Javascript in a Weekend*.

Query letters and SASEs for Prima Tech should be directed to:

Emi Nakamura, Acquisitions Editor

Lynette Quinn, Acquisitions Editor

Jody Kennen, Acquisitions Editor

Melody Layne, Acquisitions Editor

Kevin Harreld, Acquisitions Editor

Kim Spilker, Acquisitions Manager

Stacy Hiquet, Publisher

Random House Trade Group

Random House Trade Group is composed of the original Random House imprint, Modern Library, and Villard.

Assuming a mainstream commercial profile, Random House presents a preferred list of trade fiction and nonfiction titles within its wide-ranging adult trade hardcover lineup.

Random House nonfiction presents topics of popular interest in current events; history, biography, and memoirs; investigative stories and narrative nonfiction; lifestyle and arts; and popular science. Fiction accents frontlist novels; outstanding mysteries, suspense tales, and thrillers; and commercial literary works.

Random House books are often available in large-print editions, audiobooks, and electronic formats. The evocative Random House logo of a rambling home is a recognized symbol of unstinting standards in bookmaking.

Random House nonfiction encompasses *Midnight in the Garden of Good and Evil* by John Berendt; *Faith of My Fathers* by John McCain; *A Vast Conspiracy* by Jeffrey Toobin; *The Orchid Thief* by Susan Orlean; *The Greatest Generation* and *The Greatest Generation Speaks* by Tom Brokaw.

The Random House list in fiction and letters includes: *A Widow for One Year* by John Irving; *City of God* by E. L. Doctorow; *Omerta* by Mario Puzo; *The Angel of Darkness* by Caleb Carr; *Monster* by Jonathan Kellerman.

Prima Tech has played a significant role in American cultural life for the better part of a century. The series was founded in 1917 by the publishers Boni and Liveright and eight years later acquired by Bennett Cerf and Donald Klopfer. It provided the foundation for their next publishing venture, Random House. The Modern Library has been a staple of the American book trade, providing readers with affordable hardbound and paperback editions of important works of literature and thought.

Villard Books, founded in 1983, is the publisher of savvy and sometimes quirky hardcovers and paperbacks. Its list encompasses both fiction and nonfiction, including celebrity memoirs, sports, and music. Villard often produces bestsellers such as *Into Thin Air* by John Krakauer; *Aretha: From These Roots* by Aretha Franklin; and *I Ain't Got Time to Bleed* by Jesse Ventura.

The Random House Trade Group does not accept unsolicited manuscripts. Query letters and SASEs should be directed to:

Ann Godoff, Publisher—Nonfiction: contemporary issues. Commercial and literary fiction.

Katie Hall, Senior Editor—Wide range of interests consistent with the house list.

Deb Futter, Editor—General fiction.

Kate Medina, Senior Vice President, Executive Editor—Nonfiction, memoir, literary fiction.

Jonathan Karp, Vice President, Executive Editor

Lee Boudreau, Editor—fiction and narrative nonfiction.

Random House Value Publishing

Random House Value Publishing is the promotional imprint for Random House, publishing originals and reprints at exceptional prices. The categories that it publishes include fully illustrated gardening books, art books, travel books, as well as a variety of bestselling reprints in fiction and nonfiction, reference, and books on transportation and the Civil War. The philosophy is mass-market hardcovers: quality books at value prices.

Query letters and SASEs should be directed to:

Donna Lee Lurker, Editor

Nancy Davis, Executive Editor

Susanne Jaffe, Vice President and Editor in Chief

Times Books

This imprint is now a part of Henry Holt.

Villard Books

Query letters and SASEs should be directed to:

Bruce Tracy, Editorial Director

Melody Guy, Associate Editor

Pamela Cannon, Editor

READER'S DIGEST GENERAL BOOKS

Reader's Digest Children's Publishing

Reader's Digest Road, Pleasantville, NY 10570
914-238-1000

Reader's Digest General Books accents how-to/do-it-yourself and self-help in topics that cover home maintenance and repair, gardening, crafts and hobbies, cooking, and health. Reader's Digest also produces reference books in law, medicine, money management, English-language usage and vocabulary, history and geography, science and nature, religion and archaeology, travel, and general reference.

Reader's Digest General Books (founded in 1961) is a publisher of general nonfiction, most of which is conceptualized and commissioned editorially. Author credit on many of the house's books is given as the Editors of Reader's Digest; indeed, most titles are originated in-house and are written by consulting writers. Reader's Digest General Books is thus not a likely home for an original publishing project, but when prospecting assignments, the house might be worth a try for well-qualified freelance writers.

On the Reader's Digest General Books list:

Among house-authored titles are: *Deluxe Tapestry Sewing Basket; Complete Book of Embroidery; The Calligrapher's Studio; Decorating for Christmas; Papercraft School; The Rolling Tool Box; Heartland Cooking Breads; Professionals' Guide to Patient Drug Facts; Guide to Medical Cures and Treatments; The Bible Through the Ages; A Journey Down Route 66; America's First Ladies; Gift Wraps, Baskets & Bows Book.*

Reader's Digest General Books directs a wide marketing and distribution team. Query letters and SASEs should be directed to:

Christopher Cavanaugh, General Books, Editor in Chief

Reader's Digest Children's Publishing

914-244-4867

Reader's Digest Young Families Books for Children accents children's books and interactive books that inspire young imaginations. Books are distributed by Random House, Inc. Reader's Digest Young Families Books for Children is interested in children's books and stories. Query letters and SASEs should be directed to:

Linda Falken, Editorial Director

REED PUBLISHING (USA)

Reed Reference Publishing

Reed Trade Publishing

Reed Reference Publishing:

121 Chanlon Road, New Providence, NJ 07974
800-366-2665

Reed Trade Publishing:

225 Wildwood Avenue, Woburn, MA 01801
908-464-6800

R

Reed Publishing (USA), along with Reed Reference Publishing, constitutes one of the leading houses in the arena of biographical, bibliographical, and business reference materials. Reed's professional titles cover virtually the entire reference spectrum, from law, medicine, and science to education, history, and the performing arts. Reed is also a leader in electronic publishing, with many titles currently available on CD-ROM.

Reed Reference is a division of Reed Publishing (USA), an international publisher of reference works and directories for trade, institutional, corporate, and library markets that is a wing of the Reed Elsevier Group. RRP imprints include R. R. Bowker (publisher of *Literary Market Place; Books in Print*), Congressional Information Service, Martindale Hubbell (law directories), Marquis Who's Who, National Register Publishing, K. G. Sauer, Bowker-Sauer, and D. W. Thorpe.

Reed Elsevier also owns Heinemann (see separate main entry for Heinemann, along with its Digital Press and Focal Press divisions).

Reed is exploring the acquisition of new trade books that dovetail with its existing product lines. Fields of special publishing emphasis are self-help, how-to, and other directory/reference works, particularly in the business, legal, and health-care fields. Catalog areas cover epic adventure, satire, and photography; fantasy, family health, and biography; thrillers, literary works, and popular science; travel, lifestyle, psychology, and inspiration; and popular history and reference.

For prospective trade projects: Please query publisher beforehand, as this is an experimental line and is therefore subject to reorganization (not to mention complete downsizing) at any given instant.

Representative Reed trade titles: *Kalashnikovs and Zombie Cucumbers* by Nick Middleton; *Positive Parenting* by Elizabeth Hartley-Brewer; *Mind, Body, and Immunity* by Rachel Charles; *The Magistrate's Tale* by Nora Naish; *The Celibate* by Michael Arditti; *Literary Guide to Dublin* by Vivien Igoe; *Claudia Schiffer* by Karl Lagerfeld; *Bulimia* by David Haslam; *Beating the Blues* by Xandia Williams.

Distribution is overseen by Reed's in-house team via book-trade channels, direct-ordering facilities, and international marketing via Reed subsidiary facilities. RRP delivers its information worldwide in a variety of formats—books, CD-ROM, microfiche, tape leasing, and through online accessing of RRP databases.

REGNERY PUBLISHING, INC.

Harry Crocker House, Regnery Publishing
One Massachusetts Avenue, NW, Washington, DC 20001
202-216-0600, 800-462-6420
www.regnery.com

Areas of Regnery publishing interest include contemporary politics, current events, public issues, biography, history, alternative health; the house is open to projects with broad trade appeal by promotable authors with strong media CVs.

Regnery Publishing Inc. (formerly Regnery Gateway, founded in 1947) is a growing, midsize house that produces primarily nonfiction projects in hardcover and quality paper editions. Regnery Gateway was acquired by Phillips Publishing International and is part of Phillips's Eagle Publishing subsidiary, which produces public-policy periodicals and operates the Conservative Book Club. A major accent of Regnery's program is to feature books that offer a Washington-insider purview. The house is also traditionally strong in paperbound reprints for the college market. Regnery Publishing supports a strong backlist. In 1997, Regnery launched LifeLine Press, which will concentrate on alternative health books.

The Phillips corporate connection enables Regnery to promote titles through such venues as Phillips's Human Events newspaper and to take advantage of the parent company's expertise in direct-mail and special-market sales.

From the Regnery Publishing trade list: *Brighter than the Baghdad Sun: Saddam Hussein's Nuclear Threat to the United States* by Shyam Bhatia and Daniel McGrory; *Gods, Guns, and Rock & Roll* by Ted Nugent; *The Bible Is History* by Ian Wilson; *Over Before It Began* by David P. Schippers.

Indicative of this house's heritage is founder Henry Regnery's choice of his publisher's mark—the gateway that serves as colophon for books published by Regnery. This gateway is a graphic representation of the Porta Nigra in Trier, Germany, a Roman gate constructed about 300 A.D., when Trier was a colonial capital city of the Roman Empire. As such, the gateway symbolizes the passage from barbarous realms into the world of civilization.

Regnery Publishing is distributed to the trade by National Book Network. Query letters and SASEs should be directed to:

Harry Crocker, Executive Editor
www.townhall.com/eagle

DOB or sign: Are you kidding?

Education: B.A., in English and American Literature from the University of California at San Diego. M.A., in International Relations from the University of Southern California, (United Kingdom program), in London, U.K.

Employment history/editor career path: I started in journalism as an Editorial Writer for the *San Diego Union,* where I had a drill instructor as an Editor and daily deadlines.

Great training. I joined Regnery as its Editor in Chief when Al Regnery took over the company and moved it to Washington, D.C. I left to write speeches for the governor of California, and returned to publishing, and Regnery, via a short stint—about a year and a half—as Editor of the Conservative Book Club and Movie & Entertainment Book Club. While I was at the Clubs, Regnery had me work with Gary Aldrich, whose book, *Unlimited Access*, became a #1 bestseller. I worked full time for both Regnery and the Clubs for a while. Now I direct Regnery's editorial department and am an adviser to the Clubs. I also write books for other publishers. Last year I wrote *Robert E. Lee on Leadership* for Prima Publishing. My next project is a popular history of the Catholic Church.

Personal interests: In reading, I assume you mean. The English classics: Shakespeare, Boswell's Johnson, Edmund Burke, and so on. For a book of my own I've been rereading the King James version of the Bible, especially the New Testament. I like Kipling as a poet, Siegfried Sassoon for prose fiction, Orwell for nonfiction. I also like the Anglo-Catholic writers: Cardinal Newman, and, more popularly, Evelyn Waugh and Graham Greene. Among living authors, George MacDonald Fraser for novels, Craig Brown for parodies, and anything by Auberon Waugh. Other interests: History in general, British imperial and military history in particular, British politics.

What would you be doing if you were not an editor? Soldier of fortune.

What has been your most successful book that you have acquired to date? I wouldn't want to single out one author. As a rule, we've had a remarkable string of successes here.

What books have you acquired that make you the most proud? What books that you have acquired reflect the types of books you like to represent? I tend to be the proudest of the books that aren't bestsellers—because bestsellers have their own reward. Of recent books, I'm very proud of *An Education for Our Time* by Josiah Bunting III, the superintendent at VMI, which was our attempt to rewrite Cardinal Newman's *The Idea of a University* for an American 21st-century audience. We did a novel, *Speak No Evil*, coauthored by Gary Aldrich and former White House speech writer Mark Davis, that attempted to bring a bit more real-world knowledge to the genre of White House thrillers. It's an underrated book. *The Wine Sense Diet* by Annette Shafer, is one of the handsomest books we've ever done. And we brought *Bulldog Drummond* back into print—not that anyone but me noticed.

Do you represent fiction? If so, what do you look for? Exceedingly rarely. The fiction market is so stacked against non-bestselling authors that, from a business point of view, it is nearly suicidal to dabble in it. I very much wish this weren't so, but it is.

What do you want to see less of? Books with no conceivable hope of turning a profit. When writers (especially of political books, of which we do a lot) are idealists and enthusiasts. But they need to remember that book buyers don't respond to books they should read but buy books they feel they simply have to have—either because they are breaking news or are the talk of the town. Very few projects have that sort of potential. But that's what we look for.

Do you represent nonfiction? News-driving nonfiction is our bread and butter.

Do you require book proposals? Yes.

Are certain aspects of a book proposal given more weight than others? The two most important factors in evaluating a book proposal are the credibility and promotability of the author and a serious possibility of good sales. We're a marketing-driven company and respond to hard market analysis. To get noticed in today's market, you need to have a name.

What process do you use for making a decision? What is the process for acquisition, is there a committee? Yes, made up of every different segment of the company. Every proposal is torn apart, argued over, and examined from every angle. It's hard for most proposals to survive that analysis, because the odds are always, for any book project, on the side of failure. Publishing decisions are calibrations of acceptable risk.

What kinds of nonfiction books do you want to see less of? Books with no commercial potential.

Are you interested in work geared for the masses (readers of *People, The Star,* etc.)? Yes.

Are agents important? Why? Yes and no. A writer has a much better chance of getting noticed if he has an agent. But few agents, in my opinion, earn their keep. Unless the author is a Tom Clancy with complicated rights deals to work out, publishing contracts are pretty simple. Moreover, most of the books we do are projects by design, matching author and subject, so an agent is superfluous in getting a book accepted.

Do you like new writers? What should new writers do to break into the business? As in any other business, writers need to get a track record. They also need to show that they understand how to target commercial audiences with their ideas.

How should writers approach you? The standard SASE is the best way. Phone calls are the worst. E-mail submissions will be rejected the same day, which saves me time, I suppose.

What are some common mistakes writers make? What really gets on your nerves? The most common is a lack of commercial realism. Far too many writers think that because a topic is important to them—or because a topic is important for the country or the world at large—that there's an audience for it. The fact is, getting people to lay down $25 for a book is a very hard thing to do. As the remainder bins prove, books are one of the few commercial commodities that often can't even be given away. I know my church thrift shop won't accept contributions of books anymore. Most books are destined for landfills, which means they shouldn't have been made in the first place.

What can writers do to get your attention and to avoid the slush pile? They need to be experts in their field and have a strong, commercially viable idea.

What have been some of your craziest experiences with submissions? I'll pass. I don't want to encourage them.

What have been some of your best experiences with writers or in your job? Too many to name—which is rare in this business.

What, if anything, makes you different from other editors? First, Regnery Publishing is in Washington, so we're not afflicted by NYC groupthink. Second, perhaps I'm a little different because I work on both sides of the desk, as a writer as well as an editor.

Is there anything you would like to see changed in the industry? We're going to be changing soon enough with whatever e-publishing has in store.

Any advice for writers? I wouldn't want to encourage anyone to be a writer. What we need are more readers—especially of quality books. Every writer should ask himself: Just how necessary is my project? Will it add any more to the sum total of human knowledge about, say, human conflict that we don't already have from either the ancients—

Thucydides—or from the greats—Shakespeare—or from popularizers of modern research in our own time—perhaps Robert Ardrey? No author should write a book that merely gets in the way of readers going back to the real thing. And only a small handful of writers come close to making a living at it. Most would be much better off, be relieved of much frustration, be happier, and be doing more worthwhile things if they spent their spare time with their kids or planting trees. So, my advice to aspiring writers—take up golf, subscribe to *The Common Reader* book catalogue, and read good, old-fashioned, escapist adventure fiction like *Beau Gest, Captain Blood*, and *The Scarlet Pimpernel*.

R

RENAISSANCE BOOKS

Audio Renaissance

New York office:

175 Fifth Avenue, c/o SMP, New York, NY 10010

212-674-5151 (extensions: 586; 871)

e-mail: pubbooks@aol.com

California office:

5858 Wilshire Boulevard, Suite 200, Beverly Hills, CA 90036

323-939-1840   fax: 323-939-6436

Renaissance Books is a nonfiction trade publisher dedicated to an editorial mix of popular culture and serious inquiry. Subjects and categories include: biography and business, cookbooks, self-help, and spiritual growth. The house produces trade nonfiction packages as well as trivia books, coffee-table books, and pictorial volumes. Renaissance publishes in hardcover and paperback.

Renaissance Books (founded in 1997) is the book-publishing imprint sibling to Audio Renaissance, a company known for marketing innovation in audio publishing. Through the company's book imprint, Renaissance has transferred its program in the fields of self-help, motivation, and business from audio publishing into print. Renaissance Books remains dedicated to the company's historic roots and at the same time looks for projects that will expand the vision: works that reveal popular tastes and culture, ride the crest of a coming wave, and are well written, perceptive, and entertaining in and of themselves.

Bill Hartley, President and Publisher, Audio Renaissance and Renaissance Books, proffers the following outlook: Renaissance Books is an exciting new step for the company—one that is expected to mirror the philosophy that has guided the enterprise's growth as an audio publisher. The publisher projects a well-balanced mixture of nonfiction, including books on personal and spiritual growth, self-help, and motivation.

Representative titles: *Single No More: Fifty-One Ways to Meet Your Lover (Plus All the Things You Should Do So You're Ready for It When It Happens)* by Ellen Kreidman, Ph.D.; *Matt Damon: An Unauthorized Biography* by Chris Nickson; *Soap Stars to Superstars: Celebrities Who Started Out in Daytime Drama* by Annette D'Agostino; *Alfred Hitchcock Triviography & Quiz Book* by Kathleen Kaska; *The New Prince* by Dick Morris; *J. D. Salinger: A Biography* by Paul Alexander; *The Legal Edge: For Homeowners, Buyers, and Renters* by Michel James Bryant, Esq.; *TV Chefs: The Dish on the Stars of*

Your Favorite Cooking Shows by Karen Lurie; *The Best Guide to Success: How to Get Ahead in Your Career* by Barbara Somervill; *Conspiracies, Lies, and Hidden Agendas* by Mick Farren; *How to Draw Those Bodacious Bad Babes of Comics* by Frank McLaughlin and Mike Gold; *Buying and Selling Real Estate on the Internet* by Ron Raisglid, with Daniel Cubias; *Finding Your Strong Suit: How to Read Yourself, Your Partner, or Your Opponent* by Mike Was, Allan Combs, and Julie N. Combs.

Renaissance Books is distributed by St. Martin's Press. Query letters and SASEs should be directed to:

Joe McNeely, Director of Acquisitions (New York)—Self-help, motivation, business.

Richard F. X. O'Connor, Editor (California)—Popular trade nonfiction; self-help, inspiration, how-to, New Age topics; personal and spiritual growth; business and marketing.

Audio Renaissance

5858 Wilshire Boulevard, Suite 200, Los Angeles, CA 90036
323-939-1840   fax: 323-939-6436

Audio Renaissance produces audio products in a variety of nonfiction subjects. the house is a major presence in the areas of personal and spiritual growth, self-help, business, and motivation.

For the past 10 years, Audio Renaissance has been one of the leading independent audio publishers in America, publishing over 450 titles in that time. Among them: *Understanding Men's Passages by Managing Change* by Gail Sheehy; *How to Argue and Win Every Time* by Gerry Spence; *James Herriot's Favorite Dog Stories; Emotional Intelligence* by Daniel Goleman; *You Can Negotiate Anything* by Herb Cohen; *Psycho-Cybernetics* by Maxwell Maltz; *How to Meditate* by Laurence LeShan; *Think and Grow Rich* by Napoleon Hill.

Audio Renaissance typically acquires projects by licensing audio rights to works originally created in other media, primarily books. Query letters and SASEs should be directed to:

Joe McNeely, Director of Acquisitions for Audio Media, Audio Renaissance (New York)
   Born: November 23, 1956.
   Education: B.A., Fine Arts; M.A., Theater; Minor in English.
   Employment history/editor career path: I was an actor starting out for about 10 years, and when I finally realized I couldn't make a living at it, I applied for the receptionist job at Audio and got it. I have worked my way up the scale here over the years.
   Personal interests: Golf, Zen, Karate.
   What would you be doing if you were not an editor? I would hope someone would pay me to play golf, or I would be a Zen monk.
   What has been your most successful book that you have acquired to date? *Powerful Prayers* by Larry King and *Emotional Intelligence* by Daniel Goleman.
   What books have you acquired that make you the most proud? What books that you have acquired reflect the types of books you like to represent? *Seventeen Lies That Hold You Back and the Truth That Sets You Free* by Steve Chandler.
   Do you represent fiction? No.

Do you represent nonfiction? Yes, self-help, motivation, self-actualization, Eastern-minded into Western civilization.

Do you require book proposals? If so, what do you look for in evaluating a book proposal? Yes, I look for good writing, sample chapters, outline, writing style, and author credentials.

Are certain aspects of a book proposal given more weight than others? It all is given equal weight and needs to be present—author credentials, market, writing style, writing timeline, outline, sample material.

What process do you use for making a decision? What is the process for acquisition, is there a committee? Lugubrious. A manuscript goes through an editorial review board. The board will look at it to see if the merits of the book will stand up and if it will be able to hold its own on the shelves. It basically gets put through the ringer and back by the time it's finally acquired.

What kinds of nonfiction books do you want to see less of? Sixty-day knock-off books and books on fads.

Are you interested in work geared for the masses (readers of *People, The Star,* etc.)? Yes.

Are agents important? Why? Yes, I think that they are very important. Agents are becoming more and more essential to the publishing industry every day because the publishing houses are now turning into more of "printing houses." Agents are doing more of the editors' jobs every day.

Do you like new writers? What should new writers do to break into the business? To break into the business, the only thing I could say to do is Just Write. That's it. You Write. Writing is 50% about the actual writing of the material and 50% becoming a hustler or a salesman to sell your product.

How should writers approach you? With a good cover letter and a proposal. The good cover letter is essential, tell me what your book can do in one page. Do not send unsolicited manuscripts.

What are some common mistakes writers make? What really gets on your nerves? Being naïve. Everyone goes through it, but the trick is how quickly you can get over it. Endless follow-up calls are always annoying, as well as not having any patience.

What have been some of your craziest experiences with submissions? We get material that is handwritten.

What have been some of your best experiences with writers or in your job? Discovering a writer who has something important to say and helping to guide that person through the publishing process. Knowing that you have helped to refine someone's work/talent.

What, if anything, makes you different from other editors? I think that writers find the editors that they deserve. It's a marriage—for better or for worse—it could be short, it could be long. If I believe in something I will fight for it.

Is there anything you would like to see changed in the industry? I would like to see more diversity. I would like to also see less emphasis on the financial/accounting side of things, as this is becoming more and more overwhelming.

Any advice for writers? Be disciplined about your work—it's easy to work and write when you are inspired by something; the real work comes when you are not. Understand the craft of language, it gives meaning to our words.

RE/SEARCH PUBLICATIONS

Juno Books

V/Search

111 Third Avenue, #11 G, New York, NY 10003
212-604-9074   fax: 212-366-5247
www.junobooks.com   e-mail: junobooks@junobooks.com

RE/Search Publications focuses on media and the arts; cultural studies; word art and graphics; biography and memoir; erotic interfaces of all natures. RE/Search and V/Search productions are often published in oversize trade-paperback journal formats. Juno Books is a personalized trade-paperback book imprint. The press publishes a short list of new titles per year and hosts a comprehensive backlist.

A number of works from this house have achieved classic status virtually instantaneously upon release. Areas of renown include cultures of the mind and body, general mischief, literature in reprint, popular music, and film studies.

From RE/Search: *Deviant Desires: Incredibly Strange Sex; Angry Women* by Carolee Schneemann and Annie Sprinkle; *Bodies of Subversion; Modern Primitives; Dangerous Drawings; Horror Hospital Unplugged: A Queer Boys Graphic Novel;* and *Sex, Stupidity and Greed* by Ian Grey.

The V/Search list includes: *Memoirs of a Sword Swallower* by Daniel P. Mannix; *Zines! Incendiary Interviews with Independent Publishers* (2 volumes; edited by Andrea Juno and V. Vale); *Search and Destroy: An Authoritative Guide to Punk History* (edited by Andrea Juno and V. Vale).

On the Juno Books imprint: *Bodies of Subversion: The Secret History of Women and Tattoo* by Margot Mifflin; *Driving Me Wild: Nitro-Powered Outlaw Culture* by Leah Kerr; *Sex, Stupidity and Greed: The Underbelly of the American Movie Industry* by Ian Grey; *Dangerous Drawings: Interviews with Comix and Graphix Artists* (edited by Andrea Juno); *Concrete Jungle: A Pop Media Investigation of Death and Survival in Urban Ecosystems* (edited by Mark Dion and Alexis Rockman); *Angry Women in Rock* by A. Juno; *Concrete Jungle* by A. Rockman and M. Dion; *Horror Hospital Unplugged (A Graphic Novel)* by Dennis Cooper and Keith Magarson; *Bread and Wine* by Samuel R. Delany.

RE/Search, V/Search, and Juno Books distribute to the trade through Power House Books in New York City; direct marketing for selected titles is handled through a number of independent catalogers, including Fantagraphics. Query letters and SASEs should be directed to:

Andrea Juno, Executive and Editorial Director

Daniel Power, All business inquiries.

RIZZOLI INTERNATIONAL PUBLICATIONS

300 Park Avenue South, New York, NY 10010-5399
212-982-2300

Rizzoli catalogs titles in fine arts, architecture, crafts, culinary arts, decorative arts, design, fashion, the home, gardens, landscaping, travel, and photography. Rizzoli also offers selected titles in sports and the performing arts.

The Rizzoli catalog offers titles from additional publishers in the arts and literary arena, including Angel City Press, Collectors' Press, Vendome, PBC International, Villegas Editores, Ipso Facto, and Merrell.

Rizzoli International (founded in 1976) is one of the exclusive set of cosmopolitan publishers renowned for finesse in the bookmaking craft. The house interest embraces artistic realms worldwide, throughout history as well as the contemporary arena.

Rizzoli's consummately produced volumes feature graphics of the highest quality and are offered in hardback and trade paperback editions. (Please see entry for Universe Publishing.)

Titles from Rizzoli: *Fifth Avenue: The Best Address* by Jerry Patterson; *The Sensual Home* by Ilse Crawford (photographs by Martyn Thompson); *John Galliano: Romantic, Realist and Revolutionary* by Colin McDowell; *Architectural Glass Art: Form and Technique in Contemporary Glass* by Andrew Moor; *German Expressionism: Art and Society* by Stephanie Barron and Wolf-Dieter Dube; *East Meets West: Global Design for Contemporary Interiors* by Kelly Hoppen (photographs by Bill Batten); *Secret Gardens of Santa Fe* by Sydney LeBlanc (photographs by Charles Mann); *Living by Design: A Country House & Garden* by John Stefanidis (photographs by Fritz von der Schulenburg); *Diving: The World's Best Sites* by Jack Jackson.

PBC International titles: *New American Style* by Mike Strohl; *Kitchens: Lifestyle and Design* by James W. Krengel and Bernadette Baczynski; *Designing with Light: The Creative Touch* by Dr. Carol Soucer King, Ph.D.; *Color: Details and Design* by Terry Trucco; *Magazines Inside and Out* by Steven Heller and Teresa Fernandes.

Rizzoli International Publications is distributed to the trade in the United States by St. Martin's Press; Canadian distribution is handled through McClelland & Stewart.

The house acquires new projects only on an extremely selective basis. Query letters and SASEs should be directed to:

Isabel Venero, Editor—Art and general trade books.

Liz Sullivan, Senior Editor—Art, culinary arts.

David Morton, Senior Editor—Architecture.

RODALE, INC.

33 East Minor Street, Emmaus, PA 18098-0099
610-967-5171, 800-813-6627
www.rodalepress.com

Rodale, Inc. (founded in 1932), specializes in books on health and wellness; sports and fitness; gardening and organic lifestyles; home arts such as cooking, quilting, and sewing; practical spirituality and inspiration; self-improvement; and selected general interest titles. Rodale, Inc., publishes hardcover and trade paperback books and some video products.

Rodale, Inc., publishes several award-winning magazines, including *Men's Health, Prevention, Organic Gardening, Runner's World, Bicycling,* and *Backpacker.*

Rodale, Inc., published two *New York Times* bestsellers in 2000; Dr. Shapiro's *Picture Perfect Weight Loss* by Dr. Howard Shapiro and *The Wrinkle Cure* by Dr. Nicholas Perricone.

Other recent books from Rodale include: *Ann Lovejoy's Organic Garden Design School* by Ann Lovejoy; *Try and Make Me* by Ray Levy, Ph.D., and Bill O'Hanlong with Tyler Norris Goode; *The Immunity Pleasure Connection* by Carl Chametski, Ph.D., and Francis Brennan, Ph.D.; *Run with the Champions* by Marc Bloom; *Another Shot* by Joe Kita; *The Green Pharmacy Anti-Aging Prescription* by Dr. James A. Duke; and *The Joint Health Prescription* by James Rippe, M.D.

Rodale, Inc., distributes books through multiple channels: direct mail, retail sales, book clubs, and so on. St. Martin's Press distributes Rodale titles to the book trade. Query letters and SASEs should be directed to:

Jennifer Kushner, Assistant Editor

Stephanie Tade, Editor

Tami Booth, Editor in Chief, Women's Health Books—Prevention books.

Steve Salemo, Executive Editor, Men's Health Books—General interest for men, health for men, motivation for men.

Kathleen Fish, Executive Editor, Organic Living Books—Organic gardening and organic stylebooks.

Neil Wertheimer, Vice President, Publisher, Rodale Books—General interest titles, cooking, quilting, sewing, fitness, and sports.

Born: May 16, 1959.

Education: B.A., Math, from the University of Rochester; M.A., Journalism, from the University of Michigan.

Employment history/editor career path: I decided early out of college that I loved writing, not math. I started as an intern at *LA Daily News* and eventually became a full-time reporter. I then became a full-time Editor at Orange Register Company and worked there for about four years. I quickly moved on and have been an editor at Rodale for about six years now.

Personal interests: Music, jazz, cooking, eating well, nature activities, hiking, bike riding.

What would you be doing if you were not an editor? Trying to get a job as an Editor.

What has been your most successful book that you have acquired to date? *On Sex: A Man's Guide* has sold over a million copies, and *Imagine What America Could Be in the 21st Century* will be coming out in the fall.

What books have you acquired that make you the most proud? What books that you have acquired reflect the types of books you like to represent? I can't think of a book that I wasn't proud of or that hasn't helped people in some way. I'm passionate about all of the projects I work on.

Do you represent fiction? No.

Do you represent nonfiction? Yes, self-help, new ventures, parenting, men's health, fitness, spirituality, pets, household management, cooking.

Do you require book proposals? If so, what do you look for in evaluating a book proposal? 80% of our sales are through the mail, telemarketing, or the Internet. For trade

R

imprints, yes, I require a book proposal. I am looking for mostly passion and fire for a project. I can help to shape the actual text and writing, but I can't give you "fire" for the project.

Are certain aspects of a book proposal given more weight than others? The cover letter; assessing how smart you are in your area; how well do you know your competition; the table of contents needs to clever and delightful; and the actual sample writing.

What process do you use for making a decision? What is the process for acquisition, is there a committee? Yes, every two weeks we have an editorial review meeting. Editors bring forth the manuscripts that they feel are worthy of representation and the board will critically help the editor to make that decision. The board or committee consists of the marketing department, design, production, and publicity departments, as well as the publisher and editors.

What kinds of nonfiction books do you want to see less of? Spirituality is very over-published today and is sometimes badly conceived. I also do not want to see any bad fitness concepts.

Are you interested in work geared for the masses (readers of *People*, *The Star*, etc.)? Yes, we're a middle-America publisher.

Are agents important? Why? I have a very healthy respect for agents. It's very rare that I get good quality material that's unagented. Agents funnel through the manuscripts to send you the quality material.

Do you like new writers? What should new writers do to break into the business? Yes, I like new writers, but I don't like professional authors. I like passionate writers. To break into the business, I would say be passionate about your work.

How should writers approach you? With fistfuls of cash or caviar. Or, identify if I am the appropriate editor to send material to by doing your homework, and get an agent.

What are some common mistakes writers make? What really gets on your nerves? Self-centered writing, authors who say, "You can't edit my work, only I know how my sentences should look." Not being punctual.

What can writers do to get your attention and to avoid the slush pile? Make the messages in your book be understandable, be able to explain the uniqueness of your book in a couple of sentences; it always helps to have marketing skills or a marketing background.

What have been some of your craziest experiences with submissions? Walk-ups at Book Expo. I also once had to deal with a woman who said that she could mind read, and she had been mind reading O. J. Simpson's dog, who told her that O. J. did it.

What have been some of your best experiences with writers or in your job? *On Sex: A Man's Guide* was a wonderful give-and-take experience. The book became successful, I believe, because of this.

What, if anything, makes you different from other editors? I am passionate about the words, the substance, and the product and will do more than satisfy the customers, I will delight them. I used to be a designer and won many awards doing so, so this helps out in the design process.

Is there anything you would like to see changed in the industry? I think we should publish a little less and diversify the voices being heard. It's wrong that the same 12 people sell books all the time. One of the best things in the industry that is happening is that books today are beautiful. They look intelligent, interesting, glossy, and are very vibrant.

Any advice for writers? Be fearless, do not fear the keyboard. You can't be a crazed, office-pacing writer. Be passionate, have opinions about everything, be open to sensual experiences like food, music, and travel.

Ken Winston Caine, Executive Writer/former Daybreak Editor
    Sign: Sagittarius.
    Education: I have never stopped being a student.
    Employment history/editor career path: I worked as a reporter for almost 20 years. I have written books for Rodale that have sold half a million copies. I used to live in the wilderness in a solar-powered home in Santa Fe. And I have now been with Rodale for six years.
    Personal interests: Alternative and personal health.
    What would you be doing if you were not an editor? I would love to live and work in the wilderness or work in India in a hospital.
    What has been your most successful book that you have acquired to date? It's always been a team process, I don't feel as though I was the only "acquiring" editor.
    Do you represent fiction? If so, what do you look for? No.
    Do you represent nonfiction? Yes, spirituality.
    Do you require book proposals? If so, what do you look for in evaluating a book proposal? Yes. I want to know the writer's media experience, and I want to see a video showing me the writer being interviewed. I would like to see a workshop schedule, a good outline (12–40 pages), sample chapters, a bio, and I want to know that the writer knows who his or her competition is.
    Are certain aspects of a book proposal given more weight than others? Telling me what's unique about the project. You need a unique "hook." I need to know that there is indeed an audience for the book and need to see great writing that will keep me entertained.
    What process do you use for making a decision? What is the process for acquisition, is there a committee? Yes, we have a committee that consists of the editorial board, division publisher, marketing, and production. In order for a book to be acquired, it has to have an acceptance rate among the board. It has to convince about 6 to 8 people on a board consisting of only 10 to 12 people. This is hard to do.
    Are you interested in work geared for the masses (readers of *People, The Star,* etc.)? Yes, we're looking to target middle America. We're always looking for people who want to help themselves.
    Are agents important? Why? Yes, I feel that they are very important. One of the first questions that gets asked in our editorial meetings is, did the material come from an agent? Agents don't send you bad material, they know what you want to see and how to prepare the package for you. In most cases agents are easier to work with as compared to writers.
    Do you like new writers? What should new writers do to break into the business? Yes, we're always looking for new writers. To break into the business, I would say put together a great proposal. Don't *tell* me your project is unique, *show* me how it's unique. Show me your competition (despite what some may think, there is always competition for your book).
    How should writers approach you? Present material/packages to us in the mail. I also think that it's okay to do multiple submissions as long as you state that this is your intention at the end of your letter.

R

R

What are some common mistakes writers make? What really gets on your nerves? When writers do not proofread. Proofreading is more than just spell checking your document, you must actually read it. Misspelling and bad grammar will shoot a proposal down right away. Telling me that your book is the greatest book ever and that everyone will love it, we will for sure sell millions and millions of copies. Also letting me know that we will be extremely successful solely because of you and your book and that you will be willing to go on *Oprah* anytime.

What can writers do to get your attention and to avoid the slush pile? Get an agent.

What have been some of your best experiences with writers or in your job? I worked with an author named Hester Mundis who worked with Jack Hanna on a book called *Heart Songs with Animal Lovers.* It was a wonderful experience; she is a wonderful author to work with.

What, if anything, makes you different from other editors? I have spent most of my career as a writer; most editors haven't.

Is there anything that you would like to see changed in the industry? I wish we could publish more great writers rather than great writing. I wish that publishing houses could stick with writers longer. I would like to see publishing houses stop concentrating so much on the "hook" of the book rather than on the actual author.

Any advice for writers? If you are one of the people who is fortunate enough to get an editor, listen to him or her very, very carefully and ask lots of questions. Know exactly what your editor wants and make sure to get interviewed as much as possible.

Kevin Ireland, Managing Editor—New Ventures.

Born: June 26, 1952.

Education: B.A. in Music from the University of Connecticut and continuing education in publishing.

Employment history/editor career path: I started in newspapers in the 1970s in New York. I worked in the newspaper business for about 12 years. I have been with Rodale for about 8 years.

Personal interests: Athletics, exercise, building furniture, music, guitar, reading.

What would you be doing if you were not an editor? I would probably be running a small newspaper press or managing some kind of a small company.

What has been your most successful book that you have acquired to date? *Vinegar, Duct Tape, Milk Jugs & More* by the Editors of *Yankee* magazine has sold over 300,000 copies. *Martin Guitars: An Illustrated Celebration of America's Premier Guitar Maker* won the guitar book of the year award.

What books that you have acquired make you the most proud? What books that you have acquired reflect the types of books you like to represent? *Try and Make Me* by Bill O'Hanlon and Ray Levy; *Prayer, Faith, & Healing* by Winston Caine and Brian Coffman.

Do you represent fiction? No.

Do you represent nonfiction? Yes, parenting, teen publishing, relationships, romance, spirituality (most of which are small books 140–160 pages max.).

Do you require book proposals? If so, what do you look for in evaluating a book proposal? Yes, overview, competition, table of contents, sample chapters.

Are certain aspects of a book proposal given more weight than others? The overview, table of contents, and good writing.

What process do you use for making a decision? What is the process for acquisition, is there a committee? Yes, each editor will take projects he or she feels would be a good book before the editorial review committee. Rodale also does a lot of mail orders, so we do a lot of surveying.

What kinds of nonfiction books do you want to see less of? Projects that are trying to re-say something that has already been hammered to death.

Are you interested in work geared for the masses (readers of *People*, *The Star*, etc.)? No—Rodale looks for small niches and will try to meet the needs of those niches (women's and men's health issues, cooking, etc.).

Are agents important? Why? Yes, for certain types of books and for individual authors. Agents do a good job of pre-screening and giving editors high quality work.

Do you like new writers? What should new writers do to break into the business? Show a history of good writing and good publications.

How should writers approach you? Write me a simple letter or give a quick call.

What are some common mistakes writers make? What really gets on your nerves? Trying to be too clever. Not doing your homework on the material I like to see.

What can writers do to get your attention and to avoid the slush pile? Make a call to me before sending something in—ask me if the idea appeals to me and let me know it's coming.

What have been some of your craziest experiences with submissions? I once received a proposal from a man who was a priest and also worked part time for the CIA. I thought this was an odd combination.

What have been some of your best experiences with writers or in your job? Working on *Try and Make Me* has been a wonderful experience. They are wonderful authors, who have a wonderful agent with a wonderful book.

What, if anything, makes you different from other editors? I'm very concerned with saving the author's voice. My goal is to work with the author to develop a great book and have fun while doing it.

Is there anything you would like to see changed in the industry? I would like it to be more profitable. I would like to see more time for the editors to help develop the authors' and their material. We're relying more and more on agents to do editors' jobs because there is simply not enough time. I like to work with authors on editing their manuscripts for long periods of time to make it the best possible product that it can be, but sometimes it's just impossible to do so.

Any advice for writers? Try to find a fresh topic and a fresh perspective and develop a good proposal.

ROUTLEDGE (AN IMPRINT OF TAYLOR & FRANCIS BOOKS)

29 West 35th Street, New York, NY 10001-2299
212-216-7800   fax: 212-564-7854
www.routledge.com

Routledge accents current events, communications and media, cultural studies, education, self-improvement, world political and cultural studies, philosophical thought, economics, feminist theory, gender studies, history, and literary criticism. The house produces trade nonfiction and academic works.

Routledge produces adult nonfiction in the humanities and social sciences. Routledge specialties include projects that give a vanguard twist to topical issues. Routledge imprints include Theatre Arts Books.

Founded as Methuen Inc. (in 1977), and then as part of Routledge and Chapman and Hall (as a subsidiary of International Thompson Organization), the house held to the overall profile of a commercial publisher, abreast of trends in scholarship and general public interest, as it issued strong lines of trade and academic books. Routledge (with a concentration in the contemporary trade arena) and Chapman and Hall are today separate publishing companies. (Please see Chapman and Hall entry in this directory.) Routledge is now an imprint of Taylor & Francis Books.

Routledge titles: *Me Against My Brother* by Scott Peterson; *New Labour, New Language?* by Norman Fairclough; *The Almanac of British Politics,* 6th edition by Robert Waller and Bryon Criddle; *Vespasian* by Barbara Levick; *Handwriting of the Twentieth Century* by Rosemary Sassoon; *Liquid Pleasures: A Social History of Drinks in Modern Britain* by John Burnett; *Lost Innocents: A Follow-Up Study of Fatal Child Abuse* by Peter Reder and Sylvia Duncan; *Twin and Triplet Psychology: A Professional Guide to Working with Multiples* by Audrey Sandbank; *Punk Rock: So What? The Cultural Legacy of Punk Rock* by Roger Sabin; *TV Living: Television Culture and Everyday Life* by David Gauntiett and Anneaen Hill; *The Atlantic* by Paul Butel; and *101 Philosophy Problems* by Martin Cohen.

Query letters and SASEs should be directed to:

Linda Hollick, Vice President and Publisher

Bill Germano, Vice President and Publisher, Director—Humanities.

Sylvia Miller, Publishing Director—Reference.

Brendan O'Malley, Associate Editor—History.

Eric Nelson, Associate Editor—Politics.

Ilene Kalish, Editor—Sociology and women's studies.

Ken Wright, Vice President and Publishing Reference Director

Anne Davidson, Senior Editor

Richard Carlin, Editor—Music.

Joseph Miranda, Editor—Education.

David McBride, Editor—Geography/Urban studies.

Nick Street, Editor—Religion.

RUNNING PRESS BOOK PUBLISHERS

Running Press Books for Children

125 South 22nd Street, Philadelphia, PA 19103-4399
215-567-5080   fax: 215-568-2919
www.runningpress.com

Running Press shows flair in the areas of popular culture and arts, lifestyle, popular science, hobby how-to, and popular-interest reference titles. Running Press produces a singular line of specialty items that include bookstore-counter impulse-sales wares, striking free-standing exhibition units for kids' books, and a gleaming array of display and promotional titles (especially on the Courage Books imprint).

Running Press Book Publishers (founded in 1972) publishes hardcover and paper-back trade books in general nonfiction. The house, in addition, issues audiocassettes, stylized journals, diaries, bookplates, Miniature Editions, generously appointed educational-entertainment kits, and postcard books. Running Press products are associated with sleek production, as well as a sometimes humorous or insouciant air. Running Press maintains a solid backlist.

Sample Running Press titles: *Free to Be . . . You and Me,* and *Free to Be . . . a Family (a 25th Anniversary Celebration): Stories, Songs and Poems for Children and Adults to Enjoy Together* (conceived by Marlo Thomas, with introductions by Gloria Steinem and Letty Cottin Pogrebin); *The Art of Spooning: A Cuddler's Handbook* by Jim Grace and Lisa Goldblatt Grace; *The Vikings* by Fiona Macdonald; *Men Together: Portraits of Love, Commitment, and Life,* essays by Anderson Jones (photographs by David Fields); *The Expectant Father's Handbook: A Simple Guide to Your New Life* (edited by Greg Jones); *A Positive Life: Portraits of Women Living with HIV,* interviews by River Huston (photographs by Mary Berridge).

Running Press Miniature Edition books are delightful little books that fit in the palm of your hand. The list covers an astonishing range of subjects: *Passages: A Treasury of New Beginnings; Passion: Visions of Love, in Word and Image; Quotable Cats: The Quintessential Collection of Feline Wisdom; The Rolling Stone Book of Life: Wisdom for Survival* and *The Rolling Stone Book of Rock: An Alternative Treasury of Wisdom* (compiled by the Editors of Rolling Stone Press); *The Twelve Days of Christmas; The Nutcracker Keepsake Set.*

Courage Books is the promotional imprint of Running Press, producing eye-catching volumes that can be advertised by booksellers as attractive, reasonably priced items. Sample Courage titles: *Tiger Woods: A Pictorial Biography* by Hank Gola; *Diana: the People's Princess* by Peter Donnelly; *Mother Teresa: The Pictorial Biography; Streisand: The Pictorial Biography* by Diana Karanikas Harvey and Jackson Harvey; *The Flowering of American Folk Art 1776–1876* by Joan Lipman and Alice Winchester; *Mothers: A Loving Celebration* (edited by Tara Ann McFadden, with contributions by Mark Twain and Toni Morrison); *The Good Sex Book* by Dr. Paul Brown and Christine Kell.

Running Press participates in a joint publishing program with M. Shanken Communications, Inc., publishers of *Wine Spectator* and *Cigar Aficionado* magazines. Titles available: *California Wine: A Comprehensive Guide to the Wineries, Wines, Vintages and Vineyards of America's Premier Winegrowing State* by James Laube; *Ultimate Guide to Buying Wine; Guide to Great Wine Values $10 and Under; Buying Guide to Premium Cigars.*

Running Press distributes its own list. Query letters and SASEs should be directed to:

Brian Perrin, Associate Publisher

Carlo DeVito, Associate Publisher

Jennifer Worick, Editorial Director

Nancy Steele, Director of Acquisitions

Stuart Teacher, President

Running Press Books for Children

Running Press Books for Children features finely engineered pop-up books, foldouts, small-format editions, kits, coloring books, and how-to's—in stand-alone editions and numerous series.

Running Press created the Fit-A-Shape series (books for preschoolers that teach basic concepts using three-dimensional objects that fit matching shapes); the Gem series (captivating, fact-filled titles, each with vast amounts of information in a handy format); Five-Minute Mysteries (that test your powers of observation and deductive reasoning); Treasure Chests (expeditions into ancient cultures); Action Books (informative texts and components for exploring science and creating projects); Discovery Kits (read about a specific subject, such as a radio, then build your own); Book Buddy, created by Penny Dann (each title in this series features a die-cut corner where a soft-fabric Book Buddy lives); Start Collecting (each title includes a guide that explains the history of the category, famous specimens, a poster, and tips on how to begin collecting).

ST. MARTIN'S PRESS
(PART OF VERLAGSGRUPPE GEORG VON HOLTZBRINCK)

A. Wyatt Books

Bedford Books

Buzz Books

Forge

Orb

Picador USA

St. Martin's Griffin

St. Martin's Scholarly and Reference

St. Martin's Press Trade

Stonewall Inn Editions

A Thomas Dunne Book for St. Martin's Press

175 Fifth Avenue, New York, NY 10010
212-674-5151

St. Martin's publishes across the spectrum of trade nonfiction and hosts a wide range of popular and literary fiction. The house is particularly strong in a number of special areas, some with associated lines and imprints (including popular culture, international arts and letters, relationships, multicultural topics, science, business, and professional). St. Martin's is known for a strong list of scholarly and reference titles and offers a solid lineup of college textbooks. St. Martin's produces hardcover, trade paperback, and mass-market paper editions and also offers a line of calendars. The press produces a few works for younger readers.

St. Martin's Press is an international publisher with a broad and comprehensive program. St. Martin's is part of the German-based international communications conglomerate Verlagsgruppe Georg von Holtzbrinck. Within this framework, St. Martin's enjoys its long-standing tradition of editorial independence as it operates from its historic environs in Manhattan's famed Flatiron Building.

St. Martin's Press is home to an array of divisions and imprints, including Picador USA, Stonewall Inn Editions, Buzz Books, St. Martin's Griffin (a Thomas Dunne Book for St. Martin's Press), and St. Martin's Scholarly and Reference Books.

Picador USA is a St. Martin's imprint geared to the international literary and cultural scene. Picador publishes both originals and reprints. (Please see separate Picador USA subentry further on.)

St. Martin's was among the first commercial houses to highlight topflight entrants in the arena of lesbian, gay, and gender issues and interest. The house publishes noteworthy mainstream fiction and nonfiction in this vein, as well as works with a literary approach. (Please see the subentry for Stonewall Inn Editions.)

Buzz Books hooks into the current of contemporary culture. St. Martin's Griffin speaks to timely nonfiction and fiction titles in trade paperback. (Please see separate subentries elsewhere in this guide.)

A Thomas Dunne Book for St. Martin's Press represents an imprint with a personalized editorial dimension. (Please see separate subentries elsewhere in this guide.)

St. Martin's distributes its own books as well as those of such houses as Academy Editions, Amistad Press, Audio Renaissance and Renaissance Books, Boyds Mills Press, Consumer Reports Books, Rodale Press, Tor Books/Forge, Universe Publishing, and World Almanac.

Query letters and SASEs should be directed to:

Charles Spicer, Senior Editor—Commercial fiction: crime, suspense, mysteries. Nonfiction: true crime, biography, history. Titles include *The Other Mrs. Kennedy* by Jerry Oppenheimer; *Topping from Below* by Laura Reese; *The Rise and Fall of the British Empire* by Lawrence James.

Corin See, Associate Editor—reference; first novels; collection of comics; film.

Michael Connor, Assistant Editor—Pop culture, general nonfiction.

Elizabeth Beir, Editor—General nonfiction.

George Witte, Editor in Chief for St. Martin's Press: Quality literary fiction and nonfiction of literary or intellectual interest. Titles include *Farewell, I'm Bound to Leave You* by

Fred Chappell; *In the Deep Midwinter* by Robert Clark; *The River Beyond the World* by Janet Peery.

Heather Jackson, Editor—Commercial nonfiction of all stripes: health, nutrition, parenting, child care, popular reference, popular culture, psychology/self-help. Titles include *The Ten Commandments of Pleasure* by Susan Block, *The Kitchen Klutz* by Colleen Johnson.

Hope Dellon, Senior Editor—Fiction: mysteries, serious historical novels. Nonfiction: parenting, women's issues, psychology, biography. Titles include *Mary Queen of Scotland and the Isles* by Margaret George; *The Sculptress* by Minette Walters; *Beyond Jennifer and Jason* by Linda Rose.

Jennifer Weis, Executive Editor—Commercial fiction: women's, thrillers, romance. Commercial nonfiction: people books, narrative nonfiction, cookbooks, self-help, health and parenting, humor, popular culture. Projects include *Aaron Spelling: A Prime-Time Life* by Aaron Spelling.

John Sargent, Chairman, Editorial Director—Bestseller fiction, controversial current affairs.

Keith Kahla, Editor—Gay and lesbian interest, mystery and suspense, literary fiction, cartoon books, anthologies. Projects include *Murder on the Appian Way* by Steven Saylor; *Pawn to Queen Four* by Louis Eighner.

Kelley Ragland, Associate Editor—Commercial and serious nonfiction. Literary nonfiction, especially related to women's or racial issues, also including parenting, psychology, biography; essays. Popular and literary fiction: a wide range of mysteries, thrillers, suspense.

Linda McFall, Editor

Marian Lizzi, Editor—Nonfiction: popular culture, women's issues, popular history, self-improvement, and an occasional cookbook. Titles include *Funk: The Music, the People, and the Rhythm of the One* by Rickey Vincent; *Welcome to the Jungle* by Geoffrey Holtz.

Matthew J. Shear, Vice President and Publisher, Mass-Market Division—All mass-market categories in fiction and nonfiction.

Michael Denneny, Senior Editor—Literary nonfiction and fiction. Gay and lesbian subjects.

Michael Connor, Assistant Editor—Pop culture, general nonfiction.

Sally Richardson, President and Publisher, Trade Division; President, Mass Market Division.

Jennifer Enderlin, Senior Editor—Women's fiction, psychological suspense, general commercial fiction. Commercial nonfiction (sex, relationships, psychology). Projects include *To Build the Life You Want, Create the Work You Love* by Marsha Sinetar.
  Born: June 10, 1967.
  Education: B.A., in English from University of New Hampshire.
  Employment history/editor career path: Started at Putnam/Berkley in 1989; moved to NAL/Dutton in 1991; moved to SMP in 1993.
  Personal interests: Travel.

What would you be doing if you were not an editor? I'd still be reading if I weren't an editor. But maybe only 10 books a week. I'd like to work in a spa—it's the nurturing side of me.

What has been your most successful book that you have acquired to date? *High Five* by Janet Evanovich; *Never Be Lied to Again* by Dr. David Lieberman.

Do you represent fiction? If so, what do you look for? Yes. Commercial women's fiction.

Do you represent nonfiction? Yes.

Are agents important? Why? Yes. I love agents! They bring me great projects and they work hard. After all, they have to do the two hardest things on earth, seek (projects) and sell (projects).

Do you like new writers? What should new writers do to break into the business? Writers are some of the most hilarious, wonderful, inventive, intelligent people around. I feel privileged that I can work with them. On the downside, they can often be insecure, needy, unappreciative, and arrogant! But I'm sure they would say the same thing about editors.

Is there anything you would like to see changed in the industry? I would change dismal entry-level publishing salaries so that we don't lose the best and the brightest to the Internet.

Any additional thoughts? I love the fact that I get to read for a living! I love discovering new writers. I love seeing a book I've fought for, work in the marketplace. I hate the fact that every single weekend is occupied by work. People don't seem to understand that I do not read or edit in the office. Every submission is read at home, every bit of editing is done on the weekends. "Part 2" of my job begins weeknights at 7:30 P.M. and for 8 to 10 hours per day on the weekends.

Buzz Books

Productions from St. Martin's Buzz Books imprint often share the West Coast ambiance of copublisher *Buzz* magazine. Areas include: autobiography/biography, music, current culture, fiction.

Picador USA

St. Martin's Press initiated the Picador USA imprint during the last part of 1994, and the house was an immediate industry presence, with an array of titles featuring an international cast of world-class writers. Picador USA (along with its sibling Picador United Kingdom imprint) publishes in hardcover and trade paperback editions, and highlights original titles as well as reprints.

Picador marketing support encompasses dynamic full-scale promotion and advertising campaigns, author publicity, exposure via major book and literary reviews, and author tours.

Representative Picador nonfiction: *Twilight of the Wagners* by Gottfried Wagner; and *A Short History of Rudeness* by Mark Caldwell.

From the Picador fiction portfolio: *In the Deep Midwinter* by Robert Clark; *Little* by David Treuer; *Blackwater* by Kerstin Ekman; *Behind the Scenes at the Museum* by Kate Atkinson; *Winterkill* by Craig Lesley; *Bitter Grounds* by Sandra Benitez; *The Red Tent* by Anita Diament; *Quarantine* by Jim Crace; *Brain Storm* by Richard Dooling.

Backlist favorites: *The Romantic Movement: Sex, Shopping and the Novel* by Alain de Botton; *Rotten: No Irish, No Blacks, No Dogs* by John Lydon with Keith and Kent Zimmerman; *The Dog with the Chip in His Neck: Essays from NPR and Elsewhere* by Andrei Codrescu; *Voodoo Dreams: A Novel of Marie Laveau* by Jewell Parker Rhodes; *Henry and Clara* by Thomas Mellon; and *The Bird Artist* by Howard Norman.

Query letters and SASEs should be directed to:

Frances Coady, Publisher—Picador USA.

Diane Higgins, Editor—Picador USA.

Reagan Arthur, Senior Editor, Picador USA—Contemporary fiction, women's fiction, media-related pop-culture, nonfiction. Works with the Picador USA imprint. *No Logo* by Naomi Klein; *The Country Life* by Rachel Cust; *Flying Leap* by Judy Buduirz.

St. Martin's Griffin

St. Martin's Griffin publishes exclusively trade paperbacks, with a strong emphasis in crafts, cooking, nutrition and fitness, modern and contemporary fiction, current culture, biography, and travel. Griffin authors include Douglas Coupland, Studs Terkel, Doris Kearns-Goodwin, Vincent Scully, James Baldwin, and Bob Dylan. Griffin reprints a preferred selection of St. Martin's hardcover originals in trade-paper editions.

Titles from Griffin: *Bread Machine Magic* by Linda Rehberg and Lois Conway; *The Cancer Prevention Diet* by Michio Kushi; *Critical Path* by R. Buckminster Fuller; *Nancy Drew Scrapbook* by Karen Plunkett-Powell; *England's Dreaming* by Jon Savage; *Generation X* by Douglas Coupland; *Route 66* by Michael Wallis; *Vurt* by Jeff Noon; *The World's Most Famous Math Problem* by Marilyn Vos Savant.

Travel titles include the Let's Go Series, with some 24 new, updated, and revised titles a year, plus 6 map guides.

St. Martin's Press Trade

St. Martin's (founded in 1952) publishes within all major trade and popular reference categories. Combined with the house's enterprising commercial spirit, St. Martin's shows remarkable depth and strength across its entire program. The house issues a hefty seasonal frontlist and maintains a strong backlist.

Areas of St. Martin's nonfiction interest include current events, popular culture, true crime, cookbooks, business, sports, biography, self-awareness and self-improvement, popular science and psychology, travel and the outdoors, and gardening. St. Martin's instituted a collaborative editorial operation with West Coast–based *Buzz* magazine to develop high-interest titles in the contemporary current-culture arena.

In fiction and literature, St. Martin's publishes top-of-the-line commercial works and is a leader in such genres as mysteries, thrillers, suspense titles, and historical works, as well as selected science fiction and fantasy, along with some contemporary Westerns (most often in the action-adventure or suspense modes). (For more information regarding category fiction, especially science fiction, fantasy, futurist adventure, horror, and Westerns, please see separate main entry for the St. Martin's affiliate Tor Books.) The publisher's roster embraces cultural biographies and criticism, as well as poetic works and short-story collections.

Nonfiction from St. Martin's: *Fighting Fire* by Caroline Paul; *Death of a Princess: The Investigation* by Thomas Sancton and Scott Macloed; *The Excruciating History of Dentistry: Toothsome Tales and Oral Oddities from Babylon to Braces* by James Wynbrandt; *20/20 Insight: 6 Keys to Transform Relationships, Resolve Conflict, and Achieve Success* by Randy Gibbs; *Hastened to the Grave: The Gypsy Murder Investigation* by Jack Olsen; *Mama Drama: Making Peace with the One Woman Who Can Push Your Buttons, Make You Cry, and Drive You Crazy* by Denise McGregor; *Heartwiseguy: How to Live the Good Life After a Heart Attack* by Gary Cartwright; *Calculus Made Easy* by Sylvanus P. Thompson and Martin Gardner; *The Last Patrician: Bobby Kennedy and the End of the American Aristocracy* by Michael Knox Beran; *Confirmation: The Hard Evidence of Aliens Among Us* by Whitley Streiber; *Good Loving, Men's Health Life Improvement Guide #11: Keys to a Lifetime of Passion, Pleasure, and Sex* by Donna Raskin, Larry Keller, and the Editors of Men's Health Books; *Making Flawless Cabinets and Built-Ins* by Nick Engler; *Dancing with God: Americans Who Have Been Touched by the Divine* by Steve Wall; *The King's English: Guide to Modern Usage* by Kingsley Amis; *Dogs: The Ultimate Care Guide; From Aging and Barking to Paw Protectors and Weather, the Most Complete Guide to Raising a Healthy, Well-Adjusted Dog* (edited by Matthew Hoffman); *Lost Fathers: The Politics of Fatherlessness* (edited by Cynthia R. Daniels); *Crossing the Jordan: Israel's Road to Peace* by Samuel Segev; *Subterranean Kerouac: The Hidden Life of Jack Kerouac* by Ellis Amburn.

St. Martin's frontlist fiction and popular literature: *Fortunes of War* by Stephen Coonts; *Hitler's Angel: A Novel* by Kris Rusch; *Faraday's Popcorn Factory* by Sandra Lee Gould; *Sappho: The Tenth Muse* by Nancy Freedman; *Four to Score: A Stephanie Plum Novel* by Janet Evanovich; *The Stalking of Sheilah Quinn: A Legal Thriller* by Jeremiah Healy; *An Arrow's Flight: A Novel* by Mark Merlis; *In a Child's Eye: A Novel of Suspense* by Tim Wilson; *Articles of Faith: A Thriller* by Robert L. Rodin; *The Gilded Lily* by Helen Argers; *Stately Pursuits* by Katie Fforde; *Object of Your Love: Stories* by Dorothy Speak; *Going Home Again* by Howard Waldrop; *Blood Money* by Clive Egleton.

St. Martin's presents a rich and varied lineup in the arena of mystery, suspense, and thrillers. The list features stand-alone works as well as ongoing series, published in hardcover and trade paper. Dead Letter is St. Martin's sobriquet for an adventurous, eclectic, commercial mass-market paperback list of mystery and suspense, including reprints of successful hardcover titles.

Titles from St. Martin's list in mysteries, suspense fiction, and thrillers: *Invitation to a Funeral: A Tale of Restoration Intrigue* by Molly Brown; *The Doctor Digs a Grave* by Robin Hathaway; *The Mango Opera* by Tom Corcoran; *The Subtle Serpent: A Sister Fidelma Mystery* by Peter Tremayne; *Only Flesh and Bones* by Sarah Andrews; *Cutter's Run: A Brady Coyne Mystery* by William G. Tapply; *Wicked Games* by Ellen Hart; *Faithful Until Death: A Chief Inspector Barnaby Novel* by Caroline Graham; *Without Prejudice* by Nicola Williams.

S

St. Martin's Scholarly and Reference

St. Martin's Scholarly and Reference division publishes works pertinent to particular professional and academic fields and disciplines, as well as a select group of titles with mainstream-crossover potential keyed to areas of the house's core publishing program.

Areas of St. Martin's Scholarly and Reference publishing scope include: arts and humanities, the sciences, history, biography, politics and economics, regional studies and travel, essay and commentary.

Some titles here: *Auden and Isherwood: The Berlin Years* by Norman Page; *Spaghetti Westerns: Cowboys and Europeans from Karl May to Sergio Leone* by Christopher Frayling; *A Place in the Sun? Women Writers in Twentieth-Century Cuba* by Catherine Davies; *Diasporic Citizenship: Haitian Americans in Transnational America* by Michael S. Laguerre; *Past Imperfect, Future Uncertain: The United Nations at Fifty* (edited by Ramesh Thakur); *Image and Representation: Key Concepts in Media Studies* by Nick Lacey; *Art of Interruption: Realism, Photography, and the Everyday* by John Roberts; *The New Patricians: An Essay on Values and Consciousness* by R. W. K. Paterson; *Capital Accumulation and Women's Labor in Asian Economies* by Peter Custers; *Female Genesis: Creativity, Self, and Gender* by Nicole Ward Jouve.

Stonewall Inn Editions

Stonewall Inn Editions publishes works with a lesbian and gay cultural slant in hardcover and paperback editions. The house addresses such trade areas as current events and public interest, reference works, cultural affairs, literary anthologies, Stonewall Inn Studio Books (featuring graphically lavish and luxuriously produced gift volumes), and the Stonewall Inn Mysteries line. The scope of St. Martin's lesbian- and gay-interest list is not limited to works issued under the Stonewall Inn imprint.

Featured Stonewall Inn authors have included such lights as Quentin Crisp, Larry Kramer, Paul Monette, Ethan Mordden, Denise Ohio, Randy Shilts, Edmund White, and Mark Richard Zubro.

Popular titles from Stonewall Inn: *The Violet Quill Reader: The Emergence of Gay Writing After Stonewall* (edited by David Bergman); *Sportsdykes: Stories from On and Off the Field* by Susan Fox Rogers; *Dark Wind: A True Account of Hurricane Gloria's Assault on Fire Island* by John Jiler; *Another Dead Teenager* (a Paul Turner mystery) by Mark Richard Zubro; *Sacred Lips of the Bronx* (a love story) by Douglas Sadonick; *End of the Empire* (visionary romance-adventure) by Denise Ohio.

A Thomas Dunne Book for St. Martin's Press

In Thomas Dunne's more than 25 years at St. Martin's Press, he has published virtually every kind of book, from runaway bestsellers such as *The Shell Seekers* by Rosamunde Pilcher, and *River God* by Wilbur Smith, to the critically acclaimed nonfiction of Robert Kaplan and Juliet Barker. The Thomas Dunne imprint produces roughly 150 titles per year and covers a wide array of interests that include: commercial fiction, mysteries, military histories, biographies, divination systems, politics, philosophy, humor, literary fiction, and current events.

Titles from Thomas Dunne: *A Passion for Golf: Fifty Years of the Best Golf Writing* (edited by Schuyler Bishop, foreword by Arnold Palmer); *The Bordeaux Atlas and Encyclopedia of Chateaux* by Hubrecht Duijker and Michael Broadbent; *Hemingway's Chair* by Michael Palin; *West of Paradise* by Gwen Davis; *A Shoot in Cleveland: A Milan Jacovich Mystery* by Les Roberts; *The Human Sexes* by Desmond Morris; *Superhero: A Biography of Christopher Reeve* by Chris Nickson; *Reeling in Russia: An Angler's Journey* by Fen Montaigne; *Gin Lane: A Novel of Southampton* by James Brady; *Bite-Size Twain: Wit and Wisdom from the Literary Legend* (compiled by John P. Holms and Karin Baji); *Encyclopedia of Hell* by Miriam Van Scott; *The Brutal Friendship: The West and the Arab Elite* by Saïd K. Aburish.

From the Thomas Dunne line of mystery, suspense, and thriller titles: *Time and Trouble* by Gilliam Roberts; *The Audubon Quartet: A Jonathon Wilder Mystery* by Ray Sipherd; *A Death of Distinction* by Marjorie Eccles; *A Double Coffin* by Gwendoline Butler; *The House by the Side of the Road* by Jan Gleiter; *Murder on Fifth Avenue* by Michael Jahn; *Canaletto and the Case of the Westminster Bridge* by Janet Laurence; *The Shanghai Murders: A Mystery of Love and Irony* by David Rotenberg.

Query letters and SASEs should be directed to:

Thomas L. Dunne, Vice President, Executive Editor, Publisher, A Thomas Dunne Book for St. Martin's Press—Eclectic interests; projects have covered commercial women's fiction, mysteries, military histories, biographies, divination systems, politics, philosophy, humor, literary fiction, current events.

Peter Wolverton, Senior Editor and Associate Publisher, A Thomas Dunne Book for St. Martin's Press—Fiction: Commercial and popular literature, genre mysteries. Nonfiction: Wide range consistent with the Thomas Dunne list; sports—golf, football.

Carin Siegfried, Editorial Assistant, Thomas Dunne/St. Martin's Press—Literary fiction.

Ruth Cavin, Senior Editor; Associate Publisher, A Thomas Dunne Book for St. Martin's Press—Crime fiction, contemporary fiction, anecdotal science and medicine novelties (quotation books). Titles include *The Beekeeper's Apprentice* by Laurie R. King; *Whoever Fights Monsters* by Robert Ressler; *Four Hands* by Paco Ignacio Taibo II.

Sign: Libra.

Employment history/editor career path: St. Martin's Press, 1988 to present; Walker Books 1979–1988; Two Continents Publishing, 1975–1979, freelance writer, Editor, author.

Personal interests: Theater, travel, children/grandchildren, people.

What would you be doing if you were not an editor? If it weren't that family problems prevent it, I would travel. I would probably also write. But I intend to keep my day job, because I love it. They will have to throw me or carry me out.

What has been the most successful book that you have acquired to date? I would have to look at the numbers, but what comes to mind is: Nonfiction: *Whoever Fights Monsters*, Robert K. Ressler and Tom Shachtman, Fiction: *A Grave Talent*, Laurie King.

What books have you acquired that make you the most proud? What books that you have acquired reflect the types of books you like to represent? I'm proud of a great many of them. I publish almost 50 books a year and have done so for the last dozen years; it would be too difficult to list them all. The only ones I'm considerably less proud of are those that were mistakes in judgment, in the sense that I saw potential I thought could be realized but wasn't, because the author and I could not agree, or the author was not able to do what I expected. But there are only a few of those. There are also books that I am certainly not ashamed of but that I publish because I know people want them rather than that I would give them "A for Excellence." The types of books I like to represent are anything as varied, very well written, and imaginative as *Charles Todd: A Test of Wills* or *Afterzen* by Janwillem van de Wetering or *Volcano Cowboys* by Dick Thompson. I look for good books, fiction or nonfiction, that I feel are well worth reading, that others will enjoy, and that have a reasonable chance of commercial success.

Do you represent fiction? Yes, I publish fiction. Some mainstream novels, but it is difficult to launch a new mainstream novel unless something about it will help to sell it; if the author is known for something else, or if the house is very high on it and will spend money promoting it. David Corn's first novel, *Deep Background,* sold well because it's a terrific book, David had published a successful nonfiction book previously, his name is known as the longtime Washington editor of *The Nation,* he knows people whose "blurb" will impress bookstores and readers, it got terrific reviews, and David himself is a familiar on political talk shows. And even then, the book did only moderately well—but well above the usual for a first novel. Yet hope springs eternal, and if there is a wonderful book of fiction like *This Is Graceanne's Book* by P. L. Whitney or *Jenny Rose* by Mary Anne Kelly or *My Darling Elia* by Eugenie Melnyk, I publish it. Of course, all three authors have been published as mystery writers before. I have published novels from some "names"—for example, Herbert Gold, Jerome Charyn. You do keep trying if you believe in the book and the author understands not to give up that day job. Category books like mysteries are easier to get out there when the author is unknown, because people who follow the category are actively looking for new writers and protagonists. I look for individuality, imagination, a fresh voice.

What do you want to see less of? Mysteries just like a hundred others.

Do you represent nonfiction? Yes, I publish nonfiction.

Do you require book proposals? If so, what do you look for in evaluating a book proposal? I require something, either a proposal, an outline, a writing sample, or a full manuscript. I will buy nonfiction on a proposal if the subject is one I think will find an audience, the author has some kind of credentials for writing about that subject, and I have an outline and enough writing sample to be confident about the author's style. I will not buy fiction on a proposal except from authors whose work I have published previously and know well, but if an author or agent wants to submit an outline and three chapters I will be able to tell whether I want to see the complete manuscript.

Are certain aspects of a book proposal given more weight than others? I suppose in nonfiction the subject/the content. But the outline and the writing style are very important.

What process do you use for making a decision? What is the process for acquisition, is there a committee? I read the proposal or manuscript. I sometimes ask colleagues for an opinion, although I don't always. I ask for the author's track record; other books published and sales and subrights figures if any, reviews, other writing background, publicity possibilities. (A good agent gives you these without being asked.) I then discuss the book and its attributes with my boss, Tom Dunne, and we arrive at a figure for an offer, with some knowledge of what to include in any necessary negotiation. If the money is more than usual, we get an estimated P & L from sales, production, and accounting and also consult our publisher and others in the house.

What kinds of nonfiction books do you want to see less of? I want to see nothing of inspirational, religious, psychological self-help, beauty, slimming diet, celebrity bios, all that commercial stuff that I know brings in a lot of money but isn't for me.

Are you interested in work geared for the masses (readers of *People, The Star,* etc.)? No way.

Are agents important? Why? Yes, because the good ones winnow out the chaff and also know which editor is interested in what kinds of books. They understand the business and can be easier than an inexperienced author to deal with. But I also look at nonagented work.

Do you like new writers? What should new writers do to break into the business? It's not a question of like or not like. It's harder, of course; they have no following. But if their books are good and I feel they have a chance of selling, I'll be delighted. If new writers want to write fiction, they have a better shot for publication by writing category books than mainstream, but they have to listen to their own desires.

How should writers approach you? Send a proposal or manuscript addressed to me. Be prepared to wait for an answer; I get hundreds of submissions. Do not call and ask if I've read it; when I've read it, you'll know. The call just puts it off further, when it is one of many. Do not send a query letter and nothing else for a work of fiction, there's no way I can judge fiction from a query letter unless the plot description is so incredibly awful it rules out any desire to see the rest. It's easy to describe a plot, but a book made from that story can be dreadful or marvelous and there's no way a letter can indicate that.

What are some common mistakes writers make? What really gets on your nerves? If you mean in the actual writing, I can't say, except if they don't use some imagination instead of the same old same old. Some of the physical details really get on my nerves. Such as, giving me a pitch on how this book is going to be the grandest blockbuster of a bestseller I've ever published. Sending cover designs along. Not numbering the pages consecutively (numbering each chapter separately instead.) Single-spacing. Sending the book in a heavy and unwieldy binder, using expensive paper that makes the manuscript twice as heavy as good old copier paper. (Editors have to schlep the books around— home, to the baseball game, anywhere they can find a little time to read it.) Not keeping a copy for themselves in case we lose the one they sent.

What can writers do to get your attention and to avoid the slush pile? If a submission is addressed to me by my name, it will not land in the slush pile. I don't guarantee to read it all the way through, but it will get a read of a large enough section to let me know whether or not it is something I want to pursue further.

What have been some of your craziest experiences with submissions? Annoying and funny: A woman who had the whole U.S. postal system looking for a manuscript we returned, not because she didn't have a copy (that would just have been a tragedy) but because she was sure that we had stolen it and were going to make a fortune by publishing it under our name. (This, I shall say gently, was highly unlikely even if we were inclined to cheat an author.) Sad: The factory worker who drove all the way overnight from somewhere in the Midwest to deliver by hand a (quite promising) six-page or so proposal for a memoir and was then going back that night so he could go to work the next day.

What have been some of your best experiences with writers or in your job? Above all, working for and with Tom Dunne. Meeting wonderful, very generous, interesting, and varied authors, so many that I can't start naming them here.

What, if anything, makes you different from other editors? Old age.

Is there anything you would like to see changed in the industry? Yes. I would like to see the publishers take the $27,000 they spend on a full-page ad in the *New York Times* to tell us about a book that has already six million copies out and use the money to bring some fine authors to the attention they are not getting and that they deserve. I'd like to find a way of convincing the reading public how their lives will be enriched if they raise their standards of and demands for good writing.

Any advice for writers? Writing a book is more than putting words down on paper; it requires a lot of thinking, a lot of discernment, constant observation of the way people behave, reading but not aping, and the primary motive: you must want to write that book. Wanting to have a published book is not enough, and wanting to make a fortune with a bestseller is adolescent and a futile way to go about it. Don't give up your day job.

SASQUATCH BOOKS

615 Second Avenue, Suite 260, Seattle, WA 98101
206-467-4300   fax: 206-467-4301
www.sasquatchbooks.com   e-mail: books@sasquatchbooks.com

Sasquatch specializes in books on travel, regional interest, gardening, guidebooks, nature, the outdoors, and food and wine. Sasquatch is broadening its Pacific Northwest regional concentration to include California. Additional areas of Sasquatch interest include literary nonfiction, especially in subject areas related to the house's core interests.

Sasquatch Books (founded in 1979) is known for a string of small-press successes. Among these: the Best Places travel series (Northwest Best Places; Northern California Best Places), the Cascadia Gardening series, and the Art Wolfe photo books.

Books from Sasquatch: *Watertrail: The Hidden Path Through Puget Sound* by Joel W. Rogers; *The Garden in Bloom: Plants & Wisdom for the Year-Round Gardener in the Pacific Northwest* by Ann Lovejoy; *Native Peoples of Alaska: A Traveler's Guide to Land, Art, and Culture* by Jan Halliday, with Patricia J. Petrivelli and the Alaska Native Heritage Center; *Inside Passage Walking Tours: Exploring Major Ports of Call in Southeast Alaska* by Julianne Chase; *Field Guide to North American Bison: A Natural History and Viewing Guide to the Great Plains Buffalo* by Robert Stellquist; *Slug Tossing and Other Adventures of a Reluctant Gardener* by Meg Descamp.

Titles in the Best Places series: *Inside Out Oregon: A Best Places Guide to the Outdoors* by Terry Richard; *Northwest Budget Traveler: Cheap Eats, Cheap Sleeps, Affordable Adventure* (edited by Nancy Leson); *The Northwest Best Places Cookbook: Recipes from the Outstanding Restaurants and Inns of Washington, Oregon, and British Columbia* by Cynthia Nims and Lori McKean.

Sasquatch Books is distributed through a network of regional sales representatives. Jennie McDonald can be reached at Sasquatch Books, 1563 Solano Avenue, Box 364, Berkeley, CA, 94707. Query letters and SASEs should be directed to:

Gary Luke, Editorial Director

Jennie McDonald, Senior Editor

Kate Rogers, Senior Editor

SCHOLASTIC

555 Broadway, New York, NY 10012
212-343-6100

Scholastic publishes quality hardcover picture books, middle grade and young adult fiction, and some nonfiction.

The house publishes not only trade hardcover, but also educational lines in hardcover and paperback editions, and owns a solid niche in electronic publishing. In addition, Scholastic, Prep. (founded in 1920) issues magazines, operates classroom book clubs, and offers computer software.

Scholastic's high-end hardcover imprints include Blue Sky Press, Scholastic Press and Acedina Books. Cartwheel publishes board books and novelties for pre-K.

Scholastic created the Literacy Place and Solares lines: These two core-curriculum reading and language-arts programs are for English and Spanish languages. Scholastic spent six years developing these programs because the publishers believe that teachers and children need and deserve a coherent plan of skills development (including phonics), better assessment, and, of course, the best children's literature.

Wiggleworks and Wiggleworks Español for grades K–2 (a complete early literacy system) are geared to raise reading scores. These programs use books and other educational technology that help emerging readers develop fluency, confidence, and control by reading, writing, listening, and speaking.

Solares is an innovative K–6 reading and language program in Spanish. Children read a wide variety of quality fiction that includes works originally written in Spanish, as well as classics translated from English and other languages. Solares provides a solid foundation for literacy through a program of explicit, intentional skills instruction that includes phonics.

The house accepts no unsolicited manuscripts, and the acquisitions personnel deal only with published writers or agented material. Scholastic handles its own distribution. Picture book manuscripts, query letters and SASEs should be directed to:

Dianne Hess, Executive Editor

Elizabeth Szabla, Editorial Director

Tracy Mack, Senior Editor

SCRIBNER

Rawson Associates

1230 Avenue of the Americas, New York, NY 10020
212-698-7000

Scribner publishes trade fiction and nonfiction, with much of the list devoted to authoritative and accomplished writing. Scribner nonfiction covers current events, cultural history, biography, criticism, science, true crime, and popular reference. Scribner is home to Lisa Drew Books, a feature line with an especially hard-hitting commercial approach to frontlist publishing. The Rawson Associates imprint concentrates on self-awareness, health, and business books (see subentry further on). Fiction from Scribner embraces the range of commercial literary interests and tastes; the house is particularly strong (and admired) in crime fiction and hosts a number of ongoing mystery series.

Scribner often acquires hard/soft with other S&S divisions, including Touchstone, Fireside, and the Scribner Paperback Fiction imprint, as well as with Pocket Books.

The Scribner list bears the name as well as the midnight-reader's oil-lamp logo of the former Charles Scribner's Sons, Publishers, originally an independent firm (founded in 1846). The house subsequently became part of Macmillan; following the acquisition of Macmillan by Simon & Schuster, much of the Macmillan trade operation was taken over by the Scribner program. In addition, remnants of the former Atheneum imprint were added to the Scribner lineup.

Nonfiction titles from Scribner: *Wild Thoughts from Wild Places* by David Quammen; *Star Spangled Men: America's Ten Worst Presidents* by Nathan Miller; *Everyone's Children: A Pediatrician's Story of an Inner-City Practice* by Caire McCarthy, M.D.; *Clement Greenberg: A Life* by Florence Rubenfield; *Rick Bayless's Mexican Kitchen: Recipes and Techniques for World-Class Cuisine* by Rick Bayless; *Wyman's Gardening Encyclopedia* by Donald Wyman; *Spiritual Literacy: Reading the Sacred in Everyday Life* by Frederic and Mary Ann Brussat; *Our Times* (edited and with new material by Dan Rather, based on the landmark series by Mark Sullivan); *A History of American Life* (edited by Arthur M. Schlessinger, Sr., and Dixon Ryan Fox, abridged and revised by Marc C. Carnes and Arthur M. Schlessinger, Jr., with introduction by Arthur M. Schlessinger, Jr.).

Of popular note: *Coyote Medicine: Lessons from Native American Healing* by Lewis Mehl-Madrona; *Dog Eat Dog: A Very Human Book about Dogs and Dog Shows* by Jane and Michael Stern; *Don't Stand Here: Single Mothers and the Myth of the Welfare Queen* by David Zucchino; *Awakening to Zen Teachings* by Roshi Philip Kapleau; *Letitia Baldrige's More Than Manners: Raising Today's Kids to Have Good Manners & Kind Hearts* by Letitia Baldrige; *Bill James' Guide to Baseball Managers: From 1870 to Present* by Bill James; *Serious Business: Cartoons in America from Betty Boop to Toy Story* by Stefan Kanfer; *The Trouble with Testosterone, and Other Essays on the Biology of the Human Predicament* by Robert M. Sapolsky; *Jimmy Carter: A Comprehensive Biography from Plains to Post-Presidency* by Peter G. Bourne; *Prescription for Profits: How the Pharmaceutical Industry Bankrolled the Unholy Marriage Between Science and Business* by Linda Marsa.

Scribner fiction and literary writing includes: *Nobody's Girl: A Novel* by Antonya Nelson; *Blueback: A Contemporary Fable* by Tim Winton; *The Fiery Pantheon: A Novel* by Nancy Lemann; *Spending: A Novel* by Mary Gordon; *Time on My Hands: A Novel with Photographs* by Peter Delacorte; *Accordion Crimes* (novel) by E. Annie Proulx; *Sanctuary: A Tale of Life in the Woods* by Paul Monette (illustrated by Vivienne Flesher); *The Dogs of Winter* by Kem Nunn; *Off the Face of the Earth* by Aljean Harmetz; *The Rescue of Memory* by Cheryl Sucher; *Terrestrials: A Novel of Aviation* by Paul West.

Mystery, suspense, and crime fiction from Scribner (no alibis will hold if you maintain these genres are in all ways literary): *Once Too Often: An Inspector Luke Thanet Novel* by Dorothy Simpson; *A Corpse by Any Other Name: A Stokes Moran Mystery* by Neil Mc-Gaughey; *Likely to Die* by Linda Fairstein; *A Deadly Vineyard Holiday* (a Martha's Vineyard mystery) by Philip R. Craig; *Giotto's Hand* (a Jonathan Argyll mystery) by Iain Pears; *Three to Get Deadly* (a Stephanie Plum novel) by Janet Evanovich; *Doubled in Spades* (a Cassandra Swann mystery) by Susan Moody; *Past Tense* (a John Marshall Tanner novel) by Stephen Greenleaf; *Caught in a Rundown* (a novel introducing Jewel Averick and Dee Sweet) by Lisa Saxton; *Full Frontal Murder* (a mystery with Marian Larch) by Barbara Paul; *Hard Bargain* (a Cat Marsala mystery) by Barbara D'Amato.

Lisa Drew Books hones a select list in the area of current events and high-interest nonfiction, along with some popular fiction. From Lisa Drew: *Obsession: The FBI's Legendary Profiler Probes the Psyches of Killers, Rapists, Stalkers and Their Victims and Tells How to Fight Back* by John Douglas and Mark Olshaker; *The Right Women: A Journey Through the Heart of Conservative America* by Elinor Burkett; *You Won—Now What?: How Americans Can Make Democracy Work from City Hall to the White House* by Taegan D. Goddard and Christopher Riback.

Query letters and SASEs should be directed to:

Bill Rosen, Simon & Schuster Editions; Vice President and Associate Publisher—Projects include *The Woven Figure* by George F. Will; *The Middle East* by Bernard Lewis.

Gillian Blake, Senior Editor—Commercial and literary fiction and nonfiction consistent with the Scribner list. Projects include *For Colored Girls Who Have Considered Suicide/When the Rainbow Is Enuf* by Ntozake Shange.

Jane Rosenman, Senior Editor—Literary fiction, commercial nonfiction. Projects include *Good Meat* by Bruce Aidelis and Denis Kelly; *Name-Dropping* by Alan King; *There's a Word for It!* by Charles Harrington Elster.

Leigh Haber, Senior Editor—Literary fiction. Nonfiction consistent with house description. Projects include *The Year of Reading Proust* by Phyllis Rose; *The Skull of Charlotte Corday and Other Stories* by Leslie Dick; *Eating Chinese Food Naked* by Mei Ng; *Go Now* by Richard Hell.

Lisa Drew, Publisher, Lisa Drew Books—Commercial nonfiction, including high-interest history, celebrity biographies, and current affairs. Popular fiction. Titles include *George Bush: The Life of a Lone Star Yankee* by Herbert S. Parmet; *Michael and Natasha: The Life and Love of Michael II, the Last of the Romanov Tsars* by Rosemary and Donald Crawford.

Nan Graham, Vice President and Editor in Chief—American literary fiction; fiction about clashing cultures, Third World and European. Nonfiction interests include contemporary social and political issues, women's studies, historical and literary biography, and biographies of artists.

Susan Moldow, Publisher—Areas consistent with house interest. Projects include *The Illusionist* by Dinitia Smith; *The Color Code* by Taylor Hartman, Ph.D.; *Three Gospels* by Reynolds Price.

Susanne Kirk, Vice President/Senior Editor, Scribner/Simon & Schuster—Mystery and suspense fiction. Titles include *Déjà Dead* by Kathy Reichs; *Dreaming of the Bones* by

S

Deborah Crombie; *Tequila Mockingbird* by Paul Bishop; *Final Jeopardy* by Linda Fairstein; *Death on a Vineyard Beach* by Philip R. Craig.

Education: A.B., Smith College; M.S., Columbia University.

Employment history/editor career path: 25 years at Scribner; 3 years at Tuttle in Tokyo.

What would you be doing if you were not an editor? I would be a journalist.

What has been your most successful book that you have acquired to date? Patricia Cornwell's first six novels.

What books have you acquired that make you the most proud? What books that you have acquired reflect the types of book you like to represent? I specialize in crime fiction, although I am open to both general fiction and nonfiction.

Do you represent fiction? If so, what do you look for? Yes. Excellent writing and originality of voice and plot.

What do you want to see less of? Routine work. To make our small list, it must be something special.

Do you represent nonfiction? Yes.

Do you require book proposals? If so, what do you look for in evaluating book proposals? Yes, for nonfiction. Superior writing and structure. The author with the most credentials for the project.

What process do you use for making a decision? What is the process for acquisition, is there a committee? There is an editorial board of fellow editors, the editor in chief, and the publisher.

Are agents important? Why? They are essential. We only acquire through agents. Our staff is too small to handle nonagented material.

Do you like new writers? What should new writers do to break into the business? New writers should research the field, read every book on publishing, and attend writers conferences where they can meet editors and agents and get information.

How should writers approach you? Through agents only.

What are some common mistakes writers make? What really gets on your nerves? Writers must be patient even when the wait is far too long.

What can writers do to get your attention and to avoid the slush pile? Publish in magazines, with a small press, come with a personal introduction from an impartial person (bookseller, publisher, author).

Is there anything you would like to see changed in the industry? I wish we had more time to develop writers and more room for "midlist." But these are exciting times as we move into the electronic publishing age.

Rawson Associates

Rawson Associates produces selected books in health and diet, self-help, popular psychology, and business how-to. Representative Rawson projects: *Filling the Void: Six Steps from Loss to Fulfillment* by Dorothy Bullitt; *Healing the Child: A Mother's Story* by Nancy Cain; *Rejecting Mothers, Wounded Daughters* by Ann Symonds.

Query letters and SASEs should be directed to:

Eleanor Rawson, Publisher

SEAL PRESS

3131 Western Avenue, Suite 410, Seattle, WA 98121-1041
206-283-7844   fax: 206-285-9410
www.sealpress.com   e-mail: sealpress@sealpress.com

Seal Press is dedicated to promoting the work of women writers. In addition to its several successful mystery series, Seal publishes a wide range of fiction, poetry, titles in women's studies and lesbian studies, sports and the outdoors, popular culture, parenting, self-help, awareness, and health.

Seal Press books enjoy a reputation for high literary quality, and the list often features finely designed, well-produced editions in hardcover and trade paperback. Seal Press supports a hardy backlist.

Seal Press (founded in 1976) is a smaller house that has leaped into its third decade of publishing with the same enthusiasm and mission that inspired the first book to bear the Seal name. Some 150 books later, the publishing business as well as the cultural climate around feminism have changed considerably. Seal remains editorially agile and responsive to the industry's current challenges. Recent Seal books evidence the shifting signposts of feminism and an ever-expanding range of women's interests.

A new series was launched in 1995 as Listen Up: Voices from the Next Feminist Generation. This line provides a forum for young women to wield fresh brands of feminism, to acknowledge their lives as different from their mothers' and to apply their realities to an established, yet necessarily fluid, movement for social change.

Seal fiction is known for offbeat approaches to genre and gender, in addition to such mystery series as Barbara Wilson's Cassandra Reilly series and Pam Nilsen mysteries; Elisabeth Bowers's Meg Lacey series; Jean Taylor's Maggie Garrett series, and Ellen Hart's Jane Lawless mysteries.

Titles from Seal Press: *Navigating the Darwin Straits* by Edith Forbes; *Breeder* (edited by Ariel Gore and Bee Lavender); *Sex and Single Girls* (edited by Lee Damsky); *Body Outlaws* (edited by Ophira Edut); *No Hurry to Get Home: The Memoir of the* New Yorker *Writer Whose Unconventional Life and Adventures Spanned the 20th Century* by Emily Hahn; *Shy Girl* by Elizabeth Stark; *The Case of the Orphaned Bassoonists* by Barbara Wilson; and *Coming Out of Cancer: Writings from the Lesbian Cancer Epidemic* (edited by Victoria A. Brownworth).

Adventura Books is a Seal imprint that captures women's outdoor and travel experiences with some of the finest writing of its kind. Adventura blazes a literary trail and encourages the spirit of adventure in every woman. Some Adventura series titles: *Another Wilderness: Notes from the New Outdoorswoman* (edited by Susan Fox Rogers); *Femme d'Adventure: Travel Tales from Inner Montana to Outer Mongolia* by Jessica Maxwell; *Season of Adventure: Off the Beaten Track with Women over Fifty* (edited by Jean Gould).

Special Seal titles in self-help and recovery: *A Woman Like You: The Face of Domestic Violence* (interviews by Vera Anderson); *The Lesbian Health Book: Caring for Ourselves* by Jocelyn White, M.D., and Marissa C. Martinez; *Dating Violence: Young Women in Danger* (edited by Barrie Levy); *New Beginnings: A Creative Writing Guide for Women Who Have Left Abusive Partners* by Sharon Doane; *The Obsidian Mirror: An Adult Healing from Incest* by Louise M. Wisechild; *You Don't Have to Take It! A Women's Guide to*

Confronting Emotional Abuse at Work by Ginny NiCarthy, Naomi Gottlieb, and Sandra Coffman.

Seal Press is distributed to the trade by Publishers Group West. Query letters and SASEs should be directed to:

Faith Conlon, Publisher and Editor

Leslie Miller, Senior Editor

Anne Mathews, Managing Editor

SELF-COUNSEL PRESS

1704 North State Street, Bellingham, WA 98225
360-676-4530   fax: 360-676-4549

Vancouver editorial office:
1481 Charlotte Road, North Vancouver, BC Canada V7J 1H1
604-986-3366

Self-Counsel produces business how-to, legal reference, self-help, and practical popular psychology. Topical areas include entrepreneurship, the legal system and you, business training, the family, and human resources development and management. The house also produces titles geared to lifestyles and business and legal issues in Florida, Oregon, and Washington.

Self-Counsel Press (founded in 1977) is a smaller house dedicated to providing well-researched up-to-date books (primarily trade paperbacks), as well as cassettes and work kits. The company's trade motto is "Our business is helping business people succeed." Self-Counsel's expertly written books do not just tell people what to do; they show them—step by step—how to do it. Kick Start Guides is a lineup of pocket-size titles designed for business travelers. The Start and Run list shows how to start and run a number of different kinds of small-business ventures.

Self-Counsel books cover everything from business to finance, legal matters to family matters, in language that everyone can understand. Self-Counsel prides itself on delivering concise, easy-to-understand books and audio, offering the practical information you need, whether it is for helpful legal tips, succeeding in business, or personal self-help issues.

Self-Counsel also offers legal books covering national issues, as well as books covering legal matters in Florida, Oregon, and Washington. Other topics include retirement, personal self-help, and lifestyles.

From Self-Counsel: *So You Wanna Buy a Car . . . Insider Tips for Saving Money and Your Sanity* by Bruce Fuller and Tony Whitney; *Start and Run a Profitable Mail-Order Business* by Robert W. Bly; *Start and Run a Profitable Tour Guiding Business* by Barbara Braidwood, Susan Boyce, and Richard Cropp; *First-Time Sales Rep: Sound Like a Pro, Act Like a Pro, Sell Like a Pro!* by Wayne Vanwyck; *Study Smarter, Not Harder: Your Guide to Successful Learning and Studying in Any Situation* by Kevin Paul; *A Small Business Guide to Doing Big Business on the Internet* by Brian Hurley and Peter Birkwood.

Kick Start Guides is a series of handy, pocket-size guides developed for the business traveler. Each guide is written for a specific country and is designed to help readers kick-start themselves into action as soon as they arrive at their destination. The Guides are also helpful tools for entrepreneurs on the lookout for overseas business opportunities.

The Start and Run series offers step-by-step business plans and shows how to set up shop, sell products or services, hire employees, get financing, design marketing strategies, and identify legal considerations for a variety of different enterprises. The Start and Run Series includes titles keyed to bed-and-breakfast, the crafts business, freelance writing, secondhand bookstores, student-run businesses, and the gift-basket business.

Self-Counsel Press operates its own distribution services. Query letters and SASEs should be directed to:

Diana R. Douglas, President (Vancouver Office)

Ruth Wilson, Managing Editor (Vancouver Office)

SEVEN STORIES PRESS

140 Watts Street, New York, NY 10013
212-226-8760
www.sevenstories.com

Seven Stories publishes trade nonfiction, commercial literature, and popular reference works. The house's signature is a provocative edge in literature, current events, contemporary culture, biography/personality and memoirs, and inventive writing of all stripes (including classic reprints). In 2000, a Spanish-language imprint, Siete Cueulos Editorial, was founded.

Seven Stories Press was founded by publisher Dan Simon in 1996. Simon was previously cofounder (with John Oakes) of Four Walls Eight Windows (see main entry). Seven Stories' publishing assets include backlist properties formerly catalogued by Four Walls.

Some titles from Seven Stories: *Grand Central Winter: Stories from the Street* by Lee Stringer; *The Man With the Golden Arm* from *Nonconformity: Writing on Writing* by Nelson Algren; *Dark Alliance: The CIA, the Contras and the Crack Cocaine Explosion* by Gary Webb; *Profit Over People* by Noam Chomsky; *The Zinn Reader* by Howard Zinn; *Borrowed Hearts: New and Selected Stories* by Rick DeMarinis; *Like Shaking Hands with God: A Conversation About Writing* by Kurt Vonnegut and Lee Stringer; *Get Healthy Now! With Gary Null* by Gary Null; *Scandals of '51: How the Gamblers Almost Killed College Basketball* by Carley Rosen; *The Undiscovered Chekhov: Thirty-Eight New Stories* by Anton Chekhov; *Shame* by Annie Ernaux; and *The Open Media Pamphlet Series.*

Distribution to the trade for Seven Stories is handled by Publishers Group West. Query letters and SASEs should be directed to:

Jill Schoolman, Associate Editor

M. E. SHARPE

80 Business Park Drive, Armonk, NY 10504
914-273-1800   fax: 914-273-2106
www.mesharpe.com

Sharpe publishes across the range of social and political sciences, including law, literature, area studies, women's studies, multicultural studies, business, comparative politics,
and international and developmental economics. Special Sharpe focus is on Asian studies,
Slavic and Eastern Europe studies, business (international and domestic), Latin American
studies, economics, political science, history, sociology, comparative public-policy analysis, and studies of the former Soviet Union.

M. E. Sharpe (founded in 1959) is a privately held company that produces trade books,
reference books, scholarly and academic works, business books, and professional books
in hardcover and paperback.

M. E. Sharpe has long been known for its area studies program covering Russia, Eastern Europe, and Asia. Expanding on that excellent publishing tradition, Sharpe has inaugurated programs in Latin American studies, American studies, African studies, and
European studies, as well as related disciplines of comparative studies, women's studies,
and literature, to provide a comprehensive understanding of today's world.

M. E. Sharpe chooses titles and authors that will define future debates about the political, economic, and social issues faced by various global regions and their peoples. Titles
are selected by the editors to represent the most innovative and critical thinking in their
respective disciplines.

Along with the primarily scholarly works, M. E. Sharpe publishes major single and
multi-volume reference works under the Sharpe Reference imprint; books aimed at the
professional market are generally under the Sharpe Professional stamp.

The Sharpe list thus encompasses original research, policy studies, translations, reference compendiums, popular literature and classic reprints, and books that lend themselves to slots in the trade market. Sharpe started as a publisher of academic and
professional journals and by the late 1970s, had begun expansion into book publishing.

Books from Sharpe: *The Making of Modern Economics: The Lives and Ideas of the
Great Thinkers* by Mark Skousen; *The Negotiation Handbook* by Patrick J. Cleary; *Con-
sumer Economics: A Practical Overview* by Steven Soderlind; *An Introduction to the Pol-
icy Process: Theories, Concepts, and Models of Public Policy Making* by Thomas A.
Birkland; *New York Politics: A Tale of Two States* by Edward Schneier and John Brian
Murtaugh; *Russian Wondertales I. Tales of Heroes and Villains: Volume 3 of the Complete
Russian Folktale* by Editor Jack V. Haney; *The Alternative Principles of Economics* by
Stanley Bober; *The Ancient Americans: A Reference Guide to the Art, Culture, and His-
tory of Pre-Columbian North and South America* by Juan Schobinger; *Dictionary of the
Political Thought of the People's Republic of China* by Henry Yuhuai He; *Elite Politics in
Contemporary China* by Joseph Fewsmiht; *Eyewitness to Massacre: American Mission-
aries Bear Witness to Japanese Atrocities in Najing* by Editors Kaiyan Zhang and Martha
Lund Smally; *The Negotiation Handbook* by Patrick J. Cleary; *A Rainbow in the Desert:
An Anthology of Early Twentieth Century Japanese Children's Literature* by Yuki Ohta;
*and Soldiers of Fortune: The Rise and Fall of the Chinese Military-Business Complex,
1978–1998* by James Charles Mulvenon.

It also highlights titles of the practical how-to variety on its Sharpe professional list.
Sharpe sells and promotes its titles both nationally and internationally; the house is a recognized industry leader in worldwide distribution. A large part of Sharpe's sales come
from direct marketing; in addition, the house pursues a variety of means to sell its list—
such as libraries, universities, trade and institutional bookstores, and catalogs.

M. E. Sharpe orchestrates its own distribution network, including stateside regional sales representatives, library-market specialists, and international wholesalers and reps. Query letters and SASEs should be directed to:

Patricia Loo, Editorial Director and Executive Editor—Asian studies.

Patricia A. Kolb, Executive Editor—European and Russian studies, political science.

Peter M. Labella, Executive Editor—American Studies and history.

Elizabeth Granda, Editor—Economics.

Harry Briggs, Executive Editor—Management and Public Administration.

SIERRA CLUB BOOKS

Sierra Club Books for Children and Young Adults

85 Second Street, San Francisco, CA 94105
415-977-5500   fax: 415-977-5793
www.sierraclub.org/books

Sierra Club publishes works in the categories of nature, appropriate technology, outdoor activities, mountaineering, health, gardening, natural history, travel, and environmental issues. Sierra Club series include the Adventure Travel Guides, Sierra Club Totebooks, Naturalist's Guides, Natural Traveler, the John Muir Library, and Guides to the Natural Areas of the United States. Sierra Club Books has a strong division that publishes works geared to children and young adults (see subentry further on).

Founded in 1892 by John Muir, the membership of the Sierra Club has for over a century stood in the forefront of the study and protection of the earth's scenic, environmental, and ecological resources; Sierra Club Books is part of the nonprofit effort the club carries on as a public trust. The house publishes hardcover and paperback books, many of them finely illustrated.

Sierra Club Books has the proud tradition of publishing books that are worldwide messengers for the Sierra Club mission: "To explore, enjoy and protect the wild places of the Earth; to practice and promote the responsible use of the Earth's ecosystems and resources; to educate and enlist humanity to protect and store the quality of the natural and human environment; and to use all lawful means to carry out these objectives."

The books represent the finest in outdoor photographic artistry; fervent and thought-provoking discussions of ecological issues; literary masterworks by the highest-caliber naturalist authors; authoritative handbooks to the best recreational activities the natural world can offer. Today, the need to protect and expand John Muir's legacy is greater than ever—to help stop the relentless abuse of irreplaceable wilderness lands, save endangered species, and protect the global environment.

On the Sierra Club list: *Bear* by Daniel Cox and Rebecca Grambo; *Kangaroo Dreaming* by Edward Kanze; *Seasons of the Arctic* by Paul Nicklen and Hugh Brody; *The Ultimate African Wildlife* by Nigel Dennis; *A Feathered Family* by Linda Johns; *The Spirit of the Valley* by Baxter Trautman; *Made Not Born* (edited by Casey Walker); *The Stations of Still Creek* by Barbara J. Scot; *The Lost River* by Richard Bangs; *Where Vultures Feast* by Ike Okanta and Oronto Douglas; *The Waterfall's Gift* by Joanne Ryder (illustrated by

Richard Jesse Watson); *What Does the Crow Know?* by Margery Facklam (illustrated by Pamela Johnson); *Bees Dance and Whales Sing* by Margery Facklam.

The Lost Gospel of the Earth by Tom Hayden (founder of SDS, member of the Chicago Seven, and longtime California legislator), presents a passionate eco-spiritual manifesto calling for a return to the ancient belief in nature as a sacred source of wisdom.

Sierra Club Books Adventure Travel Guides (newly published or up-to-date revised editions): *Adventuring in Alaska* by Peggy Wayburn; *Adventuring in the California Desert* by Lynne Foster; *Adventuring in Southern Africa* by Allen Bechky; *Adventuring in Hawaii* by Richard McMahon; *Adventuring in British Columbia* by Isobel Nanton and Mary Simpson; *Adventuring in the Caribbean* by Carrol B. Fleming; *Adventuring in Arizona* by John Annerino.

Sierra Club Books are distributed to the book trade by Random House. Query letters and SASEs should be directed to:

Danny Moses, Editor in Chief—Nature writing; environmental issues; nonfiction literary works dealing with nature, environment, cultural anthropology, history, travel, and geography. Fiction and poetry that is clearly related to natural or environmental themes.

James Cohee, Senior Editor—Areas consistent with house list.

Sierra Club Books for Children and Young Adults

Sierra Club Books for Children and Young Adults publishes primarily nonfiction, along with selected fiction keyed to subject areas that generally reflect the overall Sierra Club house emphasis.

Titles here: *Desert Trip* by Barbara A. Steiner (illustrated by Ronald Himler); *The Empty Lot* by Dale H. Fife (illustrated by Jim Arnosky); *The Seal Oil Lamp* (retold by Dale DeArmond); *The Snow Whale* by Caroline Pitcher (illustrated by Jackie Morris); *Squishy, Misty, Damp & Muddy: The In-Between World of Wetlands* by Molly Cone; *Wild in the City* by Jan Thornhill (illustrated by the author); *Animals You Never Even Heard of* by Patricia Curtis; *Buffalo Sunrise: The Story of a North American Giant* by Diane Swanson; *In Good Hands* by Stephan R. Swinburne; *Wolf of Shadows* by Whitley Streiber.

Author-artist Barbara Bash has written and illustrated six celebrated children's titles for Sierra Club Books, including *In the Heart of the Village: The World of the Indian Banyan Tree,* the latest book in her award-winning Tree Tales series.

Sierra Club Books for Children and Young Adults is distributed to the trade by Little, Brown. Query letters and SASEs should be directed to:

Helen Sweetland, Editor in Chief—Sierra Club Children's Book Division.

SIMON & SCHUSTER (PART OF VIACOM INC.)

Fireside Books

Pocket Books

Scribner Paperback Fiction

Simon & Schuster Trade Division

Simon and Schuster Trade Paperbacks

Touchstone Books

Washington Square Press

New York offices:
1230 Avenue of the Americas, New York, NY 10020
212-698-7000
www.SimonSays.com

Simon & Schuster is a leader in consumer books, educational and academic works, business and professional publishing, and reference lines. Simon & Schuster represents an elaborate network of divisions, imprints, and publishing groups that together address virtually all publishing categories and market niches. This powerhouse of publishing operates primarily from editorial environs at several New York addresses, as well as offices in New Jersey, Virginia, San Francisco, and other United States locations.

S&S imprints and divisions include Simon & Schuster Trade Division, Simon & Schuster Children's Publishing Division, Simon & Schuster Interactive, Pocket Books, Scribner, The Free Press, Brassey's (US), Jossey-Bass, The New Lexington Press, Pfeiffer & Company, Prentice Hall, Silver Burdett Ginn, Allyn & Bacon, Computer Curriculum Corporation, Educational Management Group, and Macmillan Publishing USA.

Simon & Schuster Trade imprints, along with Scribner and Pocket Books programs and books from the Free Press, cover the commercial trade spectrum. In addition to its own trade lineup, Pocket Books maintains a traditional mass-market publishing concentration. Macmillan and Prentice Hall have a commanding presence in professional, business, and academic publishing. Simon & Schuster Children's Publishing Division is a strapping domain of books for young readers. (See separate entry.)

The Simon & Schuster Trade Division is first and foremost a publisher of popular works, with a vast list that includes such imprints as Simon & Schuster, Touchstone, and Fireside.

Pocket Books publishes commercial works in fiction and nonfiction in hardcover, trade paperback, and mass-market paperback editions, and offers movie and television tie-ins on the Tundra imprint.

Simon & Schuster operates divisions (many under the Macmillan and Prentice Hall designations) devoted primarily to business, professional, computer publishing, and educational offerings; books in the arena of hobbies, horticulture, and travel, as well as personal development, lifestyle, how-to, and general reference.

Simon & Schuster is the book-publishing flagship of Viacom-owned Paramount Communications. Viacom Inc. is an enormous communications colossus that straddles the media worlds of film, radio, television, video, electronics, and print.

Simon & Schuster (founded in 1924) was among America's largest publishing houses by the time it was acquired by Gulf & Western in 1975. Subsequent to the S&S acquisition, G&W transformed its own corporate tag to Paramount Communications, under which name it operated a megamedia conglomerate that encompassed film and television-broadcast and cable interests, videos, music, and electronic, as well as print publishing enterprises.

In 1984 Simon & Schuster acquired Prentice Hall, itself a publisher of mammoth size and proven reputation for hitting exceedingly well-targeted professional and educational markets.

S

The 1994 acquisition by Paramount of the extensive remnants of the Macmillan Publishing Group fit nicely into a corporate tradition of multifaceted change and growth. The former trade-publishing wing of Macmillan was realigned (along with other S&S properties) under the Scribner imprint in 1994; by the middle of 1995, a new trade division emerged, bearing a refreshed Macmillan logo, to concentrate on practical nonfiction, business, and popular reference.

The Paramount Publishing designation was inaugurated in 1993 to cover all Simon & Schuster and Prentice Hall divisions, as well as the operations embraced in the Paramount buyout of Macmillan Publishing Group. Many Paramount Publishing lines continued to be issued under their historic imprints. In light of established trade-name recognition and publishing tradition, in May 1994 the name of the book-publishing umbrella reverted to what it had been—and thus the house of Simon & Schuster endures.

Simon & Schuster distributes its many constituent imprints and divisions (please see subentries further on); S&S also handles distribution services for a number of smaller and midsize houses.

Simon & Schuster titles include: . . . *And the Horse He Rode In On: The People v. Kenneth Starr* by James Carville; *Titanic: Fortune and Fate: Letters, Mementos, and Personal Effects from Those Who Sailed on the Lost Ship* by Mariners' Museum; *All Through the Night: A Suspense Story* by Mary Higgins Clark; *Under a Wing: A Memoir* by Reeve Lindbergh; *To the Brink: Stockton, Malone, and the Utah Jazz's Climb to the Edge of Glory* by Michael C. Lewis; *Heaven Talks Back: An Uncommon Conversation* by Jon Macks (introduction by Jay Leno); *Dear Socks, Dear Buddy: Kids' Letters to the First Pets* by Hillary Rodham Clinton; *Charles Kuralt's American Moments* by Charles Kuralt with Peter Freundlich; *The Victors: Eisenhower and His Boys: The Men of World War II* by Stephen E. Ambrose; *The Woody: A Novel* by Peter Lefcourt; *The African Cookbook: Tastes of a Continent* by Jessica Harris; *Hundred Dollar Holiday: The Case for a More Joyful Christmas* by Bill McKibben; *Grow Something Besides Old: Seeds for a Joyful Life* by Laurie Beth Jones; *The New Encyclopedia of Modern Bodybuilding: Fully Updated and Revised* by Arnold Schwarzenegger, with Bill Dobbins; *Out of the Woods: Stories* by Chris Offutt; *Living the 7 Habits* by Stephen Covey; *Noah's Flood: The New Scientific Discoveries About the Event That Changed History* by William Ryan and Walter Pitman; *Duane's Depressed: A Novel* by Larry McMurtry; *Age Right: Turn Back the Clock with a Proven Personalized Anti-Aging Program* by Karlis Ullis, M.D., with Greg Ptacek; *The Motley Fool's Rule Breakers, Rule Makers: A Foolish Guide to Picking Stocks* by David and Tom Gardner; *The Big Bad City: A Novel of the 87th Precinct* by Ed McBain.

Query letters and SASEs should be directed to:

Charles F. Adams, Senior Editor—Commercial fiction and nonfiction.

David Rosenthal, Vice President and Publisher

Stephen Fraser, Executive Editor—Aladdin Paperbacks.

Simon & Schuster Trade Division

The Simon & Schuster logo (an iconic rendition of Jean François Millet's famous sower) signals hardcover and trade paperback books in a wide range of commercial nonfiction and fiction areas, generally selected for potential appeal to the broadest possible spectrum of mainstream and special-interest readerships.

In nonfiction, Simon & Schuster is ever a major player in such topical arenas as popular history and current affairs, popular culture, business, health, self-awareness and improvement, and popular biography and memoirs.

Nonfiction from S&S: *Apocalypse Now: Tales for a New (or at Least Very Low Mileage) Millennium* by James Finn Garner; *The Language of Names: What We Call Ourselves and Why It Matters* by Justin Kaplan and Anne Bernays; *Gods of Death: Around the World, Behind Closed Doors, Operates an Ultra Secret Business of Sex and Death, One Man Hunts the Truth About Snuff Films* by Yaron Svoray with Thomas Hughes; *The Heart of Parenting: Raising an Emotionally Intelligent Child* by John Gottman with Joan DeClaire; *The Road Less Traveled and Beyond* by M. Scott Peck; *Unlimited Power: A Black Choice* by Anthony Robbins and Joseph McClendon III; *The Dream Messenger: How Dreams of the Departed Bring Healing Gifts* by Patricia Garfield, Ph.D.; *Everywoman's Guide to Sexual Fulfillment* by Susan Quilliam; *The Assault on Parenthood: How Our Culture Undermines the Family* by Dana Mack; *John Wayne's America: The Politics of Celebrity* by Garry Wills; *Confessions of a Late-Night Talk-Show Host: The Autobiography of Larry Sanders* by Garry Shandling and David Rensin; *Susie Bright's Sexual State of the Union* by Susie Bright; *Spiritual Serendipity: Cultivating the Art of the Unexpected* by Richard Eyre; *Dreammaker: A Biography of Steven Spielberg* by Joseph McBride; *Jack Nicklaus: My Story* by Jack Nicklaus, with Ken Bowden; *Virtual Power: Living, Learning, Loving, and Positively Thriving with Your Personal Computer* by Mark Bunting; *Ben & Jerry's Double-Dip Capitalism: Lead with Your Values and Make Money Too* by Ben Cohen and Jerry Greenfield; *The Defense Is Ready: Life in the Trenches of Criminal Law* by Leslie Abramson, with Richard Flaste; *What Losing Taught Me About Winning: The Complete Book for Success in Small Business* by Fran Tarkenton.

Simon & Schuster's roster of popular fiction and literary writing include works of cultural note. Among Simon & Schuster's fiction authors are such popular and critically respected writers as Maxine Chernoff, Mary Higgins Clark, Jackie Collins, Andrei Codrescu, John Hawkes, Larry McMurtry, and Roxanne Pulitzer.

As a group these books address the mainstream popular readership; S&S titles are usually in the commercial frontlist mode, with topnotch representatives in mystery and suspense, Westerns, women's romances and family sagas, and adventure and espionage thrillers. S&S also produces literary history, biography, and memoirs; investigative narrative nonfiction; and literary inspirational works.

Fiction titles include: *Tycoon* by Harold Robbins; *The Killer's Game* by Jay Bonansinga; *Change of Heart* by Tracy Stern; *Triple Feature* by Louise Bagshawe; *Last Rites* by Philip Shelby; *Fall on Your Knees* by Ann-Marie MacDonald; *Pretend You Don't See Her* by Mary Higgins Clark; *Charity* by Paulette Callen; *Hocus: An Irene Kelly Mystery* by Jan Burke; *One, Two, Buckle My Shoe* by Jessie Hunter.

Simon & Schuster Editions (series of deluxe editions of American short-novel classics): *Bartleby the Scrivener: A Story of Wall Street* by Herman Melville; *The Country of the Pointed Firs* by Sarah Orne Jewett; *Cruddy* by Lynda Barry.

Query letters and SASEs should be directed to:

Arisa Schmidt, Associate Editor—Investigative journalism, current events, true crime thrillers.

Rosemary Ahern, Editorial Director, Washington Square Press—Serious fiction and nonfiction, both original and reprints.

Amanda Murray, Editor—Hardcover nonfiction, both narrative and practical; subjects include (but aren't limited to) popular reference, beauty, fashion, entertainment, mind/body/health, and general women's interest.

Constance Herndon, Editor—General fiction and nonfiction.

Alice Mayhew, Editorial Director, Simon & Schuster Trade Division—Politics, current events, contemporary biographies and memoirs. Projects include *Making the Most of Your Money* by Jane Bryant Quinn; *Pillar of Fire* by Taylor Branch; *In Love with Daylight* by Wilfrid Sheed; *Taking Charge* by Michael Bechloss.

Bill Rosen, Simon & Schuster Editions—Vice President and Associate Publisher for Illustrated Books for the Simon & Schuster Group. In charge of illustrated books and special projects.

Charles F. Adams, Senior Editor—Commercial fiction and nonfiction. Titles include *No Regrets* by Caroline Seebohm; *Armadillos & Old Lace* by Kinky Freidman; *Ray Had an Idea About Love* by Eddie Lewis; and *Off Stage* by Betty Comden.

Chris Lynch, Executive Editor, S&S Audio—Audio projects.

Denise Roy, Senior Editor—General nonfiction and literary nonfiction.

Geof Klosker, Editor, Nonfiction—Serious nonfiction.

Andrea Mullins, Assistant Editor—First-time fiction, black issues.

Jeff Neuman, Senior Editor—Sports stories and biographies; humor. Titles include *Year of the Cat* by Scott Fowler and Charles Chandler; *Under the Lone Star Flagstick* by Melanie Hauser; *Postcard from Hell* by Rex Dancer.

Mary Sue Rucci, Senior Editor—Commercial fiction and nonfiction. Projects include *Women Make the Best Friends* by Lois Wyse; *Shed 10 Years in 10 Weeks* by Julian Whitaker and Carol Colman; *Divided Lives: The Public and Private Struggles of Three Accomplished Women* by Elsa Walsh.

Michael Korda, Editor in Chief—Commercial fiction and nonfiction. *Flood Tide* by Clive Cussler; *Comanche Moon* by Larry McMurtry. With Charles Adams (see separate entry earlier): *Climbing the Mountain* by Kirk Douglas; *Footnotes* by Tommy Tune.

Robert Bender, Senior Editor—Popular psychology, natural history, health and fitness, literary biography; wide commercial interests (excluding New Age and celebrity stories). Titles include *Sophia Loren* by Warren G. Harris; *Curing Cancer* by Michael Waldholtz.

Simon & Schuster Trade Paperbacks
Fireside Books
Touchstone Books
Scribner Paperback Fiction

Editors at Simon & Schuster Trade Paperbacks division can acquire for the following imprints: Fireside, Touchstone, and Scribner Paperback Fiction; editors also acquire hardcover for Simon & Schuster, Scribner, and Free Press.

Fireside covers the entire slate of commercial nonfiction categories. House emphasis includes self-help, inspiration, New Age, humor, popular culture, personal finance, fitness and health, sports, games (including crossword puzzles), lifestyle and hobbies, and parenting.

Fireside Books concentrates on original nonfiction and trade paperback reprints covering the mainstream commercial field.

Simon & Schuster's Touchstone Books imprint emphasizes popular nonfiction in trade paper editions, many of which have been originally published in hardcover. Touchstone also issues selected original titles.

Selected titles from Simon & Schuster Trade Paperbacks: (Touchstone, Scribner, Paperback Fiction): *The Bible Unearthed* by Israel Finkelstein and Neil Asher Silberman; *Dreamcatcher* by Stephen King; *Amelia Earhart* by Marie K. Long and Elgen M. Long; *Resurrecting Mingus* by Jenoyne Adams; *Soul Prints* by Marc Gafni; *The End of the Rainbow* by V. C. Andrews; *6-321* by Michael Laser; *AAA 2001 Britain Road Atlas* by AAA; *Altar Music* by Christian Lore Weber; *American By Blood* by Andrew Huebner; *American Heritage Children's Dictionary* by SSI/HMI; *Angela Anaconda: My Notebook* by Kent Redeker and Barry Goldberg; *Ashes of Victory* by David Weber; *Ask a Nurse* by American Association of Colleges of Nurses; *Augusta, Gone* by Martha Tod Dudman; *Avatar* by John Passarella; *The Awesome Animated Monster Maker Math* by SSI/HMI; *Love in the Tempest of History* by Aude Yung-de Prevaux; *KarlMarx.com* by Susan Coll; *My Mother, My Friend* by Mary Marcdante; *The Burning Times* by Jeanne Kalogridis; *Be Quick—But Don't Hurry* by Andrew Hill; *The Best Baby Shower Book* by Courtney Cooke; *Beyond Valor* by Patrick O'Donnell; and *Blind Spot* by Judy Mercer.

More from Simon & Schuster Trade Paperbacks (Fireside, Simon & Schuster Libros en Español): *The Wall Street Journal Guide to Planning Your Financial Future* by Kenneth M. Morris, Alan M. Siegel, and Virginia B. Morris; *Happy Horsemanship* by Dorothy Henderson Pinch; *A Kwanzaa Keepsake: Celebrating the Holiday with New Traditions and Feasts* by Jessica B. Harris; *Drawing in 3-D with Mark Kistler; 1999 American Guide to U.S. Coins* by Charles F. French (edited by John Adler); *Raising an Emotionally Intelligent Child* by John Gottman, Ph.D. (with Joan DeClaire); *Spoken in Whispers: The Autobiography of a Horse Whisperer* by Nicci Mackay; *Coyote Medicine: Lessons from Native American Healing* by Lewis Mehl-Madrona, M.D. (foreword by Andrew Weil, M.D.)

Query letters and SASEs should be directed to:

Caroline Sutton, Senior Editor—Interests include psychology and self-help, health and medicine, American history, nature, humor, and language. Also, acquires originals for Fireside and Touchstone. Projects include *Beyond the Battlefield,* sponsored by the U.S. Civil War Center, and *Blonde Like Me* by Natlia Ilyin.

Cherise Grant, Editor—Major interests include the craft of writing, branded nonfiction, career development, education, health, self-help, American history, illustrated books, humor, pop/youth/hip hop culture, personal memoir, and home decorating. Titles include *Conquering Chaos at Work* by Harriet Schechter.

Doris Cooper, Senior Editor—Interests include narrative nonfiction, women's issues, psychology and self-help, sports and fitness (especially the outdoors), health, quirky business,

S

relationships (from romantic to familial), and literary fiction. She is also interested in clever branded books.

Kristine Puopolo, Editor—Interested in history, narrative nonfiction, writing, language and literature, culture, psychology, popular reference, and women's issues. Her tastes in fiction are literary and women's fiction. She also has a weakness for very clever humor.

Lisa Considine, Senior Editor—Has a deep and abiding interest in psychology and self-help, health, science and nature, American history, business—particularly titles related to new media—and literary fiction.

Marah Stets, Associate Editor—Major interests are in the areas of lifestyle, including food and cooking, fiction, narrative nonfiction, women's issues, psychology/self-help, parenting and childcare, and health.

Matt Walker, Associate Editor—Major interests include movies, rock, pop culture; literary fiction and literate nonfiction for Gen-X readers; chess, crosswords, and games; and offbeat science and history.

Trish Todd, Vice President and Editor in Chief—Interests include humor, self-help, childcare, health and psychology.

Marcela Landres, Associate Editor—Marcela will not rest until she finds the Latina Terry McMillan. Her interests are pop culture; New Age, especially astrology; commercial projects for the multicultural market in general and Latinos in particular; and funky projects geared toward the Girl Power market.

   Born/ Sign: September 15, 1968, or Virgo, Leo Rising, Gemini Moon, born in the year of the Monkey and the hour of the Tiger.

   Education: Barnard

   Employment history/editor career path: I started out as the Assistant to the Editor in Chief, Simon & Schuster, Trade Paperbacks, then Assistant Editor, and now Associate Editor.

   Personal interests: Anything New Age, like astrology and feng shui; cooking; dancing; working out; and reading books completely unrelated to my job.

   What would you be doing if you were not an editor? I'd be an astrologer.

   What has been your most successful book that you have acquired to date? *Move Your Stuff, Change Your Life: How to Use Feng Shui to Get Love, Money, Respect, and Happiness* by Karen Rauch Carter, Fireside. Main selection of the Book-of-the-Month Club, now in its third printing (as of April 2000), even though it was just published in January 2000.

   What books have you acquired that make you the most proud? What books that you have acquired reflect the types of books you like to represent? I'm very, very picky about what I acquire, so when I do acquire a project it's because I truly believe in it. So, I'm proud of all my books. I prefer books that are practical, reader-friendly, and results-oriented. If a reader tells me that a book I worked on changed his/her life or touched him/her in some way, then I know I've done my job right. I publish books that are for people who don't usually read and who don't live in homes with bookshelves lined with books—which describes the vast majority of Americans. I work on books about: pop culture; anything and everything New Age, especially astrology; commercial projects for the multicultural market in general and Latinos in particular; and funny projects geared toward the Girl Power market. Some examples of the kinds of books I like to publish are the earlier mentioned feng shui book, *Move Your Stuff, Change Your Life: How to Use Feng Shui to Get Love, Money, Respect and Happiness* by Karen Rauch Carter; *Your Handwriting Can Change Your Life* by Vimala Rogers; *The Gift of Shyness* by Alexander Avila; and *Sexscopes* by *Cosmopolitan's* Bedtime Astrologer columnist Stuart Hazleton. My goal is to publish books that will inspire people who haven't read a book since high school to get off their butts, buy a book, and read it.

Do you represent fiction? If so, what do you look for? Yes. In particular, I'm desperately seeking the Hispanic Terry McMillan (author of *Waiting to Exhale*). In other words, commercial fiction by Latinas for Latinas.

What do you want to see less of? Poetry and short stories. People like to write them, no one likes to buy them. However, I encourage writers to write poetry, because it makes them better writers, but they shouldn't invest their time and effort into trying to get their poetry published. Instead, writers should concentrate their efforts on writing novels and getting them published.

Do you represent nonfiction? Yes, if it's practical, reader-friendly, results-oriented nonfiction.

Do you require book proposals? If so, what do you look for in evaluating a book proposal? Yes, because how else can you determine if a writer can do the job? For nonfiction, a book proposal requires: cover letter, table of contents, outline, comparison to competition, description of author's marketing/publicity platform, list of media contacts, and a sample chapter. If the author lectures or conducts workshops/seminars, a list of author events is invaluable. For nonfiction, the manuscript does not need to be completely written at the submission stage. For fiction, the manuscript should be completely written, but please do not submit the entire manuscript. A query letter and perhaps a short sample chapter should suffice. If the editor is interested, the editor will request the remainder of the manuscript. Bear in mind that it is very unusual for a publisher to sign up an author for a work of fiction if the manuscript is only partially written.

Are certain aspects of a book proposal given more weight than others? The author's marketing/publicity platform. If a writer has a nationally syndicated newspaper column, a radio or TV show, or a friend who is a bestselling author willing to offer an advance blurb, the chances of that writer getting a book contract are exponentially better than for a writer who has no such advantage.

What process do you use for making a decision? What is the process for acquisition, is there a committee? If the proposal is for a book that is in a strong category, like self-help, and has a unique, fresh hook that will make it stand out from all the other self-help books on the market, then it is likely I'll be interested in buying it. Other determining factors include whether I think the author and I can work together well; if I think my marketing and sales colleagues will support the book; how much and how strong the competition is; and, of course, the author's writing skills or lack thereof. The vast majority of submission come in through agents, though I have acquired and pursued unagented projects. I must have the approval of even higher-ranking executives. There is no committee to speak of, but there are layers of approval one must navigate before a manuscript can be acquired.

What kinds of nonfiction books do you want to see less of? Memoirs. Everyone has a story to tell, but not everyone has a story that's publishable.

Are you interested in work geared for the masses (readers of *People, The Star,* **etc.)?** Yes. Indeed, I envision all the readers for my books to be avid readers of *TV Guide* and not much else.

Are agents important? Why? Agents are valuable but not essential. I will sign up an author who is agentless without hesitation. Agents are helpful, however, because they can teach authors about the mysterious ways of publishing. Otherwise, I find myself explaining things to agentless authors that I wouldn't have to if they had agents. Agents are also advocates for their authors, and while part of an editor's function is to be the author's advocate, at the end of the day the editor's paycheck comes from the publishing company, not the author.

Do you like new writers? What should new writers do to break into the business? I adore new writers. New writers need to educate themselves as much as possible about the industry. They need to think of the process of getting a book contract as being the same as interviewing for a job. If you think about it, a book contract represents the author being hired on a freelance basis to perform a job for the publishing company. If the author doesn't do his or her job well, we won't be hiring that author again. If the author does a great job, we'll want a more permanent relationship. Writers should take writing classes not only to improve their technique, but also to network with other writers. Teachers at writing programs are often published authors themselves and can make valuable mentors. Writing conferences and seminars are also wonderful opportunities for networking, because agents and editors often attend or speak on panels.

How should writers approach you? With as much knowledge as possible about my needs as an editor, about the needs of my publishing company, and how and if they fill those needs. Writers should also be informed on what the market is like—what's selling, what's not, and how their work fits in (or not).

What are some common mistakes writers make? What really gets on your nerves? I hate it when I receive submissions for the kinds of book I don't do. For instance, I don't do children's books. If a writer sends a children's book, I know that writer hasn't taken the time or effort to figure out who the right editor or publishing house is for the book. To me, this indicated that the writer isn't capable of or willing to go the extra mile.

What can writers do to get your attention and to avoid the slush pile? If you write the kinds of books I want to work on, send me a query letter saying you're sending me your work because you know I publish your kind of writing. For instance, I do astrology books. If you send me an astrology proposal, tell me that you're sending it to me specifically because you know I do astrology books. I guarantee I will be impressed.

What have been some of your craziest experiences with submissions? Slush can sit around for many, many months, so in an effort to help make a submission stand out in the slush pile, an author sent me a lovely box of Godiva chocolates. Despite this clever maneuver, we ended up rejecting the submission. I shared the box of chocolates with all of my colleagues but nevertheless felt guilty.

What have been some of your best experiences with writers or in your job? As one of the few Latina editors in the book business, I am constantly confronted with the fact that there is no infrastructure in place for connecting Hispanic writers with interested publishers. As a result, I have to find Latina writers in unconventional ways. For instance, *Latina* magazine recently sponsored a book reading by some Latina authors. I, of course, attended and during the Q & A session I stood up and announced to all the Latinas in the audience that I was a Latina book editor in search of Latina writers and that anyone interested in being a writer should see me and get a business card. The overwhelming and enthusiastic response was a sign of how hungry Latinas are for information about the publishing industry and was an empowering reminder of just how important my work is not only to me but to all Latinas.

What, if anything, makes you different from other editors? I'm one of the very few Latina editors in the business. My parents are both from Ecuador in South America. I was born and grew up in the projects in Queens, New York. My dad is a fireman, so I come from a blue-collar as well as an immigrant background, and I was the only real reader in a family that tended to read the *TV Guide* to the *Star* instead of books, which is an unusual background for a person in publishing.

Is there anything you would like to see changed in the industry? I would like to see more people of color working in positions of power. You are more likely to find people of color in the reception area or in the mailroom than in Editorial, Marketing, Publicity, or in the corporate level. This is tragic.

Any advice for writers? Latina writers, take note: your chances of getting a book contract for a commercial novel are exponentially better than those of your male counterparts. There is an assumption in book publishing that women buy more books than men, so books by women for women are more likely to get published. Book publishing is a female-dominated industry, after all. Latino writers should note that as a group we are following in the hugely successful footsteps of African-American writers. Look at what is being published by and for African-Americans. That is the model you should follow. To all writers, regardless of color or background: please don't call me a few days after you sent me your proposal and ask my opinion of your writing. I work long hours during the week and only have time to read proposals during the weekend. It may take a few weekends before I get to the point in my reading pile where your submission is located. I promise I will respond to you, but please allow me the necessary time in which to do so.

S

SIMON & SCHUSTER CHILDREN'S PUBLISHING DIVISION

Aladdin Paperbacks

Atheneum Books for Young Readers

Little Simon

Margaret K. McElderry Books

Nickelodeon Books and Nick Jr.

Rabbit Ears Book and Audio

Simon & Schuster Books for Young Readers

1230 Avenue of the Americas, New York, NY 10020
212-698-7000

The Simon & Schuster Children's Publishing Division features a robust lineup of nonfiction, fiction, and poetry in all age ranges, plus a rich array of picture books and specialty publications. S&S publishes books for the Spanish-language market under the Libros Colibrí imprint. Rabbit Ears Book and Audio concentrates on book-and-audio packages. The new Nickelodeon Books operation includes television show tie-in titles and general publishing projects under the Nick imprint.

The division was created subsequent to Paramount's acquisition of Macmillan. The Macmillan enterprise had itself been a major force in children's publishing. The newly forged Simon & Schuster Children's Publishing Division has cohered into a powerful performance sphere, with numerous award-winning and bestselling titles.

The Simon & Schuster Books for Young Readers imprint is a hardcover publisher that aims to create high-quality books that sell to both libraries and bookstores and become backlist staples. The imprint publishes fiction and nonfiction for all readership groups, from preschoolers through young adults. About 60 percent of the list is made up of picture books (but not board books or novelty books), nonfiction, and storybooks for older readers. The rest of the list features novels and poetry collections for middle-grade readers and young adults.

Representing the Simon & Schuster Books for Young Readers list: *Be Nice Nanette!* by Sarah Wilson; *Blue Egg Hunt* by Deborah Reber; *Bugged by Bugs* by Kiki Thorpe; *Bunny's Easter Bonnet* by Elenor Hudson; *Butterfly, Butterfly: What Colors Do You See?* by Annie Horwood; *Cats, Cats, Cats!* by Leslea Newman.

Atheneum Books for Young Readers produces picture books, fiction, and nonfiction that cover the spectrum of reader-age ranges in all genres (except for board books and novelty books). Atheneum books are often richly produced hardcover editions; works that feature illustration and photography are often packaged with fine-art quality graphics. About a third of the list consists of picture books; however, Atheneum is renowned for topnotch titles in fiction and nonfiction. Produced under Atheneum auspices are Jean Karl Books, Anne Schwartz Books, and the Libros Colibrí Spanish-language line.

From Atheneum: *Beatrice's Goat* by Page McBrier; *Born in Sin* by Evelyn Coleman; *Buddy Is a Stupid Name for a Girl* by Davis Roberts; *Countdown to Independence* by Natalie S. Bober; *Dangling* by Lillian Eige; *Darkness Before Dawn* by Sharon M. Draper; *The Devil in Ol' Rosie* by Louise Moeri.

Titles representative from Aladdin Paperbacks: *Daniel's Story* by Susan Kirby; *Bernie Magruder and the Case of the Big Stink* by Phillis Reynolds Naylor; *Blue Star Rapture* by James W. Bennett; *Animal Rescue: The Best Job There Is* by Susan E. Goodman; *Back in the Beforetime* by Jane Louise Curry; *Barnyard Song* by Rhonda Gowler Green; and *Abraham's Battle: A Novel of Gettysburg* by Sara Harrell Banks.

Margaret K. McElderry Books publishes original hardcover trade books for children. The McElderry list encompasses picture books, easy-to-read series, fiction, and nonfiction for 8- to 12-year-olds, science fiction and fantasy, and young adult fiction and nonfiction. McElderry titles: *Yolanda's Genius* by Carol Fenner; *Dog Friday* by Hilary McKay; *A Sound of Leaves* by Lenore Blegvad (illustrated by Erik Blegvad).

Aladdin Paperbacks primarily produces reprints of Simon & Schuster Publishing Division hardcover originals. The Aladdin scope covers preschoolers through young adult, including picture books, paperback reprints, novelty books, and fiction and mysteries for kids to the age of 12. Aladdin originals include selective series and media tie-ins.

Little Simon is a line devoted to novelty books and book-related merchandise. Little Simon addresses a range from birth through 8 years. Popular formats include pop-up books, board books, cloth books, bath books, sticker books, and book-and-audiocassette sets.

Nickelodeon Books and Nick Jr. are queued to Nickelodeon cable-channel programming. This line creates books and other products that cross-promote with co-licensees in the arenas of toys, home videos, CD-ROMs, and party goods.

Rabbit Ears is an award-winning entertainment company that produces children's videos. The Simon & Schuster Rabbit Ears Book and Audio lineup concentrates on a slate of tales based on the videos, retold and illustrated in high-profile new editions, accompanied by audiocassettes replete with surround-sound design and musical scores for a discerning audience. Representative performing artists involved are Rubén Blades, Holly Hunter, John Hurt, Garrison Keillor, Jack Nicholson, Meg Ryan, and Kathleen Turner; musicians include Mickey Hart, Mark Isham, Tangerine Dream, and Bobby McFerrin.

Cindy Alvarez, Editorial Director, Little Simon

Caitlyn Dlouhy, Senior Editor, Atheneum Books for Young Readers

David Gale, Editorial Director, Simon & Schuster Books for Young Readers—Middle-grade and young-adult novels, primarily. Looks for sharp writing and fresh voices. Does not want to consider standard young-adult problem novels or romances, but is interested in more unusual, hard-hitting, and literary young-adult novels.

Ellen Krieger, Vice President, Associate Publisher and Editorial Director, Aladdin Paperbacks

Emma K. Dryden, Executive Editor, Margaret K. McElderry Books

Jonathan Lanman, Editor at Large, Atheneum Books for Young Readers

Ginee Seo, Vice President and Associate Publisher, Atheneum Books for Young Readers

Kevin Lewis, Editor, Simon & Schuster Books for Young Readers in Picture books (both short texts for younger readers and longer texts for older readers), interesting and fresh nonfiction for all age groups, and middle-grade novels with a distinctive voice.

Marcia Marshall, Executive Editor, Atheneum Books for Young Readers

Margaret K. McElderry, Vice President and Publisher—Margaret K. McElderry Books

Jessica Schulte, Editor, Simon & Schuster Books for Young Readers

Kristina Peterson, President and Publisher, Simon & Schuster Children's Publishing Division

Robin Corey, Vice President and Publisher—Novelty and media tie-ins.

Stephen Geck, Vice President, Associate Publisher Simon & Schuster Books for Young Readers

Jenny Miglis, Senior Editor, Simon Spotlight

Jennifer Koch, Editorial Director, Simon Spotlight

Sheri Tan, Executive Editor, Simon Spotlight

S

Erin Molta (née McCormack), Senior Editor, Simon & Schuster/Little Simon
  Sign: Capricorn
  Education: B.A., Mount Holyoke College
  Employment history or editor career path: I started out an editorial assistant on the Scholastic Book Clubs. For six years I was at Scholastic in the Book Clubs, as an Editor for various clubs. I left to go to Hyperion/Disney, where I worked on a variety of books, both Disney character–based and not—paperback reprints, original paperback series, hardcover picture books and novels, chapter books, board books, and first readers. Now I am at Little Simon working on novelty books.
  Personal interests: I love to read (I'd be in a bad spot if I didn't, wouldn't I?) and I consider myself a pretty competent amateur photographer—up to date with all the latest in digital camera technology!
  What would you be doing if you were not an editor? Hmm . . . never really thought about it—I've always wanted to be an editor. But I suppose if that were not possible, a book reviewer or maybe write for a local newspaper or magazine.
  What has been your most successful book that you have acquired to date? *Rats* by Paul Zindel and *A Pinky Is a Baby Mouse* by Pam Munoz Ryan.
  What books have you acquired that make you the most proud? What books that you have acquired reflect the types of books you like to represent? All of them! Actually, three stand out—*Memory Jug,* which was the second novel by a new writer, Pat Martin. I enjoyed working on the first one, but this one was just remarkable and the story made me cry; it was so beautifully written. And the second one is a picture book, *Jason's Bears* by Marion Dane Bauer, which is just fabulous. A great story that speaks directly to a child with gorgeous, kid-friendly art by Kevin Hawkes. The third was a lift-the-flap book based on the Doug TV character. The author, Pam Ryan, did so much for this and it offered much more than a normal, everyday flap book. It went above and beyond a flap book.
  Do you represent fiction? If so, what do you look for? Looking for novelty book ideas: I am currently looking for novelty formats with early learning concepts—shapes, colors, opposites, alphabet, numbers, animals' feelings, words, weather, and so on. These can be incorporated into a story or as straight nonfiction. Anything that a toddler and preschooler would enjoy and want to return to again and again. The more innovative the format idea, the better—glitter, stickers, flaps, pops, sliding, apparatus, etc.
  What do you want to see less of? Stories in a board-book format. We have found that unless it is a successful picture book already and there is a demonstrated interest in making it available to a younger audience, straight picture board books are too expensive to do and they do not sell that well.
  Do you require book proposals? If so, what do you look for in evaluating a book proposal? I don't find proposals helpful, especially for the novelty-type books that I am looking for. It is time better spent to look at the whole package—entire manuscript, with any format ideas included.
  What process do you use for making a decision? What is the process for acquisition, is there a committee? It's a committee, but passion counts for a lot, so if I really like an idea, it could get by a skeptical board.
  Are you interested in work geared for the masses (readers of *People, The Star,* etc.)? Yes, yes, yes!!!

Are agents important? Why? Agents are important because I trust what is coming. If I have a stack of submissions and half are agented and the other half are unsolicited, I'll read the agented ones first because, in theory, they have been weeded out already and should have some merit.

Do you like new writers? What should new writers do to break into the business? I love new writers. I love working with and developing new talent. If a writer does not want to go the agented route, it's just a matter of being persistent and if an editor is nice enough to give you a reason why the manuscript was rejected, take heart because that usually means it was read and appreciated and you should pay attention. Try to work on the aspects that were noted.

How should writers approach you? Though it is said that presentation is the ultimate, it shouldn't be all about how it looks but also about the content. Overkill turns me off right away. A simple cover letter with the manuscript and a return envelope or e-mail address is usually enough to get me to take a look at something. Humor almost always works!

What are some common mistakes writers make? What really gets on your nerves? Not knowing the market or the publisher to whom they are submitting. Telling me that you are submitting something because your students loved it or your children or friends loved it, just sends me!! What kids are going to tell their teacher that his/her story stinks?

What can writers do to get your attention and to avoid the slush pile? A good story and an interesting format will do it, but humor always helps. Also, if you think your book is like something else that is a bestseller, tell me, and if it's better, be specific. Show that you know the market—what's out there and what kids like to read, talk about, and are fascinated by.

What have been some of your craziest experiences with submissions? I had received two manuscripts from a writer, which I rejected for several reasons. In less than a week's time, I received revises and two more manuscripts. I don't think that writer even bothered to ponder anything. It was a shame.

What have been some of your best experiences with writers or in your job? Brainstorming. I love to kick ideas back and forth and develop them into a book. Whether it is a novel or a novelty book—that is the best part of being an editor—bringing an idea to fruition.

What, if anything, makes you different from other editors? Hmm . . . well, I'm quick and thorough. Once I've signed up a book, I don't sit on revisions and I get back to an author ASAP about his or her manuscript with thoughtful comments and suggestions. I also don't beat around the bush. I will tell an author if I think something needs to be changed and why and am willing to compromise—which is good for all concerned.

Is there anything you would like to see changed in the industry? I would like to see more risks taken and to see publishers let books grow. If you think about it, it seems likely that if the venerable and bestselling Dr. Seuss were to submit his first manuscript nowadays, it might not be published. That is a scary thought, indeed.

Any advice for writers? Any way to improve the system for you? Any additional thoughts? Bottom line is that I love children's books and I love working with writers and illustrators to create books that will last on store shelves for a long time and hold a special place in children's hearts even when they grow up and have their own children.

GIBBS SMITH, PUBLISHER

P.O. Box 667, Layton, UT 84041
801-544-9800
www.gibbs-smith.com

Gibbs Smith publishes general trade nonfiction, including interior decorating, Western lifestyle, architecture, and nature. Gibbs Smith also produces a line in children's outdoor activity books and picture books. The house has a strong emphasis on home and health literature of the Western United States, including cowboy humor and poetry. The publisher's architecture program features a new work on *The Blacker House* by Randell Makinson.

The house produces books in fine hardcover and trade paper editions and offers distinctive lines of gift books keyed to the publisher's interest areas.

Gibbs Smith, Publisher (founded in 1969), is a house with a resourceful spirit. Company mission statement: To enrich and inspire humankind. Gibbs Smith looks for new projects that contribute to and refresh this spirit. Gibbs Smith believes that the single most important quality for both writer and publisher is passion: a sense of great purpose; an unusually heightened interest in the subject matter and in the task—whether it be writing or publishing. As Gibbs M. Smith writes: "It is a great privilege to work from our old barn office in the Rocky Mountains and have our books enter the literary bloodstream of the world."

High on the Gibbs Smith list: *The Lesson* by Carol Lynn Pearson (illustrated by Kathleen Peterson); *French by Design* by Betty Lou Phillips; *Art of the Boot* by Tyler Beard and Jim Arndt; *Bungalow Kitchen* by Jane Powell.

Gibbs Smith publishes a seasonal-holiday sampler modeled on Moore's classic: "Night Before Christmas." Subjects include teachers, grandmas, grandpas, dads, cats, dogs, fishermen, and golfers, in Texas, Chicago, Seattle, Florida, California.

Of interest to children and family: *Bullfrog Pops!* by Rick Walton (illustrated by Chris McAllister); *Fishing in a Brook,* by Lawson Drinkard (illustrated by Fran Lee); and *Trekking on a Trail* by Linda White (illustrated by Fran Lee).

Gibbs Smith, Publisher, distributes its own list and utilizes a network of regional sales representatives.

Query letters and SASEs should be directed to:

Gail Yngve, Editor—Interior design, poetry.

Madge Baird, V. P. Editorial—Interior design, Western, humor.

Suzanne Taylor, Senior Editor—Interior design, children's.

SOHO PRESS

853 Broadway, New York, NY 10003
212-260-1900

Soho publishes trade nonfiction and fiction. Nonfiction covers areas such as literary criticism, international affairs, and memoirs. This compact house is also distinguished for its formidable list of contemporary fiction (often with a literary bent), which includes mysteries and historical reprints. The Soho train of interest also verges into travel, autobiography, and the social sciences.

Soho Press (founded in 1986) publishes a superior roster of hardcover and softcover trade books. Many of the house's titles have achieved marked critical and commercial success, including Oprah winner and National Book Award nominee Edwidge Danticat, author of *The Farming of Bones* and *Breath, Eyes and Memory.*

Fiction and literary arts from Soho: *Gloria* by Keith Maillard; *The Gravity of Sunlight* by Rosa Shand; *Death of a Red Heroine* by Qiu Xialong; *A Far Better Rest* by Susanne Alleyn; *The Twins* by Tessa De Loo; *Adrian Mole: The Cappuccino Years* by Sue Townsend.

Soho mysteries: *The Amsterdam Cops* by Janwillem van de Wetering; *The Vault* and *The Reaper* by Peter Lovesem; *The Tattoo Murder Case* by Akimitsu Takagi (translated by Deborah Boehm); *The Whispering Wall* and *The Souvenir* by Patricia Carlon.

The Hera Series presents works of historical fiction that feature strong female characters. Hera series titles: *Lady of the Reeds* by Pauline Gedge; *Stealing Heaven: The Love Story of Heloise and Abelard* by Marion Meade.

Soho Press books are distributed to the trade by Farrar Straus & Giroux.

Query letters and SASEs should be directed to:

Juris Jurjevics, Publisher

Laura Hruska, Associate Publisher

Melanie Fleishman, Vice President, Marketing and Publicity, and Editor

S

SOURCEBOOKS, INC.

Sourcebooks Casablanca

Sourcebooks Hysteria

Sourcebooks Landmark

Sourcebooks Media Fusion

Sphinx Publishing

955 Connecticut Avenue, #5303, Bridgeport, CT 06607

Illinois office:
1935 Brookdale Road, Suite 139, Naperville, IL 60563
800-961-3900   fax: 630-961-2468

Founded in 1987, Sourcebooks' mission is to reach as many people as possible with books that will enlighten their lives. Sourcebooks grew 67 percent in 1998, and another 80 percent in 1999. Also in 1999, Sourcebooks was rated by the industry's leading trade publication, *Publishers Weekly,* as the second-fastest-growing independent publisher in America. This was the third consecutive year Sourcebooks was ranked. It also marked Sourebooks' final appearance on the list, as the company is now too large to be considered. Most recently, Sourcebooks was named one of the fastest growing private companies by *Inc.* magazine in their Inc. 500 list. Sourcebooks in the only publisher on this year's list.

Sourcebooks has strong distribution into the retail market—bookstores, gift and specialty shops whose primary product is something other than books and provides tremendous editorial, sales, marketing, and publicity support for their authors. They follow a somewhat out-of-date model for book publishing that makes their passion for books central. In short, Sourcebooks believes in authorship. They work with authors to develop great books that find and inspire a wide audience. They believe in helping develop authors' careers and recognize that a well-published, successful book is often a cornerstone. They seek authors who are as committed to success as they are.

Their fiction imprint, Sourcebooks Landmark, publishes a variety of titles. They are interested first and foremost in books that have a story to tell. They are currently only reviewing agented fiction manuscripts.

For nonfiction, they are interested in books that will establish a unique standard in their area. They look for books with a well-defined, strong target market. Their publishing list includes most nonfiction categories, including entertainment, sports, general self-help/ psychology, business (particularly small business, marketing and management), parenting, health and beauty, reference, biographies, gift books and women's issues.

They are not currently publishing children's books, but they do keep an active list of artists and illustrators.

Please direct query letters with SASE's to:

Sourcebooks, Editorial Submissions, P.O. Box 4410, Naperville, IL 60567-4410

Hillel Black, (CT) Executive Editor—Commercial and literary fiction, thrillers, suspense, love stories, historical fiction and mysteries. In nonfiction, history, biography, autobiography, science, medicine and relationship books.

Deborah Werksman, (CT) Editorial Manager—Humor, love, dating, relationships, wedding books, self-help, women's interest, and parenting.

Jennifer Fusco, (CT) Editor—Parenting, self-help, history, politics/current affairs, cookbooks, psychology and health, women's fiction, literary fiction and family sagas.

Alex Lubertozzi, (IL) Editor—Acquires books for Sourcebooks MediaFusion and Sourcebooks Landmark. Media components (audio CD's, DVD's), historical, cultural and sports stories, all genres of fiction.

Dianne Wheeler, (IL)—Division manager of Sphinx Publishing. Titles that cover legal topics to interest the lawyer customer.

STACKPOLE BOOKS

5067 Ritter Road, Mechanicsburg, PA 17055-6921
717-796-0411   fax: 717-796-0412

Stackpole specializes in nature and the outdoors, crafts and hobbies, fly fishing, sporting literature, history (especially military history), military reference, and works geared to the Pennsylvania region.

Stackpole Books publishes editions that are created lovingly, with striking design. When selecting projects to produce, the publisher determines what readers need and how these needs will be met through a proposed project's fresh perspective. Stackpole signs expert authors, juggles production schedules, and commits the personalized verve to make the dream real. Stackpole believes in perfectionism and care—when focused upon the practical—as keys to successful publishing.

Stackpole Books was established in 1933 as Stackpole & Sons, a small family-owned publishing enterprise. The house acquired Military Service Publishing Company in 1935 and has continued to grow into additional publishing areas, while remaining attuned to its original publishing vision.

On the Stackpole list: *Around the World on a Bicycle* by Thomas Stevens (with an introduction by Thomas Pauly); *The Barrier Islands* by Curtis K. Badger and Rick Kellam; *Civil War Firsts: The Legacies of America's Bloodiest Conflict* by Gerald S. Henig and Eric Niderost; *The Complete Guide to New Zealand Trout Lures* by Derek Qulliam; *From Blue to Gray: The Life of Confederate General Cadmus M. Wilcox* by Gerard A. Patterson; *Pop Flies: Bob Popovic's Approach to Saltwater Fly Design* by Ed Jaworowski and Bob Popovics; *Rocky Mountain: A Visitor's Companion* by George Wuerthner (illustrated by Douglas W. Moore); *Mountain Biking* by Susanna and German Mills; *Senator* by Samuel J. Martin; *Underground Railroad in Pennsylvania* by William J. Switala; *Whitewater Rafting* by Graeme Addison; *Bird Sounds: How and Why Birds Sing, Call, Chatter and Screech* by Barry Kent MacKay; *Homeward Bound: The Demobilization of the Union and Confederate Armies 1865–1866* by William B. Holberton; *Captain Marryat: Seaman, Writer and Adventurer* by Tom Pocock; *County Courthouses of Pennsylvania: A Guide* by Oliver Williams; *Falling Stars: A Guide to Meteors and Meteorites* by Michael Reynolds; *Guide to Military Installations,* 6th edition by Dan Cragg; *Swamp Doctor: The Diary of a Union Surgeon in the Virginia and North Caroline Marshes* by Thomas Lowry; *A Good Horse Has No Color: Searching Iceland for the Perfect Horse* by Nancy Marie Brown; *The Guide and the CEO* by M. David Detweiler; *Real Alaska: Finding Our Way in the Wild Country* by Paul Schullery; and *The Half Not Told: The Civil War in a Frontier Town* by Preston Filbert.

From the Who's Who in British History series: *Who's Who in Tudor England, 1485–1603,* vol. 1 by C.R.N. Routh; *Who's Who in Victorian Britain, 1851–1901,* vol. 1 by Roger Ellis; *Who's Who in Early Medieval England* by Christopher Tyermand; *Who's Who in Late Medieval England* by Michael Hicks.

From the Pennsylvania Trail of History Guides: *Erie Maritime Museum and U.S. Brig Niagara; Brandywine Battlefield; Pennsbury Manor; Conrad Weiser Homestead; Hope Lodge;* and *Mather Mill.*

Exploring the Appalachian Trail series titles: *Hikes in Northern New England* by Michael Kodas, Andrew Weegar, Mark Condon, and Glenn Scherer; *Hikes in Southern New England* by David Emblidge; *Hikes in the Mid-Atlantic States* by Glenn Scherer and Don Hopes; *Hikes in the Virginias* by David Lillard and Gwyn Hicks; *Hikes in the Southern Appalachians* by Doris Gove.

Stackpole distributes its own books, as well as a list of titles from United Kingdom and U.S. publishers.

Query letters and SASEs should be directed to:

S

Ed Skender, Editor—Military reference.

Judith Schnell, Editorial Director—Outdoor sports; fly fishing.

Kyle Weaver, Editor—Pennsylvania.

William C. Davis, Editor—History.

Mark Allison, Editor—Nature.

Born: 1964.

Education: B.A., English, Penn State University.

Employment history/editor career path: Started as an Editorial Assistant at Stackpole after working as a writer and proofreader.

Personal interests: Photography; reading books out of my line.

What books have you acquired that make you the most proud? What books that you have acquired reflect the types of books you like to represent? Books with a long shelf life. We want to keep an author's work in print forever.

Do you represent fiction? No.

What do you want to see less of? Imitations of successful titles, *Harvey's Penick's Little Red Book*–style treatments for subjects other than golf.

Do you represent nonfiction? Yes, exclusively.

Do you require book proposals? If so, what do you look for in evaluating a book proposal? I require a proposal or a sample chapter with a cover letter, no magic formula. I look for demonstrated expertise in the subject matter, demonstrated skill as a writer, and evidence of commitment to the project.

Are certain aspects of a book proposal given more weight than others? The writing itself and the description of what the book is all about—which must be well thought out, exact, and clearly presented.

What process do you use for making a decision? What is the process for acquisition, is there a committee? (1) Investigation and research by the editor. (2) Input from sales and marketing. (3) Review and discussion by the editorial board.

What kinds of nonfiction books do you want to see less of? Books that are heavy on design and photography/art but skimpy on content.

Are you interested in work geared for the masses (readers of *People*, *The Star*, etc.)? Our readers usually have a keen interest in the activities or subject matter our lines cover: birding, fly fishing, Civil War history, and so on.

Are agents important? Why? We usually deal directly with authors but have good working relationships with a few agents who know our lines. We sometimes get proposals from agents that are so far out of our lines that I wonder what purpose they are serving.

Do you like new writers? What should new writers do to break into the business? We publish a number of new writers, who should establish their expertise and perhaps an audience by writing for magazines and newspapers before tackling a book.

How should writers approach you? Query and proposal or query and sample chapter are the best ways. I personally don't like e-mail queries.

What are some common mistakes writers make? What really gets on your nerves? Focus on design and presentation of the book, instead of on the content.

What can writers do to get your attention and to avoid the slush pile? Straightforward presentation of the project in our line, author expertise.

What have been some of your craziest experiences with submissions? A querying author once refused to reveal the subject matter of his "top secret" project until a contract was signed.

Any advice for writers? Try to stay enthusiastic and realistic and remember that the author and publisher should be working toward the same goal.

STERLING PUBLISHING COMPANY

387 Park Avenue South, New York, NY 10016-8810
212-532-7160

Sterling emphasizes general popular reference and information books, science, nature, arts and crafts, architecture, home improvement, history, humor, health, self-help, wine and food, gardening, business and careers, social sciences, sports, pets, hobbies, drama and music, psychology, occult, and military-science books. Sterling also publishes games, puzzles, calendars, and children's books.

The current scope of the Sterling Publishing Company program includes a wide range of nonfiction practical approaches, including informative how-to books in gardening, crafts, and woodworking; books on military history; art and reference titles; and activity and puzzle books for the kids. The house (founded in 1949) hosts a formidable backlist.

Representative Sterling titles: *Body Shaping with Free Weights: Easy Routines for Your Home Workout* by Stephenie Karony and Anthony L. Ranken; *Golf Mistakes & How to Correct Them* by Oliver Heuler; *200 Perplexing Chess Puzzles* by Martin Freif; *The Little Giant Encyclopedia of Mazes* by the Diagram Group; *Space Mazes* by Roger Moreau; *Challenging False Logic Puzzles* by Norman D. Willis; *Weight Training Basics* by Robert Kennedy (publisher of *MuscleMag International*); *Gemstones of the World* by Walter Schumann; *Romantic Massage* by R. J. Nikola, L.M.T.; *Zen Wisdom: Daily Teaching from the Zen Masters* by Timothy Freke; *The Truth About Alien Abductions* by Peter Hough and Moyshe Kalman; *The Mystic Grail: The Magical World of the Arthurian Quest* by John Matthew.

On the Sterling children's book list: *Science Crafts for Kids: 50 Fantastic Things to Invent & Create* and *Nature Crafts for Kids: 50 Fantastic Things to Make with Mother Nature's Help* by Gwen Diehn and Terry Krautwurst; *The Great Rubber Stamp Book: Designing, Making, Using* by Dee Gruenig; *Cat Crafts: More Than 50 Purrfect Projects* by Dawn Cusick; *Dog Crafts: More Than 50 Grrreat Projects* by Bobbe Needham.

Query letters and SASEs should be directed to:

Sheila Barry, Acquisitions Manager

STEWART, TABORI & CHANG

115 West 18th Street, New York, NY 10111
212-519-1200   fax: 212-519-1230

Stewart, Tabori, & Chang publishes luxuriously produced titles about love, food, spirituality, divination, history, comic art, music, and Christmas. The house offers topnotch specialty merchandise such as calendars, cards, journals, and engagement books. Terrail is an imprint in collaboration with Editions Terrail that publishes a line of art books at reasonable prices. The Essential Gardens library is a line accenting a wide range of topical-interest editions. The publisher offers a solid list of new seasonal titles and supports an impeccably select backlist.

Stewart, Tabori & Chang books are produced in hardcover and trade paperback editions. Booksellers especially appreciate the quality product signified by the publisher's prancing-bison trade logo—these books on display in a bookstore can draw significant point-of-purchase interest from customers. House trade motto: "The heart and soul of illustrated books."

Stewart, Tabori & Chang (founded in 1981 by Andy Stewart, Lena Tabori, and Nai Chang), recently part of the publishing stable of Peter Brant (owner of the magazines *Interview, Art in America,* and *Antiques*), is now a division of U.S. Media Holdings, Inc.

From Stewart, Tabori & Chang: *Colors of Provence* by Michel Bicha (photographs by Heinz Angermayr); *Quick Cooking with Pacific Flavors* by Hugh Carpenter and Teri Sandison; *Goddess: A Celebration in Art and Literature* (edited by Jalaja Bonheim); *Little Moments of Happiness* by Elisabeth Brami and Philippe Bertrand; *I Ching: A Spiritual Guide* by Frits Blok; *Tangram: The Ancient Chinese Puzzle* by Joost Elffers and Michael Schuyt; *Native Americans: A Portrait, the Art and Travels of Charles Bird King, George Catlin, and Karl Bodmer* by Robert J. Moore, Jr.; *Heart & Soul: A Celebration of Black Music Style in America 1930–1978* by Bob Merlis and Davin Seay; *The Jewish Spirit: A Celebration in Stories and Art* (edited by Ellen Frankel); *The Discovery of the Nile* by Gianni Guadalupi; *Ancient Greece: The Dawn of the Western World* by Furio Durando.

The Essential Garden Library series encompasses gardening titles covering a variety of subjects and formats. Each book in the series features Stewart, Tabori & Chang quality in writing, photography, and production. Numbered chronologically, these books are uniform in height and width to stand next to one another in the reader's garden library. Some titles: *Herbs* by George Carter (photographs by Marianne Marjerus); *Getting Ready for Winter and Other Fall Tasks* by Stephen Bradley.

Stewart, Tabori & Chang distributes to the trade via Publishers Resources; in addition, the house uses a network of independent regional sales representatives.

Query letters and SASEs should be directed to:

Alexandra Childs, Assistant Editor

Linda Sunshine, Editorial Director

Mary Kalamaras, Editor

SYBEX, INC.

1151 Marina Village Parkway, Alameda, CA 94501
510-523-8233   fax: 510-523- 1766
www.sybex.com   e-mail: info@sybex.com

Sybex was founded in 1976 and is the oldest publisher of computer books, as well as the largest independent computer book publisher. Sybex also publishes a wide range of computer-based training and Web-based training products. It publishes trade computer books for all levels and all types of users. Sybex offers high-quality tutorials and references in all major software areas, including certification, programming, graphics, business applications, operating systems, and games. The company has wide distribution in all major retail bookstores, mass-market outlets, and warehouse clubs and enjoys superior worldwide distribution.

The Sybex catalog features certification titles for technical professionals, the Mastering series for beginning, intermediate, and advanced users; Strategies and Secrets for gamers; I Didn't Know You Could Do That! for intermediate users; Complete for beginning to intermediate users; Developer's Guides for professional programmers and developers; and Jumpstart and Visual Jumpstart for beginners.

Recent bestsellers include: *CCNA Study Guide* by Todd Lammle; *Mastering Windows 2000 Server,* 3rd edition, and *The Complete PC Upgrade and Maintenance Guide,* 11th edition by Mark Mianasi; *MCSE Window 2000 Core Requirements Study Guides* by James Chellis and other authors; *Pokemon Gold and Silver Pathways to Adventure* by Jason Rich.

Sybex handles its own distribution.

Query letters and SASEs should be directed to:

Jordan Gold, Vice President and Publisher—He will direct you to the appropriate associate publisher and acquisitions editor who is responsible for the particular product or topic area. Any book or series idea may be directed to his attention. He will also help you in any publishing-related matter.

THE TAUNTON PRESS (PART OF PUBLISHER'S GROUP WEST)

63 South Main Street, P.O. Box 5506, Newtown, CT 06470-5506
203-426-8171   fax: 203-426-3434
www.taunton.com

The Taunton Press is known for its high-quality, authentic books and magazines. For over 20 years, it has published leading magazines, such as *Fine Woodworking* and *Fine Gardening.* Taunton started out publishing woodworking books but then grew to include fiber arts, home design, building and remodeling, gardening, and cooking. Taunton is a small publishing company but has a strong market reach through its parent company, Publisher's Group West. Taunton currently publishes 35–40 frontlist titles each year, with an active backlist of over 250 books.

Query letters and SASEs should be directed to:

Jim Childs, Publisher

TAYLOR PUBLISHING COMPANY

1550 West Mockingbird Lane, Dallas, TX 75235
214-819-8501

Taylor presents frontlist trade books and targeted-interest practical titles in the areas of celebrity biography, health and fitness, gardening, home improvement, lifestyle, parenting, popular culture, regional, sports, and coffee-table/gift books. Taylor Publishing Company (founded in 1980) is an innovative house that is particularly adept at hitting specialty interest areas and international gift-book/display markets.

Titles from Taylor: *ESPN: The Uncensored History* by Michael Freeman; *Koufax* by Ed Oruver; *The Depressed Child* by Dr. Douglas Riley; *The Bully Pulpit: A Teddy Roosevelt Book of Quotations* (edited by H. Paul Jeffers); *The Moonlit Garden* by Scott Ogden; *The Stan DeFreitas Garden Answer Book* by Stan DeFreitas.

Backlist hits: *Spielberg: The Man, the Movies, the Mythology* by Frank Santello; *Patty Sheehan on Golf* by Patty Sheehan and Betty Hicks; *A Winning Edge* by Bonnie Blair with Greg Brown (illustrated by Doug Keith); *Count Me In, Never Give Up* by Cal Ripken, Jr.

Taylor Publishing distributes its own list and handles distribution for a variety of other houses.

Query letters and SASEs should be directed to:

Lynn A. Brooks, Publisher and Editorial Director

Michael Emmerich, Acquisitions Director

TEN SPEED PRESS/CELESTIAL ARTS/TRICYCLE PRESS

Celestial Arts

Tricycle Press

P.O. Box 7123, Berkeley, CA 94707
510-559-1600   fax: 510-524-1052
www.tenspeed.com

Ten Speed/Celestial Arts publishes practical nonfiction in cooking, business and careers, women's issues, parenting, health, self-discovery, leisure and lifestyle, humor, outdoors, house crafts, and popular reference. Tricycle Press (please see separate subentry further on) is Ten Speed/Celestial's children's division. Ten Speed Press/Celestial Arts publishes hardcover and paperback titles; the house also produces a line of posters and novelty items.

Ten Speed Press (founded in 1971) gained success with *Anybody's Bike Book* by Tom Cuthbertson—the first book the publisher produced; this classic work has been revised and updated several times and is emblematic of the type of reference book that Ten Speed Press publishes so well. With the acquisition of the Celestial Arts subsidiary (see separate subentry), the house obtained the midsize status that set the platform for subsequent expansion of the list. Throughout this growth, Ten Speed has been renowned for its small press publishing savvy.

Ten Speed/Celestial is selective in acquiring new works and procures in part on the basis of projected endurance: The hardy backlist and announcements of revised editions read as fresh and bright as many houses' new releases.

Ten Speed is noted for the individualist expression of the American culture as voiced by the house's authors. Many Ten Speed titles feature unconventional approaches to the subject matter at hand—making creativity an enduring Ten Speed/Celestial Arts hallmark.

Among its perennial sellers, Ten Speed publishes *What Color Is Your Parachute?* and other career-related works by Richard Bolles; *The Moosewood Cookbook* by Mollie Katzen (along with several additional food titles by Ms. Katzen and the Moosewood Collective).

Ten Speed titles: *Charlie Trotter Cooks at Home* by Charlie Trotter; *Mushrooms Demystified* by David Arora; *The Village Baker* by Joe Ortiz; *White Trash Cooking* by Ernest Matthew Mickler; *Why Cats Paint* by Burton Silver and Heather Busch; *Cindy Pawlcyn's Mustards Grill Cookbook* by Cindy Pawlcyn; *Caprial Cooks for Friends* by Caprial Pence; *Terra: Cooking from the Heart of Napa Valley* by Hiro Sone and Lissa Doumani; *Allergy-Free Gardening* by Thomas L. Ogren; *Man Eating Bugs* by Peter Menzel and Faith D'Aluisio.

Ten Speed Press/Celestial Arts handles its own distribution.

Query letters and SASEs should be directed to:

Kirsty Melville, Publisher

Lorena Jones, Editorial Director

Philip Wood, Founder

Aaron Warner, Editor

Celestial Arts

The Celestial Arts program homes toward titles in self-discovery, nutrition and fitness, general health, spirituality, popular psychology, relationships and healing, pregnancy and parenting, gay and lesbian issues, practical how-to, kitchen arts, and general trade nonfiction.

Celestial Arts was founded as an independent house in 1966 and was acquired by Ten Speed Press in 1983. The house produces an individual line of hardcover and trade paperback books, along with calendars, maps, poster art, personal journals, and engagement books.

On the Celestial Arts roster: *Bestfeeding* by Mary Renfrew, Chloe Fisher, and Suzanne Arms; *Living Juicy* by Sark; *Uncommon Sense for Parents with Teenagers* by Mike Riera; *Natural Superwoman* by Rosamon Richardson; *Hit Below the Belt: Facing Up to Prostate Cancer* by F. Ralph Berberich, M.D.; *Natural Alternatives to HRT Cookbook* by Marilyn Glenville; *Positively Gay* (edited by Betty Berzon, Ph.D.); *The Detox Diet* by Elson M. Haas, M.D.

Celestial Arts is distributed by Ten Speed Press/Celestial Arts.

Query letters and SASEs should be directed to:

Jo Ann Deck, Vice President, Editor

Lovena Jones, Editorial Director

Tricycle Press

Tricycle is devoted to books and posters for kids and their grown-ups. Tricycle Press was started in 1993 to unify and expand the house's children's list (previously divided between parent Ten Speed and sister Celestial Arts). Tricycle Press, in addition to its own roster of originals, catalogs appropriate backlist selections from Ten Speed and Celestial Arts.

Tricycle is committed to publishing projects that reflect the creative spirit of the parent company, Ten Speed Press, and its publishing partner, Celestial Arts.

Titles from Tricycle: *G is for Googol* by David Schwartz; *Pretend Soup* and *Honest Pretzels* by Mollie Katzen; *Hey Little Ant* by Phillip and Hannah Hoose; *The Pumpkin Blanket* by Deborah Turney Zagwyn; *We Can Work It Out: Conflict Resolution for Children* by Barbara K. Polland; *Crashed, Smashed, and Mashed: A Trip to Junkyard Heaven* by Joyce Slayton Mitchell and Steven Borns.

No query letters please. Send complete picture book manuscripts, and sample chapters and outlines for longer works, making sure to include an SASE, care of:

Nicole Geiger, Publisher

TEXAS MONTHLY PRESS

See Gulf Publishing.

THAMES AND HUDSON

500 Fifth Avenue, New York, NY 10110
212-354-3763   fax: 212-398-1252
www.thamesandhudsonusa.com

Thames and Hudson publishes popular and scholarly works, as well as college texts in the fine arts, archaeology, architecture, biography, crafts, history, mysticism, music, photography, and the sciences.

Thames and Hudson (founded in 1977) is an international producer of well-crafted nonfiction trade books in hardcover and trade paperback under its double-dolphin logo. Though a portion of the publisher's list is originated through the New York editorial office, the greater part of Thames and Hudson's titles are imports via the house's United Kingdom branch.

From Thames and Hudson: *The Most Beautiful Villages of Israel; The Most Beautiful Villages and Towns of the South; The Golden Age of Dutch Art; Looking Back at Francis Bacon; Living in the Highlands; Techno Architecture; The Dalai Lama's Secret Temple; William Blake: The Complete Illuminated Books; Practically Minimal; Chronicle of the Maya Kings and Queens; The World of King Arthur.*

Thames and Hudson is distributed to the trade by W. W. Norton. The house also offers an 800 ordering number and has in-house fulfillment services for purchases by individual consumers.

Query letters and SASEs should be directed to:

Peter Warner, President

THEATRE COMMUNICATIONS GROUP, INC.

355 Lexington Avenue, New York, NY 10017-0217
212-697-5230

Theatre Communications Group is interested in theater-related works.

TIMBERWOLF PRESS

P.O. Box 266, Allen, TX 75013
972-644-7098
www.TwolfPress.com   e-mail: info@twolfpress.com

Founded in 1994 by Patrick Seaman, Timberwolf Press started out as a software company, publishing a Windows Database version of the bestselling trade reference, the *Insider's Guide to Book Editors, Publishers, and Literary Agents* by Jeff Herman. The software was called Writer's Desktop Database for Windows and is now in its fourth annual release.

In 1995, Patrick became affiliated with the premiere Internet broadcasting company AudioNet (http://www.AudioNet.com). While searching for content to broadcast on AudioNet, Seaman asked a writing acquaintance, Jim Cline, to produce an audio version of a novel that Jim was working on at the time. In late 1995, this project gave birth to the first serialized audio-novel on the Internet. Thanks to the Internet, it received fan mail from around the world.

In 1997, Timberwolf Press expanded from a software and multimedia publishing company to the world of print publishing when it released Jim Cline's epic military science fiction novel in a hardback edition: *A Small Percentage*.

A sequel to *A Small Percentage* is in the works, as well as other science fiction and techno-thriller titles.

Query letters and SASEs should be directed to:

Eve McClellen, Senior Editor

Jennifer Mikhail, Editor at Large

Patrick Seaman, Publisher

T

TIME WARNER BOOK GROUP

Warner Books

Bulfinch Press

Hyperion Books

Little Brown & Co. (see separate entry in U.S. publishers)

Mysterious Press

Time Warner Audio Books

Warner Aspect

Time & Life Building, 1271 Avenue of the Americas, New York, NY 10020
212-522-7200
www.twbookmark.com

Warner Books publishes trade nonfiction and commercial fiction. Warner produces mass-market, trade paperback, and hardcover originals, as well as reprints. Among Warner's nonfiction categories are biography, business, cooking, current affairs, history, house and home, humor, popular culture, psychology, self-help, sports, games books, and general reference. Warner fiction accents the popular approach and includes frontlist commercial novels and works in the categories of mystery and suspense, fantasy and science fiction, action thrillers, horror, and contemporary and historical romance.

Warner Aspect is an imprint that specializes in future fiction, science fiction, and fantasy. Warner Vision books are generally high-profile mass-market releases. Books on cassette are the domain of Time Warner AudioBooks. The formerly independent Mysterious Press publishes a distinguished list of mystery, suspense, and crime novels, as well as selected crime nonfiction and reference (see separate entry).

Warner Books (founded in 1961) is a division of Time Warner Communications.

From the Warner list: *26 Nights* by Editors of *Penthouse* magazine; *A Call to Conscience* by Clayborne Carson and Kris Shepard; *A Darkness More Than Night* by Michael Connelly; *A Knock at Midnight* by Clayborne Carson and Peter Holloran; *A Midnight Clear* by Katherine Storne; *A Triumph of Souls* by Alan Dean Foster; *Almost Eden* by Dorothy Garlock; *Along Came a Spider* by James Patterson; *Andy Kaufman Revealed!* by Bob Zmuda and Matthew Scott Hansen; *Angels Flight* by Michael Connelly; *Another Dawn* by Sandra Brown; *Amanda's Wedding* by Jenny Colgan; *Blue River* by Ethan Anin; *Brain Longevity* by Dharma Singh Khalsa and Cameron Stauth; *Cane River* by Lalita Tademy; *Commitments* by Barbara Delinsky; *Champions in Courage* by Pat LaFontaine, Ernie Valutis, M.D., Chas Griffin, and Larry Weisman; *Cradle and All* by James Patterson; *Death of an Addict* by M. C. Beaton; *ESO* by Alan Brauer and Donna J. Brauer; *Extreme Management* by Mark Stevens; *Free Agent Nation* by Daniel H. Pink; *Getting Back* by William Dietrich; *Hail, Hail, the Gang's All Here!* by Ed McBrain; *Hidden Fires* by Sandra Brown; *If Not Now, When?* by Stephanie Marston; *Power Talk* by Sarah Myers McGinty, Ph.D.; and *Real Fitness for Women* by Rochelle Rice.

Warner Books handles its own distribution and distributes book products from other publishers.

Query letters and SASEs should be directed to:

Amy Einhorn, Executive Editor, Warner Trade Paperbacks—Popular culture, business, fitness, and self-help.

Betsy Mitchell, Executive Editor—Science fiction.

Caryn Karmatz Rudy, Senior Editor— Fiction, general nonfiction, and popular culture.

Claire Zion, Executive Editor, Mass Market Paperbacks—Women's fiction, including romance.

Diana Baroni, Editor—fitness/health, general fiction, nonfiction.

Jamie Raab, Senior Vice President/Publisher, Warner hardcovers—General nonfiction and fiction.

John Aherne, Associate Editor—Popular culture, fiction, general nonfiction.

Les Pockell, Associate Publisher— General nonfiction.

Rick Horgan, Vice President and Executive Editor—General nonfiction. Fiction: thrillers.

Rob McMahon, Editor—Business, fiction, sports.

Beth de Guzman, Editorial director—Mass market (fiction and nonfiction)

Sara Ann Freed, Editor in Chief—Mysterious Press—Mysteries and suspense.

Jackie Joinwe, Associate Editor—Commercial fiction, spiritual/New Age, memoir/biography.

Rick Wolff, Executive Editor, Warner Books—Business, sports, humor.

Born: July 14, 1951.

Education: Harvard '73, Long Island University, M.A., '85.

Employment history/editor career path: Warner books for the last seven years; Macmillan Books seven years before that; and Alex Hamilton Institute eight years before that.

Personal interests: I'm fairly eclectic—everything from sports to psychology to reading books. But most of my spare time is devoted to my wife and our three children. Our lives revolve around them.

What would you be doing if you were not an editor? Probably writing books instead of editing them.

What has been your most successful book that you have acquired to date? *Politically Correct Fairy Tales*—a humorous hardcover that was on the *NYT* list for close to two years and was number one for a few weeks. That book sold more than four million copies worldwide. The author was James Finn Garner.

What books have you acquired that make you the most proud? What books that you have acquired reflect the types of books you like to represent? *Pros and Cons: The Criminals Who Play in the NFL* (Warner, 1999). Also, *You Gotta Have Wa* by Robert Whiting, about the Japanese obsession with baseball (Macmillan, 1987*). Rich Dad, Poor Dad*, which is on the list right now. Financial advice from Robert Kiyosaki.

Do you represent fiction? If so, what do you look for? Yes. Strictly big-time commercial fiction. Warner has a very short fiction list, so whatever we acquire, it has to smell like a bestseller.

What do you want to see less of? Can't say. After all, *Politically Correct Fairy Tales* came in the slush pile.

Do you represent nonfiction? Yes—I handle business, sports, humor, psychology, biography, finances, and so on.

Do you require book proposals? If so, what do you look for in evaluating a book proposal? A book proposal is a *must*. I don't have the time to chat about "ideas" for a book over the phone or in e-mail.

Are certain aspects of a book proposal given more weight than others? It has to be well written by an author with top credentials, who is committed to promoting the book, and the idea behind the book has to be fresh and different.

What process do you use for making a decision? What is the process for acquisition, is there a committee? If a proposal gets past my review, I take it to the general editorial meeting to get more readings. If it makes the cut there, I take it to the publisher's review meeting for a determination of whether we should pursue it and for how much.

What kinds of nonfiction books do you want to see less of? At Warner, which is a major front-list house, unless the book can break out in a major way for us, it probably isn't right for us. That usually means most general midlist nonfiction won't work for us.

T

Are you interested in work geared for the masses (readers of *People, The Star,* etc.)? Depends on the star and how popular they are.

Are agents important? Why? Of course. To help develop proposals, to help the author understand the publishing process, and to work with the editor to make sure the book is a success.

Do you like new writers? What should new writers do to break into the business? Write for newspapers and magazines. Build from that.

How should writers approach you? Through an agent. I wish I had more time to chat with writers who aspire to be published, but unfortunately, I just don't.

What are some common mistakes writers make? What really gets on your nerves? Not promoting their books. Assuming that they can place demands on their editor and other people in the publishing house.

What can writers do to get your attention and to avoid the slush pile? Get an agent.

What have been some of your craziest experiences with submissions? I once put a clause in a contract with the author, a woman in her early 20s, that she couldn't lose her virginity until her book was published. And she signed the contract.

What have been some of your best experiences with writers or in your job? Most of them become lifelong friends and trusted colleagues. That's a major part of the job.

What, if anything, makes you different from other editors? I'm smarter and better looking than my editorial colleagues.

Is there anything you would like to see changed in the industry? I wish the production process could be speeded up with books. It seems silly to have to wait eight or nine months to get a book published after the manuscript is completed.

Any additional thoughts? One of the great aspects of book publishing is that you never know when a new talent is going to be discovered. That's what drives me—I'm always on the lookout for that next great writer.

TOR BOOKS/FORGE BOOKS

175 Fifth Avenue, 14th Floor, New York, NY 10010
212-388-0100

Tom Doherty Associates (TDA), LLC, is part of the Von Holtzbrinck Publishing Group. TDA has two main imprints, Tor and Forge, which publish general commercial fiction of nearly all types and a limited amount of nonfiction. Both imprints release books in hardcover, trade paperback, and mass market formats; in addition, TDA publishes the Orb line of trade paperback reprints in science fiction, fantasy, and horror.

Tor Books are primarily science fiction, fantasy, and horror. Young adult titles, both fiction and nonfiction, are also published under the Tor imprint; some of our YA publications are done for the educational market and we have a strong list of mass-market paperback editions of classic literature. Forge books are historical fiction, contemporary fiction, thrillers, mysteries, Westerns, and virtually all types of general fiction with the exception of romance, which we do not publish.

Recent books from the Tor imprint include: *Rhapsody* by Elizabeth Haydon; *Ender's Shadow* by Orson Scott Card; *The Marriage of Sticks* by Jonathan Carroll; *Communion*

Blood by Chelsea Quinn Yarbro; *Dragon and Phoenix* by Joanne Bertin; *Greenhouse Summer* by Norman Spinrad; *The Fox Woman* by Kij Johnson; *The Stone War* by Madeleine E. Robins; *Lodestar* by Michael Flynn; *The Light of Other Days* by Arthur C. Clarke and Stephen Baxter; *Winter's Heart* by Robert Jordan; *Faith of the Fallen* by Terry Goodkind.

Recent books from the Forge imprint include: *Vengeance* by Stuart M. Kaminsky; *Peace, War & Politics* by Jack Anderson; *Help Me Please* by Barbara D'Amato; *The Protocol* by April Christofferson; *The Flying Scotsman* by Quinn Fawcett; *The Difficult Saint* by Sharan Newman; *Thunder City* by Loren D. Estleman; *Hours of Gladness* by Thomas Fleming; *Cat in a Jeweled Jumpsuit* by Carole Nelson Douglas; *Choices* by Abigail Reed; *Furthermore!: Memories of a Parish Priest* by Andrew M. Greeley.

Proposals and query letters must include SASE for reply and should be directed to:

Beth Meacham, Executive Editor—Science fiction.

Claire Eddy, Editor—Women's fiction, romances, mysteries.

David Hartwell, Senior Editor—Science fiction.

Greg Cox, Editor—Media tie-ins.

Melissa Ann Singer, Senior Editor—Women's fiction, romances, mysteries.

Patrick Nielsen Hayden, Senior Editor—Manager of Science Fiction, horror, fantasy.

Forge Books

The books that carry the Forge emblem (a stylized flaming anvil) run the gamut of commercial fiction and nonfiction. At Forge the various genres and categories are well represented (often with frontlist sensibility), and many titles honor mainstream conventions even as they exhibit their own individualistic bent.

Fiction from Forge: *Play It Again* (detective fiction) by Stephen Humphrey Bogart (author is the son of Lauren Bacall and Humphrey Bogart); *Cat on a Blue Monday* (and other Midnight Louie mysteries) by Carole Nelson Douglas; *Steroid Blues* (suspense) by Richard La Plante (author of *Mantis* and *Leopard*); *The Cutting Hours* by Julia Grice; *Speak Daggers to Her* by Rosemary Edgehill; *Presumed Dead* by Hugh Holton; *False Promises* by Ralph Arnote.

Representing Forge nonfiction: *Zoo Book: The Evolution of Wildlife Conservation Centers* by Linda Koebner; *The October Twelve: Five Years of Yankee Glory* by Phil Rizzuto and Tom Horton; *Deke! My Thirty-Four Years in Space* by Donald K. Slayton with Michael Cassutt.

Query letters and SASEs should be directed to:

Natalia Aponte, Senior Editor—Women's fiction.

Will Smith, Editorial Assistant

J. N. TOWNSEND, PUBLISHING

12 Greenleaf Drive, Exeter, NH 03833
603-778-9883   fax: 603-772-1980
www.jntownsendpublishing.com   e-mail: jntown@mediaone.net

J. N. Townsend is a small publisher with a successful line of titles about pets, wildlife, nature, and country living. Townsend (founded in 1986) initially published in softcover format only and issued its first hardcover title in 1994. The house has thrived on the basis of short press runs and by keeping titles alive on a full backlist.

From Townsend: *Duffy: Adventures of a Collie* by Irving Townsend; *Goat Song: My Island Angora Goat Farm* by Susan Basquin; *A Cat's Life: Dulcy's Story,* as told to Dee Ready; *Who Ever Heard of a HORSE in the HOUSE?* by Jacqueline Tresl; *The Ugly Dachshund* (5th printing) by G. B. Stern; *Regards, Rodeo: The Mariner Dog of Cassi* (2nd printing) by Alan Armstrong (illustrations by Martha Armstrong).

J. N. Townsend Publishing presents the latest book by Era Zistel, *The Good Year;* she writes about her life with animals in the Catskill Mountains of New York. Other Zistel titles: *Gentle People; Wintertime Cat; Orphan; A Gathering of Cats; Good Companions.*

Celebrating a third printing is *Separate Lifetimes: A Collection* by Irving Townsend (illustrated by Judith Roberts-Rondeau); this collection of essays is particularly cherished by readers who have suffered the loss of an animal companion. *Separate Lifetimes* was the first book published by the press in 1986 as a memorial to the publisher's father.

Distributed to the trade by Alan C. Hood and Company.

Query letters and SASEs should be directed to:

Jeremy N. Townsend, Publisher

TURNER PUBLISHING, INC.

Turner Publishing has officially gone out of business.

TUTTLE PUBLISHING

153 Milk Street, 5th Floor, Boston, MA 02109
617-951-4080   fax: 617-951-4045

Tuttle Publishing is America's leading independent publisher of Asian-interest books and maps and the premier publisher of English-language books in Japan. Tuttle's imprints strive to span the East and West with market-leading books on cooking, martial arts, Eastern philosophy, spiritual development, Asian culture, design, and language learning.

Their publications include such renowned books as: *The New Nelson Japanese-English Dictionary; Bruce Lee's Striking Thoughts,* compiled and annotated by John Little; *The Henna Body Art Kit* by Aileen Marron; *Japan's Big Bang: The Deregulation and Revitalization of the Japanese Economy* by Declan Hayes; and *Zen Flesh, Zen Bones* by Nyogen Senzaki and Paul Reps.

UNITED PUBLISHERS GROUP/UPG

    Hastings House

    Gates & Bridges

    Judd Publishing

50 Washington Street, Norwalk, CT 06854
203-838-4083   fax: 203-838-4084
www.upub.com   e-mail: info@upub.com

United Publishers Group/UPG produces a number of trade nonfiction lines and selective fiction through several affiliated imprints. The group includes Hastings House (Daytrips travel guides); Gates & Bridges (works with multicultural/global themes); Judd Publishing (illustrated editions); and Rosset-Morgan Books (books with a literary or cultural perspective).

United Publishers Group (founded in 1996) and its imprints conduct their programs from offices in several locations, including Connecticut; Washington, D.C.; and Manhattan. UPG is a subsidiary of the German-based Peter Leers Group, a privately held real-estate and insurance amalgamate.

Henno Lohmeyer (UPG publisher) opened the house in fine style by acquiring several previously independent publishing firms, and by securing the United States rights to a number of international publishing properties. Plans are to build the publishing group through a number of robust boutique imprints, rather than by combining editorial operations.

From Hastings House: *The Truth About Fiction Writing* by William Appel and Denise Sterrs; *Test Your Bible Power* by Jerry Agel; *Passion for Wine: The Ultimate Guide* by Paul Lirette.

Gates & Bridges is a new imprint that features works that exemplify the essential image: "gates to new worlds . . . bridges between continents." From G&B: *Land of the Ascending Dragon: Rediscovering Vietnam* (photoessay) by Paul Martin (photographs by Seven Raymer); *The Opera Quiz Book: Everything You Always Wanted to Know About the Greatest Art Form Ever Invented by Mankind* by Michael Walsh (photographs by Henry Grossman).

United Publishers Group distributes through Publishers Group West.

Initial queries to UPG may be directed to the main-entry address.

Query letters and SASEs should be directed to:

Henno Lohmeyer, Publisher and Editor, Gates and Bridges—Works from an international perspective; regional markets; commercial and trade nonfiction.

Hy Steirman, Editor in Chief, Hastings House—Presides over Hastings House (now featuring Daytrips travel guides).

Ruina W. Judd, Editor in Chief, Judd Publishing—Illustrated books.

UNIVERSE PUBLISHING

Children's Universe

300 Park Avenue South, New York, NY 10010-5399
212-982-2300

Universe produces books in art history and appreciation, architecture and design, photography, fashion, sports, alternative culture, and performing arts. Universe Publishing also takes on selected high-interest projects in literary writing and criticism, and the occasional human- or social-interest title in illustrated format. The Universe Publishing emphasis (through individual titles and a number of successful series) is on works of popular, as well as scholarly, interest in the arts worldwide and the arts and artists of the Western and European tradition from prehistoric to contemporary times.

Universe Publishing (founded in 1956; formerly a wing of Phaidon Universe) is an affiliate division of Rizzoli International. Imprints and associated publishers include Universe, Children's Universe, Universe Calendars, Vendome, and Universe Publishing. Among Universe's products are illustrated gift books, children's books, children's paper products, calendars, address books, and diaries.

Universe titles: *The Internet Design Project: The Best of Graphic Art on the Web* by Patrick Burgoyne and Liz Faber; *All-American: A Tommy Hilfiger Style Book* by Tommy Hilfiger, with David A. Keeps; *Secrets of Skating* by Oksana Baiul; *Gymnastics: Balancing Acts* by Christina Lessa; *Camera Ready: How to Shoot Your Kids* by Arthur Elgort; *Intimate Landscapes: The Canyon Suite of Georgia O'Keeffe* by Dana Self, in association with the Kemper Museum of Contemporary Art & Design; *The Romance of California Vineyards* by Molly Chappellet (photographs by Daniel D'Agostini); *Weekends with the Impressionists: A Collection from the National Gallery of Art, Washington* by Carla Brenner.

Universe Publishing and Vendome Press combine on special series lines: Universe of Fashion; Universe of Design; Universe of Art. Beautifully printed and designed—and reasonably priced—these books are geared to appeal equally to novice and expert.

Universe of Fashion offerings are introduced by Grace Mirabella (of magazine fame); each volume deals with the works of great 20th-century couturiers. These books connect the worlds of art, couture, and society with stories of legendary designers. Titles: *Coco Chanel* by Francois Baudot; *Dior* by Marie-France Pocha; *Yves Saint Laurent* by Pierre Bergé; *Valentino* by Bernadine Morris; *Versace* by Richard Martin.

From Universe of Design: *Ferrari and Pininfarina* by Lionel Froissard; *Cartier* by Philippe Trétiack.

The Universe of Art series features shifting, distinctive approaches. Some titles focus on an important facet in the work of an individual legendary master, generally a period or place that encapsulates the essence of a lifetime's work. Titles: *Matisse in Nice* by Xavier Girard; *Renoir's Nudes* by Isabelle Cahn; *Degas Backstage* by Richard Kendall; *Cézanne in Provence* by Denis Coutagne. Other titles in this series feature celebrity authors writing on celebrated artists: *Jasper Johns* by Leo Castelli; *Andy Warhol* by Bob Colacello.

From Vendome: *House & Garden Book of Country Rooms* by Leonie Highton; *Secrets of the Harem* by Carla Coco; *Treasures from Italy's Great Libraries* by Lorenzo Crinelli; *Churches of Rome* by Pierre Grimal (photographs by Caroline Rose); *The Grand Canal* by Umberto Franzoi (photographs by Mark Smith).

Universe is distributed to the trade by St. Martin's.

Query letters and SASEs should be directed to:

Charles Miers, Publisher—Calendars, graphic products; Children's Universe projects.

Elizabeth Johnson, Senior Editor—Art, architecture, women's studies.

Children's Universe

Children's Universe produces a variety of inventive products, ranging from book-and-toy packages to storybooks, to hide-and-seek books (with moveable parts), cut-out puppets, posters, masks, and make-it-yourself gift boxes. These are finely designed books and are produced in sturdy editions to withstand carefree handling.

Books from Children's Universe: *Skateboard Monsters* by Daniel Kirk; *Ravita and the Land of Unknown Shadows* (story by Marietta and Peter Brill; illustrated by Laurie Smollett Kutscera); *Head Trips* by Sara Schwartz; *First Steps in Paint: A New and Simple Way to Learn How to Paint* by Tom Robb; *Dinosaur Cowboys Puppet Theatre* by Judy Lichtenstein; *The ABC's of Art* (with a wall frieze version) by the National Gallery of Art, London (with flash cards by the National Gallery of Art, Washington, D.C.).

VAN NOSTRAND REINHOLD

Van Nostrand Reinhold was purchased by John Wiley in 1997 and disbanded as an independent publisher.

VERSO, INC.

New York office:
180 Varick Street, New York, NY 10014-4606
212-807-9680   fax: 212-807-9152
www.versobooks.com

U.K. office:
Verso/New Left Books
6 Meard Street, London W1S 0EG
0171.437.3546   fax: 0171.734.0059
e-mail: 100434.1414@compuserve.com

Verso accents trade nonfiction and literary fiction. Areas of Verso scope include contemporary issues and culture; history and biography; investigative works; world literature and thought in translation; continental, postmodernist, and deconstructivist philosophy and criticism; humor. Verso produces hardcover and trade paperback editions, as well as occasional special merchandise lines such as calendars and cards.

Verso, Inc. (founded in 1968) is an international house; the United Kingdom headquarters operates from London offices; the downtown New York wing is responsible for Stateside promotion, marketing, sales, and distribution; the major editorial acquisitions program is centered in the UK; over the past several seasons the U.S. list has gained increasing presence.

Titles from Verso: *The World Is Not for Sale: Farmers Against Junk Food* by Jose Bove and Francoix Dufour; *Merchants and Revolution: Commercial Change, Political Conflict, and London's Overseas Traders, 1550–1653* by Robert Brenner; *Close Up: Iranian Cinema: Past, Present and Future* by Hamid Dabashi; *The Murder of Lumumba* by Ludo De Witte; *The No-Nonsense Guide to Globalization* by Wayne Ellwood; *Virtuality Check: Power Relations and Alternative Strategies in the Information Society* by Francois Fortier; *The Trial of Henry Kissinger* by Christopher Hitchens; *Flying Sparks: Growing Up on the Edge of Las Vegas* by Odette Larson; *Hollywood Flatlands: Animation, Critical*

Theory and the Avant-Garde by Esther Leslie; *Mother Millett* by Kate Millett; *The No Nonsense Guide to Fair Trade* by David Ransom; *Wanderlust: A History of Walking* by Rebecca Solnit; *Rock 'Til You Drop* by John Strausbaugh; *Private Warriors* by Ken Silverstein; and *High Art Life: British Art in the 1990's.*

Verso distributes to the trade through W. W. Norton (U.S.); Penguin Canada (Canada); and Marston Book Services (U.K. and the rest of the world).

Query letters and SASEs for the United States concerns and interests of Verso, Inc., should be directed to **Managing Editor** at the New York address. Otherwise, contact U.K. offices.

WALKER & COMPANY

Walker & Company Books for Young Readers

435 Hudson Street, New York, NY 10014
212-727-8300   fax: 212-727-0984

Walker publishes trade nonfiction and mystery fiction. Nonfiction emphasis includes science, history, health, nature, self-help, business, and entrepreneurship. Frontlist fiction accents mysteries. Walker produces a list of large-print Judaica and Christian inspirational titles; books for children range from preschool picture books to books for young adults (please see subentry for Walker & Company Books for Young Readers).

Walker & Company (established in 1959) is a concentrated powerhouse with a hard-hitting, diverse list; especially strong are Walker's market niches in history and science, health, mysteries, large-print religious and inspirational titles, and children's books that complement a broad, carefully chosen selection of adult nonfiction titles.

Walker operates on the publishing credo that what often separates the success of one book from another is the ability to execute an effective marketing strategy; what then separates one house from another is the ability to execute many such strategies—often simultaneously—season upon season.

Walker & Company was founded by the intrepid Sam Walker, who expressed the view "there cannot be a surfeit of good taste." Such faith in editorial content remains at the heart of the firm today, under the current leadership of publisher George Gibson. Underlying the house's publishing strategy is a commitment to quality of product. This two-pronged assault on the marketplace thus relies on compositional and literary depth as well as the ability to capitalize on the potential appeal of such works.

Walker nonfiction titles: *Longitude: The True Story of a Genius Who Solved the Greatest Scientific Problem of His Time* and *Galileo's Daughter* by Dava Sobel; *Cod: A Biography of the Fish That Changed the World* by Mark Kurlansky; *Monitor: The Story of the Legendary Civil War Ironclad and the Man Whose Invention Changed the Course of History* by James Tertius deKay; *Overcoming Overspending: A Winning Plan for Spenders and Their Partners* by Olivia Mellan with Sherry Christie; *The Joy of Pi* by David Blatner; *Fermat's Enigma: The Epic Quest to Solve the World's Greatest Mathematical Problem* by Simon Singh; *E = MC2: A Biography of the World's Most Famous Equation* by David Bodanis; *Burnelleschi's Dome* by Ross King.

In fiction, Walker is admired for its standout approach to category books (a significant number of which are first novels) in mysteries. (Walker discontinued its lines in such genres as Western thrillers, romances, and adventure novels.)

On the Walker list in mystery: *Killing Cassidy: A Dorothy Martin Mystery* by Jeanne M. Dams; *Eye of the Cricket: A Lew Griffin Mystery* by James Sallis; *The Wrong Dog: A Rachel Alexander and Dash Mystery* by Carol Lea Benjamin; *The Ice Pick Artist: A Carl Wilcox Mystery* by Harold Adams; *Five Card Stud: A Jake Hines Mystery* by Elizabeth Gunn.

Walker's guidelines for manuscript submission to its genre lists include valuable hints for fiction authors in general and category writers in particular; the sheet for Walker mysteries notes such tips as the editorial view that the mystery novel is a game between author and reader, an entertaining puzzle to be savored and solved; the mystery must be primary (with such nuances as romantic interest secondary); the mystery-novel story line must be rooted in the real world (and not imbued with supernatural overtones); and manuscripts should in general respect the conventions of the genre.

Authors please note: Materials submitted without a self-addressed stamped envelope (SASE) will not be returned.

Walker handles marketing, sales, and distribution for its own list.

Query letters and SASEs should be directed to:

George Gibson, Publisher—Nonfiction in all Walker areas, including science, nature, parenting, education, business, health, sourcebooks.

Jacqueline Johnson, Editor—Nonfiction.

Michael Seidman, Editor—Mysteries. No romantic suspense or horror stories.

Walker and Company Books for Young Readers

Walker and Company Books for Young Readers maintains a backlist in addition to its seasonal offerings of new books. The house caters to a variety of young-reader markets from preschooler picture books to fiction and nonfiction for young adults.

Walker titles for young readers: *Snow Day* by Moira Fain; *The Milkman's Boy* by Donald Hall (illustrated by Greg Shed); *Velcome* by Kevin O'Malley; *Grand Canyon: A Trail Through Time* by Linda Vieria (illustrated by Christopher Canyon); *Naming the Cat* by Laurence Pringle (illustrated by Katherine Potter); *Until I Met Dudley: How Everyday Things Really Work* by Roger McGough (illustrated by Chris Riddell); *Trapped by the Ice: Shackleton's Amazing Antarctic Adventure* by Michael McCurdy; *The Keeping Room* by Anna Myers.

Query letters and SASEs should be directed to:

Emily Easton, Publisher

Jim Travaglini, Editor

The above two editors acquire children's books. They are especially interested in young science, photoessays, historical fiction for middle grades, biographies, current affairs, and young-adult nonfiction.

WATSON-GUPTILL PUBLICATIONS

770 Broadway, New York, NY, 10001
646-654-5500

Watson-Guptill produces titles in art instruction and technique, graphic design, fine arts, photography, crafts, environmental and interior design, lifestyle, popular culture, architecture, music, theater, and film. Manuals and handbooks abound on the Watson-Guptill booklist, as do annual design reviews geared to these specialized fields.

Watson-Guptill's imprints include Whitney Library of Design, Amphoto, Billboard Books, Back Stage Books, and RAC Books. The publisher maintains an extensive backlist and is a leading publisher in its areas of interest. Watson-Guptill Publications (founded in 1937) is a division of Billboard Publications.

The Watson-Guptill imprint addresses art instruction and graphic design, architecture, interior design, and planning. Amphoto produces instructional volumes from leading photographers. Whitney Library of Design issues selected titles in architecture and planning. Billboard Books vends authoritative, up-to-the-minute books on every aspect of music and entertainment. Back Stage Books purveys informative reference and instruction books in the performing arts. RAC Books offers a complete line of titles for radio amateurs.

Watson-Guptill distributes its own list.

Query letters and SASEs should be directed to:

Bob Nirkind, Senior Acquisitions Editor, Billboard Books—Music, film, television.

Candace Raney, Senior Acquisitions Editor—Fine art, art technique, cartooning and comic book art.

Dale Ramsey, Editor, Back Stage Books.

Joy Aquilino, Senior Editor—Crafts.

Marian Appellof, Senior Editor—Graphic Design.

Sylvia Warren, Senior Editor—Architecture and Interior Design.

Victoria Craven, Senior Editor, Amphoto and Lifestyle.

WESTERN PUBLISHING COMPANY, INC.

Golden Books Adult Publishing Group

Golden Books Children's

850 Third Avenue, New York, NY 10022
212-753-8500

Western Publishing accents children's books and adult trade nonfiction, plus some commercial fiction. The children's program includes illustrated color picture books, coloring books, activity books, gift books, and games and puzzles. Western also produces videocassettes, electronic books, related merchandise, and toys; the house has a line of promotional/display titles as well. Western Publishing's Golden Books Adult Publishing Group publishes trade books with a family focus in nonfiction and fiction.

Western Publishing imprints include Artists & Writers Guild Books, Golden Books (for children), Goldencraft, Golden Press, Wave Books (paperbacks for teenagers), and Golden Books Adult Publishing Group.

Western Publishing (founded in 1907) is a worldwide enterprise with offices in Wisconsin, Australia, Canada, and London. Western Publishing's colorfully illustrated Golden Books for children are popular with young readers all over the globe.

Western Publishing announced plans to expand its presence in the adult trade when Richard Snyder took over the helm at Western in late 1995, subsequent to Snyder's departure from Simon & Schuster, where he had been Chief Executive Officer.

Golden Books Adult Publishing Group will publish a library of essential work that will help parents raise great kids and help all adult readers in other areas of their personal lives. In addition to titles on parents and child care, the house will feature books addressing the broader concerns of home and family—everything from health to self-help; from personal finance to spirituality; from books that instruct and enlighten to works that entertain and inspire.

Projects from Golden Books Adult Publishing Group: *Cristina Ferrare's Family Entertaining: Celebrating the Life of the Home* by Cristina Ferrare; *The Energy Break: Recharge Your Life with Autokinetics* by Bradford Keeney, Ph.D.; *A Woman's Guide to Changing Her Man (Without His Even Knowing It)* by Michele Weiner-Davis; *The 7 Habits of Highly Effective Families* by Stephen R. Covey; *Don't Be Afraid to Discipline: The Commonsense Program for Low-Stress Parenting* by Dr. Ruth Peters; *Jewish Family & Life: A Guide to Parenting* by Yosef I. Abramowitz and Rabbi Susan Silverman; *Grow Up! Take Responsibility and Make Yourself Happy* by Dr. Frank Pittman; *Lassie's Guide to a Family's Best Friend: Raising the Family Dog* by Ace Collins.

Western Publishing orchestrates its own global distribution.

Query letters and SASEs should be directed to:

Laura Yorke, Editor in Chief

JOHN WILEY & SONS

Wiley Children's Books

605 Third Avenue, New York, NY 10158-0012
212-850-6000, 800-225-5945   fax: 212-850-6088
www.wiley.com (Wiley's Web site has the latest information on new books, journals, and other publications, along with special promotions and publicity.)

Wiley is best known in the areas of (in alphabetical order): architecture and design, biography, black interests, business and management, careers, children's and young adult nonfiction, computers, finance, health, history, hospitality, investment, nature, parenting, psychology, science, and tax. The publisher maintains a reputation for publishing top-drawer professional and popular works, in addition to academically oriented works in business and the sciences. Wiley publishes in hardcover and trade paperback editions.

John Wiley & Sons (founded in 1807) is an independent, global publisher of print and electronic products, specializing in textbooks and educational materials for colleges and universities, scientific and technical books and journals, and professional and consumer books and subscription services. The company has publishing, marketing, and distribution centers in the United States, Canada, Europe, Asia, and Australia.

From the Wiley trade list: *The Book of Business Wisdom: Classic Writings by the Legends of Commerce & Industry* (edited by Peter Krass); *Forbes Great Minds of Business* (edited by Gretchen Morgenson, Senior Editor, *Forbes*); *Plain Talk: Lessons from a Business Maverick* by Ken Iverson; *The Rich and Famous Money Book: Investment Strategies of Leading Celebrities* by Jean Sherman Chatzky; *Against the Gods: The Remarkable Story of Risk* by Peter L. Bernstein; *The Nordstrom Way: The Inside Story of America's No. 1 Customer Service Company* by Robert Spector and Patrick D. McCarthy; *Women of the Street: Making It on Wall Street in the World's Toughest Business* by Sue Herera; *Back from the Brink: The Greenspan Years* by Steven K. Beckner; *The Education of a Speculator* by Victor Niederhoffer; *Jacqueline Bouvier: An Intimate Memoir* by John H. Davis; *Jerusalem in the Twentieth Century* by Martin Gilbert; *Superchefs: Signature Recipes from America's New Royalty* by Karen Gantz Zahler; *Would-Be Worlds: Breaking the Complexity Barrier with the New Science of Simulation* by John L. Casti; *Sister Power: How Phenomenal Black Women Are Rising to the Top in a Race-Conscious Society* by Patricia Reid-Merritt; *Goodbye, Descartes: The End of Logic and the Search for a New Cosmology of the Mind* by Keith Devlin.

John Wiley & Sons handles its own distribution.

Query letters and SASEs should be directed to:

Airie Dekidjier, Sr., Editor—Narrative nonfiction, business marketing, business biography, business history.

Larry Alexander, Publisher—Business/Management.

Bob Ipsen, Publisher— Computer books; technology-related topical nonfiction.

Gerard Helferich, Publisher—General interest books.

Carole Hall, Editor in Chief—African-American books.

Deborah Englander, Editor—Financial and investment subjects.

Hana Umlauf Lane, Senior Editor—History, biography.

Jeanne Glasser, Senior Editor—E-finance.

Mike Hamilton, Senior Editor—Career development, small businesses, real estate.

Tom Miller, Executive Editor—Health, self-improvement, spirituality.

Chip Rossetti, Senior Editor—Reference, biography, history, narrative nonfiction.

Steven Power, Executive Editor—Science.

Karen Hansen, Editor—Professional trade publishing.

Matthew Holt, Executive Editor

Jeff Golick, Editor—Science and reference.

Elizabeth Zack, Editor—Health.

W

Wiley Children's Books

Wiley Children's Books show the house motto: "Discovering the world up close." Wiley children's titles offer an in-depth approach to subjects at hand, be it the natural world, science and technology, or witty fun-and-game experimental projects. Branches in the Wiley children's family include the Earth-Friendly series, Janice VanCleave's science lines (including the Science for Every Kid series), Flying Start, the House of Science, and "Spend the Day" series.

Some titles: *The Mash and Smash Cookbook: Fun and Yummy Recipes Every Kid Can Make* by Marian Buck-Murray; *What Makes the Grand Canyon Grand? The World's Most Awe-Inspiring Natural Wonders* by Spencer Christian and Antonia Felix; *Science in Seconds with Toys: Over 100 Experiments You Can Do in Ten Minutes or Less* by Jean Potter; *Janice VanCleave's Insects and Spiders: Mind-Boggling Experiments You Can Turn into Science Fair Projects* by Janice VanCleave; *The New York Public Library Amazing African American History* by Diane Patrick Wexler.

Query letters and SASEs should be directed to:

Kate Bradford, Senior Editor—Professional and Trade Division: Science, nature, children's nonfiction.

WILLIAMSON PUBLISHING COMPANY

1355 Church Hill Road, P.O. Box 185, Charlotte, VT 05445
802-425-2102   fax: 802-425-2199
e-mail: info@williamsonbooks.com

Williamson's books help children succeed by helping them to discover their creative capacity. Kids Can!, Little Hands, Kaleidoscope Kids, and Good Times books encourage curiosity and exploration with irresistible graphics and open-ended instruction. The house publishes hands-on learning books in science and nature, arts and craft, cooking, social studies and more, featuring new Kaleidoscope Kids and Kids Can! titles. Its publishing program is committed to maintaining excellent quality while providing good value for parents, teachers, and children.

Williamson Publishing Company (founded in 1983) is known for a wide variety of works and viewpoints, united through an enthusiastic, upbeat, purposeful how-to approach. Williamson typically produces a small list of new titles each year and commands a comprehensive backlist.

On the Williamson list in children's activity titles and entertainingly educational books: *Alphabet Art: With A–Z Animal Art & Fingerplays* by Judy Press; *Adventures in Art: Art & Craft Experiences for 8–13 Year Olds* by Susan Milford; *Boredom Busters! The Curious Kids' Activity Book* by Avery Hart and Paul Mantell; *Hand-Print Animal Art* by Carolyn Carreiro; *Making Cool Crafts & Awesome Art! A Kids' Treasure Trove of Fabulous Fun* by Roberta Gould; *Math Plays! 80 Ways to Count & Learn* by Diane McGowan and Mark Schrooten; *Cut-Paper Play! Dazzling Creations from Construction Paper* by Sandi Henry.

Titles in parenting and the family: *Sugar-Free Toddlers: Over 100 Recipes Plus Sugar Ratings for Store-Bought Products* by Susan Watson; *The Brown Bag Cookbook: Nutri-*

tious Portable Lunches for Kids and Grown-ups by Sara Sloan; *Parents Are Teachers, Too: Enriching Your Child's First Six Years* by Claudia Jones; *Doing Children's Museums: A Guide to 265 Hands-On Museums* by Joanne Cleaver.

Indicative of Williamson trade nonfiction, in general interest and specialist fields: *The Women's Job Search Handbook: With Issues and Insights into the Workplace* by Gerri Bloomberg and Margaret Holden; *Retirement Careers: Combining the Best of Work and Leisure* by DeLoss L. Marsh; *Dining on Deck: Fine Foods for Sailing and Boating* by Linda Vail; *Building a Multi-Use Barn: For Garage, Animals, Workshop, or Studio* by John Wagner; *The Sheep Raiser's Manual* by William K. Kruesi.

Williamson Publishing distributes its own list and works through a number of regional book sales representatives.

Query letters and SASEs should be directed to:

Susan Williamson, Editorial Director

WILLOW CREEK PRESS

P.O. Box 147, 9931 Highway 70 West, Minocqua, WI 54548
800-850-9453   fax: 715-358-7010
e-mail: books@willowcreekpress.com

Willow Creek Press is a fast-growing, small press company that publishes high-quality books mainly related to pets, the outdoors, wildlife, hunting, fishing and cooking. The house is also interested in videos and calendars.

Query letters and SASEs should be directed to:

Tom Petrie, Publisher

Andrea Donner, Managing Editor

WORKMAN PUBLISHING COMPANY

Artisan

Greenwich Workshop Press

See also: Algonquin Books of Chapel Hill

708 Broadway, New York, NY 10003-9555
212-254-5900   fax: 212-254-8098
www.workmanweb.com

Workman publishes commercial nonfiction with an accent on lifestyle areas of cooking, food and wine, health and exercise, how-to, sports, pregnancy and childcare, cats, and related popular reference. The house is known for a precisely targeted selection of games and puzzles, cartoon books, and specialty merchandise such as gift books, calendars, journals, and diaries. General trade nonfiction hits the high points of most how-to/ self-help categories; business, careers, and personal finance; and quirky works that strike a contemporary note in the popular culture. Workman hosts an outstanding line of children's books.

Workman also lists titles in popular science, some science fiction and general fiction, satire and humor, self-discovery, fun and games, hobbies and handicrafts, gardening and the home, and travel. Workman produces electronic works, including software, multimedia, and interactive products; these projects are often copublished with or distributed for such firms as Turner Interactive International.

Workman imprints and divisions include Artisan and Greenwich Workshop Press (which stress lifestyle, crafts, and design). (See separate subentries.) In 1988 Workman acquired Algonquin Books of Chapel Hill, which specializes in American fiction and belletristic nonfiction.

Workman Publishing Company (started in 1967) is adept at a marketing, sales, and promotional style that features such results as eye-catching counter displays for booksellers and racks devoted entirely to Workman lines.

Highlights from Workman: *Desperation Dinners! Home-Cooked Meals for Frantic Families in 20 Minutes Flat* by Beverly Mills and Alicia Ross; *Kill Your Parents Before They Kill You: An Illustrated Manifesto for Surviving the 90s and Beyond* by Ted Rall (illustrated by the author); *Children Learn What They Live* by Dorothy Law Nolte, Ph.D., with Rachel Harris, Ph.D.; *Practical Prayers for Practically Everything* by Jay Steele and Brett Bayne; *How to Remember Jokes* by Philip Van Munching; *Official Rules of Card Games* (85th edition) by Joli Quentin Kansil and Tom Braunlich.

Calendars and diaries are often theme-keyed to other arenas of Workman publishing interest. Many calendar lines tie in with Workman's successful series in lifestyle, inspiration, nature, games and puzzles, humor, sports, cats and dogs.

Of interest to young readers and the family: *The Great Easter Egg Hunt* by Mary Packard (illustrated by Carolyn Croll); *The Secret Diary* by Elizabeth Koda-Callan; *Peek-A-Boo, Lizzy Lou! A Daytime Book and Muppet Puppet* by Lauren Attinelo (illustrated by author; puppet by Rolie Krewson); *My First Bible Brain Quest* by Melody Carlson; *Neanderthal Book & Skeleton* by Stephen Cumbaa and Barbara Hehner.

Workman Publishing Company handles its own distribution.

Query letters and SASEs should be directed to:

Peter Workman, President—Oversees entire program. Acquires in all areas consistent with list.

Suzie Bolotin, Editor in Chief—Acquires in all areas consistent with list.

Suzanne Rafer, Editor—Cookbooks, humor, family issues; children's activity books.

Artisan

Greenwich Workshop Press

Workman's Artisan division specializes in lifestyle titles; the Artisan list includes titles from the Greenwich Workshop Press imprint (crafts and the arts), as well as calendars and other specialty merchandise. Artisan and Greenwich Workshop Press together accent crafts, home, garden, and design, each with its own distinctive editorial approach and publishing lines.

On the Artisan list: *Pierre Franey Cooks with His Friends* by Pierre Franey with Claudia Franey Jensen (photographs by Martin Brigdale and Jean Cazals); *French Tarts: 50 Savory and Sweet Recipes* by Linda Dannenberg (photographs by Guy Bouchet; illustrated by Vavro); *Portobello Cookbook,* (mushroom recipes) by Jack Czarnecki (photographs by Alexandra Maldonado); *Fresh Cuts: Arrangements with Flowers, Leaves, Buds & Branches* by Edwina von Gal (photographs by John Hall; foreword by Ken Druse); *Picasso's One-Liners* (single-line drawings by Pablo Picasso); *Cowgirl Rising* (paintings by Donna Howell-Sickles; text by Peg Streep; introduction by Teresa Jordan); *The Glory of Flight: The Art of William S. Phillips* (paintings by William S. Phillips; text by Edwards Park; introduction by Stephen Coonts).

Artisan is the publisher of the Audubon Society's calendar line and distributes books for Eating Well Books (from *Eating Well* magazine).

WRIGHT GROUP/MCGRAW HILL

19201 120th Avenue, NE, Bothell, WA 98011
800-345-6073, 800-523-2371
www.wrightgroup.com

The Wright Group (founded in 1980) is a leading publisher of educational books for elementary school and junior high curricula. Wright series lines include SUNSHINE, Foundations, Heritage Readers, Woodland Mysteries, the Writing Project, Visions: African-American Experiences, the Evangeline Nicholas Collection, Story Vine, and Primarily Health.

The Wright Group publishers believe that, after the parents' role, teachers are the most important people in the life of a child. The teacher who empowers a child to read fulfills the greatest purpose.

Wright educational tools feature the "whole language" approach to reading; Wright hosts a wide range of books in science and social studies, as well as professional books for educators. The house has a full slate of books geared to the Spanish-language market.

The SUNSHINE program is a core instructional reading program with over 1,000 books for children. SUNSHINE includes fiction, nonfiction, poetry, plays, collections, traditional tales, and more. SUNSHINE features a mix of talented authors and illustrators from cultures and countries around the world. SUNSHINE is also available in Spanish.

The Foundations program introduces a powerful intervention system for use by classroom teachers. Foundations offers immediate intervention for children who are having problems learning to read and write.

Heritage Readers is an integrated literature and language-arts program for K–8 students. Heritage Readers are illustrated by renowned artists from the past and present and feature stories from the classic literary legacies of many cultures.

Woodland Mysteries is a collection of 30 high-interest novels designed especially for discouraged readers and ESL students.

The Writing Project complements and extends any language-arts program. Using their own life experience, students structure their writing from authentic writing models that incorporate various styles, forms, and functions.

W

Visions: African-American Experiences is a guide-reading program for young students that brings together a collaborative team of African-American educators, authors, and illustrators.

The Evangeline Nicholas Collection introduces students to rich multi-ethnic characters and true-to-life urban settings. Story Vine is a line that weaves tales of the American continent. These multicultural books include contemporary stories, traditional stories, and a memoir.

Primarily Health is a dynamic, hands-on health curriculum for grades K–3. Primarily Health was created by the Comprehensive Health Education Foundation with the input of children, nurses, educators, and national experts.

The Wright Group also offers professional books for teachers: *Think Big! Creating Big Books with Children* by Cynthia Johnson; *Whole Learning: Whole Child* by Joy Cowley; *Student Portfolios: A Practical Guide to Evaluation* by Lindy Vizyak; *Literacy Learning: A Revolution in Progress* by David B. Doake; *The Spelling Teacher's Book of Lists* by Joe Phenix.

The Wright Group handles its own distribution.

Query letters and SASEs should be directed to:

Amanda Balkwill, Administrative Assistant, Product Development

---

THE WRITER, INC.

Plays, Inc., Publishers

120 Boylston Street, Boston, MA 02116-4615
617-423-3157   fax: 617-423-2168

The Writer, Inc., publishes a selection of books in hardcover and paperback on all phases of writing and selling the written work; these publications are written and edited by experienced and successful authors.

Since 1887, both aspiring and professional writers have looked to *The Writer* magazine ("the pioneer magazine for literary workers") as a practical guide to instruct, inform, and inspire them in their work. *The Writer* is renowned for the annually updated reference resource *The Writer's Handbook* (edited by Sylvia K. Burack). The house also publishes *Plays: The Drama Magazine for Young People,* with an attendant list in books. (See separate subentry further on.)

Frontlist offerings: *Practical Playwriting* by David Copelin; *How to Write Your Novel* by Margaret Chittenden; *Write on Target* by Dennis E. Hensley and Holly G. Miller; *The Elements of Mystery Fiction* by William G. Tapply; *Writing & Revising Your Fiction* by Mark Wisniewski.

Reference books for writers: *The Writer's Handbook* (edited by Sylvia K. Burack); *The Thirty-Six Dramatic Situations* by Georges Polti; *Dictionary of Fictional Characters* by Martin Seymour-Smith; *The Writer's Rhyming Dictionary* by Langford Reed; *Writing Poetry: Where Poems Come from and How to Write Them* by David Kirby; *Preparing Your Manuscript* by Elizabeth Preston; *Guide to Fiction Writing* by Phyllis A. Whitney; *Writing*

Books for Young People by James Cross Giblin; *How to Write and Sell Your Articles* (edited by Sylvia K. Birrade).

The Writer distributes its own books.

Query letters and SASEs should be directed to:

Sylvia K. Burack, Editor

Plays, Inc., Publishers

Plays, Inc., Publishers is a wing of the Writer that targets younger performers in theater. This imprint's list also includes a solid slate of resource materials of value to professionals who work in the theater with children.

From Plays, Inc.: *Lively Plays for Young Actors* by Christine Hamlett; *Great American Events on Stage, Thirty Plays from Favorite Stories,* and *The Big Book of Skits* (edited by Sylvia E. Kamerman); *Plays from African Tales* and *Plays from Hispanic Tales* by Barbara Winther; *Costume: An Illustrated Survey from Ancient Times to the 20th Century* by Margot Lister; *The Puppet Book* by Claire Buchwald (illustrated by Audrey Jacubiszyn); *Mime: Basics for Beginners* by Cindie and Mathew Straub (photographs by Jeff Blanton).

WRITER'S DIGEST BOOKS/F&W PUBLICATIONS

Betterway Books

North Light Books

Story Press

1507 Dana Avenue, Cincinnati, OH 45207
513-531-2222   fax: 513-531-4744

Writer's Digest/F&W produces books to help writers, poets, artists, songwriters, and photographers develop their talent, hone their professional skills, and—of course—sell their work. The publisher pursues this mission by issuing a list of guidebooks, how-to, reference, and professional titles in hardcover and paperback editions.

Writer's Digest Books (founded in 1919) is a division of F&W Publications, publisher of *Writer's Digest* magazine. The firm was bought in 2000 by Citibank. Writer's Digest Books offers a classic and expansive list for the professional as well as aspiring writer. Story Press is an imprint geared to literary interest. North Light Books issues professional titles in fine arts and design. Betterway features a variety of topic-oriented titles in fields such as woodworking, genealogy, theater, and coaching guides. (See separate subentries.) Writer's Digest/F&W maintains a comprehensive backlist.

Writer's Digest Books

The Writer's Digest list covers virtually all commercial writing fields; many of these works are high on the professional writer's recommendation list. Writer's Digest Books features a series of annually updated resource guides, including *Writer's Market.*

From Writer's Digest Books: *Ten Steps to Publishing Children's Books: How to Develop, Revise, and Sell All Kinds of Books for Children* by Berthe Amoss and Eric Suben; *The Secrets of Close-Up Photography* by Lou Jacobs, Jr.; *Sell & Resell Your Magazine Articles* by Gordon Burgett; *Grammatically Correct: The Writer's Guide to Punctuation, Spelling, Style, Usage and Grammar* by Anne Stilman; *The Musician's Guide to Making & Selling Your Own CDs & Cassettes* by Jana Stanfield; *The Photographer's Market Guide to Photo Submission and Portfolio Formats* by Michael Willins.

Writer's Digest offers the electronic (CD-ROM) version of its classic *Writer's Market: Where & How to Sell What You Write* (edited by Kirsten C. Holm).

Additional titles are keyed to writers' needs in comedy, horror, historical fiction, science fiction, Westerns, suspense fiction, popular songwriting, business writing, and children's/young-adult books. The Howdunit series has met with particular success and features works geared for writers in the fields of mystery, suspense, and true crime.

Sample titles: *Writing the Private Eye Novel: A Handbook by the Private Eye Writers of America* (edited by Robert J. Randisi); *Malicious Intent: A Writer's Guide to How Criminals Think* by Sean P. Mactire; *Modus Operandi: A Writer's Guide to How Criminals Work* by Mauro V. Corvasce and Joseph R. Paglino; *Armed and Dangerous: A Writer's Guide to Weapons* by Michael Newton; *The Writer's Guide to Everyday Life in the Middle Ages* by Sherrilyn Kenyon; *Aliens and Alien Societies* by Stanley Schmidt.

The Story Press imprint features classic works for literary devotees (many of them in reprint), along with destined-to-be-classic new works. From Story Press: *Building Fiction: How to Develop Plot & Structure,* by Jesse Lee Kercheval; *Fast Fiction: Creating Fiction in Five Minutes,* by Roberta Allen; *Turning Life into Fiction* by Robin Hemley.

Bill Brohaugh does not wish to receive any unsolicited queries, proposals, or manuscripts at the Story Press imprint; all acquisitions for this line are editorially generated in house and activated through existing avenues.

Query letters and SASEs should be directed to:

Jack Heffron, Editor, Writer's Digest Books—How-to books for writers, how-to books for photographers.

Betterway Books

Betterway Books (founded in 1980) is a former independent that is now part of F&W Publications. Betterway is a midsize imprint in the interest areas of home-building and remodeling, resource guides and handbooks, small business and personal finance, self-help, theater crafts, collectibles, sports, and reference.

From Betterway: *A Genealogist's Guide to Discovering Your Italian Ancestors* by Lynn Nelson; *A Genealogist's Guide to Discovering Your African-American Ancestors* by Tommie Morton-Young; *Homemade Money* by Barbara Brabec; *Period Make-Up for the Stage Step by Step* by Rosemarie Swinfield; *The Woodworking Handbook* by Thomas Begnal; *Earn a Second Income from Your Woodworking* by Garth Graves; *Make Your Quilting Pay for Itself* by Sylvia Ann Landman.

Betterway Books is distributed through the network of F&W Publications, the parent company.

North Light Books

The North Light Books division of F&W Publications produces how-to books geared to the areas of drawing, painting, clip art, printing, desktop publishing, and graphic arts, along with a line of titles for young readers.

Representative North Light titles: *Painting Sunlit Still Lifes in Watercolor* by Liz Donovan; *Creating Radiant Flowers in Colored Pencil* by Gary Greene; *Creating Extraordinary Beads from Ordinary Material* by Tina Casey; *Painting the American Heartland in Watercolor* by Diane Phalen; *Graphic Design Tricks & Techniques* by Molly Joss and Lycette Nelson; *Jewelry: Fundamentals of Metalsmithing* by Tim McCreight.

North Light Books are distributed by F&W Publications; the house also catalogs the lists of Coast to Coast Books and Rockport Publishers.

Query letters and SASEs should be directed to:

Lynn Haller, Editor—Graphic design.

Rachel Wolf, Editor for Fine Arts—How-to books for fine artists and graphic designers.

ZOLAND BOOKS

384 Huron Avenue, Cambridge, MA 02138
617-864-6252   fax: 617-661-4998
www.zolandbooks.com

Zoland Books produces fiction, poetry, and art books of literary interest. A significant portion of the Zoland list accents the interrelationship between the written and visual arts. Zoland nurtures a staunch backlist.

Zoland (founded in 1987) is a small independent house that publishes 10 to 14 new titles per year, usually not geared to any particular seasonal business goals; projects are acquired on an extremely selective basis.

Zoland is distributed to the trade by Consortium Book Sales and Distribution.

Query letters and SASEs should be directed to:

Roland F. Pease, Jr., Publisher and Editor

University Presses

The University As Publisher

From Academic Press to Commercial Presence

WILLIAM HAMILTON

You nod as you glance at the ads in the book reviews, you are aware of the spots you heard or saw on radio and late-night television, and you recognize the authors from television interviews and radio call-in shows. So you know today's university presses publish much more than scholarly monographs and academic tomes.

While the monograph is—and will always be—the bread and butter of the university press, several factors over the past quarter century have compelled university presses to look beyond their primary publishing mission of disseminating scholarship. The reductions in financial support from parent institutions, library-budget cutbacks by federal and local governments, and the increasing scarcity of grants to underwrite the costs of publishing monographs have put these presses under severe financial pressure. The watchword for university presses, even in the 1970s, was survival.

While university presses were fighting for their lives, their commercial counterparts were also experiencing difficult changes. The commercial sector responded by selling off unprofitable and incompatible lists or merging with other publishers; many houses were bought out by larger concerns. Publishers began to concentrate their editorial and marketing resources on a few new titles that would generate larger revenues. Books that commercial publishers now categorized as financial risks, the university presses saw as means of entry into new markets and opportunities to revive sagging publishing programs.

Take a look through one of the really good bookstores in your area. You'll find university press imprints on regional cookbooks, popular fiction, serious nonfiction, calendars, literature in translation, reference works, finely produced art books, and a considerable number of upper-division textbooks. Books and other items normally associated with commercial publishers are now a regular and important part of university press publishing.

There are approximately 100 university presses in North America, including United States branches of the venerable Oxford University Press and Cambridge University Press. Of the largest American university presses—California, Chicago, Columbia,

Harvard, MIT, Princeton, Texas, and Yale—each publishes well over 100 books per year. Many of these titles are trade books that are sold in retail outlets throughout the world.

The medium-sized university presses—approximately 20 fit this category—publish between 50 and 100 books a year. Presses such as Washington, Indiana, Cornell, North Carolina, Johns Hopkins, and Stanford are well established as publishers of important works worthy of broad circulation.

All but the smallest university presses have developed extensive channels of distribution, which ensure that their books will be widely available in bookstores and wherever serious books are sold. Small university presses usually retain larger university presses or commissioned sales firms to represent them.

UNIVERSITY PRESS TRADE PUBLISHING

The two most common trade areas in which university presses publish are (1) nonfiction titles that reflect the research interests of their parent universities and (2) regional titles.

For example, University of Hawaii Press publishes approximately 30 new books a year with Asian or Pacific Rim themes. Typically, eight to ten of these books are trade titles. Recent titles have included Japanese literature in translation, a lavishly illustrated book on Thai textiles, books on forms of Chinese architecture, and a historical guide to ancient Burmese temples. This is a typical university press trade list—a diverse, intellectually stimulating selection of books that will be read by a variety of well-informed, responsive general readers.

For projects with special trade potential, some of the major university presses enter into copublishing arrangements with commercial publishers—notably in the fields of art books and serious nonfiction with a current-issues slant—and there seems to be more of these high-profile projects lately.

Certain of the larger and medium-sized university presses have in the past few years hired editors with experience in commercial publishing in order to add extra dimensions and impact to the portion of their program with a trade orientation.

It's too early to know whether these observations represent trends. Even if so, the repercussions remain to be seen. Obviously, with the publishing community as a whole going through a period of change, it pays to stay tuned to events.

UNIVERSITY PRESS AUTHORS

Where do university press authors come from? The majority of them are involved in one way or another with a university, research center, or public agency, or are experts in a particular academic field. Very few would list their primary occupation as author. Most of the books they write are the result of years of research or reflect years of experience in their fields.

The university press is not overly concerned about the number of academic degrees following its trade book authors' names. What matters is the author's thoroughness in addressing the topic, regardless of his or her residence, age, or amount of formal education. A rigorous evaluation of content and style determines whether the manuscript meets the university press's standards.

UNIVERSITY PRESS ACQUISITION PROCESS

Several of the other essays in this volume provide specific strategies for you to follow to ensure that your book idea receives consideration from your publisher of choice—but let me interject a cautionary note: The major commercial publishers are extremely difficult to approach unless you have an agent, and obtaining an agent can be more difficult than finding a publisher!

The commercial publishers are so overwhelmed by unsolicited manuscripts that you would be among the fortunate few if your proposal or manuscript even received a thorough reading. Your unagented proposal or manuscript will most likely be read by an editorial assistant, returned unread, or thrown on the slushpile unread and unreturned.

An alternative to the commercial publisher is the university press. Not only will the university press respond; the response will generally come from the decision maker—the acquisitions editor.

Before approaching any publisher, however, you must perform a personal assessment of your expectations for your book. If you are writing because you want your book to be on the bestseller list, go to a medium-to-large commercial press. If you are writing in order to make a financial killing, go to a large commercial publisher. If you are writing in the hope that your book will be a literary success, contribute to knowledge, be widely distributed, provide a modest royalty, and be in print for several years, you should consider a university press.

SHOULD A UNIVERSITY PRESS BE YOUR FIRST CHOICE?

That depends on the subject matter. It is very difficult to sell a commercial publisher on what appears on the surface to be a book with a limited market. For example, Tom Clancy was unable to sell *The Hunt for Red October* to a commercial publisher because the content was considered too technical for the average reader of action-adventure books. Clancy sent the manuscript to a university press that specialized in military-related topics. Naval Institute Press had the foresight to see the literary and commercial value of Clancy's work. As they say, the rest is history. Tom Clancy created the present-day techno-thriller genre and has accumulated royalties well into the millions of dollars. Once Clancy became a known quantity, the commercial publishers began courting him. All of his subsequent books have been published by commercial houses.

How do you find the university press that is suitable for you? You must research the university press industry. Start by finding out something about university presses. In addition to the listings in the directory of publishers and editors appearing in this book, most university presses are listed in *Literary Market Place*.

A far better and more complete source is *The Association of American University Presses Directory*. The AAUP directory offers a detailed description of each AAUP member press with a summary of its publishing program. The directory lists the names and responsibilities of each press's key staff, including the acquisitions editors. Each press states its editorial program—what it will consider for publication. A section on submitting manuscripts provides a detailed description of what the university press expects a proposal to contain.

Another useful feature is the comprehensive subject grid, which identifies over 125 subject areas and lists the university presses that publish in each of them.

An updated edition of *The Association of American University Presses Directory* is published every fall, and is available for a nominal charge from the AAUP central offices in New York City or through its distributor, University of Chicago Press.

Most university presses are also regional publishers. They publish titles that reflect local interests and tastes and are intended for sale primarily in the university press's local region. For example, University of Hawaii Press has over 250 titles on Hawaii. The books—both trade and scholarly—cover practically every topic one can think of. Books on native birds, trees, marine life, local history, native culture, and an endless variety of other topics can be found in local stores, including the chain bookstores.

This regional pattern is repeated by university presses throughout the country. University of Washington Press publishes several titles each year on the Pacific Northwest and Alaska. Rutgers University Press publishes regional fiction. University of New Mexico Press publishes books on art and photography, most dealing with the desert Southwest. Louisiana State University Press publishes Southern history and literature. Nebraska publishes on the American West.

Almost all university presses publish important regional nonfiction. If your book naturally fits a particular region, you should do everything possible to get a university press located in that region to evaluate your manuscript.

Do not mistake the regional nature of the university press for an inability to sell books nationally—or globally. As mentioned earlier, most university presses have established channels of distribution and use the same resources that commercial publishers use for book distribution. The major difference is that the primary retail outlets for university press books tend to be bookstores associated with universities, smaller academic bookstores, specialized literary bookstores, and independent bookstores that carry a large number of titles.

Matching books to buyers is not as difficult as you might think. Most patrons of university press bookstores know these stores are likely to carry the books they want.

Traditionally, very few university press titles are sold through major chain bookstores outside their local region. Even so, this truism is subject to change. Some of the biggest bookstore chains are experimenting with university press sections in their large superstores.

WHAT TO EXPECT AT A UNIVERSITY PRESS

You should expect a personal reply from the acquisitions editor. If the acquisitions editor expresses interest, you can expect the evaluation process to take as long as 6 to 8 months. For reasons known only to editorial staffs—commercial as well as those of university presses—manuscripts sit and sit and sit. Then they go out for review, come back, and go out for review again!

Once a favorable evaluation is received, the editor must submit the book to the press's editorial board. It is not until the editorial board approves the manuscript for publication that a university press is authorized to publish the book under its imprint.

A word about editorial boards. The imprint of a university press is typically controlled by an editorial board appointed from the faculty. Each project presented to the editorial board is accompanied by a set of peer reviews, the acquisitions editor's summary of the reviews, and the author's replies to the reviews. The project is discussed with the press's management and voted upon.

Decisions from the editorial board range from approval, through conditional approval, to flat rejection. Most university presses present to the editorial board only those projects they feel stand a strong chance of acceptance—approximately 10% to 15% of the projects submitted annually. So if you have been told that your book is being submitted to the editorial board, there's a good chance that the book will be accepted.

Once a book has been accepted by the editorial board, the acquisitions editor is authorized to offer the author a publishing contract. The publishing contract of a university press is quite similar to a commercial publisher's contract. The majority of the paragraphs read the same. The difference is most apparent in two areas—submission of the manuscript and financial terms.

University presses view publishing schedules as very flexible. If the author needs an extra 6 to 12 months to polish the manuscript, the market is not going to be affected too much. If the author needs additional time to proofread the galleys or page proofs, the press is willing to go along.

Why? Because a university press is publishing for the long term. The book is going to be in print for several years. It is not unusual for a first printing of a university press title to be available for 10 or more years. Under normal circumstances the topic will be timeless, enduring, and therefore of lasting interest.

University presses go to great lengths to ensure that a book is as close to error-free as possible. The academic and stylistic integrity of the work is foremost in the editor's mind. Not only the content but the notes, references, bibliography, and index should be flawless—and all charts, graphs, maps, and other illustrations perfectly keyed.

It does not matter whether the book is a limited-market monograph or serious nonfiction for a popular trade. The university press devotes the same amount of care to the editorial and production processes to ensure the book is as accurate and complete as possible. Which leads us to the second difference—the financial terms.

Commercial publishers follow the maxim that time is money. The goal of the organization is to maximize shareholder wealth. Often the decision to publish a book is based solely on financial considerations. If a book must be available for a specific season in order to meet its financial goals, pressure may be applied to editorial by marketing, and editorial in turn puts pressure on the author to meet the agreed-upon schedule. This pressure may result in mistakes, typos, and inaccuracies—but will also assure timely publication and provide the publisher with the opportunity to earn its expected profit. At the commercial publishing house, senior management is measured by its ability to meet annual financial goals.

University presses are not-for-profit organizations. Their basic mission is to publish books of high merit that contribute to universal knowledge. Financial considerations are secondary to what the author has to say. A thoroughly researched, meticulously documented, and clearly written book is more important than meeting a specific publication date. The university press market will accept the book when it appears.

Do not get the impression that university presses are entirely insensitive to schedules or market conditions. University presses are aware that certain books—primarily textbooks and topical trade titles—must be published at specific times of the year if sales are to be maximized. But less than 20% of any year's list would fall into such a category.

University Presses and Author Remuneration

What about advances? Royalties? Surely university presses offer these amenities—which is not to suggest they must be commensurate with the rates paid by commercial houses.

No and yes. No royalties are paid on a predetermined number of copies of scholarly monographs—usually 1,000 to 2,000.

A royalty is usually paid on textbooks and trade books. The royalty will be based on the title's sales revenue (net sales), and will usually be a sliding-scale royalty ranging from as low as 5% to as high as 15%.

As with commercial publishers, royalties are entirely negotiable. Do not be afraid or embarrassed to discuss them with your publisher. Just remember that university presses rarely have surplus funds to apply to generous advances or high royalty rates. However, the larger the university press, the more likely you are to get an advance for a trade book.

Never expect an advance for a monograph or supplemental textbook.

When Considering a University Press

When you're deciding where to submit your manuscript, keep the following in mind. University presses produce approximately 10% of the books published in the United States each year. University presses win approximately 20% of the annual major book awards. Yet university presses generate just 2% of the annual sales revenue.

So if you want to write a book that is taken seriously, that will be carefully reviewed and edited; if you want to be treated as an important part of the publishing process, and want your book to have a good chance to win an award; and if you are not too concerned about the financial rewards—then a university press may very well be the publisher for you.

Cambridge University Press

40 West 20th Street, New York, NY 10011-4211
212-924-3900, 800-872-7423

The Cambridge list includes hardcover and paperback titles of topical contemporary general interest, as well as academic import, in the fields of literature, art, music, religion, history, philosophy, economics, the classics, mathematics, and the behavioral, biological, physical, social, and computer sciences. One of publishing's old guard, Cambridge University Press (founded in 1534), is now a major international operation that holds fast to a long commitment to quality.

Cambridge University Press is the printing and publishing house of the University of Cambridge. It is a charitable enterprise required by University Statute to devote itself to printing and publishing in the furtherance of the acquisition, advancement, conservation, and dissemination of knowledge in all subjects; to the advancement of education, religion, learning, and research; and to the advancement of literature and good letters.

Special imprints include Cambridge Film Classics and the popularly priced Canto line. Cambridge also produces some titles for young readers and publishes a full range of academic and popular reference works. Cambridge is strong in the reprint area, offering editions of anthologies and compilations as well as individual classic works.

Cambridge publishes over 2,000 new titles each year.

The house hosts a strong reference list, including *The Cambridge International Dictionary of English* (edited by Paul Procter).

Cambridge University Press handles its own distribution.

Query letters and SASEs should be directed to:

Adam Black, Editor—Physical sciences.

Alan Harvey, Editor—Mathematics.

Beatrice Rehl, Editor—Arts and classics.

Christine Bartels, Editor—Linguistics.

Deborah Goldblatt, Senior Editor—ESL (English as a second language) books.

Florence Padgett, Editor—Engineering.

Frank Smith, Publishing Director—Social sciences.

Lauren Cowles, Editor—Mathematics and computer science.

Lewis Bateman, Editor—Political science.

Lothlorien Homet, Editor—Computing.

Mary Child, Editor—Social sciences.

Mary Vaughn, Publishing Director—ESL (English as a second language) books.

Matt Lloyd, Editor—Earth sciences.

Michael Penn, Editor—Life science.

Philip Laughlin, Editor—Psychology.

Scott Parris, Editor—Economics.

Terry Moore, Publishing Director—Humanities.

CLEVELAND STATE UNIVERSITY POETRY CENTER

1983 East 24th Street, Cleveland, OH 44115-2440
216-687-3986

Cleveland State University Poetry Center was begun in 1962 at Fenn College (which became Cleveland State in 1964); the center initiated its book-publishing program in 1971. The press publishes poets of local, regional, and international reach, generally under the aegis of one or another of the center's ongoing series. Under its flying-unicorn logo, CSU

Poetry Center most often publishes trade paper editions and also offers some titles in hardbound. The press generally produces a limited number of new titles each year. In addition, the house maintains a full backlist.

CSU Poetry Center presents a variety of styles and viewpoints—some with evident sociopolitical bent, others with broadly inspirational themes, and others notable for their strong individualistic inflections. The Poetry Center sponsors the Poetry Forum workshop and presents programs of public readings.

The center sponsors an annual poetry contest; please contact the CSU Poetry Center for submission guidelines.

The Largest Possible Life by Alison Lutermans, was selected by Bruce Weigl as the contest winner from 864 manuscripts submitted for the 2000 competition. The competition is extremely tough and the Poetry Center recommends that poets publish some individual poems in magazines and literary journals before submitting to this series. It is also recommended that prospective entrants review some of the work that the Poetry Center publishes.

Recent books from the Poetry Center: *The Book of Orgasms* by Nin Andrews; *Les Barricades Mystérieuses* by Jared Carter; *In Joanna's House* by Bonnie Jacobson; *Attendant Ghosts* by George Looney; *Out of Eden* by Frankie Paino; *Short History of Pets* by Carol Potter; *Obsidian Ranfla* by Anthony R. Virgil; *Buried Treasure* by Dan Bellm; *The Door Open to Fire* by Judith Vollmer.

Shorter volumes and chapbooks: *Almost Home* by Susan Grimm; *The Book of Snow* by Mary Moore; *Troubled by an Angel* by Elizabeth Murawski; *Enough Light to Steer By* by Steven Reese.

The full range of publications from CSU Poetry Center Press includes award-winning volumes from established poets and releases from accomplished new writers. On the CSU list: *Blood Stories* by Martha Ramsey; *Hurdy-Gurdy* and *Hammerlock* by Tim Seibles; *Order, or Disorder* by Amy Newman; *Refinery* by Claudia Keelan; *Fugitive Colors* by Chrystos; *Lives of the Saints and Everything* by Susan Firer; *The Long Turn Toward Light* by Cleveland poet and artist Barbara Tanner Angell; *At Redbones* by Thylias Moss; *The Sioux Dog Dance: shunk ah weh* by Red Hawk.

Poetry Center books are distributed through Partners Book Distributing, Ingram, and Spring Church Book Company.

The Poetry Center accepts unsolicited manuscripts only from November 1 to February 1 in connection with the Center's annual competition ($20 entry fee; full manuscripts only). For complete guidelines, send request plus SASE, or visit www.csuohio.edu/poetrycenter.

Query letters and SASEs should be directed to:

Rita M. Grabowski, Coordinator

Ted Lardner, Director

COLUMBIA UNIVERSITY PRESS

61 West 62nd Street, New York, NY 10023
212-459-0600

Columbia hosts a roster of specialty titles, including distinguished lines in Asian studies, literary studies, social work, history, film and earth sciences, and film and innovative publications. Columbia's publishing interest also includes current events, public issues, popular culture and fine arts, gay and lesbian studies, history, the sciences, literature, and Asian studies. Columbia University Press (established in 1893) publishes a slate of general-interest titles in addition to its established list of scholarly, academic, and scientific works. Also on the roster are a number of standard reference works geared for the institutional and academic market. The press produces books in hardcover and trade paperback editions and nurtures a healthy backlist.

Among Columbia highlights: *Losing Matt Shepard* by Beth Loffreda; *No Island Is an Island* by Carlo Ginzburg; *The Vital Illusion* by Jean Baudrillard; *Invisible Light* (edited by Diana Culbertson); *Gay Fiction Speaks* by Richard Canning; *How Brains Make Up Their Minds* by Walter Freeman; *Sexing the Brain* by Lesley Rogers; *The Theory Mess* by Herman Rapaport; *Antigone's Claim: Kinship Between Life and Death* by Judith Butler; *On Black Men* by David Marriott; *Mary Wollstonecraft: A Revolutionary Life* by Janet Todd; *East Asia at the Center* by Warren I. Cohen; *Post Soviet Russia* by Roy Medvedev; *Presidential Debates: Forty Years on High Risk TV* by Alan Schroeder; *No Return Address* by Anca Vlasopolos; *A Life of an Unknown* by Alain Corbin; *Wooden Eyes: Nine Reflections on Distance* by Carlo Ginzburg; *Future Perfect: Confronting Decisions About Genetics* by Lori B. Andrews; *Hannah Arendt* by Julia Kristeva; *Intoxicating Minds: How Drugs Work* by Ciaran Regan; *Democracy in Europe* by Larry Siedentop; *Journalism and New Media* by John V. Pavlik; *Against the Tide: The Battle for America's Beaches* by Cornelia Dean.

From Columbia reference: *The Columbia Encyclopedia* (edited by Jay Parini); *The Columbia Guide to Standard American English* by Kenneth G. Wilson.

Columbia University Press distributes its own list and handles distribution for a number of other academically oriented publishers, including East European Monographs, and Edinburgh University Press, and Kegan Paul International.

Query letters and SASEs should be directed to:

Ann Miller, Executive Editor—Pop culture and lesbian studies, religion, and medieval studies.

Robin C. Smith, Senior Executive Editor—Science.

James Raimes, Assistant Director for Reference Publishing.

Jennifer Crewe, Editorial Director—Literature, film, and Asian studies.

John Michel, Senior Executive Editor—Social work, anthropology.

Peter Dimoch, Senior Executive Editor—History and political science.

James Warren, Executive Editor—Reference.

CORNELL UNIVERSITY PRESS

Sage House, 512 East State Street, Ithaca, NY 14850
607-277-2338
www.cornellpress.cornell.edu

Cornell publishes trade nonfiction, in addition to a wide berth of academic and scholarly titles. The press's Comstock Books series continues a tradition of excellence in natural history. The ILR Press imprint focuses on labor and workplace issues. Cornell University Press (begun in 1869) is the oldest university press in the United States.

Representing the Cornell program: *The Working Class Majority: America's Best Kept Secret* by Michael Zweig; *Cathedrals of Europe* by Anne Prache; *Indians and English: Facing Off in Early America* by Karen Ordahl Kupperman; *The Twilight of Ancient Egypt: First Millennium B.C.E.* by Karol Mysliwiec; *Field Guide to the Birds of Cuba* by Orlando H. Garrido and Arturo Kirkconnell; *Women of Okinawa: Nine Voices from a Garrison Island* by Ruth Ann Keyso; *The Evidence of Things Not Said: James Baldwin and the Promise of American Democracy* by Lawrie Balfour; *Pluralism in Philosophy: Changing the Subject* by John Dekes; *The Eye's Mind: Literary Modernism and Visual Culture* by Karen Jacobs; *The Making of NAFTA: How the Deal Was Done* by Maxwell A. Cameron and Brian W. Tomlin.

Cornell University Press distributes its own list.

Query letters and SASEs should be directed to:

Bernhard Kendler, Executive Editor—Literary criticism, classics, drama and film studies, art history, archaeology.

Catherine Rice, Editor—Women's studies, cultural studies, philosophy, race studies, gay and lesbian studies, and political theory.

Frances Benson, Editor in Chief—Labor, business, sociology, anthropology.

John Ackerman, Director—European history, Slavic studies, medieval studies, music.

Peter Prescott, Editor—Life sciences, natural history, plant science, animal science, ecology, entomology, geology, zoology.

Roger Haydon, Editor—philosophy, history of science, U.S. politics, international relations, Asian and Middle Eastern studies.

DUKE UNIVERSITY PRESS

Box 90660, Durham, NC 27708-0660
919-687-3600   fax: 919-688-4391
www.duke.edu/web/dupress

Areas of Duke publishing scope include cultural studies; literary studies; Latin American and Caribbean studies; legal studies; history; East European, Soviet, and post-Soviet studies; German studies; environmental studies; and history of economics. Post-Contemporary Interventions is a series that features imaginative world-class thinkers on culture, media, and global society.

Duke University Press (founded in 1921) publishes scholarly, trade, and textbooks in hardcover and trade paperback editions and maintains a strong backlist. Duke also publishes a number of academic journals, including *MLQ: Modern Language Quarterly.*

On the Duke list: *Don't: A Reader's Guide to the Military's Anti-Gay Policy* by Janet E. Hailey; *The Brazil Reader: History, Culture, Politics* (edited by Robert M. Levine and

John J. Crocitti); *Consuming Russia: Popular Culture, Sex, and Society Since Gorbachev* (edited by Adele Marie Barker); *Bound and Gagged: Pornography and the Politics of Fantasy in America* by Laura Kipnis; *How to Have Theory in an Epidemic* by Paula A. Treichler; *Ziegfeld Girl: Image and Icon in Culture and Cinema* by Linda Mizejewski; *Chalk Lines: The Politics of Work in the Managed University* (edited by Randy Martin); *Under Western Eyes: India from Milton to Macaulay* by Balachandra Rajan; *Colonial Habits: Convents and the Spiritual Economy of Cuzco, Peru* by Kathryn Burns.

The C. Eric Lincoln Series on the Black Experience is designed to facilitate the effort to help the black experience know itself better and to share what it knows in the common interest. Representative title: *In the Name of Elijah Muhammad: Louis Farrakhan and the Nation of Islam* by Mattias Gardell.

Of popular cultural note: *The Third Eye: Race, Cinema, and Ethnographic Spectacle* by Fatimah Tobing Rony; *Vampires, Mummies, and Liberals: Bram Stoker and the Politics of Popular Fiction* by David Glover; *Pop Out: Queer Warhol* (edited by Jennifer Doyle, Jonathan Flatley, and José Esteban Muñoz); *Guilty Pleasures: Feminist Camp from Mae West to Madonna* by Pamela Robertson; *Rhythm and Noise: An Aesthetics of Rock* by Theodore Gracyk.

Duke University Press oversees its own distribution.

Query letters and SASEs should be directed to:

Kenneth A. Wissoker, Editor in Chief

F

THE FEMINIST PRESS AT THE CITY UNIVERSITY OF NEW YORK

365 Fifth Avenue, New York, NY 10016
212-360-5790

The publishing horizon at the Feminist Press includes biographies, cross-cultural studies, fiction, health and medicine, history/sociology, interdisciplinary texts, literary anthologies, art and music, resources and reference works, educational materials, children's books, and women's studies (including several notable series). The house hosts a reprint program as well as its renowned originals, and also supports several feminist journals. The Feminist Press publishes in hardcover and paperback editions and moves a backlist both heady and deep through special sales, including holiday mailings.

The Feminist Press maintains its aim to express and celebrate differences within the cultural context of humanity; in so doing the house has held the publishing forefront with a series of important works that brings fresh dimensions to the attention of readers. Founded in 1970 at the crest of the second wave of American feminism, the press led off with a list that concentrated on a program to reestablish hitherto overlooked women's literary classics, aligned with an additional focus on literature of United States working-class women. The house's agenda has expanded gradually to encompass such themes as growing up female, women artists, and the family, as well as the publication of academic and general-interest works with an international cast of authors in varied disciplines and literary forms.

Highlights from Feminist Press: *Among the White Moon Faces: An Asian-American Memoir of Homelands* by Shirley Geok-lin Lim; *The New Lesbian Studies: Into the 21st*

Century (edited by Bonnie Zimmerman and Toni A. H. McNaron); *Sisterhood Is Global: The International Women's Movement Anthology* (edited by Robin Morgan); *China for Women: Travel and Culture* (edited by Feminist Press); *Black and White Sat Down Together: Reminiscences of an NAACP Founder* by Mary White Ovington; *Motherhood by Choice: Pioneers in Women's Health and Family Planning* by Perdita Huston; *Get Smart! What You Should Know (but Won't Learn in Class) About Sexual Harassment and Sex Discrimination* by Montana Katz and Veronica Vieland; *Women Composers: The Lost Tradition Found* by Diane Peacock Jezic.

In fiction and literature: *Paper Fish* by Tina De Rosa; *Winter's Edge* by Valerie Miner; *Changes* by Ama Ata Aidoo; *Songs My Mother Taught Me* by Wakako Yamauchi; *Unspeakable Women* (edited and translated by Robin Pickering-Iazzi); a bilingual edition of *The Answer/La Repuesta* by Sor Juana Inéz de la Cruz; *Folly* by Maureen Brady; and *What Did Miss Darrington See? An Anthology of Feminist Supernatural Fiction* (edited by Jessica Amanda Salmonson).

A noteworthy Feminist Press educational project is *Women of Color and the Multicultural Curriculum* (edited by Liza Fiol-Matta and Miriam K. Chamberlain), which includes essays and course outlines.

A special-production volume from Feminist Press is *Long Walks and Intimate Talks,* with stories and poems by Grace Paley and paintings by Vera B. Williams.

Feminist Press books may be ordered directly from the publisher; the list is distributed to the trade in the United States via Consortium Book Sales & Distribution.

Query letters and SASEs should be directed to:

Jean Casella, Senior Editor

GALLAUDET UNIVERSITY PRESS

800 Florida Avenue NE, Washington DC 20002-3695
202-651-5488
http://gupress.gallaudet.edu

Gallaudet offers titles in categories such as communication, language arts, deaf culture and history, employment and law, audiology and speechreading, instructional materials, literature, parenting, and professional books, as well as a special concentration in sign language (including American Sign Language). The publisher maintains an extensive backlist.

Imprints of Gallaudet University Press include Clerc Books and Kendall Green Publications. Among areas of current publishing emphasis are audiology, sociolegal issues in special education, English as a second language (ESL), and signed children's books in English; the house also markets a line of videotapes.

The publishing program of Gallaudet University Press (founded in 1968) exemplifies the educational impulse of Gallaudet University through an accent on issues pertinent to deafness. Gallaudet University Press publishes scholarly, educational, and general-interest titles, as well as children's books.

Among Gallaudet features: *Lend Me Your Ear: Rhetorical Constructions of Deafness* by Brenda Jo Brueggemann; *Original Signs: Gesture, Sign, and the Sources of Language* by David F. Armstrong; *Sounds Like Home: Growing Up Black and Deaf in the South* by

Mary Herring Wright; *The Cry of the Gull* by Emmanuelle Laborit; *Shall I Say a Kiss?: The Courtship Letters of a Deaf Couple, 1936–1938* (edited by Lennard J. Davis); *Signs of the Times* by Edgar H. Shroyer (illustrated by Charles Floyd); *At Home Among Strangers: Exploring the Deaf Community in the United States* by Jerome D. Schein; *Never the Twain Shall Meet: Bell, Gallaudet, and the Communications Debate* by Richard Winefield; *A Deaf Adult Speaks Out* by Leo M. Jacobs; *The Politics of Deafness* by Owen Wrigley; *A Place of Their Own: Creating the Deaf Community in America* by John Vickrey Van Cleve and Barry A. Crouch.

Representing the Gallaudet backlist: *The Week the World Heard Gallaudet* by Jack R. Gannon; *Deaf President Now!* by John B. Christiansen and Sharon N. Barnartt; *No Walls of Stone: An Anthology of Literature by Deaf and Hard of Hearing Writers* (edited by Jill Jepson).

Gallaudet University Press books are distributed via Chicago Distribution Center.

Query letters and SASEs should be directed to:

Ivey Wallace, Assistant Director, Editorial

HARVARD BUSINESS SCHOOL PRESS

60 Harvard Way, Boston, MA 02163
617-783-7636   fax: 617-783-7489
www.hbsp.harvard.edu

Our mission at Harvard Business School Press is straightforward: to be the source of the most influential ideas and conversations that shape business worldwide. Yet it addresses an enormous ambition. We understand that our books, however thoughtful, provocative, and enlightening, will become influential only when their ideas are brought to bear on our daily business activities. No matter how savvy the marketing, attractive the packaging, or aggressive the sales force, at the end of the day only the ideas themselves can make a difference in the thoughts, practice, and conversations of business book readers

As the publishers of landmark books in strategy, general management, the digital economy, technology and innovation, and human resources, among other disciplines, we take a broad look at the questions businesspeople face every day and provide the answers that will have a profound impact on their lives and work. Among our most influential titles: *The Innovator's Dilemma* by Clayton Christensen; *Competing for the Future* by Gary Hamel and C. K. Prahalad; *The Age of Unreason* by Charles Handy; *The Wisdom of Teams* by Jon Katzenbach and Douglas Smith; *Human Resource Champions* by Dave Ulrich; *The Loyalty Effect* by Frederick Reichheld; *Net Gain* by John Hagel and Arthur Armstrong; *Leading Change* by John Kotter; *The Balanced Scorecard* by Robert Kaplan and David Norton; *Unleashing the Killer App* by Larry Downes and Chunka Mui; *Information Rules* by Carl Shapiro and Hal Varian; *Future Wealth* by Stan Davis and Chris Meyer; *Digital Capital* by Don Tapescott, David Ticoll, and Alex Lowy; and *The Social Life of Information* by John Seely Brown and Paul Duguid.

Established in 1984, the Press currently has more than 300 titles in print. Our publishing program combines the high standards of a university press with the aggressive marketing

H

of a trade publisher to deliver the best of contemporary thinking in business and management to the widest possible audience. Manuscripts considered for publication by the Press are reviewed by peers, a process unique in trade publishing that ensures the quality and relevance of books that carry the Harvard Business School Press imprint.

Harvard Business School Press titles are consistently recognized by publishing industry awards and annual "best book" round-ups, among them, the *Financial Times*/Booz, Allen & Hamilton Best Business Book of 1997 for *The Innovator's Dilemma* by Clayton Christensen; *Business Week*'s Ten Best Books of the Year awards; *Library Journal*'s Best Books of the Year awards; and Soundview Executive Book Summaries' Thirty Best Books of the Year. In 1994, *Business Week* hailed *Competing for the Future* by Gary Hamel and C. K. Prahalad, the "year's best management book."

Harvard Business School Press titles regularly garner significant national media attention in publications such as *Business Week;* the *Economist, Fortune, Inc.; Wired;* the *New York Times;* the *Financial Times; USA Today;* and the *Wall Street Journal.* Several books have appeared on the national *Business Week* Bestseller List, including *Competing for the Future, The Loyalty Effect, Leading Change, Net Gain, Real Time, Unleashing the Killer App, Net Worth,* and *The Innovator's Dilemma.* Press titles also regularly appear on many regional bestseller lists, including the *Denver Post, Philadelphia Inquirer,* and *San Francisco Chronicle.*

Harvard Business School Press is a business unit of Harvard Business School Publishing, a wholly owned, not-for-profit subsidiary of the Harvard Business School headquartered in Boston, Massachusetts. Harvard Business School Publishing offers material in a variety of platforms and delivery methods that reflect its extension of the educational mission of the Harvard Business School and its access to leading authors and companies. Other business units of Harvard Business School Publishing include: Harvard Business Review, Academic Cases & Reprints, Conferences, e-Learning, and Newsletters, which publishes *Harvard Management Update, Harvard Management Communications Letter,* and *The Balanced Scorecard Report.*

Query letters and SASEs should be sent to:

Carol Franco, Vice President, HBS Publishing, Director, HBS Press

Hollis Heimbouch, Executive Editor

Kirsten D. Sandberg, Executive Editor

Marjorie Williams, Editorial Director

Melinda Adams Merino, Senior Editor

Jeff Kehoe, Editor

H

HARVARD UNIVERSITY PRESS

79 Garden Street, Cambridge, MA 02174
617-495-2600   fax: 617-495-5898
www.hup.harvard.edu

Harvard's publishing categories include current events, cultural affairs, the arts, history, psychology, literary studies (including selected poetry), the sciences, legal studies, and economics. Harvard's special series have included such lines as the Twentieth Century Fund, the Global AIDS Policy Coalition, and the Developing Child series.

Harvard University Press (started in 1913) is currently the largest academic press in the United States. Harvard University Press produces a large number of trade-oriented general-interest books for an eclectic readership, while maintaining its core program to provide a balanced offering of scholarly works in a range of academic fields. Harvard's extensive list is published in hardcover and trade paperback editions.

Featured Harvard titles: *Original Subjects* by A. A. Alryes; *The 30-Minute Fitness Solution* by P. Amend; *Famous Women* by G. Boccaccio; *Gender, Emotion, and the Family* by W. N. Brownsberger; *The Harvard Guide to African American History* by R. K. Burkett; *Black Rice* by J. A. Carney; *Suspect Identities* by S. A. Cole; *Dark Paradise* by D. T. Coruwright; *Building the Invisible Orphanage* by M. A. Crenson; *On Fertile Ground* by P. T. Ellison; *How Milton Works* by S. Fish; *Law and Investment in Japan* by D. H. Foote; *Collected Papers* by S. Freeman; *Why Government Succeeds and Why It Fails* by A. Glazer; *Nearest Star* by L. Golub; *Illusion of Order* by B. E. Harcourt; *Russia and Russians* by G. Hosking; *Separate and Unequal* by B. Hutman; *Behind the Mask* by D. C. Jack; *Lucy's Legacy* by A. Jolly; *Justice as Fairness* by E. Kelly; *The Family in Greek History* by C. B. Patterson; *The Infant's World* by R. Rochat; *Dancing in the Street* by S. E. Smith; *The Ambiguity of Play* by B. Sutton-Smith; *The Craft of Zeus* by J. Svenbro; *Feeling in Theory* by R. Terada; and *Heaven Below* by G. Wacker.

Harvard University Press handles its own distribution.

The publisher will not consider unsolicited poetry or fiction.

Query letters and SASEs should be directed to:

Elizabeth Knoll, Senior Editor for the Behavioral Sciences—Behavioral sciences, earth sciences, astronomy, neuroscience, education.

Elizabeth Suttell, Senior Editor—East Asian studies.

Joyce Seltzer, Senior Executive Editor—History, contemporary affairs. Contact Joyce Seltzer at: 150 Fifth Avenue, Suite 625, New York, NY 10011, 212-337-0280.

Lindsay Waters, Executive Editor for the Humanities—Literary criticism, philosophy, film studies, cultural studies.

Margaretta Fulton, General Editor for the Humanities—Classics (including Loeb Classics), religion, music, art, Jewish studies, women's studies.

Michael A. Aronson, Senior Editor, Social Sciences—Economics, political science, sociology, law, some business.

Michael Fisher, Executive Editor for Science and Medicine—Medicine, science (except astronomy), neuroscience.

Stephanie Gouse, Paperbacks and Foreign Rights.

Kathleen McDermott, Senior Editor—History and social sciences.

H

HOWARD UNIVERSITY PRESS

2225 Georgia Avenue NW #720, Washington, DC 20059
202-238-2575   fax: 202-588-9849
www.founders.howard.edu/hupress

Customer service
P.O. Box 50283, Baltimore, MD 21211
410-516-6947

A major sector of the Howard University Press publishing scope covers issues and traditions pertaining to African Americans, other African Diasporic populations and other people of color worldwide—including cultural expressions, geopolitical topics, and historical studies. University Press (founded in 1972) produces scholarly and general nonfiction works in the areas of history, biography, economics, sociology, political science, education, contemporary affairs, communications, the arts, and literature, and produces a strong line of general-reference books. Howard University Press generally publishes a select group of new titles per year in hardcover and trade paperback editions. The press maintains a diverse backlist.

Indicative of the Howard University Press publishing program: *Barbara C. Jordan: Selected Speeches* (edited by Sandra Parham, with a foreword by Ann Richards); *Singular Like a Bird: The Art of Nancy Morejon* (edited by Miriam DeCosta-Willis); *A History of the Black Press* by Armistead Pride and Clint C. Wilson II; *Othello: New Essays by Black Writers* (edited by Mythili Kaul); *Mordecai—The Man and His Message: The Story of Mordecai Wyatt Johnson* by Richard I. McKinney; *The Jamaican Crime Scene: A Perspective* by Bernard Headley, *Basic Currents of Nigerian Foreign Policy* by Mae C. King; *We Paid Our Dues: Women Trade Union Leaders of the Caribbean* by A. Lynn Bolles; *African Americans and U.S. Policy Toward Africa* by Elliott P. Skinner; *Captain Paul Cuffe's Logs and Letters, 1808–1817: A Black Quaker's "Voice from Within the Veil"* (edited by Rosalind Wiggins); *An African Victorian Feminist: The Life and Times of Adelaide Smith Casely Hayford, 1869–1960* by Adelaide Cromwell; *Manichean Psychology: Racism and the Minds of People of African Descent* by Camara Jules Po Harrell; and *Cocoa and Chaos in Ghana* by Gwendolyn Mikell.

On the literary, cultural, and artistic front: *Social Rituals and the Verbal Art of Zora Neale Hurston* by Lynda Marion Hill; *The Dramatic Vision of August Wilson* by Sandra Shannon; *Ancient Songs Set Ablaze: The Theatre of Femi Osofisan* by Sandra L. Richards; *Black Drama in America* (edited by Darwin T. Turner); *Modern Negro Art* by James A. Porter; *The New Cavalcade: African American Writing from 1700 to the Present* (edited by Arthur P. Davis, J. Saunders Redding, and Joyce Ann Joyce).

Howard University Press handles distribution through its own in-house marketing department; fulfillment is handled through Johns Hopkins University Press.

The publisher will not consider unsolicited fiction or poetry. Please note: Howard University Press suspended operations in August 1996 and began reorganizing in 2000. Please contact the press prior to sending any correspondence, including queries.

Do Kamili Anderson, Director of the Press

H

INDIANA UNIVERSITY PRESS

601 North Morton Street, Bloomington, IN 47404-3797
812-855-4203   fax: 812-855-8507
www.iupress.indiana.edu   e-mail: iuporder@indiana.edu

Indiana University Press (founded in 1950) publishes books of serious trade interest, as well as titles directed toward scholarly and academic audiences. The press addresses such subjects as African and Afro-American studies, Russian studies, music, philosophy, regional and cultural studies, military history, political science and international affairs, popular culture and the arts, semiotics, science and technology, environmental issues and natural history, Jewish studies, paleontology, Middle East studies, classics, anthropology, and gender studies. Indiana University Press also publishes fiction in translation. IUP produces hardcover and paperback editions.

Indiana University Press issues a number of prestigious series, among them Middle East Studies, Studies in Continental Thought, Theories of Contemporary Culture, Blacks in the Diaspora, Arab and Islamic Studies, and Medical Ethics. The house is home to a variety of academic journals, including *Africa Today, Jewish Social Studies,* and a number of journals in feminist studies.

On the IUP list: *Nation Dance; Traps; A Question of Manhood, Volume 2; Stone Age Spear and Arrow Points of California and the Great Basin; My Life in Stalinist Russia; The Pennsylvania Railroad at Bay; Wildflowers of Door County; The BFI Companion to Eastern European and Russia Cinema; Armenian Folk Arts, Culture and Identity; The American Midwest; The Imperial Mantle; Government's, Citizens, and Genocide; Moses Hess and Modern Jewish Identity; Business Ethics in Healthcare; Dance and the Music of J. S. Bach; American Philosophy of Technology; The Fundamental Concepts of Metaphysics; Dictionary of Midwestern Literature; Indiana's Favorite Restaurants; Our Common Country; Australia's Lost World; Empty Figure on an Empty Stage; Women Building Chicago 1790–1990.*

Indiana University Press publishes *Guidelines for Bias-Free Writing* by Marilyn Schwartz and the Task Force on Bias-Free Language of the Association of American University Presses. IUP also recommends to potential authors the popular writing-reference stylebook *The Handbook of Nonsexist Writing* by Casey Miller and Kate Swift.

Also of high cultural concern: *The Well-Tempered Announcer: A Pronunciation Guide to Classical Music* by Robert Friedkin.

Indiana University Press distributes its own list, as well as books produced by the Indiana Historical Society and the British Film Institute; IUP also serves as regional sales representative for several other university presses.

Query letters and SASEs should be directed to:

Janet Rabinowich, Editorial Director—Russian and East European studies, African studies, Middle Eastern and Judaic studies, philosophy.

Robert Sloan, Senior Sponsoring Editor—Science, military history, U.S. history, African American studies, and religion.

Roberta Diehl, Sponsoring Editor—Gardening and railroads.

I

Marilyn Grobschmidt, Sponsoring Editor—Medical ethics, philanthropy, women's studies (history and social science), politics, and international studies.

Michael Lundell, Sponsoring Editor—Classical studies, ancient history, medieval and Renaissance studies, film, folklore, and literature.

Dee Mortensen, Sponsoring Editor—African studies, Caribbean and Black diaspora studies, philosophy, and women's studies (literary and cultural).

THE JOHNS HOPKINS UNIVERSITY PRESS

2715 North Charles Street, Baltimore, MD 21218-4363
410-516-6900
www.press.jhu.edu

The Johns Hopkins University Press (founded in 1878) issues a strong list of contemporary-interest titles and academic trade books, as well as scholarly, technical, and professional works and select course books, reference books, and books of regional interest. The Press publishes in such diverse academic areas as literary criticism, ancient studies, religious studies, political science, and history of and current trends in medicine, science, and technology. Johns Hopkins titles: *Secret Yankees: The Union Circle in Confederate Atlanta* by Thomas G. Dyer; *Fast Food: Roadside Restaurants in the Automobile Age* by John A. Jakle and Keith A. Sculle; *The Bees of the World* by Charles D. Michener; *The Democratic Invention* (edited by Marc F. Plattner and Joao Carlos Espada); *The Invention of Literature: From Greek Intoxication to the Latin Book* by Florence Dupont (translated by Janet Lloyd).

Johns Hopkins produces a number of specialty lines, such as the American Moment series of undergraduate course books in American history, the American Land Classics series of facsimile reprint editions, and Complete Roman Drama in Translation. The Johns Hopkins University Press handles its own distribution with the support of regional sales representatives.

The press will not consider unsolicited poetry or fiction.

Query letters and SASEs should be directed to:

James D. Jordan, Director—Science.

Trevor Lipscombe, Editor in Chief—Physics and Astronomy.

Henry Y. K. Tom, Executive Editor—Sociology, religious studies, economics, development, European history, sociology, political science.

Jacqueline C. Wehmueller, Executive Editor—Trade medical books for an educated general audience; books in higher education; history of medicine; reference books, clinical medicine.

Wendy Harris, Medical Editor—Medicine (hard science for medical professionals), public health, bioethics.

I

Robert Brugger, History Editor—American history, history of science and technology, regional titles, documentary editions.

Maura E. Burnett, Humanities Editor—Humanities, literary theory and criticism, classics and ancient studies, film studies, American studies, theater.

George F. Thompson, Project Editor—Geography and environmental studies, Anabaptist studies, urban planning.

LOUISIANA STATE UNIVERSITY PRESS

P.O. Box 25053, Baton Rouge, LA 70894-5053
3990 West Lakeshore Drive, Baton Rouge, LA 70803
225-578-6294

Areas of Louisiana State University Press interest include Southern history, the American Civil War, African-American history, United States history, Latin American history, European history, philosophy and politics, art, architecture and design, photography, literary voices of the South, American literature, general criticism and European literature, music, natural history, and medicine. LSU offers a wide variety of regional books (not limited to Louisiana environs), as well as concentrations in contemporary fiction, poetry, and literary criticism. The house produces hardcover and trade paperback editions and maintains a solid backlist. Louisiana State University Press (founded in 1935) publishes a primarily academic and scholarly list, along with a good number of general-interest titles.

From LSU Press: *John Marshall and the Heroic Age of the Constitution* by R. Kent Newmyer; *The Companion to Southern Literature* (edited by Joseph M. Flora, Lucinda H. Mackenthan, and Todd Taylor); *The Slave Power: The Free North and Southern Domination, 1780–1860* by Leonard L. Richards; *Notorious Woman: The Celebrated Case of Myra Clark Gaines* by Elizabeth Alexander; *Blessed Are the Peacemakers; Martin Luther King Jr., Eight White Religious Leaders, and the Letter from Birmingham Jail* by S. Jonathan Bass; *A Girl's Life: Horses, Boys, Weddings, and Luck* by Marianne Gingher; *Ignatius Rising: The Life of John Kennedy Toole* by René Pol Nevils and Deborah George Hardy; *Louisiana Faces: Images from a Renaissance,* photographs by Philip Gould, text by Jason Berry.

Fiction and poetry from LSU: *Selected Poems of Robert Penn Warren* (edited by John Burt); *Transfigurations: Collected Poems* by Jay Wright; *Family Gathering* by Fred Chappell: *Intervale: New and Selected Poems* by Betty Adcock; *The Finished Man* by George Garrett; *The Hard Blue Sky* by Shirley Ann Grau.

Louisiana State University Press oversees a distributional network that utilizes the services of regional university presses and book-distribution companies, as well as independent sales representatives. The Press will not consider unsolicited poetry or any original fiction.

Query letters and SASEs should be directed to:

Maureen G. Hewitt, Editor in Chief—all subject areas.

John Easterly, Executive Editor—Literary studies.

L

Sylvia Frank Rodriguez, Acquisitions Editor—American Civil War history, Southern history, civil rights studies.

THE MIT PRESS

5 Cambridge Center, Cambridge, MA 02142
617-253-5646

The MIT Press publishes nonfiction titles in the forefront of such fields as contemporary art, architectural studies, science, environmental studies, computer science and artificial intelligence, cognitive science and neuroscience, linguistics, and economics and finance. The house produces scholarly and professional works, in addition to educational textbooks and books for general audience. The MIT Press was founded in 1961 as the publishing wing of the Massachusetts Institute of Technology.

Representative titles from MIT Press include: *Without a Map* by Andrei Shleifer and Daniel Trustman; *The Subtlety of Emotions* by Aaron Ben-Ze'ev; *Dreamworld and Catastrophe* by Susan Buck-Morss; *The Land That Could Be* by William A. Shutkin; *After the City* by Lars Lerup; *Dialogues in Public Art* by Tom Finkelpearl; *Feeding the World* by Vaclav Smil; *Labyrinth: A Search for the Hidden Meaning of Science* by Peter Pesic; *Snap to Grid* by Peter Lunenfeld; *Changing Minds* by Andrea DiSessa; *From Gutenberg to the Global Information Infrastructure* by Christine L. Borgman; *Syntactic Structures Revisited* by Howard Lasnik; *The Things We Can Do* by Gary Cziko.

The MIT Press also publishes 40-odd specialist journals such as *The Drama Review; The Washington Quarterly,* and *October.* The Bradford Books imprint accents titles representing the frontiers of cognitive science and neuroscience.

The MIT Press distributes its own list and handles distribution for several other publishers (including Zone Books and AAAI Press).

Query letters and SASEs should be directed to:

Tom Stone, Linguistics and Cognitive Science Editor

Clay Morgan, Environmental Science Editor

Douglas Sery, Computer Science Editor

Larry Cohen, Editor in Chief

Michael Rutter, Neurosciences Editor

Robert Prior, Computer Science Editor

Roger Conover, Architecture and Design Editor

Elizabeth Murrey, Economics, Finance, and Business Editor

John Covell, Economics, Finance, and Business Editor

NAVAL INSTITUTE PRESS

United States Naval Institute, 118 Maryland Avenue, Annapolis, MD 21402-5035
410-268-6110   fax: 410-269-7940
www.usni.org

L

Naval Institute Press features trade books, in addition to the house's targeted professional and reference titles. Areas of NIP interest include how-to books on boating and navigation, battle histories, and biographies, as well as occasional selected titles in fiction (typically with a nautical adventure orientation). Specific categories encompass such fields as seamanship, naval history and literature, the Age of Sail, aviation and aircraft, World War II naval history, World War II ships and aircraft, current naval affairs, naval science, and general naval resources and guidebooks. Bluejacket Books is a trade-paperback imprint that includes time-honored classics as well as original titles. Naval Institute Press also publishes a line of historical and contemporary photographs and poster art.

Naval Institute Press, situated on the grounds of the United States Naval Academy, is the book-publishing imprint of the United States Naval Institute, a private, independent, nonprofit professional society for members of the military services and civilians who share an interest in naval and maritime affairs. USNI was established in 1873 at the Naval Academy in Annapolis; the press inaugurated its publishing program in 1898 with a series of basic guides to United States naval practice.

Titles from Naval Institute Press: *Green Berets in the Vanguard: Inside Special Forces 1953–1963* by Chalmers Archer Jr.; *Punk's War* (novel) by Ward Carroll; *Death on the Hellships: Prisoners at Sea in the Pacific War* by Gregory F. Michno; *Reluctant Allies: German-Japanese Naval Relations in World War II* by Hans-Joachim Krug, et al.; *Shield and Sword: The United States Navy and the Persian Gulf War* by Edward J. Marolda and Robert Schneller Jr.; *The Eagle Mutiny* by Richard Linnett and Roberto Loiederman; *Nelson Speaks: Admiral Lord Nelson in His Own Words* by Joseph F. Callo; *Matthew Calbraith Perry: Antebellum Sailor and Diplomat* by John H. Schroeder; *Three Days to Pearl: Incredible Encounter on the Eve of War* by Peter J. Shepherd; *The Co-Vans: U.S. Marine Advisors in Vietnam* by John Grider Miller.*Fighter Squadron at Guadalcanal* by Max Brand is a lost classic, published 50 years after the author's death. Now after more than 50 years and a string of fortunate coincidences, Brand's stirring firsthand account of the 212th Marine Fighter Squadron's operations at Guadalcanal in 1942 has been published.

The Naval Institute Guide to the Ships and Aircraft of the U.S. Fleet (17th edition) by Norman Polmar is indispensable to anyone needing technical data and program information on the contemporary U.S. Navy.

Bluejacket Books is an exciting series of fiction and nonfiction titles available in affordable paperback editions. Titles: *Around the World Submerged: The Voyage of the Triton* by Edward L. Beach; *Midway: The Battle That Doomed Japan, the Japanese Navy's Story* by Mitsuo Fuchida and Masatake Okumiya; *A Country Such As This* by James Webb; *Reminiscences* by Douglas MacArthur; *Teddy Roosevelt's Great White Fleet* by James R. Reckner.

Naval Institute Press handles its own distribution.

Query letters and SASEs should be directed to:

Eric Mills, Acquisitions Editor

Thomas J. Cutler, Senior Acquisitions Editor

Paul Wilderson, Executive Editor

NEW YORK UNIVERSITY PRESS

70 Washington Square South, New York, NY 10012
212-998-2575
www.nyupress.nyu.edu

New York University Press covers the fields of law and politics, history, American history, religion and Jewish studies, psychology, gender studies, sociology, cultural studies, media studies, literary criticism, urban studies, anthropology, race and ethnic studies, business, and New York regional affairs.

New York University Press (founded in 1916) offers a list laden with works of wide contemporary appeal for the general reader; NYU also maintains a strong presence in the scholarly and professional arena. Major series include titles catalogued under Fast Track (general-interest contemporary issues and affairs): *Critical America; Sexual Cultures: New Directions from the Center for Gay and Lesbian Studies; Cultural Front; The World of War;* The Religion, Race and Ethnicity series; *New Perspectives on Jewish Studies; Essential Papers in Jewish Studies; Essential Papers in Psychoanalysis;* and *Qualitative Studies in Psychology.* NYU publishes hardcover and paperback editions and supports a vigorous backlist.

From the NYU program: *Displays of Power: Memory and Amnesia in the America Museum* by Steven C. Dubin; *Time Square Red, Time Square Blue* by Samuel R. Delany; *Seduced by Science: How American Religion Has Lost Its Way* by Steven Goldberg; *Childhood in America* (edited by Paula Fass and Mary Ann Mason); *Battleground of Desire: The Struggle for Self Control in Modern America* by Peter N. Stearns; *Take Charge!: The Complete Guide to Senior Living in New York City* by John Vinton; *Within the Veil: Black Journalists, White Media* by Pamela Newkirk; *Still Lifting, Still Climbing: African American Women's Contemporary Activism* (edited by Kimberly Springer); *The Victorian Underworld* by Donald Thomas; *Guns in America: A Reader* (edited by Jan E. Dizard, Robert Merrill Muth, and Stephen P. Andrews); *Sex, Love, Race: Crossing Boundaries in American History* (edited by Martha Hodes); and *Tennis: A Cultural History* by Heiner Gillmeister.

NYU Press is the exclusive North American distributor for Berg Publishers, Monthly Review Press, Lawrence & Wishart, and Rivers Oram (Pandora).

NYU Press Prize winners include *The Marvelous Adventures of Pierre Baptiste: Father and Mother, First and Last* (fiction) by Patricia Eakins; and *The Alphabet of Desire* (poetry) by Barbara Hamby.

New York University Press handles distribution through its own sales office, as well as a network of regional sales and marketing representatives.

Query letters and SASEs should be directed to:

Eric Zinner, Editor-in-Chief—Literary criticism and cultural studies, media studies, history, anthropology.

Jennifer Hammer, Editor—Religion and psychology.

Stephen Magro, Editor—Sociology and politics.

OHIO UNIVERSITY PRESS

Scott Quadrangle, Athens, OH 45701
740-593-1155   fax: 740-593-4536
www.ohiou.edu/~oupress

Ohio University Press areas of interest encompass literary criticism, philosophy, African studies, history, international regional and cultural studies, and Frontier Americana; the press also publishes fiction reprints and anthologies. Poetry issued through the Swallow Press imprint certifies the house's outstanding presence in this literary niche.

Ohio University Press (established in 1964) produces scholarly and academic works, as well as a line of general-interest titles. OU Press publishes in hardcover and paperback. The house backlist is comprehensive.

On the OU Press list: *Dared and Done: The Marriage of Elizabeth Barrett and Robert Browning* by Julia Markus; *Death and Taxes: The Complete Guide to Family Inheritance Planning* by Randell C. Doane and Rebecca G. Doane; *Deprived of Unhappiness* by Sam Pickering; *Brave Are My People: Indian Heroes Not Forgotten* by Frank Waters (foreword by Vine Deloria, Jr.); *RFD* by Charles Allen Smart (foreword by Gene Logsdon); *The Watchers* by Memye Curtis Tucker; *Ruskin's Mythic Queen: Gender Subversion in Victorian Culture* by Sharon Aronofsky Weltman; *The Absent Man: The Narrative Craft of Charles W. Chesnutt; The Complete Works of Robert Browning, Volume XVI: With Variant Readings and Annotations* (edited by Susan Crowl and Roma A. King, Jr.); *Word Play Place: Essays on the Poetry of John Matthias* (edited by Robert Archambeau); *The Green Archipelago: Forestry in Preindustrial Japan* by Conrad Totman (foreword by James L. A. Webb, Jr.); *Theory of Objective Mind: An Introduction to the Philosophy of Culture* by Hans Freyer (translated, and with an introduction by Steven Grosby); *Es'kia Mphahlele: Themes of Alienation and African Humanism* by Ruth Obee; *Herero Heroes: A Socio-Political History of the Herero of Namibia, 1890–1923* by Jan-Bart Gerwald; *Theater and Martial Arts in West Sumatra: Randai and Silek of the Minangkabau* by Kirstin Pauka.

Ohio University Press oversees its own sales and distribution.

Query letters and SASEs should be directed to:

Gillian Berchowitz, Senior Editor

OXFORD UNIVERSITY PRESS

198 Madison Avenue, New York, NY 10016
212-726-6000
www.oup-usa.org

Oxford's list is especially prominent in the subject areas of current affairs, world history (both ancient and modern), and United States history. Popular and classical music constitute another area of Oxford focus; the house's books on jazz are especially well known. In addition, Oxford is strong in literary studies and historical and contemporary cultural expression.

Oxford University Press (founded in 1478) is an international publisher of trade, scholarly, professional, and reference titles in the humanities, the arts, science, medicine, and social studies in hardcover and paperback editions.

Oxford titles include: *Inroads into Burma* by Gerry Abbott; *Sport in Australian History* by Daryl Adair; *Tourism and Spatial Transformation* by G. J. Ashworth; *Tourism in Spain* by M. Barke; *The Oxford Companion to the Wines of North America* by Bruce Cass; *Rome* by Amanda Claridge; *Spain* by Roger Collins; *The Temple Tiger and More Man-Eaters of Kumaon* by Jim Corbett; *World Leisure Participation* by G. Cushman; *The Classical Cookbook* by Andrew Dalby; *The A–Z of Sailing Terms,* 2nd edition by Ian Dear; *Traditional Chinese Clothing* by Valery M. Garrett; *Trends in Outdoor Recreation, Leisure and Tourism* by W. C. Gartner; *Sou' West in Wanderer IV* by Eric C. Hiscock; *Budapest* by Michael Jacobs; *Travelers' India* by H. K. Kaul; *The Oxford Companion to Ships and the Sea* by Peter Kemp; *Yangtze River* by Madeleine Lynn; *Destinations* by Jan Morris; *The Holy Land,* 4th edition by Jerome Murphy O'Connor; *Oxford History of Board Games* by David Parlett; *The Oxford Book of Australian Travel Writing* by Roslyn Pesman; *Eisenhower and the Cold War* by Robert A. Divine; *Narrative of the Life of Frederick Douglass,* and *American Slave* by Frederick Douglass; *The American Pacific* by Arthur P. Dudden; and *Them Dark Days* by William Dusinberre.

Oxford also publishes college textbooks, Bibles, music, English as a second language (ESL) educational materials, and children's books, as well as a number of journals. The Twentieth Century Fund series accents works in the public interest that consider contemporary political, governmental, cultural, and international issues.

Oxford University Press presents the *Oxford Mark Twain* (Series Editor Shelley Fisher Fishkin). This 29-volume set collects the writings of Mark Twain, including all the original illustrations, some of which were drawn by Twain himself. Many of these works have not been readily available for decades.

Oxford's New York division is editorially independent of the British home office and handles distribution of its own list, as well as titles originating from Oxford outposts worldwide.

In 1999 Oxford began a Professional Publishing division. It publishes titles in business, psychology, and medicine for practitioner audiences.

Query letters and SASEs should be directed to:

Beth Kaufman Barry, Senior Editor—Clinical medicine.

Cynthia Read, Senior Editor—Religion, linguistics.

Donald Kraus, Senior Editor—Bibles.

Jeff House, Vice President—Medicine.

Joan Bossert, Editorial Director—Psychology, business, and medicine.

Joyce Berry, Senior Editor—Medicine, science, geology, geography, art, and architecture.

Kirk Jensen, Senior Editor—Life sciences.

Maribeth Payne, Executive Editor—Music.

Nancy Toff, Editorial Director—Trade and Young Adult reference, children's and young-adult books.

Peter Ginna, Executive Editor, Trade Department—History, commercial nonfiction consistent with house list.

Robert Miller, Senior Editor—Philosophy, classics.

Robert Rogers, Senior Editor—Chemistry.

T. Susan Chang, Senior Editor—Literature, comparative literature.

Paul S. Donnelly, Executive Editor—Business, finance, and economics—trade, college, professional, and academic trade.

PRINCETON UNIVERSITY PRESS

41 William Street, Princeton, NJ 08540
609-258-4900
www.pup.princeton.edu
U.K. office:
3, Market Place
Woodstock
Oxfordshire OX20 1SY
United Kingdom
(011) 44-1993-814500

Princeton University Press has particularly strong focus in such areas as popular culture and fine arts, current affairs, literary biography, European history, political science, economics, and natural history. Princeton University Press (founded in 1905) publishes trade and general-interest books, in addition to a list of scholarly and scientific works that span the academic spectrum. Popular Princeton lines include the Bollingen series and Princeton Science Library. Princeton publishes hardcover and paperback editions and hosts a comprehensive backlist.

Princeton titles: *Charles Taylor* by Ruth Abbey; *Sexual Identities, Queer Politics* (edited by Mark Blasius); *Financing the American Dream: A Cultural History of Consumer Credit* by Lendol Calder; *Diplomacy of Conscience: Amnesty International and Changing Human Rights Norms* by Ann Marie Clark; *Asset Pricing* by John H. Cochrane; *The Secular Mind* by Robert Coles; *Winslow Homer and the Critics: Forging a National Art 1870's* by Margaret C. Conrads; *Home Team: Professional Sports and the American Metropolis* by Michael N. Danielson; *Learning and Expectations in Macroeconomics* by George W. Evans and Seppo Honkapohja; *How the Leopard Changed Its Spots: The Evolution of Complexity* by Brian Goodwin; *The Color of School Reform, Race, Politics, and the Challenge of Urban Education* by Jeffrey R. Henig, Richard C. Hula, Marion Orr, and Desiree S. Pedescleaux; *The Necessary Nation* by Gregory Jusdanis; *The Story of Mathematics* by Richard Mankiewicz; *Suburban Warriors: The Origins of the New American Right* by Lisa McGirr; and *William Blake: The Creation of the Songs from Manuscript to Illuminated Printing* by Michael Phillips.

The Bollingen Series, established in 1941, is sponsored by the Bollingen Foundation and has been published by Princeton since 1967. Bollingen titles are works of original scholarship, translations, and new editions of classics. An ongoing Bollingen project is Mythos: The Princeton/Bollingen series in world mythology. Titles here: *Psychology of Kundalini Yoga* by C. G. Young; *On the Laws of the Poetic Art* by Anthony Hecht; *The Survival of the Pagan Gods: The Mythological Tradition and Its Place in Renaissance Humanism and Art* by Jean Seznec.

Books from the Princeton Science Library include *Infinity and the Mind* by Rudy Rucker; *A Natural History of Shells* by Geerat J. Vermeij, and *Total Eclipses of the Sun* by J. B. Zirker.

Princeton University Press handles distribution through the offices of California/Princeton Fulfillment Services, as well as regional sales representation worldwide.

Query letters and SASEs should be directed to:

Mary Murrell, Anthropology Editor

Peter Dougherty, Economics Editor

Walter Lippincott, Director

Sam Elworthy, Science Editor—Biology, earth science, and trade science.

Nancy Grubb, Executive Editor—Fine arts and art history.

Robert Kirk, Senior Editor—Natural history.

Thomas LeBien, American Studies Editor—Pre-twentieth century American history, American studies, and American religion.

Ian Malcolm, Philosophy, Political Theory, and Sociology Editor

Chuck Myers, Political Science, Law, and Classics Editor

Brigitta van Rheinberg, History and Religion Editor—Twentieth-century American history, non-American history, and Religion (Jewish and Asian studies).

Terry Vaughn, Editor in Chief

Joe Wisnovsky, Executive Editor—Physical sciences and trade science.

Richard Baggaley (U.K. office), European Publishing Director—Finance and economics.

David Ireland (U.K. office), Applied Math Editor

RUTGERS UNIVERSITY PRESS

100 Joyce Kilmer Avenue, Piscataway, NJ 08854
732-445-7762
http://rutgerspress.rutgers.edu

Rutgers subject areas include African-American studies, American history, anthropology, art and architecture, Asian-American studies, environment and ecology, European history, gay and gender studies, geography, health and medicine, history of medicine and science, literature and literary criticism, media studies, multicultural studies, New Jerseyana, peace studies, poetry, religion, and sociology.

Rutgers University Press (founded in 1936) publishes a list of general-interest trade books in addition to scholarly titles in the humanities and social sciences, as well as books with a regional American bent.

Representing the nonfiction Rutgers list: *Midnight Dreary: The Mysterious Death of Edgar Allan Poe* by John Evangelist Walsh; *Talking Leadership: Conversations with Powerful Women* (edited by Mary S. Hartman); *The Truth That Never Hurts: Writings on Race, Gender, and Freedom* by Barbara Smith; *Surviving Modern Medicine: How to Get the Best from Doctors, Family and Friends* by Peter Clarke and Susan H. Evans; *Mortal Men: Living with Asymptomatic HIV* by Richard MacIntyre (foreword by Stephen Lacey); *Heresy in the University: The Black Athena Controversy and the Responsibilities of American Intellectuals* by Jacques Berlinerblau; *How Jews Became White Folks and What That Says About Race in America* by Karen Brodkin; *Consuming Environments: Television and Commercial Culture* by Mike Budd, Steve Craig, and Clay Steinman; *Evaluating Alternative Cancer Therapies: A Guide to the Science and Politics of an Emerging Medical Field* by David Hess; *In Praise of Difference: The Emergence of a Global Feminism* by Rosiska Darcy De Oliveira; *Gone Fishin': The 100 Best Spots in New Jersey* by Manny Luftglass and Ron Bern; *Anatomy of a Miracle: The End of Apartheid and the Birth of the New South Africa* by Patti Waldmeir.

Rutgers features the Touring North America guidebook series that offers an accent on regional landscape. Titles: *Beyond the Great Divide: Denver to the Grand Canyon; Megalopolis: Washington, DC, to Boston.*

New Jerseyana from Rutgers includes *Roadside New Jersey* by Peter Genovese; *Murdered in Jersey* by Gerald Tomlinson; *Teenage New Jersey,. 1941–1975* (edited by Kathryn Grover); *The New Jersey State Constitution: A Reference Guide* by Robert F. Williams; *New Jersey Parks, Forests, and Natural Areas* by Michael P. Brown.

Rutgers University Press handles its own distribution.

Query letters and SASEs should be directed to:

David Myers, Editor—Social sciences.

Helen Hsu, Senior Editor—Sciences.

Leslie Mitchner, Associate Director and Editor in Chief—Humanities, literature, film, communications.

Suzanne Kellam, Associate Editor in the Humanities—History.

S

STANFORD UNIVERSITY PRESS

Stanford, CA 94305-2235
415-723-9598

Stanford produces a notable line of titles in the fields of new technology, the global political and natural environment, postmodern philosophy and psychology, gender studies, and international issues, as well as a number of books (many in translation) dealing with current cultural and literary theory. A major Stanford publishing concentration is in the Asian-American and Pacific Rim fields of studies.

Stanford University Press (started in 1925) produces trade and scholarly books in literature, the social sciences, religion, history, political science, anthropology, and natural science in hardcover and paperback editions.

Highlights from Stanford: *Taking Our Pulse: The Health of America's Women* by Iris F. Litt, M.D.; *The Cable Car in America* by George W. Hilton; *The Fall of the Packard Motor Car Company* by James A. Ward; *From Immigrant to Ethnic Culture: American Yiddish in South Philadelphia* by Rakhmiel Peltz; *Caught by History: Holocaust Effects in Contemporary Art, Literature, and Theory* by Ernst Van Alphen; *Desiring Women Writing: English Renaissance Examples* by Jonathan Goldberg; *The Mottled Screen: Reading Proust Visually* by Mieke Bal; *Psychoanalyzing: On the Order of the Unconscious and the Practice of the Letter* by Serge Leclaire (translated by Peggy Kamuf); *The Queer Afterlife of Vaslav Nijinsky* by Kevin Kopelson; *A Sense for the Other: The Timeliness and Relevance of Anthropology* by Marc Augé (translated by Amy Jacobs); *Freedom and Religion in the Nineteenth Century* (edited by Richard Helmstadter); *The Price of Redemption: The Spiritual Economy of Puritan New England* by Mark A. Peterson; *Traces of Dreams: Landscape, Cultural Memory, and the Poetry of Basho* by Haruo Shirane; *The Will to Orthodoxy: A Critical Genealogy of Northern Chan Buddhism* by Bernard Faure (translated by Phyllis Brooks); *Space Between Words: The Origin of Silent Reading* by Paul Saenger.

Stanford University Press books are distributed by Cambridge University Press Distribution Center.

Query letters and SASEs should be directed to:

Helen Tartar, Assistant Director—Philosophy, literary criticism and theory.

John Feneron, Managing Editor—Asian literature.

Muriel Bell, Senior Editor—Asian studies, political science, anthropology.

Norris Pope, Director—Latin American studies, history, Victorian studies, natural sciences.

SYRACUSE UNIVERSITY PRESS

621 Skytop Road, Suite 110, Syracuse, NY 13244-5290
315-443-5534   fax: 315-443-5545
e-mail: talitz@syr.edu

Syracuse University Press (founded in 1943) hosts a publishing program that accents scholarly, general, and regional (New York and New England) nonfiction interests, as well as literature and criticism. Syracuse has particular presence in Irish studies, Iroquois studies, Middle Eastern studies, studies in peace and conflict resolution, history of the medieval period, and historical American utopianism and communitarianism.

On the Syracuse list: *Crossing Highbridge: A Memoir of Irish America* by Maureen Waters; *Under the Spell of Arabia,* photographs by Mathias Oppersdorff; *Gertrude Bell: The Arabian Diaries, 1913–1914* (edited by Rosemary O'Brien); *Women in Muslim Family Law* by John L. Esposito with Natana DeLong-Bas; *The Gatekeeper: My 20 Years as a TV Censor* by Alfred R. Scdhneider with Kaye Pullen; *Prime Time Authorship: Works*

About and by Three TV Dramatists by Douglas Heil; *Gustav Stickley's Craftsman Farms: The Quest for an Arts and Crafts Utopia* by Mark Alan Hewitt; *Masterpieces of American Furniture from the Munson-Williams-Proctor Institute* (edited by Anna Tobin D'Ambrosio); *My Self, My Muse* (edited by Patricia Boyle Haberstroh); *Reading Roddy Doyle* by Caramine White; *The Scottish Connection: The Rise of English Literary Study in Early America* by Franklin E. Court; *Pleasure Zones: Bodies, Cities, Spaces* (edited by David Bell); *Does Your Government Measure Up? Basic Tools for Local Officials and Citizens* by William D. Coplin and Carol Dwyer; *The President Is at Camp David* by W. Dale Nelson; *The Man Who Stopped the Trains to Auschwitz* by David Kranzler; *Diary of an Adulterous Woman* by Curt Leviant; *TV Creators: Conversations with America's Top Producers of Television Drama* by James L. Longworth, Jr.; *Catching Dreams: My Life in the Negro Baseball Leagues* by Frazier "Slow" Robinson with Paul Bauer; *A Room of His Own: In Search of the Feminine in the Novels of Saul Bellow* by Gloria Cronin.

Titles in the Reader's Guide series: *A Reader's Guide to Walt Whitman* by Gay Wilson Allen; *A Reader's Guide to Joseph Conrad* by Frederick R. Karl; *A Reader's Guide to William Butler Yeats* by John Unterecker; *A Reader's Guide to Dylan Thomas, A Reader's Guide to James Joyce,* and *A Reader's Guide to Finnegan's Wake* by William York Tindall; *A Reader's Guide to Samuel Beckett* by Hugh Kenner.

Syracuse University Press distributes its list via its own in-house offices and utilizes a variety of distribution services worldwide.

Syracuse University Press does not wish to receive unsolicited manuscripts.

Mary Shelden Evans, Executive Editor—E-mail: msevans@syr.edu

Texas A & M University Press

John H. Lindsey Building, Lewis Street, College Station, TX, 77843-4354
979-458-3975   fax: 979-847-8752
www.tamu.edu/upress/   e-mail: d-vance@tamu.edu

Texas A&M University Press (founded in 1974) publishes scholarly nonfiction, regional studies, art, economics, government, history, environmental history, natural history, social science, United States–Mexican borderlands studies, veterinary medicine, women's studies, and military studies. A special portion of the Texas A&M list accents Texas photography, history, and literature.

Texas A & M nonfiction: *Land of the Desert Sun: Texas' Big Bend Country* by D. Gentry Steele; *Wild Edens: Africa's Premier Game Parks and Their Wildlife* by Joseph James Shomon; *Planetary Astronomy: From Ancient Times to the Third Millennium* by Ronald A. Schorn; *Stirring Prose: Cooking with Texas Authors* by Deborah Douglas; *Tejano Empire: Life on the South Texas Ranchos* by Andres Tijerina; *The Plains Indians* by Paul H. Carlson; *Sailing Ship Elissa* by Patricia Bellis Bixel; *Coercive Military Strategy* by Stephen J. Cimbala; *Shaping and Signaling Presidential Policy: The National Security Decision Making of Eisenhower and Kennedy* by Meena Bose; *Under Ice: Waldo Lyon and the Development of the Arctic Submarine* by William M. Leary; *East of Chosin: Entrapment and Breakout in Korea, 1950* by Roy E. Appleman; *Galveston and the Great West* by Earle B. Young.

Texas A&M University Press manages its own distribution network and handles distribution for several other regional academically oriented presses.

Query letters and SASEs should be directed to:

Mary Lenn Dixon, Editor in Chief—e-mail: mary-dixon@tamu.edu

Shannon Davies, Senior Editor—e-mail: smdavies@aol.com

Jim Sadkovich, Acquisitions Editor—e-mail: j-sadkovich@tamu.edu

UNIVERSITY OF ARIZONA PRESS

355 S. Euclid, Suite 103, Tucson, AZ 85719
520-621-1441   fax: 520-621-8899
www.uapress.arizona.edu

University of Arizona Press (founded in 1959) publishes works of general as well as academic interest related primarily to the scholarly emphasis of the university's programs in Southwest regional culture and natural history. Fields of publishing concentration include general nonfiction about Arizona, the American West, and Mexico; wider categories encompass the American Indian and Latin America, anthropology, and archaeology.

From the Arizona program: *Nobody's Son: Notes from an American Life* by Luis Alberto Urrea; *Shelter* by Bobby Burns (foreword by David A. Snow); *The Nearsighted Naturalist* by Ann Haymond Zwinger; *Almost an Island: Travels in Baja California* by Bruce Berger; *Old Fences, New Neighbors* by Peter R. Decker; *The Power of Kiowa Song* by Luke E. Lassiter; *The Emperor's Mirror: Understanding Cultures Through Primary Sources* by Russell J. Barber and Frances F. Berdan; *The Last Gamble: Betting on the Future in Four Rocky Mountain Mining Towns* by Katherine Jensen and Audie Blevins; *Gender, Law and Resistance in India* by Erin P. Moore; *Crossing Borders: Changing Social Identities in Southern Mexico* by Kimberley M. Grimes; *Cowbirds and Other Brood Parasites* by Catherine P. Ortega.

University of Arizona Press handles its own distribution and also distributes titles originating from the publishing programs of such enterprises and institutions as Oregon State University Press, the Arizona State Museum, and other archaeological and environmental consulting firms.

Query letters and SASEs should be directed to:

Christine Szuter, Director

UNIVERSITY OF ARKANSAS PRESS

201 Ozark Avenue, Fayetteville, AR 72701
501-575-3246
www.uark.edu/~uaprinfo   e-mail: uaprinto@cavern.uark.edu

University of Arkansas Press (begun in 1980) features titles in general humanities, biography, fiction, poetry, translation, literary criticism, history, business, regional studies, natural science, political science, and popular culture. The house issues a moderate list of new books each season (in hardcover and paperback editions), while tending a hardy backlist. University of Arkansas Press hosts an electronic-publishing program with a selection of software editions.

Indicative of the Arkansas list: *Arkansas Wildlife: A History by the Arkansas Game and Fish Commission* (edited by Keith Sutton); *Arkansas Mammals: Their History, Classification, and Distribution* by John A. Sealander and Gary A. Heidt; *We Are a People in This World: The Lakota Sioux and the Massacre at Wounded Knee* by Conger Beasley, Jr.; *Black Charlestonians: A Social History, 1822–1885* by Bernard E. Powers, Jr.; *Roberta: A Most Remarkable Fulbright* by Dorothy D. Stuck and Nan Snow; *Steamboats and Ferries on the White River: A Heritage Revisited* by Duane Huddleston, Sammie Cantrell Rose, and Pat Taylor Wood; *It's About Time: The Dave Brubeck Story* by Fred Hall, with a foreword by Gene Lees.

Titles from the Carter Collection: *Why Not the Best? The First Fifty Years; A Government as Good as Its People; An Outdoor Journal; Keeping Faith; The Blood of Abraham* by Jimmy Carter; *Everything to Gain* by Jimmy and Rosalynn Carter; *First Lady from Plains* by Rosalynn Carter.

Poetry titles: *It Will Be All Right in the Morning* by Michael Burns; *Discovery and Reminiscence: Essays on the Poetry of Mona Van Duyn* (edited by Michael Burns); *The Truth About Small Towns* by David Baker; *Meter in English: A Critical Engagement* (edited and with an introduction by David Baker).

In the area of folklore, Arkansas has produced *Roll Me in Your Arms and Blow the Candle Out* by Vance Randolph (edited by G. Legman) and *The Arkansas Folklore Sourcebook* (edited by W. K. McNeil and William M. Clements).

University of Arkansas Press distributes its own list.

Query letters and SASEs should be directed to:

Brian King, Managing Editor

John Coghlan, Acting Director and Production Manager

Karen Johnson, Manuscript Editor

Kevin Brock, Acquisitions Editor

UNIVERSITY OF CALIFORNIA PRESS

2120 Berkeley Way, Berkeley, CA 94720

Branch Office:
510-642-4247   fax: 510-643-7127
1600 Hershey Hall South Annex, UCLA, CA 90095
www.upress.edu

University of California Press (founded in 1893) publishes a solid general-interest list, in addition to its substantial contribution in academic publishing; the house maintains a broad program that encompasses scholarly and classical studies, humanities and the arts, medicine and science, the environment, popular historical and contemporary culture and issues, and language and linguistics. The press has major concentrations in such specialty areas as California and the West; the Pacific Ocean region, including the Pacific Rim; Asian studies; Oceania; and Latin America. University of California Press also produces literary fiction, letters, and poetry.

University of California titles include: *America Day by Day* by Simone de Beauvoir (translated by Carol Cosman); *The Teachings of Don Juan: A Yacqui Way of Knowledge* (The Original Teachings in a Deluxe 30th Anniversary Edition); *Ambrose Bierce and the Queen of Spades: A Novel* by Oakley Hall; *The Art of Living: Socratic Reflections from Plato to Foucault* by Alexander Nehamas; *Creating the Corporate Soul: The Rise of Public Relations and Corporate Imagery in American Big Business* by Roland Marchand; *Tiger on the Brink: Jiang Zemin and China's New Elite* by Bruce Gilley; *After Heaven: Spirituality in America Since the 1950s* by Robert Wuthnow; *Illness and Culture in the Postmodern Age* by David B. Morris; *Disaster Hits Home: New Policy for Urban Housing Recovery* by Mary C. Comerio; *A Companion to California Wines: An Encyclopedia of Wine and Winemaking from the Mission Period to the Present* by Charles L. Sullivan; *Inside Out: New Chinese Art* (edited by Gao Minglu); *Odd Man In: Norton Simon and the Pursuit of Culture* by Suzanne Muchnic; *Bob Thompson* by Thelma Golden; *The Art of Joan Brown* by Karen Tsujimoto and Jacquelynn Baas; *Beyond Reason: Art and Psychosis: Works from the Prinzhorn Collection* by Laurent Busine, Inge Jadi, Bettina Brand-Claussen, and Caroline Douglas.

University of California Press distributes its own list.

Query letters and SASEs should be directed to:

Deborah Kirshman, Editor—Fine arts.

Doris Kretchmer, Executive Editor—Natural history, biology, archaeology

Linda Norton, Editor—Literature, poetry, linguistics.

Lynne Withey, Editor—Music, Middle Eastern studies.

Kate Toll, Editor—Classics.

Monica McCormick, Editor—African studies and American studies.

Naomi Schneider, Executive Editor—Sociology, politics, gender studies, ethnic studies, Latin American studies.

Sheila Levine, Editorial Director—Asian studies and European history, food.

Stan Holwitz, Assistant Director—Anthropology, Judaica, geography.

Stephanie Fay, Editor—Fine arts.

Mary Francis, Editor—Music.

Blake Edgar, Editor—Environmental science, biology.

Eric Smoodin—Film, philosophy.

Reed Malcom—Religion, political science.

UNIVERSITY OF CHICAGO PRESS

1427 East 60th Street, Chicago, IL 60637-2954
773-702-7700   fax: 773-702-9756
www.press.uchicago.edu   e-mail: marketing@press.uchicago.edu

University of Chicago Press (founded in 1891) specializes in the arts, humanities, and social sciences. Above all a scholarly and academic house, Chicago nonetheless has a noteworthy list of books intended for a wider readership. Major areas of Chicago publishing interest are history, regional Chicago and Illinois books, literary studies, philosophy and linguistics, anthropology, archaeology, art, architecture, music, religion, business and economics, media studies, political science, sociology, psychology, education, legal studies, gender studies, popular culture, and publishing, along with selected titles in the biological and physical sciences.

Titles from University of Chicago Press: *Rock of Ages, Sands of Time* by Warren Allmon, paintings by Barbara Page; *Making Patriots* by Walter Berns; *Bushmanders and Bullwinkles: How Politicians Manipulate Electronic Maps and Census Data to Win Elections* by Mark Monmonier; *Death and the Afterlife in Ancient Egypt* by John H. Taylor; *Leonardo: The Last Supper* by Pinin Brambilla Barcilon and Pietro C. Marani, translated by Harlow Tighe; *The Chicago Guide to Your Academic Career* by John A. Goldsmith, John Komlos, and Penny Schine Gold; *Animal Minds: Beyond Cognition to Consciousness* by Donald R. Griffin; *Educating Institution* by Robin M. Hogarth; *Global Sex* by Dennis Altman; *On European Ground* by Alan Cohen; *Talk of Love: How Culture Matters* by Ann Swindler; *Reflections on Baroque* by Robert Harbison; *Skeptical Music: Essays on Modern Poetry* by David Bromwich; *Processing Politics: Learning from Television in the Internet Age* by Doris A. Graber; *Chinese Migrant Networks and Cultural Change* by Adam McKeown; *Feminisms at a Millennium* (edited by Judith A. Howard and Carolyn Allen); and *Liberace: An American Boy* by Darden Asbury Pyron.

The press publishes the professional reference work *The Chicago Manual of Style* and distributes the annually updated resource for academic writers *Association of American University Presses Directory.*

University of Chicago Press distributes its own list.

Query letters and SASEs should be directed to:

Alan Thomas, Editor—Literary criticism and theory, religious studies.

Christie Henry, Editor—Biological science.

Douglas Mitchell, Editor—Sociology, history, gay and lesbian studies.

Geoffrey Huck, Editor—Economics, linguistics, classics.

John Tryneski, Editor—Political science, law, education.

Kathleen Hansell, Editor—Music.

Linda Halorson, Editor—Reference.

Penelope Kaiserlian, Associate Director—Geography.

Susan Abrams, Editor—History of science.

Susan Bielstein, Editor—Art, architecture, classics, women's studies.

T. David Brent, Editor—Anthropology, philosophy, psychology.

UNIVERSITY OF GEORGIA PRESS

330 Research Drive, Athens, GA 30602-4901
706-369-6130   fax: 706-369-6131

University of Georgia Press (established in 1938) publishes a solid list of mainstream-interest books in addition to its specialized roster of academic, scholarly, and scientific publications. Georgia trade-book titles accent fiction and literature, biography and memoirs, history, current affairs, and regional titles; the house academic emphasis overlaps these areas of concentration, in a program that features scholarly nonfiction, poetry, short fiction, regional studies, and novels. The press publishes hardcover and trade paperback editions.

Representative of the Georgia list: *Daughter of My People* by James Kilgo; *We're Heaven Bound!: Portrait of a Black Sacred Drama* by Gregory D. Coleman; *Fiber* by Rick Bass, illustrations by Elizabeth Hughes Bass; *Lessons from the Wolverine* by Barry Lopez, illustrations by Tom Pohrt; *The Jekyll Island Cottage Colony* by June Hall Mc-Cash; *Ocmulgee Archaeology, 1936–1986* (edited by David J. Hally); *The Travels of William Bartram: Naturalist's Edition* by William Bartram (edited by Francis Harper); *Unto This Hour: A Novel* by Tom Wicker; *Civil War Stories* by Catherine Clinton; *Chained to the Rock of Adversity: To Be Free, Black, and Female in the Old South* (edited by Virginia Meacham Gould); *The Selected Letters of Louisa May Alcott* (edited by Joel Myerson and Daniel Shealy; Associate Editor Madeleine B. Stern); *From Selma to Sorrow: The Life and Death of Viola Liuzzo* by Mary Stanton; *Cornerstones of Georgia History: Documents That Formed the State* (edited by Thomas A. Scott).

Backlist favorites: *American Plants for American Gardens: Plant Ecology—The Study of Plants in Relation to Their Environment* by Edith A. Roberts and Elsa Rehmann; *Why the South Lost the Civil War* by Richard E. Beringer, Herman Hattaway, Archer Jones, and William N. Still, Jr.

The New Georgia Guide is filled with essays, tours, maps, and other resources keyed to Georgia's heritage and culture.

University of Georgia Press sponsors the Flannery O'Connor Award for Short Fiction. (Please write for entry requirements and submission guidelines.)

University of Georgia Press oversees its own distribution.

Query letters and SASEs should be directed to:

Barbara Ras, Executive Editor

UNIVERSITY OF HAWAII PRESS

2840 Kolowalu Street, Honolulu, HI 96822-1888
808-956-8257   fax: 808-988-6052
www.uhpress.hawaii.edu

Areas of University of Hawaii Press publishing interest include cultural history, economics, social history, travel, arts and crafts, costume, marine biology, natural history, botany, ecology, religion, law, political science, anthropology, and general reference; particular UHP emphasis is on regional topics relating to Hawaii, East Asia, South and Southeast Asia, and Hawaii and the Pacific.

University of Hawaii Press (started in 1947) publishes books for the general trade as well as titles keyed to the academic market. UHP also issues a series of special-interest journals. The house maintains an established backlist.

On the University of Hawaii list: *Presstime in Paradise: The Life and Times of the Honolulu Advertiser, 1856–1995* by George Chaplin; *The Elder Law Hawaii Handbook: Protecting Your Health, Wealth, and Personal Wishes* by James H. Pietsch with Lenora H. Lee; *Hawaiian Heritage Plants* by Angela Kay Kepler; *A Guide to Kona* by the Kona Historical Society; *Imperial Benevolence: Making British Authority in the Pacific Islands* by Jane Samson; *A Pocket Guide to Hawaii's Flowers* by Douglas Peebles and Leland Miyano; *In Deeper Waters: Photographic Studies of Hawaiian Deep-Sea Habitats and Life-Forms* by E. H. Chave and Alexander Malahoff; *The Rise of Asia: Economy, Society, and Politics in the Industrial Age* by Frank B. Tipton; *Readers' Guide to Intermediate Japanese: A Quick Reference to Written Expressions* by Yasuko Ito Watt and Richard Rubinger; *The Korean Alphabet: Its History and Structure* (edited by Young-Key Kim-Renaud); *Fables from the Garden* by Leslie Ann Hayashi (illustrated by Kathleen Wong Bishop); *Kauai: Ancient Place-Names and Their Stories* by Frederick Wichman.

A notable UHP series is Talanoa: Contemporary Pacific Literature, which makes writing of Pacific Islanders available to a wider audience. Sample titles here: *Deep River Talk: Collected Poems* by Hone Tuwhere; *Once Were Warriors* by Alan Duff; *Leaves of the Banyan Tree* by Albert Wendt.

The University of Hawaii Press handles its own distribution via a network that includes in-house fulfillment services as well as independent sales representatives.

Query letters and SASEs should be directed to:

Keith Leber, Acquisitions Editor—Natural history and science; e-mail: kleber@hawaii.edu

Pamela Kelley, Acquisitions Editor—Pacific studies, Southeast Asian studies, and Asian American studies; e-mail: pkelley@hawaii.edu

Patricia Crosby, Executive Editor—East Asia history, religion, art history, and social sciences; e-mail: pcrosby@hawaii.edu

Masako Ikeda, Acquisitions Editor—Hawaiiana, literature, and regional children's books; e-mail: masakoi@hawaii.edu

William Hamilton, Director

UNIVERSITY OF ILLINOIS PRESS

1325 South Oak Street, Champaign, IL 61820
217-333-0950   fax: 217-244-8082
www.press.uillinois.edu   e-mail: uipress@uillinois.edu

University of Illinois Press (founded in 1918) publishes books of general and scholarly nonfiction, with strong emphasis on American studies (especially history, literature, music), communications, film studies, folklore, gender studies, African-American studies, regional studies, ecology, law and political science, religion and philosophy, labor studies, and athletics. The press also publishes poetry.

Representative of the University of Illinois program: *African American Mayors; American Opera; Ancient Records of Egypt; Bluegrass Odyssey; Chicago and the Old Northwest; Damnedest Radical; Desirable Body; Early Encounter with Tomorrow; Elliot Coues; Enemies Within; Gold and the American Country Club; Graying of America; Haunting Violations; Holding Up More Than Half the Sky; House of Poured Out Waters; Lessons in Progress; Love, War, and the 96th Engineers; Masculine Women in America 1890–1935; Mormons and Mormonism; Murals; Passing the Torch; Salt Hour; Science or Pseudoscience; Shaping Losses; Spirit of Youth and the City Streets; Tomorrow's Eve; Vacation Stories;* and *Zion in the Courts.*

Celebrating 25 years of publishing poetry: For the past 11 years, the University of Illinois Press has been chosen as one of the publishers for the National Poetry Series. New poetry titles: *Grazing* by Ira Sadoff; *Walt Whitman Bathing* (poems) by David Wagoner; *To the Bone* (new and selected poems) by Sydney Lea; *The Tracks We Leave: Poems on Endangered Wildlife of North America* by Barbara Helfgott Hyett (illustrated by Robert W. Treanor); *The Broken World* (poems) by Marcus Cafagna; *Dance Script with Electric Ballerina* (poems) by Alice Fulton; *Bruised Paradise* (poems) by Kevin Stein.

Of literary note: *"I Cease Not to Yowl": Ezra Pound's Letters to Olivia Rossetti Agresti* (edited by Demetres P. Tryphonopoulos and Leon Surette); *Unbought Spirit: A John Jay Chapman Reader* (edited by Richard Stone); *The Urban Sublime in American Literary Naturalism* by Christophe Den Tandt; *Taking It Home: Stories from the Neighborhood* by Tony Ardizzone; *Flights in the Heavenlies* by Ernest J. Finney; *The New World* by Russell Banks; *Walter Burley in America* (photographs and essay by Mati Maldre; essay, catalog, and selected bibliography by Paul Kruty).

University of Illinois Press distributes its own list as well as books from other university publishers, including Vanderbilt University Press.

Query letters and SASEs should be directed to:

Joan Catapano, Associate Director and Editor in Chief—Women's studies, history, African American studies, film.

Ann Lowry, Journals Manager and Senior Editor—Literature.

Elizabeth G. Delany, Editor—Western Americana, religious studies, archaeology, anthropology.

Judith M. McCulloh, Executive Editor—Music, folklore, pop culture.

Richard J. Martin, Executive Editor—Political science, sociology, law, philosophy, architecture, economics.

Richard L. Wentworth, Editor—American history, black history, communications, sports history, and regional books.

Willis G. Regier, Director and Editor in Chief—Literature, Near Eastern studies, foodways.

UNIVERSITY OF IOWA PRESS

100 Kuhl House, Iowa City, IA 52242-1000
319-335-2000   fax: 319-335-2055
www.uiowa.edu/~uipress

University of Iowa Press (established in 1938) produces a solid list in selected categories that includes scholarly works, general-interest nonfiction, and regional titles in the areas of archaeology, anthropology, and history. The house also produces short stories, literary criticism, and poetry.

Iowa series include American Land and Life, the Iowa Nonfiction Series, and publications from studies in Theatre History and Culture, the annual Iowa Poetry Prize competition.

Iowa nonfiction: *King James and Letters of Homoerotic Desire* by David M. Bergeron; *Of Cabbages and Kings County: Agriculture and the Formation of Modern Brooklyn* by Marc Linder and Lawrence S. Zacharias; *Soldier Boy: The Civil War Letters of Charles O. Musser, 29th Iowa* (edited by Barry Popchock); *Sickness, Recovery, and Death: A History and Forecast of Ill Health* by James C. Riley; *After the West Was Won: Homesteaders and Town-Builders in Western South Dakota* by Paula M. Nelson; *China Dreams: Growing Up in Jewish Tientsin* by Isabelle Maynard (foreword by Albert E. Stone); *Okoboji Wetlands: A Lesson in Natural History* by Michael J. Lannoo; *Fourteen Landing Zones: Approaches to Vietnam War Literature* (edited by Philip K Jason); *Was This Heaven?: A Self-Portrait of Iowa on Early Postcards* by Lyell D. Henry, Jr.; *Beyond Homelessness: Frames of Reference* by Benedict and Jeffrey Giamo.

Iowa fiction and literature: *Shiny Objects* by Dianne Benedict; *Friendly Fire* by Kathryn Chetkovich; *Old Wives' Tales* by Susan M. Dodd; *Toward the End of the Century: Essays into Poetry* by Wayne Dodd; *Igloo Among Palms* by Rod Val Moore; *Traps* by Sondra Spatt Olsen; *The Black Velvet Girl* by C. E. Poverman; *Between the Heartbeats* (poems and prose by nurses; edited by Cortney Davis and Judy Schaefer); *Uncertainty and Plenitude: Five Contemporary Poets* by Peter Stitt.

Literary criticism and the arts are areas in which Iowa has traditionally produced a strong list. Titles here: *Metafiction: A Community of Writers* by Paul Engle and the Iowa Writer's Workshop; *Interpreting the Theatrical Past: Essays in the Historiography of Performance* by Thomas and Bruce A. Postlewait; *Bearing the Bad News: Contemporary American Literature and Culture* by Sanford Pinsker; *Self-Consciousness in African American Literature* by Madelyn Jablon; *Notations of the Wild: Ecology in the Poetry of Wallace Stevens* by Gyorgyi Voros; *Emily Dickinson's Gothic: Goblin with a Gauge* by Daneen Wardrop; *Textual and Theatrical Shakespeare: Questions of Evidence* (edited by Edward Pechter).

Winners of the Iowa Poetry Prize include *Wake* by Bin Ramke; *The Oval Hour* by Kathleen Peirce; *Try* by Cole Swensen.

University of Iowa Press books are distributed by the University of Chicago Distribution Center.

Query letters and SASEs should be directed to:

Holly Carver, Director and Editor

Prasenjit Gupta, Humanities Editor

University of Michigan Press

839 Greene Street, P.O. Box 1104, Ann Arbor, MI 48106-1104
734-764-4388, 734-936-0456
www.press.umich.edu

University of Michigan publishes trade nonfiction and works of scholarly and academic interest. Topic areas and categories include: African-American studies, anthropology, archaeology, Asian studies, classical studies, literary criticism and theory, economics, education, German studies, history, linguistics, law, literary biography, literature, Michigan and the Great Lakes region, music, physical sciences, philosophy and religion, poetry, political science, psychology, sociology, theater and drama, women's studies, disability studies, gay and lesbian studies, health policy and management.

University of Michigan Press (founded in 1930) executes a major program to publish an abundant list of textbooks, monographs, academic literature, and professionally oriented works primarily of scholarly interest. Subject areas here encompass disciplines within the behavioral and biological sciences as well as the humanities. University of Michigan Press publishes in hardcover and paperback editions. Ann Arbor Paperbacks is an imprint geared toward the general trade market.

From the Michigan list: *Tony Kushner in Conversation* (edited by Robert Vorlicky); *Approaching the Millennium: Essays on Angels in America* (edited by Deborah R. Geis and Steven F. Kruger); *Health Benefits at Work: An Economic and Political Analysis of Employment-Based Health Insurance* by Mark V. Pauly; *Purchasing Population Health: Paying for Results* by David A. Kindig; *The Body and Physical Difference: Discourses of Disability in the Humanities* (edited by David Mitchell and Sharon Snyder); *Law and the Postmodern Mind: Essays on Psychoanalysis and Jurisprudence* (edited by David Gray Carlson and Peter Goodrich); *The Cat and the Human Imagination: Feline Images from Beast to Garfield* by Katharine M. Rogers; *John Coltrane: His Life and Music* by Lewis Porter.

University of Michigan Press handles distribution through a worldwide network of independent sales representatives.

Query letters and SASEs should be directed to:

Charles Myers, Acquisitions Editor—Political science, law.

Colin Day, Director—Economics.

Ellen Bauerle, Acquisitions Editor—Classics, archaeology, history.

Ellen McCarthy, Acquisitions Editor

Ingrid Erickson, Assistant Editor, Ann Arbor Paperbacks.

Kelly Sippell, Acquisitions Editor

LeAnn Fields, Executive Editor—Literature, theater, women's studies.

Mary Erwin, Assistant Director—ESL (English as a second language), regional.

Rebecca McDermott, Acquisitions Editor

Susan Whitlock, Acquisitions Editor—Anthropology, series.

UNIVERSITY OF MINNESOTA PRESS

111 Third Avenue South, Suite 290, Minneapolis, MN 55401-2520
612-627-1970
www.upress.umn.edu

The University of Minnesota Press (founded in 1927) is a not-for-profit publisher of academic books for scholars and selected general interest titles. We do not publish original fiction or poetry. Areas of emphasis include American studies, anthropology, art and aesthetics, cultural theory, film and media studies, gay and lesbian studies, geography, literary theory, political and social theory, race and ethnic studies, sociology, and urban studies. The Press also maintains a long-standing commitment to publishing books that focus on Minnesota and the Upper Midwest, including regional nonfiction, history, and natural science.

Recent notable titles: *Postmodern Fables* by Jean-Francois Lyotard; *The Capture of Speech and Other Writings* by Michael de Certeau; *The Forty-Nine Steps* by Roberto Calasso; *Reflecting Narcissus: A Queer Aesthetic* by Steven Bruhm; *The Forgotten Queens of Islam* by Fatima Mernissi; *Shot in America: Television, the State, and the Rise of Chicano Cinema* by Chon A. Noriega; *Space, Site, Intervention: Situating Installation Art* by Erika Suderburg; *Aching for Beauty: Footbinding in China* by Wang Ping; *The Wrong Man: A True Story of Innocence on Death Row* by Michael Mello; *Homeless Mothers: Face to Face with Women and Poverty* by Deborah R. Connolly; *Fighting Words: Black Women and the Search for Justice* by Patricia Hill Collins; *The Karma of Brown Folk* by Vijay Prashad; *Race and the Hood: Conflict and Violence Among Urban Youth* by Howard Pinderhughes; *New York, Chicago, Los Angeles; America's Global Cities* by Janet L. Abu-Lughod; *Lost Minnesota: Stories of Vanished Places* by Jack El-Hai; *Northland Wildflowers: The Comprehensive Guide to the Minnesota Region* by John B. Moyle and Evelyn W, Moyle; *Stadium Games: 50 Years of Big League Greed and Bush League Boondoggles* by Jay Weiner.

University of Minnesota Press order fulfillment by the Chicago Distribution Center and in the U.K. and Europe through Plymbridge Distributors, Ltd.

Jennifer Moore, Acquisitions Editor—Anthropology, art and aesthetics, film and media studies, Native American studies.

Richard Morrison, Acquisitions Editor—American studies, cultural theory, gay and lesbian studies, humanities.

Carrie Mullen, Executive Editor—Geography, political and social theory, race and ethnic studies, sociology, urban studies.

Todd Orjala, Acquisitions Editor—Regional studies.

U

UNIVERSITY OF MISSOURI PRESS

2910 LeMone Boulevard, Columbia, MO 65201
573-882-7641   fax: 573-884-4498
www.system.missouri.edu/press

University of Missouri Press accents scholarly books, general-interest trade titles, fiction, and regional works. Specific areas within the UMP publishing range include African-American studies, cultural studies, folklore, gender studies, intellectual history, journalism, and photography. University of Missouri Press (founded in 1958) publishes in hardback and trade paper editions.

Highlights of the Missouri line: *The Collected Works of Langston Hughes* (edited by Arnold Rampersand and others); *Gettysburg to Vicksburg: The Five Original Civil War Battlefield Parks* by A. J. Meek and Herman Hataway; *In the Philippines and Okinawa: A Memoir, 1945–1948* by William S. Triplet (edited by Robert H. Ferrell); *Primo Levi and the Politics of Survival* by Frederic D. Homer; *An Airman's Odyssey: Walt Braznell and the Pilots He Led into the Jet Age* by William Braznell; *Clio's Favorites: Leading Historians of the United States, 1945–2000* by Robert Allen Rutland; *The Voice of America and the Domestic Propaganda Battles, 1945–1953* by David F. Krugler; *Reflections on a Disruptive Decade: Essays from the Sixties* by Eugene Davidson; *A Youth in the Meuse-Argonne: A Memoir, 1917–1918* by William S. Triplet (edited by Robert H. Ferrell); *Missouri's Confederate: Claiborne Fox Jackson and the Creation of Southern Identity in the Border West* by Christopher Phillips; *Can We Wear Our Pearls and Still Be Feminists? Memoirs of a Campus Struggle* by Joan D. Mandle; *The Reagan Reversal: Foreign Policy and the End of the Cold War* by Beth A. Fischer; *Boxing the Kangaroo: A Reporter's Memoir* by Robert J. Donovan.

In the UMP literary arena: *The Masks of Mary Renault: A Literary Biography* by Caroline Zilboorg; *No Visible Means of Support: Stories* by Dabney Stuart; *Transfiguring America: Myth, Ideology, and Mourning in Margaret Fuller's Writing* by Jeffrey Steele; *Rereading Conrad* by Daniel R. Schwarz; *John Updike and the Cold War: Drawing the Iron Curtain* by D. Quentin Miller; *We Who Live Apart: Stories* by Joan Connor; *Long Odds* by Gordon Weaver.

From the Give 'em Hell Harry series: *Harry S. Truman and the News Media: Contentious Relations, Belated Respect* by Franklin D. Mitchell; *Off the Record: The Private Papers of Harry S. Truman* (edited by Robert H. Ferrell); *The Truman Scandals and the Politics of Morality* by Andrew J. Dunar.

Titles in the Missouri Heritage Readers series: *The Trail of Tears Across Missouri* by Joan Gilbert; *The Osage in Missouri* by Kristie C. Wolferman; *Orphan Trails to Missouri* by Michael D. Patrick and Evelyn Goodrich Trickel.

University of Missouri Press handles its own distributional services.

Query letters and SASEs should be directed to:

Beverly Jarrett, Director and Editor in Chief

Clair Willcox, Acquisitions Editor

UNIVERSITY OF NEBRASKA PRESS

233 North 8th Street, Lincoln, NE 68588- 0255
402-472-3581   fax: 402-472-6214
http://nebraskapress.unl.edu   e-mail: pressmail@unl.edu

The program at University of Nebraska Press encompasses anthropology, environmental studies, history, literature and criticism, Native American studies, philosophy, wildlife and environment, and general reference works. The house further accents the literature and history of the Trans-Missouri West, the American Indian, contemporary and modern literary trends, sports, and the environment (especially emphasizing Western United States and American Indian tie-in topics).

University of Nebraska Press (founded in 1941) publishes general trade titles in hardcover and paperback, as well as selected scholarly nonfiction. Many UNP titles and subject areas overlap categories and thus are provided wider marketing exposure. University of Nebraska Press has successfully established niches in each of its targeted market sectors; a solid showcase of Nebraska titles has garnered book-club sales in both mainstream and specialty venues.

The University of Nebraska literary horizon features leading-edge criticism and theory, works keyed to the American West and the American Indian, and historical as well as current writers worldwide, including European women and French literature in translation; the house offers a strong selection of scholarly writings on the life and works of Willa Cather.

University of Nebraska Press produces: the Women in the West series; Western history and literature; American Indian topics; and the great outdoors. Bison Books is Nebraska's imprint for popularly oriented trade titles.

Nebraska's American Indian studies include biography and memoirs, literature and legend, society and culture, and history, as well as a line of titles for young readers. Series listed in this area are American Indian Lives, Sources of American Indian Oral Literature, Studies in the Anthropology of North American Indians, Indians of the Southeast, and The Iroquoians and Their World. The press offers the North American Indian Prose Award in conjunction with the Native American Studies Program at the University of California, Berkeley. (Detailed information is available from the publisher upon request.) A recent winner of this award is *Boarding School Seasons* by Brenda Child.

Representative of the Nebraska publishing program: *Lee the Soldier* (edited by Gary W. Gallagher); *Emily: The Diary of a Hard-Worked Woman* by Emily French (edited by Janet Lecompte); *Dust Bowl Descent* by Bill Ganzel; *Custer's Last Campaign: Mitch Boyer and the Little Bighorn Reconstructed* by John S. Gray, foreword by Robert M. Utley; *Stravinsky Retrospectives* by Ethan Haimo and Paul Johnson; *Blue Jacket: Warrior of the Shawnees* by John Sugden; *Cold Shapas Yearning* by Robert Vivian; *Voices of Wounded Knee* by William Coleman; *Grandmother's Grandchild: My Crow Indian Life* by Alma Snell; *Team Spirits: The Native American Mascots Controversy* (edited by Richard King and Charles Splingwood).

The Bison Frontiers of Imagination Series features reprints of classic speculative fiction, ranging from Edgar Rice Burroughs's *Land That Time Forgot,* to Wylie and Balmer's *When Worlds Collide*.

Query letters and SASEs should be directed to:

Dan Ross, Director

Gary Dunham, Editor in Chief

U

University of New Mexico Press

1720 Lomas Boulevard, NE, Albuquerque, NM 87131-1591
505-277-2346   fax: 505-277-9270
e-mail: unmpress@unm.edu

University of New Mexico Press (begun in 1929) is a publisher of general, scholarly, and regional trade books in hardcover and paperback editions. Among areas of strong New Mexico interest are archaeology, folkways, literature, art and architecture, photography, crafts, biography, women's studies, travel, and the outdoors. New Mexico offers a robust list of books in subject areas pertinent to the American Southwest, including native Anasazi, Navajo, Hopi, Zuni, and Apache cultures; Nuevomexicano (New Mexican) culture; the pre-Columbian Americas; and Latin American affairs. UNP also publishes works of regional fiction and belles lettres, both contemporary and classical. The press commands a staunch backlist.

Representative of the University of New Mexico Press list: *The Royal Road: El Camino Real from Mexico City to Santa Fe* by Christine Preston, Douglas Preston, and Jose Antonio Esquibel; *Howl: The Artwork of Luis Jimenez* by Camille Flores-Turney; *The Taos Society of Artists* (edited and annotated by Robert R. White); *O Brave New People: The European Invention of the American Indian* by John F. Moffitt and Santiago Sebastian; *The Iguana Killer: Twelve Stories of the Heart* by Alberto Alvaro Rios; *The Book of Memories* by Ana Maria Shua (translated by Dick Gerdes); *The Jewish Gauchos of the Pampas* by Alberto Gerchunoff (translated by Prudencio de Pereda); *A Garlic Testament: Seasons on a Small New Mexico Farm* by Stanley Crawford; *The Cold War American West* (edited by Kevin Fernlund); *Fly-Fishing in Southern New Mexico* by Rex Johnson, Jr., and Ronald Smorynki; *Houses in Time: A Tour Through New Mexico History* by Linda G. Harris (photographed by Pamela Porter); *Bone Voyage: A Journey in Forensic Anthropology* by Stanley Rhine; *Scattered Round Stones: A Mayo Village in Sonora* by David Yetman; *Reed Rubber, Bleeding Trees: Violence, Slavery, and Empire in the Upper Amazon, 1859–1933* by Michael Edward Stanfield; *The Sowing and the Dawning: Termination, Dedication, and Transformation in the Archaeological and Ethnographic Record of Mesoamerica* (edited by Shirley Boteler Mock); *Mountains of the Great Blue Dream* by Robert Leonard Reid.

New Mexico fiction/poetry titles: *How Rain Records Its Alphabet,* poems by John Tritica; *Sofia* by Joan Logghe; *No Parole Today* by Laura Tohe; *Destruction Bay* by Lisa Chavez; *Sojourner, So to Speak* (poems) by Joseph Somoza; *Crazy Woman* by Kat Horsley; *Six Directions: Haiku and Field Notes* (poems) by Jim Kacian; *The Flesh Envelope* (poems) by Susan Luzzaro; *Murder in the New Age* (mystery) by D. J. H. Jones; *Show and Tell: Identity as Performance in U.S. Latina/o Fiction* by Karen Christian; *Two Lives for Oñate* by Miguel Encinias.

University of New Mexico Press is home to the literary journal *Blue Mesa Review.* The Pasó por Aquí series makes available texts from the Nuevomexicano literary heritage (many editions in bilingual format). Diálogos is a series in Latin American studies, specializing in books with crossover potential in both academic and general markets.

U

University of New Mexico Press handles distribution for its own list and also works through regional sales representatives.

Query letters and SASEs should be directed to:

Dana Asbury, Editor—Art and photography.

David V. Holtby, Associate Director and Editor—Latin American studies.

Dianne Edwards, Assistant to the Director—Rights and permissions.

Elizabeth Hadas, Director

Larry Durwood Ball, Editor—History and anthropology.

UNIVERSITY OF NORTH CAROLINA PRESS

P.O. Box 2288, Chapel Hill, NC 27515-2288
919-966-3561   fax: 919-966-3829
http://uncpress.unc.edu   e-mail: uncpress@unc.edu

University of North Carolina Press (founded in 1922) publishes works of general nonfiction, scholarly titles, and regional books, as well as a selection of general-interest trade titles. The house has a broad array of books on a firm backlist.

University of North Carolina Press publishing interest encompasses African-American studies, American studies, British history, business history, Civil War, folklore, Latin American studies, literary studies, anthropology, nature, political science, social issues, legal history, sports and sports history, and gender studies.

North Carolina nonfiction: *North Carolina Women: Making History* by Margaret Supplee Smith and Emily Herring Wilson, foreword by Doris Betts; *Broadcasting Freedom: Radio, War, and the Politics of Race, 1938–1948* by Barbara Dianne Savage; *The Outer Banks* by Anthony Bailey; *The Mystery of Samba: Popular Music & National Identity in Brazil* by Hermano Vianna (edited and translated by John Charles Chasteen); *Henry Steele Commager: Midcentury Liberalism & the History of the Present* by Neil Jumonville; *Catesby's Birds of Colonial America* (edited by Alan Feduccia); *Rank Ladies: Gender and Cultural Hierarchy in American Vaudeville* by M. Alison Kibler; *Working with Class: Social Workers and the Politics of Middle-Class Identity* by Daniel J. Walkowitz; *Beyond Regulations: Ethics in Human Subjects Research* (edited by Nancy M. P. King, Gail E. Henderson, and Jane Stein); *Iron Confederacies: Southern Railways, Klan Violence, and Reconstruction* by Scott Reynolds Nelson; *Ancient Greek Alive* by Paula Saffire and Catherine Freis.

North Carolina highlights for 2000 include: *Coastal Plants from Cape Cod to Cape Canaveral* by Irene H. Stuckey and Lisa Lofland Gould; *Gettysburg—The First Day* by Harry W. Pfanz; *Highland Heritage: Scottish Americans in the American South* by Celeste Ray.

University of North Carolina Press handles its own distribution with the assistance of regional sales representatives.

Query letters and SASEs should be directed to:

U

David Perry, Editor in Chief—Southern regional studies, several interest books.

Elaine Maisner, Religion, Latin American studies.

Kate Torrey, Director—gender studies.

Ms. Sian Hunter, Editor—American studies, literature.

Vicky Wells, Rights and permissions.

UNIVERSITY OF OKLAHOMA PRESS
1005 Asp Avenue, Norman, OK 73019-6051
405-325-5111

University of Oklahoma Press highlights the fields of Americana, regional topics (especially the American West), anthropology, archaeology, history, military history, political science, literature, classical studies, and women's studies. University of Oklahoma Press series include the Western Frontier Library, the American Indian Literature and Critical Studies series, and the Bruce Alonzo Goff Series in Architecture.

University of Oklahoma Press (founded in 1928) publishes a wide range of scholarly nonfiction, with crossover trade titles primarily in popular history and the arts; the house's prowess is particularly renowned in the arena of the native cultures of North, Central, and South America—the extensive backlist as well as new and current offerings in these fields embrace a wellspring of over 250 titles.

On Oklahoma's nonfiction list: *The Soul of a Small Texas Town: Photographs, Memories, and History from McDade* by David Wharton; *Literature and the Visual Arts in Ancient Greece and Rome* by D. Thomas Benediktson; *Documents of American Indian Diplomacy* by Vine Deloria, Jr., and Raymond J. DeMallie; *The United States Infantry: An Illustrated History, 1775–1918* by Gregory J. W. Urwin; *Will Rogers: A Biography* by Ben Yagoda; *Frontier Children* by Linda Peavy and Ursula Smith; *The West of Billy the Kid* by Frederick Nolan; *America's National Historic Trails* by Kathleen Cordes; *Yellowstone and the Biology of Time* by Mary Meagher and Douglas B. Houston.

Works of special cultural note: *American Indians and World War II: Toward a New Era in Indian Affairs* by Alison R. Bernstein; *Voices from Exile: Violence and Survival in Modern Maya History* by Victor Montejo; *Regeneration Through Violence: The Mythology of the American Frontier, 1600–1860* by Richard Slotkin; *Let Me Be Free: The Nez Perce Tragedy* by David Lavender; *Women and Monarchy in Macedonia* by Elizabeth Carney; *The Angry Genie: One Man's Walk Through the Nuclear Age* by Karl Z. Morgan and Ken M. Peterson.

Fiction and literary titles: *Dark River: A Novel* by Louis Owens; *Survivor's Medicine: Short Stories* by Donald E. Two-Rivers; *Reading Virgil's Aeneid: An Interpretive Guide* (edited by Christing Perkell); *Cartographies of Desire: Captivity and Race in the Shaping of an American Nation* by Rebecca Blevins Faery; *Kiss of the Fur Queen: A Novel* by Tomson Highway; *The Sons of the Wind: The Sacred Stories of the Lakota* (edited by D. M. Dooling).

The University of Oklahoma Press distributes its own books and those of the University Press of Colorado, Vanderbilt University Press, and Geoscience Press with the assistance of regional sales representatives.

Query letters with SASEs should be directed to:

Jean Hurtado, Acquisitions Editor—Western history, political science.

Jeff Burnham, Acquisitions Editor—Native American studies, Latin America.

John N. Drayton, Director—Literature and literary studies, natural history.

Ron Chrisman, Acquisitions Editor—Paperbacks.

UNIVERSITY OF SOUTH CAROLINA PRESS

937 Assembly Street, Eighth Floor, Carolina Plaza, Columbia, SC 29208
803-777-5243   fax: 800-868-0740

University of South Carolina Press covers Southern studies, military history, contemporary and modern American literature, maritime history, religious studies and speech and communication, University of South Carolina Press (founded in 1944) publishes a strong academic and scholarly list, with some crossover general trade titles. The press publishes in hardcover, as well as trade paperback, and maintains an extensive backlist.

Indicative of the South Carolina program: *Heaven Is a Beautiful Place: A Memoir of the South Carolina Coast* by Genevieve C. Peterkin in conversation with William P. Baldwin; *On Literary Biography* by John Updike; *Who Is Jesus?: History in Perfect Tense* by Leander E. Keck; *The Jewish Confederates* by Robert N. Rosen*; To Loot My Life Clean: The Thomas Wolfe–Maxwell Perkins Correspondence* (edited by Matthew J. Bruccoli and Park Bucker); *O Lost: A Story of the Buried Life* by Thomas Wolfe (text established by Arlyn and Matthew J. Bruccoli); *A Memory of Trains: The Boll Weevil and Others,* text and photographs by Louis D. Rubin, Jr.; *Where the Tigers Were: Travels Through Literary Landscapes* by Don Meredith; *Crossing the Color Line: Readings in Black and White* (edited by Suzanne W. Jones); *A Naturalist's Guide to the Southern Blue Ridge Front* by L. L. Gaddy; *Before Gatsby: The First Twenty-Six Stories* by F. Scott Fitzgerald (edited by Matthew J. Bruccoli); *From the Pen of a She-Rebel: The Civil War Diary of Emilie Riley McKinley* (edited by Gordon A. Cotton).

University of South Carolina Press oversees its own distribution.

Query letters and SASEs should be directed to:

Linda Fogle, Assistant Director—Trade titles.

Barry Blose, Acquisitions Editor—Literary studies, rhetoric, religious studies, studies in social work.

Alex Moore, Acquisitions Editor—Southern history, regional studies, Civil War studies, maritime history.

UNIVERSITY OF TENNESSEE PRESS

110 Conference Center Building, Knoxville, TN 37996-4108
865-974-3321   fax: 865-974-3724

The University of Tennessee Press publishes scholarly and general interest books in American studies, in the following subdisciplines: African-American studies, Appalachian studies, literature, religion (history, sociology, anthropology, biography), folklore, history, architecture, material culture, and historical archaeology. Submissions in other fields, and submissions of poetry, textbooks, and translations, are not invited.

The University of Tennessee Press (founded in 1940) has earned a national reputation for excellence, with titles representing both traditional and cutting-edge scholarship. The press's editorial point of view reflects an awareness of social and quality-of-life issues and results in books that inform thought and policy, as well as contribute to scholarship.

Tennessee titles published in 2000 include: *The Scopes Trial: A Photographic History* by Edward Caudill, Edward J. Larson, and Jesse Fox Mayshark*; The Great Smokies: From Natural Habitat to National Park* by Daniel S. Pierce; *Ninety-Eight Days; A Geographer's View of the Vicksburg Campaign* by Warren E. Grabau; *Confederate Engineer: Training and Campaigning with John Morris Wampler* by George G. Kundahl; *After the Backcountry: Rural Life in the Great Valley of Virginia, 1800–1900* (edited by Kenneth E. Koons and Warren R. Hofstra); *Mountain Hands: A Portrait of Southern Appalachia* by Sam Venable; *Tennessee Political Humor* by Roy Herron and L. H. "Cotton" Ivy; *Cuban-Jewish Journeys* by Caroline Bettinger-Lopez; and *Partisan Linkages in Southern Politics* (edited by Michael A. Maggiotto and Gary D. Wekkin).

Books from the University of Tennessee Press are distributed by the Chicago Distribution Center.

Query letters and SASEs should be directed to:

Joyce Harrison, Acquisitions Editor

UNIVERSITY OF TEXAS PRESS

P.O. Box 7819, Austin, TX 78713-7819
512-471-7233   fax: 512-320-0668
www.utexas.edu/utpress

Areas of University of Texas Press publishing scope include international and regional studies, gender studies, Latin America, American Southwest, Native America, Texana, Mesoamerica, applied language and Latino literature (including Latin American and Middle Eastern works in translation), the environment and nature, art and architecture, classic, film studies, social sciences, and humanities.

University of Texas Press (founded in 1950) is among the largest American University presses. UTP publishes in a wide range of general nonfiction fields, offering titles of popular interest and for scholarly and academic readers produced in hardcover and trade paperback.

On the UTP nonfiction list: *Twentieth-Century Art of Latin America* by Jacqueline Barnitz; *Mexican Suite: A History of Photography in Mexico* by Olivier Debroise, translated by Stella de Sa Rego; *Galveston and the 1900 Storm* by Patricia Bellis Bixel and Elizabeth Hays Turner; *Gender and Power in Prehispanic Mesoamerica* by Rosemary Joyce; *The Lieutenant Nun: Transgenderism, Lesbian Desire, and Catalina de Erauso* by Sherry

Velasco*; Inanna, Lady of Largest Heart: Poems of the Sumerian High Priestess Enhedu-anna* by Betty DeShong Meador; *Remembering Cuba: Legacy of a Diaspora* (edited by Andrea O'Reilly Herrera); *Bulbs for Warm Climates* by Thad M. Howard; *Greek and Roman Comedy: Translations and Interpretations of Four Representative Plays* (edited by Shawn O'Bryhim); *Looking for Carrasciolendas: From a Child's World to Award Winning Television* by Aida Barrera; *Lourdes Portillo: The Devil Never Sleeps and Other Films* (edited by Rosa Linda Fregoso).

University of Texas Press handles its own distribution.

Query letters and SASEs should be directed to:

Jim Burr, Sponsoring Editor—Humanities and classics.

Bill Bishel, Sponsoring Editor—Sciences.

Theresa May, Assistant Director and Editor in Chief—Social sciences, Latin American studies.

UNIVERSITY OF WASHINGTON PRESS

P.O. Box 50096, Seattle, WA 98145-5096
206-543-4050   fax: 206-543-3932
www.washington.edu/uwpress/   e-mail: uwpord@u.washington.edu

The program at University of Washington Press is particularly strong in some of the fields of the publisher's major academic concentrations, which encompass fine arts (including a special interest in the arts of Asia), regional America (with an emphasis on Seattle and the Pacific Northwest), and Native American studies. University of Washington Press maintains a solid backlist.

University of Washington Press (established in 1920) is a midsize house with a primarily scholarly list that features select titles geared toward the general-interest trade market. The house produces books in hardcover and paperback (including reprint editions), and distributes adjunct visual resources (including videotapes, films, and filmstrips). University of Washington also handles a line of scholarly imports (primarily fine arts titles). UWP enters into joint-publication projects with a variety of museums and cultural foundations and produces a large number of fine arts books and exhibition catalogues.

On the Washington list: *Adios to Tears: The Memoirs of a Japanese Peruvian Internee in U.S. Concentration Camps* by Seiichi Higashide; *Art and Intimacy: How the Arts Began* by Ellen Dissanyake; *At the Forest's Edge: Memoir of a Physician Naturalist* by David Tirrell Hellyer; *Captured in the Middle: Tradition and Experience in Contemporary Native American Writing* by Sinder Larson; *The Eight Lively Arts: Conversations with Painters, Poets, Musicians, and the Wicked Witch of the West* by Wesley Wehr; *Glacier Ice* by Austin Post and Edward LaChapelle; *Henry M. Jackson: A Life in Politics* by Robert G. Kaufman; *Land America Leaves Wild* by Diana Wege; *Mountain Patterns: The Survival of Nuosu Culture in China* by Steven Harrel, Barno Qubumo, and Ma Erzi; *Reconciliation Road: A Family Odyssey* by John Douglas Marshall; *Sun Dogs and Eagle Down: The Indian Paintings of Bill Holm* by Steven C. Brown and Lloyd J. Avernill; and *To Fish in Common: The Ethnohistory of Lummi Indian Salmon Fishing.*

U

Weyerhaeuser Environmental Books series (under the general editorship of William Cronon) titles: *Landscapes of Promise: The Oregon Story, 1800–1940* by William Robbins; *World Fire: The Culture of Fire on Earth* and *Fire in America: A Cultural History of Wildland and Rural Fire,* both by Stephen J. Pyne.

University of Washington Press handles its own distribution via its home office and a number of regional sales representatives, as well as distributes for a number of other specialist publishers and arts institutions, including the Tate Gallery, Asian Art Museum of San Francisco, Reaktion Books, the Columbus Museum of Art, National Portrait Gallery of the Smithsonian Institution, Exhibitions International, and the Idaho State Historical Society.

Query letters and SASEs should be directed to:

Michael Duckworth, Acquisitions Editor—Asian studies, Middle East studies, Russian and East European studies.

Naomi Pascal, Associate Director and Editor in Chief—Western studies, Asian American studies, Western history, regional history.

UNIVERSITY OF WISCONSIN PRESS

2537 Daniels Street, Madison, WI 53718-6772
608-224-3890

University of Wisconsin Press catalogues such fields as African studies, autobiography, art, American studies, anthropology and folklore, biography, contemporary issues, classical studies, environmental studies, European studies, gay studies, geography, history, criminology, Latin American studies, law, literature and criticism, medicine, music, poetry, sociology, Wisconsin regional studies, and women's studies. The press hosts a steadfast backlist.

University of Wisconsin Press (founded in 1937) is a midsize house that specializes in nonfiction and scholarly books and journals, with a growing and vigorous list of crossover titles geared to mainstream trade interest.

Distribution for University of Wisconsin Press publications is through the Chicago Distribution Center; trade sales are garnered nationwide by the press's formidable lineup of regional field representatives. Query letters and SASEs should be directed to:

Raphael Kadushin, Acquisitions Editor—Gay and lesbian studies, autobiography, film studies, classics, environmental studies, history, Holocaust studies, dance and performance art.

VANDERBILT UNIVERSITY PRESS

Box 1813, Station B, Nashville, TN 37235-0001
615-322-3585   fax: 615-343-8823
www.vanderbilt.edu/vupress   e-mail: vupress@vanderbilt.edu

Y

Founded in 1940, Vanderbilt University Press is the publishing arm of one of the nation's leading research universities. The Press's primary mission is to select, produce, market, and disseminate scholarly publications of outstanding quality and originality. Vanderbilt has published titles in the humanities, social sciences, education, and regional studies for both academic and general audiences.

Notable titles include: *A Good-Natured Riot: The Birth of the Grand Ole Opry* by Charles K. Wolfe; *Emphatics* by Paul Weiss; and *Enter Rabelais, Laughing* by Barbara C. Bowen. Although its main emphasis falls in the area of scholarly publishing, Vanderbilt Press also publishes works that are of interest to the general public, including works that focus on Tennessee and the South, as well as on country music.

Query letters and SASEs should be directed to:

Michael Ames, Director

YALE UNIVERSITY PRESS

302 Temple Street, P.O. Box 209040, New Haven, CT 06520-9040
203-432-0960   fax: 203-432-0948
www.yale.edu/yup/   e-mail: yupmkt@yalevm.cis.yale.edu

The Yale publishing program offers both trade and academically oriented titles in the fields of the arts, the humanities, and the social sciences. Particular general-interest areas include contemporary issues, culture, and events; architecture, art criticism, and art history; history of America (with additional focus on the American West); literature and literary criticism; and political science, economics, and military studies. Yale produces hardcover and trade paper editions.

Yale University Press sponsors the annual Yale Younger Poets Competition and publishes the winning manuscript. Yale series include Composers of the Twentieth Century and Early Chinese Civilization.

Yale University Press (established in 1908) is at the forefront of university publishing. The house is one of the major academic houses, and Yale's commercial presence is evident in the catalogs of book clubs, as well as on national, regional, and specialty bestseller lists.

On the nonfiction list at Yale: *Secrecy: The American Experience* by Daniel Patrick Moynihan; *The New Encyclopedia of the American West* (edited by Howard R. Lamar); *Bill Evans: How My Heart Sings* by Peter Pettinger; *Sir Francis Drake: The Queen's Pirate* by Harry Kelsey; *Preempting the Holocaust* by Lawrence L. Langer; *My German Question: Growing Up in Nazi Berlin* by Peter Gay; *The Practice of Reading* by Denis Donoghue; *The Great Experiment: George Washington and the American Republic* by John Rhodehamel; *Medicine's 10 Great Discoveries* by Meyer Friedman, M.D., and Gerald W. Friedland, M.D.; *The Neighborhoods of Brooklyn,* introduction by Kenneth T. Jackson; *The Collapse of the Soviet Military* by William E. Odom; *Nietzsche and Wagner: A Lesson in Subjugation* by Joachim Kohler; *Jack Yeats* by Bruce Arnold.

Cultural criticism, literary works, and the arts: *Visionary Fictions: Apocalyptic Writings from Blake to the Modern Age* by Edward J. Ahearn; *Rethinking the Rhetorical Tradition:*

From Plato to Postmodernism by James L. Kastely; *Dryden and the Problem of Freedom: The Republican Aftermath, 1649–1680* by David B. Haley; *The Sound of Virtue: Philip Sidney's Arcadia and Elizabethan Politics* by Blair Worden; *The Letters of Gertrude Stein and Thornton Wilder* (edited by Edward M. Burns and Ulla E. Dydo with William Rice); *The Emergence of the Modern American Theater, 1914–1929* by Ronald H. Wainscott; *Utamakura, Allusion, and Intertextuality in Traditional Japanese Poetry* by Edward Kamens; *English Poems, Life of Pico, the Last Things: The Yale Edition of the Complete Works of St. Thomas More* (volume 1) (edited by Anthony S. G. Edwards, Katherine Gardiner Rodgers, and Clarence H. Miller); *Noah's Flood: The Genesis Story in Western Thought* by Norman Cohn.

Yale University Press handles its own distribution.

Query letters and SASEs should be directed to:

Charles Grench, Acquisitions Editor—Anthropology, history, Judaic studies, religion, women's issues.

Jean E. Thomson Black, Acquisitions Editor—Science and medicine.

John S. Covell, Acquisitions Editor—Economics, law, political science.

Jonathan Brent, Acquisitions Editor—Literature, philosophy, poetry, annals of Communism, Cold War studies.

Otto Bohlmann, Acquisitions Editor—Scholarly editions.

Robert T. Flynn, Acquisitions Editor—Reference books.

Susan C. Arellano, Acquisitions Editor—Behavioral and social sciences, education.

Religious, Spiritual, and Inspirational Publishers

The Writer's Journey
Themes of the Spirit and Inspiration

DEBORAH LEVINE HERMAN

If you have decided to pursue writing as a career instead of as a longing or a dream, you might find yourself falling into a pattern of focusing on the goal instead of the process. When you have a great book idea, you may envision yourself on a book-signing tour or as a guest on *Oprah* before you've written a single word.

It's human nature to look into your own future, but too much projection can get in the way of what the writing experience is all about. The process of writing is like a wondrous journey that can help you cross a bridge to the treasures hidden within your own subconscious. Some people believe that it's a way for you to link with the collective or universal consciousness, the storehouse of all wisdom and truth, as it has existed since the beginning of time.

There are many methods of writing that bring their own rewards. Some people can produce exceptional prose by using their intellect and their mastery of the writing craft. They use research and analytical skills to help them produce works of great importance and merit.

Then there are those who have learned to tap into the wellspring from which all genius flows. They are the inspired ones who write with the intensity of an impassioned lover. They are the spiritual writers who write because they have to. They may not want to, they may not know how to, but something inside them is begging to be let out. It gnaws away at them until they find a way to set it free.

Although they may not realize it, spiritual writers are engaged in a larger spiritual journey toward ultimate self-mastery and unification with God.

Spiritual writers often feel as if they're taking dictation. It is as though their thoughts have a life of their own and the mind is merely a receiver. Some people refer to this as "channeling" and believe disembodied spirits take over and write through them. Although I sincerely doubt that Gandhi or other notables have authored as many channeled books as people have been claiming, truly spiritual writing does have an other worldly feeling and can often teach the writer things he or she would otherwise not have known.

Writing opens you up to new perspectives, much like self-induced psychotherapy. Although journals are the most direct route for self-evaluation, fiction and nonfiction also serve as vehicles for a writer's growth. Writing helps the mind expand to the limits of the imagination.

Anyone can become a spiritual writer. There are many benefits from doing so, not the least of which is the development of your soul. On a more practical level, it is much less difficult to write with flow and fervor than it is to be bound by the limitations of logic and analysis. If you tap into the universal source, there is no end to your potential creativity.

The greatest barrier to becoming a spiritual writer is the human ego. We treat our words as if they were our children—only we tend to be neurotic parents. A child is not owned by a parent, but rather must be loved, guided, and nurtured until he or she can carry on, on his or her own.

The same is true for our words. If we try to own and control them like property, they will be limited by our vision for them. We will overprotect them and will not be able to see when we may be taking them in the wrong direction for their ultimate well-being.

Another ego problem that creates a barrier to creativity is our need for constant approval and our tendency toward perfectionism. We may feel the tug toward free expression, but will erect blockades to ensure appropriate style and structure. We write with a "schoolmarm" hanging over our shoulders waiting to tell us what we are doing wrong.

Style and structure are important to ultimate presentation, but that is what editing is for. Ideas and concepts need to flow like water through a running stream.

The best way to become a spiritual writer is to relax and have fun. If you are relaxed and are in a basically good mood, you'll be open to intuition. Writers tend to take themselves too seriously, which causes anxiety, which exacerbates fear, which causes insecurity, which diminishes our self-confidence and leads ultimately to mounds of crumpled papers and lost inspiration.

If you have faith in a Supreme Being, the best way to begin a spiritual writing session is with the following writer's prayer:

> Almighty God (Jesus, Allah, Great Spirit, etc.), Creator of the Universe, help me to become a vehicle for your wisdom so that what I write is of the highest purpose and will serve the greatest good. I humbly place my (pen/keyboard/Dictaphone) in your hands so that you may guide me.

Prayer helps to connect you to the universal source. It empties the mind of trash, noise, and potential writer's blocks. If you are not comfortable with formal prayer, a few minutes of meditation will serve the same purpose.

Spiritual writing as a process does not necessarily lead to a sale. The fact is that some people have more commercial potential than others, no matter how seemingly unimportant their message might be. Knowledge of the business of writing will help you make a career of it. If you combine this with the spiritual process, it can also bring you gratification and inner peace.

If you trust the process of writing and allow the journey to take you where it will, it may bring you benefits far beyond your expectations.

ABINGDON PRESS

Dimensions for Living

201 Eighth Avenue South, P.O. Box 801, Nashville, TN 37202-0801
615-749-6290

Abingdon Press is the book-publishing division of the United Methodist Publishing House (founded in 1789). Abingdon produces hardcover, trade paperback, and mass-market paperback editions, covering a wide range of religious specialty, religious trade, and popular markets. Areas of concentration include professional reference and resources for the clergy; academic and scholarly works in the fields of religious and biblical history and theory; inspirational and devotional books; and titles with contemporary spiritual and ethical themes intended for a wider readership. Abingdon's publishing presence includes software and works on CD-ROM.

Abingdon also issues several series of books for children, in addition to resources for Sunday school and general Christian education, as well as church supplies (posters, calendars, certificates, maps, buttons, music, and dramatic scripts). Dimensions for Living is an Abingdon imprint dedicated to titles with a popular orientation (see separate subentry further on). Abingdon reprints a number of its bestselling titles in mass-market paperback editions and tends a formidable backlist.

On the Abingdon list: *Best Regards: Recovering the Art of Soulful Letter Writing* (compiled by Ben Alex); *Liters & Other Born-Again Christians: Commentaries on Bleeding Hearts and Warmed Hearts Coming Together* by Sally B. Geis; *32 Ways to Be a Great Sunday School Teacher* by Delia Halverson; *Forty Days with the Messiah: Day-by-Day Reflections on the Words of Handel's Oratorio* by David Winter; *Sharing My Faith with My Friends: Youth Reaching Youth* by Duane Kemerley; *Caretakers of Our Common House: Women's Development in Communities of Faith* by Carol Lakey Hess; *Somebody's Got My Rose: A Lighthearted Look at Choir Directing* by John Yarrington.

The Grand Sweep series by J. Ellsworth Kalas is a Bible-study program that moves in canonical sequence based on Ellsworth Kalas's book *365 Days from Genesis Through Revelation*. Titles: *The Grand Sweep: Bible Study for Individuals and Groups; The Grand Sweep: Daily Response Book; The Grand Sweep: Sermon Ideas for 52 Weeks.*

Body & Soul: A Disciplined Approach to a Healthy Lifestyle is a series of programs for Christians seeking a healthful lifestyle. Body & Soul focuses on the spiritual, physical, mental, emotional, and social aspects of persons for a powerful approach to behavior change. Titles: *Health Yourself; Second Helpings; Wonderfully Healthy; Caring & Sharing; Stepping Forward.*

Serious trade books, scholarly reference, and academic and professional how-to books (as stand-alones or in sets) have long been mainstays of the Abingdon program. Academic and scholarly titles—some with crossover religious trade appeal—are represented by: *Faithful Change: The Personal and Public Challenges of Postmodern Life* by James W. Fowler; *Jews & Christians in Pursuit of Social Justice* by Randall M. Falk and Walter J. Harrelson; *Stewards of Life: Bioethics and Pastoral Care* by Sondra Ely Wheeler; *The Business Corporation & Productive Justice* by David A. Krueger with Donald W. Shriver,

A

Jr., and Laura Nash; *Environmental Ethics and Christian Humanism* by Thomas S. Derr, with James A. Nash and Richard John Neuhaus; *Listening in: A Multicultural Reading of the Psalms* by Stephen Breck Reid.

In addition to distributing its own books, Abingdon Press handles the lists of several other smaller religious publishers.

Query letters and SASEs should be directed to:

Dr. Rex D. Matthews, Editor, Academic Books—Books for Sunday and parochial schools and seminaries.

Jack Keller, Editor, Professional Books and Reference Books—Methodist doctrine and church practices for clergy and laity. Dictionaries and general reference guides relevant to Methodist history and policy.

Mary Catherine Dean, Editor, Trade Books—Nonfiction books that help families and individuals live Christian lives; contemporary social themes of Christian relevance.

Dimensions for Living

Dimensions for Living is an Abingdon imprint devoted to general-interest religious trade books on practical Christian living. Dimensions for Living publishes in the popular categories of inspiration, devotion, self-help, home, and family, as well as gift volumes. The concept behind the Dimensions for Living imprint—"quality books that celebrate life"—was developed in response to market research. The editorial approach is to combine contemporary themes with mainstream Christian theology.

Titles from Dimensions for Living: *The Essential Christmas Book: Family Crafts & Activities to Get to the Heart of Christmas* by Alan MacDonald and Janet Stickley; *365 Daily Meditations for Women* (edited by Mary Ruth Howes); *Everyday Miracles: Realizing God's Presence in Ordinary Life* by Marjorie L. Kimbrough; *The Christian Parent's Guide to Guilt-Free Parenting: Escaping the Perfect Parent Trap* by Robert and Debra Bruce, and Ellen W. Oldacre; *More Meditations to Make You Smile* by Martha J. Bechman (illustrated by John McPherson); *When You're a Christian—The Whole World Is from Missouri: Living the Life of Faith in a "Show Me" World* by James W. Moore.

Simple Pleasures books are designed to encourage, motivate, and enable individuals and families to simplify, to discover life's slower, more tranquil pace. Titles: *Simple Pleasures for Christmas; Simple Pleasures for Busy Men; Simple Pleasures for Busy Women; Simple Pleasures for Busy Families.*

Query letters and SASEs should be directed to:

Sally Sharpe, Editor, Dimensions for Living—Quality books that celebrate life and affirm the Christian faith.

AMERICAN FEDERATION OF ASTROLOGERS

6535 South Rural Road, P.O. Box 22040, Tempe, AZ 85285-2040
480-838-1751   fax: 480-838-8293
www.astrologers.com   e-mail: AFA@msn.com

American Federation of Astrologers (founded in 1938) is a specialist publisher of books in astrology for everyone from the beginner to the professional; the house also offers astrological software, charts, and other astrological aids but does not publish these.

As an organization, American Federation of Astrologers aims to further astrological education and research. AFA is an astrological membership organization, as well as a major publisher and distributor of astrological books and related supplies. AFA books are written by a variety of talented astrologers from all over the globe.

AFA encourages and promotes the science and art of astrology and advocates freedom of thought and speech in the astrological arena; the house offers a monthly membership bulletin, *Today's Astrologer,* and hosts periodic conventions. The organization's publishing program has generally produced a short list of new titles each year and supports an extensive publications backlist.

From American Federation of Astrologers: *You in a Modern World* by Doris Chase Doane; *First Survive, Then Thrive: The Journey from Crisis to Transformation* by John F. Eddington and Beth Rosato; *Phases of the Moon* by Marilyn Busteed and Dorothy Wergin; *Freudian Astrology; Lilith; Libido* by Elizabeth Greenwood; *Zodiac Explorer's Handbook* by Helene Hess; *The Living Stars* by Dr. Eric Morse; *Sun Sign Success* by Joseph Polansky; *Cosmopsychology: Engine of Destiny* by Marc Robertson; *The Book of Lovers* by Carolyn Reynolds.

Authors please note: American Federation of Astrologers wishes to consider for publication completed manuscripts only—and does not wish to consider queries, outlines, samples, or proposals. Manuscripts may be submitted along with copies on diskette (other than Macintosh), in text format.

American Federation of Astrologers distributes its own list, as well as publications of other houses.

Send completed manuscripts to:

Kris Brandt Riske, Production Manager

JASON ARONSON INC., PUBLISHERS

230 Livingston Street, Northvale, NJ 07647
201-767-4093
www.aronson.com

Jason Aronson Inc., Publishers (founded in 1965), produces a strong list of works in the field of Jewish interest, covering contemporary currents of Jewish thought as well as traditional Judaica. The house interest embraces popular, scholarly, and literary works—original titles and reprints. The well-nurtured Aronson backlist includes a lineup of established classics. (For Aronson's program in psychotherapy, please see U.S. Publishers section.)

Representative of the Aronson list: *Holy Brother: Inspiring Stories and Enchanted Tales About Rabbi Shlomo Carlebach* by Yitta Halbertstam Mandelbaum; *Pathways: Jews Who Return* by Richard H. Greenberg; *Piety and Fanaticism: Rabbinic Criticism of Religious Stringency* by Sara Epstein Weinstein; *American Torah Toons: 54 Illustrated Commentaries* by Lawrence Bush; *Ascending Jacob's Ladder: Jewish Views of Angels, Demons,*

A

and Evil Spirits by Ronald H. Isaacs; *The Jokes of Sigmund Freud: A Study in Humor and Jewish Identity* by Elliott Oring; *Einstein's God: Albert Einstein's Quest as a Scientist and as a Jew to Replace a Forsaken God* by Robert N. Goldman; *Restoring the Jews to Their Homeland: Nineteen Centuries in the Quest for Zion* by Joseph Adler; *Easy Kosher Cooking* by Rosalyn F. Manesse; *Forest of the Night: The Fear of God in Early Hasidic Thought* by Niles Elliot Goldstein; *The Faith and Doubt of Holocaust Survivors* by Reeve Robert Brenner; *Waiting for the Messiah: Stories to Inspire Jews with Hope* by Mordechai Staiman; *The Puzzle of the 613 Commandments and Why Bother* by Philip J. Caplan; *Above the Zodiac: Astrology in Jewish Thought* by Matityahu Glazerson; *The Dead Sea Scrolls: Understanding Their Spiritual Message* by Steven Fisdel; *God's Presence in History: Jewish Affirmations and Philosophical Reflections* by Emil L. Fackenheim.

Aronson supervises its own distribution, which, in addition to a network of regional and national trade-fulfillment services, features a direct-mail catalog operation. Aronson also oversees the operations of the Jewish Book Club. Query letters and SASEs should be directed to:

Arthur Kurzweil, Editor in Chief

AUGSBURG FORTRESS PUBLISHING

Fortress Press

426 South Fifth Street, P.O. Box 1209, Minneapolis, MN 55440-1209
612-330-3300, 800-426-0115
www.augsburgfortress.org

Augsburg Fortress publishes titles in popular and professional religious categories. The Augsburg Fortress list accents works of interest to general readers, in addition to books that appeal primarily to a mainstream religious readership and a solid selection of works geared to professional clergy and practitioners of pastoral counseling.

Categories include theology and pastoral care, biblical and historical academic studies, the life and tradition of Martin Luther, self-improvement and recovery, and books for younger readers from nursery and preschoolers through young adult.

The Fortress Press imprint accents issues of contemporary cultural, theological, and political impact. In addition, Augsburg Fortress produces computer software, recordings, artwork, and gift items. Augsburg Fortress also vends a line of liturgical vestments and supplies. The house is widely known for its full range of Bibles, produced in a variety of edition styles.

Augsburg Fortress's ecumenical emphasis enables the house to address a broad range of issues and views within a diversified booklist. Augsburg Fortress Publishing (founded in 1890) is a subsidiary of the Publishing House of the Evangelical Lutheran Church in America.

Representative of the Augsburg list: *Nurturing Silence in a Noisy Heart: How to Find Inner Peace* by Wayne E. Oates; *Autumn Wisdom: Finding Meaning in Life's Later Years* by James E. Miller; *The Contemplative Pastor: Returning to the Art of Spiritual Direction* by Eugene Peterson; *The Jesus Prescription for a Healthy Life* by Leonard Sweet; *Grieving the Death of a Friend* by Harold Ivan Smith; *A Year of Prayer: 365 Reflections for Spiritual Growth* by Jeanne Hinton; *Soul Weavings: A Gathering of Women's Prayers* (edited by Lyn Klug); *Wrestling with Depression: A Spiritual Guide to Reclaiming Life* by William and Lucy Hulme; *Streams of Living Water: Celebrating the Five Great Traditions of Christian Faith* by Richard J. Foster; *Love Letters from Cell 92* by Ruth-Alice von Bismarck and Ulrich Kabitz; *Dead Sea Scrolls Today* by James C. VanderKam; *The History of God: The 4,000 Year Quest of Judaism, Christianity, and Islam* by Karen Armstrong; *Breaking the Code: Understanding the Book of Revelation* by Bruce M. Metzger.

Children's selections include the line of Good News Explorers Sunday school curriculum series, the Rejoice series, and the Witness series, as well as individual titles. Samples here: *Swamped!* by Nathan Aaseng; *So I Can Read* by Dandi Mackall (illustrated by Deborah A. Kirkeeide); *Ms. Pollywog's Problem-Solving Service* by Ellen Javernick (illustrated by Meredith Johnson).

Authors should note: Augsburg Fortress prefers to receive a proposal rather than a completed manuscript; the house receives over 3,000 submissions per year—a finely honed book proposal may therefore be considered essential.

Augsburg Fortress has a potent distribution network with sales representatives operating via offices nationwide.

Fortress Press

Fortress Press focuses on the ever-changing religious worldview of the contemporary world. The Fortress list is keyed to issues of topical interest, tackled with vision and precision; these works address political and cultural issues and are often on the cusp of current religious debate. The Fortress market orientation tilts toward both the general trade and the religious trade.

Titles from Fortress Press: *God Beyond Gender: Feminist Christian God Language* by Gail Ramshaw; *The Crucifixion of Jesus: History, Myth, Faith* by Gerard S. Sloyan; *The Paradoxical Vision: A Public Theology for the Twenty-First Century* by Robert Benne; *The Spirituality of African Peoples: The Search for a Common Moral Discourse* by Peter J. Paris; *Theology for a Scientific Age: Being and Becoming—Natural, Divine, and Human* by Arthur Peacocke; *Womanism and Afrocentrism in Theology* by Cheryl J. Sanders; *X-odus: An African-American Male Journey* by Garth Kasimu Baker-Fletcher.

Query letters and SASEs should be directed to:

Marshall Johnson, Editorial Director

Robert Klausmeier, Senior Acquisitions Editor

Baháʼí Publishing Trust

Baháʼí National Center, 1233 Central Street, Evanston, IL 60201
847-251-1854, 800-999-9019 (catalog) BPTWVSBNC.org

Bahá'í Publishing Trust (founded in 1902) is a wholly owned, not-for-profit company of the National Spiritual Assembly of the Bahá'í of the United States. The house publishes books pertaining to the Bahá'í faith; interest areas include history, philosophy, self-help, juveniles, scholarly works, and multimedia materials.

The house's Bahá'í Distribution Service, located in Atlanta, Georgia, handles trade and personal order fulfillment.

Query letters and SASEs should be directed to:

Lee Minnerly, General Manager

BAKER BOOK HOUSE
Chosen Books
Fleming H. Revell
Spire Books
Wynwood Books

Twin Brooks Industrial Park, 6030 East Fulton Road, Ada, MI 49301
616-676-9185   fax: 616-676-9573
www.bakerbooks.com

Mailing address
P.O. Box 6287, Grand Rapids, MI 49516-6287

Baker Book House (founded in 1939) produces works across the spectrum of general religious subject areas (from Protestant and ecumenical perspectives). Baker Book House is a preeminent distributor in the religious-publishing field. Baker Book House distributes its own list (including its diverse imprints).

Query letters and SASEs should be directed to:

Rebecca Cooper, Assistant Editor

Baker Book House

The publishing division of Baker Book House issues titles of general trade interest, as well as a wide selection of books for ministers, students, schools, libraries, and church workers.

Highlighting the Baker program: *Ruth Bell Graham's Collected Poems* by Ruth Bell Graham; *Messenger of Hope: Becoming Agents of Revival for the Twenty-First Century* by David Bryant; *Willing to Believe: The Controversy Over Free Will* by R. C. Sproul; *Yearning Minds and Burning Hearts: Rediscovering the Spirituality of Jesus* by Glendion Carney and William Long; *A Time to Heal: John Perkins, Community Development, and Racial Reconciliation* by Stephen E. Berk; *Masterpieces of the Bible: Insights into Classical Art of Faith* by Keith White; *Teaching in Tough Times* by Judy Nichols; *Treasured Friends: Finding and Keeping True Friendships* by Ann Hibbard; *Turning Points: Deci-*

sive Moments in the History of Christianity by Mark A. Noll; *Jehovah-Talk: The Mind-Control Language of Jehovah's Witnesses* by David A. Reed.

Query letters and SASEs should be directed to:

Jim Kinney, Director of Academic Books

Rebecca Cooper, Assistant Editor

Chosen Books

Fleming H. Revell

Spire Books

This Baker wing specializes in spiritually oriented works for the popular religious audience, including a wide range of fiction. Offerings from the Revell program include the Treasury of Helen Steiner Rice line of inspirational titles. The Chosen Books imprint produces evangelical Christian books for personal growth and enrichment. Spire accents an inspirational list of personal stories told through autobiography and memoir.

From Revell: *The New Birth Order Book* by Dr. Kevin Lemani; *The Menopause Manager: Balancing Medical Knowledge and Botanical Wisdom for Optimal Health* by Mary Ann and Joseph L. Mayo; *Happily Ever After: And 21 Other Myths About Family Life* by Karen Scalf Linamen; *Love Busters: Overcoming the Habits That Destroy Romantic Love* by Willard F. Harley, Jr.; *What Kids Need Most Is Mom* by Patricia H. Rushford; *When Your Best Is Never Good Enough: The Secret of Measuring Up* by Kevin Leman; *Women of Grace* by Kathleen Morgan.

Chosen titles include: *Twilight Labyrinth: Why Does Spiritual Darkness Linger Where It Does?* by George K. Otis, Jr.; *The Love Every Woman Needs: Intimacy with Jesus* by Jan McCray; *I Give You Authority* by Charles H. Kraft; *Blessing or Curse* by Derek Prince.

On the Spire roster: *Jonathan, You Left Too Soon* by David B. Biebel; *Getting the Best of Your Anger* by Les Carter; *Making Peace with Your Past* by H. Norman Wright; *Those Turbulent Teen Years* by Jeenie Gordon.

Query letters and SASEs should be directed to:

Lonnie Hull Dufont, Acting Editorial Director

Wynwood Press

As of 1998, Wynwood Press is not an active imprint.

BEAR & COMPANY PUBLISHING

P.O. Box 2860, Santa Fe, NM 87504
505-983-5968   fax: 505-989-8386
e-mail: bearco@bearco.com

B

Bear & Company was recently acquired by Inner Traditions.

Bear & Company publishes a wide array of titles in historical and contemporary spiritual traditions, healing, and energetic medicine. Bear's list in health and medicine accents revolutionary techniques that incorporate such elements as emotion, intuition, channeling, herbs, and crystals.

Conceived over a kitchen table in the fall of 1979, Bear & Company (founded formally in 1980) originally highlighted titles in creation spirituality. The publisher has built a substantial backlist in this field (including Matthew Fox's *Original Blessing: A Primer in Creation Spirituality*)—and publishes works exhibiting an increasingly diverse spectrum of thought.

A natural outgrowth of the original Bear & Company approach is a remarkable lineup in Native American spirituality, including works that expand the interpretation of pre-Columbian traditions into the contemporary arena. Bear's benchmark title in this area is *The Mayan Factor: Path Beyond Technology* by José Argüelles.

The house insignia—a rambling bear under a full moon—marks a roster of thoughtful, vivid, and evocative explorations into who we are and where we came from, and the destiny of the species, as illuminated by the company's trade slogan: Books to celebrate and heal the Earth.

The evolving seasonal booklist demonstrates that artistry continues to waft from the Bear & Company kitchen: *Walking on the Wind: Cherokee Teachings for Harmony and Balance* by Michael Garrett; *Maya Cosmogenesis 2012: The True Meaning of the Maya Calendar End-Date* by John Major Jenkins; *The Hidden Maya: A New Understanding of Maya Glyphs* by Martin Brennan; *The Ancient Cookfire: How to Rejuvenate Body and Spirit Through Seasonal Foods and Fasting* by Carrie L'Esperance; *The Goddess in the Gospels: Reclaiming the Sacred Feminine* by Margaret Starbird; *Family of Light: Pleiadian Tales and Lessons in Living* by Barbara Marciniak.

A Bear hallmark is the divination series, which features illustrated books and sets of cards. Packages include: *The Egyptian Oracle* by Maya Heath; *The Mayan Oracle: Return Path to the Stars* by Ariel Spilsbury and Michael Bryner (illustrated by Donna Kiddie); *Inner Child Cards: A Journey into Fairy Tales, Myth & Nature* by Isha Lerner and Mark Lerner (illustrated by Christopher Guilfoil); *Medicine Cards: The Discovery of Power Through the Ways of Animals* by Jamie Sams and David Carson (illustrated by Angela Werneke).

Latest Releases: *The Mystery of the Crystal Skulls: A Real Life Detective Story of the Ancient World* by Chris Morton and Ceri Louise Thomas; *The Giza Power Plant: Technologies of Ancient Egypt* by Christopher Dunn; *PsyEarth Quest: A Prophetic Novel* by Charles Bensinger.

From Bear's bestselling backlist: *Vibrational Medicine: New Choices for Healing Ourselves* by Richard Gerber, M.D.; *The Teachings of Don Carlos: Practical Applications of the Works of Carlos Castaneda* by Victor Sanchez; *Illuminations of Hildegard of Bingen*, commentary by Matthew Fox; *The Woman with the Alabaster Jar: Mary Magdalen and the Holy Grail* by Margaret Starbird; *Bringers of the Dawn: Teachings from the Pleiadians* by Barbara Marciniak; *Gift of Power: The Life and Teachings of a Lakota Medicine Man* by Archie Fire Lame Deer and Richard Erdoes; *Liquid Light of Sex: Understanding*

Your Key Life Passages by Barbara Hand Clow; *The Earth Chronicles* (series) by Zecharia Sitchin.

Bear & Company distributes its list via a network that includes several distribution services and wholesalers.

Query letters and SASEs should be directed to:

John Nelson, Editorial Director

B

BETHANY HOUSE PUBLISHERS

11300 Hampshire Avenue South, Minneapolis, MN 55438
612-829-2500   fax: 612-829-2768

Bethany House Publishers (founded in 1956) issues hardcover and trade paperback titles in evangelical Christian fiction (with an accent on historicals) and nonfiction, as well as a powerful youth lineup. Areas of Bethany House nonfiction interest include devotional works, relationships and family, and biblical reference.

Bethany's fiction authors include such bestselling names as Janette Oke, Judith Pella, and Gilbert Morris. The program accents titles with American prairie and Western themes, historical romances, and works with contemporary settings; the house also offers boxed series sets. Among Bethany fiction features are the series by the father/daughter writing team Lynn Morris and Gilbert Morris.

The house's trade credo is: "God's light shining through good books." Bethany's traditional devotion to bookmaking is evident in its enduring backlist.

Nonfiction from Bethany: *Shop, Save, Share* by Ellie Kay; *Your Angels Guard My Steps: A 40-Day Journey in the Company of Bernard of Clairvaux* by David Hazard; *Why Revival Tarries* by Leonard Ravenhill; *Dying for a Change* by Leith Anderson; *Listening to the Voice of God: How Your Ministry Can Be Transformed* by Roger Barrier; *When Someone You Love Is Dying: Making Wise Decisions at the End of Life* by David Clark and Peter Emmett; *Who Broke the Baby?* by Jean Staker Garton; *Truth About Rock: Shattering the Myth of Harmless Music* by Steve Peters and Mark Littleton; *Reclaiming Intimacy in Your Marriage: A Plan for Facing Life's Ebb and Flow Together* by Robert and Debra Bruce; *The Soul at Rest: A Journey into Contemplative Prayer* by Tricia McCary Rhodes; *Glimpses: Seeing God in Everyday Life* by Annie Herring; *Life Keys: Discovering Who You Are, Why You Are Here, What You Do Best* by Jane A. G. Kise, David Stark, and Sandra Krebs Hirsh.

Overview of Bethany adult fiction: *The Garden at the Edge of Beyond* by Michael Phillips; *Snow: A Novel* by Calvin Miller; *Island of the Innocent* by Lynn Morris and Gilbert Morris; *A Haunting Refrain* by Patricia H. Rushford; *Passage into Light* by Judith Pella; *A Place Called Morning* by Ann Tatlock; *Honor's Pledge* by Kristen Heitzmann; *The Bridge over Flatwillow Creek* by Lance Wubbels; *Morningsong* by Patricia Rushford; *Shroud of Silence* by Carol S. Slama; *Framed* by Tracie Peterson; *Behind the Veil* by Linda Chaikin.

B

Nonfiction for youth and young adults: *What Children Need to Know When Parents Get Divorced: A Book to Read with Children Going Through the Trauma of Divorce* by William L. Coleman; *Hero Tales: A Family Treasury of True Stories from the Lives of Christian Heroes* by Dave and Neta Jackson; *Hot Topics, Tough Questions: Honest Answers to Your Hardest Questions* by Bill Myers.

Youth and young-adult fiction: *Hide Behind the Moon* by Beverly Lewis; *High Hurdles: Close Quarters* by Lauraine Snelling; *Rescue at Boomerang Bend* by Robert Elmer; *Mysterious Signal* by Lois Walfrid Johnson (the Riverboat Adventures series); *Swept Away* by Yvonne Lehman (White Dove Romances).

Bethany House distributes to the trade through Ingram, Baker & Taylor, and other wholesalers.

In accord with its current acquisitions policy, Bethany House is not considering unsolicited manuscripts or proposals.

Query letters and SASEs should be directed to:

Sharon Madison, Acquisitions Editor

COOK COMMUNICATIONS

Victor Books

Faith Marriage

Faith Parenting

Faithful Woman

Lion

Faith Kids Books

Faith Kids Toys & Media

Cook Communications, 4050 Lee Vance View, Colorado Springs, CO 80918
719-536-3271   fax: 719-536-3269

Cook Communications produces mainstream Christian religious titles in books and other media. Divisions include: Victor Books, Faith Marriage, Faith Parenting, Faithful Woman, Lion, Faith Kids Books, and Faith Kids Toys & Media.

Cook Communications and its imprints reflects the merger (in July of 1996) of Chariot Family Publishing and Scripture Press Publications/Victor Books, along with the operation's relocation from Illinois to Colorado.

The house mission is to assist in the spiritual development of people by producing and distributing consumer-driven, centrist Christian products that foster discipleship, increase understanding of the Bible, and promote the application of Christian values in everyday life.

Cook Communications products are prayerfully crafted to fit their prime audience. They are inspirational, fun, and creative and provide sound Christian education. They are easy and simple for parents, teachers, and others to use effectively. The nature of the house product and its marketing will encourage linking church and home.

Cook Communications markets lines that target broad sectors of the market: youth (primarily from the Faith Kids Brand), adult (Victor Books, Faith Marriage, Faith Parenting, and Faithful Woman), and general religious trade (Lion Publishing).

Cook Communications distribution utilizes a network of field representatives and services that includes its own in-house catalog and marketing operations.

Faith Kids Books & Toys

Faith Kids produces a strong list of titles with a religious orientation in the publishing areas of juvenile fiction, inspirational and devotional, reference (most of them works for young readers), as well as works for a general religious readership. Chariot markets a line of illustrated Bibles and illustrated inspirational and devotional readings.

As the editors of Faith Kids Books note: "We have been called by Christ to foster the spiritual development of children. That is why first, through Faith Kids Books & Toys, we focus on training children in and through the family. We exist to help parents evangelize and discipline their children as a part of everyday life as commanded in Deuteronomy 6:5–9. We will facilitate family discipleship by providing an organized Christian growth program of market-sensitive, exemplary products."

Faith Kids Books offers a wide range of reading materials for ages birth to teen. Faith Kids Toys offers gift and educational items that are inspirational and fun—toys, games, and gift products for ages birth to teen.

Lion Publishing

Lion Publishing produces works for the religious trade and serious general trade markets.

Through the Lion imprint the publisher strives to reach the spiritually inquisitive or "seeker" directly or through outreach gift giving. Such books do not presuppose any prior Christian or biblical understanding. Instead, seeker adult and children's books facilitate the spiritual development process, primarily at pre-evangelism and evangelism levels.

Query letters and SASEs should be directed to:

Shella Lapora, Editorial Assistant

Victor Books

Victor Books (founded in 1934) offer a wide range of books keyed to spiritual, religious, philosophical, and social topics for the adult, as well as educational materials and supplies.

Categories of publishing interest include family spiritual growth, women's spiritual growth, books of the Bible, Bible characters, group builder resources, and general topics. The Victor Books imprint marks the trade-directed portion of the program. Victor is the imprint that marks games and gifts for adults.

The Victor product line meets various personal needs of the market. Victor reaches evangelicals with the purpose of aiding the intended audience in its spiritual formation. Victor adult fame and media adult products facilitate fun learning of Bible truths through adult group and family interaction with such items as games, puzzles, and activities.

Query letters and SASEs should be directed to:

Shella Lapora, Editorial Assistant

Faith Marriage

Faith Marriage seeks to help married men and women grow together in their relationship with Jesus Christ by providing materials specifically aimed at deepening couples' spiritual lives. Faith Marriage seeks to build up Christian marriage so that the partners will be equipped to meet the many challenges of modern married life.

Faith Parenting

Faith Parenting is designed to help parents with the biblical mandate of passing on their Christian faith to their children. Central to this effort are books that encourage family devotions, such as the Family Night Tool Chest Line.

Faithful Woman

Faithful Woman speaks to women through their specific spiritual needs as women. As ministries by and for women have become more and more prevalent, Cook Communications saw the need for a line of books that would address the special needs women experience in their Christian walk. Faithful Woman aims to assist women in fulfilling their unique calling as members of the body of Christ.

COUNCIL OAK BOOKS

1290 Chestnut Street, Suite 2, San Francisco, CA 94109
fax: 415-931-5353
www.counciloakbooks.com   kevincob@pacbell.net

Council Oak Books, founded in 1984, is a publisher of distinguished nonfiction books based in personal, intimate history (letters, diaries, memoir); Native American history and spiritual teachings; African-American history and contemporary experience, small illustrated inspirational gift books, and unique vintage photo books and Americana. We're looking for those unique, eloquent voices whose history, teachings, and experiences illuminate our lives. No fiction, poetry, or children's books. Check our Web site at: www.counciloakbooks.com.

Titles from Council Oak: *Strongman* (edited by Robert Mainardi); *Of Unknown Origin* by Debra Levi Holtz; *Vow* by Kay Leigh Hagan; *Only the Earth Endures* by Cedrick Red Feather, with Jan Witken; *No Word for Time: The Way of the Algonquin People* by Evan T.

Pritchard; *Beyond Fear: The Toltec Guide to Freedom and Joy,* the teachings of Don Miguel Ruiz, as recorded by Mary Carroll Nelson; *Secrets from an Inventor's Notebook* by Maurice Kanbar; *When the Night Bird Sings* by Joyce Sequichie Hifler; *A Cherokee Feast of Days* by Joyce Sequichie Hifler; *Fools Crow: Wisdom and Power* by Thomas E. Mails; *The Hoop and the Tree* by Chris Hoffman; *Bloodland: A True Story of Oil, Greed, and Murder on the Osage Reservation* by Dennis McAuliffe.

Send a brief query letter describing your book, with SASE, or a full proposal including table of contents or chapter outline, sample chapter, and author bio, with either sufficient postage for return or a notation that the material may be recycled if declined. Unsolicited manuscripts cannot be returned.

Query or proposal should be directed to:

Kevin Bentley, Editor in Chief

THE CROSSING PRESS

1201 Shaffer Road, Suite B, Santa Cruz, CA 95060
fax: 831-420-1114
www.crossingpress.com   e-mail: crossing@crossingpress.com

The Crossing Press publishes a wide range of hardcover and trade paperback editions and is dedicated to publishing books, videos, and audios on natural healing, spirituality, alternative healing practices, pet care, general nonfiction, and cookbooks. Our subjects include astrology, aromatherapy, body image, meditation, shamanism, and women's issues, to name a few. It is our hope that the power of information is a catalyst for change and development, not only for the self but for the global community as well.

The Crossing Press was established in upstate New York in 1972 as a modest, indeed a veritable cottage press, run from the farmhouse of the founders, Elaine Goldman Gill and John Gill, who were teaching at Cornell University at this time. Relocated to the central California coastal region in the 1980's, the Crossing Press retains its personalized editorial touch and small press savvy.

The Crossing Press general nonfiction includes: *Essential Reiki* by Diane Stein; *Aromatherapy* by Kathi Keville and Mindy Green; *Shaman in a 9 to 5 World* by Trish Telesco; *Wind and Water: Your Personal Feng Shui Journey* by Carol Hyder; *Advanced Celtic Shamanism; A Little Book of Candle Magic; A Little Book of Pendulum Magic,* all by D. J. Conway; *Physician of the Soul: A Modern Kabbalist's Approach to Health and Healing* by Rabbi Joseph Gelberman; *Dead Mars, Dying Earth* by John Brandenburg, Ph.D., and Monica Rix Paxson; *The Herbal Medicine Maker's Handbook* by James Green; *Complete Guide to Tarot* by Cassandra Eason; *My Husband Is Gay: A Woman's Survival Guide* by Carol Grever; *Soul Proprietor: 101 Lessons from a Lifestyle Entrepreneur* by Jane Pollack; *Zen Judaism* by Rabbi Joseph Gelberman; *Crafting the Body Divine through Ritual, Movement and Body Art* by Yasmine Galenorn; *The Future of Healing: Exploring the Parallels of Eastern and Western Medicine* by Michael P. Milburn, Ph.D.; *Black Holes and Energy Pirates: How to Recognize and Release Them* by Jesse Reeder; *Essential*

Wicca by Paul Tuitean and Estelle Daniels; *Healing Spirit: True Stories from 14 Spiritual Healers* by Judith Joslow-Rodewald and Patricia West-Barker.

Titles in the kitchen arts include: *The Balanced Diet Cookbook* by Bill Taylor; *Easy French Cooking* by Carol Colbert; *Everyday Tofu* by Gary Landgrebe; *The Great Barbecue Companion* by Bruce Bjorkman; *Marinades* by Jim Tarantino; *Noodle Fusion,* by Andra Chesman and Dorothy Rankin; *Japanese Vegetarian Cooking,* by Patricia Richfield.

The Crossing Press distributes through Publisher's Group West.

The Crossing Press accepts unsolicited manuscripts. Query letters, proposals, and manuscripts (SASEs included) should be directed to:

Caryle Hirshberg, Managing Editor

CROSSROAD PUBLISHING COMPANY

Verlag Herder

370 Lexington Avenue, New York, NY 10017-6550
212-532-3650   fax: 212-532-4922

Crossroad Publishing Company (founded in 1980) publishes scholarly and general-interest titles in religion, philosophy, spirituality, and personal improvement. Crossroad offers books in spirituality, religion, and counseling for general and popular religious markets. The Crossroad Herder imprint publishes books in theology, religious studies, and religious education for professionals and active members of Catholic and mainline Protestant churches.

Crossroad and sibling imprint Crossroad Herder (formerly Herder & Herder) is a United States–based wing of the international firm Verlag Herder (founded in 1798). The programs of Crossroad and Crossroad Herder offer books by some of the most distinguished authors in the United States and abroad in the fields of theology, biblical studies, spirituality, religious education, women's studies, world religions, psychology, and counseling. Crossroad supports a strong backlist.

Crossroad and Continuum, now two completely separate entities sharing the same address, were corporate affiliates within the Crossroad/Continuum Publishing Group from 1980 through the early 1990s. Even through the dual-house years, each publisher retained its distinct identity. (For Continuum, please see the entry in the US Publishers section.)

Crossroad is an entrepreneurial house of modest size, with a tightly focused program that takes advantage of diverse marketing channels; as such, this publisher provides an excellent environment for authors looking for personalized and long-term publishing relationships.

Frontlist titles: *Sabbatical Journey: The Diary of His Final Year* by Henri J. M. Nouwen; *Henri Nouwen: A Restless Seeking for God* by Dr. Jurjen J. Beumer; *Holy Work: Be Love. Be Blessed. Be a Blessing* by Marsha Sinetar; *And Now I See. . . . A Theology of Transformation* by Robert Barron; *Children of Disobedience: The Love Story of Martin Luther and Katarina of Bora* by Asta Scheib; *Enneagram II: Advancing Spiritual Discernment* by Richard Rohr; *Reluctant Dissenter: An Autobiography* by James Patrick Shannon; *By Grace Transformed: Christianity for a New Millennium* by N. Gordon Cosby; *A Place to Hold My Shaky Heart: Reflections from Life in a Community* by Sue Mosteller; *Let It Be:*

Advent and Christmas Meditations for Women (edited by Therese Johnson Borchard); *The Catholic Funeral: The Church's Ministry of Hope* by Chris Aridas.

Selections from the backlist: *Dear Heart, Come Home: The Path of Midlife Spirituality* by Joyce Rupp; *101 Ways to Nourish Your Soul* by Mitch Finley; *Discovering the Enneagram* by Richard Rohr and Andreas Ebert; *The Great Apparitions of Mary: An Examination of the Twenty-Two Supranormal Appearances* by Ingo Swann; *Medicine Wheels: Native American Vehicles of Healing* by Roy I. Wilson; *In the Courts of the Lord: A Gay Priest's Story* by James Ferry.

An ongoing Crossroad line is the Adult Christian Education Program, which issues series titles in scripture study, theology and church history, Christian living, and world religious traditions.

Crossroad has sponsored the Crossword Women's Studies Award and the Crossroad Counseling Book Award, both of which bestow publication under the house imprimatur. (Details are available upon request from the publisher.) Crossroad distributes via Spring Arbor Distributing.

Query letters and SASEs should be directed to:

Alison Donohue, Editor

Paul McMahon, Editor

Crossroad Herder

Books published under the Crossroad Herder imprint mark the cutting edge of theology. Each volume presents fresh perspectives on a topic of interest, expands discussion on an issue of concern, and is accessible to the theologian and interested readers alike. Titles: *In Ten Thousand Places: Dogma in a Pluralistic Church* by Paul G. Crowley; *Understanding Catholic Morality* by Elizabeth L. Willems; *I Believe in the Holy Spirit* by Yves Congar; *The Holy Spirit, Lord and Giver of Life* (prepared by the Theological-Historical Commission for the Great Jubilee of the Year 2000); *Catholic Common Ground Initiative* by Cardinal Joseph Bernardin and Archbishop Oscar H. Lipscomb.

Backlist Crossroad Herder titles: *The Girard Reader* by René Girard (edited by James G. Williams); *Resurrection from the Underground: Feodor Dostoevsky* by René Girard (translated by James G. Williams); *Wrestling with God: Religious Life in Search of Its Soul* by Barbara Fiand; *Finding God in All Things* (edited by Michael J. Himes and Stephen J. Pope); *The Growth of Mysticism: Gregory the Great Through the 12th Century* by Bernard McGinn.

Query letters and SASEs should be directed to:

Michael Parker, Editor

CROSSWAY BOOKS (A DIVISION OF GOOD NEWS PUBLISHERS)

1300 Crescent Street, Wheaton, IL 60187-5883
630-682-4300   fax: 630-682-4785

Crossway produces a small list of books with an evangelical Christian perspective aimed at both the religious and general audience, including issue-oriented nonfiction, evangelical works, inspiration, and fiction. Crossway Books (founded in 1938) is a division of Good News Publishers.

From the Crossway nonfiction list: *Strength for Today: Daily Readings for a Deeper Faith* by John F. MacArthur; *Time to Get Serious: Daily Devotions to Keep You Close to God* by Tony Evans; *Ten Secrets for a Successful Family: A Perfect 10 for Homes That Win* by Adrian Rogers; *A Woman's Walk with God: A Daily Guide for Prayer and Spiritual Growth* by Sheila Cragg; *Telling the Truth: How to Revitalize Christian Journalism* by Marvin Olasky.

Representative Crossway fiction: *Code of the West* by Stephen Bly; *Fated Genes* by Harry Lee Krauss, Jr.; *The Gathering Storm* by W. E. Davis; *Wells of Glory* by Mary McReynolds.

Sample children's books: *Annie Henry and the Secret Mission* by Susan Olasky; *Children of the King* by Max Lucado; *Hattie Marshall and the Dangerous Fire* by Debra Smith.

Crossway Books is interested in nonfiction areas of books on the deeper Christian life, issues books, and a select number of academic and professional volumes. It feels called to publish fiction works that fall into these categories: historical, youth/juvenile, adventure, action, intrigue, thriller, and contemporary and Christian realism.

Crossway handles its own distribution.

Crossway Books invites query letters regarding works written from an evangelical Christian perspective. Please send a synopsis (one to two pages, double-spaced), and no more than two chapters. No entire manuscripts; such submissions will be returned.

Query letters and SASEs should be directed to:

Marvin Padgett, Vice President, Editorial

DHARMA PUBLISHING

2910 San Pablo Avenue, Berkeley, CA 94702
510-548-5407   fax: 510-548-2230
www.nyingma.org   e-mail: dharma-publishing@nyingma.org

Dharma Publishing is a specialist house active in a variety of formats. Dharma publishes trade paperbacks and journals; distribution includes subscription and mail order. Areas of interest include art, history, biography, literature, philosophy, psychology, spiritual, scholarly, cosmology, and juveniles.

Established by Tarthang Tulku in 1971, Dharma Publishing's founding purpose was twofold: to preserve Tibetan texts and art and to lay the foundation for Dharma education in the West. Incorporated as a nonprofit organization in 1975, Dharma Publishing and Press have continued to rely on a small staff of Dharma students and volunteers to accomplish its goals. All profit from sales of books and art is dedicated to the production of more books and sacred art.

Dharma's Tibetan Translation series develops appreciation of the Buddha and the qualities of enlightenment and also deepens understanding of the science of consciousness, the nature of the Bodhisattva, and the Vajrayana.

The Nyingma Psychology series is written for individuals coping with life in modern society. Books in this series offer ways to relieve anxiety, cultivate creative aspects of mind, and transform every situation into an opportunity for self-knowledge and insight. This series includes Dharma's most popular books on the development of awareness and spiritual satisfaction in daily life and work: *Gesture of Balance, Skillful Means,* and *Mastering Successful Work* by Tarthang Tulku.

Dharma's Time, Space, and Knowledge series stimulates a dynamic inquiry into knowledge. Free from doctrine and dogma, these books offer a forum for discovering the nature of mind and all phenomena.

The Crystal Mirror series is designed to introduce Westerners to the Dharma. Each volume explores a particular aspect of the development of Buddhism from the time of the Buddha to the present.

Dharma's Art, History, and Culture series offers the reader a broad view of Tibetan Buddhist culture.

The Jataka Series for Children presents the profoundly moving stories of the Buddha's previous lives adapted for a young audience. Conveying universal values of generosity, integrity, and compassion, these tales encourage ethical, caring action and provide uplifting, positive models for young people.

Dharma titles: *Teachings from the Heart: Introduction to the Dharma and One Point of Knowledge; Enlightenment Is a Choice: The Beauty of Dharma* by Tarthang Tulku; *Invitation to Enlightenment* by Matriceta and Candragomin (translated by Michael Hahn); *All Points of Knowledge* by Tarthang Tulku; *Leaves of the Heaven Tree: The Great Compassion of the Buddha* (Fields of Knowledge series); *The Stupa: Sacred Symbol of Enlightenment* (Crystal Mirror series); *Light of Knowledge: Essays on the Interplay of Knowledge, Time, and Space.*

Query letters and SASEs should be directed to:

Tarthang Tulku, President and Editor

DISCIPLESHIP RESOURCES

1908 Grand Avenue, P.O. Box 840, Nashville, TN 37202-0840
615-340-7068
www.discipleshipresources.org   e-mail: discipleshipresources@gbod.org

Discipleship Resources (founded in 1951) is the publishing component of the General Board of Discipleship, one of the major program boards of the United Methodist Church. Areas of publishing interest encompass United Methodist history, doctrine, and theology, as well as Bible study, Christian education, ethnic church concerns, evangelism, ministry of the laity, stewardship, United Methodist men, and worship.

Discipleship Resources issues a varied inventory, including books, booklets, manuals, audiovisuals, packets, and supplies directed to local church members and leaders, lay and clergy, men and women, children, youth, and adults—as well as to district and conference leaders and others serving the congregation. Some resources guide the leader of an area of work or particular program, while others are aimed toward individual study and enrichment.

Titles from Discipleship Resources: *Finding Christ, Finding Life: How to Live as a Christian in a Non-Christian World* by Von W. Unrub; *Hand in Hand: Growing Spiritually with Our Children* by Sue Downing; *Emmanuel!: Celebrating God's Presence with Us* by Timothy L. Bias; *Come to the Feast: Invitational Evangelism* by Roberto Escamilla; *Grace Note: Spirituality and the Choir* by M. Anne Burnette Hook; *Lay Speakers Lead in Worship* by Hoyt L. Hickman; *Couples Who Care* by Jane P. Ives; *Growing in Faith, United in Love* by Barb Nardi Kurtz; *Living Our Beliefs: The United Methodist Way* by Bishop Kenneth L. Carder; *Echoing the Word: The Ministry of Forming Disciples* by Grant Sperry-White; *The Faith-Sharing Congregation* by Roger K. Swanson and Shirley F. Clement.

Writers who wish to submit materials to Discipleship Resources for publishing consideration may acquire editorial guidelines upon request from the publisher. The guide includes versatile tips that are broadly applicable to manuscript preparation in general.

Discipleship Resources handles its own sales and distribution.

Query letters and SASEs should be directed to:

Alan K. Waltz, Managing Editor and Publisher

Mary Gregory, Editor in Chief

WILLIAM B. EERDMANS PUBLISHING COMPANY

Eerdmans Books for Young Readers

255 Jefferson Avenue SE, Grand Rapids, MI 49503
616-459-4591
e-mail: sales@eerdmans.com

Eerdmans publishes books of general interest; religious, academic, and theological works; books for young readers; regional history; and American religious history. The Eerdmans publishing reach offers a Christian handle on such areas as anthropology, biblical studies, and in religious approaches to biography, African American studies, church administration, music, philosophy, psychology, science, social issues, current and historical theology, and women's interests.

The Eerdmans catalog also highlights general reference works, such as Bible commentaries and theological dictionaries, as well as titles in Old and New Testament studies.

William B. Eerdmans Publishing Company (founded in 1911) is one of the largest independent nondenominational Christian religious publishers in the United States.

On the Eerdmans list: *The Pilgrim's Guide: C. S. Lewis and the Art of Witness* (edited by David Mills); *Choosing the Right College: The Whole Truth About America's 100 Top Schools* by the Intercollegiate Studies Institute; *Saint Paul Returns to the Movies: Triumph over Shame* by Robert Jewett; *Abiding: Landscape of the Soul* by David Lubbers and Stephen C. Rowe; *Toward the Renewal of Civilization: Political Order and Culture* (edited by T. William Boxx and Gary M. Quinlivan); *The Bible and Healing: A Medical and Theological Commentary* by John Wilkinson; *The Bible and the New York Times* by

Fleming Rutledge; *Imagining God: Theology and the Religious Imagination* by Garrett Green; *Lost Daughters: Recovered Memory Therapy and the People It Hurts* by Reinder Van Til; *The Foolishness of Preaching: Proclaiming the Gospel Against the Wisdom of the World* by Robert Farrar Capon; *Last Rights? Assisted Suicide and Euthanasia Debated* (edited by Michael M. Uhlmann); *Where Garden Meets Wilderness: Evangelical Entry into the Environmental Debate* by E. Calvin Beisner; *The Theology of Paul the Apostle* by James D. G. Dunn.

A special Eerdmans project is the beautifully produced *The Leningrad Codex: A Facsimile Edition* (Astrid B. Beck, Managing Editor; David Noel Freedman, General Editor; James A. Sanders, Publication Editor).

Query letters and SASEs should be directed to:

Charles van Hof, Managing Editor

Jon Pott, Editor in Chief

Eerdmans Books for Young Readers

Eerdmans publishes some regional books and other nonreligious titles. It is essentially a religious publisher whose titles range from the academic to the semi-popular. It is now publishing a growing number of books in the areas of spirituality and the Christian life. It has long specialized in biblical studies and theology and in religious approaches.

Some recent titles include: *Silent Night: The Song and Its Story* by Margaret Hodges (illustrated by Tim Ladwig); *Psalm Twenty-Three* (illustrated by Tim Ladwig); *God's Little Seeds,* written and illustrated by Bijou Le Tord; *Exodus,* written and illustrated by Brian Wildsmith; *The Blessing of the Lord,* written by Gary Schmidt (illustrated by Dennis Nolan); *Masada* by Gloria Miklowitz; *Forgive the River, Forgive the Sky* by Gloria Whelan; and *A Traitor Among Us* by Elizabeth Van Steenwyk.

Eerdmans also publishes two photo-biographies for young adults: *Princess Kai'ulani: Hope of a Nation, Heart of a People* by Sharon Linnea, and *William Bradford: Plymouth's Faithful Pilgrim* by Gary Schmidt. Eerdmans Books for Young Readers publishes picture books, middle readers, and young adult fiction and nonfiction. The house seeks manuscripts that nurture children's faith in God and that address spiritual themes in thoughtful, authentic, and imaginative ways.

Query letters and SASEs should be directed to:

Judy Zylstra, Children's Book Editor

FELDHEIM PUBLISHERS

200 Airport Executive Park, Nanuet, NY 10954
914-356-2282
www.feldheim.com   e-mail: sales@feldheim.com

Feldheim Publishers (founded in 1954) is among the leading houses in areas of publishing activity that include works of contemporary authors in the field of Orthodox Jewish thought, translations from Hebrew of Jewish classical works, dictionaries and general reference works, textbooks, and guides for Sabbaths and festivals, as well as literature for readers ages three and up (Young Readers Division). The Feldheim publishing program is expanding, and the house releases an increasing number of new titles each season. Feldheim retains a comprehensive backlist.

From Feldheim: *Gateway to Heaven* by Rabbi Naftali Hoffner; *The Halacha Bencher* by Yisroel Pinchos Bodner; *In Honor of Shabbos: Sefer Zemiros from the Jerusalem Siddur* (translated by Avraham Sutton); *Serving our Creator* by Rabbi Moshe Chaim Luzzatto (translated by Rabbi Aryeh Kaplan); *Pathways to the Way of God* by Rabbi Avraham Yaakov Katz; *Orchos Tzaddikim: The Ways of the Tzaddikim* (edited by Rabbi BenZion Sobel, translated by Rabbi Shraga Silverstein); *Torah Guide to Money Matters: For Home, Business & Everyday Life* by Rabbi S. Wagschal; *Practical Judaism* by Rabbi Yisrael Meir Lau; *The Warsaw Ghetto Diaries* by Dr. Hillel Siedman; *The Beginner's Kosher Cookbook* by Seymour Fiedler; *Facing Adversity with Faith* by M. L. Cramer.

Feldheim Publishers handles its own distribution, as well as offers books of additional publishers such as American Yisroel Chai Press and Targum Press.

Query letters and SASEs should be directed to:

Yitzchak Feldheim, President

F

FRIENDSHIP PRESS

National Council of the Churches of Christ, 475 Riverside Drive, Room 860, New York, NY 10115-0050
212-870-2383

The Friendship list encompasses religious books as well as mainstream trade titles in the public-interest realm that address contemporary topics, including: cultural pluralism, the media, global awareness, health and wholeness, technology and the environment, human rights, and world peace. Friendship also produces ecumenical religious, spiritual, inspirational, and educational program materials intended for the use of adults, youths, and children. The house offers several lines of videos, maps, notecards, and informational posters.

Friendship Press was established in 1902 as a missionary education movement in the United States and Canada. Now part of the National Council of the Churches of Christ USA, Friendship Press is a leading ecumenical publisher of educational materials for schools and parishes.

Titles from Friendship Press: *Families Valued: Parenting and Politics for the Good of All Children* by Jack Nelson-Pallmeyer; *Leader's Guide to Uprooted! Refugees and Forced Migrants* by Elizabeth C. Ferris; *Indonesia in Shadow and Light* by John Campbell-Nelson; *First, We Must Listen: Living in a Multicultural Society* (edited by Anne Leo Ellis); *Having Gifts That Differ: Profiles of Ecumenical Churches* by Peggy L. Shriver; *Swallow's Nest: A Feminine Reading of the Psalms* by Marchiene Vroon Rienstra; *Breach of Promise: Portraits of Poverty in North America* by James A. Gittings; *The Mything Link: A Study Guide on Gospel, Culture and Media* by Dave Pomeroy; *Torch in the Night: Worship Resources from South Africa* by Anne Hope; *The Indian Awakening in Latin America* (edited by Yves Materne); *The Caribbean: Culture of Resistance, Spirit of Hope* (edited by Oscar Bolioli); *Remembering the Future: The Challenge of the Churches in Europe* (edited by Robert C. Lodwick).

Friendship Press publishes a limited number of new titles per season—most of which are commissioned additions to the house's ongoing curriculum series. Friendship is, however, open to considering manuscripts by authors written from an embracing global cultural perspective.

Friendship Press distributes its own list.

Query letters and SASEs should be directed to:

Roger Burgess, Executive Director

Susan C. Winslow, Senior Editor

GLENEIDA PUBLISHING GROUP

See Baker Book House and Liguori Publications.

GOSPEL LIGHT PUBLICATIONS

Regal Books

Renew Books

2300 Knoll Drive, Ventura CA 93003
805-644-9721

Gospel Light (founded in 1933) accents titles in general religious interest, religious education, and juveniles; the house also offers video and audio selections. Divisions of Gospel Light include: Regal Books (founded in 1965), which specializes in resources for evangelism, discipleship, and Christian education; Renew Books (founded in 1997), which serves the fastest-growing segment of the Church worldwide—those experiencing awakening and renewal with an expectancy for revival.

The publisher's mission is to equip all Christians, their churches, their communities, and their world with the good news of Jesus Christ. The Gospel Light/Regal trade motto is "Bright ideas to help you grow."

Gospel Light highlights: *Stomping Out the Darkness* by Neil T. Anderson and Dave Park; *The Voice of God* by Cindy Jacobs; *The Measure of a Man* by Gene Getz; *So You're Getting Married* by H. Norman Wright; *Peace Child* by Don Richardson; *Pastors of Promise* by Jack W. Hayford; *Praying with Power* by C. Peter Wagner; *Understanding the Blood of Christ* by David Alsobrook; *Our Daily Walk* by Jack Hayford; *Explaining Blessings and Curses* by Derek Prince; *Angels, Demons & Spiritual Warfare* by Trevor Newport; *Rivers of Revival: How God Is Moving and Pouring Himself Out on His People Today* by Elmer Towns and Neil Anderson; *Stand in the Gap: How God Can Use You Where You Are to Change the World* by David Bryant; *How to Run a Life-Giving Church* by Ted Haggard and Lance Coles.

Regal titles: *Always Daddy's Girl* by H. Norman Wright; *Caring Enough to Forgive* by David Augsburger; *Autobiography of God* by Lloyd John Ogilvie; *The Delicate Art of Dancing with Porcupines* by Bob Phillips; *Communication: Key to Your Marriage* by H. Norman Wright; *I'd Speak Out on the Issues . . . If I Only Knew What to Say* by Jane Chastain; *Dream Big: The Henrietta Mears Story* (edited by Earl Roe); *Emotions: Can You Trust Them?* by Dr. James Dobson; *How to Be a Christian Without Being Religious* by Fritz Ridenour; *Healing America's Wounds* by John Dawson.

Renew titles: *As in the Days of Noah: God's Judgement on the Nations* by Johannes Facius; *Dearly Beloved . . . Letters of Faith and Encouragement to Overcoming Saints* by Paul and Gretel Haglin; *Forgive, Release and Be Free!* by Joff Day; *Don't Talk to Me Now, Lord . . . I'm Trying to Pray* by Steve Sampson; *Evicting Demonic Intruders* by Noel and Phyl Gibson.

On the Regal list of children's and youth books: *Busting Free: Helping Youth Discover Their Identity in Christ* by Neil T. Anderson and Dave Park; *What Hollywood Won't Tell You About Love, Sex, and Dating* by Susie Shellenberger and Greg Johnson.

Gospel Light oversees its own distribution.

Unsolicited manuscripts are not accepted.

Query letters and SASEs should be directed to:

Kyle Duncan, Acquisitions

HARPERSANFRANCISCO

353 Sacramento Street, Suite 500, San Francisco, CA 94111-3653
415-477-4400   fax: 415-477-4444
www.harpercollins.com/sanfran   e-mail: hcsanfrancisco@harpercollins.com

HarperSanFrancisco strives to be the preeminent publisher of the most important books across the full spectrum of religion and spiritual literature, adding to the wealth of the world's wisdom by respecting all traditions and favoring none. It publishes books in the areas of spirituality, religion, and inspiration across the full spectrum of religious traditions.

HSF focuses on books that inspire and nurture the mind, body, and spirit; explore the essential religious, spiritual, and philosophical questions; present the rich and diverse array of cultures and their wisdom traditions; and support readers in their ongoing personal discovery and enrichment.

It is the policy of HarperSanFrancisco to publish books that represent important religious groupings, express well-articulated thought, combine intellectual competence and felicitous style, add to the wealth of religious literature irrespective of creedal origin, and aid the cause of religion without proselytizing for any particular sect.

HSF has featured works by Martin Luther King, Jr., Huston Smith, Billy Graham, Mother Teresa, Marcus Borg, John Shelby Sporg, the Dalai Lama, C. S. Lewis, Matthew Fox, and Melodie Beattie. The house is corporately affiliated with the editorially independent Zondervan, subsidiary of HarperCollins (see separate Zondervan listing), which focuses on books for the evangelical Christian market.

HarperSanFrancisco is literally a division of the international HarperCollins corporate family of publisher HarperCollins Adult Trade Division (which includes imprints emanating from the HarperCollins New York offices; see HarperCollins in U.S. Publishers section). HarperSanFrancisco benefits directly from core HarperCollins marketing, sales, and power and retains its editorial and marketing independence and identity.

Frontlist trade books from HarperSanFrancisco: *The Hidden Book in the Bible* by Richard Elliott Friedman; *The Four Witnesses* by Robin Griffith-Jones; *Harper's Bible Commentary* by James L. Mays, General Editor with the Society of Biblical Literature; *Just as I Am* by Billy Graham; *Here I Stand* by John Shelby Spong; *The Next Pope* by Peter Hebblethwaite, revised and updated by Margaret Hebblethwaite; *A Search for Solitude* by Thomas Merton; *The Eyes of the Heart* by Frederick Buechner; *Essential Monastic Wisdom* by Hugh Feiss, OS.B; *Living Jesus* by Luke Timothy Johnson; *Finding Your Religion: When the Faith You Grew Up with Has Lost Its Meaning* by Rev. Scotty McLennan; *The Intimate Merton* by Thomas Merton; *The Divine Conspiracy* by Dallas Willard; *Stand and Be Counted* by David Crosby and David Bender; *The Heart Math Solution* by Doc Childre and Howard Martin, with Donna Beech; *The Living Beauty Detox Program* by Ann Loise Gittleman, M.S., C.N.S.; *Generation J* by Lisa Schiffman; *C. S. Lewis: A Companion and Guide* by Walter Hooper; *The Heart of the Tarot* by Sandra A. Thomson, E.D.D., Robert E. Mueller, Ph.D., and Signe E. Nichols, M.S.

The house invites prospective authors to correspond first via a brief query letter describing the essential character of the projected work, along with author qualifications and any previous books or professional credentials. Detailed guidelines for submissions are available upon request from the editorial department.

HarperSanFrancisco titles are distributed by HarperCollins Publishers in Scranton, Pennsylvania.

Query letters and SASEs should be directed to:

David Hennessy, Associate Editor

Elizabeth Perle, Editor at Large—Psychology/self-help; women and family, biography, alternative and complementary health; Buddhist and Jewish spirituality; lesbian and gay studies; multicultural studies.

Gideon Weil, Associate Editor

John V. Loudon, Executive Editor—Religious studies, biblical studies, psychology/personal growth, inspiration, Eastern religions, Buddhist and Christian spirituality.

Renee Sedliar, Assistant Editor

H

HARVEST HOUSE PUBLISHERS

1075 Arrowsmith, Eugene, OR 97402-9197
541-343-0123   fax: 541-342-6410

Harvest House produces religious-oriented nonfiction and fiction, Bible study and theological thought, and educational and devotional resources. Harvest House frontlist titles address topics of current interest, often with widespread implications on the social-religious front. Subjects include media, technology, politics; parenting, youth, relationships, and the family; Christian living and contemporary values; cults and the occult; personal awareness, inspiration, and spiritual growth; Christian history and heritage; and humor.

The publisher's nondenominational list features many works that offer an evangelical Christian perspective and includes a number of notably individualist author voices. Harvest House publishes books in hardcover, trade paperback, and mass-market paperback editions.

The house issues a number of strong lines directed toward the children's-and-youth market (please see separate subentry further on). Harvest House also produces books in the Spanish language, as well as audiobooks, calendars, and daily planners.

Harvest House Publishers (founded in 1974) holds the following credo for books and other product lines: "Helping people grow spiritually strong."

Nonfiction titles: *A Sanctuary for Your Soul* by Kay Arthur; *Heaven Sent* by Kathryn Andrews Fincher; *A Garden Full of Love* by Sandra Kuck; *Friends of the Heart* by Emilie Barnes and Donna Otto; *Whispers of Prayer* by Emilie Barnes; *How Big Is God's Love* by David and Helen Haidle; *Moms Who Have Changed the World* by Lindsey O'Connor; *Just Enough Light for the Step I'm on* by Stormie Omartian; *Unquenchable Love* by David and Heather Kopp; *Hidden Agendas for the New Millennium* by Dave Hunt; *Foreshadows of Wrath and Redemption* by William T. James; *Bruce and Stan's Guide to the End of the World* by Bruce Bickel and Stan Jantz; *What Every Catholic Should Ask* by Jim McCarthy; *A Friend Like You* by D. Morgan; *Hats Off to You,* also by Sandy Lynam Clough; *Stepping Out* by Pam Farrel; *A Romantic Treasury of Love* by Gay Talbott Boassy; *Celebrating Our Family* by Ruthann Winans and Linda Lee; *God Is Your Hope: His Love Never Fails* by Marie Shropshire; *Decorating Dreams on a Budget* by Yoli Brogger.

Special Harvest House project: *Simpler Times* by Thomas Kinkade, an artist renowned for light-infused paintings of nostalgic, heartwarming scenes, combines his visual talents with thoughtful narrative in this exquisitely designed gift book. More than 20 full-color paintings are accompanied by Thomas Kinkade's thoughts on living in a complex age, keeping perspective, and creating balance. Additional titles in the Lighted Path Collection include: *Home Is Where the Heart Is; Glory of Creation; I'll Be Home for Christmas, Romantic Hideaways; Beyond the Garden Gate.*

Fiction from Harvest House includes mainstream novels with a religious accent; historical adventure tales; Bible-based stories; books geared toward a women's readership (including romances); occult thrillers; mystery and suspense fiction; and futuristic works.

Biblical and historical fiction from Harvest House: *The Princess* by Lori Wick; *Island Bride* by Linda Chaikin; *Magnolia Dreams* by Virginia Gaffney; *Promise Me Tomorrow* by Lori Wick; *The Moment I Saw You* by Lisa Samson; *Captive Heart* by Linda Chaikin.

Harvest House manages its own distributional network.

Harvest House Books for Children and Young Adults

Harvest House produces a selection of books directed toward a youthful readership, as well as titles of interest to teachers and parents. The solid list encompasses board books, picture books, storybooks, interactive books, joke books, general nonfiction, and novels (including a number of successful series).

On the Harvest House children's-and-youth list *Let's Make Something Fun* by Emilie Barnes; *Nighty Night, Sleep Tight* (board book) by Michael Sparks; *The Bondage Breaker Youth Edition* by Neil T. Anderson and Dave Park; *Extremely Good Clean Jokes for Kids* by Bob Phillips.

Query letters and SASEs should be directed to:

Manuscript Coordinator

HAZELDEN PUBLISHING GROUP

Hazelden Foundation

15251 Pleasant Valley Road, P.O. Box 176, Center City, MN 55012-0176
612-257-4010
www.hazelden.org

Hazelden Publishing Group issues books for a general and professional readership in such areas as awareness, discovery, wholeness and transformation, meditation, recovery, personal and spiritual growth, self-help, spirituality, substance abuse, and compulsive behaviors. The house's backlist represents all areas of the Hazelden publishing program.

The Hazelden publications and marketing vision encompass books, pamphlets, audiocassettes and videocassettes, computer software, calendars, organizers, and books for young readers, along with a gift line.

Hazelden: A Mission in Motion. When Hazelden opened its doors nearly 50 years ago, the mission seemed simple: to rehabilitate clients and restore self-worth and dignity to their lives. Hazelden still commits to this mission as a multidimensional organization involved in public policy, research, education, evaluation, and many other areas of chemical dependency. Hazelden has become a respected leader in the chemical-dependency field and the premier publisher of bibliotherapy. As a pioneer in addiction research and education, Hazelden's clinical expertise is reflected in educational materials that cover a wide range of topics in the treatment of chemical dependency and other additions. Core to the success of the treatment process, Hazelden materials interact with clients. This matrix of materials reinforces important information to clients. Most of all, these materials are a concrete way for clients to retain the concepts they learn in treatment.

Hazelden was established as a publishing operation (in 1954, as Hazelden Educational Materials) with the hardcover release of *Twenty-Four Hours a Day* by Rich W (still in print in hardcover and paperback editions). Hazelden is a division of the Hazelden Foundation, which also operates a network of recovery centers. The publisher has a major concentration in materials related to the 12-Step approach.

In early 1994, Hazelden purchased CompCare and Parkside, two former niche publishers (both with strong backlists) in areas consistent with Hazelden's publishing range—particularly in treatment and recovery titles, as well as in the broader general-interest trade arena. Hazelden also bought PIA (Psychiatric Institute of America), a publisher with similar scope. The titles of these publishers have been folded into the Hazelden list, thereby augmenting Hazelden's preeminence in this particular publishing arena.

In addition to the aforementioned *Twenty-Four Hours a Day,* Hazelden's bestselling trade entrants include *Codependent No More* and *The Language of Letting Go* (both by Melody Beattie), and *Each Day a New Beginning.*

From Hazelden: *Denial Is Not a River in Egypt* by Sandi Bachom; *Pavement for My Pillow: A Homeless Woman's Climb from Degradation to Dignity* by Chris Kitch; *Love, Soul, and Freedom: Dancing with Rumi on the Mystic's Path: Featuring the Translations of Rumi* by Coleman Barks; *Cracking Up: Nice Day for a Brain Hemorrhage* by Peter Swet; *The Great Leap: Face-to-Face with Initiation and Growth* by Hans and Hanneke Korteweg, with Jaap Voigt; *Consuming Confessions; The Paradigm Conspiracy; Self-Esteem: A Family Affair* by Jean Illsley Clarke; *Easing the Ache: Gay Men Recovering from Compulsive Behavior* by Gay Kettlehack; *To Understand and Be Understood: A Practical Guide to Successful Relationships* by Erik Blumenthal; *Life on the Edge: Parenting a Child with ADD/ADHD* by David Spohn; *A Broken Heart Still Beats: After Your Child Dies* by Mary Semel and Anne McCracken; *The Way to Inner Freedom: A Practical Guide to Personal Development* by Erik Blumenthal.

Representing the Hazelden children's program: *The Cat at the Door and Other Stories to Live By: Affirmations for Children* by Anne D. Mather and Louise B. Weldon (illustrated by Lyn Martin); *Making the Most of Today: Daily Readings for Young People on Self-Awareness, Creativity, and Self-Esteem* by Pamela Espeland and Rosemary Wallner; *Starry Night* (written and illustrated by David Spohn).

Hazelden furnishes its titles to the bookstore trade directly and has made inroads into the gift-distribution world. Additional marketing avenues for Hazelden trade titles include the house's direct-to-the-consumer mail-order business. Hazelden books are popular items worldwide, with a foreign distribution network that includes Russia and Canada.

Other areas to which Hazelden markets include: structured care (Hazelden develops and markets print, audio, and visual materials for treatment centers, hospitals, and professional markets); prevention, education, and professional training (the publisher accesses the markets of primary and secondary schools, counselor-training programs, and community prevention and treatment programs); and corrections (the publisher addresses the needs of county, state, and federal corrections facilities).

Query letters and SASEs should be directed to:

Becky Post, Executive Editor

Betty Greydanus, Administrative Assistant

H

HEBREW PUBLISHING COMPANY

P.O. Box 222, Spencertown, NY 12165
518-392-3322   fax: 518-392-4280

Hebrew Publishing Company (established in 1901) offers a wide range of titles in such categories as reference and dictionaries; religion, law, and thought; Rabbinic literature; literature; history and biography; children's books; Hebrew-language textbooks and Hebrew culture;

Yiddish; Bible, Hebrew/English; Bible, English only; prayers and liturgy: daily, Hebrew only, and Hebrew/English; prayers and liturgy: Sabbath, high holidays, and festivals; prayers and liturgy: memorial; prayers and liturgy: Purim; general prayers and liturgy; Hanukkah items; Haggadahs; educational materials; sermons and aids of the rabbi; and calendars. The house publishes a limited number of new titles and maintains an established backlist.

On the HPC list: *Yom Kippur* by Philip Birnbaum; *Judaism as a Civilization* by Mordecai Kaplan; *Acharon Hamohikanim* (The Last of the Mohicans) by James Fenimore Cooper; *Business Ethics in Jewish Law* (Jung/Levine); *Encyclopedia of Jewish Concepts* by Philip Birnbaum; *Rahel Varnhagen: The Life of a Jewess* by Hannah Arendt; *Torah and Tradition* by Orenstein and Frankel; *Jewish Tales and Legends* by Menachem Glen.

Hebrew Publishing Company oversees its own distribution, utilizing services of independent fulfillment and distribution firms. Query letters and SASEs should be directed to:

Charles Lieber, Editor in Chief

HEBREW UNION COLLEGE PRESS
3101 Clifton Avenue, Cincinnati, OH 45220-2488
513-221-1875   e-mail: hucpress@huc.edu

Hebrew Union publishes scholarly Judaica, along with some frontlist titles of broader appeal. Within the Hebrew Union College scope are books representing a variety of divisions, institutions, and programs: Klau Library, Skirball Museum, Kuntresim (Hebrew texts copublished with Ben-Zion Dinur Center of the Hebrew University), the journals *Hebrew Union College Annual* and *American Jewish Archives,* and special-interest projects (such as books and videotapes) from HUC-UC Ethics Center.

Hebrew Union College Press (founded in 1921) publishes a select list of new titles covering a full range of its list, while tending a full backlist. HUC engages in copublishing projects with other institutions, including Harvard University Press, KTAV Publishing House, University of Alabama Press, and Yale University Press.

From Hebrew Union College Press: *"Your Voice Like a Ram's Horn": Themes and Texts in Traditional Jewish Preaching* by Marc Saperstein; *No Way Out: The Politics of Polish Jewry 1935–1939* by Emanuel Melzer; *Ideals Face Reality: Jewish Law and Life in Poland 1550–1655* by Edward Fram; *The Jews in European History: Seven Lectures* by Eberhard Jackel; *"To Write the Lips of Sleepers": The Poetry of Amir Gilboa* by Warren Bargad; *German Jews Beyond Judaism* by George L. Mosse; *The Jew in the Medieval World: A Source Book: 315–1791* by Jacob Rader Marcus; *To Worship Properly: Tensions Between Liturgical Custom and Halakhah in Judaism* by Ruth Langer; *Karaite Separatism in Nineteenth-Century Russia* by Philip Miller; *The Merit of Our Mothers: A Bilingual Anthology of Jewish Women's Prayers* (compiled by Tracy Guren Klirs); *Jewish Lore in Manichaean Cosmogony: Studies in the Book of Giants Traditions* by John C. Reeves; *The Jews of Dynastic China: A Critical Bibliography* by Michael Pollak.

HUC welcomes the submission of scholarly manuscripts in all areas of Judaica. For further information, contact Professor Michael Meyer, Chair, Publications Committee, at the publisher's address.

H

Hebrew Union College Press is distributed by Wayne State University Press. Query letters and SASEs should be directed to:

Barbara Selya, Managing Editor

HORIZON PUBLISHERS, NOW PART OF CORNERSTONE

50 South 500 West, P.O. Box 490, Bountiful, UT 84011-0490
fax: 801-295-0196
www.horizonpublishers.com   e-mail: horizonp@burgoyne.com

Horizon Publishers (founded in 1971) was purchased in August 2000 by Cornerstone Publishing & Distribution, Inc. Cornerstone will continue to distribute Horizon's list and use the Horizon Publishers imprint on selected works. The combined companies form a smaller house that produces hardcover and paperback works with emphasis in the areas of religion, inspiration, youth and adult fiction, cooking and food storage, emergency preparedness, outdoor living, music and art, marriage and family, children's books, and crafts (especially cross-stitch).

Cornerstone is a privately owned corporation with no ecclesiastical ties. The main readership of the house's theological works is Latter-Day Saint (Mormon), so most of its religious works are compatible with that doctrinal perspective, but many are aimed at a wider Christian audience. Cornerstone/Horizon's publishing interest encompasses books on doctrine and church history, children's religious teaching, inspirational and doctrinal talk tapes, religious music, and art. Its list includes religious humor, faith-promoting experiences, historical works, biographies of well-known leaders, doctrinal studies, and fiction for middle-grade, young adult, and adult readers.

The house's guidelines for authors are filled with apt advice for all writers.

Representative of the Cornerstone/Horizon list: *Organize My Kingdom : A History of Restored Priesthood* by John A. Tvedtnes; *How Greek Philosophy Corrupted the Christian Concept of God* by Richard R. Hopkins; *Prophecy: Key to the Future* by Duane S. Crowther; *One in a Billion* by Sharlee Mullins Glenn, illustrated by Rachel Hoffman-Bayles; *The Latter Day Girl Collection,* with stories for middle readers by Carol Lynch Williams and Laurel Stowe Brady; *Let's Cook Dutch! A Complete Guide for the Dutch Oven Chef* by Robert L. Ririe; *Favorite Utah Pioneer Recipes* by Marla Rawlings; *You Can Stay Alive: Wilderness Living and Emergency Survival* by Larry J. Wells and Roger G. Giles; *Journeys Beyond Life: True Accounts of Next World Experiences* by Arvin S. Gibson.

Fiction titles: *Thy Kingdom Come, Volume 1: Prodigal Journey* by Linda Paulson Adams; *Singled Out* by Eric Samuelsen; *The Wise Man in the Checkered Shirt* by Michael Drake; *Crescendo* by Terry J. Moyer.

Family-oriented books: *How to Raise Kids Without Climbing the Walls* by Larry G. Brady, Ph.D.; *Making Marriage Magnificent* by Reed and Lorena Markham; *Family Home Evenings for Dads* by Dianne Friden, Carolyn Seimers, and Barbara Thackeray.

Cornerstone/Horizon handles its own distribution. Query letters and SASEs should be directed to:

The Editorial Board

INNER TRADITIONS INTERNATIONAL

One Park Street, Rochester, VT 05767
802-767-3174   fax: 802-767-3726
www.InnerTraditions.com   e-mail: (contact name)@gotoit.com

Inner Traditions publishes across such subject areas as acupuncture, anthroposophy, aromatherapy, the arts, astrology, bodywork, cookbooks, crafts, cultural studies, earth studies, Egyptian studies, gemstones, health and healing, homeopathy, indigenous cultures, African-American traditions, inner traditions of the West and the East, myth and legend, massage, natural medicine, self-transformation, sacred sexuality, spirituality, and travel.

Inner Traditions International (founded in 1975) produces hardcover trade books and trade paperbacks, illustrated gift books, and mass-market paperback editions, as well as a line of audioworks and selected videotapes. The house also packages specialty items such as boxed sets and tarot decks.

Special imprints include Destiny Books, Destiny Recordings, Healing Arts Press, and Park Street Press. Inner Traditions en Español is a line published in the Spanish language. Inner Traditions India issues works aimed at the Indian market. The house has announced a forthcoming slate of multimedia titles in the works. Inner Traditions International publishes a medium-sized list each year and maintains a strong backlist.

The Inner Traditions imprint accents works that represent the spiritual, cultural, and mythic traditions of the world, focusing on inner wisdom and the perennial philosophies.

Inner Traditions imprint titles: *The Celtic Wisdom of Tarot* by Caitlin Matthews; *Ritual Art of India* by Ajit Mookerjee; *The Prozac Alternative: Natural Relief from Depression with St. John's Wort, Kava, and Other Alternative Therapies* by Ran Knishinsky; *The Healing Cuisine of China: 300 Recipes for Vibrant Health and Longevity* by Zhuo Zhao and George Ellis; *The Lost Treasure of the Knights Templar: Solving the Oak Island Mystery* by Steven Sora; *Renewing the Covenant: A Kabbalistic Guide to Jewish Spirituality* by Leonora Leet; *Sacred Woman, Sacred Dance: Awakening Spirituality Through Movement and Ritual* by Iris J. Stewart; *The Arthritis Bible* by Leonid Gordin, M.D., and Craig Weatherby; *Chinese Massage for Infants and Children: Traditional Techniques for Alleviating Colic, A Yoga of Indian Classical Dance: The Yogini's Mirror* by Roxanne Kamayani Gupta; *Dog's Best Friend: Journey to the Roots of an Ancient Partnership* by Ursula Birr, Gerald Krakauer, and Daniela Osiander; *The Secret Doctrine of the Kabbalah: Recovering the Key to Hebraic Sacred Science* by Leonora Leet; *The Heart of Yoga: Developing a Personal Practice* by T. K. V. Desikachar; *Soma: The Divine Hallucinogen* by David Spess; *A Brief History of Drugs: From the Stone Age to the Stoned Age* by Antonio Escohotado (translated by Ken Symington); *Advanced Bach Flower Therapy: A Scientific Approach to Diagnosis and Treatment* by Gotz Blome, M.D. Destiny Books are contemporary metaphysical titles for a popular audience, with special emphasis on self-transformation, the occult, and psychological well-being. Destiny Recordings are cassettes and compact discs of spiritual and indigenous music traditions. Destiny Audio Editions include Inner Traditions books on tape, as well as original spoken-word cassettes.

Destiny Books titles: *The Nostradamus Code: The Lost Manuscript That Unlocks the Secrets of the Master Prophet* by Ottavio Cesare Ramotti; *The Healing Power of Color:*

Using Color to Improve Your Mental, Physical, and Spiritual Well-Being by Betty Wood; *How to Read the Aura and Practice Psychometry, Telepathy, and Clairvoyance* by W. E. Butler.

Healing Arts Press publishes works on alternative medicine and holistic health that combine contemporary thought and innovative research with the accumulated knowledge of the world's great healing traditions.

Healing Arts Press books: *Traditional Reiki for Our Times: Practical Methods for Personal and Global Healing* by Amy Z. Rowland; *Hildegard von Bingen's Physica: The Complete English Translation of Her Classic Work on Health and Healing* (translated by Priscilla Throop); *Perfect Endings: A Conscious Approach to Dying and Death* by Robert Sachs; *The Estrogen Alternative: Natural Hormone Therapy with Botanical Progesterone* by Raquel Martin with Judi Gerstung, D.C.; *The Book of Ki: A Practical Guide to the Healing Principles of Life Energy* by Mallary Fromm, Ph.D.; *The Herbal Handbook: A User's Guide to Medical Herbalism* by David Hoffmann.

Park Street Press produces books on travel, psychology, consumer and environmental issues, archaeology, women's and men's studies, and fine art.

Park Street Press titles: *Sharp Spear, Crystal Mirror: Martial Arts in Women's Lives* by Stephanie T. Hoppe; *Creepy Crawly Cuisine: The Gourmet Guide to Edible Insects* by Julieta Ramos-Elorduy, Ph.D. (photographs by Peter Menzel); *Phantastica: A Classic Survey on the Use and Abuse of Mind-Altering Plants* by Louis Lewin, M.D.; *Shattering the Myths of Darwinism* by Richard Milton; *Sirens: Symbols of Seduction* by Meri Lao.

Inner Traditions en Español is the house's Spanish-language publishing program, in cooperation with Lasser Press of Mexico City. This line includes popular titles from a variety of Inner Tradition imprints.

Selections from the Inner Traditions en Español list: *Secretos Sexuales* (Sexual Secrets) by Nik Douglas and Penny Slinger; *Astrología Dinámica* (Dynamic Astrology) by John Townley; *El Cáñamo para la Salud* (Hemp for Health) by Chris Conrad.

Kits and gift packages from Inner Traditions: *The Book of Doors Divination Deck* by Athon Veggi and Allison Davidson; *The Lakota Sioux Sweat Lodge Cards* by Chief Archie Fire Lame Deer and Helene Sarks; *Leela: The Game of Self-Knowledge* by Harish Johari.

Inner Traditions supervises its own distribution. Query letters and SASEs should be directed to:

Jon Graham, Acquisitions Editor

INNISFREE PRESS

136 Roumfort Road, Philadelphia, PA 19119-1632
215-247-4085, 800-367-5872   fax: 215-247-2343
www.innisfreepress.com

Innisfree is a creative publishing forum for books that feature the areas of personal growth with spiritual and feminine dimensions. The editorial sphere encompasses self-discovery, relationships, nutrition, writing and journaling, healing and inspiration, transition and renewal, Bible study, and meditation. Innisfree acquired LuraMedia in late 1996.

From the Innisfree list: *Circle of Stones: Woman's Journey to Herself* by Judith Duerk; *Suncatcher: A Study of Madeleine L'Engle and Her Writing* by Carole Chase; *Everyday Edens: Experiences of Personal Sacred Space* by Phyllis Cole-Dai (photographs by James Murray); *The Tao of Eating* by Linda Harper; *Return to the Sea: Reflections on Anne Morrow Lindbergh's Gift from the Sea* by Anne M. Johnson; *Family Puzzles: A Private Life Made Public* by Linda Weltner; *The Woman Who Lost Her Heart: A Tale of Reawakening* by Sue O'Halloran and Susan Delattre; *Whole Earth Meditation: Ecology for the Spirit* by Joan Sauro; *Sabbath Sense: A Spiritual Antidote for the Overworked* by Donna Schaper.

LuraMedia, Inc. (founded in 1982) was known as a small house that undertook to select, design, produce, and distribute its list with care and flair; the publisher's stated goal was to provide materials that foster healing and hope, balance and justice. Effective November 15, 1996, LuraMedia was sold to Innisfree Press in Philadelphia, Pennsylvania, and the San Diego office of LuraMedia closed. LuraMedia books are available through the new company.

Innisfree distributes to the trade via Consortium. Query letters and SASEs should be directed to:

Marcia Broucek, Publisher

INTERVARSITY PRESS

InterVarsity Christian Fellowship of the USA, P.O. Box 1400, Downers Grove, IL 60515
630-734-4000   fax: 630-734-4200
www.ivpress.com   e-mail: mail@ivpress.com

InterVarsity Press publications embrace the main fields of Bible study guides, reference books, academic and theological books, and issue-oriented books of general interest to educated Christians.

Nonfiction categories in areas of contemporary religious interest include titles in self-improvement, spirituality, and interpersonal relations. The house also produces humor.

InterVarsity Press (founded in 1947) is the publishing arm of InterVarsity Christian Fellowship of the USA. The press operates within IVCF's framework and publishes interdenominational books (in hardback and paperback) under the banner "Heart. Soul. Mind. Strength."

Indicative of the InterVarsity Press nonfiction frontlist: *Making Life Work* by Bill Hybels; *The Wedge of Truth,* by Phillip E. Johnson; *Soul Craft* by Douglas Webster; *Habits of the Mind* by James W. Sire; *The Holy Spirit* by Donald Bloesch; *The Challenge of Jesus* by N. T. Wright; *Church Next* by Eddie Gibbs; *Love, Honor & Forgive* by Bill and Pam Fanel; *Never Beyond Hope* by J. I. Packer.

LifeGuide Bible Studies introduces new titles that focus on particular scriptural areas and specific books of the Bible. Other Bible studies are published each year.

I

A full set of guidelines for manuscript submission to InterVarsity Press is available upon request from the publisher.

Query letters and SASEs should be directed to:

Andrew T. Le Peau, Editorial Director

JEWISH LIGHTS PUBLISHING

P.O. Box 237, Sunset Farm Offices, Route 4, Woodstock, VT 05091
802-457-4000   fax: 802-457-4004
www.jewishlights.com

Jewish Lights Publishing shows a vigorous approach to titles "for people of all faiths, all backgrounds." Its books cover Jewish spirituality, life cycle, self-help/healing, theology, history, and contemporary culture—all within the trade motto "Words for the soul—made in Vermont." Jewish Lights offers books in hardcover, quality paperback, and gift editions.

Jewish Lights features authors at the forefront of spiritual thought. Each voice is unique, and each speaks in a way readers can hear. Jewish Lights books are judged as successful not only by whether they are beautiful and commercially successful, but by the difference they make in their readers' lives.

Jewish Lights Publishing (founded in 1990), a division of LongHill Partners, Inc., describes itself as publishing books that reflect the Jewish wisdom tradition for people of all faiths and all backgrounds. Its books really focus on the issue of the quest for the self, seeking meaning in life. They are books that help you to understand who you are and who you might become as a Jewish person, or as a person who is part of a tradition that has its roots in the Judeo-Christian world. The books deal with issues of personal growth and issues of religious inspiration.

Jewish Lights' principal goal is to stimulate thought and help all people learn about who the Jewish People are, where they come from, and what the future can be made to hold. Although people of diverse Jewish heritage are the primary audience, Jewish Lights books speak to people in the Christian world as well and will broaden their understanding of Judaism and the roots of their own faith.

Jewish Lights seeks out materials about the unity and community of the Jewish People and the relevance of Judaism to everyday life. To help in these efforts, respectful of the rich diversity of the Jewish heritage, the publisher has established an Advisory Board representing a broad range of Jewish perspectives. The Advisory Board helps seek out new material and provides insights into the publishing needs of the Jewish community.

The press publishes the award-winning Kushner Series: *Classics of Modern Jewish Spirituality* by Lawrence Kushner. A related special-edition project is *The Book of Letters: A Mystical Hebrew Alphabet* (designed by Lawrence Kushner).

From Jewish Lights: *The Book of Words: Talking Spiritual Life, Living Spiritual Talk* by Lawrence Kushner; *Eyes Remade for Wonder,* also by Lawrence Kushner; *Finding Joy: A Practical Spiritual Guide to Happiness* by Daniel L. Schwartz, with Mark Hass; *How to Claim the Spiritual Meaning of Your Bar or Bat Mitzvah Moses—The Prince, the Prophet: His Life, Legend & Message for Our Lives* by Rabbi Levi Meier, Ph.D.; *Parent-*

ing as a Spiritual Journey: Deepening Ordinary & Extraordinary Events into Sacred Occasions by Rabbi Nancy Fuchs-Kreimer; *Tears of Sorrow, Voices from Genesis: Guiding Us Through the Stages of Life* by Norman J. Cohen; *The Year Mom Got Religion: One Woman's Midlife Journey into Judaism* by Lee Meyerhoff Hendler; *Embracing the Covenant: Converts to Judaism Talk About Why & How* (edited by Rabbi Allan Berkowitz and Patti Moskovitz).

The Art of Jewish Living series from the Federation of Jewish Men's Clubs provides the following titles: *A Time to Mourn, a Time to Comfort: A Guide to Jewish Bereavement and Comfort; The Shabbat Seder;* and *Hanukkah* by Dr. Ron Wolfson.

The Jewish Thought Series from Israel's MOD Books is distributed exclusively by Jewish Lights. A part of Israel's Broadcast University Series, the books are written by leading experts and authors in their respective fields. Titles are published jointly by Tel Aviv University, the Chief Education office of the IDF, and IDF Radio. Selected series offerings: *Jerusalem in the 19th Century* by Yehoshua Ben-Arieh; *Jewish Reactions to the Holocaust* by Yehuda Bauer; *Lectures on the Philosophy of Spinoza* by Professor Yosef Ben-Shlomo; *The Spiritual History of the Dead Sea Sect* by David Flusser; *The World of the Aggadah* by Avigdor Shinan; *Human Rights in the Bible and Talmud* by Haim H. Cohn.

Children's titles and books for the family from Jewish Lights: *A Prayer for the Earth: The Story of Naamah, Noah's Wife* by Sandy Eisenberg Sasso (illustrated by Bethanne Andersen); *When a Grandparent Dies: A Child's Own Workbook for Dealing with Shiva and the Year Beyond* by Nechama Liss-Levenson; *The New Jewish Baby Book: A Guide to Choices for Today's Families* by Anita Diamant.

Jewish Lights Publishing handles its own distribution.

Query letters and SASEs should be directed to:

Stuart M. Matlins, Editor in Chief

THE JEWISH PUBLICATION SOCIETY

2100 Arch Street, 2nd floor, Philadelphia, PA 19103
215-832-0609   fax: 215-568-2017
www.jewishpub.org   e-mail: Jewishbook@aol.com

The Jewish Publication Society specializes in hardcover and trade paperback books of Jewish interest, especially traditional religious works (including the Torah), as well as relevant commentaries and resources for Jewish life.

The Jewish Publication Society (founded in 1888) upholds a commitment to the English-speaking Jewish community by publishing works of exceptional scholarship, contemporary significance, and enduring value. The publisher traditionally assumes a demanding balancing act among the various denominations of Jewish institutional life, between academic and popular interests, and between past and present visions of Judaism.

Recently published: *Swimming in the Sea of Talmud: Lessons for Everyday Living* by Michael Katz and Gershon Schwartz; *Entering the High Holy Days: A Complete Guide to the History, Prayers and Themes* by Reuven Hammer; *Matters of Life and Death: A Jew-*

J

ish Approach to Modern Medical Ethics by Elliot N. Dorff; *Adoption and the Jewish Family: Contemporary Perspectives* by Shelley Kapnek Rosenberg; *A Time to Be Born: Jewish Birth Customs and Traditions* by Michele Klein, Ph.D.; *Reading Levinas/Reading Talmud: An Introduction* by Ira F. Stone; *The Language of Truth: The Torah Commentary of the Sefat Emet* (translated and interpreted by Arthur Green); *The Shema: Spirituality and Law in Judaism* by Norman Lamm; *Engendering Judaism* by Rachael Adler; *Genesis: The Beginning of Desire* by Avivah Gottlieb Zornberg.

Indicative of JPS nonfiction: *In the Year 1096: The First Crusade and the Jews* by Robert Chazen; *Reclaiming the Dead Sea Scrolls* by Lawrence Schiffman; *On the Possibility of Jewish Mysticism in Our Time* by Gershom Scholem; *On Family and Feminism* by Blu Greenberg; *Blessings* (a prayer book) by Melanie Greenberg.

The Jewish Publication Society is a not-for-profit educational institution that distributes its own list and, through its book club, offers to its membership Judaica from other publishers as well.

Query letters and SASEs should be directed to:

Dr. Ellen Frankel, Editor in Chief, 215-564-5925, ext. 3311

Kar-Ben Copies

6800 Tildenwood Lane, Rockville, MD 20852
301-984-8733, 800-4-KARBEN   fax: 301-881-9195
Order online at: www.karben.com   e-mail: karben@aol.com

Kar-Ben Copies offers an expansive Jewish library for young children and families, as well as teachers. The Kar-Ben list encompasses presentations keyed to high holidays, Sabbath, culture and tradition, and general-interest concepts.

Kar-Ben's children's books are handsomely produced volumes that often incorporate fine illustrative work. The Kar-Ben catalog also highlights books especially for toddlers, as well as a reference line for youngsters (My Very Own Jewish Library). The house also offers audiocassettes and calendars.

Kar-Ben titles: *Kids Love Israel, Israel Loves Kids: A Travel Guide for Families* (revised edition) by Barbara Sofer; *Simchat Torah: A Family Celebration* by Judith Z. Abrams; *Hanukkah, Oh Hanukkah* (illustrated by Miriam Sagasti); *A Costume for Noah: A Purim Story* by Susan Remick Topek; *Israel Fun for Little Hands* by Sally Springer (games, riddles, puzzles, and mazes introduce young children to favorite sites in Israel); *Jewish Holiday Games for Little Hands* by Ruth Esrig Brinn (illustrated by Sally Springer); *Sammy Spider's First Passover* by Sylvia A. Rouss (illustrated by Katherine Janus Kahn); *Brainteasers from Jewish Folklore* by Rosalind Charney Kaye; *Terrible, Terrible!: A Folktale Retold* by Robin Bernstein; *Fins and Scales: A Kosher Tale* by Deborah Miller and Karen Ostrove.

A special Kar-Ben line comprises book-and-cassette packages, with accompanying leader's guides for family services keyed to the high holidays (Selichot, Rosh Hashanah,

K

and Yom Kippur). These works are written by Judith Z. Abrams, designed and illustrated by Katherine Janus Kahn, with original music by Frances T. Goldman.

Kar-Ben (founded in 1976) welcomes comments, kudos, and manuscripts.

Query letters and SASEs should be directed to:

Madeline Wikler, Editor in Chief

H. J. Kramer, Inc.

Starseed Press

P.O. Box 1082, Tiburon, CA 94920
415-435-5367   fax: 415-435-5364

Kramer covers spiritual life, interpersonal relationships, resources for good health, and self-awareness and guidance. The Starseed Press imprint publishes books for younger readers (see subentry further on). Kramer books are finely produced editions in trade paperback and hardcover. The house typically issues a small number of new titles seasonally and sustains a strong backlist.

The books H. J. Kramer publishes are contributions to an emerging world based on cooperation rather than on competition, on affirmation of the human spirit rather than on self-doubt, and on the certainty that all humanity is connected. The goal of the publishers is to touch as many lives as possible with a message of hope for a better world.

H. J. Kramer, Inc. (founded in 1984 by Hal and Linda Kramer) holds a commitment to publish books that touch the heart and open us to spirit. Kramer books, old and new, are intended to support the reader's personal vision. A number of Kramer books sell exceedingly well in the mainstream market and garner translation rights worldwide, as well as domestic book-club sales.

From Kramer: *The Last of the Dream People* by Alice Anne Parker; *Reclaiming Our Health: Exploding the Medical Myth and Embracing the Source of True Healing* by John Robbins; *Diet for a New America: How Your Food Choices Affect Your Health, Happiness, and the Future of Life on Earth,* also by John Robbins; *Way of the Peaceful Warrior: A Book That Changes Lives* by Dan Millman; *The Laughing Classroom: Everyone's Guide to Teaching with Humor and Play* by Diane Loomans and Karen Kolberg; *Personal Power Through Awareness: A Guidebook for Sensitive People* by Sanaya Roman; *Guardians of Hope; The Angels' Guide to Personal Growth* by Terry Lynn Taylor; *Soul Love: Awakening Your Heart Centers* by Sanaya Roman; *Into a Timeless Realm: A Metaphysical Adventure* by Michael J. Roads; *The Laws of Spirit: Simple, Powerful Truths for Making Life Work* by Dan Millman; *The Awakened Heart: Finding Harmony in a Changing World* by John Robbins and Ann Mortifee Biowing; *Zen* by Ray Brooks; *Moments of Union* by Hal Dramer.

The Earth Life series by Sanaya Roman, channel for Orin, is a course in learning to live with joy, sense energy, and grow spiritually. Titles include: *Living with Joy: Keys to Personal Power and Spiritual Transformation; Personal Power Through Awareness: A Guidebook for Sensitive People; Spiritual Growth: Being Your Higher Self.*

K

A Kramer hallmark is Dan Millman's renowned set of writings (including *Way of the Peaceful Warrior*) that, in addition to audiocassette rendering, has now branched into a children's series. Kramer has also published a number of works in José Silva's mind-control method.

Prospective authors please note: Kramer's list is selective and is, generally speaking, fully slated several publishing seasons in advance; Kramer and Starseed are thus essentially closed to unsolicited submissions.

The company does not accept any submissions via fax. Query letters and SASEs should be directed to:

Hal Kramer, President

Jan Phillips, Managing Editor

Linda Kramer, Publisher

Starseed Press

Starseed Press children's books from H. J. Kramer are award-winning children's books that build self-esteem, inspire nonviolence, and encourage positive values. The imprint produces illustrated works slated for trade as well as educational markets.

Starseed books embody the principles of education through the power of story and incorporate myths, legends, fables, fairy tales, folklore, and original author visions into volumes of contemporary appeal.

Titles here: *Where Does God Live?* by Holly Bea (illustrated by Kim Howard); *The Lovables in the Kingdom of Self-Esteem* by Diane Loomans (illustrated by Kim Howard); *Grandfather Four Winds and Rising Moon* by Michael Chanin (illustrated by Sally J. Smith).

The Peaceful Warrior children's series by Dan Millman (illustrated by T. Taylor Bruce) includes these titles: *Secret of the Peaceful Warrior* and *Quest for the Crystal Castle*. The series adapts the characters, lessons, and spirit of Dan Millman's international bestseller *Way of the Peaceful Warrior.*

Backlist benchmarks include *The Land of the Blue Flower* by Frances Hodgson Burnett (author of *The Secret Garden* and *The Little Princess*), in an edition illustrated by Judith Ann Griffith.

Starseed Press's mission statement reads as follows: "All children are seeds from the stars who look to adults for love, inspiration, guidance, and the promise of a safe and friendly world. We dedicate Starseed Press to this vision and to the sacred child in each of us."—Hal and Linda Kramer, publishers.

K

KTAV PUBLISHING HOUSE INC.

900 Jefferson Street, P.O. Box 624, Hoboken, NJ 07030-7205
201-963-9524   fax: 201-963-0102
www.ktav.com   e-mail: 7463.2017@compuserve.com

KTAV Publishing House (founded in 1924) features books of Jewish interest, including scholarly Judaica, sermonica, textbooks, and books for a younger readership. KTAV also markets religious educational materials (including books), as well as gifts and decorative items. Many KTAV titles in the scholarly vein relate the history of Jewish thought and culture within the context of broader issues—some of global scope—and are of appeal to the interested general reader.

KTAV's catalog embraces the categories of Judaica, Biblica, Torah study, Jewish law, contemporary Halachic thought, sermonica, Jewish history, Jewish thought, contemporary Jewry, and Torah and science.

Titles from KTAV: *Confronting the Loss of a Baby: A Personal and Jewish Perspective* by Rabbi Yamin Levy; *Modern Medicine and Jewish Ethics* by Fred Rosner; *The Guide to Jewish Films on Video* by Larry Anklewicz; *Bioethical Dilemmas: A Jewish Perspective* by J. David Bleich; *Legends of the Chinese Jews of Kaifeng* by Xu Xin; *Tell It Like It Is: Tough Choices for Today's Teens* by Ellen Frankel and Sarah Levine; *The How-to Handbook for Jewish Living* and *The Second How-to Handbook for Jewish Living* by Rabbi Kerry Olitzky and Rabbi Ronald H. Isaacs; *Let's Talk About Being Jewish: Mitzvot, Prayers, and Celebrations* by Aimee Neibart; *Praying with Spirituality* by Sol Scharfstein; *Making a Difference: Commandments and Community, Our Jewish Service Organizations and Mitzvot* by Rabbi Michal Shekel.

Representing KTAV's diverse historical and cultural perspective: *Voices in Exile: A Study in Sephardic Intellectual History* by Marc D. Angel; *Modern Medicine and Jewish Ethics* (in a revised and augmented edition) by Fred Rosner; *Roots and Boots: From Crypto-Jew in New Spain to Community Leader in the American Southwest* by Floyd S. Fierman; *The Jewish Woman in Time and Torah* by Eliezar Berkovits.

Of scholarly note: *The Metsudah Linear Chumash—Rashi: A New Linear Translation* (in five volumes) by Rabbi Avrohom Davis and Rabbi Abrohom Kleinkaufman: *Volume I: Bereshis; Volume II: Shemos; Volume III: Vayikro; Volume IV: Bamidbar; Volume V: Devarim.*

KTAV distributes its own list; in addition, the house distributes the books of Yeshiva University Press. Query letters and SASEs should be directed to:

Bernard Scharfstein, Publisher

LIGUORI PUBLICATIONS

One Liguori Drive, Liguori, MO 63057-9999
314-464-2500, 800-325-9526
www.liguori.org

Liguori Publications and its trade imprint Liguori Triumph represent a twofold approach to religious publishing. Liguori (run by Redemptionist priests) produces books and pamphlets focused on the needs of Catholic parishes and specialized religious-bookstore markets and publishes *Liguorian* magazine. Triumph Books publishes for the mainstream religious-trade-book market. Under the rubric of Liguori Faithware, the publisher supplies computer resources for Catholics.

L

Liguori initiated its book program in 1968 and met with immediate success with *Good Old Plastic Jesus* by Earnest Larsen and *Keeping Your Balance in the Modern Church* by Hugh O'Connell.

Though Liguori, America's largest producer of Catholic publications, is assuredly a business, it is primarily a ministry. Through publications—in print and through electronic media—Liguori is able to reach people in ways that are not available in ordinary day-to-day ministry. Authors interested in Liguori or Triumph may request from the publisher a brochure covering submissions guidelines.

Liguori titles: *Angels All Around Us: The Catholic Belief and Experience; Daily Strength: One Year of Experiencing the Psalms* by Victor M. Parachin; *For Men Only: Strategies for Living Catholic* by Mitch Finley; *In the Womb of God: Creative Nurturing for the Soul* by Celeste Snowber Schroeder; *A Call to Peace: 52 Meditations on the Family Pledge of Nonviolence* by James McGinnis; *Out of the Ordinary: Awareness of God in the Everyday* by Peter Verity; *The Essential Catholic Handbook: A Summary of Beliefs, Practices, and Prayers* (compiled by pastors and preachers of the Redemptorist Order); *Living Advent: A Daily Companion to the Lectionary* by Julia Dugger; *Revisiting the Journey: Adult Faith-Sharing with the Catechism of the Catholic Church* (a Redemptorist Pastoral Publication); *The Light of the World* by David Fielding.

Highlights from Liguori include *Mother Teresa: In My Own Words* by Mother Teresa; *Family Planning: A Guide for Exploring the Issues* by Charles and Elizabeth Balsam; *Sex and the Christian Teen* by Jim Auer.

Liguori Publications promotes and markets through such vehicles as catalog mailings and listings in *Liguorian* magazine, circulates bookstore and parish newsletters, and utilizes flyers and self-mailers. Authors interested in Liguori or Triumph may request from the publisher a brochure covering submission guidelines. Query letters and SASEs should be directed to:

Rev. Thomas Santa, Publisher, Editor in Chief, Book and Pamphlet Department

Triumph Books

Triumph Books emphasizes an ecumenical perspective in the religious trade market. Triumph reaches a wide readership through books in a variety of areas, including psychology, spirituality, inspiration, awareness, theology, and Christian living.

Triumph Books asserts the impact of social and cultural developments on readers' values and religious faith and reflects this stance in its selection of new titles. The publishing program accents topics of contemporary controversy and debate. Triumph was formerly part of Gleneida Publishing Group.

From Triumph: *Jesus: An Unconventional Biography* by Jacques Duquesne; *Shaking a Fist at God: Struggling with the Mystery of Undeserved Suffering* by Katharine Dell; *Happy Are They . . . Living the Beatitudes in America* by Jim Langford; *On Living Simply: The Golden Voice of John Chrysostom* (compiled by Robert Van de Weyer); *Lift Up Your Heart: A Guide to Spiritual Peace* by Fulton J. Sheen; *From a Monastery Kitchen* by Brother Victor-Antoine D'Avila-Latourrette; *A Human Search: Reflections on My Life* by Father Bede Griffiths (edited by John Swindells); *Where Does God Live? Questions and*

Answers for Parents and Children by Rabbi Marc Gellman and Monsignor Thomas Hartman; *Divine Energy: God Beyond Us, Within Us, Among Us* by Donal Dorr; *Life Doesn't Get Any Better Than This: The Holiness of Little Daily Dramas* by Robert A. Alper; *Short Prayers for the Long Day* (compiled by Giles and Melville Harcourt).

Query letters and SASEs should be directed to:

Judy Bauer, Managing Editor

LLEWELLYN PUBLICATIONS

P.O. Box 64383, St. Paul, MN 55164-0383
612-291-1970
www.llewellyn.com   e-mail: lwlpc@llewellyn.com

Traditional areas of Llewellyn publishing concentration include astrology, magick, the occult, self-improvement, self-development, spiritual science, alternative technologies, nature religions and lifestyles, spiritist and mystery religions, divination, phenomena, and tantra. These works are brought out under the lustrous Llewellyn logo: a crescent moon. Llewellyn's trade motto—"new worlds of mind and spirit"—indicates the publisher's openness to explore new territory.

Llewellyn Publications (established in 1901) is a venerable house with a historical emphasis on the practical aspects of what today may be termed New Age science—how it works, and how to do it.

Llewellyn catalogs a full stock of new seasonal releases, along with a prolific backlist in hardcover, trade paper, and mass-market editions. Llewellyn also issues tarot decks and divination kits. The house's expanded program includes Spanish-language trade paperbacks.

On the Llewellyn nonfiction list: *Astrology for the Millions* by Grant Lewi; *Auras: See Them in Only 60 Seconds!* by Mark Smith; *The Intimate Enemy: Winning the War Within Yourself* by Guy Finley and Ellen Dickstein, Ph.D.; *In the Presence of Aliens: A Personal Experience of Dual Consciousness* by Janet Bergmark; *Magical Gardens: Myths, Mulch and Marigolds* by Patricia Monaghan; *Feng Shui for Beginners: Successful Living by Design* by Richard Webster; *Peaceful Transition: The Art of Conscious Dying & the Liberation of the Soul* by Dr. Bruce Goldberg; *How to Develop and Use Psychic Touch* by Ted Andrews; *Strange but True: From the Files of* FATE *Magazine* (edited by Corine Kenner and Craig Miller); *100 Days to Better Health, Good Sex & Long Life: A Guide to Taoist Yoga* by Eric Steven Yudelove; *Experiencing the Kabbalah: A Simple Guide to Spiritual Wholeness* by Chic Cicero and Sandra Tabatha Cicero; *Enochian Magic for Beginners: The Original System of Angel Magic* by Donald Tyson; *Twelve Faces of Saturn: Your Guardian Angel Planet* by Bil Tierney; *Inner Passages, Outer Journeys: Wilderness, Healing and the Discovery of Self* by David Cumes, M.D.; *Women at the Change: The Intelligent Woman's Guide to Menopause* by Madonna Sophia Compton; *Your Pet's Horoscope* by Diana Nilsen.

Llewellyn has produced a limited number of fiction titles. Among them: *Visions of Murder* by Florence Wagner McClain; *Lilith* by D. A. Heeley; *Cardinal's Sin: Psychic Defenders Uncover Evil in the Vatican* by Raymond Buckland; *Walker Between the Worlds* by Diane DesRochers; *The Holographic Dollhouse* by Charlotte Lawrence.

Llewellyn is a specialty house and looks for projects (books and audiotapes, as well as videos and computer software) that will have extended sales viability; Llewellyn is not geared toward academic or scholarly publishing, and its products are aimed at general audiences without specialist knowledge or training. Authors may request the house's writers' guidelines, which contain valuable tips generally applicable to structuring and proposing publishing projects.

To request a copy of the Llewellyn Writers' Guidelines for book publication, send an SASE to Nancy Mostad, Acquisitions Manager. Only writers who request and adhere to the writers' guidelines will be considered for publication.

An aggressive marketer and promoter, Llewellyn publications and authors are given full house support, including the areas of arranging author interviews and appropriate advertising and subsidiary rights—often incorporated into the schedule is placement in Llewellyn's magazines (*New Times*) and primarily promotional venues (*New Worlds*). Llewellyn's marketing network encompasses distributional arrangements worldwide.

Query letters and SASEs should be directed to:

Nancy J. Mostad, Acquisitions Manager

Barbara Wright, Acquisitions Editor—Tarot and kits.

LOTUS PRESS (A DIVISION OF LOTUS BRANDS, INC.)

P.O. Box 325, Twin Lakes, WI 53181
262-889-8561   fax: 262-889-8591
Lotus Brands, Inc.:
P.O. Box 325, Twin Lakes, WI 53181

Lotus Press produces works in the fields of health, yoga, and Native American and New Age metaphysics.

Lotus Press (founded in 1981) is a division of Lotus Brands, Inc.

On the Lotus Press list: *The Healing Power of Grapefruit Seed* by Shalila Sharamon and Bodo J. Baginski; *The Healing Power of Essential Oils* by Rololphe Balz; *Abundance Through Reiki* by Paula Horan; *Ayurveda Secrets of Healing* by Maya Tiwari; *Reiki: Way of the Heart* by Walter Lubeck; *New Eden: For People, Animals, Nature* by Michael W. Fox (illustrated by Susan Seddon Boulet); *Rainforest Remedies: One Hundred Healing Herbs of Belize* by Rosita Arvigo and Michael Balick; *Stargazer: A Native American Inquiry into Extraterrestrial Phenomena* by Gerald Hausman.

Lotus Press distributes primarily through special product outlets such as health-food stores and spiritual-interest booksellers. Query letters and SASEs should be directed to:

Cathy Hoselton

LURAMEDIA, INC.

See listing for Innisfree Press.

L

M

MESORAH PUBLICATIONS, LTD.

4401 Second Avenue, Brooklyn, NY 11232
718-921-9000
www.artscroll.com   e-mail: listproc@virtual.co.il

Mesorah Publications hosts a wide-ranging program that includes works of contemporary cultural and popular interest, in addition to traditional Judaica, Bible study, liturgical materials, history, and juveniles. The Art Scroll Library series is produced with special attention to design and production.

Mesorah Publications, Ltd. (founded in 1976), publishes hardcover and paperback editions within a traditional approach, as noted by the publisher's trade motto: Mesorah Publications, helping preserve the heritage . . . one book at a time.

From Mesorah: *Schottenstein Daf Yomi Edition of the Talmud-English Makkos: Patience: Formulas, Stories and Insights* by Rabbi Zelig Pliskin; *The Jewish People: A Light unto the Nations* by Rabbi Berel Wein; *Wisdom Each Day* by Rabbi Abraham J. Twerski; *Understanding Judaism* by Rabbi Mordechai Katz; *A Look Back* by Dr. Gershon Kranzler; *Calculated Risk* by Yair Weinstein; *Take Me to the Holy Land* by Tsivia Yanofsky; *The Jewish Experience: 2000 Years* by Rabbi Nachman Zakon.

Mesorah catalogs books from such other houses as Shaar Press, Tamar Books, and OU/NCSY Publications.

Query letters and SASEs should be directed to:

Mrs. D. Schecter, Literary Editor

MOODY PRESS

820 North LaSalle Boulevard, Chicago, IL 60610-3284
312-329-2101, 800-678-8812
www.moodypress.org

In addition to general-interest religious titles (Bible-based interdenominational), Moody produces a list that includes Bibles, books for children and youths, novels, biographies, educational resources, and works for religious professionals. Moody's books are issued in clothbound editions, trade paper, and mass-market paperback. Moody also catalogs computer software, audiotapes, and videocassettes. Moody Press (founded in 1894) serves as the publishing ministry of Moody Bible Institute.

Moody produces a number of targeted and successful lines that encompass the spectrum of the house's publishing interests. This portion of the Moody program offers such series as Men of Integrity, Moody Acorns, Golden Oldies, Healing for the Heart, Quiet Time Books for Women, and Salt & Light Pocket Guides.

Representative Moody titles: *Your Eternal Reward: Triumph and Tears at the Judgment Seat of Christ* by Erwin W. Lutzer; *The Choice: America at the Crossroads of Ruin and Revival* by Sammy Tippit; *Money Management for College Students* by Larry Burkett with Todd Temple; *Seven Reasons Why You Can Trust the Bible* by Erwin Lutzer;

Something New Under the Sun: Ancient Wisdom for Contemporary Living by Ray Pritchard; *Guy Stuff: or It's OK to Ask for Directions* by Tim Smith; *God Up Close: How to Meditate on His Word* by Doug McIntosh; *Growing Little Women: Capturing Teachable Moments with Your Daughter* by Donna Miller with Linda Holland; *Raising Lambs Among Wolves: How to Protect Your Children from Evil* by Mark J. Bubeck; *The Financial Guide for the Single Parent* by Larry Burkett; *The End Is Coming* by Paul N. Benware; *The Five Love Languages of Children* by Gary Chapman and Ross Campbell, M.D.; *Spiritual Power* by Dwight L. Moody; *Exit Interviews: Revealing Stories of Why People Are Leaving the Church* by William D. Hendricks; *Traveling Light: Contentment amid the Burden of Life's Expectations* by Kurt D. Bruner.

Northfield Publishing, an imprint of Moody Press, is a line of books for non-Christians in your life, those who are exploring the Christian faith or acquaintances who identify themselves as Christians but may not be active in a local church. While remaining true to biblical principles, certain Christian wording and Scripture book references are eliminated to avoid reader confusion. Covering such areas as finances, relationships, and business, Northfield authors are professionals in their field who write with relevance and offer wide-ranging perspectives.

Some Northfield titles: *The Five Love Languages: How to Express Heartfelt Commitment to Your Mate* by Gary Chapman; *Reinventing Your Career: Surviving a Layoff and Creating New Opportunities* by Stephen P. Adams; *The Relaxed Parent: Helping Your Kids Do More as You Do Less* by Tim Smith.

Fiction from Moody includes historicals, high-tech espionage, and contemporary mysteries. Larry Burkett Products is a line of books and tapes accenting the social/financial sphere.

Query letters and SASEs should be directed to:

Jim Bell, Executive Editor

MOORINGS

As of spring 1996, Random House/Ballantine ceased publishing under the Moorings imprint.

MULTNOMAH PUBLISHERS

204 West Adams Avenue, P.O. Box 1720, Sisters, OR 97759
541-549-1144   fax: 541-549-2044

Multnomah covers the major categories of Christian trade publishing in general nonfiction and fiction.

Multnomah produces books and audiocassettes with a contemporary verve in Christian living and family enrichment, as well as lines of devotional titles and gift books.

Multnomah also offers a strong list of fiction, including contemporary and historical novels, romances, sagas, and thrillers.

Query letters and SASEs should be directed to the Editorial Department or to:

Bill Jensen, Vice President

N

THOMAS NELSON PUBLISHERS
Tommy Nelson

501 Nelson Place, P.O. Box 141000, Nashville, TN 37214-1000
615-889-9000

Thomas Nelson Publishers is an editorially independent product group of Thomas Nelson, Inc. (founded in Scotland in 1798 and purchased by Sam Moore in 1969). Thomas Nelson Publishers produces Christian trade books in hardcover and trade paperback in the areas of health, inspiration, self-help, psychology, family concerns, parenting, charismatic interest, leadership and motivation, contemporary issues and interest, and healing and recovery. Oliver-Nelson is a trade-oriented imprint.

Already among the major players in the religious-publishing arena, Nelson enjoys its current phase of corporate exuberance. The house bought Here's Life Publishers from Campus Crusade for Christ and expanded its evangelism and discipleship markets.

Nonfiction titles from Thomas Nelson: *What If Jesus Had Never Been Born?* by D. James Kennedy; *An Unchanging Faith in a Changing World* by Kenneth D. Boa and Robert M. Bowman, Jr.; *God's Gift for Mothers: Comfort and Encouragement from the Word of God; Newstart Lifestyle Cookbook: More Than 200 Heart-Healthy Recipes Featuring Whole Plant Foods* by the Weimar Institute; *Woman's Journey to the Heart of God* by Cynthia Heald; *How to Turn the Other Cheek and Still Survive in Today's World* by Dr. Suzette Haden Elgin; *101 Things God Can't Do* by Maisie Sparks; *Anchor Man: How a Father Can Anchor His Family in Christ for the Next 100 Years* by Steve Farrar; *The Leadership Genius of Jesus: Ancient Wisdom for Modern Business* by William Beausay II; *God's Plan for Your Financial Success* by Charles Ross; *The Soul Search: A Spiritual Journey to Authentic Intimacy with God* by Gary R. Collins; *God Will Make a Way: Amazing Affirmations of God's Faithfulness in Everyday Life* by Thelma Wells; *Help, I'm Laughing and I Can't Get Up: Fall-Down Funny Stories to Fill Your Heart and Lift Your Spirit* by Liz Curtis Higgs; *Lessons from a Father to His Son* by John D. Ashcroft; *Untapped Potential: Turning Ordinary People into Extraordinary Performers* by Jack Lannom; *What If the Bible Had Never Been Written?* by D. James Kennedy and Jerry Newscombe.

Nelson fiction includes historical and contemporary novels, as well as futurist thrillers. Fiction from Nelson: *Touched by an Angel: A Christmas Story* (created by Martha Williamson); *Only the River Runs Free* by Bodie and Brock Thoene; *Sins of the Fathers* by Will Cunningham; *Tidings of Comfort and Joy: A Tender Story of Love, Loss, and Reunion* by T. Davis Bunn; *Blood Money* by William Krietlew (the Lake Champlain Mysteries); *Sarah's Patchwork* by Stephanie Grace Whitson (Keepsake Legacies series).

N

A noted Nelson project is a series of family-oriented works from Carolyn Coats and Pamela Smith. Titles include *Things Your Mother Told You but You Didn't Want to Hear; Things Your Dad Always Told You but You Didn't Want to Hear;* and *My Grandmother Always Said That.*

Thomas Nelson Publishers does not accept unsolicited query letters, proposals, or manuscripts.

Tommy Nelson

Tommy Nelson is a children's-publishing division geared toward the youngest readers up through young adults. Launched as the new home for the highly successful Word Kids! and Nelson Jr. product lines, the Tommy Nelson list features such bestselling authors as Max Lucado, Frank Peretti, and Bill Myers. Tommy Nelson is particularly strong in fiction and novelty items. Series include the Itty Bitty Books line.

Nelson also issues a line of titles for young readers (currently accenting the Tommy Nelson division). The house offers a strong, select list of adult and young-adult fiction. Thomas Nelson produces magazines and journals and is among the largest publishers of Bibles and scriptural commentary in the United States. Nelson addresses the growing Christian Spanish readership in the United States and abroad through its Editorial Caribe and Editorial Betania divisions (both acquired in 1994). Thomas Nelson also owns the editorially independent Word Publishing (see separate main entry in this directory). The overall corporate banner for the various divisions in this enterprise is Nelson Word Publishing Group.

Thomas Nelson's publishing philosophy: To grow through fairness and integrity in distinctive service to all. Thomas Nelson's purpose: To publish, produce, and market products that honor God and serve humanity and to enhance shareholder value.

Representative titles: *The Crippled Lamb* by Max Lucado; *The Legend of Annie Murphy* by Frank Peretti; *The Parable of the Sunflower* by Liz Curtis Biggs; *Whose Eyes Are These?* by Elizabeth Burman; *Cyber: The Pharaoh's Tomb* by Sigmund Brouwer; *God Loves You* (a pop-up book) by Vlasta Van Kempen.

Thomas Nelson handles its own distribution. Query letters and SASEs should be directed to:

Laura Minchew, Editor for Tommy Nelson

NEWCASTLE PUBLISHING COMPANY

Has been purchased by Career Press.

NEW LEAF PRESS
Master Books

P.O. Box 726, Green Forest, AR 72638
870-438-5288   fax: 870-438-5120
e-mail: mbnlp@cswnet.com

Areas of New Leaf publishing include Christian living, prophecy and eschatology, theology, applied Christianity, Bible study, family/home/marriage, friendship and love, education, evangelism, devotional works (including daily readings), and humor. Master Books is the house's imprint for its children's, as well as creation science, titles. The house has a solid backlist.

New Leaf Press (founded in 1975) publishes primarily for the Christian religious market, with some trade-religious crossover titles. New Leaf produces in hardcover and paperback (trade paper and mass-market); many New Leaf books are priced economically.

On the New Leaf list: *First Comes Love, Then Comes Money* by Roger Gibson; *First Thing Monday Morning* by Dianna Booher; *Reasons for Believing: A Seeker's Guide to Christianity* by Frank Harper; *Recapturing Your Dreams* by David Shibley; *Bible Comes Alive,* volume 2 by Drs. Clifford and Barbara Wilson; *The Fragrance of Christmas* by Dan and Dave Davidson; *A Cup of Devotion with God* also by Dan and David Davidson; *Success Without Guilt* by Robert Strand; *When Hollywood Says Yes, How Can America Say No?* by Gene Wolfenbarger; *Alike in Love: When Opposites Attract* by Tim and Beverly LaHaye; *The Pursuit of Beauty* by Katie Luce; *Wounded Soldier* by John Steer; *Swept Away* by Ron Auch.

Master titles: *Buried Alive* by Dr. Jack Cuozzo; *The Great Alaskan Dinosaur Adventure* by Buddy Davis, Mike Liston, and John Whitmore; *Darwin's Enigma: Ebbing the Tide of Naturalism* by Luther Sunderland; *Fossils Facts & Fantasies* by Joe Taylor; *Bombus Finds a Friend* and *A Bombus Creativity Book* by Elsie Larson Elizabeth Haidle; *Skeletons in Your Closet* by Dr. Gary Parker; *The Great Dinosaur Mystery Solved!* by Ken Ham; *That Their Words May Be Used Against Them* by Henry Morris.

New Leaf Press distributes its own list; New Leaf also provides distribution services for other publishers with related market outlooks.

Query letters and SASEs should be directed to:

Roger Howerton, Acquisitions

Numata Center

2620 Warring Street, Berkeley, CA 94704
510-843-4128   fax: 510-845-3409
www.slip.net/~numata

Numata Center for Buddhist Translation and Research is a nonprofit organization established by Mr. Yehan Numata, founder of the Mitutoyo Corporation, international manufacturer of precision measuring instruments.

Numata has undertaken the translation and publication of the Chinese Buddhist canon, as well as additional works, in finely produced English-language editions.

Numata engages a variety of scholars and writers to participate in this landmark program, and the initial volumes have been received heartily by the library market, as well as by specialty and trade booksellers.

Sample titles: *The Lotus Sutra* (translated by Kubo Tsugunari and Yuyama Akira); *The Summary of the Great Vehicle* (translated by John P. Keenan); *Letters of Master Rennyo* (translated by Minor Rogers); *Essentials of the Eight Traditions* (translated by Leo Pruden).

The BDK Tripitaka Translation Project covers the entire Buddhist Canon, translated by internationally known scholars, using the Taisho Edition of the Chinese Tripitaka. The First Series consists of 139 titles in 108 volumes. Query letters and SASEs should be directed to:

Reverend Seishin Yamashita, President

ONJINJINKTA PUBLISHING

909 S.E. Everett Mall Way A120, Everett, WA 98208
425-290-7809   fax: 425-290-7789
www.rippledon.com   e-mail: peter@onjinjinkta.com

Onjinjinkta publishes a strong, diverse list of fiction and nonfiction titles in mass-market, trade paperback, and hardcover. Onjinjinkta's publishing model, instituted by bestselling author Betty J. Eadie, is to safeguard the message inherent in most nonfiction against the impingement of less authorial concerns. We also consider nonfiction work with very specific audiences by authors with expressed interest in becoming highly involved in their own marketing. Among its nonfiction categories, which include self-help, popular culture, humor, and current affairs, Onjinjinkta is especially strong in spiritual titles. The result is a nonfiction list that demonstrates an exceptional sensitivity to a book's content, independent of concerns traditionally imposed by a larger publisher. Onjinjinkta's fiction accents popular trends, though it will often conclude with resolutions that tend to enlighten. All Onjinjinkta titles are directed to uplift and inspire the human spirit.

Query letters and SASEs should be directed to:

Bret Sable, Assistant Editor

Peter Orullian, Editor

PAULIST PRESS, INC.

997 Macarthur Boulevard, Mahwah, NJ 07430
201-825-7300   fax: 201-825-6921
e-mail: info@paulistpress.com

Paulist Press publishes Roman Catholic as well as ecumenical titles in Bible study, biography, women's studies, spirituality, current issues, self-help and personal growth, Catholicism, liturgy, theology, philosophy, ethics, Jewish-Christian relations, world religions, youth ministry, and education. The Paulist list ranges from popularly oriented traditionalist works to provocative frontiers of religious thought. In addition to books, Paulist offers a multimedia line.

Choices & Community: The Three Faces of Christian Ethics by Russell B. Connors, Jr., and Patrick T. McCormick; *Handbook for Spiritual Directors* by Julie M. Douglas; *Evolution and Eden: Balancing Original Sin and Contemporary Science* by Jerry D. Korsmeyer; *What Price Prejudice?: Christian Antisemitism in America* by Frank E. Eakin, Jr.; *Christian Mysticism East and West: What the Masters Teach Us* by Maria Jaoudi; *Walking in Virtue: Moral Decisions and Spiritual Growth in Daily Life* by John W. Crossin, O.S.F.S.; *Moods of the Soul: Spiritual Enrichment Through the Psalms* by Ronald Quillo; *Spiritlinking Leadership: Working Through Resistance to Organizational Change* by Donna J. Markham; *Taming Monster Moments: Tips for Turning on Soul Lights to Help Children Handle Fear and Danger* by Daniel Porter (illustrated by Cheryl Nathan); *The Good Life: Where Morality and Spirituality Converge* by Richard N. Gula, S.S.; *The Intrareligious Dialogue* by Raiman Panikkar.

Query letters and SASEs should be directed to:

Susan Heyboer O'Keefe, C.S.P., Children's Book Editor

Maria L. Maggi, Managing Editor

P

THE PILGRIM PRESS

United Church of Christ

See also: United Church Press

700 Prospect Avenue, East Cleveland, OH 44115-1100
216-736-3364   fax: 216-736- 2207
e-mail: pilgrim@ucc.org

Pilgrim Press is a Christian-related imprint that focuses on three areas: theological ethics (including science, technology, and medicine); human identity, relationships, and sexuality (including feminist and gay/lesbian issues); and activist spirituality (having a social dimension).

Pilgrim Press (begun in 1645 and established in the United States in 1895) is the book-publishing banner of the publishing wing of the United Church of Christ. United Church Press is a Pilgrim imprint geared primarily toward the inspirational readership.

Pilgrim's trade motto: Books at the Nexus of Religion and Culture.

The house has a tradition of publishing books and other resources that challenge, encourage, and inspire, crafted in accordance with fine standards of content, design, and production.

Indicative of the Pilgrim list: *Amistad: The Slave Uprising Aboard the Spanish Schooner* by Helen Kromer; *Celebrating Her: Feminist Ritualizing Comes of Age* by Wendy Hunter Roberts; *Crossing the Soul's River: A Rite of Passage for Men* by William O. Roberts, Jr.; *Now That You're Out of the Closet, What About the Rest of the House?* by Linda Handel; *Forgiving Our Grownup Children* by Dwight Lee Wolter; *Prayers for the Common Good* by A. Jean Lesher; *Just Peacemaking: Ten Practices for Abolishing War* by Glen Stassen; *Meditations on the Way of the Cross* by Mother Teresa of Calcutta and Brother Roger of Taize; *The Wealth or Health of Nations: Transforming Capitalism from Within* by Carol Johnston; *Sacred Texts and Authority* by Jacob Neusner; *The Great Commandment: A Theology of Resistance and Transformation* by Eleanor H. Haney.

The Pilgrim Library of World Religions is a series designed for both classroom and general use, written by authorities in each tradition. The series addresses how five great world religions—Judaism, Hinduism, Buddhism, Islam, and Christianity—approach a certain critical issue. Titles include: *God* (edited by Jacob Neusner). Projected titles include: *Evil and Suffering; Women and Families; Death and the Afterlife; Sacred Texts and Authority.* A representative title from Pilgrim Library of Ethics: *Abortion: A Reader* (edited by Jacob Neusner).

The Pilgrim Press oversees its own distribution.

Query letters and SASEs should be directed to:

Timothy Staveteig, Publisher

PRESBYTERIAN PUBLISHING CORPORATION

100 Witherspoon Street, Louisville, KY 40202
800-227-2872, 800-541-5113
www.pcusa.org/ppc/

The Presbyterian Publishing Corporation, denominational publisher of the Presbyterian Church (USA), publishes under the imprints Westminster/John Know Press and Geneva Press. PPC's three primary objectives are: (1) To develop and publish high-quality, useful resources for congregations, both within the PC (USA) and ecumenically, (2) To expand the scope of the Westminster John Know Press academic publishing program in order to better facilitate the training of clergy and scholars, and (3) To publish books for lay and general readers that "contribute to the broader conversation about religion, society, and moral values."

With a publishing heritage that dates back over 160 years, PPC publishes more than 100 new works each year, while maintaining a backlist of more than 1,000 titles sold around the world. PPC, located in Louisville, Kentucky, and with offices in the United Kingdom and the Netherlands, characterizes its publishing program with the theme "Challenging the Mind, Nourishing the Soul."

Query letters and SASEs should be directed to:

Davis Perkins, Editor in Chief

REGAL BOOKS

See Gospel Light Publications.

St. Anthony Messenger Press and Franciscan Communications

1615 Republic Street, Cincinnati, OH 45210
513-241-5615   fax: 513-241-1197
www.AmericanCatholic.org

Areas of St. Anthony Messenger publishing interest include Franciscan topics, Catholic identity, family life, morality and ethics, parish ministry, pastoral ministry, prayer helps, sacraments, saints and Christian heroes, Scripture, seasonal favorites, small-group resources, spirituality for every day, children's books, and youth ministry. The house produces books (hardcover and paperback, many in economically priced editions), magazines, audiotapes, and videocassettes, as well as educational programs and an award-winning Web site

St. Anthony Messenger Press (founded in 1970) and Franciscan Communications publishes Catholic religious works and resources for parishes, schools, and individuals. The house also owns the video/print imprints Ikonographics and Fischer Productions.

Titles: *A Retreat with John the Evangelist: That You May Have Life* by Raymond E. Brown, S.S.; *A Retreat with Mark: Embracing Discipleship* by Stephen C. Doyle, O.F.M.; *Living God's Word: Reflections on the Weekly Gospels: Cycle A* by David Knight; *Thresholds to Prayer* by Kathy Coffey; *Jesus of the Gospels: Teacher, Storyteller, Friend, Messiah* by Arthur E. Zannoni; *Jesus' Plan for a New World: The Sermon on the Mount* by Richard Rohr, O.F.M., with John Bookser Feister; *Following Francis of Assisi: A Spirituality for Daily Living* by Patti Normile; *Journeys into Matthew: 18 Lessons of Exploration and Discovery* by Raymond Apicella; *Marriage and the Spirituality of Intimacy* by Leif Kehrwald; *God Is Close to the Brokenhearted: Good News for Those Who Are Depressed* by Rachael Callahan, C.S.C., and Rea McDonnell, S.S.N.D.; *Harvest Us Home: Good News as We Age* by Rachel Callahan, C.S.C., and Rea McDonnell, S.S.N.D.; *The Blessing Candles: 58 Simple Mealtime Prayer-Celebrations* by Gaynell Bordes Cronin and Jack Rathschmidt, *Thomas Merton's Paradise Journey: Writings on Contemplation* by William H. Shannon; *The Lay Contemplative: Testimonies, Perspectives, Resources* (edited by Virginia Manss and Mary Frolich); *Twelve Tough Issues: What the Church Teaches—And Why* by Archbishop Daniel E. Pilarczyk; *The Sun and Moon over Assisi: A Personal Encounter with Francis and Clare* by Gerard Thomas Straub; *Can You Find Jesus? Introducing Your Child to the Old Testament; Can You Find Followers? Introducing Your Child to Disciples* by Philip D. Gallery and Janet L. Harlow; *Mary's Flowers: Gardens, Legends and Meditations* by Vincenzina Krymow.

A special St. Anthony Messenger Press project is A Retreat With . . . , a series that features the words of such historical figures as Thomas Merton, Gerard Manley Hopkins, and Hildegard of Bingen. Did you ever wonder what it would be like to make a retreat with some great holy person from history? Authors weave the mentor's own words into seven days of prayer, dialogue, and deepening acquaintance. Selected titles: *A Retreat with Pope John XXIII: Opening the Windows to Wisdom* by Alfred McBride, O. Praem.; *A Retreat with Francis de Sales, Jane de Chantal and Aelred of Rievaulx: Befriending Each*

Other in God by Wendy M. Wright; *A Retreat with Francis and Clare of Assasi: Following Our Pilgrim Hearts* by Murray Bodo, O.F.M., and Susan Saint Sing; A *Retreat with Thomas Merton: Becoming Who We Are* by Dr. Anthony T. Padovano.

St. Anthony Messenger Press also offers music CDs, computer software, videos, and audiocassettes.

St. Anthony Messenger Press distributes books through Ingram, Spring Arbor, Riverside Distributors, Appalachian Inc., Baker & Taylor, and ABS/Guardian.

Query letters and SASEs should be directed to:

Lisa Biedenbach, Managing Editor

SHAMBHALA PUBLICATIONS

Horticultural Hall, 300 Massachusetts Avenue, Boston, MA 02115-4544
617-424-0030   fax: 617-236-1563
www.shambhala.com   e-mail: editors@shambhala.com

Shambhala publishes hardcover and paperback titles in creativity, philosophy, psychology, medical arts and healing, mythology, folklore, religion, art, literature, cooking, martial arts, and cultural studies. Shambhala generally issues a modest list of new titles each year and tends a flourishing backlist; the house periodically updates some of its perennial sellers in revised editions.

The house packages a number of distinct lines, including gift editions and special-interest imprints. Shambhala Dragon Editions accents the sacred teachings of Asian masters. Shambhala Centaur Editions offers classics of world literature in small-sized gift editions. The New Science Library concentrates on titles relating to science, technology, and the environment. Shambhala copublishes C. G. Jung Foundation Books with the C. G. Jung Foundation for Analytical Psychology. Shambhala Redstone Editions are fine-boxed sets composed of books, postcards, games, art objects, and foldouts. Shambhala Lion Editions are spoken-word audiotape cassette presentations.

Shambhala Publications is a foremost representative of the wave of publishers specializing in the arena of contemporary globalized spiritual and cultural interest. Since Shambhala's inception (the house was founded in 1969), the field has blossomed into a still-burgeoning readership, as underscored by the many smaller independent presses and large corporate houses that tend this market.

From Shambhala: *The Book of Five Rings* by Miyamota Musashi, translated by Thomas Cleary; *A Brief History of Everything,* 2nd edition by Ken Wilber; *The Light of Dawn: Daily Readings from the Holy Quar'an* by Camille Adams Helminski; *The Pocket Rumi Reader* (edited by Kabir Helminski); *The Art of War: A New Translation* (edited by Denma Translation Group); *Dakini's Warm Breath: The Feminine Principal in Tibetan Buddhism* by Judith Simmer-Brown; *Glimpses of Abhidharma* by Chogyam Trungpa; *Making Friends with Death: A Buddhist Guide to Encountering Mortality* by Judith Lief; *Kabbalah: The Way of the Jewish Mystic* by Perle Epstein; *Seeking the Heart of Wisdom: The Path of Insight Meditation* by Joseph Goldstein and Jack Kornfield; *Visible Here and Now: The Buddha's Teachings on the Rewards of Spiritual Practice* by Ayya Khema; *Ap-*

preciate Your Life: The Essence of Zen Practice (edited by Eve Myonen Marko); *Awakening to Zen: The Teachings of Roshi Philip Kapleau; Circles of Care: How to Set Up Quality Home Care for Our Elders* by Ann Cason; *Enlightened Journey: Buddhist Practice as Daily Life* by Tulku Thondup; and *Freedom, Love, and Action* by J. Krishnamurti.

Features from Shambhala's strong backlist: *Hard Travel to Sacred Places* by Rudolph Wurlitzer; *The Beat Book: Poems and Fiction from the Beat Generation* (compiled by Anne Waldman; foreword by Allen Ginsberg); *The Erotic Spirit: An Anthology of Poems of Sensuality, Love, and Longing* (edited by Sam Hamill); *Spiritual Path, Sacred Place: Myth, Ritual, and Meaning in Architecture* by Thomas Barrie; *The Female Ancestors of Christ* by Ann Belford Ulanov; *The Forbidden Self: Symbolic Incest and the Journey Within* by John Perkins; *Same-Sex Love: And the Path to Wholeness* (edited by Robert H. Hopke, Karen Lofthus Carrington, and Scott Wirth).

Shambhala Redstone Editions offers these items specially boxed: *José Guadalupe Posada: Mexican Popular Prints* (edited by Julian Rothstein); *A Gambling Box* (edited by Kate Pullinger); *Surrealist Games* (compiled by Alistair Brotchie; edited by Mel Gooding).

Shambhala distributes to the trade via Random House. Shambhala services individual and special orders through its own house fulfillment department.

Query letters and SASEs should be directed to:

Peter Turner, President and Executive Editor

Sam Bercholz, Chairman and Editor in Chief

Mai Shaikhanuar-Cota, Managing Editor

Emily Hilburn-Sell, Senior Editor

Kendra Crossen Burroughs, Editor

Joel Segel, Associate Editor

Emily Bower, Editor

Eden Steinberg, Associate Editor

Beth Frankl, Associate Editor

Kerrie-Beth Mello, Production Editor

Jael Riordan, Editorial Assistant

S

SIGNATURE BOOKS

564 West 400 North Street, Salt Lake City, UT 84116-3411
801-531-1483   fax: 801-531-1488
www.signaturebooksinc.com

The Signature list emphasizes contemporary literature, as well as scholarly works relevant to the Intermountain West. Signature Books (established in 1981) publishes subjects that range from outlaw biographies and Mormonism to speculative theology, from demographics to humor. In addition to a wide range of nonfiction, Signature publishes novels and collections of poetry. The common objective of the selections on Signature's roster is to provide alternatives to the institutional agendas that underlie many of the publications in the region.

Indicative of Signature nonfiction: *Salamander: The Story of the Mormon Forgery Murders* by Linda Sillitoe and Allen Roberts (George J. Throckmorton, forensic analysis); *Remembering Brad: On the Loss of a Son to AIDS* by H. Wayne Schow; *The Sanctity of Dissent* by Paul James Toscano; *Waiting for the World's End: The Diaries of Wilford Woodruff* (edited by Susan Staker); *A Sculptor's Testimony in Bronze and Stone: Sacred Sculpture of Avard T. Fairbanks; "Wild Bill" Hickman and the Mormon Frontier* by Hope A. Hilton.

Representative of Signature fiction and popular literature: *Aspen Marooney* by Levi S. Peterson; *The Backslider,* also by Levi S. Peterson; *Beyond the River: A Novel* by Michael Fillerup; *Bright Angels and Familiars: Contemporary Mormon Stories* (edited by Eugene England); *Canyon Interludes: Between White Water and Red Rock* by Paul W. Rea; *An Environment for Murder* by Rod Decker; *Imagination Comes to Breakfast: Poems* by Kathy Evans; *Love Chains: Stories* by Margaret Blair Young; *My New Life* by Ron Molen; *Secrets Keep: A Novel* by Linda Sillitoe; *Stone Spirits: Poems* by Susan Elizabeth Howe; *Washed by a Wave of Wind: Science Fiction from the Corridor* (edited by M. Shayne Bell); *The Tabernacle Bar* (novel) by Susan Plamer; *The Way We Live: Stories by Utah Women* (edited by Ellen Fagg); *No Man Knows My Pastries: The Secret (Not Sacred) Recipes of Sister Enid Christensen; Marketing Precedes the Miracle: More Cartoons* by Calvin Grondahl.

Signature Publications oversees distribution of its titles via in-house ordering services and a national network of wholesalers.

Signature Books does not accept unsolicited manuscripts.

Query letters and SASEs should be directed to:

Ron Priddcs, Director

TYNDALE HOUSE PUBLISHERS

351 Executive Drive, Carol Stream, IL 60188
630-668-8300   fax: 630-668-3245

Tyndale offers a comprehensive program in Christian living: devotional, inspirational, and general nonfiction, from a nondenominational evangelical perspective. They publish the bestselling LEFT BEHIND series. Tyndale's publishing interest also encompasses religious fiction. The house offers a strong line of Bibles. Tyndale House Publishers (founded in 1962) produces hardcover, trade paperback, and mass-market paperback originals, as well as reprints. Tyndale also catalogs audio and video products.

From Tyndale: *Are We Living in the End of Times?* by Jerry Jenkins; *The Control Freak* by Les Parrott; *The 5 Love Needs of Men and Women* by Gary and Barbara Rosberg; *Reunited* by Judy Baer, Jan Duffy, Peggy Stoks, and Jeri Odell; *The Silence* by Jim Kraus; *The Atonement Child* by Francine Rivers; *Soul Harvest* by Tim LaHaye and Jerry B. Jenkins; *Give Them Wings* by Carol Kuykendall; *Seven Keys to Spiritual Renewal* by Stephen Arterburn and Dr. David Stoop; *Breathless* by Gary R. Collins, Ph.D.; *Too Young to Die* by Gordon McLean; *Chart Watch* by Bob Smithouser and Bob Waliszewski; *Beyond Words* by Ron DiCianni; *Bound by Honor* by Gary Smalley and Greg Smalley; *Bold Purpose* by Dan Allender and Tremper Longman; *Into Abba's Arms* by Sandra D. Wilson, Ph.D.; *601 Quotes About Marriage and Family* by William and Nancie Carmichael.

In a publishing partnership with the American Association of Christian Counselors, Tyndale offers books written by leading Christian counselors that integrate counseling principles and biblical theology as they offer authoritative analysis and research for the Professional Counseling Library. Titles: *Counseling Children Through the World of Play* by Daniel Sweeney, Ph.D.; *Psychology, Theology, and Spirituality in Christian Counseling* by Mark R. McMinn; *Counseling Through the Maze of Divorce* by George Ohlschlager; *Treating Sex Offenders* by Daniel Henderson; *Brief Counseling* by Gary J. Oliver; *Treating Victims of Sexual Abuse* by Diane Langberg.

Tyndale fiction includes mainstream novels as well as a number of inspirational romance series, including works set in Revolutionary War and Civil War milieus. The house is interested in evangelical Christian-theme romance in other historical periods (including Regency), as well as those with a humorous twist.

Tyndale fiction list: The Left Behind Series by Lattaye/Jenkins; *Unspoken* by Francine Rivers; *Out of the Shadows* by Sigmund Broower; *Safely Home* by Randy Alcorn; *Ribbon of Years* by Robin Lee Hatcher.

The Tyndale program of books for children and young adults is in a transitional phase; currently, the house is not interested in fiction geared for this younger age group.

Tyndale House oversees its own distribution. Tyndale also distributes books from Focus on the Family.

Tyndale does not accept unsolicited manuscripts. For manuscript submissions, send SASE to the Manuscript Review Committee, requesting a copy of the committee's writers' guidelines—and query first.

Query letters and SASEs should be directed to:

Jon Farrar, Adult nonfiction.

Ginny Williams, Acquisitions Editor

Jon Farrar, Adult nonfiction.

Linda Washington, Children's and gift.

Jan Stob, Adult fiction

Anne Goldsmith, Women's fiction and romance.

Union of American Hebrew Congregations/UAHC Press

Union of American Hebrew Congregations, 633 Third Avenue, New York, NY 10017
212-650-4120   fax: 212-650-4119
http:// uahcpress.com   e-mail: press@uahc.org

Union of American Hebrew Congregations/UAHC Press publishes in the areas of religion (Jewish), Reform Judaism, textbooks, audiovisual materials, social action, biography, and life cycles and holidays. In trade categories, UAHC Press accents juvenile fiction and adult nonfiction books, as well as titles in basic Judaism and inspirational works. The house catalogs books, audiocassettes, videotapes, and multimedia products.

The UAHC Press provides the highest quality in religious educational materials and has done so for well over 100 years. The publications of the press are suitable for all ages, from preschool through adult, for use in both the classroom and at home. The publishers are committed to providing their readers with the foremost in materials and service, to be a continuing resource for books, publications, audiocassettes, videotapes, and multimedia.

Founded in 1873, UAHC Press is a division of Union of American Hebrew Congregations. The UAHC Press publishing program includes the *Reform Judaism* magazine.

Indicative of UAHC Press interest: *Jewish Dimensions of Social Justice: Tough Moral Choices of Our Time* by Albert Vorspan and David Saperstein; *The Matzah Ball Fairy* by Carla Heymsfeld (illustrated by Vlad Guzner); *America: The Jewish Experience* by Sondra Leiman; *Where We Stand: Jewish Consciousness on Campus* (edited by Allan L. Smith); *A Jerusalem Mystery* by Aaron Frankel; *What Crucified Jesus? Messianism, Pharisaism, and the Development of Christianity* by Ellis Rivkin; *Tzedakah: Can Jewish Philanthropy Buy Jewish Survival?* by Jacob Neuser; *A Shabbat Reader: Universe of Cosmic Joy* (edited by Dov Peretz Elkins); *Judaism and Spiritual Ethics* by Niles E. Goldstein and Steven S. Mason.

Children's titles from UAHC: *Hello, Hello, Are You There God?* by Molly Cone (illustrated by Rosalind Charney Kaye); *The God Around Us* by Mira Pollak Brichto (illustrated by Selina Alko); *Let There Be Lights!* by Camille Kress (illustrated by the author); *Who Knows Ten? Children's Tales of the Ten Commandments* by Molly Cane (illustrated by Robin Brickman); *The Big Book of Great Teaching Ideas: For Jewish Schools, Youth Groups, Camps, and Retreats* by Shirley Barish (illustrated by Ann D. Koffsky); *Drawing Your Way Through the Jewish Holidays* by Eleanor Schick (illustrated by the author).

UAHC Press handles its own distribution. Query letters and SASEs should be directed to:

Kenneth Gesser, Publisher

Rabbi Hara Person, Editor

U

UNITED CHURCH PRESS (A DIVISION OF THE PILGRIM PRESS)

700 Prospect Avenue East, Cleveland, OH 44115
216-736-3700   fax: 216-736-3703

United Church Press is a publishing imprint of the United Church of Christ. It was formed in 1957 after the Evangelical Reformed Church and the Congregational Christian Church merged to become the United Church of Christ.

The first resources published under the United Church Press imprint were Christian education curriculum. Today, the United Church Press publishes books for clergy, lay leaders, and Christians who want to increase their faith and spirituality through inspirational yet cutting-edge resources. United Church Press publishes books on such topics as women's issues, racial/ethnic issues, sexuality issues, and family concerns. In addition, it continues to publish Christian education curriculum.

United Church Press has introduced a delightful and meaningful set of picture books for young children. The Word and Picture Books are the perfect "first Bible" books for infants and toddlers up to four years of age. Titles include: *Come to Jesus; Jesus, a Special Baby; Jesus Goes Fishing; Breakfast at the Lake; Loving Shepherd;* and *The First Church.*

United Church oversees its own distribution. Query letters and SASEs should be directed to:

Kim Sadler, Editor, United Church Press

Sidney Fowler, Curriculum Editor, United Church Press

VEDANTA PRESS

Vedanta Society of Southern California, 1946 Vedanta Place, Hollywood, CA 90068
323-960-1728
www.vedanta.com   e-mail: info@vedanta.com

Vedanta's publishing interest includes meditation, religions and philosophies, and women's studies. In addition to its list of titles imported from the East (primarily from Indian publishers), Vedanta's program embraces works of Western origin. The publisher catalogs titles from other publishers and also sells audiotapes and videotapes.

The house publishes books on the philosophy of Vedanta, with an aim to engage a wide variety of temperaments, using a broad spectrum of methods, in order to attain the realization of each individual personality's divinity within. Vedanta Press (founded in 1947) is a subsidiary of the Vedanta Society of Southern California.

Backlist from the press: *How to Know God: The Yoga Aphorisms of Patanjali* (translated by Swami Prabhavananda and Christopher Isherwood); *The Upanishads: Breath of the Eternal* (translated by Swami Prabhavananda and Frederick Manchester); *Women Saints: East and West* (edited by Swami Ghanananda and Sir John Stewart-Wallace); *The Sermon on the Mount According to Vedanta* by Swami Prabhavananda; *Seeing God Everywhere: A Practical Guide to Spiritual Living* by Swami Shraddhananda; *Six Lighted Windows: Memories of Swamis in the West* by Swami Yogeshananda. Vedanta publishes many classic Vedic works in a variety of editions and translations. Among them: *Bhagavad Gita: The Song of God* (translated by Swami Prabhavananda and Christopher Isherwood; introduction by Aldous Huxley).

Vedanta Press handles its own distribution.

Vedanta's books originate in house, though the publisher is open to considering additional projects that may fall within its program. Vedanta does not wish to receive unsolicited manuscripts. Before you submit a query letter, be sure your book is within our niche. We don't do personal spiritual biographies and subjects outside the Vedanta tradition. Please do your research before writing to us or, for that matter, any publisher. Query letters and SASEs should be directed to:

Bob Adjemian, Manager

V

WEISER BOOKS

P.O. Box 612, York Beach, ME 03910-0612
207-363-4393   fax: 207-363-5799
e-mail: weiser@weiserbooks.com

Areas of Weiser publishing interest include self-transformation, alternative healing methods, meditation, metaphysics, consciousness, magic, astrology, tarot, astral projection, Kabbalah, earth religions, Eastern philosophy and religions, Buddhism, t'ai chi, healing, and Tibetan studies.

The publisher has observed the many paths that lead to personal transformation and strives to publish books to help many different people find the path that is right for them. Weiser Books specializes in books relating to all facets of the secret and hidden teachings worldwide.

Frontlist Weiser titles characteristically revamp age-old themes into new and vibrant works of contemporary sensibility. In addition to new titles, Weiser publishes classic references and tracts in reprint; Weiser also offers a particularly distinguished selection of titles pertinent to the life and works of Aleister Crowley, as well as a strong line of Gurdjieff studies. The house publishes in hardcover and paperback editions and maintains a thriving backlist. Weiser Books was founded in 1955.

Weiser Books handles its own distribution and distributes selected titles from other houses; the Weiser distribution catalog lists titles from over 200 publishers. Weiser Books is the exclusive distributor of Nicolas-Hays, Inc., titles, as well as Binkey Kok. Weiser utilizes the services of several national trade distributors.

Query letters and SASEs should be directed to:

Eliot Stearnes, Editor

WESTMINSTER/JOHN KNOX PRESS

Presbyterian Church (USA),100 Witherspoon Street, Louisville, KY 40202-1396
502-569-5000
www.ppcpub.org   e-mail: www.pcusa.org/ppc

Westminster/John Knox publishes general-interest religious trade books, as well as academic and professional works in biblical studies, theology, philosophy, ethics, history, archaeology, personal growth, and pastoral counseling. Among Westminster/John Knox series are Literary Currents in Biblical Interpretation, Family Living in Pastoral Perspective, Gender and the Biblical Tradition, and The Presbyterian Presence: The Twentieth-Century Experience.

Westminster/John Knox Press represents the publications unit of the Presbyterian Church (USA). The house unites the former independents Westminster Press and John Knox Press, which were originally founded as one entity in 1838, then separated into distinct enterprises, and again merged as WJK following the reunion of the Northern and Southern Presbyterian Churches in 1983.

Selected titles from Westminster/John Knox: *Dark the Night, Wild the Sea* by Robert McAfee Brown; *Speaking the Truth in Love: Prophetic Preaching to a Broken World* by J. Philip Wogaman; *Our Testament Wisdom: An Introduction* (revised and enlarged) by James L. Crenshaw; *Theology of the Prophetic Books: The Death and Resurrection of Israel* by Donald E. Gowan; *Honor and Shame in the Gospel of Matthew* by Jerome H. Neyrey; *Jesus as a Figure in History: How Modern Historians View the Man from Galilee* by Mark Allan Powell; *Athena's Disguises: Mentors in Everyday Life* by Susan Ford Wiltshire; *Both Feet Planted in Midair: My Spiritual Journey* by John McNeill; *Equipping the Saints: Teacher Training in the Church* by Sara Covin Juengst; *Survival or Revival: Ten Keys to Church Vitality* by Carnegie Samuel Calian; *We Have Seen the Lord!: The Passion and Resurrection of Jesus Christ* by William Barclay.

WJK's Studies in the Family, Religion, & Culture series offers informed and responsible analyses of the state of the American family from a religious perspective and provides practical assistance for the family's revitalization. Titles: *For the Love of Children: Genetic Technology and the Future of the Family* by Ted Peters; *Religion, Feminism, and the Family* (edited by Anne Carr and Mary Steward Van Leeuwen); *Faith Traditions and the Family* (edited by Phyllis D. Airhart and Margaret Lamberts Bendroth).

Westminster/John Knox distributes its list through Spring Arbor. The house also represents titles from other publishers, including Orbis Books, Pilgrim Press, Saint Andrew Press of Scotland, and Presbyterian Publishing Corporation.

Query letters and SASEs should be directed to:

Angela Jackson, Assistant Editor

WISDOM PUBLICATIONS

199 Elm Street, Somerville, MA 02144
617-776-7416   fax: 617-776-7841
www.wisdompubs.org   e-mail: info@wisdomoubs.org

Wisdom Publications centers on Buddhism, Tibet, and related East–West themes. The house offers books and its acclaimed Tibetan Art Calendar. Wisdom Publications (founded in 1975) was initiated by Lama Thubten Yeshe around the time he established the international Foundation for the Preservation of the Mahayana Tradition (FPMT).

Wisdom Publications, a not-for-profit publisher, is dedicated to making available authentic Buddhist works for the benefit of all. The house publishes translations of the sutras and tantras, commentaries and teachings of past and contemporary Buddhist masters, and original works by the world's leading Buddhist scholars. Wisdom Publications was named as one of the top 10 fastest-growing small publishers in the country (the company has been in the United States since 1989) by *Publishers Weekly* (November 18, 1996).

Wisdom titles are published in appreciation of Buddhism as a living philosophy and with the commitment to preserve and transmit important works from all the major Buddhist traditions. Wisdom products are distributed worldwide and have been translated into a dozen foreign languages.

Wisdom publishes the celebrated Tibetan Art Calendar, containing 13 full-color reproductions of the world's finest Indo-Tibetan thangka paintings, accompanied by detailed iconographical descriptions.

Wisdom highlight: *The Good Heart: A Buddhist Perspective on the Teachings of Jesus by the Dalai Lama* (introduced by Fr. Laurence Freeman).

Wisdom Publications is distributed to the trade in the United States and Canada by National Book Network (NBN). Query letters and SASEs should be directed to:

Timothy J. McNeill, Publisher

WORD PUBLISHING

Word Publishing is now an imprint of Thomas Nelson.

YESHIVA UNIVERSITY PRESS

500 West 185th Street, New York, NY 10033
212-960-5400

Yeshiva University Press (founded in 1960) produces a select list that includes original academic works, as well as titles of mainstream reader interest; the house also produces scholarly Judaica in reprint editions.

Representing the Yeshiva University list: *Free Enterprise and Jewish Law: Aspects of Jewish Business Ethics* by Aaron Levine; *All About Jewish Holidays and Customs* by Morris Epstein; *The Biblical and Historical Background of the Jewish Holy Days* by Abraham P. Bloch; *Jewish Woman in Jewish Law* by Moshe Meiselman; *Modern Medicine and Jewish Ethics* by Dr. Fred Rosner; *Judaism and Psychology: Halakhic Perspectives* by Moshe Halevi Spero; *Faith and Doubt: Studies in Traditional Jewish Thought* by Norman Lamm; *Honor Thy Father and Mother: Filial Responsibility in Jewish Law and Ethics* by Gerald Blidstein.

Books from Yeshiva University Press are distributed through KTAV Publishing House.

Query letters and SASEs should be directed to the editorial offices of KTAV Publishing House (please see entry for KTAV in this section of the directory).

ZONDERVAN PUBLISHING HOUSE

5300 Patterson Avenue SE, Grand Rapids, MI 49530
616-698-6900   fax: 616-698-3439
www.zondervan.com

Zondervan produces both fiction and nonfiction books that address contemporary issues in spirituality and counseling; inspirational novels; juveniles; humor; Bibles; and Bible study guides. As well as books, Zondervan has entries in the form of computer software, audiotape, and videotape. Zondervan Publishing House (founded in 1931) is among the most potent publishers specializing in evangelical Christian titles.

As the publisher notes: "In the everyday commerce of speech, words should be selected as carefully as treasured jewels. The right word at the right time uplifts, inspires, corrects, and instructs. Since 1931, through the power of words, Zondervan Publishing House has brought positive and redemptive change into the lives of people worldwide. Zondervan publishes its 2,000 bestselling and award-winning Bibles, books, audio books, videos, software, multimedia, and gift products to promote biblical principles and to meet the needs of people."

Zondervan's public persona includes eye-catching bookseller floor displays, posters, advertising schedules, and tie-ins via other media outlets. Zondervan authors are among the most enterprising in this area of publishing. Zondervan's HarperCollins connection (the house has been an editorially independent subsidiary of HarperCollins since 1988) makes for a brawny marketing arm, and Zondervan's readership and distribution are extraordinary.

From Zondervan: *Amhearst Mystery: Caught in the Act* by Gayle Roper; *Anatomy of a Lie* by Diane Komp, M.D.; *Blessing* by Trask/Goodall; *Book of God for Children* by Walter Wangerin, Jr.; *Business Basics from the Bible* by Bob Briner; *Christian Men Who Hate Women* by Dr. Margaret Rinck; *Epiphany* by Paul McCusker; *Faith Lesson/Prophets, Kings* by Ray Vander Laal; *God's Outrageous Claims* by Lee Strobel; *His Victorious Indwelling* by Nick Harrison; *I'm Alive and Doctor's Dead* by Sue Buchanan; *Interactions: Essential Christianity* by Bill Hybels; *Love Beyond Reason* by John Ortberg; *Mary's First Christmas* by Walter Wangerin, Jr.; *More Precious Than Silver* by Joni Eareckson Tada; *Nirv Kids Book of Devotions* by Mark Littleton; *Present Time/Lost Prophet* by John Schmidt.

Zondervan distributes its own titles to the general market, the book trade, and the CBA.

Zondervan asks that interested authors write to request submissions guidelines before submitting manuscripts or other material.

Z

Canadian Publishers

Canadian Book Publishing and the Canadian Market

Greg Ioannou

Canadian and United States writers who are considering submitting inquiries to Canadian publishers should keep a few important points in mind. In most cases, Canadian book publishers are looking for material of Canadian interest. However, this does not mean they are not interested in queries from writers who reside in or are native to other countries.

Indeed, a rich current in the Canadian publishing stream features the Canadian experience from outlander or expatriate perspectives. Canadian reader interests are also keyed into a number of broader market sectors, such as North American pop culture or British Commonwealth concerns.

Appropriate queries (see the listings for these publishers) will be considered. Keep in mind the markets as well as the mandates of each house.

Publishing in Canada is markedly different from the industry in the United States. A large percentage of Canadian-owned publishing houses are small- to medium-sized, with net sales that may seem low to those accustomed to the standards of the U.S. marketplace. (Remember, the English-language Canadian market is only one-tenth the size of the United States market.)

Canada *is* a separate market, and some writers are able to sell the Canadian rights to their books separately from the U.S. rights. Before you sign a contract for "North American rights," consider whether your book would likely sell enough copies in Canada that it would be of interest to a Canadian publisher.

Don't just blithely sell the Canadian rights to a hockey book or a biography of a Canadian celebrity (such as Faye Wray or Neil Young or Peter Jennings) to a U.S. publisher for the blanket "foreign rights" or "world English-language rights" rate—the Canadian rights alone may be worth more than the U.S. or rest of the worldwide rights are!

The Canadian government directly subsidizes the book industry to help ensure that Canadian writers get their works published domestically and to keep the national market from being overwhelmed by the publishing giants to the south. The government grant system makes possible a greater independence on the part of Canadian-owned houses, which comprise the creative heart of publishing in Canada.

Never send an unsolicited manuscript to a Canadian publisher. Many Canadian publishers will send them back unopened because of a court ruling that forced Doubleday Canada to pay a writer thousands of dollars in compensation for losing the only copy of an unsolicited manuscript. Send query letters only!

It is a nice touch for American writers to remember that Canada is *not* part of the United States, so Canadian publishers cannot use U.S. stamps to return anything you send them. Use International Reply Coupons (available at any post office) instead.

ANVIL PRESS

MPO Box 3008, Vancouver, BC V63 3X5, Canada
604-876-8710
www.anvilpress.com

Anvil Press began in 1988 as the publisher for *sub-TERRAIN Magazine.* In 1991, it expanded into the book-publishing field with the mandate to discover and nurture new talent in Canada. It now publishes six titles a year and sponsors the three-day International Novel Contest every September (more information about the contest is available on its Web site: www.anvilpress.com). Although it does occasionally publish nonfiction, Anvil specializes in contemporary literary fiction, poetry, and drama; it does not publish genre fiction.

Recent Anvil titles include: *Snatch* by Judy Macinnes, Jr.; *Skin* by Bonnie Bauman; and Lyle Neff's book of poetry, *Full MagPie Dodge.*

For fiction/nonfiction submissions, Anvil requests a brief, one-page synopsis of the entire manuscript and 20–30 pages of the manuscript itself. For poetry, 8–12 poems should be submitted. Anvil requests the entire manuscript for works of drama, unless excessively long. Anvil only publishes Canadian authors. Only manuscripts accompanied by an SASE will be considered. Query letters and SASEs should be directed to:

Brian Kaufman, Publisher

BEACH HOLME PUBLISHING

226-2040 West 12th Avenue, Vancouver, BC V6J 2G2, Canada
604-733-4868   www.beachholme.bc.ca

Beach Holme Publishing, so-named in honor of the owner's house, is a small Vancouver publisher with a mandate "to promote indigenous creative writing to the wider Canadian public." Its literary roots began with its former incarnation, Press Porcepic, which published such renowned authors as Dorothy Livesay and James Reaney. Porcepic Books began as an imprint of Beach Holme and continues to build its own niche in the Canadian literary heritage with newer talents like Evelyn Lau and Jane Urquhart. Novels, plays, poetry, and short fiction are all featured under the Porcepic Books imprint. Beach Holme also publishes young adult fiction (Sandcastle Books).

Titles typical of the list: *What the Small Day Cannot Hold* by Susan Musgrave; *Ondine's Curse* by Steven Manners; *Villa Four* by Bernadette Dyer; *Cold Clear Morning* by Lesley Choyce; and *The Self-Completing Tree* by Dorothy Livesay.

Under its new imprint, Prospect Books, Beach Holme publishes creative nonfiction. Beach Holme Publishing only produces work by Canadian authors resident in Canada; foreign manuscripts will not be considered and should be directed elsewhere. Query letters and SASEs should be directed to:

Michael Carroll, Publisher

CORMORANT BOOKS

R.R. 1, Dunvegan, ON K0C 1J0, Canada
613-527-3348   fax: 613-527-2262
www.cormorant.com   e-mail: cormorant@glen-net.ca

Cormorant Books publishes a small, select list of literary fiction and trade nonfiction. This small press also produces several works of fiction in translation.

Notables from the Cormorant catalogue: *Lives of the Saints* by Nino Ricci; *Kitchen Music* by Charles Foran; *Gaff Topsails* by Patrick Kavanagh; *The Good Body* by Bill Gaston; *Purple Forsky* by Carol Bruneau; *Drowning in Darkness* by Peter Oliva.

Recent nonfiction titles: *Living in the World as If It Were Home* by Tim Lilburn; *A Very Large Soul: Selected Letters from Margaret Laurence to Canadian Writers* (edited by J. A. Wainwright); *Invisible Among the Ruins: Field Notes of a Canadian in Ireland* by John Moss.

Query letters and SASEs should be directed to:

Barbara Glen, Assistant to the Publisher

Jan Geddes, Publisher

COTEAU BOOKS

401, 2206 Dewdney Avenue, Regina, SK S4R 1H3, Canada
306-777-0170   fax: 306-522-5152
www.coteaubooks.com   e-mail: coteau@coteaubooks.com

Coteau Books publishes a range of Canadian works, with a particular focus on the literary genres—novels, short fiction, poetry, drama, and juvenile fiction. Coteau presents an annual list that reflects literary quality across the country, including First Nations authors, with a focus on prairie voices of all kinds. Nonfiction work, especially memoir, is a growing interest as well.

Coteau has recently launched a new poetry series called Open Eye, with the intent to feature new, young poetic voices and attract a broad readership to the genre.

The Coteau list features such titles as the international short fiction anthology *Two Lands Two Visions* (edited by Janice Kulyk Keefer and Solomea Pavlychko); Open Eye poetry title *My Flesh the Sound of Rain* by Heather MacLeod; *The Intrepid Polly McDoodle,* the second in a juvenile novel series by Edmonton author Mary Woodbury.

Recent titles include Governor-General's Award–winner Anne Szumigalski's greatest hits, *On Glassy Wings* which received the Canadian Authors Association Poetry Prize; Barbara Nickels's first poetry book, *The Gladys Elegies* which was awarded the Pat Lowther Memorial Prize as the best book of poetry by a woman; and the short fiction collection *In the Misleading Absence of Light* by Regina author Joanne Gerber (which has received five national and provincial awards to date).

Coteau also publishes the annual daybook *Herstory: The Canadian Women's Calendar* compiled annually by the Saskatoon Women's Calendar Collective.

Queries and SASEs should be directed to:

Nik Burton, Managing Editor, Regina

Douglas & McIntyre Publishers

Douglas & McIntyre Children's Division

Firefly Books

1615 Venables Street, Vancouver, BC V5L 2H1, Canada
604-254-7191

Toronto office:
585 Bloor Street West, 2nd Floor, Toronto, ON M6G 1K5
416-537-2501

D

Douglas & McIntyre Publishers (founded in 1964) offers a publishing program with Canadian emphasis—often with a specifically British Columbian inflection. The house produces hardcover and paperback books in both fiction and nonfiction. Nonfiction areas of interest include native art, current affairs, history, travel, and nature studies. Douglas & McIntyre fiction tends toward literary works, serious popular fiction, and tales of mystery and suspense.

Nonfiction titles: *Haida Art* by George F. MacDonald; *Cold as Charity: The Truth Behind the High Cost of Giving* by Walter Stewart; *Politically Speaking* by Judy Rebick and Kiké Roach; *HeartSmart Chinese Cooking* by Stephen Wong and the Heart & Stroke Foundation of Canada; *Working Dollars: The VanCity Savings Story* by Herschel Hardin; *Mike Harcourt: A Measure of Defiance* by Michael Harcourt, with Wayne Skene; *The Immortal Beaver: The World's Greatest Bush Plane* by Sean Rossiter; *Bishop's: The Cookbook* by John Bishop; *Back to the Front: An Accidental Historian Walks the Trenches of World War I* by Stephen O'Shea; *Toni Cavelti: A Jeweller's Life* by Max Wyman.

Fiction and literary works: *Bachelor Brothers' Bedside Companion* by Bill Richardson (illustrated by Rose Cowles); *eye wuz here: 30 women writers under 30* (edited by Shannon Cooley); *The Lesser Blessed* by Richard VanCamp; *Let the Drums Be Your Heart: New Native Voices* (edited by Joel T. Maki); *Local Colour: Writers Discovering Canada* (edited by Carol Martin); *A Story as Sharp as a Knife: An Introduction to Classical Haida Literature* by Robert Bringhurst; *Notes from the Century Before: A Journal from British Columbia* by Edward Hoagland (illustrated by Claire Van Vliet).

The Greystone Books imprint offers travel guides, one-day getaways, regional histories, sports books (especially hockey), and titles in hiking, camping, and outdoor recreation. Representative titles from Greystone: *Cowgirls* by Candace Savage; *British Columbia: A Natural History* by Richard Cannings and Sydney Cannings; *Hockey the NHL Way: The Basics* by Sean Rossiter; *The Nature of Shorebirds: Nomads of the Wetlands* by Harry Thurston; *The Nature of Penguins: Birds of Distinction* by Jonathan Chester; *Orca: Visions of the Killer Whale* by Peter Knudtson; *Courting Saskatchewan: A Celebration of Winter*

Feasts, Summer Loves and Rising Brooks by David Carpenter; *Day Trips from Vancouver* by Jack Christie; *Fishing in the West* by David Carpenter; *52 Weekend Activities Around Vancouver* by Sue Lebrecht and Judi Lees.

Douglas & McIntyre handles its own distribution, as well as purveys books from additional houses and institutions including Canadian Museum of Civilization, the Mountaineers, the New Press, Sierra Club Books, and Thames and Hudson.

Query letters and SASEs should be directed to the **Acquisitions Editor;** correspondence will be redirected in house.

Douglas & McIntyre Children's Division

Within its children's division, Douglas & McIntyre offers several special imprints. Groundwood Press publishes titles for preschoolers through young adults. Earthcare Books is an environmental series for middle-grade readers, which includes *For the Birds* written by Canadian novelist Margaret Atwood. First Discovery is a series of nature books for toddlers and early readers. Rounding out Douglas & McIntyre's juveniles list are fiction for young adults, picture books, the Walker imprint's nonfiction and picture books (some of which are targeted for appeal to the entire family), and Meadow Mouse paperbacks.

On the list: *So You Love to Draw: Every Kid's Guide to Becoming an Artist* by Michael Seary (illustrated by Michel Bisson); *Jade and Iron: Latin American Tales from Two Cultures* (translated by Hugh Hazelton; edited by Patricia Aldana; illustrated by Luís Garay); *A Completely Different Place* by Perry Nodelman (fiction for ages 10–13); *Mary Margaret's Tree* by Blair Drawson (picture book for ages 3–6); *Beaver the Tailor: A How-to Picture Book* by Lars Klinting (for ages 5–7); *The Rooster's Gift* by Pam Conrad (illustrated by Eric Beddows) (picture book for ages 4–8); *Steel Drums and Ice Skates* by Dirk Mclean (illustrated by Ho Che Anderson) (picture book for ages 6–9); *Sarah and the People of Sand River* by W. D. Valgardson (illustrated by Ian Wallace) (picture book for ages 5–9); *Enchantment in the Garden* by Shirley Hughes (ages 8 and up).

Query letters and SASEs should be directed to the **Acquisitions Editor;** correspondence will be redirected in house. The Toronto office handles fiction and children's books; the rest of the Douglas & McIntyre list is issued from the Vancouver office.

Firefly Books

3680 Victoria Park Avenue, Willowdale, ON M2H 3K1, Canada
416-499-8412, 800-387-5085

Firefly produces trade nonfiction in areas that include popular biography, popular science, lifestyles, the natural world, hobbies and crafts, gardening, food, sports, recreation, and health.

Representative of the Firefly list: *All Fired Up! Year Round Grilling and Barbecuing* by John and Margaret Howard; *The Wild Food Gourmet: Fresh and Savory Food from Nature* by Anne Gardon; *Clueless in the Kitchen: A Cookbook for Teens and Other Beginners* by

Evelyn Raab; *The Art of Perennial Gardening: Creative Ways with Hardy Flowers* by Patrick Lima (photographs by John Scanlan); *Dry-Land Gardening: A Xeriscaping Guide for Dry-Summer Cold-Winter Climates* by Jennifer Bennett; *Butterflies of the World* by Valerio Sbordoni and Saverio Forestiero; *High Above the Canadian Rockies: Spectacular Aerial Photography* by Russ Heinl; *Restoring Houses of Brick and Stone* by Nigel Hutchins; *Caring for Your Parents in Their Senior Years: A Guide for Grown-Up Children* by William Molloy, M.D.; *Coaching: Winning Strategies for Every Level of Play* by Dave Chambers.

Firefly Books handles its own distribution. Query letters and SASEs should be directed to:

Lionel Koffler, President

FITZHENRY & WHITESIDE LTD.

195 Allstate Parkway, Markham, ON L3R 4T8, Canada
905-477-9700   fax: 905-477-9179

Fitzhenry & Whiteside Ltd. (founded in 1966) specializes in trade nonfiction and children's books. The firm also offers a textbook list and a small list of literary/fiction works.

Fitzhenry & Whiteside nonfiction tittles range throughout Canadian history, biography, native studies, nature, and antiques and collectibles. The children's book list includes early readers, picture books, and middle-grade and young adult novels.

From Fitzhenry & Whiteside nonfiction: *Trees in Canada* by John Laird Farrar; *What Time of Day Was That?* by Dale Patterson; *Under Sydenham Skies* by Cornelia Baines; and *The Canadian Geographic Quiz Book* by Doug MacLean.

Fitzhenry & Whiteside fiction and literature: *The Poetry of Lucy Maud Montgomery* (edited by Kevin McCabe and Alexandra Heibron); *North with Franklin* by John Wilson; *New Canadian Poetry* (edited by Evan Jones).

On the children's list: *Sea Otter Inlet* by Celia Godkin; *A Screaming Kind of Day* by Rachna Gilmore and Gordon Suave; *The Follower* by Richard Thompson and Martin Springett; *Next Stop!* by Sarah Ellis and Ruth Ohi; *More Frogs for Dinner* by Frieda Wishinsky; *Mina's Spring of Colors* by Rachna Gilmore; and *Lost in Spain* by John Wilson.

Fitzhenry & Whiteside distributes its own list and provides distribution services in Canada for a number of United States publishers.

Query letters and SASEs should be directed to:

Sharon Fitzhenry, President and Publisher

Gail Winskill, Children's Book Publisher

GOOSE LANE EDITIONS

469 King Street, Fredericton, NB E3B 1E5, Canada
506-450-4251   fax: 506-459-4991

Goose Lane Editions is a small Canadian publishing house that specializes in literary fiction, poetry, and a select list of nonfiction titles. It does not publish commercial fiction, genre fiction, or confessional works of any kind. Occasionally, one of its books will appeal to young adults, but it does not publish books specifically for that market, nor does it publish books for children.

Recent Goose Lane titles: *16 Categories of Desire* by Douglas Glover; *A Personal Calligraphy* by Mary Pratt; *A Fit Month for Dying* by M. T. Dohaney; and *Strange Heaven* by Lynn Coady.

As a member of the Literary Press group, Goose Lane Editions has a Canada-wide sales force serving the book trade. In addition, the company employs several regional sales representatives to nontraditional outlets such as gift stores. Academic sales are handled by Irwin Publishing. General Distribution Services takes care of order fulfillment.

Goose Lane considers submissions from outside Canada only rarely, and only when both the author and the material have significant Canadian connections and the material is of extraordinarily high interest and literary merit. Writers should submit a synopsis, outline, and sample (30–50 pages) with an SASE if in Canada; international authors should include an SAE and international reply coupons with submission. Please query by mail or phone before submitting; direct queries to:

Laurel Boone, Acquisitions Editor

G

HARLEQUIN ENTERPRISES LIMITED

Worldwide Library

225 Duncan Mill Road, Don Mills, ON M3B 3K9, Canada
416-445-5860

The Harlequin Enterprises home base in Ontario, Canada, issues the greater portion of Harlequin Books series, while the New York office issues several Harlequin series, as well as the Silhouette list (please see listing for Harlequin Books in the directory of United States publishers and editors). Harlequin Enterprises Limited also publishes the Worldwide Library, which accents titles in the mystery/suspense and thriller mode.

Harlequin Books (Canada)

The Harlequin series of romance novels published in Canada, like their American counterparts, each stake out particular market-niche segments of reader interest within the overall categories of romance fiction and women's fiction.

The editorial acquisitions departments for Harlequin Romance and Harlequin Presents are located at the operation's United Kingdom offices (the address for which is listed further on). Following are overviews of some of the editorial guidelines supplied to authors:

Mira Books is dedicated to mainstream single-title women's fiction in hardcover and mass-market paperback editions. Mira titles assume no particular genre designation, though the works are considered to be of interest to a primarily women's readership. Mira Books hosts a wide variety of authors and approaches.

Harlequin Temptation introduces strong, independent heroines and successful, sexy heroes who overcome conflict inherent to their heated relationships and in the end decide to marry. The books in this series are known for their wit as well as emotional strength.

Harlequin Temptations are sensuous romances about choices . . . dilemmas . . . resolutions . . . and, above all, the fulfillment of love. The most highly charged and most sensual Harlequin series.

Harlequin Superromance is a line of longer, contemporary romance novels. Realistic stories with emotional depth and intensity . . . more involving plots . . . more complex characters. Superromance women are confident and independent, yet eager to share their lives.

Harlequin Superromances are the longest books of the Harlequin series (approximately 350 manuscript pages) and therefore require a more complex plot and at least one fully developed subplot. This series is generally mainstream in tone, with romance, of course, being the propelling theme. Love scenes may be explicit, so long as they exhibit good taste.

Detailed information is available upon request from the publisher. Harlequin will send prospective authors full editorial guidelines with suggested heroine and hero profiles, as well as information pertaining to manuscript length, setting, and sexual approach and content.

Make sure your query is clear as to which line it is intended for: Harlequin Romance, Harlequin Presents, Harlequin Temptation, Harlequin Superromance, or Harlequin Duets

Query letters and SASEs should be directed to:

Amy Moore, Editor—Mira Books.

Birgit David Todd, Senior Editor—Harlequin Temptation.

Brenda Chin, Editor—Harlequin Temptation, Duets.

Dianne Moggy, Editorial Director—Mira Books.

Laura Shin, Editor—Harlequin Superromance.

Bev Sotelov, Editor—Harlequin Superromance.

Paula Eykelhof, Senior Editor—Harlequin Superromance.

Susan Sheppard, Editor—Harlequin Temptation, Duets.

Zilla Soriano, Editor—Harlequin Superromance.

Martha Keenen, Associate Editor—Mira Books.

Harlequin Mills & Boon

Harlequin Presents

Harlequin Romance

Mills & Boon/Harlequin Enterprises Ltd.

Eton House, 18-24 Paradise Road, Richmond, Surrey TW9 1SR, United Kingdom

Acquisitions for Harlequin Romance and Harlequin Presents are through the United Kingdom offices. Query the offices to request a set of editorial guidelines supplied to prospective authors.

Harlequin Romance is the original line of romance fiction, the series that started it all—over 35 years ago. These are warm, contemporary novels, filled with compassion and sensitivity, written by world-famous authors.

Harlequin Presents is overall the bestselling Harlequin line, published in 16 different languages and sold in almost every country of the world. This line features heartwarming romance novels about bright, capable women who are taking charge of their own lives, set in exotic locales.

To query the U.K. divisions, write (and enclose SASE) in care of the Editorial Department (especially to request guidelines), or direct inquiries to the following individual editors:

Lesley Stonehouse, Senior Editor—Silhouette.

Karin Stoecker, Editorial Director—All Mills & Boon series.

Linda Fildew, Senior Editor—Historical Romance and Mira.

Samantha Bell, Senior Editor—Mills and Boons Enchanted and Harlequin Romance.

Sheila Hodgson, Senior Editor—Medical.

Tessa Shapcott, Senior Editor—Harlequin Presents (contemporary romances).

Worldwide Library

Worldwide Mystery

Gold Eagle Books

The Worldwide Library division of Harlequin Enterprises hosts two major imprints, Worldwide Mystery and Gold Eagle Books. Worldwide Library emphasizes genre fiction in the categories of mystery and suspense, action-adventure, futuristic fiction, war drama, and post-holocaust thrillers. The house gives its titles (primarily mass-market paperbacks) solid marketing and promotional support.

The Worldwide Mystery imprint specializes in mainstream commercial mystery and detective fiction in reprint. This imprint has not been issuing previously unpublished, original fiction; however, Worldwide is not to be overlooked as a resource regarding potential reprint-rights sales in this field. The house generally keeps lines of popular writers' ongoing series in print for a number of seasons, sometimes indefinitely.

Titles in reprint at Worldwide: *Zero at the Bone* by Mary Willis Walker; *Time of Hope* by Susan B. Kelly; *The Hour of the Knife* by Sharon Zukowski; *Murder Takes Two* by Bernie Lee; *Hard Luck* by Barbara D'Amato; *A Fine Italian Hand* by Eric Wright.

Gold Eagle Books is known for a fast-and-furious slate of men's action and adventure series with paramilitary and future-world themes. Series include Deathlands, the Destroyer, the Executioner, and Stony Man. Gold Eagle also publishes Super Books keyed to the various series—longer novels with more fully developed plots. Prospective authors should be familiar with the guidelines and regular characters associated with each series.

Query letters and SASEs should be directed to:

Feroze Mohammed, Senior Editor and Editorial Coordinator—Gold Eagle Books.

Heather Locker—Associate Editor

HOUSE OF ANANSI PRESS

34 Lesmill Road, Toronto, ON M3B 2T6, Canada
416-445-3333   fax: 416-445-5967
www.anansi.ca

House of Anansi Press is a literary press, founded in 1967 by Dennis Lee and David God-frey, with a mandate to publish innovative literary works in fiction, nonfiction, and poetry by Canadian writers. Anansi acquired a reputation early on for its editors' ability to spot talented writers who push the boundaries and challenge the expectations of the literary community. This continues to be a part of the press's mandate, while it also maintains its rich backlist and keeps important works by Canadian writers in print.

Anansi has published works by such Canadian luminaries as Northrop Frye, Margaret Atwood, Michael Ondaatje, and Dennis Lee. The house emphasizes literary fiction, trade nonfiction, poetry, politics, philosophy, social thought, literary criticism, theory, autobi-ography, biography, and women's studies. Anansi also publishes *Alphabet City,* an edgy annual journal of cultural theory, literature, philosophy, and architecture.

Representative of the list: *The Real World of Technology* by Ursula M. Franklin; *Becoming Human* by Jean Vanier; *Mean* by Ken Babstock; *The Plight of Happy People in an Ordinary World* by Natalee Caple; and *Ruin and Beauty* by Patricia Young.

Query letters and SASEs should be directed to:

Adrienne Leahey, Assistant Editor

Martha Sharpe, Publisher

INSOMNIAC PRESS

192 Spadina Avenue, Suite 403, Toronto, ON M5T 2C2, Canada
416-504-6270   fax: 416-504-9313
www.insomniacpress.com

Insomniac Press, established in 1992, publishes a small, eclectic list of books, most of which have an experimental bent. Though focused primarily on literary fiction, Insom-niac also produces select nonfiction and popular trade titles.

Poetry and graphic novels round out the catalog of this unique press. Nonfiction areas of interest include: architecture, social commentary, political science, business, personal fi-nance, travel and food, black studies, and pop culture. Insomniac also publishes literature of gay and lesbian interest and is celebrated for its high-caliber spoken word anthologies.

I

Works representative of the nonfiction list: *The Uncommon Investor* by Benjamin Gallander; *Get Stuffed Toronto* by Julie Crysler; *Black Like Who?* by Rinaldo Walcott; *Room Behavior* by Rob Kovitz.

A sampler of titles from the literary line-up: *Written in the Skin* by Rob McLennan (with photographs by Jules deNiverville); *Silver* by Matthew Remski; *The Quilted Heart* by R. M. Vaughan; *Bull* by Mark Sinnett; *Guilty* by Sky Gilbert; *The Heart Is Its Own Reason* by Natalee Caple; *Carnival* (edited by Peter McPhee); *Desire High Heels Red Wine* by Timothy Archer, Sky Gilbert, Sonja Mills, and Margaret Webb; *Hard Candy* by Jill Battson; *Paul's Case* by Lynn Crosbie.

Insomniac does not accept unsolicited manuscripts; send queries and SASEs to:

Mike O'Connor, Publisher

KEY PORTER BOOKS LTD.

70 The Esplanade, 3rd Floor, Toronto, ON M5E 1R2, Canada
416-862-7777

Key Porter Books Ltd. (founded in 1981) is a midsize house that publishes a primarily nonfiction list with a Canadian twist. Key Porter produces titles in current affairs, science and health, travel, the environment, ecology, politics, sports, and a solid line of money books and entrepreneurial guides. In addition, the house offers coffee-table and gift editions, as well as occasional fiction and literary works.

Frontlist Key Porter titles are provided full promotional support that spotlights targeted review venues, national media exposure, magazine advertising (including co-op arrangements), and foreign-rights sales. The house maintains a strong backlist.

Among Key Porter highlights: *Walking on Land* by Farley Mowat; *Can Asians Think?* by Kishore Mahbubani; *The Hiding Place* by Trezza Azzopardip; *The Dog Rules* by William Thomas; *When Eve Was Naked* by Josef Skvorecky; *The Truth About Love* by Patrick Roscoe; *The Jasmine Man* by Lola Lemire Tostevin; *Always Give a Penny to a Blind Man* by Eric Wright; *Odjig: The Art of Daphne Odjig 1966–2000* by Daphne Odjig with Carol Podedworny; *Civilians* by Felipe Fernandez-Armstrong.

Susan Renouf, President and Editor in Chief

Key Porter Kids

Key Porter Kids is an imprint that specializes in works for younger readers, including pop-ups, board books, storybooks, novels, and reference works. The house publishes science books for children under the imprint Greeyde Pencier/Books from Owl. Some titles from this division are cross-cataloged with the house's core list.

Titles include: *Bubblegum Delicious Alligator Pie* (collector's edition), and *Jelly Belly* by Dennis Lee; *The Deep Cold River Story* by Tabatha Southey (illustrated by Sue Savor); *New Animal Discoveries* by Ronald Orenstein (foreword by Jane Goodall); *Ancient Adventures for Modern Kids* (illustrated by John Mardon and Vesna Krstanovich); *The Little Women Pop-up Dollhouse.*

Key Porter Kids also publishes the Young Readers' Classics Series, which includes: *Heidi; The Secret Garden; Anne of Green Gables; Little Women* and, most recently, *Black Beauty* (retold by Barbara Greenwood and illustrated by Rennie Benoit).

Key Porter handles its own distribution.

McGill-Queen's University Press

Montreal office:

McGill University, 3430 McTavish Street, Montreal, QC H3A 1X9, Canada

514-398-3750

www.mcgill.ca/mqup   e-mail: mqup@mqup.mcgill.ca

Kingston office:

Queen's University, Kingston, ON K7L 3N6, Canada

fax: 613-533-6822

mqup@post.queensu.ca

Publications from McGill-Queen's University Press include works in architecture, biography, British studies, business history, Canadian history, Canadian politics, economics, environment, French history, housing policy, international history, Irish history, Judaica, literature and literary criticism, Loyalist history, native studies, philosophy, political economy, psychology, Quebec history, sociology, urban geography, women's studies, poetry, and general-interest works primarily in areas of current interest in international and cultural affairs. McGill-Queen's publishes no hard sciences.

McGill-Queen's University Press (founded in 1969) produces trade books with scholarly market crossover, as well as titles geared specifically for the academic market. The press is a conjoint publishing endeavor of Queen's University (Kingston) and McGill University (Montreal). Many McGill-Queen's books have a Canadian subject slant; in addition, the house is strong in a variety of fields in the international arena, as well as in the social sciences and humanities. McGill-Queen's publishes in the French and English languages.

On the McGill-Queen's list: *Marguerite Bourgeoys and Montreal 1640–1665* by Patricia Simpson; *Canada Enters the Nuclear Age: A Technical History of Atomic Energy of Canada Limited as Seen from Its Research Laboratories* by E. Critoph et al.; *Degrees of Freedom: Canada and the United States in a Changing World* (edited by Keith Banting, George Hoberg, and Richard Simeon); *The Secession of Quebec and the Future of Canada* by Robert A. Young; *A Long Way from Home: The Tuberculosis Epidemic Among the Inuit* by Pat Sandiford Grygier; *The Virtual Marshall McLuhan* by Donald F. Theall; *Stranger Gods: Salman Rushdie's Other Worlds* by Roger Y. Clark; *The Distant Relation: Time and Identity in Spanish American Fiction* by Eoin S. Thomson; *Canada, Latin America, and the New Internationalism* by Brian J. R. Stevenson; *Bullets on the Water: Canadian Refugee Stories* by Ivaylo Grouev; *French Socialists Before Marx* by Pamela Pilbeam; *The Future of NATO* by Charles-Philippe David and Jacques Levesque; *English Immigrant Voices* by Wendy Cameron; *Alejandro Melaspina: Portrait of a Visionary* by John Kendrick.

M

The McGill-Queen's literary purview embraces criticism, memoir, biography, and letters. Offerings here: *Lying About the Wolf: Essays in Culture and Education* by David Solway; *Aesthetics* by Colin Lyas; *African Exploits: The Diaries of William Stairs 1887–1892* (edited by Roy MacLaren); *The Cassock and the Crown: Canada's Most Controversial Murder Trial* by Jean Monet; *Cold Comfort: My Love Affair with the Arctic* by Graham W. Rowley; *Mapping Our Selves: Canadian Women's Autobiography* by Helen M. Buss; *The Birth of Modernism: Ezra Pound, T. S. Eliot, W. B. Yeats, and the Occult* by Leon Surette;

Distribution for McGill-Queen's University Press is handled by General Distribution Services in Canada and by Cornell University Press (Cup Services) in the United States.

Query letters and SASEs should be directed to:

Aurele Parisien, Editor (Montreal)

Donald H. Akenson, Editor (Kingston)

Joan Harcourt, Editor (Kingston)

John Zucchi, Editor (Montreal)

Philip J. Cercone, Director of Press and Acquisitions Editor (Montreal)

Roger Martin, Editor (Kingston)

McGraw-Hill Ryerson Limited

300 Water Street, Whitby, ON L1N 9B6, Canada
905-430-5116

McGraw-Hill Ryerson Limited prides itself on being one of the "liveliest Canadian publishers." Though founded on its educational division, McGraw-Hill Ryerson also has a thriving trade arm. This division publishes general interest books by, about, and for Canadians.

Notable from the McGraw-Hill list: *No Guts No Glory: How Canada's Greatest CEOs Built Their Empires* by David Olive and *How Much Is Enough?* by Diane McCurdy.

McGraw-Hill Ryerson concentrates on personal finance, management, and small business books. The SOHO series offers solutions for those in the small office/home office sector.

Query letters and SASEs should be directed to:

Lynda Walthert, Assistant to the Publisher

NC Press Limited

345 Adelaide Street West, Toronto, ON M5V 1R5, Canada
416-593-6284

NC Press publishes a broad range of topics covering the spectrum of general trade interest in areas such as cooking, health, Canadian history, politics, poetry, art and performance, literature and literary criticism, folkways and lifeways, the natural world, self-help, and popular psychology.

NC Press Limited (incorporated in 1970) is a trade publisher of Canadian books dedicated to the social, political, economic, and spiritual health of the human community. This is a small press—currently publishing a frontlist of 6 to 10 new books each year—with an expansive vision: "To make a difference." NC Press thus strives to present complex ideas in ways accessible to a wide readership. Among NC Press books are numerous literary-award winners. The press has served as agent for non-Canadian publishers and catalogs a substantial backlist.

In 1988 Gary Perly, president of Perly's Maps, purchased a majority interest in NC Press Limited; the house now produces the Perly's map and atlas series, which offers a strong line of urban atlases and street guides to such environs as Toronto, Montreal, and Quebec City.

NC Press nonfiction: *Ninety-Nine Days: The Ford Strike in Windsor in 1945* by Herb Colling; *Living and Learning with a Child Who Stutters: From a Parent's Point of View* by Lise G. Cloutier-Steele; *Eating Bitterness: A Vision Beyond Prison Walls* by Arthur Solomon; *A Woman in My Position: The Politics of Breast Implant Safety* by Linda Wilson, with Dianne Brown.

Literary and works of cultural note: *Voices from the Odeyak* by Michael Posluns; *Folktales of French Canada* by Edith Fowke; *One Animal Among Many: Gaia Goats and Garlic* by David Walter-Toews; *Images: Thirty Stories by Favorite Writers* (compiled and with paintings by Len Gibbs).

NC Press books are distributed via the publisher's network, which involves independent sales representatives worldwide and the fulfillment services of University of Toronto Press.

Query letters and SASEs should be directed to:

Caroline Walker, President and Publisher

ORCA BOOK PUBLISHERS

P.O. Box 5626, Station B, Victoria, BC V8R 6S4, Canada
250-380-1229   fax: 250-380-1892
www.orcabook.com   e-mail: orca@orcabook.com

Orca publishes an eclectic mix of children's picture books and juvenile and young adult fiction. At the present, Orca only considers manuscripts by Canadian authors.

Pick of the Orca list: *Draugr* by Arthur G. Slade; *The Moccasin Goalie* by William Brownridge; *A Fly Named Alfred* by Don Trembath; *A Time to Choose* by Martha Attema; *Belle's Journey* by Marilyn Reynolds.

Orca is eagerly seeking picture book manuscripts in the following areas: stories derived from the author's own childhood experiences, carefully researched historical tales, and modern stories situated within Canada but with universal appeal. Manuscripts should be limited to 2,500 words in length.

In the juvenile and young adult fiction genres, Orca seeks manuscripts that meet the following criteria: regional stories, challenging language and themes, stories based on historical subjects, or contemporary stories that are issue-oriented. These manuscripts should be between 20,000 and 45,000 words in length.

For picture books, submit a manuscript without artwork unless you are a trained artist; do not send any originals. For juvenile or young adult projects, send a query first, along with a synopsis and the first few chapters. All submissions should include an SASE. Do not query by e-mail or fax.

These and other guidelines can be found on the Orca Web site.

Query letters and SASEs should be directed to:

Maggie deVries, Children's Book Editor—Picture books, chapter books, juvenile fiction.

Bob Tyrrell, Publisher—Teen fiction.

PENGUIN BOOKS CANADA LIMITED

10 Alcorn Avenue, Suite 300, Toronto, ON M4V 3B2, Canada
416-925-2249
www.penguin.ca

Penguin Books Canada Limited operates independently of its American affiliate Penguin/Putnam USA. Founded in 1974, Penguin Canada's mandate is to publish Canadian authors; the house does so with fine style, covering a mother lode of original trade nonfiction, as well as a golden seam of mainstream and category fiction and literary works.

Penguin Canada purveys, via its catalog and distribution network, featured titles from the parent company's various international divisions, including Penguin USA, Viking Australia, and Viking UK. The house also distributes for W. W. Norton and Faber and Faber UK. The Viking Canada and Penguin Puffin and Viking are the house's juvenile imprints.

From the Penguin Canada list: *Kit's Law* by Donna Morrissey; *The Girl in the Picture* by Denise Chong; *Titans* by Peter C. Newman; *Paper Shadows* by Wayson Choy; *Parenting with Wit & Wisdom* by Barbara Coloroso; *Notes from the Hyena's Belly* by Nega Mezlekia; *Dagmar's Daughter* by Kim Echlin; *Cold Is the Grave* by Peter Robinson; *The Saratine Mosaic* by Guy Gavriel Kay; and *Home from the Vinyl Café* by Stuart McLean.

Penguin Books Canada's titles are distributed by Canbook Distribution.

Query letters and SASEs should be directed to:

Barbara Berson, Children's Books and Fiction Editor

Cynthia Good, Publisher/President

Diane Turbide, Editorial Director

PLAYWRIGHTS CANADA PRESS

54 Wolseley Street, Toronto, ON M5T A5, Canada
416-703-0201   fax: 416-703-0059
e-mail: angela@puc.ca *or* orders@puc.ca

Playwrights Canada Press is an award-winning drama publisher. The press publishes 12 to 15 titles annually, specializing in Canadian plays and selected drama theory and history.

Recent titles include *The Drawer Boy* by Michael Healey; *It's All True* by Jason Sherman; *Perfect Pie* by Judith Thompson; and *The Duchess* by Wallace Simpson.

U.S. Distributor: Theatre Communications Group.

Query letters and SASEs should be directed to:

Angela Reberio, Publisher/Editor

POLESTAR BOOK PUBLISHERS

c/o Raincoast Books, 8680 Cambie Street, Vancouver, BC V6P 6M9, Canada
604-323-7100   fax: 604-323-7109

Polestar Book Publishers produces literary and commercial titles aimed at a wide readership. Polestar encourages "culturally significant writing" through its First Fiction series, which publishes the work of new authors. Polestar also maintains a poetry list. Popular nonfiction rounds out the Polestar catalog, with an emphasis on sports, dogs, science, and food.

Books representative of the trade list: *Country on Ice* by Doug Beardsley; *Home Run* by Michael McRae; and *Great Canadian Scientists* by Barry Shell. Literary line-up: *Love Medicine* by Gregory Scofield; *Diss/Ed Banded Nation* by David Nandi Odhiambo; *Pool-Hopping* by Anne Fleming.

Polestar publishes Canadian authors only. It does not accept illustrated children's books.

Query letters and SASEs should be directed to:

Lynn Henry, Managing Editor

THE PORCUPINE'S QUILL

68 Main Street, Erin, ON N0B 1T0, Canada
519-833-9158
www.sentex.net/~pql/new.html

The Porcupine's Quill is a leading Canadian small press producing a hand-picked list of literary works (short story collections, novels, juvenile fiction, and poetry) by both emerging and veteran writers. The press is proud to have produced several books that have been shortlisted for awards, including the prestigious Governor General's Award. The Porcupine's Quill also produces a selection of trade and critical works, as well as a handful of books on the visual arts.

The Porcupine's Quill roster includes: *A Kind of Fiction* by P. K. Page; *An Artist's Garden* by G. Brender a Brandis; *Done Legend* by Richard Outram; *Southern Stories* by Clark Blaise.

Now a popular destination for submissions, the Porcupine's Quill is swamped with manuscripts; as such, it does not accept unsolicited work. Instead, the Porcupine's Quill often seeks out writers whose work has appeared in literary magazines such as *The New Quarterly.* All submissions should include an SASE, short biography, and bibliography. They should be directed to:

John Metcalf, Senior Editor

Tim Inkster, Publisher

RAINCOAST BOOKS

8680 Cambie Street, Vancouver, BC V6P 6M9, Canada
604-323-7100   fax: 604-323-2600
www.raincoast.com   e-mail: info@raincoast.com

Raincoat Books publishes intelligent, topical, and beautifully designed books of a regional, national, and international nature in the areas of food, travel, creative nonfiction, picture books, arts and photography, pop culture, biography, and the outdoors. Raincoast also has launched a new national fiction imprint publishing Canadian novels, short fiction, and young adult.

Raincoast has recently acquired Polestar Books, which will remain an imprint and continue to publish poetry, history, feminist works, and sports titles.

Titles published by Raincoast: *Harry Potter I–III* by J. K. Rowling; *Fire into Ice* by Verne Frolick; *The Mermaids Muse* by Dave Bouchard; *Shocking Beauty* by Thomas Hobbs; *Zest for Life* by Diane Clement; and *The Sensualist* by Barbara Hodgson.

Queries and SASEs should be directed to:

Lynn Henry, Managing Editor

Joy Gugeler, Editorial Director—Fiction

Michelle Benjamin, Associate Publisher

RANDOM HOUSE CANADA

One Toronto Street, Suite 300, Toronto, ON M5C 2V6, Canada
416-364-4449
www.randomhouse.ca

A division of Random House of Canada Limited, Random House Canada produces a select list of trade fiction and nonfiction. Publications include Canadian and international titles, with a major concentration on books that appeal to the Canadian market.

Nonfiction areas include popular topical interest and current events, cooking, lifestyle and the arts, history and politics, biography and memoir, travel narrative, popular science, and business and economics. Nonfiction titles include *The Water in Between* by Kevin Patterson; *Bones* by Elaine Dewar; *The Lion, the Fox, and the Eagle* by Carol Off; *Hot Sour Salty Sweet* by Jeffrey Alford and Naomi Duguid; *The Nature of Economies* by Jane Jacobs; and *Anti Diva* by Carole Pope.

The Random House Canada fiction program is known for its mix of established literary titans and exciting new talent. The list includes Canadian authors such as Douglas Coupland, Katherine Govier, Paul Quarrington, John MacLachlan Gray, Elyse Friedman, Billie Livingston and Pulitzer Prize–winner Carol Shields. Internationally, Random House Canada publishes authors that include Julian Barnes, Peter Carey, Eleanor Bailey, Barry Lopez, Graham Swift and Booker Prize–winners Graham Swift and Arundhati Roy.

Query letters and SASEs should be directed to:

Anne Collins, Vice President and Publisher

SOMERVILLE HOUSE BOOKS LIMITED

380 Yonge Street, Suite 5000, Toronto, ON M4N 3N1, Canada
416-488-5938   fax: 416-488-5506
www.sombooks.com   e-mail: sombooks@goodmedia.com

Somerville House specializes in interactive books and kits for young readers. In 1997, Somerville House announced a joint-venture partnership with Penguin Putnam Inc. In 1999, Somerville House became the official youth publisher of the NHL. These new efforts continue to produce the same kind of fun and educational children's titles typical of the Somerville list.

Titles: *The Holographic Night Sky Book & Kit* by Kenneth Hewitt-White; *The Titanic Book and Submersible Model* by Susan Hughes and Steve Santini; *A Century of Hockey Heroes* by James Duplacey and Eric Zweig; *Chess for Kids* by Kevin F. R. Smith and Daniel C. Macdonald; *The Tiny Perfect Dinosaur Series: Tyrannosaurus Rex* by John Acorn and Dale Russell; and *The Bones Book & Skeleton* by Stephen Cumbaa.

Children's nonfiction submissions are welcome. Please include an SASE. Due to the volume of submissions, Somerville House discards materials after three months if insufficient postage is enclosed. Direct all queries to:

Harry Endrulat, Manager, Editorial and Product Development

STODDART PUBLISHING COMPANY LTD.

34 Lesmill Road, Don Mills, ON M3B 2T6, Canada
416-445-3333

Stoddart Publishing maintains a hold on the mainstream of commercial publishing. Stoddart nonfiction categories include humor, history, military history, politics, hockey, finance, biography, environment, nutrition, and business and consumer guides. Stoddart also features a solid fiction line that publishes only literary fiction, not poetry. Stoddart Publishing (founded in 1984) is the trade-publishing arm of General Publishing Company. The house produces a wide range of titles with a Canadian orientation or by Canadian authors.

Nonfiction from Stoddart: *Water* by Marc DeVillers; *From Naked Ape to Superspecies* by David Suzuki and Holly Dressel; *Ultimate Hockey* by Trans Weir, Jeff Chapman, and Glenn Weir; *Ortona: Canada's Epic World War II Battle* by Mark Zuehlke.

Stoddart fiction and literature: *Olivo Oliva* by Phillippe Poloni; *The Long Stretch* by Linden MacIntyre; *Visible Amazement* by Gale Zoe Garnett.

Stoddart orchestrates its own distributional network worldwide and handles distribution for books issued by a number of other houses, including House of Anansi Press, the Boston Mills Press, and Cormorant Books. In the United States, Stoddart distributes to the trade through General Distribution Services, Inc.

Stoddart does not accept complete manuscripts. However, it will consider submission of up to two chapters. Query letters and SASEs should be directed to:

Don Bastian, Managing Editor

Stoddart Juveniles

Stoddart publishes a children's program with an emphasis on Canadian works. Stoddart's young-adult paperbacks list includes the Gemini and Junior Gemini lines. Stoddart Young Readers are for preschoolers through young adults and include picture books, pop-up books, fairy tales, and science titles for young adults.

TUNDRA BOOKS

P.O. Box 1030, Plattsburgh, NY 12901, USA
416-598-4786

Tundra specializes in children's books of high literary and artistic quality, including picture books, award-winning fiction, and nonfiction. The company's fiction list includes: *Jacob Two-Two Meets the Hooded Fang* by Mordecai Richler; *The Only Outcast* by Julie Johnston; *The Forest Family* by Joan Bodger. Nonfiction for young adults includes: *The Dancer Who Flew: A Memoir of Rudolf Nureyev* by Linda Maybarduk; and *Catching Fire: The Story of Firefighting* by Gena Gorrell. Picture books include: *High Flight* by Linda Granfield, illustrated by Michael Martchenko; *Sinbad* by Ludmila Zeman; and *Dippers* by Barbara Nichol, with illustrations by Barry Moser.

We do not accept unsolicited manuscripts.

UNIVERSITY OF BRITISH COLUMBIA PRESS

2029 West Mall, Vancouver, BC V6T 1Z2, Canada
604-822-4161
www.ubcpress.ubc.ca   e-mail: info@ubcpress.ubc.ca

Categories of University of British Columbia Press interest include Canadian culture and history, political science, Asian studies, native studies with an accent on the Northwest Coast, Pacific Rim studies, global geography, fisheries and forestry, environmental studies, Northern studies, and Canadian sociology.

University of British Columbia Press (founded in 1971) publishes academic books, as well as general-interest works, with an emphasis on Canadian subjects.

On the University of British Columbia Press list: *Citizens Plus: Aboriginal Peoples and the Canadian State* by Alan C. Cairns; *Un/Covering the North: News Media and Aboriginal People* by Valerie Alia; *Houser: The Life and Work of Catherine Bauer* by Peter Oberlander and Eva Newbrun; *Invisible and Inaudible in Washington* by Edelgard Mahant and Graeme S. Mount; *Aboriginal Education* (edited by Marlene Brant Castellano, Lynne Davis, and Louise Lahache); *Feminists and Party Politics* by Lisa Young; and *Fatal Consumption: Rethinking Sustainable Development* (edited by Robert Woollard and Aleck Ostry).

University of British Columbia Press distribution is handled by Raincoast Books (custserv@raincoast.com).

Query letters and SASEs should be directed to:

Jean Wilson, Associate Director, Editorial

UNIVERSITY OF TORONTO PRESS

10 Saint Mary Street, Suite 700, Toronto, ON M4Y 2W8, Canada
416-978-2239   fax: 416-978-4738

University of Toronto Press publishes in a range of fields, including history and politics; women's studies; health, family, and society; law and crime; economics; workplace communication; theory/culture; language, literature, semiotics, and drama; medieval studies; Renaissance studies; Erasmus; Italian-language studies; East European studies; classics; and nature. The list includes topical titles in Canadian studies, native studies, sociology, anthropology, urban studies, modern languages, and music, as well as travel and touring guides.

University of Toronto Press produces titles for the general trade, as well as academic works. UTP issues a series of specialist journals of note, including *Scholarly Publishing*. The house produces no original contemporary fiction or poetry.

Representing the University of Toronto nonfiction list: *The Butterflies of Canada* by Ross A. Layberry, Peter W. Hall, and J. Donald Lafontaine (with specimen plates by John T. Fowler); *Working for Wildlife: The Beginning of Preservation in Canada* by Janet Foster; *The Illuminated Page: Ten Centuries of Manuscript Painting in the British Library* by Janet Backhouse; *Conduct Unbecoming: The Story of the Murder of Canadian Prisoners of War in Normandy* by Howard Margolian; *The Socially Concerned Today* by John Kenneth Galbraith; *Kaiser and Führer: A Comparative Study of Personality and Politics* by Robert G. L. Waite; *Werewolf! The History of the National Socialist Guerrilla Movement 1944–1946* by Perry Biddiscombe; *The Science of War: Canadian Scientists and Allied Military Technology During the Second World War* by Donald H. Avery; *The Mystery of the Eye and the Shadow of Blindness* by Rod Michalko; *Into the Daylight: A Wholistic Approach to Healing* by Calvin Morrisseau; *Unfinished Dreams: Community Healing and the Reality of Aboriginal Self-Government* by Wayne Warry; *Looking White People in the Eye: Gender, Race, and Culture in Courtrooms and Classrooms* by Sherene H. Razack; *Making Work Making Trouble: Prostitution as a Social Problem* by Deborah R. Brock.

U

Publications in the arts and literature: *Power to Rise: The Story of the National Ballet of Canada* by James Neufeld; *Painting Place: The Life and Work of David B. Milne* by David P. Silcox; *Modern Furniture in Canada 1920–1970* by Virginia Wright; *Paths of Desire: Images of Exploration and Mapping in Canadian Women's Writings* by Marlene Goldman; *Allusion: A Literary Graft* by Allan H. Pasco; *Discoveries of the Other: Alterity in the Work of Leonard Cohen, Hubert Aquin, Michael Ondaatje, and Nicole Brossard* by Winifred Siemerling; *The Logic of Ecstasy: Canadian Mystical Painting 1920–1940* by Ann Davis; *Northern Voices: Inuit Writing in English* (edited by Penny Petrone); *Sounding Differences: Conversations with Seventeen Canadian Women Writers* by Janice Williamson; *The Political Writings of Mary Wollstonecraft* (edited by Janet Todd).

University of Toronto Press oversees a distributional network encompassing offices and sales agents worldwide; the house handles titles from other book publishers as well as for institutions such as Royal Ontario Museum and Canadian Museum of Nature.

Query letters and SASEs should be directed to:

Gerald Hallowell, Editor—Canadian history and Canadian literature.

Joan Bulger, Editor—Art and classics, architecture.

Kieran Simpson, Editor—Department of Directories.

Ron Schoeffel, Senior House Editor—Romance languages, native languages, religion and theology, education, philosophy.

Suzanne Rancourt, Editor—Medieval studies, medieval and Old English literature.

Virgil Duff, Executive Editor—Social sciences, scholarly medical books, law and criminology, women's studies.

WHITECAP BOOKS

351 Lynn Avenue, North Vancouver, BC V7J 2C4, Canada
604-980-9852   fax: 604-980-8197
www.whitecap.ca

Whitecap Books, established in 1977, was created with one thing in mind: "survival." As such, Whitecap Books is a commercial press, with a strong marketing program to showcase its publications.

Whitecap produces trade nonfiction, with a strong focus on cookbooks by chefs, gardening, large-format photography, and books on local interest subjects. Whitecap also maintains a children's list of nonfiction and fiction.

Representative titles include: *The Lazy Gourmet* by Susan Mendelson; *The Blooming Great Gardening Book* by Steve Whysall; *Secret Coastline* by Andrew Scott; and *Hiking Ontario's Heartland* by Shirley Teasdale.

Books from the children's list: *Whose House Is This?* by Wayne Lynch; *Gilbert de la Frogponde* by Jennifer Rae (illustrated by Rose Cowles).

Query letters and SASEs should be directed to:

Leanne McDonald, Foreign Rights and Acquisitions Associate

PART TWO

Directory of Literary Agents

What Makes This Agent Directory Special?

Jeff Herman

No other listing of literary agents comes anywhere close to this one. We don't just tell you who the agents are and where to find them; we get the agents to actually talk to you and reveal a slice of their personalities. These surveys also reveal what each agent wants to represent (and doesn't want to); when and where they were born and educated; their career history; and their agenting track record. Memorize some of these tidbits and you can be something of a gossip.

About 200 exceptionally well-qualified agents are included in this listing. Each year I invite the 200-plus members of the Association of Author Representatives, as well as a couple dozen excellent nonmember agents, to be in the book. As you might expect, many of the most successful agents are not overly hungry for unsolicited new submissions, and some of them therefore do not wish to participate. We listed no one against their wishes, and allowed all of our agent contributors to be as terse or expansive as they pleased. I made the best effort to include only legitimate agencies. Please let me know about any negative experiences you encounter, though I hope there won't be any.

AEI ATCHITY EDITORIAL/ENTERTAINMENT INTERNATIONAL

9601 Wilshire Boulevard, Box 1202, Beverly Hills, CA 90210
323-932-0407   fax: 323-932-0321
www.AEIonline.com   e-mail: webAEI@aol.com

Agents: Literary Manager: Kenneth Atchity, President; Chi-Li Wong, Partner and Vice President of Development and Production; Andrea McKeown, Executive Vice President; Brenna Lui (Development); Jennifer Pope (Submissions).

Born: Atchity: Eunice, Louisiana.

Education: B.A., Georgetown; Ph.D. in Comparative Literature, Yale.

Career history: Professor of comparative literature (classics, medieval, Renaissance), Occidental College (1970–1987); Instructor, UCLA Writer's Program (1970–1987). Author of 13 books, including *A Writer's Time: A Guide to the Creative Process, from Vision Through Revision* (Norton), *The Mercury Transition: Career Change Through Entrepreneurship* (Longmeadow), and *Writing Treatments That Sell* (with Chi-Li Wong; Owl Books). Producer of 20 films for video, television, and theater, including *Champagne for Two* and *The Rose Café* (Cinemax-HBO), *Amityville: The Evil Escapes* (NBC), *Shadow of Obsession* (NBC), and *Falling Over Backwards.*

Hobbies/personal interests: Collecting autographed editions, pitchers; tennis; travel.

Areas most interested in agenting: Nonfiction: Strong mainstream nonfiction, especially true and heroic stories with TV or film potential; business books, especially with entrepreneurial orientation; previously published books with solid sales records. Fiction: Mainstream commercial novels (action, horror, thrillers, suspense, mainstream romance, espionage, outstanding science fiction with strong characters) that can also be made into TV or feature films. Scripts: For TV: strong female leads. For film: All kinds, especially action, romantic comedy, thrillers, science fiction, and horror.

Areas not interested in agenting: Drug-related; fundamental religious; category romance; category mystery or Western; poetry; children's; "interior" confessional fiction.

If not agenting, what would you be doing? If I weren't a literary manager, writer, and producer, I'd be doing the same thing and calling it something else.

Best way to initiate contact: Query letter with SASE.

Client representation by category: Nonfiction, 45%; Fiction, 45%; Screenplays, 10%.

Commission: 15% of all domestic sales, 25–30% foreign. If we exercise our option to executive produce a project for film or television, commission on dramatic rights sale is refunded.

Number of titles sold last year: 18.

Rejection rate (all submissions): 95%.

Most common mistakes authors make: The most costly and time-consuming mistake is remaining ignorant of where your work fits into the market and of whom your reader might be. Sending the kind of work (romances, light mysteries, episodic scripts) we're specifically not looking for.

Description of the client from Hell: He or she is so self-impressed that it's impossible to provide constructive criticism; makes his package impossible to open; and provides a return envelope too small to be used.

A

Description of a dream client: He or she comes in with an outstanding novel that's both high concept and castable, plus an outline for two more; and is delighted to take commercial direction on the writing and the career.

Why did you become an agent? Nearly two decades of teaching comparative literature and creative writing at Occidental College and the UCLA Writers Program, reviewing for the *Los Angeles Times* Book Review, and working with the dreams of creative people through DreamWorks (which I co-founded with Marsha Kinder) provided a natural foundation for this career. I made the transition from academic life through producing, but continued my publishing-consulting business by connecting my authors with agents. As I spent more and more time developing individuals' writing careers, as well as working directly with publishers in my search for film properties, it became obvious that literary management was the next step. True or fiction, what turns me on is a good story.

Comments: Dream big. Don't let anyone define your dream for you. Risk it. The rewards in this new career are as endless as your imagination, and the risks, though real, are not greater than the risk of suffocating on a more secure career path. Begin by learning all you can about the business of writing, publishing, and producing, and recognizing that as far off and exalted as they may seem, the folks in these professions are as human as anyone else. We're enthusiasts, like you: Make us enthused!

Representative titles: *I Ain't Got Time to Bleed: Reworking the Body Politic from the Bottom Up* and *Do I Stand Alone? Going to the Mat Against Political Pawns & Media Jackals* by Governor Jesse Ventura (Pocket Books); *The Amazing World of Ripley's Believe It or Not* (Black Dog & Leventhal) and *Ripley's Guide to America the Beautiful and Bizarre* by Julie Mooney (Frommer's); *I Don't Have to Make Everything All Better* (Viking/Penguin) and *Married for Better, Not Worse: The Fourteen Secrets to a Happy Marriage* by Gary and Joy Lundberg (Viking); *The Rag Street Journal: A Guide to Thrift Shops in North America* (Holt/Owl Books) and *Valuable Vintage* by Elizabeth Mason (Clarkson Potter); *Till Debt Do Us Part* by Bud Poduska (Deseret Books); *Dictionary for Investors* by Howard Bonham (Adams Media); *Heavenly Answers to Earthy Questions* by Joyce H. Brown (NAL/Dutton); *The Secret Castle* by Carole S. Hughes (St. Martin's Press); *Attention to Detail: A Gentleman's Guide to Professional Etiquette* by Clinton T. Greenleaf, III (Series; Adams Media); *When Hope Can Kill* by Dr. Lucy Papillon (Everywhere Press); *Thank God It's Monday Morning* by Tim Hoerr (Celebrity Press); *Simply Heavenly: The Monastery Vegetarian Cookbook* by Abbot George Burke (Macmillan).

Fiction titles include: *Meg* by Steve Alten (Doubleday/Bantam); *The Trench* (Kensington); *The Last Valentine* (Doubleday), *Ticket Home,* and *The Piano Man* by James Michael Pratts (St. Martin's Press); *Sins of the Mother* by Cheryl Saban (Dove); *River of Summer* and *Without Mercy* by Lois Gilberts (Dutton/Onyx); *A Midnight Carol* by Patricia K. Davis (St. Martin's Press); *The Cruelest Lie* by Milt Lyle (AEI-Calcasieu); *Gold Fever* by Dr. Tom Stern (AEI-Titan); *Insurrection Red, Force Gold and Black Light* by Michael Murray (Putnam/Signet); *Spirits of the High Mesa* by Floyd Martinez (Arte Público Press); *Veiled Journey* and *Lioness* by Shirley Palmer (Mira) (AEI Consulting); *The Hong Kong Sanction* by Mitchell Rossi (Pinnacle).

Film sales include *Henry's List of Wrongs* (New Line/AEI and Zide Perry), *The Kill Martin Club* (Warner Bros./AEI & Ben Stiller's Red Hour), *Life, or Something Like It*

(New Regency/AEI & John David), *Eulogy for Joseph Way* (Warner Bros./AEI and John Wells), *American Dream* (Columbia/AEI and Donald DeLine), *Joe Somebody* (Fox 2000/AEI and Kopelson), *Sherman's March* (Fox/NBC and Kopelson), *Glory Days* (Fox pilot), and *The Loop* (Fox pilot) by John Scott Shepherd; *Meg* by Steve Alten (Walt Disney /AEI and Zide-Perry); *Midnight Carol* by Patricia Davis (HBO; AEI, and Pace); *180 Seconds at Willow Park* by Rich Lynch (New Line, AEI, and Zide-Perry); *The Columbia Malignancy: The Marc Gardner Story* (HBO; AEI, and Zide-Perry); *Sign of the Watcher* by Brett Bartlett (Propaganda Films/AEI and Zide-Perry); *They Called Them Grifters* by Alice McMillen (USA/AEI).

ALL-IN-ONE LITERARY AGENCY

1800 Northern Blvd., Suite 315, Roslyn, NY 11576
516-484-7501   fax: 516-484-0825

Agent: Antonin Masek, M.D.
   Born: 1948, Prague, Czech Republic.
   Education: Medical school at the University of Geneva, Switzerland. I am a specialist in obstetrics and gynecology.
   Career history: I continue to own an ob-gyn clinic in Geneva, overseen by doctors who report to me. I have practiced medicine in several countries. I am semi-retiring in the United States. I say "semi-retiring" because, in 1999, I joined several partners in establishing a U.S.-based literary agency/publishing firm/distributor/bookstore, all in one.
   Hobbies/personal interests: Reading, writing, tennis, opera, cooking, painting, martial arts.
   Areas most interested in agenting: Novels, novellas.
   If not agenting, what would you be doing? Establishing hospitals in developing countries.
   Best way to initiate contact: Regular mail, with a character description and a detailed plot skeleton. We need to know how your book/story ends. All of this should fit into about three pages.
   Reading-fee policy: No, it's completely free and if our publishing subsidiary decides to publish you, it is also completely free.
   Commission: No commission—I'm a major shareholder of the publisher.
   Number of titles sold last year: 4.
   Most common mistakes authors make: A poorly constructed synopsis.
   Why did you become an agent? To find new ways for new authors.
   Comments: Visit www.399Novel.com.

ALTAIR LITERARY AGENCY

141 Fifth Avenue, Suite 8N, New York, NY 10010
212-505-3320

A

Agents: Nicholas Smith, Andrea Pedolsky

Born: Smith: 1952, St. Louis, Missouri. Pedolsky: 1951, New York, New York.

Education: Smith: Languages, Vassar, 1973–1974; Arts Management, SUNY/Purchase, 1985. Pedolsky: B.A., American Studies, CUNY/Queens College, M.S., Library Science, Columbia University.

Career history: Smith: Bookseller, Editor, Publisher, Marketing and Sales Manager (publishing), Director, New Product Development (packager/agency); Independent Agent; Agent/Co-Founder Altair Literary Agency. Pedolsky: Editor, reference and professional books, Neal Schuman Publishers, 1978–1988; Acquisitions Editor, Director of Editorial Development and Production, Amacom Books; Executive Editor (created and launched) Peterson's/Pacesetter Books, 1994–1996; Agent/Co-Founder Altair Literary Agency. Also, Editor/Co-Editor/Co-Author of *Continuing Education for Businesspeople, The Small Business Sourcebook,* and *Creating a Financial Plan.*

Hobbies/personal interests: Smith: Music, reading, museums (art, science, and natural history exhibitions), travel, history. Pedolsky: Art, reading, walking, travel, old cities.

Areas most interested in agenting: Smith: Nonfiction adult: American history (especially colonial era), archaeology, Asian art and history, biography (prominent and/or historical figures only), business (especially management, careers, and personal finance), business history and biography, exploration, fine art, health reference, history (a wide variety of eras, subjects, and places), illustrated books (especially topic-centered photography books), industrial design, medicine (history of), museum exhibition–related books (science, art, natural history, history, and other topics), music (only history, biography, or reference), narrative nonfiction (topic-centered only), natural history and nature, reference (especially dictionaries, words, and quote books), science (especially illustrated and/or history of), theology, and invention (especially history of). Pedolsky: Art (biography, history of), biography (prominent and historical figures); business and careers (howto and narrative); contemporary issues (must have direct experience with, expertise in, and/or a publication history with the topic), creative nonfiction health (especially women's—must have expertise in, and/or a publication history, with the topic); history; illustrated books; multicultural topics, personal finance (must have expertise in, and/or a publication history with, the topic); pop culture, psychology (must have expertise in, and/or a publication history); religion (history of, new ideas about); spirituality (must have a practice and /or have articles and/or books written); sports (must have expertise in and/or a publication history with the topic); women's issues (must have expertise in).

Fiction: Smith: Historical fiction (especially pre-20th century settings), literary historical mysteries. Pedolsky: Literary, new, experimental.

Children's books: Smith: Activity books only (science, nature, technology, or natural history only).

Areas not interested in agenting: Smith: True crime, memoir, romance.

Best way to initiate contact: Nonfiction: a well-thought out and composed query letter, citing your related credentials and why you are the best person to write your book, and/or a complete proposal. We will only respond and/or return materials when you include an SASE. Fiction: a query letter, including a brief, compelling synopsis of the story, and a bio/c.v. with writing credits. We will only respond and/or return materials when you include an SASE.

Client representation by category: Nonfiction, 80%; Fiction, 20%.

Commission: 15% domestic; 20% foreign.

Rejection rate (all submissions): 90%.

Most common mistakes authors make: Not demonstrating, either through your proposal or synopsis, that you have the background, knowledge, savvy, and ability to write your proposed book. Also, failing to understand and demonstrate how you can help your potential publisher to take advantage of the marketplace for your book. Another common mistake is querying by telephone or fax.

Description of the client from Hell: There have not been many. Those who come to mind have little or no understanding of the book marketplace and require too much hand-holding.

Description of a dream client: First and foremost, be a great writer and storyteller. Be someone who has the knowledge, skill, creativity, and expertise to write and support your book; who understands the collaborative aspects of working with an agent and editor; who takes responsibility for meeting deadliness; and who has a sense of humor.

Why did you become an agent? Smith: I love ideas and books, enjoy encountering interesting authors, with both, and particularly like to bring authors and editors together over a great book—then mediate the process to everyone's benefit. Pedolsky: When I was an editor, I had to confine and align my acquiring efforts to a particular house's list and interests. It became clear to me that if I wanted to work with a variety of authors with unique voices, styles, and concerns, being an agent was the way to go.

Representative titles: *Facing the Fifties* by Gordon Ehlers, M.D., and Jeffrey Miller (M. Evans); *First You Shave Your Head* by Geri Larkin (Ten Speed/Celestial Arts); *Getting Started in Internet Auctions* by Alan Elliott (John Wiley & Sons); *How to Say It . . . in Careers* by Robbie Miller Kaplan (Prentice Hall); *Khrushchev's Shoe* by Roy Underhill (Perseus); *Make Your Kid a Millionaire* by Kevin McKinley (Simon & Schuster); *Making Peace with Your Things* by Cindy Glovinsky (St. Martin's Press); *Say It Like Shakespeare!* by Tom Leech (McGraw Hill); *Still Waters Run Deep* by Marti Olsen Lancey (Workman); *The Bio Tech Investor's Bible* by George Wolff (John Wiley & Sons); *The Brand Marketing Checklist* by Brad VanAuken (AMACOM); *The Choices We Made* by Angela Bonavoglia (Four Walls Eight Windows); *The Light at the End of the Tunnel . . . Is an Oncoming Train* by Stephen Wicks (Andrews McMeel).

MIRIAM ALTSHULER LITERARY AGENCY

53 Old Post Road North; Red Hook, NY 12571

Agent: Miriam Altshuler

Born: New York City.

Education: B.A., Middlebury College.

Career history: Agent for 11 years at Russell & Volkening. Started my own agency in 1994.

Hobbies/personal interests: Skiing, horses, the outdoors, my children, reading.

Areas most interested in agenting: Literary and commercial fiction, narrative nonfiction, popular culture.

A

Areas not interested in agenting: No sci-fi, Westerns, romance, horror, genre mysteries.
Best way to initiate contact: Query letter with SASE.
Reading-fee policy: No reading fee.
Client representation by category: Nonfiction, 50%; Fiction, 50%.
Commission: 15% books and movies; 20% foreign; 17.5% England.

AMICUS LITERARY AGENCY

3202 East Greenway, Suite 1307-182, Phoenix, AZ 85032
602-569-2481   fax: 602-569-2265
e-mail: bookwoman@qwest.net

Agent: Rose Stadler
Education: B.S.W., University of Minnesota, 1979; M.S.W., Arizona State University (May 1997).
Career history: Over 20 years in social work, counseling, college instructor.
Hobbies/personal interests: Writing, camping, photography, amateur astronomy.
Areas most interested in agenting: Mainstream, good literary fiction, mysteries/thrillers, current events, and nonfiction.
Areas not interested in agenting: No cookbooks, poetry, Westerns, or science fiction. Absolutely no pornography or satanic trash. No longer take children's literature.
If not agenting, what would you be doing? Stand-up comedy, teaching social work, teaching writing, more social work, counseling or therapist, writing, writing, and more writing.
Best way to initiate contact: A good query letter and the first 50 pages or first 3 chapters, with SASE for fiction. Query letter only for nonfiction with SASE. No bubble-wrap packaging, as I live in Arizona and it results in melted plastic slime. Use a sturdy box and always enclose SASE. No SASE, no response. OK to e-mail me but not more than one page; no attachments, please.
Reading-fee policy: No reading fee.
Client representation by category: Fiction, 50%; Nonfiction, 50%.
Commission: 15% domestic, 20% foreign.
Rejection rate (all submissions): 95%.
Most common mistakes authors make: Several come to mind: don't call me at four in the morning and expect me to remember your name, much less anything coherent. Don't send me something that I don't handle, it's a waste of my time and yours. Don't convince me that I will absolutely love something if I read it all the way through. Don't beg, don't grovel, and don't slip me something under the stall door if you see me at a conference. Please don't tell me that I absolutely, have to, must read it because if I don't, you will stop taking your medication, and it will be my fault when you do your swan dive off a storage shed. Don't send unsolicited manuscripts. Always include SASE if you want a response. Please put your name, address, and phone number on the query letter.
Description of the client from Hell: The CFH is an arrogant bully, know-it-all, overly concerned about advances and royalties, likes to yell at agents and publishers, threatens

A

bodily harm and lawsuits if his or her work doesn't sell, won't take criticism, doesn't meet deadlines, calls daily for an update, becomes depressed and/or suicidal, needs a financial adviser or marriage counselor, lists agent on a loan application, is selfish, is antisocial, or may have his own page in the DSM-IV-R. Since this is a self-imposed career, I do not have to work with unpleasant individuals and will send them packing should they become annoying, demanding, hysterical, or unethical.

Description of a dream client: Persistent, tenacious, has an unsinkable attitude, gets the work done on time, doesn't give me excuses or delays, provides copies and appropriate samples when needed, believes in his or her work, and is pleasant to work with. I respect and admire the people I work with and we share mutual goals; therefore, we utilize a teamwork approach to see their work published.

How did you become an agent? One of my students sat on my front porch for three days and begged. At the same time, someone happened to write an article about writing in the local paper, and I returned the phone call. The next day there were 87 messages. I saw a need in Phoenix and took it from there. I discovered that I don't have to live in L.A. or New York to make things happen.

Why did you become an agent? For someone with an unquenchable thirst for books and a 20-year affair with the literary world, it was the right thing to do at the time. Besides, I love a good challenge.

What can a writer do to enhance their chances of getting you as an agent? Make me laugh, convince me that you're better than the average bear. The three P's—polished, professional, and proofread—are most important.

How would you describe what you actually do for a living? Interesting question: days vary from picking up the mail, hauling it to my car by camel, schlepping it to my house by mule, piling it up in the living room, reading, answering mail, logging in mail, logging out mail, sitting at the computer for days, waiting in line at the post office to return packages; answering my e-mails, faxing phone lines, making calls, listening to bad music while on hold, talking to clients, talking to editors, calling publishing houses, getting more mail, answering more calls, writing letters and proposals, writing columns and/or articles, attending conferences and seminars, teaching several courses at the local community college, being a guest speaker for various groups, chatting, talking, writing, corresponding, hand-holding, buffering rejections, jumping for joy with a sale, negotiating advances and royalties (income), promoting authors, arranging book signings and tours, handling contracts, reading and answering more mail, more reading, traveling, schmoozing, more chatting, more promotions, and getting to wear blue jeans most of the days I don't leave the house; some days I don't get home before midnight. Nothing is routine about this job, but I love it and can't see myself doing anything different. I'm a self-starter and I like it that way.

BETSY AMSTER LITERARY ENTERPRISES
P.O. Box 27788, Los Angeles, CA 90027-0788
323-662-1987

A

Agent: Betsy Amster

Education: B.A., University of Michigan.

Career history: Before opening my agency in 1992, I spent ten years as an Editor at Vintage Books and Pantheon and two years as Editorial Director of the Globe Pequot Press.

Hobbies/personal interests: Reading, movies, art, swimming, hiking, poking into odd corners of L.A.

Areas most interested in agenting: Literary fiction; narrative nonfiction (social issues, history, adventure, travel); psychology and self-help; women's issues; health; parenting; popular culture; clever gift books by illustrators who can also write.

Areas not interested in agenting: Children's or YA titles; commercial women's fiction; category romance, science fiction, fantasy, Westerns, horror; genre mysteries; computers; poetry.

If not agenting, what would you be doing? I'd be a lawyer.

Best way to initiate contact: No phone calls or faxes. For fiction, please send the first three pages of your manuscript; for nonfiction, please send a query letter or your proposal. No response without an SASE.

Reading-fee policy: No reading fee.

Commission: 15%.

Number of titles sold last year: 25.

Most common mistakes authors make: Nonfiction: Failing to research the competition. Fiction: Submitting a first draft.

Description of a dream client: Writes well, takes direction gracefully, moves easily from book to book. Meets deadlines. Rises to the challenge of helping the publisher promote the book. Knows the difference between a big problem and a little one. Calls and faxes only during business hours. Likes to laugh. A mensch!

Why did you become an agent? I can't keep my nose out of books.

What can a writer do to enhance their chances of getting you as an agent? If you're writing nonfiction, read the books on how to write a book proposal. If you're writing fiction, join (or start) a writers' group in order to get feedback on your work. Study story structure. Be prepared to go through drafts and drafts. Ripeness is all.

How would you describe what you actually do for a living? I'm constantly on the lookout for writers whose work moves or enlightens me, which means I read everything in sight. Once I take writers on, I work with them to make sure that their proposal or manuscript is polished and persuasive. I keep track of which editors are doing what types of books and make sure that I understand their taste. I jump up and down on the phone with editors (or in their offices or over lunch) to share my enthusiasm for my clients' work. I nudge publishers as required, to see that they live up to their promises.

Representative titles: *The Green Suit* by Dwight Allen (Algonquin); *The Road to Esmeralda* by Joy Nicholson (St. Martin's); *Esperanza's Box of Saints* by Maria Amparo Escandon (Scribner); *The Backbone of the World: A Year Along the Continental Divide* by Frank Clifford (Broadway); *The Victoria's Secret Catalog Never Stops Coming . . . and Other Lessons I Learned from Breast Cancer* by Jennie Nash (Scribner); *The Flag of Yoshio Shimizu: A Daughter Discovers Her Father's War* by Louise Steinman (Algonquin); *Dogtionary* by Sharon Montrose (Viking Studio); *Fun with Mommy and Me* by Dr.

Cindy Nurik (Dutton); *Getting Married When It's Not Your First Time* by Pamela Hill Nettleton (Quill).

A

MARCIA AMSTERDAM AGENCY

41 West 82nd Street, New York, NY 10024
212-873-4945

Agent: Marcia Amsterdam
    Education: B.A., English and Journalism, Brooklyn College.
    Career history: Editor; agent (1960–present).
    Hobbies/personal interests: Reading, theater, movies, art, travel, discovering wonderful new writers.
    Areas most interested in agenting: An eclectic list of mainstream and category fiction and popular nonfiction. I enjoy medical and legal thrillers, character-driven science fiction, mysteries, horror, historical romance, contemporary women's fiction, and quality young-adult fiction.
    Areas not interested in agenting: Children's books, poetry, short stories, technical books, thrillers about drug cartels.
    If not agenting, what would you be doing? Reading published books more, traveling more.
    Best way to initiate contact: A query letter (with SASE).
    Reading-fee policy: No reading fee.
    Client representation by category: Nonfiction, 20%; Fiction, 70%; Children's, 10%.
    Commission: 15% domestic; 20% on foreign sales and movie and television sales (split with subagents); 10% on screenplays.
    Number of titles sold last year: A fair number.
    Rejection rate (all submissions): Alas, most.
    Most common mistakes authors make: Spelling and grammar still count, as does a comfortable, legible typeface.
    Description of the client from Hell: I wouldn't know. I've never had one.
    Description of a dream client: One who trusts the reader, is professional, is adaptable, has a sense of humor, and has confidence in my judgment.
    Why did you become an agent? When I was an editor, other editors often came to me for suggestions about books they were working on. I found that I enjoyed giving editorial and career advice. One editor said, "You keep selling my books. Why don't you become an agent?" So I did.
    Representative titles: *Dark Morning* (Kensington); *Flash Factor* (Kensington); *Moses Goes to School* (Farrar, Straus & Giroux); *Rosey in the Present Tense* (Walker & Co.); *The Haunting* by Ruby Jean Jensen (Kensington).

ARCADIA

31 Lake Place, North Danbury, CT 06810
203-797-0993

A

Agent: Victoria Gould Pryor

Born: 1945, New York City.

Education: B.A., Pembroke College in Brown University (Modern Lit./History); M.A. (Modern Lit.), NYU.

Career history: John Cushman Agency, Sterling Lord Agency, Harold Matson Agency, Literistic Ltd., Arcadia.

Hobbies/personal interests: Science, medicine, nature, gardening, classical music and singing, current/foreign affairs, reading, children, education, law, art, business.

Areas most interested in agenting: Literary and commercial fiction. Nonfiction: science/medicine, current affairs, any book that is intriguing and wonderful or one that could be said to change a reader's life (how's that for a challenge!).

Areas not interested in agenting: Children's/YA, science fiction and fantasy, humor, how-to and self-help (unless they're of the life-changing variety); horror.

If not agenting, what would you be doing? I'd be an unhappy and prosperous doctor or lawyer, a happy and starving woodworker, or, if I could sing far better than I do, an ecstatic and prosperous Wagnerian opera singer.

Best way to initiate contact: Detailed query letter with sample materials and SASE.

Reading-fee policy: No reading fee.

Client representation by category: Nonfiction, 75%; Fiction, 25%.

Commission: 15% for new clients.

Number of titles sold last year: 10.

Rejection rate (all submissions): 99.9%.

Most common mistakes authors make: Long, rambling pitch letters; not studying the market and knowing one's niche; showing work half-cocked; forgetting the SASE. Fiction writers who submit supplementary material to show how timely their manuscript is. (If the agent isn't in touch with what's happening in the world, why would you want him or her to represent you?)

What gets you excited? A professionally prepared presentation leaps out from whatever else is on one's desk at the time. It is thorough, thoughtful, intelligent, provocative and highly enticing. It grabs you in the heart and gut, demands your respect, and will not let you say no.

Description of the client from Hell: The client from Hell delivers extremely late or not at all and insists on calling after hours or on weekends, usually to deliver complex information that should be put in writing. He/she knows best, whatever information or advice is offered, and demands that rules that apply to all other authors be set aside for his/her work. Fortunately, I don't represent anyone who resembles this.

Description of a dream client: The dream client, like almost all of my current clients, behaves professionally, delivers top writing on time, and is a mensch.

Why did you become an agent? The luck of the draw; I stumbled into the perfect field for me, which combined a love of reading, people, and business with a little law and social work thrown in on the side.

Comments: It's a jungle out there. Prepare yourself for anything and everything. Have a sturdy spouse—preferably one who is independently wealthy or at least works full time—and a sturdier ego. Work hard, have a high threshold for frustration and a well-developed sense of adventure and humor. You'll need it all.

Representative titles: *Gangbusters: The Destruction of America's Last Mafia Dynasty* by Ernest Volkman (Faber & Faber); *Listening Now* by Anjana Appachana (Random House); *Prescriptions for Living* by Dr. Bernie Siegel (HarperCollins); *Rachel's Passage* by Paula Reid (HarperCollins); *Talking to the Enemy* by Arner Mandelman (Oberon); *The Enlightened Stepmother* by Perdita Kirkness Norwood with Teri Wingender (Avon); *Time, Love, Memory: A Great Biologist and His Quest for the Origins of Behavior* by Jonathan Weiner (Knopf); *Why We Hurt: The Origins of Human Pain* by Dr. Frank T. Vertosick, Jr. (Harcourt).

AUTHENTIC CREATIONS LITERARY AGENCY

875 Lawrenceville-Suwanee Road, Suite 310-306, Lawrenceville, GA 30043
770-339-3774   fax: 770-339-7126
www.authenticcreations.com
e-mail: Ron@authenticcreations.com

Agent: Mary Lee Laitsch
  Born: Baraboo, Wisconsin.
  Education: B.S., Education, University of Wisconsin.
  Career history: Taught library science. Established my literary agency in 1995.
  Hobbies/personal interests: Family, reading, crafts, and sewing.
  Areas most interested in agenting: Fiction: Adventure, historical, murder mysteries, romance, suspense, and, of course, literary fiction. Nonfiction: Business, crafts, how-to, humor, political, sports, true crime, and women's issues.
  Areas not interested in agenting: Poorly crafted works.
  If not agenting, what would you be doing? I totally enjoy what I am doing and cannot imagine getting into any other line of work.
  Best way to initiate contact: Query letter with SASE.
  Reading-fee policy: No reading fee.
  Client representation by category: Nonfiction, 40%; Fiction, 60%.
  Commission: 15% domestic, 20% foreign.
  Number of titles sold last year: The exact number of manuscripts sold varies from year to year. The only constant is that each year has seen a steady increase over the number of manuscripts sold during the previous year.
  Rejection rate (all submissions): 98%.
  Description of the client from Hell: We have clients from all over the world, but none of them, to our knowledge, comes from Hell. We attempt to treat all of our clients as the unique and talented artists they are and in return expect them to respect our professional opinion on how to get their books published. So far this system has worked out well for us.
  Description of a dream client: A talented writer who has carefully proofread the manuscript before submitting it to us.
  Why did you become an agent? I enjoy working with new writers to develop their initial works into publishable manuscripts.
  Comments: It takes an enormous amount of dedication and effort to write a marketable manuscript. It takes the same effort by the literary agent to find just the right publisher. We

A

prefer to establish a long-term relationship with those authors who appreciate and respect the contributions made by each half of what then will become a successful partnership.

LORETTA BARRETT BOOKS, INC.

101 Fifth Avenue, 11th floor, New York, NY 10003
212-242-3420

Agent: Loretta Barrett
  Education: B.A./M.A., University of Pennsylvania
  Career history: Social Studies Teacher, then Editor-in-Chief of Anchor Books and Vice President and Executive Editor at Doubleday & Co., and a literary agent since 1990.
  Hobbies/personal interests: Skiing, traveling, reading.
  Areas most interested in agenting: Nonfiction: Spirituality, biography, popular science, self-help, health/fitness, psychology, narrative, women's issues, ethnic issues. Fiction: Mainstream contemporary, ethnic, family saga, mystery/suspense, contemporary romance, thriller/espionage.
  Areas not interested in agenting: Science fiction, fantasy, cookbooks, poetry, children's books.
  Best way to initiate contact: Send a well-written query letter with an SASE.
  Client representation by category: Nonfiction, 70%; Fiction, 30%.
  Commission: 15%.
  Rejection rate (all submissions): 95%.
  Most common mistakes authors make: Not providing enough background information on their own writing, work, or experience.
  How did you become an agent? I was an Executive Editor at Doubleday and decided I wanted to work more directly with authors. I have been doing so for over 10 years and love it.
  Why did you become an agent? I love working directly with writers and helping them develop their projects.
  What can a writer do to enhance their chances of getting you as an agent? For nonfiction, submit a detailed marketing plan and as much background information as possible. For fiction, provide background information, not just a synopsis of the manuscript.
  How would you describe what you actually do for a living? I would describe what I do as being a midwife. I help authors give life to their books and help find homes for them.
  What do you think about editors? A good editor is worth his or her weight in gold.
  What do you think about publishers? It concerns me that so many American publishers are owned by conglomerates, which means fewer houses for authors to approach for publication, and it also seems to limit competition. I also think a good publisher is worth his or her weight in gold.
  Representative titles: *The Shadow Negotiation: How Women Can Master the Hidden Agendas That Determine Bargaining Success* by Deborah Kolb and Judith Williams, Ph.D. (Simon & Schuster); *Terrible Honesty: Mongrel Manhattan in the 1920's* by Ann Douglas (Farrar, Straus & Giroux); *The Age of Spiritual Machines* by Ray Kurzweil

(Viking); *Line of Sight* by Jack Kelly (Hyperion); *If You Can't Be Free, Be a Mystery: Myths and Meanings of Billie Holiday* by Farah Griffin (Free Press); *The Last Lover* by Laura Van Wormer (Mira); *Voices Carry* by Mariah Stewart (Pocket); *Inviting God to Your Wedding* by Martha Williamson (Harmony); *Witness to Hope: The Biography of Pope John Paul II* by George Weigel (Harper Collins).

B

THE WENDY BECKER LITERARY AGENCY

530-F Grand Street, Suite 11-H, New York, NY 10002
212-228-5940 (telephone/fax)
e-mail: dulf86a@prodigy.com or DanWen@prodigy.net

Agent: Wendy Becker
   Career history: Associate Editor, McGraw-Hill. Editor, John Wiley & Sons. Agency begun in 1994.
   Areas most interested in agenting: Nonfiction (trade): business, biography, history, current events, parenting/psychology.
   Areas not interested in agenting: Poetry, literary fiction, short stories, children's books, anything in the college market.
   Best way to initiate contact: Query letter (with SASE), to include outline, table of contents, author resume, and up to three sample chapters. Do not call. Do not send complete manuscripts.
   Reading-fee policy: No reading fee.
   Client representation by category: Nonfiction, 80%; Fiction, 20%.
   Commission: 15%.
   Most common mistakes authors make: Never approach an agent initially via telephone, because there is no way to properly evaluate an author without seeing his or her work.

MEREDITH BERNSTEIN LITERARY AGENCY, INC.

2112 Broadway, Suite 503A, New York, NY 10023
212-799-1007 or 212-799-1145

Agents: Meredith Bernstein, Elizabeth Cavanaugh
   Born: Bernstein: July 9, 1946; Hartford, Connecticut; Cavanaugh: October 16, 1962.
   Education: Bernstein: B.A., University of Rochester, 1968; Cavanaugh: B.A., Literature and Creative Writing, Ohio University, Athens, Ohio.
   Career history: Bernstein: Many jobs before becoming an Agent: freelance reader, Story Editor, and worked for another agency for five years before starting my own in 1981. Cavanaugh: Before working in publishing, I held a number of positions that were "book"-related, including working for a period as a librarian; began in publishing with the Bernstein Agency in the mid-1980s and was instrumental in the development of our foreign rights activity.

B

Hobbies/personal interests: Bernstein: I am a collector of vintage and contemporary costume jewelry and clothing, so fashion is a strong interest; sports of all kinds; almost any cultural event (I'm an avid theatergoer); spending time with friends; travel, adventure, and personal-growth work. Cavanaugh: I am interested in all forms of art and love museums, movies, dance, music (I studied the violin for 10 years), and, of course, reading. I am also an avid cook, love gardening, and am currently renovating a 70-year-old house. I am a strong environmentalist and love animals and nature, and enjoy camping, hiking, and canoeing.

Areas most interested in agenting: Bernstein: Nonfiction: psychology, self-help, health/fitness, memoir, current events, business, biography, celebrity. Cavanaugh: narrative nonfiction, parenting, pop-science, general nonfiction, mysteries, literary fiction, mainstream fiction.

Areas not interested in agenting: Bernstein: Children's books, westerns (men's), sci-fi. Cavanaugh: science fiction, children's, poetry, or screenplays.

If not agenting, what would you be doing? Bernstein: 1. (1) Curating the American Craft Museum; (2) Replacing Oprah; (3) Running a top fashion house in Paris. Cavanaugh: It would most likely involve some aspect of books or publishing (maybe editing or even writing), or perhaps be as far afield as environmental science or catering.

Best way to initiate contact: A query letter with SASE.

Reading-fee policy: No reading fee.

Client representation by category: Nonfiction, 50%; Fiction, 50%.

Commission: 15% domestic; 20% on foreign sales (split with subagents).

Number of titles sold last year: A lot!

Rejection rate (all submissions): Unsure, but probably fairly high because we must truly believe in the projects we represent and, therefore, are selective about what we request to see.

Most common mistakes authors make: Bernstein: Poor presentation, no SASE. Cavanaugh: Poorly researched projects (which includes not knowing the market in terms of what is already on the shelves for the type of book they are writing), sloppy presentation.

Description of the client from Hell: Bernstein: Pushy, demanding, inflexible, calls too much, sloppy presentation of material, egomaniacal. Cavanaugh: Someone who does not take a professional approach to his or her career and who does not appreciate the role of an agent.

Description of a dream client: Bernstein: Professional, courteous, sees our relationship as teamwork, respects how hard I work for him/her. Cavanaugh: A great writer whose talent and passion for his/her work brings the project to life and who wants us to work together to reach his/her potential.

How did you become an agent? Bernstein: Sold my first book overnight! almost 25 years ago.

Why did you become an agent? Bernstein: I was born to do this! Cavanaugh: As an agent, the diversity of projects I represent allows me to work within the creative process in many different genres and with many different publishers.

How would you describe what you actually do for a living? Bernstein: I actualize the experience of the authors' dreams.

B

What do you think about editors? Bernstein: I wish they would stop becoming agents!

What do you think about publishers? Bernstein: This is a long conversation that I'd be happy to have over drinks!

Comments: Bernstein: The saddest thing for me about publishing today is that "the bottom line is king." I see so many beautiful pieces of work that I am told are "too small." In the old days, there was "a wing and a prayer"—the loss of that belief system is a failure to envision.

Representative titles: *Romances* by Smeron Sale a.k.a. Dinah McCau, Ana Leigh, Sandra Hill and Janis Reems Hudson; *When Broken Glass Floats* by Chanrithy Him (W. W. Norton); *The Bone Density Diet* by Dr. Kessler (Ballantine); *The Nature of Animal Healing* by Dr. Martin Goldstein (Knopf); *The Whole Truth* by Nancy Pickard (Pocket); *Hormone Deception* by Lindsay Berkson (Contemporary); *The Swampwalker's Journal* by David Carroll (Houghton-Mifflin).

PAM BERNSTEIN & ASSOCIATES INC.

790 Madison Avenue, Suite 310, New York, NY 10021
212-288-1700   fax: 212-288-3054

Agent: Pam Bernstein

Career history: Pam Bernstein was with the William Morris Agency for 15 years. In 1993 she founded Pam Bernstein & Associates, Inc.

Hobbies/personal interests: Reading, skiing, sailing, horseback riding, cooking, gardening.

Areas most interested in agenting: Women's fiction—both literary and commercial. Thrillers, commercial nonfiction; psychological, health, spiritual, relationships.

Areas not interested in agenting: Science fiction and horror.

Best way to initiate contact: Send a brief query letter explaining the work and author's background.

Reading-fee policy: No reading fee.

Client representation by category: Nonfiction, 50%; Fiction, 50%.

Commission: 15%.

Number of titles sold last year: 20.

Rejection rate (all submissions): 90%.

Most common mistakes authors make: Repeated phone calls, poorly typed letters.

Description of the client from Hell: The person with unrealistic dreams about his talent, his advance, and his importance with his publisher. It takes time to build an author's career.

Description of a dream client: A warm, appreciative, talented writer who understands that we both have different roles in this relationship, and who respects the differences.

Why did you become an agent? I love the creative process of working with authors—reading, selling, finding the right marriage of editor and author.

Representative titles: *A Jury of Her Peers* by Jean Hanff Korlity (Crown); *Angry All the Time* by Scott Wetzler (HarperCollins); *Friends for Life: Mothers and Their Adult*

Daughters by Susan Jonas and Marilyn Nissenson (Morrow); *Recovery of Sacred Psychology* by Peter Rinehart (Addison-Wesley); *The Virgin Homeowner* by Janice Papolos (Norton); *Tumbling* by Diane Whetstone (William Morrow); *The Misdiagnosed Child* by Demitri and Janice Papolos (Broadway); *The Sabbathday River* by Jean Hanff Korelitz (Farrar, Straus and Giroux); *The Wholeness of a Broken Heart* by Katie Singer (Riverhead/Penguin, Putnam); *Yoga Baby* by Dr. DeAnson Parker (Broadway). *Bipolar Child* by Janice and Demitri Papolos (Broadway); *The Barefoot Contessa Cookbook* by Ina Garten (Clarkson Potter);

DANIEL BIAL AGENCY

41 West 83rd Street, Suite 5-C, New York, NY 10024
212-721-1786

Agent: Daniel Bial

Education: B.A., English, Trinity College.

Career history: Editor for 15 years, including 10 years at HarperCollins. Founded agency in 1992.

Hobbies/personal interests: Travel, cooking, music, parenting.

Areas most interested in agenting: Nonfiction: popular reference, business, popular culture, science, history, humor, Judaica, sports, psychology, cooking. Fiction: quality fiction, mysteries.

Areas not interested in agenting: Nonfiction: academic treatises, crafts, gift books. Fiction: romances, horror, medical thrillers, children's books, poetry, novels by authors with no publishing credits.

Best way to initiate contact: Query letter with SASE.

Reading-fee policy: No reading fee.

Client representation by category: Nonfiction, 90%; Fiction, 10%.

Commission: 15% domestic; 20% foreign.

Number of titles sold last year: 18.

Most common mistakes authors make: A surprising number of writers devote time in their query letter to telling me about their previous failures. They essentially reject themselves.

What gets you excited? Savvy writers research their field and rate the competition's strengths and weaknesses. They highlight why their book will be new, different, better. They explain why they are the best writer on the topic. And they display an enthusiasm that suggests it will survive all the ups and downs of the publishing process.

Description of the client from Hell: Clients from Hell are almost always wrapped up in private grievances and needs. They talk when they should listen, try force when they should use tact, and get involved in personal gamesmanship when much of publishing calls for team play. They suspect the worst and often cause crises simply through their own closed-mindedness.

Description of a dream client: Dream clients produce trim, tight, ready-to-sell material. They know the business and how to get ahead. They recognize the importance of marketing and that good intentions don't sell books—hard work does. They take pride in their work and their relationships.

Why did you become an agent? I became an agent for the same reason I first became an editor: because I loved the discovery of new authors and books, loved helping create a sellable project, and loved negotiating big advances. I switched desks because I wanted to be my own boss.

B

DAVID BLACK LITERARY AGENCY

156 5th Avenue, Suite 608, New York, NY 10010
212-242-5080   fax: 212-924-6609

Agents: David Black, Gary Morris, Susan Rainhofer, Laureen Rawland, and Joy E. Tutela
   Areas most interested in agenting: Nonfiction, politics, sports, current events, science, fitness, women's issues, music, business and history, fiction, literary fiction, commercial fiction.
   Areas not interested in agenting: Poetry, screenplays, children's.
   Best way to initiate contact: Query letter with SASE enclosed. No faxes, no e-mails.
   Commission: 15%.
   Representative titles: *Tuesdays with Morrie* by Mitch Albom (Doubleday); *Body for Life* by Bill Phillips (Harper Collins); *Isaac's Storm* by Erik Larson (Crown).

BLEECKER STREET ASSOCIATES, INC.

532 LaGuardia Place, New York, NY 10012
212-677-4492   fax: 212-388-0001

Agent: Agnes Birnbaum
   Place of Birth: Budapest, Hungary, but have lived most of my life in the United States.
   Education: Educated in Europe and America.
   Career history: Spent 16 years as an Editor before starting my own agency in 1984. Was Senior Editor at Pocket Books and NAL; Editor in Chief of Award Books, later a part of Berkley.
   Hobbies/personal interests: Reading, classical music, movies, theater, travel.
   Areas most interested in agenting: Nonfiction: history, biography, science, investigative reporting, health, women's issues, popular psychology, nature and outdoor writing, true adventure, New Age/spirituality. In fiction: mystery and suspense thrillers; women's novels—very much, including romances; literary fiction.
   Areas not interested in agenting: Poetry, science fiction, Westerns, children's books film/TV scripts, plays, professional and academic books.
   If not agenting, what would you be doing? I'd still be an editor.
   Best way to initiate contact: With a short letter about the book and the author. An SASE is a must.
   Reading-fee policy: We have no reading fee.

B

Client representation by category: Nonfiction, 65%; Fiction, 35%.

Commission: 15% on domestic sales; 25% on foreign and film/TV if a co-agent is used (who gets 10% commission)—it's 15% on foreign and film/TV if Bleecker is the sole agent.

Titles sold last year: 45.

Rejection rate (all submissions): 90% (alas!).

Most common mistakes authors make: They call or fax; send handwritten, ungrammatical letters; they tell you the book is great because their husband/mother/children all loved it.

Description of the client from Hell: The writer with unreasonable and unrealistic expectations; people who don't know the market they're writing for; someone who is unprofessional—late in delivery of work, refuses to make editorial changes, falls apart from rejection of critiques. The person who asks for a personal meeting prior to sending in material for professional evaluation.

Description of a dream client: The writer with talent and creative new ideas. A person who is passionate about his or her work, is willing to self-promote, understands the pros and cons of the business behind the books.

Why did you become an agent? I love books. I enjoyed being an editor and I wanted to go into business for myself. This was the logical next profession that still involved reading and writers.

What can writers do to enhance their chances of getting you as agent? They can send a great short letter (an art form in itself)—a writer who knows how to convince me the idea is salable by listing facts instead of adjectives. The author who has proven expertise on the topic of his/her book and is familiar with the market for it, knows the competition, and can point out how his/her book is wonderfully different.

How would you describe what you actually do for a living? Wonderful fun—I really enjoy what I do. And I think I'm good at it. I'm good at the negotiating process, good at helping writers shape their work. Bleecker has an excellent track record with first-time authors, for example.

What do you think about editors? I like them. I used to be one so I can relate to their problems and points of view. It's helpful when an agent who was once on the other side of the desk can anticipate the objections in the deal-making process and have the answers handy in advance.

What do you think about publishers? They can be too tough on writers. However, ultimately I think that publishers and authors share a common goal: a terrific book that is also successful.

Comments: I wish that beginning writers read more on the topic of genre they themselves are working in. Bestselling authors are especially worthwhile to dissect and study—there are inevitably good reasons why someone attracts a large following.

Representative titles: *Boys into Men: Raising African-American Male Teenagers* by Nancy Boyd-Franklin, Ph.D., and A. J. Franklin, Ph.D. (Dutton/Plume); *The Women's Pharmacy* by Julie Catalano (Dell); *Strange Skies* by Patricia Barnes-Svarney and Thomas Svarney (Fireside/Touchstone); *Bright Minds—Poor Grades* by Michael Whitley, Ph.D. (Perigee/Putnam); *The Encyclopedia of the Occult* by Brad Steiger (Gale); *How Hitler Could Have Won WWII* by Bevin Alexander (Crown); *Ophelia Speaks* by Sara Shandler

(Harper); *The Irish Manor House Murder* by Dicey Deere (St. Martins); *Angel's Crime* by Preston Pairo (NAL); *Smart Guide to Time Management* by Lisa Rogak (Wiley); *Her Father's Daughter* by Mollie Poupeney (Random House).

BOOK ENDS, LLC

136 Long Hill Road, Gillette, NJ 07933
908-604-2652
www.bookends-inc.com

Agents: Jessica Faust, Jacky Sach

Born: Faust: March 24, 1971, Minnesota; Sach: June 9, 1964, United Kingdom.

Education: Faust: B.A. in Journalism from Marquette University. Sach: B.A. in English from Oneonta, New York.

Career history: Faust: Berkley Publishing: 1994–1998 (Associate Editor); Macmillan Publishing 1998–1999 (Senior Editor). Sach: Berkley Publishing/Penguin Putnam: 1986–2000.

Hobbies/personal interests: Faust: Walking my dog, running, travel, cooking, gardening, yard sales, and flea markets. Sach: Playing with my dog, reading, running, cooking, gardening, backpacking, camping, outdoor enthusiast.

Areas most interested in agenting: Faust: Romance and mysteries, women's fiction, nonfiction; business, relationships, self-help, psychology, parenting, pets, health. Sach: Literary fiction, mysteries, spirituality, self-help, suspense/thriller fiction.

Areas not interested in agenting: Faust: Children's, science fiction, and fantasy. Sach: Children's, science fiction and fantasy, textbooks.

If not agenting, what might you be doing? Faust: I would be an editor. I spent seven years in publishing as an acquisitions editor and I loved every minute of it. There is no doubt in my mind that if I were to leave agenting, it would only be because I've made a decision to re-join a publishing house. Sach: Writing, editing, or service work of some capacity.

Best way to initiate contact: Query letters are accepted via snail mail and e-mail. However, if you know the material you are submitting fits a category our agency represents, feel free to send along the entire manuscript or just a partial. Always include a brief query letter, outlining your book and giving your credentials as a writer, a synopsis of the book, and an SASE. The agency does not accept e-mail attachments and will only look at short letters.

Client representation by category: Nonfiction, 60%; Fiction, 40%.

Commission: 15% English language; 20% British and foreign translation; 15% television, movie, and so on.

Number of titles sold last year: 10.

Rejection rate (all submissions): 40%.

Most common mistakes authors make: Faust: Not including a query letter. I don't know how many times I'll request a manuscript after getting an e-mail or snail mail query, only to receive the material and nothing else. I get hundreds of submissions and queries a month and can't always remember which I've requested and which were just sent to me.

B

It is important to remind me in a short letter not only that I've requested your material, but who you are, what your background is, and a brief two-sentence synopsis of your book. Sach: Clients forget that we look at hundreds of submissions and cannot always keep track of random communications and submissions. I appreciate a potential client who is clear with every piece of communication with me, detailing who the client is, what the client is sending me, conversations we may have had, dates submission were sent, and titles of submissions.

Description of the client from Hell: Faust: The client from Hell already knows everything there is to know and doesn't need an agent or an editor. She usually thinks the book is perfect just as she wrote it and will refuse to accept any editorial suggestions her agent or editor might make. In addition, her primary goal is to be a star and she expects her editor and agent to make her one, without doing any work herself. Sach: The client from Hell thinks he/she has written the perfect book that needs no help whatsoever and is resistant to changes and input from editors and agents. This client also thinks that everything should be dropped immediately for him/her and has no understanding of time and patience. The client from Hell is egotistical, self-centered, and impatient.

Description of a dream client: Faust: My dream client understands the need for an editor or an agent. She/he knows that her book is not perfect and relishes the look of a second pair of eyes, someone who isn't so close to the characters that she can't see their flaws. She takes the time to know the industry and asks questions of things she doesn't understand. The dream client writes because she loves to write, not just because she wants to be published. And whether she is published or not, she is always writing. Sach: My dream client understands the symbiotic relationship between writers and agents/editors. The client is open to suggestion and change and wants his/her book to be the best it can be. The client relies on the hard-earned experience and knowledge of his/her editors and agents, while communicating his/her own ideas, dreams, and suggestions. The dream client is patient and eager to learn and grow. The dream client wants a thriving/positive relationship with her/his agent and strives first and foremost to make the best book possible. The dream client also is willing to learn about the publishing industry: I believe that a knowledgeable client is a good client. The dream client is a writer at heart. She/he is most interested in writing; getting published is a wonderful benefit but not the reason she writes. Most of all, the client writes, writes, writes!

How did you become an agent? Faust: In 1999, Jacky Sach and I were sitting in her Brooklyn apartment discussing our jobs and careers when, out of the blue, I wondered if she would ever consider starting a business. Boom! Five months later we were the proud owners of BookEnds, LLC, a book packaging company. After just a short year in business we were proud to say we had sold 10 books, but for some reason neither of us felt we were getting what we wanted from the business That's when it hit us. What we really missed was working with the authors. We missed the romance and intrigue (literally) of working on fiction and nonfiction and helping an author to craft the work she created. That's when we decided it was time to present ourselves as agents. We'd already had a number of requests for representation so in 2001 we made it official. Sach: I'll rely on my partner's (Jessica Faust's) words for this one. Well said!

Why did you become an agent? Faust: I really love working with authors. I love helping them shape the book, and I love brainstorming during its inception. While I was able to achieve these things as an editor, I felt hemmed in by the confines of the publishing house. As an agent I can take on almost any project that interests me because I have a huge variety of publishing houses to offer it to. Sach: I love reading and I love representing writers. I love the idea of helping someone fulfill a dream and build a career in writing. I also enjoy the creative input I have as an agent.

What can writers do to enhance their chances of getting you as their agent? Faust: I'm looking for writers with new and terrific ideas. While I'll always consider looking at a writer who describes her work as the next Nora Roberts, I would much rather find that writer whom everyone else describes themselves as the next of. I want to find a mystery series with a detective that no one has thought of and a romance I lose myself in and can't put down. If you're a nonfiction writer, I'm looking for someone with a platform. I want someone who has ideas of his own and speaks and writes and promotes those ideas. To him the book is just another platform, not the only platform. Sach: Originality.

How would you describe what you do for a living? Faust: I am an advocate for the author. It is my job to coach the author (as needed) through writing the book and then negotiate the contract and deal with the publishing house on his or her behalf. Sach: Author advocate.

What do you think about editors? Faust: Since I was an editor for many years, I think they are wonderful. I have a good relationship with many editors, and 90 percent of them do their job out of love. They love books and they love helping an author shape his or her manuscript. Unfortunately, an editor is often restrained by the confines of the company she works for. Not all publishing houses handle cozy mysteries or historical romances, and for that reason an editor is not always able to take on a project she loves. It is a frustrating job at times, and editors are often given a bad rep for these reasons. Sach: I think today's editors are extremely overworked. A large percentage of them are wonderful, dedicated, hardworking individuals who have an honest desire to find a great writer and develop that writer's career—not just for the bestseller status but for the joy of producing something notable. I believe there are many talented editors out there.

What do you think about publishers? Faust: They are businessmen and while what they deal with is often considered art, the publishers themselves only look at it from a business perspective. This is an important thing for all writers to remember. Sach: There are fewer publishers left, as consolidation becomes more frequent—I wish there were more publishers! I wish the bottom line didn't weigh as heavily as it does. I wish writing as an art were more appreciated. But all in all, I do think publishers are doing a good job of getting writers out there. Although I do wish there were more opportunities for new writers and the publishers were more willing to take big chances. . . . I also think many publishers feel this way themselves.

Comments: Faust: There are so many amazing writers out there with wonderful stories to tell, but those who really hit home with me are the writers who are doing it from the heart. They are writing about something they know and writing because of their love for writing. I love being an agent and I'm looking forward to, more than anything, working and meeting so many new and terrific writers and helping them make their dreams come true. Sach: What rocks my world is when I know I am reading the truth; when the truth just rings out from the plate, whether it's a novel or a nonfiction work, honesty speaks to me. That moment when you read something and you know it is absolutely right, completely perfect . . . nothing is more beautiful than that.

Representative titles: *The Complete Idiot's Guide to Hinduism* by Linda Johnsen (Macmillan); *The Complete Idiot's Guide to Women's History* by Sonia Weiss with Lorna Rinear (Macmillan); *Critical Lives Presents Che Guevera* by Eric Luther (Macmillan); *Court TV's You Be the Judge* by Patrick J. Sauer (Warner); *To My Daughter on the Birth of Her First Child* by BookEnds, LLC (Hyperion); *To My Daughter on Her Wedding Day* by BookEnds, LLD (Hyperion).

B

ANDREA BROWN LITERARY AGENCY, INC.

P.O. Box 1027, Montara, CA 94037

Agents: Andrea Brown; Laura Rennert, Associate Agent
   Born: Rennert: 12/16/64, Bethesda, Maryland.
   Education: Brown: B.A., Journalism and English, Syracuse University. Rennert: B.A., Cornell University, M.A., University of Virginia; Ph.D. University of Virginia (English Literature).
   Career history: Brown: Editorial Assistant, Dell; Editorial Assistant, Random House; Assistant Editor (all children's books) Knopf, started agency in 1981. Rennert: Faculty member in English department of universities in the United States and in Japan for eight years. Freelance Editor for four years. Associate Agent at Andrea Brown Literary Agency for four years.
   Hobbies/personal interests: Brown: Golf, theater, gardening, travel, my cats.
   Areas most interested in agenting: Brown: Easy-readers, anything humorous, science activity books, high-tech nonfiction for all ages. Rennert: Picture books, middle-grade and young adult fiction, historical fiction, photography, I am also looking for talented illustrators who are also writers.
   Areas not interested in agenting: Brown: Don't send adult books; we specialize in children's books and still get flooded with adult proposals. No rhyming picture books. Rennert: I am an omnivorous reader and an omnivorous agent. We do, however, represent primarily children's books.
   If not agenting, what might you be doing? Brown: I've been an agent so long now, I can't imagine doing anything else, though it's often so frustrating these days. Rennert: If I weren't an agent, I would continue my career as a professor of English Literature and as a scholar.
   Best way to initiate contact: Brown: Query letter with SASE only. Rennert: A query letter and four chapters of work or a query and a complete picture book manuscript.
   Client representation by category: Brown: Children's, 99% (Nonfiction, 50%; Fiction, 50%). Rennert: Nonfiction, 3%; Fiction, 2%; Children's, 95%.
   Commission: 15% domestic; 20% foreign.
   Number of titles sold last year: Brown: Not for public consumption—more than last year. Rennert: 40 books for agency.
   Rejection rate (all submissions): Brown: 95%.
   Most common mistakes authors make: Brown: Faxing queries. I hate that. Or long calls, asking lots of questions before I'm interested. And calling after I've already said no. Or re-sending with minor changes after we have rejected it. It closes the door on any fu-

ture interest I may have in the writer. Rennert: The most common mistakes are not knowing the comparables and competition. If you are going to write picture books, for example, then you should be reading *a lot* of picture books.

Description of the client from Hell: Brown: One who has to talk to his agent on a daily basis, always thinks his work is perfect as it is, and that the editor is always wrong. Rennert: The client from Hell wants frequent phone updates and constant handholding. Because we specialize in children's books, we have more clients and make more deals than adult agents. The sheer volume of manuscripts and deals with which we are involved takes up much of our time during and after business hours, and the client from Hell is one who doesn't understand that much of our time is spent on the business of promoting and selling books.

Description of the dream client: Brown: One who works hard and takes his career seriously; he respects that an agent has many clients to represent, but still remembers to mention that he appreciates the time and effort taken on his behalf. Rennert: My dream client is one who is devoted to the craft of writing, who welcomes editorial input, and who is willing to revise and, if necessary, revise again. My dream client understands that the work of selling books takes a lot of time and dedication, and he welcomes e-mail updates and communication, interspersed with the occasional phone call.

Why did you become an agent? Brown: I fell into the children's book field and loved it. But, I loved working with authors and illustrators and creating good books for kids. I saw that authors needed more representation in the changing children's books field, and I was the first to represent both children's book authors *and* illustrators. That was 1981, and now authors need agents more than ever. Rennert: I became an agent because of my love of the written word and of books. I wanted to be passionate about what I do and to work with people who are passionate about what they do.

What can writers do to enhance their chances of getting you as their agent? Brown: Doing their homework in the children's book field as to appropriate age group, category, length, and so on. If writers come off as knowledgeable and professional (and can write and think commercially), I'm more likely to take them on. Writing well is not enough. Rennert: If a writer can move me to laughter or to tears, then I usually think very carefully about taking her or him on as a client. I look for writers with whom I can have a long-term relationship and with whom I can grow.

How would you describe what you do for a living? Rennert: I am involved in the creative process, working with writers to help them realize the full potential of their vision and to perfect their craft. I use my relationships with publishers to help find the best home for each writer's work, and then I negotiate the best deal possible for my authors.

Comments: Brown: Unfortunately, everyone thinks it is easy to write for children. Actually, it is the toughest form of writing to do, especially picture books. In a few words, a writer must tell a perfect story with a fresh writing voice. It takes rare talent to pull it off well. It's more important to write from the child within you than to have three children and think you can write. Many people make this mistake. A children's writer must have the passion and voice to get published. Name brands sell, and it's tougher than ever to get a new writer published. Good writing is not enough. Writers must think in a commercial way and plan to promote their books. And don't waste your time trying to get an agent if you just have one picture book. Agents need writers committed to a long-term career writing for children.

Representative titles: *"K" Is for Kitten* by Niki Leopold, illustrated by Susan Jeffers (Penguin/Putnam); *Escape from Heart* by Lynette Stark (Harcourt); *Paul McCartney: I Saw Him Standing There* by Jorie Gracen (Billboard Books/Watson Guptil); *How People Learned to Fly* by Fran Hodgkins and illustrated by Tru Kelley (HarperCollins).

B

CURTIS BROWN LTD.

Ten Astor Place, New York, NY 10003
212-473-5400

Agents: Ellen Geiger, Elizabeth Harding, Ginger Knowlton, Laura Blake Peterson, Douglas Stewart, Mitchell Waters

The following information pertains to ELLEN GEIGER:
Born: New York, NY.
Education: Graduate Degree in Anthropology.
Career history: Former PGS Executive before becoming a literary agent.
Hobbies/personal interests: Tennis, reading, growing perfect tomatoes, eating out, travel, film, theatre, arts.
Areas most interested in agenting: Nonfiction of all kinds, especially narrative, and high-quality commercial and literary fiction, cutting-edge issues, journalists, Asia and Asian American subjects, religion, science, history.
Areas not interested in agenting: Romance, New Age, children's, poetry, cookie-cutter thrillers, right-wing propaganda of any kind.
Best method to initiate contact: Query letter with SASE, sample chapters (if novel), or proposal (if nonfiction). Absolute best way is a referral from an existing client.
If not agenting, what would you be doing? I'll always be an agent.
Client representation by category: Nonfiction: 75%; Fiction: 25%.
What is your commission structure? 15% domestic; 20% Canadian/overseas.
Rejection rate (all submissions): 95%.
Most common mistakes authors make: Sending a whole manuscript with a query letter without being requested, sloppy mistakes and typos in proposals, calling repeatedly for status reports, telling me what a great *film* their book will make.
Description of the client from Hell: Someone who can't be pleased, no matter what happens. An overanxious author who calls or e-mails all the time; suspicious authors who can't trust their agents.
Description of the dream client: A writer who is talented, patient, hard working, self-confident. A writer with a track record of some sort. A genius who is also a nice person.
How did you become an agent? I was mentored into the business by a top agent.
Why did you become an agent? It's immensely satisfying to bring good work to the public.
What can a writer do to enhance their chances of getting you as an agent? Write a dynamite query letter, have some expertise on the subject (if nonfiction) or a publishing track record (if fiction).

How would you describe what you actually do for a living? Among other clichés: mine for gold, storm the barricades, pour oil on the waters, throw caution to the winds, tilt at windmills.

What do you think about editors? They are under tremendous pressure to justify their acquisitions before their Editorial Boards. They are also seriously understaffed and cannot do the kind of in-depth editing and handholding they'd like to.

What do you think about publishers? They should all tilt at the shrine of St. Oprah for popularizing literature and creating new readers.

Comments: I love it when unusual books become hits, like *Tuesdays with Morrie* or *Longitude*. This happens often enough in publishing to give me hope.

Representative titles: *Body Transformation* by Dr. Scott Connelly (Putnam); *Lillian Gish* by Charles Affron (Scribner); *God At The Edge* by Nile Goldstein (Bell Tower); *Murder With Puffins, Flammgos, etc.* by Donna Andrews (St. Martin's Press).

The following information pertains to ELIZABETH HARDING:

Education: B.A. in English, University of Michigan (Ann Arbor)

Areas most interested in agenting: Children's literature.

Best method to initiate contact: Query letter or sample chapters.

Client representation by category: Children's: 100%.

Commission: 15% domestic; 20% foreign; 15% dramatic

The following information pertains to GINGER KNOWLTON:

Born: Before the 60's; Princeton, New Jersey.

Education: Questionable, navy brat quality.

Career history: I worked in a factory assembling display cases in Mystic, CT, for a time. Gained numerous pounds one summer working in a bakery in Mendocino, CA. I've taught preschool and I directed an infant and toddler childcare center. That means I organized a lot of fundraisers. I started working at Curtis Brown in 1986.

Areas most interested in agenting: Middle grade and teenage novels.

Areas not interested in agenting: I prefer to remain open to all ideas.

Best method to initiate contact: A simple, straightforward letter with a return envelope works well.

If not agenting, what might you be doing? I love my job, but if I had the luxury of not having to work, I would play tennis even more than I already do; I would tend my gardens more fastidiously; and I would spend more time playing with others.

Client representation by category: Nonfiction: 5%; Fiction 5%; Children's 90%.

Commission: 15% domestic; 20% foreign.

Rejection rate (all submissions): 98%.

Most common mistakes authors make: Expecting an answer within a week, but mostly poor quality writing.

Description of the client from Hell: Happy to report that I still don't have first-hand experience with a "client from Hell" so once again I will refrain from describing one (for fear of a self-fulfilling prophecy).

Description of a dream client: A professional author who respects my job as I respect his, who will maintain an open dialogue so we may learn from each other and continue to grow, who is optimistic and enthusiastic, and who continues to write books worthy of publication.

How did you become an agent? I asked Dad for money for graduate school. He offered me a job at Curtis Brown instead.

What do you think about editors? I have a lot of respect for editors and I think they have an incredibly difficult job. As in all professions, some are more gifted than others.

B

The following information pertains to LAURA BLAKE PETERSON:

Education: B.A. Vassar College.

Career history: 1986–present, Curtis Brown, Ltd.

Hobbies/personal interests: Gardening, pets, regional equestrian competitions.

Areas most interested in agenting: Exceptional fiction, narrative nonfiction, young adult fiction, anything outstanding.

Areas not interested in agenting? Fantasy, science fiction, poetry.

Best way to initiate contact: The best way is through a referral from either a client of mine or an editor with whom I work.

Client representation by category: Nonfiction: 25%; Fiction: 60%; Children's 15%.

Commission: 15% domestic; 20% foreign.

Rejection rate (all submissions): 98%.

Common mistakes authors make: Calling, rather than sending a query letter.

Description of the client from Hell: An author who calls incessantly, preventing me from accomplishing anything on his or her behalf.

Description of the dream client: A talented writer who know the idiosyncrasies of the publishing business yet nonetheless remains determined to be a part of it; a writer with the skills and patience to participate in an often frustrating and quirky industry.

Why did you become an agent? I love language. I can't imagine a better job than helping to bring a skilled writer to the attention of the book-buying public.

If not agenting, what might you be doing? Teaching, gardening, who knows?

What can a writer do to enhance their chances of getting you as an agent? Do their homework. Find out what I (or whoever they're contacting) like to read and represent, what books I've sold in the past, etc., Reading this survey!

The following information pertains to DOUGLAS STEWART:

Born: 1971, Wisconsin

Education: B.A., Vassar College.

Areas most interested in agenting: Literary fiction, serious nonfiction.

Areas not interested in agenting: Romance, how-to, health, children's, spirituality.

Best way to initiate contact: Query letter and one sample chapter (fiction), or just a query letter (nonfiction).

Client representation by category: Nonfiction: 50%; Fiction: 50%.

Rejection rate (all submissions): 98%.

Representative titles: *Shadow Baby* by Alison McGhee (Harmony Books); *Lit Life* by Kurt Wenzel (Random House); *Mountain City* by Gregory Martin (FSG/North Point); *Ghostwritten* by David Mitchell (Random House); *Humanity* by Jonathan Glover (Yale University Press); *The Colors of Nature* by Alison Deming and Laucet Savog (Milkweed)

B

The following information pertains to MITCHELL WATERS:

Born: Brooklyn, New York; 6/19/57.

Education: M.A., English Lit. Fordham University.

Hobbies/personal interests: Tennis, theatre, opera.

Areas most interested in agenting: Literary fiction, narrative nonfiction, mystery, suspense, health, social sciences, gay & lesbian fiction, and nonfiction.

Areas not interested in agenting: Science fiction, romance.

Best way to initiate contact: Query letter.

Client representation by category: Nonfiction: 60%; Fiction: 35%; Children's 5%.

Commission: 15% domestic sales.

Number of titles sold last year: 25.

Rejection rate (all submissions): 95%.

Most common mistakes authors make: Frequent follow-up phone calls.

Why did you become an agent? To be an advocate for talented writers.

If not agenting, what might you be doing? Teaching literature.

What can a writer do to enhance their chances of getting you as an agent? Be patient, but remind me they are there.

PEMA BROWNE LTD.

Pine Road, HCR Box 104B, Neversink, NY 12765
914-985-2936 or 914-985-2062   fax: 914-985-7635

Agents: Pema Browne (Pema rhymes with Emma), Perry Browne

Education: Pema: Moore College of Art, University of PA; Barnes Foundation; Perry: Syracuse University, B.A., English/Communications.

Career history: Pema: Artist/Painter; exhibited widely, in three N.Y. city shows; art buyer. Perry: Radio/TV DJ; commercials.

Hobbies/personal interests: Travel.

Areas most interested in agenting: Solid adult literary fiction and nonfiction. Children's, all genres from novelty, picture books, novels and nonfiction.

Areas not interested in agenting: Poetry and pornography.

Best way to initiate contact: One-page query letter with SASE (no checks).

Reading-fee policy: No reading fee.

Client representation by category: Nonfiction, 35%; Fiction, 35%; Children's, 30%.

Commission: 15% manuscripts; 20% author/illustrations; 30% illustrations; 10% screenplays.

Number of titles sold last year: 32.

Rejection rate (all submissions): 98%.

Description of the client from Hell: We do not handle anyone who would fit that description.

Description of a dream client: Authors who have integrity and professionalism and continue to polish their skills. Those who present well-thought-out proposals and neat manuscripts.

B

Representative titles: *Career ReExplosion—Reinvent Yourself in Thirty Days* by Joseph Grappo (Berkley); *Healing the Trauma of Past Lives* by Thelma B. Freedman, Ph.D. (Kensington/Carol); *Athena's Conquest* by Noelle Gracy (Regnery/Kensington); *Rodeo Hearts* by Patricia Ellis (Contemporary/Kensington); *A Family Affair* by Cathleen Claire (Regnery/Kensington); *Dead and Breakfast* by Susan Scott (Cora Verlag); *River of No Return* by Linda Cargill (Cora Verlag); *Abracadabra, You're Dead!* by Betty Headapohl (Cora Verlag); *Math Easy Fun Series* by Lynette Long (John Wiley & Sons); *Three Little Puppies and the Big Bad Flea,* illustrated by Charles Jordan; *Tale of a Tail,* illustrated by John Sandford; *Fairy Poems* by Laura Ingalls Wilder, compiled by Stephen Hines, illustrated by Richard Hull.

SHEREE BYKOFSKY ASSOCIATES, INC.

16 West 36th Street, New York, NY 10018
212-244-4144

Agent: Sheree Bykofsky
　Born: September, 1956; Queens, New York.
　Education: B.A., State University of New York, Binghamton; M.A., Columbia University (English and Comparative Literature).
　Career history: Executive Editor/Book Producer, the Stonesong Press (1984–1996); Freelance Editor/Writer (1984); General Manager/Managing Editor, Chiron Press, 1979–1984. Author and co-author of a dozen books, most notably *The Complete Idiot's Guide to Getting Published* (Alpha/Macmillan).
　Hobbies/personal interests: Tournament Scrabble, poker, racquetball, movies, bridge.
　Areas most interested in agenting: Popular reference, adult nonfiction (hardcovers and trade paperbacks), quality fiction (highly selective).
　Areas not interested in agenting: Genre romances, science fiction, Westerns, occult and supernatural, children's books.
　If not agenting, what would you be doing? Writing and editing.
　Best way to initiate contact: Send a well-written, detailed query letter with an SASE. Please, no phone calls.
　Reading-fee policy: No reading fee.
　Client representation by category: Nonfiction, 80%; Fiction, 20%.
　Commission: 15%.
　Number of titles sold last year: 100.
　Rejection rate (all submissions): 90%.
　Most common mistakes authors make: Excessive hubris, not explaining what the book is about; paranoia (we're not going to steal your idea); sloppy grammar, punctuation, and spelling.
　Description of the client from Hell: I only take on an author if I feel we can work well together.
　Description of a dream client: One who is not only a talented writer but who is a professional in every sense—from writing the proposal to promoting the book. Also, one

who appreciates my hard work on his or her behalf. I love when authors read my book, *The Complete Idiot's Guide to Getting Published.*

How did you become an agent? I managed a small textbook publishing company. Then I was a book producer and author, then an agent.

Why did you become an agent? It suits me, and I feel I have the talent and experience to do it well.

Comments: In addition to being an agent, I have been a book packager and author. This gives me and my clients a perspective that most agents do not have. Often, I match my clients with publishers' ideas.

Representative titles: *365 Ways to Become a Millionaire Without Being Born One* by Brian Koslow (Dutton); *All Aboard: The Comprehensive Guide to North American Train Travel* by Jim Loomis (Prima); *Love Types: Discover Your Romantic Style and Find Your Soul Mate* by Alexander Avila (Avon); *Multicultural Manners* by Norine Dresser (Wiley); *No Human Involved* by Barbara Seranella (St. Martin's, fiction); *Race Manners* by Bruce Jacobs (Arcade); *Ten-Minute Life Lessons for Kids* by Jamie Miller (HarperCollins); *The Bearded Lady* by Sharlee Dieguez (Hill Street); *The Complete Idiot's Guide to Getting Published* by Sheree Bykofsky (Alpha/Macmillan); *Dealers, Healers, Brutes & Saviors* by Gerald and Susan Meyers (Wiley); *In All the Wrong Places* by Donna Anders (Pocket); *22 Ways to Creating a Meaningful Work Place* by Tom Terez (Adams); *Breast Cancer Survival Manual* by John Link, M.D. (Holt); *Create Your Own Luck* by Azriela Jaffe (Adams); *The Baghavad Gita for Westerners* by Jack Hawley (New World Library); *Tripping* by Charles Hayes (Viking); *The Toltec Way* by Susan Gregg (Renaissance); *Christmas Windows in New York: A Pictorial Look at 100 Years of Christmas Windows* by Sheryll Bellman (Rizzoli); *Emotional Vampires: Dealing with People Who Drain You in 90 Seconds or Less* by Nicholas Boothman (Workman).

CAMBRIDGE LITERARY ASSOCIATES

25 Green Street, Newburyport, MA 01950
978-499-0374

Agent: Michael Valentini, member AAR.
  Born: August 3, 1965; Somerville, Massachusetts.
  Education: B.A., 1987; M.A., 1992, Harvard University.
  Career History: Reporter/Writer, Commercial Record; Reporter, Beacon Press; Free-lance Magazine Writer; Freelance Ghostwriter.
  Hobbies/personal interest: Travel, biking, skiing, sailing, film.
  Areas most interested in agenting: Priority: True life, novels, action adventure.
  Areas not interested in agenting: New Age.
  If not agenting, what would you be doing? Working as an editor for a publishing house.
  Client representation by category: Nonfiction: 20%; Fiction: 60%; Children's 5%; Textbooks: 2%; Short Story: 13%.
  Commission: 15% domestic, 20% foreign.

Number of titles sold last year: 15

Rejection rate (all submissions): 85%–90%.

Most common mistakes authors make: Vague and unprofessional query letters, no SASE, braggadocio by beginners.

Description of the client from Hell: Unpublished and wants an advance on his first novel. This same type expects an auction and is disappointed if he doesn't get one.

Description of the dream client: He/she writes well, is realistic about his/her chances, and appreciates every read.

Why did you become an agent? Lifelong love of books and literature.

Comments: We at Cambridge understand that we are dealing with something precious—our client's dreams—and we treat them accordingly.

Representative titles: *The Global Negotiator* by Jeswald Salacuse (St. Martin's); *Stepliving for Teens* by Dr. Joel Block and Dr. Susan Bartell (Penguin); *The Unexpected Storm* by Steven Manchester (Hellgate Press).

MARIA CARVAINIS AGENCY, INC.

1350 Avenue of the Americas, Suite 2905, New York, NY 10019

212-245-6365   fax: 212-245-7196

e-mail: mcamariacarvainisagency.com

Agent: Maria Carvainis

Born: March 24, 1946; Brisbane, Australia.

Education: B.A., City College of New York, 1967.

Career history: Maria Carvainis established the Maria Carvainis Agency, Inc. in 1977 and the agency has expanded and been profitable for 23 years. Prior to 1977, she worked for 10-plus years in the publishing industry as an Editor and then Senior Editor at Macmillan Publishing, Basic Books, Avon Books, and Crown Publishing. She has been active in the Association of Authors' Representatives, serving as a Board Member, Treasurer, and Chair of the AAR Contracts Committee, and currently is a member of the AAR Royalty Committee.

Hobbies/personal interests: Reading literary fiction, biographies, and mysteries; gardening, gourmet cooking, wine appreciation, and international travel. Maria is a Conservator of the New York Republic Library, Member of Literary Partners, Board Member of the Bidwell House Museum, and devotee of Vintage English cars, especially Bentleys.

Areas most interested in agenting: The agency represents both fiction and nonfiction, with special interest in general fiction/mainstream, literary fiction, mystery and suspense, thrillers, fantasy, historical works, young adult, contemporary women's fiction, biography and memoirs, health and self-help, business, finance, psychology, and popular science.

Areas not interested in agenting: Science fiction.

If not agenting, what would you be doing? I have never considered an alternative profession.

Best way to initiate contact: An articulate and succinct query letter with SASE. Include a one- or two-paragraph description of the project, mention writing credits, if any, and describe where your project fits in the marketplace. In additional, identify what material is available: complete manuscript, sample chapters, or synopsis.

Reading-fee policy: No reading fee.

Client representation by category: Nonfiction, 35%; Fiction, 65%.

Commission: 15% domestic, 20% foreign.

Number of titles sold last year: Confidential.

Rejection rate (all submissions): 99%, but new original writers should never be discouraged by the statistics.

Most common mistakes authors make: The writer views his/her query as a form letter. The writer claims more for his/her project than it delivers.

Description of a dream client: A writer who is intelligent, has original ideas, and is informed about the marketplace, in addition to having the ability to write and willingness to rewrite.

How did you become an agent? I wanted to be an entrepreneur and used my 10 years of editorial experience to do so.

Why did you become an agent? After 10-plus years on the corporate side of the desk, I found myself more identified with the authors and their interests than with the corporate mission. Furthermore, I wanted to be an independent businessperson, responsible only to my clients and myself. I was willing to take a risk for greater personal and financial rewards and have had the satisfaction of helping many writers fulfill their aspirations and establish careers.

What can a writer do to enhance their chances of getting you as an agent? The writer should be able to crystallize the originality of his/her work. Clarity is a sign of competence and confidence.

How would you describe what you actually do for a living? I believe that I am a long-term business partner with the writer to build a successful career. Each writer has unique strengths. My job is to complement the author. Authors vary in how much creative direction they need. The author who is still building a readership can often benefit from editorial direction as he/she shapes the next project. The agent's role always involves vigorously trying to sell a project she represents because she believes in the author. After the sale, it is all about negotiating the best contract and protecting the author's rights.

What do you think about editors? Editors today vary tremendously in their abilities. Because the corporate structure uses agents as readers or screeners of material, the editor is primarily in an acquisition role, often spending more time in meetings than in working with authors and manuscripts.

What do you think about publishers? There is tremendous confusion in the industry among publishers. The great uncertainty is whether the traditional role of a publisher has value or whether a publisher is simply a content provider. And the emergence of electronic commerce and the electronic book, combined with globalized consolidation, seems at times to totally preoccupy them.

Comments: The loss of the code of honor that existed between authors, agents, and publishers is a disturbing consequence of the major changes confronting everyone who works in the publishing industry today. As a result, the book is becoming more of a commodity in the entertainment marketplace.

Representative titles: *The Switch* by Sandra Brown (Warner Books); *The Guru Guide to Entrepreneurship* by Joseph H. Boyett and Jimmie T. Boyett (John Wiley & Sons); *Bearing Witness* by Michael Kahn (TOR/Forge); *Dead of Winter* by P. J. Parrish (Kensington); *Fame: The Power and Cost of a Fantasy* by Sue Erikson Bloland (Viking); *Heroin* by Charlie Smith (W. W. Norton); *More Than a Mistress* by Mary Balogh (Delacorte); *Fish Tank Sonata* by Arthur Tress (Bulfinch).

C

MARTHA CASSELMAN, LITERARY AGENT

P.O. Box 342, Calistoga, CA 94515
707-942-4341

Agent: Martha Casselman
   Born: New York City.
   Education: B.A., English and Education, Jackson College of Tufts University; attended Radcliffe Publishing Procedures Course.
   Career history: Magazines, Editorial Assistant, Copyeditor, Editor (*Good Housekeeping, Show* magazine, *Holiday* magazine); Freelance Editor and Reader (Book-of-the-Month Club, Viking, etc.)—in New York before moving to California in 1976.
   Hobbies/personal interests: Can you believe—reading? (Belongs to a reading group.)
   Areas most interested in agenting: Food books, some nonfiction, other exciting books too wonderful to turn away.
   Areas not interested in agenting: Poetry, textbooks, religion, fiction, children's, or full scripts.
   If not agenting, what would you be doing? It changes. I can't remember not being an agent.
   Best way to initiate contact: Write a brief letter (with SASE), and be straightforward about what other contacts are being made; make proposal/query so good it's impossible for me not to go after it (but expect long-distance return calls to be collect if you make a query by phone). Reminder: No return postage means no response. Sorry.
   Reading-fee policy: No reading fee.
   Client representation by category: Nonfiction, 98%; Fiction, 2%.
   Commission: 15%, plus some copying, overnight mail expenses; 20% if using subagents.
   Number of titles sold last year: Confidential.
   Rejection rate (all submissions): 99%.
   Most common mistakes authors make: Not doing their marketing homework: What are the other books out there? Do an evaluation, neither knocking nor over-praising. How is this book going to get reader/buyers, with all the other books in competition with it?
   What gets you excited? Be good writers; be tuned in to promotional opportunities or create them; join professional organizations, local (better, national); seek out radio/TV contacts and appearances. Your publisher will be able to build on those.
   Description of the client from Hell: My sympathies are increasingly with authors, except when authors simply don't want to listen to reality (please don't shoot the messenger—when it's me, anyway).
   Comments: It's not getting any easier.

CASTIGLIA LITERARY AGENCY

1155 Camino Del Mar, Suite 510, Del Mar, CA 92014
858-755-8761   fax: 858-755-7063

Agents: Julie Castiglia, Winifred Goldon
   Education: Educated in England.
   Career history: Published writer (three book titles—hundreds of magazine articles, essays, poetry in literary anthologies), Freelance Editor (10 years), agent (last 13 years).
   Hobbies/personal interests: Traveling, hiking, skiing, gardening, animals, decorative arts books.
   Areas most interested in agenting: Mainstream, literary, and ethnic fiction. Nonfiction: psychology, science and health, biography, women's issues, niche books, contemporary issues, narrative nonfiction, and how-to.
   Areas not interested in agenting: Horror and science fiction; formula romance.
   If not agenting, what would you be doing? Writing and traveling.
   Best way to initiate contact: Query letter with SASE.
   Reading-fee policy: No reading fee.
   Client representation by category: Nonfiction, 50%; Fiction, 50%.
   Commission: 15% domestic; 20% foreign.
   Number of titles sold last year: 15.
   Rejection rate (all submissions): 95%.
   Most common mistakes authors make: Not attending writers' conferences or workshops before they submit to an agent. Not looking at *Books in Print* before writing their proposal. Submitting fiction before it's polished.
   Description of the client from Hell: Loquacious, untrustworthy, grumpy, promises but does not perform, doesn't meet deadlines. Talks but doesn't write!
   Description of a dream client: Trustworthy, intelligent, hardworking, understands the eccentricities of the business. Trusts my judgment. Meets deadlines. Doesn't make mountains out of molehills.
   Why did you become an agent? I've always loved books and knew the publishing business well, having sold my own three books and edited other writers' work. It was a natural step.
   What can a writer do to enhance their chances of getting you as an agent? I prefer potential clients to be referred by editors, professional writers, or clients. Otherwise, the query letter has to knock my socks off.
   Comments: I'd love to pontificate, but I don't have time!
   Representative titles: *Power of Attraction* by Geraldine Sullivan and Saffi Crawford (Ballantine); *Desperate Remedies* by Dr. Curt Freed and Simon LeVay (W. H. Freeman); *Romance Revival* by Doug Keister and Appol Gellner (Penguin); *M&M* by John Peak (St. Martin's); *Mark Twain for Dummies* by Kent Rasmussen (IDG Books); *Wicca Cookbook* by Jamie Wood and Tara Seefeldt (Ten Speed); *Scent of Orange Blossoms* by Kitty Morse (Ten Speed); *Literary Babyname Book* by Tershina d' Elgin (Berkley); *Powder Duff Derby* by Gene Nora Jesson (Source Books); *The Ethics of Star Trek* by Judith Bared, Ph.D., with Ed Robertson (Harper Collins); untitled novel by April Sinclair (Hyperion).

C

Wm Clark Associates

325 West 13th Street, New York, NY 10014
212-675-2784   fax: 212-349-1658
www.wmclark.com
e-mail: wcquery@wmclark.com

Agent: William Clark
  Born: Roanoke, Virginia.
  Education: College of William and Mary.
  Career history: Virginia Bargear Agency (1992–1993), William Morris Agency (1993–1997).
  Areas most interested in agenting: Mainstream literary fiction and quality nonfiction, especially memoirs, popular culture, and current events.
  Areas not interested in agenting: Horror, science fiction, fantasy, children's or young adult, how-to.
  If not agenting, what would you be doing? I would be a Buddhist monk.
  Best way to initiate contact: E-mail queries (to wcquery@wmclark.com) are encouraged and preferred and are usually considered and responded to more quickly than those sent via regular mail. E-mail queries should include a general description of the work, a synopsis/outline, biographical information, and publishing history, if any. I will respond whether or not I am interested in your work or idea, or if I feel it is not right for me.
  Client representation by category: Nonfiction, 40%; Fiction, 60%.
  Number of titles sold last year: 28.
  Rejection rate (all submissions): 95%.
  Commission: 15% domestic, 20% foreign.
  Description of the client from Hell: I have no clients from Hell.
  Description of the dream client: A client who understands his or her role in the publication of the book beyond actually writing the book.
  Representative titles: *River Town* by Peter Hessler (HarperCollins); *Light House* by William Monahan (Riverhead); *Born to Rent* by David Eddie (Riverhead); *Tennant's Rock* by Steve McGiffen (Picador); *Gig* by Marisa Bowe, John Bowe, and Sabin Streeter (Crown); *The Heat of Lies* by Jonathan Stone (St. Martin's Press); *Tha Doggfather* by Snoop Dogg (William Morrow); *God, Dr. Buzzard, and the Bolito Man* by Cornelia Bailey, with Christena Bledsoe (Doubleday); *Mark Hampton: The Art of Friendship* by Duane Hampton; *The Vogue Photographic Archive* by Lisa Lovatt-Smith.

Clausen, Mays & Tahan Literary Agency

249 West 34th Street, New York, NY 10001
212-239-4343   fax: 212-239-5248
e-mail: CMTassist@aol.com

Agents: Stedman Mays, Mary M. Tahan
  Education: Mays: M.A., English, University of Virginia. Tahan: M.A., Near East Studies, New York University.

Areas most interested in agenting: (Mostly nonfiction): women's issues, relationships, men's issues, parenting, spirituality, religion, history, memoirs, biography, autobiography, true stories, medical, health/nutrition, psychology, how-to, business/financial, fashion/beauty, style, humor, novels (both genre and literary); rights for books optioned for TV movies and feature films.

Areas not interested in agenting: Although the majority of our list is nonfiction, we are actively looking for novels.

Best way to initiate contact: A query letter (containing proposed book concept and author bio) or brief proposal (containing the following sections: Concept, Market Analysis, Competition, Publicity, Author's Credentials, and Outline), including self-addressed stamped envelope for return of materials. Do not fax queries or proposals.

Reading-fee policy: No reading fees.

Client representation by category: Nonfiction, 95%; Fiction, 5%.

Commission: 15%.

Rejection rate (all submissions): 95%.

Description of a dream client: An author with a vision who listens to constructive suggestions. (It is also important for an author to be willing to promote the book aggressively, resourcefully, and creatively. Publishers look for authors skilled at generating publicity.)

Why did you become an agent? Love publishing—learn with every book.

Representative titles: *The Science and Art of Tracking* by Tom Brown (Berkley); *The Naked Civil Servant* (Penguin) and *Resident Alien: The New York Diaries* (Alyson), both titles by Quentin Crisp; *Loving Him Without Losing You* by Beverly Engel (John Wiley & Sons); *Does This Make Me Look Fat?* by Leah Feldon (Villard/Random House); *The Rules* and *The Rules II,* both titles by Ellen Fein and Sherrie Schneider (Warner Books); *What Men Want* and *Marry Me!* both titles by Bradley Gerstman, Esq., Christopher Pizzo, CPA, and Richard Seldes, M.D. (Harper Collins); *What the IRS Doesn't Want You to Know: A CPA Reveals the Tricks of the Trade* by Martin Kaplan and Naomi Weiss (Villard—revised annually); *How to Write a Movie in 21 Days* by Viki King (Harper Collins); *On Acting* by Sanford Meisner (Vintage/Random House); *Estrogen* by Lila Nachtigall, M.D., and Joan Heilman (HarperCollins, now in its third edition*); Jackson Pollock: An American Saga* by Steven Naifeh and Gregory White Smith (Clarkson Potter, awarded the Pulitzer Prize); *The Official RENT-A-HUSBAND Guide to a Safe, Problem-Free Home* by Kaile R. Warren, Jr., and Jane Craig (Broadway/Doubleday).

RUTH COHEN, INC.

P.O. Box 2244, La Jolla, CA 92038
858-456-5805

Agent: Ruth Cohen

Areas most interested in agenting: *Very selective* women's fiction (contemporary themes of modern women), mysteries (different settings with fascinating characters), juvenile literature (quality picture books, middle-grade fiction/nonfiction, young-adult novels, thrillers (no drugs or Mafia).

Areas not interested in agenting: Films, scripts, poetry, books in rhyme or verse, science fiction, Westerns, how-to books.

Best way to initiate contact: Send a query letter (with SASE), which also includes the opening 10 to 15 pages of the manuscript. *Please, no unsolicited full manuscripts.*

Reading-fee policy: No reading fee. Charge for foreign mailings and copying manuscripts.

Client representation by category: Nonfiction, 5%; Fiction, 60%; Children's, 35%.

Commission: 15% domestic; 20% foreign.

Number of titles sold last year: 71

C

Description of the client from Hell: There aren't really any clients from Hell. There are clients who grow disappointed and who despair of the publishing world as it merges and alters and leaves fewer opportunities for new writers to succeed in work they love—writing.

Description of a dream client: Clients who understand that our combined efforts generally will advance both our careers, and that patience and stamina are the preferred attributes for getting published well—now and always.

Comments: Keep trying—and keep trying to detach yourself from your own writing so that you can view it objectively. Then reassess, revise, rework, and resubmit.

FRANCES COLLIN, LITERARY AGENT

P.O. Box 33, Wayne, PA 19087-8033
610-254-0555

Agent: Fran Collin

Areas not interested in agenting: Cookbooks, gardening books, illustrated books (coffee-table books, that is).

If not agenting, what would you be doing? Haven't a clue.

Best way to initiate contact: Query letter by mail with SASE, unless recommended by editors, writers (clients), or other professionals, in which case, telephone. NO faxes please. No e-mail unless invited to do so.

Client representation by category: Nonfiction, 49%; Fiction, 49%; Textbooks, 1%; Poetry, 1%.

Commission: 15% on U.S. deals; 20% on foreign, translation, film, and permissions.

Rejection rate (all submissions): 99.44/100%.

How did you become an agent? Went for an interview to a large agency as secretary and never looked back.

Why did you become an agent? I discovered that I could be paid for introducing my writer friends to editors—that is, I found that there was a profession devoted to my avocation.

CREATIVE MEDIA AGENCY INC.

240 West 35th Street, Suite 500, New York, NY 10001
212-560-0909

Agent: Paige Wheeler

Born: 1967 in Richmond, Virginia.

Education: Boston University.

Career history: Euromoney Publications, London; Harlequin/Silhouette Books; Artists Agency Inc.; Creative Media Agency Inc.

Areas most interested in agenting: Fiction—commercial fiction, women's fiction, romance, mysteries, thrillers. Nonfiction—popular reference, self-help, how-to, pop culture, women's issues.

Areas not interested in agenting: Horror, sci-fi, fantasy, Westerns, children's, and biographies.

Best way to initiate contact: Send a query letter with an SASE.

Reading-fee policy: No reading fee.

Client representation by category: Nonfiction, 40%; Fiction, 60%.

Commission: 15% domestic, 20% foreign.

Rejection rate (all submissions): 90%.

Description of the client from Hell: Uncooperative, impatient—doesn't understand the nature of publishing.

Description of a dream client: Cooperative, patient, brilliant, willing to work as a partner to build a solid career.

Why did you become an agent? It is a great combination of many talents. You are an editor, salesperson, and businessperson simultaneously.

Representative titles: *Targeting the Job You Want* by Kate Wendleton (Career Press); *Cosmically Chic* by Greg Polkosnik (Andrews McMeel); *Made in America: The People Behind the Brands That Made America Great* by John Gove (Berkley); *A Star to Sail By* by Susan Delaney (Onyx/NAL); *Qualified for Murder* by Roberta Islerb (Berkley); *Once Upon a Time in Great Britain* by Melanie Wentz (St. Martin's Press); *Compass of Health* by Kihyon Kim (New Page Press).

CROSSMAN LITERARY AGENCY

65 East Scott, Suite 12J, Chicago, IL 60610
312-664-6470   fax: 312-664-7137
crossmanla@aol.com

Agent: Nancy Crossman

Career history: V.P.; Editorial Director; Associate Publisher, Contemporary Books, Inc.

Areas most interested in agenting: General nonfiction, self-help, gift books.

Areas not interested in agenting: Children's or young adult titles; fiction; poetry.

Best way to initiate contact: Query with synopsis and SASE.

Reading-fee policy: No reading fee.

Commission: 15%.

Number of titles sold last year: 25.

Most common mistakes authors make: Not doing their marketing and competition homework.

Description of a dream client: Professional, works as a team player, talented, and is passionate about his/her work.

Why did you become an agent? After 16 years as the director of a publishing house, I left so that I could work on a variety of projects that personally interested me.

What can a writer do to enhance their chances of getting you as an agent? Be patient and have a good sense of humor.

Representative titles: *The Cake Mix Doctor* by Anne Byrn (Workman); *Meditations for Mothers* by Beth Wilson Saavedra (Andrews McMeel); *Breast Fitness: An Optimal Exercise and Health Plan for Reducing Your Risk of Breast Cancer* by Drs. Anne McTiernan, Julie Gralow, and Lisa Talbott (St. Martin's Press); *The Pocket Parent* by Gail Reichlin and Caroline Winkler (Workman); *The New Success Rules for Women* by Susan Abrams (Prima).

RICHARD CURTIS ASSOCIATES, INC.

171 East 74th Street, New York, NY 10021
212-772-7363

Agent: Richard Curtis

Born: June 23, 1937.

Education: B.A., American studies, Syracuse University; M.A., American studies, University of Wyoming.

Career history: Foreign Rights Manager, Scott Meredith Literary Agency (1959–1966); freelance author (1967–1975); started own agency (1975); incorporated Richard Curtis Associates, Inc. (1979); first President of Independent Literary Agents Association (1980); Treasurer (1991–1995) and President (1995–1997) of Association of Authors' Representatives.

Hobbies/personal interests: Watercolor painting, softball, racquetball, classical music.

Areas most interested in agenting: Commercial nonfiction, including business, history, biography, narrative nonfiction, celebrity biographies, medical, sports. Literary and commercial fiction. Thrillers, science fiction, romance. Pop culture. The media and entertainment. Software/multimedia.

Areas not interested in agenting: Everything not in the above categories.

If not agenting, what would you be doing? A pianist, an artist, a catcher for the New York Mets, a linebacker for the New York Giants, a volleyball player on a California beach, a psychotherapist, a rabbi, a playwright.

Best way to initiate contact: One-page query letter plus no more than a one-page synopsis of proposed submission. Must be accompanied by an SASE or we won't reply. No faxed queries, no e-mail queries. No submission of material unless specifically requested. If requested, submission must be accompanied by an SASE, or we assume you don't want your submission back.

Reading-fee policy: No reading fee.

Client representation by category: Nonfiction, 75%; Fiction, 25%.

Commission: 15% on basic sale to domestic publisher; 15% on dramatic rights (movies, television, audio, multimedia); 20% on British and foreign publication rights.

Number of titles sold last year: Approximately 150.

Rejection rate (all submissions): 99.9%.

Most common mistakes authors make: Phone queries instead of a letter. Want to see us before we've read material. Don't proofread their work.

Description of the client from Hell: High PITA factor. PITA stands for Pain In The Ass. Divide commissions earned into time dealing with complaints.

Description of a dream client: Low PITA factor.

Why did you become an agent? Love authors, love publishers, love books, love being in the middle.

Comments: The average published book today has the shelf life of a tomato. That's because the distribution system, making books fully returnable for credit, is completely outmoded. Now electronic delivery of text, as well as print on demand presses, have created the potential for an exciting alternative publishing industry. To meet that demand, Richard Curtis has launched e-reads, an online publisher/book retailer, to reissue previously published books. Contact info@e-reads.com.

Representative titles: *A Gathering of Spies* by John Altman (Putnam); *Stop Teaching Our Kids to Kill* by David Grossman and Gloria DeGaetano (Crown); *The Lustration 4 Fantasy Novels* by Greg Reyes (Del Rey).

D

LIZA DAWSON ASSOCIATES

240 West 35th Street, New York, NY 10001
Rebecca Kurson: 212-629-9212 Liza Dawson: 212-465-9071

Agents: Liza Dawson, Rebecca Kurson.

Born: Kurson: 1970.

Education: Dawson: B.A. in History from Duke University; graduate of Radcliffe's Publishing Procedure Course. Kurson: B.A. in English, University of Chicago; M.A. in Writing, New York University.

Career history: Dawson: Pocket Books, Editor; William Morrow, Executive Editor and Vice President; G. P. Putnam Executive Editor. Founded Liza Dawson Associates in 1998. Kurson: Worked in editorial department FSG from 1995 to 1999. With Liza since June 1999.

Hobbies/personal interests: Kurson: Gardening, animals, working.

Areas most interested in agenting: Dawson: Commercial fiction for the intelligent reader, literary fiction that has narrative drive, lively history, self-help (health, parenting, psychology, spirituality, women's issues) by authors who have credentials, and memoirs written with distinction. Kurson: Nonfiction, narratives about nature or science, anything about animals, vegetarian lifestyle, sports, and business.

Areas not interested in agenting: Dawson: Poetry, Westerns, category romances, genre science fiction, sports. Kurson: Commercial fiction, romance, sci-fi, New Age.

If not agenting, what would you be doing? Writing about animals and the environment.

Best method to initiate contact: Dawson: Query letter with an SASE. Kurson: Referral by current client or friend. Query letter with SASE is fine. Do Not Call.

Reading-fee policy: Dawson: No reading fee. Kurson: No reading fee.

Client representation by category: Dawson: Nonfiction, 50%; Fiction, 50%. Kurson: Nonfiction, 60%; Fiction, 39%; Children's, 1%.

Commission: Dawson: 15% domestic; 20% foreign. Kurson: 15% domestic; 20% foreign; 10% periodicals.

Number of titles sold last year: Kurson: I began sending out proposals in September and sold three books and a film option.

Rejection rate (all submissions): Kurson: 95%.

Most common mistakes authors make: Kurson: Repeated phone calls or e-mails.

Description of a dream client: Kurson: Smart, patient, and full of ideas.

How did you become an agent? Kurson: I was a restless editor. A wise move.

Why did you become an agent? Kurson: It's thrilling to work with writers.

What can a writer do to enhance their chances of getting you as an agent? Dawson: Have a strong writing talent; have obsession, follow-through, deep knowledge of your area of expertise, and entertaining conversation. Kurson: Do your homework. Send me something only if it's the kind of book I'm looking for.

How would you describe what you actually do for a living? Kurson: Eating lunch and making pitches over the phone. Lots of line editing.

What do you think about editors? Kurson: Most are very smart, just overworked.

What do you think about publishers? Kurson: Often monolithic.

Comments: Dawson: A good agent should help shape your material to make it appealing to publishers. She should return phone calls, answer questions, and not make hyperbolic promises about your destiny as the next John Grisham. She should talk intelligently about which publisher might be right for your book. She should be committed enough to your book and career that she'll not lose heart when your manuscript is rejected by the first four houses. Kurson: Editorial boards and endless meetings can be disastrous.

Representative titles: *Back Roads* by Tawni O'Dell (Viking); *E-Investing* by Jackie Day Packel (Macmillan); *Everyday Dangers and Disasters* by Kate Kelly (Dutton); *Loser* by Paul Collins (St. Martin's Press); *Ordinary Horror* by David Searey (Viking); *Organize Yourself Series* by Ronnie Eisenberg (Hyperion); *The Murder of Tutankhamen* by Dr. Bob Brier (Kushner-Locke Productions); *Grace* by Roberts Wood (Dutton); *Edinburgh* by Alex Chee (Welcome Rain); *Autobiography of Olympia Dukakis* (Harper Collins).

DeFiore and Company, Author Services

853 Broadway, New York, NY 10003
212-505-7979   fax: 212-505-7779
e-mail: submissions@defioreandco.com

Agent: Brian DeFiore
  Born: August 15, 1956, New York City.
  Education: B.A., English, Queens College.

Career history: 1981–88, Editor, St. Martin's Press; 1988–1990, Senior Editor, Dell Publishing; 1990–1992, VP, Editorial Director, Delacorte Press; 1992–1997, VP, Editor in Chief, Hyperion; 1997–1998, Senior Vice President, Random House Trade Books, Publisher, Villard.

Hobbies/personal interests: Movies, theater, cooking, being a good dad.

Areas most interested in agenting: Commercial fiction, suspense fiction, modern fiction, business books, finance books, self-help, inspiration, health, memoir, biography, entertainment, cooking, sports, psychology.

Areas not interested in agenting: Romance, science fiction, poetry.

If not agenting, what would you be doing? I'd be a psychotherapist.

Best way to initiate contact: By query: either by letter or e-mail. The query should be kept to one page and should describe the book and the author's credentials for writing it, including not only educational background, if that is important, but the life experiences important to the writing of the book. If sending via e-mail, please do not use attachments—which I will not open (because of possible virus infection . . .).

Reading-fee policy: We do not charge reading fees.

Client representation by category: Nonfiction, 66%; Fiction, 33%.

Commission: 15% domestic; 20% foreign.

Number of titles sold last year: 15.

Rejection rate (all submissions): 95%.

Most common mistakes authors make: There are two: first is to pitch me several different sorts of projects at once, as if that demonstrates a broad range. That actually gives the impression of someone who does not have a passionate idea or direction; it is much more effective to make one strong pitch for the project that he or she loves the most. After I'm excited by that and want to take the client on, I'll want to hear about others. The second mistake is when people argue with me over an initial negative reaction instead of questioning why I had it. For example, if I say I don't want to take a project on because there are too many similar books in the market, instead of arguing that I'm mistaken and that your book is different, take a step back and think: This is the reaction a professional had to my material. What can I add to the proposal to demonstrate that this book is unique?

Description of the client from Hell: Someone who hears but doesn't listen and who refuses to accept the reality of what the publishing business is, versus some fantasy about what it should be.

Description of a dream client: Someone whose ideas turn me on and whose skill with words inspires me. Someone who has a unique perspective on the world or on the tiniest piece of it. Writers who understand that they must take an active role in the process of publishing their work but do not insist on controlling it—who are willing to work hard and keep the faith.

How did you become an agent? After 15 years in training as an Editor, Editor in Chief, and Publisher of major New York publishing houses, I started up the business myself early in 1999, in New York's Union Square.

Why did you become an agent? After 15 years on the publishing side of things, as first an Editor, then Editor in Chief, then Publisher, I was getting frustrated with having my work life become more about corporate infighting and posturing than about creative development of material and the building of authors' careers. I thought I'd have more fun and creative satisfaction on this side of the business.

What can a writer do to enhance their chances of getting you as an agent? Write a very persuasive query letter that demonstrates competence, creativity, and wherewithal. Then, if I respond to the query, demonstrate a high level of business and personal courtesies. Agents and their clients have a very intense and intimate relationship. If the early contact seems strained, difficult, unreasonably demanding— then I may well take a "life is too short" attitude toward taking the client on.

How would you describe what you actually do for a living? I nurture the creative spirit in writers, work with them on shaping their material in a form most attractive to the modern publishing world, then I find the most effective and lucrative way of presenting their work to the media community, and finally, I handle the business affairs relating to the work.

What do you think about editors? Having been one myself for most of my career, I have great respect for what they do and great sympathy for the difficulty they have in working inside complex corporate structures. They are overworked, understaffed, and often unappreciated, but they are the lifeblood of any publishing operation. These days corporations give much more clout to their sales and marketing people than they do their editors—without honoring the fact that they would have little to sell or market unless their editors brought in great material.

What do you think about publishers? I think that the people who constitute "publishers" are for the most part good, professional people who respect good writing, have good intentions, and are creative and enthusiastic supporters of authors and their work. I think that, these days, the huge corporate structures in which most individual publishing companies are but a small piece, foster an environment in which, too often, the most creative and powerful executives have to focus their energies on the survival of their divisions rather than on the careers of individual authors. That's unfortunate.

Comments: Despite the fact that we've seen enormous changes in the publishing industry in the last few years—and that those changes seem to me just the beginning of cataclysmic changes to come—I think that this is actually a good time for writers and for creative material. While big publishing companies keep consolidating and trimming costs and staff, small presses are thriving, Internet book sellers are exploding, books are being sold through every sort of retailer, new online magazines (and print magazines) enter the market every month, new beautiful superstores open all the time. And most important, more and more books are being sold everywhere. The problems of the industry have to do with the distribution of profit, not with whether a huge profitable market exists. It does. I'm a firm believer in the power of the free marketplace, and I believe that the industry shake-ups will continue and that the publishing industry as we know it may be unrecognizable 10 years from now, but that as long as people demand to read good books—and every indication is that that demand is *increasing*—then the industry will reshape itself to meet the demands of that market. Whether that new shape will include only one enormous foreign-owned publishing company or thousands of small ones, it's impossible to say—but whatever happens, good writing will be read and authors will need strong, intelligent representation in order to maneuver the new landscape of the business.

Representative titles: *The Mailroom* by David Rensin (Ballantine); *Shooting Doctor Jack* by Norman Green (HarperCollins); *Hard Feelings* by Jason Starr (Vintage); *Life Is Not a Stress Rehearsal* by Loretta LaRoche (Broadway); *The Angel of Hyde Park* by Nina Roosevelt Gibson and Joel Engel (William Morrow); *The Fourth Mega-Market* by Ralph Acampora (Hyperion).

DH LITERARY, INC.

P.O. Box 990, Nyack, NY 10960
212-753-7942
e-mail: dhendin@aol.com

Agent: David Hendin

Born: December 16, 1945.

Education: B.S., Biology, Education, University of Missouri (1967); M.A., Journalism, University of Missouri (1967).

Career history: United Feature Syndicate/United Media; Senior Vice President and Chief Operating Officer of United Feature Syndicate; President and Chief Operating Officer of World Almanac, Pharos Books (1970–1993). Author of 11 nonfiction books, including *Death as a Fact of Life* (Norton, Warner), *The Life Givers* (Morrow), and co-author of *The Genetic Connection* (Morrow, Signet).

Hobbies/personal interests: Archaeology.

Areas most interested in agenting: Strong nonfiction,. I also represent comic strips and columns for newspaper syndication (very selectively).

Areas not interested in agenting: Fiction submissions By Referral Only.

If not agenting, what would you be doing? Excavating ruins in the Middle East or teaching journalism at a university (both of which I've done).

Best way to initiate contact: E-mail: dhendin@aol.com

Reading-fee policy: No reading fee. We're members of the AAR.

Client representation by category: Nonfiction, 85%; Fiction, 10%; Textbooks, 5%.

Commission: 15%.

Number of titles sold last year: 15.

Rejection rate (all submissions): 99.9%.

Most common mistakes authors make: Send too much material before being asked; don't write a good query letter; don't enclose SASE; start the query by telling me they have 14 unpublished projects . . .

Description of the client from Hell: I have no clients from Hell.

Description of a dream client: Great ideas, prompt delivery, at least a passing interest in the business side of publishing.

Why did you become an agent? I have been a newspaper columnist, book author, and President of a publishing company. Becoming an agent was the next logical extension of my professional life—not to mention that some of my best friends are writers!

Comments: Writers—send me your fabulous ideas. I have a relatively small number of clients and love to work on projects I like.

Representative titles: *Age of Anxious Anxiety* by Tom Tiede (Grove/Atlantic); *Doc in the Box* by Elaine Viets (Dell); *Miss Manners' History of American Etiquette* by Judith Martin (W. W. Norton & Co.).

DHS LITERARY, INC.

2528 Elm Street, 2nd floor, Dallas, TX 75226
214-363-4422   fax: 214-363-4423
e-mail: submissions@dhsliterary.com

Agents: David Hale Smith, Seth Robertson
Born: Smith: July 9, 1968. Robertson: March 4, 1974.
Education: Smith: B.A., English, Kenyon College, 1990. Robertson: B.A., English, B.A. in Spanish, University of Virginia, 1996.
Career history: Copyeditor, one year, Southwest NewsWire, Inc., Dallas; Assistant Agent/Agent, three years. Smith: Dupree/Miller & Associates, Dallas; founded DHS Literary Agency, March 1994. Robertson: English teacher, one year, Instituto Norteamericano, Santiago, Chile; started at DHS Literary in January 1998.
Hobbies/personal interests: Smith: Reading, writing, camping, hiking, travel. Robertson: Reading, writing, travel, photography.
Areas most interested in agenting: Smith: Mainstream fiction: thrillers, suspense, mystery, and historical fiction; literary fiction. Business nonfiction. Multicultural interests. Pop culture, music, film and television, technology. General nonfiction and gift books. Robertson: Nonfiction: narrative nonfiction, biography, true crime, pop culture, travel/adventure, health, humor, music. Fiction: literary fiction, thrillers, suspense, mysteries.
Areas not interested in agenting: Smith: Short stories, poetry. Robertson: Romance, fantasy, poetry.
If not agenting, what would you be doing? Smith: I am in awe of good writers, and I have always wanted to be one. I know some pretty good stories, and I plan on taking a crack at writing them down someday. I would also like to sail around the world with my family one day.
Best way to initiate contact: E-mail queries to submissions@dhsliterary.com. No file attachments please.
Reading-fee policy: No reading fee.
Client representation by category: Nonfiction, 65%; Fiction, 35%.
Commission: 15% domestic sales; 25% on foreign (via subagents).
Number of titles sold last year: About 30.
Rejection rate (all submissions): 98%.
Most common mistakes authors make: The biggest mistake we see people making is coming on too strong without backing up their claims of "sure-fire" success. We think that people must be aggressive to get noticed in this business—but if you're all style and no substance, it is a waste of everybody's time. Another common blunder we see is just a general lack of preparedness. Spend some time learning about the business, before contacting agents and publishers.

Description of the client from Hell: Unprofessional people who think that once they have an agent, their role in placing and selling their work is finished. We had a client who made the mistake of thinking this agency was his personal secretarial and counseling firm, without ever realizing that all the time we spent talking to him and doing his busy-work was time we couldn't spend selling his stuff. He is no longer a client.

Description of a dream client: A professional in every phase of the business, who believes that the agent-author relationship is a team endeavor. A successful publishing experience is the result of a collaborative effort. We work extremely hard for our clients—and we work even harder for those who make it easier for us to do our job by working with us, not against us.

Why did you become an agent? Smith: I have always loved books, reading good ones, and talking about them with other people—that's the best part of the job. When I learned that agents get to see the good stuff even before the publishers do, that's where I wanted to be. Robertson: I love being able to work with books in a variety of ways. As an agent, I have the opportunity not only to make sales pitches and negotiate contracts, but also to brainstorm and work creatively with our clients.

What might you be doing if you weren't an agent? Robertson: I would probably still be working with writers and books, perhaps as an editor.

What can a writer do to enhance their chances of getting you as an agent? See our description of the "dream client." We actually have an "Ideal Client Profile": talented, passionate, professional, progressive thinker, articulate communicator, and financially independent. If you fit that profile, we want to hear from you.

Comments: Always read the book first, then go see the movie!

Representative titles: *Deadbeat* by Leo Atkins (Berkley Prime Crime); *First Son: George W. Bush and the Bush Family Political Dynasty in America* by Bill Minutaglio (Times Books/Random House); *Food and Mood* by Elizabeth Somer (Henry Holt & Co.); *God Is a Bullet* by Boston Teran (Knopf); *Shooting at Midnight* by Greg Rucka (Bantam hardcover); *Stealth Health* by Evelyn Tribole (Viking); *Take Time for Your Life* by Cheryl Richardson (Broadway).

SANDRA DIJKSTRA LITERARY AGENCY

PMB 515, 1155 Camino Del Mar, Del Mar, CA 92014-2605
858-755-3115 ext. 18   fax: 858-792-1494
e-mail: sdla@dijkstraagency.com

Agent: Sandra Dijkstra

Born: Dijkstra: New York, NY.

Education: B.A., Adelphi (English); M.A., UC Berkeley (Comparative Literature); Ph.D., UC San Diego (French Literature).

Career history: University professor, literary agent.

Hobbies: Reading, films.

Areas most interested in agenting: Quality fiction (commercial and literary); narrative nonfiction; history; psychology; health; business; spiritual; self-help; children's literature (commercial and literary).

Areas not interested in agenting: Westerns, romances, fantasy, poetry, science fiction, screenplays.

If not agenting, what would you be doing? Dijkstra: I would be an editor and/or college professor.

Best way to initiate contact: *We no longer accept unsolicited manuscripts.* We will only consider those manuscripts recommended to us by our authors, published professionals, and contacts.

Reading-fee policy: No reading fee.

Client representation by category: Nonfiction, 50%; Fiction, 40%; Children's, 10%.

Commission: 15% domestic and film; 20% foreign.

Number of titles sold last year: 40.

Rejection rate (all submissions): 70%–80%.

Description of the client from Hell: The client from Hell is never satisfied and has expectations that exceed all possibilities of realization.

Description of a dream client: The dream client trusts his/her agent, asks the right questions, and offers useful support material. He or she does not e-mail and/or call daily. This client calls on need and keeps us apprised of progress. These clients are professionals who understand that we are their partners and advocates and help us to represent their best interests.

Why did you become an agent? To publish books that make a difference and to help writers realize their dreams.

What do you think about editors? Overworked and underpaid. They are by and large, dedicated and passionate about authors and books.

What do you think about publishers? In a perfect world, they would have more support, more money, and more time! Publishers should be "making public the book, in the fullest sense," which they do only some of the time.

Comments: Many writers and readers continue to believe in the importance of words and thoughts and messages and stories—all of which make us more civilized!

What are some common mistakes authors make? Incessant phoning to check on the status of their submissions.

What can a writer do to enhance their chances of getting you as an agent? They should try to find a bookseller, author, or publisher to recommend them to us. They should also try to publish their work in magazines—forcing us to chase them!

How would you describe what you actually do for a living? I read and hope to fall in love. I talk on the phone and prepare editors to fall in love (and then pay for the privilege to publish what they've fallen in love with). I support talent with all my heart and brainpower.

Representative titles: *The Bonesetter's Daughter* by Amy Tan (Putnam); *The Seven Stories of Love: And How to Choose Your Happy Ending* by Marcia Millman (William Morrow); *The Diary of V* by Debra Kent (Warner Books); *The Twentieth Wife* by Indu Sundaresan (Pocket Books); *Racing the Antelope: What Animals Teach Us About Run-*

ning and Life by Bern Heinrich (HarperCollins); *Red Poppies* by Alai, translated by Howard Goldblatt (Houghton Mifflin).

DONADIO & OLSON

121 West 27th Street, Suite 704, New York, NY 10001

Agent: Neil Olson
    Best way to initiate contact: Query with 50 pages, synopsis, SASE.
    Reading-fee policy: No reading fee.
    Client representation by category: Nonfiction, 40%; Fiction, 60%.
    Commission: 15% domestic; 20% foreign.

D

JIM DONOVAN LITERARY

4515 Prentice, Suite 109, Dallas, TX 75206
214-696-9411

Agent: Jim Donovan
    Born: December 6, 1954.
    Education: B.S., University of Texas.
    Career history: In books since 1981 as a bookstore Manager; chain-store Buyer; published writer (*Dallas: Shining Star of Texas,* 1994, Voyageur Press; *The Dallas Cowboys Encyclopedia,* 1996, Carol Publishing; *Elvis Immortal,* 1997, Legends Press; *Custer and the Little Bighorn,* 2001, Voyager Press). Freelance Editor; and Senior Editor, Taylor Publishing, six years. Literary Agent since 1993.
    Areas most interested in agenting: Any book with something fresh to say, whether it's fiction or nonfiction.
    Areas not interested in agenting: Children's, poetry, short stories, romance, religious/spiritual, technical books, computer books.
    If not agenting, what would you be doing? A publisher.
    Best way to initiate contact: Nonfiction: Query with synopsis and SASE. Fiction: Query with 2–5 page synopsis, first 30–40 pages, and SASE.
    Reading-fee policy: No reading fee.
    Client representation by category: Nonfiction, 75%; Fiction, 25%.
    Commission: 15%.
    Number of titles sold last year: About 24.
    Rejection rate (all submissions): 97%.
    Most common mistakes authors make: The top 10 query letter turnoffs: (1) Don't use a form letter that begins with "To whom it may concern" or "Dear editor." (2) Don't say your writing is better than bestselling writers'. (3) Don't mention your self-published books unless they've sold several thousand copies. (4) Don't refer to your "fiction novel." (5) Don't brag about how great or how funny your book is. (6) Don't quote rave reviews from your relatives, friends, or editors whom you've paid. (7) Don't tell the agent how

you're positive your book will make both of you rich. (8) Don't say it's one of five novels you've finished. (9) Don't tell the editor that he'll be interested because it will make a great movie. (10) Don't ask for advice or suggestions (if you don't think it's ready, why should they?).

What gets you excited? Provide a clear, well-thought-out query letter or proposal that describes the book, and for nonfiction, why there's a need for it, how it does something better than or different from the competition, and why the author is the perfect person to write the book.

What do you think about editors? Editors are the miners of the publishing world—they spend days and nights digging through endless layers of worthless material for the occasional golden nugget. Anything the agent or the writer can do to make their job easier is greatly appreciated, so I stress that to potential writers.

Comments: Most aspiring authors don't want to put in the time and effort necessary to become published—they think that if they attend enough writers' conferences and read enough books on how to become published that somehow, through some form of osmosis or alchemy, they will become published. I'm not interested in working with someone who doesn't understand that the key to publication is revision . . . and more revision . . . and more revision.

Representative titles: *All About "All About Eve,"* by Sam Staggs (St. Martin's); *Beyond Viagra* by Dr. Gerald Melchiode (Henry Holt & Co.); *Corporate Cults* by Dave Arnott (AMACOM); *Dark and Bloody Ground* by Tom Ayres (Taylor); *Daytona* by Ed Hinton (Warner); *I Watched a Wild Hog Eat My Baby (and Vice Versa)* by Bill Sloan (Prometheus); *Royal and Ancient* by Curt Sampson (Villard); *The Junction Boys* by Jim Dent (St. Martin's); *Sales Proposals for Dummies* by Bob Kantin (IDG Books).

DUNHAM LITERARY

156 Fifth Avenue, Suite 625, New York, NY 10010-7002
fax: 212-929-0904
www.dunhamlit.com

Agent: Jennie Dunham
   Born: April 1969.
   Education: Princeton University, Anthropology major, Magna Cum Laude.
   Career history: One year at John Brockman Associates, one year at Mildred Marmur Associates, six years at Russell & Volkening, started Dunham Literary in August 2000.
   Hobbies/personal interests: Book arts and paper making, movies, photography, Old English, language and linguistics, feminist/woman's studies, travel, science history, health, religion.
   Areas most interested in agenting: Quality fiction, nonfiction, and children's.
   Areas not interested in agenting: Romance, science fiction, poetry, horror, Westerns, and individual short stories. Also, we don't represent plays or screenplays (but we do represent books into movies and plays).
   Best way to initiate contact: Write a letter describing the project and the author's qualifications for the project and enclose the customary self-addressed stamped envelope

for a response. If the project seems as if we might be interested, we will request it. Please do not send sample material unless requested. We have lots of information on our Web site about submissions and what we're interested in.

Client representation by category: Fiction, 25%; Nonfiction, 25%; Children's, 50%.

Commission: 15% domestic, motion picture, and other dramatic contracts; 20% foreign contracts.

Number of titles sold last year: 25.

Rejection rate (all submissions): We reject the vast majority of query letters sent to us, but we read each one and respond usually within a week. So many people write to us with books about topics that we don't handle. Just doing this little bit of research will substantially increase a writer's chance of finding the right match with an agent.

Description of the client from Hell: A client who says one thing and does another, who doesn't trust an agent's advice, who doesn't know or pay attention to the market, and who tries to tell an agent how to handle his or her business.

Description of the dream client: A client who is productive, dedicated, talented, successful, interesting, and pleasant and is a good client. It's also good if the client wins awards and is a self-promoter.

Common mistakes made by authors: In this day of computers, it's a mistake to send a form query letter without a specific person's name in the salutation. Also, sometimes writers address agents familiarly as if they knew them, which really should be reserved for people who do know them personally. The grammar, spelling, and punctuation should all be correct. It's really best to send the query letter in writing rather than to call first and ask to send it. That does not constitute a solicited manuscript.

Why did you become an agent? As an agent I like helping authors to bring their books to the world. In this sense I like to think of myself as a midwife of creativity or someone who can make a writer's dream come true. I like the variety of book projects I handle as an agent. I receive great satisfaction in protecting authors by negotiating contracts for them. Ever since my first job as an agent, I knew that this was what I wanted for a career.

If not agenting, what might you be doing? Maybe I would be an anthropologist or a professor of English, folklore, or communications. If I won the lottery, I'd travel a lot more and probably set up a residence where people could come to pursue their creative (but serious) pursuits.

What can a writer do to enhance their chances of getting you as an agent? Professionalism, good writing, good ideas, and the willingness to work with an agent to manage the writer's career make us enthusiastic about a client. More people try to write bestsellers than good books, and if they concentrated on writing a good book, they'd be closer to having a bestseller. We look closely at a writer's previous experience, especially in magazines and books.

Comments: It takes talent and hard work to capture human truths in words, and to me that is what makes good writing, fiction and nonfiction, vital to our lives.

Representative titles: *Fake Liar Cheat* by Tod Goldberg (Pocket Books); *Molly* by Nancy Jones (Crown); *Skin Game* by Caroline Kettlewell (St. Martin's); *365 Goddess* by Patricia Telesco (Harper San Francisco); *Magick Made Easy* by Patricia Telesco (Harper San Francisco); *Letters of Intent,* edited by Meg Daly and Anna Bondoc (Free Press); *A*

Positive Life by River Huston and Mary Berridge (Running Press); *Hidden Witness* by Jackie Napolean Wilson (St. Martin's Press); *The Wonderful Wizard of Oz* (pop-up) by Robert Sabuda (Little Simon); *A Little Princess,* retold and illustrated by Barbara McClintock (HarperCollins); *In the Shade of the Nispero Tree* by Carmen T. Bernier-Grand (Orchard); *Lincoln,* illustrated by David Johnson (Scholastic).

D

HENRY DUNOW LITERARY AGENCY

22 West 23rd Street, New York, NY 10023
212-645-7606   fax: 212-645-7614
e-mail: dunowlit@interport.net

Agents: Henry Dunow, Jennifer Carlson, Cheryl Pientka, Kyung Cho.
  Born: November 1, 1952, New York.
  Education: B.A., Bennington College.
  Career history: Curtis Brown, Ltd., Harold Ober Associates; Henry Dunow Literary Agency, founded 1997.
  Areas most interested in agenting: Quality fiction and nonfiction.
  Areas not interested in agenting: Science fiction.
  Best way to initiate contact: Query LETTER, not e-mailed query.
  Reading-fee policy: No fee.
  Client representation by category: Nonfiction, 40%; Fiction, 60%.
  Commission: 15% domestic; 20% foreign.
  Rejection rate (all submissions): 95%.
  Comments: Keep your mind on the work, not on the market.
  Representative authors: Robert Hellenga, William Kotzwinkle, Elizabeth McCracken, Susan Power, Kirkpatrick Sale, Melanie Thernstrom, Marianne Wiggins, Heidi Jularits, Aimee Bender, Jean Thompson, Marisa Silver, David Schickler, Stephen Amidor, Kevin Baker.

JANE DYSTEL LITERARY MANAGEMENT

One Union Square West, Suite 904, New York, NY 10003
212-627-9100

Agent: Jane Dystel
  Education: B.A., New York University. Attended, but did not graduate from Georgetown Law.
  Career history: Permissions Editor at Bantam Books; Managing & Acquisitions Editor at Grosset & Dunlap; Publisher of *World Almanac* and founder of World Almanac publications; Partner at Acton and Dystel Inc.; Partner at Acton, Dystel, Leone and Jaffe; Founder and Owner of Jane Dystel Literary Management.
  Hobbies/personal interests: Golf, gardening, cooking, ice skating, travel, Jewish studies.

Areas most interested in agenting: Literary and commercial fiction; serious nonfiction.

Areas not interested in agenting: Poetry.

If not agenting, what would you be doing? I'd be in some area of law or public service.

Best way to initiate contact: Submit a query letter accompanied by an outline and a couple of sample chapters (with SASE).

Reading-fee policy: No reading fee.

Client representation by category: Nonfiction, 80%; Fiction, 20%.

Commission: 15%.

Number of titles sold last year: 90.

Rejection rate (all submissions): 95%.

Most common mistakes authors make: Flashy, self-important letters full of hype and cuteness. Authors who refer to their work as "fictional novels." Most common and costly mistakes have to do with bad grammar, sloppy presentation, illegible material (exotic fonts or single spacing), and lack of proofreading.

What gets you excited? Intelligent, well-written queries that show originality.

Description of the client from Hell: Someone who calls incessantly, wanting updates and handholding. Someone who whines about everything. Someone who is dishonest and unpleasant.

Description of a dream client: Someone who is talented and asks intelligent questions. Someone who is patient and understanding of the fact that selling books can be a slow process. Someone who takes rejection in his or her stride.

Why did you become an agent? Having worked in many other areas of publishing, it seemed like an exciting new field to explore. I was intrigued by the increasing importance of the agent–author relationship in the publishing world.

Comments: People should read more and read better books.

Representative titles: *Simplify Your Work Life* by Elaine St. James; *Keep It Simple, Stupid* by Judge Judy (Sheindlin); *Water Carry Me* by Thomas Moran; *Boy Meets Grill* by Bobby Flay; *Taken for a Ride* by Bill Vlasic and Brad Stertz; *The Eight Human Talents* by Gurmukh; *The Sparrow* by Mary Russell; *The Italian Country Table* by Lynne Rosetto Kasper; *Pride* by Lorene Cary; *China Boy* by Gus Less; *The Will* by Reed Arvin; *A Spoonful of Ginger* by Nina Simonds.

ANN ELMO AGENCY, INC.

60 East 42nd Street, New York, NY 10165
212-661-2880

Agent: Lettie Lee

Areas most interested in agenting: Nonfiction, romance, juvenile.

Areas not interested in agenting: Poetry.

Best way to initiate contact: Query letter.

Commission: 15%, no reading fee.

Mary Evans, Inc.

242 East 5th Street, New York, NY 10003
212-979-0880

Agents: Mary Evans, Tanya McKinnon
  Education: Columbia, Tufts University.
  Areas most interested in agenting: Fiction (commercial and literary); Nonfiction (health, psychology, history, narrative, anything that interests us).
  If not agenting, what would you be doing? Tanya McKinnon has an M.A. in Cultural Anthropology and Mary Evans would have been a lawyer.
  Best way to initiate contact: Please send us a query letter and sample chapter in the mail.
  Client representation by category: Nonfiction, 50%; Fiction, 50%.
  Commission: 15%; 20% for foreign rights.
  Number of titles sold last year: 20.
  Rejection rate (all submissions): 75%.
  Why did you become an agent? We love working with writers editorially and helping writers to build new careers.

First Books

3000 Market Street, N.E., #527, Salem, OR 97301
503-588-2224
www.firstbooks.com

Agent: Jeremy Solomon
  Born: Chicago, Illinois.
  Education: B.A., University of Wisconsin-Madison; Graduate, Radcliffe Publishing Course, Harvard University; NYU Film School; M.B.A., Wharton School of Business, University of Pennsylvania.
  Areas most interested in agenting: Mainstream fiction and nonfiction.
  Areas not interested in agenting: Religious or spiritual works, poetry, screenplays, romance novels, Westerns, short stories. Extremely violent novels, especially *not!*
  If not agenting, what would you be doing? A family practice physician.
  Best way to initiate contact: Write a good query letter, no more than 2 pages long. Include SASE.
  Reading-fee policy: No reading fee.
  Client representation by category: Nonfiction, 60%; Fiction, 20%; Children's, 20%.
  Commission: 15%–20%, depending on the right.
  Number of titles sold last year: 30.
  Rejection rate (all submissions): 99%.
  Most common mistakes authors make: Not including an SASE in their submission; being rude to us on the phone.
  Description of the client from Hell: An unpleasant person who doesn't write well.

Description of a dream client: One who writes well, is a dear to work with, and makes us a lot of money.

Why did you become an agent? To work with writers and to have my own business.

Comments: Write us a clear, compelling 1–2 page letter about your book. Include SASE. Do not call or fax us. Do not send us an e-mail. Do not send chapters. Just the query letter with SASE. Include your phone number if you'd like.

Representative titles: *How Murray Saved Christmas* by Mike Reiss (Penguin-Putnam); *Northwest Style* by Ann Wall Frank (Chronicle Books); *So Many Strange Things* by Charise Mericle (Little Brown & Co.); *Sugars That Heal* by Emil Mondoa, M.D. (Ballantine); *The Same Phrase Describes My Marriage and My Breasts: Before the Kids They Used to Be a Cute Couple* by Amy Krouse Rosenthal (Andrews McMeel); *Trading to Win* by Ari Kiev (John Wiley & Sons); *When I Grow Up* by Charise Mericle (Chronicle Books).

JOYCE A. FLAHERTY, LITERARY AGENT

816 Lynda Court, St. Louis, MO 63122
314-966-3057

Agent: Joyce A. Flaherty

Born: Milwaukee, Wisconsin.

Education: University of Wisconsin, Madison; Webster University, St. Louis, B.A. and postgraduate work.

Career history: Executive Director of large chamber of commerce, Public Relations Consultant—for national clients, authors' tours, and so on, President of St. Louis Writers Guild.

Hobbies/personal interests: Bird watching, visiting bookstores, reading and collecting books, attending opera and theater.

Areas most interested in agenting: Women's fiction, mysteries, thrillers, commercial novels that are unique. A large assortment of fiction and nonfiction.

Areas not interested in agenting: Children's books, collections of columns, articles, poetry or short stories, science fiction, fantasy, New Age.

If not agenting, what would you be doing? A bookstore owner.

Best way to initiate contact: Query letter including first chapter, short synopsis, or outline—be sure to include an SASE.

Reading-fee policy: No reading fee.

Client representation by category: Nonfiction, 20%; Fiction, 80%.

Commission: 15%.

Number of titles sold last year: 55.

Rejection rate (all submissions): 99%.

Most common mistakes authors make: Using "gimmicky" letters rather than a straightforward approach that tells us what their work actually is. Not including an SASE for our response and to return the materials. Not letting us know if it's a simultaneous submission to other agents. Professional letters always stand out and we appreciate receiving them.

Description of the client from Hell: We don't have any—we're very happy with our clients!

F

Description of a dream client: Authors who meet deadlines and are great writers, as well as flexible and patient. A sense of humor helps, as well as a professional attitude.

How did you become an agent? By having publishers as marketing clients and authors as special events clients. Also, though an independent agent, I did some co-agenting with two established New York agents during my first year of business.

Why did you become an agent? I have always respected authors and loved books. My father was a songwriter, recorded by famous singers and musicians, and I learned at an early age what it meant to have excellent representation as he did with ASCAP. I'm not musical, but I have a business, marketing, and public relations background and since I was a paid journalist from my teens on and served as President of the St. Louis Writers' Guild, I understood the frustrations of authors and had the very real desire to help them.

What can a writer do to enhance their chances of getting you as an agent? We appreciate professionalism as well as good manners. We love authors who love to write as a career and present work that stands out in a tough, crowded market.

How would you describe what you actually do for a living? Represent authors by selling their books as wisely as possible, often discovering a new talent as well as guiding long-term clients in career decisions. I negotiate contracts and also sell subsidiary rights. My clients know that I care about many of their concerns and mediate if there is a problem or misunderstanding with a publisher and/or editor. I'm responsible for collecting monies due to authors and making sure that contracts are fulfilled.

What do you think about editors? I think very highly of most editors. They have always had heavy workloads but even more so today, with so many publishing mergers but fewer editors to do more work. Good editors always respect the author's viewpoint and will be happy to compromise. There should be a healthy give and take.

What do you think about publishers? They are bottom-line people and those who care about publishing good books always stand out and are loyal to their authors and help promote authors' careers. Good publishers provide good royalty statements that give detailed, accurate information and they pay promptly.

Comments: I have been an independent agent since June of 1980, so 2001 is our 21st year. My memberships include the Association of Authors' Representatives, the Authors' Guild, Mystery Writers of America, and Romance Writers of America. Although the market is truly tight, I believe that good books will continue to be published and that writers should only present their best work and be persistent in finding the right agent and publisher.

Representative titles: *Toasts for Every Occasion* by Jennifer Rahel Conover (New American Library); *Murder of a Sweet Old Lady* by Denise Swanson (New American Library); *Falcon's Angel,* by Judith E. French (Ballantine); *Highland Bride,* by Hannah Howell (Kensington); *IDA Lou's Story* by Susan E. Kirby (Simon & Schuster).

THE FOGELMAN LITERARY AGENCY

7515 Greenville Avenue, Suite 712, Dallas, TX 75231
214-361-9956   fax: 214-361-9553
www.Fogelman.com

Agents: Evan M. Fogelman, Linda M. Kruger

Born: Fogelman: May 1, 1960.

Education: Fogelman: B.A. with honors (1982), Juris Doctor (1985), Tulane University; Stanford Publishing Course. Kruger: B.A., Media Theory and Criticism, University of Texas at Austin (1989).

Career history: Fogelman: Entertainment attorney, book reviewer, author publicist. Kruger: Has been with the agency since its inception.

Hobbies/personal interests: Fogelman: Enjoying the company of my wife and children, laughter, French bulldogs, distance running, history, issues of constitutional law, investing. Kruger: Walking, dogs, reading, home projects, movies.

Areas most interested in agenting: Fogelman: Nonfiction, novels targeted to women buyers. Kruger: All categories of romance. I work primarily with published authors of the romance genre. Nonfiction: subjects that target a female audience, pop culture, some self-help, mainly commercial nonfiction.

Areas not interested in agenting: Fogelman: Poetry, short stories, science fiction, historical fiction, action adventure, New Age. Kruger: Poetry, short stories, true Westerns, science fiction, historical fiction, action adventure, New Age, mysteries.

If not agenting, what would you be doing? Fogelman: I'd be in the oil business. Book deals are often a lot like wildcat oil wells, actually. Kruger: Taking way too many pictures of my two Labs.

Best way to initiate contact: Fogelman: E-mail or snail mail. Kruger: A query letter with SASE will be responded to within five business days. Published authors are invited to call. No unsolicited material, please. Please check out our Web site at www .Fogelman.com.

Reading-fee policy: No reading fee.

Client representation by category: Fogelman: Nonfiction, 50%; Fiction, 50%. Kruger: Nonfiction, 10%; Fiction, 90%.

Commission: 15% domestic, including all agency-negotiated subsidiary-rights deals; 10% foreign.

Number of titles sold last year: Fogelman: 75-plus; Kruger: 50-plus.

Rejection rate (all submissions): Fogelman: 99.5%; Kruger: 99.5%.

Most common mistakes authors make: Fogelman: Seeking representation too early in the process. If you're a new novelist, finish the book first. If you're a nonfiction writer, do a formal proposal first. Kruger: When a writer cannot tell me what type of a book he or she has written. One writer described his books as (and this is an actual quote): "a non-genre erotic contemporary mainstream men's fantasy action/adventure romantic sexual comedy novel, or, if you really need a category, call it Romance Novel, Male Division." In helping a writer categorize his or her book, I always ask one question: If you had one copy of your manuscript and you had to put it on one bookshelf at the bookstore, where would it go? Also, I hate unsolicited material.

Description of the client from Hell: Fogelman: One who would rather complain to me about how unfair publishing is instead of finishing his book; one who screams for all the rest of us to make our deadlines, yet demands an extension on every contracted manuscript delivery date. Kruger: A writer who does not realize that this is a creative, yet professional, business.

Description of a dream client: Fogelman: Anyone who loves to write more than he likes to tell others, "I'm a writer." Kruger: Someone who keeps the lines of communication open. This is a two-way relationship. As for the creative process, my dream client creates characters and then releases those characters to tell the story.

How did you become an agent? Kruger: I met Evan Fogelman when he opened the doors to the agency. His enthusiasm and love of the business were contagious and my schooling and background made agenting second nature for me. Fogelman: As an entertainment lawyer, I started negotiating book deals and became enthralled.

Why did you become an agent? Fogelman: I completely enjoy the crossroads of art and commerce. Kruger: There are many reasons I became an agent, but what keeps me in this business is the chance to work with such creative individuals. This is an exciting business, one unlike any other profession. The atmosphere of our agency is always entertaining and challenging. I wouldn't change a thing.

How would you describe what you actually do for a living? Kruger: I wear many hats. I'm an editor, a listener, a cheerleader, a reader, a salesman, a negotiator. At times, I am a pit bull and at other times, I let silence work for me. Fogelman: Well, it's rather like the oil business: Plan for hitting paydirt and carve up a royalty and rights pie!

What do you think about editors? Kruger: As long as they are acquiring my clients' books, I love them. Fogelman: What—are you a comedian? I love editors. Without them, I wouldn't have a job.

What do you think about publishers? Kruger: As long as they're publishing my clients' books, I love them. Fogelman: I like Linda's answer.

Comments: Fogelman: Don't underestimate either e-technologies or e-commerce. From a contractual standpoint, I expect most media developers—publisher and bookseller included—to continue to rush toward e-gold in the cyberspace hills.

Representative titles: The Agency's clients include: Terri Brisbin, Lisa Cach, Alice Duncan, Anne Eames, Elizabeth Eliot, Jane Graves, Leann Harris, Candice Hern, Victoria Chancellor, Caroline Rose Hunt, Joni Johnston, Karon Karter, April Kihlstrom, Sylvie Kurtz, Karen Leabo, Delia Parr, Pam McCutcheon, Laurel O'Donnell, Gwen Pemberton, Susan Plunkett, Louise B. Raggio, Laura Renken, Larry Shriner, Teresa Southwick, Crystal Stovall, Katherine Sutcliffe, RaeAnne Thayne, Ronda Thompson, and Cathy Yardley.

FORTHWRITE LITERARY AGENCY

23852 West Pacific Coast Hwy. #701, Malibu, CA 90265
310-456-5698   fax: 310-456-6589

Agent: Wendy Keller
  Born: Chicago, Illinois.
  Education: Arizona State University.
  Career history: Agent since 1988, founded ForthWrite 1989.
  Hobbies/personal interests: Mothering my daughter, epée fencing, reading, gardening, and agenting.
  Areas most interested in agenting: Business (sales, management, marketing, and finance), self-help, pop psych, health/alternative health, metaphysical/perennial wisdom.

Areas not interested in agenting: Everything but those listed above as interests!

Best way to initiate contact: E-mail query first.

Reading-fee policy: No reading fee.

Client representation by category: Nonfiction, 100%.

Commission: 15% life of property; 20% foreign we place.

Number of titles sold last year: 12.

Rejection rate (all submissions): 99.999%.

Most common mistakes authors make: (1) Telling me their book is better than anything ever published so far! (2) Not recognizing that there have to be more than three other people in the United States interested in their topic for me to sell it.

Description of the client from Hell: I don't take on "clients" from Hell! But there are apparently thousands of unpublished "authors" from Hell! They're the ones who didn't research their topic before writing; don't understand there are competitive books, *or* start their query letter with "I'm a bestseller to be!"

Description of a dream client: My list of authors.

Why did you become an agent? I like writing and sales, but I stay in it because little compares to the thrill of finding a brilliant idea.

If not agenting, what might you be doing? Dusting ancient glass displays at the Met.

What can a writer do to enhance their chances of getting you as an agent? Research your competition and be prepared to adapt your concept if necessary to make it worth more money.

How would you describe what you actually do for a living? I spend 5,000 hours each day on the phone, sleep a while, and go back to my desk.

What do you think about editors? Editors have a huge responsibility to weed out the good stuff agents send and (hopefully) publish what's *great* under very stressful conditions.

Comments: If you're a writer who wants to get published and you've spent the time to read this book, write your idea, and know how your book contributes to this crowded market, good for you. But if you haven't done your research—that is, you don't know *who* will buy your book and why, buy this guide; but before you discourage yourself and waste our time and yours, find out what your book contributes: Is it new? Different? Better? More? How does it compare to all the other similar books? Why will anyone buy it? Why? Find an agent when you can answer that question because you won't before.

Representative titles: *Bringing Home the Business* by Kim Gordon (Perigee/Putnam); *Sensational Smoothies* by Cherie Calbom (Warner Books); *Growing Your Business in Emerging Markets* by John Caslione and Andrew Thomas (Greenwood Publishing); *Secrets of Word of Mouth Marketing* by Genge Silvermon (AMACOM).

JEANNE FREDERICKS LITERARY AGENCY, INC.

221 Benedict Hill Road, New Canaan, CT 06840

phone/fax: 203-972-3011

e-mail: jfredrks@optonline.net

Agent: Jeanne Fredericks

Born: April 19, 1950.

Education: B.A., Mount Holyoke College, 1972; Radcliffe Publishing Procedures Course; M.B.A., New York University Graduate School of Business Administration, 1979.

Career history: Assistant to Editorial Director and Foreign/Subsidiary Rights Director, Basic Books (1972–1974); Managing Editor and Acquisitions Editor, Macmillan (1974–1980); Editorial Director, Ziff-Davis Books (1980–1981); Literary Agent, Susan P. Urstadt Agency (1990–1996); Acting Director, Susan P. Urstadt Agency (1996–1997); established own agency, February 1997. Member of AAR.

Hobbies/personal interests: Family activities, tennis, skiing, swimming, N.I.A., yoga, reading, cooking, traveling, biking, gardening, casual entertaining, antiquing, and pets.

Areas most interested in agenting: Practical, popular reference by authorities, especially in health, sports, science, business, cooking, parenting, travel, antiques and decorative arts, gardening, women's issues, plus an occasional outstanding novel.

Areas not interested in agenting: Horror, occult fiction, true crime, juvenile, textbooks, poetry, essays, plays, short stories, science fiction, pop culture, computers and software guides, politics, pornography, overly depressing or violent topics, memoirs that are more suitable for one's family or that are not compelling enough for the trade market, romance, manuals for teachers.

If not agenting, what would you be doing? A trade book publisher or a writer.

Best way to initiate contact: Please query (with SASE) by mail, with outline, description of project, author biography, sample writing. No phone calls. No fax. E-mail queries should be short and without attachments.

Reading-fee policy: No reading fee.

Client representation by category: Nonfiction, 98%; Fiction, 2%.

Commission: 15% domestic (20% movie, TV, video); 20% foreign (if direct); 25% foreign (if with co-agent).

Number of titles sold last year: 20.

Rejection rate (all submissions): 95%.

Most common mistakes authors make: Calling me to describe their proposed books and giving far too much detail. I'd much rather see that potential clients can write well before I spend valuable phone time with them. Also, claiming to have the only book on a subject when a quick check on the Internet reveals that there are competitive titles.

Description of the client from Hell: An arrogant, pushy, self-centered, unreliable writer who doesn't understand publishing or respect my time, and who vents his or her anger in an unprofessional way.

Description of a dream client: A creative, cooperative, professional writer who is an expert in his/her field and who can offer information and guidance that is new and needed by a sizable audience.

Why did you become an agent? I enjoy working with creative writers who need my talents to find the right publishers for their worthy manuscripts and to negotiate fair contracts on their behalf. I'm still thrilled when I open a box of newly published books by one of my authors, knowing that I had a small role in making it happen. I'm also ever hopeful that the books I represent will make a difference in the lives of many people.

What can a writer do to enhance their chances of getting you as an agent? Show me that they have thoroughly researched the competition and can convincingly explain why their proposed books are different, better, and needed by large, defined audiences. Be polite, patient, and willing to work hard to make their proposals ready for submission.

What do you think about editors? Having been on the editorial side of publishing for about 10 years, I have great respect for the demands on the time of a busy editor. I therefore try to be targeted and to the point when I telephone them and provide them with a one-page pitch letter that gives them the essence of what they need to make a proposal to management. I also make sure that the proposals I represent are focused, complete, and professional to make it easy for an editor to grasp the concept quickly and have a good sense of what the book will be like and why it will sell well. With few exceptions, editors value the creativity and hard work of authors and are intelligent and well meaning. Since they are often overwhelmed with manuscripts, paperwork, and meetings, though, they sometimes neglect some of their authors and need an agent's nudging and reminders.

Representative titles: *Complete Idiot's Guide to Antiques* by Emyl Jenkins (Macmillan); *Gaining Ground: Creating Big Gardens in Small Spaces* by Maureen Gilmer; *Homeology* by Carolyn Janik; *Mastering the Inner Game* by David Kauss, Ph.D.; *Melanoma* by Catherine Poole and Dupont Guerry, M.D.; *Mother-Daughter Kosher Cooking* by Evelyn and Judi Rose (William Morrow & Co.); *New Mother's Organizer* by Helene Stalian (Chronicle Books); *The Best Hikes of Colorado* by Christina Williams (Altitude); *The Art of Dried Flowers* by Michael and Jan Gertley; *The Book of Five Rings for Executives* by Donald Krause; *The Office Romance: Playing with Fire Without Getting Burned* by Dennis Powers, Esq.; *Whole Healing* by Elliott Dacher, M.D.

F

SARAH JANE FREYMANN LITERARY AGENCY

59 West 71st Street, Suite 9B, New York, NY 10023
212-362-9277   fax: 212-501-8240

Agent: Sarah Jane Freymann

Born: London, England.

Education: Although educated mostly in New York, I went to a French school, the Lycée Francais, which is why I am fluent in many languages; and I traveled a great deal from a very early age.

Career history: My first job was with the United Nations; I also worked as a model and as an editor.

Hobbies/personal interests: Spiritual journeys; adventures of all kinds that ultimately provide insight, growth, and a greater appreciation of our world; wondrous food shared with good friends and family; experiencing different cultures and lifestyles; opera; my daughter.

Areas most interested in agenting: Nonfiction: Spiritual, psychology, self-help; women's/men's issues; health (conventional and alternative); cookbooks; narrative nonfiction; natural science, nature; memoirs, biography; cutting-edge current events; multicultural issues; popular culture. Fiction: quality mainstream and literary fiction.

Areas not interested in agenting: Science fiction, fantasy, horror, genre romance, genre mysteries, screenplays, anything channeled.

If not agenting, what would you be doing? Embarking on a teaching career teaching proprioceptive writing, working with children and adolescents, roaming the world in search of beautiful islands.

Best way to initiate contact: Via a query letter (with SASE). Not by phone. Not by fax.

Reading-fee policy: No reading fee.

Client representation by category: Nonfiction, 85%; Fiction, 15%.

Commission: 15% domestic; 20% foreign.

Rejection rate (all submissions): 85%.

Most common mistakes authors make: Please do not fax queries or call us and attempt to describe your work over the telephone. Please enclose an SASE and let us know if you have submitted to more than one agent.

Description of the client from Hell: I wouldn't know—we've never had one.

Description of a dream client: One who not only writes beautifully, with passion and intelligence, but who is also a nice human being—a "mensch." Someone with a sense of humor. Someone who has the patience and willingness to rewrite and rework his or her material, if necessary. And last, but not least, a client who has the confidence not to call us too often and who realizes that if we spend all our time talking to him or her on the phone, we won't have that time to spend selling his or her work.

Why did you become an agent? Probably in the genes. I'm a natural matchmaker and a physician's daughter. I like to think that, thanks to my intervention, this author and that publisher met, formed a relationship, and that I am the midwife to this wonderful book.

What can a writer do to enhance their chances of getting you as an agent? Submit a strong, clear, well-written query letter that sells both the book and its author, with the promise of substance rather than hype.

How would you describe what you actually do for a living? I'm a treasure hunter constantly in search of hidden gems and undiscovered talent; I'm an editor who helps clients shape their manuscripts and proposals; I'm a matchmaker, a deal-maker, and a negotiator; and finally, I'm a believer with the conviction that books (in whatever form they're published) are still our most powerful magic.

What do you think about editors? I love editors. They are intelligent, surprisingly idealistic, well informed, incredibly hardworking, devoted to their books and to their authors, and some of my dearest friends.

What do you think about publishers? Like so many industries, publishing is in transition. The last few years have seen publishing becoming more corporate and bottom line–oriented . . . And less willing to take risks. That being said, however, exciting new writers and wonderful books are being published all the time and, I believe, they will continue to be.

Comments: Even though agents have had to respond to the current realities of the publishing world accordingly, we remain the bridge between the creative and the commercial; between the world of the writer and the world of the publisher. This makes an agent's job pretty tricky, because we have to be aware of how the industry works: know which editors are looking for what kinds of books . . . What the competition is . . . What the sales possibilities are . . . And how to pitch the publisher in an arresting and compelling way.

But at the same time, we still have to be willing to be seduced: by a writer's passion, by an extraordinary story, by memorable characters, by powerful ideas. We have to be willing to take a chance on a project or a writer we believe in. This requirement to be a clear-headed businessperson and a dreamer is a balancing act, but in order to represent clients in the best way possible, it's a requirement.

Representative titles: *Writing the Soul Alive: The Proprioceptive Method* by Linda Trichter Metcalf and Tobin Simon (Random/Ballantine); *A Big Free Happy Unusual Life: Self-Expression and Creativity for Those Who Have Time for Neither* by Nina Wise (Random/Broadway Books); *A Crew of One: True Stories of a Solitary Deep-Sea Angler* by Carlos Bentos (Tarcher); *More Prayers on My Pillow: Words of Comfort, Hope and Faith for Teenage Girls* by Celia Straus (Random/Ballantine); *Great Food the John Ash Way* by John Ash (Random/Clarkson Potter); *Eye of the Whale: From Baja to Siberia with the World's Largest Mammal* by Dick Russell (Simon & Schuster); *Grassroots Zen* by Perle Besserman and Manfred Steger (Tuttle); *Mexican Inns and Haciendas: Spirit, Style, Design* by Meba Levick (Chronicle).

MAX GARTENBERG, LITERARY AGENT

521 Fifth Avenue, Suite 1700, New York, NY 10175
212-292-4354

Agent: Max Gartenberg
 Born: New York City.
 Education: B.A., New York University; M.A., Brown University.
 Career history: As an English major with a graduate degree, I drifted into college teaching, then realized that I wanted to be where the action was, not where it had been in the past. I was living in the Midwest when that lightning bolt struck—about the same time I had to go to New York on family business. The rest is commentary.
 Areas most interested in agenting: Although I will occasionally take on a new novelist whose talent seems to me superior, fiction writers might be well advised to look elsewhere. I am most interested in solid nonfiction—books that present fresh and significant information or viewpoints—regardless of subject area, whether for trade, paperback, or reference.
 Areas not interested in agenting: I am not interested in category fiction, novelty books, and personal memoirs.
 Contact methods: With a one- or two-page, first-class letter describing any relevant background information, accompanied by an SASE if the writer wishes for any sort of reply. I usually don't read sample pages or chapters if these are included. And I am absolutely turned off by cold calls and faxed queries.
 Reading-fee policy: No reading fee.
 Commission: 15% on initial sale; thereafter, 10% on sales in the United States, 15–20% elsewhere.
 Rejection rate (all submissions): 95%.
 Most common mistakes authors make: What most turns me off is a solicitation that tells me almost nothing about the writer or his material but requests detailed information

about myself and my services, which is readily available in such books as the *Writer's Guide.*

What gets you excited? A sense that the writer knows his subject, has reviewed the literature that has come before, and has written a book that is genuinely fresh and new.

Description of the client from Hell: The client who demands unceasing attention, who is never satisfied with the deal I bring him (he always has friends whose agents got twice as much), who delivers his manuscript late and in such disorder that the publisher rejects it and demands return of the advance—and who, on top of everything, blames me for the mess. This is not an imaginary character.

Description of a dream client: A writing professional who can be counted on to produce a well-made, literate, enlightening, and enjoyable book with a minimum of *Sturm und Drang*. Fortunately, this is not an imaginary character, either.

Why did you become an agent? I love good books. They are the pillars of our civilization. It is a privilege to work with those who create them.

Representative titles: *A History of Warfare in China* by Ralph D. Sawyer (Westview Press); *Great Exploration Hoaxes* by David Roberts (Modern Library); *Stealing Secrets, Telling Lies* by James Gannon (Brassey's); *A to Z of Earth Scientists* by Alexander E. Gates, Ph.D., and Gayle S. Martinko (Facts on File).

THE SEBASTIAN GIBSON AGENCY

P.O. Box 13350, Palm Desert, CA 92255-3350
760-837-3726   fax: 760-322-3857

Agent: Sebastian Gibson

Born: December 8, 1950.

Education: B.A., cum laude, UCLA; L.L.B., magna cum laude, University College Cardiff, Great Britain; J.D., University of San Diego School of Law.

Career history: Author of two novels, six screenplays, the lyrics and music to a stage musical, and hundreds of copyrighted songs. Author of published legal articles in both the United States and England. Performed as a stage musician on tour in the United States and Europe, and in a national television special. Obtained law degrees in both the United States and Great Britain. Practiced law in San Diego for four years, subsequently in England and the Middle East, and in 1984 began the Law Offices of Sebastian Gibson in Palm Springs, California. Presently practice law and represent literary and entertainment clients and models from law offices in Palm Springs, California.

Hobbies/personal interests: Reading well-written books, traveling to book fairs, discovering new talent.

Areas most interested in agenting: All categories of fiction, particularly novels with interesting characters and well-woven plots. Especially interested in psychological thrillers, historical novels, mystery/suspense and action/adventure or espionage with romance subplots and interesting twists, crime/police with humorous/gritty elements, medical dramas, women's fiction, sagas, and any well-written novel with unusual characters.

Nonfiction with unusual approaches or written by celebrities, cookbooks or photography with a novel twist, humorous diet books, controversial issues, biographies, current affairs, "kiss and tell" books, and women's issues. What really gets us excited is when we read something fresh and new, with a genre all its own, or a story told in a way that has never been told before. If it grabs our imagination, it will grab the imagination of a publisher and the buying public as well.

Areas not interested in agenting: Poetry, textbooks, essays, short stories, how-to books, books in verse, computer, gardening, pornography, autobiographies by non-celebrities, drug recovery.

If not agenting, what would you be doing? Sipping piña coladas on a beach in Greece, far away from telephones, car phones, beepers, pagers, and computers.

Best way to initiate contact: Fiction: Send query letter or book proposal with outline and the first three chapters or up to 50 pages with an SASE. Proposals and sample chapters without postage will be trashed. No disks, please. Sample chapters should already be edited and without typographical errors or incorrect grammar.

Reading-fee policy: No reading fee as such. We do, however, request a bush-league, small potato, hardly worth mentioning but ever so popular contribution to our efforts of $10 per submission to pay for guard dogs to keep other agents away from our authors, to send those delightfully tacky pens and coasters that publishers like so much, and to pay for all those cocktails at the pools in Palm Springs and Las Vegas where we do our reading (eat your hearts out, you agents who winter in New York). Seriously, each year we receive more and more submissions, and to give each one the time it deserves increases our overhead dramatically.

Client representation by category: Nonfiction, 30%; Fiction, 60%; Children's, 10%.

Commission: 10% domestic; 20% foreign (split with foreign agents).

Rejection rate (all submissions): 95%–98%.

Most common mistakes authors make: Sending first drafts, no SASE, faxing queries, incessant calls, autobiographies, and travel memoirs of trips to Orlando or Tijuana.

What gets you excited? Bribes. Seriously, book proposals and manuscripts already well edited and thoughtfully and creatively written.

Description of the client from Hell: We don't have any over-demanding clients with unrealistic expectations. Five years ago we buried them all alive in killer anthills in the desert. Recently, one was dug up and found to still be typing away.

Description of a dream client: A bestselling author who leaves his or her present uncaring agent for the personal care our agency can provide.

Why did you become an agent? With my background in music and literature, as well as interests in Europe and the law, it was a natural progression to add a literary agency to our law firm.

Comments: The world needs more good books. An author with something to say that pulls on one's emotions and sparks one's interest can have a profound effect on others. Share your strength, your intellect, and don't be afraid to bare the soul of your characters, as long as it's done in an interesting way. Remember, many publishers read only the first few pages before they lose interest or are distracted. The dialogue in those first pages should fly off the page and grab the reader.

G

IRENE GOODMAN LITERARY AGENCY

521 Fifth Avenue, New York, NY 10175
212-682-1978   fax: 212-490-6502

Agent: Irene Goodman
  Born: November 29, 1949; Detroit, Michigan.
  Education: B.A., University of Michigan, 1971; M.A., University of Michigan, 1973.
  Career history: Editorial Assistant at T. Y. Crowell, 1975–1976; Assistant at Kirby McCauley Agency, 1976–1978; established own agency in 1978.
  Hobbies/personal interests: Theater, opera, cooking, Nantucket, the Berkshires, Doonesbury, figure skating (watching, not doing), politics, movies, hanging out with small children, watching cooking shows on weird cable channels.
  Areas most interested in agenting: All types of women's fiction, romance novels, mysteries, biographies, some popular nonfiction.
  Areas not interested in agenting: Literature, esoteric nonfiction, techno-thrillers, macho genre books, psychobabble, feminist diatribes. I don't handle children's books because I like to leave something sacred.
  If not agenting, what would you be doing? When I was in my 20s, I was considering two career options: pursuing an advanced degree in medieval studies and studying gourmet cooking in Paris. The third option was to come to New York and go into book publishing, which is obviously what I did.
  Best way to initiate contact: The very best way is through a referral by a client.
  Reading-fee policy: No reading fee.
  Client representation by category: Nonfiction, 5%; Fiction, 95%.
  Commission: 15% until the author sells a book for $100,000 or more, or until the author brings in $100,000 in a calendar year, then the commission goes to 10% on those titles.
  Number of titles sold last year: 40.
  Rejection rate (all submissions): 98%.
  Most common mistakes authors make: The biggest problem is a general one and it concerns the sheer volume. No one I know in the business can seriously devote any real attention to the "slush pile," simply because there is too much of it. While we look at everything, we do it very rapidly, often giving only seconds to each piece.
  Description of the client from Hell: Someone who wants me to be mother, psychiatrist, best friend, sounding board, loan officer, editor, accountant, and lawyer—all rolled into one. I am none of those things in my work. What I am is an agent.
  Description of a dream client: I have several real dream clients. It is my privilege to work with them. Here's what they all have in common: They work hard, they don't whine, they have a terrific sense of humor, they are intelligent, they have lives and expect me to have one, and—oh, yes—they have talent. They are responsible for themselves, they know how to say thank you, they know how to laugh at themselves (and at me occasionally, when I deserve it), and they like to give people the benefit of the doubt. They enrich my life and give as much back to me as I give to them.
  Why did you become an agent? I became an agent because it was my destiny. That sounds pompous, but consider this: I don't like working in large companies because I

can't tolerate the politics. I like to be a part of a working community, but I also need to fly solo. Autonomy is stimulating to me; it motivates me to get things done. I love making deals, I love books, and I love having an equal partnership with a very talented author. Bureaucracy makes me crazy, and I love being in a position where I can cut through it.

Representative titles: *Thursdays at Eight* by Debbie Macomber (Mira); *Springwater Wedding* by Linda Lael Miller (Pocket Books); *The Secret Wife of King George IV* by Diane Haeger (St. Martin's).

GRAYBILL & ENGLISH, LLC

1920 N Street, NW, Suite 620, Washington, DC 20036-1619
202-861-0106   fax: 202-457-0662
www.GraybillandEnglish.com

Agents: Nina Graybill, Jeff Kleinman, Elaine English, Lynn Whittaker

Born: Kleinman: September 28, 1965, Cleveland, Ohio; Whittaker: October 24, 1951.

Education: Graybill: Graduated from George Washington law school in 1987. Kleinman: B.A. with High Distinction, University of Virginia (English/Modern Studies). M.A., University of Chicago (Italian Language/Literature); Whittaker: Undergraduate in English and Political Science at University of Georgia, Masters in English, University of Georgia, graduate work in Political Science at MIT and Harvard.

Career history: Graybill: I am an attorney specializing in publishing and entertainment law and a literary agent. Graybill & English began in 1997. Prior to becoming a lawyer, I was a freelance Editor and writer, working on presidential and congressional investigations and commissions, the final one being the House-Senate Iran-Contra Committee in 1987. I am also the co-author of six cookbooks. Kleinman: After graduating from the University of Virginia, I lived in Italy for about three years, studying the Italian Renaissance. Previously an Associate at the art and literary law firm of Kaufman & Silverberg in Washington, D.C., I am now counsel to the law firm of Graybill & English. Whittaker: Many years as an Editor and Publications Director in academic and educational publishing, several years a publisher and Editor in Chief of a small press, co-author of two women's history books.

Hobbies/personal interests: Graybill: Reading, cooking, antiques, design and architecture, art. Kleinman: Art, history, horses (train dressage and event horses).

Areas most interested in agenting: Graybill: Narrative nonfiction, very readable serious nonfiction (e.g., health, psychology, science, culture and race, history, politics), some light nonfiction, literary/commercial fiction, and limited mystery and suspense. Kleinman: Perspective nonfiction, health, parenting, aging, nature, pets, how-to, and so on. Narrative nonfiction, especially books with a historical bent, but also travel, nature, ecology, politics, military, espionage, cooking, romance, equestrian, pets, memoir, biography. Fiction, very well written, character-driven novels; some science fiction and fantasy, suspense, thrillers; otherwise mainstream commercial and literary fiction. Whittaker: Creative and narrative nonfiction of all kinds; serious nonfiction, especially history and

G

biography; nature and science writing; literary fiction; mysteries; how-to/self-help; celebrity. Subjects of particular interest include women's topics and issues, U.S. history, multicultural and African-American subjects, race relations, dogs, sports, health/nutrition, psychology, business/career, pop culture, writing. Also, academics who can write for trade market.

Areas not interested in agenting: Graybill: Children's, genre fiction (except some mysteries and suspense), poetry, New Age, spirituality, screenplays, stage plays. Kleinman: Mysteries, romance, Westerns, children's poetry, plays, screenplays. Whittaker: Children's/young adult, romance, Westerns, science fiction, screenplays, and scripts.

If not agenting, what would you be doing? Graybill: I am also an attorney, a sometime cookbook writer, and a part-time interior design consultant. Kleinman: If I weren't an agent, I'd probably be practicing intellectual property law.

Best way to initiate contact: Graybill: Query letter, with a one-page synopsis and sample chapters for fiction, and a proposal or detailed explanation of the book and a bio for nonfiction, and an SASE. Kleinman: Written or e-mail. Nonfiction: cover letter, proposal, including author credentials and sample chapter and/or outline. Fiction: cover letter and the first few pages of the novel. Whittaker: A query letter that outlines your book and your credentials, sent by regular mail or e-mail (no attachments please). Okay to send sample of up to 30 pages with mailed query letter. I also love to meet writers at writing conferences and to hear from writers who have heard me speak on panels. And I love getting referrals.

Reading-fee policy: AAR members; no reading fee.

Client representation by category: Nonfiction, 80%; Fiction, 20%.

Commission: 15% domestic; 25% foreign and first serial.

Rejection rate (all submissions): 95%.

Most common mistakes authors make: Graybill: Over-hyped letters about how wonderful they and their certain-to-be bestselling book are; query letters and first pages (even paragraphs) of a manuscript that are full of typos, grammatical errors, misspellings (which to me indicates a lack of professionalism). Kleinman: Groveling—agents are professionals, and they expect writers to act professionally as well; providing too much information—telling me too much about the project, rather than being able to succinctly summarize it; and sending me a poorly formatted, difficult-to-read manuscript. Whittaker: Handing me a list of 10 books they're writing and asking me to choose which ones I'd like to see. Querying me about types of books I don't represent.

Description of the client from Hell: Graybill: I try to spot these coming and step aside: Writers with an overblown sense of their talent and value, writers who don't want to put in the time and hard work a proposal or a manuscript requires. I don't mind big egos or artistic temperament, I just ask that there be some valid underpinnings for them. Kleinman: The client from Hell doesn't listen, doesn't incorporate suggestions, and believes that the world "owes" him (or her) a bestseller.

Description of the dream client: Graybill: Dream clients are enthusiastic, eager to make their work even better, considerate, prompt, and very, very talented. Kleinman: Someone who writes beautifully; who has marketing savvy and ability; who is friendly, accessible, easy to work with, and fun to talk to and can follow directions and guidance without taking offense, realizing that an agent's job is to help make the end product even better than it already was.

How did you become an agent? Kleinman: My law firm shared offices with an agency, and I did several book contracts. Gradually, I started reading manuscripts, talking to writers, and before long, there I was—a literary agent.

Why did you become an agent? Graybill: I became a lawyer/agent because I wanted to combine my interest and background in books and writing with my new law degree. Kleinman: Agentry is a great marriage of law and writing—both of which I'm very interested in. Whittaker: I've loved to read all my life and believe in the power of books to affect people's lives. I like the combination of solitary work (reading, thinking, evaluating, editing) and social interaction (with writers, editors, booksellers, and others in the book world). I love my clients and enjoy learning from them, making them happy by selling their work, and giving them whatever advice and support they need to develop their careers. I also really enjoy the eclectic variety of books I share with my clients.

What can writers do to enhance their chances of getting you as an agent? Graybill: If a writer gets referred by someone I know, I will look at his or her project a little more closely than I might a stranger's. But mostly, I am interested in a query letter offering a fresh treatment of an intriguing topic by someone with the appropriate credentials to write such a book. In the case of fiction, I look for writers who, their natural talent aside, have read many, many good books in their area of interest, such as literary fiction or mysteries, and who have studied fiction writing enough—through reading, courses, workshops, writing groups—to understand the demands of their chosen type of fiction. Kleinman: *Enhance your credentials.* Get published. Show me (so I can show a publisher) that you're a good risk for publication. If you don't have any eye-opening credentials, then be sure that the writing is as strong and as fresh as you can make it. Whittaker: Most of all, be good writers. Also, have books on topics I love. Teach me about something new.

How would you describe what you actually do for a living? Kleinman: Soothe egos.

What do you think about editors? Graybill: I really admire strong, hands-on editors who understand what a book and its author are about and only seek to make it better, and those who stay actively involved throughout the entire process, from acquisition through launch. Kleinman: I think that too often they're overworked and underpaid, and often don't have the time to really "connect the dots" in a manuscript or a proposal—so it's crucial that we (the writer and I) connect the dots for them.

What do you think of publishers? Graybill: I've never heard any writers say that their publishers did enough to promote their books. I am distressed about the takeover of so many publishers by a few conglomerates because the competition among publishers is far less intense and the emphasis is on trendy books that sell in huge numbers at the expense of smaller but worthwhile books. Kleinman: Probably by the time this book comes out, there will only be one publisher left.

Comments: Kleinman: From personal experience, I know how frustrating it can be to work with literary agents; your manuscript disappears for months at a time, only to return to you with a polite little "Sorry, not for us" scrawled on your original cover letter. Or an agent agrees to take you on, and a year goes by with no word—only to have your manuscript returned to you with "Sorry, I'm just not enthusiastic enough about this one." Was it submitted to publishers? If not, just what was your agent doing for the past year? Who knows? Don't expect that from me. My turnaround time, at the moment, is about two months for fiction solicited manuscripts and about three weeks for nonfiction proposals.

Representative titles: *The 50 Greatest Women in Broadcasting* by American Women in Radio & Television (Andrews McMeel); *Herblock: A Cartoonist's Life* by Herbert Block (Times Books/Random House); *Madam Secretary: A Biography of Madeleine Albright* by Thomas Blood (Thomas Dunne/St. Martin's Press); *The Lost Ships* by Dr. Mensun Bound (Simon & Schuster); *Mom I Want a Pet* by Mary Jane Checchi (St. Martin's Press); *The Anxiety Cure: An Eight Step Program* by Robert DuPont, Elizabeth DuPont Spencer, and Caroline DuPont (John Wiley & Sons); *A Biography of Elijah Muhammad* by Karl Evanzz (Pantheon); *From Nero's Nagging Mother to Catherine's Stable of Studs: A Treasury of Royal Scandals* by Michael Farquhar (Penguin); *The Sanctuary Garden* by Tricia Clark McDowell and C. Forrest (Simon & Schuster/Fireside); *Walrus on My Table* by Anthony Guglielmo and Cari Lynn (St. Martin's Press); *From Chaos to Calm: Effective Parenting for Challenging Children* by Janet Heininger, Ph.D., and Sharon Weiss, M.Ed. (Perigee/Berkley); *James Dean: The Biography* by Val Holley (St. Martin's Press); *America's Great Black Jockeys* by Edward Hotaling (Prima); *Stirring the Mud: On Swamps, Bogs, and Human Imagination* by Barbara Hurd (Beacon Press); *If Men Were Angels* by Karaim Reed (Norton); *The Complete Guide to African-American Baby Names* by Linda Keister (Dutton); *Meltdown on Main Street: Why Small Business Is Leading the Revolution Against Big Government* by Richard Lesher (Dutton); *The Buying of the President* by Charles Lewis (Avon); *When Divas Confess* by Marcia Lieberman and Paul Griffiths (Universe/Rizzoli); *Fathering Words: The Making of an African American Writer* by Ethelbert Miller (Thomas Dunne Books/St. Martin's); *Your Cockatiel's Life* by Nikki Moustaki (Prima); *The Persia Café* by Melany Neilson (St. Martin's Press); *101 Tax Loopholes for the Middle Class* by Sear Smith (Broadway Books); *The Great Awakening: A History of Psychology and Spirituality in Modern Culture* by Dr. Eugene Taylor (Counterpoint Books); *The Secret History of the CIA* by Joseph Trento (Prima); *The Encyclopedia of Heaven* and *The Encyclopedia of Hell* by Miriam Van Scott (St. Martin's Press); *Radio Priest: Charles Coughlin, the Father of Hate Radio* by Donald Warren (The Free Press); *Spiritual Intelligence* by Richard Wolman (Harmony Books/Random House).

G

ASHLEY GRAYSON LITERARY AGENCY

1342 18th Street, San Pedro, CA 90732
310-514-0267

Agents: Ashley Grayson, Carolyn Grayson, Dan Hooker

Born: C. Grayson: Los Angeles, California. Hooker: Los Angeles, California.

Education: A. Grayson: B.S., Physics. C. Grayson: B.A., English, Wellesley College; M.B.A., Marketing, UCLA. Hooker: B.A., Spanish, UCLA.

Career history: A. Grayson: Computer sales, Management Consultant, Literary Agent. C. Grayson: Market Research Analyst; Consultant and Managing Editor for marketing consulting firm. Hooker: Several jobs before coming to agenting. Agenting the last 10 years. Published writer of about a dozen short stories and articles.

Hobbies/personal interests: C. Grayson: Reading, gardening, travel, snorkeling, golf, investing, wine, cooking. Hooker: Writing, reading, checking out bookstores wherever I go, sports, strange low-budget movies.

Areas most interested in agenting: A. Grayson: Commercial and literary fiction, historical novels, suspense, thrillers, young adult, science fiction. I read widely and would be happy to have a top-of-category work in just about any area. I am willing to read an occasional published book in German for possible sale in the U.S./UK markets. I am also the agent for a number of entertainment companies and Web sites that wish to spin their properties into books. C. Grayson: Mainstream commercial fiction. Some literary fiction. Women's fiction: mainstream and romance (historical and contemporary). Mystery, suspense, thrillers, crime and true crime, horror. Children's and young adult fiction. Would like to take on more nonfiction: travel, gardening, cooking, health, some self-help, how-to, pop culture, bio/autobiographies, creative nonfiction. Hooker: Commercial fiction; mysteries; thrillers; suspense; hard science fiction; contemporary fantasy; horror; young adult and middle-grade; quality fiction by outstanding new voices. Nonfiction: Popular subjects and treatment with high commercial potential.

Areas not interested in agenting: A. Grayson: I believe I can obtain an optimal business deal for virtually any book on any topic if one or more buyers can be identified. I am unlikely to be an effective crusader to locate a single publisher for narrow-focused works on politics, diet and health, and religion. Books from recognized leaders in these areas, however, are of interest. C. Grayson: No poetry. No screenplays. No short stories. No novellas. Not interested in action/adventure, war books, novelty, New Age, psychic phenomena, textbooks, professional books, social issues, religion. Hooker: Epic fantasy, poetry, religion, New Age, short stories, novellas.

If not agenting, what would you be doing? A. Grayson: I would probably be running a software or Net-based company. C. Grayson: Ad agency executive; landscape architect; interior designer; living on the beach in Hawaii. Hooker: Writing, which I do anyway, as time permits.

Best way to initiate contact: Published authors can fax or call to discuss their needs. An intelligent query letter is the best way for an unpublished writer to apply. C. Grayson: By referral or query letter with synopsis and SASE. Hooker: Concise query letter that tells me about your book and about your writing background.

Reading-fee policy: No reading fee.

Client representation by category: A. Grayson: Nonfiction, 15%; Fiction, 65%; Children's, 20%. C. Grayson: Nonfiction, 10%; Fiction, 50%; Children's, 40%. Hooker: Nonfiction, 5%; Fiction, 75%; Children's, 20%.

Commission: 15%, U.S. and Canada; 20%, international; 10%, film/TV plus subagent/legal fees.

Number of titles sold last year: More than 100. C. Grayson: Difficult to answer because we sell most of the foreign rights for clients' works ourselves, so we have sold some books six or more times in a year.

Rejection rate (all submissions): Greater than 95%. Hooker: 99%.

Most common mistakes authors make: A. Grayson: Unrealistic and outrageous claims for the quality of the work or the potential audience for the work are frequent. Errors of grammar in cover letters are surprisingly common. C. Grayson: Query letters that are too much hype and/or contain too little information about the book(s). Giving incomplete information regarding previous works. Do not query more than one person in our agency! Do not send your query by certified mail with signature required. And there is no need to send one sheet of paper in a 9" × 13" envelope.

What gets you excited? A. Grayson: A personal recommendation by a bestselling author never hurts. Really, mastery of the topic and craftsmanship in writing are key. C. Grayson: Show they understand their craft and the market and are professional.

Description of the client from Hell: A. Grayson: Of course, we don't represent any clients from Hell, but such a person is more interested in the celebrity of being an author than in actually writing books. Those who feel that grammar and spelling are for the little people to fix; who call after working hours, are late on delivery, or want to borrow money. Anyone who won't work on the next book until the first (or second) one sells. Anyone who calls up weekly and asks, "How about a book about (insert the news event of the week)—would that be worth a lot of money?" Any client who also wants to second-guess his/her agent. C. Grayson: One who tries to do my job; calls three times a day; thinks she/he is my only client.

Description of a dream client: C. Grayson: One who keeps writing wonderful books; is in command of his or her craft; is willing to accept editorial advice, either from us and/or from editors; is creative, respectful, loyal, and dependable. A. Grayson: The dream client always has a few ideas simmering for the next book or two. S/he always listens to input and feedback, but ultimately decides what to do and how to do it because the client both respects the market and upholds his or her standards of art and technique. We seek productive authors with a proven audience whose works we can sell in multiple territories and across different media: books to film and TV.

Why did you become an agent? A. Grayson: I love to read books and sell new ideas. The real reason I became an agent is that Judy-Lynn Del Rey (the late founder of the Del Rey imprint at Random House) told me in 1976 that I should. She had great insight—I'm still having a great time. C. Grayson: The joy of discovering new talent and seeing the books in print. Hooker: As an aspiring writer, I wanted to learn about the publishing business, but I didn't want to move to New York to work in a publishing house. I found a good agency near my home, and they gave me a chance. Turned out I really liked agent stuff.

What can writers do to enhance their chances of getting you as an agent? Hooker: Develop your own "voice," one that can only be identified as yours, and tell the reader about life and people in that voice. Be dedicated and patient. Don't overhype your marketability; I can figure that out. Be more than good—be damn good.

Comments: A. Grayson: Our international success is expanding our reputation as the agent's agents; we represent a number of European agents in the United States/United Kingdom and U.S.-based agents in the rest of the world. C. Grayson: We also represent several French and German publishers for U.S./UK rights and can read and speak French, German, and Spanish in the agency. Hooker: I always like to connect with talented writers who aren't afraid to express their unique perspectives on this world of ours. Determination and a professional attitude are absolute requirements, too.

Representative titles: *Candle* by John Barnes (TOR); *Headcrash* by Bruce Bethke (Warner); *Hokkaido Popsicle* by Isaac Adamson (Avon); *I Was a Sixth Grade Alien* by

Bruce Coville (Archway, also to Hodder Children's Books, U.K.); *In My Enemy's House* by Carol Matas (Simon & Schuster Books for Young Readers); *Mars Crossing* by Geoff Landis (TOR); *Mary Louise Loses Her Manners* by Diane Cuneo (Doubleday); *Move Your Stuff, Change Your Life* by Karen Rauch Carter (Fireside); *Spooksville* by Christopher Pike (Ediciones B, Spain); *The Grave* by Christopher Pike (Archway); *The Return* by Buzz Aldrin and John Barnes (Forge); *The Voyage of the Space Beagle* by A. E. van Vogt (Plaza & Janes, Spain); *The World of Null-A* by A. E. van Vogt (Amber Publishing, Poland); *Virtual Design* by Ann Lawrence (Dorchester).

SANFORD J. GREENBURGER ASSOCIATES, INC.

55 Fifth Avenue, New York, NY 10003
212-206-5000   fax: 212-463-8718
www.Greenburger.com

Agents: Heide Lange, Vice President; Faith Hamlin, Beth Vesel, Theresa Park, Daniel Mandel, Nancy Stender, Peter Harrison McGuigan, Peter Harrison, International Rights Agent.

> **Best way to initiate contact:** Query letter with SASE.
> **Client representation by category:** Nonfiction, 60%; Fiction, 40%.
> **Commission:** 15% domestic; 20% international.
> **Number of titles sold last year:** Hundreds.

The following information pertains to HEIDE LANGE:

> **Born:** July 21, 1949.
> **Education:** B.A., Hunter College, CUNY.
> **Career history:** I started working at the agency while attending college. As Sanford Greenburger's assistant, I was fortunate to learn the business from a "publishing gentleman" with an international reputation, and it's been my home for 28 years. My books have generally reflected my background, interests, and stages in my life. Married, two children, I've handled general nonfiction, from art, which was my college major (*Drawing on the Right Side of the Brain* was my first bestseller), to relationships and sex (*The G Spot*), pregnancy and childbirth, parenting, women's health and other issues, current events, controversy, biographies, memoirs, journalism, some general reference, how-to, self-improvement.
> **Hobbies/personal interests:** Reading, gardening, bicycling, rollerblading and my other activities I can share with the family before our children go off to college (in a flash it seems).
> **Areas most interested in agenting:** See above and representative titles below, but basically, if an author is passionate about and experienced in the subject he or she is writing about, I'm prepared to be enticed by it.
> **Areas not interested in agenting:** Category fiction, children's books.
> **Why did you become an agent?** The fact that I love to read was really my entry into this business, and sometimes I still can't believe I can make money doing what I love. That, and the clients I can help to realize their dreams, makes this very gratifying work.

Representative titles: *Let Me Hear Your Voice: A Family's Triumph Over Autism* by Catherine Maurice (Knopf); *Emotional Wisdom* by Jean Grasso Fitzpatrick (Viking); *Raising Your Spirited Child* by Mary Kurcinka (HarperCollins); *Swim With The Dolphins: How Women Can Succeed in Corporate America on Their Own Terms* by Connie Glaser and Barbara Smalley (Warner); *The Multi-Orgasmic Man: How Any Man Can Experience Multiple Orgasms and Dramatically Enhance His Sexual Relationship* by Mantak Chia and Douglas Abrams Arava (HarperSanFrancisco); *The Random House Word Menu* by Stephen Glazier (Random House); *Life's Big Instruction Book: The Almanac of Indispensable Information* by Carol Madigan and Ann Elwood (Warner); *Encyclopedia of the Renaissance,* edited by Paul Grendler (Scribner); *Lauren Groveman's Kitchen: Nurturing Foods for Family and Friends* by Lauren Groveman (Chronicle); *Italian Food and Drink: An A to Z Guide* by John Mariani (Broadway Books); *A Cold Stay in Hell: One Woman's' Tale of Courage and Survival on Mount McKinley* by Ruth Ann Kocour as told to Michael Hodgson (St. Martin's); *Rains All The Time: A Social History of Weather in the Pacific Northwest* by David Laskin (Sasquatch Books); *Darwin's Orchestra: An Almanac of Nature in History and the Arts* by Michael Sims (Holt); *Red Hour Glass* by Gordon Grice (Delacorte); *The Coldest Winter Ever* by Sister Souljah (Pocket).

The following information pertains to FAITH HAMLIN:

Education: Boston University—Speech Therapy and Psychology.

Career history: Parent to two children; bookstore buyer/manager; sales rep for several publishers; sales manager for Macmillan, Atheneum, Scribner, Free Press; agent for 12 years.

Areas most interested in agenting: Most nonfiction, especially health, medical, psychology, parenting, women's issues, sports, biography/autobiography, business, science, humor, the arts, and books by journalists.

Areas not interested in agenting: Adult fiction, except mysteries.

Representative titles: *Organizing From the Inside Out* by Julie Morgenstern (Henry Holt); *Time Management from the Inside Out* by Julie Morgenstern (Henry Holt); *Change Your Brain, Change Your Life* by Daniel Amen, M.D. (Times Books); *Healing ADD from the Inside Out* by Daniel Amen, M.D. (Putnam); *The Mood Cure and The Diet Cure* by Julia Ross (Viking); *The Coming Nuclear War* by Helen Caldicott (The Free Press); *Plane Insanity* by Elliot Hester (St. Martin's Press); *The Life You Imagine* by Derek Jeter with Jack Curry (Derek Jeter is represented by IMG) (Crown); *Unguarded* by Lenny Wilkens with Terry Pluto (Simon & Schuster); *Archimede's Bathtub* by David Perkins (Norton).

The following information pertains to BETH VESEL:

Education: UC Berkley—B.A. in English with a minor in Political Science; Graduate work in Comparative Literature—UC Berkley.

Career history: Agent at Greenburger since 1988. Worked for Gloria Loomis prior to that.

Areas most interested in agenting: Entertaining literary fiction, original, relevant serious psychology.

Areas not interested in agenting: Category/genre fiction.

Why did you become an agent? Because I love books and care about authors.

If not agenting, what might you be doing? I would be a writer.

Representative titles: *Kiddie Drug Madness* by Larry Diller (Basic Books); *The Un-raveling* by Martin Roper (Henry Holt); *Finding Your Own North Star* by Martha Beck (Crown); *Transference* by Keith Ablow (St. Martin's).

The following information pertains to THERESA PARK:

Education: B.A., University of California, Santa Cruz; J.D., Harvard Law School.

Career history: Previously an attorney with Cooley Godward (Palo Alto, California), joined Sanford J. Greenburger Associates in 1994.

Areas most interested in agenting: Commercial fiction, serious nonfiction, including cultural studies, science, history, multicultural/cross-cultural issues, memoir, social narrative, serious psychology, event-driven narrative works, Asian-American work.

Areas not interested in agenting: Science fiction, humor, diet books.

If not agenting, what might you be doing? I don't know—I love being an agent so much that I can't imagine doing anything else right now.

What can writers do to enhance their chances of getting you as their agent? Be professional, send concise, effective query letters.

Why did you become an agent? I love books, I love to work with people, and I love to do deals! Also, with my background as a transfunctional lawyer, it seemed like the right area of publishing to get into. One of the best things about being a lawyer was having clients—I enjoy getting to know people and working closely with them on their manuscripts and proposals; the personal reward of watching a client's career blossom is the best part of my job.

Representative titles: *The Notebook, Message in a Bottle, A Walk to Remember, The Rescue* by Nicholas Sparks (Warner Books); *Remaking Eden: Cloning and Beyond in a Brave New World* by Lee Silver (Avon Books); *The Eighth Continent: Life, Death, and Discovery in the Lost World of Madagascar* by Peter Tyson (Morrow); *Bloodlines: From Ethnic Pride to Ethnic Terrorism* by Vamik Volkan, M.D. (Farrar, Straus & Giroux); *The Family Virtues Guide* by Linda Kavelin Popv with Dan Popv and John Kaelin (Dutton Signet); *The Simple Living Guide* (Broadway Books) and *Simple Loving: A Path to Deeper, More Sustainable Relationships* by Janet Luhrs (Viking/Penguin); *Handyman* by Linda Nichols (Delacorte); *My Spy: Memoir of a CIA Wife* by Bina Cay Kiyonaga (Avon Books); *Voodoo Science: The Road From Foolishness to Fraud* by Robert L. Park (Oxford University Press); *Dante's Inferno* by Sarah Lovett (Simon & Schuster); *P.E.A.C.E.* by Guy Holmes (Simon & Schuster).

The following information pertains to DAN MANDEL:

Education: B.S. Cornell University

Career history: Associate, Diane Cleaver, Inc.

Areas most interested in agenting: Fiction, new media, politics, and popular culture.

If not agenting, what might you be doing? I would, of course, be a writer.

Representative titles: *Kiss Me Judas* by Will Christopher Baer (Viking); *Tao of the Dumpster* by Dirk Jamison (Warner); *New York Diary* by Daniel Drennan (Ballantine); *Guerrilla Girls' Bedside Companion to the History of Western Art* by the Guerrilla Girls (Penguin/Viking).

The following information pertains to NANCY STENDER:

Born: 1964, Montana.

Education: B.A., English & Philosophy, Macalester College.

Career history: Bookseller/book buyer, Hungry Mind Bookstore; Book buyer, Borders Books & Music.

Areas most interested in agenting: Self-help, parenting, psychology, memoir, biography, history, current affairs, gender & cultural studies, narrative nonfiction.

Areas not interested in agenting: Horror, romance.

Description of the dream client: Honest, polite, well-prepared, organized, and flexible.

Why did you become an agent? I love to sell and to edit writing. This job combines the best of both worlds.

Representative titles: *Claim Your Inner Grown-Up: 4 Essential Steps to Authentic Adulthood* by Ashley David Prend, A.C.S.W.; *Coping with Chronic Heartburn: What You Need To Know About Acid Reflux and GERD* by Elaine Fantle Shimberg; *Technology at the Speed of Stupid: A Handbook for Thriving in the New E-conomy* by Dan Burke and Alan Morrison.

The following information pertains to PETER HARRISON MCGUIGAN:

Areas most interested in agenting: Narrative nonfiction, science, adventure, and literary and controversial fiction.

What can writers do to enhance their chances of getting you as their agent? Have patience.

Representative titles: *No Apparent Danger* by Victoria Bruce (HarperCollins); *Sonic Boom* by John Alderman (Perseus); *The Official Iron Chef Companion* (Beverly Books); *A Brief History of the Smile* by Angus Trumble (Basic Books); *The Bird Conservation Handbook* by American Bird Conservatory (W. H. Freeman).

G

GREY LITERARY ENTERPRISES, INC.

6214 Bayshore Boulevard, Tampa, FL 33611-5024

813-624-9466   fax: 813-839-0986

e-mail: lgrey1@tampabay.rr.com

Agent: Lawrence Grey

Born: April 5, 1955, New York City.

Education: B.A., magna cum laude, Hofstra University; Medical degree, SUNY Downstate Medical Center, New York City; Post-graduate medical training in surgery, urology, and pathology. Board certified in surgery, 1988. Additional studies in literature and foreign language.

Career history: I practiced medicine for about a dozen years, privately, eventually becoming a leader in my area of expertise, surgical reconstruction of male genitalia, and surgical and pharmacological correction of erectile dysfunction. I made a fortune and got extremely bored. I continue to practice medicine, but strictly on a pro bono basis at the time of this writing. I have authored three novels and edited many more, written numerous medical articles, several short stories, and have done a great deal of ghost writing. Finally, I have done marketing on a corporate level with substantial success.

Hobbies/personal interests: Writing; working on a fourth novel. I still do ghost writing and editing. I am an instrument-rated, multi-engine pilot, and owner of twin engine aircraft. I am a companion to my wonderful wife (first wife!), Muriel Lavallee-Grey, M.D., and our two beloved Doberman Pinschers, Sam and Stormy.

Areas most interested in agenting: I like commercial fiction, horror, hardcore murder mysteries, and medical thrillers. I will review and consider any quality fiction. In the area of nonfiction, I accept only medical and health-related subjects, but no quackery or books about enemas to cure brain cancer.

Areas not interested in agenting: No porno. No hate books. No feminist manifestos. No historical novels. No fundamental religious stuff.

If not agenting, what would you be doing? I would continue to do the other things I do and do them more.

Best way to initiate contact: Fiction: query letter, three-page synopsis, first fifty pages. Nonfiction: solid, well-constructed proposal.

Client representation by category: Nonfiction, 15%; Fiction, 85%.

Commission: 15% domestic; 20% foreign.

Number of titles sold last year: 3. New agency.

Rejection rate (all submissions): 90%.

Most common mistakes authors make: They call, they nag, they impose, they compare themselves to Hemingway, they push, they prod, they poke, they compare themselves to Henry Miller, they pester, they pound, etc. But even if these are the most common mistakes, they are rare enough that my job is still a pleasure. And most prospective clients are rather nice.

Description of the client from Hell: Gargantuan ego, miniscule talent, immature, demanding, impulsive, phones often, faxes multiple pages at a time, and suffers with halitosis and flatulence. He/she is middle-aged, single, lives with parents, picks nose, and doesn't like dogs. Have not had one of these yet, but I know it will happen.

Description of a dream client: The dream client has talent, patience, trust, maturity, character, wings, etc.

How did you become an agent? The forces of nature nudged me into the publishing business.

Why did you become an agent? I love books, reading, learning, and other people who love books, reading, and learning. The excitement of finding smashing new talent makes each day worthwhile.

What do you think about editors? Underloved, maybe underpaid. It's a tough job and I'm glad they do it.

What can writers do to enhance their chances of getting you as an agent? Follow instructions, have manners, communicate in writing, and accept constructive criticism. Do not send form letters or pages stained with coffee or body fluids.

Representative titles: I consider this information to be confidential and so state in my contracts.

G

Comments: Strictly self-serving, fundamentally dishonest, ass-kissing people suck. There are a lot of them. Some are very successful. You know how they got there. Understanding, kind people with goodness (not greatness) rock everyone's world. So do people who put people before money. They are fairly rare, but I know some. Dogs rock my world, as do other animals, and nature.

THE CHARLOTTE GUSAY LITERARY AGENCY

10532 Blythe Avenue, Los Angeles, CA 90064
fax: 310-559-2639

Agent: Charlotte Gusay
   Education: B.A., English Literature/Theater; M.A., English.
   Career history: Taught in secondary schools for several years. Interest in filmmaking developed. Founded (with partners) a documentary film company in the early 1970s. Soon became interested in the fledgling audio-publishing business. Became the Managing Editor for the Center for Cassette Studies/Scanfax, producing audio programs, interviews, and documentaries. In 1976 founded George Sand, Books, in West Hollywood, one of the most prestigious and popular bookshops in Los Angeles. It specialized in fiction and poetry, sponsored readings and events. Patronized by the Hollywood community's glitterati and literati, George Sand, Books, was the place to go when looking for the "best" literature and quality books. It was here that the marketing of books was preeminent. It closed in 1987. Two years later the Charlotte Gusay Literary Agency was opened.

   Hobbies/personal interests: Gardens and gardening, magazines (a magazine junkie), good fiction reading, anything French, anything Greek.
   Areas most interested in agenting: I enjoy both fiction and nonfiction. Prefer commercial, mainstream—but quality—material. Especially like books that can be marketed as film material. Also material that is innovative, unusual, eclectic, nonsexist. Will consider literary fiction with crossover potential. TCGLA is a signatory to the Writers' Guild and so represents screenplays and screenwriters selectively. I enjoy unusual children's books and illustrators but have begun to limit children's projects.
   Areas not interested in agenting: Does not consider science fiction or horror, poetry or short stories (with few exceptions), or the romance genres per se.
   If not agenting, what would you be doing? I would write a book called *Zen and the Art of Gardening with a Black Thumb* (I'm kidding!). I would travel to Istanbul and become a foreign agent. I would finish all of Proust. I would re-read Jane Austen. Work on my French. Study Greek. Play the piano. Tap dance.
   Best way to initiate contact: Send one-page query letter with SASE. Then if we request your material (book, proposal, whatever it is), note the following guidelines: For fiction: Send approximately the first 50 pages and a synopsis, along with your credentials (i.e., list of previous publications, and/or list of magazine articles, and/or any pertinent information, education, and background.) For nonfiction: Send a proposal consisting of an overview, chapter outline, author biography, sample chapters, marketing and audience research, and survey of the competition. Important note: Material will not be returned without an SASE. Second important note: Seduce me with humor and intelligence.

Reading fee policy: No reading fee. No editorial fees. When a client is signed, the client and I share 50/50% out-of-pocket expenses. In certain cases, I charge a nominal processing fee—especially when considering unsolicited submissions—decided upon as and when queries arrive in my office.

Client representation by category: Nonfiction, 40%; Fiction, 15%; Children's, 10%; Books to Film/Screenplays: 35%.

Commission: 15% books; 10% screenplays.

Most common mistakes authors make: Clients must understand the role of agents and that agents represent only the material they feel they can best handle. Potential clients must understand that any given agent may or may not be an editor, a sounding board, a proposal writer, or guidance counselor. Because of the enormous amount of submissions, queries, and proposals, the agent most often has only the time to say yes or no to your project. Above all, when clients don't understand why in the world I can't respond to a multiple submission with regard to their "900-page novel" within a few days, all I can do is shake my head and wonder if that potential client realizes I am human.

Description of the client from Hell: The one who does not understand the hard work we do for our clients. Or the one who refuses to build a career in a cumulative manner, but rather goes from one agent to the next and so on. Or the one who circulates his or her manuscript without cooperating with his agent. Or the one who thinks it all happens by magic. Or the one who does not understand the nuts and bolts of the business.

Description of the dream client: The one who cooperates. The one who appreciates how hard we work for our clients. The one who submits everything on time, in lean, edited, proofed, professional copies of manuscripts and professionally prepared proposals. The one who understands the crucial necessity of promoting his/her own books until the last one in the publisher's warehouse is gone. The one who works hard on his or her book selling in tandem with the agent. The author–agent relationship, like a marriage, is a cooperative affair, and it's cumulative. The dream client will happily do absolutely whatever is necessary to reach the goal.

How did you become an agent? With a great entrepreneurial spirit, cold calls, seat-of the pants daring, 12 years in the retail book business (as founder and owner of a prestigious book shop in LA), and 20 years of business experience, including producing films and editing spoken-word audio programs; agenting is the most challenging and rewarding experience I've ever had.

Why did you become an agent? I became an agent because I know how to sell books and movies. Above all, I am knowledgeable and experienced, and I love agenting.

How would you describe what you actually do for a living? My job is essentially that of a bookseller. I sell books. To publishers, producers, and ultimately to the retail book trade. Sometimes, I develop a book idea. Sometimes, I develop someone's story, help the writer get a proposal written. I've even written proposals myself because I believed strongly in the book, or the person's story, or the salability of an idea. For fiction writers with potential, I sometimes make cursory suggestions, but most often I help them to find a professional editor to work on their novel *before* it is submitted to a publishing house.

What do you think about editors? Editors are overworked and underpaid. Therefore, if you wish to have the best chance of having your work accepted, you must do their work for them and don't complain. That is the reality of the editor's milieu. Editors are usually very smart. Most always, if they're any good, they are temperamental, and they know their particular publisher's market. If interested, they know how to make your work fit into their list. Do what your editor (and agent) tells you. No argument.

What do you think about publishers? Publishers are having a very difficult time these days. The "conglomeratizing" of the publishing business is extremely worrisome and publishers are feeling the pressure. However, publishers are always looking for the next great writer, the next great book, and a way to make both successful. (That means making money.)

Comments: Be professional. Be courteous. Be patient. Understand that we are human. Pay careful attention to the kinds of projects we represent. Query us only if you feel your project fits with our Agency profile. Know what we are overworked, always swamped with hundreds of queries. Know that we love and understand writers. Take us to lunch. Send flowers (just kidding).

Representative titles: *Imperial Mongolian Cooking: Recipes from the Kingdoms of Genghis Khan* by Marc Cramer (Hippocrene Publishers). Films: *Love Groucho: Letters from Groucho Marx to His Daughter Miriam.* Edited by Miriam Marx Allen (Faber & Faber, Straus & Giroux U.S., and Faber & Faber U.K.), sold to CBS; *A Place Called Waco: A Survivor's Story* by David Thibodeau and Leon Whiteson (Public Affairs/ Perseus Book Group), sold to Fox.

REECE HALSEY AGENCY

8733 Sunset Blvd. Suite 101, Los Angeles, CA 90069
310-652-2409   fax: 310-652-7593

Agent: Dorris Halsey
Reece Halsey Agency, North
98 Main Street #704, Tiburon, CA 94920
415-789-9191   fax: 415-789-9177
e-mail: bookgirl@worldnet.att.net

Agent: Kimberley Cameron
   Education: Halsey: Educated in France. Cameron: Marlborough School, Humboldt State University, Mount St. Mary's College.
   Career history: Halsey: Worked with her husband, Reece, who was head of the literary department at William Morris. They opened this office in 1957. Cameron: Former publisher, Knightsbridge Publishing Company. Has been working with Dorris Halsey since 1993.
   Hobbies/personal interests: Reading for the sheer pleasure of it.
   Areas most interested in agenting: Literary fiction, writing that we feel is exceptional in its field.
   Areas not interested in agenting: Children's fiction, poetry.
   If not agenting, what would you be doing? Reading.

Best way to initiate contact: Ms. Halsey works with referrals only. Please send an SASE with all queries to Kimberley Cameron at Reece Halsey North.

Reading-fee policy: No reading fee.

Client representation by category: It depends completely on the material we decide to represent. It changes often. The most accurate breakdown is: Nonfiction, 30%; Fiction, 70%.

Commission: 15% domestic; 20% foreign.

Number of titles sold last year: We don't feel this should be public information.

Rejection rate (all submissions): 98%.

Most common mistakes authors make: We are always impressed by politeness, in a well-written letter or otherwise. Their most costly mistake is using too many rhetorical adjectives to describe their own work.

Description of the client from Hell: One who calls too often and asks, "What's new?"

Description of a dream client: A patient author who understands the publishing business and knows what it takes to get a book sold.

Why did you become an agent? We both love books and what they have to teach us. We both understand how important and powerful the written word is and appreciate what it takes to be a good writer.

Note: Dorris Halsey has the distinguished honor of representing the Aldous Huxley Estate. HarperCollins is publishing all his works, marking the centennial of his birth (1894–1963). Dorris has sold many celebrity biographies, nonfiction works, and fiction to most major houses and smaller houses, including Knightsbridge.

Comments: This business, especially today, is all uphill. We work extremely hard at what we're doing, and the love of books is what keeps us going. I don't think many agents do what they do every day for the money. We feel an exceptional amount of responsibility for our authors, and I just wish they could see and hear what we do for them. We have the highest regard for the process of writing and do the best we can with the material in our hands. What more can one do?

H

JEANNE K. HANSON LITERARY AGENCY

6708 Cornelia Drive, Edina, MN 55435
952-920-8819 phone and fax
e-mail: jkhlit@aol.com

Agent: Jeanne K. Hanson

Born: August 12, 1944.

Education: B.A. in Philosophy and English, Wellesley College; M.A.T. in English and Education, Harvard; M.A., Journalism, University of Minnesota; Radcliffe Publishing Course.

Career history: Teacher for 2 years; Journalist for 15 years; Literary Agent for 16 years.

Hobbies/personal interests: Running, reading, weight lifting.

Areas most interested in agenting: Nonfiction books written by journalists.

Areas not interested in agenting: Genre fiction; celebrity books; memoirs.

If not agenting, what would you be doing? Probably being a writer.

Best way to initiate contact: Query letter with a table of contents and 1–3 pages of sample writing from the book.

Client representation by category: Nonfiction, 98%; Fiction, 2%.

Commission: 15% with no extra fees.

Number of titles sold last year: 20.

Rejection rate (all submissions): 99%.

Most common mistakes authors make: Large multiple submissions (agents can just tell); self-absorbed authors who may be a little nuts, even.

Description of the client from Hell: Someone who is really late delivering the book to the publisher; someone who sends me a proposal sealed so tightly with layers and layers of paper and tape that it takes forever to open it!

Description of a dream client: A great journalist who understands how to write for an audience and how to analyze trends; a professor who really, really knows something really interesting and can write about it in a way that doesn't sound like a classroom lecture.

How did you become an agent? I wrote a book and liked my agent.

Why did you become an agent? Because I love books and love doing deals for them that make everybody happy!

What can writers do to enhance their chances of getting you as an agent? Have a great idea.

How would you describe what you actually do for a living? Getting to yes.

What do you think about editors? Nice.

What do you think about publishers? O.K.

Representative titles: *Cancer Club* by Christine Clifford (Putnam); *Frolicking Fauna* by Roger Knutson (W. H. Freeman).

THE HARDY AGENCY

3020 Bridgway, #204, Sausalito, CA 94965
415-898-2414

Agents: Michael Vidor, Anne Sheldon

Born: Vidor: December 20, 1949, Michigan. Sheldon: 1958, California.

Education: Vidor: B.A., Western Michigan/Wayne State. Sheldon: West Valley College/San Jose State.

Career history: Vidor: Marketing and Advertising; co-founded the Hardy Agency in 1990. Sheldon: Publisher, Enchanté Publishing; Publishing and Marketing Consultant; co-founded the Hardy Agency, 1990.

Hobbies/personal interests: Vidor: Sailing, photography, travel, Baja. Sheldon: Music, film, gardening, and cooking.

Areas most interested in agenting: Fiction: contemporary to commercial. Nonfiction: history, sociology, contemporary issues, pop culture.

Areas not interested in agenting: Vidor: No children's, romance, science fiction, Westerns, mysteries.

If not agenting, what might you be doing? Vidor: Promoting and marketing books, perhaps selling pencils. Sheldon: I'd be a landscape architect or I'd live on the beach somewhere.

Best way to initiate contact: Query letter and first two chapters.

Client representation by category: Nonfiction, 20%; Fiction, 80%.

Commission: 15% domestic, 20% foreign and film.

Number of titles sold last year: 8.

Rejection rate (all submissions): 99%.

Most common mistakes authors make: Vidor: Talking too much rather than showing me through their work. Sheldon: Sending us material that doesn't fall into a category we represent and not knowing what our submission requirements are. Not working to further their own career and having nothing to tell us about what they've accomplished.

Description of the client from Hell: Vidor: Someone who doesn't understand how the business works and would expect me to execute on his or her behalf based on his or her misguided perceptions. One who is writing simply for the money. An impatient individual with emotional triggers. Sheldon: One who mistakes publishing as an easy business and doesn't recognize the amount of work done by those who are ultimately successful.

Description of the dream client: Vidor: Hardworking, dedicated to the craft and to promoting oneself. Professional in every sense of the word. Sheldon: One who has become an expert on the publishing business and who has done the work, both from a publishing and a marketing standpoint.

How did you become an agent? Vidor: Fell in love with my partner. Sheldon: It was the result of an epiphany.

Why did you become an agent? Vidor: Combination of passion for the arts, a writer's super-ego, and masochistic tendencies. Sheldon: Because I love great books.

What can writers do to enhance their chances of getting you as an agent? Vidor: Have good interpersonal skills and a working knowledge of the business. Sheldon: They should make sure the work is complete and polished. They should be fully engaged in moving their career forward; attending conferences, belonging to a writer's group, placing short stories in literary journals, entering contests, and getting nominated for awards. Then tell us about those things.

How would you describe what you do for a living? Vidor: I promote writing and the translation of art. Sheldon: I steer the careers of writers.

What do you think about editors? Vidor: Tough job. Good ones are few and far between. Sheldon: Great editors are priceless. But the success or failure of any book is the responsibility of its author.

What do you think about publishers? Vidor: The same. Most have little real desire to be the gatekeeper of an essence of life: the written word. Sheldon: Publishing is an industry in constant flux. Some publishers are amazingly great, some are merely printers. All of them offer something; the key is knowing what that is and approaching the right publishers for any given project. Not all of publishing resides in New York.

Comments: Vidor: Never give up. Do the right thing. The truth will set you free. Move forward or die. "Our contemporary Western society, in spite of its material, intellectual and political progress, is increasingly less conductive to mental health, and tends to undermine the inner security, happiness, reason and the capacity for love in the individual; it tends to turn him into an automaton who pays for his human failure with increasing mental sickness, and with despair hidden under a frantic drive for work and so-called pleasure." (Erich Fromm). "Let us be kinder to one another." (Aldous Huxley's last words).

Representative titles: *Pay It Forward* by Catherine Ryan Hyde (Simon & Schuster/film to Warner Brothers); *Defending Andy* by Marilyn Azevedo (Health Communications); *Electric God* by Catherine Ryan Hyde (Simon & Schuster/film to Propaganda Film).

HARRIS LITERARY AGENCY

P.O. Box 6023, San Diego, CA 92166
619-697-0600   fax: 619-697-0610
www.harrisliterary.com   e-mail: hlit@adnc.com

Agent: Barbara J. Harris
Born: Madison, Wisconsin.
Education: B.S., University of Wisconsin, Madison; M.A., San Diego State University.
Career history: Literary Editor; Speech/Language Pathologist; Literary Agent.
Hobbies/personal interests: Reading, running, sailing, golf, swimming, bicycling, and skiing.
Areas most interested in agenting: Mainstream fiction, thriller, mystery, humor, science fiction, children's, young adult, historical fiction. Nonfiction: true story, how-to books, adventure, historical, medical, self-help.
Areas not interested in agenting: Poetry, textbooks, essays, short stories, fantasies, Westerns, erotica, horror.
If not agenting, what would you be doing? I would be sailing off into the sunset with a good book—one that I had published, of course!
Best way to initiate contact: Query letter with SASE, e-mail.
Reading-fee policy: No reading fee.
Client representation by category: Nonfiction, 35%; Fiction, 60%; Children's, 5%; Textbooks, 0%.
Commission: 15% domestic; 20% foreign. Client provides submission materials and postage or maximum of $250 advance expense for submissions material and postage.
Number of titles sold last year: 10.
Rejection rate (all submissions): 95%.
Most common mistakes authors make: They do not follow our guidelines and have poorly written query letters and/or synopses.
Description of the client from Hell: We do not tolerate this client, but if you insist: He/she calls for constant updates, ignores constructive advice, has unrealistic expectations, and demands instant attention and gratification.
Description of a dream client: We do welcome this client with open arms: He/she is a team player who understands the game, accepts critique, and is patient and cooperative.
Why did you become an agent? Having done editing for a number of years, I observed excellent material go unpublished and thought I could better serve authors by promoting their works to publishers.
What can writers do to enhance their chances of getting you as an agent? They must make a good first impression. Be concise and legible and follow submission guidelines.

Comments: Ralph Waldo Emerson wrote, "Talent alone cannot make a writer." I agree and, therefore, would like to add my advice: "Persevere."

Representative titles: *The Men's Club* by Gottlieb and Mawn (Pathfinder); *Sweep of the Second Hand* by Dean Monti (Academy of Chicago); *Caught in the Web* by Ron Joseph (Beijia Publishing); *Meltdown* by Rick Slater (Beijia Publishing); *Trojan Horse* by Nigel Mitchell (Beijia Publishing); *The Protocol* by Keith Barton (Beijia Publishing); *A Cure by Death* by Brian Dorner (Beijia Publishing); *The Family Man* by Michael Patterson (Mac/Adam/Cage); *Power to the Suckers* by Larry Forness, Ph.D. (Prometheus Books); *The Power of Your Mind Unleashed* by Tom Foster (Pathfinder).

JOHN HAWKINS & ASSOCIATES

71 West 23rd Street, Suite 1600, New York, NY 10010
212-807-7040   fax: 212-807-9555

Agents: J. Warren Frazier, Anne Hawkins, William Reiss, Elly Sidel

Born: Reiss: September 14, 1942.

Education: Frazier: Princeton. Reiss: B.A., Kenyon College. Sidel: B.A., Bennington College. Hawkins: A.B., Bryn Mawr College.

Career history: Reiss: Freelance Researcher; Editorial Assistant to Lombard Jones (a graphic designer and Editor); Encyclopedia Editor, Funk & Wagnall's Standard Reference Library; Literary Agent. Sidel: I have had a long, varied career in publishing, film, and television, as well as raising two children as a single mom and working as a certified chemical-dependency counselor at Hazeldon in Minnesota. Also Vice President of Movies and Mini-Series, Warner Brothers Television Director of Special Projects, CBS Entertainment, New York; Vice President of Production, 20th Century Fox Film Corporation; Senior Editor, Bantam Books; Manager of Subsidiary Rights, Bantam Books, and so on.

Hobbies/personal interests: Sidel: Reading; going to the ballet, movies, theater; hanging out; playing with friends and family; walking; swimming; politics; travel. Hawkins: Music, collecting tribal art, hiking, gardening—almost any excuse to be outdoors.

Areas most interested in agenting: Frazier: Fiction: literary and commercial, mysteries, suspense. Nonfiction: biography, travel, natural history, science. Reiss: Biographies, nonfiction historical narratives, archaeology, science fiction and fantasy, mysteries and suspense, true-crime narrative, natural history, children's fiction, adult fiction. Sidel: Literary and commercial fiction, including mysteries and novels touching on women's issues and narrative nonfiction. Hawkins: Fiction: literary and commercial, including quite a bit of mystery and suspense. Nonfiction: A wide variety of narrative nonfiction, particularly history, biography, science, public policies, and women's issues. I especially enjoy working with academicians writing serious nonfiction for the trade market.

Areas not interested in agenting: Frazier: Romance. Reiss: Romance novels, poetry, plays. Sidel: Cookbooks, children's, science fiction. Hawkins: Genre men's military, horror, romance, and juvenile fiction; "how-to" nonfiction. Fiction: children's books, romance, horror, Westerns. Nonfiction: cookbooks, "how-to." Other: poetry, plays, screenplays.

If not agenting, what might you be doing? Hawkins: Hard to say, since I really love being a literary agent. Other dream jobs might be working as a curator in a major museum

H

or running an experimental nursery for exotic trees, shrubs, and perennials. Sidel: Travel around the world.

Best way to initiate contact: Frazier: Letter with personality, one-half page synopsis of book with first 3–4 chapters. Reiss: Telephone or send a letter describing project, with a few sample pages to provide a sense of writing style. Sidel: The very best way of contact is through a referral or a query letter (with SASE). Hawkins: Concise query letter, brief author bio, one-page synopsis, opening chapter(s) of book (no more than 50 pages), SASE.

Reading-fee policy: No reading fee.

Client representation by category: Frazier: Nonfiction, 50%; Fiction, 50%. Hawkins: Nonfiction, 40%; Fiction, 60%.

Commission: 15% domestic; 20% foreign.

Rejection rate (all submissions): 95%.

Most common mistakes authors make: Sidel: Someone who is too pushy and aggressive and won't take no for an answer. Hawkins: Two extremes here—the under-promoter and the over-promoter. The under-promoter throws together a sloppy query package with a rambling, unconvincing letter and/or sample chapters riddled with errors. The over-promoter makes extravagant claims about the project—"a sure pick for Oprah's Book Club" or "guaranteed to be a #1 national bestseller." It's hard to take either seriously.

Description of the client from Hell: Sidel: A pushy, demanding, inflexible, argumentative, dumb person with unrealistic expectations.

Description of a dream client: Sidel: A talented, flexible, creative professional writer who understands that this is a process. Someone with a sense of humor and a Pulitzer Prize. Hawkins: The dream client takes the trouble to educate her/himself about the realities of the publishing business and enters the process armed with good sense, good manners, and hood humor.

Why did you become an agent? Sidel: A good way to integrate all of my professional and personal experience, use my contacts, and work with ideas and smart, creative people, as well as earn a living.

What can writers do to enhance their chances of getting you as an agent? Hawkins: As a practical matter, projects directly referred by people I know always rise to the top of the pile, since they are more likely to be a good fit with my taste and areas of expertise. But there's also the occasional cold-call query letter that shows so much personality, intelligence, and professionalism that I'm predisposed to like the sample materials. An agent and an author work together for a long time, and I want to feel that I will enjoy representing the writer as much as his/her work.

Representative titles: *Confessions of an Ugly Stepsister* by Gregory Maguire (Regan Books/Harper); *Copper Elephant* by Adam Rapp (Front Street); *Hart's War* by John Katzenbach (Ballantine); *Trespassing* by John Hanson Mitchell (Perseus Books).

HEACOCK LITERARY AGENCY

707 Seventh Street, Tularosa, NM 88352
505-585-2475

Agent: Rosalie Grace Heacock

  Born: Girard, Kansas.

  Education: B.A., Fine Arts/Literature (cum laude), California State University, Northridge, 1971; M.A., Humanities, (magna cum laude), California State University, Dominguez Hills, 1991.

  Career history: Editor, Green Hut Press, Valencia, California, 1975; Editor, Kids & Company, Los Angeles, California, 1977; Heacock Literary Agency, founded in 1978, by James B. Heacock and Rosalie Grace Heacock.

  Areas most interested in agenting: Well-written books.

  Areas not interested in agenting: Science fiction, horror, true crime, category fiction.

  Best way to initiate contact? Please send a query letter with self-addressed, stamped envelope enclosed. Letters without return postage cannot be answered, as we receive around 250 queries per week. Prefer no multiple queries, please.

  Client representation by category: Nonfiction. 80%; Fiction, 5%; Children's, 5%.

  Commission: 15% domestic; 25% foreign.

  Number of titles sold last year: 18–20.

  Rejection rate (all submissions): 95%.

  How did you become an agent? Two good friends (living abroad) could not get an agent and asked me to submit their work. I found the process so fascinating that I could not resist plunging into the field of literary representation.

  Why did you become an agent? I became an agent because I cherish ideas, have a keen curiosity, and love good books.

  What can writers do to enhance their chances of getting you as their agent? It is a matter of timing, which is beyond the writer's control. If my list is full (which is approaching at this time), I will reluctantly reject good material so that I may perform a better service for those currently under representation. This has nothing to do with the author, but rather with timing.

  What do you think about editors? I respect them and appreciate their dedication.

H

RICHARD HENSHAW GROUP

132 West 22nd Street, 4th Floor, New York, NY 10011
212-414-1172   fax: 212-727-3279

Agent: Rich Henshaw

  Born: September 18, 1964; New York, New York.

  Education: B.A., Franklin and Marshall College.

  Career history: Independent since 1995; 1987–1995, Agent and Director of Foreign Rights, Richard Curtis Associates; 1992–1995, Partner in the Content Company, an agency specializing in new media.

  Hobbies/personal interests: My family, books, cooking, wine, travel, skiing.

  Areas most interested in agenting: Mainstream and genre fiction, including mysteries and thrillers, science fiction, fantasy, horror, historical, literary, and women's and romance. Nonfiction areas of interest are business, celebrity biography, computer, current events, health, history, how-to, movies, popular culture, popular reference, popular science, psychology, self-help, cooking, and sports. I am also interested in working with books that lend themselves to adaptation to alternative media formats.

Areas not interested in agenting: Fiction: children's, young adult, Westerns, poetry, short stories. Nonfiction: coffee table books, cookbooks, scholarly books.

If not agenting, what would you be doing? I might start my own publishing company.

Best way to initiate contact: Query letter and first 50 pages (with SASE) for fiction. Query letter (with SASE) for nonfiction. I also accept queries by e-mail, not to exceed one page. My e-mail address is: submissions@Henshaw.com.

Reading-fee policy: No reading fee.

Client representation by category: Nonfiction, 30%; Fiction, 70%.

Commission: 15% domestic; 20% foreign.

Number of titles sold last year: 18.

Rejection rate (all submissions): 97%.

Most common mistakes authors make: No SASE. Unpolished manuscripts. Bound manuscripts. Slick queries that say little about the characters, plot, subject, or style of the work.

Description of the client from Hell: Blames agent for all pitfalls in the publishing process. Never expresses gratitude or appreciation for a job well done.

Description of a dream client: Informed, courteous, loyal, professional.

Why did you become an agent? Since I wrote my first (terrible) short story in college and attempted to market it, I've been fascinated by the creative process involved in writing and the manner in which books and other intellectual property are commercially exploited. I've always been an agent and I can't imagine doing anything else.

Representative titles: *Peg Allen's Community Cookbook* by Peg Allen (Clarkson Potter); *The Well-Trained Mind* by Susan Wise Bauer and Jessie Wise (W. W. Norton); *The Shadow Dancer* by Margaret Coel (Berkley Prime Crime); *Bad Lawyer* by Stephen Solomita (Penzler/Carroll and Graf); *The Singing of the Dead* by Dana Stabenow (St. Martin's Press); *Nothing Gold Can Stay* by Dana Stabenow (Dutton); *Silk and Song* by Dana Stabenow (Warner/I Publish).

H

THE JEFF HERMAN AGENCY, LLC

332 Bleecker Street, New York, NY 10014
212-941-0540   fax: 212-941-0614
www.jeffherman.com   e-mail: jeff@jeffherman.com

Agents: Jeff Herman, Deborah Levine Herman, Amanda A. White

Born: J. Herman: December 17, 1958; Long Island, New York. D. L. Herman: October 4, 1958; Long Island, New York. A. White: April 12, 1979, Marion, Ohio.

Education: J. Herman: Liberal Arts, B.S., Syracuse University, 1981. D. L. Herman: Too much. B.A., Ohio State University, Master's of Journalism, Ohio State University Graduate School in a dual degree with the College of Law. Got Juris Doctorate, passed the bar, and have been in recovery ever since. A. White: Jeff Herman University (I am currently a student at Ohio State University).

Career history: J. Herman: Publicity Department—Schocken Books, Account Executive for a public relations agency, founded my own PR agency, founder of literary agency in 1988. D. L. Herman: An Assistant Attorney General for Ohio, private litigator—civil matters, writer neophyte, rejection-letter expert (recipient), ghostwriter, author, book proposal/book doctor/literary agent/rejection-letter expert (purveyor). A. White: Employed with the Jeff Herman Agency since 1997.

Hobbies/personal interests: J. Herman: Moments of solitude in quiet places, with no demands other than my next breath. Eating when hungry. D. L. Herman: My three children, low-brow entertainment, yard sales, antiques, flea markets, oil painting, karaoke, gossip magazines, celebrities, spiritual development, horses, my pets. A. White: Watching any and all sports, spending time with family and friends, decorating.

Areas most interested in agenting: J. Herman: I could answer this, but by tomorrow, I'll change my mind. D. L. Herman: Popular culture, unique nonfiction. I like books that usher in the trends rather than trail behind. A. White: Nonfiction—relationships, sports, psychology, self-help, anything with celebrity tie-ins.

Areas not interested in agenting: J. Herman: As above. D. L. Herman: Anything pompous, judgmental, or boring. Autobiographies are difficult to place, but they can be used as the backdrop for exceptional projects. No matter how wonderful or tragic your life might be, it will take a lot for it to compete as straight autobiography. A. White: No fiction, poetry, children's.

If not agenting, what would you be doing? J. Herman: I'd get a job with Fed Ex. A. White: Hopefully, I would have won the lottery and I would be spending most of my time relaxing on the beach, but if I haven't won the lottery I would probably teach English to high school students.

Best way to initiate contact: J. Herman: Letters, e-mails, faxes. D. L. Herman: Query letter sent to my attention through our Midwest office: P.O. Box 307540, Columbus, OH 43230. A. White: Send a query letter with SASE to our Midwest office, or 1–2 page e-mail.

Reading-fee policy: J. Herman: As per AAR rules, we don't charge any.

Client representation by category: J. Herman: Nonfiction, 90%; Children's Textbooks, 10%. D. L. Herman: Nonfiction, 95%. A. White: Nonfiction, 100%.

Commission: 15% on domestic sales; still 10% for foreign.

Number of titles sold last year: 25.

Rejection rate (all submissions): In the high 90s.

Most common mistakes authors make: J. Herman: Muddling their pitch. D. L. Herman: Asking me to sell myself to them. I'm too busy. Being rude or demanding on the phone. We all answer phones to cover each other. Those of you who try to get past our screening process by behaving like royalty might just find yourself talking to me and pitching yourself right into embarrassment. Another mistake is to try to pitch by phone unless we know you or are related to you. This is a hard-copy business; follow protocol. A. White: Calling to get a status report two days after the material has been sent, then continuing to call. Not sending an SASE with their material and then wondering why it was not returned to them. Pitching your idea to me over the phone or leaving your entire pitch on voice mail.

Description of the client from Hell: J. Herman: There are several archetypes that come to mind, such as: Manic ego—maniacs who really don't have much to sell other than their own wind, people who nag me so that I either have to fire them or make them a close relative. People who interminably obsess about what others were "supposed" to do for them or did to them. D. L. Herman: Someone who views his or her writing as a destination and not a process. We can each be messengers of the greater light. The trick is to know when to get out of the way. There are no real clients from Hell because, if they are too arrogant to accept direction, I send them back to the Universe for further polishing and education. A. White: One who calls continuously. People who think that the world revolves around them and their schedules. We all are very busy and have schedules to keep as well. People who want to pitch their ideas to me over the phone. People who constantly whine and complain.

Description of a dream client: J. Herman: They know how to punch a hole through unfortunate circumstances and walk through to the other side. And they know how to see and embrace a good thing. D. L. Herman: Someone who listens to and finds his or her own inner voice. This is where the best writing is found. A person like this understands that time and space are not always what we want them to be. Sometimes the Universe has its own agenda. A. White: Someone who listens and is very polite, open-minded, and self-motivated. A sense of humor is always appreciated.

How did you become an agent? J. Herman: I started by pitching manuscripts written by my public relations clients. I would just cold-call publishers and get editors on the phone. I didn't know that made me a literary agent until much later.

Why did you become an agent? J. Herman: I have a weak back and strong eyes. D. L. Herman: To learn to become a writer. Then I married Jeff Herman to ensure representation. He still makes me put it in writing! A. White: Because the publishing industry fascinates me and Jeff Herman told me I could do it.

What can writers do to enhance their chances of getting you as an agent? J. Herman: Don't give up. D. L. Herman: Focus on writing from a business perspective. If no one would ever buy your book, how can we possibly sell it for you? If your project is well-thought-out and commercially meaningful, you have as much chance as anyone else does. A. White: Write me a query letter that will do one of two things: (1) Make me laugh, (2) Make me say "Wow!" If this approach does not work, try sending me gifts.

How would you describe what you actually do for a living? J. Herman: I help get books published. A. White: Read, Read, Talk, Talk, then read and talk some more.

What do you think about editors? J. Herman: That's a tough job, because there are so many people they have to answer to, so many people they have to cover for, so many they have to appease, and so many details to attend to. They are underappreciated.

What do you think about publishers? J. Herman: Ask me again next year.

Comments: J. Herman: Seriously, none of this is rocket science. Please enjoy what you do, and educate yourself about what it takes to succeed.

Representative titles: *Dare to Win* by Mark Victor Hansen and Jack Canfield (Berkley); *Joe Montana on the Art and Magic of Playing Football* by Joe Montana (Henry Holt); *A Setback Is a Setup for a Comeback* by Willie Jolley (St. Martin's Press); *The Aladdin Factor* by Mark Victor Hansen and Jack Canfield (Berkley*); Blackroots: An African American Guide to Tracing the Family Tree* by Tony Burroughs (Simon & Schuster); *Driving Your Woman Wild in Bed* by Staci Keith (Warner Books); *The People's Religion: American Faith in the 90's* by George Gallup, Jr., and Jim Castelli (Macmillan); *The*

Writer's Guide to Book Editors, Publishers, and Literary Agents by Jeff Herman (Prima Publishing); *The Power Strategies of Jesus Christ* by Harry Olsen, Ph.D. (Revel/Wynwood); *The Breastfeeding Sourcebook* by M. Sara Rosenthal (Lowell House); *50 Ways to Raise Cash Fast* by Chris Molles (Dell); *Write the Perfect Book Proposal* by Jeff and Deborah Herman (John Wiley & Sons); *The Cheerleader's Guidebook* by Cindy Villareal (HarperCollins); *Pocket Guide to Saints* by Annette Sandoval (Dutton); *The Living Foods Diet* by Brian Clement and Theresa DiGeronimo (Prima Publishing); *Wedding Vows* by Diane Warner (Career Press); *Getting Your Kid Off Ritalin* by David Stein, Ph.D. (Jossey-Bass); *The Angry Child* by Timothy Murphy (Random House); *How to Get Clients: A Program to Build Your Business* by Jeff Slutsky (Warner Books); *Million Dollar Consulting: How to Grow Your Consulting Business* by Alan Weiss (McGraw-Hill); *Power Public Relations: A Writer's Guide* by Merry Aronson and Donald Spetner (Macmillan); *The Secrets of Power Negotiating* by Roger Dawson (Career Press); *The Complete Idiot's Guide to Investing Like a Pro* by Ed Koch and Debra DeSalvo (Macmillan); *E-Fear: Protecting Yourself in the Digital World* by Ira Winkler (Prentice Hall).

STEPHANIE VON HIRSCHBERG LITERARY AGENCY, LLC

565 Fifth Avenue, 18th floor, New York, NY 10017
212-486-8216 fax 212-865-1494

Agent: Stephanie von Hirschberg

Born: December 18, 1950; Pretoria, South Africa.

Education: B.A., English, Comparative Literature, magna cum laude, Finch College; M.A., English Literature, St. John's University.

Career history: I began my career as an Editor at Doubleday working on fiction and general nonfiction. In 1984, I joined *New Woman* magazine because I wanted to do more hands-on editorial work. For the next 14 years, I worked on all kinds of stories—psychology, celebrities, finance, health, careers. I wrote articles, surveys, a book review column, and an alternative health column. I also freelanced as a book editor. In 1994, I received the Editor of the Year award from the American Society of Journalists and Authors, in recognition of my support of writers. I am co-author of the off-Broadway play *We Are Your Sisters,* an adaptation of a biography of African-American women in the nineteenth century. In 1998, I moved to *Reader's Digest* to work on narrative and dramatic nonfiction stories. I launched my literary agency in 1999.

Hobbies/personal interests: Reading, animals, ecology, jazz.

Areas most interested in agenting: Psychology, medicine, mind-body practices, self-help, religion (ecumenical), mythology, biography, nature, environmental issues, animals, true-life adventure, teen girls, literary fiction, mainstream women's fiction.

Areas not interested in agenting: Children's books, horror.

If not agenting, what would you be doing? I'd probably be a farmer (organic foods only) and run a small publishing company out of my barn.

Best way to initiate contact: Send a query letter with an SASE; for novels, please include a 10–15 page sample.

Reading-fee policy: No reading fee.

Client representation by category: Nonfiction, 75%; Fiction, 25%.

Commission: 15%; 25% if a co-agent is involved (e.g., for film or foreign rights).

Number of titles sold last year: 3.

Rejection rate (all submissions): 98%.

Most common mistakes authors make: Not doing enough homework about the competition and similar books. Poorly written queries and proposals.

Description of a dream client: Someone who is talented, highly motivated, appreciates editorial suggestions, and has a sense of humor and a positive, realistic outlook.

Why did you become an agent? I love books and the whole, crazy business of publishing. Also, I enjoy being a catalyst—developing talent, bringing great stories and ideas into the world, making dreams come true.

What can writers do to enhance their chances of getting you as an agent? Recommendations from writers I've worked with, from established writers, and from directors of writing workshops count for a lot.

Representative titles: *Secrets of the Tsil Café* by Thomas Fox Averill (Blue Hen/Penguin/Putnam); *Book of Cain* by Herb Chapman (Carroll & Graf); *The Best Food Processor Cookbook Ever* by Norene Gilletz (Whitecap Canada).

THE KARPFINGER AGENCY

357 West 20th Street, New York, NY 10011
212-662-7607

Agent: Olivia B. Blumer

Born: Long Island.

Education: Goucher College.

Career history: Doubleday—Editorial, Rights, Publicity (10 years); Atheneum, Rawson, Scribner, Macmillan—Rights Director (5 years); Warner—Rights and Editorial; Agent 4+ years.

Hobbies/personals interests: Tennis, gardening, travel, flea markets, cooking, poker, reading.

Areas most interested in agenting: Quality fiction, some food, gardening, self-help. Inspiration, how-to, narrative nonfiction, memoir, quality nonfiction.

Areas not interested in agenting: Science fiction, poetry, children's.

If not agenting, what might you be doing? Gardening, antiquing/junking, travel, reading for pleasure.

Best way to initiate contact: Via mail (letter of inquiry).

Client representation (by category): Nonfiction, 75%; Fiction, 25%.

Commission: 15% domestic; 20% foreign.

Number of titles sold last year: 10.

Rejection rate (all submissions): 90+%.

What are some common mistakes writers make? Fiction: I hate plot summaries; give me the full picture. Nonfiction: Someone who hasn't researched the competition or analyzed the market.

Description of the client from Hell: Whiney, unprofessional, never says "And how are you?," calls constantly for no reason, just attention.

Description of the dream client: Treats his or her career like a job; in other words, is professional. Considerate of my boundaries, that is, doesn't call me constantly, doesn't call me at home, is self-reliant, has a sense of humor.

Why did you become an agent? Ran out of patience with corporate life. Agenting is more creative, with fewer meetings and less time wasted. I wanted to invest in myself.

How would you describe what you do for a living? I'm a matchmaker.

What do you think about editors? Some good, some bad. All are under the gun.

What do you think about publishers? Some good, some bad. Wish there were more up-and-coming small presses.

Representative titles: *A Year by the Sea* by Anderson (Doubleday/Broadway); *Hot Sour Salty Sweet* by Alford and Dugvid (Artisan/Workman); *Let Evening Come* by Morrison (Doubleday); *Miratolis* by Cokal (Blue Hen/Putnam).

Natasha Kern Literary Agency, Inc.

P.O. Box 2908, Portland, OR 97208-2908
503-297-6190
www.natashakern.com

Agent: Natasha Kern

Born: 1945; Lindsey, California.

Education: University of North Carolina, Chapel Hill; Columbia University, New York; graduate work, New York University.

Career history: Publicist and Editor for New York publishers and Acquisitions Editor for New York agents prior to founding her own agency in 1986.

Hobbies/personal interests: Gardening, travel, animals and birds, yoga, shamanism, new physics, performing arts, history, geology, and, of course, storytelling and reading.

Areas most interested in agenting: Fiction: commercial and literary, mainstream women's, romances, historicals, thrillers, suspense, and mysteries, mainstream sci-fi. Nonfiction: investigative journalism, health, science, women's issues, parenting, spirituality, psychology, business, self-help, gardening, current issues, gay topics, animals/nature, controversial subjects, and narrative nonfiction, fiction: magical realism.

Areas not interested in agenting: Fiction: horror and fantasy, true crime, short stories, children's or young adult. Nonfiction: sports, cookbooks, poetry, coffee-table books, computers, technical, scholarly or reference, stage plays, scripts, screenplays, or software.

If not agenting, what would you be doing? I did everything else I ever wanted to do before becoming an agent. Agenting is truly a calling for me, and I would not be as happy doing anything else. It is a case of "Do what you love (and are good at) and the money follows." I also have a deep commitment to bringing new knowledge, new ideas, and new writing into the world. I believe storytelling is powerful and a great book truly can change the world.

Best way to initiate contact: Send a one-page query letter with an SASE. Include a brief summary, genre, submission history (publishers/agents), estimated word count, your

K

writing credits, information about how complete the project is, name of past or present agent (if any). For nonfiction, include your credentials for writing your book, your targeted audience, and whether a proposal is available. Do not send sample chapters or manuscripts unless requested. An online query submission form is available on our Web site (www.natashakern.com).

Reading-fee policy: No reading fee charged.

Client representation by category: Nonfiction, 40%; Fiction, 60%.

Commission: 15% domestic and film; 20% foreign.

Number of titles sold last year: 43.

Rejection rate (all submissions): 99% unsolicited; 85% solicited partials, proposals, and manuscripts. From 4,000 queries every year, approximately 10 writers are accepted for representation. Write a good query! We are selective, but we do want to find successful writers of the future.

Most common mistakes authors make: Not describing their material or project adequately. Querying by fax, phone, or e-mail. Sending unrequested material. Exaggerated claims or credentials. Comparing themselves favorably to current bestselling authors. Lack of professionalism. Omitting the end from a synopsis.

What gets you excited? In nonfiction, the author's expertise and a passionate belief in the subject are important, as well as a well-defined audience for the book. In fiction, I look for a wonderful, fresh authorial voice, a page-turning plot, character depth, well-structured chapters, emotional resonance, and strong imaginative prose. In fiction, the writing is everything.

Description of the client from Hell: I do not have any clients like this. All of my clients are people I respect and admire as individuals as well as writers. They are committed to their own success, and I am committed to helping them to achieve it. They understand the complex tasks involved in agenting, including sales, negotiations, editorial, arbitration, foreign and film rights, and so forth, and we work as a team to ensure the best outcome for their work. Usually, problem clients who are difficult to work with are identified before a contract is signed.

Description of a dream client: One who participates in a mutually respectful business relationship, is clear about needs and goals, and communicates about career planning. If we know what you need and want, we can help you to achieve it. A dream client has a gift for language and storytelling, a commitment to a writing career, a desire to learn and grow, and a passion for excellence. This client understands that many people have to work together for a book to succeed and that everything in publishing takes far longer than one imagines. Trust and communication are truly essential. How wonderful that so many of my clients are dream clients.

Why did you become an agent? When I left New York, I knew that I wanted to stay in publishing. However, editorial work was not sufficiently satisfying by itself. I knew I could acquire and develop salable properties and that my background gave me expertise in sales and running a company. I wanted to work with people long-term and not just on a single project or phase of one. Plus, I had an entrepreneurial temperament and experience negotiating big-money deals from raising venture capital for high-tech firms. When I developed literary projects for other agents that did not sell, I knew I could sell them myself—so I did. I've never regretted that decision. Agenting combined my love of books,

K

my affinity for deal making, and my preference for trusting my own intuition. I sold 28 books the first year the agency was in business.

What can writers do to enhance their chances of getting you as an agent? In nonfiction, the author's passionate belief in the subject as well as expertise and a defined audience are appealing. Be a client who is willing to listen, learn, and work hard to succeed. If there are writing problems, I will get this author help, in order to produce a salable proposal. In fiction, I look for a wonderful, fresh, authorial voice, a page-turning plot that really does keep me up at night after a long day, well-structured chapters, and imaginative prose. A writer who can pull me into another point of view and another world I don't want to leave. In fiction, the writing is everything. We are glad to encourage promising writers who still need to master some aspects of craft, if they are willing to work with an editor.

How would you describe what you actually do for a living? Unpublished writers often think an agent's job is sales and negotiations. I am often involved in a book's development from the initial concept through preparation of a proposal; editorial advice; selection of appropriate editors; submissions; negotiations; troubleshooting publication problems, including reviewing publicity planning, distribution concerns, creating a Web site, and working with private publicists; long-term career planning and strategies; handling an author's financial affairs, auditing royalty statements, collecting unpaid monies, dealing with tax documents and legal issues of many kinds; subsidiary sales, including foreign rights, film rights, audio, video, and other rights; handling career crises or conflicts with publishers; assisting authors in earning a livelihood with their writing; providing expertise at writers' conferences; educating clients about the publishing industry and its vicissitudes; keeping in touch with editors and their acquisitions interests or concerns about clients; attending industry events like Book Expo; meeting personally with clients, editors, and others in the industry; answering hundreds of e-mails each week; talking on the phone a lot; reading the work of clients and prospective clients and to keep up with trends; working with office staff and upgrading corporate procedures and technical support; supervising the bookkeeper and accountants; arranging articles and interviews for trade publications, and so on. It's a long day.

What do you think about editors? Editors are indispensable and every writer should be blessed with a good one. It is one of my primary goals to match each client with the editor who is perfect for him or her. I often succeed and the result is magical, like all great collaborations: Fred Astaire and Ginger Rogers; Maxwell Perkins and Thomas Wolfe; Gilbert & Sullivan. Writers are more successful in great partnerships. No one can be objective about his or her own work or realistically expect to recognize all of his or her own flaws. Most artistic endeavors require a coach—a voice coach, a dance teacher, a master painter. Writing is no exception. There are gifted editors, both private editors and those at publishing houses, who can turn a strong manuscript into a great one, a gifted author into a bestselling one. I want all my clients to have that opportunity.

What do you think about publishers? They are going to have some interesting times ahead in the volatile new world of publishing, with challenges at every turn. Developing new talent and valuing the writers who are creating their long-term success would seem to be prerequisites for meeting these challenges.

Comments: Believe in yourself and your own gifts. Keep in mind that the challenge for every writer is twofold—to have something to say and to have the mastery of the craft

K

to say it well. Study and practice plotting, pacing, point of view, and so forth—so you can express exactly what you want to say. Nothing is more important than being true to your own artistic vision and understanding the requirements of the medium you have chosen to express it, whether you are writing a symphony, a haiku, or a novel. Keep in mind that in imitating other writers, you can only be second-rate at being them. Expressing your own inner thoughts, feelings, and stories in your own way is the only path to real success. Your world, your history, your experiences, your insights cannot be duplicated by anyone else. Bring us in to share your vision, your imagination. No one can do it better than you can, because the truth of your uniqueness is what you are here to offer everyone else. It is what moves us and takes us outside of our own lives when we read what you have written.

Representative titles: *American Apartheid: The Jim Crow Story* by Jerrold Packard (St. Martin's Press); *Biological Exuberance* by Bruce Bagemihl (St. Martin's Press); *Healthy Baby/Toxic World* by Melody Milam Potter and Erin Milam (New Harbinger); *Hope Is the Thing with Feathers* by Christopher Cokinos (Tarcher); *Identity Is Destiny* by Laurence Ackerman (Berrett-Koehler); *The Ecological Garden* by Toby Hemenway (Chelsea Green); *The Quiet Game* by Greg Iles (Dutton); *The Skull Mantra* by Eliot Pattison (St. Martin's Press); *The Shepherd's Voice* by Robin Lee Hatcher (Waterbrook); *Daughter of God* by Lewis Perdue (Forge/TOR); *The Piper's Sons* by Bruce Fergusson (Dutton); *The Nephilim* by Lynn Marzulli (Zondervan); *The Sacred Bedroom* by Jon Robertson (New World Library).

KIDDE, HOYT & PICARD

335 East 51st Street, New York, NY 10022
212-755-9461   fax: 212-223-2501

Agent: Kay Kidde; Laura Langlie, Associate Agent
   Born: Kidde: August 30, 1930; Langlie: January 21, 1964.
   Education: Kidde: Chatham Hall, Virginia (1948); B.A., Vassar College (1952). Langlie: University of Iowa.
   Career history: Kidde: Has taught, worked as Editor, Senior Editor at NAL, Putnam/Coward McCann, Harcourt. Langlie: Assistant to the Publisher at Carroll & Graf Publishers, Inc.; Associate Production Manager at Kensington Publishing Corporation.
   Hobbies/personal interests: Kidde: Published poet, writer; ocean swimming, sailing. Langlie: Theater-going, film-watching, cooking, and reading.
   Areas most interested in agenting: Kidde: Mainstream/literary fiction, mainstream nonfiction, romantic fiction, mystery. Langlie: General nonfiction, biographies, mainstream/literary fiction, nature writing, mystery and suspense fiction, historical romances.
   Areas not interested in agenting: Male adventure, porn, science fiction, young adult, juvenile, poetry, unpublished short stories.
   If not agenting, what would you be doing? Kidde: Writing more. Langlie: Somehow, I'd be involved with authors and publishing. This always has been what I've wanted to do.
   Best way to initiate contact: Write a query letter (with SASE), preferably one to three pages, including a synopsis, past publishing credits, and other writing experience.

K

Reading-fee policy: No reading fee. Author is responsible for photocopying, some long-distance telephone and fax expenses, and postage expenses for manuscripts being returned to the author.

Client representation by category: Nonfiction, 25%; Fiction, 75%.

Commission: 15% for new clients.

Number of titles sold last year: 15.

Rejection rate (all submissions): 90%.

Most common mistakes authors make: Kidde: Insistence; the coy, undisciplined, lack of straight presentation of selves. Langlie: An incomplete presentation of their book projects. Presumptuousness.

Description of the client from Hell: The prospective client from Hell is one who is pushy, loud, not a stylist, unpublished.

How did you become an agent? I started as an editor and found myself more on the author's side.

Why did you become an agent? Kidde: Because I love good books. Langlie: I enjoy putting people together. I'm a good matchmaker in business.

How would you describe what you actually do for a living? Help to get good authors of value out there.

What do you think about editors? I admire many of them.

What do you think of publishers? I admire many, but feel they're selling out to commercialism only, in some cases.

Comments: Go for good values; go for love, style, and reality. Kidde: I love a good story and a well-told novel with people in it to whom I can look up, who are witty and sympathetic, admirable.

Representative titles: *Cracking Up* by Peter Swet (Hazeldon); *Don't Talk to Strangers* by Bethany Campbell (Bantam); *February Light* by Heather T. Remoff (St. Martin's Press); *Hen Frigates* by Joan Druett (Simon & Schuster); *Letters to the Editor,* edited by Gerard Stropnidky, Tom Byrn, James Goode, and Jerry Matheny (Touchstone/Simon & Schuster); *Presumption of Guilt* by Lelia Kelly (Kensington); *The Judas Glass* by Michael Cadnum (Carroll & Graf); *The Street Where She Lived* by Mark Miano (Kensington); *Where Roses Grow Wild* by Patricia Cabot (St. Martin's Press).

THE KNIGHT AGENCY

P.O. Box 550648, Atlanta, GA 30355
404-816-9620   fax: 404-237-3439
e-mail: deidremk@aol.com

Agent: Deidre Knight

Career history: Background in film production and marketing/sales. Established the Knight Agency in 1996. Member of the AAR, the Author's Guild, and Romance Writers of America.

Hobbies/personal interests: Music, playing Hammond Organ and keyboard, reading, travel, and films.

K

Areas most interested in agenting: Romance and women's fiction; most areas of non-fiction, including personal finance, business, parenting, careers, religion, music, pop culture, health, self-help, narrative nonfiction, and popular reference.

Areas not interested in agenting: Science fiction, fantasy, mystery, action-adventure, New Age, occult.

If not agenting, what would you be doing? Something entrepreneurial and creative, such as running a small press or a film production company. Music management has always appealed to me, too.

Best way to initiate contact: Send a one-page query letter with SASE prior to submitting material. Queries without return postage cannot be answered, nor can we accept e-mail queries with attached documents. Please do not call or fax.

Reading-fee policy: No reading fee.

Client representation by category: Nonfiction, 50%; Fiction, 50%.

Commission: 15% domestic; 20–25% foreign.

Number of titles sold last year: 40.

Rejection rate (all submissions): 99%.

Most common mistakes authors make: Calling or faxing rather than sending a query letter. Interviewing me up front about my qualifications. Querying me about categories I don't represent. Forgetting return postage with their query letter. Boasting about having written "the next bestseller." Submitting work that isn't their best or isn't as well developed as it needs to be.

Description of the client from Hell: Calls and e-mails constantly for updates. Faxes incessantly, most often with needless information. Isn't receptive to my input and suggestions. Rude and unappreciative, never thanking me for my hard work. Generally doesn't respect my time. Impatient with the publishing process.

Description of a dream client: Hardworking, reliable, loyal, and informed. Respectful of my time and efforts on his or her behalf. Appreciative of what I do. Receptive to feedback. A team player. Realistic in his or her publishing goals and committed to a long-term process of building a career.

How did you become an agent? My husband is a writer, and I became aware of the agenting profession through him. For a long time I thought this would make a terrific career for me, and in 1996 I decided to make "the leap." It's gone very well for me and has proved to be the right career choice. Now my husband has me for an agent, which is an added benefit!

Why did you become an agent? I've always been a salesperson, as well as a voracious reader. Agenting combines both of those qualities perfectly.

What can writers do to enhance their chances of getting you as an agent? Present a nonfiction proposal that is thoroughly conceived and well-written, including market analysis and promotional opportunities, full chapter outlines, and competition. I'm open to a very wide range of nonfiction ideas, so send me a well-developed proposal and show me why it will sell—you'll grab my attention. In fiction, I'm looking for strong writers of romance, women's fiction, and commercial fiction. I also love books that combine both literary and commercial elements (think Alex Garland's *The Beach* or Donna Tartt's *The Secret History*).

K

How would you describe what you actually do for a living? I've often told people that I am the "Jerry Maguire of books." I look for terrific books and authors, then represent them to appropriate publishers, with the end goal of finding the right match. I negotiate all elements of the author's deal and thoroughly review and negotiate his or her contract. I then serve as that author's liaison with his or her publishing house and editor in all business-related matters, including negotiating future offers. More important, I help plan that author's career well beyond the first book. Our mutual goal is to develop a successful writing career, not merely to publish a single book.

Representative titles: *Beyond Success* by Brian Biro (Penguin Putnam); *True North* by Beverly Brandt (St. Martin's Press); *Lone Rider* by Lauren Bach (Warner Books); *A Beginner's Guide to Day Trading Online* by Toni Turner (Adams Media); *Healing Hearts* by Cheryl Wolverton (Harlequin); *How'dja Get That Job? Over 100 Careers in the Music Business* by Tanja Crouch (Barron's); *Simply Living* by Cecil Murphey (Westminster John Knox Press); *This Joint Is Jumpin': A History of Swing Music and Dance* by Tanja Crouch (TV Books); *The Highlander's Touch* by Karen Marie Moning (Bantam Dell).

LINDA KONNER LITERARY AGENCY

10 West 15th Street, Suite 1918, New York, NY 10011
212-691-3419

Agent: Linda Konner
   Born: Brooklyn, New York.
   Education: B.A., Brooklyn College, Modern Languages; M.A.T., Fordham University, Sociology and Urban Education.
   Career history: 1976–1981, Editor at *Seventeen* magazine; 1981–1983, Managing Editor, and 1983–1985, Editor in Chief at *Weight Watchers Magazine;* 1985–1986, Entertainment Editor at *Redbook;* 1986–1993, Entertainment Editor at *Woman's World* magazine; 1996–present, Literary Agent. Author of eight books.
   Hobbies/personal interests: Movies, theater, travel, exploring New York City.
   Areas most interested in agenting: Nonfiction only: especially health, self-help, fitness and nutrition, relationships, parenting, pop psychology, celebrities, how-to, career, and personal finance.
   Areas not interested in agenting: Fiction, children's.
   If not agenting, what would you be doing? Writing books, in particular, a book I can't sell for the life of me, called *Apartners: Living Apart and Loving It* (my honey of 22 years and I are not married and don't live together).
   Best way to initiate contact: Send a brief query letter along with SASE.
   Reading-fee policy: No reading fee.
   Client representation by category: Nonfiction, 100%.
   Commission: 15% domestic, 25% foreign (my foreign rights subagents collect 15%).
   Number of titles sold last year: About 16.
   Rejection rate (all submissions): 90%.
   What gets you excited? See description of a dream client.

K

Description of the client from Hell: Doesn't follow through. Says he/she will turn in a proposal promptly/do a rewrite promptly/come up with ideas for the next book but then never does. Shmoozes endlessly with me on the phone, either out of loneliness or to get my help coming up with a new idea. Thinks that "fun" multicolored proposals with lots of (needless) visuals are great (they do not save an otherwise poor idea or poor writing).

Description of a dream client: One who writes well and has a steady stream of good, commercial nonfiction ideas. An expert in his/her field (or has access to one). Not afraid to think big. Has a sense of the marketplace—what's happening in the publishing world and what is likely to sell. Follows directions. Turns things around promptly. Keeps phone conversations brief and to the point. Appreciates the efforts I'm making on his or her behalf.

Why did you become an agent? I wanted a change from book writing. I had successfully sold and negotiated contracts for several books of my own and my friends (often getting better deals for myself than my agents had gotten), and I enjoyed the process. Also, I had always had many more good book ideas than I ever had the time to write myself, and now I can see some of my ideas (such as *The Wedding Dress Diet*) blossom into books written by other talented people, who may be good writers but don't have a concrete book idea at the moment.

Representative titles: *Date Like a Man . . . to Get the Man You Want* by Myreah Moore and Jodie Gould (HarperCollins); *Quality of Life: How to Get It, How to Keep It* by Genna Murphy and Shauna Ries (Eagle Brook/William Morrow); *The Force Program: The Healthy Way to Fight Cancer* (Ballantine). *In Search of Our Ancestors* by Megan Smolenyak (Adams Media, PBS Companion book).

BARBARA S. KOUTS, LITERARY AGENT

P.O. Box 560, Bellport, NY 11713
631-286-1278

Agent: Barbara S. Kouts
  Born: October 24, 1936.
  Education: B.A., English, New York University; M.A., English, SUNY at Stony Brook.
  Career history: Freelance editorial work at book publishers and magazines; began working in literary agency 1980; founded own agency in 1991.
  Hobbies/personal interests: Walking, swimming, reading, bicycle riding, gardening, spending time with my family and friends.
  Areas most interested in agenting: Children's, literary novels, psychology, parenting, interpersonal relationships. Mysteries. Novels with depth in ideas and characters. Health, sports, and gardening.
  Areas not interested in agenting: Science fiction and romance novels.
  If not agenting, what would you be doing? Traveling, sailing around the world, working with children, reading, and writing.
  Best way to initiate contact: Query letter and description of project (with SASE).
  Reading-fee policy: No reading fee (only photocopying expenses).
  Client representation by category: Nonfiction, 20%; Fiction, 20%; Children's, 60%.
  Commission: 15%.

K

Number of titles sold last year: Lost count!

Rejection rate (all submissions): 90% of new submissions and queries.

Most common mistakes authors make: Calling on the phone over and over again to find out about everything! Constantly! Sending sloppy and unprofessional work!

What gets you excited? They are professional in all aspects of their query letter and phone conversations. Real pros stand out!

Description of the client from Hell: Expecting much too much—instant reads, instant dollars, instant attention! A feeling of nontrust, quibbling over everything.

Description of a dream client: Hardworking, reliable, consistent in writing, willing to rewrite and revise, kind and considerate. Upbeat and cheerful.

How did you become an agent? Studied English literature, studied editorial procedures. Worked for a book publisher and a magazine publisher.

Why did you become an agent? Great love of books! And good reads! I love to see a manuscript turn into a published book.

How would you describe what you actually do for a living? I work for a writer to better his or her career. I work to serve writers.

What do you think about editors? I admire a good editor and there are many in the field now.

What do you think about publishers? A good publisher publishes good books, books of fine quality!

Comments: Keep on writing—never give up! "To one's own self be true." Hakuna matata.

Representative titles: *Dancing on the Edge* by Han Nolan; *Sacajawea* by Joseph Bruchac; *Cinderella Skeleton* by Robert San Souci; *Froggy's First Christmas* by Jonathan London.

IRENE KRAAS AGENCY

256 Rancho Alegre, Santa Fe, NM 87505
505-474-6212   fax: 505-474-6216

Agent: Irene W. Kraas

Born: August 16, is this necessary?

Education: B.A., Psychology; M.Ed., Educational Psychology.

Career history: Career Counselor; Management Consultant and Trainer to business, universities, and government; Literary Agent (1990–present).

Hobbies/personal interests: Reading, hiking, and enjoying life.

Areas most interested in agenting: At the moment the agency is looking for psychological thrillers, mysteries, and sci-fi. Material by unpublished authors will be accepted in those areas only. Published authors seeking representation may contact me regarding material in any area except children's picture books and chapter books.

Areas not interested in agenting: Any other than those listed above. For published authors, please send query or call.

If not agenting, what would you be doing? I've done what I've wanted all along and this is the ultimate. However, if I had to choose, I would be a rich publisher and publish all those great books that I've had rejected!

K

Best way to initiate contact: Send me a short cover letter, the first 50 pages of a completed manuscript, and return postage. Please, no query letters!!

Reading-fee policy: No reading fee.

Client representation by category: Nonfiction, 5%; Fiction, 95%; Children's, 20%.

Commission: 15%.

Number of titles sold last year: Varies from year to year.

Rejection rate (all submissions): 99%.

Most common mistakes authors make: No cover letter or no return postage. Envelope too small. I can ignore everything if it's a great manuscript.

Description of the client from Hell: I'll take the fifth, thanks.

Description of a dream client: A great writer who trusts me to do the very best for him or her.

Why did you become an agent? I went from 20 years in business consulting to becoming the great American writer to agenting. I love using my business acumen in helping first-time authors get a break.

How would you describe what you actually do for a living? I read, read, read. Then sell, sell, sell.

What do you think about editors? Mostly they are top-notch people interested in good writing.

What do you think about publishers? Well, let's just say they don't always see the picture clearly and don't always have the writer's best interests in mind. But that's why we have agents!

Representative titles: *Any Kind of Luck* by William Jack Sibley (Kensington); *A Matter of Profit* by Hilari Bell (Avon); *The Genealogy Handbook* by Dawn Bradley Berry (Lowell House); *The Edge on the Sword* by Rebecca Tingle (Putnam); *Amateur Genealogist's Guide to the Family History Library in Salt Lake City* by Dawn Bradley Berry (Lowell House); *Singing Camels of Navohar* by Hillari Bell (ROC); *Songs of Power* by Hillari Bell (Hyperion, young adult); *St. Germain (Untitled) #14* by Chelsea Quinn Yarbro (Forge, young adult).

LEIGHTON & COMPANY, INC.

7 Washington Street, Beverly, MA 01915
978-921-0887 fax: 978-921-0223
www.leightonreps.com e-mail: leighton@leightonreps.com

Agent: Leighton O'Connor

Born: August 11, 1963; Salem, Massachusetts.

Education: Some college.

Career history:. Commercial photographer and photographers' and illustrators' representatives.

Hobbies/personal interests: Racing sailboats, ski racing, snowboarding, hiking, camping, and walking.

Areas most interested in agenting: Children's picture books.

K

Areas not interested in agenting: Anything that isn't a children's picture book.
If not agenting, what would you be doing? Sailing around the world.
Best way to initiate contact: Send an e-mail with a short synopsis of the story.
Reading-fee policy: No reading fee.
Commission: 12.5%–25%.
Rejection rate (all submissions): 95%.
Most common mistakes authors make: They spell my name wrong.
Description of the client from Hell: No clients from Hell. . . . I don't kiss and tell.
Description of a dream client: Lots of books with lots of money.
Why did you become an agent? I like to wear a headset.

PAUL S. LEVINE LITERARY AGENCY

1054 Superba Avenue, Venice, CA 90291-3940
310-450-6711   fax: 310-450-0181
e-mail: pslevine@ix.netcom.com

Agent: Paul S. Levine
Born: March 16, 1954; New York.
Education: B.Comm., Concordia University, Montreal; M.B.A., York University, Toronto; J.D., USC.
Career history: Attorney for almost 20 years.
Areas most interested in agenting: Commercial fiction and nonfiction.
Areas not interested in agenting: Science fiction and children's and young adult books.
If not agenting, what would you be doing? Practicing entertainment law.
Best way to initiate contact: Query by snail mail (with SASE), e-mail, fax.
Reading-fee policy: No reading fee.
Client representation by category: Nonfiction, 60%; Fiction, 40%.
Commission: 15%.
Number of titles sold last year: 20.
Rejection rate (all submissions): 95%.
Most common mistakes authors make: Writing bad query letters.
What gets you excited? See description of a dream client.
Description of the client from Hell: One who calls, faxes, e-mails, or otherwise tries to contact me every day. One who constantly needs reassurance that each rejection letter does not mean the client's project lacks merit and that the client is an awful person.
Description of a dream client: The opposite of above.
Why did you become an agent? I have loved the book business ever since I started practicing law in 1980. My first client was a major book publisher.
What can writers do to enhance their chances of getting you as an agent? Contact me in a professional manner. Be referred by an existing client, colleague, or friend.
How would you describe what you actually do for a living? I represent writers—book authors, screenwriters, television writers, and writer-producers.

L

What do you think about editors? I love them.

What do you think about publishers? I love them, too.

Comments: I always tell my clients that the only thing that I know how to write is a contract—I envy writers who can actually write.

THE LITERARY GROUP INTERNATIONAL

270 Lafayette Street, Suite 1505, New York, NY 10012

212-274-1616   fax: 212-274-9876

www.theliterarygroup.com   e-mail: litgrpfw@aol.com

Austin office:

8202 Emberwood Drive, Austin, TX 78757

hornfischer@mail.utexas.edu

Agents: Jim Hornfischer (Austin office), Frank Weimann (New York office), and Andrew Stuart (New York office)

    Born: Hornfischer: 1965; Salem, Massachusetts.

    Education: Hornfischer: B.A., Colgate University (Phi Beta Kappa); M.B.A., University of Texas at Austin.

    Career history: Hornfischer: Editorial positions in the McGraw-Hill general books division (1987–1989) and the HarperCollins adult trade division (1989–1992). Agent, Literary Group International, (1993–present).

    Hobbies/personal interests: Weimann: Ice hockey.

    Areas most interested in agenting: Weimann: Categories include: sports, science, how-to, mystery, romance, suspense, African-American subjects, politics, memoirs, history. Hornfischer: All types of high-quality narrative nonfiction, current events, military history, U.S. history, world history, political subjects, science, medicine/health, business/management/finance, academic writing and research that has a general-interest audience. Quality literary and mainstream fiction.

    Areas not interested in agenting:: Poetry, science fiction, romances.

    If not agenting, what would you be doing? Weimann: This is all I ever wanted to do.

    Best way to initiate contact: The ideal way to initiate contact is by sending us a clear, concise, compelling query letter.

    Reading-fee policy: No reading fee.

    Client representation by category: Weimann: Nonfiction, 60%; Fiction, 35%; Children's, 5%. Hornfischer: Nonfiction, 90%; Fiction, 10%.

    Commission: 15% domestic; 20% foreign.

    Number of titles sold last year: Weimann: 75. Hornfischer: 55.

    Rejection rate (all submissions): Weimann: 99%. Hornfischer: The vast majority.

    Most common mistakes authors make: The most common mistake is to insist on meeting with us. It is what's on the page that counts, not a wonderful personality.

    Description of the client from Hell: The worst thing a client can do, in my mind, is to constantly bombard the agency and/or publisher with needless phone calls.

L

Description of a dream client: Most of our authors fit into this category. A dream client is someone who is willing to put his or her faith and confidence into our hands and trust that we will do what is in his or her best interest.

How did you become an agent? My first client, Thomas "Hollywood" Henderson, asked me to represent him after publishers loved his story and hated the proposal I wrote for him.

Why did you become an agent? Very simple—I don't have the ability to write books but have the ability to help those who can.

How would you describe what you do for a living? I have the greatest job in the world.

What can writers do to enhance their chances of getting you as their agent? It is important to us that a writer is willing to rely on our experience and take career suggestions from us. Hornfischer: Thinks big, drinks from the glasses that are half full, even her grocery lists have narrative momentum, keeps an open ear for useful editorial advice and invariably runs with it in brilliant and surprising ways.

What do you think about editors? I believe editors are the most overworked and underpaid people in the creative arts.

What do you think about publishers? Where would we be without them?

Representative titles: Weinmann: *Rocket Boys* by Homer Hickam (Delacorte); *Bird Watching* by Larry Bird (Warner). Hornfischer: *Flags of Our Fathers* by James Bradley with Ron Powers (Bantam); *The First American* by H. W. Brands (Doubleday); *The "Jewish Threat"* by Joseph Bendersky (Basic); *The Man Who Flew the Memphis Belle* by Col. Robert K. Morgan with Ron Powers (Dutton); *The Bullet Meant for Me* by Jan Reid (Broadway); *The Myth of the Great War* by John Mosier (HarperCollins); *Lady Bird* by Jan Jarboe-Russell (Scribner); *T.R.: The Last Romantic* by H. W. Brands (Basic). Stuart: *The Last Dive* by Bernie Choudhury (HarperCollins); *The Darwin Awards* by Wendy Northcutt (Dutton).

TONI LOPOPOLO LITERARY MANAGEMENT

8837 School House Lane, Coopersburg, PA 18036
215-679-0560   fax: 215-679-0561
e-mail: LopopoloBooks@aol.com

Agent: Toni Lopopolo
  Born: Los Angeles, CA; July 18th, 19XX.
  Education: M.A.
  Career history: 1972–1973, Publicity Associate, Bantam Books; 1973–1975, Paperback Marketing Manager, Houghton-Mifflin; 1975–1981, Executive Editor, Macmillan; 1981–1990, Executive Editor, St. Martin's Press; 1990–Present, Literary Agency.
  Hobbies/personal interests: Reading, house restoration, my dogs, opera, antiques.
  Areas most interested in agenting: Good mysteries with unusual protagonists like Latin-American, Italian-American, and so on. Also, nonfiction on today's most important subjects.

L

Areas not interested in agenting: Try me.

If not agenting, what might you be doing? I'd like to go back to teaching.

Best way to initiate contact: Terrific query letter and excellent credentials.

Client representation by category: Nonfiction, 75%; Fiction, 25%.

Commission structure: 15% unless the client has already found a publisher, then 10%.

Number of titles sold last year: 12.

Rejection rate (all submissions): 95%.

Common mistakes authors make: People who have not done their homework to learn how to solicit an agent, in other words, mastering the skills that make up the craft of writing fiction or nonfiction, phoning to ask the most basic questions; mastering the query letter, the SASE; giving their credentials for writing the book they want to submit, not knowing what a proposal is, or a synopsis, and so on.

Description of the client from Hell: The terminally insecure.

Description of the dream client: The true professional writers who trust and believe in their agent and themselves.

How did you become an agent? I worked for an agent, then opened up my own shop.

Why did you become an agent? Becoming an agent was a natural follow-up to a long publishing career. The love of good books.

How would you describe what you do for a living? I search for talented writers and manage their careers. This includes a lot of editing.

What can writers do to enhance their chances of getting you as their agent? For fiction writers, mastering the skills that make up the craft of book-length fiction. Informing me of what they have published, where and how long they have studied. Submitting an excellent proposal for nonfiction, mastering the editing process.

What do you think about editors? Because I worked as an editor for many years, I am very empathetic to their workload and plight in the machinery of a publishing house. Many are great talents.

What do you think about publishers? If you look inside a bookstore, you can see how many books they are pumping out a year; and there the books live or die. Without much help from the publishers, people are getting wise and a lot of self-publishing is going on, some of it quite successful. The publishers are pretty much still in the dark ages with the publishing process. Hope they can catch up soon.

Comments: Why do so many people think that writing is a skill they learned by the third grade? Just because you can carry a tune does not mean you can sing like Pavarotti. Just because you can type does not mean you can write a novel. The craft must be studied, practiced, and mastered. And because you have managed to sit still long enough to fill hundreds of pages with words, the world owes you absolutely nothing.

Representative titles: *Self-Promotion for Creative People* by Lee Silber (Crown); *Meridian Therapy* by Gloria Arenson (Simon & Schuster).

LOWENSTEIN ASSOCIATES INC.

121 West 27th Street, Suite 601, New York, NY 10001
212-206-1630   fax: 212-727-0280

Agents: Barbara Lowenstein, Nancy Yost, Eileen Cope

Born: Lowenstein: New York. Yost: California.

Education: Yost: B.A., Comparative Literature, UNLV. Cope: Degrees in Political Science and Journalism.

Career history: Lowenstein: 25 years as head of Lowenstein Associates. Yost: Most recent: Agent, Lowenstein (since 1990); Contracts Department, Random House; Editor, Avon Books. Cope: Was an Editor with the Putnam Berkley Group.

Hobbies/personal interests: Lowenstein: Adventure travel. Yost: Reading, snorkeling/scuba, rollerblading, movies, opera, antiquing.

Areas most interested in agenting: Lowenstein: Fiction: literary and commercial fiction. Nonfiction: business, relationships, narrative travel, adventure travel, current affairs, health and science, biography and autobiography. Yost: Crime fiction, women's fiction, popular science, culture, natural sciences, women's issues, some health, "how-to," nonfiction, light reference, up-market thrillers, and commercial fiction. Cope: Literary and multicultural fiction, comparative religions, psychology, ethics, contemporary social issues, contemporary ethnic and cultural issues, Asian studies, anthropology, sexuality, politics, and the arts (particularly music, theater, and art history).

Areas not interested in agenting: Yost: No Westerns, sci-fi, political nonfiction, no textbooks. Cope: All category fiction, children's, and young adult.

If not agenting, what would you be doing? Lowenstein: Extreme sports. Yost: I'd either be raising puppies between scuba classes or be a personal shopper for shoes.

Best way to initiate contact: Lowenstein: Query letter with SASE. Yost: The old way (sorry!)—by query letter. Cope: Please send a query letter and C.V. with an SASE.

Reading-fee policy: No reading fee.

Number of titles sold last year: 40–50

Client representation by category: Lowenstein: Nonfiction, 75%; Fiction, 25%. Yost: Nonfiction, 25%; Fiction, 75%. Cope: Nonfiction, 60%; Fiction, 40%.

Commission: 15% U.S.; 20% foreign; 15% film.

Rejection rate (all submissions): Lowenstein: 90%. Yost: 95%.

Most common mistakes authors make: Yost: Sending material that (a) I don't represent, (b) is in rough draft and needs extensive revisions.

Description of the client from Hell: Lowenstein: One who doesn't deliver or delivers an unpublishable manuscript. Yost: It's all in the attitude—some symptoms, though, include: over-aggressive phone calls, incomplete communication of desires, opinions leading to resentment and miscommunication, unrealistic expectations, phoning at home on weekends, surly manners.

Description of a dream client: Lowenstein: Delivers a great proposal, is professional, and then delivers a terrific book; cooperates with the publisher and brings something to the process of marketing; is good on television and is willing to work like Hell to get the book sold without driving everyone nuts! Yost: Creative, industrious, knowledgeable about one's area of "expertise"/genre. Oh, you can be currently on the bestseller list, and your brother is head of Ingram, Barnes & Noble, and Borders, while your father is head of a major movie studio and wants to produce all of your books.

How did you become an agent? Yost: As an editor, I was "recruited" by my current employer with the promise of being able to play in everyone's backyard instead of just one.

Why did you become an agent? Lowenstein: Love books. Yost: I love books, and I like to help authors find the right "fit" for a good career. Also, I love the challenge of always getting better and knowing there's always more to learn—about the business of publishing and life in general.

What can writers do to enhance their chances of getting you as an agent? Yost: Writing marketable books—that is, know your genre; and any referrals by published writers/editors/industry professionals are useful, too.

How would you describe what you actually do for a living? Yost: Part salesperson, part editor, part lawyer, part therapist, part pit-bull, part cheerleader.

What do you think about editors? Yost: Hardworking (overworked!) and, mostly, very dedicated to books.

What do you think about publishers? Yost: That answer depends on the house.

Comments: Yost: Not enough room in your book for my rants!!

Representative titles: *Moonlight on the Avenue of Faith* by Gina Nahai; *10 Great Choices That Empower Black Women's Lives* by Grace Cornish; *The Reed Reader* by Ishmael Reed; *Do or Die* by Grace Edwards; *This Is How Love Works* by Steven Carter; *Searching for Intruders: Interconnected Stories* by Stephen Raleigh Byler; *Mosquito War* by V. A. McAllister (TOR); *A Whole World of Trouble* by Helen Chappell (Simon & Schuster); *A Finer End* by Deborah Crombie (Bantam); *The Lost Cases of Arthur Conan Doyle* by Womack Hines (Berkley); *Writ of Execution* by Perri O'Shaughnessy (Delacorte/Dell); *Awakening the Buddha Within* by Lama Surya Das; *The Red Moon* by Kuwana Haulsey (Villard); *Dalai Lama, My Son: A Mother's Story* by Diki Tsering; *To Repel Ghosts* by Kevin Young; *American Character: The Curious History of Charles Fletcher Lummis and the Rediscovery of the Southwest* by Mark Thompson (Arcade); *Emotional Alchemy: How the Mind Can Heal the Heart* by Tara Bennett-Goleman (Crown); *The Baby Whisperer: How to Calm, Connect & Communicate with Your Baby* by Tracy Hogg and Melinda Blau.

LUKEMAN LITERARY MANAGEMENT LTD.

249 West 34th Street, New York, NY 10001
www.Lukeman.com

Agents: Noah Lukeman, Amye Dyer

Education: Lukeman: B.A., Brandeis; High Honors, English and Creative Writing, cum laude. Dyer: B.A. in English, Texas Christian University, M.A. in Creative Writing, Emerson University.

Career history: Lukeman: worked in editorial at William Morrow, Farrar Straus & Giroux, and Delphinium Books prior to becoming an agent. Dyer: seven years' editorial experience at Warner Books and HarperCollins; have worked with numerous bestselling authors.

Areas most interested in agenting: Lukeman: Open to many categories. Dyer: Open to many categories, but most interested in parenting, gardening, design, yoga, spirituality, and women's fiction.

L

M

Areas not interested in agenting: Poetry, children's books, juvenile or young adult; genre romance, science fiction, Western, or mystery.

Best way to initiate contact: Preferably, a one-page query letter by e-mail (Queries@Lukeman.com), NO attachments. Or, regular mail query letter with SASE.

Reading-fee policy: No reading fee.

Client representation by category: Nonfiction, 50%; Fiction, 50%.

Commission: 15%.

Number of titles sold last year: 40.

Rejection rate (all submissions): 99%.

Description of the client from Hell: Pushy, impatient, controlling.

Why did you become an agent? To help writers.

Comments: I suggest you visit the Web site (www.Lukeman.com) to find out more about the types of books we represent and especially to read our preferences about how to query. I also suggest you look at my book *The First Pages* if you want to know our thoughts about writing. You can read a sample chapter on our Web site (www .Lukeman.com).

Representative titles: *30 Days to a More Spiritual Life* by Shana Aborn (Doubleday); *Art Deco New York* by David Garrard Lowe (Watson Guptill, essays); *Cold* by John Smolens (Harmony Books, novel); *How to Teach Your Dog to Talk* by Captain Haggerty (Simon & Schuster/Fireside); *Inside Riker's: The First Look Inside the World's Largest Penal Colony* by Jennifer Wynn (St. Martin's Press); *Muhammad Ali's Greatest Fight* by Howard Bingham and Max Wallace (M. Evans & Co.); *Teaching Creative Writing* by Carol Bly (Anchor Vintage, illustrated); *The First Five Pages: A Writer's Guide to Staying Out of the Rejection Pile* by Noah Lukeman (Simon & Schuster/Fireside); *Wake of the Perdido Star* by Gene Hackman and Daniel Lenihan (Newmarket Press, story collection).

DONALD MAASS LITERARY AGENCY

160 West 95th Street, Suite 1B, New York, NY 10025
212-866-8200   fax: 212-866-8181

Agents: Donald Maass, Jennifer Jackson, Michelle Brummer

Born: Maass: 1953; Columbus, Georgia; Jackson: 1971; Cambridge, New York. Brummer: 1972; Zama, Japan.

Education: Maass: B.A., St. Lawrence University, 1975; Jackson: B.A., St. Lawrence University, 1993. Brummer: B.A., University of Georgia, 1995.

Career history: Maass: 1977–1978, Editor, Dell Publishing; 1979, Agent, Scott Meredith Literary Agency, Inc.; 1980, founded Donald Maass Literary Agency. Jackson: 1993–present, Donald Maass Literary Agency. Brummer: 1995–1996, Assistant Store Manager, B. Dalton Super Store, and Assistant Publicist. L. Cade; 1996–1997, Editorial Assistant; 1997–1998, Assistant Agent; 1998–1999, Assistant Agent and Rights Associate.

Hobbies/personal interests: Maass: Reading, theater, sailing, squash, antiques, stock market. Jackson: cooking, cross-stitch, books, writing, Web-page design, RPGs. Brummer: Books, film, travel, photography, and creating mosaics.

M

Areas most interested in agenting: Maass: Fiction specialist. Concentration in science fiction, fantasy, mystery, suspense, horror, frontier, mainstream, and literary. Jackson: Fiction specialist in all genres, especially romance, women's fiction, mystery, suspense, thrillers, science fiction, and fantasy. Brummer: Fiction: literary, mainstream, science fiction, fantasy, horror, and historical romances.

Areas not interested in agenting: Maass: Pop psychology, how-to, true crime, humor/novelty, juvenile. Jackson: Nonfiction, poetry, and children's books.

If not agenting, what would you be doing? Maass: Oh, Lord, it's too late to think about that now. Brummer: In a different world, I would own an independent bookstore.

Best way to initiate contact: Send a concise, one-page query letter (with SASE) that includes a description of the book and any prior book or short story credits.

Reading-fee policy: No reading fee.

Client representation by category: Fiction, 100%. Jackson: Nonfiction, 1%; Fiction, 99%.

Commission: 15% domestic; 20% foreign.

Number of titles sold last year: Maass: 75. Jackson: 30.

Rejection rate (all submissions): 99%.

Most common mistakes authors make: Long summaries. You need only three things to hook me on your story: setting, protagonist, problem. Brevity is also good in your bio and career plans.

Description of a dream client: Patient, passionate, dedicated to craft, writes for the joy of it, works well with others, enjoys the publishing game.

Why did you become an agent? Maass: I love books, and I believe that fiction matters. Brummer: Of course, I love books, so discovering new authors is as exciting as it is rewarding. It is wonderful to be part of the process of bringing books to print. Jackson: It grew very naturally out of my love for books and storytelling. I've never looked back.

Comments: Maass: I currently serve on the Board of Directors of the AAR. Interested writers may want to read my book *The Career Novelist* published in 1996 by Heinemann. Brummer: While writing is a creative process, publishing is a business. If you view it as such, your professional relationships with others in publishing (e.g., editors, agents, publicists) will be more fruitful.

Representative titles: *The Inconstant Moon* by Pierce Askegren (Penguin/Putnam, Albe Shiloh, Inc.); *The Most Suitable Duchess* by Patricia Bray (Kensington); *The Tutankhamun Prophecies* by Maurice Cotterell (Inner Traditions); *SugarPlum Surprise* by Donna Girmarc (Penguin Putnam/ Berkley); *Angel of Destruction* by Susan Matthews (Penguin Putnam/ROC); *The Highwayman* by Anne Kelleher (Penguin Putnam/Berkley); *Technogenesis* by Syne Mitchell (Penguin Putnam/ROC); *His Gentling Touch* by Patricia Rosemoor (Harlequin Intrigue); *The Blue Stocking* by Melynda Skinner (Kensington); *Nailed* by Lucy Taylor (Penguin Putnam/Onyx).

CAROL MANN AGENCY

55 Fifth Avenue, New York, NY 10003
212-206-5635 Mann; 212-206-5636 Fitzgerald; 212-206-5637 Esersky.

M

Agents: Carol Mann, Gareth Esersky, Jim Fitzgerald

Born: Mann: July 23, 1949; Cambridge, Massachusetts. Esersky: June 3, 1951; Hanover, New Hampshire. Fitzgerald: El Paso, Texas.

Education: Mann: University High, Chicago; Smith College. Esersky: B.A., Goucher College; M.A. (and Ph.D. studies), Tufts University. Fitzgerald: Jesuit High School, El Paso; Regis College, Denver; University of Colorado, Boulder.

Career history: Mann: Teacher, the Brearley School; educational marketing, Avon Books. Esersky: Editor (Dell, Putnam Berkley, Simon & Schuster), Author (*Please Read This for Me* [Morrow]; *List Yourself for Pregnancy; List Yourself for Parenting* [Andrews McMeel]); and Book Packager. Fitzgerald: Teacher (Indian High School, Santa Fe); Editor (*New York Times,* Doubleday, St. Martin's Press); Author (four books, ranging from *The Ronald Reagan Paperdoll Book* to *The Joys of Smoking*); Book Packager/Designer; Agent.

Hobbies/personal interests: Mann: Tennis, film, social history. Fitzgerald: Member of the National Railroad Historical Society; model railroading; crossword puzzles; photo slide shows; collages (manual and electronic); poetry (both read and written); singer Hazel Dickens, Metallica, and Spanish Prayer in Colonial America. Esersky: Yoga; creative nonfiction; film and theater; family life.

Areas most interested in agenting: Mann: Fiction: Authors Paul Auster, Marita Golden. Nonfiction: history, psychology, health and fitness, alternative medicine, sociology, anthropology, political science, American social history, popular culture, biography, memoir, true crime. Esersky: Parenting, popular psychology, inspiration/religion, narrative nonfiction, self-discovery, Judaica, health, nutrition, popular culture. Fitzgerald: Fiction: First-time authors, such as Douglas Coupland and Rachel Resnick; Spanish authors, such as Ray Loriga and Alberto Fueguet. Nonfiction: Music, biography, socio-pop-culture; alternative travel books; anthropology; memoir; Buddhism and enlightened thought; and last but not least, humor (HA-HA).

Areas not interested in agenting: Mann: Any genre fiction (i.e., romance, historicals, mysteries, etc.), children's books, and/or illustrated books. Esersky: Politics and history, fiction, children's books, illustrated books. Fitzgerald: Health; gardening; mysteries, how-to, self-help, cookbooks.

If not agenting, what would you be doing? Esersky: Be an editor, do research, or write. Fitzgerald: Working in conjunction with Jesuits or raising money for a Kurt Cobain Memorial in Rio de Janeiro.

Best way to initiate contact: With a query letter and SASE. No phone or fax queries. No unsolicited manuscripts (query first). Esersky: Query letter with description of proposed work and author information; SASE. No unsolicited manuscripts; query first. Fitzgerald: With a query letter and SASE. No phone, fax, or e-mail queries. No unsolicited manuscripts. (Query letters first.)

Reading-fee policy: No reading fee.

Client representation by category: Mann: Nonfiction, 85%, Fiction, 15%. Esersky: Nonfiction, 80%, Fiction, 20%. Fitzgerald: Nonfiction, 60%; Fiction, 30%; other, 10%.

Commission: 15%.

Number of titles sold last year: Fitzgerald: 15.

Rejection rate (all submissions): Fitzgerald: 98%.

M

Description of the client from Hell: Fitzgerald: A client who fails to communicate all the information that he or she may know. The biggest example is if a particular property has been shopped before and to whom.

Description of a dream client: Mann: Nonfiction: Someone who has extensive experience and credentials in his or her field and is willing to self-promote. Fiction: Stronger writers who have previously had their work published by a (big or small) trade house and/or in a serious literary journal, *Granta, Paris Review, Story,* and so forth. Esersky: Nonfiction: Someone with strong credentials and experience who is a willing self-promoter. An articulate, positive, interested individual who is willing to do the work it takes to get successfully published. Fitzgerald: Someone who is honest, trusts in you, communicates, delivers when expected, doesn't expect a million dollars, doesn't complain, is realistic, reads other books in his/her genre, and looks ahead.

Why did you become an agent? Fitzgerald: Having been an editor within a house for over two decades, I saw the book publishing business going the way of the television and movie businesses. Talent was being bought and not employed. Editors were no longer expected to be championed for ideas, they were not lauded for excellent line work or editorial skills but for their financial acumen instead. Their business smarts and savvy were valued more by the house. It was time to get out and return to do what I did best and that is preparing the idea and letting others market and sell it.

What can writers do to enhance their chances of getting you as an agent? Esersky: Generate good, thoughtful, persuasive proposals; know your market and do research about the publishing industry (a little knowledge can go a long way).

Comments: Mann: If you want to write professionally (i.e., for a living), know your market, learn about the process, and be willing to self-promote as you would in any job. Fitzgerald: In five years the traditional publishing business will be half of what it is now. The Internet and the electronic by-products thereon are the new information and enjoyment sources that people are not only gravitating toward but enjoying more. Ask yourself, what do you enjoy more? A good movie or a good book? It is important for publishers to continue to change and remain ahead of the curve. Yes, there will be books, but will they only be instructional manuals for the DVDs that are pocketed in the back? Will the virtual reality experience overcome all the others? Will we even recognize the language that we are now using? @ used to be seen only on ledger sheets designating the exact cost of something. What does it now represent? The electric language world is now here. Notice how the syntax of what you write by hand is completely different from when you use a keyboard. The challenge for everyone involved in this game is to stay creative and ahead of the accountants.

Representative titles: *Bringing Heaven Down to Earth* by Rabbi Tzvi Freeman (Adams Media); *Easy to Love, Difficult to Discipline* by Dr. Becky Bailey (Morrow); *Just Plain Folks* by Lorrain Johnson and Sue Coleman; *Meditation Made Easy* by Lorin Roche (HarperSanFrancisco); *Meditation Secrets for Women* (HarperSanFrancisco); *Monica's Untold Story* by Anonymous; *Radical Healing* by Dr. Rudolph Ballantine (Harmony); *Stop Cancer Before It Starts* by the American Institute for Cancer Research (St. Martin's Press); *The Fire of Discontent* by Jeffrey Jones (Hazeldon); *Timbuktu* by Paul Auster

(Holt). Mann: *The Unexpected Legacy of Divorce* by Dr. Judith Wallerstein (Hyperion); *E=MC²* by David Bodanis (Walker); *The Last Days: A Son's Story of Sin and Segregation at the Dawn of the New South* by Charles Marsh (Basic); *The Protein Power Lifeplan* by Drs. Mike and Mary Dan Eades (Warner); *The Holocaust Kid* by Sonia Pilcer (Persea); *Escape Your Shape* by Edward Jackowski, Ph.D. (Pocket Books); *Peaceful Parents, Peaceful Kids* by Naomi Drew (Kensington). Fitzgerald: *Hell's Angel* by Sonny Barger (William Morrow); *Digital Hustlers* by Casey Kait and Stephen Weiss (Regan/Harper Collins); *Songs from the Heart* by Jonathan Baird (St. Martin's).

MANUS & ASSOCIATES LITERARY AGENCY, INC.

375 Forest Avenue, Palo Alto, CA 94301
650-470-5151   fax: 650-470-5159
www.ManusLit.com   e-mail: ManusLit@ManusLit.com

Agents: Janet Wilkens Manus, Jillian W. Manus, Jandy Nelson, Stephanie Lee, and Laura Bradford.

Born: Janet Wilkens Manus: Hartford, Connecticut. Jillian Manus: New York City, April 26—That's all you get. Nelson: November 25, 1965; New York. Lee: August 6, Palo Alto, California; Bradford: February 6, San Francisco, California.

Education: Janet Wilkens Manus: Bachelor's and Master's degrees. Jillian Manus: NYU Film School and life. Nelson: B.A., Cornell University; M.F.A., Brown University. Lee: B.A. in Literature, Stanford University. Bradford: B.A. in Literature, UC San Diego.

Career history: Janet Wilkens Manus: Formerly, Foreign Rights Agent for British and foreign publishers; East Coast Rep for the Guinness Book of World Records. Jillian Manus: TV agent at ICM, Director of Development at Warner Bros. & Universal Studios, VP of Production for Dino Delaurentis, VP of Media Acquisitions at Trender AG in Zurich, Associate Publisher of two national magazines dealing in entertainment and technology sections. Nelson: Teacher (creative writing, drama); Theater Artist; Casting Director (film, TV, theater). Lee: I worked in this office during college and never left. Bradford: Bookstore Manager, Career Counselor, Creative Magazine Editor.

Hobbies/personal interests: Janet Wilkens Manus: Travel, arts, football, interrelating with three adult daughters, two grandsons, and husband. Jillian Manus: Boxing, Tae Kwon Do, ballet, gymnastics, critiquing, movies, water skiing; personal interests: all sports, political efforts, child rearing, and children's health and welfare. Nelson: Books, film, theater, hiking, traveling, festivity, poetry. Lee: Movies, books, music, pop culture, sculpture, kitsch, camping. Bradford: Travel, writing, books, skiing, swimming, football games, adopting causes, caffeine, competition. I once jumped out of an airplane.

Areas most interested in agenting: Janet Wilkens Manus: True crime with TV/film potential; issue-based true crime; parenting; food books (cookbooks and food memoirs); unique mysteries. Jillian Manus: Women's commercial literary fiction, fiction that I can successfully sell into the movie/TV marketplace, health and nutrition, sports, prescriptive self-help and self-esteem, biographies/memoirs, dramatic narrative fiction, politics,

M

parenting, high-concept suspense/thrillers, child rearing. Nelson: Literary fiction, multicultural fiction, memoirs, thrillers, commercial fiction, women's fiction; narrative nonfiction; women's issues; intelligent, prescriptive self-help; health; pop culture. Lee: Commercial literary fiction, dark/quirky fiction, prescriptive self-help memoirs, narrative nonfiction, Gen X/Gen Y issues, young voices. Bradford: Commercial fiction, mysteries, sexy thrillers, historical contemporary, category romance, memoirs, prescriptive self-help, health issues.

Areas not interested in agenting: Janet Wilkens Manus: Romance, science fiction, poetry, espionage, textbooks, computer books, Westerns, magazine articles. Jillian Manus: Romantic novels, horror, sci-fi/fantasy, children's, Westerns, textbooks, cookbooks, craft books, travel, poetry, magazine queries and articles, computers, technology. Nelson: Romance, fantasy, sci-fi, Westerns, horror, poetry, children's, cookbooks, craft books, screenplays. Lee: Romance, fantasy, science fiction, Westerns, horror, children's, poetry, screenplays, mystery, magazine articles, gift books, cookbooks. Bradford: Screenplays, poetry, magazine articles, gift books, fantasy, science fiction, horror, children's, cookbooks.

If not agenting, what would you be doing? Janet Wilkens Manus: Secret service agent, educator. Jillian Manus: I would love to be a teacher, an honest politician, a child psychologist, or an Olympic gymnast. Nelson: Teaching, climbing Mt. Everest, being a rock star! Lee: Writing, editing, filmmaking, or launching a new magazine. Bradford: I don't know, can I be James Bond?

Best way to initiate contact: Fiction: Send a compelling pitch letter with the first 30 pages and an SASE. Nonfiction: Send a compelling pitch letter and bio, and an SASE. Please do not query call.

Reading-fee policy: No reading fee.

Client representation by category: Janet Wilkens Manus: Nonfiction, 70%; Fiction, 30%. Lee: Nonfiction, 40%; Fiction, 60%; Bradford: Nonfiction, 25%; Fiction, 75%. Jillian Manus: Nonfiction, 60%; Fiction, 40%. Nelson: Nonfiction, 50%; Fiction, 50%.

Commission: 15% for domestic publication and worldwide motion pictures and TV; 25% for foreign publication, only if co-agented.

Number of titles sold last year: A lot!

Rejection rate (all submissions): 95%.

Most common mistakes authors make: Janet Wilkens Manus: Calling instead of writing with their bio and proposal (nonfiction) or three chapters (fiction). Jillian Manus: They call instead of introducing themselves and their projects in queries. Nelson: They call instead of querying.

Description of a dream client: Janet Wilkens Manus: A talented writer who is a team player. Jillian Manus: A great writer who works well in a team effort. Nelson: An awesome and disciplined writer with a delightful disposition. Lee: An enthusiastic and well-rounded writer who plays well with others. Bradford: Communicative, productive, ambitious, filled with enthusiasm and originality.

How did you become an agent? Janet Wilkens Manus: My husband (a publishing lawyer) talked me into it. Jillian Manus: My mother talked me into it! Nelson: I badgered Jillian Manus. Lee: I badgered Jandy Nelson. Bradford: I badgered Stephanie Lee.

M

Why did you become an agent? Janet Wilkens Manus: I love books and think it is a wonderful calling. Jillian Manus: Because I love working with writers, as I truly respect their dedication and craft. Nelson: To work with writers and to help bring writing into the world that will move, enrich, inspire, and delight the reading public. Lee: Because books are magical and working with writers is equally so. Bradford: I started as a writer. Actually, I had just begun tiptoeing my way through the publishing world, trying to find a place to plant myself, when I met an agent at a conference. She told me what it was that agents did and whammo! I was hooked. Nothing else would feel this right.

What can writers do to enhance their chances of getting you as an agent? Fiction: We rely on the quality of the writing. Nonfiction: It is helpful for a nonfiction writer to have a platform and additional avenues of distribution, such as lecture circuits, seminars, and so forth.

How would you describe what you actually do for a living? Janet Wilkens Manus: I keep my eyes open, nurture, and enjoy. Jillian Manus: I search, nurture, sell, and celebrate. Nelson: Rejoicing in writers and their words. Lee: Treasure hunting. Bradford: I search for diamonds in the rough.

What do you think about editors? Janet Wilkens Manus: A talented and caring editor means everything. Jillian Manus: I think savvy editors are worth their weight in gold. Nelson: They are the wizards behind the curtains.

What do you think about publishers? Janet Wilkens Manus: I respect them for having a tough time in the present climate of publishing. Jillian Manus: I respect and pity them at the same time. Bradford: Keeping an eye on the bottom line in a subjective and charged creative atmosphere is a formidable job and one I do not envy.

Representative titles: *Catfish and Mandala* by Andrew Pham (Farrar, Straus & Giroux); *Getting It Right: How Working Mothers Successfully Take Up the Challenge of Life, Family, and Career* by Dr. Laraine Zappert (Pocket Books); *The World of Normal Boys* by K. M. Soehnlien (Kensington); *Breast Cancer Beyond Convention: Alternative Therapies for Women with Breast Cancer* ed. by Mary Tagliaferri, Debu Tripathy, and Isaac Cohen (Pocket Books); *Life's an Open Book: Bibliotherapy a Novel Approach to Living* (Riverhead); *The Territory of Men: One Woman's Trespass* by Joelle Fraser (Random House); *Dream of the Walled City* by Lisa Huang Fleischman (Pocket Books); *The One-Minute Millionaire* by Mark Victor Hansen and Robert Allen (Harmony/Three Rivers); *The Last City Room* by Al Martinez (St. Martin's Press); *Matt Makes a Run for the Border* by Texas icon, chef Matt Martinez (Lebhar-Friedman).

MARCH TENTH, INC.

4 Myrtle Street, Haworth, NJ 07641
201-387-6551

Agent: Sandra Choron
  Born: March 10, 1950; New York City.
  Education: B.A., Lehman College, New York.

M

Career history: As an Editor, Publisher, Author, and Book Producer, I have had experience in all aspects of book publishing at both large (Dell) and small (Hawthorn) firms.

Hobbies/personal interests: Popular culture, music, folk art, painting.

Areas most interested in agenting: Popular culture, history, general nonfiction, music, commercial fiction, fine fiction, self-help (those without credentials need not apply), biography, new trends, novelties.

Areas not interested in agenting: Genre fiction, techno-thrillers, politics, personal memoirs of people who never did anything interesting, special interest, picture books, short fiction, poetry.

If not agenting, what would you be doing? Writing.

Best way to initiate contact: Submit a query letter (with SASE).

Reading-fee policy: No reading fee.

Client representation by category: Nonfiction, 95%; Fiction, 5%.

Commission: 15% domestic; 20% foreign or dramatic rights.

Number of titles sold last year: 15.

Rejection rate (all submissions): 90%.

Most common mistakes authors make: They fail to describe the project in a concise way. They fail to state their credentials. I don't like being hyped. Facts and sales ammunition are great, but if there are three exclamation points in your first paragraph, my BS-detector goes crazy!

Description of the client from Hell: Someone who is convinced that "everyone" will buy his book.

Description of a dream client: Tall, dark. . . .

How did you become an agent? It's a long story . . .

Why did you become an agent? As an editor, my interests always exceeded the capabilities of any one publisher. Agenting allows me to work in many different areas.

What can writers do to enhance their chances of getting you as an agent? Know your audience.

How would you describe what you actually do for a living? I make books happen.

What do you think about editors? They come in too many shapes and sizes to generalize.

What do you think about publishers? See above.

Comments: Publishing a book is an incredibly gratifying experience. It can also be unbelievably grueling. Enter at your own risk.

Representative titles:; *Bruce Springsteen Songs* by Bruce Springsteen (Avon); *If: Questions for the Game of Life* (4 volumes) by James Saywell and Evelyn McFarlane (Villard); *Shock Value* by John Waters (Thunder's Mouth/Marlowe); *Strong for Potatoes* by Cynthia Thayer (St. Martin's Press, fiction); *This Business We Shall Overcome* by Dave Marsh (Simon & Schuster).

MARGRET MCBRIDE LITERARY AGENCY

7744 Fay Avenue, Suite 201, La Jolla, CA 92037
858-454-1550   fax: 858-454-2156
www.mcbrideliterary.com

M

Agent: Margret McBride

   Career history: Random House, Ballantine Books, Warner Books.

   Areas most interested in agenting: Mainstream business, fiction, and nonfiction.

   Areas not interested in agenting: Children's books, poetry, genre and category romance, scientific/professional (non-trade) books, textbooks, magazine articles.

   If not agenting, what would you be doing? I would be a Prima Ballerina.

   Best way to initiate contact: Query letter via U.S. mail with an SASE.

   Reading-fee policy: No reading fee.

   Client representation by category: Nonfiction, 75%; Fiction, 25%.

   Commission: 15% domestic; 25% foreign.

   Number of titles sold last year: 25.

   Rejection rate (all submissions): 96%.

   Most common mistakes authors make: Trying to get an appointment before materials have been reviewed. They don't realize that time is precious and we use our time wisely.

   Description of the client from Hell: An author who won't revise when it is needed. Any author not courteous to me and my staff.

   Description of a dream client: One who sends gifts. An author who respects himself/herself and is a professional in every step of the process. One who realizes it is all about the reader, not the author.

   How did you become an agent? An author came to me and asked me to sell his books. I sold 50 over a period of 10 years.

   Why did you become an agent? Couldn't fight destiny.

   What can a writer do to enhance their chances of getting you as an agent? Have a great platform.

   How would you describe what you actually do for a living? I look for something to become enthusiastic about and then I sell it.

   What do you think about editors? I think their names should be on the covers of the books with the authors. Obviously, I think highly of them.

   What do you think about publishers? Publishers vary, from totally brilliant to 10 years behind the times.

   Representative titles: *High Five: The Magic of Working Together* by Ken Blanchard, Sheldon Bowles, Don Carew, and Eunice Parisi-Carew (William Morrow); *Fish! A Remarkable Way to Boost Morale and Improve Results* by Stephen C. Lundin, Harry Paul, and John Christianson (Hyperion); *Thirteen Senses* by Victor Villasenor (Rayo Books); *Loving Your Unborn Child to Health and Happiness: A Psychological and Spiritual Guide to Birthing a Healthy Baby* by Frederick Wirth, Jr., M.D. (Regan Books); *The Art of Shen Ku* by Zeek (Perigee); *Special Circumstances* by Sheldon Siegel (Bantam); *The Wit and Wisdom of Cal Thomas* by Cal Thomas (Barbour Publishing).

McINTOSH AND OTIS, INC.

353 Lexington Avenue, 15th Floor, New York, NY 10022
212-687-7400

M

Agents: Juvenile Department: Tracey Adams; Adult Department: Eugene Winick, Sam Pinkus, Elizabeth Winick.

Career history: McIntosh and Otis, Inc., has been representing authors since the early 1920s and has one of the oldest juvenile departments of any agency.

Areas most interested in agenting: Material that is fresh, original, and special in some way.

Best way to initiate contact: Adult and juvenile fiction or nonfiction, send a query letter and sample chapter (include SASE). For picture books, send the entire manuscript.

Reading-fee policy: No reading fee.

Commission: 15%.

CLAUDIA MENZA LITERARY AGENCY

1170 Broadway Suite 807, New York, NY 10001
212-889-6850

Agent: Claudia Menza

Career history: 1969–1973, Assistant Editor, *Evergreen Review;* 1973–1983, various titles, Managing Editor before leaving, Grove Press; 1983–present, President, Claudia Menza Literary Agency; published writer; member, Academy of American Poets; member, Italian American Writer's Association; member, P.E.N.

Areas most interested in agenting: African-American studies, African-American fiction, avant garde fiction, serious nonfiction, photography books, feature film screenplays and treatments (as well as TV).

Areas not interested in agenting: Science fiction, poetry, plays, mysteries, thrillers.

If not agenting, what would you be doing?: Being a publisher.

Best way to initiate contact: Query letter with SASE. No phone calls.

Reading-fee policy: No reading fee.

Client representation by category: Nonfiction, 50%; Fiction, 50%.

Commission: 15% on all rights represented, except in case of a co-agent's involvement when it's 20%. Co-agents are used for film, dramatic, foreign rights. We do not reduce commissions.

Rejection rate (all submissions): 70%.

Most common mistakes authors make: Sending unrequested samples with query letters. Calling us to solicit interest in their manuscripts. Calling us three times a week to see if we've read it yet, three weeks after sending us a manuscript. Not including an SASE with submission—letters get filed, manuscripts are recycled, no phone calls are made.

Description of the client from Hell: A constant nudge that calls three times a week for updates on a book's submission status.

Description of a dream client: A client who understands the intimacy and collaboration of the author–agent relationship.

Why did you become an agent? I love books. I love writers.

Representative titles: *Dark Eros* (edited by Reginald Martin, St. Martin's Press); *Icons and Dolls* by Jack Mitchell (Amphoto Art); *Naming the New World* by Calvin

M

Baker (St. Martin's Press); *Sam and the Tigers* by Julius Lester (Dial Books for Young Readers); *Toni Morrison Explained: A Reader's Road Map to the Novels* by Ron David (Random House); *The Advocate* by Bill Mesce, Jr., and Steven G. Szilagyi (Bantam Books); *Sweet Swing Blues on the Road* by Wynton Marsalis and Frank Stewart (W. W. Norton and Thunders Mouth Press).

Doris S. Michaels Literary Agency, Inc.

1841 Broadway, Suite 903, New York, NY 10023
212-265-9474   fax: 212-265-9480
www.dsmagency.com

Agent: Doris S. Michaels; Faye Bender, Associate Agent
  Born: Michaels: May 1955; Lodi, California.
  Education: B.A., English and German Literature, University of California at Santa Cruz; M.A.T., German and English, University of California at Berkeley; Certificate in Computer Technology, Columbia University; Certificate in Book and Magazine Publishing, Summer Publishing Institute, New York University. Bender: B.A., Wellesley College.
  Career history: Acquisitions Editor for Prentice Hall, 1982–1984; Technology Consultant and Trainer for PHINET and Prudential-Bache, 1984–1987; International Information Center Manager for Union Bank of Switzerland, based in Zurich, 1987–1992; independent Literary Agent based in NYC, 1994–present. Bender: Associate, Nicholas Ellison, Inc.
  Hobbies/personal interests: Reading, music, especially listening to classical music and playing the violin. Sports, especially mountain biking, skiing, and swimming. Computers. Bender: Hiking, camping, archaeology.
  Areas most interested in agenting: Fiction: commercial fiction, literary fiction, women's fiction, novels with strong screen potential. Adult nonfiction (hardcovers and trade paperbacks): Biographies, business, classical music, sports, women's issues. Multimedia electronic works for computers. Bender: Commercial fiction, literary fiction, women's fiction, serious nonfiction, politics, popular culture, biography.
  Areas not interested in agenting: Science fiction, fantasy, mysteries, thrillers, romances, Westerns, occult and supernatural, horror stories, poetry, textbooks, religion, film scripts, cookbooks, diet books, short stories, articles, humor, professional manuals. Bender: Any genre work, religion, poetry.
  If not agenting, what would you be doing? Touring as a concert violinist. Bender: I'd be working on an archaeological dig in Central America or ensconced in the purgatory that is graduate school.
  Best way to initiate contact: E-mail: mail@dsmagency.com. Please, no calls.
  Reading-fee policy: No reading fee.
  Client representation by category: Nonfiction, 50%; Fiction, 50%.
  Commission: 15%.
  Number of titles sold last year: 30.
  Rejection rate (all submissions): 98%.
  Most common mistakes authors make: They send an unprofessional query letter. Bender: Typos in a query letter, calling to confirm receipt (chances are, we received it).

M

Description of the client from Hell: I only work with clients with whom I can develop a good working relationship. Bender: An author who doesn't appreciate the enormous amount of work that goes into getting a book published.

Description of a dream client: Someone who has talent, understands the publishing process, appreciates the hard work I do, and listens carefully. Bender: Someone who has the talent to develop a fresh idea and the insight to think of me.

How did you become an agent? After attending New York University's Summer Publishing Institute, I began my own agency in 1994.

Why did you become an agent? I enjoy reading good fiction and the process of helping talented writers get published.

How would you describe what you actually do for a living? I seek out talented writers and help them get published. I work closely with them to help them grow and build their careers. My time is spent maintaining the connections that I have with some of the industry's top editors, reading the projects of my clients and projects from potential clients, and giving my best efforts to ensure the production of high-quality work and the most professional image possible for my agency.

What do you think about editors? The best editors are those who respond in a timely manner to submissions. They are willing to negotiate contracts to ensure the best deal possible for all parties concerned. They are passionate about their projects, and they are willing to work closely with both the author and me as a team to help build the author's career.

Representative titles: *E-Writing: 21st Century Tools for Effective Communication* by Dianna Booher (Pocket Books); *Don't Send a Resume and Other Contrarian Rules to Help Land a Great Job* by Jeffrey J. Fox (Hyperion); *Loyalty Marketing for the Internet Age: The Art and Science of Relationship Marketing on the Web* by Kathleen Sindell (Dearborn); *In the River Sweet* by Patricia Henley (Pantheon); *50 Blue Cats for Dad: How People with Synesthesia Color Their Worlds* by Patricia Duffy (W. H. Freeman); *Pink Think: Or How to Become a Woman in Many Uneasy Lessons* by Lynn Peril (Harper Collins).

MOUNTAINVIEW LITERARY ASSOCIATES

P.O. Box 50580, Phoenix, AZ 85076-0580
e-mail: mountainviewliterary@lycos.com

Agent: Olivia Newport
    Born: Bishop, California, in May.
    Education: B.A. in English and Business Management. M.A. in Business Management, minor Liberal Arts.
    Career history: Associate Agent for a wonderful, creative talent agency for more than 10 years.
    Hobbies/personal interests: Traveling, reading, and digging for dinosaur fossils in my backyard.

Areas most interested in agenting: Adult fiction, textbooks and other educational material, and all nonfiction books (including children's).

Areas not interested in agenting: Scripts, children's fiction, poetry, erotic material.

Best way to initiate contact: E-mail queries are wonderful. Your query should include a short synopsis, the intended market, and a brief bio listing your writing credits. If you have no writing credits, do not be afraid to say so. We won't hold it against you.

Client representation by category: Nonfiction, 40%; Fiction, 40%; Textbooks, 20% (We're hoping to increase this number).

Commission: 15% domestic; 20% foreign.

Number of titles sold last year: Cannot list, due to working under another agency.

Rejection rate (all submissions): Can't say, the agency is too new.

What are common mistakes that authors make? Submitting a manuscript (or sample chapters) before it is requested. Sending attachments with e-mail. I never open attachments—I delete the entire message without reading it.

Description of the client from Hell: Hmmm! I've never experienced a "client from Hell." If a client warrants that description, he/she won't be a client very long.

Description of the dream client: A writer who is respectful of my time—and sends me lots of holiday presents.

Why did you become an agent? For the love of good books. We also produce textbooks and educational materials because of the need for quality education in the world.

What can writers do to enhance their chances of getting you as an agent? Get an e-mail address!

How would you describe what it is you do for a living? We sell books that scream to be published. We develop educational material for elementary through university level schools.

Comments: In addition to being a literary agency, we also produce educational material. We are looking for writers interested in developing textbooks and other education projects. Please note: You must be an authority on the subject, with education to back it up. You do not, however, need to have a completed manuscript to work with us. We do not charge fees of any kind. This means no reading, mailing, telephone reimbursement, or photocopying charges. We make our money on commissions only. For this reason, we will not respond if you do not include an e-mail address or proper postage. No metered envelopes—real stamps only, please.

JEAN V. NAGGAR LITERARY AGENCY

216 East 75th Street, 1E, New York, NY 10021
212-794-1082

Agents: Jean V. Naggar, Anne Engel, Frances Kuffel, and Alice Tasman

Born: Kuffel: 1956; Missoula, Montana. Tasman: May 26, 1967; Philadelphia, Pennsylvania.

Education: Naggar: B.A., with honors, London University. Engel: Bachelor of Laws, London University. Kuffel: B.A., English, B.A., Religious Studies, University of Montana;

N

M.F.A., Creative Writing, Cornell University. Tasman: B.A., Brown University, 1989; M.F.A., Sarah Lawrence College, 1994.

Career history: Naggar: Writer, Editor, Translator, Book Reviewer. Engel: 20 years as an Editor in British publishing houses. Kuffel: Way too many years of graduate school and teaching college composition. The year 2000 was my twelfth year at the Agency. Tasman: Jean V. Naggar Literary Agency in sub-rights and agenting my own list from 1995–present.

Hobbies/personal interests: Naggar: Parenting, reading, music, business, travel, cooking. Wide-ranging other interests that do not include sports and politics. Engel: Looking at cities, cooking, and entertaining. Kuffel: History, ballet, and cooking.

Areas most interested in agenting: Naggar: Fiction: strong, well-written mainstream fiction, literary fiction, contemporary, suspense, historical fiction, mysteries. Nonfiction: biography, literary autobiography or memoirs, science for the layperson, psychology, and sophisticated self-help. Engel: Science, biography. Kuffel: History, biography, voice-driven, literary mysteries. I'd love to find a clever historical mystery; women's fiction that's *not* about boyfriends, husbands, having children, or drinking coffee with other women. Tasman: Literary/commercial nongenre fiction, literary thrillers, multicultural nonfiction, celebrity biographies.

Areas not interested in agenting: Naggar: Sports, politics, category fiction, most science fiction, KGB/South American drug-cartel espionage. Engel: Fiction, children's books. Kuffel: Science fiction, coffee-table books, self-help. Tasman: Science fiction, fantasy fiction, romance, self-help.

If not agenting, what would you be doing? Kuffel: Correcting college freshmen essays or being a secretary. On the other hand, maybe I'd be living in Montana and have a dog and be able to read books. Tasman: I would probably, most likely, be handling film rights for a small agency or working in the production office of a film company.

Best way to initiate contact: Naggar: Query letter. Engel: An enthusiastic, balanced letter. Kuffel: Query letter. Tasman: Query letter.

Reading-fee policy: No reading fee.

Client representation by category: Naggar: Nonfiction, 45%; Fiction, 45%; Children's, 10%. Engel: Nonfiction, 100%. Kuffel: Nonfiction, 33%; Fiction, 33%, Children's, 33%. Tasman: Nonfiction, 5%; Fiction, 90%; Children's, 5%.

Commission: 15% domestic; 20% international. Tasman: 15% of advance; 10% of sub-rights sales. Kuffel: 15% domestic; 20% international.

Number of titles sold last year: Naggar: 47. Kuffel: 15. Tasman: This is my first year agenting.

Rejection rate (all submissions): 96%. Tasman: 75%. Kuffel: 99%.

Most common mistakes authors make: Naggar: Not doing any background research on agents before contacting; asking, Do you want to see my work? without describing it; calling every five minutes to check up on things—a sure precursor of the client from Hell! Kuffel: Sending an entire manuscript without invitation. Calling rather than querying. Writing a query letter that explains what a novel means rather than what the plot is. Gimmicky presentations, including little gifts or food with the material, or fussy, ungainly packaging. Tasman: Too many calls before we've agreed to take them on.

Description of the client from Hell: Naggar: An author who has chosen me as an agent but never quite trusts me. Kuffel: There are three personality traits that, singly or in combination, create this specimen: suspicion, paranoia, and ego. Add to that the naiveté of thinking that he or she can expect to make a living from writing, and any agent is facing a really bad phone call. Some of the more common topics of conversation include: threatening financial insolvency if I don't sell his or her book RIGHT NOW; asking, when informed of where a manuscript has been sent, "Is the editor important?"; not trusting that I know what I'm doing when I urge revisions, or don't demand answers when the seasonal or particular editor's timing is wrong, or when I refuse to send out literary novels multiply; responding to offers, "Is that all?"; constantly comparing his/her career against other writer-friends (if there is such a thing), with the unsubtle implication that shortfalls are my fault; offering to write submission letters for me since I obviously "don't get" what I'm trying to sell; asking, "Could I send the manuscript to you in Montana so you can read it on vacation?"; that imperative and chilling statement "Just have your assistant . . ." Tasman: A client who asks to read and/or write his or her submission letter. Weekly and daily calls and/or e-mails. An unpublished author who asks if he or she can quit his or her job. An unemployed client. An unpublished author who is banking on a six-figure advance.

Description of a dream client: Naggar: Talented, appreciative, intelligent, knowledgeable. Kuffel: The dream client is sensitive. He or she thinks about my reasons for doing things, realizes I have 44 other clients who need attention; trusts me. The *real* dream client is riotously funny, well-read, earthy, has seen something of the real world, has a private income and a private life. He or she gives witty, expensive Christmas presents and urges me to take my two weeks of vacation. Tasman: A client who lets you do your job; a relationship based in trust and faith. A client who isn't afraid to move on to the next project. A client who doesn't nag; who is patient and realizes his or her job is temporarily finished—now it's your turn to roll up your sleeves; get to it.

How did you become an agent? Tasman: I was getting my M.F.A. at Sarah Lawrence College. I worked as an intern for the Wendy Well Agency. I was extremely interested in books and film. Wendy strongly suggested I look for a job in sub-rights, which is where I started at this agency. Kuffel: I started as the general assistant in the office and after a while I was given some sub-rights to handle. After three years, I started a small list and continued to be Jean Naggar's assistant. I gradually wore her down and I gradually got better at selling.

Why did you become an agent? Naggar: I love reading and respect writers. I enjoy being an advocate for writers I respect. Kuffel: I couldn't stand the thought of reading eighteenth-century poetry any longer and my parents insisted I had to get a real job. I like books so I answered some ads in the *Times*. I got hired. Tasman: I love books and people. I thought I wanted to be a writer but realized that I am much more effective and fulfilled being part of someone else's creative process.

What can writers do to enhance their chances of getting you as an agent? Tasman: Give me time to thoroughly assess their work! Kuffel: Writers ought to ask themselves from the outset, Who cares? Reality check your subject, style, and audience. Naggar: Present themselves well, have patience to wait out my heavy reading schedule, and make no early outrageous claims for their work.

N

How would you describe what you actually do for a living? Tasman: I represent writers; I am the liaison between a writer and a publisher. I read manuscripts, edit manuscripts, pitch manuscripts to editors, and place them with the appropriate publishing house. Kuffel: "I'm the dirty middle man." "I'm the one who returns your phone calls because I still have a job after the last corporate shuffle." "I'm the one who keeps you from selling your soul and all your rights to the Devil." Naggar: Indulge my reading enthusiasms and then enlist the world to take pleasure with me! Read and negotiate strong contracts. Supervise and set in motion every possible venue to enhance a client's career.

What do you think about editors? Tasman: I am grateful for editors; I think they're important. Kuffel: I like editors, but I don't think they have much power. Acquisitions are made by committee and even editing is often done by committee. They're at the mercy of marketing people who too often dictate acquisitions. And corporate life being what it is, there's no recourse. Sometimes I end up feeling as bad for the editor who's disappointed about not being able to offer on a project as I do for the writer or myself. We, at least, get another shot. Still, editors are what give the publishing conglomerates a human face. They are very smart, very hip, and work harder than lumberjacks.

What do you think about publishers? Tasman: Ditto. Kuffel: I think I answered that.

Comments: Kuffel: Stop whining and get a real job—the world does not owe you a living you can perform in your pajamas! Tasman: How damn difficult it is to find a home for literary fiction and good quality fiction in general!

Representative titles: *Down on Ponce* by Fred Willard (Longstreet); *Easy as One Two Three* by Phillip DePoy (Dell); *Fiddle Fever* by Sharon Doucet (Simon & Schuster Children's Books); *Go West Young F***d-Up Chick* by Rachel Resnick (St. Martin's Press); *I'm Afraid You're Afraid* by Melinda Muse (Hyperion); *Medea* by Neil McMahon (Harper-Collins); *Remember the Alamo* by D. Anne Love (Holiday House); *Last Breath* by Peter Stark (Ballantine); *Princess Naughty and the Voodoo Cadillac* by Fred Willard (Longstreet); *Teaching Maggie* by Lee Reilly (Ruminator Books); *The Puppeteer's Apprentice* by Anne Lowe (Margaret McElderry Books); *A Life in the Trees* by Fred Heafale (Riverhead).

THE CRAIG NELSON COMPANY

115 West Eighteenth Street, Fifth Floor, New York, NY 10011
212-929-3242   fax: 212-929-3667
e-mail: litagnt@aol.com

Agent: Craig Nelson
   Born: February 6, 1955; Manion, Indiana.
   Career history: Twenty years in the book industry, previously Executive Editor and Vice President of Random House, Hyperion, and HarperCollins.
   Hobbies/personal interests: Third World travel, being frightened.
   Areas most interested in agenting: Dramatic nonfiction, storytelling, history, biography, current affairs, psychology and science, literary fiction with an "outsider" perspective, gripping thrillers based on the author's own experiences.

Areas not interested in agenting: Category mystery, romance, sci-fi, fantasy, domestic dramas, and excessively fanciful New Age/spiritual tomes.

If not agenting, what would you be doing? I'd give up all my real estate and pare down to the absolute essentials, and put them in a box. Then I'd wander the globe, just me and my box.

Best way to initiate contact: Query first (e-mail preferred; fax forbidden). If snail mail, include an SASE.

Reading-fee policy: No reading fee.

Client representation by category: Nonfiction, 75%; Fiction, 25%.

Commission: 15% domestic, 20% foreign.

Number of titles sold last year: 15.

Rejection rate (all submissions): I'd guess 1,000 to 1.

Most common mistakes authors make: Most novice writers don't do the research to find out what agents work in their category, not realizing that publishing is a very specialized business. I don't know anything about the mass-market original mysteries, romance, and other category fiction, and I don't know anything about children's literature, cookbooks, or scientific and technical publications, so I can't work in those fields.

Why did you become an agent? As a book company editor I had 15 bestsellers, and every single one of them did great things for their authors, agents, and publishers . . . but not their editor.

What can writers do to enhance their chances of getting you as an agent? In nonfiction, follow the rules of attention-grabbing journalism (well outlined in James Stewart's book *Follow the Story*). In fiction, do something groundbreaking, so that when it's published two years from now, it'll be fresh and original.

How would you describe what you actually do for a living? (1) Convince authors to make their manuscripts salable. (2) Convince publishers to take a chance. (3) Provide a haven in a heartless world. (4) Remember that "life is just a bowl of cherries," . . . and so forth and so on.

A New Author's Literary Agency

2480 Lawn Drive, East Meadow, NY 11554
fax: 516-484-0825

Agent: Nandasiri Jasentuliyana
  Born: November 23, 1938; Sri Lanka.
  Education: LL.B. University of London, U.K.; LL.M. McGill University, Montreal, Canada; visiting lecturer at Princeton, Stanford, and Columbia Universities.
  Career history: Deputy to the Director General, United Nations, Vienna (1994 to date); Director, UN Office for Outer Space Affairs (1988 to date).
  Hobbies: Writing, reading, theater, opera.
  Areas most interested in agenting: Novels, novellas.
  Areas not interested in agenting: Nonfiction.

N

Best way to initiate contact: A complete synopsis by regular mail. The synopsis should clearly identify the protagonist and the antagonist (hero and anti-hero) and also delineate the problem, confrontation, and solution. Please, no cliffhangers. The synopsis should be 2–3 pages long, should summarize the progress of key chapters, and should provide us with a description of all your central characters. The history of the central characters and how it motivates "present-day" behavior should also be detailed.

Reading fee: No reading fee.

Commission: 10% across the board.

Number of titles sold last year: No comment.

Most common mistakes authors make: Bad synopsis.

Description of the client from Hell: Haven't had the pleasure yet.

How did you become an agent? Six months ago, I accepted an invitation to become a member of the board of directors of a publishing firm. Essentially, what this means is that if I like a book, my chances of getting it published are very significant in at least one place.

What can writers do to enhance their chances of getting you as an agent? Have the ability to produce a solid synopsis.

NEW BRAND AGENCY GROUP
A DIVISION OF ALTER-ENTERTAINMENT LLC

370 Jefferson Drive, Suite 204, Deerfield Beach, FL 33442
954-764-3331   fax: 954-725-6461
www.literaryagent.net   e-mail: AgentNB@aol.com

Agents: Eric D. Alterman, Mark D. Ryan, Cricket Pechstein

Born: Alterman: April 4, 1963; New Jersey. Ryan: March 17, 1971; Miami. Pechstein: I'm proud to say that I am a descendent of nineteenth-century Floridians who chose to raise their families in the splendor and independence of isolated Florida in a time when the only folks in the mosquito-ridden state were considered savages, crooks, or crazies. Which is to say, I come from tough stock.

Education: Alterman: Undergraduate, Tufts University; Law School: Washington College of Law, American University. Ryan: Ambassador University, Psychology. Pechstein: University of Florida during an era of Vietnam War protests, sex, drugs, and rock and roll. I've gained my formal writing education through conferences, workshops, and seminars, learning from such writers as Michael Connelly, Daniel Keyes, Peter Matthiessen, Barbara Parker, Anne Perry, Sol Stein, John Updike, and so on.

Career history: Alterman: Attorney, owner-operator of radio broadcasting company, legal and marketing consulting, literary agent. Ryan: Weed-puller, lawn-cutter, actor (Baltimore Orioles commercial—age 10), bag boy, stock clerk, dishwasher, busboy, prep cook, cashier, aircraft parts painter, shipper/receiver, telemarketer, door-to-door salesman, tree-trimmer, logger, greenhouse worker, heavy equipment operator, general construction worker, window installer, chemist/metallurgist, quality control inspector, developmentally delayed residential instructor, behavior specialist, group home manager, residential program director, author, public speaker (positive parenting and child abuse prevention), freelance reader/editor, literary agent. Pechstein: Following 15 years as a toiling business owner, I spun my creativity into business clients (more money than adventure). For a time I even slaved daily as the editor of a national full-color slick magazine. In 1991 I established Possibilities Press to support small publishers with writing, editing, design, and production services.

Hobbies/personal interests: Alterman: Guitar, golf, reading. Ryan: New ideas and new experiences, people-watching, motorcycle racing, outdoor activity (this is starting to sound like a personal ad), movies, reading and writing and talking about writing, having fun at writers' conferences. Pechstein: Yeah, yeah, yeah, reading and writing. What else? To keep me banging on all eight cylinders I hike the forgotten places in Florida; soak up sun, shade, and vegetation; canoe the wild waters; and basically allow my senses to swim in Mother Nature.

Areas most interested in agenting: Fiction and nonfiction with bestseller or high commercial potential. Projects with national and/or international appeal that will sell at least 25,000 copies. Nonfiction: business/management/success/leadership, psychology /self-help, gift/novelty, popular culture. Fiction: adult and young adult thrillers, mysteries, suspense, horror, mainstream, historical.

Areas not interested in agenting: Star-Trek novels, genre romance, hard-core science fiction and fantasy, nonfiction sports, erotica, technical writing, screenplays, poetry, knitting, regional books, short story collections, and personal manifestos. Also, books accompanied by query letters that say "Just Read It" or "Send me 20 dollars and I'll send you the manuscript."

If not agenting, what would you be doing? Ryan: I know this sounds hokey, but I can't imagine myself doing anything else. Pechstein: Oh, I suppose I'd be running Possibilities Press, producing books for small and independent publishers. Alterman: I might be sitting around somewhere spending all day reading published books instead of unpublished books (it wouldn't be as fun).

Best way to initiate contact: For nonfiction please send a cover letter, SASE, and proposal with the following sections: overview, marketing, competition, author biography, sample chapters. For fiction send a cover letter, SASE, 1–2 page synopsis (double-spaced), and the first 50 pages. For both fiction and nonfiction, position your book with a large-scale perspective in regard to theme and content. Compare and contrast your work to similar titles published over the last 10 years. This lets us know you are well-read and likely to be writing original work for an identifiable market. Tell us why you are the best person to write and promote your book. Put yourself and your writing style into the query—it doesn't have to be a stale business letter. If you want to go the extra mile, include blurbs from published authors in your genre, an article about your subject showing its timeliness or popularity, and so on. Another plus is a promo photo or audio/video clips. There are some terrific books out there on preparing queries and proposals. Use them. If a project is well-developed, we're much more likely to be enthusiastic about it. Our response time is always less than two weeks.

Reading-fee policy: No reading fee.

N

Category percentages: Nonfiction, 50%; Children's, 25% (no picture books); Textbooks, 0%.

Commission: 15% domestic; 20% foreign

Number of titles sold last year: Enough that we've stopped counting—see representative titles listed below.

Rejection rate (all submissions): 99%.

Most common mistakes authors make: Follow submission instructions and take your time. Don't forget the SASE. Use 12-point font and double space. And use a decent printer. Remember, good agents are salespeople. They can sense, immediately, if you know what you're talking about—by simply skimming your cover letter (they've reviewed tens of thousands of them). Don't think your work is a masterpiece just because Aunt Gladys says so. Be sure that many other eyes—well-educated, discerning eyes—have reviewed your manuscript before it lands in our office. Preferably other writers (published writers are ideal), and, if you can afford it, a reputable freelance editor.

Description of the client from Hell: Alterman: Doesn't take care in checking his/her manuscript for errors; doesn't include SASE with submissions; expects publishers to respond overnight; forgets my birthday. Ryan: Any best-selling author (with interesting things to say), not with New Brand. Clients who leave messages at three A.M., drunk. Pechstein: Clients who call at 7:30 on a Sunday morning or dump a string of obscenities (the spoiled brat). Agenting is work, but it is supposed to be fun, too.

Description of a dream client: Alterman: Polite bestselling author who remembers my birthday. Ryan: Blond hair . . . blue eyes . . . Okay, okay. Has long-term publication goals and studies the industry before seeking representation. Perceives our relationship as a partnership. Rewards my enthusiasm with trust and patience. Pechstein: Someone who is so enthusiastic about his or her writing that I can't help but be enthusiastic, too. Writers who are willing to join me in investing in the future of their writing with their time and their energy. Those who recognize that everyone has to pitch in and market the book if it's to reach its readers.

How did you become an agent? Ryan: Shortly after I realized that I wasn't going to become a bestselling author in one year or less, I met Eric. A few days later, he asked me to be his partner. Pechstein: Working in publishing for the last 11 years as a writer, editor, book designer, and publisher, I was asked more times than I can count, "Why aren't you an agent? You understand things. You'd be so good." I always had some objection. But Mark Ryan spent the time to hammer on me about it, and my objections vaporized into the wind.

Why did you become an agent? Alterman: At some point in her or his career, every lawyer must ask the question, Is there some other way I might make a living? I love working with new writers who have lots of energy and a drawer full of fresh ideas. Ryan: Eric hates it when I say this, but . . . I originally became an agent so I could get my own books published. Along the way I discovered that agenting is, on many levels, more rewarding than being a published author. There are no guarantees in this business, but every day you are faced with a choice: Take responsibility for your success and learn more about the industry, or leave it to chance. Pechstein: It just seemed like the next logical step.

What can writers do to enhance their chances of getting you as an agent? Imagine us (Mark, Cricket, and Eric), sitting next to each other in front of 200 submissions with the intent of selecting 2 of those projects for representation. Some of those submissions are from authors who have been previously represented by agents; have already published books with major publishing houses; have self-published and sold tens of thousands of copies; have paid professional editors thousands of dollars for editing; have strong promotional platforms (radio, TV, newspaper, magazines, workshops and seminars, extensive client mailing lists); have M.F.A. degrees; have a background in publishing (previously agents, editors, etc.). Take your competition seriously. Follow your fifth-grade teacher's advice and do your homework—the same way that we do. Spend time in places where you will grow—bookstores, workshops, critique groups, reading groups, conferences, and so on. Network. Read every book on craft and marketing you can find. Study your market and target your submissions. Remember that neatness and spelling *do* count. Finally, keep writing. Regularly. Distinctly. Then find an agent who believes in you—with the knowledge, connections, and energy to make things happen.

How would you describe what you actually do for a living? Ryan: Agents sell books, and the best agents use every tactic (within reason, conscience, and the law) to get it done. Agents view the author/agent relationship as a partnership; offer strong contacts with publishers; help authors discover and develop their niches; help massage proposals and books into clean, tight, marketable copy; add credibility to their authors' work; are aware of the tastes and eccentricities of individual editors and publishers; give authors new book ideas; are energetic and persistent; return calls and correspondence promptly; sort out unexpected catastrophes; help develop speaking platforms and offer marketing support; are always learning, stretching, growing; aren't afraid to fight for their authors. Pechstein: A literary agent is, among other things, an author's accomplice, advocate, ally, anchor, champion, coach, commando, compass, conductor, confessor, confidante, consultant, counsel, cover, cowboy, critic defender, dragon-slayer, drummer, editor, envoy, evangelist, expert, financial adviser, fire-eater, flesh peddler, fortune teller, go-between, guardian angel, hand-holder, handler, harmonizer, helper, henchman, interpreter, jungle guide, keeper, knight, liaison, lobbyist, magician, mediator, medicine man, musketeer, negotiator, ombudsman, partisan, partner, pearl-diver, pilot, prophet, promoter, protector, psychic, referee, representative, scout, scrapper, shaman, sharpshooter, shoulder to cry on, shrink, sounding board, steward, Superman or Superwoman, surrogate, swordsman, sympathizer, tower of strength, umpire, warrior, witch doctor, and wizard.

What do you think about editors? Ryan: Editors are overworked and underpaid. They receive a tremendous volume of submissions, and often become jaded as a result. They want to be recognized for the projects they have developed. And they want the next bestseller as bad as you and I do. Pechstein: Having been one, I have walked a mile in their shoes. I understand the investment they make in each book and the belief they must have in a book in order to take it on.

What do you think about publishers? Ryan: Publishers pay my bills. I like them a lot. Pechstein: Again, having walked at least a short distance in their shoes, I understand the investment they make in each book and the belief they must have in a book in order to take it on.

Comments:. Choose your agent carefully. Editors interview new agents to determine whether they are worth developing a long-term relationship with. Editors sense, quickly, which agents are most likely to succeed, the same way good agents quickly sense which authors are most likely to succeed. Three things make an editor want to work with an agent: Trust—Editors want to do business with agents who are open, down to earth, sincere, and reliable. Passion—The best agents work only/mostly with projects they are very passionate about (partly because they couldn't live with themselves if they didn't, and partly because it lets them pitch each project with confidence and excitement). Enthusiasm is contagious. Competence—Most important, editors want to work with agents who are familiar with protocol; can spot bestselling or highly commercial properties; are able to help authors discover and develop their niches; and deliver clean, tight projects well-suited to their lists.

Representative titles: *24/7 and 99-Einstein* by Jim Brown (Ballantine); *The Marriage Plan: How to Marry Your Soul Mate in a Year or Less* by Aggie Jordan, Ph.D. (Broadway/Bantam); *The Finnegan Zwake Mystery Series* by Michael Dahl (Pocket/Scholastic); *The Young Shakespeare Mystery Series* (Hyperion); *The Misfits Inc. Mystery Series* by Mark Delaney (Peachtree); *Money-Tree Marketing* by Pat and Jennifer Bishop (AMACOM); *Eat or Be Eaten* by Phil Porter (Prentice-Hall); *Creative Selling* by Dave Donelson (Entrepreneur Books); *101 Weird Ideas to Promote Top Performance* by John Putzier (AMACOM); *Father to Son* by Harry Harrison (Workman); *The Walrus Was Paul: The Great Beatle Death Clues of 1969* by Gary Patterson (Simon & Schuster); *The Dog's Drugstore* by Dr. Richard Redding and Myrna Weibel, D.V.M. (St. Martin's); *The Women's Guide to Legal Issues* by Nancy Jones (Renaissance); *The Scooter Spy Mystery Series* by Michael Dahl (Pocket).

NEW ENGLAND PUBLISHING ASSOCIATES, INC.

P.O. Box 5, Chester, CT 06412
860-345-7323   fax: 860-345-3660
www.nepa.com   e-mail: nepa@nepa.com

Agents: Elizabeth Frost-Knappman, Edward W. Knappman

Born: EFK: October 1, 1943. EWK: November 17, 1943.

Education: EFK: B.A., Anthropology, George Washington University (1965); graduate work at University of Wisconsin and New York University. EWK: B.A., History, George Washington University (1965); M.S., Journalism, Columbia University (1966).

Career history: EFK: Senior Editor, William Morrow; Senior Editor, Doubleday; Editor, William Collins & Sons (London); Associate Editor, Natural History Press. Author of *Courtroom Drama: Women's Suffrage in America, Women's Rights on Trial, World Almanac of Presidential Quotations, ABC-CLIO History of Women's Progress in America,* and *The Quotable Lawyer.* EWK: Publisher of Facts on File; Executive Vice President of Facts on File. Editor of *Great World Trials, Great American Trials, American Jobs Abroad* (with V. Harlow), and *Sex, Sin, and Mayhem.*

Hobbies/personal interests: EFK: Swimming, knitting, gardening, and tennis. EWK: Reading in the areas of history and politics and keeping up with computer developments.

Areas most interested in agenting: EFK: Women's subjects, science, biographies, current events, literature. EWK: Reference, history, business, information, self-help, biographies, narrative nonfiction.

Areas not interested in agenting: Personal memoirs, fiction, children's books, screenplays.

If not agenting, what would you be doing? EFK: Traveling. EWK: Traveling.

Best way to initiate contact: Send a well-thought-out proposal with a sample chapter and resume. Check our submission guidelines page at www.nepa.com and follow them.

Reading-fee policy: No reading fee.

Client representation by category: Nonfiction, 90%.

Commission: 15%, unless co-agents must be employed for dramatic or foreign rights.

Number of titles sold last year: 65.

Rejection rate (all submissions): 95%.

Most common mistakes authors make: It's important to put in the time and effort to perfect a proposal. The key is to carefully research your competition, not just in the bookstores, but in the libraries, union catalog, and *Books in Print.*

Most common mistakes authors make: Make substitutions in materials; call too soon for a decision; treat the competition too cavalierly.

Description of the client from Hell: Phone addicts and prospective clients who e-mail us their manuscripts without an okay.

Description of a dream client: Professional, flexible about revisions, patient, friendly.

How did you become an agent? In 1982 EFK found it easier to be a parent while working from home, starting a new business.

Why did you become an agent? After many years as an editor (EFK) and publisher (EWK), we wanted to start our own business and move midway between Boston and New York City. Our combined literary agency, book-producing business, and consulting operations allow us to do this. What started as a small business in 1983 has grown to a good-sized one, with five employees to serve clients.

What can writers do to enhance their chances of getting you as an agent? Follow our guidelines for preparing proposals; request a sample proposal if you need a model; make certain your qualifications match the book you wish to write; make your sample chapters the best literary quality you can.

How would you describe what you actually do for a living? Read, edit, query editors, submit your work to publishers, negotiate the best possible sale and contracts, make subsidiary rights sales (foreign, dramatic), do all bookkeeping for the life of your book, problem solve day in, day out.

What do you think about editors? Editors are well-read, hardworking, underpaid people who are under constant pressure to turn a profit for the conglomerates that employ them.

What do you think about publishers? Working with most publishers today is like dealing with the Department of Agriculture. No one has sufficient power, efficiency is not at a premium, and decisions are arbitrary. So authors would be wise not to try to go it alone.

Comments: The world of publishing has changed so radically in the last 30 years that the business is difficult for authors, agents, and editors alike. Presses want the same genre or brand-name books. Advances are less competitive than ever before. Fortunately, each year start-ups and new imprints emerge to breathe new life into our industry, taking more chances on a first book or a writer without a "platform." Still, our advice to authors is, Don't give up your day job.

Representative titles: *Book of Management Wisdom* (Wiley); *Cigars, Whiskey, & Winning* (Prentice Hall); *Dust* (University of California Press); *Eudora Welty: A Writer's Life* (Doubleday); *How to Live Well Off Your Investments* (Adams); *Ice Blink: The Tragic Fate of Sir John Franklin's Lost Polar Expedition; Penguin Dictionary of American English Usage* (Penguin); *Speaking of Love* (Random House); *Susan Sontag: The Making of an Icon* (Norton); *The ASPCA Complete Pet Care Manual* (Penguin); *The Learning Disabilities Trap* (Contemporary Books); *The Prettiest Feather* (Bantam); *The Puzzle Club Mysteries* (Concordia); *Why I Believe in God: And Other Reflections by Children* (Prima); *William Faulkner: A to Z* (Facts On File); *The Murder Channel* (John Wiley & Sons); *How to Plan an Elegant Wedding in Six Months or Less* (Prima); *Every Heart Attack Is Preventable* (Lifeline-Regnery); *The Feel Good Curriculum* (Perseus); *The Urban Tree Book* (Crown).

BETSY NOLAN LITERARY AGENCY

3426 Broderick Street, San Francisco, CA 94123
415-922-7794   fax: 415-922-7795

Agent: Betsy Nolan
   Areas not interested in agenting: Romance, juvenile, poetry, science fiction.
   Best way to initiate contact: Letter with SASE.
   Client representation by category: Nonfiction, 50%; Fiction, 50%.
   Commission: 15%.

NORTHRUP LITERARY & ENTERTAINMENT AGENCY

4505 New Dawn Court, Lutz, FL 33549
813-926-2431 faxes by appointment only, please.
www.MarcysAgency.homestead.com/Northrup.html
e-mail: AntiquarianMHN@aol.com

Send all screenplays to:
PET-A-BEE Global Films, Inc.
P.O. Box 77711
Washington, DC 20013-7711
301-218-4374
K. J. Vigue II   e-mail: PETABEE310866@aol.com

Agent: Marcy H. Northrup. Sissy Myers (e-mail: LitEntAgent@verizonmail.com)
   Born: October 7, 1964, born in Manhattan, resided in Greenpoint, Brooklyn, New York, moved to Staten Island, then California before settling in Florida during the late

'70s. Myers: September 8, 1966, born in Brooksville, Florida. I traveled the United States and eventually settled in Florida during the mid '70s.

Career history: Educator; Vice President, and Founder of a private school for children, preschool through eighth grade; Director of Foreign Exchange, Marketing Executive, Business Owner, Writer, Editor.

Hobbies/personal interests: My other full-time job is as a single parent for my three children. . . . Reading is a passion of mine. . . . Loitering at Barnes and Noble with a cup of café and cocoa. Myers: Spending time with my two sets of twins (ages 2 and 5) and my 9-year-old. Some of my interests include the art of trompe l'oeil, arts and crafts, stenciling, and research.

Areas most interested in agenting: Marcy Northrup and Sissy Myers represent celebrities, entertainers, and high-profile individuals. We are very involved with books written by celebrities and authorized biographies.

If not agenting, what would you be doing? Marcy: If I wasn't able to work as an agent, I'd probably write and open up a publishing company. Sissy: If agenting wasn't a career option for me, I'd very much enjoy focusing on my love of art, education, and children.

Best way to initiate contact: Feel free to contact us via e-mail or snail mail. No need to send an SASE. We will foot the bill if we are interested.

Reading-fee policy: No reading fee.

Commission: 15% on domestic sales.

Rejection rate (all submissions): Unfortunately, we have to reject a high percentage, due to writers sending manuscripts that aren't conductive to our specialization.

Common mistakes authors make: Marcy: Sending us manuscripts outside of our area of expertise. Sissy: Sending unsolicited manuscripts.

Description of the client from Hell: We enjoy all of our clients and work with them as a team.

Description of a dream client: It's always a plus when the client provides us with information requested in a timely manner.

How did you become an agent? It was a sneaky metamorphosis. One minute I was a writer, then an editor, and next thing I knew, I was sending out rejection notices. (Just kidding.)

Why did you become an agent? I love everything that has to do with books. Being around people who share my passion energizes me.

What can writers do to enhance their chances of getting you as an agent? Research the market and have a solid story to tell.

How would you describe what you actually do for a living? Northrup Literary & Entertainment Agency offers exclusive representation and promotion to celebrities, entertainers, and high-profile authors worldwide. Our primary function is to represent the author and sell his work at the best terms possible.

What do you think about editors? We thank God every day for them.

What do you think about publishers? We have a great working relationship with many publishers.

Comments: Marcy: I love every aspect of this business: writing, editing, sculpting and refining the treatments, contracting, and honing the relationships with publishers, editors, and authors. Advising and counseling our clients on the development of their careers is a source of energy for us. Sissy: It is a pleasure to do business with such talented authors and celebrities. Cultivating relationships with our clients and working in conjunction with the editors and publishers to bring a project to fruition give me great joy.

N

THE RICHARD PARKS AGENCY

138 East 16th Street, Suite 5B, New York, NY 10003
212-254-9067

Agent: Richard Parks
  Education: B.A., Duke University; M.A., University of North Carolina
  Career history: Curtis Brown, Ltd. (1970–1978); United Artists Corporation (1978–1981); Alexander, Smith & Parks (1981–1988); the Richard Parks Agency (1989–present).
  Best way to initiate contact: Fiction: by referral only. Nonfiction: by referral or query letter with SASE.
  Reading-fee policy: No reading fee.
  Client representation by category: Nonfiction, 50%; Fiction, 50%.
  Commission: 15% domestic, 20% foreign.
  Most common mistakes authors make: No calls, e-mail, or faxed queries, please.

JAMES PETER ASSOCIATES, INC.

P.O. Box 670, Tenafly, NJ 07670
201-568-0760   fax: 201-568-2959
e-mail: bertholtje@compuserve.com

Agent: Bert Holtje
  Born: February 24, 1931.
  Education: B.S.; M.A., Experimental Psychology.
  Career history: Founded James Peter Associates, Inc., in 1971. Author of 27 published books.
  Hobbies/personal interests: Amateur radio, W2TQS.
  Areas most interested in agenting: All nonfiction.
  Areas not interested in agenting: Fiction, children's and young adult books, poetry.
  If not agenting, what would you be doing? Be an architect.
  Best way to initiate contact: Send a brief query, author bio, and writing sample with SASE.
  Reading-fee policy: No.
  Client representation by category: Nonfiction, 100%.
  Commission: 15% domestic, 20% foreign.
  Number of titles sold last year: 37.
  Rejection rate (all submissions): N/A.
  Most common mistakes authors make: Trying to convince me that "everyone" will buy their books.

Description of the client from Hell: The writer who constantly sees the writer-publisher relationship in adversarial terms.

Description of a dream client: One who has a clear understanding of his or her strengths and weaknesses and who sees writing as an art as well as a business.

How did you become an agent? First, I wrote and published 27 books. As much as I enjoy writing, I also enjoy the business side. It was a natural progression.

Why did you become an agent? I enjoy both the editorial side as well as the business side of the business. Never a dull or uninteresting moment!

What can writers do to enhance their chances of getting you as an agent? Have carefully conceived ideas that are of commercial value.

How would you describe what you actually do for a living? Make things happen for talented people.

What do you think about editors? I love them!

What do you think about publishers? I love them!

Representative titles: *Balance of Power: Power and Politics from the Era of McCarthy to the Age of Gingrich* by James C. White, Former Speaker, U.S. House of Representatives (Turner Publishing); *Disaster at the Pole: A Harrowing Tale of Arctic Endurance and Survival* by Wilbur Cross (Lyons Press); *Elizabeth I: C.E.O.* by Alan Axelrod (Prentice Hall); *The Encyclopedia of American Spies and Counterspies* by Timothy Maga (Facts on File); *The Penguin Dictionary of American Folklore* by Harry Oster and Alan Axelrod (Penguin); *Unsolved Mysteries of Science* by John Malone (John Wiley & Sons); *Encyclopedia of the American West* (3 volumes), Zenda Inc. (Macmillan); *Walkin' the Line: A Journey from the Past to the Present Along the Mason Dixon Line* by William Ecenbarger (M. Evans & Co.); *Hepatitis C: The Silent Killer* by Carol Turkington (Contemporary Books).

P

PINDER LANE & GARON-BROOKE ASSOCIATES, LTD.

159 West 53rd Street, Suite 14-E, New York, NY 10019
212-489-0880
e-mail: pinderl@interport.net

Agents: Dick Duane, Nancy Coffey (Consulting Agent), Robert Thixton

Career history: Duane: Agent since 1960, co-owner; also packages feature films, handles movie tie-ins, and has an extensive advertising background. Thixton: Agent since 1975, co-owner. Coffey: Agent since 1992; previously Editorial Adviser to Editor in Chief at Putnam Berkley Publishing; Editorial Director, Ballantine Books and Avon Books.

Areas most interested in agenting: In general, any intriguing well-written book, either fiction or nonfiction. Fiction: Commercial and literary fiction, including thrillers, technothrillers, adventure, romance, science fiction/fantasy, and some young adult fiction. Nonfiction: personal lifestyle, including cookbooks, pop culture, historical biographies, investigative reporting, and natural history.

Areas not interested in agenting: None.

Best way to initiate contact: A one-page query letter briefly describing the author's work. A positive response can be expected within four weeks of submission of a query. There will be no response if the agency is not interested in seeing further material.

P

Reading-fee policy: No charge for requested material.

Client representation by category: Nonfiction, 25%; Fiction, 75%.

Commission: 15% domestic; 30% foreign.

Number of titles sold last year: 20.

Rejection rate (all submissions): 95%.

Most common mistakes authors make: Telling the agency that they are considering several other agencies and they will "let you know." Our agency doesn't audition and that type of potential client will not be signed. Any material submitted to our agency must be on an exclusive basis while we take the time to read and evaluate a manuscript.

Description of the client from Hell: An author who calls asking why his or her book hasn't sold after a very short submission time. An author who does not know the state of the publishing industry, who does not do research "on the shelves" in bookstores. The market is very tough out there, and a writer should be as objectively tough on his or her manuscripts as publishers are when they respond to a submission.

Description of a dream client: The author who listens to his or her agent concerning rewrites and editorial work and knows the state of the publishing marketplace. An author who will rewrite and edit, regardless of how many times it is required, knowing that it is critical to have the manuscript in the best possible shape before submitting it to publishers. An author who understands that not all books are sold the "first-time out."

Why did you become an agent? The agents at Pinder Lane & Garon-Brooke Associates, Ltd., have an enduring love of literature in all its forms. To be able to nurture a writer's career strikes us as the most desirable job anyone, anywhere, could have.

What can writers do to enhance their chances of getting you as an agent? They should listen to comments our agents make about their work without becoming defensive. A willingness to listen to suggestions in order to make a manuscript better and salable is the only attitude possible and is often the deciding factor in whether or not a client is signed.

What do you think about editors? In today's changing publishing world, many editors' jobs go beyond what their traditional editorial efforts have been in the past.

Comments: The future of book publishing will be so closely aligned to other media that agents will have to have expertise in all fields of films, television, Internet, electronic, and other new media in order to negotiate the best contracts for their clients. Because our agents have cross-media experience in all areas of publishing, promotion, advertising, and other related fields, we feel Pinder Lane & Garon-Brook Associates, Ltd., is uniquely positioned as a literary/media agency for the publishing industry.

Representative titles: *An Army of Children* by Evan H. Rhodes (Bastei Lube); *Bezique* by Greg Wilson (Robert Hale, Ltd.); *Fertile Ground* by Ben Mezrich (HarperCollins); *Getting to the Good Part* by Lolita Files (Warner Books); *Jealousy* by Nancy Friday (M. Evans & Co.); *Kennedy Weddings* by Jay Mulvaney (St. Martin's Press); *Nobody's Safe* by Richard Steinberg (Doubleday); *Protect & Defend* by Eric Harry (Berkley); *Reaper* by Ben Mezrich (HarperCollins); *Scenes from a Sistah* by Lolita Files (Warner Books); *Shattered Bone* by Chris Stewart (M. Evans & Co.); *The Devil Is a Virgin* by Evan H. Rhodes (Bastei Lube); *The Invasion* by Eric Harry (Berkley); *The Ladies of Covington Send Their Love* by Joan Medlicott (Tom Dunne); *The Third Consequence* by Chris Stewart (M. Evans

& Co.); *Threshold* by Ben Mezrich (HarperCollins); *The 4 Phase Man* by Richard Stein-bery (Doubleday); *Jackie—The Clothes of Camelot* by Jay Mulvaney (St. Martin's Press).

PMA LITERARY AND FILM MANAGEMENT, INC.

132 West 22nd Street, 12th Floor, New York, NY 10011
212-929-1222
www.pmalitfilm.com   e-mail: pmalitfilm@aol.com

Agents: Peter Miller, Delin Cormeny

Born: Miller: Atlantic City, New Jersey. Cormeny: March 30, 1970, in Olathe, Kansas.

Education: Miller: B.A., Monmouth College. Cormeny: B.S. in Journalism, with honors, from University of Kansas; additional courses at the Universita di Pavia (Pavia, Italy), University of Zimbabwe (Harare, Zimbabwe).

Career history: Miller: Founded Writers House, a literary agency, 1972; founded the Peter Miller Agency, 1974; incorporated agency in 1981; founded PMA Literary and Film Management, Inc., 1992. Founded 21st Century Lion, Inc. (a production company) in 1996. Have now been in business for almost 30 years. Cormeny: Reporter and Copy Editor for various newspapers; Manager of Development at Hill-Fields Entertainment (Los Angeles); Fulbright Scholar (Harare, Zimbabwe); Newswire Editor (Harare, Zimbabwe).

Hobbies/personal interests: Miller: Traveling, gourmet food and wine, reading, fishing, playing with my daughters (Liseanne and Margo). Cormeny: Sea kayaking, camping, snow skiing, scuba diving, dressage, travel, woodworking.

Areas most interested in agenting: Miller: Action/suspense fiction, thrillers and legal thrillers, history, serious journalism, current events, pop culture. Cormeny: Ethnic fiction, women's fiction, literary and commercial crossover fiction, narrative nonfiction, serious journalism, quirky pop culture, fiction/nonfiction with international bent, "fringe" fiction/nonfiction, historical fiction, suspense.

Areas not interested in agenting: Miller: Poetry, pornography, children's books. Cormeny: Poetry, children's books, science fiction, traditional business books.

What might you be doing if you weren't an agent? Miller: A publisher or film producer, executive at a film studio. Cormeny: Most likely, I'd be working abroad as a reporter or with an NGO or the foreign service.

Best way to initiate contact: Miller: Send a query to my attention, detailing the essence of the book and why it is commercial, along with a biography of the author. Cormeny: Query me via e-mail or snail mail; include a short letter, one-page synopsis of your project, and a brief author bio.

Reading-fee policy: No.

Client representation by category: Miller: Nonfiction, 20%; Fiction, 60%; Screenplays, 30%. Cormeny: Nonfiction, 30%; Fiction, 70%.

Commission: Miller: Domestic 15%; film rights 10–15%; foreign rights 20–25%. Cormeny: Domestic rights 15%; film rights 10–15%; foreign rights 20–25%.

Number of titles sold last year: Miller: 20. Cormeny: 15.

Rejection rate (all submissions): Miller: 90–95%. Cormeny: 90–95%.

Most common mistakes authors make: Miller: Many authors express a negative attitude toward agents and the publishing industry in general. What a way to win your potential agent's confidence! Cormeny: Don't send me everything you've ever written. Select the best and send that. If I love it, I'll ask to see more. Please include a one-page synopsis; a two-sentence description isn't enough.

Description of the client from Hell: Miller: The client who sends you a handwritten manuscript and calls you every day to see if you have read it. Cormeny: The writer who sends 1,500 pages of his/her unfinished manuscript and expects you to come up with a detailed evaluation, a suggested ending, a guaranteed six-figure book deal, and a feature film deal . . . within two weeks.

Description of a dream client: Miller: A client who trusts your judgment and lets you work for him or her. After all, I've been selling books for almost 30 years and I've sold over 800, so I must be doing something right. Cormeny: A consistently creative, motivated, and professional writer with vision; someone who is serious about his/her craft and is constantly striving to improve it. Someone who thinks big and works hard.

Why did you become an agent? Miller: I had always wanted to be involved with films and I figured out early on that a great way to find properties was in the book world. I'm glad it happened this way because I think I'm good at it. I love my work. Cormeny: It lets me keep one foot in the creative side of the industry and the other in the business side. I love editing as much as I love closing deals, and it's never the same thing twice.

What can writers do to enhance their chances of getting you as an agent? Miller: Submit a professional, well-thought-out query letter with a polished synopsis and/or manuscript presentation. Cormeny: Do your homework—convince me your book is commercially viable. Research similar titles, authors, or topics; pay attention to market trends. Also, proofread, proofread, proofread! Then proofread again. Each grammatical error is a red flag.

How would you describe what you actually do for a living? Miller: Dealmaker. Cormeny: I'm part editor and part dealmaker.

How would you describe what you actually do for a living? I'm an artistic persuasive. I sell words, intellectual properties.

How did you become an agent? Cormeny: A series of accidents and good luck.

What do you think of editors? Miller: They're brilliant, God-like, and I highly respect them. Cormeny: Editors have the toughest jobs in the business. They are overworked, underpaid, and constantly under pressure to find the next literary sensation. They have to answer to everyone—writers, agents, publishers, marketing gurus, and publicists—and if the books they love don't live up to projected sales, they can suddenly find themselves editing their resumes.

What do you think about publishers? Miller: Publishers are in the business to make money! Cormeny: I worry about the frontlist mentality publishers seem to have adopted. Only those books the major houses can publish in extraordinary numbers are getting bought these days, and a number of small treasures have been overlooked as a result. Publishers don't seem to want to work at growing authors any more; they're looking for instant bestsellers. Ultimately, it's the readers who suffer.

Comments: Miller: Writers, write *on!* Cormeny: The most difficult part of this business by far, is watching terrific novels get rejected. We have a number of wonderfully compelling books that have been praised—yet rejected—and are sitting on our shelves collecting dust. Ultimately, market forces dictate the kinds of books publishing houses will take on, and as a result, commercial viability generally wins out over literary merit. While we understand the dynamics of the business and the constraints of the publishing houses, it doesn't make it any easier to go into a bookstore and see less-than-stellar works selling like crazy while some of our modest poignant authors aren't even given a chance.

Representative titles:). *Miss Julia Takes Over* by Ann Ross (Viking); *Satin Doll* by Karen E. Quinones Miller (Simon & Schuster); *Brothers* by Freddie Lee Johnson, III (One World/Ballantine); *The New York Cabbie Cookbook* by Mary Ellen Winston and Holly Garrison (Running Press); *Dream in Color* by Darlene Johnson (HarperCollins); *The Unwanted* by Kien Nguyen (Little Brown); *No Finish Line: The Marla Runyan Story* by Marla Runyan (G. P. Putnam's Sons); *Buddha's Child* by former South Vietnam Prime Minister Nguyen Cao Ky and Marvin J. Wolf (St. Martin's Press); *Chocolate for a Woman's Blessings* by Kay Allenbaugh (Fireside, Simon & Schuster); *Walking to Canterbury* by Jerry Ellis (Ballantine); *Quilts Are Forever* by Kathy Lamancusa (Fireside and Simon & Schuster); *Kursk Down!* by Clyde Burleson (Warner Books); *Tolkien on Leadership* by Joe Tye (Prentice Hall); *Final Verdict: The Simple Truth in the Killing of JFK* by Vincent Bulgliosi (W. W. Norton); *The Secret Universe of Names* by Roy Feinsen (Overlook Press).

AARON PRIEST LITERARY AGENCY

708 Third Avenue, 23rd Floor, New York, NY 10017
212-818-0344   fax: 212-573-9417

Agents: Lisa Erbach Vance, Paul V. Cirone

Born: Vance: Chicago, Illinois. Cirone: 6/4/74, Brooklyn, New York.

Education: Vance: B.A., English Literature, Northwestern University, Academic honors. Cirone: B.A., English, New York University.

Career history: Vance: Management Trainee at Random House, Inc. Foreign Rights Associate at Crown Publishing Group. Cirone: Five-year Assistant and apprentice to Molly Friedrich.

Hobbies/personal interests: Cirone: Audiophile, weight training, films, and, of course, reading.

Areas most interested in agenting: Vance: Novels—literary and/or commercial and narrative nonfiction. I'm particularly interested in women's fiction and bold, riveting thrillers. I also love historical novels and mystery/suspense with truly unique plots and characters. I'm always hungry for thoughtful books—beyond the previous categories. I'm more interested in quality than category. Cirone: Literary fiction, multicultural, gay and lesbian, Latin American, and African-American fiction among others. Narrative-driven nonfiction; I love "magical realism" and some horror as well. Also, historical fiction and literary thrillers.

Areas not interested in agenting: Vance: Genre romance, cozy mysteries, horror, fantasy/science fiction, "New Age"—fiction or nonfiction, poetry, screenplays, young adult/children's, health/diet, how-to. Cirone: Genre mystery, genre romance, commercial thrillers, self-help books, prescriptive nonfiction.

If not agenting, what might you be doing? Cirone: I might be an English teacher, still in school, or a disc jockey.

Best method to initiate contact: Vance: Query letter that includes a good synopsis of the work and/or a statement about the themes the book explores—no longer than 2–3 pages. Include first chapter, if desired. An SASE is not required. If I'm interested, I will respond within three weeks. I will not respond if not interested. Cirone: Query letter.

Reading-fee policy: No reading fee.

Client representation by category: Vance: Nonfiction, 15%; Fiction, 85%. Cirone: Nonfiction, 20%; Fiction, 80%.

Commission: Vance: 15%. Domestic sales; 10% on all foreign sales (plus additional 10% for foreign sub-agents). Cirone: 15%.

Number of titles sold last year: Cirone: Sold my first novel in July 2000.

Rejection rate (all submissions): Vance: 99%. Cirone: 90%.

Most common mistakes authors make: Bad grammar—especially using the phrase "fictional novel." An unfocused description or not enough description of the work. Gimmicks or excessive cuteness, let your personality shine through, but please don't play games with me. Microscopic type size in query letters.

Description of the client from Hell: One who is demanding—as opposed to cooperative. One who is paranoid—publishing is not a conspiracy against writers!

Description of a dream client: Vance: One who takes editorial suggestions well. One who understands that successful publication requires a team effort—that the author's job doesn't end when the manuscript is accepted. One whose creativity doesn't stop with the written word. One who is positive. Cirone: One who is amenable to some editorial guidance, is personable, and is passionate about writing.

How did you become an agent? Vance: Years of working as Aaron Priest's assistant, plus a background in foreign rights. Cirone: I began as an intern at Aaron Priest and worked my way through the ranks.

Why did you become an agent? A passion for books, coupled with a desire to be as involved in publishing as possible. An agent has to understand all aspects of the business and know a lot of people—it's challenging, thrilling, and great fun! Cirone: Because I love to read and because after five years of being an apprentice to Molly Friedrich, I was inspired to try my hand at it.

How would you describe what you actually do for a living? Vance: I see myself as a career-builder. I am dedicated to those who are dedicated to writing, and my objective is to see the "big picture" for my clients, as well as manage the details. I'm looking for writers who are ready and ripe for growth, whether they are already published or not. Cirone: An agent is responsible for shepherding writers toward publication, to get them the right relationship with the most appropriate editors/publishers.

What do you think about editors? Cirone: I think some are fiercely intelligent, passionate about books, and crucial to a book's publication.

What do you think about publishers? Cirone: I think publishers are obviously corporate-minded, so that can be frustrating. But for the most part, I have to believe that they have the books' best interests in mind.

Representative titles: *Tell No One* by Harlan Coben (Delacorte); *The Magic of Ordinary Days* by Ann Howard Creel (Viking); *Acid Test* by Ross LaManna (Ballantine); *Mother to Mother* by Sindiwe Magma (Beacon); New Mystery Series by G. M. Ford (Avon); *Peace Like a River* by Leif Enger (Grove Atlantic).

SUSAN ANN PROTTER, LITERARY AGENT

110 West 40th Street, Suite 1408, New York, NY 10018
212-840-0480

Agent: Susan Ann Protter
   Education: B.A., 1961; M.A., NYU, 1965.
   Career history: French teacher, Lawrence High School, Cedarhurst, New York, 1963–1964; Publishing Assistant, *Report Magazine,* New York, 1964–1965; Associate Director, Subsidiary Rights Department, Harper & Row Publishers Inc., 1966–1970; Consultant, Addison-Wesley Publishers, Reading, Massachusetts, 1970–1971; founded Susan Ann Protter agency, 1971.
   Hobbies/personal interests: Sailing, film, opera, travel, languages.
   Areas most interested in agenting: Fiction: thrillers, mysteries, science fiction. Nonfiction: women's health, parenting, popular psychology, true crime, medicine, biography, advice, how-to.
   Areas not interested in agenting: Star Trek, Star Wars, romance, Westerns, children's books.
   Best way to initiate contact: Query letter (with SASE).
   Reading-fee policy: No reading fee.
   Client representation by category: Nonfiction, 45%; Fiction, 55%.
   Commission: 15%.
   Number of titles sold last year: 15.
   Rejection rate (all submissions): 96%.
   Most common mistakes authors make: Spend first paragraph of letter apologizing for taking up your time or telling you that they are unaware of the proper way to write a manuscript.
   Description of the client from Hell: Calls all the time and tells me how to run my business.
   Description of a dream client: A creative, disciplined writer with an ability to write with a clear audience in mind, who takes editorial comments and criticism constructively, and delivers on time.
   Comments: Don't give up. Rewrite and then rewrite again.
   Representative titles: *A Cat on Stage Right* by Lydia Adamson (Dutton); *Breastfeeding and the Working Mother, Revised Edition* by Diane Mason and Diane Ingersoll (St. Martin's Press); *Dr. Nightingale Dances with Lions* by Lydia Adamson (Signet); *Einstein's Bridge* by John G. Cramer (Avon); *Freeware* by Rudy Rucker (Avon); *Mass Hate* by Neil J. Kressel (Plenum); *Shadow Heart* by Lynn Armistead McKee (Signet/Onyx); *The Fifth Element* by Terry Bisson (Harper Prism, novelization); *The Gift* by Patrick O'Leary (Tor); *The Science Fiction Century* (edited by David G. Hartwell) (BOMC and Tor).

P

SUSAN RABINER LITERARY AGENCY, INC.

240 West 35th Street, Suite 500, New York, NY 10001-2506
fax: 212-279-0932
e-mail: fortrab@idt.net

Agent: Susan Rabiner

Career history: Former Editorial Director and Vice President of Basic Books, the serious nonfiction division of HarperCollins Publishers, Senior Editor at Pantheon Books, St. Martin's Press, Oxford University Press.

Areas most interested in agenting: Serious nonfiction, history, science, biography, business, economics, politics, law, psychology, and so on.

Areas not interested in agenting: Fiction, self-help, New Age.

Best way to initiate contact: E-mail a query, snail mail a proposal or sample chapters.

Client representation by category: Nonfiction, 95%; Textbooks, 5%.

Commission: 15% domestic; 20% foreign.

Number of titles sold last year: 15.

Rejection rate (all submissions): 70%.

Why did you become an agent? I became an agent after 25 years as an editor because I felt that authors needed help conceptualizing their projects editorially before they showed them to publishers.

Representative titles: *The Chinese in America* by Irish Chang (Viking-Penguin); *Atom: A Space Odyssey* by Lawrence Krauss (Little Brown & Co.); *Philosophy from the Inside* by Colin McGrinn (HarperCollins); *Winning the Talent Wars* by Bruce Tulgas (W. W. Norton); *Hirohito and the Making of Modern Japan* by Herb Bix (HarperCollins); *Cathy Lavender: The Western Women's Readers* by Lillian Schlissel (HarperCollins); *Guppy Love: The Culture of Sex and Mating* by Lee Dujatkin (The Free Press); *Tragedy and Triumph: The Story of Postwar Europe* by Will Hitchcock (Broadway Books); *The Seven Sins of Memory* by Daniel Schacter (Houghton Mifflin).

RAINES & RAINES

71 Park Avenue, New York, NY 10016
212-684-5160

Agents: Theron Raines, Joan Raines, Keith Korman

Best way to initiate contact: One-page letter (with SASE).

Reading-fee policy: No reading fee.

Commission: 15% domestic, 20% foreign.

Rejection rate (all submissions): Most.

Representative titles: *Active Faith* by Reed; *Ball Four* by Bouton and Shector; *Brain Quest* by Feder; *Complete Book of Bread* by Clayton; *Deliverance* by James Dickey; *Die Hard* by Thorp; *Forrest Gump* by Groom; *How to Eat Fried Worms* by Rockwell; *Hush* by

Nykanen; *Mountains of Tibet* by Gerstein; *My Dog Skip* and other books by Willie Morris; *Ordinary Men* by Browning; *Orphans of the Living* by Toth; *Puttermesser Papers* by Ozick; *Safe, Not Sorry* by Metaksa; *The Contender* by Lipsyte; *The Destruction of the European Jews* by Hilberg; *The Great Reckoning* by Davidson and Rees-Mogg; *The Strange Death of Vincent Foster* by Ruddy; *The Uses of Enchantment* and other books by Bruno Bettelheim; *The Wealth Equation* by Tanous; *What the Dead Remember* by Greene.

HELEN REES LITERARY AGENCY

123 North Washington Street, Boston, MA 02114
617-723-5232, ext. 233   fax: 617-723-5211

Agent: Helen Rees
   Born: October 2, 1936.
   Education: B.A., History, George Washington University.
   Career history: Director of Office of Cultural Affairs, City of Boston (1978–1982); Literary Agent (1983–present).
   Hobbies/personal interests: Horseback riding, opera, theater, hiking.
   Areas most interested in agenting: Literary fiction, history, psychology, business.
   Areas not interested in agenting: Children's books, young adult, science fiction, poetry, cookbooks, gardening books, photography.
   Best way to initiate contact: Query letter (with SASE) with three chapters and a synopsis.
   Reading-fee policy: No reading fee.
   Commission: 15% domestic; 20% foreign.
   Number of titles sold last year: 15.
   Rejection rate (all submissions): 85%.
   Most common mistakes authors make: In a query letter, they unrealistically hype their material.
   Description of the client from Hell: Someone who sends a manuscript over and calls an hour later to see if I've read it.
   Description of a dream client: Someone who listens and is talented.
   Representative titles: *Reasonable Doubt* by Alan Dershowitz; *Reengineering the Corporation* by Michael Hammer and James Champy; *Shiny Water* by Anna Salter; *The New War* by Senator John Kerry.

JODY REIN BOOKS, INC.

7741 South Ash Court, Littleton, CO 80122
303-694-4430
www.jodyreinbooks.com

Agent: Jody Rein

Career history: Spent 13 years in publishing at Contemporary Books, Bantam Doubleday Dell, and Morrow/Avon Books. Incorporated Jody Rein Books in 1994.

Areas most interested in agenting: Very commercial nonfiction written by people who have both media contacts/experience and true expertise in their chosen subject matter. An amazing work of literary fiction by an award-winning short-story writer.

Areas not interested in agenting: Category fiction (mystery, romance, science fiction, horror, etc.), poetry, children's books.

Best way to initiate contact: A recommendation from someone I trust. A one-page query letter.

Reading-fee policy: No reading fee.

Client representation by category: Nonfiction, 85%; Fiction, 15%.

Commission: 15%.

Number of titles sold last year: 11.

Rejection rate (all submissions): 90–95%.

Most common mistakes authors make: Fax me; e-mail me; send me something I know nothing about; call me; say, "I can write about anything!"; say, "Well, I don't really know if this has been done before . . . ."

Description of the client from Hell: Not someone I would do business with! (An author who expects a perfect publishing experience but doesn't expect to do any work on his own.)

Description of a dream client: Someone with a fabulous idea and the requisite writing experience, life experience, education, and passion to pull it off. Plus, media experience and contacts. Plus, a real willingness to do whatever he or she can to work with the agent and publisher to make his or her book a bestseller. Plus, respect for himself or herself, for the book, for the publisher, and for me.

Why did you become an agent? I had been in the publishing business at an executive level for 13 years when I moved to Denver. I love this business. Being an agent was the only way to stay in the business, working with the top professionals in New York—and still live in the Rocky Mountains.

Comments: You can find good agents anywhere in the country, but make sure you protect yourself by doing adequate research. Ask the agent who wants to represent you if she has New York experience, how you would work together, and so on. But don't ask these questions until she has offered to represent you. If she doesn't want to sell your work, it doesn't matter what her experience is.

Representative titles: *Beethoven's Hair* by Russell Martin; *Patrick O'Brien: A Life Revealed* by Dean King; *Stopping at Every Lemonade Stand* by James Vollbracht; *Think Like a Genius: The Ultimate User's Manual for Your Brain* by Todd Siler; *You Mean I'm Not Lazy, Stupid, or Crazy?: A Self-Help Book for Adults with Attention Deficit Disorder* by Kate Kelly and Peggy Ramundo.

THE AMY RENNERT AGENCY

98 Main Street #302, Tiburon, CA 94920
415-789-8955   fax: 415-789-8944

Agent: Amy Rennert

Areas most interested in agenting: Narrative nonfiction, especially memoirs; business; pop culture; health; adventure; sports; psychology; food; wine; and travel. Literary fiction, mysteries, suspense.

Areas not interested in agenting: Religious fundamentalism, gag gifts, romance novels, science fiction.

Best way for a client to initiate contact: Query with a cover letter and a proposal for nonfiction with one sample chapter; cover letter, and 50–75 pages of sample writing for fiction. We don't need to see a query letter first.

Reading-fee policy: No reading fee.

Client representation by category: Nonfiction, 75%; Fiction, 20%; Children's, 5%.

Commission: 15% domestic; 20% foreign.

Number of titles sold last year: 25.

Rejection rate (all submissions): 95%.

Most common mistakes authors make: Some common mistakes include not taking enough care in writing a good cover letter, not enclosing a self-addressed envelope (of appropriate size with appropriate postage) for return of materials wanted back, sending out manuscripts that aren't the absolutely best material they can produce, and faxing over revised pages three days after the package has arrived.

Description of client from Hell: The client from Hell can't spell, calls the office repeatedly, expects and demands more than is possible, and is interested in publication only for the money or the ego rush.

Description of dream client: The dream client is professional in all dealings, knows the rules of submission, and learns a little or a lot about the publishing business from workshops and writing consultants before approaching the agency. Dream clients don't need money desperately right now but are interested in a career of growing through their writing and letting their hard work and fate lead them in the right direction. Also, the dream client *has patience and says thank you.*

Why did you become an agent? For the opportunity to bring books that matter into the world, so that I could use both my editorial and my business skills, so that I didn't have to work for anybody else, and so that I could help writers achieve their dreams while realizing my own.

What do you think about publishers? I think that most of them are smart and market savvy, and that they are too pressured by the bottom line these days. I like to hear the reasons that they love or do not love specific books—but what you have to keep in mind is that just a specific agent might not be right for an ultimately successful project, so a publisher may not be the one to bring it to market. Perseverance is the key.

Representative titles: *Blood Washes Blood* by Frank Viviano (Pocket Books); *A Slant of Sun* (Norton) and *Into the Tangle of Friendship* (Houghton Mifflin) by Beth Kephart; *Anatomies: A Novella and Stories* by Anndee Hochman (Picador); *Salon.com's Wanderlust,* edited by Don George (Villard); *Red House* by Sarah Messer (Viking); *Waiting: True Confessions of a Waitress* (HarperCollins); *The Rebel Rules: Daring to Be Yourself in Business* by Chip Conely (Simon & Schuster/Fireside); *The Mother's Guide to Sex* by Anne Semans and Cathy Winks (Times Books); *A Bright Red Scream* by Marilee Strong (Viking); *Harvests of Joy* by Robert Mondavi (Harcourt Brace); *Muhammed Ali: Ring-*

side, edited by John Miller and Aaron Kenedi (Bulfinch); *The Poison Sky: A Jack Liffey Mystery* by John Shannon (Berkley).

R

THE ANGELA RINALDI LITERARY AGENCY

P.O. Box 7877, Beverly Hills, CA 90212-7665
310-842-7665   fax: 310-837-8143
e-mail: e2arinaldi@aol.com

Agent: Angela Rinaldi

Career history: Editor at NAL/Signet, Pocket Books, Bantam, Manager Book Publishing, the *Los Angeles Times.*

Areas most interested in agenting: Literary and commercial fiction, narrative nonfiction, prescriptive and pro-active self-help.

Areas not interested in agenting: Cookbooks, category romance, Westerns, science fiction, young adult, poetry, screenplays, children's, sports, coffee-table books, software.

Best way to initiate contact: Send a query with SASE. Fiction: send first 100 pages; and nonfiction, query first or send proposal; please allow 4–6 weeks response time. Do *not* fax queries or send Certified Mail.

Client representation by category: Nonfiction, 60%; Fiction, 40%.

Commission: 15% domestic; 20% foreign.

Representative titles: *Who Moved My Cheese?* by Dr. Spencer Johnson (Putnam); *The Seventh Sin* by Eben Paul Perison (NAL/Signet); *Blind Spot* by Stephanie Kane (Bantam); *The Thyroid Solution* by Dr. Ridha Arem (Ballantine); *Leadership Lessons from the Civil War* by Thomas Wheeler (Doubleday); *The Starlite Drive In* by Marjorie Reynolds (William Morrow); *Stepwives* by Lynn Oxhorn Ringwood, Louise Oxhorn, and Marjorie Krausz (Simon & Schuster).

ANN RITTENBERG LITERARY AGENCY, INC.

1201 Broadway, Suite 708, New York, NY 10001
212-684-6936   fax: 212-684-6929
e-mail: ARLAInc@banet.net

Agent: Ann Rittenberg

Born: New York, New York, 1957.

Education: B.A., Eckerd College.

Career History: 1979-1980, St. Petersburg Times; 1980-1986, Editor, Athenum Publishers; 1986-1992, Agent, Julian Bach Agency; 1992-present, President, Ann Rittenberg Literary Agency, Inc.

Hobbies/personal interests: Gardening, travel, ballet/theater, entertainment, cabaret, New York.

Areas most interested in agenting: Literary fiction, upmarket contemporary women's fiction, biography/autobiography/memoir, cultural history, social history, and serious narrative nonfiction.

Areas not interested in agenting: Sci-fi, genre fiction, romance, how-to, gift books.

If not agenting, what would you be doing? Traveling the world, playing tennis and golf, studying art and languages, writing literary criticism—in other words, pursuing leisure activities! There's no other job I'd want to have.

Best way to initiate contact: Write me a letter.

Client representation by category: Nonfiction: 50%; Fiction: 50%.

Commission: 15% domestic, 15% film (split with sub agent), 20% foreign.

Number of titles sold last year: A dozen.

Rejection rate (all submissions): 98%.

Most common mistakes authors make: When a writer says, "I've just finished a novel . . . ," I wonder why he or she hasn't put it through another draft before approaching agents. I also don't like letters that focus more on marketing than they do on the work.

Description of the client from Hell: One who doesn't want to revise his or her work until after it's sold to a publishing house. One who never calls, then complains about lack of attention.

Description of a dream client: All of my clients are dream clients. They are hardworking, enthusiastic, dedicated to writing, convinced that the work comes first, conscious that the author-agent relationship flourishes when it is a partnership based on mutual respect and trust.

Why did you become an agent? When I worked in a publishing house, I saw that it wasn't politic to put the author's needs before the needs of the publicity department, the sales department, the rights department, even the book-ordering department. That didn't seem right to me, and I became an agent so I could advocate for authors.

What can writers do to enhance their chances of getting you as an agent? Keep their letters short.

How would you describe what you actually do for a living? Advocating for authors, with all that entails: Coping with an avalanche of paperwork and a cacophony of telephone calls, faxes, and e-mails; meeting editors, film producers, and foreign publishers and staying current with their interests and the demands of the marketplace. I also spend a lot of time talking to clients so I can get to know them and their hopes and needs as well as their work, and I strategize about when to submit work, how to get the best work out of a writer, how to raise a writer's profile, and how to get the publishers to focus on how to best publish each book I represent.

What do you think about editors? I think they are smart, wonderful, creative, caring people who are swamped by work and the demands of the corporations so many of them work for.

What do you think about publishers? They're too big and are inefficient as a result of streamlining and merging in a quest for economic efficiency. Some of them are too small, and while they can give personal attention at every stage in a way that the big publishers can't, their distribution arrangements can be a source of frustration.

Representative titles: *A Short History of Rudeness* by Mark Caldwell (Picador); *Altars in the Street* by Melody Chavis (Harmony); *Every Day* by Elizabeth Richards

(Pocket); *First Cut: A Season in the Human Anatomy Lab* by Albert Howard Carter III (Picador); *Rescue* by Elizabeth Richards (Pocket); *Shizuko's Daughter* by Kyoko Mori (Holt); *Someone Else's Child* by Nancy Woodruff (Simon & Schuster); *The Poetry of Sight* by Avis Berman (Clarkson Potter/Crown); *Mystic River* by Dennis Lehare (William Morrow & Co.).

JUDITH RIVEN, LITERARY AGENT/EDITORIAL CONSULTANT

250 West 16th, #4F, New York, NY 10011
212-255-1009

Agent: Judith Riven

Education: B.A.; M.A., English Literature.

Career history: Majority of experience as an Acquiring Editor for several major trade publishers. Independent Agent since mid-1993.

Areas most interested in agenting: Medical/health—both conventional and alternative approaches. Ideally prefer a thoughtful combination of psychology, science, and intelligent self-help. Women's issues, cookbooks, personal finance, business, social issues, and narrative nonfiction.

Areas not interested in agenting: Sci-fi, romance, Westerns, serial killers.

Best way to initiate contact: Query letters only. SASE a must! No faxes.

Reading-fee policy: None.

Client representation by category: Nonfiction, 95%; Fiction, 5%.

Commission: 15% of all moneys; 10% of foreign (foreign agent commissions at 15% for a total of 25%).

Number of titles sold last year: 20.

Rejection rate (all submissions): 95%.

Most common mistakes authors make: Trumpeting their great abilities instead of letting the material and their credentials and experience speak for themselves.

Description of the client from Hell: Someone who is overly needy, unrealistic about expectations, and unable to maintain an objective perspective on what publishers can do.

Description of a dream client: One who works in a collaborative fashion; who is motivated, is inner-directed, and is able and willing to actively participate in the publishing process but who understands how to take direction. Also, the ideal client has high aspirations and strong abilities and is willing to work to realize them. Must appreciate that today's publishing world offers proportionately few chances for great success.

Why did you become an agent? Wanted to work independently yet continue to help develop book projects—also, I enjoy the negotiation process.

What can writers do to enhance their chances of getting you as an agent? For nonfiction—know their market, have clearly thought out what they can do to target and reach it.

Representative titles: *Mom's Marijuana* by Dan Shapiro (Harmony/Vintage); *Nightmusic* by Harrison Wignall (Harcourt Brace); *Strollercize* by Elizabeth Trindade and Victoria Shaw (Three Rivers Press).

LINDA ROGHAAR LITERARY AGENCY, INC.

133 High Point Drive, Amherst, MA 01002
413-256-1921   fax: 413-256-2636
www.lindaroghaar.com   e-mail: Lroghaar@aol.com

Agent: Linda L. Roghaar

Born: September 11, 1947; Winchester, Massachusetts.

Education: B.A., Religion, Miami University (Ohio), 1969; M.A., Liberal Studies, Vanderbilt University, 1997.

Career history: I've worked in publishing since 1974, first as a Book-Seller and Bookstore Manager, then as a publishers' Sales Rep. Established the agency in 1997.

Areas most interested in agenting: I am generalistic, and I focus on nonfiction.

Areas not interested in agenting: Children's, horror, science fiction.

If not agenting, what would you be doing? Selling books in another division of the publishing industry.

Best way to initiate contact: Query letter with SASE.

Reading-fee policy: No reading fee.

Client representation by category: Nonfiction, 90%; Fiction, 10%.

Commission: 15% domestic, 20% foreign.

Rejection rate (all submissions): 97%.

Most common mistakes authors make: Announcing that they have a "sure best-seller," not telling me exactly what it is they are writing about ("This is such a great idea, I'm not going to tell you!"), calling me to tell me about the book. Sending an incomplete, confusing package, not enough postage, or a metered envelope.

Description of a dream client: Someone who is friendly, patient, organized. A sense of humor always helps, along with a realistic perspective of his or her place in publishing. Someone who has thought through his or her idea (for nonfiction) or polished his or her manuscript (for fiction) before contacting me.

How did you become an agent? I've been an entrepreneur for so long. I researched the industry, wrote a business plan, and opened up my doors. My 25 years of experience in the publishing business have been invaluable, and I use much of my experience in my everyday dealings with writers and publishers.

Why did you become an agent? I love making the connection between writer and publisher and seeing worthy projects find their way into print. Years ago, I made that connection between the bookstore customer and a book, and then for many years as a publisher's rep between publisher and bookseller. Now, it's between writer and publisher, and it's a natural progression for me. I really love my work!

What can writers do to enhance their chances of getting you as an agent? Present the material in a clear, complete package.

What do you think about editors? Overall, a delightful and interesting group of people who deal remarkably well with the frustrations of their jobs.

What do you think about publishers? I can't discuss publishers without dividing them into two groups: The Big Guys (maybe by the time you read this, it will be One Big Guy) and the Independents. The Big Guys: they can really get things done and continue to produce quality lists. My biggest frustration with them is this—they want something new and different but with a track record. They are less likely to take chances and therefore miss some very good opportunities. The Independents: they publish some of the most interesting and important books today and now, finally, are getting better review attention. The quality of their production is excellent, and each book gets a lot of in-house attention. My frustrations are less precise and timely publishing schedules, long lead times to decide on a manuscript, smaller advances. Generally, though, at all publishing houses everyone is overworked, a bit frantic, and totally committed to his or her work.

Representative titles: *Off the Grid* by Susan and Satya Kuner (Rodale); *Owls Aren't Wise and Bats Aren't Blind* by Warner Shedd (Harmony); *A Place Like Any Other* by Molly Wolf (Doubleday).

THE ROSENBERG GROUP

2800 Harlanwood Drive, Fort Worth, TX 76109
www.rosenberggroup.com

Agents: Michael A. Rosenberg; Barbara Collins Rosenberg

Born: MAR: Patterson, N.J.; BCR: The Bronx, N.Y.

Education: MAR: B.S., University of Colorado, Political Science and English. BCR: B.A., Montclair State University, Theater and English.

Career history: MAR: Executive Editor at Harcourt English for eight years. BCR: Senior Acquisitions Editor for eight years at Harcourt.

Areas most interested in agenting: MAR: Any commercial nonfiction, any college textbooks for first and second year courses. BCR: Romance, women's fiction, mystery, literary fiction, sports fiction.

Areas not interested in agenting: MAR: Scholarly, children's, small market books in general. BCR: Inspirational, and paranormal science fiction, espionage, children's.

If you weren't agenting, what might you be doing? Something to do with books and ideas.

Best way to initiate contact: Query letter via snail mail. *No* faxes. *No* e-mails.

Client representation by category: MAR: Nonfiction, 85%; Fiction, 5%; Textbooks, 10%. BCR: Nonfiction, 5%; Fiction, 95%.

Commission: 15% domestic.

Number of titles sold last year: 25.

Rejection rate (all categories): 95%.

Most common mistakes authors make: Soliciting multiple products in multiple genres in multiple writing forms

Description of the client from Hell: We have been in publishing for too long to allow the "client from Hell" through our door.

Description of the dream client: Dream clients have done their research and spent the time to hone their craft before seeking representation.

How did you become an agent? We have always thought of publishing as an accidental career.

Why did you become an agent? We are fascinated and challenged by the marketplace. We are inherently author sophisticates and driven by the wonderful sense of dignity that comes when you find that special project.

What can writers do to enhance their chances of getting you as their agent? Make a conscious effect to understand the sales, marketing, and promotion sides of commercial publishing. Know where their book fits in the market.

How would you describe what it is you actually do for a living? We help authors navigate the treacherous waves of a writer's career.

What do you think about editors? They're overworked and underpaid.

What do you think about publishers? We are very optimistic. We think there will be more opportunities for writers in the next five years from publishers of all sizes, than there ever have been before.

Comments: Please check our Web site before querying us: www.rosenberggroup.com.

Representative titles: Fiction: *The Rag and Bone Shop* by Jeff Rackham, Ph.D. (Zoland); *The Promise* by Dee Davis (Leisure); *Law Dogs* by J. Lee Butts (Berkley). Nonfiction: *My Twice Loved Life: A Memoir* by Donald M. Murraq (Ballantine); *Doing College* by Sherrie Nist, Ph.D., and Jodi Holschhub, Ph.D. (Ten Speed Press). College Textbooks: *Alternative Currents: Perspectives from Cyberspace and the Popular Press* by Carol Lea Clark (Houghton Mifflin); *The Curious Writer* by Bruce Balknser, Ph.D. (Allyn & Bacon).

R

CAROL SUSAN ROTH, LITERARY REPRESENTATION

1824 Oak Creek Drive, Suite 416, Palo Alto, CA 94304
650-323-3795
e-mail: carol@authorsbest.com

Agent: Carol Susan Roth

Born: October 22, 1947; New Brunswick, New Jersey.

Education: B.A., New York University; M.A., East West Counseling and Psychotherapy; California Institute of Integral Studies, San Francisco. Stanford University Professional Publishing Program, Mark Victor Hansen, "Building Your Speaking and Publishing Empire."

Career history: Trained as a psychotherapist specializing in motivational training seminars. More than a decade producing and promoting public events (100+) with the "who's who" in personal growth, spirituality, health, and business (bestselling authors, including John Gray, Scott Peck, Bernie Siegal, Thomas Moore). In 1987, produced the first Spirituality and Business Conference—"The Heart of Business"—with more than a dozen multimillionaire entrepreneurs who had followed their hearts to great success.

Hobbies/personal interests: Warm-water sailing, Siddha yoga, the Dalai Lama.

Areas most interested in agenting: Nonfiction only; specialty is spirituality, health, personal growth, business. I represent many first-time authors, as well as clients who have been published before and several who have been published with 20 to 30 books each.

Areas not interested in agenting: Sorry, *no fiction*. Any book written by an author without credentials, groundbreaking new content, charisma, and dedication to making it a bestseller.

If not agenting, what would you be doing? Book development, marketing strategy, and promotion for authors (which I also do now).

Best way to initiate contact: Please send your query and proposal with several sample chapters and a marketing plan with SASE. Also, your media kit, seminar brochures, videos.

Reading-fee policy: No reading fee. Consulting available for proposal development, marketing strategy, and promotion. I also refer out to book doctors/ghostwriters.

Client representation by category: Nonfiction, 100%.

Commission: 15%. I arrange for the publisher to set up separate accounts so the author is paid directly.

Number of titles sold last year: 18.

Rejection rate (all submissions): 95%.

Most common mistakes authors make: They don't realize that publishing is a fiercely competitive business, that their book is seen as a product by editors.

Description of the client from Hell: An author without credentials, exciting new content, or charisma who thinks that becoming a bestselling author is a hobby.

Description of a dream client: My clients! They have hearts. They inspire and educate me. Hardworking—willing to do whatever it takes—brilliant and fun.

Why did you become an agent? I promoted many authors on their way to the bestseller lists. It was thrilling. I find it even more exciting to work directly with authors, collaborating with them to develop their work and their careers.

What can writers do to enhance their chances of getting you as an agent? Be original! Be willing to work hard to develop your celebrity and your audience. Love yourself, your work, your world.

How would you describe what you actually do for a living? I am a matchmaker. My job is to intimately know the book business, so that I can match authors with the editors who will embrace them, but also to create opportunities and book ideas for my clients.

What do you think about editors? I deeply respect great editors. They are the vital link in bringing my clients' work to the public.

What do you think about publishers? Publishers all have their own personality or flavor. It's great fun identifying and matching what they want with my authors' expertise.

Comments: I want to make you a star if you have a great message that serves humanity on this beautiful blue pearl Earth.

Representative titles: *Two Questions* by Michael Ray (Scribner); *Healing Zen* by Ellen Birx (Viking); *Yoga RX* by Larry Payne (Broadway); *Kindling the Celtic Spirit* by Mar Freeman (HarperSanFrancisco); *Changewave Investing 2.0* by Tobin Smith (Doubleday/Currency); *Investing in Biotech* by Jim McCamant (Perseus); *Extreme Success* by Frank McKinney (John Wiley & Sons); *Power Yoga for Dummies* by Doug Swenson (Hungry Minds); *Networking for Dummies* by Donna Fisher (Hungry Minds); *Advertising for Dummies* by Gary Dahl (Hungry Minds); *Career Change for Dummies* by Carol McMelland (Hungry Minds); *Drums for Dummies* by Jeff Strong (Hungry Minds).

THE PETER RUBIE LITERARY AGENCY

240 W. 35th Street, Suite 500, New York, NY 10001
212-279-1776
www.prlit.com

Agents: Peter Rubie; Associate Agents: Jennifer Dechiara and June Clark
    Born: Rubie: May 3, 1950.
    Education: Rubie: Journalism degree, NCTJ, England.
    Career history: Rubie: Fleet Street newspapers (England); BBC radio news (England); Fiction Editor, Walker & Co. (New York City); book doctor (New York City); literary agent; published novelist, and nonfiction writer. Adjunct Professor at New York University.
    Hobbies/personal interests: Rubie: Movies, chess, politics/world affairs, music, science.
    Areas most interested in agenting: Pop culture, business, history, pop science, strong narrative nonfiction, Judaica, New Age, children's books, literate thrillers, literate crime novels, literate science fiction and fantasy, literary fiction. We intend to bridge the gap between traditional publishing and e-publishing.
    If not agenting, what would you be doing? Writing full time.
    Best way to initiate contact: Query letter with SASE and a proposal.
    Reading-fee policy: No reading fee.
    Client representation: Nonfiction, 75%: Fiction, 25%.
    Commission: 15% domestic; 20% foreign.
    Number of titles sold last year: Rubie: 50.
    Rejection rate (all submissions): 95%.
    Most common mistakes authors make: Overly cute approach, putting form over substance, unrealistic view of publishing, and being unprofessional.
    Description of the client from Hell: Unprofessional, unreal expectations, no knowledge of the publishing industry, calls every day for news, does not listen to advice, and a control freak.
    Description of a dream client: Knows the market and how to present his or her material; takes editorial input well; has patience. Calls every six weeks or so, works with agent as part of an effective team, responsive, responsible, thoroughly professional.
    Why did you become an agent? To help discover new talent and help further the careers of established writers. As a writer, I try to be the sort of agent I would like to have.
    Comments: I wish more writers considered themselves professionals and looked at their careers accordingly. To understand my philosophy of writing, read my book *The Elements of Storytelling* (John Wiley, 1996).
    Representative titles: *Toward Rational Exuberance* by Mark Smith (Farrar, Straus & Giroux); *How the Tiger Lost Its Stripes* by Cory Meacham (Harcourt Brace); *How to Keep Your Cool with Your Kids* by Lou Makarowski (Perigee); *On Night's Shore* by Randall Silvis (St. Martin's Press); *Jew Boy* by Alan Kaufman (Fromm); *Glass Harmonica* by Louise Monkey (ACE); *The Emperor and the Wolf* by Stuart Galbrayth (Farber)

R

RUSSELL & VOLKENING, INC.

50 West 29th Street, Suite 7, New York, NY 10001
212-684-6050   fax: 212-889-3026

Agent: Joseph Regal

Education: English, magna cum laude, Columbia College.

Career history: Professional musician after college, been at Russell & Volkening for 10 years.

Hobbies/personal interests: Music (classical, rock, funk, blues, jazz, and so on), sports (basketball, tennis), art, anthropology, photography, science, philology, spirituality, travel, and design.

Areas most interested in agenting: I am interested in good stories, whether fiction (commonly called "literary") or nonfiction. I am especially interested in exotic cultures with which I am unfamiliar—be they Pakistani, Greek, Irish, Thai, inner city Cleveland, or the American South. In nonfiction, those stories tend to be narratives from science, history, and memoir—even photobooks and cookbooks. I look for voice more than subject.

Areas not interested in agenting: I don't handle genre: no romance, science fiction, or horror. Nor do I handle self-help, diet books, or prescriptive nonfiction.

If not agenting, what might you be doing? I'd be a musician, physicist, or priest.

Best way to initiate contact: Send a query letter with SASE, and if it's fiction, send a synopsis and the first five pages.

Client representation by category: Nonfiction, 50%; Fiction, 50%.

Commission: 15% commission, except on foreign contracts, which are 20%.

Number of titles sold last year: 13.

Rejection rate (all submissions): 99%.

Most common mistakes authors make: Because of the tremendous drain on our time and resources, the little things mean a lot when we look at query letters. It is truly astounding how many people send poorly written letters, rife with typos and grammatical errors. Why would we show your work more respect than you do? If you can't write a good letter, we're not going to be too enthusiastic about the prospects for the book.

Description of the client from Hell: There is no client from Hell. The relationship between author and agent is like any other: it flourishes when there are clear ground rules each party respects. If boundaries are transgressed, it is up to one party to communicate that to the other. While no one's perfect (including me), this almost always works.

Description of a dream client: Dream clients show me the same respect, patience, enthusiasm, and care I show them and their work.

How did you become an agent? Pretty much by accident; I was singing in a band in New York City and needed a day job. Since I loved books, I wanted to get into publishing and was lucky enough to land at a very fine agency. I had planned to remain an assistant, but within my first year I fell in love with three novels the other agents were rejecting and was allowed to offer my assistance to the writers. I sold all three (eventually) and found myself hooked.

Why did you become an agent? I love books and the next best thing to being a mother is a midwife. I enjoy being involved in every stage of the publishing process and find it very satisfying to think that I have made a contribution through my advocacy of writers I admire.

What can writers do to enhance their chances of getting you as their agent? Good writing is what it always comes down to. Sometimes there might be something special that makes a difference if we're on the fence—a fascinating career, the support of a famous writer, incredible life experiences, being a 25-year-old ex-cover girl—but in the end, we'll take on anyone if the writing moves us.

How would you describe what you actually do for a living? I juggle: at any given moment I'm a talent scout, editor, psychologist, art consultant, lawyer, or schmoozologist.

What do you think about editors? I don't have any thoughts about editors as a group. As with any group, there are good, bad, and indifferent. I do know it's not an easy job balancing the needs of your publishing house, your authors, and your passions.

What do you think about publishers? I think the publishing industry is slightly out of touch with the real world. When all you do is read books for a living, you can lose sight of how the average reader comes to books and how little time most people have for reading. This is manifested in different ways, but most obviously in marketing and publicity. In what other industry would the newest, least experienced employees be in charge of promoting a product? Of course, that's if the product is actually promoted, which quite often it isn't—especially if it's literary fiction, which needs the most promotion but often gets the least. Publishers need to re-imagine the whole promotional structure; a sea change is possible, but only if people believe it is possible.

Comments: It's a very exciting time for books; I feel that the threat of electronic publishing has helped awaken publishers from their collective slumber. Because of e-books and the Internet, everyone has begun to think about publishing in a slightly different way. I don't think most publishers or agents (including me) have grasped fully what the information revolution will mean—certainly not the end of books, as some fear—but there is a lot of energy now, and positive things are happening. One of the most cheering aspects is that publishers have begun to realize how important it is that they establish themselves as a brand, an arbiter of quality, in a world where any author can put his or her work online and invite people to read it and buy it. If the means of delivery and distribution begins to slip away, it ironically places a greater emphasis on some of the old-fashioned aspects of publishing, editorial work in particular. One nice benefit has been a slight renaissance in the publishing of literary fiction, but there are bound to be other unexpected results. Where does that leave you? Do good work. Strive for excellence. Take pleasure in the work itself. The world will still recognize quality; it's only a question of how long it takes.

Representative titles: *Back When We Were Grownups* by Anne Tyler (Knopf); *The Pickup* by Nadine Gordimer (FSG); *Warriors of God* by James Reston, Jr. (Doubleday); *No Certain Rest* by Jim Lehrer (Random House); *Daddy Says* by Ntozake Shange (Simon & Schuster); *Conscious Style Home* by Danny Seo (St. Martin's Press); *Turning on the Girls* by Cheryl Benard (FSG); *The Many Aspects of Mobile Home Living* by Martin Clark (Knopf); *The Beatles in Rishikesh* by Paul Saltzman (Viking Studio); *The Games*

We Played by Steven Cohen (Simon & Schuster); *Places in the Dark* by Thomas H. Cook (Bantam).

THE SAGALYN LITERARY AGENCY

4825 Bethesda Avenue, Suite 302, Bethesda, MD 20814
301-718-6440

Agent: Raphael Sagalyn
    Areas most interested in agenting: Adult fiction and nonfiction.
    Areas not interested in agenting: Cookbooks, children's, and poetry.
    Best way to initiate contact: Send a query letter outlining your professional experience and a brief synopsis by e-mail to: agency@sagalyn.com.
    Representative titles: *The Fortune Tellers* by Howard Kurtz (Free Press); *The Breach* by Peter Baker (Scribner); *The Future of Success* by Robert Reich (Knopf); *The Mind of the CEO* by Jeffrey Clarten (Basic Books); *The Cutout* by Francine Mathews (Bantam).

VICTORIA SANDERS LITERARY AGENCY

241 Avenue of the Americas, New York, NY 10014
212-633-8811

Agent: Victoria Sanders
    Born: Hollywood, California.
    Education: B.F.A., New York University, 1983; J.D., Benjamin N. Cardoza School of Law, 1988.
    Career history: WNET/Channel 13 (PBS); Simon & Schuster Inc.; Carol Mann Agency; Charlotte Sheedy Agency; founded own agency in 1992.
    Areas most interested in agenting: Fiction: literary and commercial. Nonfiction: history, biography, politics, sociology, psychology. Special interests: African-American, Latin, women's, gay and lesbian work.
    Areas not interested in agenting: Hard science, children's, textbooks, and poetry.
    If not agenting, what would you be doing? A producer.
    Best way to initiate contact: Query letter with SASE.
    Reading-fee policy: No reading fee.
    Client representation by category: Nonfiction, 50%; Fiction, 50%.
    Commission: 15% straight; 20% if co-agented foreign; 20% Film and TV commission is 15%.
    Number of titles sold last year: 21.
    Rejection rate (all submissions): 90%.
    Most common mistakes authors make: Don't query if you are unsure or hesitant about submitting without additional information on the agency or current clients.
    Why did you become an agent? It's the best of both worlds. I get to read manuscripts and negotiate deals. I came from L.A. and film and, after getting a law degree, realized

that the best part of the entertainment business was in bridging the gap between the writer or artist and the producer or publisher. I love being the representative and friend of my clients.

Representative titles: *Untitled Folktales Collection* by Zora Neale Hurston; *The Justus Girlz* by Slim Lambright; *Mars 2050* by Michael Hatzer; *Crowns: Portraits of Black Women in Church Hats* by Craig Marberry and Michael Cunningham.

SCHIAVONE LITERARY AGENCY, INC.

236 Trails End, West Palm Beach, FL 33413-2135
phone/fax: 561-966-9294
e-mail: profschia@aol.com

Agent: James Schiavone, Ed.D.

Born: New York City.

Education: B.S., M.A., New York University. Ed.D. Nova University. Professional Diploma, Columbia University.

Career history: Professor Emeritus of Developmental Skills at the City University of New York; Literary Agent.

Areas most interested in agenting: Celebrity biography; autobiography; memoirs; nonfiction. Fiction: mainstream, commercial, and literary; thrillers and mysteries; romances, historical. Children's: all genres of fiction and nonfiction.

Areas not interested in agenting: Poetry; short stories.

If not agenting, what would you be doing? Teaching graduate courses in the psychology of reading; writing nonfiction.

Best way to initiate contact: Queries only via post. Include brief bio-sketch, synopsis, previous books published. Nonfiction: Send full-blown proposal. No response without SASE. No phone calls, faxes. One-page e-mail queries are acceptable, absolutely NO attachments.

Reading-fee policy: No reading fee.

Client representation by category: Nonfiction, 51%; Fiction, 41%; Children's, 5%; Textbooks, 3%.

Commission: 15% domestic; 20% foreign.

Number of titles sold last year:. 17.

Rejection rate (all submissions): 90%.

Most common mistakes authors make: Failure to query first; no SASE; sends unsolicited manuscript; expects agency to download entire manuscript via e-mail; makes initial contact via phone/fax.

Description of a dream client: One who is a published, successful author.

How did you become an agent? It was a natural segue from academia.

Why did you become an agent? I have enjoyed a lifetime love of books and reading. I served as a reading specialist in schools and colleges and authored five trade books and three textbooks. I enjoy representing creative people and helping them to sell their work.

How would you describe what you actually do for a living? Sell creative work of authors/clients to major publishing houses; negotiate contracts; handle business details—enabling authors to concentrate on the craft of writing.

What do you think about editors? I have been fortunate in working with the best editors in the industry. Generally, they are conscientious, indefatigable, and sincere in bringing an author's work to press. Agenting would be impossible without them.

What do you think about publishers? They are the backbone of the industry. I am grateful for the serious consideration they give to my highly selective submissions.

Comments: While I prefer working with authors published by major houses, I do encourage submissions from highly creative, talented first-time authors.

SUSAN SCHULMAN—A LITERARY AGENCY

454 West 44th Street, New York, NY 10036
fax: 212-581-8830 and 2 Bryan Plaza, Washington Depot, CT 06794
e-mail: Schulman@aol.com

Agent: Susan Schulman

Areas most interested in agenting: Books for, by, and about women; psychology, popular culture, and contemporary history. Literary fiction. Children's books.

Areas not interested in agenting: Romance, fantasy, and humor.

Best way to initiate contact: The best contact is through personal recommendation or a letter of inquiry, including a synopsis of the work and an SASE. We accept queries via e-mail at schulman@aol.com.

Reading-fee policy: No reading fee. We are a member of the AAR.

Commission: 15% new clients; 20% for foreign sales.

Rejection rate (all submissions): I regret that most submissions are returned for work or forwarded to another agent. About 3% of the unsolicited submissions become active.

Client Representation by category: Nonfiction, 60%; Fiction, 20%; Children's, 20%.

Most common mistakes authors make: The most common mistakes are calling to inquire about their letter of inquiry or to pitch their project over the phone, and failure to include SASE.

Why did you become an agent? I love business and I love to read. Literary representation is like Christmas to me. Each new package offers the potential to enjoy the read and to sell it so others may as well.

What can writers do to enhance their chances of getting you as an agent? We appreciate writers who have done their homework—writers who have taken the time to educate themselves on the publishing industry and a bit about the process of literary representation. We seek enthusiastic self-starters.

Representative titles: *Why Is This Happening to Me Again?* by Alan Down (Simon & Schuster); *Corporate (IR) Responsibilities* by Lawrence Mitchell (Yale University Press); *True Balance* by Sonia Choquette (Random House); *Into the A, B, Sea* by

Deborah Rose (Scholastic Press); *Boys and Girls Learn Differently* by Michael Gurian (Jossey-Bass).

SEBASTIAN LITERARY AGENCY

172 E. Sixth Street, #2005, St. Paul, MN 55101-1978
651-224-6670
e-mail: harperlb@aol.com

Agent: Laurie Harper

Born: September 1954.

Education: Business and finance, with pre-law studies.

Career history: The literary agency was founded in 1985. It evolved simultaneously with the closing of my small Bay Area regional publishing company (Sebastian Publishing), which published gift books, selling to B. Dalton, Waldenbooks, and independents throughout the West Coast. After I placed books with other publishers for authors I could not publish, I discovered my strengths as an agent. I briefly experienced the author's side of publishing by writing a media biography of a legendary radio personality (*Don Sherwood: The Life and Times of the World's Greatest Disc Jockey,* Prima Publishing, 1989), which enjoyed 12 weeks on the *San Francisco Chronicle*'s bestseller list. Prior to publishing, I was in banking (operations and lending) with a major California bank for eight years. I frequently consult with authors.

Hobbies/personal interests: Reading; games; outdoor activities, including skiing, sailing, rollerblading, shooting hoops, bike riding.

Areas most interested in agenting: Narrative nonfiction across a broad spectrum, though not family memoirs; consumer reference; health/nutrition/medical issues; psychology/sociology, current affairs/journalism, business (management, careers, business stories), and various books/topics that target mainstream educated readers.

Areas not interested in agenting: Mainstream fiction is being nominally considered, though it is not a big part of my list. No genre fiction. No poetry, children's, original screenplay material, gift books, religious, academic, or scholarly.

If not agenting, what would you be doing? I would most likely be in contract law, perhaps working for the Authors Guild.

Best way to initiate contact: Please note that I am taking on few new clients at this time. Send a query letter explaining the project, who you are, and why you are doing this book. Feel free to include the proposal, outline, and a sample chapter. And, of course, the SASE. I do not want phone calls unless the author has been referred to me by a client or colleague.

Reading-fee policy: No reading fee or editorial fee. I do charge my clients a one-time $100 fee, which is a nominal contribution to phone and postage expenses incurred prior to a first sale.

Client representation by category: Nonfiction, 99%; Fiction, 1%.

Commission: 15% domestic; 20% foreign.

Number of titles sold last year: It usually averages about 20.

Rejection rate (all submissions): 95%. The majority of new clients come from referrals from my clients or industry professionals and colleagues. However, every submission is read and considered on its own merit.

Most common mistakes authors make: It is a costly mistake to use anything other than the current year's resource material when exploring potential agents, due to the constant changes in the industry. It is also counterproductive to query without providing the agent with sufficient orientation and information. We are reading the proposal cold. The author has to make it make sense; give it a proper framework. Demonstrate that you know the market for your book; what's been published, how your book fits into the scheme of things. You must answer the obvious questions: Who cares? Why? Are these book-buying people? How many are there? Can anyone find them? What do you specifically have to offer a publisher who would invest in this project? Publishing is, after all, first and foremost a business . . . not an endowment for the arts or for hobbyists.

Description of the client from Hell: The first thing has to be unrealistic expectations; financial and promotional expectations that are simply not realistic for as-yet-unproved authors. For previously unpublished authors, it's understandable that they don't know the industry, but it is incumbent upon each prospective author to inform him/herself on the basics. Attend some conferences; do some reading; talk to other published authors. I'm happy to coach an author about strategy or problem solving, to help plan out a realistic publishing career path, but the agent can't be in charge of teaching Publishing 101. Another difficulty comes if the author expects the agent to perform miracles: We can't sell what isn't salable. It is the author's responsibility to consider and reflect upon the feedback given by agents and publishers, and to use that to improve the manuscript's potential for publication. I expect my clients to be mature professional adults, capable of approaching this process positively and constructively. No whining allowed.

Comments: The challenge facing every author and publisher (and therefore agent) is how to reach a readership, how to get people to buy this particular book. It isn't a matter of "Put it out there and they will come." Accordingly, my decisions about which authors to partner with are based on many elements. Aside from the book itself, I consider the talents of the writer and what the writer brings to the marketing and promotion of that book. I also have to balance my overall client list. And certainly I evaluate the timing of your book for the specific category and market. The best advice I can give a writer is to only write the books you have to write, that book for which you have passion, skill, and ability to promote and market over many years. As an agent I am focused on books and authors that can compete at a national level for readers' precious attention.

Representative titles: *The Ten Smartest Decisions a Woman Can Make After Forty* by Tina Tessina, Ph.D. (Renaissance Books); *Bald in the Land of Big Hair: A True Story* by Joni Rogers (HarperCollins); *The Other Side of Eden: Life with John Steinbeck* by Nancy Steinbeck (Prometheus); *Latticework: The New Investing* (Texere) and *The Essential Warren Buffett* by Robert Hagstrom (Wiley); *A Dance for Emilia* by Peter S. Beagle (Dutton); *The Third Age: 6 Principles for Growth and Renewal After Forty* by William Sadler, Ph.D. (Perseus); *Too Nice for Your Own Good* by Duke Robinson (Warner); *Executive Thinking,* by Leslie Kossoff (Davies-Black Publishing); *Natural Beauty from the Garden* by Janice Cox (Henry Holt); *Champions of Silicon Valley* by Charles Sigismund (Wiley).

THE SEYMOUR AGENCY

475 Minor Street, Canton, NY 13617
315-386-1831   fax: 315-386-1037
Pages.slic.com/mseymour.com   e-mail: mseymour@slic.com

Agents: Mary Sue Seymour, Michael J. Seymour

Born: Mary Sue: September 21, 1952; Michael: August 19, 1948.

Education: Mary Sue: B.S., State University of Potsdam, New York; postgraduate work with Potsdam State, Ithaca College, Azusa Pacific College. Michael: B.S., Siena College, New York; M.S., St. Lawrence University; M.A., SUNY at Potsdam.

Career history: Mary Sue: Taught 11 years in the public school system; professional artist; currently teach part time; freelance writer published in several national magazines. Michael: Taught over 20 years; columnist for newspaper group and Regional Editor for a magazine; Coast Guard captain—runs fishing charter service seasonally. Assistant Agent at the Seymour Agency.

Hobbies/personal interests: Mary Sue: Piano, reading, alpine skiing, swimming, hiking, camping, camping in the Adirondacks (!). Michael: Fishing, hunting—and then there's writing about fishing and hunting.

Areas most interested in agenting: Christian romance, Christian self-help, romance, Westerns, and general nonfiction.

Areas not interested in agenting: Short stories, screenplays, poetry, or anything that conflicts with our faith in God.

If not agenting, what would you be doing? Mary Sue: Writing and painting. Michael: Writing and guiding full time.

Best way to initiate contact: Short query letter and first 50 pages of novel or nonfiction proposal summary.

Reading-fee policy: No.

Client representation by category: Nonfiction, 40%; Fiction, 50%; Children's, 5%; Textbooks, 5%.

Commission: 12.5% published authors; 15% unpublished.

Number of titles sold last year: Several.

Rejection rate (all submissions): 90%.

Description of the client from Hell: Never had one.

Description of the dream client: A dream client is one who writes a lot, uses suggestions, is enthusiastic about his/her writing, appreciates what we try to do for him/her, and sends us a book we can sell.

How did you become an agent? We listed ourselves in a writer's guide and sold a four-book contract with our first submission. I guess it was just meant to be.

Why did you become an agent? I love books—reading and learning, and I enjoy each of the diverse challenges of publishing. Books are fundamental to our society, and I take pride in being part of their contribution. There is enormous satisfaction from creating a successful team—making the right match between author and publisher, negotiating a fair contract that promotes a successful venture, and assisting in every way to build long-lasting relationships.

S

What can writers do to enhance their chances of getting you as an agent? Being professionally polite, and a sense of humor doesn't hurt either.

How would you describe what you actually do for a living? Attend conferences such as the RWA Step Back in Time Conference held in Williamsburg, VA, in 1999, the Romantic Times Convention held in Toronto in 1999, Ottowa Romance Writers Brunches in 1999 and 2000, and the Fiction from the Heartland Writers Conference in Kansas City in 2001. Work seven days a week, try to keep our clients feeling good about themselves, work with contracts and royalties, and keep accurate records of all of the above.

What do you think about editors? Editors are professionals who know their stuff. They work long hours and bring too much work home (any is too much).

Comments: Writing comes from deep within ourselves—it's a reflection of us as people. We write about our friends, our experiences, and our own thoughts. Therefore, it's not surprising that when our novel is rejected, we take it personally. It means we're not "good" people. We've opened up our innermost thoughts to strangers and these people denied their worth. I can understand why so many writers feel this way. But the reality of the situation is, writing is a business and business is about making money. If an agent rejects your work, he/she feels her company can't make money on it. If an editor rejects your work, he/she feels her company can't make money on it. Because a book isn't a moneymaker doesn't mean it's bad. I've seen some intriguing toys developed for Christmas marketing that I wouldn't want my name on. Yet they made a lot of money. Separate your self-esteem from commercialism. They're two different things. Thousand of musicians are out of work in this country, but that doesn't diminish the quality of their music. Not everyone who writes gets his or her book published, but no one can distinguish who will and who won't.

Representative titles: *Spanish Bride* by Ammanda McCabe (New American Library); 2 untitled books by Ammanda McCabe (New American Library); *Dark Knight* by Tori Phillips (Harlequin Historicals); *Eye of the Cat* by Audra McWilliams (Macmillan); *Pennytown Justice* by Audra McWilliams (Macmillan); untitled novel by Farrah Spence (Hawk Publishers); *Nokoa's Woman* by Gayce Rogers (Five Star Macmillan Hardcover); *Wild Rose of York* by Betty Davidson (Berkley); *Papa Was a Boy in Gray* by Mary Schaller (Thomas Publications).

THE ROBERT E. SHEPARD AGENCY

4111 18th Street, Suite 3, San Francisco, CA 94114
415-255-1097
www.shepardagency.com   e-mail: query@shepardagency.com

Agent: Robert Shepard

Education: B.A. and M.A., English, University of Pennsylvania.

Career history: I've spent 18 years in and around the publishing world. For nearly nine of them, I worked in the trade division of Addison-Wesley, a respected publisher that has since been merged-and-acquired out of existence. My work on the editorial, sales, and marketing sides of publishing and later as a consultant has given me a good understanding of the "business" side, as well as excellent working relationships with scores of acquisitions editors. But after more than seven years in my own practice as an agent, I'm especially proud of the close rapport I've established with authors—one reason I've chosen to keep my agency small. With dozens of books in print, I'm now working with several clients for the second or third time.

Hobbies/personal interests: Hiking, biking, trains, raptors, and diagramming sentences.

Areas most interested in agenting: I represent only nonfiction, and under that heading I've cultivated two separate categories of books. The first consists of works driven by an exceptionally strong, unified, literary narrative—books intended to make complex ideas accessible to a wider public; to shed new light on aspects of history, society, or popular culture; or to provide fresh insights into people, places, or concepts we may think of as commonplace. On this side of the practice, my subject headings include history, contemporary affairs and politics, science for laypeople, sexuality, urbanism, and sports. The other general category of books I represent tends to be driven less by narrative and more by hard information; on this side, I have a core interest in personal finance and investing, business, and series-oriented works in travel, music, and popular culture. It's safe to say that I'm interested in neither the most commercial nor the most abstruse kinds of books; but I'm happy to represent works that change readers' minds, that may require a somewhat more intellectually curious audience, or about which someone might say, "I never thought this would be an interesting subject, but this book was a super read!"

Areas not interested in agenting: I never handle fiction, poetry, screenplays, or textbooks, and in general I'm not interested in autobiographical works—even when they relate in some way to my regular categories. (In other words, I most likely wouldn't represent a book on your sailing trip through the South Pacific, during which you played the clarinet; but I might represent a history of that region—or a biography of Benny Goodman). Robert E. Shepard Agency titles are usually aimed at a broad audience, so that highly specialized works (such as ones that examine religious writings in detail, or whose intended readers are mainly in a single profession) are not appropriate. As a general rule, I'm also not interested in works in New Age spirituality, self-help, or recovery.

If not agenting, what would you be doing? It could go one of three ways: Either I would go back and get that Ph.D. and write papers on 19th-century authors who were extremely prominent in their day but paradoxically have become totally obscure (probably due to bad marketing), or I would be conducting a symphony orchestra, or I would be riding trains somewhere in an attempt to escape my job as publisher of a distinguished literary nonfiction house. I'm not picky.

Best way to initiate contact: Never call or fax; neither will speed consideration of your proposal. I encourage authors to mail a query letter or proposal or to e-mail a relatively brief query describing the proposed work, its intended audience, and the author's own credentials and reason for writing on this subject. Don't just refer me to a Web site; I want to see how you present your ideas in the succinct form demanded by a query letter, whether by mail or e-mail. Please do not attach any computer files to e-mail messages; for security purposes, they'll be deleted. If you use regular mail, always enclose a postage-paid return envelope capable of holding everything you sent me, without which you will not receive a reply.

Reading-fee policy: No reading fee.

S

Client representation by category: Nonfiction, 100%.

Commission: 15% domestic, 20% for "subagented" foreign rights.

Number of titles sold last year: 10. I have deliberately kept the practice small in order to devote time to my clients. I am happy to see proposals from new authors or from authors whose previous works may have been in genres other than general nonfiction. However, your credentials and expertise should be suited to the kind of book you're proposing.

Rejection rate (all submissions): 99%.

Most common mistakes authors make: A big one is failing to share the proposal with a friend, another writer, or a trusted adviser before sending it out. Authors who work in a vacuum risk losing perspective. In the many months you've been working on your book proposal—and very often they really do take that long to write—has your focus shifted inadvertently? Have you failed to discuss some aspect of your topic that an agent or editor might find fascinating—simply because you're too immersed in writing to realize you'd missed it? Have you cited a date or name incorrectly, making yourself look careless even though you really do know your facts? A trusted adviser, particularly one with experience in writing books, can help you improve your proposal or even catch mistakes before you send it to agents. Not to sound like the English teacher I sometimes think I should have been, but bad spelling and grammar often guarantee rejection slips, too. Proofread your work, and if you don't trust your proofreading skills, find someone you do trust to help you. I also counsel authors to avoid proposal clichés. A big one is "there's no competition for my book." You should always try to find works that others might consider competitive, and then describe what's new, different, and better about yours. Finally, there are two important housekeeping issues: Always enclose a return envelope large enough to hold your material, with the proper postage (without which you won't get a response); and always provide your return address.

Description of the client from Hell: One who's good at selling an agent or editor on a book but doesn't want to actually write it. Writing is tough and an agent tries to help, but in the end the responsibility is the author's.

Description of a dream client: One who is passionate about writing, passionate about his or her subject, and appreciative when things go right.

Why did you become an agent? I love books and believe they can and should still be central to our cultural life, even in an era when they're being joined by new sources of entertainment and information all the time. But the consolidations of leading publishers during the 1990s resulted in the loss of many editors, the very people who traditionally worked the closest with authors, helped them craft better books, and made sure that the marketing got done. The vast majority of today's editors are as talented and dedicated as ever but find themselves with more books to edit and less time to spend with authors. So although authors create the intellectual property that fuels our culture, they can feel lost in the publishing shuffle, confused by business aspects of their writing careers, and even disillusioned by the paradoxical demand of publishers to write "fresh" books that nonetheless don't deviate much from the constraints of established categories. I see my role as an agent as that of a mentor and advocate for my clients and their work, as a diplomat who can moderate the author–publisher relationship, as a business adviser who watches over royalty statements, and, in the end, as someone who helps authors feel good about the writing experience, so they can write more books in the future. The good news is that, when everything works as it should, the wealth of media outlets available to us in the Internet age means books can be more rather than less influential.

What can writers do to enhance their chances of getting you as an agent? Go to a good, independent bookstore. It's essential for authors to have some perspective on their work, and that means knowing all about books that are similar, or that an agent might mistake as being similar, and (in another vein) being able to talk about authors you respect whose work is in some ways akin to yours. There's nothing more helpful to me than a short overview that answers questions like these: Why did you write this book? What need does it fill? What audience do you envision? What are some books like yours, even if they are terrible (and say why)? Why are you the right person to write this book? What would you like your work to achieve that hasn't been achieved before? Browsing in bookstores, and buying and reading a few recent works, can be very helpful as you answer those questions. I recommend libraries, too, but it's essential to stay current.

Representative titles: *Wine and War: The French, the Nazis, and the Battle for France's Greatest Treasure* by Don and Petie Kladstrup (Broadway Books); *Talking Money: Everything You Need to Know About Your Finances and Your Future* by Jean Chatzky (Warner Books); *Word Freak: Heartbreak, Triumph, Genius and Obsession in the World of Competitive Scrabble* by Stefan Fatsis (Houghton Mifflin); *Between Sodom and Eden: A Gay Journey Through Today's Changing Israel* (Columbia University Press); *Legacy of the Prophet: Despots, Democrats, and the New Politics of Islam* by Anthony Shadid (Westview Press); *The Uncle Book: Everything You Need to Know to Be a Kid's Favorite Relative* by Jesse Cogan (Marlow & Co.); *Your Stock Options* by Alan Ungar and Mark Sakanshi (HarperCollins); *Sidewalk Critic: Lewis Mumford's Writings on New York,* edited by Robert Wojtowicz (Princeton Architectural Press).

S

WENDY SHERMAN ASSOCIATES, INC.

450 Seventh Avenue, Suite 3004, New York, NY 10123
212-279-9027   fax: 212-279-8863
e-mail: wendy@wsherman.com

Agent: Wendy Sherman
  Born: New York City.
  Education: Bachelor Degree in Special Education.
  Career history: Agent at Aaron Priest Agency until 1999. VP Executive Director Henry Holt, VP Associate Publisher Owl Books, VP Sales and Sub-Rights (1988–1999).
  Hobbies/personal interests: Reading, skiing, walking, traveling.
  Areas most interested in agenting: Quality fiction, thrillers, suspense, narrative nonfiction, practical nonfiction, memoir, human drama.
  Areas not interested in agenting: Sci-fi, fantasy, horror.
  If not agenting, what would you be doing? I could be back in corporate publishing but choose not to be.
  Best way to initiate contact: Query letter to agency.

Reading-fee policy: No.

Client representation by category: Nonfiction, 50%; Fiction, 50%.

Commission: 15% domestic; 20% foreign.

Number of titles sold last year: Established in November 1999. New agency, sold 12 books in 2000.

Rejection rate (all submissions): 99%.

Most common mistakes authors make: The most common mistake is impatience. We receive dozens of queries per day and read them all. In addition, it's important to remember that it's finding the right agent for the books that counts, not just finding any agent.

Description of the client from Hell: The client from Hell is unreasonably demanding and doesn't trust my judgment and 20 years of experience.

Description of a dream client: All of my clients (so far) are dream clients. They thoroughly trust my experience, appreciate my efforts on their behalf, and have been supportive of my launching a new business. In addition, my clients have been well rewarded with excellent contracts with excellent publishers.

How did you become an agent? I left Henry Holt and worked for the Aaron Priest Agency for nine months, learning from these successful agents. Then I struck out on my own.

Why did you become an agent? 20+ years as a publisher led me to this career. I sold subsidiary rights for most of my career and love selling and negotiating. When I left Henry Holt, I wanted to stay in the biz but work for myself and my clients.

How would you describe what you actually do for a living? Find new talent and bring it to the best possible/most enthusiastic editor. Also, work with published writers who may need my services.

What do you think about editors? They have a very tough job today. Finding great manuscripts, convincing colleagues to support the projects; dealing with too much work and a lot of pressure.

What do you think about publishers? Tough to make money these days. We need to work together.

Comments: I absolutely love being an agent. It pulls together everything I've done in a 20-year career. If thoughts like this sound like Pollyanna, so be it. It's all true. Every submission gets opened like it's Christmas. I think, "This could be the one." But let's face it, it's usually not. Yet I never lose my optimism. Publishing today is tougher than ever before. I know. I was there. There are enormous obstacles to getting books published. Everyone from the author to the agent to the editor and the publisher has to work together. The challenge as an agent is to take on what you can sell. Not just take on clients to say you have them. That said, I am very selective.

S

JACQUELINE SIMENAUER LITERARY AGENCY, INC.

P.O. Box 1039, Barnegat, NJ 08005

609-607-1780

Agents: Fran Pardi, Jacqueline Simenauer

Born: Simenauer: February 23, 1949; New York. Pardi: 1949; Pittsburgh, Pennsylvania.

Education: Simenauer: Fordham University; Pardi: B.A. in English.

Career history: Simenauer: Editor, World Wide Features, Inc.; President, Psychiatric Syndication Service, Inc.; freelance writer and co-author: *Beyond the Male Myth* (Times Books); *Husbands and Wives* (Times Books); *Singles: The New Americans* (Simon & Schuster); *Not Tonight Dear* (Doubleday); *Singles Guide to Cruise Vacations* (Prima Publishing). Pardi: Strong journalism background; freelance writer, and editor.

Hobbies/personal interests: Simenauer: Cruising the world. Pardi: Music, reading, dance, theater.

Areas most interested in agenting: Simenauer: I like a wide range of strong commercial nonfiction books that include medical, health/nutrition, popular psychology, how-to/self-help, parenting, women's issues, spirituality, men's issues, relationships, social sciences, fashion, beauty, business, computers, reference. Pardi: Cookbooks, medical books.

Areas not interested in agenting: Poetry, crafts, children's books, fiction.

If not agenting, what would you be doing? Simenauer: Become an entrepreneur. Pardi: Probably sitting on a beach or in front of a fireplace reading published books, as opposed to unpublished books.

Best way to initiate contact: Simenauer: I prefer a query letter with SASE. Pardi: Query letter with SASE.

Reading-fee policy: No reading fee.

Client representation by category: Nonfiction, 100%—We are a nonfiction agency.

Commission: 15%.

Rejection rate (all submissions): Simenauer: 95%. Pardi: 98%.

Most common mistakes authors make: Simenauer: Call and tell you that other agents are interested and want to know what you will do for them if they decide to go with you (and this is before you have even had a chance to see their material). Pardi: Cute gimmicks or self-platitudes. What's on the paper is the only thing that matters.

Description of the client from Hell: Simenauer: One who keeps calling for all sorts of reasons. Doesn't send SASE, yet demands material back. Calls collect. Calls with long-winded query and expects you to make decision over the phone. Sends in handwritten, illegible query. Pardi: The one who thinks I can read 250 pages a minute and keeps calling back to check on status. This is one case where the squeaky wheel does not get oiled. It just gets annoying.

Description of a dream client: Simenauer: Sends in a terrific outline—well-written, great idea, easy to work with. Follows through. Has patience and loyalty. Pardi: The one who trusts that I will do everything in my power to represent the book without being badgered.

Why did you become an agent? Simenauer: I have been an articles editor, journalist, freelance writer, and coauthor. Agenting seemed the next step. Pardi: I sort of fell into it but quickly realized it does satisfy my "readaholic" compulsion. The only time I am not reading is when I am driving (although I do manage to absorb a few paragraphs at traffic lights).

Comments: Simenauer: I think my background as a freelance writer and coauthor makes me even more sympathetic to struggling writers. I understand what it feels like to see your name on a book jacket and appear on a major TV show, and if I can help you achieve your dream, then it becomes mine as well. But understand that it takes a great deal of perseverance to go from an idea to a proposal strong enough to get the attention of the publishing world. I hear good ideas all day long, yet few ever go anywhere. Pardi: I love to be surprised when I read a manuscript, and I love to become emotionally involved. Also, I am a little partial to Pittsburgh Steelers fans.

MICHAEL SNELL LITERARY AGENCY

P.O. Box 1206, Truro, MA 02666-1206
508-349-3718

Agents: Michael Snell, President; Patricia Snell, Vice President

Born: Michael: August 16, 1945; Denver, Colorado. Patricia: March 6, 1951; Boston, Massachusetts.

Education: Michael: B.A., DePauw University, Phi Beta Kappa. Patricia: Pratt Institute, Fine Arts.

Career history: Michael: Editor, Wadsworth Publishing Company (1967–1978); Executive Editor, Addison-Wesley (1978–1979); Owner, Michael Snell Literary Agency (1979–present). Patricia: Financial Officer; Editor; Executive V.P., H. Michael Snell, Inc. (1986–present).

Hobbies/personal interests: Michael: Tennis, golf, shell-fishing, fishing, gardening. Patricia: Tennis, organic vegetable and flower gardening.

Areas most interested in agenting: Nonfiction books that offer readers genuine, tangible benefits, especially practical, applied self-help and how-to titles in all areas: health and fitness, parenting, relationships, sex, travel, gardening, sports, psychology, communication, writing and publishing, pet care, and training. Michael specializes in business, management, leadership, finance, computers, technology, entrepreneurship, motivation, careers at all levels, from professional/reference to low-level how-to. Both Michael and Patricia emphasize books by women for women on all subjects, from workplace issues and entrepreneurship and management to dating, marriage, relationships, communication, sex, and parenting.

Areas not interested in agenting: Personal memoirs, science fiction, children's books, noncommercial fiction.

If not agenting, what would you be doing? Almost any creative career (painting, sculpture, fiction-writing, teaching) where something solid and valuable arises from applying skill and endures long after you die. Then, again, it's nice to get paid for your accomplishments.

Best way to initiate contact: New authors can obtain a brochure, "How to Write a Book Proposal," by sending an SASE. We also urge prospective clients to read our 1997 book *From Book Idea to Bestseller* (Prima Publishing). Keep query letters concise and focused: your topic, your credentials, and your intended audience. Always include an SASE for response. We only consider new clients on an exclusive basis.

Reading-fee policy: No, we work strictly on a commission basis.

Client representation by category: Nonfiction, 90%; Fiction, 10%.

Commission: 15% of all income from primary and subsidiary rights, with higher percentages arranged for developmental editing, rewriting, line editing, collaborating, and ghostwriting.

Number of titles sold last year: 40.

Rejection rate (all submissions): 93%.

Most common mistakes authors make: Authors who do not respect the etiquette that multiple queries are okay but multiple submissions are not. Too many ambitious would-be authors engage in their quest for an agent as if they were looking for a plumber rather than a mentor and friend. They forget that we invest valuable time, expertise, and resources every minute we spend reacting to, critiquing, developing, editing, and shaping a project. Manipulation, playing one agent off against another, while gaining value from both, usually backfires. It certainly derails the crucial building of a trusting relationship.

Description of the client from Hell: Subject experts who assume expertise in writing and publishing and do not appreciate that they can learn from our 40 years of book development experience. Eager authors who do not take the time to develop the full potential of their books and grow impatient with the inherently slow, deliberate nature of book publishing. Writers so intent on making money that they forget that bestsellers benefit readers' lives first and foremost and make money only when they solve problems and change readers' lives. Hastiness, inattention to detail, manipulativeness, greediness, dishonesty and lack of integrity, and humorlessness drive us crazy, just as they drive any businessperson crazy.

Description of a dream client: Anyone, regardless of his or her background and area of expertise, who takes time to listen and learn about project development and publishing; who takes time to develop and write a valuable book proposal and manuscript; who enters into a relationship with us in a spirit of partnership; who works hard but patiently; who, above all, maintains a sense of perspective and humor. The dream client displays all the traits we expect from friends and family: trust, honesty, integrity, respect, and a genuine caring. Without those qualities, no relationship can flourish. With them, all the hard work can pay off for all concerned—author, agent, editor, and publisher.

How did you become an agent? I reached a point after 13 years as an editor working for a corporation where more time was consumed in organizational politics and meetings than in working with writers, words, and manuscripts. Skills gained in publishing enabled us to hang out our own shingle, focus on authors and their books, and broaden our interests and relationships. Now, in a sense, we work with and for 200 authors and 50 different publishing houses.

Why did you become an agent? A lifelong love of writing and books, a belief that books can make a big difference in people's lives. In business terms, good books satisfy needs, provide tangible benefits, and solve problems. In a human sense, a successfully published book brings the same personal satisfaction a parent gets from the birth of a child or a gardener from a bountiful harvest. How amazing to do work that brings constant, daily joy! Agenting satisfies all three major needs: personal, financial, and spiritual (in the broadest sense of the word).

What can writers do to enhance their chances of getting you as an agent? Approach us with enthusiasm and confidence but also with a certain amount of humility. Ask vital

S

questions about your project and listen closely to our answers. If you want to know about our credentials and track record, read our book *From Book Idea to Bestseller* (Prima), where you'll not only learn about our approach, but will also meet over 50 of our clients in the book's examples. Treat us as you would any potential business partner, but bear in mind that publishing is a people business, where success hinges on qualities you cannot put in a contract: loyalty, trustworthiness, and love. Love? Yes, when we (or an editor) fall in love with a book, we (or the publisher) will work our tails off to help make it succeed.

How would you describe what you actually do for a living? Three words: development, development, development. A query arrives, we send back developmental advice. A proposal results, we offer suggestions for developing its full potential. We sell the book to a publisher, we develop the author's relationship with an editor. Even after a client has published 3 or 5 or 30 books, development and continued growth dominate our daily activities. Marketing and contract negotiation are the easy parts. Adding value takes a whale of a lot of time and energy.

What do you think about editors? These days, fewer editors actually edit. They often function as traffic cops, buying projects and putting them into production. To deal with that trend, we and our authors must fill the gap, shouldering responsibility for developmental editing. Still, we love editors. Without them, we could not generate income for ourselves and our writers. Everything we say about relationship-building between an agent and client applies to agent–editor and author–editor relationships.

What do you think about publishers? The huge houses have become more bureaucratic and slow. The newer, more entrepreneurial houses are quicker, more personal, more aggressive. Both the conglomerate and the independent offer pros and cons to authors. Still, it has gotten more difficult to find the right home for the right book.

Comments: You want to hear us rant and rave? Push either of these "Hot Buttons": Marketing and Technology. Increasingly, the marketing folks at publishing companies carry all the clout, giving thumbs up or thumbs down to a book an editor loves and wants to buy. But these people couldn't land or hold a marketing position with a real business. They wouldn't recognize a well-written manuscript if it whacked them upside the head; they assume a writer's next book will sell less than her first book; they judge a book by its cover; they market what they do publish with all the skill and enthusiasm of toothpaste salespeople. If someone made us king of the world, we'd give smart, experienced editors with good judgment and instincts all the decision-making power, and we'd tell the marketing department to get creative, get to work, and sell their butts off. Technology! Fax! E-mail! Hurry, hurry, hurry, I need it yesterday! Oh, all these machines are fine, they make a writer's job a lot easier, but a computer does not make a writer one IQ point smarter, and a fax or e-mail message does not make a communication one iota more urgent. If we could wave a magic wand, we'd make all aspiring book authors type their queries and proposals and manuscripts on old standard upright typewriters (with carbon paper!). The queries would get shorter, the proposals more concise, the manuscripts more carefully crafted. Okay, that's extreme. But don't let your machines seduce you into thinking you no longer need to slow down, take your time, think about it, and do it right. Machines may make you speedier, but they do not add quality, just quickness and quantity. P.S. If you're not having fun in this crazy business, you really ought to be doing something else with your life.

Representative titles: *The Innovator's Tale* by Craig Hickman (John Wiley & Sons); *Speed Dreams* (NASCAR) by Joy Ahuja (Kensington); *As Told by Water* by David James Duncan (Sierra Club/Random House); *How to Say It to the One You Love* by Paul Coleman (Prentice Hall); *The Innovative Woman* by Norma Carr-Ruffino (Career Press); *Why Didn't I Think of That?* by Charles McCoy (Prentice Hall); *The Complete Idiot's Guide to Real Estate Investing* by Stu Rider (Macmillan); *Great Party!* by Anne-Stuart Hamilton (Prentice Hall); *Streetwise Guide to Internet Marketing* by Barry Feig (Adams Media); *9 Ways to Profit from New Products* by Don Debelak (Entrepreneur); *Leadership Secrets of Elizabeth I* by Shawn Higgins (Perseas); *25 Stupid Mistakes Dog Owners Make* by Janine Adams (Lowell House); *Bullet Proof Your Business* by Deb Traurso (Bloomberg Press)

SPECTRUM LITERARY AGENCY, INC.

111 Eighth Avenue, Suite 1501, New York, NY 10011
212-691-7556

Agent: Lucienne Diver

Education: Degree in English/Writing and Anthropology, summa cum laude, State University of New York, Potsdam.

Hobbies/personal interests: Hobbies: reading, writing, painting, mandolin, theater. Personal interests: forensics, anthropology.

Areas most interested in agenting: Fantasy, science fiction, mysteries, romance, suspense. Primarily adult commercial fiction.

If not agenting, what would you be doing? I considered going to graduate school for forensic anthropology. Publishing won out!

Best way to initiate contact: Query letter with brief synopsis and SASE.

Reading-fee policy: No reading fee.

Most common mistakes authors make: The biggest turn-off is ego. An author convinced that his or her first novel will break all sales records the first week on the shelves is likely to be disappointed and difficult to work with. One very basic mistake is the failure to include an SASE with a submission. Most agencies and publishing houses will not even look at material that does not come with a response envelope. Many writers underestimate the importance of the cover letter, which is, after all, the first impression the reader gets.

Description of the client from Hell: Has unrealistic expectations (first novel will break all sales records and be made into a major motion picture grossing billions). It happens, but not daily.

Description of a dream client: Someone who has taken the time to learn something of the business and who can make informed decisions.

Why did you become an agent? I love books, was always excited by the prospect of a job in publishing, and love working with intelligent, creative people.

S

PHILIP G. SPITZER LITERARY AGENCY

50 Talmage Farm Lane, Easthampton, NY 11937
516-329-3650   fax: 516-329-3651

Agent: Philip Spitzer
   Born: August 6, 1939, New York City.
   Education: M.A., New York University Graduate Institute of Book Publishing; M.A., French, University of Paris, France.
   Career history: New York University Press, 1961–1962; McGraw Hill Book Company, trade sales, Sales Promotion Manager, art book department, 1963–1966; John Cushman Associates/Curtis Brown Ltd. Literary Agency, 1966–1969; Philip G. Spitzer Literary Agency, 1969–present.
   Hobbies/personal interests: Sports and travel.
   Areas most interested in agenting: Fiction: literary and suspense. Quality nonfiction, including sports, biography, current events.
   Areas not interested in agenting: Most category fiction, most how-to.
   If not agenting, what might you be doing? Book sales representative.
   Best way to initiate contact: Query letter with SASE.
   Reading fee policy: No reading fee.
   Client representation by category: Nonfiction, 40%; Fiction, 60%.
   Commission: 15% domestic; 20% foreign.
   Rejection rate (all submissions): 95%.
   Most common mistakes authors make: Telephoning is a mistake.
   Description of the client from Hell: Daily phone calls; impossible to satisfy; if book doesn't sell—either to publisher or subsequently in bookstores—agent is to blame.
   Description of the dream client: Informed, respectful, and loyal.
   Why did you become an agent? An opportunity to work closely with both authors and publishers.
   Representative titles: *House of Sand and Fog* by Andre Dubus III (Norton, Vintage); *Bitterroot* by James Lee Burke (Simon & Schuster); *Split Second* by Alex Kava (Mira Books); *The Final Season* by Tom Stanton (St. Martin's Press); *City of Bones* by Michael Connelly (Little, Brown & Co.).

S

STEELE-PERKINS LITERARY AGENCY

26 Island Lane, Canandaigua, NY 14424
716-396-9290   fax: 716-396-3579

Agent: Pattie Steele-Perkins
   Education: B.A., English, Nazareth College, M.S., Communications, Syracuse University, New House School.
   Career history: 15 years as a TV Producer; 14 years as a Literary Agent.

What subjects/categories are you most enthusiastic about agenting? Romance and women's fiction.

What subjects are you not interested in agenting? Science fiction.

What is the best way to contact you? Synopsis and three chapters.

Client representation by category: Fiction, 100%.

Commission: 15%.

What are some common mistakes writers make? The biggest mistake potential clients make is not researching the marketplace before searching for an agent.

Description of the client from Hell: The unpublished author who calls every day and e-mails twice a day.

Description of the dream client: The published author who is so busy writing books she doesn't know I'm alive except at contract time.

What can writers do to enhance their chances of getting you as an agent? Writers should study the marketplace and submit work to those agents who specialize in the author's genre.

What do you think of editors? Editors love books and are in constant search of "The Book."

ROBIN STRAUS AGENCY, INC.

229 East 79th Street, New York, NY 10021
212-472-3282

Agent: Robin Straus

Education: B.A., Wellesley College; M.B.A., New York University.

Career history: Little, Brown, Editorial; Doubleday, Subsidiary Rights; Random House, Subsidiary Rights; Wallace & Sheil Agency, Agent; founded Robin Straus Agency in 1983. American representative for Andrew Nurnberg Associates Ltd., Jonathan Clowes Ltd., and Margaret Hanbury, out of London.

Areas most interested in agenting: General high-quality fiction and nonfiction.

Areas not interested in agenting: Genre fiction: science fiction, mysteries, romances, horror. No screenplays or books for children.

Best way to initiate contact: Letter, sample material, biographical information, and prior submission history—and SASE (stamped, no metered postage) for everything sent, which should be under one pound.

Reading-fee policy: No reading fee.

Client representation by category: Nonfiction, 65%; Fiction, 30%; Children's, 5% (only those written by my adult book writers).

Commission: 15% domestic, 20% foreign.

Number of titles sold last year: Authors represented include: Thomas Flanagan, fiction; Andrew Hacker, nonfiction; J. G. Ballard, fiction; Brian Aldiss, fiction; Frederick Turner, nonfiction; James Villas, cookbook; David Burnham, nonfiction; Alex Garland, fiction; Theodore Zeldin, nonfiction; Colin Eisler, nonfiction; Thomas Lickona, nonfiction; Antony Beevor, nonfiction; Michele Hernandez, nonfiction; Stephen Fox, nonfiction;

S

Gustaw Herling, fiction and nonfiction; Anne Willan, cookbooks; Sheila Kohler, fiction, Peter Watson, nonfiction; David Doubilet, nonfiction and photography.

Rejection rate (all submissions): 99.5%.

Most common mistakes authors make: Faxing material, and a long synopsis (sample pages tell us much more).

The John Talbot Agency

540 West Boston Post Road, Mamaroneck, NY 10543
914-381-9463
www.johntalbotagency.com

Agent: John Talbot

Education: B.A., DePauw University.

Career history: I am a Literary Agent and former book Editor with 16 years of experience in corporate book publishing. Prior to becoming an Agent, I spent seven years as a Senior Editor with the Putnam Berkley Group, where I edited such *New York Times* bestselling authors as Tom Clancy, W. E. B. Griffin, and Jack Higgins, as well as rising literary stars like Tom Perrotta, author of *Election* (Putnam), the novel upon which the Matthew Broderick movie was based, and Fred Haefele, author of *Rebuilding the Indian: A Memoir* (Riverhead). I published national bestsellers in hardcover, trade paperback, and mass market paperback, along with five *New York Times* Notable Books. I began my career at Simon & Schuster and worked at Pocket Books and Putnam Berkley before moving on to the Anita Diamant Literary Agency and then forming my own agency. I represent clients who write in all genres, with literary fiction, narrative fiction, and suspense being my areas of emphasis. I am a member of the Authors Guild.

Hobbies/personal interests: Sailing, boating, and related water sports. I am a published poet and have had a novel optioned for film. Church is a growing influence in my life.

Areas most interested in agenting: I am most enthusiastic about agenting literary fiction, narrative nonfiction, and novels of suspense. In fiction, I am looking for the fresh and occasionally edgy voice, no matter the subject or genre. Writers with minority backgrounds and unusual experiences and perspectives interest me, as do, perhaps conversely, writers of what Sue Miller calls domestic realism. Previous publication in literary journals and magazines is a big plus. Narrative nonfiction can cover almost any subject, but adventure and personal journey are particular interests of mine. *Rebuilding the Indian* (see above) is a good example of both. Newspaper and magazine experience can be helpful in this area; many books are generated from concepts first tried out in articles.

Areas not interested in agenting: I do not represent children's books, science fiction, fantasy, Westerns, poetry, or screenplays.

If not agenting, what would you be doing? I'd be writing full time, teaching, or working via the Internet.

Best way to initiate contact: Clients for both fiction and nonfiction should send a query letter, outline, and 10 sample pages to my attention, along with a self-addressed stamped envelope for reply, with enough postage for the material to be returned if you want it returned. Do not send postmarked envelopes, as the postmark will not be valid outside your area. Please do not send original manuscripts or artwork.

Reading-fee policy: I do not charge reading fees.

Client representation by category: Nonfiction, 30%; Fiction, 70%.

Commission: 15% on all domestic sales, including film and subsidiary sales. Commissions on foreign rights sales vary; they are usually 20% but can go to 25%, depending on co-agent.

Number of titles sold last year: I sold approximately 25 titles last year.

Rejection rate (all submissions): My acceptance rate for cold queries has been 1 in 500.

Most common mistakes authors make: A phone pitch or queries by fax or e-mail. Labeling fiction as mainstream. Telling me you have several more unpublished novels. Sending an obvious form letter. Telling me about your personal life and writing habits instead of describing the book itself. Suggesting your own marketing plans and cover design. Including parts of other agents' or editors' rejection letters. Using referrals from people I don't know.

Description of the client from Hell: The client from Hell doesn't respect my time. He or she fails to recognize the publisher's justly proprietary attitude toward marketing, book design, and other facets of publication. He or she won't take suggestions for change, no matter how small or well-reasoned, complains about writing, and treats being published as a right instead of the opportunity and privilege that it is.

Description of a dream client: Dream clients respect my personal and professional lives. They trust me. They are open to input from their editor. They love to read and they love to write. They are enthusiastic about their ideas and about what they do.

Why did you become an agent? Becoming an agent was a natural progression from being an editor. It's the same type of work, but I'm able to spend less time in meetings and more time working with authors. I can also handle a more eclectic range of material, and I get to work with editors throughout the industry who share my passions and enthusiasms.

What can writers do to enhance their chances of getting you as an agent? Try to respect my time. Make sure your proposal is clear, succinct, and well organized. Make sure the rest of your material is finished and ready to go if I'm interested.

How would you describe what you actually do for a living? I help authors manage their careers for the long-term. I find and put projects that I'm passionate about into the hands of equally enthusiastic editors.

What do you think about editors? Editors without a doubt are the hardest working and most idealistic people in book publishing.

What do you think about publishers? Publishers represent the best opportunity for gifted writers to get wide distribution, readership, and money in what is an often difficult business.

Representative titles: Fiction: *Frontera Street* by Tanya Maria Barrientos (NAL); *Deep Sound Channel* and *Thunder in the Deep* by Joe Buff (Bantam); *SexGeek* by Gary S. Kadet (Forge); *Render Safe* by Jodie Larsen (Berkley); *Feeding the Rat* by Clint McKinzie (Bantam); *Lily of the Valley* and *Around Again* by Suzanne Strempek Shea (Pocket Books); *Forgive the Moon* by Maryanne Stahl (NAL); *Night Angel Nine* by Peter Telep (Berkley); *Burden* by Tony Walters (St. Martin's Press). Nonfiction: *The Dr. Atkins' Age-Defying Diet Revolution* by Sheila Buff (St. Martin's Press); *Girlfriends' Secrets: Insider Info, Extraordinary Tips, and True Confessions About Cosmetic Surgery* by Charlee

Ganny (Renaissance); *The Encyclopedia of Pirates and Piracy* by David Jacobs (Facts on File); *Inez: A Memoir* by Clarence Major (John Wiley & Sons); *The Complete Idiot's Guide to Fantasy Football* by Michael Zimmerman (Macmillan).

SUSAN TRAVIS LITERARY AGENCY

1317 North San Fernando Boulevard, #175, Burbank, CA 91504
818-557-6538

Agent: Susan Travis

Education: B.A., English Literature, University of California, Berkeley.

Career history: Prior to establishing my agency in 1995, I spent four years with the Margret McBride Literary Agency, most recently as an Associate Agent. Before joining the Margret McBride Agency, I worked in the Managing Editorial Department of Ballantine Books, New York.

Areas most interested in agenting: I represent fiction and nonfiction and truly enjoy working on both. For fiction, I am currently representing literary and mainstream fiction and am interested in reading just about anything, provided the writing is good and there is depth to the work. My nonfiction interests encompass a wide area. In the past, I've handled cookbooks, self-help/psychology, health, and business. I would like to receive more nonfiction submissions for books targeted at a general audience, not those aimed at an exclusive or limited market.

Areas not interested in agenting: I do not represent children's or young-adult works, poetry, screenplays, fantasy, or horror.

Best way to initiate contact: Fiction: A query letter that gives a brief synopsis or overview of the project and any pertinent information about the author. The letter should be concise. My interest is usually piqued more by a description of the underlying themes in a project rather than a blow-by-blow plot summary. The first 15–20 pages of the manuscript may be enclosed with the query. Nonfiction: A query letter giving a brief overview of the project and a brief description of the author's credentials or expertise. Or, a complete proposal may be sent. If the manuscript is complete, the author should query first rather than sending the entire manuscript. An SASE with correct postage must be enclosed for a reply and return of material.

Reading-fee policy: No reading or marketing fees.

Client representation by category: Nonfiction, 70%; Fiction, 30%.

Commission: 15% domestic, 20% foreign.

Rejection rate (all submissions): 95%.

Most common mistakes authors make: Verbal/telephone queries seldom work. If an author is trying to market writing, then let the writing speak for itself. Authors have to make the effort to pitch their work using the written word. One of the most costly mistakes an author can make is to market work prematurely. I usually base decisions on an as is basis, not on the hidden potential. Unpolished manuscripts can rarely compete with those by authors who have taken the extra time to polish their projects and make a professional submission.

Description of a dream client: Dream clients are those who are professional, businesslike yet friendly, who appreciate input and advice but don't require constant handholding.

UNITED TRIBES

240 West 35th Street, #500, New York, NY 10001
212-244-4166
e-mail: janguerth@aol.com

Agent: Jan-Erik Guerth
 Born: 1965, in a Volkswagen Beetle.
 Education: M.Ph. in Cultural Studies from New York University.
 Career history: Comedian (one of five funny Germans!), journalist, radio producer, film distributor, before discovering my true passion—publishing.
 Areas most interested in agenting: Only nonfiction—including "Spirituality in Everyday Life"; ethical, social, gender, and cultural issues; comparative religion; self-help and wellness; science and arts; history and politics; nature and travel; and any fascinating future trends and other serious nonfiction.
 Areas not interested in agenting: Depends on each project, but most certainly not agriculture, animals, military/war, sports, and needlework.
 Best way to initiate contact: Outline with one sample chapter, resume, and SASE.
 Reading-fee policy: No reading fee.
 Client representation by category: Nonfiction, 100%.
 Commission: 15%; 20% on foreign rights sales.
 Description of the client from Hell: Has two little horns on forehead, hides bushy tail and horse's hoof, and smells of sulfur and roses.
 Description of a dream client: Has been reported missing.

THE RICHARD R. VALCOURT AGENCY, INC.

177 East 77th Street PPHC, New York, NY 10021

Agent: Richard R. Valcourt
 Born: November 29, 1941; Fall River, Massachusetts.
 Education: B.A., Roger Williams College; M.A., New York University; ABD, City University Graduate School; L.L.B., LaSalle Extension University.
 Career history: Radio-television Journalist (1961–1980); Program Administration, City University of New York (1980–1995); Instructor, Department of Political Science, Hunter College (1981–1995); founded Richard Valcourt Agency (1995), Consulting Faculty, American Military University (1996–present). Editor in Chief, *International Journal of Intelligence* (1998–present), Executive Editor (1986–1998).

V

Areas most interested in agenting: Now represent exclusively professional and scholarly works in international relations, national security, and related aspects of United States government and politics.

Areas not interested in agenting: All works not included in the above category.

Best way to initiate contact: Letter of inquiry (with SASE), brief biography, summary of material.

Reading-fee policy: No reading fee. May charge for photocopying, mailing, and phone calls if excessive.

Client representation by category: Nonfiction, 100%.

Commission: 15% domestic, 20% foreign.

Rejection rate (all submissions): 99.5%.

What can writers do to enhance their chances of getting you as an agent? Be experienced practitioners, academics, or journalists in the fields I represent.

RALPH M. VICINANZA, LTD.

111 8th Avenue, Suite 1501, New York, NY 10011

Agent: Sharon Friedman

Education: B.A., English, Queens College; J.D., Cornell Law School.

Career history: Formerly an attorney in New York City; worked as agent for nine years (first at John Hawkins Associates).

Hobbies/personal interests: Martial arts.

Areas most interested in agenting: Literary and commercial fiction, science, business, biography, health.

Areas not interested in agenting: Science fiction, fantasy, mysteries, genre romance.

Best way to initiate contact: Query letter via e-mail or regular mail.

Reading-fee policy: No reading fee.

Client representation by category: Nonfiction, 50%; Fiction, 40%; Children's, 10%.

Commission: 15%.

Representative titles: *A Handbook for Living* by His Holiness Dalai Lama and Dr. Howard Cutler; *Bad Medicine* by Ron Querry (Bantam); *Complexonomics* by Roger Lewin and Birute Regine (Simon & Schuster); *Nothing but the Rent* by Sharon Mitchell (Dutton); *The ABC's of Family Values* by Steven Lewis (Dutton); *The Alternative Medicine Handbook* by Barrie Cassileth (Norton); *White Crosses* by Larry Watson (Pocket).

V

THE VINES AGENCY, INC.

648 Broadway, Suite 901, New York, NY 10012
212-777-5522   fax: 212-777-5978
e-mail: tva@mindspring.com

Agent: James C. Vines

Born: May 1, 1966; Huntsville, Alabama.

Education: Auburn University.

Career history: Raines & Raines, Literary Agent, 1989–1992; Virginia Barber Literary Agency, Literary Agent, 1993–1995; The Vines Agency, Inc., Literary Agent, 1995–present.

Hobbies/personal interests: Sailing, music.

Areas most interested in agenting: Quality commercial fiction, thrillers, women's fiction, quality commercial nonfiction, adventure, relationship books.

Areas not interested in agenting: If it's well written, I want to see it.

If not agenting, what would you be doing? I am an agent because I can't be anything else.

Best way to initiate contact: Query letter with one-page letter describing the story, along with SASE.

Reading-fee policy: No reading fees whatever.

Client representation by category: Nonfiction, 50%; Fiction, 50%.

Commission: 15% domestic, 20% foreign.

Number of titles sold last year: 30.

Rejection rate (all submissions): I reject 80% of the "over the transom" submissions I receive.

Most common mistakes authors make: Writing 12-page cover letters (single-spaced); sending chapters from the middle of the novel, claiming "those are the best"; and calling to see if I've had a chance to read the material yet.

Description of the client from Hell: I do not represent hellish clients.

Description of a dream client: See my list of authors under "Representative titles."

How did you become an agent? I had met some brilliant authors who needed a good business manager, and I couldn't find anything else in this world nearly as exciting as helping them to develop their careers.

Why did you become an agent? I love great authors and want to help them reach their goals.

What can writers do to enhance their chances of getting you as an agent? Write on subjects about which you are passionate. Research the marketplace to make sure the same book hasn't already been written by somebody else. Don't pack your manuscript in plastic "peanuts" that will require us to vacuum the office after opening the box containing your manuscript.

How would you describe what you actually do for a living? I identify the largest and best audience for a book and then arrange deals on the author's behalf with the publishers and film producers best positioned to deliver that book to its audience.

What do you think about editors? I love editors, if they're good.

What do you think about publishers? The right publisher for the right author is a dream come true.

Comments: Please don't write for the money because if you do write for the money, you'll be intolerable once you finally get it.

Representative titles: *The Warmest December* by Bernice L. McFadden (Dutton/Plume); *The Surrendered Wife* by Laura Doyle (Simon & Schuster); *The Fourth Wall* by

Beth Saulnier (Warner Books); *Naked Came the Phoenix* by Marcia Talley et al. (St. Martin's Press); *Meltdown* by James Powlik (Delecorte); *Miami Twilight* by Tom Coffey (Pocket Books); *California Fire and Life* by Don Winslow (Knopf Publishing); *Hunting with Hemingway* by Hilary Hemingway (Riverhead Books); *America the Beautiful* by Moon Unit Zappa (Scribner); *Cross Dressing* by Bill Fitzhugh (HarperCollins); *The Bottoms* by Joe Lansdale (Warner Books & New Line Cinema).

WALES LITERARY AGENCY, INC.

108 Hayes Street, Seattle, WA 98109
206-284-7114   fax: 206-284-0190
e-mail: waleslit@aol.com

Agent: Elizabeth Wales
   Born: March 30, 1952.
   Education: B.A., Smith College; graduate work in English and American Literature at Columbia University.
   Career history: Worked in the trade sales departments at Oxford University Press and Viking Penguin; worked in city government and served a term on the Seattle school board; also worked as a Bookseller and Publisher's Representative.
   Areas most interested in agenting: A wide range of narrative nonfiction and literary fiction titles. Especially interested in nonfiction projects that could have a progressive cultural or political impact. In fiction, looking for talented mainstream storytellers, both new and established. Especially interested in writers from the Northwest, Alaska, the West Coast, and what have become known as the Pacific Rim countries.
   Areas not interested in agenting: Children's books, almost all genre projects (romance, historicals, true crime, horror, action/adventure), how-to, self-help.
   Best way to initiate contact: Send query letter with writing sample(s) and a brief description of the book project with SASE to the agency for consideration.
   Reading-fee policy: No reading fee.
   Client representation by category: Nonfiction, 60%; Fiction, 40%.
   Commission: 15% domestic.
   Number of titles sold last year: 14.
   Rejection rate (all submissions): Most of our projects and authors come from referrals, but several times a year we "discover" a beauty of a book from the submissions pile.
   Why did you become an agent? For the adventure and the challenge; also, I am a generalist—interested in variety.
   Comments: I am particularly interested in writers who are dedicated to writing and/or who have a particularly compelling story to tell.
   Representative titles: *May-I-Help-You.com: The Best Customer Service on the Web* by Robert Spector (Perseus Books); *Skipping Towards Gomorrah: Sin in America* by Dan Savage (Dutton); *Laying Waste* by Duff Wilson (HarperCollins).

V

T. C. WALLACE, LTD.

425 Madison Avenue
New York, NY 10017
212-759-8600   fax: 212-759-9428
e-mail: TCWallace@mindspring.com

Agent: Tom Wallace
Born: Vienna, Austria, December 13, 1933.
Education: B.A., Yale, 1955; M.A., History, 1957.
Career history: Putnam, 1959–1962; Henry Holt & Co., 1962–1981; W. W. Norton & Co., 1982–1987; Literary Agent, 1987–present.
Areas most interested in agenting: Nonfiction: history, biography, memoir, current events, serious journalism. Fiction: serious rather than light, British rather than American.
Areas not interested in agenting: "Pop" fiction and "pop" nonfiction.
If not agenting, what would you be doing? Teaching or writing.
Contact methods: Please do not contact unless recommended by a client, a publisher, or an editor known to me.
Reading-fee policy: No.
Commission: 15%.
Number of titles sold last year: 15.
Rejection rate (all submissions): 95%.
Client representation by category: Nonfiction, 90%; Fiction, 10%.
Description of the client from Hell: I don't represent such writers!
Description of the dream client: A cross between John Updike, Arthur Schlesinger, Jan Morris, and Simon Winchester. You might throw in a Michael Gobroyd and John Keeyan as well.
How did you become an agent? I chose to.
Why did you become an agent? I felt that after nearly 30 years as an editor (Putnam, Holt, Norton), I knew how and where to place serious nonfiction and serious fiction.
What can writers do to enhance their chances of getting you as an agent? Come to see me *after* being invited.
How would you describe what you actually do for a living? Working in the Vineyard, and getting the best possible contracts for writers I admire intensely
What do you think about editors? Some are my best friends. Others . . . I wouldn't cross the street to enumerate their inadequacies: bad judgment, inefficiency, and lack of personal conviction (i.e., "balls"). Most are overworked and underpaid. Some are God's gift to serious writers.
What do you think about publishers? Some are becoming (or already are) mindless, paper-publishing bureaucrats who should be in any business not called book publishing. Others are serious and competent and let editors get on with publishing good books. I fear the former outnumber the latter.
Representative titles: *The Sword and the Shield* by Christopher Andrew (Basic Books); *The Higher Angel* by Roy Lorrus (Oxford University Press); *Yankee Doodle*

W

Dandy by John Dizikes (Yale University Press); *Myself When I Am Real* by Charles Ofingun (Oxford University Press); *See the Treasure of All Things* by Jonathan Golthorne Hardy (Indiana); *Gentleman Spy* by Peter Grose (Houghton Mifflin); *Operation Rollback* by Peter Grose (Houghton Mifflin); *Madonna—Who Is She Really?* by Barbara Victor (Chiff Street Books); *The Rise of Democracy in America (1776–1860)* by Sean Wilerts (W. W. Norton); *Players* by Steve Levine (Random House).

John A. Ware Literary Agency

392 Central Park West, New York, NY 10025

Agent: John A. Ware
  Born: May 21, 1942.
  Education: B.A., Philosophy, Cornell University; graduate work, English Literature, Northwestern University.
  Career history: Editor, eight years, Doubleday & Company; Literary Agent, one year, James Brown Associates/Curtis Brown Ltd.; founded John A. Ware Literary Agency in 1978.
  Hobbies/personal interests: Music, choral singing and blues bands, Italy.
  Areas most interested in agenting: Biography and history; investigative journalism, social commentary, and contemporary affairs; bird's eye views of phenomena; literary and suspense fiction; Americana and folklore; nature and science.
  Areas not interested in agenting: Technothrillers and women's romances, men's action-adventure; how-to's, save the area of medicine and health; guidebooks and cookbooks; science fiction, personal memoirs.
  If not agenting, what would you be doing? Teaching philosophy or working as a sportswriter, or in some position in race relations.
  Best way to initiate contact: Query letter only with SASE.
  Reading-fee policy: No reading fee. Only for Xeroxing, authors' copies of galleys and books, and unusual mailing expenses.
  Client representation by category: Nonfiction, 80%; Fiction, 20%.
  Commission: 15% on all sales, save foreign, which are 20%.
  Rejection rate (all submissions): 90%.
  Description of the client from Hell: Untrusting, and accordingly, nudging.
  Description of a dream client: Professional at all aspects of his or her chosen writing area; trusting; in possession of a sense of humor.
  Why did you become an agent? I like working with writers, editorially and otherwise, outside the corporate realms of meetings and red tape, inside of which I worked as an editor.
  Comments: In what remains of our genteel world of books, I would encourage a shoring up of the realm of common courtesy, returning phone calls, saying please and thank you, and so forth and so on.
  Representative titles: *An Unreturned Pilgrim: Biography of Bishop James A. Pike* by David Robertson (Knopf); *The Water and the Blood* by Nancy E. Turner (Regan/Harper-

Collins); *The Immortal Class: Bike Messengers and the Cult of Human Power* by Travis Hugh Culley (Villard/Random House); *Going, Going, Gone* by Jack Womack (Atlantic Monthly Press); *The Warbler's Call: The Disappearance of America's Songbirds* by Kenneth A. Brown (W. H. Freeman).

WATERSIDE PRODUCTIONS, INC.

The Waterside Building, 2191 San Elijo Avenue, Cardiff-by-the-Sea, CA 92007-1839
760-632-9190   fax: 760-632-9295
www.waterside.com

Agents: David Fugate, Margot Maley, Matthew Wagner

Education: Fugate: B.A., Literature, University of California at San Diego. Maley: Literature, University of California at San Diego. Wagner: B.A., Literature/Creative Writing, University of California at Santa Cruz.

Career history: Fugate: Agent with Waterside Productions since 1994. Maley: Literary Agent with Waterside since 1992. Wagner: I've been a library clerk, a bookbinder, a bookstore clerk, and a Buyer. I've been a Literary Agent for eight years.

Hobbies/personal interests: Fugate: Travel, basketball, skiing, reading, and independent films. Maley: Skiing, tennis, biking, cooking, reading, running. Wagner: Yoga, tennis, golf, lots of reading.

Areas most interested in agenting: Fugate: Computer books and compelling nonfiction in many areas, including pop culture, business, technology, sports, and cyberculture. Wagner: Computer books, Internet-specific programming titles, sports, culture and technology, general how-to, business, and management.

Areas not interested in agenting: Fugate: New Age, children's, romance, poetry, short stories. Maley: Fiction, New Age, religious. Wagner: Fiction, poetry, self-help.

If not agenting, what would you be doing? Fugate: I would be the sixth man for some mediocre professional basketball team in Greece, or a nomadic ski bum, or a project-development person in Tarantino's production company, or on the editorial side of the publishing industry. Maley: I would be leading safaris in East Africa. Wagner: Editor, publisher, or packager. I would love to run a bookstore someday.

Best way to initiate contact: Query letter or proposal. Maley: Query letter or proposal. Wagner: Query letter.

Reading-fee policy: No reading fee.

Client representation by category: Fugate: Nonfiction, 100%. Maley: Nonfiction, 100%. Wagner: Nonfiction, 95%; Textbooks, 5%.

Commission: 15% domestic, 20% film, 25% foreign.

Number of titles sold last year: Fugate: 110. Maley: 110. Wagner: 150.

Rejection rate (all submissions): 95%.

Most common mistakes authors make: Fugate: Those whom I can tell haven't researched their market thoroughly have little chance of success. I'm also turned off by anyone who wants to meet with me before showing me any of their materials. Maley: A poorly written proposal or query letter or too many phone calls to check on the status of their proposal. Wagner: Telling me the book is sure to sell several million copies because the market is everyone. Insufficient market research.

Description of the client from Hell: Fugate: The client from Hell is unprofessional, is reactionary, isn't willing to put in the work to produce a quality book or proposal, fails to meet deadlines, and overestimates his or her value in the marketplace consistently. Maley: A rude, arrogant, pushy, and impatient person who has completely unrealistic expectations. Wagner: Someone prone to projection who thinks he or she is always right.

Description of a dream client: Fugate: A talented writer who is professional, understands the business, meets deadlines, is easy to work with, and has good relationships with his or her editors. Maley: A great writer with good ideas who meets deadlines and is friendly and pleasant to deal with. Wagner: Professional, open-minded, creative, honest, and disciplined.

Why did you become an agent? Fugate: I like books, words, and ideas. Maley: Growing up, I always seemed to have either a book or a phone in my hand. Wagner: Probably because I can talk really fast. Also, I love books and like dealing with writers and publishers. It helps to be on the cutting edge.

Comments: Fugate: Check out our Web site at www.waterside.com for information about our authors, publishers we work with, and the Waterside Publishing Conference, held annually in San Diego.

Representative titles: Maley: *Flash Action Script FX and Design* by Bill Sanders (Coriolis); *Dreamweaver Magic* by Al Sparber and Sherry London (New Riders Press); *Rookie Dad* by Susan Fox (Simon & Schuster); *.Com Success* by Sally Richards (Sybex); *The Salt Solution* by Herb Boynton (Avery Press); *Fed Up! Dr. Oliver's Ten Step No Diet Fitness Plan* by Dr. Wendy Oliver (Contemporary Books). Wagner: *KISS Guide to Windows* by Rich Levin (Dorling Kindersly); *Poor Richard's Building Online Communities* by Margy Levine Young (Top Floor Publishing); *MCSD in a Nutshell: The Visual Basic Exams* by James Foxall (O'Reilly & Associates); *PC's for Dummies* by Dan Gookin (Hungry Minds). Fugate: *The JavaScript Bible* by Danny Goodman (Hungry Minds); *The Flash 5 Bible* by Rob Reinhardt and Jon Warren Lentz (Hungry Minds); *Fire in the Valley* by Paul Freiberger and Michael Swaine (McGraw Hill); *Maximum Linux Security* by Anonymous (Sams Publishing); *Evil Geniuses in a Nutshell* by Illiad (O'Reilly & Associates).

WIESER & WIESER, INC.

25 East 21st Street, New York, NY 10010
212-260-0860

Agents: Olga B. Wieser, Jake Elwell
   Born: Elwell: July 23, 1964; Milton, Massachusetts.
   Education: Elwell: B.A., Lake Forest College.
   Career history: O. Wieser: NYU Press; Agent since 1975. Elwell: House painter; high school English teacher; Wieser & Wieser: Assistant, 1989–1994; Agent, 1994–present.

Hobbies/personal interests: Elwell: Antiques, book collecting, hockey, fishing, travel.

Areas most interested in agenting: O. Wieser: Well-written, challenging books of all kinds. Strong commercial and literary fiction; holistic, medical, and psychological issues are of particular interest. Elwell: Commercial fiction, including mysteries, historicals, military, suspense, romance. Nonfiction backed by a strong author profile: history, true crime, biography, Americana, books about New England.

Areas not interested in agenting: O. Wieser: Category romance; historicals. Elwell: Science fiction, self-published books that did poorly.

If not agenting, what would you be doing? O. Wieser: Writing. Elwell: Teaching, traveling, trying to be a writer, painting houses.

Best way to initiate contact: Through a referral from someone we know well or by mail with a well-presented outline and opening 50 pages with SASE. Please, no phone or faxed queries.

Reading-fee policy: No reading fee.

Client representation by category: Nonfiction, 45%; Fiction, 50%; Children's, 5%.

Commission: 15% domestic; 20% foreign.

Number of titles sold last year: 50.

Rejection rate (all submissions): 97%.

Most common mistakes authors make: Showing material that is incomplete in planning or presentation. Pitches that try to shock or impress with coolness. We avoid faxed proposals, spiral (or otherwise) bound manuscripts, and solicitations that include past rejection letters from agents and editors (yes, it happens!) like the plague.

Description of the client from Hell: Pitches numerous, disparate ideas and expects reaction/action on all of them. Never is satisfied.

Description of a dream client: Knowledgeable of the realities of publishing (good and bad). Appreciative, receptive to our input, resourceful, and trustworthy.

Why did you become an agent? O. Wieser: There's no job more rewarding, enriching, and exciting. Elwell: I like working in an entrepreneurial setting, and I love books. And there's nothing like playing a role in bringing a book to life.

Representative titles: *1978: When Baseball Was Still Baseball* by Bert Randolph Sugar (Taylor); *Angels and Demons* by Dan Brown (Pocket); *Cutting* by Steven Levenkron (Norton); *Grinning in His Mashed Potatoes* by Margaret Moseley (Berkley Prime Crime); *Hocus Corpus* by James Tucker (Signet); *Kill Grandma for Me* by Jim DeFelice (Pinnacle); *Roots of the Rich and Famous* by Robert Davenport (Taylor); *Rules of Command* by C. A. Mobley (Berkley); *Smoke and Murder* by Harry Paul Lonsdale (Avon/Twilight); *Sounding Drum* by Larry Jay Martin (Kensington); *The Cammi Granato Story* by Thom Loverro (Lerner); *The Captain's Courtship* by Kate Huntington (Zebra); *The Kamikazes* by Edwin P. Hoyt (Burford Books); *The Last Hostage* by John J. Nance (Doubleday).

Writer's House

21 West 26th Street, New York, NY 10010
212-685-2400   fax: 212-685-2605

Agents: Steven Makl, Susan Ginsburg, Fran Lebowitz, Karen Solem, Michele Rubin, Albert J. Zuckerman, Merrilee Heifetz, Amy Berkower, Jennifer Lyons, Susan Cohen, Simon Lipskar.

Born: Ginsburg: New York. Lebowitz: Baltimore, Maryland. Lyons: August 30, 1961, New York City. Cohen: June 27, 1958.

Education: Ginsburg: Yale University. Zuckerman: D.F.A., Dramatic Literature, Yale. Lebowitz: Franklin and Marshall College; University of Maryland. Heifetz: B.A., Sarah Lawrence College. Solem: Graduated Wheaton College, 1972. Lyons: B.A., Sarah Lawrence College; M.A., Middlebury College. Cohen: B.A., Princeton University.

Career history: Ginsburg: Editor in Chief, Atheneum; Executive Editor, St. Martin's; Executive Editor, Simon & Schuster/Pocket Books. Zuckerman: Naval officer; Foreign Service officer, U.S. State Department; Assistant Professor of Playwriting, Yale Drama School; winner of Stanley Drama Prize for best new American play of 1964; author of two published novels and of *Writing the Blockbuster Novel;* writer for *The Edge of Night* on TV; Broadway producer. Lebowitz: Lowenstein Associates; William Morris Agency. Heifetz: Teaching writing to children; Literary Agent. Solem: Editor in Chief at Silhouette Books, Editor in Chief/Associate Publisher of Harper Paperbacks. Lyons: Began as an Assistant to Joan Daves. Became Director in 1995. I also work as a senior Writer's House Agent. Cohen: 20 years at Writer's House.

Hobbies/personal interests: Zuckerman: Helping writers; tennis, antique textiles and furniture. Lebowitz: Dangerous sports. Heifetz: Cooking, art, sports. Lyons: Dance, rare books, travel.

Areas most interested in agenting: Ginsburg: Fiction: commercial fiction of any type and literary fiction that is accessible. Nonfiction: broad range of topics chosen purely by interest and marketability. Narrative nonfiction, women's issues, science, biography/autobiography, cookbooks. Zuckerman: Fiction: wonderful novels of all kinds, especially those accessible and attractive to a large readership. Nonfiction: history, biography, narrative nonfiction. Lebowitz: Middle-grade and young adult novels, popular culture books, adult novels. Heifetz: Fiction with an edge, distinctive mysteries, wonderful women's fiction, well-written but commercial fantasy; exceptional young adult fiction. Solem: Commercial fiction, including women's fiction, romance novels, mysteries, and thrillers. I would like to see more nonfiction in the areas of animals and nature, gardening, and spirituality. I am very interested in handling more (I already do some) religious and inspirational fiction and nonfiction. Lyons: Literary and commercial fiction, memoir and anthology, narrative nonfiction, parenting, illustrated packaged international authors, literary estates. Cohen: Children's books; both authors and illustrators; adults, selected number of nonfiction projects.

Areas not interested in agenting: Ginsburg: Children's books, science fiction. Zuckerman: Scholarly, professional. Lebowitz: Financial and self-help. Heifetz: Men's adventure. Solem: Western novels, science fiction, children's books, and academic nonfiction. Lyons: Romance, limited science fiction. Cohen: Science fiction, fantasy, educational, inspirational, academic, financial, business.

If not agenting, what would you be doing? Heifetz: Living in Italy. Solem: I'd be back in corporate publishing or starting a small press. Lyons: I would work in the arts, perhaps as a curator of a literary series such as the one at Symphony Space or the 92nd Street Y. I would also teach.

Best way to initiate contact: Ginsburg: Through written correspondence—query letter (with SASE). Zuckerman: An interesting, intelligent letter (with SASE). Lebowitz: Letter (with SASE), a synopsis, and several sample chapters. Heifetz: Letter (with SASE). Solem: Query letter with or without sample material. Lyons: Send a query letter and three sample chapters. Cohen: Query letter.

Reading-fee policy: No reading fee.

Client representation by category: Agency as a whole has about 500 clients. Ginsburg: 40–50 clients; Nonfiction, 60%; Fiction, 40%. Zuckerman: About 70 clients; Nonfiction, 50%; Fiction, 50%. Lebowitz: Nonfiction, 20%; Fiction, 80%; Children's, 70%. Heifetz: Nonfiction, 10%; Fiction, 80%; Children's, 10%. Solem: Nonfiction, 5%; Fiction, 90%;. Lyons: Nonfiction, 50%; Fiction, 45%, Children's, 5%. Cohen: Nonfiction, 15%; Fiction, 5%; Children's, 80%.

Commission: 15% domestic and film; 20% foreign.

Number of titles sold last year: Agency: More than 400. Lebowitz: About 40. Solem: About 100. Lyons: 65. Cohen: 100.

Rejection rate (all submissions): 50%. Cohen: 90%.

Most common mistakes authors make: Lebowitz: Calling the agency soon after sending a submission. Heifetz: Harassing the agent. But I don't let the authors I represent make mistakes. Solem: If they write fiction, indicating that they are all across the board, moving from genre to genre without the ability to focus and develop their work. Lyons: They call too often, demand too much too quickly, and are anxious about everything. They try to be "cute" instead of being straightforward. They send submissions in strange formats and colors. No need for that. Cohen: Telling me they were referred by someone I've never heard of, sending photos of themselves, sending unprofessional illustrations with their stories.

Description of the client from Hell: Heifetz: I don't have any. Solem: Writers who have no realistic sensibility about their work or the market they are attempting to write for. Writers who demand constant handholding and who are ambitious to the point of aggression with their editor/publisher. Lyons: A writer who doesn't have any sense of boundaries and who has not bothered to learn the very basics of publishing. I expect professional behavior. I don't do well with demanding and ungrateful people. Working together is a partnership and requires mutual respect.

Description of a dream client: Heifetz: Talented, professional, pleasant to deal with, prolific. Solem: Writers who have a career plan—who know what they're doing and are capable of focusing their writing as their career begins to build. Writers who communicate with both their editor/publisher and me. Someone who is ambitious and has a clear/realistic sense of direction. A terrific writer. Lyons: A writer who is professional. I work with authors who are well prepared, polite, and understanding of the process. A good client understands that agenting is a tough business and that agents only have limited amounts of time during the day to be interrupted. Authors should be focused about what they are writing about.

How did you become an agent? Lyons: My father is a publisher. He began the Lyons Press about 15 years ago. Prior to that, he was an English professor and nonfiction editor at Crown Publishing. He introduced me to publishing at an early age, and I had the bug. Also, I met Joan Daves, who represented six Nobel Prize–winning authors, right after graduate school. She immediately took me into the company, which is a part of Writer's House, LLC. Cohen: I started at an entry-level position, became an agent's assistant, and after learning how to represent authors, started doing so.

Why did you become an agent? Heifetz: I like reading and I like writers. Solem: I wanted more independence and the flexibility that comes from being self-employed but wanted to continue to work with authors to see the best possible books published. With 25 years' publishing experience on the other side of the desk, I believe I have a lot to offer. Lyons: I like the combination of reading, writing, doing publicity and legal work, and working with authors.

How would you describe what you actually do for a living? Cohen: I help authors navigate the world of trade publishing.

Comments: Well-known clients are: Octavia E. Butler, Nora Roberts, F. Paul Wilson, Tim Willocks, Ridley Pearson, Ann Martin, Francine Pascal, James Howe, Bruce Sterling, Joan D. Vinge, Cynthia Voigt, Colin Wilson, Robin McKinley, Ed Humes, Robert Anton Wilson, Lora Brody, Jane Feather, Joan Johnston, Ken Follett, Michael Lewis, Stephen Hawking, V. C. Andrews, Linda Howard, Paula Danziger, Banana Yoshimoto, Barbara Delinsky, Eileen Goudge, Sydney Omarr, David Berlinski, Jessica Harris, Leigh and Leslie Keno, Neil Gairman, Laurell Hamilton, Rosanne Cash.

Representative titles: *Black Holes and Baby Universes* by Stephen Hawking (Bantam); *Coast Road* by Barbara Delinsky (Simon & Schuster, first in a three-book mystery series); *Inner Harbor* by Nora Roberts (Berkley); *Inside Intel* by Tim Jackson (Dutton); *Monitor* by James DeKay (Walker); *Neverwhere* by Neil Gaiman (Avon); *Style and the Man* by Alan Flusser (Harper); *Sunflower* by Martha Powers (Simon & Schuster); *The First Wives' Club* by Olivia Goldsmith (Simon & Schuster); *The Hammer of Eden* by Ken Follett (Crown); *The Swan Maiden* by Susan King (Penguin Putnam); *Tired of Nagging (30 Days to Positive Parenting)* by Virginia Stowe with Andrea Thompson; *Trail Fever* by Michael Lewis (Knopf). Cohen: *MacLean Trilogy* by Janice Johnson (Harlequin); *The World* by Roni Schotter (Atheneum); *Rocket Sheep* by Nancy Shaw (Houghton Mifflin); *The Pickle Museum* by Debbie Tilley (Harcourt); *Irish Anthology* by Kathleen Krull (Hyperion).

THE ZACK COMPANY, INC.

243 West 70th Street, Suite 8D, New York, NY 10023-4366
www.zackcompany.com

Agent: Andrew Zack
  Born: 1966; Massachusetts.
  Education: B.A., English and Political Science, University of Rochester, 1988.
  Career history: I began my publishing career on the retail side as the Evening Manager of an independent bookstore in Massachusetts. While attending the University of Rochester in Rochester, New York, I continued working on the retail side at the university's Barnes & Noble bookstore. Later, I served as an Editor on several student publica-

tions, including two years as the Managing Editor of the university yearbook, *Interpres*. I graduated in 1988 with a B.A. and the summer following attended the Radcliffe Publishing Course at Harvard University, an intensive publishing "boot camp" led by numerous publishing veterans. In September of 1988, I began work at Simon & Schuster Trade Division as a Foreign Rights Assistant, where I worked with S&S's foreign subagents in the licensing of foreign editions. Not long thereafter, I moved to Warner Books as an Editorial Assistant. While there, I edited a number of titles and began acquiring on my own. I was substantively involved in the editing of several bestsellers, including the Batman movie tie-in and two *Headlines* titles by Jay Leno. I next worked at Donald I. Fine, Inc., as an Assistant Editor and Rights Associate. Within six months, I was promoted to Associate Editor and Rights Manager. I acquired numerous titles and sold subsidiary rights to the entire Fine list, including serial, book club, reprint, large print, film, and television. I also served as liaison with Fine's British and foreign subagents. The Berkley Publishing Group was my next home, my having been recruited as an Editor. I was eventually responsible for more than 40 titles and brought a number of first-time authors to the list. I left Berkley during a corporate downsizing and entered the world of freelance. As a freelance Editor, I worked with a number of different clients, including several literary agencies and major publishers such as the Berkley Publishing Group, Donald I. Fine, Inc., Avon Books, Dell Publishing, and Tom Doherty Associates. I also reviewed for *Kirkus* and the Book-of-the-Month Club. I became a Literary Agent in September of 1993, joining the then recently formed Scovil Chichak Galen Literary Agency as a full Agent. I launched the Andrew Zack Literary Agency in March of 1996, which I then incorporated as the Zack Company, Inc., in May 1997.

Hobbies/personal interests: Indoor rowing, biking, film, investing, computers, jazz, reading, racquetball.

Areas most interested in agenting: History, particularly military history and intelligence services history; politics and current affairs works by established journalists and political writers; science and technology—how they affect society and business—by established journalists or experts in their fields; narrative accounts of how big breakthroughs were achieved and accounts of how big disasters occurred; natural sciences for the layman—geology, paleontology, biology, and so on; biography/autobiography about or by newsworthy individuals; personal finance and investing; commercial fiction (but not women's fiction); thrillers in every shape and form—international, serial killer, medical, scientific/technological/computer, psychological, erotic, military, environmental, legal; mysteries and crime novels—less cozy, more hard-edged but not necessarily hard-boiled; action novels, but not genre action/adventure.

Areas not interested in agenting: Women's fiction, romance novels, and anything that is primarily aimed at readers of women's fiction; genre horror novels; humor, unless by an *established* humorist/columnist/comedian; Star Trek novels by other than established Star Trek authors.

If not agenting, what would you be doing? I would likely still be an editor, or I might have gone to law school and pursued a career in entertainment law.

Best way to initiate contact: First, visit our Web site at www.theZackcompany.com. Nonfiction: Query letter with resume and a 2–3 page introduction to the project. Fiction:

Query, with history of previously published works, if any. Always include SASE for response/the return of any material. No phone calls, faxes, or e-mails please.

Reading-fee policy: No reading fee.

Client representation by category: Nonfiction, 35%; Fiction, 65%. (I want more nonfiction by leading authorities in their areas of expertise.)

Commission: 15% domestic, 20% foreign.

Rejection rate (all submissions): 99.95%.

Most common mistakes authors make: Phoning instead of writing; having a poorly written synopsis; making repeated telephone calls to check on the status of their submissions; not sending an SASE.

Description of the client from Hell: The client from Hell has probably published two or three, or maybe three or four, books. They are likely fiction but might be nonfiction. He or she has "fired" his or her previous agent because his or her career is going nowhere and that is, of course, the agent's fault. He or she is looking for an agent who can "make things happen"; and just to make sure those things happen, he or she calls a minimum of three or four times a week for updates. He or she regularly pitches ideas to his or her old editor, to the point where that editor calls me and asks me to stop my client from doing this constantly. The client is convinced that his or her ideas are future bestsellers and can't understand why no one agrees with him or her. He or she wants instant feedback from me or his editor and never once considers that I may have other clients or that the editor may have books on production schedules ahead of the client's. The client sends proposals via e-mail and doesn't understand why there isn't an instant response (the one downside to e-mail is that it creates a presumption that, because it's almost instantaneous in delivery, the reply to it should be instantaneous). Bottom line: The client from Hell is someone who believes his or her needs outweigh everyone else's—his agent's, his editor's, his publicist's, and those of all of the other authors with whom those people may be working.

Description of a dream client: The dream client acts like a professional. He or she prepared his material according to publishing standards. He or she keeps me updated on the progress of the work and on his or her career. He or she sends me an updated biography when something significant happens, as well as copies of reviews of published books if they reach him or her before they get to my office. He or she calls with news, or faxes, or e-mails me with news, but generally is aware that time spent "chatting" is time that could be spent selling his or her works. And, of course, he or she is a *New York Times* bestselling author.

Why did you become an agent? I had been in the publishing business as an editor and subsidiary rights salesperson for a number of years. I had the opportunity to move into representation with a start-up firm that held a lot of promise. It seemed to be the next, natural step in my career.

What can writers do to enhance their chances of getting you as an agent? Nonfiction writers have to be recognized experts in their subject areas or proven journalists who have written with great success about a number of different subjects. Novelists should be, first and foremost, real wordsmiths. Understand how to write, not just type. Then, know your marketplace. The combination of good writing and a commercial story will always sell.

How would you describe what you actually do for a living? I represent authors in the sale of their works to publishers, film studios, audio companies, and so on. That means reviewing materials to see if I believe there is a market for them, locating the best markets for them, concluding the sale, negotiating the contract on behalf of my client, and continuing to follow up with the buyer to ensure that the process goes well and that the buyer is using the best efforts to make the work a success.

What do you think about editors? In today's publishing world, editors have become more like product managers. Because of the demands on them to meet with marketing, publicity, and art departments, there is little time to brainstorm with their authors, to help develop the work. In addition, technology has made it mechanically easier to write books, which has resulted in an explosion in the number of books that are submitted. The sheer amount of reading required has made it that much more difficult for editors to look for "diamonds in the rough." Instead, they are looking for more "perfect" books that need little editorial work.

What do you think about publishers? Publishers today are looking for the biggest bang for their buck. They seem more willing to spend $100,000–$1 million on a book and put a big push behind it than to spend $10,000–$25,000 on several books and advertise and promote these books. I would guess that even with a $100,000 advance, publishers are going to do a lot less to push a book than an author might want. Publishers are loath to spend money to make money and will only invest heavily in promotion if there is a large advance involved. This forces agents and authors to seek larger and larger advances, which frequently do not earn out, which in some cases means the publisher loses money. When the publisher loses money, that means it is less likely to take risks and, strangely enough, it is the smaller books that are seen as risks, not the big-money books. This makes it more and more difficult for first-time authors to be sold, unless publishers perceive the author as the "next big thing." In the end, if he or she is not the "next big thing," and the publisher loses money on the book, it is very likely the author will have a very difficult time selling his or her second book. There is a vicious cycle at work, but it is generally one that was started by publishers and can only be ended by publishers.

Comments: The agent–author relationship is a business partnership. The agent has his or her role and the author has his or her role. Neither is an employee of the other. Interestingly enough, I never hear about agents or authors hiring each other, but I hear about them firing one another all the time. Agents, obviously, are businesspeople. Authors need to be businesspeople, too. Authors should do their best to be as informed as possible about the nature of the publishing business. They should subscribe to *Publishers Weekly*, or at least read it in the library every week. They should talk to their local independent bookseller (and if they really want to learn a few things, they should get a part-time job working in a bookstore). My best client is an educated client. I find that the hardest thing about the agent-author relationship is communication. E-mail has become an important mode of communication for me. It's quick and easy and almost instantaneous as a form of communication. Authors should be able to ask their agents all the questions they want, and if an author's agent disagrees with that, it's time to find another agent. But authors also need to recognize that every minute spent on the phone with them is a minute that could be spent selling their projects. As long as an author understands the job he or she has and the job

Z

the agent has in the author-agent relationship, the business partnership will flourish and be profitable.

Representative titles: *Star Trek—Spock vs. the Sequel: Did I Say That?* starring Leonard Nimoy and John de Lancie (Simon & Schuster Audio); *Homeschooling on the Internet* by Laura Maery Gold (Prima); *Sir Apropos, of Nothing* by Peter David (Pocket Books); *Star Risk* (two-book deal) by Chris Bunch (ROC); *J. K. Lasser's Invest Online* by Laura Maery Gold and Dan Post (John Wiley & Sons); *Doubleoon* by Jay Amber (Forge Books); *Reed's Promise* by John Clarkson (Forge Books); *Evil Whispers* by Owl Goingback (Signet); *Beyond Valor: World War II Rangers and Airborne Reveal the Heart of Combat* by Patrick O'Donnell (Free Press; Random House Audio*); Toward the Rising Sun: World War II's Veterans Reveal the Heart of Combat in the Pacific* by Patrick O'Donnell (Free Press); *Promise of Glory* by C. X. Moreau (Forge Books, Blackstone Audiobooks).

PART THREE

Road Maps to Your Success

Over the Transom and into Print

Maximizing Your Chances in the Battle of the UNs (Unagented/Unsolicited Submissions)

JEFF HERMAN

Most major publishing houses claim to have policies that prevent them from even considering unagented/unsolicited submissions. *Unagented* means that the submission was not made by a literary agent. *Unsolicited* means that no one at the publisher asked for the submission.

It's possible that you, or people you know, have already run into this frustrating roadblock. You may also be familiar with the rumor that it's more difficult to get an agent than it is to get a publisher—or that no agent will even consider your work until you *have* a publisher. On the surface, these negatives make it seem that you would have a better shot at becoming a starting pitcher for the Yankees, or living out whatever your favorite improbable fantasy might be.

But, as you will soon learn, these so-called policies and practices are often more false than true; especially if you develop creative ways to circumvent them.

I have dubbed the above obstacle course the Battle of the UNs. If you're presently unagented/unsolicited, you're one of the UNs. Welcome! You're in good company. Nobody is born published. There is no published author who wasn't at one time an UN. Thousands of new books are published each year, and thousands of people are needed to write them. You can be one of them.

In this chapter I'll show you how to win the Battle of the UNs. But first let me clarify an important distinction. When I use the word *win* here, I don't mean to say that you'll necessarily get your work published. What I mean is: You'll gain reasonable access to the powers-that-be for your work, and you'll learn how to increase the odds—dramatically—that your work will in fact be acquired.

Please be realistic. For every published writer, there are, at minimum, several thousand waiting in line to get published. "Many are called, but few are chosen."

It's completely within your power to maximize your chances of getting published. It's also within your power to minimize those chances. There are reasons why some highly talented people habitually underachieve, and those reasons can often be found within them. If you fail, fail, and fail, you should look within yourself for possible answers. What can you do to turn it around? If you find some answers, then you haven't failed at all, and the lessons you allow yourself to learn will lay the groundwork for success in this and in other endeavors.

Having an agent greatly increases the likelihood that you will be published. For one thing, on the procedural level, an established agent can usually obtain relatively rapid (and serious) consideration for his or her clients. One basic reason for this is that editors view agents as a valuable screening mechanism—that is, when a project crosses the editor's desk under an agent's letterhead, the editor knows it's undergone vetting from someone in the industry who is familiar with the applicable standards of quality and market considerations.

I usually recommend that unpublished writers first make every attempt to get an agent before they start going directly to the publishers. It's significantly easier to get an agent than it is to get a publisher—not the other way around. Most agents I know are always on the lookout for fresh talent. Finding and nurturing tomorrow's stars is one of our functions.

However, one of my reasons for writing and researching this book is to reveal to you that, as a potential author, not having an agent does not necessarily disqualify you from the game automatically. Before I show you ways to win the Battle of the UNs, I'd like you to have a fuller understanding of the system.

You Are the Editor

Imagine that you're an acquisitions editor at one of America's largest publishing firms in New York City. You have a master's degree from an Ivy League college and you, at least, think you're smarter than most other people. Yet you're earning a lot less money than most of the people who graduated with you. Your classmates have become lawyers, accountants, bankers, and so forth, and they all seem to own large, well-appointed apartments or homes—whereas you, if you fall out of bed, might land in the bathtub of your minuscule New York flat.

On the other hand, you love your job. For you, working in publishing is a dream come true. As in other industries and professions, much of your satisfaction comes from advancement—getting ahead.

To move up the career ladder, you'll have to acquire at least a few successful titles each year. To find these few good titles, you'll be competing with many editors from other publishers, and perhaps even with fellow editors within your own firm. As in any other business, the people who make the most money for the company will get the choice promotions and the highest salaries. Those who perform less impressively will tend to be passed over. (Of course, being a good editor and playing politics well are also important.)

There are two tried-and-true sources for the titles that publishers acquire: literary agents and direct solicitations.

Literary Agents

As an editor on the move, you'll cultivate relationships with many established literary agents. You'll want them to know what you like and what you don't like. And, by showing these agents you're disposed to acquiring new titles to build your position in the company, you'll encourage these agents to send you projects they think are right for you.

When you receive material from agents, you usually give it relatively fast consideration—especially if it's been submitted simultaneously to editors at other houses, which is usually the case. When something comes in from an agent, you know it's been screened and maybe even perfected. An established agent rarely wastes your time with shoddy or inappropriate material. They couldn't make a living that way because they'd quickly lose credibility with editors.

Direct Solicitations

If you're an ambitious editor, you won't just sit back passively and wait to see what the agents might bless you with. When you're resourceful, the opportunities are endless. Perhaps you'll contact your old American history professor and ask her to do a book showcasing her unique perspectives on the Civil War.

Or maybe you'll contact that young, fresh fiction writer whose short story you just read in a leading literary journal. You might even try reaching that veteran United States senator who just got censured for sleeping with his young aides.

One place you'll tend *not* to use is the "slush pile." This is the room (more like a warehouse) where all the unagented/unsolicited submissions end up. Looking through the slush pile isn't a smart use of your limited time and energy. The chances that anything decent will be found there are much less than 1 percent. You have less-than-fond memories of your first year in the publishing business, when, as an editorial assistant (which was basically an underpaid secretarial job), one of your tasks was to shovel through the slush. Once in a great while, something promising could be found; but most of the stuff wasn't even close. At first, you were surprised by how unprofessional many of the submissions were. Many weren't addressed to anyone in particular; some looked as if they had been run over by Mack trucks; others were so poorly printed they were too painful for tired eyes to decipher—the list of failings is long.

No, the slush pile is the last place—or perhaps no place—to find titles for your list.

Now you can stop being an editor and go back to being whoever you really are. I wanted to show you why the system has evolved the way it has. Yes, though it's rational, it's cold and unfair; but these qualities aren't unique to publishing.

You're probably still wondering when I'm going to get to that promised modus operandi for winning the Battle of the UNs. Okay, we're there.

OUT OF THE SLUSH

The following steps are intended to keep you out of the infamous slush pile. Falling into the slush is like ending up in jail for contempt of court; it's like being an untouchable in India; it's like being Frank Burns on *M*A*S*H*. My point is that nobody likes the Slushables. They're everyone's scapegoat and nobody's ally.

Once your work is assigned to the slush pile, it's highly unlikely that it will receive effective access. Without access, there can be no acquisition. Without acquisition, there's no book.

Let's pretend that getting published is a board game. However, in this game you can control the dice. Here are several ways to play.

Get the Names!

If you submit to nobody, it will go to nobody. Sending it to "The Editors," "Gentlemen," or the CEO of a $100-million publishing house equals sending it to no one.

Use the directory in this book to get the names of the suitable contacts.

In addition to using this directory, there are two other proven ways to discover who the right editors may be:

1. Visit bookstores and seek out recent books that are in your category. Check the Acknowledgments section of each one. Many authors like to thank their editors here (and their agents). If the editor is acknowledged, you now have the name of someone who edits books like yours. (Remember to call to confirm that the editor still works at that publishing house).

2. Simply call the publisher and ask for the editorial department. More often than not, the phone will be answered by a young junior editor who will say something like "Editorial." Like people who answer phones everywhere, these people may sound as if they are asleep, or they may sound harried, or even as if they're making the most important declaration of their lives. Luckily for you, publishers plant few real secretaries or receptionists in their editorial departments, since it's constantly reconfirmed that rookie editors will do all that stuff for everyone else—and for a lot less money! Hence, real editors (although low in rank) can immediately be accessed.

Returning to the true point of this—once someone answers the phone, simply ask, "Who edits your business books?" (Or whatever your category is.) You can also ask who edited a specific and recent book that's similar to yours. Such easy but vital questions will bring forth quick and valuable answers. Ask enough times and you can build a list of contacts that competes with this book.

Don't Send Manuscripts Unless Invited to Do So!

Now that you're armed with these editors' names, don't abuse protocol (editors yell at *me* when you do—especially when they know where you've gotten their name). Initiate contact by sending a letter describing your work and encouraging the editor to request it. This letter, commonly referred to as a query letter, is in reality a sales pitch, or door-opener. (Please see the material in this book about query letters for a full overview of this important procedure.) In brief, the letter should be short (less than 1½ pages); easy to read and to the point; personalized; and well printed on good professional stationery. Say what you have, why it's hot, why you're a good prospect, and what's available for review upon request.

In addition to the letter, it's okay to include a résumé/bio that highlights any writing credits or relevant professional credentials; a brief summary (2–3 pages) if the book is nonfiction, or a brief synopsis if it's fiction; a photo, if you have a flattering one; and promotional materials. Be careful: At this stage your aim is merely to whet the editor's appetite; you don't want to cause information overload. Less is more.

Also include a self-addressed stamped envelope (SASE). This is an important courtesy; without it, you increase your chances of getting no response. Editors receive dozens of these letters every week. Having to address envelopes for all of them would be very time-consuming. And at 33 cents a pop, it's not worth doing. The SASE is generally intended to facilitate a response in the event of a negative decision. If the editor is intrigued by your letter, he may overlook the missing SASE and request to see your work—but don't count on it.

You may be wondering: If I have the editor's name, why not just send her my manuscript? Because you're flirting with the slush pile if you do. Even though you have the editor's previously secret name, you're still an UN; and UNs aren't treated kindly. An editor is inundated with reams of submissions, and her problem is finding good stuff to publish. If you send an unsolicited manuscript, you'll just be perceived as part of that problem. She'll assume you're just another slushy UN who needs to be sorted out of the way so she can go on looking for good stuff. A bad day for an editor is receiving a few trees' worth of UN manuscripts; it deepens her occupational neurosis.

On the other hand, a professional letter is quite manageable and is, at least, likely to be read. It may be screened initially by the editor's assistant, but will probably be passed upstairs if it shows promise.

If the editor is at all intrigued by your letter, she will request to see more material, and you will have earned the rank of being solicited. Even if your work is not ultimately acquired by this editor, you will have at least challenged and defeated the UNs' obstacle course by achieving quality consideration. Remember: Many people get published each year without the benefits of being agented or initially solicited.

It's okay, even smart, to query several editors simultaneously. This makes sense because some editors may take a very long time to respond, or, indeed, may never respond. Querying editors one at a time might take years. If more than one editor subsequently requests and begins considering your work, let each one know that it's not an exclusive. If an editor requests an exclusive, that's fine—but give him a time limit (4 weeks is fair).

Don't sell your work to a publisher before consulting everyone who's considering it and seeing if they're interested. If you do sell it, be sure to give immediate written and oral notification to everyone who's considering it that it's no longer available.

The query-letter stage isn't considered a submission. You only need to have follow-up communications with editors who have gone beyond the query stage, meaning those who have requested and received your work for acquisition consideration. If you don't hear back from an editor within 6 weeks of sending her your letter, it's safe to assume she's not interested in your work.

If you send multiple queries, don't send them to more than one editor at the same house at the same time. If you don't hear back from a particular editor within 6 weeks of your submission, it's probably safe to query another editor at that house. One editor's reject is another's paradise; that's how both good and bad books get published.

We've just covered a lot of important procedural ground; so don't be embarrassed if you think you've forgotten all of it. This book won't self-destruct (and now, presumably, you won't either).

Cold Calls Breed Cold Hearts

One more thing: It's best not to cold-call these editors. Don't call them to try to sell them your work. Don't call them to follow up on query letters or submissions. Don't call them to try to change their minds.

Why? Do you like it when someone calls you in the middle of your favorite video to sell you land in the Nevada desert, near a popular nuclear test site?

Few people like uninvited and unscheduled sales calls. In some businesses, such as public relations, calling contacts is a necessary part of the process—but not in publishing. Furthermore, this business is based on hard copy. You may be the greatest oral storyteller since Uncle Remus, but if you can't write it effectively and engagingly, nobody is going to care. You'll end up soliciting their hostility. Of course, once they *are* interested in you on the basis of your hard copy, your oral and physical attributes may be of great importance to them.

On the other hand, some people are so skilled on the telephone that it's a lost opportunity for them not to make maximum use of it as a selling method. If you're one of these extremely rare and talented people, you should absolutely make use of whatever tools have proven to work best for you.

Everything I've said is my opinion. This is a subjective industry, so it's likely—no, it's for certain—that others will tell you differently. It's to your advantage to educate yourself to the fullest extent possible (read books, attend workshops, and so forth)—and in the end, to use your own best instincts about how to proceed. I'm confident that my suggestions are safe and sound; but I don't consider them to be the beginning and the end. The more you know, the simpler things become; the less you know, the more complex and confusing they are.

BREAKING THE RULES

Taken as a whole, this book provides a structure that can be considered a set of guidelines, if not hard-and-fast rules. Some people owe their success to breaking the rules and swimming upstream—and I can certainly respect that. Often such people don't even know they're breaking the rules; they're just naturally following their own unique orbits (and you'll find a few illustrations of this very phenomenon elsewhere in these essays). Trying to regulate such people can often be their downfall.

On one hand, most of us tend to run afoul when we stray from established norms of doing business; on the other hand, a few of us can't succeed any other way (Einstein could have written an essay about that). If you're one of those few, hats off to you! Perhaps we'll all learn something from your example.

Keep reading!

Write the Perfect
Query Letter

DEBORAH LEVINE HERMAN

JEFF HERMAN

The query is a short letter of introduction to a publisher or agent, encouraging him or her to request to see your fiction manuscript or nonfiction book proposal. It is a vital tool, often neglected by writers. If done correctly, it can help you to avoid endless frustration and wasted effort. The query is the first hurdle of your individual marketing strategy. If you can leap over it successfully, you're well on your way to a sale.

The query letter is your calling card. For every book that makes it to the shelves, there are thousands of worthy manuscripts, proposals, and ideas knocked out of the running by poor presentation or inadequate marketing strategies. Don't forget that the book you want to sell is a product that must be packaged correctly to stand above the competition.

A query letter asks the prospective publisher or agent if she would like to see more about the proposed idea. If your book is fiction, you should indicate that a manuscript or sample chapters are available on request. If nonfiction, you should offer to send a proposal and, if you have them, sample chapters.

The query is your first contact with the prospective buyer of your book. To ensure that it's not your last, avoid common mistakes. The letter should be concise and well written. You shouldn't try to impress the reader with your mastery of all words over three syllables. Instead, concentrate on a clear and to-the-point presentation with no fluff. Think of the letter as an advertisement. You want to make a sale of a product, and you have very limited space and time in which to reach this goal.

The letter should be only one page long if possible. It will form the basis of a query package that will include supporting materials. Don't waste words in the letter describing material that can be included separately. Your goal is to pique the interest of an editor who has very little time and probably very little patience. You want to entice her to keep reading and ask you for more.

The query package can include a short résumé, media clippings, or other favorable documents. Do not get carried away, or your package will quickly come to resemble junk mail. Include a self-addressed stamped envelope (SASE) with enough postage to return your entire package. This will be particularly appreciated by smaller publishing houses and independent agents.

For fiction writers, a short (one- to five-page), double-spaced synopsis of the manuscript will be helpful and appropriate.

Do not waste money and defeat the purpose of the query by sending an unsolicited manuscript. Agents and editors may be turned off by receiving manuscripts of 1,000+ pages that were uninvited and not even remotely relevant to what they do.

The query follows a simple format (which can be reworked according to your individual preferences): (1) lead; (2) supporting material/persuasion; (3) biography; and (4) conclusion/pitch.

YOUR LEAD IS YOUR HOOK

The lead can either catch the editor's attention or turn him off completely. Some writers think getting someone's attention in a short space means having to do something dramatic. Editors appreciate cleverness, but too much contrived writing can work against you. Opt instead for clear conveyance of thoroughly developed ideas and get right to the point.

Of course, you don't want to be boring and stuffy in the interest of factual presentation. You'll need to determine what is most important about the book you're trying to sell, and write your letter accordingly.

You can begin with a lead similar to what you'd use to grab the reader in an article or a book chapter. You can use an anecdote, a statement of facts, a question, a comparison, or whatever you believe will be most powerful.

You may want to rely on the journalistic technique of the inverted pyramid. This means that you begin with the strongest material and save the details for later in the letter. Don't start slowly and expect to pick up momentum as you proceed. It will be too late.

Do not begin a query letter like this: "I have sent this idea to 20 agents/publishers, none of whom think it will work. I just know you'll be different, enlightened, and insightful, and will give it full consideration." There is no room for negatives in a sales pitch. Focus only on positives—unless you can turn negatives to your advantage.

Some writers make the mistake of writing about the book's potential in the first paragraph without ever stating its actual idea or theme. Remember, your letter may never be read beyond the lead; so make that first paragraph your hook.

Avoid bad jokes, clichés, unsubstantiated claims, and dictionary definitions. Don't be condescending; editors have egos, too, and have power over your destiny as a writer.

SUPPORTING MATERIAL: BE PERSUASIVE

If you are selling a nonfiction book, you may want to include a brief summary of hard evidence, gleaned from research, that will support the merit of your idea. This is where you convince the editor that your book should exist. This is more important for nonfiction than it is for fiction, where the style and storytelling ability are paramount. Nonfiction writers must focus on selling their topic and their credentials.

You should include a few lines showing the editor what the publishing house will gain from the project. Publishers are not charitable institutions; they want to know how they can get the greatest return on their investment. If you have brilliant marketing ideas, or know of a well-defined market for your book where sales will be guaranteed, include this rather than other descriptive material.

In rereading your letter, make sure you have shown that you understand your own idea thoroughly. If it appears half-baked, the editors won't want to invest time fleshing out your thoughts. Exude confidence so that the editor will have faith in your ability to carry out the job.

In nonfiction queries, you can include a separate table of contents and brief chapter abstracts. Otherwise, it can wait for the book proposal.

Your Biography Is No Place for Modesty

In the biographical portion of your letter, toot your own horn, but in a carefully calculated, persuasive fashion. Your story of winning the third-grade writing competition (it was then that you knew you wanted to be a world-famous writer!) should be saved for the documentary done on your life after you reach your goal.

In the query, all you want to include are the most important and relevant credentials that will support the sale of your book. You can include, as a separate part of the package, a résumé or biography that will elaborate further.

The separate résumé should list all relevant and recent experiences that support your ability to write the book. Unless you're fairly young, your listing of academic accomplishments should start after high school. Don't overlook hobbies or non-job-related activities if they correspond to your book story or topic. Those experiences are often more valuable than academic achievements.

Other information to include: any impressive print clippings about you; a list of your broadcast interviews and speaking appearances; and copies of articles and reviews about any books you may have written. This information can never hurt your chances and could make the difference in your favor.

There is no room for humility or modesty in the query letter and résumé. When corporations sell toothpaste, they list the product's best attributes and create excitement about the product. If you can't find some way to make yourself exciting as an author, you'd better rethink your career.

Here's the Pitch

At the close of your letter, ask for the sale. This requires a positive and confident conclusion with such phrases as "I look forward to your speedy response." Such phrases as "I hope" and "I think you will like my book" sound too insecure. This is the part of the letter where you go for the kill.

Be sure to thank the reader for his or her attention in your final sentence.

FINISHING TOUCHES

When you're finished, reread and edit your query letter. Cut out any extraneous information that dilutes the strength of your arguments. Make the letter as polished as possible so that the editor will be impressed with you as well as with your idea. Don't ruin your chances by appearing careless; make certain your letter is not peppered with typos and misspellings. If you don't show pride in your work, you'll create a self-fulfilling prophecy; the editor will take you no more seriously than you take yourself.

Aesthetics are important. If you were pitching a business deal to a corporation, you would want to present yourself in conservative dress, with an air of professionalism. In the writing business, you may never have face-to-face contact with the people who will determine your future. Therefore your query package is your representative.

If an editor receives a query letter on yellowed paper that looks as if it's been lying around for 20 years, he or she will wonder if the person sending the letter is a has-been or a never-was.

You should invest in a state-of-the-art letterhead—with a logo!—to create an impression of pride, confidence, and professionalism. White, cream, and ivory paper are all acceptable, but you should use only black ink for printing the letter. Anything else looks amateurish.

Don't sabotage yourself by letting your need for instant approval get the best of you. Don't call the editor. You have invited him or her to respond, so be patient. Then prepare yourself for possible rejection. It often takes many nos to get a yes.

One more note: This is a tough business for anyone—and it's especially so for greenhorns. Hang in there.

QUERY TIPS

If you have spent any time at all in this business, the term *query letter* is probably as familiar to you as the back of your hand. Yet, no matter how many courses you've attended and books you've read about this important part of the process, you may still feel inadequate when you try to write one that sizzles. If it's any consolation, you're far from being alone in your uncertainties. The purpose of the query letter is to formally introduce your work and yourself to potential agents and editors. The immediate goal is to motivate them to promptly request a look at your work, or at least a portion of it.

In effect, the letter serves as the writer's first hurdle. It's a relatively painless way for agents and editors to screen out unwanted submissions without the added burden of having to manhandle a deluge of unwanted manuscripts. They are more relaxed if their in-boxes are filled with 50 unanswered queries, as opposed to 50 uninvited 1000-page manuscripts. The query is a very effective way to control the quality and quantity of the manuscripts that get into the office. And that's why you have to write good ones.

The term *query letter* is part of the lexicon and jargon of the publishing business. This term isn't used in any other industry. I assume it has ancient origins. I can conjure up the image of an English gentleman with a fluffy quill pen composing a most civilized letter to a prospective publisher for the purpose of asking for his work to be read and, perchance, published. Our environments may change, but the nature of our ambitions remain the same.

Let's get contemporary. Whenever you hear the term *query letter* you should say to yourself "pitch" or "sales" letter. Because that's what it is. You need the letter to sell.

QUERY LETTER TIPS

- *Don't be long-winded.* Agents/editors are receiving lots of these things, and they want to mow through them as swiftly as possible. Ideally, the letter should be a single page with short paragraphs. (I must admit I've seen good ones that are longer than a page.) If you lose your reader, you've lost your opportunity.
- *Get to the point; don't pontificate.* Too many letters go off on irrelevant detours, which makes it difficult for the agent/editor to determine what's actually for sale— other than the writer's soapbox.
- *Make your letter attractive.* When making a first impression, the subliminal impact of aesthetics cannot be overestimated. Use high-quality stationery and typeface. The essence of your words are paramount, but cheap paper and poor print quality will only diminish your impact.
- *Don't say anything negative about yourself or your attempts to get published.* Everyone appreciates victims when it's time to make charitable donations, but not when it's time to make a profit. It's better if you can make editors/agents think that you have to fight them off.

Q & A: MORE QUERY LETTER TIPS

Q: Why can't I bypass the query hurdle by simply submitting my manuscript?
A: You may—and no one can litigate against you. But if you submit an unsolicited manuscript to a publisher, it's more likely to end up in the so-called slush pile and may never get a fair reading. If sent to an agent, nothing negative may come of it. However, most agents prefer to receive a query first.

Sending unsolicited nonfiction book proposals is in the gray zone. Proposals are much more manageable than entire manuscripts, so editors/agents may not particularly mind. But you may want to avoid the expense of sending unwanted proposals. After all, the query is also an opportunity for you to screen out those who clearly have no interest in your subject. Also, you shouldn't be overly loose with your ideas and concepts.

These pointers, in combination with the other good information in this book and all the other available resources, should at least give you a solid background for creating a query letter that sizzles.

The Knockout Nonfiction Book Proposal

JEFF HERMAN

The nonfiction book proposal is very similar to a sales brochure; viewed as such, and given its due and primary importance in the process of editorial acquisition and book publishing in general, mastery of proposal writing will give you more than a mere leg up: It will invariably make the difference between success and failure.

Before agents and publishers will accept a work of fiction (especially from a newer writer), they require a complete manuscript. However, nonfiction projects are different: A proposal alone can do the trick. This is what makes nonfiction writing a much less speculative and often more lucrative endeavor (relatively speaking) than fiction writing.

You may devote five years of long evenings to writing a 1,000-page fiction manuscript, only to receive a thick pile of computer-generated rejections. Clearly, writing nonfiction doesn't entail the same risks. On the other hand, writing fiction is often an emotionally driven endeavor in which rewards are gained though the act of writing, and are not necessarily based on rational, practical considerations. Interestingly, many successful nonfiction writers fantasize about being fiction writers.

Fiction writing, whether it be pulp or literary, is one of the most creative things a person can do. And there is a market for fiction: Millions of Americans read fiction voraciously. As is covered elsewhere in this book, the fiction market has a category structure through which agents and publishers can be approached.

Nevertheless, as an author, you should understand that writing nonfiction is the easier road to getting published.

As you'll learn, the proposal's structure, contents, and size can vary substantially, and it's up to you to decide the best format for your purposes. Still, the guidelines given below serve as excellent general parameters. In addition, a topnotch excellent model proposal is featured in the next chapter.

APPEARANCE COUNTS

- Your proposal should be printed in black ink on clean, letter-sized (8 1/2" × 11"), white paper.
- Avoid slick-surfaced computer paper. Be sure to type or print out your manuscript on bond paper—and to separate and trim the pages if they are generated from a fanfold tractor-fed printer.
- Letter-quality printing is by far the best. Make sure the ribbon or toner or ink cartridge is fresh and that all photocopies are dark and clear enough to be read easily. Be wary of old manual typewriters—have the proposal retyped on up-to-date equipment if necessary. Publishing is an image-driven business, and you will be judged, perhaps unconsciously, on the physical and aesthetic merits of your submission.
- Always double-space, or you can virtually guarantee reader antagonism—eyestrain makes people cranky.
- Make sure your proposal appears fresh and new and hasn't been dog-eared, marked-up, and abused by previous readers. No editor will be favorably disposed if she thinks that everyone else on the block has already sent you packing. You want editors to suppose that you have lots of other places you can go, not nowhere else to go.
- Contrary to common practice in other industries, editors prefer not to receive bound proposals. If an editor likes your proposal, she will want to photocopy it for her colleagues, and your binding will only be in the way. If you want to keep the material together and neat, it's best to use a paper clip; if it's a lengthy proposal, maybe it will work best to clip each section together separately.

THE TITLE PAGE

The title page should be the easiest part, but it can also be the most important, since, like your face when you meet someone, it's what is seen first.

Try to think of a title that's attractive and effectively communicates your book's concept. A descriptive subtitle, following a catchy title, can help to achieve both goals. It's very important that your title and subtitle relate to the book's subject, or an editor might make an inaccurate judgment about your book's focus and automatically dismiss it. For instance, if you're proposing a book about gardening, don't title it *The Greening of America*.

Examples of titles that have worked very well are:

How to Win Friends and Influence People by Dale Carnegie

Think and Grow Rich by Napoleon Hill

Baby and Child Care by Dr. Benjamin Spock

How to Swim with the Sharks Without Being Eaten Alive by Harvey Mackay

And, yes, there are notable exceptions: An improbable title that went on to become a perennial success is *What Color Is Your Parachute?* by Richard Bolles. Sure, you may gain freedom and confidence from such exceptional instances, and by all means let your imagination graze during the brainstorming stage. However, don't bet on the success of an arbitrarily conceived title that has nothing at all to do with the book's essential concept or reader appeal.

A title should be stimulating and, when appropriate, upbeat and optimistic. If your subject is an important historic or current event, the title should be dramatic. If a biography, the title should capture something personal (or even controversial) about the subject. Many good books have been handicapped by poorly conceived titles, and many poor books have been catapulted to success by good titles. A good title is good advertising. Procter & Gamble, for instance, spends thousands of worker-hours creating seductive names for its endless array of soap-based products.

The title you choose is referred to as the "working title." Most likely, the book will have a different title when published. There are two reasons for this: (1) A more appropriate and/or arresting title may evolve with time; and (2) the publisher has final contractual discretion over the title (as well as a lot of other things).

The title page should contain only the title; your name, address, and telephone number—and the name, address, and phone number of your agent, if you have one. The title page should be neatly and attractively spaced. Eye-catching and tasteful computer graphics and display-type fonts can contribute to the overall aesthetic appeal.

OVERVIEW

The overview portion of the proposal is a terse statement (one to three pages) of your overall concept and mission. It sets the stage for what's to follow. Short, concise paragraphs are usually best.

BIOGRAPHICAL SECTION

This is where you sell yourself. This section tells who you are and why you're the ideal person to write this book. You should highlight all your relevant experience, including media and public-speaking appearances, and list previous books and/or articles published by and/or about you. Self-flattery is appropriate—so long as you're telling the truth. Many writers prefer to slip into the third person here, to avoid the appearance of egomania.

MARKETING SECTION

This is where you justify the book's existence from a commercial perspective. Who will buy it? For instance, if you're proposing a book on sales, state the number of people who earn their livings through sales; point out that thousands of large and small companies are sales-dependent and spend large sums on sales training, and that all sales professionals are perpetually hungry for fresh, innovative sales books.

Don't just say something like "My book is for adult women and there are more than fifty million adult women in America." You have to be much more demographically sophisticated than that.

COMPETITION SECTION

To the uninitiated, this section may appear to be a set-up to self-destruction. However, if handled strategically, and assuming you have a fresh concept, this section wins you points rather than undermines your case.

The competition section is where you describe major published titles with concepts comparable to yours. If you're familiar with your subject, you'll probably know those titles by heart; you may have even read most or all of them. If you're not certain, check *Books in Print*—available in virtually every library—which catalogues all titles in print in every category under the sun. Don't list everything published on your subject—that could require a book in itself. Just describe the leading half-dozen titles or so (backlist classics as well as recent books) and *explain why yours will be different.*

Getting back to the sales-book example, there is no shortage of good sales books. There's a reason for that—there's a big market for sales books. You can turn that to your advantage by emphasizing what a substantial, insatiable demand there is for sales books. Your book will feed that demand with its unique and innovative sales-success program. Salespeople and companies dependent on sales are always looking for new ways to enhance sales skills (it's okay to reiterate key points).

PROMOTION SECTION

Here you suggest possible ways to promote and market the book. Sometimes this section is unnecessary. It depends on your subject and on what, if any, realistic promotional prospects exist.

If you're proposing a specialized academic book such as *The Mating Habits of Octopi*, the market is a relatively limited one, and elaborate promotions would be wasteful. But if you're proposing a popularly oriented relationship book along the lines of *The Endless Orgasm in One Easy Lesson*, the promotional possibilities are also endless. They would include most major electronic broadcast and print media outlets, advertising, maybe even some weird contests. You want to guide the publisher toward seeing realistic ways to publicize the book.

CHAPTER OUTLINE

This is the meat of the proposal. Here's where you finally tell what's going to be in the book. Each chapter should be tentatively titled and clearly abstracted. Some successful proposals have fewer than one hundred words per abstracted chapter; others have several hundred words per chapter. Sometimes the length varies from chapter to chapter. There are no hard-and-fast rules here; it's the dealer's choice. Sometimes less is more; at other times a too-brief outline inadequately represents the project.

At their best, the chapter abstracts read like mini-chapters—as opposed to stating "I will do . . . and I will show . . . " Visualize the trailer for a forthcoming movie; that's the tantalizing effect you want to create. Also, it's a good idea to preface the outline with a table of contents. This way, the editor can see your entire road map at the outset.

Sample Chapters

Sample chapters are optional. A strong, well-developed proposal will often be enough. However, especially if you're a first-time writer, one or more sample chapters will give you an opportunity to show your stuff, and help dissolve an editor's concerns about your ability to actually write the book, thereby increasing the odds that you'll receive an offer—and you'll probably increase the size of the advance, too.

Nonfiction writers are often wary of investing time to write sample chapters since they view the proposal as a way of avoiding speculative writing. This can be a shortsighted position, however, for a single sample chapter can make the difference between selling and not selling a marginal proposal. Occasionally a publisher will request that one or two sample chapters be written before making a decision about a particular project. If the publisher seems to have a real interest, writing the sample material is definitely worth the author's time, and the full package can then be shown to additional prospects too.

Many editors say that they look for reasons to reject books, and that being on the fence is a valid reason for rejecting a project. To be sure, there are cases where sample chapters have tilted a proposal on the verge of rejection right back onto the playing field!

Keep in mind that the publisher is speculating that you can and will write the book upon contract. A sample chapter will go far to reduce the publisher's concerns about your ability to deliver a quality work beyond the proposal stage.

What Else?

There are a variety of materials you may wish to attach to the proposal to further bolster your cause. These include:

- Laudatory letters and comments about you.
- Laudatory publicity about you.
- A headshot (not if you look like the Fly, unless you're proposing a humor book or a nature book).
- Copies of published articles you've written.
- Videos of TV or speaking appearances.
- Any and all information that builds you up in a relevant way; but be organized about it—don't create a disheveled, unruly package.

LENGTH

The average proposal is probably between 15 and 30 double-spaced pages, and the typical sample chapter an additional 10 to 20 double-spaced pages. But sometimes proposals reach 100 pages, and sometimes they're 5 pages total. Extensive proposals are not a handicap.

Whatever it takes!

MODEL SUCCESSFUL NONFICTION BOOK PROPOSAL

What follows is a genuine proposal that won a healthy book contract. It's excerpted from *Write the Perfect Book Proposal* by Jeff Herman and Deborah Adams (John Wiley & Sons), and includes an extensive critique of its strongest and weakest points. All in all, it's an excellent proposal and serves as a strong model.

The book is titled *Heart and Soul: A Psychological and Spiritual Guide to Preventing and Healing Heart Disease* and is written by Bruno Cortis, M.D. This project was sold to the Villard Books division of Random House. Every editor who saw this proposal offered sincere praise. Ironically, several of these editors regretted not being able to seek the book's acquisition. From the outset I was aware this might happen. The past few years have given us numerous unconventional health and healing books—many of which are excellent. Most publishers I approached felt that their health/spirituality quota was already full and that they would wind up competing with themselves if they acquired any more such titles.

Experienced agents and writers are familiar with the market-glut problem. In many popular categories it's almost endemic. If you're prepared for this reality from the outset, there are ways to pave your own road and bypass the competition. Dedicated agents, editors, and writers want to see important books published regardless of what the publishers' lists dictate. Further, it is not necessary for every publisher to want your book (though that is the proven way to maximize the advance). In the end, you need only the right publisher and a reasonable deal. Let's look at the title page from the book proposal.

Note: Readers of *Writer's Guide* who wish to do more research on the topic of book proposals may be referred to *Write the Perfect Book Proposal: 10 Proposals That Sold and Why* by Jeff Herman and Deborah Adams (John Wiley & Sons). This work contains samples of successful book proposals along with commentary and coaching on techniques writers employ to develop book projects agents find salable—and publishers marketable.

HEART AND SOUL

(This is a good title. It conjures up dramatic images similar to a soulful blues melody. And it has everything to do with what this proposal is about. The subtitle is scientific and provides a clear direction for the patients.)

**Psychological and Spiritual Guide to
Preventing and Healing Heart Disease
by
Bruno Cortis, M.D.
Book Proposal**

**The Jeff Herman Agency, Inc.
Midwest Editorial Office
731 East Broad Street
Columbus, OH 43205
telephone: 212-941-0540**

(The title page is sufficient overall. But it would have been better if the software had been available to create a more striking cover sheet. To a large degree, everything does initially get judged by its cover.)

OVERVIEW

(One minor improvement here would have been to shift the word "Overview" to the center of the page—or otherwise styling the typeface for such headings and subheadings throughout the proposal to make them stand out from the body text.)

Heart disease is the number-one killer of Americans over the age of 40. The very words can sound like a death sentence. Our heart, the most intimate part of our body, is under siege. Until now, most experts have advised victims of the disease, as well as those who would avoid it, to change avoidable risk factors, like smoking, and begin a spartan regimen of diet and exercise. But new research shows that risk factors and lifestyle are only part of the answer. In fact, it is becoming clear that for many patients, emotional, psychological, and even spiritual factors are at least as important, both in preventing disease and in healing an already damaged heart.

(This is a powerful lead paragraph. The author knows there are a lot of books out there about heart disease. The first paragraph of the overview immediately distinguishes this book proposal and draws attention to "new research." Anything that is potentially cutting edge is going to catch the eye of a prospective publisher.)

Like *Love, Medicine, and Miracles* by Bernie Siegel, which showed cancer patients how to take charge of their own disease and life, *Heart and Soul* will show potential and actual heart patients how to use inner resources to form a healthy relationship with their heart, actually healing circulatory disorders and preventing further damage.

(The preceding paragraph contains the central thesis for the project, and it is profoundly important. In retrospect, this could have worked exceedingly well as the first paragraph of the proposal, thereby immediately setting the table.) This is a clever comparison to a highly successful book. It indicates an untapped market that has already proven itself in a similar arena. Instead of merely making unsubstantiated claims based on the success of Dr. Siegel's work, the author shows what this book will do to merit the same type of attention.)

The author, Bruno Cortis, M.D., is a renowned cardiologist whose experience with hundreds of "exceptional heart patients" has taught him that there is much more to medicine than operations and pills.

(It is good to bring the author's credentials into the overview at this juncture. A comparison has been made with a highly successful and marketable doctor/author—which will immediately raise questions as to whether this author has similar potential. The author anticipates this line of editorial reasoning and here makes some strong statements.)

Dr. Cortis identifies three types of heart patients:

- Passive Patients, who are unwilling or unable to take responsibility for their condition. Instead, these patients blame outside forces, withdraw from social contacts, and bewail their fate. They may become deeply depressed, and tend to die very soon.
- Obedient Consumers, who are the "A" students of modern medicine. Following doctors' orders to the letter, these patients behave exactly as they are supposed to, placing their fates in the hands of the experts. These patients tend to die exactly when medicine predicts they will.
- Exceptional Heart Patients, who regard a diagnosis of heart disease as a challenge. Although they may have realistic fears for the future, these patients take full responsibility for their situation and actively contribute to their own recovery. While they may or may not follow doctors' orders, these patients tend to choose the therapy or combination of therapies that is best for them. They often live far beyond medical predictions.

(This is an exceptional overview—especially where it defines the three patient types.)

It is Dr. Cortis' aim in this book to show readers how to become exceptional heart patients, empowering them to take responsibility for their own health and well-being.

(The remaining paragraphs of this overview section show a highly focused and well-thought-out plan for the book. The writing collaborator on this project had to condense and assimilate boxes and boxes of material to produce this concise and to-the-point overview that leaves no questions unanswered. Although it took a great deal of effort for the writer to write such a good proposal, there is no struggle for the editor to understand exactly what is being proposed and what the book is going to be about.)

Although Dr. Cortis acknowledges the importance of exercise, stress management, and proper nutrition—the standard staples of cardiac treatment—he stresses that there is an even deeper level of human experience that is necessary in order to produce wellness. Unlike other books on heart disease, *Heart and Soul* does not prescribe the same strict diet and exercise program for everyone. Instead it takes a flexible approach, urging readers to create their own unique health plan by employing psychological and spiritual practices in combination with a variety of more traditional diet and exercise regimens.

While seemingly revolutionary, Dr. Cortis' message is simple: You can do much more for the health of your heart than you think you can. This is true whether you have no symptoms or risk factors whatsoever, if you have some symptoms or risk factors, or if you actually already have heart disease.

MARKET ANALYSIS

Heart and Soul could not be more timely. Of the $1\frac{1}{2}$ million heart attacks suffered by Americans each year, nearly half occur between the ages of 40 and 65. Three fifths of these heart attacks are fatal. While these precise statistics may not be familiar to the millions of baby boomers now entering middle age, the national obsession with oat bran, low-fat foods, and exercising for health, shows that the members of the boomer generation are becoming increasingly aware of their own mortality.

(The writer would be well advised to ease off the use of the term baby boomer. It is so often used in book proposals that many editors are undoubtedly sick of it—and some have said so. It might have been better merely to describe the exceptional number of people in this pertinent age bracket—without attempting to sound trendy. Good use of facts, trends, and the public's receptivity to what some would characterize as an unorthodox treatment approach.)

This awareness of growing older, coupled with a widespread loss of faith in doctors and fear of overtechnologized medicine, combine to produce a market that is ready for a book emphasizing the spiritual component in healing, especially in reference to heart disease.

Most existing books on the market approach the subject from the physician's point of view, urging readers to follow doctor's orders to attain a healthy heart. There is very little emphasis in these books on the patient's own responsibility for wellness or the inner changes that must be made for the prescribed regimens to work. Among the best known recent books are:

(Not a big deal in this instance—but ordinarily it would be better to have identified this portion of the proposal as the competition section, and set it off under a separate heading.)

Healing Your Heart, by Herman Hellerstein, M.D., and Paul Perry (Simon & Schuster, 1990). Although this book, like most of the others, advocates proper nutrition, exercise, cessation of smoking and stress reduction as the road to a healthy heart, it fails to provide the motivation necessary to attain such changes in the reader's lifestyle. Without changes in thinking and behavior, readers of this and similar books will find it difficult, if not impossible, to follow the strict diet and exercise program recommended.

In *Heart Talk: Preventing and Coping with Silent and Painful Heart Disease* (Harcourt Brace Jovanovich, 1987), Dr. Peter F. Cohn and Dr. Joan K. Cohn address the dangers of "silent" (symptomless) heart disease. While informative, the book emphasizes only one manifestation of heart disease, and does not empower readers with the motivational tools needed to combat that disease.

(This section is termed the market analysis, which in this proposal actually departs from the approach of the typical marketing section of most proposals. Instead of telling the publisher how to sell the book, the writing collaborator (see the About the Authors section below) shows special insight into the target audience. The key is that this analysis is not merely a statement of the obvious. This type of in-depth analysis of the potential reader can be very persuasive.)

The Trusting Heart, by Redford Williams, M.D. (Times Books, 1989), demonstrates how hostility and anger can lead to heart disease while trust and forgiveness can contribute to wellness. While these are important points, the holistic treatment of heart disease must encompass other approaches as well. The author also fails to provide sufficient motivation for behavioral changes in the readers.

(The author does a good job of demonstrating the invaluable uniqueness of this particular project—especially important when compared with the strong list of competitors.)

The best book on preventing and curing heart disease is Dr. Dean Ornish's *Program for Reversing Heart Disease* (Random House, 1990). This highly successful book prescribes a very strict diet and exercise program for actually reversing certain types of coronary artery disease. This still-controversial approach is by far the best on the market; unfortunately, the material is presented in a dense, academic style not easily accessible to the lay reader. It also focuses on Dr. Ornish's program as the "only way to manage heart disease," excluding other, more synergistic methods.

(The writer collaborator directly analyzed the competition, highlighting the most relevant books on the market without listing each one directly. Although you do not want to present the editor with any unnecessary surprises, if there are too many similar books out in your particular subject area, you might want to use this approach. The writer confronts the heaviest competition directly by finding specific distinguishing factors that support the strength of their proposed project.)

APPROACH

Heart and Soul will be a 60,000- to 70,000-word book targeted to health-conscious members of the baby boom generation. Unlike other books on heart disease, it will focus on the "facts of the connection between the mind and the body as it relates to heart disease, showing readers how to use that connection to heal the heart." The book will be written in an informal but authoritative style, in Dr. Cortis' voice. It will begin with a discussion of heart disease and show how traditional medicine fails to prevent or cure it. Subsequent chapters will deal with the mind-body connection, and the role in healing of social support systems, self-esteem, and faith. In order to help readers reduce stress in their lives, Dr. Cortis shows how they can create their own "daily practice" that combines exercise, relaxation, meditation, and use of positive imagery. Throughout the book, he will present anecdotes that demonstrate how other Exceptional Heart Patients have overcome their disease and gone on to lead healthy and productive lives.

In addition to a thorough discussion of the causes and outcomes of coronary artery disease, the book will include tests and checklists that readers may use to gauge their progress, and exercises, ranging from the cerebral to the physical, that strengthen and help heal the heart. At the end of each chapter readers will be introduced to an essential "Heartskill" that will enable them to put the advice of the chapter into immediate practice.

Through example and encouragement *Heart and Soul* will offer readers a variety of strategies for coping with heart disease, to be taken at once or used in combination. Above all an accessible, practical book, *Heart and Soul* will present readers with a workable program for controlling their own heart disease and forming a healthy relationship with their hearts.

(This is a good summary statement of the book.)

ABOUT THE AUTHORS

Bruno Cortis, M.D., is an internationally trained cardiologist with more than 30 years' experience in research and practice. A pioneer of cardiovascular applications of lasers and angioscopy, a Diplomate of the American Board of Cardiology, contributor of more than 70 published professional papers, Dr. Cortis has long advocated the need for new dimensions of awareness in health and the healing arts. As a practicing physician and researcher, his open acknowledgment of individual spirituality as the core of health puts him on the cutting edge of those in traditional medicine who are beginning to create the medical arts practices of the future.

(This is a very good description of the author. The writing collaborator establishes Dr. Cortis as both an expert in his field and a compelling personality. All of this material is relevant to the ultimate success of the book.)

Dr. Cortis has been a speaker at conferences in South America, Japan, and Australia, as well as in Europe and the United States. His firm, Mind Your Health, is dedicated to the prevention of heart attack through the development of human potential. Dr. Cortis is the cofounder of the Exceptional Heart Patients program. The successful changes he has made in his own medical practice prove he is a man not only of vision and deeds, but an author whose beliefs spring from the truths of daily living.

(A formal vita follows in this proposal. It is best to lead off with a journalistic-style biography and follow up with a complete and formal résumé—assuming, as in this case, the author's professional credentials are inseparable from the book.)

Kathryn Lance is the author of more than 30 books of nonfiction and fiction (see attached publications list for details). Her first book, *Running for Health and Beauty* (1976), the first mass-market book on running for women, sold half a million copies. *The Setpoint Diet* (1985), ghosted for Dr. Gilbert A. Leveille, reached the *New York Times* bestseller list for several weeks. Ms. Lance has written widely on fitness, health, diet, and medicine.

(Though she wasn't mentioned on the title page, Lance is the collaborator. This brief bio and the following résumé reveal a writer with virtually impeccable experience. Her participation served to ensure the editors that they could count on the delivery of a high-quality manuscript. Her bio sketch is also strong in its simplicity. Her writing credits are voluminous, but she does not use up space here with a comprehensive listing. Instead she showcases only credits that are relevant to the success of this particular project.)

(Comprehensive author résumés were also attached as addenda to the proposal package.)

HEART AND SOUL
by
Bruno Cortis, M.D.
Chapter Outline

(Creating a separate page [or pages] for the entire table of contents is a useful and easy technique to enable the editor to gain a holistic vision for the book before delving into the chapter abstracts. In retrospect, we should have had one here.)

(The following is an exceptional outline because it goes well beyond the lazy and stingy telegraph approach that many writers use, often to their own detriment. [Telegrams once were a popular means of communication that required the sender to pay by the word.] Here each abstract reads like a miniature sample chapter unto itself. It proves that the writers have a genuine command of their subject, a well-organized agenda, and superior skills for writing about it. Together they are a darn good team. Whatever legitimate reasons a publisher may have had for rejecting this proposal, it had nothing to do with its manifest editorial and conceptual merits. Some writers are reluctant to go this editorial distance on spec. However, if you believe in your project's viability and you want to maximize acquisition interest and the ultimate advance, you'll give the proposal everything you've got.)

Contents

Introduction: Beating the Odds: Exceptional Heart Patients
(See sample chapter.)

CHAPTER ONE. YOU AND YOUR HEART

Traditional medicine doesn't and can't "cure" heart disease. The recurrence rate of arterial blockage after angioplasty is 25%–35%, while a bypass operation only bypasses the problem, but does not cure it. The author proposes a new way of looking at heart disease, one in which patients become responsible for the care and well-being of their hearts, in partnership with their physicians. Following a brief, understandable discussion of the physiology of heart disease and heart attack, further topics covered in this chapter include:

(This is a good technique for a chapter abstract. The writer organizes the structure as a listing of chapter topics and elaborates with a sample of the substance and writing approach that will be incorporated into the book. The editor cannot, of course, be expected to be an expert on the subject, but after reading this abstract will come away with a good sense of the quality of the chapter and the depth of its coverage.)

Heart disease as a message from your body. Many of us go through life neglecting our bodies' signals, ignoring symptoms until a crisis occurs. But the body talks to us and it is up to us to listen and try to understand the message. The heart bears the load of all our physical activity as well as our mental activity. Stress can affect the heart as well as any other body system. This section explores the warning signs of heart disease as "messages" we may receive from our hearts, what these messages may mean, and what we can do in response to these messages.

Why medical tests and treatments are not enough. You, the patient, are ultimately responsible for your own health. Placing all faith in a doctor is a way of abdicating that responsibility. The physician is not a healer; rather, he or she sets the stage for the patient's body to heal itself. Disease is actually a manifestation of an imbalance within the body. Medical procedures can help temporarily, but the real solution lies in the patient's becoming aware of his own responsibility for health. This may involve changing diet, stopping smoking, learning to control the inner life.

(Although the abstracts are directed to the editor who reviews the proposal, the writer incorporates the voice to be used in the book by speaking directly to the reader. This is an effective way to incorporate her writing style into the chapter-by-chapter outline.)

Getting the best (while avoiding the worst) of modern medicine. In the author's view, the most important aspect of medicine is not the medication but the patient/physician relationship. Unfortunately, this relationship is often cold, superficial, professional. The patient goes into the medical pipeline, endures a number of tests, then comes out the other end with a diagnosis, which is like a flag he has to carry for life. This view of disease ignores the patient as the *main* component of the healing process. Readers are advised to work with their doctors to learn their own blood pressure, blood sugar, cholesterol level, and what these numbers mean. They are further advised how to enlist a team of support people to increase their own knowledge of the disease and learn to discover the self-healing mechanisms within.

How to assess your doctor. Ten questions a patient needs to ask in order to assure the best patient-doctor relationship.

Taking charge of your own medical care. Rather than being passive patients, readers are urged to directly confront their illness and the reasons for it, asking themselves: How can I find a cause at the deepest level? What have I learned from this disease? What is good about it? What have I learned about myself? Exceptional heart patients don't allow themselves to be overwhelmed by the disease; rather, they realize that it is most likely a temporary problem, most of the time self-limited, and that they have a power within to overcome it.

Seven keys to a healthy heart. Whether presently healthy or already ill of heart disease, there is a great deal readers can do to improve and maintain the health of their hearts. The most important component of such a plan is to have a commitment to a healthy heart. The author offers the following seven keys to a healthy heart: respect your body; take time to relax every day; accept, respect, and appreciate yourself; share your deepest feelings; establish life goals; nourish your spiritual self; love yourself and others unconditionally. Each of these aspects of heart care will be examined in detail in later chapters.

Heartskill #1: *Learning to take your own pulse.* The pulse is a wave of blood sent through the arteries each time the heart contracts; pulse rate therefore provides important information about cardiac function. The easiest place to measure the pulse is the wrist: place your index and middle finger over the underside of the opposite wrist. Press gently and firmly until you locate your pulse. Don't use your thumb to feel the pulse, because the thumb has a pulse of its own. Count the number of pulse beats in fifteen seconds, then multiply that by four for your heart rate.

This exercise will include charts so that readers can track and learn their own normal pulse range for resting and exercising, and be alerted to irregularities and changes that may require medical attention.

(The inclusion of this technique shows how specific and practical information will be included in the book—important for a nonfiction book proposal. Editors look for what are called the program aspects of a book, because they can be used in promotional settings—and may also be the basis for serial-rights sales to magazines.)

CHAPTER TWO. YOUR MIND AND YOUR HEART

This chapter begins to explore the connection between mind and body as it relates to heart disease. Early in the chapter readers will meet three Exceptional Heart Patients who overcame crushing diagnoses. These include Van, who overcame a heart attack (at age 48), two open heart surgeries, and "terminal" lung cancer. Through visualization techniques given him by the author, Van has fully recovered and is living a healthy and satisfying life. Goran, who had a family history of cardiomyopathy, drew on the support and love of his family to survive a heart transplant and has since gone on to win several championships in an Olympics contest for transplant patients. Elaine, who overcame both childhood cancer and severe heart disease, is, at the age of 24, happily married and a mother. The techniques used by these Exceptional Heart Patients will be discussed in the context of the mind-body connection.

(The authors do not save the good stuff for the book. If you have interesting case studies or anecdotes, include them in your abstracts: The more stimulating material you can include, the more you can intrigue your editor. In general, this chapter-by-chapter synopsis is exceptionally detailed in a simplified fashion, which is important for this type of book.)

How your doctor views heart disease: Risk factors v. symptoms. Traditional medicine views the risk factors for heart disease (smoking, high blood cholesterol, high blood pressure, diabetes, obesity, sedentary lifestyle, family history of heart disease, use of oral contraceptives) as indicators of the likelihood of developing illness. In contrast, the author presents these risk factors as *symptoms* of an underlying disease, and discusses ways to change them. Smoking, for example, is not the root of the problem, which is, rather, fear, tension, and stress. Smoking is just an outlet that the patient uses to get rid of these basic elements which he or she believes are uncontrollable. Likewise high cholesterol, which is viewed by the medical establishment as largely caused by poor diet, is also affected by stress. (In a study of rabbits on a high-cholesterol diet, narrowing of arteries was less in rabbits that were petted, even if the diet remained unhealthful.) Other elements besides the traditional "risk factors," such as hostility, have been shown to lead to high rates of heart disease.

A mind/body model of heart disease. It is not uncommon to hear stories like this: they were a very happy couple, married 52 years. Then, suddenly, the wife developed breast cancer and died. The husband, who had no previous symptoms of heart disease, had a heart attack and died two months later. All too often there is a very close relationship between a traumatic event and serious illness. Likewise, patients may often become depressed and literally will themselves to die. The other side of the coin is the innumerable patients who use a variety of techniques to enlist the mind-body connection in helping to overcome and even cure serious illnesses, including heart disease.

Rethinking your negative beliefs about heart disease. The first step in using the mind to help to heal the body is to rethink negative beliefs about heart disease. Modern studies have shown that stress plays a most important role in the creation of heart disease, influencing all of the "risk factors." Heart disease is actually a disease of self, caused by self, and is made worse by the belief that we are its "victims." Another negative and incorrect belief is that the possibilities for recovery are limited. The author asserts that these beliefs are untrue, and that for patients willing to learn from the experience, heart disease can be a path to recovery, self-improvement, and growth.

The healing personality: tapping into your body's healing powers. Although the notion of a "healing personality" may sound contradictory, the power of healing is awareness, which can be achieved by anyone. The author describes his own discovery of spirituality in medicine and the realization that ultimately the origin of disease is in the mind. This is why treating disease with medicine and surgery alone does not heal: because these methods ignore the natural healing powers of the body/mind. How does one develop a "healing personality"? The starting point is awareness of the spiritual power within. As the author states, in order to become healthy, one must become spiritual.

Writing your own script for a healthy heart. Before writing any script, one must set the stage, and in this case readers are urged to see a cardiologist or physician and have a thorough checkup. This checkup will evaluate the presence or absence of the "risk factors," and assess the health of other body organs as well. Once the scene is set, it is time to add in the other elements of a healthy heart, all of which will be explored in detail in the coming chapters.

Making a contract with your heart. We see obstacles only when we lose sight of our goals. How to make out (either mentally or on paper) a contract with one's heart that promises to take care of the heart. Each individual reader's contract will be somewhat different; for example, someone who is overweight might include in the contract the desire that in six months she would weigh so much. The point is to set realistic, achievable goals. Guidelines are provided for breaking larger goals down into small, easily achievable, steps. Creating goals for the future makes them a part of the present in the sense that it is today that we start pursuing them.

What to say when you talk to yourself. In the view of the author, the greatest source of stress in life is negative conversations we have with ourselves. These "conversations," which go on all the time without our even being aware of them, often include such negative suggestions as "When are you going to learn?" "Oh, no, you stupid idiot, you did it again!" When we put ourselves down we reinforce feelings of unworthiness and inadequacy, which leads to stress and illness. Guidelines are given for replacing such negative self-conversation with more positive self-talk, including messages of love and healing.

Heartskill #2: *Sending healing energy to your heart.* In this exercise, readers learn a simple meditation technique that will help them get in touch with their natural healing powers and begin to heal their hearts.

CHAPTER THREE. THE FRIENDSHIP FACTOR: PLUGGING INTO YOUR SOCIAL SUPPORT SYSTEM

Heart disease is not an isolated event, and the heart patient is not an isolated human being. Among the less medically obvious "risk factors" involved in coronary disease are social isolation. In this chapter the author discusses the importance of maintaining and strengthening all the social support aspects of the patient's life, including family, friendship, community, and sex. He shows how intimacy and connection can be used not just for comfort but as actual healing tools.

Sexual intimacy: the healing touch. Following a heart attack, many patients may lose confidence due to a fear of loss of attractiveness or fear of death. Citing recent studies, the author points out that there is a difference between making sex and making love. The desire for sex is a human need and is not limited to healthy people. Anybody who has had a heart problem still has sexual needs and ignoring them may be an additional cause of stress. Guidelines for when and how to resume sexual activity are offered. Other topics covered in this chapter include:

Keeping your loved ones healthy, and letting them keep you healthy

How you may be unwittingly pushing others out of your life

The art of nondefensive, nonreactive communication

Accepting your loved ones' feelings and your own

How to enlist the support of family and friends

Joining or starting your own support group

Heartskill #3: *Mapping your social support system*

CHAPTER FOUR. OPENING YOUR HEART: LEARNING TO MAKE FRIENDS WITH YOURSELF

In addition to enlisting the support of others, for complete healing it is necessary for the patient to literally become a friend to himself or herself. This may entail changing old ways of thinking and responding, as well as developing new, healthier ways of relating to time and other external stresses. In this chapter the author explores ways of changing Type A behavior, as well as proven techniques for dealing with life's daily hassles and upsets. An important section of the chapter shows readers how to love and cherish the "inner child," that part of the personality that needs to be loved, to be acknowledged, and to have fun. Equally important is the guilt that each of us carries within, and that can lead not only to unhealthy behaviors but also to actual stress. The author gives exercises for learning to discover and absolve the hidden guilts that keep each of us from realizing our true healthy potential. Topics covered in this chapter include:

A positive approach to negative emotions

Checking yourself out on Type A behavior: a self-test

Being assertive without being angry

Keeping your balance in the face of daily hassles and major setbacks

Making a friend of time

Identifying and healing your old childhood hurts

Letting go of hurts, regrets, resentments, and guilt

Forgiving yourself and making a new start

The trusting heart

Heartskill #4: *Forgiveness exercise*

CHAPTER FIVE. IDENTIFYING AND ELIMINATING STRESS IN YOUR LIFE

The science of psychoneuroimmunology is beginning to prove that the mind and body are not only connected, but inseparable. It has been demonstrated that changes in life often precede disease. Lab studies have shown that the amount of stress experienced by experimental animals can induce rapid growth of a tumor that would ordinarily be rejected. For heart patients, the fact of disease itself can become another inner stress factor that may worsen the disease and the quality of life. One out of five healthy persons is a "heart reactor," who has strong responses under stress that induce such unhealthful physiological changes as narrowing of the coronary arteries, hypertrophy of the heart muscle, and high blood pressure. In this chapter the author shows readers how to change stress-producing negative beliefs into constructive, rational beliefs that reduce stress. Included are guidelines to the five keys for controlling stress: diet, rest, exercise, attitude, and self-discipline.

Why you feel so stressed-out

Where does emotional stress come from and how does it affect your heart?

Your stress signal checklist

Staying in control

Calculating your heart-stress level at home and on the job

Stress management

Heartskill #5: *Mapping your stress hotspots*

CHAPTER SIX. YOUR FAITH AND YOUR HEART

As the author points out, there are few studies in the field of spirituality and medicine, because physicians, like most scientists, shy away from what is called "soft data." Soft data are anything outside the realm of physics, mathematics, etc.: the "exact sciences." As a physician, the author has grown ever more convinced of the body's natural healing power, which is evoked through mind and spirit. No matter how "spirit" is defined, whether in traditional religious terms or as a component of mind or personality, the truth is that in order to become healthy, it is necessary to become spiritual.

In a 10-month study of 393 coronary patients at San Francisco General Hospital, it was proven that the group who received outside prayer in addition to standard medical treatment did far better than those who received medical treatment alone. Those in the experimental group suffered fewer problems with congestive heart failure, pneumonia, cardiac arrests, and had a significantly lower mortality rate. This chapter explores the possible reasons for this startling result and illuminates the connection between spirit and health.

The difference between spirituality and religion. A discussion of the differences between traditional views of spirituality and the new holistic approach that sees mind, body, and spirit as intimately connected and interdependent.

Faith and heart disease. The healing personality is that of a person who takes care of his own body. He may also use such other "paramedical" means to get well as physical exercise, a proper diet, prayer, meditation, positive affirmations, and visualization techniques. The author surveys these techniques that have been used for centuries to contribute to the healing of a wide variety of diseases. Other topics exploring the connection between faith and a healthy heart include:

Tapping into your personal mythology

Forgiving yourself for heart disease

Keeping a psychological-spiritual journal

Heartskill #6: *Consulting your inner advisor*

CHAPTER SEVEN. PUTTING IT ALL TOGETHER: HOW TO DEVELOP YOUR OWN DAILY PRACTICE FOR A HEALTHY HEART

Daily Practice as defined by the author is a personalized program in which readers will choose from among the techniques offered in the book to create their own unique combination of mental and physical healing exercises. Each component of the daily practice is fully explained. The techniques range from the familiar—healthful diet and exercise—to the more spiritual, including prayer, meditation, and visualization. Included are examples of use of each of these techniques as practiced by Exceptional Heart Patients.

The benefits of daily practice

Meditation: how to do it your way

Stretching, yoga, and sensory awareness

Hearing with the mind's ear, seeing with the mind's eye

The psychological benefits of exercise

Healthy eating as a meditative practice

The healing powers of silent prayer

Creating your own visualization exercises

Creating your own guided-imagery tapes

Using other types of positive imagery

Heartskill #7: *Picking a practice that makes sense to you*

CHAPTER EIGHT. LEARNING TO SMELL THE FLOWERS

In our society, pleasure is often regarded as a selfish pursuit. We tend to feel that it is not as important as work. And yet the key element in health is not blood pressure, or cholesterol, or blood sugar; instead it is peace of mind and the ability to enjoy life. Indeed, this ability has been proven to prevent illness. In this chapter the author focuses on the ability to *live* in the moment, savoring all that life has to offer, from the simple physical pleasures of massage to the more profound pleasures of the spirit. Topics covered in this chapter include a discussion of Type B behavior, which can be learned. The secrets of this type of behavior include self-assurance, self-motivation, and the ability to relax in the face of pressures. The author shows how even the most confirmed Type A heart patient can, through self-knowledge, change outer-directed goals for inner ones, thus achieving the emotional and physical benefits of a Type B lifestyle. Other topics discussed in this chapter include:

Getting the most out of the present moment

Taking an inventory of life's pleasures

Counting down to relaxation

Hot baths, hot showers, hot tubs and saunas

Touching; feeding the skin's hunger for human touch

Pets, plants, and gardens as healing helpers

Heartskill #8: *Building islands of peace into your life*

CHAPTER NINE. CREATING YOUR FUTURE

The heart may be viewed in many different ways: as a mechanical pump, as the center of circulation, as the source of life. The author suggests viewing the heart above all as a spiritual organ, the center of love, and learning to figuratively fill it with love and peace. A *positive* result of heart disease is the sudden knowledge that one is not immortal, and the opportunity to plan for a more worthwhile, fulfilling life in the future. In this final chapter, Dr. Cortis offers guidelines for setting and achieving goals for health—of mind, body, and spirit. For each reader the goals, and the means to achieve them, will be different. But as the author points out, this is a journey that everyone must take, patients as well as doctors, readers as well as the author. No matter how different the paths we choose, we must realize that truly "our hearts are the same."

The Art of Happiness

Choosing your own path to contentment

Goals chosen by other exceptional heart patients

Developing specific action steps

Reinforcing and rethinking your life goals

Finding your own meaning in life and death

Heartskill #9: *Helping others to heal their hearts*

RECOMMENDED READING

APPENDIX I. FOR FRIENDS AND FAMILY: HOW TO SUPPORT AN EXCEPTIONAL HEART PATIENT

APPENDIX II. ON FINDING OR STARTING A SELF-HELP GROUP

APPENDIX III. ABOUT THE EXCEPTIONAL HEART PATIENT PROJECT

AUTHOR'S NOTES

ACKNOWLEDGMENTS

INDEX

(Appendixes are always a valuable bonus.)

(It is great to be able to include an actual endorsement in your proposal package. Quite often, writers state those from whom they intend to request endorsements—but do not actually have them lined up. Perhaps unnecessary to say, but valuable to reiterate, is that editors and agents are not overly impressed by such assertions. They do, however, nod with respect to those authors who demonstrate that they can deliver on their claims. The inclusion of at least one such blurb creates tremendous credibility.)

GERALD G. JAMPOLSKY, M.D.
Practice Limited to Psychiatry
Adults and Children
21 Main Street
Tiburon, California 94920
(415) 435-1622

April 1, 1998

Mr. Jeff Herman
The Jeff Herman Agency, Inc.
140 Charles Street, Suite 15A
New York, NY 10014

Dear Jeff:
You may use the following quote for Bruno's book:

> *"Dr. Bruno Cortis writes from the heart—for the heart. This is a much-needed and very important book."*

Gerald Jampolsky, M.D.
Coauthor of *Love Is the Answer*

With love and peace,

Jerry

Gerald Jampolsky, M.D.

(The author, Dr. Cortis, is very well connected in his field. He solicited promises from several prominent persons to provide cover endorsements like this one. Having these promises to provide such blurbs at the time I marketed the proposal further enhanced the agency's sales position.)

Rejected . . . Again

The Process and the Art of Perseverance

Jeff Herman

Trying to sell your writing is in many ways similar to perpetually applying for employment; it's likely you will run into many walls. And that can hurt. But even the Great Wall of China has a beginning and an end—for it's simply an external barrier erected for strategic purposes. In my experience, the most insurmountable walls are the ones in our own heads. Anything that is artificially crafted can and will be overcome by people who are resourceful and determined enough to do it.

Naturally, the reality of rejection cannot be completely circumvented. It is, however, constructive to envision each wall as a friendly challenge to your resourcefulness, determination, and strength. There are many people who got through the old Berlin Wall because for them it was a challenge and a symbol—a place to begin, not stop.

The world of publishing is a potentially hostile environment, especially for the writer. Our deepest aspirations can be put to rest without having achieved peace or satisfaction. But it is within each of us to learn about this special soil, and blossom to our fullest. No rejection is fatal until the writer walks away from the battle leaving the written work behind, undefended and unwanted.

WHY MOST REJECTION LETTERS ARE SO EMPTY

What may be most frustrating are the generic word-processed letters that say something like: "not right for us." Did the sender read any of your work? Did he or she have any personal opinions about it? Could she not have spared a few moments to share her thoughts?

As an agent, it's part of my job to reject the vast majority of the submissions I receive. And, with each rejection, I know I'm not making someone happy. On the other hand, I don't see spreading happiness as my exclusionary purpose. Like other agents and editors, I make liberal use of the generic rejection letter.

Here's why: Too much to do, too little time. There just isn't sufficient time to write customized, personal rejection letters. To be blunt about it, the rejection process isn't a profit center; it does consume valuable time that otherwise could be used to make profits. The exceptions to this rule are the excessive-fee-charging operations that make a handsome profit with each rejection.

In most instances, the rejection process is "giveaway" time for agents and editors since it takes us away from our essential responsibilities. Even if no personal comments are provided with the rejections, it can require many hours a week to process an ongoing stream of rejections. An understaffed literary agency or publishing house may feel that it's sufficiently generous simply to assign a paid employee the job of returning material as opposed to throwing it away. (And some publishers and literary agencies do in practice simply toss the greater portion of their unsolicited correspondence.) Agents and editors aren't Dear Abby, though many of us wish we had the time to be.

Therefore, your generic rejection means no more and no less than that particular agent/editor doesn't want to represent/publish you and (due to the volume of office correspondence and other pressing duties) is relaying this information to you in an automated, impersonal way. The contents of the letter alone will virtually never reveal any deeper meanings or secrets. To expect or demand more than this might be perceived as unfair by the agent/editor.

Know When to Hold, Know When to Fold

It's your job to persevere. It's your mission to proceed undaunted. Regardless of how many books about publishing you've read, or how many writers' conferences you've attended, it's up to no one but you to figure out how and when to change your strategy if you want to win at the book-publishing game.

If your initial query results are blanket rejects, then it may be time to back off, reflect, and revamp your query presentation or overall approach. If there are still no takers, you may be advised to reconceive your project in light of its less-than-glorious track record. Indeed, there might even come a time for you to use your experience and newfound knowledge of what does and doesn't grab attention from editors and agents—and move on to that bolder, more innovative idea you've been nurturing in the back of your brain.

An Authentic Success Story

Several years ago, two very successful, though unpublished, gentlemen came to see me with a nonfiction book project. My hunch was that it would make a lot of money. The writers were professional speakers and highly skilled salespeople, so I arranged for them to meet personally with several publishers, but to no avail.

All told, we got more than 20 rejections—the dominant reason being that editors thought the concept and material weak. Not ones to give up, and with a strong belief in their work and confidence in their ability to promote, the authors were ultimately able to sell the book for a nominal advance to a small Florida publishing house—and it was out there at last, published and in the marketplace.

As of this writing, *Chicken Soup for the Soul,* by Jack Canfield and Mark Victor Hansen, has sold millions of copies and has been a *New York Times* bestseller for several years straight. Furthermore, this initial success has generated many bestselling sequels.

We all make mistakes, and the book rascals in New York are definitely no exception. Most importantly, Canfield and Hansen didn't take no for an answer. They instinctively understood that all those rejections were simply an uncomfortable part of a process that would eventually get them where they wanted to be. And that's the way it happened.

A RELENTLESS APPROACH TO SELLING YOUR BOOK

I once heard a very telling story about Jack Kerouac, one from which we can all learn something. Kerouac was a notorious literary figure who reached his professional peak in the 1950s. He's one of the icons of the Beat Generation and is perhaps best remembered for his irreverent and manic travel-memoir-as-novel *On the Road.*

Sales Tales from the Beat Generation

The story I heard begins when Kerouac was a young and struggling writer, ambitiously seeking to win his day in the sun. He was a charismatic man and had acquired many influential friends. One day Kerouac approached a friend who had access to a powerful publishing executive. Kerouac asked the friend to hand-deliver his new manuscript to the executive, with the advice that it be given prompt and careful consideration.

When the friend handed the manuscript to the executive, the executive took one glance and began to laugh. The executive explained that two other people had hand-delivered the very same manuscript to him within the last few weeks.

What this reveals is that Kerouac was a master operator. Not only did he manage to get his work into the right face, but he reinforced his odds by doing it redundantly. Some might say he was a manipulator, but his works were successfully published, and he did attain a measure of fame in his own day, which even now retains its luster.

. . . AND FROM THE BEATEN

I will now share a very different and more recent story. It starts in the 1940s, when a bestselling and Pulitzer Prize–winning young-adult book was published. Titled *The Yearling*, this work was made into an excellent movie starring Gregory Peck. The book continues to be a good backlist seller.

In the 1990s a writer in Florida, where *The Yearling*'s story takes place, performed an experiment. He converted the book into a raw double-spaced manuscript and changed the title and author's name—but the book's contents were not touched. He then submitted the entire manuscript to about 20 publishers on an unagented/unsolicited basis. I don't believe the submissions were addressed to any specific editors by name.

Eventually this writer received many form rejections, including one from the book's actual publisher. Several publishers never even responded. A small house in Florida did offer to publish the book.

What is glaringly revealed by this story? That even a Pulitzer Prize–winning novel will never see the light of day if the writer doesn't use his brain when it's time to sell the work.

HOW TO BEAT YOURSELF—AND HOW NOT TO

People who are overly aggressive do get a bad rap. As an agent and as a person, I don't like being hounded by salespeople—whether they're hustling manuscripts or insurance policies. But there are effective ways to be heard and seen without being resented. Virtually anyone can scream loud enough to hurt people's ears. Only an artist understands the true magic of how to sell without abusing those who might buy. And each of us has the gift to become an artist in his or her own way.

Here's an example of what not to do:

It's late in the day and snowing. I'm at my desk, feeling a lot of work-related tension. I answer the phone. It's a first-time fiction writer. He's unflinchingly determined to speak endlessly about his work, which I have not yet read. I interrupt his meaningless flow to explain courteously that, while I will read his work, it's not a good time for me to talk to him. But he will not let me go; he's relentless. Which forces me to be rude and cold as I say "bye" and hang up. I then resent the thoughtless intrusion upon my space and time. And I may feel bad about being inhospitable to a stranger, whatever the provocation.

Clearly the above scenario does not demonstrate a good way to initiate a deal. I'm already prejudiced against this writer before reading his work.

Here's a more effective scenario:

Same conditions as before. I answer the telephone. The caller acknowledges that I must be busy, and asks for only 30 seconds of my time. I grant them. He then begins to compliment me; he's heard I'm one of the best, and so forth. I'm starting to like this conversation; I stop counting the seconds. Now he explains that he has an excellent manuscript that he is willing to give me the opportunity to read, and would be happy to send it right over. He then thanks me for my time and says good-bye. I hang up, feeling fine about the man; I'll give his manuscript some extra consideration.

In conclusion, relentless assertiveness is better than relentless passivity. But you want your style to be like Julie Andrews's singing voice in *The Sound of Music*, as opposed to a 100-decibel boombox on a stone floor.

The Literary Agency from A to Z
How Literary Agents Work

Jeff Herman

Literary agents are like stockbrokers, marketing or sales directors, or real estate agents: They bring buyers and sellers together, help formulate successful deals, and receive a piece of the action (against the seller's end) for facilitating the partnership.

Specifically, literary agents snoop the field for talented writers, unearth marketable nonfiction book concepts, and discover superior fiction manuscripts to represent. Simultaneously, agents cultivate their relationships with publishers.

When an agent detects material she thinks she can sell to a publisher, she signs the writer as a client, works on the material with the writer to maximize its chances of selling, and then submits it to one or more appropriate editorial contacts.

The agent has the contacts. Many writers don't know the most likely publishers; even if the writers do have a good overview of the industry, and even some inside contacts, the typical agent knows many more players and also knows which editors like to see what material. And the agent may even be aware of finesse elements such as recent shifts in a publisher's acquisition strategy.

HOW AGENTS WORK FOR THEIR CLIENTS

A dynamic agent achieves the maximum exposure possible for the writer's material, which greatly enhances the odds that the material will be published—and on more favorable terms than a writer is likely to yield.

Having an agent gives the writer's material the type of access to the powers-that-be that it might otherwise never obtain. Publishers assume that material submitted by an agent has been screened and is much more likely to fit their needs than the random material swimming in the slush pile.

If and when a publisher makes an offer to publish the material, the agent acts on the author's behalf and negotiates the advance (the money paid up front), table of royalties, control of subsidiary rights, and many other important and marginal contract clauses that may prove to be important down the line. The agent acts as the writer's advocate with the publisher for as long as the book remains in print or licensing opportunities exist.

The agent knows the most effective methods for negotiating the best advance and other contract terms, and is likely to have more leverage with the publisher than the writer does.

There's more to a book contract than the advance-and-royalty schedule. There are several key clauses that you the writer may know little or nothing about but would accept with a cursory perusal in order to expedite the deal. Striving to close any kind of agreement can be intimidating if you don't know much about the territory; ignorance is a great disadvantage during a negotiation. An agent, however, understands every detail of the contract and knows where and how it should be modified or expanded in your favor.

Where appropriate, an agent acts to sell subsidiary rights after the book is sold to a publisher. These rights can include: serial rights, foreign rights, dramatic and movie rights, audio and video rights, and a range of syndication and licensing possibilities. Often, a dynamic agent will be more successful at selling the subsidiary rights than the publisher would be.

THE AGENT'S PERSPECTIVE

No agent sells every project she represents. Even though authors are signed on the basis of their work's marketability, agents know from experience that some projects with excellent potential are not necessarily quick-and-easy big-money sales. And, yes, each and every agent has at least on occasion been as bewildered as the author when a particularly promising package receives no takers. Some projects, especially fiction, may be marketed for a long time before a publisher is found (if ever).

THE AUTHOR'S EXPECTATIONS

What's most important is that you the author feel sure the agent continues to believe in the project and is actively trying to sell it.

For his work, the agent receives a commission (usually 15%) against the writer's advance and all subsequent income relevant to the sold project.

Although this is an appreciable chunk of your work's income, the agent's involvement should end up netting you much more than you would have earned otherwise. The agent's power to round up several interested publishers to consider your work opens up the possibility that more than one house will make an offer for it, which means you'll be more likely to get a higher advance and also have more leverage regarding the various other contractual clauses.

The writer-agent relationship can become a rewarding business partnership. An agent can advise you objectively on the direction your writing career should take. Also, through her contacts, an agent may be able to get you book-writing assignments you would never have been offered on your own.

SCOUT FOR THE BEST AGENT FOR YOU

There are many ways to get an agent; your personal determination and acumen as a writer will be one of your most important assets. The best way to gain access to potential agents is by networking with fellow writers. Find out which agents they use, and what's being said about whom. Maybe some of your colleagues can introduce you to their agents, or at least allow you to drop their names when contacting their agents. Most agents will be receptive to a writer who has been referred by a current and valued client.

This book features a directory of literary agencies, including their addresses, the names of specific agents, and agents' specialty areas, along with some personal remarks and examples of recent titles sold to publishers.

QUERY FIRST

The universally accepted way to establish initial contact with an agent is to send a query letter. Agents tend to be less interested in—if not completely put off by—oral presentations. Be sure the letter is personalized: Nobody likes generic, photocopied letters that look like they're being sent to everyone.

Think of the query as a sales pitch. Describe the nature of your project and offer to send additional material—and enclose a self-addressed stamped envelope (SASE). Include all relevant information about yourself—along with a résumé if it's applicable. When querying about a nonfiction project, many agents won't mind receiving a complete proposal. But you might prefer to wait and see how the agent responds to the concept before sending the full proposal.

For queries about fiction projects, most agents prefer to receive story-concept sheets and/or plot synopses; if they like what they see, they'll request sample chapters or ask you to send the complete manuscript. Most agents won't consider manuscripts for incomplete works of fiction, essentially because few publishers are willing to do so.

If you enclose an SASE, most agents will respond to you, one way or another, within a reasonable period of time. If the agent asks to see your material, submit it promptly with a polite note stating that you'd like a response within 4 weeks on a nonfiction proposal, or 8 weeks on fiction material. If you haven't heard from the agent by that time, write or call to find out the status of your submission.

CIRCULATE WITH THE FLOW

You're entitled to circulate your material to more than one agent at a time, but you're obligated to let each agent know that such is the case. If and when you do sign with an agent, immediately notify other agents still considering your work that it's no longer available.

At least 200 literary agents are active in America, and their individual perceptions of what is and isn't marketable will vary widely—which is why a few or even several rejections should never deter writers who believe in themselves.

BUYER AND SELLER REVERSAL

When an agent eventually seeks to represent your work, it's time for her to begin selling herself to you. When you're seeking employment, you don't necessarily have to accept the first job offer you receive; likewise, you do not have to sign immediately with the first agent who wants you.

Do some checking before agreeing to work with a particular agent. If possible, meet the agent in person. A lot can be learned from in-person meetings that can't be gathered from telephone conversations. See what positive or negative information you can find out about the agent through your writers' network. Ask the agent for a client list and permission to call certain clients. Find out the agent's specialties.

Ask for a copy of the agent's standard contract.* Most agents today will want to codify your relationship with a written agreement; this should protect both parties equally. Make sure you're comfortable with everything in the agreement before signing it. Again, talking with fellow writers and reading books on the subject are excellent ways to deepen your understanding of industry practices.

When choosing an agent, follow your best instincts. Don't settle for anyone you don't perceive to be on the level, or who doesn't seem to be genuinely enthusiastic about you and your work.

SELF-REPRESENTATION: A FOOL FOR A CLIENT?

Agents aren't for everyone. In some instances, you may be better off on your own. Perhaps you actually do have sufficient editorial contacts and industry savvy to cut good deals by yourself. If so, what incentive do you have to share your income with an agent?

Of course, having an agent might provide you the intangible benefits of added prestige, save you the hassles of making submissions and negotiating deals, or act as a buffer through whom you can negotiate indirectly for tactical reasons.

You might also consider representing yourself if your books are so specialized that only a few publishers are potential candidates for them. Your contacts at such houses might be much stronger than any agent's could be.

ATTORNEYS: LITERARY AND OTHERWISE

Some entertainment/publishing attorneys can do everything an agent does, though there's no reason to believe they can necessarily do more. A major difference between the two is that the lawyer may charge you a set hourly fee or retainer, or any negotiated combination thereof, instead of an agency-type commission. In rare instances, writer-publisher disputes might need to be settled in a court of law, and a lawyer familiar with the industry then becomes a necessity.

* Please see sample agency contract in this book.

BOTTOM-LINE CALCULATIONS

The pluses and minuses of having an agent should be calculated like any other business service you might retain—it should benefit you more than it costs you. Generally speaking, the only real cost of using an agent is the commission. Of course, using the wrong agent may end up causing you more deficits than benefits; but even then you may at least learn a valuable lesson for next time.

Your challenge is to seek and retain an agent who's right for you. You're 100% responsible for getting yourself represented, and at least 50% responsible for making the relationship work for both of you.

Points of Inquiry from the Writer's Side

Questions and Answers About Agents, Editors, and the Publishing Industry

JEFF HERMAN

In the course of my ongoing participation in publishing workshops, seminar presentations, and panels at writers' conferences, there are certain questions that arise time and again. Many of these requests for information go straight to the heart of the world of book publishing.

The following questions are asked from the gut and replied to in kind. In order to be of value to the author who wishes to benefit from an insider view, I answer these serious queries in unvarnished terms, dispensing with the usual sugarcoating in order to emphasize the message of openness and candor.

Q: Is it more difficult to get an agent than it is to get a publisher?
A: I believe it's substantially easier to get an agent than it is to get a publisher.

The primary reason for this is that no agent expects to sell 100% percent of the projects she chooses to represent. Not because any of these projects lack merit (though some of them may), but because only so many titles are published per year—and many excellent ones just won't make the cut. This is especially true for fiction by unknown or unpublished writers, or for nonfiction in saturated categories. As a result, many titles will be agented but never published.

Naturally, a successful agent prefers to represent projects that she feels are hot and that publishers will trample each other to acquire. But few if any agents have the luxury of representing such sure-bet projects exclusively. In fact, the majority of their projects may be less than "acquisition-guaranteed," even though they are of acquisition quality. The agent assumes that many of these projects will eventually be sold profitably, but probably doesn't expect all of them to be. Every experienced agent knows that some of the best cash cows were not easily sold.

Make no mistake—it's not easy to get a reputable agent. Most agents reject 98% of the opportunities that cross their desks. They accept for representation only material they believe can be sold to a publisher. That is, after all, the only way for them to earn income and maintain credibility with publishers. If an agent consistently represents what a publisher considers garbage, that will become her professional signature—and her undoing as an agent.

But don't despair. This is a subjective business, composed of autonomous human beings. One agent's reject can be another's gold mine. That's why even a large accumulation of rejections should never deter you as a writer. Some people get married young, and some get married later!

Q: Is there anything I can do to increase my odds of getting an agent?
A: Yes.

First consider the odds quoted in the previous answer. The typical agent is rejecting 98% of everything he sees. That means he's hungry for the hard-to-find 2% that keeps him in business. If you're not part of that 2%, he'll probably have no use for you or your project. Your challenge is to convince him that you're part of that select 2%.

Q: What do agents and editors want? What do they look for in a writer? What can I do to become that kind of writer?
A: Let's back up a step or two and figure out *why* agents want to represent certain projects and *why* editors want to buy them. This industry preference has little to do with quality of writing as such.

Many highly talented writers never get published. Many mediocre writers do get published—and a number of them make a lot of money at it. There are reasons for this. The mediocre writers are doing things that more than compensate for their less-than-splendid writing. And the exceptional writers who underachieve in the publishing arena are (regardless of their talents) most likely doing things that undermine them.

In other words, being a good writer is just part of a complex equation. Despite all the criticism the educational system in the United States has received, America is exceedingly literate and has a mother lode of college graduates and postgraduates. Good, knowledgeable writers are a dime a dozen in this country. *Profitable* writers, however, are a rare species. And agents and editors obviously value them the most. Once more: Being an excellent writer and a financially successful writer don't necessarily coincide. Ideally, of course, you want to be both.

To maximize your success as a writer, you must do more than hone your ability to write; you must also learn the qualifiers and the disqualifiers for success. Obviously you wish to employ the former and avoid the latter. Publishing is a business, and agents tend to be the most acutely business-oriented of all the players. That's why they took the risk of going into business for themselves (most agents are self-employed).

If you wish, wear your artist's hat while you write. But you'd better acquire a business hat and wear it when it's time to sell. This subtle ability to change hats separates the minority of writers who get rich from the majority who do not. In my opinion, rich writers didn't get rich from their writing (no matter how good it is); they got rich by being good at business.

Many good but not-so-wealthy writers blame various internal or external factors for their self-perceived stagnation. My answer to them is: Don't blame anyone, especially yourself. To lay blame is an abdication of power. In effect, when you blame, you become a car with an empty gas tank, left to the elements. The remedy is to fill the tank yourself. Learn to view mistakes, whether they be yours or those of the people you relied upon, as inconvenient potholes—learning to move around them will make you an even better driver. Remember the old credo: only a poor workman blames his tools.

Observe all you can about those who are successful—not just in writing, but in all fields—and make their skills your skills. This is not to insist that making money is or should be your first priority. Your priorities, whatever they are, belong to you. But money is a widely acknowledged and sought-after emblem of success.

If an emphasis on personal gain turns you off, you may of course pursue other goals. Many successful people in business find the motivation to achieve their goals by focusing on altruistic concepts—such as creating maximum value for as many people as possible. Like magic, money often follows value even if it wasn't specifically sought. If you're unfortunate enough to make money you don't want, there's no need to despair: There are many worthy parties (including charities) that will gladly relieve you of this burden.

Here are specific ways to maximize your ability to get the agent you want:

- *Don't start off by asking what the agent can do for you.* You're a noncitizen until the agent has reason to believe that you may belong to that exclusive 2% club the agent wants to represent. It's a mistake to expect the agent to do anything to sell herself to you during that initial contact. You must first persuade her that you're someone who's going to make good money for her business. Once you've accomplished that, and the agent offers you representation, you're entitled to have the agent sell herself to you.
- *Act like a business.* As you're urged elsewhere in this book, get yourself a professional letterhead and state-of-the-art office equipment. While rarely fatal, cheap paper and poor-looking type will do nothing to help you—and in this business you need all the help you can give yourself.

Virtually anyone—especially the intellectually arrogant—is apt to be strongly affected on a subliminal level by a product's packaging. People pay for the sizzle, not the steak. There is a reason why American companies spend billions packaging, naming, and advertising such seemingly simple products as soap. We would all save money if every bar of soap were put into a plain paper box and just labeled "Soap." In fact, the no-frills section does sell soap that way—for a lot less. But few people choose to buy it that way. Understand this human principle, without judging it, and use it when packaging yourself.

- *Learn industry protocol.* I never insist that people follow all the rules. As Thomas Jefferson wisely suggested, a revolution every so often can be a good thing. But you should at least know the rules before you break them—or before you do anything.

  For instance: Most agents say they don't like cold calls. I can't say I blame them. If my rejection rate is 98%, I'm not going to be enthusiastic about having my ear talked off by someone who is more than likely part of that 98%. Just like you, agents want to use their time as productively as possible. Too often, cold calls are verbal junk mail. This is especially true if you are a writer selling fiction; your hard copy is the foot you want to get through the door.

Speaking for myself, most cold calls have a neutral effect on me (a few turn me off, and a few rouse my enthusiasm). I try to be courteous, because that's how I would want to be treated. I will allow the caller to say whatever he wants for about one minute before I take over to find out what, if anything, the person has in the way of hard copy. If he has some, I invite him to send it with an SASE. If he doesn't have any, I advise him to write some and then send it. Usually I don't remember much about what he said on the phone; I may not even remember that he called. But that doesn't matter; it's the hard copy that concerns me at first. This is the way it works with most agents. We produce books, not talk.

An agent's time is an agent's money (and therefore his clients' money). So don't expect any quality access until the agent has reason to believe you're a potential 2 percenter. If you're the CEO of General Motors, for instance, and you want to write a book, then all you need to do is call the agent(s) of your choice and identify yourself; red carpets will quickly appear. But the vast majority of writers have to learn and follow the more formalized procedures.

- *As explained elsewhere in this book, view the query letter as a sales brochure.* The best ones are rarely more than 1 1/2–2 pages long and state their case as briefly and efficiently as possible.

Here are the most common query mistakes:

1. Long, unfocused paragraphs.
2. Pontificating about irrelevancies (at least matters that are irrelevant from the agent's perspective).
3. Complaining about your tribulations as a writer. We all know it's a tough business, but nobody likes losers—least of all shrewd agents. Always be a winner when you're selling yourself, and you'll be more likely to win.

Most agents are hungry for that golden 2%, and they dedicate a great deal of time shoveling through mounds of material looking for it. You must be the first to believe that you are a 2 percenter, and then you must portray yourself that way to others. Reality begins in your own head, and is manifested primarily through your own actions—or lack thereof.

Every agent and editor has the power to reject your writing. But only you have the power to be—or not to be—a writer.

Q: Should I query only one agent at a time?
A: Some of my colleagues disagree with me here, but I recommend querying five to ten agents simultaneously, unless you already have your foot in the door with one. I suggest this because some agents will respond within 10 days, while others may take much longer, or never respond at all. Going agent by agent can eat up several months of valuable time before a relationship is consummated. And then your work still has to be sold to a publisher.

To speed up this process, it's smart to solicit several agents at a time, though you should be completely up front about it. If you go the multiple-submissions route, be sure to mention in your query letters to each agent that you are indeed making multiple submissions (though you needn't supply your agent list).

When an agent responds affirmatively to your query by requesting your proposal or manuscript, it's fine then to give the agent an exclusive reading. However, you should impose a reasonable time frame—for instance, 2 weeks for a nonfiction proposal and 4 weeks for a large manuscript. If it's a nonexclusive reading, make sure each agent knows that's what you want. And don't sign with an agent before talking to all the agents who are reading your work. (You have no obligation to communicate further with agents who do not respond affirmatively to your initial query.)

Most agents make multiple submissions to publishers, so they should be sensitive and respectful when writers have reason to use the same strategy agents have used with success.

Q: How do I know if my agent is working effectively for me? When might it be time to change agents?

A: As I remarked earlier, agents don't necessarily sell everything they represent, no matter how persistent and assertive they may be. In other words, the fact that your work is unsold doesn't automatically mean that your agent isn't doing his job. To the contrary, he may be doing the best job possible, and it may be incumbent upon you to be grateful for these speculative and uncompensated efforts.

Let's say 90 days pass and your work remains unsold. What you need to assess next is whether your agent is making active and proper attempts to sell your work.

Are you receiving copies of publisher rejection letters regarding your work? Generally, when an editor rejects projects submitted by an agent, the work will be returned within a few weeks, along with some brief comments explaining why the project was declined. (In case you're wondering, the agent doesn't have to include a SASE; the editors *want* agent submissions.) Copies of these rejection letters should be sent to you on a regular basis, as they are received by the agent. While no one expects you to enjoy these letters, they at least document that your agent is circulating your work.

If you have received many such rejection letters within these 90 days, it's hard to claim that your agent isn't trying. If you've received few or none, you might well call the agent for a status report. You should inquire as to where and when your work has been submitted, and what, if anything, the results of those submissions have been. In the end, you will have to use your own best judgment as to whether your agent is performing capably or giving you the run-around.

If it ever becomes obvious that your agent is no longer seriously trying to sell your work (or perhaps never was), you should initiate a frank discussion with the agent about what comes next. If the agent did go to bat for you, you should consider the strong possibility that your work is presently unmarketable, and act to preserve the agent relationship for your next project. Remember, if your work remains unsold, your agent has lost valuable time and has made no money.

If the evidence clearly shows that your agent has been nonperforming from day one, then your work has not been tested. You should consider withdrawing it and seek new representation.

Agent-hopping by authors is not rampant, but it's not uncommon either. Often the agent is just as eager as you—or more so—for the break-up to happen. One veteran colleague once told me that when he notices he hates to receive a certain client's phone calls, then it's time to find a graceful way to end the relationship.

The wisdom of agent-jumping must be assessed on a case-by-case basis. The evidence shows that many writers have prospered after switching, while others have entered limbo or even fallen far off their previous pace.

Before you decide to switch agents, you should focus on why you are unhappy with your current situation. It may be that if you appeal to your agent to discuss your specific frustrations—preferably in person, or at least by phone—many or all of them can be resolved, and your relationship will be given a fresh and prosperous start.

Agents are not mind readers. You only have one agent, but your agent has many clients. It is therefore mostly your responsibility as a writer client to communicate your concerns and expectations effectively to your agent. Your relationship may require only occasional adjustments, as opposed to a complete break-up.

Q: Who do agents really work for?

A: Themselves! Always have and always will.

True, agents serve their clients, but their own needs and interests always come first. Of course, this is the way it is in any business relationship (and in too many personal ones). You should never expect your lawyer, accountant, or stockbroker (and so on) to throw themselves into traffic to shield you from getting hit.

As long as the interests of the agent and the writer are in harmony, everything should work out well. However, on occasion the writer may have expectations that could be detrimental to the agent's own agenda (not to mention state of mind). Writers must never lose sight of the truth that publishers are the agent's most important customers. Only a foolish agent would intentionally do serious damage to her relationships with individual editors and publishing houses. It should be further noted that there is, therefore, a fine line that an agent will not cross when advocating for her clients.

Q: What do agents find unattractive about some clients?

A: Agents are individuals, so each will have his own intense dislikes. But, generally speaking, there is a certain range of qualities that can hamper any and all aspects of an agent's professional association with a client—qualities that often have similarly negative effects in realms other than publishing. Here's a litany of displeasing client types and their characteristics.

- *The Pest.* Nobody likes a nag, whether at home or at the office. A squeaky wheel may sometimes get the grease—not that anyone likes the effect—but more often they get the shaft.
- *The Complainer.* Some people can never be satisfied, only dissatisfied. It seems to be their mission in life to pass along their displeasure to others. These folks are never any fun—unless you're an ironic observer.
- *The BS Artist.* These clients believe everything even remotely connected with themselves is the greatest—for example, their fleeting ideas for books should win them millions of dollars up front. Of course, if they actually produce the goods, then the BS part of the term doesn't apply to them.
- *The Screw-Up.* These clients miss trains, planes, and deadlines. Their blunders can create major hassles for those who count on them.

- *The Sun God.* Some people believe they are more equal than others, and will behave accordingly. It's a real pleasure to see Sun Gods humbled.
- *The Liar.* Need I say more?

Sometimes these wicked traits combine, overlap, and reinforce themselves in one individual to create what an agent may rate as a veritable client from hell. Enough said on this subject for now, except that I would be remiss if I did not insist that no trade or professional class is immune to this nefarious syndrome—not even literary agents.

Q: How does someone become an agent?

A: For better or worse, anyone in America can declare themselves an agent—at any time. But what someone says and what they do are different things. Legitimate literary agents earn most or all of their income from commissions. The less-than-legitimate agencies most often depend on reading and management fees for their cash, with few if any actual book sales to their credit.

Most agents earn their stripes by working as editors for publishers. But that is by no means the only route, nor is it necessarily the most effective training ground. Good agents have emerged from a variety of environments and offer a broad range of exceptional credentials. What's most important is the mix of skills they bring to their agenting careers, such as: (1) Strong relationship skills—the ability to connect with people and earn their confidence. (2) Sales and marketing skills—the ability to get people to buy from them. (3) Persuasion and negotiating skills—the ability to get good results in their dealings. (4) An understanding of the book market and what publishers are buying. (5) An ability to manage many clients and projects at the same time.

Q: Who owns book publishing?

A: Many decades ago, book-publishing entities were customarily founded by individuals who had a passion for books. Though they obviously had to have business skills to make their houses survive and thrive, money was not necessarily their primary drive (at least not in the beginning), or they would have chosen more lucrative endeavors.

The vestiges of these pioneers can be found in the family names still extant in the corporate designations of most of today's publishing giants. But apart from the human-sounding names, these are very different companies today. Much of the industry is owned by multinational, multibillion-dollar conglomerates who have priorities other than the mere publication of books. The revenues from book operations are barely noticeable when compared with such mass-market endeavors as movies, TV/cable, music, magazines, sports teams, and character licensing. Stock prices must rise, and shareholders must be optimally satisfied for these firms to feel in any way stable.

Q: How does this type of ownership affect editors and the editorial-acquisition process?

A: This rampant corporate ownership translates into an environment in which book editors are pressured to make profitable choices if their careers are to prosper. At first look, that doesn't sound radical or wrongheaded, but a downside has indeed developed—editors are discouraged from taking risks for literary or artistic rationales that are ahead of the market curve, or even with an eye toward longer-term development and growth of a particular writer's readership.

The bottom line must be immediately appeased by every acquisition, or the non-performing editor's career will crumble. The editor who acquires blockbusters that the culturally elite disdain is an editor who is a success. The editor whose books lose money but are universally praised by critics is an editor who has failed.

Of course, the above comparison is extreme. Most editors are not single-minded money-grubbers, and do their best to acquire meaningful books that also make commercial sense. Where the cut becomes most noticeable is for the thousands of talented fiction writers who will never write big money-makers. While slots still exist for them, large publishers are increasingly reluctant to subsidize and nurture these marginally profitable writers' careers. Commercially speaking, there are better ways to invest the firm's resources.

Q: What, if any, are a writer's alternatives?

A: Yes, the big kids are dominant on their own turf and intend to extend their claim to as much of book country as they can. But this isn't the end of the story. The heroes are the thousands of privately owned "Mom and Pop" presses from Maine to Alaska who only need to answer to themselves. Every year, small presses, new and old, make an important contribution to literate culture with books that large publishers won't touch. It's not uncommon for some of these books to become bestsellers. University presses also pump out important (and salesworthy) books that would not have been published in a rigidly commercial environment.

Q: Is there anything positive to say about the current situation?

A: I don't mean to imply that the corporate ownership of the bulk of the book industry is absolutely bad. Indeed, it has brought many benefits. Publishers are learning to take better advantage of state-of-the-art marketing techniques and technologies, and have more capital with which to do it. The parent entertainment and communications firms enable the mainstream commercial publishers to cash in on popular frenzies, as with dinosaur mania, the latest and most salacious scandals, fresh interest in the environment or fitness, or celebrity and other pop-culture tie-ins, such as *Gump* and *Madonna* books.

The emergence of superstores enables more books to be sold. The stores create very appealing environments that draw much more traffic than conventional old-style bookstores. Many people who hang out at the superstores were never before motivated to go book shopping. But once they're in one of these well-stocked stores—whether at the bookshelves, ensconced in a reading-seat or perched by a steaming mug at an in-store cafe—they're likely to start spending.

The unfortunate part is that many small independent bookshops cannot compete with these new venues. However, many others are finding clever ways to hang on, by accenting special reader-interest areas or offering their own individual style of hospitality.

Q: How profitable is publishing?

A: One way to measure an industry's profitability is to look at the fortunes of those who work in it. By such a measure, the book business isn't very profitable, especially when compared to its twentieth-century sisters in entertainment and information industries: movies, television, music, advertising, and computers. Most book editors require a two-income family if they wish to raise children comfortably in New York or buy a nice home. The vast majority of published authors rely upon their day jobs or spouse's earnings.

A handful of authors make annual incomes in the six and seven figures, but it's often the movie tie-ins that get them there, and in turn push even more book sales.

A fraction of book editors will climb the ranks to the point at which they can command six-figure incomes, but most never attain this plateau. Almost all of those writers just starting in the business earn barely above the poverty level for their initial publishing endeavors—if that.

A well-established literary agent can make a lot of money. The trick is to build a number of backlist books that cumulatively pay off healthy commissions twice a year, while constantly panning for the elusive big-advance books that promise short-term (and perhaps long-term) windfalls.

In many ways, the agents are the players best positioned to make the most money. As sole proprietors they're not constrained by committees and can move like lightning. When everything aligns just right, the agent holds all the cards by controlling access to the author (product) and the publisher (producer).

The publishing companies themselves appear at least adequately profitable, averaging about 5% to 10% return on revenues (according to their public balance sheets). The larger companies show revenues of between $1 billion and $2 billion, sometimes nudging higher.

These are not sums to sneeze at. But most of those sales derive from high-priced non-bookstore products like textbooks and professional books. Large and midsize publishers alike are dependent upon their cash-cow backlist books for much of their retail sales. These books entail virtually no risk or investment, since their customer base is essentially locked in for an indefinite period, and the publisher has long ago recouped the initial investment. Many backlist books are legacies from editors and business dynamics that current employees may know nothing about.

The real risk for the current regime is their *frontlist*, which is the current season's crop. Large houses invest tens of millions of dollars to acquire, manufacture, market, and distribute anywhere from 50 to a few hundred "new" books. A small number of big-ticket individual titles will by themselves represent millions of dollars at risk. Most titles will represent less than $50,000 in risk on a pro-rata basis.

In practice, most of these frontlist titles will fail. The publisher will not recoup its investment and the title will not graduate to the exalted backlist status. But, like the fate of those innumerable turtle eggs laid in the sand, it's expected that enough spawn will survive to generate an overall profit and significant backlist annuities well into the future.

In the fairness of a broader picture, it is known that most motion pictures and television shows fail, as do most new consumer products (such as soap or soft drinks) that have engendered enormous research-and-development costs. It's the ones that hit—and hit big—that make the odds worth enduring for any industry.

Free Versus Fee
The Issue of Literary Agency Fees

Jeff Herman

Many literary agencies charge a fee to read unsolicited manuscripts, although the majority of well-established agencies don't charge such fees—yet.

There's a good deal of internal debate within the literary agency community about the ethics of charging reading fees, especially since many highly reputable agents have begun to charge relatively modest fees. Effective January 1, 1996, no members of the Association of Authors' Representatives are permitted to charge any kind of fees. While this addition to the organization's Canon of Ethics had an effect on only a fraction of its membership, it is too early to see whether the formerly fee-charging members put more stock in their fees or in their membership. (Fee-charging agencies, numbering a few hundred, are currently nonmembers of the AAR.)

Fees per se are a gray area, not necessarily right or wrong—though some *are* clearly wrong. The correctness of fee assessment must be judged on a case-by-case basis. How much is the fee? What's being provided in return for the fee? And, most importantly, what is the writer being led to believe he's getting for the fee?

Fees Range from $25 to Several Hundred Dollars and Up

When a reputable agency does charge a fee, it's usually modest—$50 to $100 for reading a complete manuscript. These agencies excuse their fees by maintaining that they're merely breaking even on such charges, since the fees cover the costs of reading the manuscript cover-to-cover and providing a detailed and useful critique—even if the work is rejected (which it usually is).

It's morally incumbent upon these agencies to make it abundantly clear to the writer that payment of the fee guarantees only a fair reading and constructive comments, and does *not* mean that the writer will be offered representation. Better yet, these agencies might even reveal approximately what percentage of prospective writer-clients are in fact offered representation.

A much more controversial scenario involves agencies that charge writers hundreds of dollars for single readings, or into the thousands of dollars for what is portrayed as in-depth editorial feedback or additional literary services. It's obvious that among these agencies are those who reap significant profits simply by reading and, almost always, rejecting manuscripts written by often-vulnerable writers.

These agencies defend themselves by asserting that, even though they reject more than 95% of the manuscripts, their extensive critiques greatly enhance the writer's chances of success down the line. Many writers claim that the critiques from some of these firms, while indeed wordy, aren't overly useful. Attending a weekend writing workshop might well be a better use of the money—that's for the writer to decide.

Some fee-charging agencies require monthly or yearly retainers (typically running into at least several hundred dollars annually). The usual justification is that, particularly when handling new writers, the agency incurs enormous expenses and, in exchange for expending their efforts and skills on long-shot (but worthy) properties, they more than earn their money.

That may be—but how can a writer be sure there is honest application behind the operation, and not just perfunctory rendering of generic services? One eye-opening giveaway may be when, in response to a query for a nonfiction book or a short synopsis or chapter selection for a novel, a contract is almost instantly sent to the writer, along with a fee schedule.

Well, then: Get a friend to send in another copy of the same material (with only the author name and address changed) and watch what happens. Barring inadvertent office miscues, if there's a contract in the offing, there's another clue for you. Maybe even send in a sheaf of printed-out gibberish and see if that earns an offer of agent representation (in exchange for cash). If it does, it's time to say "Bingo!"—and time to move on in your search for an agent.

It should be noted that established, reputable literary agencies customarily bill their clients (or are reimbursed) for such amenities as manuscript copying, messenger service, and express correspondence and deliveries. But such fees are spelled out and agreed to in an agency-representation agreement, and there are no highly visible (or invisible) items (such as those sometimes termed "management fees") over and above the agency commission on sale of the author's literary properties.

Is the Critique Worth the Cash?

Many agents resent those agents who charge fees. They feel that the entire profession's image is negatively affected by such practices, and that it's wrong for agents to earn money from anything other than commissions.

Agents who do not charge reading fees are unlikely to spend much time reading and analyzing a manuscript once they've decided to reject it. The writer is likely to receive only a terse computer-generated rejection letter. It may sometimes appear that the manuscript hasn't even been read, since many agents do stop reading if the first few pages are a turn-off. On a bad-to-mediocre day, an agent may view all manuscripts as junk mail until proven otherwise.

It is therefore understandable that battle-weary writers are tempted by the siren song of fee-charging agencies. At least they promise to acknowledge that there's a living, breathing writer alive within you, and their customized comments on official stationery are like manna—yes it's just another rejection, but one with candy on top.

WHO CHARGES FOR WHAT— WITH NO GUARANTEES?

Just because someone charges for a service does not make him an impostor or knave. Conversely, just because someone is an excellent literary advisor with a string of impressive credits does not mean she will be able to turn your idea into a big-money plum— regardless of how well-honed the writing is.

This is a complicated issue, one that does not subscribe to cut-and-dried guidelines. Yes, there are combination editor/agents as well as editorial services that charge fees up front and have respectable, even estimable track records. The question for the potential client is how to separate the scamsters from the worthy professionals.

For that there is no easy answer. It is almost a given that, in order to be able to judge whether an editorial service is of topnotch commercial quality, the writer is probably superbly accomplished (on some level) already. Freelance editors, ghostwriters, and publishing consultants have been known to remark that their best and most appreciative clients are often those whose original writing ideas or other materials show the most professionalism to begin with.

Some flourishing freelance editors and book doctors (believe it or not) actually turn down a potential client's work (even if the editor isn't rich) unless they think the client's material has a solid shot at eventual publication. It may be in the consultant's best interest to concentrate on gigs that will earn that freelancer visible publishing credits and the prospect of happy referrals down the road—rather than glomming short-term bucks from someone who'll complain when their fantasy of literary glory is shot down in a shrapnel haze of computer-generated rejection sheets, regardless of how well the consultant has served the project.

One key here is that for the most part these freelance editors, literary advisors, book doctors, and publishing consultants do not represent themselves as literary agents per se. However, when these freelancers have a range of publishing contacts, they may be able to refer or recommend a project to an agent or publisher of their acquaintance. Again—it's a delicate task to weed out the riffraff from the respected professionals, and there can be no guarantees.

I will not pass judgment on the propriety of literary agencies that charge reading fees. But if I were a writer, I'd first try my luck with the many excellent agencies that don't charge anything.

For further insight into this issue, please read the chapter titled "The Literary Agent Trade Association," which includes the Association of Authors' Representatives Canon of Ethics.

A SAMPLE SEDUCTION . . .

The following is an actual pitch letter from a fee-charging agency with only the names and other identifying information changed. Such correspondence is typical of the alluring invitations writers often receive in response to their agent submissions. There's nothing illegal about this reverse solicitation, nor, in all fairness, should such a practice automatically be deemed morally reprehensible. It's possible that a worthwhile service is indeed being provided for the money requested. However, $1,650 (or $500 or $3,000) is real money.

If a writer chooses to explore this route, there are preliminary steps I strongly advise following:

1. Ask for references. You're being asked to shell out hundreds of dollars to a virtual stranger. Get to know those who would eat your money.
2. Ask for a list of titles sold. Find out whether the so-called agency actually has an agenting track record. Or is this particular operation just a high-priced reading service with an agency facade?
3. Better yet, call or write to non–fee-charging agents and ask them to recommend book doctors, collaborative writers, or editorial freelancers whom they use to shape and develop their own clients' works. This may be a better place to spend your money.

THE WE-CHARGE-A-FEE AGENCY
Candyland, USA 77777

April 1, 19§§

Ms. Desi Parrot
123 Hungry Street
Birdland, USA 00000

Dear Ms. Parrot:

I read with interest your letter of April 1, synopsis and excerpts from your novel, *The Child-Eater*, for which you are proposing agency representation. As you know, we specialize in this genre; from my experience, I can tell you that there is definite interest by publishers in novels like yours.

We believe that every writer can benefit from representation by a full-service literary agency in providing up-to-date information on editorial/media buying trends, associations with editors and producers, and in dealing with options, contract terms, advances, royalties and ancillary rights. The odds against publication by an unrepresented writer are considerable. We have the experience to identify markets for your writing, anticipate where problems are likely to arise, and work as an advocate for your ambitions and interests.

The first step towards representation and publication is a careful reading and market analysis of your material. This involves an evaluation of the literary and commercial prospects of your work by an experienced editor. If the material is immediately marketable, we will proceed to a representation contract and undertake to sell your work worldwide. If editing is needed, we will provide specific guidelines and unlimited consultative services to you in the revising or polishing of your work. Our goal is to help you become a published author.

If you have had minimal or no trade sales (i.e., book-length fiction), our consulting fee is $1,650.00. As you know, some agencies advertise free appraisals, but these "come-ons" mask the services of very high-priced editing services with little influence in the market. We do not charge monthly representation fees and your initial fee is refunded upon sale of the work. You may pay by check or money order, or by Visa, MasterCard or Discover; please include card number and expiration date and note that there is an additional five (5) percent charge for the use of credit cards. The fee is fully refundable upon sale of the manuscript.

We are accepting a limited number of new clients and look forward to reading your complete manuscript. Please read and sign the enclosed Material Submission Release Form. Once we make a sale for you, we will accept further material on our professional commission terms, eliminating all fees. Please drop me a line, Ms. Parrot, if I can answer any questions. I look forward to being of service to you with *The Child-Eater*.

Sincerely,

Doreem On

Doreem On,
President

When the Deal Is Done

How to Thrive After Signing
a Publishing Contract

JEFF HERMAN

Congratulations! You've sold your book to an established publishing house. You've gained entry to the elite club of published authors. You'll discover that your personal credibility is enhanced whenever this achievement is made known to others. It may also prove a powerful marketing vehicle for your business or professional practice.

Smell the roses while you can. Then wake up and smell the coffee. If your experience is like that of numerous other writers, once your book is actually published, there's a better-than-even chance you'll feel a bit of chagrin. Some of these doubts are apt to be outward expressions of your own inner uncertainties. Others are not self-inflicted misgivings—they are most assuredly ticked off by outside circumstances.

Among the most common author complaints are: (1) Neither you nor anyone you know can find the book anywhere. (2) The publisher doesn't appear to be doing anything to market the book. (3) You detest the title and the jacket. (4) No one at the publishing house is listening to you. In fact, you may feel that you don't even exist for them.

As a literary agent, I live through these frustrations with my clients every day, and I try to explain to them at the outset what the realities of the business are. But I never advocate abdication or pessimism. There are ways for every author to substantially remedy these endemic problems. In many cases this means first taking a deep breath, relaxing, and reaching down deep inside yourself to sort out the true source of your emotions. When this has been accomplished, it's time to breathe out, move out, and take charge.

What follows are practical means by which each of these four most common failures can be preempted. I'm not suggesting that you can compensate entirely for what may be a publisher's defaults; it's a tall order to remake a clinker after the fact. However, with lots of smarts and a little luck you can accomplish a great deal.

A Philosophy to Write By

Let me introduce a bit of philosophy that applies to the writer's life as well as it does to the lives of those who are not published. Many of you may be familiar with the themes popularized by psychotherapists, self-awareness gurus, and business motivators that assert the following: To be a victim is to be powerless—which means you don't have the ability to improve your situation. With that in mind, avoid becoming merely an author who only complains and who remains forever bitter.

No matter how seriously you believe your publisher is screwing up, don't fall into the victim trap. Instead, find positive ways to affect what is or is not happening for you.

Your publisher is like an indispensable employee whom you are not at liberty to fire. You don't have to work with this publisher the next time; but this time it's the only one you've got.

There are a handful of perennially bestselling writers, such as John Grisham, Anne Rice, Mary Higgins Clark, and Michael Crichton, whose book sales cover a large part of their publisher's expense sheet. These writers have perhaps earned the luxury of being very difficult, if they so choose (most of them are reportedly quite the opposite).

But the other 99.98% of writers are not so fortunately invested with the power to arbitrate. No matter how justified your stance and methods may be, if you become an author with whom everyone at the publishing house dreads to speak, you've lost the game.

The editors, publicists, and marketing personnel still have their jobs, and they see no reason to have you in their face. In other words: Always seek what's legitimately yours, but always try to do it in a way that might work *for* you, as opposed to making yourself persona non grata till the end of time.

Attacking Problem No. 1: Neither You nor Anyone You Know Can Find the Book Anywhere

This can be the most painful failure. After all, what was the point of writing the book and going through the whole megillah of getting it published if it's virtually invisible?

Trade book distribution is a mysterious process, even for people in the business. Most bookstore sales are dominated by the large national and regional chains, such as Waldenbooks, B. Dalton, Barnes & Noble, and Crown. No shopping mall is complete without at least one of these stores. Publishers always have the chain stores in mind when they determine what to publish. Thankfully, there are also a few thousand independently owned shops throughout the country.

Thousands of new titles are published each year, and these books are added to the seemingly infinite number that are already in print. Considering the limitations of the existing retail channels, it should be no surprise that only a small fraction of all these books achieves a significant and enduring bookstore presence.

Each bookstore will dedicate most of its visual space to displaying healthy quantities of the titles they feel are safe sells: books by celebrities and well-established authors, or books that are being given extra-large printings and marketing budgets by their publishers, thereby promising to create demand.

The rest of the store will generally provide a liberal mix of titles, organized by subject or category. This is where the backlist titles reside and the lower-profile newer releases try to stake their claims. For instance, the business section will probably offer two dozen or so sales books. Most of the displayed titles will be by the biggest names in the genre, and their month-to-month sales probably remain strong, even if the book was first published several years ago.

In other words, there are probably hundreds of other sales books written in recent years that, as far as retail distribution is concerned, barely made it out of the womb. You see, the stores aren't out there to do you any favors. They are going to stock whatever titles they feel they can sell the most of. There are too many titles chasing too little space.

It's the job of the publisher's sales representative to lobby the chain and store buyers individually about the merits of her publisher's respective list. But here too the numbers can be numbing. The large houses publish many books each season, and it's not possible for the rep to do justice to each of them. Priority will be given to the relatively few titles that get the exceptional advances.

Because most advances are modest, and since the average book costs about $20,000 to produce, some publishers can afford to simply sow a large field of books and observe passively as some of them sprout. The many that don't bloom are soon forgotten, as a new harvest dominates the bureaucracy's energy. Every season, many very fine books are terminated by the publishing reaper. The wisdom and magic these books may have offered is thus sealed away, disclosed only to the few.

I have just covered a complicated process in a brief fashion. Nonetheless, the overall consequences for your book are in essence the same. Here, now, are a few things you may attempt in order to override such a stacked situation. However, these methods will not appeal to the shy or passive:

- Make direct contact with the publisher's sales representatives. Do to them what they do to the store buyers—sell 'em! Get them to like you and your book. Take the reps near you to lunch and ballgames. If you travel, do the same for local reps wherever you go.
- Make direct contact with the buyers at the national chains. If you're good enough to actually get this kind of access, you don't need to be told what to do next.
- Organize a national marketing program aimed at local bookstores throughout the country.

There's no law that says only your publisher has the right to market your book to the stores. (Of course, except in special cases, all orders must go through your publisher.) For the usual reasons, your publisher's first reaction may be "What the hell are you doing?" But that's okay; make them happy by showing them that your efforts work. It would be wise, however, to let the publisher in on your scheme up front.

If your publisher objects—which she may—you might choose to interpret those remarks as simply the admonitions they are, and then proceed to make money for all. This last observation leads to ways you can address the next question.

ATTACKING PROBLEM NO. 2: THE PUBLISHER DOESN'T APPEAR TO BE DOING ANYTHING TO MARKET THE BOOK

If it looks as if your publisher is doing nothing to promote your book, then it's probably true. Your mistake is being surprised and unprepared.

The vast majority of titles published receive little or no marketing attention from the publisher beyond catalog listings. The titles that get big advances are likely to get some support, since the publisher would like to justify the advance by creating a good seller.

Compared to those in other Fortune 500 industries, publishers' in-house marketing departments tend to be woefully understaffed, undertrained, and underpaid. Companies like Procter & Gamble will tap the finest business schools, pay competitive salaries, and strive to nurture marketing superstars. Book publishers don't do this.

As a result, adult trade book publishing has never been especially profitable, and countless sales probably go unmade. The sales volumes and profits for large, diversified publishers are mostly due to the lucrative—and captive—textbook trade. Adult trade sales aren't the reason that companies like Random House can generate more than $1 billion in annual revenues.

Here's what you can do:

Hire your own public relations firm to promote you and your book. Your publisher is likely to be grateful and cooperative. But you must communicate carefully with your publishing house.

Once your manuscript is completed, you should request a group meeting with your editor and people from the marketing, sales, and publicity departments. You should focus on what their marketing agenda will be. If you've decided to retain your own PR firm, this is the time to impress the people at your publishing house with your commitment, and pressure them to help pay for it. At the very least, the publisher should provide plenty of free books.

Beware of this common problem: Even if you do a national TV show, your book may not be abundantly available in bookstores that day—at least not everywhere. An obvious answer is setting up 800 numbers to fill orders, and it baffles me that publishers don't make wider use of them. There are many people watching *Oprah* who won't ever make it to the bookstore, but who would be willing to order then and there with a credit card. Infomercials have proven this.

Not all talk or interview shows will cooperate, but whenever possible you should try to have your publisher's 800 number (or yours) displayed as a purchasing method in addition to the neighborhood bookstore. If you use your own number, make sure you can handle a potential flood.

If retaining a PR firm isn't realistic for you, then do your own media promotions. There are many good books in print about how to do your own PR. (A selection of relevant titles may be found in this volume's Suggested Resources section.)

ATTACKING PROBLEM NO. 3:
YOU DETEST THE TITLE AND JACKET

Almost always, your publisher will have final contractual discretion over title, jacket design, and jacket copy. But that doesn't mean you can't be actively involved. In my opinion you had better be. Once your final manuscript is submitted, make it clear to your editor that you expect to see all prospective covers and titles. But simply trying to veto what the publisher comes up with won't be enough. You should try to counter the negatives with positive alternatives. You might even want to go as far as having your own prospective covers professionally created. If the publisher were to actually choose your version, the house might reimburse you.

At any rate, don't wait until it's after the fact to decide you don't like your cover, title, and so forth. It's like voting: Participate or shut up.

ATTACKING PROBLEM NO. 4:
NO ONE AT THE PUBLISHING HOUSE
SEEMS TO BE LISTENING TO YOU

This happens a lot—though I bet it happens to certain people in everything they do. The primary reasons for this situation are either (1) that the people you're trying to access are incompetent; (2) that you're not a priority for them; or (3) that they simply hate talking to you.

Here are a few things you might try to do about it:

- If the contact person is incompetent, what can he or she really accomplish for you anyway? It's probably best to find a way to work around this person, even if he begins to return your calls before you place them.
- The people you want access to may be just too busy to give you time. Screaming may be a temporary remedy, but eventually they'll go deaf again. Obviously their time is being spent somewhere. Thinking logically, how can you make it worthwhile for these people to spend more time on you? If being a pain in the neck is your best card, then perhaps you should play it. But there's no leverage like being valuable. In fact, it's likely that the somewhere else they're spending their time is with a very valuable author.
- Maybe someone just hates talking to you. That may be their problem. But, as many wise men and women have taught, allies are better than adversaries. And to convert an adversary is invaluable. Do it.

CONCLUSION

This essay may come across as cynical. But I want you to be realistic and be prepared. There are many publishing success stories out there, and many of them happened because the authors made them happen.

For every manuscript that is published, there are probably a few thousand that were rejected. To be published is a great accomplishment—and a great asset. If well tended, it can pay tremendous dividends.

Regardless of your publisher's commitment at the outset, if you can somehow generate sales momentum, the publisher will most likely join your march to success and allocate a substantial investment to ensure it. In turn, they may even assume all the credit. But so what? It's to your benefit.

Mastering Ghostwriting and Collaboration

Gene Busnar

If you're looking for a writing career with a never-ending source of opportunities, you might consider ghostwriting or collaborating on books. I've learned that there's an almost inexhaustible supply of would-be coauthors who are convinced that they're sitting on a bestseller—be it some kind of unique personal experience, a revolutionary new way of growing tulips, or a secret of the universe that's going to improve our lives.

Many of these unheralded giants are driven by an inflated sense of their own vision and self-importance. But, fortunately, quite a few potential collaborators actually do have commercially viable nonfiction book ideas. All they need is a professional writer to take care of a few "minor details," which can be paraphrased as follows:

- I have the ideas, but lack the writing skills.
- I don't have the time to write the book myself.
- I don't have an agent or book-publishing contacts.

Now, if these were the only reasons people needed collaborators or ghostwriters, this business would be a lot simpler. Anyone with a great story or a wonderful idea for a how-to book could hire a professional writer to put things in proper literary form. In theory, the book's content—its very soul—already exists, so the writer's job should be relatively simple.

Unfortunately, things usually don't turn out that way. Professional ghostwriters and collaborative writers are expected to know what book companies are buying at any given time, and to anticipate the inherent problems in a particular book idea—especially if it's being sold in proposal form.

A publisher or agent may come to you with a fully conceived project by an articulate, promotable coauthor. But this is relatively rare—especially when you are in the early stages of your career.

There have been times when I've had to reshape the idea, change the principal's voice and language around, and find a better title for the book. If you happen to possess these skills, coauthors shouldn't be all that hard to find. But first you have to get some publishing credits under your belt.

If you haven't yet published a book, try writing articles for magazines and local newspapers. But don't expect your first assignments to pay well. Think of them as vehicles that can propel you to a higher level.

It may be possible to short-circuit the steps most authors go through by coming up with an innovative book concept and putting together a proposal that indicates you can deliver the goods. But the skimpier and less relevant your credits, the more you'll be expected to prove before people will treat you with consideration—much less shell out some serious bucks for your effort.

Maybe you've heard inspirational stories of people who struck it rich on their first try. Such cases are rare. The vast majority of successful nonfiction writers work extremely hard at improving their craft and building their business—over the course of a number of projects and years.

For this chapter, I've chosen to focus mostly on the business aspects of collaboration and ghosting—since this is an area where many talented new writers need help. Frankly, I think it's ridiculous to enter such a difficult and competitive field unless you possess the necessary talent. So before you go any further, it might be worthwhile to take a few minutes to think about some of the issues on this talent-evaluation questionnaire:

Do You Have What It Takes?

1. What experience do you have (professional or otherwise) as a writer?
2. Have you ever received feedback about your writing from an agent or editor?
3. What was the thrust of that feedback?
4. Have you ever won any contests or received any writing awards? List them.
5. Have you worked with a teacher or mentor who encouraged you to pursue a professional writing career?
6. Are you open to constructive criticism of your writing?
7. Can you think of an instance where such criticism helped you to improve your writing?
8. Do your writing talents fit into a commercial category?
9. If not, are you willing to take steps to present them in more commercial ways?
10. What about your writing sets it apart from or makes it superior to that of your competitors?

If you honestly feel the talent is there, you may be off to a running start. But remember, even the greatest talent doesn't guarantee success.

It's a truism that many fine writers aren't good at business, but that's not surprising. Most people enter this field because they like to write—not because they expect to get rich.

If money is the primary motivation, you'd be better advised to seek out a career in law, copywriting, or any number of more financially lucrative fields. Still, if you're going to succeed—or at least survive—you'd better accept the fact that business and marketing skills are at least as important as literary talent. This is especially true in collaborative and ghostwriting work—fields that require a good deal of negotiation and personal interaction.

If you want to write just for pleasure, that's one thing. But the moment you decide to earn money at your craft, you become a businessperson. If you want to make it professionally, start thinking of yourself not just as a writer—but as someone who's in the *business* of writing. Here are four suggestions to help point your career in that direction:

1. Take a business-minded approach.
2. Present yourself powerfully.
3. Position yourself advantageously.
4. Price your services for profit.

TAKE A BUSINESS-MINDED APPROACH

Don't make the mistake of thinking that, because you're good, clients will find you. You've got lots of competitors out there who are aggressively pursuing work, so you can't afford to be too laid-back. It's part of your job to make potential clients aware of you. These include not only cowriters, but agents and editors who can direct projects your way.

Most successful nonfiction writers do all sorts of things to generate work and develop new contacts. No matter where you are in your career, you might want to consider devoting time and energy to the following activities:

- Join professional societies and attend their meetings.
- Associate with as many agents, editors, and potential collaborators as possible.
- Stay in touch with peers who have similar interests.
- Sign up for relevant courses, lectures, and seminars—especially those conducted by reputable people in your field.
- Read trade publications.
- Keep up with economic and other trends that influence our business.

In the final analysis, your success as a writer can hinge as much on how creative you are in your business as it does on your actual work. That's why it's essential that you understand and assume responsibility for the business side of your writing career as early in the game as possible.

PRESENT YOURSELF POWERFULLY

Whenever you submit a manuscript, proposal, or résumé to an editor, agent, or potential collaborator, it's essential to look at those presentation materials from the other person's point of view. When you present your work to people in a position to buy your services, you're selling yourself as well as the materials at hand.

Professionalism in your work and manner communicates that you are someone people ought to take seriously—even if they don't buy the immediate project. The creation of a professional image includes the following:

Looking Like a Pro

- Appropriate and well-organized materials.
- Dependability and promptness.
- A willingness to accept critical feedback.

Of all these factors, an openness to criticism and tolerance for rejection may be the most difficult. Here, especially, you need to get out of your own skin for a moment and imagine how you'd feel if you were an agent or an editor. One of the toughest things is telling other people that their work doesn't measure up—whatever the reason.

Criticism and rejection can be even more difficult when you're on the receiving end. Still, when you communicate a willingness to accept constructive criticism, you invite feedback that can help you make valuable refinements in your presentation. At the same time, you let people know that they're dealing with a confident professional—one who has a genuine interest in meeting their needs.

POSITION YOURSELF ADVANTAGEOUSLY

One key to presenting yourself professionally is giving potential clients a clear-cut picture of what you do. Since your potential clients have the option of choosing the writer who best fills their specific needs, it's your job to see to it that you occupy that particular niche in their minds. In advertising, this concept is called positioning. It's a principle that applies especially well to the business of writing.

Positioning saves your potential clients a good deal of time. You can assume that anyone who's in a position to give you paying work has certain requirements and categories in mind. It's your job to meet those criteria. If you don't, someone else will.

Many good writers are capable of collaborating or ghosting in a number of areas. Unfortunately, that's not what most agents and editors want to hear. Their lives are already too cluttered up with superfluous people and irrelevant information. If you try to hit them with all your credentials at once, they may find it difficult to remember anything about you.

Once you have an idea of what specific clients are looking for, you can present only the information that is most relevant. The best way to make that determination is to research potential clients before you approach them.

Let's say, for example, that you want to ghostwrite political autobiographies, and you're trying to interest an agent who specializes in that area. He asks you to send some samples of your work. How do you decide which materials to include and which ones to leave out?

As a rule, the best presentations are the most concise. That's why it's best to present potential clients with only those materials that relate to the job at hand. As you develop more of a relationship with agents and editors, you can make them aware of your other skills. But be careful not to overwhelm them with too much material.

If you tell an agent who perceives you as a political writer that you also have skills in the medical area, he may file that information away for future reference. But if a call for a medical writer comes in, he's most likely to go with someone who has positioned herself or himself primarily in that area.

Of course, there are exceptions to the rule. For example, the agent may not be able to get the medical writer he or she wants at that particular moment. The memory that you had some background in that area may surface—and suddenly your phone is ringing.

PRICE YOUR SERVICES FOR PROFIT

You may have never thought about it in this light, but in most professions, pricing is determined by positioning and perception rather than by any objective measure.

Have you ever wondered, for example, why your car mechanic charges $20 an hour, while your attorney can charge $200 an hour?

The reasons for this huge difference in pricing can't be measured in any real terms. But the fact is, nobody would pay $200 an hour to get their car fixed. And if an attorney asked for a mere $20 an hour, you'd probably question the guy's competence.

Unfortunately, pricing guidelines in the book-writing business are not nearly so well established as in lawyering or repairing cars. That's why it's essential to establish yourself as a businessperson who puts a high value on your hours.

Personally, I see no objective reason why the services of a good writer should be worth less than those of a mediocre attorney. But because writing is thought of as a glamour profession, people sometimes expect you to work for nothing—especially when you start out. Let them know that you're in this business for profit—not glamour.

I'll never forget how offended one celebrity became when I told him that I actually expected to be paid—and paid well—for working with him on his book proposal. This made a profound impression on me, and I've since made it a policy to regard people who take this attitude as a threat to my very survival.

In writing—as in any business—there are times when it may be worthwhile to accept a low-paying project. Just make sure that you have a clear idea of what's in it for you.

I've listed six compensating factors that can offset a low price. You may want to use them as negotiating points in deciding whether or not to accept a particular project:

What to Ask for When the Price Is Wrong

- The prominent appearance of your name on the cover and in all publicity for the book.
- A generous allowance for expenses and supplies.
- Greater creative freedom.
- A larger portion of the advance up front.
- A better deal on subsidiary or ancillary rights.
- A larger number of author's copies of the book.

Most writers take on work for a combination of three reasons: to make money; to be creative and expressive; and to build credibility—which will hopefully lead to making more money.

Once you accept these as the general business goals of collaboration and ghostwriting, it behooves you to look for projects that are fulfilling, well-paying, and career enhancing.

If you can find a project that meets all three of these criteria, go for it. If a project allows you to achieve any two of these goals, it's certainly worth considering. One out of three would be a marginal call at best. But if the project doesn't satisfy any of these three tests, the decision is simple.

Forget it, and move on to something more rewarding.

Fiction Dictionary

JAMIE M. FORBES

In book publishing, people describe works of fiction as they relate to categories, genres, and other market concepts, which, coming from the mouths of renowned industry figures, can make it sound as if there's a real system to what is actually a set of arbitrary terminology. Categories are customarily viewed as reflecting broad sectors of readership interest. Genres are either subcategories (classifications within categories) or types of stories that can pop up within more than one category—though *genre* and *category* are sometimes used interchangeably.

For instance, suspense fiction (as a broad category) includes the jeopardy story genre (typified by a particular premise that can just as easily turn up in a supernatural horror story). Or, again within the suspense fiction category, there's the police procedural (a subcategory of detective fiction, which is itself a subcategory of suspense that is often spoken of as a separate category). The police procedural can be discussed as a distinct genre with its own special attributes; and there are particular procedural genre types, such as those set in the small towns of the American plains or in a gritty urban environment. As a genre-story type, tales of small-town American life also surface in the context of categories as disparate as literary fiction, horror stories, Westerns, and contemporary and historical romance.

As we can see, all of this yakety-yak is an attempt to impose a sense of order onto what is certainly a muddy creative playing field.

The following listing of commonly used fiction descriptives gives an indication of the varieties of writing found within each category. This is not meant to be a strict taxonomy. Nor is it exhaustive. The definitions associated with each category or genre are fluid and personalized in usage, and can seem to vary with each author interview or critical treatise, with each spate of advertising copy or press release, or can shift during the course of a single editorial conference. One writer's "mystery" may be a particular editor's "suspense," which is then marketed to the public as a "thriller."

Then too, individual authors do come up with grand, original ideas that demand publication and thereby create new categories, or decline to submit to any such designation. But that's another story—maybe yours.

ACTION ADVENTURE

The action-oriented adventure novel is best typified in terms of premise and scenario trajectory. These stories often involve the orchestration of a journey that is essentially exploratory, revelatory, and (para)military. There is a quest element—a search for a treasure in whatever guise—in addition to a sense of pursuit that crosses over into thrillerdom. From one perspective, the action-adventure tale, in story concept if not explicit content, traces its descent from epic-heroic tradition.

In modern action-adventure we are in the territory of freebooters, commandos, and mercenaries—as well as suburbanites whose yen for experience of the good life, and whose very unawareness in the outback, takes them down dangerous trails. Some stories are stocked with an array of international terrorists, arms-smugglers, drug-dealers, and techno-pirates. Favorite settings include jungles, deserts, swamps, and mountains—any sort of badlands (don't rule out an urban environment) that can echo the perils that resound through the story's human dimension.

There can be two or more cadres with competing aims going for the supreme prize— and be sure to watch out for lots of betrayal and conflict among friends, as well as the hitherto unsuspected schemer among the amiably bonded crew.

Action-adventures were once thought of as exclusively men's stories. No more. Writers invented new ways to do it, and the field is now open.

COMMERCIAL FICTION

Commercial fiction is defined by sales figures—either projected (prior to publication, even before acquisition) or backhandedly through actual performance. Commercial properties are frontlist titles, featured prominently in a publisher's catalog and given good doses of publicity and promotion.

An agent or editor says a manuscript is commercial, and the question in response is apt to be: How so? Many books in different genres achieve bestseller potential after an author has established a broad-based readership and is provided marketing support from all resources the publisher commands.

Commercial fiction is not strictly defined by content or style; it is perhaps comparative rather than absolute. Commercial fiction is often glitzier, more stylishly of the mode in premise and setting; its characters strike the readers as more assuredly glamorous (regardless of how highbrow or lowlife).

A commercial work offers the publisher a special marketing angle, which changes from book to book or season to season—this year's kinky kick is next year's ho-hum. For a new writer in particular, to think commercially is to think ahead of the pack and not jump on the tail-end of a bandwagon that's already passed. If your premise has already played as a television miniseries, you're way too late.

Commercial works sometimes show elements of different categories, such as detective fiction or thrillers, and may cut across or combine genres to reach out toward a vast readership. Cross-genre books may thus have enticing hooks for the reading public at large; at the same time, when they defy category conventions they may not satisfy genre aficionados. If commercial fiction is appointed by vote of sales, most popular mysteries are commercial works, as are sophisticated bestselling sex-and-shopping oh-so-shocking wish-it-were-me escapades.

CRIME FICTION

Related to detective fiction and suspense novels, in subject matter and ambiance, are stories centered on criminal enterprise. Crime fiction includes lighthearted capers that are vehicles in story form for portrayal of amusingly devious aspirations at the core of the human norm. Crime stories can also be dark, black, *noir*, showing the primeval essence of tooth-and-nail that brews in more than a few souls.

Some of the players in crime stories may well be cops of one sort or another (and they are often as corrupt as the other characters), but detection per se is not necessarily the story's strong suit. It is just as likely that, in the hands of one of the genre's masters, the reader's lot will be cast (emotionally at least) in support of the outlaw characters' designs.

DETECTIVE FICTION

Varieties of detective fiction include police procedurals (with the focus on formal investigatory teamwork); hard-boiled, poached or soft-boiled (not quite so tough as hard-boiled); and the cozy (aka tea-cozy mysteries, manners mysteries, manor house mysteries).

Detectives are typically private or public pros; related professionals whose public image at least involves digging under the surface (reporters, journalists, computer hackers, art experts, psychotherapists, and university academics including archaeologists); or they may be rank amateurs who are interested or threatened via an initial plot turn that provides them with an opportunity (or the necessity) to assume an investigatory role.

The key here is that the detective story involves an ongoing process of discovery that forms the plot. Active pursuit of interlocking clues and other leads is essential—though sometimes an initial happenstance disclosure will do in order to kick off an otherwise tightly woven story.

The manifold denominations of modern detective fiction (also called mysteries, or stories or novels of detection) are widely considered to stem from the detective tales composed by the nineteenth-century American writer Edgar Allan Poe. Though mysterious tracks of atmosphere and imagery can be traced in the writings of French symbolists (Charles Baudelaire was a big fan of Poe), the first flowering of the form was in Britain, including such luminaries as Arthur Conan Doyle, Agatha Christie, and Dorothy L. Sayers. Indeed, in one common usage, a traditional mystery (or cozy) is a story in the mode initially established by British authors.

The other major tradition is the American-grown, hard-boiled detective story, with roots in the tabloid culture of America's industrial growth and the associated institutions of yellow journalism, inspirational profiles of the gangster-tycoon lifestyle, and social-action exposés.

The field continues to expand with infusions of such elements as existentialist character conceits, the lucidity and lushness of magic-realists, and the ever-shifting sociopolitical insights that accrue from the growing global cultural exchange.

Occasionally detective fiction involves circumstances in which, strictly speaking, no crime has been committed. The plot revolves around parsing out events or situations that may be construed as strange, immoral, or unethical (and are certainly mysterious), but which are by no means considered illegal in all jurisdictions.

FANTASY FICTION

The category of fantasy fiction covers many of the story elements encountered in fables, folktales, and legends; the best of these works obtain the sweep of the epic and are touched by the power of myth. Some successful fantasy series are set within recognizable museum-quality frames, such as those of ancient Egypt or the Celtic world. Another strain of fantasy fiction takes place in almost-but-not-quite archaeologically verifiable regions of the past or future, with barbarians, nomads, and jewel-like cities scattered across stretches of continental-sized domains of the author's imagination.

Fair game in this realm are romance, magic, and talking animals. Stories are for the most part adventurous, filled with passion, honor, vengeance—and *action*. A self-explanatory subgenre of fantasy fiction is termed sword-and-sorcery.

HORROR

Horror has been described as the simultaneous sense of fascination and terror, a basic attribute that can cover significant literary scope. Some successful horror writers are admired more for their portrayal of atmosphere than for attention to plot or character development. Other writers do well with the carefully paced zinger—that is, the threat-and-delivery of gore; in the hands of skilled practitioners, sometimes not much more is needed to produce truly terrifying effects.

The horror genre has undergone changes—there is overall less reliance on the religiously oriented supernatural, more utilization of medical and psychological concepts, more sociopolitical and cultural overtones, and a general recognition on the part of publishers that many horror aficionados seek more than slash-and-gore. Not that the readers aren't bloodthirsty—it is just that in order to satisfy the cravings of a discerning audience a writer must create an augmented reading experience.

The horror itself can be supernatural in nature, psychological, paranormal, or techno (sometimes given a medical-biological slant that verges on sci-fi), or can embody personified occult/cultic entities. In addition to tales of vampires, were-creatures, demons, and ghosts, horror has featured such characters as the elemental slasher/stalker (conceived with or without mythic content), a variety of psychologically tormented souls, and just plain folks given over to splatterhouse pastimes. Whatever the source of the horror, the tale is inherently more gripping and more profound when the horrific beast, force, or human foe has a mission, is a character with its own meaningful designs and insights—when something besides single-minded bloodlust is at play.

At times the horror premise is analogous to a story of detection (especially in the initial setup); often the horror plot assumes the outlines of the thriller (particularly where there is a complex chase near the end); and sometimes the horror-story scenario ascribes to action-adventure elements. However, rather than delineating a detailed process of discovery (as in a typical mystery) or a protracted hunt throughout (as in the thriller), the horror plot typically sets up a final fight to the finish (until the sequel) that, for all its pyrotechnics and chills, turns on something other than brute force.

LITERARY FICTION

The term *literary* describes works that feature the writer's art expressed at its most refined levels; literary fiction describes works of literature in such forms as the novel, novella, novelette, short story, and short-shorts (also known as flash fiction). In addition to these fictional formats, literary works include poetry, essays, letters, dramatic works, and superior writing in all nonfiction varieties covering such areas as travel, food, history, current affairs, and all sorts of narrative nonfiction as well as reference works.

Literary fiction can adhere to the confines of any and all genres and categories, or suit no such designation. A work of fiction that is depicted as literary can (and should) offer the reader a multidimensional experience. Literary can designate word selection and imagery that is careful or inspired, or that affects an articulated slovenliness. A literary character may be one who is examined in depth, or is sparsely sketched to trenchant effect. Literature can postulate philosophical or cultural insights, and portray fresh ideas in action. Literary works can feature exquisitely detailed texture or complete lack of sensory ambiance.

Structurally, literary fiction favors story and plot elements that are individualistic or astonishingly new rather than tried-and-true. In some cases the plot as such does not appear important, but beware of quick judgment in this regard: Plotting may be subtle, as in picking at underlying psychology or revelation of character. And the plot movement may take place in the reader's head, as the progressive emotional or intellectual response to the story, rather than demonstrated in external events portrayed on paper.

To say that a work is literary can imply seriousness. Nonetheless many serious works are not particularly sober, and literary reading should be a dynamic experience—pleasurably challenging, insightful, riveting, fun. A work that is stodgy and boring may not be literary at all, for it has not achieved the all-important aim of being fine reading.

Obviously, a book that is lacking with respect to engaging characters, consciousness of pace, and story development but features fancy wordplay and three-page sentences is hardly exemplary of literary mastery. Though such a work may serve as a guidepost of advanced writing techniques for a specialized professional audience, it is perhaps a more limited artifice than is a slice-and-dice, strip-and-whip piece that successfully depicts human passion and offers a well-honed story.

Commercial literature, like commercial fiction in general, is essentially a back-definition; commercial literature indicates works of outstanding quality written by authors who sell well, as opposed to just plain literature, which includes writers and works whose readership appeal has not yet expanded beyond a small core. Noncommercial literary works are staples of the academic press and specialized houses, as well as selected imprints of major trade publishers.

When a literary author attracts a large readership, or manages to switch from the list of a tiny publisher to a mammoth house, the publisher might decide a particular project is ripe for a shot at the big-time and slate the writer for substantial attention, accompanied by a grand advance. If you look closely, you'll note that literary authors who enter the commercial ranks are usually not just good writers: Commercial literary works tap into the cultural pulse, which surges through the editorial avenues into marketing, promotion, and sales support.

In day-to-day commercial publishing discourse, to call a piece of work literary simply means it is well written. As a category designation, literary fiction implies that a particular book does not truly abide by provisos of other market sectors—though if the work under discussion does flash some category hooks, it might be referred to in such catch-terms as a literary thriller or literary suspense.

Mainstream Fiction

A mainstream work is one that can be expected to be at least reasonably popular to a fairly wide readership. In a whim of industry parlance, to various people in publishing the label mainstream signifies a work that is not particularly noteworthy on any count— it's a work of fiction that's not literary according to circumscribed tastes; and not something easily categorized with a targeted, predictable base of readership. Maybe not particularly profitable, either, especially if the publishing house is bent on creating bestsellers. A mainstream work may therefore be seen as a risky proposition rather than a relatively safe bet.

Let this be a cautionary note: In some publishing minds, a plain-and-simple mainstream book signifies midlist, which equals no sale. In a lot of publishing houses, midlist fiction, even if it's published, gets lost; many commercial trade houses won't publish titles they see as midlist (see **Midlist Fiction**).

A mainstream work may be a good read—but if that's all you can say about it, it's a mark against its prospects in the competitive arena. When a story is just a good story, the publisher doesn't have much of a sales slant to work with; in publishing terms that makes for a dismal enough prognosis for an editor or agent to pass.

If a manuscript has to sell on storytelling merits or general interest alone, it most likely won't sell to a major publisher at all. If mainstream fiction is what you've got, the writer is advised to return to the workshop and turn the opus into a polished piece with a stunning attitude that can be regarded as commercial, or redesign the story line into a category format such as mystery, suspense, or thriller. A mainstream mystery or mainstream thriller may contain characters who aren't too wacko and milieus that aren't overly esoteric. Such works are eminently marketable, but you might suppress the mainstream designation in your query and just call your work by its category or genre moniker.

If you've got the gifts and perseverance to complete a solid story, and you find yourself about to say it's a mainstream book and no more, you'll be further along faster if you work to avoid the midlist designation. Think commercially and write intrepidly.

Please note: Many editors and agents use the term *mainstream fiction* more or less synonymously with (see **Commercial Fiction**).

MIDLIST FICTION

Midlist books are essentially those that do not turn a more-than-marginal profit. That they show a profit at all might testify to how low the author's advance was (usually set so the publisher can show a profit based on projected sales). Midlist books may be category titles, literary works, or mainstream books that someone, somewhere believed had commercial potential (yet to be achieved).

The midlist is where no one wants to be: You get little if any promotion, few reviews, and no respect. Why publish this kind of book at all? Few publishers do. A midlist book was most likely not intended as such; the status is unacceptable unless the writer is being prepped for something bigger, and is expected to break through *soon*. When a writer or series stays midlist too long, they're gone—the publishers move on to more profitable use of their resources.

If the publishers don't want you, and the readers can't find you, you're better off going somewhere else too. (See **Commercial Fiction** or any of the other category designations.)

MYSTERY

Many people use the term *mystery* to refer to the detective story (see **Detective Fiction**). When folks speak of traditional mysteries, they often mean a story in the British cozy mold, which can be characterized—but not strictly defined—by an amateur sleuth (often female) as protagonist, a solve-the-puzzle story line, minimal body count (with all violence performed offstage), and a restrained approach to language and tone. Sometimes, however, a reference to traditional mysteries implies not only cozies but also includes stories of the American hard-boiled school, which are typified by a private eye (or a rogue cop), up-front violence as well as sex, and vernacular diction.

On the other hand, mysteries are seen by some to include all suspense fiction categories, thereby encompassing police procedurals, crime capers, thrillers, even going so far afield as horror and some fantasy fiction.

In the interests of clarity, if not precision, here we'll say simply that a mystery is a story in which something of utmost importance to the tale is unknown or covert at the outset and must be uncovered, solved, or revealed along the way. (See **Crime Fiction, Detective Fiction, Fantasy Fiction, Horror, Suspense Fiction**, and **Thriller**.)

ROMANCE FICTION

The power of love has always been a central theme in literature, as it has in all arts, in all life. For all its importance to the love story genre, the term *romance* does not pertain strictly to the love element. The field can trace its roots through European medieval romances that depicted knights-errant and women in distress, which were as much tales of spiritual quest, politics, and action as love stories. The Romantic movement of the nineteenth century was at its heart emblematic of the heightened energy lent to all elements of a story, from human passion, to setting, to material objects, to psychological ramifications of simple acts.

Thanks to the writers and readers of modern romances, they've come a long way from the days of unadulterated heart-stopping bodice-rippers with pampered, egocentric heroines who long for salvation through a man. Today's romance most often depicts an independent, full-blooded female figure in full partnership with her intended mate.

Modern romance fiction is most assuredly in essence a love story, fueled by the dynamics of human relationships. From this core, writers explore motifs of career and family, topical social concerns, detective work, psychological suspense, espionage, and horror, as well as historical period pieces (including European medieval, Regency, and romances set in the American West) and futuristic tales. Romance scenarios with same-sex lovers are highlighted throughout the ranks of vanguard and literary houses, though this theme is not a priority market at most trade publishers or romance-specialist presses.

Among commercial lead titles tapped for bestseller potential are those books that accentuate the appeal of romance within the larger tapestry of a fully orchestrated work. (See also **Women's Fiction**.)

SCIENCE FICTION

Take humankind's age-old longings for knowledge and enlightenment and add a huge helping of emergent technology, with the twist that science represents a metaphysical quest—there you have the setup for science fiction. Though the basic science fiction plot may resemble that of action-adventure tales, thrillers, or horror stories, the attraction for the reader is likely to be the intellectual or philosophical questions posed, in tandem with the space-age glitter within which it's set. In terms of character interaction, the story line should be strong enough to stand alone when stripped of its technological trimmings.

In the *future fiction* genre, the elements of science fiction are all in place, but the science tends to be soft-pedaled, and the story as a whole is character-based. In a further variation, the post-apocalyptic vision presents the aftermath of a cataclysm (either engendered by technology or natural in origin) that sets the survivors loose on a new course that demonstrates the often-disturbing vicissitudes of social and scientific evolution. Such scenarios are generally set in the not-too-distant future, are usually earth-based, or barely interstellar, with recognizable (but perhaps advanced) technology as the norm.

Purity of genre is at times fruitless to maintain or define. Is Mary Shelley's *Franken-stein* a science fiction tale or a horror story, or is it primarily a literary work? Is Jules Verne's *20,000 Leagues Under the Sea* science fiction or a technothriller—or a futuristic action-adventure?

Stories of extraterrestrial exploration, intergalactic warfare, and other exobiological encounters are almost certain to be placed within the science fiction category, until the day
when such endeavors are considered elements of realism.

SUSPENSE FICTION

Suspense fiction embraces many literary idioms, with a wide range of genres and subdivisions categorized under the general rubric of suspense. Indeed, in broad terms, all
novels contain suspense—that is, if the writer means for the reader to keep reading and
reading, and reading on . . . way into the evening and beyond.

Suspense fiction has no precise formula that specifies certain character types tied to a
particular plot template. It is perhaps most applicable for a writer to think of suspense as a
story concept that stems from a basic premise of situational uncertainty. That is: Something horrible is going to happen! Let's read! Within suspense there is considerable latitude regarding conventions of style, voice, and structure. From new suspense writers,
editors look for originality and invention and new literary terrain, rather than a copycat
version of last season's breakout work.

However, that said, writers should note that editors and readers are looking for works in
which virtually every word, every scene, every blip of dialog serves to heighten suspense.
This means that all imagery—from the weather to social setting, to the food ingested by
the characters—is chosen by the writer to induce a sense of unease. Each scene (save
maybe the last one) is constructed to raise questions or leave something unresolved.
Every sentence or paragraph contains a possible pitfall. A given conversational exchange
demonstrates edgy elementals of interpersonal tension. Everything looks rosy in one
scene? Gotcha! It's a setup to reveal later what hell lurks underneath. Tell me some good
news? Characters often do just that, as a prelude to showing just how wrong things can
get.

The *jeopardy* story (or, as is often the case, a *woman-in-jeopardy* story) reflects a
premise rather than being a genre per se. A tale of jeopardy—a character under continu-
ous, increasing threat and (often) eventual entrapment—can incorporate what is otherwise a psychological suspense novel, a medical thriller, an investigatory trajectory, or a
slasher-stalker spree.

Additional subdivisions here include *romantic suspense* (in which a love relationship
plays an essential or dominant role—see **Romance Fiction**); *erotic suspense* (which is not
necessarily identical to neurotic suspense); and *psychological suspense* (see immediately
below).

SUSPENSE, PSYCHOLOGICAL

When drifts of character, family history, or other psychodynamics are central to a suspense story's progress and resolution, the tale may aptly be typified as psychological.
Sometimes superficial shticks or gimmicks suffice (such as when a person of a certain
gender turns out to be cross-dressed—surprise!), but such spins work best when the suspense is tied to crucial issues the writer evokes in the characters' and readers' heads and
then orchestrates skillfully throughout the story line.

There are, obviously, crossover elements at play here, and whether a particular work is presented as suspense, psychological suspense, or erotic suspense can be more of an advertising-copywriting decision than a determination on the part of editor or author.

THRILLER

The thriller category is exemplified more by plot structure than by attributes of character, content, or story milieu. A thriller embodies what is essentially an extended game of pursuit—a hunt, a chase, a flight worked fugue-like through endless variations.

At one point in the history of narrative art, thrillers were almost invariably spy stories, with international casts and locales, often set in a theater of war (hot or cold). With shifts in political agendas and technical achievement in the real world, the thriller formula has likewise evolved. Today's thriller may well involve espionage, which can be industrial or political, domestic or international. There are also thrillers that favor settings in the realms of medicine, the law, the natural environs, the human soul, and the laboratory; this trend has given rise to the respective genres of legal thriller, medical thriller, environmental thriller, thrillers with spiritual and mystical themes, and the technothriller—assuredly there are more to come.

The thriller story line can encompass elements of detection or romance, and certainly should be full of suspense; but these genre-specific sequences are customarily exposi-tional devices, or may be one of many ambient factors employed to accentuate tension within the central thriller plot. When you see a dust jacket blurb that depicts a book as a mystery thriller, it likely connotes a work with a thriller plot trajectory that uses an inves-tigatory or detective-work premise to prepare for the chase.

WESTERN FICTION

The tradition of Western fiction is characterized as much by its vision of the individualist ethic as it is by its conventional settings in the frontier milieu of the American West during the period from the 1860s to the 1890s, sometimes extending into the early 1900s. Though the image of the lone, free-spirited cowpoke with an internalized code of justice has been passed down along the pulp-paper trail, it has long been appreciated by his-torians that the life of the average itinerant ranch-hand of the day was anything but glamorous, anything but independent.

Whatever the historical record, editors by and large believe readers don't want to hear about the lackluster aspects of saddle tramps and dust-busting ruffians. Nevertheless, there have been inroads by books that display the historically accurate notions that a good chunk of the Western scene was inhabited by women and men of African American heritage, by those with Latino cultural affinities, by Asian expatriates, and European immigrants for whom English was a second language, as well as a diversity of native peoples.

Apart from the traditional genre Western, authors are equipped for a resurgence in a variety of novels with Western settings, most notably in the fields of mystery, crime, ac-tion-adventure, suspense, and future fiction. Among the newer Western novels are those replete with offbeat, unheroic, and downright antiheroic protagonists; and the standardized big-sky landscape has been superseded by backdrops that go against the grain.

Family sagas have long included at least a generation or two who drift, fight, and homestead through the Western Frontier. In addition, a popular genre of historical romance is set in the American West (see **Romance Fiction**).

Many contemporary commercial novels are set in the Western U.S., often featuring plush resorts, urban and suburban terrain, as well as the remaining wide country. The wide variety of project ideas generated by writers, as well as the reader response to several successful ongoing mystery series with Western elements, indicates a lively interest out there.

WOMEN'S FICTION

When book publishers speak of women's fiction, they're not referring to a particular genre or story concept (even if they think they are). This category—if it is one—is basically a nod to the prevalence of fiction readers who are women. Women's fiction is a marketing concept. As an informal designation, women's fiction as a matter of course can be expected to feature strong female characters and, frequently, stories offered from a woman's perspective.

As for the writers of books in this category—many (if not most) are women, but certainly not all of them are; the same observation applies to readers. Men can and do read these works too—and many professional male writers calculate potential readership demographics (including gender) as they work out details of story and plot.

In essence, what we've got is storytelling that can appeal to a broad range of readers but may be promoted principally to the women's market. It makes it easier to focus the promotion and to pass along tips to the publisher's sales representatives.

Many women writers consider their work in abstract compositional terms, regardless of to whom it is marketed. Other women writers may be publicized as cultural pundits, perhaps as feminists, though they don't necessarily see their message as solely women-oriented. Are they women writers or simply writers? So long as sales go well, they may not even care.

Some women writers adopt the genderless pose of the literary renegade as they claw their way through dangerous domains of unseemly characterization, engage in breakthrough storytelling techniques, and explore emergent modes of love. (After all, how can a force of nature be characterized by sex?) Any and all of these female wordsmiths may find themselves publicized as women authors.

Romantic fiction constitutes one large sector of the women's market, for many of the conventions of romance tap into culturally significant areas of the love relationship of proven interest to women bookbuyers.

Descriptive genre phrases pop in and out of usage; some of them trip glibly from the tongue and are gone forevermore, while others represent established literary norms that endure: kitchen fiction, mom novels, family sagas, domestic dramas, historical romances, chick lit, lipstick fiction, erotic thrillers. When these popular titles are written and/or promoted in ways intended to pique the interest of women readers, whatever else they may be, they're automatically women's fiction.

Mirror, Mirror . . .

Self-Publishing and Vanity Publishing—Advantages and Differences

JEFF HERMAN

Achieving publication through the sale of an author's work to a major commercial trade publisher may not always be feasible, possible, or even the most desirable route into the literary marketplace for a given project. Some books may be excellent candidates for the list of a smaller press with artfully targeted audiences (such as business, religious, or literary house), while others fall naturally into the publishing sphere of the university press, or the array of independent scientific, professional, and scholarly publishers that cater to specialist interests.

Literary success is all about reaching the audience that best appreciates the work at hand; commercial success by definition is keyed to finding and selling to that primary readership economically, and expanding the readership base as cost-efficiently as possible.

Certain publishing options have special appeal to entrepreneurial authors—and others who, at least in theory, wish to control the outcome of their book to the greatest possible degree. Some authors wish to have final say over the creative and editorial content of the product; they prefer to oversee the means of production, manufacture, and distribution; and they plan to step lively as they orchestrate their own publicity and promotional endeavors. Assuming these various tasks, responsibilities, and risks should result in programs wherein the author–publisher stands to gain the greatest rate of financial return possible.

Such ventures, when appropriate, can be accomplished on the cheap; other projects may well justify the investment of money and labor of the same order that a publisher might put into a comparable project. Alternate publishing options are also available for those who wish to subsidize publication through firms that produce books and offer attendant publishing services more or less on order.

Self-publishing (often with the assistance of independent contractors and consultants) and publishing through the offices of a vanity press may sound similar in concept, but important distinctions must be recognized—these pertain as much to business practices of individual companies as they do to traditions associated with the author-as-self-publisher and the subsidy publisher.

VANITY PUBLISHING

Vanity publishing is more formally referred to as subsidy publishing (primarily in the promotional literature of its practitioners). In this context the term *subsidy* does not, of course, mean that the publication of a book is subsidized by a governmental or corporate agency, or funded by an arts or humanities council. Though this form of publishing does have many variations, in the strictest usage it is the author who subsidizes publication by paying the press to publish his or her book.

Vanity publishing is a controversial industry. Sometimes it's a perfectly legitimate means of seeing one's writings in print, and the author is fully satisfied with the results. However, there are many instances in which the author has misunderstood the process and is terribly disappointed—and in the hole for a lot of money.

Few conventional commercial publishers will engage in anything that smacks of vanity publishing. (*Note*: An author who promises to buy back many copies of a published book, and to spend a lot of his or her own money on marketing, can often induce even the most prestigious publishing house to publish a book that it would not otherwise have published.)

There are a number of companies, some quite large and well established, that function solely as vanity presses. Many of these publishers promote their services by means of a variety of outlets, including brochures sent through the mail to lists-of-the-likely, and classified as well as display advertisements in selected publications. *Writer's Digest* magazine is one of the more logical and frequently used advertising channels; and the classified section of the *New York Times Book Review* has over the years logged quite a roster of listings for vanity houses and allied services.

Know Exactly What Services Will Be Provided

In vanity or subsidy publishing, the way the arrangement often works is that the writer pays a flat fee to have a set number of books produced. Some subsidy publishers provide worthy editorial, production, design, marketing, and distribution assistance. Some make exaggerated claims regarding the value and caliber of these services—whereas others make no such claims at all, maintaining that these functions are the author's responsibility.

Over the years some practitioners of the vanity trade have discovered that they snag more customers when they can glibly deflect any discussion of the possible pitfalls of the process—even in response to a potential customer's direct questions. In addition, with increased volume and increasingly cheaper production costs (and standards), the profit margin is all that much higher. For the foregoing reasons, an uninformed and less-than-curious consumer is the vanity house's most valued customer.

In all cases, the more the writer knows about the publishing process in general—and is aware of the limited or nonexistent clout a vanity press has regarding book distribution—the better situated the author is to determine any advantages one particular subsidy publisher's program may have over another's, as well as how subsidy publishing stacks up against other available options, such as self-publishing.

Among several worst-case vanity press scenarios is one wherein the publisher simply prints the books and delivers them casually to the writer's doorstep—yours to do with as you please, thank you; we're out of it now—no marketing or distribution services provided. The writer could probably have engaged a printing house to do virtually the same thing for a fraction of the cost.

In another popular variation of the vanity-publishing approach, the contractual fee is set at a price that provides the publisher with a healthy profit even without the sale of so much as one copy of the published title—even though numerous (but decidedly perfunctory and ineffectual) promotion and marketing services are specified in the contract.

In this case, the publisher may have little motivation to promote or market a given published work. However, according to the terms of the agreement, the publisher will derive further income from any sales, even if the sales are really due to the successful independent marketing efforts of the paying writer.

Well within the bounds of everyday hard-nosed business practices perhaps, and a secure way to turn a profit if done right. So long as the vanity house's contractual obligations are met in full, the question here is rather the nature of the publisher's come-on. Visions of potential glamour and literary recognition that subsidy house brochures proclaim may not be dark and devious schemes to lure the naive (doesn't all advertising trade in similar notions?); however, such forms of hype appear calculated to offer shadows and gray areas in which hitherto obscure fantasies of the potential customer may feel free to take full beguiling shape.

If the writer knows up front exactly what he or she can and can't expect from the vanity publisher, then everything is square. But if the company has encouraged or knowingly allowed the writer to have unrealistic expectations, then a crime has been committed—morally and ethically at least, if not legally. Vanity publishers that grossly mislead writers while taking their money are guilty of fraud. In 1990, one of the largest vanity presses in the country lost a million-dollar class-action suit, and hundreds of hoodwinked writers were granted refunds.

Even so, most suits against vanity presses are based on the assertion of fraud in the execution of contractual services, and any rewards to the author clients are small potatoes compared with the kind of money conceivably involved if the complainant can prove a claim of fraud in the inducement of an agreement—a complaint that, no matter how heartfelt, is most difficult to substantiate.

Beware of Sharks!

The following correspondence is genuine, though all names and titles have been altered. My purpose for exposing these ever-so-slightly personalized form letters isn't to condemn or ridicule anyone. I simply wish to show how some subsidy publishers hook their clients. Again, as long as the writer truly understands the facts, no one has the right to cast any stones at this particular publishing option.

SHARK HOUSE PUBLISHERS

Mr. Bourne Bate
Brooklyn Bridge
East River, NY 00000

Dear Mr. Bate:

Your manuscript *A Fish's Life* is written from an unusual perspective and an urgent one. In these trying economic times which have created despair and anguish, one must give thought to opportunities, and this upbeat and enthusiastic book makes us realize that those opportunities are out there! My capsule critique: Meticulous aim! With a surgeon's precision we're taught how to work through everything from raising money to targeting areas. There is a sharp eye here for all of the nuances, studded with pointers and reasoning, making it a crucial blueprint.

What can I say about a book like this? It stopped me in my tracks. I guess all I can do is thank you for letting me have the opportunity to read it.

The editors that read this had a spontaneous tendency to feel that it was imbued with some very, very good electricity and would be something very special for our list and saw such potential with it that it was given top priority and pushed ahead of every other book in house. The further problem is that publishing being an extremely rugged business, editorial decisions have to be based on hard facts which sometimes hurt publishers as much as authors. Unfortunately, we just bought several new nonfiction pieces . . . yet, I hate to let this one get away. Publishing economics shouldn't have anything to do with a decision, but unfortunately it does and I was overruled at the editorial meeting.

Still I want you to know that this is a particularly viable book and one that I really would love to have for our list. Further, this might be picked up for magazine serialization or by book clubs because it is so different. Our book *Enraptured* was serialized six times in *International Inquirer* and sold to Andorra. *The Devil Decided* sold well over 150,000 copies, and we have a movie option on it. *Far Away* serialized in *Places* magazine and *Cure Yourself* was taken by a major book club.

I really want this book for our list because it will fit into all the areas that we're active in. Therefore, I'm going to make a proposition for you to involve yourself with us. What would you think of the idea of doing this on a cooperative basis? Like many New York publishers these days, we find that sometimes investors are interested in the acquisition of literary properties through a technique which might be advantageous under our tax laws. There is no reason that the partial investor cannot be the writer, if they so choose. Tax advantages may accrue.

I'd be a liar if I promised you a best seller, but I can guarantee that nobody works as hard promoting a book as we do: nag paperback, book clubs, magazines, and foreign publishers with our zeal and enthusiasm. We do our PR work and take it seriously because this is where we're going to make the money in the long run. One of our authors hired a top publicist on his own for $50,000. He came limping back to us saying they didn't do the job that we did, and which we don't charge for. This made our office feel very proud of all our efforts.

I feel that your book deserves our efforts because it is something very special. Think about what I've written you, and I will hold the manuscript until I hear from you. I truly hope that we can get together because I really love this book and believe it is something we can generate some good action for vis-à-vis book clubs, foreign rights, etc., because it is outstanding and has tremendous potential.

Sincerely,

Eda U. Live

Eda U. Live
Executive Editor

The writer of *A Fish's Life* wrote back to Shark House (all names have been changed) and informed the vanity press that he did not want to pay any money to the publisher to have his book published. The vanity house responded with the following letter. This publisher has probably learned from experience that some exhausted writers will return to them with open wallets after fruitless pursuit of a conventional commercial publishing arrangement.

SHARK HOUSE PUBLISHERS

Mr. Bourne Bate
Brooklyn Bridge
East River, NY 00000

Dear Mr. Bate:

I have your letter in front of me and I want you to know that I think very highly of the book. Before I go any further, I want to tell you that it is a topnotch book and it hits the reader.

In order for us to do a proper job with a book, there is a great deal of PR work involved and this is very costly. To hire an outside agent to do a crackerjack job would cost you upwards of $50,000. Yet, here we do not charge for it because it is part of our promotion to propel a book into the marketplace and it is imperative that this be done. The author has to be booked on radio and TV, stores have to be notified, rights here and abroad have to be worked on, reviewers contacted, autograph parties, and myriad details.

In view of this, why did I ask you to help with the project? I think the above is self-explanatory especially when we are in the midst of a revolution between books and television. Publishers are gamblers vying for the same audience. Just because a publisher loves a book is no guarantee that the public is going to love it. In times when bookstores are more selective in the number of books they order, the best of us tremble at the thought of the money that we must put out in order to make a good book a reality.

Be that as it may, I have just come from another editorial meeting where I tried to re-open the case for us, but unfortunately, the earlier decision stands.

As a result, I have no choice but to return the manuscript with this letter. I would also like to tell you that you must do what the successful writers do. Keep sending it out. Someone will like it and someone will buy it.

I wish you every success. Live long and prosper.

Sincerely,

Eda U. Live

Eda U. Live
Executive Editor

SELF-PUBLISHING

Vanity publishing shouldn't be confused with self-publishing. If you can't find a commercial house to publish your book (or don't want them to), you can publish it yourself. In fact, many successful titles that eventually found their ways onto mainstream publishers' trade lists were initially self-published. As already mentioned, the basic production costs of doing it yourself should be much less than paying a vanity house essentially to "self-publish" it for you.

The key to the productiveness of this choice is the answer to the question: What will you do with the books after you've printed them?

It's exceptionally difficult (but not impossible) for a sole proprietor to achieve meaningful bookstore distribution—though you should at least check out the option of commissioning one of the regional or small press distribution services who send catalogs and offer representation on regional or nationwide basis.

On the other hand, if you're a born promoter who can achieve ample media visibility, or if you have an active seminar business, you can sell numerous copies of your book via back-of-the-room sales and 800 numbers.

Your per-unit profits will be many times greater than your per-unit royalties would have been if you'd used a commercial publisher. Once your up-front production costs have been met, your reprint costs can be very low (depending on quantity ordered); and the profit margin can be relatively astronomic if manufacturing volume can be matched closely to projected sales figures. As publishing houses well know, marketing and promotional efforts can entail the outlay of significant amounts of money, so discretion and prudence should be watchwords here.

If the author knows the intended audience well and has written a work geared to that familiar readership, that author may prove far more adept at reaching that readership than a given publishing house's expert but thinly spread staff would have been.

One more cautionary note about vanity houses is pertinent here: With publication under a vanity arrangement, even an ambitious author's promotional and marketing agenda may prove to be futile. Please realize that the names of the largest and most successful vanity presses are well known to booksellers and book reviewers. The jacket design and overall slack production quality of the typical vanity house's package is likely to draw snickers and sneers from industry professionals and may be more than subliminally noticeable even to casual browsers. If a bookstore were to stock such a shoddy item, it might reflect poorly on the quality of an outlet's other stock.

In a reverse-case scenario of name recognition, when faced with a volume issued under an ignominious vanity imprimatur, most bookstores or critics will have nothing to do with the work in question. If on close inspection the work is indeed worthy, it's too bad—it's all over already; a bookstore buyer or book reviewer won't even take it that far.

You're much better off with a well-packaged product under a newly minted name of your own devise that, though it may be unrecognized, at least has no one soured on it yet.

Self-publishing can be not only a boon in itself; it can be an asset with potential windfall ramifications. Successful self-publishers have licensed trade distribution rights to their books to major publishers in deals that have turned tidy profits for one and all.

The Author–Agent Agreement

Jeff Herman

The author–agent relationship is a business relationship. Substantial sums and complex deals may be involved. It's to everyone's advantage to explicitly codify the rules and parameters of the relationship in a brief, plain-English agreement. It's true that the author–agent relationship can become unusually cozy. Still, there's no reason why even the best of friends can't have written business agreements without diminishing their mutual trust and affection. From at least one perspective, explicitly written agreements can be seen to go hand in hand with—and serve to underscore or amplify—existing bonds of confidence, faith, and friendship.

Some agents prefer oral understandings and handshakes, but most use a standard written agreement. It's unlikely that any two agencies will use the same agreement, but most agreements overlap each other closely in their intent and spirit.

There are several aspects of the author–agent arrangement covered by the typical agreement. Here are some of the major points of consideration, along with some key questions you might reflect on as you peruse the materials your prospective agent has submitted to you:

1. *Representation*

What precisely will the agency be representing? Will it be a per-project representation? Or will it include all future works as well? Will it automatically cover all non-book sales, such as magazine or newspaper articles? The extent of the representation should be spelled out so that there are no memory lapses or misunderstandings down the line.

2. *Agency Commission*

The agency will receive a commission for all sales it makes against the work's advance, and on any subsequent income derived from royalties and the licensing of various rights. According to a recent study by the Authors' Guild, most agencies charge new clients 15% for domestic sales. Many agencies charge 20%–30% for foreign sales, since the commission often has to be split with local subagents (the agent in the foreign country who actually expedites the sale).

3. *Duration and Potential Termination of the Agreement*

When does the agreement end? How can the author or agency act to terminate the agreement? What happens after it's terminated?

Are agency agreements negotiable? Probably. It's a case-by-case situation. Don't be afraid to question, or attempt to reword, some aspects of the agreement. It will be better if such discussions are held in a friendly manner, directly between you and the agent. As a cautionary note: it is a common observation that the involvement of third parties— especially lawyers—can backfire and ignite issues that are irrelevant to the traditional ground rules of the author–agent understanding. It's fine to consult a lawyer, but you should be the point person.

The following is the standard agreement that I use with my clients. It's provided for your reference. It's not the only way an agreement can be or should be.

SAMPLE LETTER OF AGREEMENT

This Letter of Agreement between THE JEFF HERMAN AGENCY, LLC, ("Agency") and _____ ("Author"), entered into on *(date)*, puts into effect the following terms and conditions:

REPRESENTATION

- The Agency is hereby exclusively authorized to seek a publisher for the Author's work, hereby referred to as the "Project," on a per-project basis. The terms and conditions of this Agreement will pertain to all Projects the Author explicitly authorizes the Agency to represent, through oral and written expression, and that the Agency agrees to represent. Separate Agreements will not be necessary for each single project, unless the terms and conditions differ from this Agreement.

COMMISSION

- If the Agency sells the Project to a publisher, the Agency will be the Agent-of-Record for the Project's income-producing duration and will irrevocably keep 15% of all the Author's income relevant to sold Project. The due Agency commission will also pertain to all of the Project's subsidiary rights sales, whether sold by the Agent, Author, or Publisher. In the event the agency uses a subagent to sell foreign or film rights, and the subagent is due a commission, the Agency commission for such will be 10%, and the subagent's commission will not be more than 10%. All Project income will be paid by the publisher to the Agency. The Agency will pay the Author all due monies within a reasonable time, upon receipt and bank clearance, with full accounting provided. The Agency will not be required to return any legitimately received commissions should the Author–Publisher contract be terminated or if the Author's work is unacceptable to the Publisher. There will be an Agency Clause in the Author–Publisher contract stating the Agency's status, the wording of which shall be subject to Author approval. These terms will be binding on the Author's estate in the event of his/her demise.

EXPENSES

- The Agency will be entitled to receive reimbursement from the Author for the following specific expenses relevant to its representation of the Project: Manuscript/proposal copying costs; long-distance telephone calls and faxes between Author and Agency; necessary overnight deliveries and local messenger costs; postage and handling for manuscripts, foreign shipping and communications costs. An itemized accounting and records of all such items will be maintained by the Agency and will be shown to the Author. No significant expenses (in excess of $25.00) will be incurred without the Author's prior knowledge and consent. The Agency will have the option to either bill the Author for these expenses, regardless of whether or not the Project in question is sold to a publisher, or to charge such expenses against the Author's account.

PROJECT STATUS

- The Agency agrees to forward to the Author copies of all correspondence received from publishers in reference to the Author's Project(s).

REVISIONS

- This Agreement can be amended or expanded by attaching Rider(s) to it, if all parties to this agreement concur with the terms and conditions of the Rider(s) and sign them.

TERMINATION

- This Agreement can be terminated in writing by any party to it by writing to the other parties, at any time following its execution. However, the Agency shall remain entitled to due commissions which may result from Agency efforts implemented prior to the termination of this Agreement, and will remain entitled to all other due monies as stated in this Agreement. Termination of the Agency representation of one or more Author Projects will not imply termination of this Agreement, unless such is specifically requested in writing.

Signatures below by the parties named in this Agreement will indicate that all parties concur with the terms and conditions of this Agreement.

_____	_____
THE JEFF HERMAN AGENCY, INC.	AUTHOR
	Social Security No.:
	Date of birth:

Specific project(s) being represented at this time:

Q & A

Q: If you, Mr. Herman, were the writer, what are some of the key points that would most concern you about an agent's agreement?

A: If I were a writer, I would prefer to see the following incorporated into my agreement with the literary agency:

1. I would want the representation to be on a per-project basis. I would not want to be automatically obligated to be represented by the agent on my next project.
2. I would want a liberal termination procedure. If at any point after signing the agreement I change my mind, I want the ability to immediately end the relationship.

Of course, I realize that the agent will be entitled to his commission relevant to any deals I accept that result from his efforts on the project's behalf—even if the deal is consummated after my termination of the agent.

The Collaboration Agreement

JEFF HERMAN

Any book that is written by two or more writers is a collaborative effort. Such collaborative endeavors are predominately nonfiction works, though collaborative fiction is by no means unheard of (typically a novel featuring a celebrity author that is for the most part written by someone else, or two bestselling novelists looking to synergize their reader base). There are several reasons why a writer might choose to collaborate with another, as opposed to writing the book alone.

The most common reasons are:

- A person may have the essential expertise, professional status, and promotability to author a book, but may lack time, ability, and/or interest to do the actual writing. Therefore, retaining someone to do the writing is a sensible—even preferable— alternative.
- Some nonfiction projects, especially academic or professionally oriented ones, cover a broad range of material, and few individuals may have the requisite depth to write the book unilaterally. Therefore, two or more writers with complementary specializations may team up. For exceptionally technical books, such as medical texts, there can be several collaborators.

Many writers earn handsome incomes writing other people's books. When they are collaborative writers, their names are flashed along with the primary author of the project (and given second billing, usually preceded by "and," "with," or "as told to"). If they are true ghostwriters, they may well have the same level of input and involvement as collaborators, but will generally receive no public recognition for their work (other than perhaps a subtle pat on the back in the acknowledgments section).

WHAT ARE COLLABORATION AGREEMENTS?

As with any business relationship, it's wise for the collaborators to enter into a concise agreement (written in plain English) that spells out all the terms and conditions of the relationship—especially each party's respective responsibilities and financial benefits.

A collaboration agreement can run from 1 to more than 20 pages, depending on how much money is at issue and the complexity of the other variables. Most of the time we in the industry can keep these agreements down to an easy-to-read 2 pages. It's probably not necessary to go to the expense of retaining a lawyer for this task. If you have an agent, he can probably draw up an agreement for you, or at least show you several samples.

The following is a sample collaboration agreement that is similar to ones used by many of my clients.

(*Disclaimer*: This sample collaboration agreement is intended only as a reference guide.)

SAMPLE COLLABORATION AGREEMENT

This collaboration agreement (Agreement), entered into on [*date*], by and between John Doe (John) and Jane Deer (Jane), will put into effect the following terms and conditions, upon signing by both parties.

(1) Jane will collaborate with John in the writing of a book about [*subject or brief description goes here*].

(2) In consultation with John, Jane will prepare a nonfiction book proposal and sample chapter for the purpose of selling the book to a publisher.

(3) Jane and John will be jointly represented by [*name of literary agent/agency*].

(4) John will be the book's spokesperson. John's name will appear first on the cover and in all publicity, and his name will be more prominently displayed than Jane's.

(5) Following the sale of the project proposal to a publisher, if, for any reason, Jane does not wish to continue as a collaborator, she shall be entitled to [*monetary amount goes here*] against the book's first proceeds in consideration of her having written the successful proposal, and she will forfeit any future claims against the book and any connection thereto.

(6) Jane's and John's respective estates will be subject to the terms and conditions of this Agreement, in the event of either's demise.

(7) John agrees to indemnify and hold Jane harmless from any liability, claim, or legal action taken against her as a result of her participation in the book proposal or book. Such exoneration includes but is not limited to costs of defending claims including reasonable counsel fees. John agrees that any funds derived from sale of the proposal or book may be utilized to pay such claims.

(8) This Agreement can be amended or expanded by attaching riders to it, if such riders are signed by Jane and John.

(9) No other claims or representations are made by either party; both agree that this Agreement fully integrates their understanding. No other representations, promises, or agreements are made except as may be in writing and signed by the party to be held responsible.

(10) Jane shall receive the first [*monetary amount goes here*] of the book's proceeds when sold to a publisher. John shall receive the next [*monetary amount goes here*]. All income thereafter shall be evenly received (50/50). All subsidiary rights income shall be split 50/50.

(11) John will own the book's copyright.

(12) John will be responsible for paying expenses relevant to the preparation of the proposal (photocopying; telephone; deliveries; travel, etc.). Upon the book's sale to a publisher and the receipt of the first part of the advance, John will be reimbursed for 50% of these expenses by Jane. John and Jane will equally split (50/50) costs relevant to writing the book following its sale to a publisher.

Jane Deer   John Doe

_____   _____

Q & A

Q: What about agent representation if it's a collaborative effort?
A: There are two possibilities:

1. *The same agent will represent both parties.* However, this requires the agent to be equal in her dealings with both parties. For instance, the agent should avoid tilting toward John while he's negotiating the collaboration agreement with Jane. What I do is provide both parties with accurate advice, and then step aside as they—hopefully—work things out between themselves and then come back to me with all issues resolved.

   More important: the agent should not "double-dip." In other words, my commission will only pertain to the work's income. I will not touch any money that one collaborator may pay to the other, even if such payments exceed the work's advance.

2. Some collaborations can be coagented. Each collaborator may already have a different agent. Or it may be felt that there will be a conflict of interest for the same agent to represent both parties.

   When this happens, both agents will negotiate the collaboration agreement with each other in behalf of their respective clients. All parties will then work out a strategy to determine which agent is to be out front selling and negotiating the deal. Each agent will receive a commission only against her client's respective share.

As with any other business relationship, collaboration agreements generally have the best chance to produce a productive and successful outcome when they reasonably and realistically reflect the rights, responsibilities, special talents, and good interests of all involved parties.

Making It Happen

Deborah Levine Herman

Nothing is better than having your first book published. You may want to believe that spouses, friends, children, and world peace are more important, but when you see your name and your words in print it is nothing short of ego ecstasy.

Your publisher gives you a release date and you wait expectantly for the fanfare, but unless you're well known already (and remember, this is your first book), chances are your publisher will devote only modest publicity to your book.

It will be exciting if you are asked to do radio or television interviews, but do not expect Oprah fresh out of the gate. There are exceptions, of course, but it's important for you to know that most books don't receive extensive publisher support. It may not seem logical that a publisher would take you all the way to the mountain and not help you climb your way to the top, but it is the reality of the business. The reality is that the destiny of your book remains largely in your hands. With the right combination of drive, know-how, and chutzpah, you can make it happen for yourself.

IDEAS FOR MAKING IT HAPPEN

Here are some ideas for making it happen.

You can always hire a publicist. If you have the means, there are many publicists who can help you promote your book and who will do a lot of the work for you. You will have many great bragging opportunities when you work it into conversations that your *publicist* is setting your book tour.

Publicists are expensive and don't always deliver. You may want to check out our book *Make It Big Writing Books* to become publicist-savvy. This book contains interviews with top publicists, as well as some great promotion ideas. You can also read about how some bestselling authors made it to the top.

If you don't take the publicist route, you can do many things for yourself. Work with your publisher's publicity department. Its staff members may not invest their time and resources, but they should support your efforts.

As soon as you know the approximate date your book will be released to the bookstores, start your campaign. Ask your publicity department for review copies of your book and create a target list of possible magazines, newsletters, Web sites, and newspapers that might want to review your book. Don't sit on this. Magazines work months in advance. If your book is coming out in April, you should be contacting magazines as early as you possibly can; six months in advance isn't too soon. March is way too late. If you can't get review copies, you should still find ways to query the magazines. You may be able to get copies of your book covers and provide sample chapters.

It will be helpful for you to create an attractive publicity packet. You will need a biography of yourself, a good photograph, a copy of the book cover or the material your publisher uses to sell your book to the bookstores, a news release about your book, and any other relevant information. Do not forget to put in contact information. Book endorsements are also great, if you have them.

This packet can be used for magazines and any other print media, as well as for television and radio. If you want to spare some expense, create a one-page information sheet that you can fax to prospects whom you also contact by phone. Lists of radio stations are available in the reference department of your public library. Radio interviews can be done by phone. The key is to create a hook that will entice a radio producer to use you on his or her show. Think in terms of a short explanatory sentence that captures the essence of your book in as few words as possible.

For book signings, contact the promotions person at the bookstores you target. If you plan to visit various cities on a self-designed book tour, contact bookstores and local media well in advance so they can publicize the event. Maximize your visit to each city with a coordinated plan that will help promote your signing.

If your book is fiction, you can arrange for events in which you read portions of your book for an audience. Venues are available beyond the bookstores, but you will need to be creative in determining what they are.

If your book is nonfiction, create a topic stemming from your book that can be the subject of a workshop or lecture. Many venues are available that could help you publicize the event. Don't worry if you don't make money through lectures. If you are part of a seminar company, the exposure it will give your book in the promotional materials alone will be valuable.

Be creative. Don't let your ego trick you into believing you are above the hard work it takes to make a book successful. Roll up your sleeves. If you are passionate about your book, you are the one who can best "make it happen."

The Path to Publication in the New Millennium

MORRIS ROSENTHAL

Imagine sending a query letter offering an unfinished manuscript to eight publishers and receiving four positive responses within the week. Or, out of the blue, the managing editor of a major imprint contacting you to ask whether you need a publisher for your work? These scenarios may sound like an advertisement in a writer's magazine intended to separate you from your money, but they actually happened to me, thanks to the Internet.

WHY PUBLISH ON THE INTERNET?

The vast majority of writers today have exchanged their typewriters for personal computers, but their sole focus remains sending that double-spaced manuscript off to New York City with an SASE. That's a shame, because by simply skipping down an extra item in the File menu of your word processor, you can save that document as HTML, a form ready for instant publication on the Internet. "Why should I give my work away for free?" you argue. "What if someone steals it?"

Your primary challenge, as an unpublished writer, is getting people to read your work and respond to it. After all, you need to convince editors and agents that you really know your market, but how can you do that if your market has never heard of you? Whether you write plumbing books or poetry, an audience for your work exists on the Internet, and if you can fix people's leaky pipes or hearts, they will show their appreciation. The main pay-offs of Web publishing for the unknown writer are reader feedback and traffic (visitors to your site).

Testimonial e-mails from visitors to your site can carry real weight with an acquisitions editor. In fact, McGraw-Hill used excerpts from nine such letters as a marketing tool on the back cover of my first published book, *The Hand-Me-Down PC*. Feedback from Web surfers is valuable for another reason; this audience isn't tied to you by friendship or blood. Even criticism is useful because these people *are* your market, and compliments from Mom are rarely as uplifting as those from a complete stranger. Traffic on your site can be used to prove that you do have an audience and, even more important for smaller publishers, that you know how to promote yourself. By the way, a copyright is a copyright, so if someone does plagiarize your work, take it as a compliment and threaten to sue.

WHAT TO PUT ON YOUR SITE

Building a Web site is something that anyone can do. Before you rush out and buy the latest book on the subject, try setting up a free Web site using one of the online providers, like Geocities, which will lead you through the process step by step. This doesn't have to be your permanent site. In fact, there are many good reasons to host your site on a commercial server for anywhere from $10 to $50 per month, but the main point is to get started. Unlike paper publishing, Web publishing is flexible by its very nature. If you make a spelling mistake, want to change something you said, add a picture, or even close down the site, you can do it instantly any time of the day or night!

The critical components (2 Cs) for any Web site are content and contact—content is the work you want people to see and contact is the means through which they can react to it, normally e-mail. As I said, it only takes one click of the mouse to save your manuscript in Web format, but you might want to produce material specifically targeted for the Web. Many people who surf the Web are looking for answers, so if you write nonfiction, you could offer to answer readers' e-mailed questions about your subject of expertise. This can take some time, but you will definitely learn what your audience is interested in rather than what you think they are interested in. This "hands-on" experience really carries weight with editors.

For example, back in 1995 I signed up for a $14.95/month Internet account with a national service that was later acquired by AOL. Learning that it came with space for a Web site, I posted a short guide titled "Troubleshooting and Repairing Clone PCs," which I had previously written for some co-op students I had trained. My primary motivation in posting the computer material was to attract people to read the short fiction and poetry I had also posted on the site. People who didn't find an answer to their problems but who thought I might be able to help them began sending me questions. Recognizing that this was "content," I began adding a new question and answer to the Web site each night. This section of the site, titled "The Midnight Question," became the most popular draw during the years that I maintained it and had a large number of repeat visitors. That original short guide and the material from the "Midnight Question" became the core of my first published book.

Many journalists now depend on the Internet for material to fill out their articles, and the questions and answers I posted on my site brought me two generous helpings of free publicity. The first was a front-page story in *The Investor's Business Daily,* which described me as a "Digital Age Dear Abby" and the second was an interview and a link on the *Dateline MSNBC* site, which sent 10,000 visitors to my site in a single day. These cases may be extreme, but I continue to receive regular exposure in both online and traditional publications due to material I have posted online.

When it comes to fiction and poetry, you have little choice other than to publish whole works on the Web. In some documented cases, individuals began by Web publishing a novel, responded to reader demand by self-publishing their own books, and eventually landed real publishing contracts, but this kind of success is rare. Publishing fiction and poetry on the Internet is less likely to bring an unknown author the kind of instant exposure that can result from a well-planned information site, but the feedback, when it comes, is all the more welcome for that reason. The modest successes I've experienced with fiction on the Web, like having a short story picked up for a printed zine or adopted onto a genre site, have worked wonders for my bruised fiction ego.

Once I got an e-mail from a guy with a corporate return address, asking if I could send him my online novel, which was then posted in twenty-six individual HTML documents, as a Word file. I wrote back asking why he wanted the novel in Word format when he could already get it in any Web browser. He replied, "Nothing sinister, I'm reading it at the office and if it's in Word, I can act like I'm working."

GETTING PEOPLE TO COME TO YOUR SITE

"Even if you build it, they won't come unless you tell them it's there!"
—Morris Rosenthal

From Fortune 500 ghost sites to Aunt Millie's home page with pictures of the cat, the Web is crowded with sites that nobody visits. As you have read in many sections of this book, publishing is a business, and in business you can't escape from marketing. The good news is that on the Web, the only type of marketing you need is free, as long as you provide the labor. This marketing of your site can be broken into three basic areas: search engines and directories, link trading (including Web rings), and discussion groups.

Search engines and directories, once very different beasts, have been integrated to the point where I'll treat them as one subject. Examples of these are: Yahoo, Altavista, Infoseek, Excite, Lycos, Webcrawler, Snap, and so on. The pure search engine concept is one in which you type certain key words into a box and the search engine returns some or all of the sites containing those key words in one combination or another, depending on the search conditions you apply. A pure directory is a hierarchical catalog in which you choose a general subject, like "Arts and Humanities," and continually narrow down your search in layer after layer of categories until you reach "Bronze casting techniques in Ancient Greece." The key is for you to get listed in the major search engines and directories, and not to get taken in by an ad for a service that will list you in 1,000 search engines for $19.95. Most search traffic is directed by a handful of search engines and directories, primarily those listed herein. Make sure that you submit to any search engines and directories that *you* use, and just hope that your potential readers think the same way.

If you want to be published, you must undertake one exercise in market research: try to put yourself in the shoes of your target audience and search the Web for the sort of work you hope to publish. You'll quickly get a feel for the type of key words you should include on your pages, not to mention valuable insight into the "competition," which makes up an important part of any sales pitch to a traditional publisher. You may be astounded by the number of sites that already offer almost exactly what you had planned to offer, but don't be discouraged. In publishing, the bigger the existing market, the more likely a publisher will want to produce another title for it. Competing with other Web sites will help you hone your skills for the big battle, which is competing with other books.

Getting listed in search engines is easy. Simply go to the search engine site, look for a link that says "Submit your URL" or "Add your site," and click on it. This will bring you to a submissions page where you type in the address of your new Web page. Take note of any search engine you visit so that you can return in two weeks to see if it listed you, and resubmit if it didn't. Repeat as needed. Directories take a little more thought and persistence. You need to carefully choose which category you want to be listed in, and again, the best way to do this is to pretend you are a potential reader looking for whatever it is you write about. Directory entries are handled by human beings rather than by automated software, so only a small number of submissions are ever actually looked at. Sound familiar? Some directories even offer a guaranteed consideration of your site for a flat fee, around $100, but Yahoo is the only one I would even consider paying, and then only for a commercial site.

A link is essentially an address holder that shows up in most browsers as an underlined word or phrase. Link exchanges work on the old principle of "You scratch my back, I'll scratch yours." You find another site with content related to your own site, and you and the other webmaster negotiate an exchange of links via e-mail. When visitors to your site click on a link you have made to another site, they're gone. I'm not a big fan of link exchanges because they can easily get out of hand to the point where your site is no more than a revolving door. If you provide good content and make sure you are listed in the big search engines, people who maintain "all links" sites, essentially small targeted directories, will eventually find and link you. WebRings, on the other hand, are a nice way to join an online community of people who share your writing interests. For an index of WebRings and how to join, visit www.webring.com.

Discussion groups and news groups are a highly targeted way to announce the existence of your site. There are tens of thousands of public news or use groups, not to mention those discussion groups hosted on individual sites. Odds are, somebody out there is interested in what you are doing. It was by way of a technology discussion group that I received an unsolicited offer from a major imprint to publish a book based on my online material, although I eventually turned them down in favor of McGraw-Hill. The editor was apparently in the habit of checking the group for new trends or potential material, and a message I had posted to the group about new online material brought her to my site.

This Is the Future

Maybe you secretly hate your computer, though you avoid thinking about it while you're working for fear it will read your mind and trash your documents. There will always be room for a small number of eccentrics whose quirks are part and parcel of their attraction, but it's a tough role to break in with. The Internet is the future, and a Web strategy will be an integral part of any query letter in the coming years. The best way to learn about the Web and its potential is to get online and experiment with it. Even if you never post material to the Internet, you will need to understand how the publishing industry uses this tool.

Lest you think, "This is all great and fine for writing about technology, but what about my special field?" let me relate a final anecdote. For the past couple of years I've worked on translations of my great-grandmother's Hebrew books and wanted to get a short piece published about how she came to learn Hebrew in 1860s Latvia. This is definitely not "high tech" stuff. A Web search conducted with Altavista turned up a list of possible publications, and I sent queries to those that listed e-mail addresses for the editor. Of the three or four responses, I submitted the article, via e-mail, to the most enthusiastic, where it was accepted for publication in the next issue. The edited copy was sent for my approval, via e-mail, and the only time paper or postage entered the process was when the publisher sent me five complimentary copies of the magazine.

Once you have a Web site of your own, you'll wonder how you lived without one. For example, you can access your own material from any Internet-connected computer in the world! No more missed opportunities because the dog ate the manuscript and the editor you met on vacation wants to see it yesterday. I have written and submitted material for publication from a friend's computer on the other side of the Atlantic, and with e-mail, you'll never worry about missing a phone call. A popular Web site can actually pay! You can sell self-published books to people for less than the cost of the inkjet cartridge they would use up printing it or you can sell yourself as a consultant, speaker, writer, and so on. Last but not least, you can sign up as an AMAZON associate, referring your visitors to AMAZON.COM for books you suggest, have reviewed, or have written. Currently, AMAZON is putting over $100 per month into my pocket, which more than pays the freight for a commercial Web site.

Morris Rosenthal
www.daileyint.com

Time Management

Deborah Levine Herman

It is probably more difficult for writers who do not have a separate day job to manage time and to meet deadlines. If you are a full-time writer, you are not confined to a structured day and have to be self-disciplined and self-motivated.

If you are by nature a methodical writer who keeps an orderly home and an efficient calendar, is always prompt, and never misses appointments, I truly envy you. If you are like me, all of the above require great effort and are probably much more challenging than writing itself.

I love any kind of creative endeavor and am passionate about writing. I am also easily distracted. If I am not under deadline, I work at home and am just as likely to wallpaper my house as I am to write a book proposal, query letter, or fiction piece. As you know, there are many things a writer can be doing between assignments to further his or her career. You can write, research, plan, or promote existing projects. You can also promote yourself to gain a forum for your ideas and future projects. Unfortunately, I sometimes like to procrastinate to the point that I am not even aware of how much time I may be wasting.

I do not recommend the unofficial Deborah Herman method of kamikaze writing. As my career has developed, I have been learning to improve my time management techniques. I am a work in progress but I can share what works for me.

TIME MANAGEMENT TECHNIQUES

If writing is what you do, you need to treat it as a job. It is fine if you want to think about it all the time and define yourself by it. But it is important for you to delineate between the work of writing and your life. Otherwise you will wind up looking at the basic activities of life management as something akin to playing hooky from what you really "should" be doing. There are even times when I view housework as a treat because I am stealing time from my work. For anyone who knows me, that is truly a pitiful concept.

You need to set up a schedule that allows you to leave your work behind. If you commit to a deadline, you are going to need to evaluate approximately how many work hours you will need to do the job. Some people write quickly and prolifically, and some write as if they are constipated. You have to be honest in determining how much time you will need for actual writing, and how much time you will need to pace, twist your hair, or play solitaire on your PC until you are able to focus. You don't need to feel guilty if you have some writing rituals, but be sure to consider them as part of your overall schedule.

It is best if you schedule your writing and writing-related activities at the same time every day. Writing is a very concentration-intensive activity so you may not be able to devote eight straight hours to it. If you can be productive for two hours, that may be enough time per day. If you need to do more, I suggest you work in two-hour blocks with a substantial break in between them. You need to listen to your own writing rhythms. Sometimes I can work for two to three hours that seem like one hour, and other times one hour can seem like ten. As long as you are setting aside the same time each day, you will be able to be consistently productive and will use your time well.

When you finish your writing or writing-related activities for the day or business week, forget about them. Have a life. Have fun. Get some exercise. Stretch. Take care of your home and laundry. Do the things everyone else does to create balance. Writing takes a lot out of you emotionally, physically, and mentally. You do not want to use up your energy all at once, or you will become miserable and will no longer love to write. If you do not love to write, get out of the business. Writing is not glamorous. Sometimes it can be tedious and grueling. But if you can't imagine doing anything else with your life, make sure to be good to yourself so that you can be effective.

Do not wait for inspiration to strike before you write. If you have chosen writing as a profession, you need to be professional. You can't just wait for the right mood to strike before you get down to business. If you wake up feeling a little down, don't give into it. Kick yourself in the rear and get to your desk or computer.

Do not listen to your inner voice if it tells you your work stinks. There is nothing that will mess up your writing schedule more than your little inner demons. Go to work anyway or you will never make any progress. The unfortunate thing about writing is that we do not get the kind of instant feedback we would get at a standard job. If we do a good job, no one is there to tell us so, and we do not believe our friends and family anyway. If we do a bad job we may not know it and will still not believe anyone who tells us so. We work in a vacuum. So plod along. You will get the feedback you need when you obtain contracts for your work or when you hand in the completed manuscripts to your publisher.

The irony about writing as a profession is that we need such strong egos and are probably among the least-secure members of the human population. So view yourself as a business producing a product. As long as it meets acceptable standards for the marketplace, do not worry if it is not perfect. Once you relax about the work, you will see how much more productive you can be. You may even find you enjoy the process and produce higher-quality work. If you relax within the schedule you have created, you give yourself the chance to develop your craft and hone your skills and voice. Whether you are a ghostwriter, a novelist, or a specialist in nonfiction, you will develop a signature style. You can't do this if you are so uptight that you can't breathe.

So managing your time is really a state of mind. There are many books that will teach you specific techniques for organization, calendar usage, and time management to the minute. But for writers, the most important factor is how you feel about your writing, your career, and your life. If you seek balance and want to be productive, you will create a system that works for you. If you want to drive yourself crazy and wind up drinking yourself to an early grave so you can be immortalized as an "arteest," let your time manage you. I vote for balance. I love to be free-spirited and eccentric. It is my most comfortable persona. But when I am under deadline I do not think the anxiety is worth it. I also do not think it is worth it to have my house ready to be condemned, my children running away to Grandma's, and my husband ready to commit justifiable homicide. So take control of your time and see what a difference it will make.

The State of Book Publishing, Today and Tomorrow

Jeff Herman

For several years the big question for everyone in publishing has been: "How will the Internet affect the book business?"

I'm going to go out on a limb here and say that new technologies don't and won't matter, because it's all about delivery and production systems. It has nothing to do with the evolution of the creative process or the measure of America's appetite for reading books. Whether you're composing your verse with a chisel on a limestone tablet or orally dictating to a computer that will immediately generate your hard copy (or cyber copy), it's still all about creating.

Cassettes and LPs quickly disappeared when CDs appeared. But the producers, distributors, and artists remained the same. Napster did threaten to overthrow the status quo by enabling consumers to acquire products without having to pay, but that was obviously illegal and unsustainable.

One day consumers may routinely buy and read books without touching a piece of paper (*Star Trek*'s Captain Picard was deemed eccentric for his tendency to read books the "old-fashioned" way). Yet what hasn't been clearly explained is why this, in and of itself, is revolutionary.

A revolution is when the existing power structure is abruptly overthrown and replaced by something much different. Do we see that happening? It's true that anyone with a computer can virtually self-publish his or her book in cyberspace. But then how do you get people to know about it and motivate them to buy it? Online self-publishing saves you the trouble and expense of printing and storing thousands of copies in your garage, all on spec, but one hundred thousand words written by WHO? is likely to be forever lost in cyberspace.

The only really important issue is working out a reasonable compensation structure for writers, as publishers shift their front- and backlists to electronic "books."

We need to pay closer attention to the fallout from the "globalization" of America's publishing infrastructure, which began more than 10 years ago and has managed to consolidate the largest piece of the publishing pie into a few hands, most of which are as American as a Volkswagen. Independently owned "boutique" houses will always emerge and thrive, but they can act only from the margins. The sky hasn't fallen, but the atmosphere is different.

In the past, most books were acquired not so much for their immediate success, but because it was hoped they would nourish the "backlist," which was the surest way for a publisher to bolster its existence into the future. But that isn't today's publishing model. The large houses and the bookstore chains want megaselling, supernova brands, not a smorgasbord of delicacies. You can almost see these words written across the proverbial transoms of editors' offices: "Only bestselling writers need apply."

This is not to suggest that the midlist book is dead; far from it. Publishers can't afford to kill the midlist. But they are disrespecting it by refusing to adequately support it. The race is on to consolidate resources and place bets on the Derek Jeters of publishing. That's what gets noticed and rewarded by the corporate overlords.

But here's a silly little secret: If large houses stopped betting the farm on flaky blockbusters and mostly concentrated on feeding their healthy backlists with smart midlist acquisitions, they would be much more profitable today and tomorrow, and many more writers could make decent money from writing. And there would be a lot more good books to sell, buy, and read.

Yet an even more systemic issue pre-exists today's regime: We are a nation of readers. Tens of millions of us avidly read *People Magazine* and many other mass-market publications each week. But only a tiny fraction of this dedicated readership routinely buys books. What a shame, especially for writers, since an expanding market would mean more book contracts.

Why? There are many reasons, but I believe the most important one is historical. Two hundred years ago only a few people could actually read, and the vast majority of the population was functionally illiterate. Furthermore, only a few people could actually afford to buy books. It follows that book publishing, at its very genesis, could and would only serve the nation's most affluent and educated layer, which formed a narrow slice of the whole.

Things are much different today, and most of us are decent and active readers. But publishing as an institution has never caught up with the fact that the "rest of us" now read and have a few bucks. In fact, the most profitable book sectors, like mass-market romance, are treated as proletarian baggage, even though they subsidize many of the million-dollar acquisition mistakes made by the "smart" people.

The day that book publishers can see the *National Enquirer* as a role model instead of a joke, editors will all be earning healthy six-figure incomes, bookstores will be as common as drugstores, and many more writers will actually be writing during the day

Energize Your
Nonfiction

KATHERINE RAMSLAND

As the O. J. Simpson trial heated up, the defense team debated over the evidence. Each lawyer wondered how the jury would process complicated information like blood analysis, but it was DNA expert Barry Scheck who had an idea that shifted the strategy. Based on what he said, O. J.'s lead lawyer, Johnnie Cochran, quickly constructed a case that resulted in one of the most controversial verdicts in legal history—and gained his client's freedom.

Do you want to know what Scheck said?

Then you're hooked. Read on.

Essentially, Scheck knew what good writers know. While the other lawyers were arguing over how to manage the case, he got up and offered one simple finding from psychological research: People transform testimony into a story that makes sense to them. They build a narrative and absorb all subsequent information through it, so the key to winning a case is to tell the best story.

For submitted pieces of writing, such a stylized narrative can also make the difference between a sale and a rejection letter.

CAPOTE'S INSIGHT

Even nonfiction can be told in the framework of story. Truman Capote is credited with being the founding father of what he called "the nonfiction novel," subsequently dubbed "the new journalism" and currently known as creative or narrative nonfiction. To gather material for such an endeavor, Capote investigated the 1959 mass murder of the Clutter family in a small Kansas town. Rather than follow the example of journalists, listing names and facts, he decided to take the same information and tell it as story—as if he were writing a novel. To his mind, journalism was an underexplored medium, and he aimed for "a narrative form that employed all the techniques of fictional art, but was nevertheless immaculately factual." The result was *In Cold Blood*, and after that, popular journalism was never the same.

Some people mistakenly believe that narrative nonfiction is limited to literary efforts, but, in fact, editors prefer that certain types of commercial nonfiction also have the structure and momentum of storytelling. I recently read a book about the biology of snakes that began with a suspenseful hunt through the rain forest for the world's largest rattler.

Many devices assist in this process, but I believe the three most important ones are:

1. The hook
2. Writing in scenes
3. Character development

Let's take them one at a time.

THE HOOK

Otherwise known as the "lead," the first line or paragraph should lure readers and then thrust them right into the piece. Letting readers know that Scheck said one simple thing that made all the difference in a sensational case, without giving away what it was, is calculated to inspire sufficient curiosity in readers to make them want to find out.

When I wrote an undercover exposé of the vampire subculture in America, *Piercing the Darkness*, I started with a mystery: New York reporter Susan Walsh had been investigating "vampire cults" when she inexplicably disappeared. I set out to see what I could discover. The hint of violence, the mystery, and the sexy image of the vampire combined to provide the initial hook.

A successful hook informs readers about what they're going to learn, as well as injects them with the desire to at least read a little longer. To learn how to devise a hook for nonfiction, look at the first paragraph of a few suspense novels. That should give you some good ideas.

SCENES

The drama and pace of a given piece are often accomplished through scenes. Let's go back to Capote's strategy: While a reporter in 1959 might have written, "Four bodies were discovered today in the Clutter family home," Capote went through all of the records and interviewed everyone involved so that he could reconstruct what it would have been like to walk into this silent home, to sense that something happened there, and then to come upon the bodies, one by one. He provides a full description of the house, the eerie atmosphere, the fear that police officers felt as they walked slowly from room to room, and their disgust over what the killers had done to these fine people. The same information gets conveyed but not the same effect. You, the reader, are there with the officers. You feel what they felt at the moment they felt it.

Scenes generally involve setting, dialogue, a feeling tone (suspense, conflict, resolution), deepening of character, and information. These should advance the story while keeping readers fully involved.

When I first researched ghost-hunting equipment for *Trick or Treat?*, I decided to show how I learned about it, piece by piece, out on the Gettysburg battlefield at night. I wanted readers to feel the suspense I'd felt about whether something would actually happen, as well as the surprise and amazement I experienced when something did. My companions were real characters, and the setting on a covered bridge was perfect, so I had action, dialogue, a sense of time and place, information about how the equipment worked, and a steady feeling of both curiosity and fear driving the scene. By the scene's end, I had changed, psychologically and emotionally, and that led to further exploration.

Scenes are the building blocks of any story. This is how writers "show" rather than "tell," and vivid scenes can move the narrative, as well as keep the tale impressed in the reader's mind for a long time afterward.

CHARACTER DEVELOPMENT

We read books like *Midnight in the Garden of Good and Evil* partly because we encounter true-to-life quirky characters. What's it like to have breakfast with a guy who ties flies to his jacket and carries enough poison in his pocket to contaminate the water supply for the entire city of Savannah? Or to meet a Voodooienne in a cemetery, who instructs you to drop dimes into the dirt of a new grave? Stories are about who something happens to and who else is a player. Good character development can sometimes even make up for poor plotting.

I once worked with a woman writing her memoirs who wanted to talk about a meeting with someone, but all she could say about him was that he was "nice," had brown hair, and wore a suit. She recalled nothing else. The man was lifeless, faceless, and without character. Because of that, there was no way to make the scene come alive. To develop characters, you need to describe the finest nuances of their physical appearance, as well as show how their personality is revealed in their posture, the way they dress, the lines in their faces, and the kind of jokes they tell. External and internal elements should work together to yield a vivid portrait.

As much as possible, put the person into some kind of action that will further draw out his or her character. In *Cemetery Stories*, my book on people who have a close association with graveyards, I met a woman who said that death comes to her in various forms. She lived in a purple and black house in New Orleans, was tall and thin, and wore only black. There's no doubt that she had layers of character for me to work with, so rather than just sit and interview her, I invited her to accompany me to a cemetery, where I was seeking a religious relic that healed people. Not only did I have an interesting setting, but walking among the aboveground monuments of the decadent city of New Orleans brought out more from this woman than a face-to-face Q&A session might have done. To make that book work to the best narrative advantage, I needed to bring out the layers of the people who immersed themselves in cemetery lore.

Choose people who are suspense stories in and of themselves. The more complicated, the less easy they are to predict and readers will be curious to know what they will do next.

COMBINING THE THREE

Opening a book is always tough, but I try to develop a scene from something that will also serve as a hook. When I wrote *Prism of the Night: A Biography of Anne Rice*, I discovered that she had a childhood penchant for changing her name. This was partly due to her romantic imagination and partly to the fact that at birth she had been given the resoundingly awful name Howard Allen. On the first day of class, she was so horrified that her classmates would discover her true name that when the nun asked her mother for it, the child blurted out, "It's Anne."

Now I could have related the anecdote simply and left it at that, but instead I decided to make this into a scene that would show who she was, as well as how the incident happened. I placed her in her modest home on St. Charles Avenue, anticipating going to school. I walked her through New Orleans' Garden District, with all of its mansions, and then into the deteriorating Irish Channel to her Catholic school. (I went to each of these places to get the full sensory effect.) Then I walked her into the small classroom, holding her mother's hand and becoming aware for the first time of other kids watching her. Even at her young age, she knew how mortified she would be if they heard that wretched name, so she grew desperate enough to step in front of her mother and assert herself. I took what could have been one factual sentence and turned it into several pages of suspense, setting, and character development, in a scene that was something of a pivotal point in Rice's life—and forever after, Howard Allen was Anne.

Other creative devices can energize nonfiction, but the three that I've described here are sure winners. As Barry Scheck noted, people respond to story.

Web Sites for Authors

One of the most valuable aspects of the World Wide Web for writers is that it provides the opportunity to explore the world of publishing. This annotated list of Web sites offers descriptions of some of the most useful sites for writers. For your convenience, sites are grouped according to the following categories:

- Publishing Resources
- Poetry Resources
- Screenwriting Resources
- Horror Resources
- Children's Literature Resources
- Mystery Resources
- Science Fiction Resources
- Western Resources
- Funding Resources
- Publishing Resources

PUBLISHING RESOURCES

1001 WAYS TO MARKET YOUR BOOKS
http://www.bookmarket.com/1001bio.html

1001 Ways to Market Your Books is a site that offers a book marketing newsletter, consulting services, and book marketing updates. Other topics include success letters, author bios, sample chapters, and tables of contents.

@WRITERS: FOR WRITERS ON THE INTERNET
http://www.geocities.com/Athens/6346/body.html`

The @writers site includes information about markets, links to myriad Internet resources, and reviews of writing-related books. It also provides a technical Q&A section to answer questions about hardware, software, and the Internet. Also available is a chat room and monthly newsletter subscription.

AMERICAN BOOKSELLERS ASSOCIATION
http://www.bookweb.org

The American Booksellers Association is a trade association representing independent bookstores nationwide. The site links members to recent articles about the industry and features Idea Exchange discussion forums.

ASSOCIATION OF AMERICAN PUBLISHERS, INC.
http://www.publishers.org/home/index.htm

The Association of American Publishers "is the principal trade association of the book publishing industry." The site includes information and registration for annual meetings and conferences, industry news, info about book publishing, industry stats and issues, and copyright data.

ASSOCIATION OF AUTHOR'S REPRESENTATIVES, INC.
http://www.bookwire.com/aar

The Association of Author's Representatives, Inc., is "an organization of independent literary and dramatic agents." It is a member-only site that offers information about finding an agent, Internet links, a newsletter and a canon of ethics.

AUTHORLINK
http: //www.authorlink.com

This information service for editors, literary agents, and writers boasts more than 165,000 loyal readers per year. Features include a "Manuscript Showcase" that contains 500+ ready to publish, evaluated manuscripts.

THE AUTHOR'S GUILD
http://www.authorsguild.org/

For more than 80 years the Guild has been the authoritative voice of American writers . . . its strength is the foundation of the U.S. literary community. This site features contract advice, a legal search, information on electronic rights and how to join the organization, a bulletin index, publishers row, a listing of board members, and current articles regarding the publishing field. There is also a link for Back-in-print.com, an online bookstore featuring out-of-print editions made available by their authors.

AYLAD'S CREATIVE WRITING GROUP
http://www.publication.com/aylad

This site provides a forum for "people to get their work read and critiqued by fellow writers in a friendly atmosphere." The service is free and all writing forms are welcome. The site includes links to other resources for writers.

BOOKLIST
http://www.ala.org/booklist/index.html

Booklist is a "digital counterpart of the American Library Association's *Booklist* magazine." In the site is a current selection of reviews, feature articles, and a searchable cumulative index. Review topics include books for youth, adult books, media, and reference materials. The site also includes press releases, the best books list, and subscription information.

BOOKNOTE
http://www.booknote.com

Booknote specializes in custom designed Web sites for authors, book titles, literary agents, and publishers. Their award-winning sites are individually designed to capture the creativity of the unique individuals they feature. They also extensively target market each site to all relevant special-interest or news groups on the Web to increase both the person's recognition and World Wide Web sales.

BOOKNOTES
http://www.booknotes.org/right.htm

Based on the book and television program, *Booknotes* on C-SPAN, this site allows one to learn about the authors who have appeared on the program, read transcripts from the program, watch RealVideo clips from authors who were featured in this book, preview the upcoming *Booknotes* schedule, listen to recent *Booknotes* programs in their entirety in RealAudio, and learn about the publishing industry in general. The site also features message boards and a link to the C-SPAN bookstore.

THE BOOK REPORT
http://www.bookwire.com/tbr/

The Book Report is "where readers meet readers and readers meet writers." It is a conversational site where visitors may talk about a book they have recently read or get tips on great new books from other visitors. The site also includes book reviews and transcriptions of exclusive chats with authors.

BOOKREPORTER
http://www.bookreporter.com/brc/index.asp

Bookreporter is a site that offers book reviews and a perspectives section that deals with topics such as when a book becomes a movie. It features a daily quote by a famous author.

BOOKTALK
http://www.booktalk.com/

This site is a Publishing insider's page where you'll find out who's hot and what's up. It features links to get in touch with authors, agents, and publishers, as well as a slush pile and bookstores.

BOOKWIRE
http://www.bookwire.com/

Partners with *Publishers Weekly, Literary Market Place,* and the *Library Journal,* among others, BookWire is a site that offers book industry news, reviews, original fiction, author interviews, and guides to literary events. The site features publicity and marketing opportunities for publishers, authors, booksellers, and publicists; and it includes a list of the latest BookWire press releases.

BOOKZONE
http://www.bookzone.com/

BookZone was created "to increase book sales and profits for publishers." The site features a Super Catalog of books, thousands of book-related links, industry insights and resources, publishing news, and site hosting, development, and online marketing.

THE CHILDREN'S BOOK COUNCIL
http://www.cbcbooks.org/

"CBC Online is the Web site of the Children's Book Council—encouraging reading since 1945." It provides a listing of articles geared toward publishers, teachers, librarians, booksellers, parents, authors, and illustrators—all those who are interested in the children's book field.

COFFEEHOUSE FOR WRITERS

http://www.coffeehouse4writers.com

The Coffeehouse for Writers is an "online writer's colony; a place where writers—from novice to professional—gather to critique, advise, and encourage each other." The site provides links to other resources for writers and a list of suggested books.

CRITIQUE PARTNER CONNECTIONS

http://www.petalsoflife.com/cpc.html

A user of Critique Partner Connections pays a one-time fee of $15.00 to be matched with a fellow writer for the purpose of critiquing one another's work. Maintainers of this site strive to match people with similar interests and critique styles.

THE EDITORIAL EYE

http://www.eei-alex.com

The Editorial Eye Web site consists of a sampler of articles originally printed in the newsletter by the same name. The articles discuss techniques for writing, editing, design, and typography, as well as information on industry trends and employment. The *Eye* has been providing information to publications professionals for 18 years.

THE ECLECTIC WRITER

http://www.eclectics.com/writing/writing.html

This site is an information source for those interested in crime, romance, horror, children's, technical, screen, science fiction, fantasy, mystery, and poetry writing. It features articles, a fiction writers character chart, resources by genre, reference materials, research, general writing resources, online magazines and journals, writing scams, awards, and a writing related fun page.

THE EDITOR'S PEN

http://www.pathway.net/dwlcey/default.htm

The Editor's Pen site exists to connect "sites for and about Writers, Editors, and Indexers." It includes links to lists of freelancers and online dictionaries. Other interesting links include an "Edit challenge" and "Quotable words of editorial wisdom."

Encyclopaedia Britannica

http://www.eb.com/

This service is subscription-based and allows the user to search the Encyclopaedia Britannica. New users can try a "sample search."

Forwriters.com

http://www.forwriters.com/

This "mega-site" provides numerous links to writing resources of all kinds. It lists conferences, markets, agents, commercial services, and more. The "What's New" feature allows the user to peruse what links have recently been added under the various categories.

Granta

http://www.granta.com/

The Granta Web site offers information about the most current issue of this highly regarded literary journal. The introduction is an explanation and background info about the topic around which the issue is based. The contents of the issue are listed and visitors to the site may read a sample from the issue, as well as obtain subscription and ordering information. It also offers similar information about back issues and a readers' survey.

Hungry Mind Review

http://www.bookwire.com/hmr

The *Hungry Mind Review* is a national magazine that presents essays, author interviews, children's book reviews, nonfiction reviews, a section on poetics, and poetry reviews. *Hungry Mind Review* is also offered in a print version, in which each issue is built around a particular theme.

Inkspot

http://www.inkspot.com

Inkspot provides articles, how-to tips, market information, and networking opportunities. Special features include a FAQ for beginners, classifieds, and a section for young writers. Information is sorted by genre.

Inner Circle

http://www.geocities.com/SoHo/Lofts/1498/circlefaq.htm

The Fictech Inner Circle was started in April 1997 as "a means for writers—especially new and unpublished writers—to correspond through e-mail with others of similar interest." Membership is free and provides the opportunity to communicate with over 1,500 writers from around the globe.

INTERNATIONAL ONLINE WRITERS ASSOCIATION
http://www.project-iowa.org

IOWA's purpose is to "offer help and services to writers around the world through shared ideas, workshops, critiques, and professional advice." Services include real-time monthly workshops, real-time weekly critiques, and periodic round robins. The site also includes a library of essays, poems, short stories, and novel chapters.

INTERNET WRITING WORKSHOP
http://www.geocities.com/1kaus/workshop/index.html

The Internet Writing Workshop exists to "create an environment where works in progress can be passed around and critiqued, to help us improve these works and to improve as writers," as well as to provide support for writers. The service is membership-based and includes a variety of genres.

LIBRARY JOURNAL DIGITAL
http://www.bookwire.com/ljdigital/

Library Journal Digital is a site that offers articles about news in the publishing industry, editorials, a calendar of events, video reviews, audiobook reviews, bestseller news, and a job search section.

LITERARY MARKET PLACE
http://www.literarymarketplace.com/

The Literary Market Place Web site offers information about publishers, which are categorized by U.S. book publishers, Canadian book publishers, and small presses, as well as literary agents, including illustration and lecture agents. The site also offers trade services and resources.

LOCAL WRITERS WORKSHOP
http://members.tripod.com/~lww_2/introduction.htm

The Local Writers Workshop is an Internet forum for works in progress, especially those "in the early stages of revision." The creators of this membership-based site pride themselves on its community ethic.

MIDWEST BOOK REVIEW

http://www.execpc.com/~mbr/bookwatch/mbr/pubinfo.html

Responsible for *Bookwatch* a weekly television program that reviews books, videos, music, CD-ROMs, and computer software, as well as five monthly newsletters for community and academic library systems, and much more, the Midwest Book Review was founded in 1980. This site features its reviews.

MISC.WRITING

http://www.scalar.com/mw

"Misc.writing is a Use Net newsgroup that provides a forum for discussion of writing in all its forms—scholarly, technical, journalistic, and mere day-to-day communication." Web site resources include a writer's bookstore and market information.

THE NATIONAL WRITERS UNION

http://www.nwu.org

The National Writers Union is the trade union for freelance writers of all genres. The Web site provides links to various service of the union, including grievance resolution, insurance, job information, and databases.

PAINTED ROCK

http://www.paintedrock.com/memvis/memvis1.htm

"Painted Rock provides services to nonpublished writers, published writers, and readers." Free features on the site include information on a free 12-week Artist's Way program, message boards, goal writing groups, writing topics, a book discussion group, a research listserv, and *The Rock* online magazine. In addition to their free services, the site offers paid online writing classes, a subscription-based newsletter, and two bookstores, as well as advertising, promotion for authors, and Web site hosting and design.

PARA PUBLISHING

http://www.parapublishing.com/

The Para Publishing Book Publishing Resources page offers "the industry's largest resources/publications guide," a customized book writing/publishing/promoting information kit, as well as current and back issues of their newsletter. The site also includes research links, a listing of suppliers, and mailing lists.

PEN American Center

http://www.pen.org/

PEN is an International "membership organization of prominent literary writers and editors. As a major voice of the literary community, the organization seeks to defend the freedom of expression wherever it may be threatened, and to promote and encourage the recognition and reading of contemporary literature." The site links to information about several PEN sponsored initiatives, including literary awards.

Publishers Weekly Online

http://www.publishersweekly.com

Publishers Weekly Online offers news about the writing industry in general, as well as special features about reading and writing in general and genre writing. The site also includes news on children's books, book-selling, interviews, international book industry news, and industry updates.

Pure Fiction

http://www.purefiction.com/start.htm

Based in London and New York, Pure Fiction is a Web site "for anyone who loves to read— or aspires to write—best-selling fiction." The site includes reviews, previews, writing advice, an online bookshop, a writers' showcase, Internet links, and more. It also offers a mailing list.

ReadersNdex

http://www.ReadersNdex.com/

ReadersNdex is a searchable site designed to give "access to the most up-to-date information about your favorite authors and titles, regardless of publisher affiliation." Books on ReadersNdex are cross-referenced by author, title, subject, and publisher, and may be purchased through the bookstore, the Tattered Cover, or from the publisher. The Bookshelf section is designed for browsing the available books. The site also includes a Reading Room where magazines and reviews may be read; links to the Web sites of participating publishers; and the searchable index of books.

Reference Shelf

http://Alabanza.com/kabacoff/Inter-Links/reference.html

The Reference Shelf site provides quick access to words, facts, and figures useful when writing and fact-checking. A special "words" section features dictionaries, acronym finders, and links to computer-jargon.

R. R. Bowker

http://www.bowker.com/

R. R. Bowker is a site that offers a listing of books in print on the Web, books out of print, an online directory of the book publishing industry, a data collection center for R. R. Bowker publications, and a directory of vendors to the publishing community.

Sensible Solutions for Getting Happily Published

http://www.happilypublished.com/

This site, Sensible Solutions for Getting Happily Published, is "designed to help writers, publishers, self-publishers, and everyone else who cares about reaching readers, including editors, agents, booksellers, reviewers, industry observers and talk show hosts . . . and aims to help books get into the hands of the people they were written for." It includes information about finding a publisher, ways for publishers to raise revenues, the self-publishing option, how to boost a book's sales, and sensible solutions for reaching readers.

SharpWriter.Com

http://www.sharpwriter.com/

SharpWriter.Com is a practical resources page for writers of all types—a "writer's handy virtual desktop." Reference materials include style sheets, dictionaries, quotations, and job information. The Office Peacemaker offers to resolve grammar disputes in the workplace.

Shaw Guides, Inc., Writer's Conferences

http://www.shawguides.com/

Shaw Guides: Writers Conferences is a subscription-based listing of sponsors and the following month's writers conferences calendar. The Shaw Site for Writers Conferences allows the user to search for information about 400 conference and workshops worldwide. An e-mail service can be used to get updates about conferences that meet user criteria for dates, topics, and locations. Other resources include Quick Tips, links to organizations, and information about residencies and retreats.

Small Publishers of North America

http://www.spannet.org/home.htm

Small Publishers of North America is a site for "independent presses, self-publishers, and savvy authors who realize if their books are to be successful, they must make them so." The site offers pages for "fun, facts, and financial gain." They offer a newsletter.

United States Copyright Office
http://lcweb.loc.gov/copyright/

The United States Copyright Office site allows the user to find valuable information about copyright procedures and other basics. In addition, the user can download publications and forms, then link to information about international copyright laws.

A Web of On-Line Dictionaries
http://www.geocities.com/WestHollywood/Castro/6101/dic/diction1.html

This index of online dictionaries includes 165 different languages and gives preference to free resources. A new feature allows the user to translate words from any European language to any other.

Webster Dictionary
http://www.m-w.com/netdict.htm

Like its paper counterpart, this web-based dictionary provides definition to words and phrases sought by users. For word lovers, features like "Word of the Day" and "Word Game of the Day" are included as well.

The WELL
http://www.well.com/

The WELL (Whole Earth 'Lectronic Link) is an online gathering place that its creators call a "literate watering hole for thinkers from all walks of life."

Women Who Write
http://members.aol.com/jfavetti/womenww/www.html

Women Who Write is a "collage of women based all over the United States with a passion for writing." The site provides useful links and a large dose of encouragement to women writers of all experience levels.

WriteLinks
http://www.writelinks.com/

The site provides an array of services, including workshops, personalized tutoring, and critique groups. "WriteLinks is designed to be of value to all writers, regardless of their experience, genre, or focus."

WRITE PAGE AUTHOR LISTING INFORMATION

http://www.writepage.com/pageinfo.htm

This site offers authors a chance to create their own Web sites with the help of Callie Goble. It answers many of the questions that one might have about such an enterprise, such as "How long CAN my page be?" "How long does it take to get listed?" "What sort of exposure will my books get?" "What does the competition charge?" and much more.

WRITERSPACE

http://www.writerspace.com/

"Writerspace specializes in the design and hosting of Web sites for authors. We also provide Web services for those who may already have Web sites but wish to include more interactivity in the way of bulletin boards, chat rooms, contests, and e-mail newsletters." The site also features an author spotlight, contests, workshops, mailing lists, bulletin boards, chat rooms, romance links, a guestbook, and information on adding your link, Web design, Web hosting, their clients, and rates.

THE WRITERS' BBS

http://www.writers-bbs.com/home.shtml

The Writers' BBS is intended for "authors, poets, journalists, and readers" and high-lights writers' chat rooms, discussion forums, and an e-zine for beginning writers called "Fish Eggs for the Soul." It also includes games, personal ads, copyright information, mailing lists, Internet links, an adults-only section, and the online King James Bible.

THE WRITERS CENTER

http://www.writer.org/center/aboutwc.htm

The Writers Center is a Maryland-based nonprofit that "encourages the creation and distribution of contemporary literature," On the Web site, they provide information on their 200+ yearly workshops and links to their publication *Poet Lore and Writer's Carousel.*

WRITERS GUILD OF AMERICA WEST

http://www.wga.org

The WGA West site provides information about the Guild and its services, such as script registration. Other links to writing resources are provided as well.

WRITERS NET

http://www.writers.net/

Writes Net is a site that "helps build relationships between writers, publishers, editors, and literary agents." It consists of two main sections, The Internet Directory of Published Writers, which includes a list of published works and a biographical statement, and The Internet Directory of Literary Agents, which lists areas of specialization and a description of the agency. Both are searchable and include contact information. It is a free service that hopes to "become an important, comprehensive matchmaking resource for writers, editors, publishers, and literary agents on the Internet."

WRITERS ON THE NET

http://www.writers.com

"Writers on the Net is a group of published writers and experienced writing teachers building an online community and resource for writers and aspiring writers." A subscription to the mailing list provides a description and schedule of classes provided by the site and a monthly newsletter.

THE WRITER'S RETREAT

http://www.angelfire.com/va/dmsforever/index.html

The objectives of The Writer's Retreat are "to provide a meeting place for writers everywhere, to provide market information, to list relevant Internet links, to list inspirational and motivational information and quotations for writers of all races, creeds, and backgrounds, and to have and provide fun while doing it!"

WRITER'S TOOLBOX

http://www.geocities.com/Athens/6346/body.html

The site contains a "diverse and ever-growing collection of Internet resources for writers." The resources are categorized for many types of writers, from technical writers and PR professionals to fiction and drama writers. The site also includes links to software for writers and business resources.

WRITERS WRITE

http://www.writerswrite.com

This "mega-site" provides myriad resources, including a searchable database of online and print publications in need of submissions. The Writers Write chat room is open 24 hours for live discussion.

The Zuzu's Petals Literary Resource

http://www.zuzu.com

The Zuzu's Petals Literary Resource is a site that focuses on a comprehensive list of writers' resource links and information. It includes a bookstore, discussion forums, its literary magazine, *Zuzu's Petals Quarterly Online,* art news that reports on news in the literary world, and contests.

Poetry Resources

Atlantic Unbound Poetry Pages

http://www.theatlantic.com/atlantic/atlweb/poetry/poetpage.htm

The Atlantic Unbound Poetry Pages are brought to you from the *Atlantic Monthly,* a literary magazine. The Web site offers reviews of new poetry, a discussion forum, and the Audible Anthology, which is a collection of poetry sound files, poetry articles, links, and poetry from the *Atlantic Monthly* online zine. It is a searchable site and offers poetry and literature links.

Electronic Poetry Center

http://wings.buffalo.edu/epc/

There are perhaps more poetry Web sites online than any other literary genre, so picking one representative site is really quite pointless. But we do recommend the Electronic Poetry Center at the University of New York at Buffalo, which is the heart of the contemporary poetry community online, having been around since the early days of gopher space, practically the Dark Ages in computer time. Of particular note is the active and well-respected poetics mailing list, the large collection of audio files, and extensive listing of small press poetry publishers.

Inkspot Resources for Poets

http://www.inkspot.com/ss/genres/poetry.html

Inkspot Resources for Poets offers many Internet poetry links, a poets' chat forum, contests, general resources such as a glossary of poetic terms, mailing lists, courses available, critique groups and workshops for poets, and articles and essays on writing poetry.

THE INTERNATIONAL LIBRARY OF POETRY

http://www.poetry.com

The International Library of Poetry Web site offers information about its writing competitions, which focus on "awarding large prizes to poets who have never before won any type of writing competition." The site also includes Internet links, a list of past winners, anthologies of winning poems, and chat rooms.

NATIONAL POETRY ASSOCIATION

http://www.nationalpoetry.org/

The National Poetry Association Web site, supported in part by Grants for the Arts and Maya Angelou, offers an online poetry journal called *Poetry USA,* and aims to "promote poets and poetry to wider audiences by all possible means, serving both the literary community and the general public." The site is dedicated to the memory of William Burroughs, Allen Ginsberg, Denise Levertov, and Jack Micheline. It includes information about the National Poetry Association's current projects and offers contests for poets.

PERIHELION ROUND TABLE DISCUSSIONS

http://www.webdelsol.com/Perihelion/p-discussion3.htm

The Perihelion Round Table Discussions is a site that brings the thoughts of established poets and editors on issues of the Internet and its effect on poetry and the writing of poetry. There is also a discussion area where readers and visitors may add their insight to the discussions.

POETRY FROM THE MINING CO.

http://poetry.miningco.com/

Poetry from the Mining Co. offers links to such poetry resources as online contests and workshops, zines and anthologies, poets from the classical period to the twentieth century, multilingual and poetry translations, festivals and live poetry events, audio poetry archives, publishers, and online catalogs. The site offers a poetry newsletter, bulletin board, chat room, bookstore, and "gossip on the poetry word circuit." It also includes "an alphabetical listing and links to online lit zines, anthologies, and the online sites of print poetry magazines."

POETRY SOCIETY OF AMERICA

http://www.poetrysociety.org/

The Poetry Society of America Web site includes information about the newest developments in the Poetry in Motion project, which posts poetry to seven million subway and bus riders in New York City, Chicago, Baltimore, Portland, and Boston. It also includes news about poetry awards, seminars, the tributes in libraries program, poetry in public program, and poetry festivals.

POETS & WRITERS

http://www.pw.org/

Poets & Writers is an online resource for creative writers that includes publishing advice, message forums, contests, a directory of writers, literary links, information on grants and awards, news from the writing world, trivia, and workshops.

SCREENWRITING RESOURCES

HOLLYWOOD SCRIPTWRITER

http://www.hollywoodscriptwriter.com/about/tr.html

Hollywood Scriptwriters is an international newsletter that offers articles on craft and business "to give screenwriters the information they need to work at their careers." The site includes low-budget and indie markets available for finished screenplays, as well as a listing of agencies who are currently accepting submissions from readers of Hollywood Scriptwriter. According to Hollywood Scriptwriter, "people like Harold Ramis, Francis Ford Coppola, and Larry Gelbart have generously given of their time, knowledge, and experiences to share with HS's readers."

SCREAMING IN THE CELLULOID JUNGLE

http://www.celluloidjungle.com/

Screaming in the Celluloid Jungle is a screenwriting site that offers message boards, script sales archives, industry news, box office stats, and a writer's forum. Other topics include agents, production companies, a glossary of screenwriting and production terms, articles, producing, and directing.

THE SCREENWRITER'S HOME PAGE

http://home.earthlink.net/~scribbler/

The Screenwriter's Home Page offers "articles and interviews by people who work, day in and day out, in the movie business." Its aim is to help "not only with writing, but with the reality of the entertainment world." It includes agent listings, best ways to have your script rejected, professionals' thoughts on screenwriting, and industry news.

SCREENWRITERS & PLAYWRIGHTS HOME PAGE

http://www.teleport.com/~cdeemer/scrwriter.html

The Screenwriters & Playwrights Home Page "is designed to meet the special needs of screenwriters and playwrights." Features of the site include screenwriting basics, marketing tips, screenplay formats, agent listings, pitches and query letters, producer listings, writing for actors, and tips from pros. It also offers a free newsletter and Internet resources.

SCREENWRITER'S RESOURCE CENTER

http://www.screenwriting.com

The Screenwriters Resource Center aims to "provide links to products and services for screenwriters, compiled by the staff at the National Creative Registry." It includes links to many screenwriting sites and offers advice and copyright words of warning for writers posting original work on the Internet.

SCREENWRITER'S UTOPIA

http://www.screenwritersutopia.com/

Screenwriter's Utopia includes "helpful hints for getting screenplays produced, script development services, and contest information." The site includes a screenwriters' work station, tool kit, agent listings, and creative screenwriting magazines. Interviews with the screenwriters of *Sleepless in Seattle, Blade,* and *The Crow: City of Angels* are featured, and other interviews archived. The site also includes chat rooms, message boards, a writer's directory, and a free newsletter.

HORROR RESOURCES

CLASSIC HORROR AND FANTASY PAGE

http://home6.swipnet.se/~w-60478/

The Classic Horror and Fantasy Page aims to "collect links to every work of classic horror and fantasy fiction available on the Internet. The main purpose of this page is not to display the works themselves, but rather to direct the reader to other sites where the works are housed." Some of the authors and works that the site includes are Sir Richard Burton, *The Arabian Nights,* 1850 (translation); Johann Wolfgang von Goethe, *Faust,* 1808; and Edgar Allan Poe, *Collected Works.*

Dark Echo Horror

http://www.darkecho.com/darkecho/index.html

Dark Echo Horror features interviews, reviews, a writers workshop, dark links, and a newsletter. Articles relate to topics such as the perception and psychology of the horror writer, the "best" horror, and reviews of dark erotica. The site also offers information and links to fantasy writing.

HorrorNet

http://www.horrornet.com/

HorrorNet was created "purely as a way of giving horror fiction a well-needed boost of exposure. My goal here is to provide the most comprehensive Web site for lovers of horror and suspense fiction." The site includes new book releases, events, message boards, a chat room, links, articles, interviews, book reviews, and original fiction.

Horror Writers Association

http://www.horror.org/

The Horror Writers Association (HWA) was formed to "bring writers and others with a professional interest in horror together, and to foster a greater appreciation of dark fiction in general." Bestower of the Bram Stoker Awards, HWA offers a newsletter, late-breaking market news, informational e-mail bulletins, writers' groups, agents, FAQ, and links.

Masters of Terror

http://www.mastersofterror.cjb.net/

Masters of Terror offers information about horror fiction, book reviews, new authors, horror movies, author message boards, HorrorNet chat room, and a reference guide and critique of horror fiction that features some 500 authors and 2,500 novels. The site also includes exclusive author interviews, book and chapbook reviews, and horror news.

CHILDREN'S LITERATURE RESOURCES

CHILDREN'S WRITING RESOURCE CENTER
http://www.write4kids.com/

"Whether you're published, a beginner, or just someone who's always dreamt of writing for kids," here you'll find a free library of how-to information, opportunities to chat with other children's writers and illustrators, links to research databases, articles, tips for beginners, secrets for success as a children's writer, message boards, a children's writing survey, the chance to ask questions of known authors, and the opportunity to register in their guestbook to receive free e-mail updates filled with news and tips. The site also features a listing of favorite books, Newberry Medal Winners, Caldecott Award Winners, current bestsellers, and a link to its own children's bookshop.

THE SOCIETY OF CHILDREN'S BOOK WRITERS AND ILLUSTRATORS
http://www.scbwi.org/

This Web site "has a dual purpose: It exists as a service to our members, as well as offering information about the children's publishing industry and our organization to non-members." It features a listing of events, awards and grants, publications, information for members, information on how to become a member, and a site map.

MYSTERY RESOURCES

AMERICAN CRIME WRITERS LEAGUE
http://members.aol.com/theACWL/

The American Crime Writers League was established "by a group of writers who wanted a private forum for exchanging ideas, complaining about almost anything, and trying to understand this decidedly wacky business." The site includes information about interviews, conference information, agents' home telephone numbers, reviews, interviews, and more.

CLOCKTOWER FICTION

http://www.clocktowerfiction.com/

Clocktower Fiction aims to "provide free quality original fiction for avid readers." Clocktower Fiction publishes *Outside: Speculative and Dark Fiction,* which is a free-lance, paying online publication that is published three times a year. The site provides links to grammar, writing, and other writers' resources, and covers a variety of genres, including mystery, science fiction, macabre, suspense thrillers, and noir fiction.

CLUELASS HOME PAGE

http://www.cluelass.com

The ClueLass Home Page offers awards for mystery fiction and nonfiction, information about conferences and conventions, and mystery groups for writers and fans. It includes information about markets, other contests, reference material, and online support, as well as listings of mystery magazines and newsletters, an international directory of mystery booksellers and publishers, and factual links about crime, forensics, and investigation.

THE MYSTERIOUS HOME PAGE

http://www.webfic.com/mysthome/mysthome.htm

The Mysterious Home Page is "a guide to mysteries and crime fiction on the Internet." The site offers newsgroups, mailing lists, information on conferences and conventions, publishers, book dealers, interactive fiction, reviews, and electronic mysteries.

MYSTERY AND DETECTIVE FICTION SITES

http://umbc7.umbc.edu/~lharris/mystsite.htm

The Mystery and Detective Fiction Sites page offers a listing of resources from Animals in Mysteries to True Crime. Other focus areas of the site include authors' interviews and articles, characters, chat lines, conventions, discussion groups, newsletters, e-zines, mailing lists, online mysteries, publishers, reviews, and bookstores.

MYSTERY ON-LINE

http://www.webinspect.com/mystery.htm

Mystery On-Line is a site that is a work-in-progress of a mystery novel on the Web. Amateur and published writers may submit chapters for the Mystery On-Line continuing story. Each month a new chapter is selected and published on the site from the submissions. The site also includes mystery writing links, book reviews, and a link to the online bookstore.

THE MYSTERY WRITERS' FORUM

http://www.zott.com/mysforum/default.html

The Mystery Writers' Forum consists of "mystery writers and aspiring mystery authors who are sharing our trials, tribulations, and research problems and triumphs on a supportive, threaded bulletin board system." The site includes a bookstore, Internet links, and cyber crime references.

MYSTERY WRITERS OF AMERICA

http://www.mysterywriters.org

Mystery Writers of America "helps to negotiate contracts, watches development in legislation and tax law, sponsors symposia and mystery conferences, and publishes books." The site includes mystery links, awards, a calendar of events, writers' discussions, and a new online mystery every day. It was established to promote and protect "the interests and welfare of mystery writers and to increase the esteem and the literary recognition given to the genre."

SHORT MYSTERY FICTION SOCIETY

http://www.thewindjammer.com/smfs/

The Short Mystery Fiction Society "seeks to actively recognize writers and readers who promote and support the creative art form of short mysteries in the press, in other mystery organizations, and through awards." The site offers a newsletter and other resources.

SISTERS IN CRIME

http://www.sinc-ic.org

Sisters in Crime is a Web site devoted to "combat discrimination against women in the mystery field, educate publishers and the general public as to inequities in the treatment of female authors, raise awareness of their contribution to the field, and promote the professional advancement of women who write mysteries." The site includes information about local chapters of Sisters in Crime and offers mystery links and online bookstores.

Science Fiction Resources

Science Fiction and Fantasy Workshop
http://pages.prodigy.com/sfworkshop/

The Science Fiction and Fantasy Workshop was established "to provide workshop experience through the mail, and to put writers in contact with others in the same situation." The site offers a newsletter that includes articles on topics such as world-building, laws of magic, alien creation, working with editors, and a market column.

Science Fiction and Fantasy Writers of America
http://www.sfwa.org

The official Web site of the Science Fiction and Fantasy Writers of America offers information about the organization, its members, affiliated publications, an art gallery, and various awards.

SFNovelist
http://www.sfnovelist.com/index.html

SFNovelist is "an online writing group dedicated to novelists who write 'hard science' SF." It is a highly structured and organized system of the exchange of science fiction manuscripts for consideration by other writers. Its goals are to: 'become in the marketplace a premier source of novelists who write 'believable/hard science'' SF; garner the attention of SF publishers, SFWA, and other writers' organizations for SF novelists; develop a cadre of strong novelists, most of whom become published. Behind every great writer is usually a group of fellow writers who are equally serious about their writing; establish a presence at major SF writer conferences and conventions; and provide services and information to members that will help them in their search for self-improvement and in getting published, including contacts with other known writers and publishers and sources of distribution and marketing.

Speculative Vision
http://www.jps.net/starmage/vision.html

Speculative Vision is a site that offers selections of original science fiction, a music conservatory with TV and movie MIDI files, a discussion board, and Internet links. The

Resource Network section contains information about publishers, webzines, general science fiction resources, and TV and film news.

WESTERN RESOURCES

WESTERN WRITERS OF AMERICA, INC.
http://www.westernwriters.org
"WWA was founded in 1953 to promote the literature of the American West and bestow Spur Awards for distinguished writing in the Western field." The site offers information about Old West topics, a listing of past Spur Award winners, and opportunities to learn about WWA and the Spur Award, to apply for membership in WWA, to subscribe to *Roundup Magazine,* or to contact Western authors whose work interests you.

FUNDING RESOURCES

THE ART DEADLINE
http://custwww.xensei.com/adl/
The Art Deadline is a "monthly newsletter providing information about juried exhibitions and competitions, call for entries/proposals/papers, poetry and other writing contests, jobs, internships, scholarships, residencies, fellowships, casting calls, auditions, tryouts, grants, festivals, funding, financial aid, and other opportunities for artists, art educators, and art students of all ages. Some events take place on the Internet."

THE AT-A-GLANCE GUIDE TO GRANTS
http://www.adjunctadvocate.com/nafggrant.html
The At-A-Glance Guide to Grants offers information about grants, including a glossary of terms in grant forms, sample contracts, links to grant-related sites, a database of funding opportunities, and related agencies, foundations, and organizations. The site also includes a tutorial section that includes information about how to write a proposal and how to win a grant.

THE AUTHORS REGISTRY

http://www.webcom.com/registry/

Musicians have ASCAP and BMI, now writers have The Authors Registry. Formed in 1996, this not-for-profit organization collects fees and royalties from publishers and distributes them to authors whose works are being used. The registry also acts as a nonexclusive licenser of author-controlled rights. Log on to their site and search an extensive author directory or add your own name.

BOOKZONE

http://www.bookzone.com

This site offers information on writing, marketing, business and legal issues for publishing professionals. Forums, publishing news, online subscriptions to journals "at the guaranteed lowest prices on the Web. For design, development, e-commerce solutions, promotion and exposure, BookZone is the busiest and best Web host for publishers, authors, and other publishing professionals."

THE FOUNDATION CENTER

http://fdncenter.org/

The Foundation Center Web site is dedicated to assisting writers in finding grants. They offer "over 200 cooperating sites available in cities throughout the United States. Of particular note is its large online library with a wonderful interactive orientation to grant seeking. You'll even find application forms for several funding sources here."

NATIONAL WRITERS UNION

http://www.nwu.org/

"The union for freelance writers working in U.S. markets. . . . We are a modern, innovative union offering grievance resolution, industry campaigns, contract advice, health and dental plans, member education, job banks, networking, social events, and much more."

WESTERN STATES ARTS FEDERATION

http://www.westaf.org/

The WSAF is a "nonprofit arts service organization dedicated to the creative advancement and preservation of the arts. Focused on serving the state arts agencies, arts organizations, and artists of the West, WSAF fulfills its mission by engaging in innovative approaches to the provision of programs and services, and focuses its efforts on strengthening the financial, organizational, and policy infrastructure of the arts in the West."

Glossary

A

abstract   A brief sequential profile of chapters in a nonfiction book proposal (also called a **synopsis**); a point-by-point summary of an article or essay. In academic and technical journals abstracts often appear with (and may serve to preface) the articles themselves.

adaptation   A rewrite or reworking of a piece for another medium, such as the adaptation of a novel for the screen. (*See* **screenplay**.)

advance   Money paid (usually in installments) to an author by a publisher prior to publication. The advance is paid against royalties: If an author is given a $5,000 advance, for instance, the author will collect royalties only after the royalty moneys due exceed $5,000. A good contract protects the advance if it should exceed the royalties ultimately due from sales.

advance orders   Orders received before a book's official publication date, and sometimes before actual completion of the book's production and manufacture.

agent   The person who acts on behalf of the author to handle the sale of the author's literary properties. Good literary agents are as valuable to publishers as they are to writers; they select and present manuscripts appropriate for particular houses or of interest to particular acquisitions editors. Agents are paid on a percentage basis from the moneys due their author clients.

American Booksellers Association (ABA)   The major trade organization for retail booksellers, chain and independent. The annual ABA convention and trade show offers a chance for publishers and distributors to display their wares to the industry at large, and provides an incomparable networking forum for booksellers, editors, agents, publicists, and authors.

American Society of Journalists and Authors (ASJA)   A membership organization for professional writers. ASJA provides a forum for information exchange among writers and others in the publishing community, as well as networking opportunities. (*See* **Dial-a-Writer**.)

anthology   A collection of stories, poems, essays, and/or selections from larger works (and so forth), usually carrying a unifying theme or concept; these selections may be written by different authors or by a single author. Anthologies are compiled as opposed to written; their editors (as opposed to authors) are responsible for securing the needed reprint rights for the material used, as well as supplying (or providing authors for) pertinent introductory or supplementary material and/or commentary.

attitude   A contemporary colloquialism used to describe a characteristic temperament common among individuals who consider themselves superior. Attitude is rarely an esteemed attribute, whether in publishing or elsewhere.

auction   Manuscripts a literary agent believes to be hot properties (such as possible bestsellers with strong subsidiary rights potential) will be offered for confidential bidding from multiple publishing houses. Likewise, the reprint, film, and other rights to a successful book may be auctioned off by the original publisher's subsidiary rights department or by the author's agent.

audio books   Works produced for distribution on audio media, typically audiotape cassette or audio compact disc (CD). Audio books are usually spoken-word adaptations of works originally created and produced in print; these works sometimes feature the author's own voice; many are given dramatic readings by one or more actors, at times embellished with sound effects.

authorized biography   A history of a person's life written with the authorization, cooperation, and, at times, participation of the subject or the subject's heirs.

author's copies/author's discount   Author's copies are the free copies of their books the authors receive from the publisher; the exact number is stipulated in the contract, but it is usually at least 10 hardcovers. The author will be able to purchase additional copies of the book (usually at 40% discount from the retail price) and resell them at readings, lectures, and other public engagements. In cases where large quantities of books are bought, author discounts can go as high as 70%.

author tour   A series of travel and promotional appearances by an author on behalf of the author's book.

autobiography   A history of a person's life written by that same person, or, as is typical, composed conjointly with a collaborative writer ("as told to" or "with"; *see* **coauthor**, **collaboration**) or **ghostwriter**. Autobiographies by definition entail the authorization, cooperation, participation, and ultimate approval of the subject.

B

backlist   The backlist comprises books published prior to the current season and still in print. Traditionally, at some publishing houses, such backlist titles represent the publisher's cash flow mainstays. Some backlist books continue to sell briskly; some remain bestsellers over several successive seasons; others sell slowly but surely through the years. Although many backlist titles may be difficult to find in bookstores that stock primarily current lists, they can be ordered either through a local bookseller or directly from the publisher.

backmatter   Elements of a book that follow the text proper. Backmatter may include the appendix, notes, glossary, bibliography and other references, list of resources, index, author biography, offerings of the author's and/or publisher's additional books and other related merchandise, and colophon.

bestseller   Based on sales or orders by bookstores, wholesalers, and distributors, best-sellers are those titles that move in the largest quantities. Lists of bestselling books can be local (as in metropolitan newspapers), regional (typically in geographically keyed trade or consumer periodicals), or national (as in *USA Today*, *Publishers Weekly*, or the *New York Times*), as well as international. Fiction and nonfiction are usually listed separately, as are hardcover and paperback classifications. Depending on the list's purview, additional in-dustry-sector designations are used (such as how-to/self-improvement, religion and spiri-tuality, business and finance); in addition, bestseller lists can be keyed to particular genre or specialty fields (such as bestseller lists for mysteries, science fiction, or romance nov-els, and for historical works, biography, or popular science titles)—and virtually any other marketing category at the discretion of whoever issues the bestseller list (for in-stance African-American interest, lesbian and gay topics, youth market).

bibliography   A list of books, articles, and other sources that have been used in the writing of the text in which the bibliography appears. Complex works may break the bib-liography down into discrete subject areas or source categories, such as General History, Military History, War in the Twentieth Century, or Unionism and Pacifism.

binding   The materials that hold a book together (including the cover). Bindings are generally denoted as hardcover (featuring heavy cardboard covered with durable cloth and/or paper, and occasionally other materials) or paperback (using a pliable, resilient grade of paper, sometimes infused or laminated with other substances such as plastic). In the days when cloth was used lavishly, hardcover volumes were conventionally known as clothbound; and in the very old days, hardcover bindings sometimes featured tooled leather, silk, precious stones, and gold and silver leaf ornamentation.

biography   A history of a person's life. (*See* **authorized biography**, **autobiography**, **unauthorized biography**.)

blues (or bluelines)   Photographic proofs of the printing plates for a book. Blues are re-viewed as a means to inspect the set type, layout, and design of the book's pages before it goes to press.

blurb   A piece of written copy or extracted quotation used for publicity and promotional purposes, as on a flyer, in a catalog, or in an advertisement (*See* **cover blurbs**).

book club   A book club is a book-marketing operation that ships selected titles to sub-scribing members on a regular basis, sometimes at greatly reduced prices. Sales of a work to book clubs are negotiated through the publisher's subsidiary rights department (in the case of a bestseller or other work that has gained acclaim, these rights can be auctioned off). Terms vary, but the split of royalties between author and publisher is often 50%/50%. Book club sales are seen as blessed events by author, agent, and publisher alike.

book contract   A legally binding document between author and publisher that sets the terms for the advance, royalties, subsidiary rights, advertising, promotion, publicity—plus a host of other contingencies and responsibilities. Writers should therefore be thoroughly familiar with the concepts and terminology of the standard book-publishing contract.

book distribution   The method of getting books from the publisher's warehouse into the reader's hands. Distribution is traditionally through bookstores, but can include such means as telemarketing and mail-order sales, as well as sales through a variety of special-interest outlets such as health-food or New Age venues, sports and fitness emporiums, or sex shops. Publishers use their own sales forces as well as independent salespeople, wholesalers, and distributors. Many large and some small publishers distribute for other publishers, which can be a good source of income. A publisher's distribution network is extremely important, because it not only makes possible the vast sales of a bestseller but also affects the visibility of the publisher's entire list of books.

book jacket   (*See* **dust jacket**.)

book producer or **book packager**   An individual or company that can assume many of the roles in the publishing process. A book packager or producer may conceive the idea for a book (most often nonfiction) or series, bring together the professionals (including the writer) needed to produce the book(s), sell the individual manuscript or series project to a publisher, take the project through to manufactured product—or perform any selection of those functions, as commissioned by the publisher or other client (such as a corporation producing a corporate history as a premium or giveaway for employees and customers). The book producer may negotiate separate contracts with the publisher and with the writers, editors, and illustrators who contribute to the book.

book review   A critical appraisal of a book (often reflecting a reviewer's personal opinion or recommendation) that evaluates such aspects as organization and writing style, possible market appeal, and cultural, political, or literary significance. Before the public reads book reviews in the local and national print media, important reviews have been published in such respected book-trade journals as *Publishers Weekly*, *Kirkus Reviews*, *Library Journal*, and *Booklist*. A gushing review from one of these journals will encourage booksellers to order the book; copies of these raves will be used for promotion and publicity purposes by the publisher and will encourage other book reviewers nationwide to review the book.

Books in Print   Listings, published by R. R. Bowker, of books currently in print; these yearly volumes (along with periodic supplements such as *Forthcoming Books in Print*) provide ordering information including titles, authors, ISBN numbers, prices, whether the book is available in hardcover or paperback, and publisher names. Intended for use by the book trade, *Books in Print* is also of great value to writers who are researching and market-researching their projects. Listings are provided alphabetically by author, title, and subject area.

bound galleys   Copies of uncorrected typesetter's page proofs or printouts of electronically produced mechanicals that are bound together as advance copies of the book (compare **galleys**). Bound galleys are sent to trade journals (*See* **book review**) as well as to a limited number of reviewers who work under long lead times.

bulk sales   The sale at a set discount of many copies of a single title (the greater the number of books, the larger the discount).

byline   The name of the author of a given piece, indicating credit for having written a book or article. Ghostwriters, by definition, do not receive bylines.

C

casing   Alternate term for binding (*See* **binding**).

category fiction   Also known as genre fiction. Category fiction falls into an established (or newly originated) marketing category (which can then be subdivided for more precise target marketing). Fiction categories include action-adventure (with such further designations as military, paramilitary, law enforcement, romantic, and martial arts); crime novels (with points of view that range from deadpan cool to visionary, including humorous capers as well as gritty urban sagas); mysteries or detective fiction (hard-boiled, soft-boiled, procedurals, cozies); romances (including historicals as well as contemporaries); horror (supernatural, psychological, or technological); thrillers (tales of espionage, crisis, and the chase), Westerns, science fiction, and fantasy. (*See* **fantasy fiction**, **horror**, **romance fiction**, **science fiction**, **suspense fiction**, and **thriller**.)

CD or **computer CD**   High-capacity compact discs for use by readers via computer technology. **CD-ROM** is a particular variety; the term is somewhere between an acronym and an abbreviation—CD-ROMs are compact computer discs with read-only memory, meaning the reader is not able to modify or duplicate the contents. Many CDs are issued with a variety of audiovisual as well as textual components. When produced by publishers, these are sometimes characterized as books in electronic format. (*See* **multimedia**.)

children's books   Books for children. As defined by the book-publishing industry, children are generally readers aged 17 and younger; many houses adhere to a fine but firm editorial distinction between titles intended for younger readers (under 12) and young adults (generally aged 12 to 17). Children's books (also called juveniles) are produced according to a number of categories (often typified by age ranges), each with particular requisites regarding such elements as readability ratings, length, and inclusion of graphic elements. Picture books are often for very young readers, with such designations as toddlers (who do not themselves read) and preschoolers (who may have some reading ability). Other classifications include easy storybooks (for younger school children); middle-grade books (for elementary to junior high school students); and young adult (abbreviated YA, for readers through age 17).

coauthor   One who shares authorship of a work. Coauthors all have bylines. Coauthors share royalties based on their contributions to the book. (Compare **ghostwriter**.)

collaboration   Writers can collaborate with professionals in any number of fields. Often a writer can collaborate in order to produce books outside the writer's own areas of formally credentialed expertise (for example, a writer with an interest in exercise and nutrition may collaborate with a sports doctor on a health book). Though the writer may be billed as a coauthor (*See* **coauthor**), the writer does not necessarily receive a byline (in which case the writer is a **ghostwriter**) Royalties are shared, based on respective contributions to the book (including expertise or promotional abilities as well as the actual writing).

colophon   Strictly speaking, a colophon is a publisher's logo; in bookmaking, the term may also refer to a listing of the materials used, as well as credits for the design, composition, and production of the book. Such colophons are sometimes included in the back-matter or as part of the copyright page.

commercial fiction   Fiction written to appeal to as broad-based a readership as possible.

concept   A general statement of the idea behind a book.

cool   A modern colloquial expression that indicates satisfaction or approval, or may signify the maintenance of calm within a whirlwind. A fat contract for a new author is definitely cool.

cooperative advertising (co-op)   An agreement between a publisher and a bookstore. The publisher's book is featured in an ad for the bookstore (sometimes in conjunction with an author appearance or other special book promotion); the publisher contributes to the cost of the ad, which is billed at a lower (retail advertising) rate.

copublishing   Joint publishing of a book, usually by a publisher and another corporate entity such as a foundation, a museum, or a smaller publisher. An author can copublish with the publisher by sharing the costs and decision making and, ultimately, the profits.

copyeditor   An editor, responsible for the final polishing of a manuscript, who reads primarily in terms of appropriate word usage and grammatical expression, with an eye toward clarity and coherence of the material as presented, factual errors and inconsistencies, spelling, and punctuation. (*See* **editor**.)

copyright   The legal proprietary right to reproduce, have reproduced, publish, and sell copies of literary, musical, and other artistic works. The rights to literary properties reside in the author from the time the work is produced—regardless of whether a formal copyright registration is obtained. However, for legal recourse in the event of plagiarism or other infringement, the work must be registered with the U.S. Copyright Office, and all copies of the work must bear the copyright notice. (*See* **work-for-hire**.)

cover blurbs   Favorable quotes from other writers, celebrities, or experts in a book's subject area, which appear on the dust jacket and are used to enhance the book's point-of-purchase appeal to the potential book-buying public.

crash   Coarse gauze fabric used in bookbinding to strengthen the spine and joints of a book.

curriculum vitae   (abbreviated **c.v.**) Latin expression meaning "course of life"—in other words, the **résumé** (which see).

D

deadline   In book publishing, this not-so-subtle synonym is used for the author's due date for delivery of the completed manuscript to the publisher. The deadline can be as much as a full year before official publication date, unless the book is being produced quickly to coincide with or follow up a particular event.

delivery   Submission of the completed manuscript to the editor or publisher.

Dial-a-Writer   Members of the American Society of Journalists and Authors may be listed with the organization's project-referral service, Dial-a-Writer, which can provide accomplished writers in most specialty fields and subjects.

direct marketing   Advertising that involves a "direct response" (which is an equivalent term) from a consumer—for instance an order form or coupon in a book-review section or in the back of a book, or mailings (direct-mail advertising) to a group presumed to hold a special interest in a particular book.

display titles   Books that are produced to be eye-catching to the casual shopper in a bookstore setting are termed display titles. Often rich with flamboyant cover art, these publications are intended to pique bookbuyer excitement about the store's stock in general. Many display titles are stacked on their own freestanding racks; sometimes broad tables are laden with these items. A book shelved with its front cover showing on racks along with diverse other titles is technically a display title. Promotional or **premium** titles are likely to be display items, as are mass-market paperbacks and hardbacks with enormous bestseller potential. Check your local bookstore and find a copy of this edition of *Writer's Guide*—if not already racked in display manner, please adjust the bookshelf so that the front cover is displayed poster-like to catch the browser's eye (that's what *we* do routinely).

distributor   An agent or business that buys books from a publisher to resell, at a higher cost, to wholesalers, retailers, or individuals. Distribution houses are often excellent marketing enterprises, with their own roster of sales representatives, publicity and promotion personnel, and house catalogs. Skillful use of distribution networks can give a small publisher considerable national visibility.

dramatic rights   Legal permission to adapt a work for the stage. These rights initially belong to the author but can be sold or assigned to another party by the author.

dust jacket (also **dustcover** or **book jacket**)   The wrapper that covers the binding of hardcover books, designed especially for the book by either the publisher's art department or a freelance artist. Dust jackets were originally conceived to protect the book during shipping, but now their function is primarily promotional—to entice the browser to actually reach out and pick up the volume (and maybe even open it up for a taste before buying)—by means of attractive graphics and sizzling promotional copy.

dust-jacket copy   Descriptions of books printed on the dust-jacket flaps. Dust-jacket copy may be written by the book's editor, but is often either recast or written by in-house copywriters or freelance specialists. Editors send advance copies (*see* **bound galleys**) to other writers, experts, and celebrities to solicit quotable praise that will also appear on the jacket. (*See* also **blurb**.)

E

editor   Editorial responsibilities and titles vary from house to house (often being less strictly defined in smaller houses). In general, the duties of the editor-in-chief or executive editor are primarily administrative: managing personnel, scheduling, budgeting, and defining the editorial personality of the firm or imprint. Senior editors and acquisitions editors acquire manuscripts (and authors), conceive project ideas and find writers to carry them out, and may oversee the writing and rewriting of manuscripts. Managing editors have editorial and production responsibilities, coordinating and scheduling the book through the various phases of production. Associate and assistant editors edit; they are involved in much of the rewriting and reshaping of the manuscript, and may also have acquisitions duties. Copyeditors read the manuscript and style its punctuation, grammar, spelling, headings and subheadings, and so forth. Editorial assistants, laden with extensive clerical duties and general office work, perform some editorial duties as well—often as springboards to senior editorial positions.

Editorial Freelancers Association (EFA)   This organization of independent professionals offers a referral service, through both its annotated membership directory and its job phone line, as a means for authors and publishers to connect with writers, collaborators, researchers, and a wide range of editorial experts covering virtually all general and specialist fields.

el-hi   Books for elementary and/or high schools.

endnotes   Explanatory notes and/or source citations that appear either at the end of individual chapters or at the end of a book's text; used primarily in scholarly or academically oriented works.

epilogue   The final segment of a book, which comes "after the end." In both fiction and nonfiction, an epilogue offers commentary or further information, but does not bear directly on the book's central design.

F

fantasy   Fantasy is fiction that features elements of magic, wizardry, supernatural feats, and entities that suspend conventions of realism in the literary arts. Fantasy can resemble prose versions of epics and rhymes, may be informed by mythic cycles or folkloric material derived from cultures worldwide. Fantasy fiction may be guided primarily by the author's own distinctive imagery and personalized archetypes. Fantasies that involve heroic-erotic roundelays of the death-dance are often referred to as the sword-and-sorcery subgenre.

film rights   Like **dramatic rights**, these belong to the author, who may sell or option them to someone in the film industry—a producer or director, for example (or sometimes a specialist broker of such properties)—who will then try to gather the other professionals and secure the financial backing needed to convert the book into a film. (*See* **screenplay**.)

footbands   (*See* **headbands**.)

footnotes   Explanatory notes and/or source citations that appear at the bottom of a page. Footnotes are rare in general-interest books, the preferred style being either to work such information into the text or to list informational sources in the bibliography.

foreign agents   Persons who work with their United States counterparts to acquire rights for books from the U.S. for publication abroad. They can also represent U.S. publishers directly.

foreign market   Any foreign entity—a publisher, broadcast medium, etc.—in a position to buy rights. Authors share royalties with whoever negotiates the deal, or keep 100% if they do their own negotiating.

foreign rights   Translation or reprint rights that can be sold abroad. Foreign rights belong to the author but can be sold either country-by-country or en masse as world rights. Often the U.S. publisher will own world rights, and the author will be entitled to anywhere from 50% to 85% of these revenues.

foreword   An introductory piece written by the author or by an expert in the given field (*see* **introduction**). A foreword by a celebrity or well-respected authority is a strong selling point for a prospective author or, after publication, for the book itself.

Frankfurt Book Fair   The largest international publishing exhibition—with five hundred years of tradition behind it. The fair takes place every October in Frankfurt, Germany. Thousands of publishers, agents, and writers from all over the world negotiate, network, and buy and sell rights.

Freedom of Information Act   Ensures the protection of the public's right to access to public records—except in cases violating the right to privacy, national security, or certain other instances. A related law, the Government in the Sunshine Act, stipulates that certain government agencies announce and open their meetings to the public.

freight passthrough   The bookseller's freight cost (the cost of getting the book from the publisher to the bookseller). It is added to the basic invoice price charged the bookseller by the publisher.

frontlist   New titles published in a given season by a publisher. Frontlist titles customarily receive priority exposure in the front of the sales catalog—as opposed to backlist titles (usually found at the back of the catalog), which are previously published titles still in print.

frontmatter   The frontmatter of a book includes the elements that precede the text of the work, such as the title page, copyright page, dedication, epigraph, table of contents, foreword, preface, acknowledgments, and introduction.

fulfillment house   A firm commissioned to fulfill orders for a publisher—services may include warehousing, shipping, receiving returns, and mail-order and direct-marketing functions. Although more common for magazine publishers, fulfillment houses also serve book publishers.

G

galleys   Printer's proofs (or copies of proofs) on sheets of paper, or printouts of the electronically produced setup of the book's interior—the author's last chance to check for typos and make (usually minimal) revisions or additions to the copy (*see* **bound galleys**).

genre fiction   (*See* **category fiction**.)

ghostwriter   A writer without a byline, often without the remuneration and recognition that credited authors receive. Ghostwriters often get flat fees for their work, but even without royalties, experienced ghosts can receive quite respectable sums.

glossary   An alphabetical listing of special terms as they are used in a particular subject area, often with more in-depth explanations than would customarily be provided by dictionary definitions.

H

hardcover   Books bound in a format that uses thick, sturdy, relatively stiff binding boards and a cover composed (usually) of cloth spine and finished binding paper. Hardcover books are conventionally wrapped in a dust jacket. (*See* **binding**, **dust jacket**.)

headbands   Thin strips of cloth (often colored or patterned) that adorn the top of a book's spine where the signatures are held together. The headbands conceal the glue or other binding materials and are said to offer some protection against accumulation of dust (when properly attached). Such bands, placed at the bottom of the spine, are known as footbands.

hook   A term denoting the distinctive concept or theme of a work that sets it apart—as being fresh, new, or different from others in its field. A hook can be an author's special point of view, often encapsulated in a catchy or provocative phrase intended to attract or pique the interest of a reader, editor, or agent. One specialized function of a hook is to articulate what might otherwise be seen as dry albeit significant subject matter (academic or scientific topics; number-crunching drudgery such as home bookkeeping) into an exciting, commercially attractive package.

horror   The horror classification denotes works that traffic in the bizarre, awful, and scary in order to entertain as well as explicate the darkness at the heart of the reader's soul. Horror subgenres may be typified according to the appearance of were-creatures, vampires, human-induced monsters, or naturally occurring life forms and spirit entities— or absence thereof. Horror fiction traditionally makes imaginative literary use of paranormal phenomena, occult elements, and psychological motifs. (*See* **category fiction**, **suspense fiction**.)

how-to books   An immensely popular category of books ranging from purely instructional (arts and crafts, for example) to motivational (popular psychology, self-awareness, self-improvement, inspirational) to get-rich-quick (such as in real estate or personal investment).

hypertext   Works in hypertext are meant to be more than words and other images. These productions (ingrained magnetically on computer diskette or CD) are conceived to take advantage of readers' and writers' propensities to seek out twists in narrative trajectories and to bushwhack from the main path of multifaceted reference topics. Hypertext books incorporate documents, graphics, sounds, and even blank slates upon which readers may compose their own variations on the authored components. The computer's capacities to afford such diversions can bring reader and hypertext literateur so close as to gain entry to each other's mind-sets—which is what good books have always done.

I

imprint   A separate line of product within a publishing house. Imprints run the gamut of complexity, from those composed of one or two series to those offering full-fledged and diversified lists. Imprints as well enjoy different gradations of autonomy from the parent company. An imprint may have its own editorial department (perhaps consisting of as few as one editor), or house acquisitions editors may assign particular titles for release on appropriate specialized imprints. An imprint may publish a certain kind of book (juvenile or paperback or travel books), or have its own personality (such as a literary or contemporary tone). An individual imprint's categories often overlap with other imprints or with the publisher's core list, but some imprints maintain a small-house feel within an otherwise enormous conglomerate. The imprint can offer the distinct advantages of a personalized editorial approach, while availing itself of the larger company's production, publicity, marketing, sales, and advertising resources.

index   An alphabetical directory at the end of a book that references names and subjects discussed in the book and the pages where such mentions can be found.

instant book   A book produced quickly to appear in bookstores as soon as possible after (for instance) a newsworthy event to which it is relevant.

international copyright   Rights secured for countries that are members of the International Copyright Convention (*see* entry below for **International Copyright Convention**) and respect the authority of the international copyright symbol, ©.

International Copyright Convention   Countries that are signatories to the various international copyright treaties. Some treaties are contingent upon certain conditions being met at the time of publication, so an author should inquire before publication into a particular country's laws.

introduction   Preliminary remarks pertaining to a piece. Like a foreword, an introduction can be written by the author or an appropriate authority on the subject. If a book has both a foreword and an introduction, the foreword will be written by someone other than the author; the introduction will be more closely tied to the text and will be written by the book's author. (*See* **foreword.**)

ISBN (International Standard Book Number)   A 10-digit number that is keyed to and identifies the title and publisher of a book. It is used for ordering and cataloging books and appears on all dust jackets, on the back cover of the book, and on the copyright page.

ISSN (International Standard Serial Number)   An 8-digit cataloging and ordering number that identifies all U.S. and foreign periodicals.

J

juveniles   (*See* **children's books.**)

K

kill fee   A fee paid by a magazine when it cancels a commissioned article. The fee is only a certain percentage of the agreed-on payment for the assignment (no more than 50%). Not all publishers pay kill fees; a writer should make sure to formalize such an arrangement in advance. Kill fees are sometimes involved in work-for-hire projects in book publishing.

L

lead   The crucial first few sentences, phrases, or words of anything—be it a query letter, book proposal, novel, news release, advertisement, or sales tip sheet. A successful lead immediately hooks the reader, consumer, editor, or agent.

lead title   A frontlist book featured by the publisher during a given season—one the publisher believes should do extremely well commercially. Lead titles are usually those given the publisher's maximum promotional push.

letterhead   Business stationery and envelopes imprinted with the company's (or, in such a case, the writer's) name, address, and logo—a convenience as well as an impressive asset for a freelance writer.

letterpress   A form of printing in which set type is inked, then impressed directly onto the printing surface. Now used primarily for limited-run books-as-fine-art projects. (*See* **offset.**)

libel   Defamation of an individual or individuals in a published work, with malice afore-thought. In litigation, the falsity of the libelous statements or representations, as well the intention of malice, has to be proved for there to be libel; in addition, financial damages to the parties so libeled must be incurred as a result of the material in question for there to be an assessment of the amount of damages to be awarded to a claimant. This is con-trasted to slander, which is defamation through the spoken word.

Library of Congress   The largest library in the world is in Washington, D.C. As part of its many services, the LOC will supply a writer with up-to-date sources and bibliogra-phies in all fields, from arts and humanities to science and technology. For details, write to the Library of Congress, Central Services Division, Washington, DC 20540.

Library of Congress Catalog Card Number   An identifying number issued by the Library of Congress to books it has accepted for its collection. The publication of those books, which are submitted by the publisher, are announced by the Library of Congress to libraries, which use Library of Congress numbers for their own ordering and cataloging purposes.

Literary Market Place (LMP)   An annual directory of the publishing industry that con-tains a comprehensive list of publishers, alphabetically and by category, with their ad-dresses, phone numbers, some personnel, and the types of books they publish. Also included are various publishing-allied listings, such as literary agencies, writer's confer-ences and competitions, and editorial and distribution services. *LMP* is published by R. R. Bowker and is available in most public libraries.

literature   Written works of fiction and nonfiction in which compositional excellence and advancement in the art of writing are higher priorities than are considerations of profit or commercial appeal.

logo   A company or product identifier—for example, a representation of a company's initials or a drawing that is the exclusive property of that company. In publishing usage, a virtual equivalent to the trademark.

M

mainstream fiction   Nongenre fiction, excluding literary or avant-garde fiction, that ap-peals to a general readership.

marketing plan   The entire strategy for selling a book: its publicity, promotion, sales, and advertising.

mass-market paperback   Less-expensive smaller-format paperbacks that are sold from racks (in such venues as supermarkets, variety stores, drugstores, and specialty shops) as well as in bookstores. Also referred to as rack (or rack-sized) editions.

mechanicals   Typeset copy and art mounted on boards to be photocopied and printed. Also referred to as pasteups.

midlist books   Generally mainstream fiction and nonfiction books that traditionally formed the bulk of a publisher's list (nowadays often by default rather than intent). Midlist books are expected to be commercially viable but not explosive bestsellers—nor are they viewed as distinguished, critically respected books that can be scheduled for small print runs and aimed at select readerships. Agents may view such projects as a poor return for the effort, since they generally garner a low-end advance; editors and publishers (especially the sales force) may decry midlist works as being hard to market; prospective readers often find midlist books hard to buy in bookstores (they have short shelf lives). Hint for writers: Don't present your work as a midlist item.

multimedia   Presentations of sound and light, words in magnetically graven image—and any known combination thereof as well as nuances yet to come. Though computer CD is the dominant wrapper for these works, technological innovation is the hallmark of the electronic-publishing arena, and new formats will expand the creative and market potential. Multimedia books are publishing events; their advent suggests alternative avenues for authors as well as adaptational tie-ins with the world of print. Meanwhile, please stay tuned for virtual reality, artificial intelligence, and electronic end-user distribution of product.

multiple contract   A book contract that includes a provisional agreement for a future book or books. (*See* **option clause**.)

mystery stories or **mysteries** (*See* **suspense fiction**.)

N

net receipts   The amount of money a publisher actually receives for sales of a book: the retail price minus the bookseller's discount and/or other discount. The number of returned copies is factored in, bringing down even further the net amount received per book. Royalties are sometimes figured on these lower amounts rather than on the retail price of the book.

New Age   An eclectic category that encompasses health, medicine, philosophy, religion, and the occult—presented from an alternative or multicultural perspective. Although the term has achieved currency relatively recently, some publishers have been producing serious books in these categories for decades.

novella   A work of fiction falling in length between a short story and a novel.

O

offset (offset lithography)   A printing process that involves the transfer of wet ink from a (usually photosensitized) printing plate onto an intermediate surface (such as a rubber-coated cylinder) and then onto the paper. For commercial purposes, this method has replaced letterpress, whereby books were printed via direct impression of inked type on paper.

option clause/right of first refusal In a book contract, a clause that stipulates that the publisher will have the exclusive right to consider and make an offer for the author's next book. However, the publisher is under no obligation to publish the book, and in most variations of the clause the author may, under certain circumstances, opt for publication elsewhere. (*See* **multiple contract**.)

outline Used for both a book proposal and the actual writing and structuring of a book, an outline is a hierarchical listing of topics that provides the writer (and the proposal reader) with an overview of the ideas in a book in the order in which they are to be presented.

out-of-print books Books no longer available from the publisher; rights usually revert to the author.

P

package The package is the actual book; the physical product.

packager (*See* **book producer**.)

page proof The final typeset copy of the book, in page-layout form, before printing.

paperback Books bound with a flexible, stress-resistant, paper covering material. (*See* **binding**.)

paperback originals Books published, generally, in paperback editions only; sometimes the term refers to those books published simultaneously in hardcover and paperback. These books are often mass-market genre fiction (romances, Westerns, Gothics, mysteries, horror, and so forth) as well as contemporary literary fiction, cookbooks, humor, career books, self-improvement, and how-to books—the categories continue to expand.

pasteups (*See* **mechanicals**.)

permissions The right to quote or reprint published material, obtained by the author from the copyright holder.

picture book A copiously illustrated book, often with very simple, limited text, intended for preschoolers and very young children.

plagiarism The false presentation of someone else's writing as one's own. In the case of copyrighted work, plagiarism is illegal.

preface An element of a book's frontmatter. In the preface, the author may discuss the purpose behind the format of the book, the type of research upon which it is based, its genesis, or underlying philosophy.

premium Books sold at a reduced price as part of a special promotion. Premiums can thus be sold to a bookseller, who in turn sells them to the bookbuyer (as with a line of modestly priced art books). Alternately, such books may be produced as part of a broader marketing package. For instance, an organization may acquire a number of books (such as its own corporate history or biography of its founder) for use in personnel training and as giveaways to clients; or a nutrition/recipe book may be displayed along with a company's diet foods in non-bookstore outlets. (*See* **special sales.**)

press agent   (*See* **publicist.**)

press kit   A promotional package that includes a press release, tip sheet, author biography and photograph, reviews, and other pertinent information. The press kit can be put together by the publisher's publicity department or an independent publicist and sent with a review copy of the book to potential reviewers and to media professionals responsible for booking author appearances.

price   There are several prices pertaining to a single book: The invoice price is the amount the publisher charges the bookseller; the retail, cover, or list price is what the consumer pays.

printer's error (PE)   A typographical error made by the printer or typesetting facility, not by the publisher's staff. PEs are corrected at the printer's expense.

printing plate   A surface that bears a reproduction of the set type and artwork of a book, from which the pages are printed.

producer   (*See* **book producer.**)

proposal   A detailed presentation of the book's concept, used to gain the interest and services of an agent and to sell the project to a publisher.

public domain   Material that is uncopyrighted, whose copyright has expired, or is uncopyrightable. The last includes government publications, jokes, titles—and, it should be remembered, ideas.

publication date (or **pub date**)   A book's official date of publication, customarily set by the publisher to fall 6 weeks after completed bound books are delivered to the warehouse. The publication date is used to focus the promotional activities on behalf of the title—in order that books will have had time to be ordered, shipped, and be available in the stores to coincide with the appearance of advertising and publicity.

publicist (press agent)   The publicity professional who handles the press releases for new books and arranges the author's publicity tours and other promotional venues (such as interviews, speaking engagements, and book signings).

publisher's catalog   A seasonal sales catalog that lists and describes a publisher's new books; it is sent to all potential buyers, including individuals who request one. Catalogs range from the basic to the glitzy, and often include information on the author, on print quantity, and the amount of money slated to be spent on publicity and promotion.

publisher's discount   The percentage by which a publisher discounts the retail price of a book to a bookseller, often based in part on the number of copies purchased.

Publishers' Trade List Annual A collection of current and backlist catalogs arranged alphabetically by publisher, available in many libraries.

Publishers Weekly (PW) The publishing industry's chief trade journal. *PW* carries announcements of upcoming books, respected book reviews, interviews with authors and publishing-industry professionals, special reports on various book categories, and trade news (such as mergers, rights sales, and personnel changes).

Q

quality In publishing parlance, the word *quality* in reference to a book category (such as quality fiction) or format (quality paperback) is a term of art—individual works or lines so described are presented as outstanding products.

query letter A brief written presentation to an agent or editor designed to pitch both the writer and the book idea.

R

remainders Unsold book stock. Remainders can include titles that have not sold as well as anticipated, in addition to unsold copies of later printings of bestsellers. These volumes are often remaindered—that is, remaining stock is purchased from the publisher at a huge discount and resold to the public.

reprint A subsequent edition of material that is already in print, especially publication in a different format—the paperback reprint of a hardcover, for example.

résumé A summary of an individual's career experience and education. When a résumé is sent to prospective agents or publishers, it should contain the author's vital publishing credits, specialty credentials, and pertinent personal experience. Also referred to as the curriculum vitae or, more simply, vita.

returns Unsold books returned to a publisher by a bookstore, for which the store may receive full or partial credit (depending on the publisher's policy, the age of the book, and so on).

reversion-of-rights clause In the book contract, a clause that states that if the book goes out of print or the publisher fails to reprint the book within a stipulated length of time, all rights revert to the author.

review copy A free copy of a (usually) new book sent to print and electronic media that review books for their audiences.

romance fiction or **romance novels** Modern or period love stories, always with happy endings, which range from the tepid to the torrid. Except for certain erotic-specialty lines, romances do not feature graphic sex. Often mistakenly pigeonholed by those who do not read them, romances and romance writers have been influential in the movement away from passive and coddled female fictional characters to the strong, active modern woman in a tale that reflects areas of topical social concern.

royalty   The percentage of the retail cost of a book that is paid to the author for each copy sold after the author's advance has been recouped. Some publishers structure royalties as a percentage payment against net receipts.

S

sales conference   A meeting of a publisher's editorial and sales departments and senior promotion and publicity staff members. A sales conference covers the upcoming season's new books, and marketing strategies are discussed. Sometimes sales conferences are the basis upon which proposed titles are bought or not.

sales representative (sales rep)   A member of the publisher's sales force or an independent contractor who, armed with a book catalog and order forms, visits bookstores in a certain territory to sell books to retailers.

SASE (self-addressed stamped envelope)   It is customary for an author to enclose SASEs with query letters, with proposals, and with manuscript submissions. Many editors and agents do not reply if a writer has neglected to enclose an SASE with correspondence or submitted materials.

satisfactory clause   In book contracts, a publisher will reserve the right to refuse publication of a manuscript that is not deemed satisfactory. Because the author may be forced to pay back the publisher's advance if the complete work is found to be unsatisfactory, in order to protect the author the specific criteria for publisher satisfaction should be set forth in the contract.

science fiction   Science fiction includes the hardcore, imaginatively embellished technological/scientific novel as well as fiction that is even slightly futuristic (often with an after-the-holocaust milieu—nuclear, environmental, extraterrestrial, genocidal). An element much valued by editors who acquire for the literary expression of this cross-media genre is the ability of the author to introduce elements that transcend and extend conventional insight.

science fiction/fantasy   A category fiction designation that actually collapses two genres into one (for bookseller-marketing reference, of course—though it drives some devotees of these separate fields of writing nuts). In addition, many editors and publishers specialize in both these genres and thus categorize their interests with catchphrases such as sci-fi/fantasy.

screenplay   A film script—either original or one based on material published previously in another form, such as a television docudrama based on a nonfiction book or a movie thriller based on a suspense novel. (Compare with **teleplay**.)

self-publishing   A publishing project wherein an author pays for the costs of manufacturing and selling his or her own book and retains all money from the book's sale. This is a risky venture but one that can be immensely profitable (especially when combined with an author's speaking engagements or imaginative marketing techniques); in addition, if successful, self-publication can lead to distribution or publication by a commercial publisher. Compare with **subsidy publishing**.

self-syndication   Management by writers or journalists of functions that are otherwise performed by syndicates specializing in such services. In self-syndication, it is the writer who manages copyrights, negotiates fees, and handles sales, billing, and other tasks involved in circulating journalistic pieces through newspapers, magazines, or other periodicals that pick up the author's column or run a series of articles.

serial rights   Reprint rights sold to periodicals. First serial rights include the right to publish the material before anyone else (generally before the book is released, or coinciding with the book's official publication)—either for the U.S., a specific country, or for a wider territory. Second serial rights cover material already published, either in a book or another periodical.

serialization   The reprinting of a book or part of a book in a newspaper or magazine. Serialization before (or perhaps simultaneously with) the publication of the book is called first serial. The first reprint after publication (either as a book or by another periodical) is called second serial.

series   Books published as a group either because of their related subject matter (such as a biographical series on modern artists or on World War II aircraft) and/or single authorship (a set of works by Djuna Barnes, a group of books about science and society, or a series of titles geared to a particular diet-and-fitness program). Special series lines can offer a ready-made niche for an industrious author or compiler/editor who is up to date on a publisher's program and has a brace of pertinent qualifications and/or contacts. In contemporary fiction, some genre works are published in series form (such as family sagas, detective series, fantasy cycles).

shelf life   The amount of time an unsold book remains on the bookstore shelf before the store manager pulls it to make room for newer incoming stock with greater (or at least untested) sales potential.

short story   A brief piece of fiction that is more pointed and more economically detailed as to character, situation, and plot than a novel. Published collections of short stories—whether by one or several authors—often revolve around a single theme, express related outlooks, or comprise variations within a genre.

signature   A group of book pages that have been printed together on one large sheet of paper that is then folded and cut in preparation for being bound, along with the book's other signatures, into the final volume.

simultaneous publication   The issuing at the same time of more than one edition of a work, such as in hardcover and trade paperback. Simultaneous releases can be expanded to include (though rarely) deluxe gift editions of a book as well as mass-market paper versions. Audio versions of books are most often timed to coincide with the release of the first print edition.

simultaneous (or multiple) submissions   The submission of the same material to more than one publisher at the same time. Although simultaneous submission is a common practice, publishers should always be made aware that it is being done. Multiple submissions by an author to several agents is, on the other hand, a practice that is sometimes not regarded with great favor by the agent.

slush pile   The morass of unsolicited manuscripts at a publishing house or literary agency, which may fester indefinitely awaiting (perhaps perfunctory) review. Some publishers or agencies do not maintain slush piles per se—unsolicited manuscripts are slated for instant or eventual return without review (if an SASE is included) or may otherwise be literally or figuratively pitched to the wind. Querying a targeted publisher or agent before submitting a manuscript is an excellent way of avoiding, or at least minimizing the possibility of, such an ignoble fate.

software   Programs that run on a computer. Word-processing software includes programs that enable writers to compose, edit, store, and print material. Professional-quality software packages incorporate such amenities as databases that can feed the results of research electronically into the final manuscript, alphabetization and indexing functions, and capabilities for constructing tables and charts and adding graphics to the body of the manuscript. Software should be appropriate to both the demands of the work at hand and the requirements of the publisher (which may contract for a manuscript suitable for on-disk editing and electronic design, composition, and typesetting).

special sales   Sales of a book to appropriate retailers other than bookstores (for example, wine guides to liquor stores). This classification also includes books sold as premiums (for example, to a convention group or a corporation) or for other promotional purposes. Depending on volume, per-unit costs can be very low, and the book can be custom-designed. (*See* **premiums**.)

spine   That portion of the book's casing (or binding) that backs the bound page signatures and is visible when the volume is aligned on a bookshelf among other volumes.

stamping   In book publishing, the stamp is the impression of ornamental type and images (such as a logo or monogram) on the book's binding. The stamping process involves using a die with raised or intaglioed surface to apply ink stamping or metallic-leaf stamping.

subsidiary rights   The reprint, serial, movie and television, as well as audiotape and videotape rights deriving from a book. The division of profits between publisher and author from the sales of these rights is determined through negotiation. In more elaborately commercial projects, further details such as syndication of related articles and licensing of characters may ultimately be involved.

subsidy publishing   A mode of publication wherein the author pays a publishing company to produce his or her work, which may thus appear superficially to have been published conventionally. Subsidy publishing (alias vanity publishing) is generally more expensive than self-publishing, because a successful subsidy house makes a profit on all its contracted functions, charging fees well beyond the publisher's basic costs for production and services.

suspense fiction   Fiction within a number of genre categories that emphasize suspense as well as the usual (and sometimes unusual) literary techniques to keep the reader engaged.

Suspense fiction encompasses novels of crime and detection (regularly referred to as mysteries—these include English-style cozies; American-style hard-boiled detective stories; dispassionate law-enforcement procedurals; crime stories); action-adventure; espionage novels; technothrillers; tales of psychological suspense; and horror. A celebrated aspect of suspense fiction's popular appeal—one that surely accounts for much of this broad category's sustained market vigor—is the interactive element: The reader may choose to challenge the tale itself by attempting to outwit the author and solve a crime before detectives do, figure out how best to defeat an all-powerful foe before the hero does, or parse out the elements of a conspiracy before the writer reveals the whole story.

syndicated column   Material published simultaneously in a number of newspapers or magazines. The author shares the income from syndication with the syndicate that negotiates the sale. (*See* **self-syndication**.)

syndication rights   (*See* **self-syndication**, **subsidiary rights**.)

synopsis   A summary in paragraph form, rather than in outline format. The synopsis is an important part of a book proposal. For fiction, the synopsis portrays the high points of story line and plot, succinctly and dramatically. In a nonfiction book proposal, the synopsis describes the thrust and content of the successive chapters (and/or parts) of the manuscript.

T

table of contents   A listing of a book's chapters and other sections (such as the front-matter, appendix, index, and bibliography) or of a magazine's articles and columns, in the order in which they appear; in published versions, the table of contents indicates the respective beginning page numbers.

tabloid   A smaller-than-standard-size newspaper (daily, weekly, or monthly). Traditionally, certain tabloids are distinguished by sensationalism of approach and content rather than by straightforward reportage of newsworthy events. In common parlance, *tabloid* is used to describe works in various media (including books) that cater to immoderate tastes (for example, tabloid exposé, tabloid television; the tabloidization of popular culture).

teleplay   A **screenplay** geared toward television production. Similar in overall concept to screenplays for the cinema, teleplays are nonetheless inherently concerned with such TV-loaded provisions as the physical dimensions of the smaller screen, and formal elements of pacing and structure keyed to stipulated program length and the placement of commercial advertising. Attention to these myriad television-specific demands are fundamental to the viability of a project.

terms   The financial conditions agreed to in a book contract.

theme   A general term for the underlying concept of a book. (*See* **hook**.)

thriller   A thriller is a novel of suspense with a plot structure that reinforces the elements of gamesmanship and the chase, with a sense of the hunt being paramount.

Thrillers can be spy novels, tales of geopolitical crisis, legal thrillers, medical thrillers, technothrillers, domestic thrillers. The common thread is a growing sense of threat and the excitement of pursuit.

tip sheet   An information sheet on a single book that presents general publication information (publication date, editor, ISBN, etc.), a brief synopsis of the book, information on relevant other books (sometimes competing titles), and other pertinent marketing data such as author profile and advance blurbs. The tip sheet is given to the sales and publicity departments; a version of the tip sheet is also included in press kits.

title page   The page at the front of a book that lists the title, subtitle, author (and other contributors, such as translator or illustrator), as well as the publishing house and sometimes its logo.

trade books   Books distributed through the book trade—meaning bookstores and major book clubs—as opposed to, for example, mass-market paperbacks, which are often sold at magazine racks, newsstands, and supermarkets as well.

trade discount   The discount from the cover or list price that a publisher gives the bookseller. It is usually proportional to the number of books ordered (the larger the order, the greater the discount), and typically varies between 40% and 50%.

trade list   A catalog of all of a publisher's books in print, with ISBNs and order information. The trade list sometimes includes descriptions of the current season's new books.

trade (quality) paperbacks   Reprints or original titles published in paperback format, larger in dimension than mass-market paperbacks, and distributed through regular retail book channels. Trade paperbacks tend to be in the neighborhood of twice the price of an equivalent mass-market paperback version and about half to two-thirds the price of hardcover editions.

trade publishers   Publishers of books for a general readership—that is, nonprofessional, nonacademic books that are distributed primarily through bookstores.

translation rights   Rights sold either to a foreign agent or directly to a foreign publisher, either by the author's agent or by the original publisher.

treatment   In screenwriting, a full narrative description of the story, including sample dialogue.

U

unauthorized biography   A history of a person's life written without the consent or collaboration of the subject or the subject's survivors.

university press   A publishing house affiliated with a sponsoring university. The university press is generally nonprofit and subsidized by the respective university. Generally, university presses publish noncommercial scholarly nonfiction books written by academics, and their lists may include literary fiction, criticism, and poetry. Some university presses also specialize in titles of regional interest, and many acquire projects intended for commercial book-trade distribution.

unsolicited manuscript   A manuscript sent to an editor or agent without being requested by the editor/agent.

V

vanity press   A publisher that publishes books only at an author's expense—and will generally agree to publish virtually anything that is submitted and paid for. (See **subsidy publishing**.)

vita   Latin word for "life." A shortened equivalent term for *curriculum vitae* (*See* **résumé**).

W

word count   The number of words in a given document. When noted on a manuscript, the word count is usually rounded off to the nearest 100 words.

work-for-hire   Writing done for an employer, or writing commissioned by a publisher or book packager who retains ownership of, and all rights pertaining to, the written material.

Y

young-adult (YA) books   Books for readers generally between the ages of 12 and 17. Young-adult fiction often deals with issues of concern to contemporary teens.

young readers or **younger readers**   Publishing terminology for the range of publications that address the earliest readers. Sometimes a particular house's young-readers' program typifies books for those who do not yet read; which means these books have to hook the caretakers and parents who actually buy them. In certain quirky turns of everyday publishing parlance, *young readers* can mean anyone from embryos through young adults (and "young" means *you* when you want it to). This part may be confusing (as is often the case with publishing usage): Sometimes *younger adult* means only that the readership is allegedly hip, including those who would eschew kid's books as being inherently lame and those who are excruciatingly tapped into the current cultural pulse, regardless of cerebral or life-span quotient.

Z

zombie (or **zombi**)   In idiomatic usage, a zombie is a person whose conduct approximates that of an automaton. Harking back to the term's origins as a figure of speech for the resurrected dead or a reanimated cadaver, such folks are not customarily expected to exhibit an especially snazzy personality or be aware of too many things going on around them; hence some people in book-publishing circles may be characterized as zombies.

Suggested Resources

SELF-PUBLISHING RESOURCES

The Art of Self-Publishing
by Bonnie Stahlman Speer
Reliance Press
60-64 Hardinge Street
Deniliquin, NSW, 2710
Australia
e-mail: reliance@reliancepress.com.au

Book Production: Composition, Layout, Editing & Design. Getting It Ready for Printing.
by Dan Poynter
Para Publishing
PO Box 8206-240
Santa Barbara, CA 93118-8206
805-968-7277   fax: 805 968-1379
Cellular: 805-680-2298
e-mail: DanPoynter@aol.com
75031.3534@compuserve.com

Business and Legal Forms for Authors and Self-Publishers
by Tad Crawford
Allworth Press
10 East 23rd Street, Suite 210
New York, NY 10010
212-777-8395

The Complete Guide to Self-Publishing: Everything You Need to Know to Write, Publish, Promote and Sell Your Own Book
by Tom Ross, Marilyn J. Ross
Writers Digest Books
1507 Dana Avenue
Cincinnati, OH 45207
513-531-2222   fax: 531-531-4744

The Complete Self-Publishing Handbook
by David M. Brownstone, Irene M. Franck
Plume
375 Hudson Street
New York, NY 10014
212-366-2000

The Economical Guide to Self-Publishing:
How to Produce and Market Your Book on a Budget
by Linda Foster Radke, Mary E. Hawkins (Editor)
Five Star Publications
PO Box 6698
Chandler, AZ 85246-6698
480-940-8182

Exports/Foreign Rights, Selling U.S. Books Abroad
by Dan Poynter
Para Publishing
PO Box 8206-240
Santa Barbara, CA 93118-8206
805-968-7277   fax: 805968-1379
Cellular: 805-680-2298
e-mail: DanPoynter@aol.com
75031.3534@compuserve.com

A Guide to Successful Self-Publishing
by Stephen Wagner
Prentice Hall Direct
240 Frisch Court
Paramus, NJ 07652
201-909-6200

How to Make Money Publishing from Home: Everything You Need to Know to
Successfully Publish: Books, Newsletters, Greeting Cards, Zines, and Software
by Lisa Shaw
Prima Publishing
3000 Lava Ridge Ct.
Roseville, CA 95661
916-787-7000   fax: 916-787-7001
e-mail: sales@primapub.com

How to Publish, Promote, and Sell Your Own Book
by Robert Lawrence Holt
St. Martin's Press
175 Fifth Avenue
New York, NY 10010
212-674-5151

How You Can Become a Successful Self-Publisher in America and Elsewhere
by Paul Chika Emekwulu
Novelty Books
PO Box 2482
Norman, OK 73070
Tel/Fax: 405-447-9019
e-mail: novelty@telepath.com

The Publish It Yourself Handbook (25th Anniversary Edition)
by Bill Henderson (Introduction)
W. W. Norton & Co.
500 Fifth Avenue
New York, NY 10110
212-354-5500

Publish Your Own Novel
by Connie Shelton, Lee Ellison (Editor)
Intrigue Press
PO Box 27553
Philadelphia, PA 19118
800-996-9783

The Self-Publisher's Writing Journal
by Lia Relova
Pumpkin Enterprises
12 Packet Road
Palos Verdes, CA 90275
e-mail: princesslia@hotmail.com

The Self-Publishing Manual: How to Write, Print & Sell Your Own Book
by Dan Poynter
Para Publishing
PO Box 8206-240
Santa Barbara, CA 93118-8206
805-968-7277   fax: 805-968-1379
Cellular: 805-680-2298
e-mail: DanPoynter@aol.com
75031.3534@compuserve.com

Smart Self-Publishing: An Author's Guide to Producing a Marketable Book
by Linda G. Salisbury
Tabby House
4429 Shady Lane
Charlotte Harbor, FL 33980-3024
941-629-7646   fax: 941-629-4270,

A Simple Guide to Self-Publishing: A Step-by-Step Handbook to Prepare, Print, Distribute & Promote Your Own Book—3rd Edition
by Mark Ortman
Wise Owl Books
PO Box 29205
Bellingham, WA 98228
360-671-5858
e-mail: publish@wiseowlbooks.com

The Woman's Guide to Self-Publishing
by Donna M. Murphy
Irie Publishing
301 Boardwalk Drive, PO Box 273123
Fort Collins, CO 80527-3123
970-482-4402   fax: 970 482-4402
e-mail: iriepub@verinet.com

INDUSTRY RESOURCES

30 Steps to Becoming a Writer: And Getting Published: The Complete Starter Kit for Aspiring Writers
by Scott Edelstein
Writers Digest Books
1507 Dana Avenue
Cincinnati, OH 45207
513-531-2222   fax: 531-531-4744

1001 Ways to Market Your Books: For Authors and Publishers: Includes over 100 Proven Marketing Tips Just for Authors
by John Kremer
Open Horizons
PO Box 205
Fairfield IA 52556

1,818 Ways to Write Better & Get Published
by Scott Edelstein
Writers Digest Books
1507 Dana Avenue
Cincinnati, OH 45207
513-531-2222   fax: 531-531-4744

2000 Poet's Market: 1,800 Places to Publish Your Poetry (Poet's Market, 2000)
by Chantelle Bentley (Editor)
Writers Digest Books
1507 Dana Avenue
Cincinnati, OH 45207
513-531-2222   fax: 531-531-4744

2000 Writer's Market: 8,000 Editors Who Buy What You Write (Writers Market 2000)
Electronic version also available
by Kirsten Holm (Editor), Donya Dickerson (Editor)
Writers Digest Books
1507 Dana Avenue
Cincinnati, OH 45207
513-531-2222   fax: 531-531-4744

The Art and Science of Book Publishing
by Herbert S. Bailey, Jr.
Ohio University Press
Scott Quadrangle
Athens, Ohio 45701

The Author's Guide to Marketing Your Book:
From Start to Success, for Writers and Publishers
by Don Best, Peter Goodman
Stone Bridge Press
PO Box 8208
Berkeley, CA 94707
800-947-7271   fax: 510-524-8711
e-mail: sbporter@stonebridge.com

An Author's Guide to Publishing
by Michael Legat
Robert Hale Ltd.
Clerkenwell House 45-47
Clerkenwell Green, London
England EC1R 0HT
0171-251-2661

Book Editors Talk to Writers
by Judy Mandell
John Wiley & Sons
605 Third Avenue
New York, NY 10158-0012
212-850-6000   fax: 212-850-6088
e-mail: info@wiley.com

Book Promotion for Virgins: Answers to a New Author's
Questions About Marketing and Publicity
by Lorna Tedder
Spilled Candy Publications
PO Box 5202
Niceville FL 32578-5202
850-897-4644
e-mail: orders@spilledcandy.com

Book Publishing: The Basic Introduction
by John P. Dessauer
Continuum Publishing Group
370 Lexington Avenue
New York, NY 10017
212-953-5858

Breaking into Print: How to Write and Publish Your First Book
by Jane L. Evanson, Luanne Dowling
Kendall/Hunt Publishing Company
4050 Westmark Drive, PO Box 1840
Dubuque, Iowa 52004-1840
800-228-0810, 319-589-1000

The Career Novelist: A Literary Agent Offers Strategies for Success
by Donald Maass
Heinemann
22 Salmon Street
Port Melbourne Vic. 3207
Australia
e-mail: customer@hi.com.au

The Case of Peter Rabbit: Changing Conditions of Literature for Children
by Margaret MacKey
Garland Publishing
29 W. 35th Street
New York, New York 10001-2299
212-216-7800   fax: 212-564-7854
e-mail: info@taylorandfrancis.com

Children's Writer's & Illustrator's Market, 2000:
800 Editors & Art Directors Who Buy Your Writing & Illustrations
by Alice Pope (Editor)
Writers Digest Books
1507 Dana Avenue
Cincinnati, OH 45207
513-531-2222   fax: 531-531-4744

The Complete Guide to Book Publicity
by Jodee Blanco
Allworth Press
10 East 23rd Street, Suite 210
New York, NY, 10010
212-777-8395

The Complete Guide to Writer's Groups, Conferences, and Workshops
by Eileen Malone
John Wiley & Sons
605 Third Avenue
New York, NY 10158-0012
212-850-6000   fax: 212-850-6088
e-mail: info@wiley.com

The Complete Guide to Writing Fiction and Nonfiction—And Getting It Published
by Patricia Kubis, Robert Howland, Pat Kubis, Bob Howland
Prentice Hall Direct
240 Frisch Court
Paramus, NJ 07652
201-909-6200

A Complete Guide to Writing for Publication
by Susan Titus Osborn (Editor)
ACW Press
5501 N. 7th Ave., # 502
Phoenix, AZ 85013
877-868-9673
e-mail: editor@acwpress.com

The Complete Idiot's Guide to Getting Published
by Sheree Bykofsky, Jennifer Basye Sander
MacMillan
201 West 103rd Street
Indianapolis, IN 46290
317-581-3500

The Complete Idiot's Guide to Getting Your Romance Published
by Julie Beard
Alpha Books
4500 E. Speedway, Suite 31
Tucson, AZ 85712
800-528-3494   fax: 800770-4329

The Copyright Permission and Libel Handbook: A Step-by-Step Guide for Writers, Editors, and Publishers
by Lloyd J. Jassin, Steve C. Schecter
John Wiley & Sons
605 Third Avenue
New York, NY 10158-0012
212-850-6000   fax: 212-850-6088
e-mail: info@wiley.com

Desktop Publishing & Design for Dummies
by Roger C. Parker
IDG Books Worldwide
IDG Books Worldwide, Inc.
919 E. Hillsdale Blvd., Suite 400
Foster City, CA 94404-2112
800-762-2974

The Directory of Poetry Publishers: 1999–2000
(Directory of Poetry Publishers, 15th Ed.)
by Len Fulton (Editor)
Dustbooks
PO Box 100
Paradise CA 95967
530-877-6110, 800-477-6110   fax: 530-877-0222

Directory of Small Press/Magazine
Editors & Publishers 1999–2000: Press Editors & Publishers
by Len Fulton (Editor)
Dustbooks
PO Box 100
Paradise CA 95967
530-877-6110, 800-477-6110   fax: 530-877-0222

The Editors Speak: 500 Top Book Editors Tell You
Who They Are, What They Want, and How to Win Them Over
by Jeff Herman
Career Press
3 Tice Road
PO Box 687
Franklin Lakes, NJ 07417
201-848-0310

Formatting & Submitting Your Manuscript (Writer's Market Library Series)
by Jack Neff
Writers Digest Books
1507 Dana Avenue
Cincinnati, OH 45207
513-531-2222   fax: 531-531-4744

From Book Idea to Bestseller: What You Absolutely,
Positively Must Know to Make Your Book a Success
by Michael Snell, Kim Baker (Contributor), Sunny Baker (Contributor)
Prima Publishing
3000 Lava Ridge Ct.
Roseville, CA 95661
916-787-7000   fax: 916-787-7001
e-mail: sales@primapub.com

From Pen to Print: The Secrets of Getting Published Successfully
by Ellen M. Kozak
Henry Holt
115 West 18th Street
New York, NY 10011
212-886-9200   fax: 212-633-0748
e-mail: publicity@hholt.com

Get Published: Top Magazine Editors Tell You How
by Diane Gage
Henry Holt
115 West 18th Street
New York, NY 10011
212-886-9200   fax: 212-633-0748
e-mail: publicity@hholt.com

Getting Your Book Published for Dummies
by Sarah Parsons Zackheim
IDG Books Worldwide
IDG Books Worldwide, Inc.
919 E. Hillsdale Blvd., Suite 400
Foster City, CA 94404-2112
800-762-2974

Getting Your Manuscript Sold: Surefire Writing
and Selling Strategies That Will Get Your Book Published
by Cynthia Sterling, M. G. Davidson
Empire Publishing Service
PO Box 717
Madison, NC 27025-0717
336-427-5850   fax: 336-427-7372

How to Be Your Own Literary Agent: The Business of Getting a Book Published
by Richard Curtis
Houghton Mifflin Co.
222 Berkeley Street
Boston, MA 02116-3764
617-351-5000

How to Get Happily Published (5th ed.)
by Judith Appelbaum
HarperCollins
10 East 53rd Street
New York, NY 10022-5299
212-207-7000

How to Publish, Promote, and Sell Your Own Book
by Robert Lawrence Holt
St. Martin's Press
175 Fifth Avenue
New York, NY 10010
212-674-5151

How to Write Irresistible Query Letters
by Lisa Collier Cool
Writers Digest Books
1507 Dana Avenue
Cincinnati, OH 45207
513-531-2222   fax: 531-531-4744

How to Write & Sell Your First Novel
by Oscar Collier
Writers Digest Books
1507 Dana Avenue
Cincinnati, OH 45207
513-531-2222   fax: 531-531-4744

How to Write What You Want and Sell What You Write
by Skip Press
Career Press
3 Tice Road
PO Box 687
Franklin Lakes, NJ 07417
201-848-0310

In the Company of Writers: A Life in Publishing
by Charles Scribner
Scribner
1230 Avenue of the Americas
New York, NY 10020
212-698-7000

The Insider's Guide to Getting an Agent
by Lori Perkins
Writers Digest Books
1507 Dana Avenue
Cincinnati, OH 45207
513-531-2222   fax: 531-531-4744

The Joy of Publishing
by Nat G. Bodian
Open Horizons
PO Box 205
Fairfield IA 52556

Literary Agents: A Writer's Introduction
by John F. Baker
IDG Books Worldwide
IDG Books Worldwide, Inc.
919 E. Hillsdale Blvd., Suite 400
Foster City, CA 94404-2112
800-762-2974

Making It in Book Publishing
by Leonard Mogel
IDG Books Worldwide
IDG Books Worldwide, Inc.
919 E. Hillsdale Blvd., Suite 400
Foster City, CA 94404-2112
800-762-2974

Marketing Strategies for Writers
by Michael H. Sedge
Allworth Press
10 East 23rd Street, Suite 210
New York, NY 10010
212-777-8395

Merriam-Webster's Manual for Writers and Editors
Merriam Webster
47 Federal Street
PO Box 281
Springfield, MA 01102
413-734-3134   fax: 413-731-5979
e-mail: mwsales@m-w.com

Negotiating a Book Contract: A Guide for Authors, Agents and Lawyers
by Mark L. Levine
Moyer Bell Ltd
Kymbolde Way
Wakefield, Rhode Island 02879
401-789-0074, 888-789-1945   fax: 401-789-3793
e-mail: sales@moyerbell.com

Novel & Short Story Writer's Market, 2000:
2,000 Places to Sell Your Fiction (Novel and Short Story Writer's Market, 2000)
by Barbara Kuroff (Editor), Tricia Waddell (Editor)
Writer's Digest Books
1507 Dana Avenue
Cincinnati, OH 45207
513-531-2222   fax: 531-531-4744

Poet Power! The Practical Poet's Complete
Guide to Getting Published (and Self-Published)
by Thomas A. Williams
Venture Press
PO Box 1582
Davis, CA 95617-1582
530-756-2309   fax: 530-756-4790
e-mail: wmaster@ggweb.com

The Prepublishing Handbook: What You
Should Know Before You Publish Your First Book
by Patricia J. Bell
Cats Paw Press
9561 Woodridge Circle
Eden Prairie, MN 55347
952-941-5053   fax: 952-941-4759
e-mail: catspawpre@aol.com

Publish to Win: Smart Strategies to Sell More Books
by Jerrold R. Jenkins, Anne M. Stanton
Rhodes & Easton
35 Clark Hill Road
Prospect, CT 06712-1011
 203-758-3661   fax: 603-853-5420
e-mail: biopub@aol.com

Secrets of a Freelance Writer: How to Make $85,000 a Year
by Robert W. Bly
Henry Holt
115 West 18th Street
New York, NY 10011
212-886-9200   fax: 212-633-0748
e-mail: publicity@hholt.com

The Shortest Distance Between You and a Published Book
by Susan Page
Broadway Books

This Business of Books: A Complete Overview
of the Industry from Concept Through Sales
by Claudia Suzanne, Carol Amato (Editor), Thelma Sansoucie (Editor)
Wambtac
17300 17th Street, #J276
Tustin, CA 92780
800-641-3936   fax: 714-954-0793
e-mail: bookdoc@wambtac

This Business of Publishing: An Insider's View of Current Trends and Tactics
by Richard Curtis
Allworth Press
10 East 23rd Street, Suite 210
New York, NY 10010
212-777-8395

What Book Publishers Won't Tell You:
A Literary Agent's Guide to the Secrets of Getting Published
by Bill Adler
Citadel Press
3300 Business Drive
Sacramento, CA 95820
916-456-6000   fax: 916-732-2070

Write the Perfect Book Proposal: 10 Proposals That Sold and Why
by Jeff Herman, Deborah M. Adams
John Wiley & Sons
605 Third Avenue
New York, NY 10158-0012
212-850-6000   fax: 212-850-6088
e-mail: info@wiley.com

*Writer's Guide to Book Editors, Publishers, and Literary Agents, 2000–2001: Who They
Are! What They Want! and How to Win Them Over!* (Serial)
by Jeff Herman
Prima Publishing
3000 Lava Ridge Ct.
Roseville, CA 95661
916-787-7000   fax: 916-787-7001
e-mail: sales@primapub.com

*A Writer's Guide to Overcoming Rejection: A Practical Sales Course for the As Yet
Unpublished*
by Edward Baker
Summerdale Publishing Ltd.

*Writer's International Guide to Book Editors, Publishers, and Literary Agents: Make the
Whole English-Speaking Publishing World Yours with This One-of-a-Kind Guide*
by Jeff Herman
Prima Publishing
3000 Lava Ridge Ct.
Roseville, CA 95661
916-787-7000   fax: 916-787-7001
e-mail: sales@primapub.com

The Writer's Legal Guide (2nd ed.)
by Tad Crawford, Tony Lyons
Allworth Press
10 East 23rd Street, Suite 210
New York, NY 10010
212-777-8395

The Writer's Market Companion
by Joe Feiertag, Mary Carmen Cupito
Writer's Digest Books
1507 Dana Avenue
Cincinnati, OH 45207
513-531-2222   fax: 531-531-4744

You Can Make It Big Writing Books:
A Top Agent Shows How to Develop a Million-Dollar Bestseller
by Jeff Herman, Deborah Levine Herman, Julia DeVillers
Prima Publishing
3000 Lava Ridge Ct.
Roseville, CA 95661
916-787-7000   fax: 916-787-7001
e-mail: sales@primapub.com

Index

INSTRUCTIONS FOR CD–ROM DELUXE EDITION USERS

Running the CD No installation is required. The only files transferred to your hard disk are the ones you choose to copy or install.

Windows 95 or higher Because there is no install routine, running the CD in Windows is a breeze, especially if you have AutoRun enabled. Simply insert the CD in the CD-ROM drive, close the tray, and wait for the CD to load.

If you have disabled AutoRun, do the following to run the CD:

1. Insert the CD in the CD-ROM drive.
2. From the Start menu, select Run.
3. In the Open text box, type D:\cdinstaller.exe (where D:\ is the CD-ROM drive).
4. Select OK.

This CD contains:

- **Writer's Desktop Database.** This powerful tool contains the complete 2002–2003 edition of Jeff Herman's *Writer's Guide to Book Editors, Publishers, and Literary Agents*. In addition, the database contains expense and communications logs, as well as a title tracker to help you organize your existing works.
- **Writer's Guide Writer's Web Sites.** This assortment of Internet links will enable you to tap into the valuable writing resources available online.
- **Writer's Guide Shareware.** A collection of useful tools, utilities and add-ons that includes software programs ranging from electronic thesauri to rhyming dictionaries.

Writer's Guide Shareware The Writer's Guide Shareware includes file trees for each of the sections contained on the CD—Writer's Tools, Business Cards, Utilities, and Address Books. Click one of these buttons to view the selection of programs available. Depending on the software title you select any number of the following options may be available:

- **Install.** Use this option to install the selected software on to your hard disk. Choosing this option begins the install routine associated with the program. Be sure to follow installation instructions as they appear.
- **Explore.** This option enables you to view the contents of the CD by using either the Windows Explorer.

Using the Writer's Desktop Database Once you've installed the Writer's Desktop Database, check out the powerful Help menu at any time for instructions on every feature or tips on how to use the program more efficiently.

Following are some basic instructions to help run your first search of the database. For this example, we will pretend that you have written a mystery novel and are looking for a publisher or agent.

- Choose the Type of Search (in the upper center portion of the opening window) you wish to perform. For this example, click on Publisher/Agency.
- Next, choose the specific Category to search (headings with empty white boxes in the bottom half of the screen) by using the scroll bar to move to the right until you see the Interests header and double-click on the first white box under it. (For future searches use the other headers for different kinds of searches.)
- The Field Search Wizard will appear. Type in the word or words you want to search for (to use AND and OR searches see the Help section). Type in the word *mystery* and click OK.
- Next, click on the Search button or just press the Enter key.
- You should see a long list of publishers and agents that handle mystery books. Double-click on any of these to view their specific information.
